Cumulative Areas under the Standard Normal Curve (*continued*)

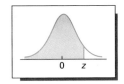

z	0.00	0.01	0.02	0.03	0.04	0.05	0.06	0.07	0.08	0.09
0.0	0.5000	0.5040	0.5080	0.5120	0.5160	0.5199	0.5239	0.5279	0.5319	0.5359
0.1	0.5398	0.5438	0.5478	0.5517	0.5557	0.5596	0.5636	0.5675	0.5714	0.5753
0.2	0.5793	0.5832	0.5871	0.5910	0.5948	0.5987	0.6026	0.6064	0.6103	0.6141
0.3	0.6179	0.6217	0.6255	0.6293	0.6331	0.6368	0.6406	0.6443	0.6480	0.6517
0.4	0.6554	0.6591	0.6628	0.6664	0.6700	0.6736	0.6772	0.6808	0.6844	0.6879
0.5	0.6915	0.6950	0.6985	0.7019	0.7054	0.7088	0.7123	0.7157	0.7190	0.7224
0.6	0.7257	0.7291	0.7324	0.7357	0.7389	0.7422	0.7454	0.7486	0.7518	0.7549
0.7	0.7580	0.7611	0.7642	0.7673	0.7704	0.7734	0.7764	0.7794	0.7823	0.7852
0.8	0.7881	0.7910	0.7939	0.7967	0.7995	0.8023	0.8051	0.8078	0.8106	0.8133
0.9	0.8159	0.8186	0.8212	0.8238	0.8264	0.8289	0.8315	0.8340	0.8365	0.8389
1.0	0.8413	0.8438	0.8461	0.8485	0.8508	0.8531	0.8554	0.8577	0.8599	0.8621
1.1	0.8643	0.8665	0.8686	0.8708	0.8729	0.8749	0.8770	0.8790	0.8810	0.8830
1.2	0.8849	0.8869	0.8888	0.8907	0.8925	0.8944	0.8962	0.8980	0.8997	0.9015
1.3	0.9032	0.9049	0.9066	0.9082	0.9099	0.9115	0.9131	0.9147	0.9162	0.9177
1.4	0.9192	0.9207	0.9222	0.9236	0.9251	0.9265	0.9279	0.9292	0.9306	0.9319
1.5	0.9332	0.9345	0.9357	0.9370	0.9382	0.9394	0.9406	0.9418	0.9429	0.9441
1.6	0.9452	0.9463	0.9474	0.9484	0.9495	0.9505	0.9515	0.9525	0.9535	0.9545
1.7	0.9554	0.9564	0.9573	0.9582	0.9591	0.9599	0.9608	0.9616	0.9625	0.9633
1.8	0.9641	0.9649	0.9656	0.9664	0.9671	0.9678	0.9686	0.9693	0.9699	0.9706
1.9	0.9713	0.9719	0.9726	0.9732	0.9738	0.9744	0.9750	0.9756	0.9761	0.9767
2.0	0.9772	0.9778	0.9783	0.9788	0.9793	0.9798	0.9803	0.9808	0.9812	0.9817
2.1	0.9821	0.9826	0.9830	0.9834	0.9838	0.9842	0.9846	0.9850	0.9854	0.9857
2.2	0.9861	0.9864	0.9868	0.9871	0.9875	0.9878	0.9881	0.9884	0.9887	0.9890
2.3	0.9893	0.9896	0.9898	0.9901	0.9904	0.9906	0.9909	0.9911	0.9913	0.9916
2.4	0.9918	0.9920	0.9922	0.9925	0.9927	0.9929	0.9931	0.9932	0.9934	0.9936
2.5	0.9938	0.9940	0.9941	0.9943	0.9945	0.9946	0.9948	0.9949	0.9951	0.9952
2.6	0.9953	0.9955	0.9956	0.9957	0.9959	0.9960	0.9961	0.9962	0.9963	0.9964
2.7	0.9965	0.9966	0.9967	0.9968	0.9969	0.9970	0.9971	0.9972	0.9973	0.9974
2.8	0.9974	0.9975	0.9976	0.9977	0.9977	0.9978	0.9979	0.9979	0.9980	0.9981
2.9	0.9981	0.9982	0.9982	0.9983	0.9984	0.9984	0.9985	0.9985	0.9986	0.9986
3.0	0.99865	0.99869	0.99874	0.99878	0.99882	0.99886	0.99889	0.99893	0.99897	0.99900
3.1	0.99903	0.99906	0.99910	0.99913	0.99916	0.99918	0.99921	0.99924	0.99926	0.99929
3.2	0.99931	0.99934	0.99936	0.99938	0.99940	0.99942	0.99944	0.99946	0.99948	0.99950
3.3	0.99952	0.99953	0.99955	0.99957	0.99958	0.99960	0.99961	0.99962	0.99964	0.99965
3.4	0.99966	0.99968	0.99969	0.99970	0.99971	0.99972	0.99973	0.99974	0.99975	0.99976
3.5	0.99977	0.99978	0.99978	0.99979	0.99980	0.99981	0.99981	0.99982	0.99983	0.99983
3.6	0.99984	0.99985	0.99985	0.99986	0.99986	0.99987	0.99987	0.99988	0.99988	0.99989
3.7	0.99989	0.99990	0.99990	0.99990	0.99991	0.99991	0.99992	0.99992	0.99992	0.99992
3.8	0.99993	0.99993	0.99993	0.99994	0.99994	0.99994	0.99994	0.99995	0.99995	0.99995
3.9	0.99995	0.99995	0.99996	0.99996	0.99996	0.99996	0.99996	0.99996	0.99997	0.99997

A *t* Table

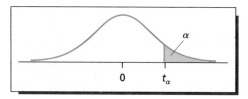

df	$t_{.100}$	$t_{.050}$	$t_{.025}$	$t_{.01}$	$t_{.005}$	$t_{.001}$	$t_{.0005}$
1	3.078	6.314	12.706	31.821	63.657	318.31	636.62
2	1.886	2.920	4.303	6.965	9.925	22.326	31.598
3	1.638	2.353	3.182	4.541	5.841	10.213	12.924
4	1.533	2.132	2.776	3.747	4.604	7.173	8.610
5	1.476	2.015	2.571	3.365	4.032	5.893	6.869
6	1.440	1.943	2.447	3.143	3.707	5.208	5.959
7	1.415	1.895	2.365	2.998	3.499	4.785	5.408
8	1.397	1.860	2.306	2.896	3.355	4.501	5.041
9	1.383	1.833	2.262	2.821	3.250	4.297	4.781
10	1.372	1.812	2.228	2.764	3.169	4.144	4.587
11	1.363	1.796	2.201	2.718	3.106	4.025	4.437
12	1.356	1.782	2.179	2.681	3.055	3.930	4.318
13	1.350	1.771	2.160	2.650	3.012	3.852	4.221
14	1.345	1.761	2.145	2.624	2.977	3.787	4.140
15	1.341	1.753	2.131	2.602	2.947	3.733	4.073
16	1.337	1.746	2.120	2.583	2.921	3.686	4.015
17	1.333	1.740	2.110	2.567	2.898	3.646	3.965
18	1.330	1.734	2.101	2.552	2.878	3.610	3.922
19	1.328	1.729	2.093	2.539	2.861	3.579	3.883
20	1.325	1.725	2.086	2.528	2.845	3.552	3.850
21	1.323	1.721	2.080	2.518	2.831	3.527	3.819
22	1.321	1.717	2.074	2.508	2.819	3.505	3.792
23	1.319	1.714	2.069	2.500	2.807	3.485	3.767
24	1.318	1.711	2.064	2.492	2.797	3.467	3.745
25	1.316	1.708	2.060	2.485	2.787	3.450	3.725
26	1.315	1.706	2.056	2.479	2.779	3.435	3.707
27	1.314	1.703	2.052	2.473	2.771	3.421	3.690
28	1.313	1.701	2.048	2.467	2.763	3.408	3.674
29	1.311	1.699	2.045	2.462	2.756	3.396	3.659
30	1.310	1.697	2.042	2.457	2.750	3.385	3.646
40	1.303	1.684	2.021	2.423	2.704	3.307	3.551
60	1.296	1.671	2.000	2.390	2.660	3.232	3.460
120	1.289	1.658	1.980	2.358	2.617	3.160	3.373
∞	1.282	1.645	1.960	2.326	2.576	3.090	3.291

Essentials of Business Statistics

THIRD EDITION

The McGraw-Hill/Irwin Series: Operations and Decision Sciences

BUSINESS STATISTICS

Aczel and Sounderpandian,
Complete Business Statistics,
Seventh Edition

ALEKS Corporation,
ALEKS for Business Statistics,
First Edition

Alwan,
Statistical Process Analysis,
First Edition

Bowerman, O'Connell, and Murphree
Business Statistics in Practice,
Fifth Edition

Bowerman, O'Connell, Orris, and Murphree
Essentials of Business Statistics,
Third Edition

Bryant and Smith,
Practical Data Analysis: Case Studies in Business Statistics, Volumes I, II, and III*

Cooper and Schindler,
Business Research Methods,
Tenth Edition

Doane, Mathieson, and Tracy,
Visual Statistics,
Second Edition, 2.0

Doane and Seward,
Applied Statistics in Business and Economics,
Second Edition

Doane and Seward,
Essential Statistics in Business and Economics,
Second Edition

Gitlow, Oppenheim, Oppenheim, and Levine,
Quality Management,
Third Edition

Kutner, Nachtsheim, Neter, and Li,
Applied Linear Statistical Models,
Fifth Edition

Kutner, Nachtsheim, and Neter,
Applied Linear Regression Models,
Fourth Edition

Lind, Marchal, and Wathen,
Basic Statistics for Business and Economics,
Sixth Edition

Lind, Marchal, and Wathen,
Statistical Techniques in Business and Economics,
Fourteenth Edition

Merchant, Goffinet, and Koehler,
Basic Statistics Using Excel for Office XP,
Fourth Edition

Olson and Shi,
Introduction to Business Data Mining,
First Edition

Orris,
Basic Statistics Using Excel and MegaStat,
First Edition

Siegel,
Practical Business Statistics,
Fifth Edition

Wilson, Keating, and John Galt Solutions, Inc.,
Business Forecasting,
Fifth Edition

Zagorsky,
Business Information,
First Edition

QUANTITATIVE METHODS AND MANAGEMENT SCIENCE

Hillier and Hillier,
Introduction to Management Science,
Third Edition

Stevenson and Ozgur,
Introduction to Management Science with Spreadsheets,
First Edition

Kros,
Spreadsheet Modeling for Business Decisions,
First Edition

*Available only through McGraw-Hill's PRIMIS Online Assets Library.

Bruce L. Bowerman

Miami University

Richard T. O'Connell

Miami University

J. B. Orris

Butler University

Emily S. Murphree

Miami University

Essentials of Business Statistics

THIRD EDITION

with major contributions by

Steven C. Huchendorf

University of Minnesota

Dawn C. Porter

University of Southern California

Patrick J. Schur

Miami University

Boston   Burr Ridge, IL   Dubuque, IA   New York   San Francisco   St. Louis
Bangkok   Bogotá   Caracas   Kuala Lumpur   Lisbon   London   Madrid   Mexico City
Milan   Montreal   New Delhi   Santiago   Seoul   Singapore   Sydney   Taipei   Toronto

 McGraw-Hill
Irwin

ESSENTIALS OF BUSINESS STATISTICS

Published by McGraw-Hill/Irwin, a business unit of The McGraw-Hill Companies, Inc., 1221 Avenue of the Americas, New York, NY, 10020. Copyright © 2010, 2008, 2004 by The McGraw-Hill Companies, Inc. All rights reserved. No part of this publication may be reproduced or distributed in any form or by any means, or stored in a database or retrieval system, without the prior written consent of The McGraw-Hill Companies, Inc., including, but not limited to, in any network or other electronic storage or transmission, or broadcast for distance learning.

Some ancillaries, including electronic and print components, may not be available to customers outside the United States.

This book is printed on acid-free paper.

1 2 3 4 5 6 7 8 9 0 VNH/VNH 0 9

ISBN   978-0-07-337368-3
MHID 0-07-337368-0

Vice president and editor-in-chief: *Brent Gordon*
Editorial director: *Stewart Mattson*
Publisher: *Tim Vertovec*
Executive editor: *Steve Schuetz*
Senior developmental editor: *Wanda J. Zeman*
Marketing manager: *Scott S. Bishop*
Senior project manager: *Harvey Yep*
Full service project manager: *Mike Ryder, Macmillan Publishing Solutions*
Lead production supervisor: *Michael R. McCormick*
Lead designer: *Matthew Baldwin*
Senior photo research coordinator: *Jeremy Cheshareck*
Photo researcher: *Ira C. Roberts*
Senior media project manager: *Greg Bates*
Cover designer: *Matthew Baldwin*
Cover image: *©Ingram Publishing/AGE Fotostock*
Typeface: *10/12 Times New Roman*
Compositor: *Macmillan Publishing Solutions*
Printer: *R. R. Donnelley, Jefferson City*

Library of Congress Cataloging-in-Publication Data

Essentials of business statistics / Bruce L. Bowerman . . . [et al.].—3rd ed.
  p. cm.—(The McGraw-Hill/Irwin series : operations and decision sciences)
  Includes index.
  ISBN-13: 978-0-07-337368-3 (alk. paper)
  ISBN-10: 0-07-337368-0 (alk. paper)
  1. Commercial statistics. I. Bowerman, Bruce L.
HF1017.B6554 2010
519.5--dc22

                                        2008050182

Brief Table of Contents

Chapter 1   2
An Introduction to Business Statistics

Chapter 2   48
Descriptive Statistics: Tabular
and Graphical Methods

Chapter 3   114
Descriptive Statistics: Numerical Methods

Chapter 4   170
Probability

Chapter 5   206
Discrete Random Variables

Chapter 6   242
Continuous Random Variables

Chapter 7   284
Sampling Distributions

Chapter 8   308
Confidence Intervals

Chapter 9   346
Hypotheses Testing

Chapter 10   394
Statistical Inferences Based on Two Samples

Chapter 11   440
Experimental Design and Analysis of Variance

Chapter 12   470
Chi-Square Tests

Chapter 13   498
Simple Linear Regression Analysis

Chapter 14   568
Multiple Regression and Model Building

Appendix A   632
Statistical Tables

Appendix B   653
Counting Rules

Appendix C   655
The Hypergeometric Distribution

**Answers to Most Odd-Numbered
Exercises**   656

References   663

Photo Credits   664

Index   665

Chapter 15   On Website
Process Improvement Using Control Charts

Appendix D   On Website
Two-Way Analysis of Variance

Table of Contents

Chapter 1

An Introduction to Business Statistics

1.1 ▦ Populations and Samples   3

1.2 ▦ Selecting a Random Sample   4

1.3 ▦ Ratio, Interval, Ordinal, and Nominative Scales of Measurement (Optional)   17

1.4 ▦ An Introduction to Survey Sampling (Optional)   18

1.5 ▦ More About Data Acquisition and Survey Sampling (Optional)   20

MINITAB, Excel, and MegaStat for Statistics   29

Appendix 1.1 ▦ Getting Started with MINITAB   29

Appendix 1.2 ▦ Getting Started with Excel   36

Appendix 1.3 ▦ Getting Started with MegaStat   41

Appendix 1.4 ▦ Introduction to Internet Exercises   46

Chapter 2

Descriptive Statistics: Tabular and Graphical Methods

2.1 ▦ Graphically Summarizing Qualitative Data   49

2.2 ▦ Graphically Summarizing Quantitative Data   56

2.3 ▦ Dot Plots   68

2.4 ▦ Stem-and-Leaf Displays   70

2.5 ▦ Crosstabulation Tables (Optional)   75

2.6 ▦ Scatter Plots (Optional)   81

2.7 ▦ Misleading Graphs and Charts (Optional)   84

Appendix 2.1 ▦ Tabular and Graphical Methods Using MINITAB   94

Appendix 2.2 ▦ Tabular and Graphical Methods Using Excel   102

Appendix 2.3 ▦ Tabular and Graphical Methods Using MegaStat   110

Chapter 3

Descriptive Statistics: Numerical Methods

3.1 ▦ Describing Central Tendency   115

3.2 ▦ Measures of Variation   125

3.3 ▦ Percentiles, Quartiles, and Box-and-Whiskers Displays   136

3.4 ▦ Covariance, Correlation, and the Least Squares Line (Optional)   144

3.5 ▦ Weighted Means and Grouped Data (Optional)   150

3.6 ▦ The Geometric Mean (Optional)   154

Appendix 3.1 ▦ Numerical Descriptive Statistics Using MINITAB   162

Appendix 3.2 ▦ Numerical Descriptive Statistics Using Excel   164

Appendix 3.3 ▦ Numerical Descriptive Statistics Using MegaStat   168

Chapter 4
Probability

4.1 ▦ The Concept of Probability   171

4.2 ▦ Sample Spaces and Events   173

4.3 ▦ Some Elementary Probability Rules   180

4.4 ▦ Conditional Probability and Independence   187

4.5 ▦ Bayes' Theorem (Optional)   198

Chapter 5
Discrete Random Variables

5.1 ▦ Two Types of Random Variables   207

5.2 ▦ Discrete Probability Distributions   208

5.3 ▦ The Binomial Distribution   219

5.4 ▦ The Poisson Distribution (Optional)   230

Appendix 5.1 ▦ Binomial and Poisson Probabilities Using MINITAB   238

Appendix 5.2 ▦ Binomial and Poisson Probabilities Using Excel   239

Appendix 5.3 ▦ Binomial and Poisson Probabilities Using MegaStat   241

Chapter 6
Continuous Random Variables

6.1 ▦ Continuous Probability Distributions   243

6.2 ▦ The Uniform Distribution   245

6.3 ▦ The Normal Probability Distribution   248

6.4 ▦ Approximating the Binomial Distribution by Using the Normal Distribution (Optional)   266

6.5 ▦ The Exponential Distribution (Optional)   270

6.6 ▦ The Normal Probability Plot (Optional)   273

Appendix 6.1 ▦ Normal Distribution Using MINITAB   279

Appendix 6.2 ▦ Normal Distribution Using Excel   281

Appendix 6.3 ▦ Normal Distribution Using MegaStat   282

Chapter 7
Sampling Distributions

7.1 ▦ The Sampling Distribution of the Sample Mean   285

7.2 ▦ The Sampling Distribution of the Sample Proportion   298

Appendix 7.1 ▦ Simulating Sampling Distributions Using MINITAB   307

Chapter 8
Confidence Intervals

8.1 ▦ z-Based Confidence Intervals for a Population Mean: σ Known   309

8.2 ▦ t-Based Confidence Intervals for a Population Mean: σ Unknown   317

8.3 ▦ Sample Size Determination   325

8.4 ▦ Confidence Intervals for a Population Proportion   329

8.5 ▦ A Comparison of Confidence Intervals and Tolerance Intervals (Optional)   336

Appendix 8.1 ▦ Confidence Intervals Using MINITAB   342

Appendix 8.2 ▦ Confidence Intervals Using Excel   344

Appendix 8.3 ▦ Confidence Intervals Using MegaStat   345

Chapter 9
Hypothesis Testing

9.1 ▦ The Null and Alternative Hypotheses and Errors in Hypothesis Testing   347

9.2 ▦ z Tests about a Population Mean: σ Known   353

9.3 ▦ t Tests about a Population Mean: σ Unknown   366

9.4 ▦ z Tests about a Population Proportion   371

9.5 ▦ Type II Error Probabilities and Sample Size Determination (Optional)   376

9.6 ▦ The Chi-Square Distribution (Optional)   382

9.7 ▦ Statistical Inference for a Population Variance (Optional)   383

Appendix 9.1 ▦ One-Sample Hypothesis Testing Using MINITAB   389

Appendix 9.2 ▦ One-Sample Hypothesis Testing Using Excel   391

Appendix 9.3 ▦ One-Sample Hypothesis Testing Using MegaStat   392

Chapter 10
Statistical Inferences Based on Two Samples

10.1 ▦ Comparing Two Population Means by Using Independent Samples: Variances Known   395

10.2 ▦ Comparing Two Population Means by Using Independent Samples: Variances Unknown   401

10.3 ▦ Paired Difference Experiments   409

10.4 ▦ Comparing Two Population Proportions by Using Large, Independent Samples   417

10.5 ▦ Comparing Two Population Variances by Using Independent Samples   423

Appendix 10.1 ▦ Two-Sample Hypothesis Testing Using MINITAB   434

Appendix 10.2 ▦ Two-Sample Hypothesis Testing Using Excel   437

Appendix 10.3 ▦ Two-Sample Hypothesis Testing Using MegaStat   438

Chapter 11
Experimental Design and Analysis of Variance

11.1 ▦ Basic Concepts of Experimental Design   441

11.2 ▦ One-Way Analysis of Variance   444

11.3 ▦ The Randomized Block Design   455

Appendix 11.1 ▦ Experimental Design and Analysis of Variance Using MINITAB   466

Appendix 11.2 ▦ Experimental Design and Analysis of Variance Using Excel   467

Appendix 11.3 ▦ Experimental Design and Analysis of Variance Using MegaStat   468

Chapter 12
Chi-Square Tests

12.1 ▦ Chi-Square Goodness of Fit Tests   471

12.2 ▦ A Chi-Square Test for Independence   480

Appendix 12.1 ▦ Chi-Square Tests Using MINITAB   490

Appendix 12.2 ▦ Chi-Square Tests Using Excel   493

Appendix 12.3 ▦ Chi-Square Tests Using MegaStat   495

Chapter 13
Simple Linear Regression Analysis

13.1 ▦ The Simple Linear Regression Model and the Least Squares Point Estimates   499

13.2 ▦ Model Assumptions and the Standard Error   514

13.3 ■ Testing the Significance of the Slope and *y*-Intercept   517

13.4 ■ Confidence and Prediction Intervals   525

13.5 ■ Simple Coefficients of Determination and Correlation   530

13.6 ■ Testing the Significance of the Population Correlation Coefficient (Optional)   536

13.7 ■ An F Test for the Model   537

13.8 ■ Residual Analysis (Optional)   540

13.9 ■ Some Shortcut Formulas (Optional)   554

Appendix 13.1 ■ Simple Linear Regression Analysis Using MINITAB   563

Appendix 13.2 ■ Simple Linear Regression Analysis Using Excel   564

Appendix 13.3 ■ Simple Linear Regression Analysis Using MegaStat   566

Chapter 14

Multiple Regression and Model Building

14.1 ■ The Multiple Regression Model and the Least Squares Point Estimates   569

14.2 ■ Model Assumptions and the Standard Error   581

14.3 ■ R^2 and Adjusted R^2 583

14.4 ■ The Overall F Test   585

14.5 ■ Testing the Significance of an Independent Variable   587

14.6 ■ Confidence and Prediction Intervals   591

14.7 ■ Using Dummy Variables to Model Qualitative Independent Variables   594

14.8 ■ Model Building and the Effects of Multicollinearity   606

14.9 ■ Residual Analysis in Multiple Regression   614

Appendix 14.1 ■ Multiple Regression Analysis Using MINITAB   625

Appendix 14.2 ■ Multiple Regression Analysis Using Excel   627

Appendix 14.3 ■ Multiple Regression Analysis Using MegaStat   629

Appendix A

Statistical Tables   632

Appendix B

Counting Rules   653

Appendix C

The Hypergeometric Distribution   655

Answers to Most Odd-Numbered Exercises   656

References   663

Photo Credits   664

Index   665

Chapter 15   Process Improvement Using Control Charts   On Website

Appendix D   Two-Way Analysis of Variance   On Website

About the Authors

Bruce L. Bowerman   Bruce L. Bowerman is professor of decision sciences at Miami University in Oxford, Ohio. He received his Ph.D. degree in statistics from Iowa State University in 1974, and he has over 40 years of experience teaching basic statistics, regression analysis, time series forecasting, survey sampling, and design of experiments to both undergraduate and graduate students. In 1987 Professor Bowerman received an Outstanding Teaching award from the Miami University senior class, and in 1992 he received an Effective Educator award from the Richard T. Farmer School of Business Administration. Together with Richard T. O'Connell, Professor Bowerman has written 15 textbooks. These include *Business Statistics in Practice,* Fifth Edition; *Forecasting and Time Series: An Applied Approach; Forecasting, Time Series, and Regression: An Applied Approach* (also coauthored with Anne B. Koehler); and *Linear Statistical Models: An Applied Approach.* The first edition of *Forecasting and Time Series* earned an Outstanding Academic Book award from *Choice* magazine. Professor Bowerman has also published a number of articles in applied stochastic processes, time series forecasting, and statistical education. In his spare time, Professor Bowerman enjoys watching movies and sports, playing tennis, and designing houses.

Richard T. O'Connell   Richard T. O'Connell is associate professor of decision sciences at Miami University in Oxford, Ohio. He has more than 35 years of experience teaching basic statistics, statistical quality control and process improvement, regression analysis, time series forecasting, and design of experiments to both undergraduate and graduate business students. He also has extensive consulting experience and has taught workshops dealing with statistical process control and process improvement for a variety of companies in the Midwest. In 2000 Professor O'Connell received an Effective Educator award from the Richard T. Farmer School of Business Administration. Together with Bruce L. Bowerman, he has written 15 textbooks. These include *Business Statistics in Practice,* Fifth Edition; *Forecasting and Time Series: An Applied Approach; Forecasting, Time Series, and Regression: An Applied Approach* (also coauthored with Anne B. Koehler); and *Linear Statistical Models: An Applied Approach.* Professor O'Connell has published a number of articles in the area of innovative statistical education. He is one of the first college instructors in the United States to integrate statistical process control and process improvement methodology into his basic business statistics course. He (with Professor Bowerman) has written several articles advocating this approach. He has also given presentations on this subject at meetings such as the Joint Statistical Meetings of the American Statistical Association and the Workshop on Total Quality Management: Developing Curricula and Research Agendas (sponsored by the Production and Operations Management Society). Professor O'Connell received an M.S. degree in decision sciences from Northwestern University in 1973, and he is currently a member of both the Decision Sciences Institute and the American Statistical Association. In his spare time, Professor O'Connell enjoys fishing, collecting 1950s and 1960s rock music, and following the Green Bay Packers and Purdue University sports.

James Burdeane "Deane" Orris J. B. Orris is a professor of management science at Butler University in Indianapolis, Indiana. He received his Ph.D. from the University of Illinois in 1971, and in the late 1970s with the advent of personal computers, he combined his interest in statistics and computers to write one of the first personal computer statistics packages—MICROSTAT. Over the past 20 years, MICROSTAT has evolved into MegaStat which is an Excel add-in statistics program. He wrote an Excel book, *Essentials: Excel 2000 Advanced,* in 1999 and *Basic Statistics Using Excel and MegaStat* in 2006. Professor Orris also has done work in neural networks, spreadsheet simulation, and statistical analysis for many research projects. He has taught statistics and computer courses in the College of Business Administration of Butler University since 1971. He is a member of the American Statistical Association and is past president of the Central Indiana Chapter. In his spare time, Professor Orris enjoys reading, working out, and working in his woodworking shop.

Emily S. Murphree Emily S. Murphree is Associate Professor of Statistics in the Department of Mathematics and Statistics at Miami University in Oxford, Ohio. She received her Ph.D. degree in statistics from the University of North Carolina and does research in applied probability. Professor Murphree received Miami's College of Arts and Science Distinguished Educator Award in 1998. In 1996, she was named one of Oxford's Citizens of the Year for her work with Habitat for Humanity and for organizing annual Sonia Kovalevsky Mathematical Sciences Days for area high school girls. Her enthusiasm for hiking in wilderness areas of the West motivated her current research on estimating animal population sizes.

Dedication

Bruce L. Bowerman
To my wife, children, sister, and other family members:
Drena
Michael, Jinda, Benjamin, and Lex
Asa and Nicole
Susan
Fiona and Radeesa
Daphne, Chloe, and Edgar
Gwyneth and Tony

Richard T. O'Connell
To my wife and children:
Jean
Christopher and Bradley

J. B. Orris
To my children:
Amy and Bradley

Emily S. Murphree
To Kevin and the Math Ladies

FROM THE AUTHORS

In *Essentials of Business Statistics, Third Edition,* we provide a modern, practical, and unique framework for teaching the first course in business statistics. This framework features case study and example driven discussions of all basic business statistics topics. In addition, we have endeavored to make this book the most clearly written, motivating, and easy-to-use business statistics text available. We have rewritten many of the discussions in this third edition and taken great pains to explain concepts simply from first principles. Therefore, the only prerequisite for this book is high school algebra.

New to the third edition are:

- **A shorter and simpler introduction to business processes and an expanded treatment of data acquisition and sampling (in Chapter 1).** In order to make Chapter 1 easier to cover, the third edition has a shortened and simplified introduction to business processes. This introduction is now part of a discussion of sampling in Section 1.2. In addition, Chapter 1 contains an expanded section (Section 1.5) that discusses more advanced aspects of data acquisition and survey sampling.

- **Two chapters on descriptive statistics.** Whereas previous editions covered all of descriptive statistics in a single chapter, the third edition breaks this material into two, shorter chapters. In addition, the explanations of all descriptive statistics topics have been simplified and clarified. Chapter 2, which discusses the graphical and tabular methods of descriptive statistics, begins with the analysis of qualitative data and has new material on frequency polygons, ogives, and contingency tables. Chapter 3, which discusses the numerical methods of descriptive statistics, contains new material on covariance, correlation, and the least squares line. Both chapters utilize a substantial number of new examples, exercises, cases, and data sets, including **The Jeep Case** and **The Household Income Case.**

- **Use of the cumulative normal table in the discussion of the normal distribution in Chapter 6 and throughout the rest of the book.** Because use of the cumulative normal table makes many normal curve calculations easier and is consistent with the way that most statistical software systems give normal curve probabilities, the third edition uses this table for all normal curve applications. A very complete cumulative normal table is given on the front pages of the book, in Chapter 6, and in Table A.3 of Appendix A. (A table giving areas under the standard normal curve from 0 to z is given in Table A.11 of Appendix A.) Normal probability plots are discussed in an optional section of Chapter 6.

- **A clearer and more motivating discussion of sampling distributions in Chapter 7.** Chapter 7 begins with a new case: **The Risk Reduction Case: Game Shows and Stock Returns.** This case motivates students to think about the properties of sampling distributions in a "fun" and familiar context.

- **A clearer and more motivating introduction to confidence intervals in Chapter 8.** Chapter 8 begins with an intuitive example that illustrates a practical application of a confidence interval for a population mean. Then, using this example as a springboard, Chapter 8 develops the logic behind and a formula for a confidence interval for a population mean (as well as other confidence interval formulas). One new real-world case exercise in Chapter 8 is **The Air Traffic Control Case.**

- **A simpler and streamlined discussion of hypothesis testing in Chapter 9.** As in the second edition, the basic hypothesis testing chapter uses a seven-step procedure that breaks hypothesis testing down into small, easy-to-understand steps and clearly shows how to use the book's hypothesis testing summary boxes. In addition, the material on hypothesis tests for a population mean has been simplified and streamlined for the fifth edition. A motivating new case—**The Valentine's Day Chocolate Case**—is used throughout the discussion of hypothesis testing.

- **Clearer and simpler chapters on regression analysis.** Chapter 13 discusses simple linear regression analysis, including an introduction to residual analysis. Chapter 14 discusses multiple regression analysis, including the use of dummy variables, model building, and analyzing residuals from a multiple regression model. Chapters 13 and 14 contain significantly simplified presentations of the simple linear regression model, multiple regression models, the least squares point estimates, and confidence and prediction intervals.

- **Increased coverage of Excel, Minitab, and MegaStat (an Excel add-in package included on the text's CD-ROM).** Throughout the third edition we provide an abundant number of outputs from all three packages in both examples and exercises that allow students to concentrate on statistical interpretations. This use of outputs is particularly prominent in areas where hand calculations are impossible or impractical and where having students run their own programs (while theoretically optimal) would, because of time constraints, not allow them to see a wide variety of applications. These areas include descriptive statistics, ANOVA, regression, and time series forecasting. In addition, appendices at the end of each chapter demonstrate how to use Excel, Minitab, and Megastat. Additional capabilities of all three packages are demonstrated, and the screen captures illustrating the use of the packages are more colorful and easier to read.

We now discuss three attributes that make *Essentials of Business Statistics* an effective learning tool.

Business improvement through statistical analysis. The ultimate goal of statistical analysis in business is business improvement. This theme is the foundation for the case studies and examples in this text, many of which are based on actual, real-world situations. For example, consider the following synopses of three case studies.

- **The Cheese Spread Case:** The marketer of a soft cheese spread wishes to replace the spout on its plastic dispenser with a less expensive spout. The company uses confidence intervals to conclude that demand for the spread will remain high enough to make using the new spout profitable.
- **The Trash Bag Case:** A leading producer of trash bags uses hypothesis testing to convince the standards and practices division of a major television network that advertising claims about its newest trash bag are valid.
- **The Fuel Consumption Case:** A natural gas company is able to avoid paying fines to a pipeline transmission system by using regression analysis to accurately predict its city's natural gas needs.

In each of these cases, statistical analysis leads to an informed action (replace the spout, advertise the claim, and use the regression prediction procedure) that results in business improvement. Furthermore, we continue this theme throughout the presentation of all statistical techniques in this book. To emphasize the text's theme of business improvement, icons **BI** are placed in the page margins to identify when an important business conclusion has been reached using statistical analysis. Each conclusion is also highlighted in yellow for additional clarity.

A unique continuity of presentation and use of case studies. *Essentials of Business Statistics* features a unique continuity of presentation that integrates different statistical areas. This integration is achieved by an early emphasis on the difference between the population and the sample and by a continuing use of practical, realistic case studies that span not only individual chapters but also groups of chapters. Specifically, Chapter 1 shows how to select random (or approximately random) samples from populations and processes by introducing three case studies as examples and by presenting additional case studies as exercises. Then in Chapters 2 and 3 we show how to use statistics to describe the important aspects of these samples. We continue to employ these case studies through the probability and sampling distribution chapters until we use confidence intervals and hypothesis tests to make statistical inferences. Furthermore, we introduce new case studies in each and every chapter. For example, we introduce several case studies in our presentation of simple linear regression and then extend these case studies in the multiple regression and model building chapter to show how regression is used in the description, prediction, and control of business variables.

A real emphasis on the importance of variation. *Essentials of Business Statistics* emphasizes that since businesses must satisfy individual customers, the analysis of individual population observations—which is achieved by analyzing population variation—is as important as analyzing the population mean. Our treatment of variation begins in Chapter 1, where we intuitively examine the variation of sample data. In Chapter 2 we continue by graphically portraying the sample data, and in Chapter 3 we use the empirical rule to estimate tolerance intervals containing different percentages of population observations. For example, we use the empirical rule in the

- **Payment Time Case** to describe the variation of individual bill payment times around the estimated mean bill payment time for a new electronic billing system.
- **Car Mileage Case** to describe the variation of individual gas mileages around the estimated mean mileage obtained by a new midsize car. (We also show how EPA mileage window stickers give similar information for new cars.)

Our emphasis on variation continues throughout the book. For example, in Chapter 8 we clearly distinguish between a confidence interval for a population mean and a tolerance interval for a given percentage of individual population measurements. In Chapters 13 and 14 we show how prediction intervals can be used to evaluate the predictive capabilities of different regression models. In addition, we demonstrate how prediction intervals can be used to assess whether individual population observations are "unusual" enough to suggest the need for business improvement. Finally, in Chapter 15 (on the Website) we present a complete discussion of statistical process control and improvement (including the six sigma philosophy adopted by Motorola, Inc., and a number of other prominent U.S. companies). Furthermore, in all of these chapters we use practical case studies to illustrate the ideas being presented.

Bruce L. Bowerman
Richard T. O'Connell
J. B. Orris
Emily S. Murphree

HOW ARE CHAPTERS ORGANIZED

Chapter Contents

Each chapter begins with a list of section topics that are covered in the chapter.

●●● CHAPTER 1

An Introduction to Business Statistics

Chapter Introductions

Each chapter opens with a preview showing how the statistical topics to be discussed apply to real business problems. The continuing case examples that run throughout the book are briefly introduced along with the techniques that will be used to analyze them.

Chapter Outline

1.1 Populations and Samples
1.2 Selecting a Random Sample
1.3 Ratio, Interval, Ordinal, and Nominative Scales of Measurement (Optional)

The subject of **statistics** involves the study of how to collect, summarize, and interpret data. **Data** are numerical facts and figures from which conclusions can be drawn. Such conclusions are important to the decision-making processes of many professions and organizations. For example, government officials use conclusions drawn from the latest data on unemployment and inflation to make policy decisions. Financial planners use recent trends in stock market prices to make investment decisions. Businesses decide which products to develop and market by using data that reveal consumer preferences. Production supervisors use manufacturing data to evaluate, control, and improve product quality. Politicians rely on data from public opinion polls to formulate legislation and to devise campaign strategies. Physicians and hospitals use data on the effectiveness of drugs and surgical procedures to provide patients with the best possible treatment.

In this chapter we begin to see how we collect and analyze data. As we proceed through the chapter, we introduce several case studies. These case studies (and others to be introduced later) are revisited throughout later chapters as we learn the statistical methods needed to analyze the cases. Briefly, we will begin to study three cases:

The Cell Phone Case. A bank estimates its cellular phone costs and decides whether to outsource management of its wireless resources by studying the calling patterns of its employees.

The Car Mileage Case. To determine if it qualifies for a federal tax credit based on fuel economy, an new bottle design for one of its popular soft drinks.

Case Studies

The text provides a unique use of case studies that span individual chapters and groups of chapters. Cases are used to introduce the concepts, to demonstrate the methods, and to provide students with motivating exercises. These case studies help students see how statistics is used in business and can be used to improve processes.

EXAMPLE 10.6 The Repair Cost Comparison Case   Ⓒ

Using the data in Table 10.2, and assuming that the population of paired repair cost differences is normally distributed, a 95 percent confidence interval for $\mu_d = \mu_1 - \mu_2$ is

$$\left[\bar{d} \pm t_{.025} \frac{s_d}{\sqrt{n}} \right] = \left[-.8 \pm 2.447 \frac{.5033}{\sqrt{7}} \right]$$
$$= [-.8 \pm .4654]$$
$$= [-1.2654, -.3346]$$

Here $t_{.025} = 2.447$ is based on $n - 1 = 7 - 1 = 6$ degrees of freedom. This interval says that Home State Casualty can be 95 percent confident that μ_d, the mean of all possible paired differences of the repair cost estimates at garages 1 and 2, is between $-\$126.54$ and $-\$33.46$. That is, we are 95 percent confident that μ_1, the mean of all possible repair cost estimates at garage 1, is between $126.54 and $33.46 less than μ_2, the mean of all possible repair cost estimates at garage 2.

TO PROMOTE STUDENT LEARNING?

Figures and Tables

Throughout the text, charts, graphs, tables, and spreadsheets are used to illustrate statistical concepts. These visuals help stimulate student interest and clarify the text explanations.

FIGURE 2.7   A Frequency Histogram of the 65 Payment Times

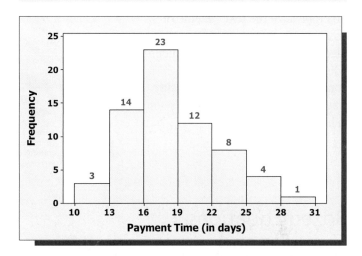

TABLE 13.1	The Fuel Consumption Data ● FuelCon1

Week	Average Hourly Temperature, x (°F)	Weekly Fuel Consumption, y (MMcf)
1	28.0	12.4
2	28.0	11.7
3	32.5	12.4
4	39.0	10.8
5	45.9	9.4
6	57.8	9.5
7	58.1	8.0
8	62.5	7.5

FIGURE 13.2   Excel Output of a Scatter Plot of y versus x

	A	B	C	D	E	F	G	H
1	TEMP	FUELCONS						
2	28	12.4						
3	28	11.7						
4	32.5	12.4						
5	39	10.8						
6	45.9	9.4						
7	57.8	9.5						
8	58.1	8						
9	62.5	7.5						
10								
11								
12								
13								
14								

Exercises

Many of the exercises in the text use real data. Data sets on the CD-ROM are identified by icon in the text. Within each chapter, exercises are broken into two part—"Concepts" and "Methods and Applications." The methods and applications exercises vary in rigor from routine calculations to fairly sophisticated case study analysis. In addition, there are Internet exercises to help students make use of the Internet for gathering and using real data and supplementary exercises at the ends of chapters.

2.7 Below we give pizza restaurant preferences for 25 randomly selected college students.
  ● PizzaPizza

Godfather's	Little Caesar's	Papa John's	Pizza Hut	Domino's	Papa John's
Papa John's	Papa John's	Pizza Hut	Pizza Hut	Papa John's	Domino's
Little Caesar's	Domino's	Domino's	Godfather's	Pizza Hut	Papa John's
Pizza Hut	Pizza Hut	Papa John's	Papa John's	Godfather's	Papa John's
Domino's					

a Find the frequency distribution and relative frequency distribution for these data.
b Construct a percentage bar chart for these data.
c Construct a percentage pie chart for these data.
d Which restaurant is most popular with these students? Least popular?

Business Improvement Icons

To emphasize the text's theme of business improvement, **BI** icons are placed in the page margins to identify when an important business conclusion has been reached using statistical analysis. Each conclusion is highlighted in yellow.

EXAMPLE 3.5 The Payment Time Case

The MINITAB output in Figure 3.6 gives a histogram of the 65 payment times, and the MINITAB output in Figure 3.7 tells us that the mean and the median of the payment times are 18.108 days and 17 days, respectively. Because the histogram is not highly skewed to the right, the sample mean is not much greater than the sample median. Therefore, using the mean as our measure of central tendency, we estimate that the mean payment time of all bills using the new billing system is 18.108 days. This is substantially less than the typical payment time of 39 days that had been experienced using the old billing system.

Boxed Equations, Formulas and Definitions

Each chapter contains easy-to-find boxes that will help students identify and understand the key ideas in the chapter.

A **frequency distribution** is a table that summarizes the number (or **frequency**) of items in each of several nonoverlapping classes.

A t Test about a Population Mean: σ Unknown

Define the test statistic

$$t = \frac{\bar{x} - \mu_0}{s/\sqrt{n}}$$

and assume that the population sampled is normally distributed. We can test H_0: $\mu = \mu_0$ versus a particular alternative hypothesis at level of significance α by using the appropriate critical value rule, or, equivalently, the corresponding p-value.

Alternative Hypothesis	Critical Value Rule: Reject H_0 If	p-Value (Reject H_0 If p-Value $< \alpha$)
H_a: $\mu > \mu_0$	$t > t_\alpha$	The area under the t distribution curve to the right of t
H_a: $\mu < \mu_0$	$t < -t_\alpha$	The area under the t distribution curve to the left of t
H_a: $\mu \neq \mu_0$	$\lvert t \rvert > t_{\alpha/2}$—that is, $t > t_{\alpha/2}$ or $t < -t_{\alpha/2}$	Twice the area under the t distribution curve to the right of $\lvert t \rvert$

Here t_α, $t_{\alpha/2}$, and the p-values are based on $n - 1$ degrees of freedom.

STUDENT LEARNING?

Chapter Ending Material

The end of each chapter includes a chapter summary, a comprehensive glossary of terms, and important formula references.

Chapter Summary

We began this chapter by presenting and comparing several measures of **central tendency.** We defined the **population mean,** and we saw how to estimate the population mean by using a **sample mean.** We also defined the **median** and **mode,** and we compared the mean, median, and mode for symmetrical distributions and for distributions that are skewed to the right or left. We then studied measures of **variation** (or *spread*). We defined the **range, variance,** and **standard deviation,** and we saw how to estimate a population variance and standard deviation by using a sample. We learned that a good way to interpret the standard deviation when a population is (approximately) normally distributed is to use the **Empirical Rule,** and we studied **Chebyshev's Theorem,** which gives us intervals containing reasonably large fractions of

the population units no matter what the population's shape might be. We also saw that, when a data set is highly skewed, it is best to use **percentiles** and **quartiles** to measure variation, and we learned how to construct a **box-and-whiskers plot** by using the quartiles.

After learning how to measure and depict central tendency and variability, we presented several optional topics. First, we discussed several numerical measures of the relationship between two variables. These included the **covariance,** the **correlation coefficient,** and the **least squares line.** We then introduced the concept of a **weighted mean** and also explained how to compute descriptive statistics for **grouped data.** Finally, we showed how to calculate the **geometric mean** and demonstrated its interpretation.

Glossary of Terms

box-and-whiskers display (box plot): A graphical portrayal of a data set that depicts both the central tendency and variability of the data. It is constructed using Q_1, M_d, and Q_3. (page 138)
central tendency: A term referring to the middle of a population or sample of measurements. (page 115)
Chebyshev's Theorem: A theorem that (for any population) allows us to find an interval that contains a specified percentage of the individual measurements in the population. (page 131)

coefficient of variation: A quantity that measures the variation of a population or sample relative to its mean. (page 133)
correlation coefficient: A numerical measure of the linear relationship between two variables that is between −1 and 1. (page 146)
covariance: A numerical measure of the linear relationship between two variables that depends upon the units in which the variables are measured. (page 145)

Excel/MINITAB/ MegaStat® Tutorials

The end-of-chapter appendices contain helpful tutorials that teach students about the use of Excel, MINITAB, and MegaStat. These tutorials include step-by-step instructions for entering and saving data, retrieving information, and performing statistical analysis.

Construct a scatter plot of sales volume versus advertising expenditure as in Figure 2.24 on page 81 (data file: SalesPlot.xlsx):

- Enter the advertising and sales data in Table 2.20 on page 81 into columns A and B—advertising expenditures in column A with label "Ad Exp" and sales values in column B with label "Sales Vol." **Note: The variable to be graphed on the horizontal axis must be in the first column (that is, the left-most column) and the variable to be graphed on the vertical axis must be in the second column (that is, the rightmost column).**
- Click in the range of data to be graphed, or select the entire range of the data to be graphed.
- Select **Insert : Scatter : Scatter with only Markers**
- The scatter plot will be displayed in a graphics window. Move the plot to a chart sheet and edit appropriately.

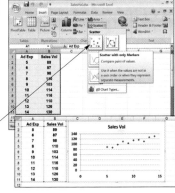

There are two software tools included on the Student CD that are referred to in the text: *MegaStat for Excel 2007* and *Visual Statistics 2.2*.

MegaStat®

MegaStat is a full-featured Excel add-in that is included on the Student CD with this text. It performs statistical analyses within an Excel workbook. It does basic functions such as descriptive statistics, frequency distributions, and probability calculations as well as hypothesis testing, ANOVA, and regression.

MegaStat output is carefully formatted and ease-of-use features include Auto Expand for quick data selection and Auto Label detect. Since MegaStat is easy to use, students can focus on learning statistics without being distracted by the software. MegaStat is always available from Excel's main menu. Selecting a menu item pops up a dialog box. A normal distribution is shown here. MegaStat works with all recent versions of Excel including Excel 2007.

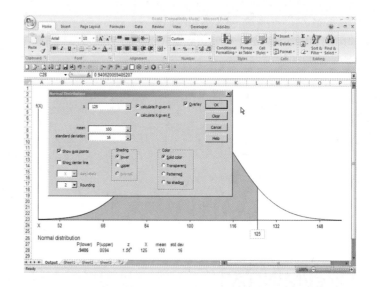

Visual Statistics

Visual Statistics 2.2 by Doane, Mathieson, and Tracy is a software program for teaching and learning statistics concepts. It is unique in that it allows students to learn the concepts through interactive experimentation and visualization. There is a Visual Statistics (VS) icon included in the margins in some chapters to point out topics where the student can enrich his or her learning by looking at the related material in the Visual Statistics chapter.

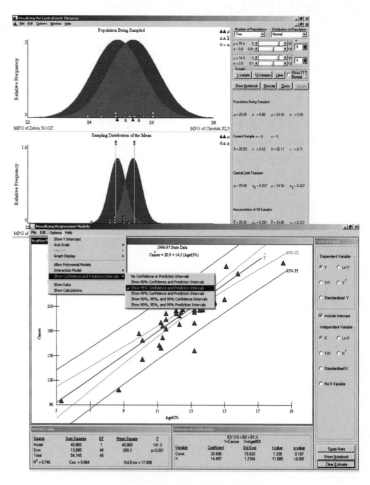

FOR USE WITH THIS TEXT?

MINITAB®/SPSS®/JMP®

Minitab® Student Version 14, SPSS® Student Version 15, and JMP Student Edition 6 are software tools that are available to help students solve the business statistics exercises in the text. Each is available in the student version and can be packaged with any McGraw-Hill business statistics text.

McGraw-Hill Connect™ Business Statistics

McGraw-Hill *Connect Business Statistics* is an online assignment and assessment system customized to the text and available as an option for students. With *Connect Business Statistics,* instructors can deliver assignments, quizzes, and tests online. The system utilizes the exercises from the text both in a static one-problem-at-a-time fashion as well as algorithmically where problems generate multiple data possibilities and answers. In addition, instructors can edit existing questions and author entirely new problems.

You choose or create the problems. Assignments are graded automatically, and the results are stored in your private gradebook. You can track individual student performance by question, assignment, or in comparison to the rest of the class. Detailed grade reports are easily integrated with Learning Management Systems, such as WebCT and Blackboard.

McGraw-Hill Connect Business Statistics is also available with the interactive online version of the text—*Connect Plus Business Statistics.* Like *Connect Business Statistics, Connect Plus Business Statistics* provides students with online assignments and assessments, plus 24/7 online access to an eBook, an identical, online edition of the printed text, to aid them in successfully completing their work, wherever and whenever they choose.

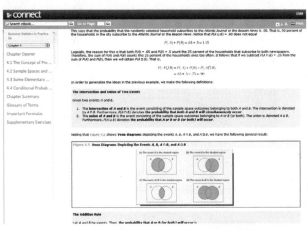

ALEKS®

ALEKS is an assessment and learning system that provides individualized instruction in Business Statistics. Available from McGraw-Hill/Irwin over the World Wide Web, ALEKS delivers precise assessments of students' knowledge, guides them in the selection of appropriate new study material, and records their progress toward mastery of goals.

ALEKS interacts with students much as a skilled human tutor would, moving between explanation and practice as needed, correcting and analyzing errors, defining terms and changing topics on request. By accurately assessing their knowledge, ALEKS focuses precisely on what to learn next, helping them master the course content more quickly and easily.

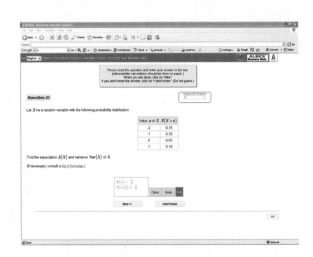

TO AID STUDENT LEARNING?

Save money. Go Green. McGraw-Hill eBooks

Green . . . it's on everybody's mind these days. It's not only about saving trees, it's also about saving money. At 55% of the bookstore price, McGraw-Hill eBooks are an eco-friendly and cost-saving alternative to the traditional printed textbook. So, you do some good for the environment and . . . you do some good for your wallet.

CourseSmart

CourseSmart is a new way to find and buy eTextbooks. CourseSmart has the largest selection of eTextbooks available anywhere, offering thousands of the most commonly adopted textbooks from a wide variety of higher education publishers. CourseSmart eTextbooks are available in one standard online reader with full text search, notes and highlighting, and email tools for sharing notes between classmates. Visit www.CourseSmart.com for more information on ordering.

Online Learning Center: www.mhhe.com/bowermaness3e

The Online Learning Center (OLC) is the text website with online content for both students and instructors.

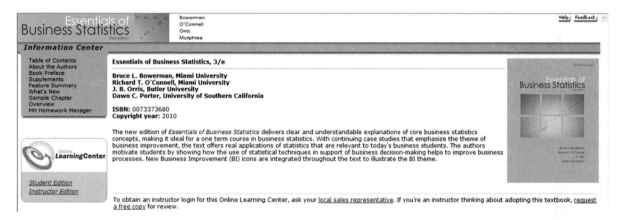

Instructor Content

- Instructor's Manual
- Test Bank
- PowerPoint
- Image Library
- Visual Statistics Walkthrough
- MegaStat User's Guide
- Instructor Updates and Errata

Student Content

- Quizzes
- PowerPoint
- Data Sets
- MegaStat User's Guide
- Appendices
- Updates and Errata
- Screencam Tutorials

WebCT/Blackboard/eCollege

All of the material in the Online Learning Center is also available in portable WebCT, Blackboard, or e-College content "cartridges" provided free to adopters of this text.

Business Statistics Center (BSC): www.mhhe.com/bstat/

The BSC contains links to statistical publications and resources, software downloads, learning aids, statistical websites and databases, and McGraw-Hill/Irwin product websites, and online courses.

WHAT RESOURCES ARE AVAILABLE FOR INSTRUCTORS?

Instructor's Resources CD-ROM (ISBN: 0077246799)

This resource allows instructors to conveniently access the instructor's Solutions Manual, Test Bank in Word and EZ Test formats, Instructor PowerPoint slides, data files, and data sets.

Online Learning Center: www.mhhe.com/bowermaness3e

The Online Learning Center (OLC) provides the instructor with a complete Instructor's Manual in Word format, the complete Test Bank in both Word files and computerized EZ Test format, Instructor PowerPoint slides, text art files, an introduction to ALEKS®, an introduction to McGraw-Hill Connect Business Statistics™, access to the eBook, and more.

EZ Test

All test bank questions are available in an EZ Test electronic format. Included are a number of multiple-choice, true/false, and short-answer questions and problems. The answers to all questions are given, along with a rating of the level of difficulty, Bloom's taxonomy question type, and AACSB knowledge category.

AACSB Statement

The McGraw-Hill Companies is a proud corporate member of AACSB International. Understanding the importance and value of AACSB accreditation, Bowerman/O'Connell/Orris/Murphree *Essentials of Business Statistics 3e* has connected questions in the test bank to the six general knowledge and skill guidelines found in the AACSB standards.

WHAT RESOURCES ARE AVAILABLE FOR STUDENTS?

Student CD-ROM

The Student CD-ROM packaged with each copy of the text includes a number of resources for student self-study and tools for working the exercises in the text. These resources include:

- Data sets
- Visual Statistics
- MegaStat® for Excel 2007

The Online Learning Center contains additional resources for student use, including self quizzes, PowerPoint slides, and Screencam tutorials. The Screencam tutorials provide instruction on using Excel, MegaStat, and Minitab.

Acknowledgments

We wish to thank many people who have helped to make this book a reality. We thank Drena Bowerman, who spent many hours cutting and taping and making trips to the copy shop, so that we could complete the manuscript on time. We thank Professor Steven Huchendorf of the University of Minnesota. Professor Huchendorf provided a substantial number of new exercises for the third edition and helped tremendously in the development and writing of the section on covariance, correlation, and the least squares line in Chapter 3 and the section on normal probability plots in Chapter 6. We thank Professor Patrick Schur of Miami University. Professor Schur did superb work—both for this and previous editions—in providing solutions to the exercises. Professor Schur also provided excellent advice and assistance whenever needed. We thank Professor Dawn Porter of the University of Southern California. Professor Porter, who is the coauthor of *Essentials of Business Statistics, Second Edition,* helped tremendously in the writing of Section 1.5. Although Professor Porter did not work on this third edition, we thank her for her contributions to the second edition and regard her as a valued friend and colleague. We thank Professor Ken Krallman of Miami University, who did a superb job in helping us to write the book's new Excel, MINITAB, and MegaStat appendices. We thank Professor Denise Krallman of Miami University. Professor Krallman developed the test bank and provided sound advice in helping us to improve this edition. We thank Professor Susan Cramer of Miami University. Professor Cramer also provided sound advice in helping us to improve this edition. We thank Professor Michael L. Hand of Willamette University, who is a coauthor of the second edition of *Business Statistics in Practice*. Although Professor Hand did not work on this essentials text, we thank him for his contributions to the former book and regard him as a valued friend and colleague. Finally, we thank Professor Anne Koehler of Miami University. Professor Koehler wrote the original version of the MINITAB and Excel appendices included in the text. We cannot thank Professor Koehler enough for her selfless work, which is a hallmark of her career.

We also wish to thank the people at McGraw-Hill/Irwin for their dedication to this book. These people include executive editor Steve Schuetz, who is an extremely helpful resource to the authors; executive editor Dick Hercher, who persuaded us initially to publish with McGraw-Hill/Irwin and who continues to offer sound advice and support; senior developmental editor Wanda Zeman, who has shown great dedication in all of her work (Wanda's many excellent ideas and timeless attention to detail have been instrumental in the improvement of this book); and senior project manager Harvey Yep, who has very capably and diligently guided this book through its production, and who has been a tremendous help to the authors. We also thank our former executive editor Scott Isenberg for the tremendous help he has given us in developing all of our McGraw-Hill business statistics books.

Many reviewers have contributed to this book, and we are grateful to all of them. They include

Ajay K. Aggarwal, Millsaps College

Sung K. Ahn, Washington State University

Eugene Allevato, Woodbury University

Mostafa S. Aminzadeh, Towson University

Randy J. Anderson, California State University–Fresno

Lihui Bai, Valparaiso University

Robert J Banis, University of Missouri–St. Louis

Ron Barnes, University of Houston–Downtown

John D. Barrett, University of North Alabama

Jeffrey C. Bauer, University of Cincinnati–Clermont

Imad Benjelloun, Delaware Valley College

Doris Bennett, Jacksonville State University

Mirjeta S. Beqiri, Gonzaga University

Richard Birkenbeuel, University of Dubuque

Arnab Bisi, Purdue University

Mary Jo Boehms, Jackson State Community College

Pamela A. Boger, Ohio University–Athens

Stephen J. Bukowy, University of North Carolina–Pembroke

Philip E. Burian, Colorado Technical University–Sioux Falls

Derek Burnett, North Central Association of Colleges and Schools

Scott Callan, Bentley College

Giorgio Canarella, California State University–Los Angeles

Margaret Capen, East Carolina University

Priscilla Chaffe-Stengel, California State University–Fresno

Moula Cherikh, Virginia State University

Ali A. Choudhry, Florida International University

Richard Cleary, Bentley College

Bruce Cooil, Vanderbilt University

Mark Cotton, Park University

Sam Cousley, University of Mississippi

Teresa A Dalton, University of Denver

Nit Dasgupta, University of Wisconsin–Eau Claire

Nandita Das, Wilkes University

Gerald DeHondt, Oakland University

Michael DeSantis, Alvernia College

Jay Devore, California Polytechnic State University

Boyan N. Dimitrov, Kettering University

Cassandra DiRienzo, Elon University

Anne Drougas, Dominican University

Jerry W. Dunn, Southwestern Oklahoma State University

Hossein Eftekari, University of Wisconsin–River Falls

Hammou Elbarmi, Baruch College

Erick M. Elder, University of Arkansas–Little Rock

Hamid Falatoon, University of Redlands

Soheila Fardanesh, Towson University

Nicholas R. Farnum, California State University–Fullerton

James Flynn, Cleveland State University

Lillian Fok, University of New Orleans

Tom Fox, Cleveland State Community College

Daniel Friesen, Midwestern State University

Robert Gallagher, Regis College

Charles A. Gates, Jr., Olivet Nazarene University

Jose Gavidia, College of Charleston

Linda S. Ghent, Eastern Illinois University

Allen Gibson, Seton Hall University

Scott D. Gilbert, Southern Illinois University

Michael R. Gordinier, Washington University–St. Louis

Nicholas Gorgievski, Nichols College

Daesung Ha, Marshall University

TeWhan Hahn, University of Idaho

Salih A. Hakeem, North Carolina Central University

Nicholas G. Hall, Ohio State University

Jamey Halleck, Marshall University

Clifford B. Hawley, West Virginia University

Rhonda L. Hensley, North Carolina A&T State University

Mickey Hepner, University of Central Oklahoma

Christiana Hilmer, San Diego State University

Zhimin Huang, Adelphi University

C. Thomas Innis, University of Cincinnati

Paul H. Jacques, Western Carolina University

Chun Jin, Central Connecticut State University

Craig Johnson, Brighan Young University

Nancy K. Keith, Missouri State University

Jong Kim, Portland State University

Risa Kumazawa, Georgia Southern University

Marcia J. Lambert, Pitt Community College–Greenville

Andrea Lange, Brooklyn College

David A. Larson, University of South Alabama

John Lawrence, California State University–Fullerton

Lee Lawton, University of St. Thomas

Bryan Lee, Missouri Western State University

John D. Levendis, Loyola University–New Orleans

Hui Li, Eastern Illinois University

Barbara Libby, Walden University

Richard S. Linder, Ohio Wesleyan University

David W. Little, High Point University

Edward Markowski, Old Dominion University

Christopher B. Marme, Augustana College

Mamata Marme, Augustana College

Rutilio Martinez, University of Northern Colorado

Jerrold H. May, University of Pittsburgh

Ralph D. May, Southwestern Oklahoma State University

Lee McClain, Western Washington University

Richard A. McGowan, Boston College

Christy McLendon, University of New Orleans

John M. Miller, Sam Houston State University

Nelson C. Modeste, Tennessee State University

Robert Mogull, California State University–Sacramento

Jason Molitierno, Sacred Heart University

Daniel Monchuck, University of Southern Mississippi

Mihail Motzev, Walla Walla College

Tariq Mughal, University of Utah

Thomas Naugler, Johns Hopkins University

Tapan K. Nayak, George Washington University

Quinton J. Nottingham, Virginia Tech University

Ceyhun Ozgur, Valparaiso University

Edward A. Pappanastos, Troy University

Linda M. Penas, University of California–Riverside

Dane K. Peterson, Missouri State University–Springfield

Michael D. Polomsky, Cleveland State University

Thomas J. Porebski, Triton Community College

Tammy Prater, Alabama State University

Robert S. Pred, Temple University

John Preminger, Tulane University

Bharatendra Rai, University of Massachusetts–Dartmouth

Gioconda Quesada, College of Charleston

Sunil Ramlall, University of St. Thomas

Steven Rein, California Polytechnic State University

Donna Retzlaff-Roberts, University of South Alabama

David Ronen, University of Missouri–St. Louis

Christopher M. Rump, Bowling Green State University

Said E. Said, East Carolina University

Fatollah Salimian, Salisbury University

Hedayeh Samavati, Purdue University–Fort Wayne

Yvonne Sandoval, Pima Community College

Sunil Sapra, California State University–Los Angeles

Patrick J. Schur, Miami University

Carlton Scott, University of California–Irvine

William L. Seaver, University of Tennessee

Scott Seipel, Middle Tennessee State University

Sankara N. Sethuraman, Augusta State University

Sunit N. Shah, University of Virginia

Kevin Shanahan, University of Texas–Tyler

Arkudy Shemyakin, University of St. Thomas

John L. Sherry, Waubonsee Community College

Charlie Shi, Daiblo Valley College

Joyce Shotick, Bradley University

Mike Shurden, Lander University

Plamen Simeonov, University of Houston Downtown

Philip Sirianni, State University of New York–Binghamton

Rafael Solis, California State University–Fresno

Toni M. Somers, Wayne State University

Erl Sorensen, Bentley College

Donald Soucy, University of North Carolina–Pembroke

Ronald L. Spicer, Colorado Technical University–Sioux Falls

Mitchell Spiegel, Johns Hopkins University

Arun Srinivasan, Indiana University–Southeast

Timothy Staley, Keller Graduate School of Management

David Stoffer, University of Pittsburgh

Rungrudee Suetorsak, State University of New York–Fredonia

Yi Sun, California State University–San Marcos

Courtney Sykes, Colorado State University

Lee Tangedahl, University of Montana

Dharma S. Thiruvaiyaru, Augusta State University

Patrick Thompson, University of Florida

Emmanuelle Vaast, Long Island University

Lee J. Van Scyoc, University of Wisconsin–Oshkosh

James O. van Speybroeck, St. Ambrose University

Raydel Tullous, University of Texas–San Antonio

Alexander Wagner, Salem State College

Ed Wallace, Malcolm X College

Elizabeth J. Wark, Springfield College

Allen Webster, Bradley University

Thomas Wier, Northeastern State University

Susan Wolcott-Hanes, Binghamton University

Louis A. Woods, University of North Florida

Mari Yetimyan, San Jose State University

William F. Younkin, Miami University

Oliver Yu, Santa Clara University

Jack Yurkiewicz, Pace University

Duo Zhang, University of Missouri–Rolla

Xiaowei Zhu, University of Wisconsin–Milwaukee

Zhen Zhu, University of Central Oklahoma

We also wish to thank the error checkers, Jacquelynne McLellan, Frostburg University, Lawrence Moore, Alleghany College of Maryland, and Lou Patille, Keller Graduate School of Management, who were very helpful. Most importantly, we wish to thank our families for their acceptance, unconditional love, and support.

Essentials of Business Statistics

THIRD EDITION

An Introduction to Business Statistics

Chapter Outline

1.1 Populations and Samples

1.2 Selecting a Random Sample

1.3 Ratio, Interval, Ordinal, and Nominative Scales of Measurement (Optional)

1.4 An Introduction to Survey Sampling (Optional)

1.5 More About Data Acquisition and Survey Sampling (Optional)

The subject of **statistics** involves the study of how to collect, summarize, and interpret data. **Data** are numerical facts and figures from which conclusions can be drawn. Such conclusions are important to the decision-making processes of many professions and organizations. For example, government officials use conclusions drawn from the latest data on unemployment and inflation to make policy decisions. Financial planners use recent trends in stock market prices to make investment decisions. Businesses decide which products to develop and market by using data that reveal consumer preferences. Production supervisors use manufacturing data to evaluate, control, and improve product quality. Politicians rely on data from public opinion polls to formulate legislation and to devise campaign strategies. Physicians and hospitals use data on the effectiveness of drugs and surgical procedures to provide patients with the best possible treatment.

In this chapter we begin to see how we collect and analyze data. As we proceed through the chapter, we introduce several case studies. These case studies (and others to be introduced later) are revisited throughout later chapters as we learn the statistical methods needed to analyze the cases. Briefly, we will begin to study three cases:

The Cell Phone Case. A bank estimates its cellular phone costs and decides whether to outsource management of its wireless resources by studying the calling patterns of its employees.

The Marketing Research Case. A bottling company investigates consumer reaction to a new bottle design for one of its popular soft drinks.

The Car Mileage Case. To determine if it qualifies for a federal tax credit based on fuel economy, an automaker studies the gas mileage of its new midsize model.

1.1 Populations and Samples ● ● ●

Statistical methods are very useful for learning about populations, which can be defined in various ways. We begin with the following definition:

A **population** is a set of existing units (usually people, objects, or events).

Examples of populations include (1) all of last year's graduates of Dartmouth College's Master of Business Administration program, (2) all consumers who bought a cellular phone last year, (3) all accounts receivable invoices accumulated last year by the Procter & Gamble company, (4) all Buick LaCrosses that were produced last year, and (5) all fires reported last month to the Tulsa, Oklahoma, fire department.

We usually focus on studying one or more characteristics of the population units.

Any characteristic of a population unit is called a **variable.**

For instance, if we study the starting salaries of last year's graduates of the Dartmouth College MBA program, the variable of interest is starting salary. If we study the gasoline mileages obtained in city driving by last year's Buick LaCrosse, the variable of interest is gasoline mileage in city driving.

We carry out a **measurement** to assign a **value** of a variable to each population unit. For example, we might measure the starting salary of an MBA graduate to the nearest dollar. Or we might measure the gasoline mileage obtained by a car in city driving to the nearest one-tenth of a mile per gallon by conducting a mileage test on a driving course prescribed by the Environmental Protection Agency (EPA). If the possible measurements are numbers that represent quantities (that is, "how much" or "how many"), then the variable is said to be **quantitative.** For example, starting salary and gasoline mileage are both quantitative. However, if we simply record into which of several categories a population unit falls, then the variable is said to be **qualitative** or **categorical.** Examples of categorical variables include (1) a person's gender, (2) the make of an automobile, and (3) whether a person who purchases a product is satisfied with the product.[1]

---

[1] Optional Section 1.3 discusses two types of quantitative variables (ratio and interval) and two types of qualitative variables (ordinal and nominative).

If we measure each and every population unit, we have a **population of measurements** (sometimes called **observations**). If the population is small, it is reasonable to do this. For instance, if 150 students graduated last year from the Dartmouth College MBA program, it might be feasible to survey the graduates and to record all of their starting salaries. In general:

> If we examine all of the population measurements, we say that we are conducting a **census** of the population.

Often the population that we wish to study is very large, and it is too time-consuming or costly to conduct a census. In such a situation, we select and analyze a subset (or portion) of the population units.

> A **sample** is a subset of the units in a population.

For example, suppose that 8,742 students graduated last year from a large state university. It would probably be too time-consuming to take a census of the population of all of their starting salaries. Therefore, we would select a sample of graduates, and we would obtain and record their starting salaries. When we measure the units in a sample, we say that we have a **sample of measurements.**

We often wish to describe a population or sample.

> **Descriptive statistics** is the science of describing the important aspects of a set of measurements.

As an example, if we are studying a set of starting salaries, we might wish to describe (1) how large or small they tend to be, (2) what a typical salary might be, and (3) how much the salaries differ from each other.

When the population of interest is small and we can conduct a census of the population, we will be able to directly describe the important aspects of the population measurements. However, if the population is large and we need to select a sample from it, then we use what we call **statistical inference.**

> **Statistical inference** is the science of using a sample of measurements to make generalizations about the important aspects of a population of measurements.

For instance, we might use a sample of starting salaries to **estimate** the important aspects of a population of starting salaries. In the next section, we begin to look at how statistical inference is carried out.

1.2 Selecting a Random Sample ● ● ●

Random samples   If the information contained in a sample is to accurately reflect the population under study, the sample should be **randomly selected** from the population. To intuitively illustrate random sampling, suppose that a small company employs 15 people and wishes to randomly select two of them to attend a convention. To make the random selections, we number the employees from 1 to 15, and we place in a hat 15 identical slips of paper numbered from 1 to 15. We thoroughly mix the slips of paper in the hat and, blindfolded, choose one. The number on the chosen slip of paper identifies the first randomly selected employee. Then, still blindfolded, we choose another slip of paper from the hat. The number on the second slip identifies the second randomly selected employee.

Of course, it is impractical to carry out such a procedure when the population is very large. It is easier to use a *random number table*. To show how to use such a table, we must more formally define a random sample.[2]

> A **random sample** is selected so that, on each selection from the population, every unit remaining in the population on that selection has the same chance of being chosen.

To understand this definition, first note that we can randomly select a sample *with or without replacement.* If we **sample with replacement,** we place the unit chosen on any particular selection back into the population. Thus we give this unit a chance to be chosen on any succeeding

---

[2]Actually, there are several different kinds of random samples. The type we will define is sometimes called a *simple random sample.* For brevity's sake, however, we will use the term *random sample.*

selection. In such a case, all of the units in the population remain as candidates to be chosen for each and every selection. Randomly choosing two employees with replacement to attend a convention would make no sense because we wish to send two different employees to the convention. If we **sample without replacement,** we do not place the unit chosen on a particular selection back into the population. Thus we do not give this unit a chance to be selected on any succeeding selection. In this case, the units remaining as candidates for a particular selection are all of the units in the population except for those that have previously been selected. **It is best to sample without replacement.** Intuitively, because we will use the sample to learn about the population, sampling without replacement will give us the fullest possible look at the population. This is true because choosing the sample without replacement guarantees that all of the units in the sample will be different (and that we are looking at as many different units from the population as possible).

In the following example, we illustrate how to use a random number table, or computer-generated random numbers, to select a random sample.

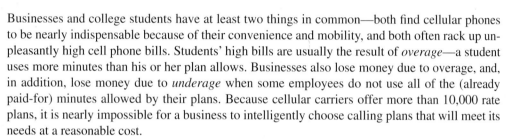

Businesses and college students have at least two things in common—both find cellular phones to be nearly indispensable because of their convenience and mobility, and both often rack up unpleasantly high cell phone bills. Students' high bills are usually the result of *overage*—a student uses more minutes than his or her plan allows. Businesses also lose money due to overage, and, in addition, lose money due to *underage* when some employees do not use all of the (already paid-for) minutes allowed by their plans. Because cellular carriers offer more than 10,000 rate plans, it is nearly impossible for a business to intelligently choose calling plans that will meet its needs at a reasonable cost.

Rising cell phone costs have forced companies having large numbers of cellular users to hire services to manage their cellular and other wireless resources. These cellular management services use sophisticated software and mathematical models to choose cost-efficient cell phone plans for their clients. One such firm, MobileSense Inc. of Westlake Village, California, specializes in automated wireless cost management. According to Doug L. Stevens, Vice President of Sales and Marketing at MobileSense, cell phone carriers count on overage and underage to deliver almost half of their revenues. As a result, a company's typical cost of cell phone use can easily exceed 25 cents per minute. However, Mr. Stevens explains that by using MobileSense automated cost management to select calling plans, this cost can be reduced to 12 cents per minute or less.

In this case we consider a bank that wishes to decide whether to hire a cellular management service to choose its employees' calling plans. While the bank has over 10,000 employees on a variety of calling plans, the cellular management service suggests that by studying the calling patterns of cellular users on 500-minute plans, the bank can accurately assess whether its cell phone costs can be substantially reduced.

The bank has 2,136 employees on a 500-minute-per-month plan with a monthly cost of $50. The overage charge is 40 cents per minute, and there are additional charges for long distance and roaming. It would be extremely time-consuming to analyze in detail the cell phone bills of all 2,136 employees. Therefore, the bank will estimate its cellular costs for the 500-minute plan by analyzing the cell phone bills of 100 randomly selected employees on this plan. According to the cellular management service, if the cellular cost per minute for the random sample of 100 employees is over 18 cents per minute, the bank should benefit from automated cellular management of its calling plans.

In order to randomly select the sample of 100 cell phone users, the bank will make a numbered list of the 2,136 users on the 500-minute plan. This list is called a **frame.** The bank can then use a **random number table,** such as Table 1.1(a), to select the needed sample. To see how this is done, notice that any single-digit number in the table is assumed to have been randomly selected from the digits 0 to 9. Any two-digit number in the table is assumed to have been randomly selected from the numbers 00 to 99. Any three-digit number is assumed to have been randomly

[3]The authors would like to thank Mr. Doug L. Stevens, Vice President of Sales and Marketing, at MobileSense Inc., Westlake Village, California, for his help in developing this case.

TABLE 1.1   Random Numbers

(a) A portion of a random number table

33276	85590	79936	56865	05859	90106	78188
03427	90511	69445	18663	72695	52180	90322
92737	27156	33488	36320	17617	30015	74952
85689	20285	52267	67689	93394	01511	89868
08178	74461	13916	47564	81056	97735	90707
51259	63990	16308	60756	92144	49442	40719
60268	44919	19885	55322	44819	01188	55157
94904	01915	04146	18594	29852	71585	64951
58586	17752	14513	83149	98736	23495	35749
09998	19509	06691	76988	13602	51851	58104
14346	61666	30168	90229	04734	59193	32812
74103	15227	25306	76468	26384	58151	44592
24200	64161	38005	94342	28728	35806	22851
87308	07684	00256	45834	15398	46557	18510
07351	86679	92420	60952	61280	50001	94953

(b) MINITAB output of 100 different, four-digit random numbers between 1 and 2136

705	1131	169	1703	1709	609
1990	766	1286	1977	222	43
1007	1902	1209	2091	1742	1152
111	69	2049	1448	659	338
1732	1650	7	388	613	1477
838	272	1227	154	18	320
1053	1466	2087	265	2107	1992
582	1787	2098	1581	397	1099
757	1699	567	1255	1959	407
354	1567	1533	1097	1299	277
663	40	585	1486	1021	532
1629	182	372	1144	1569	1981
1332	1500	743	1262	1759	955
1832	378	728	1102	667	1885
514	1128	1046	116	1160	1333
831	2036	918	1535	660	
928	1257	1468	503	468	

selected from the numbers 000 to 999, and so forth. Note that the table entries are segmented into groups of five to make the table easier to read. Because the total number of cell phone users on the 500-minute plan (2,136) is a four-digit number, we arbitrarily select any set of four digits in the table (we have circled these digits). This number, which is 0511, identifies the first randomly selected user. Then, moving in any direction from the 0511 (up, down, right, or left—it does not matter which), we select additional sets of four digits. These succeeding sets of digits identify additional randomly selected users. Here we arbitrarily move down from 0511 in the table. The first seven sets of four digits we obtain are

$$0511 \quad 7156 \quad 0285 \quad 4461 \quad 3990 \quad 4919 \quad 1915$$

(See Table 1.1(a)—these numbers are enclosed in a rectangle.) Since there are no users numbered 7156, 4461, 3990, or 4919 (remember only 2,136 users are on the 500-minute plan), we ignore these numbers. This implies that the first three randomly selected users are those numbered 0511, 0285, and 1915. Continuing this procedure, we can obtain the entire random sample of 100 users. Notice that, because we are sampling without replacement, we should ignore any set of four digits previously selected from the random number table.

While using a random number table is one way to select a random sample, this approach has a disadvantage that is illustrated by the current situation. Specifically, since most four-digit random numbers are not between 0001 and 2136, obtaining 100 different, four-digit random numbers between 0001 and 2136 will require ignoring a large number of random numbers in the random number table, and we will in fact need to use a random number table that is larger than Table 1.1(a). Although larger random number tables are readily available in books of mathematical and statistical tables, a good alternative is to use a computer software package, which can generate random numbers that are between whatever values we specify. For example, Table 1.1(b) gives the MINITAB output of 100 different, four-digit random numbers that are between 0001 and 2136 (note that the "leading 0's" are not included in these four-digit numbers). If used, the random numbers in Table 1.1(b) identify the 100 employees that should form the random sample.

After the random sample of 100 employees is selected, the number of cellular minutes used by each employee during the month (the employee's *cellular usage*) is found and recorded. The 100 cellular-usage figures are given in Table 1.2. Looking at this table, we can see that there is substantial overage and underage—many employees used far more than 500 minutes, while many others failed to use all of the 500 minutes allowed by their plan. In Chapter 3 we will use these 100 usage figures to estimate the cellular cost per minute for the 500-minute plan.

TABLE 1.2	A Sample of Cellular Usages (in minutes) for 100 Randomly Selected Employees								
● CellUse										
75	485	37	547	753	93	897	694	797	477
654	578	504	670	490	225	509	247	597	173
496	553	0	198	507	157	672	296	774	479
0	822	705	814	20	513	546	801	721	273
879	433	420	521	648	41	528	359	367	948
511	704	535	585	341	530	216	512	491	0
542	562	49	505	461	496	241	624	885	259
571	338	503	529	737	444	372	555	290	830
719	120	468	730	853	18	479	144	24	513
482	683	212	418	399	376	323	173	669	611

Approximately random samples In general, to take a random sample we must have a list, or **frame,** of all the population units. This is needed because we must be able to number the population units in order to make random selections from them (by, for example, using a random number table). In Example 1.1, where we wished to study a population of 2,136 cell phone users who were on the bank's 500-minute cellular plan, we were able to produce a frame (list) of the population units. Therefore, we were able to select a random sample. Sometimes, however, it is not possible to list and thus number all the units in a population. In such a situation we often select a **systematic sample,** which approximates a random sample.

EXAMPLE 1.2 The Marketing Research Case: Rating a New Bottle Design[4]

The design of a package or bottle can have an important effect on a company's bottom line. For example, an article in the September 16, 2004, issue of *USA Today* reported that the introduction of a contoured 1.5-liter bottle for Coke drinks (including the reduced-calorie soft drink Coke C2) played a major role in Coca-Cola's failure to meet third-quarter earnings forecasts in 2004. According to the article, Coke's biggest bottler, Coca-Cola Enterprises, "said it would miss expectations because of the 1.5-liter bottle and the absence of common 2-liter and 12-pack sizes for C2 in supermarkets."[5]

In this case a brand group is studying whether changes should be made in the bottle design for a popular soft drink. To research consumer reaction to a new design, the brand group will use the "mall intercept method,"[6] in which shoppers at a large metropolitan shopping mall are intercepted and asked to participate in a consumer survey. Each shopper will be exposed to the new bottle design and asked to rate the bottle image. Bottle image will be measured by combining consumers' responses to five items, with each response measured using a 7-point "Likert scale." The five items and the scale of possible responses are shown in Figure 1.1. Here, since we describe the least favorable response and the most favorable response (and we do not describe the responses between them), we say that the scale is "anchored" at its ends. Responses to the five items will be summed to obtain a composite score for each respondent. It follows that the minimum composite score possible is 5 and the maximum composite score possible is 35. Furthermore, experience has shown that the smallest acceptable composite score for a successful bottle design is 25.

In this situation, it is not possible to list and number each and every shopper at the mall while the study is being conducted. Consequently, we cannot use random numbers (as we did in the cell phone case) to obtain a random sample of shoppers. Instead, we can select a **systematic sample.** To do this, every 100th shopper passing a specified location in the mall will be invited to participate in the survey. Here, selecting every 100th shopper is arbitrary—we could select

[4]This case was motivated by an example in the book *Essentials of Marketing Research* by W. R. Dillon, T. J. Madden, and N. H. Firtle (Burr Ridge, IL: Richard D. Irwin, 1993). The authors also wish to thank Professor L. Unger of the Department of Marketing at Miami University for helpful discussions concerning how this type of marketing study would be carried out.

[5]Theresa Howard, "Coke Says Earnings Will Come Up Short," *USA Today,* September 16, 2004, p. 801.

[6]This is a commonly used research design. For example, see the Burke Marketing Research website at http://burke.com/about/inc_background.htm, Burke Marketing Research, March 26, 2005.

FIGURE 1.1　**The Bottle Design Survey Instrument**

Please circle the response that most accurately describes whether you agree or disagree with each statement about the bottle you have examined.

Statement	Strongly Disagree						Strongly Agree
The size of this bottle is convenient.	1	2	3	4	5	6	7
The contoured shape of this bottle is easy to handle.	1	2	3	4	5	6	7
The label on this bottle is easy to read.	1	2	3	4	5	6	7
This bottle is easy to open.	1	2	3	4	5	6	7
Based on its overall appeal, I like this bottle design.	1	2	3	4	5	6	7

TABLE 1.3　**A Sample of Bottle Design Ratings (Composite Scores for a Systematic Sample of 60 Shoppers)**
🌑 Design

34	33	33	29	26	33	28	25	32	33
32	25	27	33	22	27	32	33	32	29
24	30	20	34	31	32	30	35	33	31
32	28	30	31	31	33	29	27	34	31
31	28	33	31	32	28	26	29	32	34
32	30	34	32	30	30	32	31	29	33

every 200th, every 300th, and so forth. By selecting every 100th shopper, it is probably reasonable to believe that the responses of the survey participants are not related. Therefore, it is reasonable to assume that the sampled shoppers obtained by the systematic sampling process make up an *approximate* random sample.

During a Tuesday afternoon and evening, a sample of 60 shoppers is selected by using the systematic sampling process. Each shopper is asked to rate the bottle design by responding to the five items in Figure 1.1, and a composite score is calculated for each shopper. The 60 composite scores obtained are given in Table 1.3. Since these scores range from 20 to 35, we might infer that *most* of the shoppers at the mall on the Tuesday afternoon and evening of the study would rate the new bottle design between 20 and 35. Furthermore, since 57 of the 60 composite scores are at least 25, we might estimate that the proportion of all shoppers at the mall on the Tuesday afternoon and evening who would give the bottle design a composite score of at least 25 is $57/60 = .95$. That is, we estimate that 95 percent of the shoppers would give the bottle design a composite score of at least 25.

In Chapter 3 we will see how to estimate a typical composite score, and we will further analyze the composite scores in Table 1.3.

In some situations, we need to decide whether a sample taken from one population can be employed to make statistical inferences about another, related population. Often logical reasoning is used to do this. For instance, we might reason that the bottle design ratings given by shoppers at the mall on the Tuesday afternoon and evening of the research study would be representative of the ratings given by (1) shoppers at the same mall at other times, (2) shoppers at other malls, and (3) consumers in general. However, if we have no data or other information to back up this reasoning, making such generalizations is dangerous. In practice, marketing research firms choose locations and sampling times that data and experience indicate will produce a representative cross-section of consumers. To simplify our presentation, we will assume that this has been done in the bottle design case. Therefore, we will suppose that it is reasonable to use the 60 bottle design ratings in Table 1.3 to make statistical inferences about *all consumers.*

To conclude this section, we emphasize the importance of taking a random (or approximately random) sample. Statistical theory tells us that, when we select a random (or approximately random) sample, we can use the sample to make valid statistical inferences about the sampled population. However, if the sample is not random, we cannot do this. A classic example occurred prior to the presidential election of 1936, when the *Literary Digest* predicted that Alf Landon would defeat Franklin D. Roosevelt by a margin of 57 percent to 43 percent. Instead, Roosevelt won the election in a landslide. *Literary Digest*'s error was to sample names from telephone books and club membership rosters. In 1936 the country had not yet recovered from the Great Depression, and many unemployed and low-income people did not have phones or belong to clubs. The *Literary Digest*'s sampling procedure excluded these people, who overwhelmingly voted for Roosevelt. At this time, George Gallup, founder of the Gallup Poll, was beginning to establish his survey business. He used an approximately random sample to correctly predict Roosevelt's victory.

As another example, today's television and radio stations, as well as newspaper columnists, use **voluntary response samples.** In such samples, participants self-select—that is, whoever wishes to participate does so (usually expressing some opinion). These samples overrepresent people with strong (usually negative) opinions. For example, the advice columnist Ann Landers once asked her readers, "If you had it to do over again, would you have children?" Of the nearly 10,000 parents who *voluntarily* responded, 70 percent said that they would not. An approximately random sample taken a few months later found that 91 percent of parents would have children again. We further discuss random sampling in optional Section 1.5.

Sampling a process   A population is not always defined to be a set of *existing* units. Often we are interested in studying the population of all of the units that will be or could potentially be produced by a process.

> A **process** is a sequence of operations that takes inputs (labor, materials, methods, machines, and so on) and turns them into outputs (products, services, and the like).

Processes produce output *over time*. For example, this year's Buick LaCrosse manufacturing process produces LaCrosses over time. Early in the model year, General Motors might wish to study the population of the city driving mileages of all Buick LaCrosses that will be produced during the model year. Or, even more hypothetically, General Motors might wish to study the population of the city driving mileages of all LaCrosses that could *potentially* be produced by this model year's manufacturing process. The first population is called a **finite population** because only a finite number of cars will be produced during the year. Any population of existing units is also finite. The second population is called an **infinite population** because the manufacturing process that produces this year's model could in theory always be used to build "one more car." That is, theoretically there is no limit to the number of cars that could be produced by this year's process. There are a multitude of other examples of finite or infinite hypothetical populations. For instance, we might study the population of all waiting times that will or could potentially be experienced by patients of a hospital emergency room. Or we might study the population of all the amounts of grape jelly that will be or could potentially be dispensed into 16-ounce jars by an automated filling machine. To study a population of potential process observations, we sample the process—often at equally spaced time points—over time. This is illustrated in the following case.

EXAMPLE 1.3 The Car Mileage Case: Estimating Mileage

In 2008 the U.S. Department of Energy (DOE) and the Environmental Protection Agency (EPA) emphasized the importance of auto fuel economy. *The Fuel Economy Guide,* available at the DOE website, discusses the effects of gasoline consumption on U.S. energy security and the economy as follows.[7]

> **Buying a more fuel efficient vehicle can help strengthen our national energy security by reducing our dependence on foreign oil.** More than half of the oil used to produce the gasoline you put in your tank is imported. The United States uses about 20 million barrels of oil per day, two-thirds of which is used for transportation. Petroleum imports cost us about $5.2 billion a week—that's money that could be used to fuel our own economy.

The *Guide* also discusses the effects of gasoline consumption on global climate change:[8]

> Burning fossil fuels such as gasoline and diesel adds greenhouse gases, mostly carbon dioxide (CO_2), to the Earth's atmosphere. Large-scale increases in greenhouse gases in the Earth's atmosphere can lead to global climate change. Vehicles with lower fuel economy burn more fuel, creating more CO_2. Your vehicle creates about 20 pounds of CO_2 (170 cu. ft.) per gallon of gasoline it consumes. Therefore, you can reduce your contribution to global climate change by choosing a vehicle with higher fuel economy.

[7] http://www.fueleconomy.gov/
[8] http://www.fueleconomy.gov/

| TABLE 1.4 | A Sample of 50 Mileages (Time Order Is Given by Reading Down the Columns from Left to Right) 🔵 GasMiles |

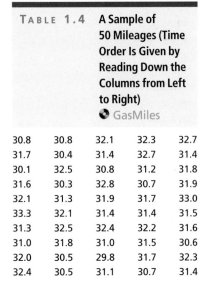

30.8	30.8	32.1	32.3	32.7
31.7	30.4	31.4	32.7	31.4
30.1	32.5	30.8	31.2	31.8
31.6	30.3	32.8	30.7	31.9
32.1	31.3	31.9	31.7	33.0
33.3	32.1	31.4	31.4	31.5
31.3	32.5	32.4	32.2	31.6
31.0	31.8	31.0	31.5	30.6
32.0	30.5	29.8	31.7	32.3
32.4	30.5	31.1	30.7	31.4

FIGURE 1.2   A Runs Plot of the 50 Mileages

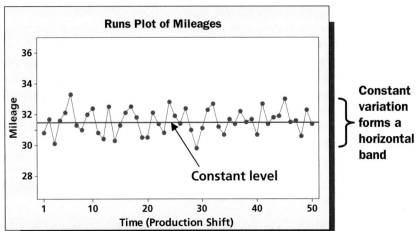

By choosing a vehicle that achieves 25 miles per gallon rather than 20 miles per gallon, you can prevent the release of about 17 tons (260,000 cu. ft.) of greenhouse gases over the lifetime of your vehicle.

In this case study we consider a tax credit offered by the federal government to automakers for improving the fuel economy of gasoline-powered midsize cars. According to *The Fuel Economy Guide—2008 Model Year*, virtually every midsize car equipped with an automatic transmission has an EPA combined city and highway mileage estimate of 26 miles per gallon (mpg) or less.[9] Furthermore, the EPA has concluded that a 5 mpg increase in fuel economy is significant and feasible.[10] Therefore, suppose that the government has decided to offer the tax credit to any automaker selling a midsize model with an automatic transmission that achieves an EPA combined city and highway mileage estimate of at least 31 mpg.

Consider an automaker that has recently introduced a new midsize model with an automatic transmission and wishes to demonstrate that this new model qualifies for the tax credit. In order to study the population of all cars of this type that will or could potentially be produced, the automaker will choose a sample of 50 of these cars. Furthermore, because the midsize cars are produced over time, the automaker will choose the sample by randomly selecting one car from those produced during each of 50 consecutive production shifts. Once selected, each car is to be subjected to an EPA test that determines the EPA combined city and highway mileage of the car. This mileage is obtained by testing the car on a device similar to a giant treadmill. The device is used to simulate a 7.5-mile city driving trip and a 10-mile highway driving trip, and the resulting city and highway mileages are used to calculate the EPA combined mileage for the car.[11]

Suppose that when the 50 cars are selected and tested, the sample of 50 EPA combined mileages shown in Table 1.4 is obtained. (Note that these mileages are given in time order.) Examining Table 1.4, we see that the car mileages range from 29.8 mpg to 33.3 mpg. Based on this, is it reasonable to conclude that most of the new midsize cars produced during the model year will obtain between 29.8 mpg and 33.3 mpg? The answer is yes if the automaker's manufacturing process for the new midsize model is operating consistently over time. That is, this process must be in a state of **statistical control.**

A process is in **statistical control** if it does not exhibit any unusual process variations. Often, this means that the process displays a **constant amount of variation** around a **constant,** or horizontal, **level.**

---

[9]The "26 miles per gallon (mpg) or less" figure relates to midsize cars with an automatic transmission *and* at least a 4-cylinder, 2.4-liter engine (such cars are the most popular midsize models). Therefore, when we refer to a midsize car with an automatic transmission in future discussions, we are assuming that the midsize car also has at least a 4-cylinder, 2.4-liter engine.

[10]The authors wish to thank Jeff Alson of the EPA for this information.

[11]Since the EPA estimates that 55 percent of all driving is city driving, it calculates combined mileage by adding 55 percent of the city mileage test result to 45 percent of the highway mileage test result.

In Chapter 15 (on this book's Website), we discuss a systematic method for studying processes called **statistical process control (SPC),** and we explain how to determine whether a process is in statistical control. For now, we note that we can begin to assess statistical control by constructing a **runs plot** (sometimes called a **time series plot**).

A **runs plot** is a graph of individual process measurements versus time.

Figure 1.2 shows a runs plot of the car mileages. (Some people call such a plot a **line chart** when the plot points are connected by line segments as in Figure 1.2.) Here we plot each car mileage on the vertical scale versus its corresponding time index on the horizontal scale. For instance, the first car mileage (30.8) is plotted versus time equals 1, the second car mileage (31.7) is plotted versus time equals 2, and so forth. The runs plot suggests that the car mileages exhibit a relatively constant amount of variation around a relatively constant level. That is, the center of the car mileages can be pretty much represented by a horizontal line (constant level)—see the line drawn through the plotted points—and the spread of the points around the line is staying about the same (constant variation). Note that the plot points tend to form a horizontal band. Therefore, the car mileages seem to be in statistical control.

In general, assume that we have sampled a process at different time points and made a runs plot of the resulting sample measurements. If the plot indicates that the process is in statistical control, and if it is reasonable to believe that the process will remain in control, then it is probably reasonable to regard the sample measurements as an approximately random sample from the population of all possible process measurements. Furthermore, since the process is remaining in statistical control, the process performance is *predictable*. This allows us to make statistical inferences about the population of all possible process measurements that will or potentially could result from using the process. For example, assuming that the manufacturing process for the new midsize model will remain in statistical control, it is reasonable to conclude that most cars produced by this process will obtain between 29.8 mpg and 33.3 mpg. Furthermore, we will soon see how we can estimate the new model's "typical" EPA combined mileage. The estimate obtained is the EPA combined city and highway mileage estimate for the new midsize model. In Chapters 2 through 8 we study precise methods for making this estimate. For now, note that the horizontal line drawn through the "middle" of the plot points in Figure 1.2 intersects the vertical axis at about 31.5 mpg. This intuitively implies that a "typical" new midsize car will obtain a mileage that exceeds the tax credit standard of 31 mpg. Therefore, it seems that the new midsize model might qualify for the tax credit.

To emphasize the importance of statistical control, suppose that the automaker had observed the car mileages that are plotted versus time in Figure 1.3. These car mileages also range between 29.8 mpg and 33.3 mpg. However, we could not infer from this that most cars of this type will obtain between 29.8 mpg and 33.3 mpg. This is because the downward trend in the runs plot of Figure 1.3 indicates that the car manufacturing process is out of control and will soon produce cars with mileages below 29.8 mpg. Another example of an out-of-control process is illustrated in Figure 1.4. Here, the car mileages seem to fluctuate around a constant level but with increasing variation (notice that the plotted mileages fan out as time advances). In general, if a process is not in statistical control, we must use the methods of Chapter 15 to bring it into control before we can make statistical inferences about the population of all possible process measurements.

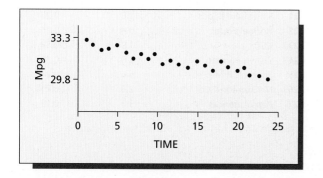

FIGURE 1.3   **A Runs Plot of Car Mileages: The Process Level Is Decreasing**

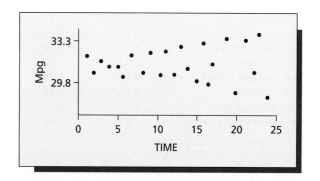

FIGURE 1.4   **A Runs Plot of Car Mileages: The Process Variation Is Increasing**

Exercises for Sections 1.1 and 1.2

CONCEPTS

connect™

1.1 Define a *population.* Give an example of a population that you might study when you start your career after graduating from college.

1.2 Define what we mean by a *variable,* and explain the difference between a quantitative variable and a qualitative (categorical) variable.

1.3 Below we list several variables. Which of these variables are quantitative and which are qualitative? Explain.
  a The dollar amount on an accounts receivable invoice.
  b The net profit for a company in 2008.
  c The stock exchange on which a company's stock is traded.
  d The national debt of the United States in 2008.
  e The advertising medium (radio, television, or print) used to promote a product.

1.4 Explain the difference between a census and a sample.

1.5 Explain each of the following terms:
  a Descriptive statistics.   **c** Random sample.
  b Statistical inference.   **d** Process.

1.6 Explain why sampling without replacement is preferred to sampling with replacement.

METHODS AND APPLICATIONS

1.7 The **Forbes 2000** is a ranking of the world's biggest companies (measured on a composite of sales, profits, assets and market values) by the editors of *Forbes* magazine. In Table 1.5 we give the best-performing U.S. companies in the food, drink, and tobacco industry from the **Forbes 2000** as listed on the *Forbes* magazine website on February 1, 2007. Consider the random numbers given in the random number table of Table 1.1(a) on page 6. Starting in the upper left corner of Table 1.1(a) and moving down the two leftmost columns, we see that the first three two-digit numbers obtained are

33   03   92

Starting with these three random numbers, and moving down the two leftmost columns of Table 1.1(a) to find more two-digit random numbers, use Table 1.1 to randomly select five of these companies to be interviewed in detail about their business strategies. Hint: Note that we have numbered the companies in the *Forbes* list from 1 to 27. ● BestPerf

1.8 Table 1.6 gives the most admired company in each of 30 industries for 2006 as listed by *Fortune* magazine. Starting in the upper right corner of the random number table of Table 1.1(a) (page 6)

TABLE 1.5　**Forbes 2000 Best-Performing Food, Drink, and Tobacco Companies**　● BestPerf

	Company	Sales (Billions $)	Profits (Billions $)		Company	Sales (Billions $)	Profits (Billions $)
1	Altria Group	68.9	10.44	15	Tyson Foods	26.0	0.35
2	PepsiCo	32.6	4.08	16	Dean Foods	10.5	0.33
3	Coca-Cola	23.1	4.87	17	Wm Wrigley Jr.	4.2	0.52
4	Archer Daniels	35.8	1.02	18	Hershey	4.8	0.49
5	Anheuser-Busch	15.0	1.84	19	Constellation Brands	4.6	0.31
6	General Mills	11.4	1.31	20	Molson Coors Brewing	5.5	0.14
7	Sara Lee	19.1	0.55	21	Smithfield Foods	11.8	0.28
8	Coca-Cola Enterprises	18.7	0.51	22	Hormel Foods	5.4	0.25
9	Reynolds American	8.3	0.99	23	UST	1.9	0.53
10	Kellogg	10.2	0.98	24	Brown-Forman	2.0	0.38
11	ConAgra Foods	14.4	0.78	25	Pilgrim's Pride	5.6	0.24
12	HJ Heinz	8.7	0.68	26	McCormick & Co	2.6	0.21
13	Campbell Soup	7.6	0.8	27	PepsiAmericas	3.7	0.19
14	Pepsi Bottling Group	11.9	0.47				

Source: Forbes.com, February 1, 2007
http://www.forbes.com/lists/2006/18/0612000_The-Forbes-2000_IndName_10.html

TABLE 1.6   The Most Admired Company in Each of 30 Industries for 2006   ● MostAdm

	Company	Industry		Company	Industry
1	Anheuser-Busch	Beverages	16	Nordstrom	General Merchandisers
2	Apache	Mining, Crude Oil Production	17	Northwestern Mutual	Insurance: Life, Health
3	Berkshire Hathaway	Insurance: P&C	18	Procter & Gamble	Household and Personal Products
4	Continental Airlines	Airlines	19	Qualcomm	Network Communications
5	DuPont	Chemicals	20	SBC Communications	Telecommunications
6	Exxon Mobil	Petroleum Refining	21	Texas Instruments	Semiconductors
7	General Electric	Electronics	22	Toyota Motor	Motor Vehicles
8	Henry Schein	Wholesalers: Health Care	23	United Parcel Service	Delivery
9	Home Depot	Specialty Retailers	24	United Technologies	Aerospace and Defense
10	Illinois Tool Works	Industrial & Farm Equipment	25	Walgreen	Food & Drug Stores
11	International Paper	Forest & Paper Products	26	Walt Disney	Entertainment
12	Intl. Business Machines	Computers	27	Wells Fargo	Mega-Banks
13	Jacobs Engineering Group	Engineering, Construction	28	Worthington Industries	Metals
14	Johnson & Johnson	Pharmaceuticals	29	WPS Resources	Energy
15	Nestle	Consumer Food Products	30	Google	Internet Services and Retailing

Source: Data excerpted from "FORTUNE: America's Most Admired Companies 2006," CNNMoney.com,
http://money.cnn.com/magazines/fortune/mostadmired/2006/industries (accessed August 30, 2007). Copyright © 2007 Time Inc. All rights reserved.

FIGURE 1.5   The Video Game Satisfaction Survey Instrument

Statement	Strongly Disagree						Strongly Agree
The game console of the XYZ-Box is well designed.	1	2	3	4	5	6	7
The game controller of the XYZ-Box is easy to handle.	1	2	3	4	5	6	7
The XYZ-Box has high-quality graphics capabilities.	1	2	3	4	5	6	7
The XYZ-Box has high-quality audio capabilities.	1	2	3	4	5	6	7
The XYZ-Box serves as a complete entertainment center.	1	2	3	4	5	6	7
There is a large selection of XYZ-Box games to choose from.	1	2	3	4	5	6	7
I am totally satisfied with my XYZ-Box game system.	1	2	3	4	5	6	7

and moving down the two rightmost columns, we see that the first three two-digit numbers obtained are

$$88 \qquad 22 \qquad 52$$

Starting with these three random numbers, and moving down the two rightmost columns of Table 1.1(a) to find more two-digit random numbers, use Table 1.1 to randomly select four of these industries for further study.   ● MostAdm

1.9   THE VIDEO GAME SATISFACTION RATING CASE   ● VideoGame

A company that produces and markets video game systems wishes to assess its customers' level of satisfaction with a relatively new model, the XYZ-Box. In the six months since the introduction of the model, the company has received 73,219 warranty registrations from purchasers. The company will randomly select 65 of these registrations and will conduct telephone interviews with the purchasers. Specifically, each purchaser will be asked to state his or her level of agreement with each of the seven statements listed on the survey instrument given in Figure 1.5. Here, the level of agreement for each statement is measured on a 7-point Likert scale. Purchaser satisfaction will be measured by adding the purchaser's responses to the seven statements. It follows that for each consumer the minimum composite score possible is 7 and the maximum is 49. Furthermore, experience has shown that a purchaser of a video game system is "very satisfied" if his or her composite score is at least 42.

a   Assume that the warranty registrations are numbered from 1 to 73,219 in a computer. Starting in the upper left corner of Table 1.1(a) and moving down the five leftmost columns, we see that the first three five-digit numbers obtained are

$$33276 \qquad 03427 \qquad 92737$$

Starting with these three random numbers and moving down the five leftmost columns of Table 1.1(a) to find more five-digit random numbers, use Table 1.1 to randomly select the numbers of the first 10 warranty registrations to be included in the sample of 65 registrations.

TABLE 1.7	Composite Scores for the Video Game Satisfaction Rating Case 🌐 VideoGame			
39	44	46	44	44
45	42	45	44	42
38	46	45	45	47
42	40	46	44	43
42	47	43	46	45
41	44	47	48	
38	43	43	44	
42	45	41	41	
46	45	40	45	
44	40	43	44	
40	46	44	44	
39	41	41	44	
40	43	38	46	
42	39	43	39	
45	43	36	41	

TABLE 1.8	Waiting Times (in Minutes) for the Bank Customer Waiting Time Case 🌐 WaitTime					
1.6	6.2	3.2	5.6	7.9	6.1	7.2
6.6	5.4	6.5	4.4	1.1	3.8	7.3
5.6	4.9	2.3	4.5	7.2	10.7	4.1
5.1	5.4	8.7	6.7	2.9	7.5	6.7
3.9	.8	4.7	8.1	9.1	7.0	3.5
4.6	2.5	3.6	4.3	7.7	5.3	6.3
6.5	8.3	2.7	2.2	4.0	4.5	4.3
6.4	6.1	3.7	5.8	1.4	4.5	3.8
8.6	6.3	.4	8.6	7.8	1.8	5.1
4.2	6.8	10.2	2.0	5.2	3.7	5.5
5.8	9.8	2.8	8.0	8.4	4.0	
3.4	2.9	11.6	9.5	6.3	5.7	
9.3	10.9	4.3	1.3	4.4	2.4	
7.4	4.7	3.1	4.8	5.2	9.2	
1.8	3.9	5.8	9.9	7.4	5.0	

b Suppose that when the 65 customers are interviewed, their composite scores are obtained and are as given in Table 1.7. Using the data, estimate limits between which most of the 73,219 composite scores would fall. Also, estimate the proportion of the 73,219 composite scores that would be at least 42.

1.10 THE BANK CUSTOMER WAITING TIME CASE 🌐 WaitTime

A bank manager has developed a new system to reduce the time customers spend waiting to be served by tellers during peak business hours. Typical waiting times during peak business hours under the current system are roughly 9 to 10 minutes. The bank manager hopes that the new system will lower typical waiting times to less than six minutes.

A 30-day trial of the new system is conducted. During the trial run, every 150th customer who arrives during peak business hours is selected until a systematic sample of 100 customers is obtained. Each of the sampled customers is observed, and the time spent waiting for teller service is recorded. The 100 waiting times obtained are given in Table 1.8. Moreover, the bank manager feels that this systematic sample is as representative as a random sample of waiting times would be. Using the data, estimate limits between which the waiting times of most of the customers arriving during peak business hours would be. Also, estimate the proportion of waiting times of customers arriving during peak business hours that are less than six minutes.

1.11 In an article titled "Turned Off" in the June 2–4, 1995, issue of *USA Weekend,* Dan Olmsted and Gigi Anders reported on the results of a survey conducted by the magazine. Readers were invited to write in and answer several questions about sex and vulgarity on television. Olmsted and Anders summarized the survey results as follows:

Nearly all of the 65,000 readers responding to our write-in survey say TV is too vulgar, too violent, and too racy. TV execs call it reality.

Some of the key survey results were as follows:

Survey Results

- 96% are very or somewhat concerned about SEX on TV.
- 97% are very or somewhat concerned about VULGAR LANGUAGE on TV.
- 97% are very or somewhat concerned about VIOLENCE on TV.

Note: Because participants were not chosen at random, the results of the write-in survey may not be scientific.

a Note the disclaimer at the bottom of the survey results. In a write-in survey, anyone who wishes to participate may respond to the survey questions. Therefore, the sample is not random and we say that the survey is "not scientific." What kind of people would be most likely to respond to a survey about TV sex and violence? Do the survey results agree with your answer?

b If a random sample of the general population were taken, do you think that its results would be the same? Why or why not? Similarly, for instance, do you think that 97 percent of the general population is "very or somewhat concerned about violence on TV"?

c Another result obtained in the write-in survey was as follows:

• Should "V-chips" be installed on TV sets so parents could easily block violent programming?

YES 90%   NO 10%

If you planned to start a business manufacturing and marketing such V-chips (at a reasonable price), would you expect 90 percent of the general population to desire a V-chip? Why or why not?

1.12 THE COFFEE TEMPERATURE CASE ● Coffee

According to the website of the Association of Trial Lawyers of America,[12] Stella Liebeck of Albuquerque, New Mexico, was severely burned by McDonald's coffee in February 1992. Liebeck, who received third-degree burns over 6 percent of her body, was awarded $160,000 in compensatory damages and $480,000 in punitive damages. A postverdict investigation revealed that the coffee temperature at the local Albuquerque McDonald's had dropped from about 185°F before the trial to about 158° after the trial.

This case concerns coffee temperatures at a fast-food restaurant. Because of the possibility of future litigation and to possibly improve the coffee's taste, the restaurant wishes to study and monitor the temperature of the coffee it serves. To do this, the restaurant personnel measure the temperature of the coffee being dispensed (in degrees Fahrenheit) at half-hour intervals from 10 A.M. to 9:30 P.M. on a given day. The following table gives the 24 temperature measurements obtained in the time order that they were observed. Here, time equals 1 at 10 A.M. and 24 at 9:30 P.M.

Time		Coffee Temperature	Time		Coffee Temperature	Time		Coffee Temperature
(10:00 A.M.)	1	163°F	(2:00 P.M.)	9	159°F	(6:00 P.M.)	17	158°F
	2	169		10	154		18	170
	3	156		11	167		19	155
	4	152		12	161		20	162
(12:00 noon)	5	165	(4:00 P.M.)	13	152	(8:00 P.M.)	21	156
	6	158		14	165		22	167
	7	157		15	161		23	155
	8	162		16	154		24	164 ● Coffee

Figure 1.6 gives the MINITAB output of a runs plot of the coffee temperatures.

a Do the 24 coffee temperatures appear to be in statistical control? Explain.

b Estimate limits between which most of the temperatures of the restaurant's coffee would fall.

FIGURE 1.6 **MINITAB Runs Plot of Coffee Temperatures (for Exercise 1.12)**

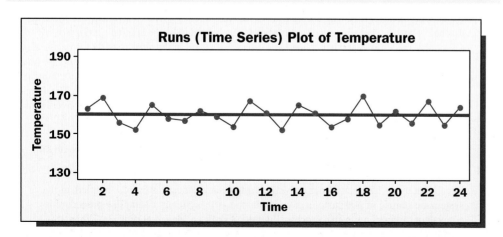

[12]http://www.atla.org, Association of Trial Lawyers of America, June 16, 2006.

TABLE 1.9	Trash Bag Breaking Strengths 🌑 TrashBag		
48.5	52.5	50.7	49.4
52.3	47.5	48.2	51.9
53.5	50.9	51.5	52.0
50.5	49.8	49.0	48.8
50.3	50.0	51.7	46.8
49.6	50.8	53.2	51.3
51.0	53.0	51.1	49.3
48.3	50.9	52.6	54.0
50.6	49.9	51.2	49.2
50.2	50.1	49.5	51.4

FIGURE 1.7   Excel Runs Plot of Breaking Strengths (for Exercise 1.13)

	A	B	C	D	E	F	G	H	I	J
1	Strength									
2	48.5									
3	52.3									
4	53.5									
5	50.5									
6	50.3									
7	49.6									
8	51.0									
9	48.3									
10	50.6									
11	50.2									
12	52.5									
13	47.5									
14	50.9									
15	49.8									
16	50.0									
17	50.8									
18	53.0									
19	50.9									
20	49.9									
21	50.1									

FIGURE 1.8   MegaStat Runs Plot of Waiting Times (for Exercise 1.14)

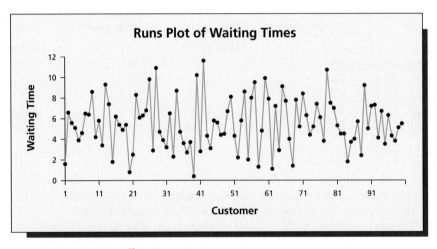

1.13   THE TRASH BAG CASE[13]   🌑 TrashBag

A company that produces and markets trash bags has developed an improved 30-gallon bag. The new bag is produced using a specially formulated plastic that is both stronger and more biodegradable than previously used plastics, and the company wishes to evaluate the strength of this bag. The *breaking strength* of a trash bag is considered to be the amount (in pounds) of a representative trash mix that when loaded into a bag suspended in the air will cause the bag to sustain significant damage (such as ripping or tearing). The company has decided to carry out a 40-hour pilot production run of the new bags. Each hour, at a randomly selected time during the hour, a bag is taken off the production line. The bag is then subjected to a *breaking strength test*. The 40 breaking strengths obtained during the pilot production run are given in Table 1.9, and an Excel runs plot of these breaking strengths is given in Figure 1.7.

a Do the 40 breaking strengths appear to be in statistical control? Explain.

b Estimate limits between which most of the breaking strengths of all trash bags would fall.

1.14   THE BANK CUSTOMER WAITING TIME CASE   🌑 WaitTime

Recall that every 150th customer arriving during peak business hours was sampled until a systematic sample of 100 customers was obtained. This systematic sampling procedure is equivalent to sampling from a process. Figure 1.8 shows a MegaStat runs plot of the 100 waiting times in Table 1.8. Does the process appear to be in statistical control? Explain.

---

[13]This case is based on conversations by the authors with several employees working for a leading producer of trash bags. For purposes of confidentiality, we have withheld the company's name.

1.3 Ratio, Interval, Ordinal, and Nominative Scales of Measurement (Optional) ● ● ●

In Section 1.1 we said that a variable is **quantitative** if its possible values are **numbers that represent quantities** (that is, "how much" or "how many"). In general, a quantitative variable is measured on a scale having a **fixed unit of measurement** between its possible values. For example, if we measure employees' salaries to the nearest dollar, then one dollar is the fixed unit of measurement between different employees' salaries. There are two types of quantitative variables: **ratio** and **interval.** A **ratio variable** is a quantitative variable measured on a scale such that ratios of its values are meaningful and there is an inherently defined zero value. Variables such as salary, height, weight, time, and distance are ratio variables. For example, a distance of zero miles is "no distance at all," and a town that is 30 miles away is "twice as far" as a town that is 15 miles away.

An **interval variable** is a quantitative variable where ratios of its values are not meaningful and there is not an inherently defined zero value. Temperature (on the Fahrenheit scale) is an interval variable. For example, zero degrees Fahrenheit does not represent "no heat at all," just that it is very cold. Thus, there is no inherently defined zero value. Furthermore, ratios of temperatures are not meaningful. For example, it makes no sense to say that 60° is twice as warm as 30°. In practice, there are very few interval variables other than temperature. Almost all quantitative variables are ratio variables.

In Section 1.1 we also said that if we simply record into which of several categories a population (or sample) unit falls, then the variable is **qualitative** (or **categorical**). There are two types of qualitative variables: **ordinal** and **nominative.** An **ordinal variable** is a qualitative variable for which there is a meaningful **ordering**, or **ranking**, of the categories. The measurements of an ordinal variable may be nonnumerical or numerical. For example, a student may be asked to rate the teaching effectiveness of a college professor as excellent, good, average, poor, or unsatisfactory. Here, one category is higher than the next one; that is, "excellent" is a higher rating than "good," "good" is a higher rating than "average," and so on. Therefore, teaching effectiveness is an ordinal variable having nonnumerical measurements. On the other hand, if (as is often done) we substitute the numbers 4, 3, 2, 1, and 0 for the ratings excellent through unsatisfactory, then teaching effectiveness is an ordinal variable having numerical measurements.

In practice, both numbers and associated words are often presented to respondents asked to rate a person or item. When numbers are used, statisticians debate whether the ordinal variable is "somewhat quantitative." For example, statisticians who claim that teaching effectiveness rated as 4, 3, 2, 1, or 0 is *not* somewhat quantitative argue that the difference between 4 (excellent) and 3 (good) may not be the same as the difference between 3 (good) and 2 (average). Other statisticians argue that as soon as respondents (students) see equally spaced numbers (even though the numbers are described by words), their responses are affected enough to make the variable (teaching effectiveness) somewhat quantitative. Generally speaking, the specific words associated with the numbers probably substantially affect whether an ordinal variable may be considered somewhat quantitative. It is important to note, however, that in practice numerical ordinal ratings are often analyzed as though they are quantitative. Specifically, various arithmetic operations (as discussed in Chapters 2 through 14) are often performed on numerical ordinal ratings. For example, a professor's teaching effectiveness average and a student's grade point average are calculated.

To conclude this section, we consider the second type of qualitative variable. A **nominative variable** is a qualitative variable for which there is no meaningful ordering, or ranking, of the categories. A person's gender, the color of a car, and an employee's state of residence are nominative variables.

Exercises for Section 1.3

CONCEPTS

1.15 Discuss the difference between a ratio variable and an interval variable.

1.16 Discuss the difference between an ordinal variable and a nominative variable.

METHODS AND APPLICATIONS

1.17 Classify each of the following qualitative variables as ordinal or nominative. Explain your answers.

Qualitative Variable	Categories
Statistics course letter grade	A　B　C　D　F
Door choice on *Let's Make A Deal*	Door #1　　Door #2
Television show classifications	TV-G　TV-PG　TV-14　TV-MA
Personal computer ownership	Yes　No
Restaurant rating	*****　****　***　**　*
Income tax filing status	Married filing jointly　Married filing separately Single　Head of household　Qualifying widow(er)

1.18 Classify each of the following qualitative variables as ordinal or nominative. Explain your answers.

Qualitative Variable	Categories
Personal computer operating system	DOS　Windows XP　Windows 2000　Windows Vista
Motion picture classifications	G　PG　PG-13　R　NC-17　X
Level of education	Elementary　Middle school　High school　College Graduate school
Rankings of top 10 college football teams	1　2　3　4　5　6　7　8　9　10
Exchange on which a stock is traded	AMEX　NYSE　NASDAQ　Other
Zip code	45056　90015　etc.

1.4 An Introduction to Survey Sampling (Optional) ● ● ●

Random sampling is not the only kind of sampling. Methods for obtaining a sample are called **sampling designs,** and the sample we take is sometimes called a **sample survey.** In this section we explain three sampling designs that are alternatives to random sampling—**stratified random sampling, cluster sampling,** and **systematic sampling.**

One common sampling design involves separately sampling important groups within a population. Then, the samples are combined to form the entire sample. This approach is the idea behind **stratified random sampling.**

In order to select a **stratified random sample,** we divide the population into nonoverlapping groups of similar units (people, objects, etc.). These groups are called **strata.** Then a random sample is selected from each stratum, and these samples are combined to form the full sample.

It is wise to stratify when the population consists of two or more groups that differ with respect to the variable of interest. For instance, consumers could be divided into strata based on gender, age, ethnic group, or income.

As an example, suppose that a department store chain proposes to open a new store in a location that would serve customers who live in a geographical region that consists of (1) an industrial city, (2) a suburban community, and (3) a rural area. In order to assess the potential profitability of the proposed store, the chain wishes to study the incomes of all households in the region. In addition, the chain wishes to estimate the proportion and the total number of households whose members would be likely to shop at the store. The department store chain feels that the industrial city, the suburban community, and the rural area differ with respect to income and the store's potential desirability. Therefore, it uses these subpopulations as strata and takes a stratified random sample.

Taking a stratified sample can be advantageous because such a sample takes advantage of the fact that units in the same stratum are similar to each other. It follows that a stratified sample can provide more accurate information than a random sample of the same size. As a simple example, if all of the units in each stratum were exactly the same, then examining only one unit in each stratum would allow us to describe the entire population. Furthermore, stratification can make a sample easier (or possible) to select. Recall that, in order to take a random sample, we must have a frame, or list, of all of the population units. Although a frame might not exist for the overall population, a frame might exist for each stratum. For example, suppose nearly all the households in the department store's geographical region have telephones. Although there might not be a telephone directory for the overall geographical region, there might be separate telephone directories for the industrial city, the suburb, and the rural area. Although we do not discuss how to analyze data from a stratified random sample in this text, we do so in Appendix F (Part I) on the CD-ROM that accompanies Bowerman, O'Connell, and Murphree (2009). For a more complete discussion of stratified random sampling, see Mendenhall, Schaeffer, and Ott (1986).

Sometimes it is advantageous to select a sample in stages. This is a common practice when selecting a sample from a very large geographical region. In such a case, a frame often does not exist. For instance, there is no single list of all registered voters in the United States. There is also no single list of all households in the United States. In this kind of situation, we can use **multistage cluster sampling.** To illustrate this procedure, suppose we wish to take a sample of registered voters from all registered voters in the United States. We might proceed as follows:

Stage 1: Randomly select a sample of counties from all of the counties in the United States.

Stage 2: Randomly select a sample of townships from each county selected in Stage 1.

Stage 3: Randomly select a sample of voting precincts from each township selected in Stage 2.

Stage 4: Randomly select a sample of registered voters from each voting precinct selected in Stage 3.

We use the term *cluster sampling* to describe this type of sampling because at each stage we "cluster" the voters into subpopulations. For instance, in Stage 1 we cluster the voters into counties, and in Stage 2 we cluster the voters in each selected county into townships. Also, notice that the random sampling at each stage can be carried out because there are lists of (1) all counties in the United States, (2) all townships in each county, (3) all voting precincts in each township, and (4) all registered voters in each voting precinct.

As another example, consider sampling the households in the United States. We might use Stages 1 and 2 above to select counties and townships within the selected counties. Then, if there is a telephone directory of the households in each township, we can randomly sample households from each selected township by using its telephone directory. Because *most* households today have telephones, and telephone directories are readily available, most national polls are now conducted by telephone.

It is sometimes a good idea to combine stratification with multistage cluster sampling. For example, suppose a national polling organization wants to estimate the proportion of all registered voters who favor a particular presidential candidate. Because the presidential preferences of voters might tend to vary by geographical region, the polling organization might divide the United States into regions (say, Eastern, Midwestern, Southern, and Western regions). The polling organization might then use these regions as strata, and might take a multistage cluster sample from each stratum (region).

The analysis of data produced by multistage cluster sampling can be quite complicated. We explain how to analyze data produced by one- and two-stage cluster sampling in Appendix F (Part 2) on the CD-ROM that accompanies Bowerman, O'Connell, and Murphree (2009). This appendix also includes a discussion of an additional survey sampling technique called *ratio estimation.* For a more detailed discussion of cluster sampling and ratio estimation, see Mendenhall, Schaeffer, and Ott (1986).

In order to select a random sample, we must number the units in a frame of all the population units. Then we use a random number table (or a random number generator on a computer) to make the selections. However, numbering all the population units can be quite time-consuming. Moreover, random sampling is used in the various stages of many complex sampling designs (requiring the numbering of numerous populations). Therefore, it is useful to have an alternative to random sampling. One such alternative is called **systematic sampling.** In order to systematically select a sample of n units without replacement from a frame of N units, we divide N by n and round the result down to the nearest whole number. Calling the rounded result ℓ, we then randomly select one unit from the first ℓ units in the frame—this is the first unit in the systematic sample. The remaining units in the sample are obtained by selecting every ℓth unit following the first (randomly selected) unit. For example, suppose we wish to sample a population of $N = 14{,}327$ allergists to investigate how often they have prescribed a particular drug during the last year. A medical society has a directory listing the 14,327 allergists, and we wish to draw a systematic sample of 500 allergists from this frame. Here we compute $14{,}327/500 = 28.654$, which is 28 when rounded down. Therefore, we number the first 28 allergists in the directory from 1 to 28, and we use a random number table to randomly select one of the first 28 allergists. Suppose we select allergist number 19. We interview allergist 19 and every 28th allergist in the frame thereafter, so we choose allergists 19, 47, 75, and so forth until we obtain our sample of 500 allergists. In this scheme, we must number the first 28 allergists, but we do not have to number the rest because we can "count off" every 28th allergist in the directory. Alternatively, we can measure the approximate amount of space in the directory that it takes to list 28 allergists. This measurement can then be used to select every 28th allergist.

Exercises for Section 1.4

CONCEPTS

connect

1.19   When is it appropriate to use stratified random sampling? What are strata, and how should strata be selected?

1.20   When is cluster sampling used? Why do we describe this type of sampling by using the term *cluster?*

1.21   Explain how to take a systematic sample of 100 companies from the 1,853 companies that are members of an industry trade association.

1.22   Explain how a stratified random sample is selected. Discuss how you might define the strata to survey student opinion on a proposal to charge all students a $100 fee for a new university-run bus system that will provide transportation between off-campus apartments and campus locations.

1.23   Marketing researchers often use city blocks as clusters in cluster sampling. Using this fact, explain how a market researcher might use multistage cluster sampling to select a sample of consumers from all cities having a population of more than 10,000 in a large state having many such cities.

1.5 More About Data Acquisition and Survey Sampling (Optional) ◉ ◉ ●

Businesses pondering expansion plans, marketing campaigns, and potential new products are eager to make "data-based" decisions. In previous sections we have assumed that businesses collect their own data by using one of the sampling techniques outlined. However, sometimes they can exploit data already gathered by public or private sources. The Internet is an obvious place to search for electronic versions of government publications, company reports, and business journals; but there is also a wealth of information available in the reference section of a good library or in county courthouse records.

If a business needs information about incomes in the Northeastern states, a natural source is the U.S. Census Bureau's website at http://www.census.gov. By following various links posted on the home page, you can find income and demographic data for specific regions of the country. Other useful websites for economic and financial data are listed in Table 1.10. All of these are trustworthy sources.

However, given the ease with which anyone can post documents, pictures, weblogs, and video on the World Wide Web, not all sites are equally reliable. If we were to use a search engine from Google, Netscape, Yahoo, Ask.com, or AltaVista (just to name a few) to find information about the price of a two-bedroom apartment in Manhattan, we would be inundated by millions of "hits." (In fact, a recent search on Google using the keywords "price 2 bedroom apartments Manhattan" yielded 1,040,000 sites.) Some of the sources will be more useful, exhaustive, and error-free than others. Fortunately, the search engines prioritize the lists and provide the most relevant and highly used sites first.

Obviously, performing such Web searches costs next to nothing and takes relatively little time, but the trade-off is that we are also limited in terms of the type of information we are able to find. Another option may be to use a private data source. Most companies keep employee records, for example, and retail establishments retain information about their customers, products, and advertising results. Manufacturing companies may collect information about their processes and defect propagation in order to monitor quality. If we have no affiliation with these companies, however, these data may be more difficult to obtain.

Another alternative would be to contact a data collection agency, which typically incurs some kind of cost. You can either buy subscriptions or purchase individual company financial reports

TABLE 1.10   Examples of Public Economic and Financial Data Sites

Title	Website	Data Type
Global Financial Data	http://www.globalfindata.com/	Annual data on stock markets, inflation rates, interest rates, exchange rates, etc.
National Bureau of Economic Research Macrohistory Database	http://www.nber.org/databases/macrohistory/contents/index.html	Historic data on production, construction, employment, money, prices, asset market transactions, foreign trade, and government activity
Federal Reserve Economic Data	http://www.stls.frb.org/fred/	Historical U.S. economic and financial data, including daily U.S. interest rates, monetary and business indicators, exchange rate, balance of payments, and regional economic data
Bureau of Labor Statistics	http://stats.bls.gov/	Data concerning employment, inflation, consumer spending, productivity, safety, labor demographics, and the like
WebEc Economics Data	http://netec.wustl.edu/WebEc/	One of the best complete economics data links including both international and domestic data categorized by area and country
Economic Statistics Briefing Room	http://www.whitehouse.gov/fsbr/esbr.html	Links to the most currently available values of federal economic indicators on eight categories

Source: Prepared by Lan Ma and Jeffrey S. Simonoff. The authors provide no warranty as to the accuracy of the information provided.

from agencies like Dun & Bradstreet, Bloomberg, Dow Jones & Company, Travel Industry of America, Graduate Management Admission Council, and the Educational Testing Service. If you need to collect specific information, some companies, such as ACNielsen and Information Resources, Inc., can be hired to collect the information for a fee.

Experimental and observational studies   There are many instances when the data we need are not readily available from a public or private source. The data might not have been collected at all or they may have been collected in a statistically unsound manner. In cases like these, we need to collect the data ourselves. Suppose we work for a soft drink producer and want to assess consumer reactions to a new bottled water. Since the water has not been marketed yet, we may choose to conduct taste tests, focus groups, or some other market research. Projecting political election results also requires information that is not readily available. In this case, exit polls and telephone surveys are commonly used to obtain the information needed to predict voting trends. New drugs for fighting disease are tested by collecting data under carefully controlled and monitored experimental conditions. In many marketing, political, and medical situations of these sorts, companies hire outside consultants or statisticians to help them obtain appropriate data. Regardless of whether newly minted data are gathered in-house or by paid outsiders, this type of data collection requires much more time, effort, and expense than are needed when data can be found from public or private sources.

When initiating a study, we first define our variable of interest, or **response variable.** Other factors, or **independent variables,** that may be related to the variable of interest will also be measured. When we are able to set or manipulate the values of these independent variables, we have an **experimental study.** For example, a pharmaceutical company might wish to determine the most appropriate daily dose of a cholesterol-lowering drug for patients having cholesterol levels over 240 mg/dL, a level associated with a high risk of coronary disease (http://www.americanheart.org/presenter.jhtml?identifier=4500). The company can perform an experiment in which one sample of patients receives a placebo; a second sample receives some low dose; a third a higher dose; and so forth. This is an experiment because the company controls the amount of drug each group receives. The optimal daily dose can be determined by analyzing the patients' responses to the different dosage levels given.

When analysts are unable to control the factors of interest, the study is **observational.** In studies of diet and cholesterol, patients' diets are not under the analyst's control. Patients are often unwilling or unable to follow prescribed diets; doctors simply observe what patients eat and then look for associations between the independent variable diet and the response variable cholesterol. Observational studies are often based upon **surveys.** For example, the National Longitudinal Survey of Young Men and the National Longitudinal Survey of Youth, two well-known surveys, explore the effects of labor market shifts on a large group of white males. Over a 15-year period, the subjects enrolled in the study were interviewed annually and the observational data gathered on their work and educational histories were tracked.

Types of survey questions   Survey instruments can use **dichotomous** ("yes or no"), **multiple-choice,** or **open-ended** questions. Each type of question has its benefits and drawbacks. Dichotomous questions are usually clearly stated, can be answered quickly, and yield data that are easily analyzed. However, the information gathered may be limited by this two-option format. If we limit voters to expressing support or disapproval for stem-cell research, we may not learn the nuanced reasoning that voters use in weighing the merits and moral issues involved. Similarly, in today's heterogeneous world, it would be unusual to use a dichotomous question to categorize a person's religious preferences. Asking whether respondents are Christian or non-Christian (or using any other two categories like Jewish or non-Jewish; Muslim or non-Muslim) is certain to make some people feel their religion is being slighted. In addition, this is a crude way and unenlightening way to learn about religious preferences.

Multiple-choice questions can assume several different forms. Sometimes respondents are asked to choose a response from a list (for example, possible answers to the religion question could be Jewish; Christian; Muslim; Hindu; Agnostic; or Other). Other times, respondents are asked to choose an answer from a numerical range. We could ask the question:

"In your opinion, how important are SAT scores to a college student's success?"

Not important at all   1   2   3   4   5   Extremely important

These numerical responses are usually summarized and reported in terms of the average response, whose size tells us something about the perceived importance. The Zagat restaurant survey (http://www.zagat.com) asks diners to rate restaurants' food, décor, and service, each on a scale of 1 to 30 points, with a 30 representing an incredible level of satisfaction. Although the Zagat scale has an unusually wide range of possible ratings, the concept is the same as in the more common 5-point scale.

Open-ended questions typically provide the most honest and complete information because there are no suggested answers to divert or bias a person's response. This kind of question is often found on instructor evaluation forms distributed at the end of a college course. College students at Georgetown University are asked the open-ended question, "What comments would you give to the instructor?" The responses provide the instructor feedback that may be missing from the initial part of the teaching evaluation survey, which consists of numerical multiple-choice ratings of various aspects of the course. While these numerical ratings can be used to compare instructors and courses, there are no easy comparisons of the diverse responses instructors receive to the open-ended question. In fact, these responses are often seen only by the instructor and are useful, constructive tools for the teacher despite the fact that they cannot be readily summarized.

Survey questionnaires must be carefully constructed so they do not inadvertently bias the results. Because survey design is such a difficult and sensitive process, it is not uncommon for a pilot survey to be taken before a lot of time, effort, and financing go into collecting a large amount of data. Pilot surveys are similar to the beta version of a new electronic product; they are tested out with a smaller group of people to work out the "kinks" before being used on a larger scale. Determination of the sample size for the final survey is an important process for many reasons. If the sample size is too large, resources may be wasted during the data collection. On the other hand, not collecting enough data for a meaningful analysis will obviously be detrimental to the study. Fortunately, there are several formulas that will help decide how large a sample should be, depending on the goal of the study and various other factors.

Types of surveys   There are several different survey types, and we will explore just a few of them. The **phone survey** is particularly well known (and often despised). A phone survey is inexpensive and usually conducted by callers who have very little training. Because of this and the impersonal nature of the medium, the respondent may misunderstand some of the questions. A further drawback is that some people cannot be reached and that others may refuse to answer some or all of the questions. Phone surveys are thus particularly prone to have a low **response rate.**

> The **response rate** is the proportion of all people whom we attempt to contact that actually respond to a survey. A low response rate can destroy the validity of a survey's results.

The popular television sitcom *Seinfeld* parodied the difficulties of collecting data through a phone survey. After receiving several calls from telemarketers, Jerry replied in exasperation,

> "I'm sorry; I'm a little tied up now. Give me your home number and I'll call you back later. Oh! You don't like being called at home? Well, now you know how I feel."

Numerous complaints have been filed with the Federal Trade Commission (FTC) about the glut of marketing and survey telephone calls to private residences. The National Do Not Call Registry was created as the culmination of a comprehensive, three-year review of the Telemarketing Sales Rule (TSR) (http://www.ftc.gov/donotcall/). This legislation allows people to enroll their phone numbers on a website so as to prevent most marketers from calling them.

Self-administered surveys, or **mail surveys,** are also very inexpensive to conduct. However, these also have their drawbacks. Often, recipients will choose not to reply unless they receive some kind of financial incentive or other reward. Generally, after an initial mailing, the response rate will fall between 20 and 30 percent (http://www.pra.ca/resources/rates.pdf). Response rates can be raised with successive follow-up reminders, and after three contacts, they might reach between 65 and 75 percent. Unfortunately, the entire process can take significantly longer than a phone survey would.

Web-based surveys have become increasingly popular, but they suffer from the same problems as mail surveys. In addition, as with phone surveys, respondents may record their true reactions incorrectly because they have misunderstood some of the questions posed.

A personal interview provides more control over the survey process. People selected for interviews are more likely to respond because the questions are being asked by someone face-to-face. Questions are less likely to be misunderstood because the people conducting the interviews are typically trained employees who can clear up any confusion arising during the process. On the other hand, interviewers can potentially "lead" a respondent by body language that signals approval or disapproval of certain sorts of answers. They can also prompt certain replies by providing too much information. **Mall surveys** are examples of personal interviews. Interviewers approach shoppers as they pass by and ask them to answer the survey questions. Response rates of around 50 percent are typical (http://en.wikipedia.org/wiki/Statistical_survey#Survey_methods). Personal interviews are more costly than mail or phone surveys. Obviously, the objective of the study will be important in deciding upon the survey type employed.

Errors occurring in surveys   In general, the goal of a survey is to obtain accurate information from a group, or sample, that is representative of the entire population of interest. We are trying to estimate some aspect (numerical descriptor) of the entire population from a subset of the population. This is not an easy task, and there are many pitfalls. First and foremost, the *target population* must be well defined and a *sample frame* must be chosen.

> The **target population** is the entire population of interest to us in a particular study.

Are we intending to estimate the average starting salary of students graduating from any college? Or from four-year colleges? Or from business schools? Or from a particular business school?

> The **sample frame** is a list of sampling units (people or things) from which the sample will be selected. It should closely agree with the target population.

Consider a study to estimate the average starting salary of students who have graduated from the business school at Miami University of Ohio over the last five years; the target population is obviously that particular group of graduates. A sample frame could be the Miami University Alumni Association's roster of business school graduates for the past five years. Although it will not be a perfect replication of the target population, it is a reasonable frame.

We now discuss two general classes of survey errors: **errors of nonobservation** and **errors of observation.** From the sample frame, units are randomly chosen to be part of the sample. Simply by virtue of the fact that we are taking a sample instead of a census, we are susceptible to *sampling error.*

Sampling error is the difference between a numerical descriptor of the population and the corresponding descriptor of the sample.

Sampling error occurs because our information is incomplete. We observe only the portion of the population included in the sample while the remainder is obscured. Suppose, for example, we wanted to know about the heights of 13-year-old boys. There is extreme variation in boys' heights at this age. Even if we could overcome the logistical problems of choosing a random sample of 20 boys, there is nothing to guarantee the sample will accurately reflect heights at this age. By sheer luck of the draw, our sample could include a higher proportion of tall boys than appears in the population. We would then overestimate average height at this age (to the chagrin of the shorter boys). Although samples tend to look more similar to their parent populations as the sample sizes increase, we should always keep in mind that sample characteristics and population characteristics are not the same.

If a sample frame is not identical to the target population, we will suffer from an *error of coverage.*

Undercoverage occurs when some population units are excluded from the process of selecting the sample.

Undercoverage was the problem dooming the *Literary Digest* poll of 1936. Although millions of Americans were included in the poll, the large sample size could not rescue the poll results. The sample represented those who could afford phone service and club memberships in the lean Depression years; but in excluding everyone else, it failed to yield an honest picture of the entire American populace. Undercoverage often occurs when we do not have a complete, accurate list of all the population units. If we select our sample from an incomplete list, like a telephone directory or a list of all Internet subscribers in a region, we automatically eliminate those who cannot afford phone or Internet service. Even today, 7 to 8 percent of the people in the United States do not own telephones. Low-income people are often underrepresented in surveys. If underrepresented groups differ from the rest of the population with respect to the characteristic under study, the survey results will be biased.

Often, pollsters cannot find all the people they intend to survey, and sometimes people who are found will refuse to answer the questions posed. Both of these are examples of the **nonresponse** problem. Unfortunately, there may be an association between how difficult it is to find and elicit responses from people and the type of answers they give.

Nonresponse occurs whenever some of the individuals who were supposed to be included in the sample are not.

For example, universities often conduct surveys to learn how graduates have fared in the workplace. The alumnus who has risen through the corporate ranks is more likely to have a current address on file with his alumni office and to be willing to share career information than a classmate who has foundered professionally. We should be politely skeptical about reports touting the average salaries of graduates of various university programs. In some surveys, 35 percent or more of the selected individuals cannot be contacted—even when several callbacks are made. In such cases, other participants are often substituted for those who cannot be contacted. If the substitutes and the originally selected participants differ with respect to the characteristic under study, the survey will be biased. Furthermore, people who will answer highly sensitive, personal, or embarrassing questions might be very different from those who will not.

As discussed in Section 1.2, the opinions of those who bother to complete a voluntary response survey may be dramatically different from those who do not. (Recall the "Dear Abby" question about having children.) The viewer voting on the popular television show *American Idol* is another illustration of **selection bias,** since only those who are interested in the outcome of the show will bother to phone in or text message their votes. The results of the voting are not representative of the performance ratings the country would give as a whole.

Errors of observation occur when data values are recorded incorrectly. Such errors can be caused by the data collector (the interviewer), the survey instrument, the respondent, or the data collection process. For instance, the manner in which a question is asked can influence the response. Or the order in which questions appear on a questionnaire can influence the survey results. Or the data collection method (telephone interview, questionnaire, personal interview, or direct observation) can influence the results. A **recording error** occurs when either the respondent or interviewer incorrectly marks an answer. Once data are collected from a survey, the results are often entered into a computer for statistical analysis. When transferring data from a survey form to a spreadsheet program like Excel, Minitab, or Megastat, there is potential for entering them incorrectly. Before the survey is administered, the questions need to be very carefully worded so that there is little chance of misinterpretation. A poorly framed question might yield results that lead to unwarranted decisions. Scaled questions are particularly susceptible to this type of error. Consider the question "How would you rate this course?" Without a proper explanation, the respondent may not know whether "1" or "5" is the best.

If the survey instrument contains highly sensitive questions and respondents feel compelled to answer, they may not tell the truth. This is especially true in personal interviews. We then have what is called **response bias.** A surprising number of people are reluctant to be candid about what they like to read or watch on television. People tend to overreport "good" activities like reading respected newspapers and underreport their "bad" activities like delighting in the *National Enquirer's* stories of alien abductions and celebrity meltdowns. Imagine, then, the difficulty in getting honest answers about people's gambling habits, drug use, or sexual histories. Response bias can also occur when respondents are asked slanted questions whose wording influences the answer received. For example, consider the following question:

Which of the following best describes your views on gun control?

1   The government should take away our guns, leaving us defenseless against heavily armed criminals.

2   We have the right to keep and bear arms.

This question is biased toward eliciting a response against gun control.

Exercises for Section 1.5

CONCEPTS

1.24   Consider a medical study that is being performed to test the effect of smoking on lung cancer. Two groups of subjects are identified; one group has lung cancer and the other one doesn't. Both are asked to fill out a questionnaire containing questions about their age, sex, occupation, and number of cigarettes smoked per day. What is the response variable? Which are the factors, or independent variables? What type of study is this (experimental or observational)?

1.25   Explain each of the following terms:
    a Undercoverage   **b** Nonresponse   **c** Response bias

1.26   A market research firm sends out a Web-based survey to assess the impact of advertisements placed on a search engine's results page. About 65 percent of the surveys are answered and sent back. What types of errors are possible in this scenario?

Chapter Summary

This chapter has introduced the idea of using **sample data** to make **statistical inferences**—that is, drawing conclusions about populations and processes by using sample data. We began by learning that a **population** is a set of existing units that we wish to study. We saw that, since many populations are too large to examine in their entirety, we often study a population by selecting a **sample,** which is a subset of the population units. Next we learned that, if the information contained in a sample is to accurately represent the population, then the sample should be **randomly selected** from the population, and we saw how **random numbers** can be used to select a **random sample.** We also learned that selecting a random sample requires a **frame** (that is, a list of all of the population units) and that, since a frame does not always exist, we sometimes select a **systematic sample.**

We continued this chapter by studying **processes.** We learned that to make statistical inferences about the population of all possible values of a variable that could be observed when using a process, the process must be in **statistical control.** We learned that a process is in statistical control if it does not exhibit any unusual process variations, and we demonstrated how we might sample a process and how to use a runs plot to try to judge whether a process is in control.

Next, in optional Section 1.3 we studied different types of quantitative and qualitative variables. We learned that there are two types of **quantitative variables—ratio variables,** which are measured on a scale such that ratios of its values are meaningful and there is an inherently defined zero value, and **interval variables,** for which ratios are not meaningful and there is no inherently defined zero value. We also saw that there are two types of qualitative variables—**ordinal variables,** for which there is a meaningful ordering of the categories, and **nominative variables,** for which there is no meaningful ordering of the categories.

We concluded this chapter with optional Sections 1.4 and 1.5. Section 1.4 discusses **survey sampling.** In this section we introduced **stratified random sampling,** in which we divide a population into groups (**strata**) and then select a random sample from each group. We also introduced **multistage cluster sampling,** which involves selecting a sample in stages, and we explained how to select a **systematic sample.** Section 1.5 gives a further discussion of data acquisition and survey sampling. In this section we introduced some potential problems encountered when conducting a sample survey—**undercoverage, nonresponse, response bias,** and **slanted questions.**

Glossary of Terms

categorical (qualitative) variable: A variable having values that indicate into which of several categories a population unit belongs. (pages 3, 17)

census: An examination of all the units in a population. (page 4)

cluster sampling (multistage cluster sampling): A sampling design in which we sequentially cluster population units into subpopulations. (page 19)

data: Numerical facts and figures from which conclusions can be drawn. (page 3)

descriptive statistics: The science of describing the important aspects of a set of measurements. (page 4)

errors of nonobservation: Sampling error related to population units that are not observed. (page 23)

errors of observation: Sampling error that occurs when the data collected in a survey differ from the truth. (page 23)

experimental study: A statistical study in which the analyst is able to set or manipulate the values of the independent variables. (page 21)

finite population: A population that contains a finite number of units. (page 9)

frame: A list of all of the units in a population. This is needed in order to select a random sample. (page 7)

independent variable: A variable (or factor) that may be related to the response variable. (page 21)

infinite population: A population that is defined so that there is no limit to the number of units that could potentially belong to the population. (page 9)

interval variable: A quantitative variable such that ratios of its values are not meaningful and for which there is not an inherently defined zero value. (page 17)

measurement: The process of assigning a value of a variable to each of the units in a population or sample. (page 3)

nominative variable: A qualitative variable for which there is no meaningful ordering, or ranking, of the categories. (page 17)

nonresponse: A situation in which population units selected to participate in a survey do not respond to the survey instrument. (page 24)

observational study: A statistical study in which the analyst is not able to control the values of the independent variables. (page 21)

ordinal variable: A qualitative variable for which there is a meaningful ordering or ranking of the categories. (page 17)

population: A set of existing units (people, objects, events, or the like) that we wish to study. (page 3)

process: A sequence of operations that takes inputs and turns them into outputs. (page 9)

qualitative (categorical) variable: A variable having values that indicate into which of several categories a population unit belongs. (pages 3, 17)

quantitative variable: A variable having values that are numbers representing quantities. (pages 3, 17)

random number table: A table containing random digits that is often used to select a random sample. (page 5)

random sample: A sample selected so that, on each selection from the population, every unit remaining in the population on that selection has the same chance of being chosen. (page 4)

ratio variable: A quantitative variable such that ratios of its values are meaningful and for which there is an inherently defined zero value. (page 17)

response bias: Bias in the results obtained when carrying out a statistical study that is related to how survey participants answer the survey questions. (page 25)

response rate: The proportion of all people whom we attempt to contact that actually respond to a survey. (page 23)

response variable: A variable of interest that we wish to study. (page 21)

runs plot: A graph of individual process measurements versus time. Also called a **time series plot.** (page 11)

sample: A subset of the units in a population. (page 4)

sample frame: A list of sampling units from which a sample will be selected. It should closely agree with the target population. (page 23)

sampling error: The difference between the value of a sample statistic and the population parameter; it occurs because not all of the elements in the population have been measured. (page 24)

sampling without replacement: A sampling procedure in which we do not place previously selected units back into the population and, therefore, do not give these units a chance to be chosen on succeeding selections. (page 5)

sampling with replacement: A sampling procedure in which we place any unit that has been chosen back into the population to give the unit a chance to be chosen on succeeding selections. (page 4)

selection bias: Bias in the results obtained when carrying out a statistical study that is related to how survey participants are selected. (page 24)

statistical control: A state in which a process does not exhibit any unusual variations. Often this means that the process displays a constant amount of variation around a constant, or horizontal, level. (page 10)

statistical inference: The science of using a sample of measurements to make generalizations about the important aspects of a population. (page 4)

statistical process control (SPC): A method for analyzing process data in which we monitor and study the process variation. The goal is to stabilize (and reduce) the amount of process variation. (page 11)

strata: The subpopulations in a stratified sampling design. (page 18)

stratified random sampling: A sampling design in which we divide a population into nonoverlapping subpopulations and then select a random sample from each subpopulation (stratum). (page 18)

survey: An instrument employed to collect data. (page 22)

systematic sample: A sample taken by moving systematically through the population. For instance, we might randomly select one of the first 200 population units and then systematically sample every 200th population unit thereafter. (pages 7, 19)

target population: The entire population of interest in a statistical study. (page 23)

undercoverage: A situation in sampling in which some groups of population units are underrepresented. (page 24)

variable: A characteristic of a population unit. (page 3)

voluntary response survey: A survey in which respondents self-select. (page 9)

Supplementary Exercises

1.27 Some television stations attempt to gauge public opinion by posing a question on the air and asking viewers to call to give their opinions. Suppose that a particular television station asks viewers whether they support or oppose a proposed federal gun control law. Viewers are to call one of two 800 numbers to register support or opposition. When the results are tabulated, the station reports that 78 percent of those who called are opposed to the proposed law. What do you think of the sampling method used by the station? Do you think that the percentage of the entire population that opposes the proposed law is as high as the 78 percent of the sample that was opposed?

1.28 In early 1995, *The Milwaukee Sentinel,* a morning newspaper in Milwaukee, Wisconsin, and *The Milwaukee Journal,* an afternoon newspaper, merged to form *The Milwaukee Journal Sentinel.* Several weeks after the merger, a Milwaukee television station, WITI-TV, conducted a telephone call-in survey asking whether viewers liked the new *Journal Sentinel.* The survey was "not scientific" because any viewer wishing to call in could do so.

On April 26, 1995, Tim Cuprisin, in his "Inside TV & Radio" column in the *Journal Sentinel,* wrote the following comment:

WE DIDN'T CALL: WITI-TV (Channel 6) did one of those polls—which they admit are unscientific—last week and found that 388 viewers like the new *Journal Sentinel* and 2,629 don't like it.

We did our own unscientific poll on whether those Channel 6 surveys accurately reflect public opinion. The results: a full 100 percent of the respondents say absolutely, positively not.

Is Cuprisin's comment justified? Write a short paragraph explaining your answer.

1.29 Table 1.11 gives the "35 best companies to work for" as rated by *Fortune* magazine in February, 2007. Use random numbers to select a random sample of 10 of these companies. Justify that your sample is random by carefully explaining how you obtained it. List the random numbers you used and show how they gave your random sample.

TABLE 1.11 **Fortune's 35 Best Companies to Work for in February 2007 (for Exercise 1.29)**

Rank	Company	Rank	Company
1	Google	19	Alston & Bird
2	Genentech	20	Quik Trip
3	Wegmans Food Markets	21	Griffin Hospital
4	Container Store	22	Valero Energy
5	Whole Foods Market	23	Vision Service Plan
6	Network Appliance	24	Nordstrom
7	S.C. Johnson & Son	25	Ernst & Young
8	Boston Consulting Group	26	Arnold & Porter
9	Methodist Hospital System	27	Recreational Equip.
10	W.L. Gore & Associates	28	Kimley-Horn & Associates
11	Cisco Systems	29	Edward Jones
12	David Weekley Homes	30	Russell Investment Grp.
13	Nugget Market	31	Adobe Systems
14	Qualcomm	32	Plante & Moran
15	American Century Invest.	33	Intuit
16	Starbucks Coffee	34	Umpqua Bank
17	Quicken Loans	35	Children's Healthcare of Atlanta
18	Station Casinos		

Source: "100 Best Companies to Work for 2007," CNNMoney.com, http://money.cnn.com/magazines/fortune/bestcompanies/2007/, (accessed August 30, 2007).

connect

FIGURE 1.9   Runs Plot of Daily Percentages of
             Customers Waiting More Than One
             Minute to Be Seated (for Exercise 1.30)

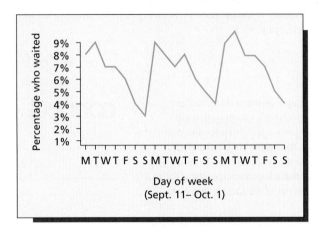

Day of week
(Sept. 11– Oct. 1)

TABLE 1.12   The Average Basic Cable Rates in the
             U.S. from 1995 to 2005
             ● BasicCable

Year	Average Basic Cable Rate
1995	23.07
1996	24.41
1997	26.48
1998	27.81
1999	28.92
2000	30.37
2001	32.87
2002	34.71
2003	36.59
2004	38.14
2005	39.63

Source: Kagan Research, LLC. From the Broadband Cable Financial Data-
book 2004, 2005 (copyright). *Cable Program Investor,* Dec. 16, 2004,
March 30, 2006, and other publications, http://www.census.gov/
compendia/statab/information_communications/

FIGURE 1.10   Runs Plot of the Average Basic Cable Rates in the U.S. from 1995 to 2005
              (for Exercise 1.31)

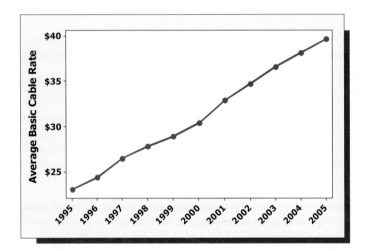

1.30 In the article "Accelerating Improvement" published in *Quality Progress,* Gaudard, Coates, and Freeman describe a restaurant that caters to business travelers and has a self-service breakfast buffet. Interested in customer satisfaction, the manager conducts a survey over a three-week period and finds that the main customer complaint is having to wait too long to be seated. On each day from September 11 to October 1, a problem-solving team records the percentage of patrons who must wait more than one minute to be seated. A runs plot of the daily percentages is shown in Figure 1.9.[14] What does the runs plot tell us about how to improve the waiting time situation?

1.31 Table 1.12 presents the average basic cable television rate in the United States for each of the years 1995 to 2005. Figure 1.10 gives a runs plot of these data. Describe how the average basic cable rates are changing over time.   ● BasicCable

1.32 Figure 1.11 gives a runs plot of the Cleveland Indians' winning percentages from 1915 (when the team was renamed as the "Indians") to 2004. Many longtime Indians fans believe that the April 1959 trade of Rocky Colavito, a feared home-run hitter, for Detroit's Harvey Kuehn, a good average hitter without exceptional power, sent the team into a decline that lasted more than 30 years. Does the runs plot provide any evidence to support this opinion? Why or why not?

[14]The source of Figure 1.9 is M. Gaudard, R. Coates, and L. Freeman, "Accelerating Improvement," *Quality Progress,*
October 1991, pp. 81–88. © 1991 American Society for Quality Control. Used with permission.

FIGURE 1.11   **Runs Plot of the Cleveland Indians' Winning Percentages from 1915 through 2004 (for Exercise 1.32)**

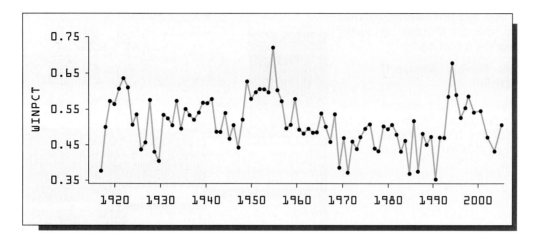

MINITAB, Excel, and MegaStat for Statistics

In this book we use three types of software to carry out statistical analysis—MINITAB Version 15, Excel 2007, and MegaStat. MINITAB is a computer package designed expressly for conducting statistical analysis. It is widely used at many colleges and universities and in a large number of business organizations. Excel is, of course, a general-purpose electronic spreadsheet program and analytical tool. The analysis ToolPak in Excel includes many procedures for performing various kinds of basic statistical analyses. MegaStat is an add-in package that is specifically designed for performing statistical analysis in the Excel spreadsheet environment. The principal advantage of Excel is that, because of its broad acceptance among students and professionals as a multipurpose analytical tool, it is both well known and widely available. The advantages of a special-purpose statistical software package like MINITAB are that it provides a far wider range of statistical procedures and it offers the experienced analyst a range of options to better control the analysis. The advantages of MegaStat include (1) its ability to perform a number of statistical calculations that are not automatically done by the procedures in the Excel ToolPak and (2) features that make it easier to use than Excel for a wide variety of statistical analyses. In addition, the output obtained by using MegaStat is automatically placed in a standard Excel spreadsheet and can be edited by using any of the features in Excel. MegaStat can be copied from the CD-ROM included with this book. MINITAB, Excel, and MegaStat, through built-in functions, programming languages, and macros, offer almost limitless power. Here, we will limit our attention to procedures that are easily accessible via menus without resort to any special programming or advanced features.

Commonly used features of MINITAB 15, Excel 2007, and MegaStat are presented in this chapter along with an initial application—the construction of a runs plot of the gas mileages in Table 1.4. You will find that the limited instructions included here, along with the built-in help features of all three software packages, will serve as a starting point from which you can discover a variety of other procedures and options. Much more detailed descriptions of MINITAB 15 can be found in other sources, in particular in the manual *Meet MINITAB 15 for Windows*. This manual is available in print and as a .pdf file, viewable using Adobe Acrobat Reader, on the MINITAB Inc. website (http://www.minitab.com/support/docs/rel15/MeetMinitab.pdf). Similarly, there are a number of alternative reference materials for Microsoft Excel 2007. Of course, an understanding of the related statistical concepts is essential to the effective use of any statistical software package.

Appendix 1.1 ■ Getting Started with MINITAB

We begin with a look at some features of MINITAB that are common to most analyses. When the instructions call for a sequence of selections from a series of menus, the sequence will be presented in the following form:

Stat : Basic Statistics : Descriptive Statistics

This notation indicates that Stat is the first selection from the Minitab menu bar, next Basic Statistics is selected from the Stat pull-down menu, and finally Descriptive Statistics is selected from the Basic Statistics pull-down menu.

Starting MINITAB   Procedures for starting MINITAB may vary from one installation to the next. If you are using a public computing laboratory, you may have to consult local documentation. For typical MINITAB installations, you will generally be able to start MINITAB with a sequence of selections from the Microsoft Windows Start menu something like the following:

- Select **Start : Programs : Minitab : Minitab 15 Statistical Software English**

You can also start MINITAB with a previously saved MINITAB worksheet (like GasMiles.MTW or one of the many other data files from the CD-ROM included with this text) from the Windows Explorer by double-clicking on the worksheet's icon.

After you start MINITAB, the display is partitioned into two working windows. These windows serve the following functions:

- The "Session window" is the area where MINITAB commands and basic output are displayed.
- The "Data window" is an Excel-like worksheet where data can be entered and edited.

Help resources   Like most Windows programs, MINITAB includes online help via a Help menu. The Help feature includes standard Contents and Search entries as well as Tutorials that introduce MINITAB concepts and walk through some typical MINITAB sessions. Also included is a StatGuide that provides guidance for interpreting statistical tables and graphs in a practical, easy-to-understand way.

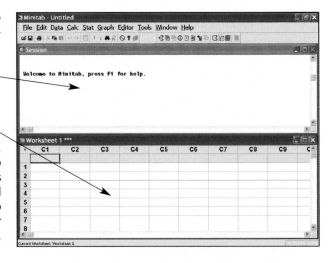

Entering data (entering the gasoline mileage data in Table 1.4 on page 10) from the keyboard:

- In the Data window, click on the cell directly below C1 and type a name for the variable—say, Mpg—and press the Enter key.
- Starting in row 1 under column C1, type the values for the variable (gasoline mileages from Table 1.4 on page 10) down the column, pressing the Enter key after each number is typed.

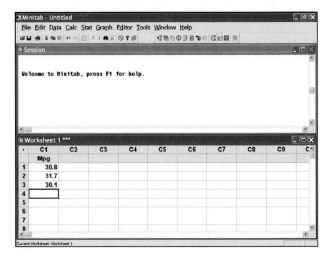

Saving data (saving the gasoline mileage data):

- Select **File : Save Current Worksheet As**

- In the "Save Worksheet As" dialog box, use the "Save in" drop-down menu to select the destination drive and folder. (Here we have selected a folder named Data Files on the Local C drive.)

- Enter the desired file name in the File name box. Here we have chosen the name GasMiles. MINITAB will automatically add the extension .MTW.

- Click the Save button in the "Save Worksheet As" dialog box.

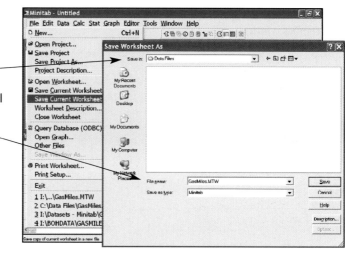

Retrieving a MINITAB worksheet containing the gasoline mileage data in Table 1.4 (data file: GasMiles. MTW):

- Select **File : Open Worksheet**

- In the Open Worksheet dialog box, use the "Look in" drop-down menu to select the source drive and folder. (Here we have selected a folder named Data Files on the Local C drive.)

- Enter the desired file name in the File name box. (Here we have chosen the MINITAB worksheet GasMiles.MTW.)

- Click the Open button in the Open Worksheet dialog box.

- MINITAB may display a dialog box with the message, "A copy of the content of this file will be added to the current project." If so, click OK.

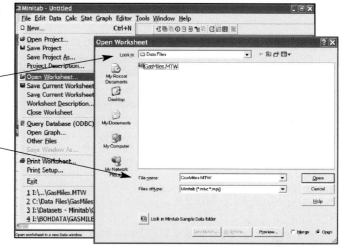

Creating a runs (or time series) plot similar to Figure 1.2 on page 10 (data file: GasMiles.MTW):

- Select **Graph : Time Series Plot**

- In the Time Series Plots dialog box, select Simple, which produces a time series plot of data that is stored in a single column, and click OK.

- In the "Time Series Plot—Simple" dialog box, enter the name of the variable, Mpg, into the Series window. Do this either (1) by typing its name or (2) by double-clicking on its name in the list of variables on the left side of the dialog box. Here, this list consists of the single variable Mpg in column C1.

- Click OK in the "Time Series Plot—Simple" dialog box.

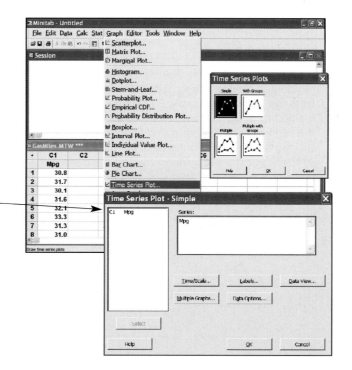

- **The runs (or time series) plot** will appear in a graphics window.

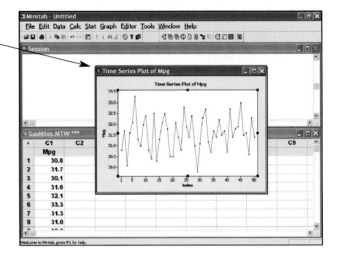

- **The graph can be edited** by right-clicking on the portion you wish to edit. For instance, here we have right-clicked on the data region.
- Selecting "Edit Data Region" from the pop-up window gives a dialog box that allows you to edit this region. The x and y scales, x and y axis labels, title, plot symbols, connecting lines, data region, figure region, and so forth can all be edited by right-clicking on that particular portion of the graph.

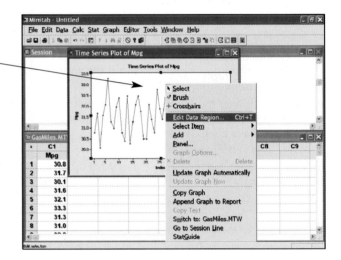

- For instance, after right-clicking on the data region and then selecting "Edit Data Region" from the pop-up menu, the Edit Data Region dialog box allows us to edit various attributes of this region. As shown, selecting Custom and clicking on the background color arrow allow us to change the background color of the data region.

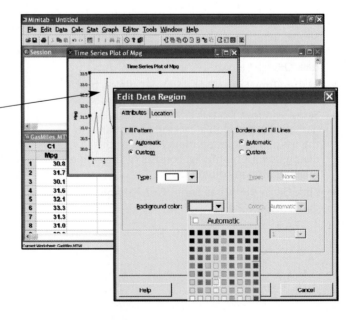

Printing a high-resolution graph similar to Figure 1.2 on page 10 (data file: GasMiles.MTW):

- Click in the graphics window to select it as the active window.
- Select **File : Print Graph** to print the graph.
- Select the appropriate printer and click OK in the Print dialog box.

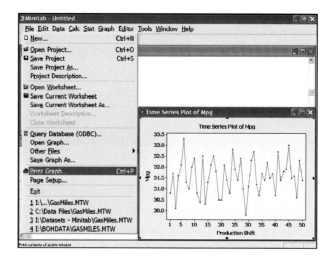

Saving the high-resolution graph:

- Click on the graph to make the graphics window the active window.
- Select **File : Save Graph As**
- In the "Save Graph As" dialog box, use the "Save in" drop-down menu to select the destination drive and folder (here we have selected the DVD/CD-RW drive).
- Enter the desired file name in the File name box (here we have chosen the name MileagePlot). MINITAB will automatically add the file extension .MGF.
- Click the Save button in the "Save Graph As" dialog box.

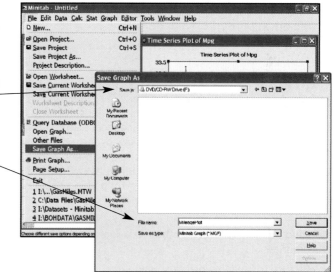

Printing data from the Session window (shown) or Data window (data file: GasMiles.MTW):
To print selected output from the Session window:

- Use the mouse to select the desired output or text (selected output will be reverse-highlighted in black).
- Select **File : Print Session Window**
- In the Print dialog box, the Print range will be the "Selection" option. To print the entire session window, select the Print range to be "All."
- Select the desired printer from the Printer Name drop-down menu.
- Click OK in the Print dialog box.

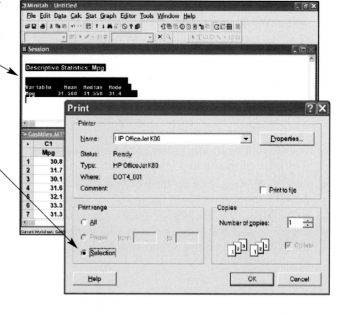

To print the contents of the Data window (that is, to print the MINITAB worksheet):

- Click in the Data window to select it as active.
- Select **File : Print Worksheet**
- Make selections as desired in the Data Window Print Options dialog box, add a title in the Title window if desired, and click OK.
- Select the desired printer from the Printer Name drop-down menu and click OK in the Print dialog box.

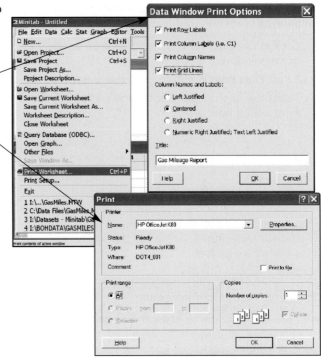

Including MINITAB output in reports   The immediately preceding examples show how to print various types of output directly from MINITAB. Printing is a useful way to capture a quick hard-copy record of an analysis result. However, you may prefer at times to collect selected analysis results and arrange them with related narrative documentation in a report that can be saved and printed as a unit. This is easily accomplished by copying selected MINITAB results to the Windows clipboard and by pasting them into your favorite word processor. Once copied to a word processor document, MINITAB results can be documented, edited, resized, and rearranged as desired into a cohesive record of your analysis. The following sequence of examples illustrates the process of copying MINITAB output into a Microsoft Word document.

Copying session window output to a word processing document:

- Be sure to have a word processing document open to receive the results.
- Use the scroll bar on the right side of the Session window to locate the results to be copied and drag the mouse to select the desired output (selected output will be reverse-highlighted in black).
- Copy the selected output to the Windows clipboard by clicking the Copy icon on the MINITAB toolbar or by right-clicking on the selected text and then selecting Copy from the pop-up menu.
- Switch to your word processing document by clicking the button on the Windows task bar (here labeled MS Word Report.doc).
- Click in your word processing document to position the cursor at the desired insertion point.
- Click the Paste button on the word processing power bar or right-click at the insertion point and select Paste from the pop-up menu.
- Return to your MINITAB session by clicking the MINITAB button on the Windows task bar.

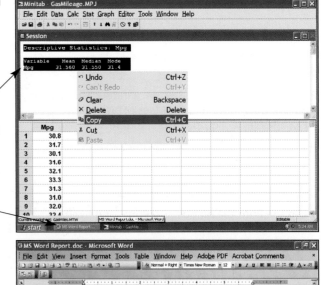

Copying high-resolution graphics output to a word processing document:

- Be sure to have a word processing document open to receive the results.
- Copy the selected contents of the high-resolution graphics window to the Windows clipboard by right-clicking in the graphics window and by then clicking Copy Graph on the pop-up menu.
- Switch to your word processing document by clicking the button on the Windows task bar (here labeled MS Word Report.doc).
- Click in your word processing document to position the cursor at the desired insertion point.
- Click the Paste button on the word processor power bar or right-click at the insertion point and select Paste from the pop-up menu.
- Return to your MINITAB session by clicking the MINITAB button on the Windows task bar.

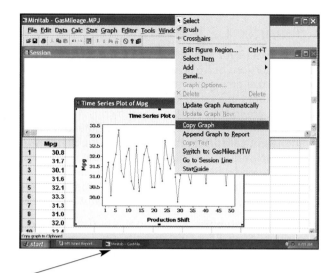

Results Here is how the copied results might appear in Microsoft Word. These results can be edited, resized, repositioned, and combined with your own additional documentation to create a cohesive record of your analysis.

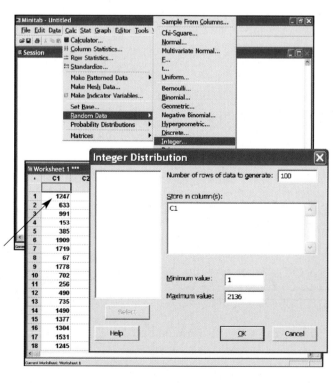

We complete this appendix by demonstrating how MINITAB can be used to generate a set of **random numbers**.

To create 100 random numbers between 1 and 2136 similar to those in Table 1.1(b) on page 6:

- Select **Calc : Random Data : Integer**
- In the Integer Distribution dialog box, enter 100 into the "Number of rows of data to generate" window.
- Enter C1 into the "Store in column(s)" window.
- Enter 1 into the Minimum value box and enter 2136 into the Maximum value box.
- Click OK in the Integer Distribution dialog box.

The 100 random numbers will be placed in the Data window in column C1. These numbers are generated with replacement. Repeated numbers would be skipped if the random numbers are being used to sample without replacement.

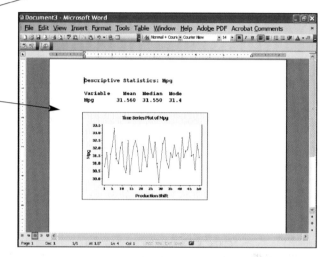

Appendix 1.2 ■ Getting Started with Excel

Because Excel 2007 may be new to some readers, and because the Excel 2007 window looks quite different from previous versions of Excel, we will begin by describing some characteristics of the Excel 2007 window. Previous versions of Excel employed many drop-down menus. This meant that many features were "hidden" from the user, which resulted in a steep learning curve for beginners. In Excel 2007, Microsoft tried to reduce the number of features that are hidden in drop-down menus. Therefore, Excel 2007 displays all of the applicable commands needed for a particular type of task at the top of the Excel window. These commands are represented by a tab-and-group arrangement called the **ribbon**—see the right side of the illustration of an Excel 2007 window below. The commands displayed in the ribbon are regulated by a series of **tabs** located near the top of the ribbon. For example, in the illustration below, the **Home tab** is selected. If we selected a different tab, say, for example, the **Page Layout tab,** the commands displayed by the ribbon would be different.

We now briefly describe some basic features of the Excel 2007 window:

1 **Office button:** By clicking on this button, the user obtains a menu of often-used commands—for example, Open, Save, Print, and so forth. This is very similar to the "File menu" in older versions of Excel. However, some menu items are unique to Excel 2007. This menu also provides access to a large number of Excel options settings.

2 **Tabs:** Clicking on a tab results in a ribbon display of features, commands, and options related to a particular type of task. For example, when the *Home tab* is selected (as in the figure below), the features, commands, and options displayed by the ribbon are all related to making entries into the Excel worksheet. As another example, if the *Formula tab* is selected, all of the features, commands, and options displayed in the ribbon relate to using formulas in the Excel worksheet.

3 **Quick Access toolbar:** This toolbar displays buttons that provide shortcuts to often-used commands. Initially, this toolbar displays Save, Undo, and Redo buttons. The user can customize this toolbar by adding shortcut buttons for other commands (such as New, Open, Quick Print, and so forth). This can be done by clicking on the arrow button directly to the right of the Quick Access toolbar and by making selections from the "Customize" drop-down menu that appears.

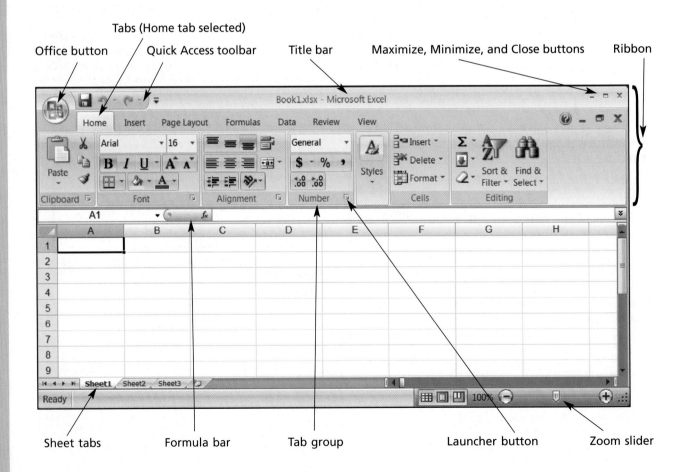

4   **Title bar:** This bar shows the name of the currently active workbook and contains the Quick Access toolbar as well as the Maximize, Minimize, and Close buttons.

5   **Ribbon:** A grouping of toolbars, tabs, commands, and features related to performing a particular kind of task—for example, making entries into the Excel spreadsheet. The particular features displayed in the ribbon are controlled by selecting a *tab.* If the user is working in the spreadsheet workspace and wishes to reduce the number of features displayed by the ribbon, this can be done by right-clicking on the ribbon and by selecting "Minimize the Ribbon." We will often Minimize the Ribbon in the Excel appendixes of this book in order to focus attention on operations being performed and results being displayed in the Excel spreadsheet.

6   **Sheet tabs:** These tabs show the name of each sheet in the Excel workbook. When the user clicks a sheet tab, the selected sheet becomes active and is displayed in the Excel spreadsheet. The name of a sheet can be changed by double-clicking on the appropriate sheet tab and by entering the new name.

7   **Formula bar:** When a worksheet cell is selected, the formula bar displays the current content of the cell. If the cell content is defined by a formula, the defining formula is displayed in the formula bar.

8   **Tab group:** This is a labeled grouping of commands and features related to performing a particular type of task.

9   **Launcher button:** Some of the tab groups have a launcher button—for example, the Clipboard, Font, Alignment, and Number tab groups each have such a button. Clicking on the launcher button opens a dialog box or task pane related to performing operations in the tab group.

10 **Zoom slider:** By moving this slider right and left, the cells in the Excel spreadsheet can be enlarged or reduced in size.

We now look at some features of Excel that are common to many analyses. When the instructions call for a sequence of selections, the sequence will be presented in the following form:

Select **Home : Format : Row Height**

This notation indicates that we first select the Home tab on the ribbon, then we select Format from the Cells Group on the ribbon, and finally we select Row Height from the Format drop-down menu.

For many of the statistical and graphical procedures in Excel, it is necessary to provide a range of cells to specify the location of data in the spreadsheet. Generally, the range may be specified either by typing the cell locations directly into a dialog box or by dragging the selected range with the mouse. Though, for the experienced user, it is usually easier to use the mouse to select a range, the instructions that follow will, for precision and clarity, specify ranges by typing in cell locations. The selected range may include column or variable labels—labels at the tops of columns that serve to identify variables. When the selected range includes such labels, it is important to select the "Labels check box" in the analysis dialog box.

Starting Excel   Procedures for starting Excel may vary from one installation to the next. If you are using a public computing laboratory, you may wish to consult local documentation. For typical Excel installations, you will generally be able to start Excel with a sequence of selections from the Microsoft Windows Start menu something like the following:

Start : Microsoft Office XP : Microsoft Office Excel 2007

You can also start Excel with a previously saved Excel spreadsheet (like GasMiles.xlsx or one of the other data files from the CD-ROM included with this text) from the Windows Explorer by double-clicking on the spreadsheet file's icon.

After starting Excel, the display will generally show a blank Excel workbook.

Help resources Like most Windows programs, Excel includes online help via a Help menu that includes search capability as well as a table of contents. To display the Help menu, click on the "Question Mark" button in the upper right corner of the ribbon.

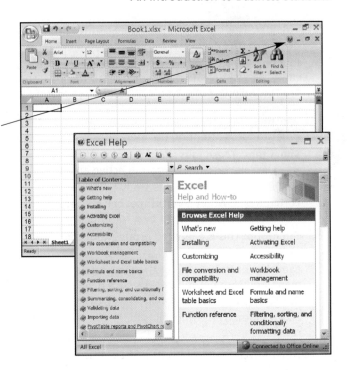

Entering data (entering the gas mileages in Table 1.4 on page 10) from the keyboard (data file: GasMiles.xlsx):

- In a new Excel workbook, click on cell A1 in Sheet1 and type a label—that is, a variable name—say, Mileage, for the gasoline mileages.

- Beginning in cell A2 (directly under the column label Mileage) type the mileages from Table 1.4 on page 10 down the column, pressing the Enter key following each entry.

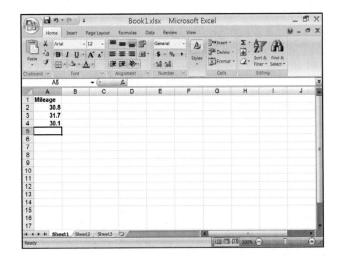

Saving data (saving the gasoline mileage data):

- To begin, click on the **Office** button.
- Select **Save As : Excel Workbook**
- In the "Save As" dialog box, use the "Save in" drop-down menu to select the destination drive and folder. Here we have selected a folder called Data Files on the Local C drive.
- Enter the desired file name in the "File name" box. Here we have chosen the name GasMiles. Excel will automatically add the extension .xlsx.
- Click the Save button in the "Save As" dialog box.

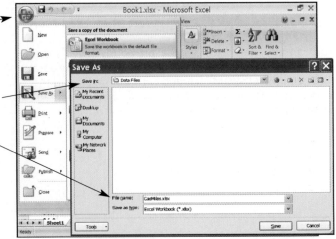

Retrieving an Excel spreadsheet containing the gasoline mileages in Table 1.4 on page 10 (data file: GasMiles.xlsx):

- Select **Office : Open**
  That is, click on the Office button and then select Open.

- In the Open dialog box, use the "Look in" drop-down menu to select the source drive and folder. Here we have selected a folder called Data Files on the Local C drive.

- Enter the desired file name in the "File name" box. Here we have chosen the Excel spreadsheet GasMiles.xlsx.

- Click the Open button in the Open dialog box.

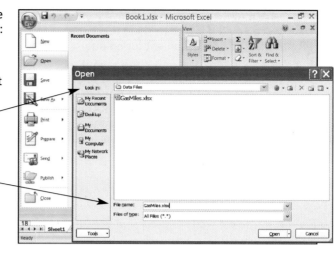

Creating a runs (time series) plot similar to Figure 1.2 on page 10 (data file: GasMiles.xlsx):

- Enter the gasoline mileage data into column A of the worksheet with label Mileage in cell A1.

- Click on any cell in the column of mileages, or select the range of the data to be charted by dragging with the mouse. Selecting the range of the data is good practice because—if this is not done—Excel will sometimes try to construct a chart using all of the data in your worksheet. The result of such a chart is often nonsensical. Here, of course, we have only one column of data—so there would be no problem. But, in general, it is a good idea to select the data before constructing a graph.

- Select **Insert : Line : 2-D Line : Line with Markers**
  Here select the Insert tab and then select Line from the Charts group. When Line is selected, a gallery of line charts will be displayed. From the gallery, select the desired chart—in this case a 2-D Line chart with markers. The proper chart can be selected by looking at the sample pictures. As an alternative, if the cursor is held over a picture, a descriptive "tooltip" of the chart type will be displayed. In this case, the "Line with Markers" tooltip was obtained by holding the cursor over the highlighted picture.

- When you click on the "2-D Line with Markers" icon, the chart will appear in a graphics window and the Chart Tools ribbon will be displayed.

- To prepare the chart for editing, it is best to move the chart to a new worksheet called a "chart sheet." To do this, click on the **Design** tab and select **Move Chart**.

- In the Move Chart dialog box, select the "New sheet" option, enter a name for the new sheet—here, "Runs Plot"—into the "New sheet" window, and click OK.

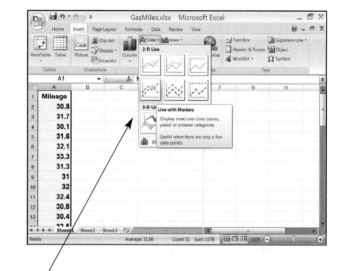

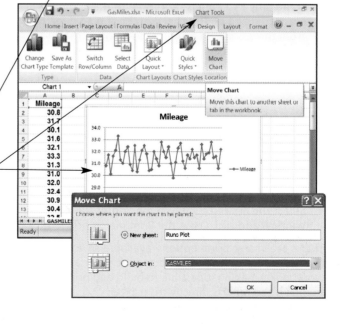

- The Chart Tools ribbon will be displayed and the chart will be placed in a chart sheet in a larger format that is more convenient for editing.

- In order to edit the chart, select the **Layout** tab from the Chart Tools ribbon. By making selections from the ribbon, many chart attributes can be edited. For instance, when you click on Axes as shown, various options for formatting the horizontal and vertical axes can be selected.

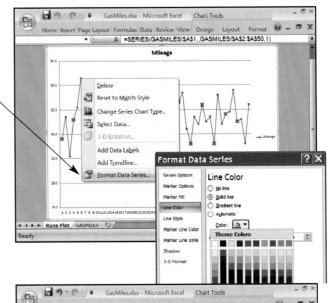

- A chart can also be edited by right-clicking on the portion of the chart that we wish to revise. For instance, in the screen shown, we have right-clicked on one of the plotted data points. When this is done, we obtain a menu as shown. If we select "Format Data Series," we obtain a dialog box that provides many options for editing the data series (the plotted points and their connecting lines). For example, if (as shown) we select

Line Color : Solid Line

and then click on the Color arrow button, we obtain a drop-down menu that allows us to select a desired color for the connecting lines between the plotted points. We can edit other portions of the chart in the same way.

- Here we show an edited runs plot. This revised chart was constructed from the original runs plot created by Excel using various options like those illustrated above. This chart can be copied directly from the worksheet (simply right-click on the graph and select Copy from the pop-up menu) and can then be pasted into a word processing document.

The chart can be printed from this worksheet as follows:

- Select **Office : Print**
  That is, click on the Office button and then select Print.

- Select the desired printer in the Printer Name window and click OK in the Print dialog box.

There are many print options available in Excel for printing—a selected range, selected sheets, or an entire workbook—making it possible to build and print fairly sophisticated reports directly from Excel.

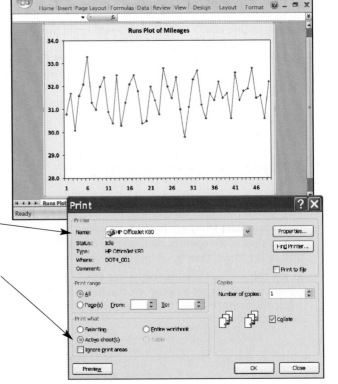

Printing a spreadsheet with an embedded graph:

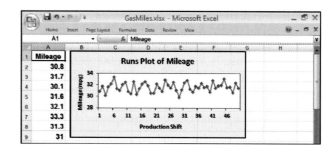

- Click outside the graph to print both the worksheet contents (here the mileage data) and the graph. Click on the graph to print only the graph.

- Select **Office : Print**
  That is, click on the Office button and then select Print.

- Select the desired printer in the Printer Name window and click OK in the Print dialog box.

Including Excel output in reports   The preceding example showed how to print selected analysis results from Excel. Printing is a useful way to capture a quick hard-copy record of an analysis result, and Excel offers a variety of options for building sophisticated reports. However, you may at times prefer to collect selected analysis results and arrange them with related narrative in a word processing document that can be saved and printed as a unit. You can simply copy Excel results—selected spreadsheet ranges and graphs—to the Windows clipboard. Then paste them into an open word processing document. Once copied to a word processing document, Excel results can be documented, edited, resized, and rearranged as desired into a cohesive record of your analysis. The cut and paste process is quite similar to the MINITAB examples at the end of Appendix 1.1.

Generating random numbers in Excel   We complete this appendix by demonstrating how Excel can be used to generate a set of **random numbers** (as in Table 1.1(b) on page 6).

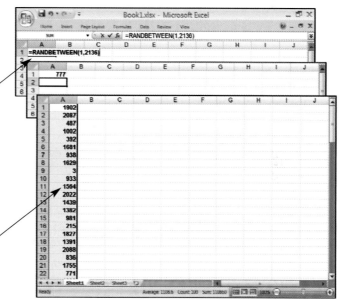

To create 100 random numbers between 1 and 2136 similar to those in Table 1.1(b):

- Type the cell formula

      =RANDBETWEEN(1,2136)

  into cell A1 of the Excel worksheet and press the Enter key. This will generate a random integer between 1 and 2136, which will be placed in cell A1.

- Using the mouse, copy the cell formula for cell A1 down through cell A100. This will generate 100 random numbers between 1 and 2136 in cells A1 through A100 (note that the random number in cell A1 will change when this is done—this is not a problem).

- The random numbers are generated with replacement. Repeated numbers would be skipped if the random numbers are being used to sample without replacement.

Appendix 1.3 ■ Getting Started with MegaStat

MegaStat, which was developed by Professor J. B. Orris of Butler University, is an Excel add-in that performs statistical analyses within an Excel workbook. Instructions for installing MegaStat can be found on the CD-ROM that accompanies this text.

- After installation, you can access MegaStat by clicking on the Add-Ins tab (on the ribbon) and by then selecting MegaStat from the Add-Ins group of menu commands. When you select MegaStat, the MegaStat menu appears as shown in the screen. Most of the menu options display submenus. If a menu item is followed by an ellipsis (...), clicking it will display a dialog box for that option.

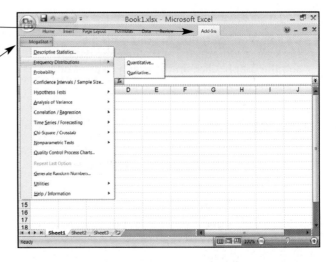

- A dialog box allows you to specify the data to be used and other inputs and options. A typical dialog box is shown in the screen.

- After you have selected the needed data and options, click OK. The dialog box then disappears, and MegaStat performs the analysis.

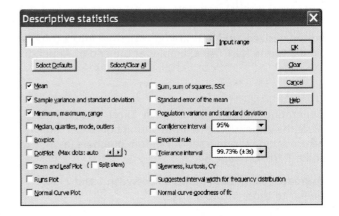

Before we look at specific dialog boxes, we will describe some features that are common to all of the options. MegaStat use is intuitive and very much like other Excel operations; however, there are some features unique to MegaStat.

Data selection   Most MegaStat dialog boxes have fields where you select input ranges that contain the data to be used. Such a field is shown in the dialog box illustrated above—it is the long horizontal window with the label "Input range" to its right. Input ranges can be selected using four methods:

1 **Pointing and dragging with the mouse.** Simply select the desired data by left-clicking on the first data item and by dragging the cursor to select the rest of the data as illustrated below.

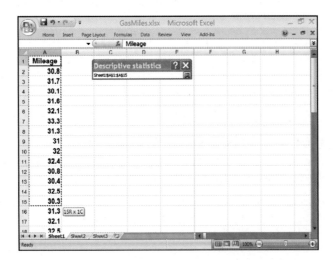

Since the dialog box pops up on the screen, it may block some of your data. You can move a dialog box around on the screen by placing the mouse pointer over the title bar (the colored area at the top) and by then clicking and holding the left mouse button while dragging the dialog box to a new location. You can even drag it partially off the screen.

You will also notice that when you start selecting data by dragging the mouse pointer, the dialog box will collapse to a smaller size to help you see the underlying data. It will automatically return to full size when you release the mouse button. You can also collapse and uncollapse the dialog box manually by clicking the collapse (-) button at the right end of the field. Clicking the button again will uncollapse the dialog box. (Never use the X button to try to collapse or uncollapse a dialog box.)

2   **Using MegaStat's AutoExpand feature.** Pointing and dragging to select data can be tedious if you have a lot of data. When you drag the mouse down it is easy to overshoot the selection, and then you have to drag the mouse back until you get the area correctly selected. AutoExpand allows rapid data selection without having to drag through the entire column of data. Here's how it works:

- Make sure the input box has the focus (that is, click in it to make the input box active). An input box has the focus when the insertion pointer is blinking in it.
- Click in one cell of the column you want. If more than one column is being selected, drag the mouse across the columns.
- Right-click over the input field or left-click the label "Input range" to the right of the input box. The data range will expand to include all of the rows in the region where you selected one row.

This procedure is illustrated below. In the left screen, we have left-clicked on one cell in the column of data labeled Mileage. In the right screen, we see the result after we right-click over the input field or left-click on the label "Input range." Notice that the entire column of data has been selected in the right screen. This can be seen by examining the input field or by looking at the column of data.

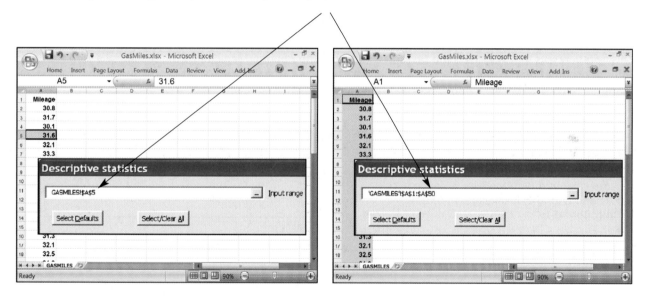

With a little practice you find this is a very efficient way to select data. The only time you cannot use it is when you want to use a partial column of data. You should also be aware that the AutoExpand stops when it finds a blank cell; thus any summations or other calculations at the bottom of a column would be selected.

Note: When using the above methods of data selection, you may select variables in an alternating sequence by holding the CTRL key while making multiple selections.

3   **Typing the name of a named range.** If you have previously identified a range of cells using Excel's name box, you may use that name to specify a data range in a MegaStat dialog box. This method can be very useful if you are using the same data for several different statistical procedures.

4   **Typing a range address.** You may type any valid Excel range address (for example, $A$1:$A$101) into the input field. This is the most cumbersome way to specify data ranges, but it certainly works.

Data labels   For most procedures, the first cell in each input range can be a label. If the first cell in a range is text, it is considered a label; if the first cell is a numeric value, it is considered data. If you want to use numbers as variable labels, you must enter the numbers as text by preceding them with a single quote mark—for instance, '2. Even though Excel stores times and dates as numbers, MegaStat will recognize them as labels if they are formatted as time/date values. If data labels are not part of the input range, the program automatically uses the cell immediately above the data range as a label if it contains a text value. If an option can consider the entire first row (or column) of an input range as labels, any numeric value in the row will cause the entire row to be treated as data. Finally, if the program detects sequential integers (1,2,3...) in a location where you might want labels, it will display a warning message. Otherwise, the rule is this: **Text cells are labels, numeric cells are data.**

Output   When you click OK on a MegaStat dialog box, it performs some statistical analysis and needs a place to put its output. It looks for a worksheet named Output. If it finds one, it goes to the end of it and appends its output; if it doesn't find an Output worksheet, it creates one. MegaStat will never make any changes to the user's worksheets; it only sends output to its Output sheet.

MegaStat makes a good attempt at formatting the output, but **it is important to remember that the Output sheet is just a standard Excel worksheet and can be modified in any way by the user.** You can adjust column widths and change any formatting that you think needs improvement. You can insert, delete, and modify cells. You can copy all or part of the output to another worksheet or to another application such as a word processor.

When the program generates output, it adjusts column widths for the current output. If you have previous output from a different option already in the Output sheet, the column widths for the previous output may be altered. You can attempt to fix this by manually adjusting the column widths. Alternatively, you can make it a practice to always start a new output sheet. The **Utilities menu** has options for **deleting the Output sheet, for making a copy of it, and for starting a new one.**

An example   We now give an example of using MegaStat to carry out statistical analysis. When the instructions call for a sequence of selections, the sequence will be presented in the following form:

Add-Ins : MegaStat : Probability : Counting Rules

This notation says that Add-Ins is the first selection (from the ribbon); MegaStat is the second selection from the Add-Ins group of menu commands; next Probability is selected from the MegaStat drop-down menu; and finally Counting Rules is selected from the Probability submenu.

Creating a runs plot of gasoline mileages similar to Figure 1.2 on page 10 (data file: GasMiles.xlsx):

- Enter the mileage data in Table 1.4 on page 10 into column A with the label Mileage in cell A1 and with the 50 mileages in cells A2 through A51.

- Select **Add-Ins : MegaStat : Descriptive Statistics**

- In the Descriptive statistics dialog box, enter the range $A$1:$A$51 into the Input range box. The easiest way to do this is to use the MegaStat AutoExpand feature. Simply select one cell in column A (say, cell A4, for instance) by clicking on the cell. Then, either right-click in the Input range box or left-click on the label "Input range" to the right of the Input range box.

- Place a checkmark in the Runs Plot checkbox.

- Click OK in the Descriptive Statistics dialog box.

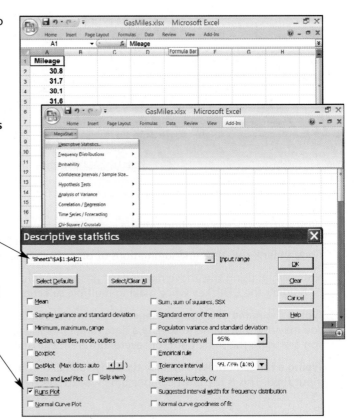

MegaStat places the resulting analysis (in this case the runs plot) in an Output worksheet. This is a standard Excel worksheet, which can be edited using any of the usual Excel features. For instance, by right-clicking on various portions of the runs plot graphic, the plot can be edited in many ways. Here we have right-clicked on the plot area. By selecting Format Plot Area, we are able to edit the graphic in a variety of ways.

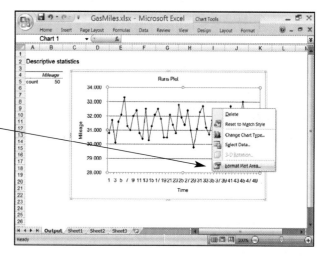

In the Format Plot Area dialog box, we can add color to the runs plot and edit the plot in many other ways.

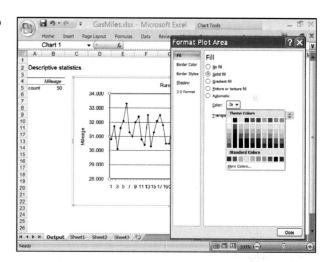

Alternatively, we can edit the runs plot by selecting

Chart Tools : Layout

By making selections from the Labels, Axes, and Background groups, the plot can be edited in a variety of ways. For example, in the screen shown we have selected the Show Plot Area button in the Background group. This gives us many options for editing the plot area of the graphic.

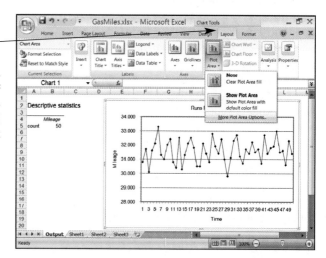

We complete this appendix by demonstrating how MegaStat can be used to generate a set of random numbers.

To create 100 random numbers between 1 and 2136 similar to those in Table 1.1(b) on page 6:

- Select **Add-Ins : MegaStat : Generate Random Numbers...**

- In the Random Number Generation dialog box, enter 100 into the "Number of values to be generated" window.

- Click the right arrow button to select 0 Decimal Places.

- Select the Uniform tab, and enter 1 into the Minimum box and enter 2136 into the Maximum box.

- Click OK in the Random Number Generation dialog box.

The 100 random numbers will be placed in the Output sheet. These numbers are generated with replacement. Repeated numbers would be skipped for random sampling without replacement.

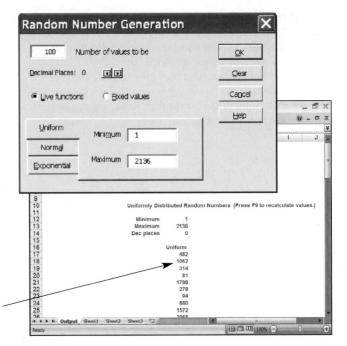

Appendix 1.4 ■ Introduction to Internet Exercises

The Internet and the World Wide Web provide a rich source of data and information on a limitless variety of subjects, among them government statistics, data about firms, and data about consumers. Though you probably have experience using the Internet, in this book we will use the Internet as a source of data for statistical analysis. We do this through Internet exercises in many chapters of this book. These exercises will ask you to go to a website, find appropriate data (and perhaps copy it), and then analyze the data.

The BSC: The McGraw-Hill/Irwin Business Statistics Center   The BSC is a collection of Internet-based resources for teaching and learning about business statistics. It includes links to statistical publications, websites, software, and data sources. To go to the BSC, enter the Web address http://www.mhhe.com/business/opsci/bstat/ into your browser. There are also links to the BSC on the CD-ROM included with this text. To see a list of databases accessible through the BSC, click on the Data Bases button on the BSC home screen. Updated links to data and additional Internet exercises can also be found at this text's website— http://www.mhhe.com/business/opsci/bowerman/.

1.33   Internet Exercise

The website maintained by the U.S. Census Bureau provides a multitude of social, economic, and government data. In particular, this website houses selected data from the most recent *Statistical Abstract of the United States* (http://www.census.gov/compendia/ statab/). Among these selected features are "Frequently Requested Tables" that can be accessed simply by clicking on the label.

a   Go to the U.S. Census Bureau website and open the "Frequently Requested Tables" from the *Statistical Abstract.* Find the table of "Consumer Price Indexes by Major Groups." Construct runs plots of (1) the price index for all items over time (years), (2) the price index for food over time, (3) the price index for fuel oil over time, and (4) the price index for electricity over time. For each runs plot, describe apparent trends in the price index.

b   By opening the "Frequently Requested Tables" from the *Statistical Abstract,* find the table of "Crimes

I n Chapter 1 we saw that although we can sometimes take a census of an entire population, we often must randomly select a sample from a population. When we have taken a census or a sample, we typically wish to describe the observed data set. In particular, we describe a sample in order to make inferences about the sampled population.

In this chapter we begin to study **descriptive statistics,** which is the science of describing the important characteristics of a data set. The techniques of descriptive statistics include **tabular and graphical methods,** which are discussed in this chapter, and **numerical methods,** which are discussed in Chapter 3. We will see that, in practice, the methods of this chapter and the methods of Chapter 3 are used together to describe data. We will also see that the methods used to describe quantitative data differ somewhat from the methods used to describe qualitative data. Finally, we will see that there are methods—both graphical and numerical—for studying the relationships between variables.

We will illustrate the methods of this chapter by describing the cell phone usages, bottle design ratings, and car mileages introduced in the cases of Chapter 1. In addition, we introduce two new cases:

C

The Payment Time Case: A management consulting firm assesses how effectively a new electronic billing system reduces bill payment times.

The Client Satisfaction Case: A financial institution examines whether customer satisfaction depends upon the type of investment product purchased.

2.1 Graphically Summarizing Qualitative Data ● ● ●

Frequency distributions When data are qualitative, we use names to identify the different categories (or classes). Often we summarize qualitative data by using a frequency distribution.

A **frequency distribution** is a table that summarizes the number (or **frequency**) of items in each of several nonoverlapping classes.

EXAMPLE 2.1 Describing 2006 Jeep Purchasing Patterns

Jeep dealerships sold four different models in 2006—Jeep Commander, Jeep Grand Cherokee, Jeep Liberty, and Jeep Wrangler. At the beginning of each new model year, a dealership must decide how many vehicles of each model should be stocked in order to meet customer demand without tying up too much money in unneeded inventory. According to the sales managers at several Greater Cincinnati Jeep dealers, the most important factor influencing their stocking decisions for a new model year is the pattern of customer purchases in the prior model year. In order to study customer purchasing patterns in 2006, the sales manager for a Cincinnati Jeep dealership compiled a list of all 251 vehicles his dealership sold in 2006. These data are given in Table 2.1—in the table C = Commander, G = Grand Cherokee, L = Liberty, and W = Wrangler. (Note that Jeep introduced three new models in 2007—Jeep Compass, Jeep Patriot, and Jeep Wrangler Unlimited. Each sales manager we interviewed believed that these new models were aimed at new market segments, and that the pattern of sales for the four 2006 models would still help them to make stocking decisions for 2007.)

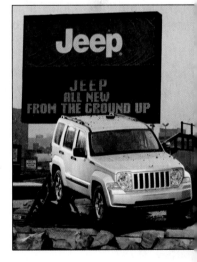

Unfortunately, the raw data in Table 2.1 do not reveal much useful information about the pattern of Jeep sales in 2006. In order to summarize the data in a more useful way, we can construct a frequency distribution. To do this we simply count the number of times each model appears in Table 2.1. We find that Commander (C) appears 71 times, Grand Cherokee (G) appears 70 times, Liberty (L) appears 80 times, and Wrangler (W) appears 30 times. The frequency distribution for the Jeep sales data is given in Table 2.2—it is a list of each of the four models along with their corresponding counts (or frequencies). The frequency distribution shows us how sales are distributed among the four models. The purpose of the frequency distribution is to make the data easier to understand—certainly looking at the frequency distribution in Table 2.2 is more informative than looking at the raw data in Table 2.1. We see that Jeep Liberty is the most popular model, Jeep Commander and Jeep Grand Cherokee are both slightly less popular than Jeep Liberty, and Jeep Wrangler is (by far) the least popular model.

TABLE 2.1   2006 Sales at a Greater Cincinnati Jeep Dealership   ● JeepSales

W	L	L	W	G	C	C	L	C	L	G	W	C
L	L	G	L	C	C	G	C	C	G	C	L	W
G	L	G	C	C	C	C	C	G	G	L	G	G
L	G	L	L	G	L	C	W	G	L	G	L	G
G	L	C	L	C	L	L	L	C	G	L	C	L
C	G	C	C	C	C	C	C	C	G	C	C	W
L	L	C	G	L	C	C	L	L	G	G	L	L
G	G	G	L	C	L	L	G	L	C	C	L	G
C	L	L	G	G	L	W	W	L	C	C	C	G
G	W	L	L	C	G	C	C	W	C	L	L	L
L	L	C	C	G	L	L	W	C	G	G	C	L
W	G	G	W	G	C	W	W	G	L	L	G	
L	L	L	C	C	G	C	L	G	G	G	L	
G	G	C	G	W	G	L	L	L	C	C	L	
W	L	W	G	W	C	W	C	W	C	L	C	
G	C	G	L	L	C	L	L	G	G	G	L	
L	C	G	L	C	L	W	L	L	C	G	C	
W	W	W	C	C	C	G	G	L	G	C	G	
W	C	C	W	L	G	W	L	L	L	G	G	
G	G	W	L	L	C	L	G	G	W	G	G	

TABLE 2.2   A Frequency Distribution of Jeeps Sold at a Greater Cincinnati Dealer in 2006
● JeepTable

Jeep Model	Frequency
Commander	71
Grand Cherokee	70
Liberty	80
Wrangler	30
	251

TABLE 2.3   Relative Frequency and Percent Frequency Distributions for the Jeep Sales Data
● JeepPercents

Jeep Model	Relative Frequency	Percent Frequency
Commander	71/251 = .2829	28.29%
Grand Cherokee	.2789	27.89%
Liberty	.3187	31.87%
Wrangler	.1195	11.95%
	1.0	100%

When we wish to summarize the proportion (or fraction) of items in each class, we employ the **relative frequency** for each class. If the data set consists of n observations, we define the relative frequency of a class as follows:

$$\textbf{Relative frequency} \text{ of a class} = \frac{\text{frequency of the class}}{n}$$

This quantity is simply the fraction of items in the class. Further, we can obtain the **percent frequency** of a class by multiplying the relative frequency by 100.

Table 2.3 gives a relative frequency distribution and a percent frequency distribution of the Jeep sales data. A **relative frequency distribution** is a table that lists the relative frequency for each class, and a **percent frequency distribution** lists the percent frequency for each class. Looking at Table 2.3, we see that the relative frequency for Jeep Commander is $71/251 = .2829$ (rounded to four decimal places) and that (from the percent frequency distribution) 28.29% of the Jeeps sold were Commanders. Similarly, the relative frequency for Jeep Wrangler is $30/251 = .1195$ and 11.95% of the Jeeps sold were Wranglers. Finally, the sum of the relative frequencies in the relative frequency distribution equals 1.0, and the sum of the percent frequencies in the percent frequency distribution equals 100%. These facts will be true for any relative frequency and percent frequency distribution.

Bar charts and pie charts   A **bar chart** is a graphic that depicts a frequency, relative frequency, or percent frequency distribution. For example, Figure 2.1 gives an Excel bar chart of the Jeep sales data. On the horizontal axis we have placed a label for each class (Jeep model), while the vertical axis measures frequencies. To construct the bar chart, Excel draws a bar (of fixed width) corresponding to each class label. Each bar is drawn so that its height equals the frequency corresponding to its label. Because the height of each bar is a frequency, we refer to Figure 2.1 as

FIGURE 2.1   Excel Bar Chart of the Jeep Sales Data

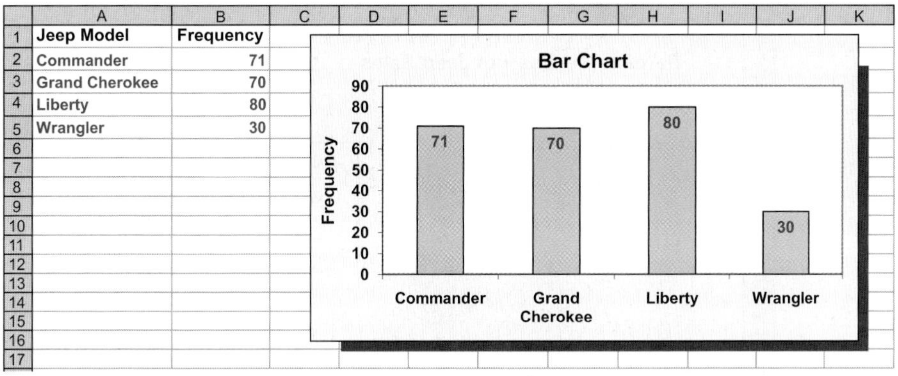

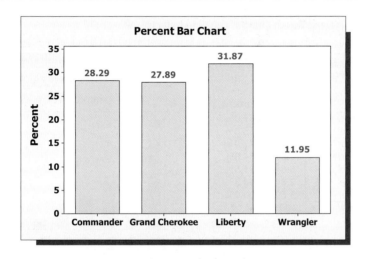

FIGURE 2.2   Minitab Percent Bar Chart of the Jeep Sales Data

a **frequency bar chart.** Notice that the bars have gaps between them. When data is qualitative, the bars should always be separated by gaps in order to indicate that each class is separate from the others. The bar chart in Figure 2.1 clearly illustrates that, for example, the dealer sold more Jeep Libertys than any other model and that the dealer sold far fewer Wranglers than any other model.

If desired, the bar heights can represent relative frequencies or percent frequencies. For instance, Figure 2.2 is a Minitab **percent bar chart** for the Jeep sales data. Here the heights of the bars are the percentages given in the percent frequency distribution of Table 2.3. Lastly, the bars in Figures 2.1 and 2.2 have been positioned vertically. Because of this, these bar charts are called **vertical bar charts.** However, sometimes bar charts are constructed with horizontal bars and are called **horizontal bar charts.**

A **pie chart** is another graphic that can be used to depict a frequency distribution. When constructing a pie chart, we first draw a circle to represent the entire data set. We then divide the circle into sectors or "pie slices" based on the relative frequencies of the classes. For example, remembering that a circle consists of 360 degrees, the Jeep Liberty (which has relative frequency .3187) is assigned a pie slice that consists of .3187(360) = 115 degrees (rounded to the nearest degree for convenience). Similarly, the Jeep Wrangler (with relative frequency .1195) is assigned a pie slice having .1195(360) = 43 degrees. Similarly, the Jeep Commander is assigned a pie slice having 102 degrees and Jeep Grand Cherokee is assigned a pie slice having 100 degrees. The resulting pie chart (constructed using Excel) is shown in Figure 2.3. Here we have labeled the pie slices using the percent frequencies. The pie slices can also be labeled using frequencies or relative frequencies.

The Pareto chart (optional)   Pareto charts are used to help identify important quality problems and opportunities for process improvement. By using these charts we can prioritize

FIGURE 2.3   **Excel Pie Chart of the Jeep Sales Data**

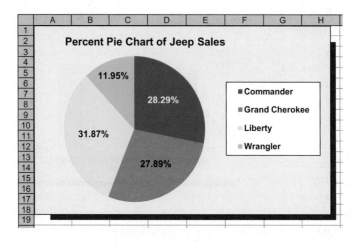

FIGURE 2.4   **Excel Frequency Table and Pareto Chart of Labeling Defects**   ◑ Labels

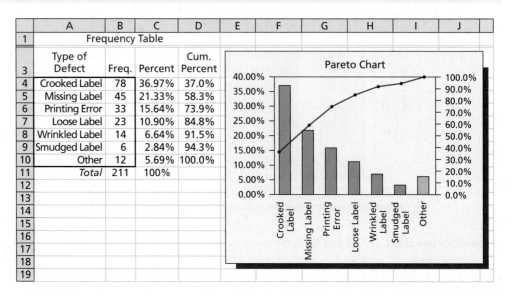

problem-solving activities. The Pareto chart is named for Vilfredo Pareto (1848–1923), an Italian economist. Pareto suggested that, in many economies, most of the wealth is held by a small minority of the population. It has been found that the **"Pareto principle"** often applies to defects. That is, only a few defect types account for most of a product's quality problems.

To illustrate the use of Pareto charts, suppose that a jelly producer wishes to evaluate the labels being placed on 16-ounce jars of grape jelly. Every day for two weeks, all defective labels found on inspection are classified by type of defect. If a label has more than one defect, the type of defect that is most noticeable is recorded. The Excel output in Figure 2.4 presents the frequencies and percentages of the types of defects observed over the two-week period.

In general, the first step in setting up a **Pareto chart** summarizing data concerning types of defects (or categories) is to construct a frequency table like the one in Figure 2.4. Defects or categories should be listed at the left of the table in *decreasing order by frequencies*—the defect with the highest frequency will be at the top of the table, the defect with the second-highest frequency below the first, and so forth. If an "other" category is employed, it should be placed at the bottom of the table. The "other" category should not make up 50 percent or more of the total of the frequencies, and the frequency for the "other" category should not exceed the frequency for the defect at the top of the table. If the frequency for the "other" category is too high, data should be collected so that the "other" category can be broken down into new categories. Once the frequency and the percentage for each category are determined, a cumulative percentage for each category is computed. As illustrated in Figure 2.4, the cumulative percentage for a particular category is the sum of the percentages corresponding to the particular category and the categories that are above that category in the table.

A Pareto chart is simply a bar chart having the different kinds of defects or problems listed on the horizontal scale. The heights of the bars on the vertical scale typically represent the frequency of occurrence (or the percentage of occurrence) for each defect or problem. The bars are arranged in decreasing height from left to right. Thus, the most frequent defect will be at the far left, the next most frequent defect to its right, and so forth. If an "other" category is employed, its bar is placed at the far right. The Pareto chart for the labeling defects data is given in Figure 2.4. Here the heights of the bars represent the percentages of occurrences for the different labeling defects, and the vertical scale on the far left corresponds to these percentages. The chart graphically illustrates that crooked labels, missing labels, and printing errors are the most frequent labeling defects.

As is also illustrated in Figure 2.4, a Pareto chart is sometimes augmented by plotting a **cumulative percentage point** for each bar in the Pareto chart. The vertical coordinate of this cumulative percentage point equals the cumulative percentage in the frequency table corresponding to the bar. The cumulative percentage points corresponding to the different bars are connected by line segments, and a vertical scale corresponding to the cumulative percentages is placed on the far right. Examining the cumulative percentage points in Figure 2.4, we see that crooked and missing labels make up 58.3 percent of the labeling defects and that crooked labels, missing labels, and printing errors make up 73.9 percent of the labeling defects.

Technical note   The Pareto chart in Figure 2.4 illustrates using an "other" category that combines defect types having low frequencies into a single class. In general, when we employ a frequency distribution, a bar chart, or a pie chart and we encounter classes having small class frequencies, it is common practice to combine the classes into a single "other" category. Classes having frequencies of 5 percent or less are usually handled this way.

Exercises for Section 2.1

CONCEPTS

2.1   Explain the purpose behind constructing a frequency or relative frequency distribution.

2.2   Explain how to compute the relative frequency and percent frequency for each class if you are given a frequency distribution.

2.3   Find an example of a pie chart or bar chart in a newspaper or magazine. Copy it, and hand it in with a written analysis of the information conveyed by the chart.

connect™

METHODS AND APPLICATIONS

2.4   A multiple-choice question on an exam has four possible responses—(a), (b), (c), and (d). When 250 students take the exam, 100 give response (a), 25 give response (b), 75 give response (c), and 50 give response (d).
   a   Write out the frequency distribution, relative frequency distribution, and percent frequency distribution for these responses.
   b   Construct a bar chart for these data using frequencies.

2.5   Consider constructing a pie chart for the exam question responses in Exercise 2.4.
   a   How many degrees (out of 360) would be assigned to the "pie slice" for response (a)?
   b   How many degrees would be assigned to the "pie slice" for response (b)?
   c   Construct the pie chart for the exam question responses.

2.6   The following is a partial relative frequency distribution of consumer preferences for four products—W, X, Y, and Z.

Product	Relative Frequency
W	.15
X	—
Y	.36
Z	.28

   a   Find the relative frequency for product X.
   b   If 500 consumers were surveyed, give the frequency distribution for these data.
   c   Construct a percent frequency bar chart for these data.
   d   If we wish to depict these data using a pie chart, find how many degrees (out of 360) should be assigned to each of products W, X, Y, and Z. Then construct the pie chart.

2.7   Below we give pizza restaurant preferences for 25 randomly selected college students.
● PizzaPizza

Godfather's	Little Caesar's	Papa John's	Pizza Hut	Domino's	Papa John's
Papa John's	Papa John's	Pizza Hut	Pizza Hut	Papa John's	Domino's
Little Caesar's	Domino's	Domino's	Godfather's	Pizza Hut	Papa John's
Pizza Hut	Pizza Hut	Papa John's	Papa John's	Godfather's	Papa John's
Domino's					

a Find the frequency distribution and relative frequency distribution for these data.
b Construct a percentage bar chart for these data.
c Construct a percentage pie chart for these data.
d Which restaurant is most popular with these students? Least popular?

2.8   Fifty randomly selected adults who follow professional sports were asked to name their favorite professional sports league. The results are as follows where MLB = Major League Baseball, MLS = Major League Soccer, NBA = National Basketball Association, NFL = National Football League, and NHL = National Hockey League.   ● ProfSports

NFL	NBA	NFL	MLB	MLB	NHL	NFL	NFL	MLS	MLB
MLB	NFL	MLB	NBA	NBA	NFL	NFL	NFL	NHL	NBA
NBA	NFL	NHL	NFL	MLS	NFL	MLB	NFL	MLB	NFL
NHL	MLB	NHL	NFL	NFL	NFL	MLB	NFL	NBA	NFL
MLS	NFL	MLB	NBA	NFL	NFL	MLB	NBA	NFL	NFL

a Find the frequency distribution, relative frequency distribution, and percent frequency distribution for these data.
b Construct a frequency bar chart for these data.
c Construct a pie chart for these data.
d Which professional sports league is most popular with these 50 adults? Which is least popular?

2.9   **a** On March 11, 2005, the Gallup Organization released the results of a CNN/USA Today/Gallup national poll regarding Internet usage in the United States. Each of 1,008 randomly selected adults was asked to respond to the following question:

> As you may know, there are Web sites known as "blogs" or "Web logs," where people sometimes post their thoughts. How familiar are you with "blogs"—very familiar, somewhat familiar, not too familiar, or not at all familiar?

The poll's results were as follows: Very familiar (7%); Somewhat familiar (19%); Not too familiar (18%); Not at all familiar (56%).[1] Use these data to construct a bar chart and a pie chart.

b On February 15, 2005, the Gallup Organization released the results of a Gallup UK poll regarding Internet usage in Great Britain. Each of 1,009 randomly selected UK adults was asked to respond to the following question:

> How much time, if at all, do you personally spend using the Internet—more than an hour a day, up to one hour a day, a few times a week, a few times a month or less, or never?

The poll's results were as follows: More than an hour a day (22%); Up to an hour a day (14%); A few times a week (15%); A few times a month or less (10%); Never (39%).[2] Use these data to construct a bar chart and a pie chart.

2.10   The National Automobile Dealers Association (NADA) publishes *AutoExec* magazine, which annually reports on new vehicle sales and market shares by manufacturer. As given on the *AutoExec* magazine website in May 2006, new vehicle market shares in the United States for 2005 were as follows[3]: Daimler-Chrysler 13.6%, Ford 18.3%, GM 26.3%, Japanese (Toyota/Honda/Nissan) 28.3%, other imports 13.5%.   ● AutoShares05
a Construct a percent frequency bar chart and a percentage pie chart for the 2005 auto market shares.
b Figure 2.5 gives a percentage bar chart of new vehicle market shares in the United States for 1997. Use this bar chart and your results from part *a* to write an analysis explaining how new vehicle market shares in the United States have changed from 1997 to 2005.   ● AutoShares97

2.11   On January 11, 2005, the Gallup Organization released the results of a poll investigating how many Americans have private health insurance. The results showed that among Americans making less than $30,000 per year, 33% had private insurance, 50% were covered by Medicare/Medicaid, and 17% had no health insurance, while among Americans making $75,000 or more per year, 87% had

---

[1]Source: Copyright © 2005 Gallup Inc. Used with permission, http://gallup.com/poll/content/default.aspx?ci=15217
[2]Source: Copyright © 2005 Gallup Inc. Used with permission, http://gallup.com/poll/content/default.aspx?ci=14947
[3]Source: www.autoexecmag.com, May 15, 2006.

FIGURE 2.5   An Excel Bar Chart of U.S. Automobile Sales in 1997 (for Exercise 2.10)
               ● AutoShares97

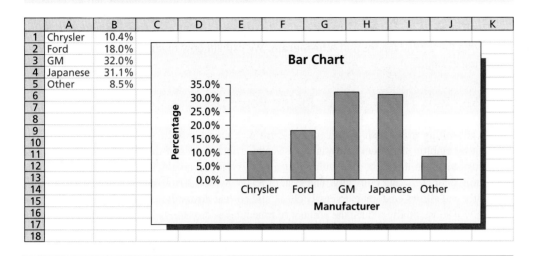

FIGURE 2.6   A Pareto Chart for Incomplete Customer Calls (for Exercise 2.12)

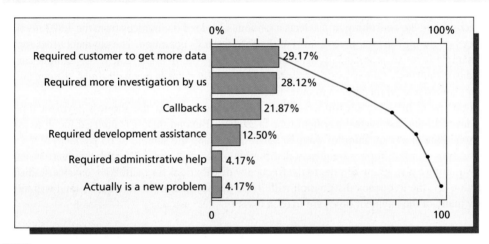

private insurance, 9% were covered by Medicare/Medicaid, and 4% had no health insurance.[4] Use bar and pie charts to compare health coverage of the two income groups.

2.12   In an article in *Quality Progress,* Barbara A. Cleary reports on improvements made in a software supplier's responses to customer calls. In this article, the author states:

> In an effort to improve its response time for these important customer-support calls, an inbound telephone inquiry team was formed at PQ Systems, Inc., a software and training organization in Dayton, Ohio. The team found that 88 percent of the customers' calls were already being answered immediately by the technical support group, but those who had to be called back had to wait an average of 56.6 minutes. No customer complaints had been registered, but the team believed that this response rate could be improved.

As part of its improvement process, the company studied the disposition of complete and incomplete calls to its technical support analysts. A call is considered complete if the customer's problem has been resolved; otherwise the call is incomplete. Figure 2.6 shows a Pareto chart analysis for the incomplete customer calls.

a   What percentage of incomplete calls required "more investigation" by the analyst or "administrative help"?

b   What percentage of incomplete calls actually presented a "new problem"?

c   In light of your answers to *a* and *b*, can you make a suggestion?

[4]Source: http://gallup.com/poll/content/default.aspx?ci=14581

2.2 Graphically Summarizing Quantitative Data ● ● ●

Frequency distributions and histograms   We often need to summarize and describe the shape of the distribution of a population or sample of measurements. Such data is often summarized by grouping the measurements into the classes of a frequency distribution and by displaying the data in the form of a **histogram.** We explain how to construct a histogram in the following example.

EXAMPLE 2.2 The Payment Time Case: Reducing Payment Times[5]

Major consulting firms such as Accenture, Ernst & Young Consulting, and Deloitte & Touche Consulting employ statistical analysis to assess the effectiveness of the systems they design for their customers. In this case a consulting firm has developed an electronic billing system for a Hamilton, Ohio, trucking company. The system sends invoices electronically to each customer's computer and allows customers to easily check and correct errors. It is hoped that the new billing system will substantially reduce the amount of time it takes customers to make payments. Typical payment times—measured from the date on an invoice to the date payment is received—using the trucking company's old billing system had been 39 days or more. This exceeded the industry standard payment time of 30 days.

The new billing system does not automatically compute the payment time for each invoice because there is no continuing need for this information. Therefore, in order to assess the system's effectiveness, the consulting firm selects a random sample of 65 invoices from the 7,823 invoices processed during the first three months of the new system's operation. The payment times for the 65 sample invoices are manually determined and are given in Table 2.4. If this sample can be used to establish that the new billing system substantially reduces payment times, the consulting firm plans to market the system to other trucking firms.

Looking at the payment times in Table 2.4, we can see that the shortest payment time is 10 days and that the longest payment time is 29 days. Beyond that, it is pretty difficult to interpret the data in any meaningful way. To better understand the sample of 65 payment times, the consulting firm will form a frequency distribution of the data and will graph the distribution by constructing a histogram. Similar to the frequency distributions for qualitative data we studied in Section 2.1, the frequency distribution will divide the payment times into classes and will tell us how many of the payment times are in each class.

Step 1: Find the number of classes   One rule for finding an appropriate number of classes says that the number of classes should be the smallest whole number K that makes the quantity 2^K greater than the number of measurements in the data set. For the payment time data we have 65 measurements. Because $2^6 = 64$ is less than 65 and $2^7 = 128$ is greater than 65, we should use $K = 7$ classes. Table 2.5 gives the appropriate number of classes (determined by the 2^K rule) to use for data sets of various sizes.

Step 2: Find the class length   We find the length of each class by computing

$$\text{Class length} = \frac{\text{largest measurement} - \text{smallest measurement}}{\text{number of classes}}$$

TABLE 2.4   A Sample of Payment Times (in Days) for 65 Randomly Selected Invoices   ◗ PayTime

22	29	16	15	18	17	12	13	17	16	15
19	17	10	21	15	14	17	18	12	20	14
16	15	16	20	22	14	25	19	23	15	19
18	23	22	16	16	19	13	18	24	24	26
13	18	17	15	24	15	17	14	18	17	21
16	21	25	19	20	27	16	17	16	21	

---

[5]This case is based on a real problem encountered by a company that employs one of our former students. For purposes of confidentiality, we have withheld the company's name.

TABLE 2.5	Recommended Number of Classes for Data Sets of n Measurements*
Number of Classes	Size, n, of the Data Set
2	$1 \leq n < 4$
3	$4 \leq n < 8$
4	$8 \leq n < 16$
5	$16 \leq n < 32$
6	$32 \leq n < 64$
7	$64 \leq n < 128$
8	$128 \leq n < 256$
9	$256 \leq n < 528$
10	$528 \leq n < 1{,}056$

*For completeness sake we have included all values of $n \geq 1$ in this table. However, we do not recommend constructing a histogram with fewer than 16 measurements.

TABLE 2.6	Seven Nonoverlapping Classes for a Frequency Distribution of the 65 Payment Times
Class 1	10 days and less than 13 days
Class 2	13 days and less than 16 days
Class 3	16 days and less than 19 days
Class 4	19 days and less than 22 days
Class 5	22 days and less than 25 days
Class 6	25 days and less than 28 days
Class 7	28 days and less than 31 days

Because the largest and smallest payment times in Table 2.4 are 29 days and 10 days, the class length is $(29 - 10)/7 = 2.7143$. This says that, in order to include the smallest and largest payment times in the seven classes, each class must have a length of at least 2.7143. To obtain a more convenient class length, we round this value. Often the class length is rounded to the precision of the measurements, although this is a matter of preference. For instance, because the payment times are measured to the nearest day, we will round the class length from 2.7143 to 3 days.

Step 3: Form nonoverlapping classes of equal width　We can form the classes of the frequency distribution by defining the **boundaries** of the classes. To find the first class boundary, we find the smallest payment time in Table 2.4, which is 10 days. This value is the lower boundary of the first class. Adding the class length of 3 to this lower boundary, we obtain $10 + 3 = 13$, which is the upper boundary of the first class and the lower boundary of the second class. Similarly, the upper boundary of the second class and the lower boundary of the third class equal $13 + 3 = 16$. Continuing in this fashion, the lower boundaries of the remaining classes are 19, 22, 25, and 28. Adding the class length 3 to the lower boundary of the last class gives us the upper boundary of the last class, 31. These boundaries define seven nonoverlapping classes for the frequency distribution. We summarize these classes in Table 2.6. For instance, the first class—10 days and less than 13 days—includes the payment times 10, 11, and 12 days; the second class—13 days and less than 16 days—includes the payment times 13, 14, and 15 days; and so forth. Notice that the largest *observed* payment time—29 days—is contained in the last class. In cases where the largest measurement is not contained in the last class, we simply add another class. Generally speaking, the guidelines we have given for forming classes are not inflexible rules. Rather, they are intended to help us find reasonable classes. Finally, the method we have used for forming classes results in classes of equal length. Generally, forming classes of equal length will make it easier to appropriately interpret the frequency distribution.

Step 4: Tally and count the number of measurements in each class　Having formed the classes, we now count the number of measurements that fall into each class. To do this, it is convenient to tally the measurements. We simply list the classes, examine the payment times in Table 2.4 one at a time, and record a tally mark corresponding to a particular class each time we encounter a measurement that falls in that class. For example, since the first four payment times in Table 2.4 are 22, 19, 16, and 18, the first four tally marks are shown below. Here, for brevity, we express the class "10 days and less than 13 days" as "$10 < 13$" and use similar notation for the other classes.

Class	First 4 Tally Marks	All 65 Tally Marks	Frequency
$10 < 13$		III	3
$13 < 16$		THL THL IIII	14
$16 < 19$	II	THL THL THL THL III	23
$19 < 22$	I	THL THL II	12
$22 < 25$	I	THL III	8
$25 < 28$		IIII	4
$28 < 31$		I	1

TABLE 2.7   Frequency Distributions of the 65 Payment Times

Class	Frequency	Relative Frequency	Percent Frequency
10 < 13	3	3/65 = .0462	4.62%
13 < 16	14	14/65 = .2154	21.54
16 < 19	23	.3538	35.38
19 < 22	12	.1846	18.46
22 < 25	8	.1231	12.31
25 < 28	4	.0615	6.15
28 < 31	1	.0154	1.54

FIGURE 2.7   A Frequency Histogram of the 65 Payment Times

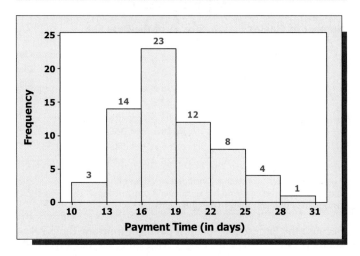

After examining all 65 payment times, we have recorded 65 tally marks—see the bottom of page 57. We find the **frequency** for each class by counting the number of tally marks recorded for the class. For instance, counting the number of tally marks for the class "13 < 16," we obtain the frequency 14 for this class. The frequencies for all seven classes are summarized in Table 2.7. This summary is the **frequency distribution** for the 65 payment times. Table 2.7 also gives the *relative frequency* and the *percent frequency* for each of the seven classes. The **relative frequency** of a class is the proportion (fraction) of the total number of measurements that are in the class. For example, there are 14 payment times in the second class, so its relative frequency is $14/65 = .2154$. This says that the proportion of the 65 payment times that are in the second class is .2154, or, equivalently, that $100(.2154)\% = 21.54\%$ of the payment times are in the second class. A list of all of the classes—along with each class relative frequency—is called a **relative frequency distribution.** A list of all of the classes—along with each class percent frequency—is called a **percent frequency distribution.**

Step 5: Graph the histogram   We can graphically portray the distribution of payment times by drawing a **histogram.** The histogram can be constructed using the frequency, relative frequency, or percent frequency distribution. To set up the histogram, we draw rectangles that correspond to the classes. The base of the rectangle corresponding to a class represents the payment times in the class. The height of the rectangle can represent the class frequency, relative frequency, or percent frequency.

We have drawn a **frequency histogram** of the 65 payment times in Figure 2.7. The first (left-most) rectangle, or "bar," of the histogram represents the payment times 10, 11, and 12. Looking at Figure 2.7, we see that the base of this rectangle is drawn from the lower boundary (10) of the first class in the frequency distribution of payment times to the lower boundary (13) of the second class. The height of this rectangle tells us that the frequency of the first class is 3. The second histogram rectangle represents payment times 13, 14, and 15. Its base is drawn from the lower boundary (13) of the second class to the lower boundary (16) of the third class, and its height tells us that the frequency of the second class is 14. The other histogram bars are constructed similarly. Notice that there are no gaps between the adjacent rectangles in the histogram. Here, although the payment times have been recorded to the nearest whole day, the fact that the histogram bars touch each other emphasizes that a payment time could (in theory) be any number on the horizontal axis. In general, histograms are drawn so that adjacent bars touch each other.

Looking at the frequency distribution in Table 2.7 and the frequency histogram in Figure 2.7, we can describe the payment times:

1   None of the payment times exceeds the industry standard of 30 days. (Actually, all of the payment times are less than 30—remember the largest payment time is 29 days.)

2   The payment times are concentrated between 13 and 24 days (57 of the 65, or $(57/65) \times 100 = 87.69\%$, of the payment times are in this range).

3   More payment times are in the class "16 < 19" than are in any other class (23 payment times are in this class).

FIGURE 2.8 A Percent Frequency Histogram of the 65 Payment Times

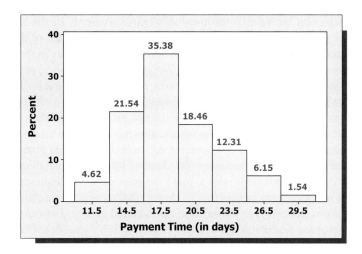

Notice that the frequency distribution and histogram allow us to make some helpful conclusions about the payment times, whereas, looking at the raw data (the payment times in Table 2.4) did not.

A **relative frequency histogram** and a **percent frequency histogram** of the payment times would both be drawn like Figure 2.7 except that the heights of the rectangles represent, respectively, the relative frequencies and the percent frequencies in Table 2.7. For example, Figure 2.8 gives a percent frequency histogram of the payment times. This histogram also illustrates that we sometimes label the classes on the horizontal axis using the **class midpoints.** Each class midpoint is exactly halfway between the boundaries of its class. For instance, the midpoint of the first class, 11.5, is halfway between the class boundaries 10 and 13. The midpoint of the second class, 14.5, is halfway between the class boundaries 13 and 16. The other class midpoints are found similarly. The percent frequency distribution of Figure 2.8 tells us that 21.54% of the payment times are in the second class (which has midpoint 14.5 and represents the payment times 13, 14, and 15).

In the following box we summarize the steps needed to set up a frequency distribution and histogram:

Constructing Frequency Distributions and Histograms

1 Find the number of classes. Generally, the number of classes K should equal the smallest whole number that makes the quantity 2^K greater than the total number of measurements n (see Table 2.5 on page 57).

2 Compute the **class length:**

$$\frac{\text{largest measurement} - \text{smallest measurement}}{K}$$

If desired, round this value to obtain a more convenient class length.

3 Form nonoverlapping classes of equal length. Form the classes by finding the **class boundaries.** The lower boundary of the first class is the smallest measurement in the data set. Add the class length to this boundary to obtain the next boundary. Successive boundaries are found by repeatedly adding the class length until the upper boundary of the last (Kth) class is found.

4 Tally and count the number of measurements in each class. The **frequency** for each class is the count of the number of measurements in the class. The **relative frequency** for each class is the fraction of measurements in the class. The **percent frequency** for each class is its relative frequency multiplied by 100%.

5 Graph the histogram. To draw a **frequency histogram,** plot each frequency as the height of a rectangle positioned over its corresponding class. Use the class boundaries to separate adjacent rectangles. A **relative frequency histogram** and a **percent histogram** are graphed in the same way except that the heights of the rectangles are, respectively, the relative frequencies and the percent frequencies.

Although we have given a procedure for determining the number of classes, it is often desirable to let the nature of the problem determine the classes. For example, to construct a histogram describing the ages of the residents of a certain city, it might be reasonable to use classes having 10-year lengths (that is, under 10 years, 10–19 years, 20–29 years, 30–39 years, and so on). In general, when constructing a histogram, the **area** of the rectangle positioned over a particular class should represent the **relative proportion of measurements in the class. When we use equal class lengths, this can be accomplished by making the height of the rectangle over a particular class represent the relative proportion of measurements in the class** (as described in the previous summary box for constructing histograms). This is because the area of a rectangle is its base multiplied by its height and because, if we are using equal class lengths, then the bases of all the rectangles over the various classes are the same.

It is best to use equal class lengths whenever the raw data (that is, all the actual measurements) are available. However, sometimes histograms are drawn with unequal class lengths—particularly when we are using published data as a source. Economic data and data in the social sciences are often published in the form of frequency distributions having unequal class lengths. In such a case, we must vary the rectangle heights to make the areas of the rectangles represent the relative proportions of measurements in the classes. How to do this is discussed in Exercise 2.85. Also discussed in this exercise is how to deal with **open-ended** classes. For example, if we are constructing a histogram describing the yearly incomes of U.S. households, an open-ended class could be households earning over $500,000 per year.

As an alternative to using the method we have described to construct a frequency distribution and histogram by hand, we can use statistical software packages such as MINITAB, Excel, and MegaStat. Each of these packages will automatically define histogram classes for the user. However, these automatically defined classes will not necessarily be the same as those that would be obtained using the manual method we have previously described. Furthermore, the various packages define classes by using different methods. (Descriptions of how the classes are defined can often be found in help menus.) For example, Figure 2.9 gives a MINITAB frequency histogram of the payment times in Table 2.4. Here, MINITAB has defined 11 classes and has labeled five of the classes on the horizontal axis using midpoints (12, 16, 20, 24, 28). It is easy to see that the midpoints of the unlabeled classes are 10, 14, 18, 22, 26, and 30. Moreover, the boundaries of the first class are 9 and 11, the boundaries of the second class are 11 and 13, and so forth. MINITAB counts frequencies as we have previously described. For instance, one payment time is at least 9 and less than 11, two payment times are at least 11 and less than 13, seven payment times are at least 13 and less than 15, and so forth. Figure 2.10 gives a MegaStat percent frequency histogram of the gas mileages in Table 1.4. Here, MegaStat has defined eight classes and has labeled the classes on the horizontal axis using class boundaries. For instance, the boundaries of the first class are 29.5 and 30.0, the boundaries of the second class are 30.0 and 30.5, and so forth.

| FIGURE 2.9 | A MINITAB Frequency Histogram of the Payment Times with Automatic Classes: The Payment Time Distribution Is Skewed to the Right | FIGURE 2.10 | A MegaStat Percent Frequency Histogram of the Gas Mileages with Automatic Classes: The Gas Mileage Distribution Is Symmetrical and Mound Shaped |

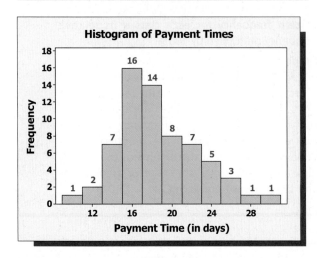

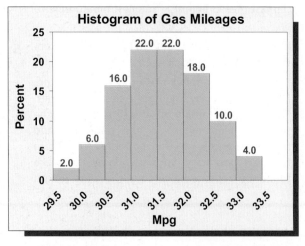

MegaStat also counts frequencies as we have previously described—that is, one gas mileage (or 2.0 percent of the 50 mileages) is at least 29.5 and less than 30.0, three gas mileages (or 6.0 percent of the 50 mileages) are at least 30.0 and less than 30.5, and so forth. Finally, Figure 2.11 gives an Excel frequency distribution and histogram of the bottle design ratings in Table 1.3. Excel labels histogram classes using their upper class boundaries. For example, the boundaries of the second class are 20 and 22, the boundaries of the third class are 22 and 24, and so forth. The first class corresponds to bottle design ratings that are 20 or less, while the last class corresponds to ratings more than 36. Excel's method for counting frequencies differs from those of MINITAB and MegaStat (and, therefore, also differs from the way we counted frequencies by hand in Example 2.2). Excel assigns a frequency to a particular class by counting the number of measurements that are greater than the lower boundary of the class and less than or equal to the upper boundary of the class. For example, one bottle design rating is greater than 20 and less than or equal to (that is, at most) 22. Similarly, 15 bottle design ratings are greater than 32 and at most 34.

In Figures 2.9 and 2.10 we have used MINITAB and MegaStat to automatically form histogram classes. It is also possible to use these software packages to form histogram classes that are defined by the user. We explain how to do this in the appendixes at the end of this chapter. Because Excel does not always automatically define acceptable classes, the classes in Figure 2.11 are a modification of Excel's automatic classes. We also explain this modification in the appendixes at the end of this chapter.

Some common distribution shapes   We often graph a frequency distribution in the form of a histogram in order to visualize the *shape* of the distribution. If we look at the histogram of payment times in Figure 2.9, we see that the right tail of the histogram is longer than the left tail. When a histogram has this general shape, we say that the distribution is **skewed to the right.** Here the long right tail tells us that a few of the payment times are somewhat longer than the rest. If we look at the histogram of bottle design ratings in Figure 2.11, we see that the left tail of the histogram is much longer than the right tail. When a histogram has this general shape, we say that the distribution is **skewed to the left.** Here the long tail to the left tells us that, while most of the bottle design ratings are concentrated above 25 or so, a few of the ratings are lower than the rest. Finally, looking at the histogram of gas mileages in Figure 2.10, we see that the right and left tails of the histogram appear to be mirror images of each other. When a histogram has this general shape, we say that the distribution is **symmetrical.** Moreover, the distribution of gas mileages appears to be piled up in the middle or **mound shaped.**

Mound-shaped, symmetrical distributions as well as distributions that are skewed to the right or left are commonly found in practice. For example, distributions of scores on standardized tests such as the SAT and ACT tend to be mound shaped and symmetrical, whereas distributions of scores on tests in college statistics courses might be skewed to the left—a few students don't study and get scores much lower than the rest. On the other hand, economic data such as income data are often skewed to the right—a few people have incomes much higher than most others. Many other distribution shapes are possible. For example, some distributions have two or more peaks—we will give an example of this distribution shape later in this section. It is often very useful to know the shape of a distribution. For example, knowing that the distribution of bottle design ratings is skewed to the left suggests that a few consumers may have noticed a problem with the design that others didn't see. Further investigation into why these consumers gave the design low ratings might allow the company to improve the design.

Frequency polygons   Another graphical display that can be used to depict a frequency distribution is a **frequency polygon.** To construct this graphic, we plot a point above each class midpoint at a height equal to the frequency of the class—the height can also be the class relative frequency or class percent frequency if so desired. Then we connect the points with line segments. As we will demonstrate in the following example, this kind of graphic can be particularly useful when we wish to compare two or more distributions.

EXAMPLE 2.3 Comparing the Grade Distributions for Two Statistics Exams

Table 2.8 lists (in increasing order) the scores earned on the first exam by the 40 students in a business statistics course taught by one of the authors several semesters ago. Figure 2.12 gives a percent frequency polygon for these exam scores. Because exam scores are often reported by using 10-point grade ranges (for instance, 80 to 90 percent), we have defined the following classes: $30 < 40$, $40 < 50$, $50 < 60$, $60 < 70$, $70 < 80$, $80 < 90$, and $90 < 100$. This is an example of letting the situation determine the classes of a frequency distribution, which is common practice when the situation naturally defines classes. The points that form the polygon have been plotted corresponding to the midpoints of the classes (35, 45, 55, 65, 75, 85, 95). Each point is plotted at a height that equals the percentage of exam scores in its class. For instance, because 10 of the 40 scores are at least 90 and less than 100, the plot point corresponding to the class midpoint 95 is plotted at a height of 25 percent.

Looking at Figure 2.12, we see that there is a concentration of scores in the 85 to 95 range and another concentration of scores around 65. In addition, the distribution of scores is somewhat skewed to the left—a few students had scores (in the 30s and 40s) that were quite a bit lower than the rest.

This is an example of a distribution having two peaks. When a distribution has multiple peaks, finding the reason for the different peaks often provides useful information. The reason for the two-peaked distribution of exam scores was that some students were not attending class regularly. Students who received scores in the 60s and below admitted that they were cutting class, whereas students who received higher scores were attending class on a regular basis.

After identifying the reason for the concentration of lower scores, the instructor established an attendance policy that forced students to attend every class—any student who missed a class was

TABLE 2.8	Exam Scores for the First Exam Given in a Statistics Class ● FirstExam			
32	63	69	85	91
45	64	69	86	92
50	64	72	87	92
56	65	76	87	93
58	66	78	88	93
60	67	81	89	94
61	67	83	90	96
61	68	83	90	98

FIGURE 2.12   A Percent Frequency Polygon of the Exam Scores

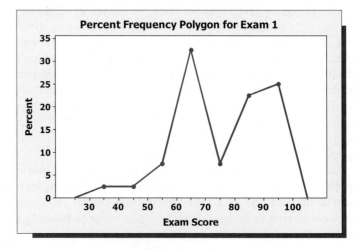

TABLE 2.9	Exam Scores for the Second Statistics Exam—after a New Attendance Policy ● SecondExam			
55	74	80	87	93
62	74	82	88	94
63	74	83	89	94
66	75	84	90	95
67	76	85	91	97
67	77	86	91	99
71	77	86	92	
73	78	87	93	

FIGURE 2.13   Percent Frequency Polygons of the Scores on the First Two Exams in a Statistics Course

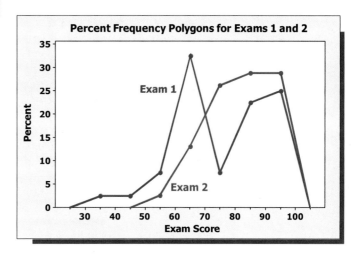

to be dropped from the course. Table 2.9 presents the scores on the second exam—after the new attendance policy. Figure 2.13 presents (and allows us to compare) the percent frequency polygons for both exams. We see that the polygon for the second exam is single-peaked—the attendance policy[6] eliminated the concentration of scores in the 60s, although the scores are still somewhat skewed to the left.

Cumulative distributions and ogives   Another way to summarize a distribution is to construct a cumulative distribution. To do this, we use the same number of classes, the same class lengths, and the same class boundaries that we have used for the frequency distribution of a data set. However, in order to construct a **cumulative frequency distribution,** we record for each class *the number of measurements that are less than the upper boundary of the class.* To illustrate this idea, Table 2.10 gives the cumulative frequency distribution of the payment time distribution summarized in Table 2.7 (page 58). Columns (1) and (2) in this table give the frequency distribution of the payment times. Column (3) gives the **cumulative frequency** for each class. To see how these values are obtained, the cumulative frequency for the class $10 < 13$ is the number of payment times less than 13. This is obviously the frequency for the class $10 < 13$, which is 3. The cumulative frequency for the class $13 < 16$ is the number of payment times less than 16, which is obtained by adding the frequencies for the first two classes—that is, $3 + 14 = 17$. The cumulative frequency for the class $16 < 19$ is the number of payment times less than 19— that is, $3 + 14 + 23 = 40$. We see that, in general, a cumulative frequency is obtained by summing the frequencies of all classes representing values less than the upper boundary of the class.

TABLE 2.10   A Frequency Distribution, Cumulative Frequency Distribution, Cumulative Relative Frequency Distribution, and Cumulative Percent Frequency Distribution for the Payment Time Data

(1) Class	(2) Frequency	(3) Cumulative Frequency	(4) Cumulative Relative Frequency	(5) Cumulative Percent Frequency
$10 < 13$	3	3	$3/65 = .0462$	4.62%
$13 < 16$	14	17	$17/65 = .2615$	26.15
$16 < 19$	23	40	.6154	61.54
$19 < 22$	12	52	.8000	80.00
$22 < 25$	8	60	.9231	92.31
$25 < 28$	4	64	.9846	98.46
$28 < 31$	1	65	1.0000	100.00

[6]Other explanations are possible. For instance, all of the students who did poorly on the first exam might have studied harder for the second exam. However, the instructor's 30 years of teaching experience suggests that attendance was the critical factor.

FIGURE 2.14   A Percent Frequency Ogive of the Payment Times

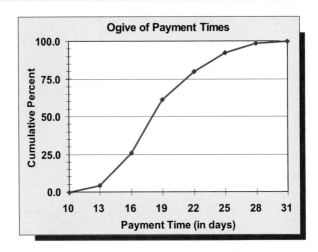

Column (4) gives the **cumulative relative frequency** for each class, which is obtained by summing the relative frequencies of all classes representing values less than the upper boundary of the class. Or, more simply, this value can be found by dividing the cumulative frequency for the class by the total number of measurements in the data set. For instance, the cumulative relative frequency for the class $19 < 22$ is $52/65 = .8$. Column (5) gives the **cumulative percent frequency** for each class, which is obtained by summing the percent frequencies of all classes representing values less than the upper boundary of the class. More simply, this value can be found by multiplying the cumulative relative frequency of a class by 100. For instance, the cumulative percent frequency for the class $19 < 22$ is $.8 (100) = 80$ percent.

As an example of interpreting Table 2.10, 60 of the 65 payment times are 24 days or less, or, equivalently, 92.31 percent of the payment times (or a fraction of .9231 of the payment times) are 24 days or less. Also, notice that the last entry in the cumulative frequency distribution is the total number of measurements (here, 65 payment times). In addition, the last entry in the cumulative relative frequency distribution is 1.0 and the last entry in the cumulative percent frequency distribution is 100%. In general, for any data set, these last entries will be, respectively, the total number of measurements, 1.0, and 100%.

An **ogive** (pronounced "oh-jive") is a graph of a cumulative distribution. To construct a frequency ogive, we plot a point above each upper class boundary at a height equal to the cumulative frequency of the class. We then connect the plotted points with line segments. A similar graph can be drawn using the cumulative relative frequencies or the cumulative percent frequencies. As an example, Figure 2.14 gives a percent frequency ogive of the payment times. Looking at this figure, we see that, for instance, a little more than 25 percent (actually, 26.15 percent according to Table 2.10) of the payment times are less than 16 days, while 80 percent of the payment times are less than 22 days. Also notice that we have completed the ogive by plotting an additional point at the lower boundary of the first (leftmost) class at a height equal to zero. This depicts the fact that none of the payment times are less than 10 days. Finally, the ogive graphically shows that all (100 percent) of the payment times are less than 31 days.

Exercises for Section 2.2

CONCEPTS

connect™

2.13   Explain
   a   Why we construct a frequency distribution and a histogram for a data set.
   b   The difference between a frequency histogram and a frequency polygon.
   c   The difference between a frequency polygon and a frequency ogive.

2.14   Explain how to find
   a   The frequency for a class.
   b   The relative frequency for a class.
   c   The percent frequency for a class.

2.15 Explain what each of the following distribution shapes looks like. Then draw a picture that illustrates each shape.
  a Symmetrical and mound-shaped.
  b Double-peaked.
  c Skewed to the right.
  d Skewed to the left.

METHODS AND APPLICATIONS

2.16 Consider the following data:　　● HistoData

36	39	36	35	36	20	19
47	40	42	34	41	36	42
40	38	33	37	22	33	28
38	38	34	37	17	25	38

  a Find the number of classes needed to construct a histogram.
  b Find the class length.
  c Define nonoverlapping classes for a frequency distribution.
  d Tally the number of values in each class and develop a frequency distribution.
  e Draw a histogram for these data.
  f Develop a percent frequency distribution.

2.17 Consider the frequency distribution of exam scores given below.

Class	Frequency
90 < 100	12
80 < 90	17
70 < 80	14
60 < 70	5
50 < 60	2

  a Develop a relative frequency distribution and a percent frequency distribution.
  b Develop a cumulative frequency distribution and a cumulative percent frequency distribution.
  c Draw a frequency polygon.
  d Draw a frequency ogive.

THE MARKETING RESEARCH CASE　　● Design

Recall that 60 randomly selected shoppers have rated a new bottle design for a popular soft drink. The data are given below.

34	33	33	29	26	33	28	25	32	33
32	25	27	33	22	27	32	33	32	29
24	30	20	34	31	32	30	35	33	31
32	28	30	31	31	33	29	27	34	31
31	28	33	31	32	28	26	29	32	34
32	30	34	32	30	30	32	31	29	33

Use these data to work Exercises 2.18 and 2.19.

2.18 **a** Find the number of classes that should be used to construct a frequency distribution and histogram for the bottle design ratings.
  b If we round up to the nearest whole rating point, show that we should employ a class length equal to 3.
  c Define the nonoverlapping classes for a frequency distribution.
  d Tally the number of ratings in each class and develop a frequency distribution.
  e Draw the frequency histogram for the ratings data, and describe the distribution shape.　　● Design

2.19 **a** Construct a relative frequency distribution and a percent frequency distribution for the bottle design ratings.
  b Construct a cumulative frequency distribution and a cumulative percent frequency distribution.
  c Draw a frequency ogive for the bottle design ratings.　　● Design

2.20 Table 2.11 gives the 25 most powerful celebrities and their annual pay as ranked by the editors of *Forbes* magazine and as listed on the Forbes.com website on February 25, 2007.　　● PowerCeleb
  a Develop a frequency distribution for the celebrity pay data and draw a histogram.
  b Develop a cumulative frequency distribution and a cumulative percent frequency distribution for the celebrity pay data.
  c Draw a percent frequency ogive for the celebrity pay data.

TABLE 2.11   **The 25 Most Powerful Celebrities as Rated by *Forbes* Magazine**   ● PowerCeleb

Power Ranking	Celebrity Name	Pay ($mil)	Power Ranking	Celebrity Name	Pay ($mil)
1	Tom Cruise	67	14	Paul McCartney	40
2	Rolling Stones	90	15	George Lucas	235
3	Oprah Winfrey	225	16	Elton John	34
4	U2	110	17	David Letterman	40
5	Tiger Woods	90	18	Phil Mickelson	47
6	Steven Spielberg	332	19	J.K. Rowling	75
7	Howard Stern	302	20	Brad Pitt	25
8	50 Cent	41	21	Peter Jackson	39
9	Cast of *The Sopranos*	52	22	Dr. Phil McGraw	45
10	Dan Brown	88	23	Jay Leno	32
11	Bruce Springsteen	55	24	Celine Dion	40
12	Donald Trump	44	25	Kobe Bryant	31
13	Muhammad Ali	55			

Source: http://www.forbes.com/2006/06/12/06celebrities_money-power-celebrities-list_land.html (accessed February 25, 2007).

FIGURE 2.15   **Excel Frequency Histogram of the 65 Satisfaction Ratings (for Exercise 2.21)**

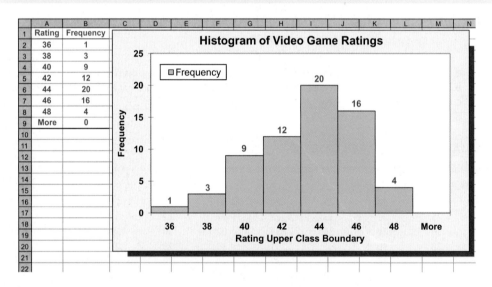

2.21   THE VIDEO GAME SATISFACTION RATING CASE   ● VideoGame

Recall that Table 1.7 (page 14) presents the satisfaction ratings for the XYZ-Box video game system that have been given by 65 randomly selected purchasers. Figure 2.15 gives the Excel output of a histogram of these satisfaction ratings.

a Describe where the satisfaction ratings seem to be concentrated.

b Describe and interpret the shape of the distribution of ratings.

c Write out the eight classes used to construct this histogram.

d Construct a cumulative frequency distribution of the satisfaction ratings using the histogram classes.

2.22   THE BANK CUSTOMER WAITING TIME CASE   ● WaitTime

Recall that Table 1.8 (page 14) presents the waiting times for teller service during peak business hours of 100 randomly selected bank customers. Figure 2.16 gives the MINITAB output of a histogram of these waiting times that has been constructed using automatic classes.

a Describe where the waiting times seem to be concentrated.

b Describe and interpret the shape of the distribution of waiting times.

c What is the class length that has been automatically defined by MINITAB?

d Write out the automatically defined classes and construct a cumulative percent frequency distribution of the waiting times using these classes.

FIGURE 2.16   **MINITAB Frequency Histogram of the 100 Waiting Times Using Automatic Classes (for Exercise 2.22)**

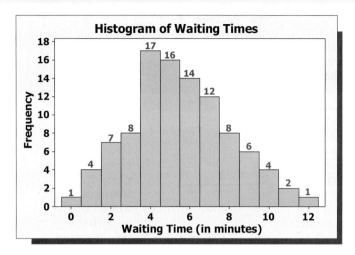

FIGURE 2.17   **MegaStat Percent Frequency Histogram of the 40 Breaking Strengths Using Automatic Classes (for Exercise 2.23)**

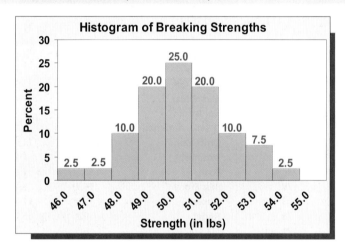

2.23   THE TRASH BAG CASE   TrashBag

Recall that Table 1.9 (page 16) presents the breaking strengths of 40 trash bags selected during a 40-hour pilot production run. Figure 2.17 gives the MegaStat output of a percent frequency histogram of these breaking strengths that has been constructed using automatic classes.

a Describe where the breaking strengths seem to be concentrated.

b Describe and interpret the shape of the distribution of breaking strengths.

c What is the class length that has been automatically defined by MegaStat?

d Write out the automatically defined classes and construct a percent frequency ogive for the breaking strengths using these classes.

2.24   Table 2.12 gives the franchise value and 2006 revenues for each of the 30 teams in major league baseball as reported by *Forbes* magazine and as listed on the Forbes.com website on February 25, 2007.   MLBTeams

a Develop a frequency distribution and a frequency histogram for the 30 team values. Then describe the distribution of team values.

b Develop a percent frequency distribution and a percent frequency histogram for the 30 team revenues. Then describe the distribution of team revenues.

c Draw a percent frequency polygon for the 30 team values.

TABLE 2.12   Major League Baseball Team Valuations and Revenues as Given on the Forbes.com Website on February 25, 2007 (for Exercise 2.24)   ⬤ MLBTeams

Rank	Team	Value ($mil)	Revenues ($mil)	Rank	Team	Value ($mil)	Revenues ($mil)
1	New York Yankees	1026	277	16	Texas Rangers	353	153
2	Boston Red Sox	617	206	17	Cleveland Indians	352	150
3	New York Mets	604	195	18	Chicago White Sox	315	157
4	Los Angeles Dodgers	482	189	19	Arizona Diamondbacks	305	145
5	Chicago Cubs	448	179	20	Colorado Rockies	298	145
6	Washington Nationals	440	145	21	Detroit Tigers	292	146
7	St Louis Cardinals	429	165	22	Toronto Blue Jays	286	136
8	Seattle Mariners	428	179	23	Cincinnati Reds	274	137
9	Philadelphia Phillies	424	176	24	Pittsburgh Pirates	250	125
10	Houston Astros	416	173	25	Kansas City Royals	239	117
11	San Francisco Giants	410	171	26	Milwaukee Brewers	235	131
12	Atlanta Braves	405	172	27	Oakland Athletics	234	134
13	Los Angeles Angels @ Anaheim	368	167	28	Florida Marlins	226	119
14	Baltimore Orioles	359	156	29	Minnesota Twins	216	114
15	San Diego Padres	354	158	30	Tampa Bay Devil Rays	209	116

Source: http://www.forbes.com/lists/2006/33/Rank_1.html (accessed February 25, 2007).

TABLE 2.13   The Best-Performing Retailers from the *Forbes* List of "The 400 Best Big Companies" as Listed on the Forbes.com Website on February 27, 2007   ⬤ ForbesBest

Company	Five-Year Total Return (%)	Sales ($bil)	Net Income ($mil)	Company	Five-Year Total Return (%)	Sales ($bil)	Net Income ($mil)
Aaron Rents	31.2	1.3	74	Fastenal	20.2	1.7	193
Abercrombie & Fitch	24.1	3.1	389	Lowe's Cos	7.1	47.3	3,180
Advance Auto Parts	21.5	4.6	235	MarineMax	26.9	1.2	39
Aeropostale	10.5	1.3	85	Nordstrom	39.6	8.2	636
Amer Eagle Outfitters	29.6	2.6	345	O'Reilly Automotive	14.4	2.2	177
AnnTaylor Stores	22.6	2.3	149	Office Depot	19.7	14.9	487
Bed Bath & Beyond	3.3	6.1	579	Petsmart	27.8	4.1	179
Best Buy	12.4	32.6	1,246	Pool	30.6	1.9	100
CarMax	18.2	6.9	178	Ross Stores	16.7	5.4	220
Charming Shoppes	22.0	3.0	103	Staples	17.0	17.3	927
Children's Place	13.1	1.8	73	Target	9.2	56.7	2,607
Claire's Stores	36.0	1.4	171	TJX Cos	8.5	17.1	821
CVS	16.2	41.5	1,358	United Auto Group	23.5	11.1	125
Dick's Sporting Goods	66.2	2.9	99	Walgreen	3.8	47.4	1,751
Dress Barn	29.3	1.3	86				

Source: http://www.forbes.com/lists/2007/88/biz_07platinum_The-400-Best-Big-Companies-Retailing_7Company.html (accessed February 27, 2007).

2.25 *Forbes* magazine publishes a list of "The 400 Best Big Companies" as selected by the magazine's writers and editors. Table 2.13 gives the best companies in the retailing industry as given by this list on the Forbes.com website on February 27, 2007.   ⬤ ForbesBest

a Develop a frequency distribution and a frequency histogram for the five-year total return percentages. Describe the distribution of these percentages.

b Develop a percent frequency histogram for the sales values and then describe this distribution.

c Develop a relative frequency ogive for the net incomes.

2.3 Dot Plots ◦ ● ●

A very simple graph that can be used to summarize a data set is called a **dot plot.** To make a dot plot we draw a horizontal axis that spans the range of the measurements in the data set. We then place dots above the horizontal axis to represent the measurements. As an example, Figure 2.18(a) shows a dot plot of the exam scores in Table 2.8. Remember, these are the scores for the first exam given before implementing a strict attendance policy. The horizontal axis spans exam

F I G U R E   2 . 1 8   **Comparing Exam Scores Using Dot Plots**

(a) **Dot Plot of Scores on Exam 1: Before Attendance Policy**

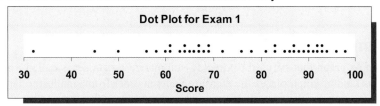

(b) **Dot Plot of Scores on Exam 2: After Attendance Policy**

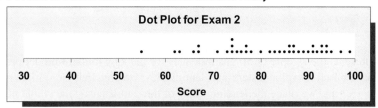

scores from 30 to 100. Each dot above the axis represents an exam score. For instance, the two dots above the score of 90 tell us that two students received a 90 on the exam. The dot plot shows us that there are two concentrations of scores—those in the 80s and 90s and those in the 60s. Figure 2.18(b) gives a dot plot of the scores on the second exam (which was given after imposing the attendance policy). As did the percent frequency polygon for exam 2 in Figure 2.13, this second dot plot shows that the attendance policy eliminated the concentration of scores in the 60s.

Dot plots are useful for detecting **outliers,** which are unusually large or small observations that are well separated from the remaining observations. For example, the dot plot for exam 1 indicates that the score 32 seems unusually low. How we handle an outlier depends on its cause. If the outlier results from a measurement error or an error in recording or processing the data, it should be corrected. If such an outlier cannot be corrected, it should be discarded. If an outlier is not the result of an error in measuring or recording the data, its cause may reveal important information. For example, the outlying exam score of 32 convinced the author that the student needed a tutor. After working with a tutor, the student showed considerable improvement on exam 2. A more precise way to detect outliers is presented in Section 3.3.

Exercises for Section 2.3

CONCEPTS

2.26   When we construct a dot plot, what does the horizontal axis represent? What does each dot represent?

2.27   If a data set consists of 1,000 measurements, would you summarize the data set using a histogram or a dot plot? Explain.

METHODS AND APPLICATIONS

2.28   The following data consists of the number of students who were absent in a professor's statistics class each day during the last month.   ● AbsenceData

2	0	3	1	2	5	8	0	1	4
1	10	6	2	2	0	3	6	0	1

Construct a dot plot of these data, and then describe the distribution of absences.

2.29   The following are the revenue growth rates for the 30 fastest-growing companies as listed March 16, 2005, on the *Fortune* magazine website.   ● RevGrowth

93%	43%	91%	49%	70%	44%	71%	70%	52%	59%
33%	40%	60%	35%	51%	48%	39%	61%	25%	87%
87%	46%	38%	30%	33%	43%	29%	38%	60%	32%

Source: Fortune.com (accessed March 16, 2005).

Develop a dot plot for these data and describe the distribution of revenue growth rates.

2.30　The yearly home run totals for Babe Ruth during his career as a New York Yankee are as follows (the totals are arranged in increasing order): 22, 25, 34, 35, 41, 41, 46, 46, 46, 47, 49, 54, 54, 59, 60. Construct a dot plot for these data and then describe the distribution of home run totals.
　　　　🌐 RuthsHomers

2.4 Stem-and-Leaf Displays ● ● ●

Another simple graph that be used to quickly summarize a data set is called a **stem-and-leaf display.** This kind of graph places the measurements in order from smallest to largest, allowing the analyst to simultaneously see all of the measurements in the data set and see the shape of the data set's distribution.

EXAMPLE 2.4 The Car Mileage Case

Table 2.14 presents the sample of 50 gas mileages for the new midsize model previously introduced in Chapter 1. To develop a stem-and-leaf display, we note that the sample mileages range from 29.8 to 33.3 and we place the leading digits of these mileages—the whole numbers 29, 30, 31, 32, and 33—in a column on the left side of a vertical line as follows:

```
29 |
30 |
31 |
32 |
33 |
```

This vertical arrangement of leading digits forms the **stem** of the display. Next, we pass through the mileages in Table 2.14 one at a time and place each last digit (the tenths place) to the right of the vertical line in the row corresponding to its leading digits. For instance, the first three mileages—30.8, 31.7, and 30.1—are arranged as follows:

```
29 |
30 | 8 1
31 | 7
32 |
33 |
```

We form the **leaves** of the display by continuing this procedure as we pass through all 50 mileages. After recording the last digit for each of the mileages, we sort the digits in each row from smallest to largest and obtain the stem-and-leaf display that follows:

```
29 | 8
30 | 1 3 4 5 5 6 7 7 8 8 8
31 | 0 0 1 2 3 3 4 4 4 4 4 5 5 6 6 7 7 7 8 8 9 9
32 | 0 1 1 1 2 3 3 4 4 5 5 7 7 8
33 | 0 3
```

As we have said, the numbers to the left of the vertical line form the stem of the display. Each number to the right of the vertical line is a leaf. Each combination of a stem value and a leaf value

TABLE 2.14	A Sample of 50 Mileages for a New Midsize Model 🌐 GasMiles			
30.8	30.8	32.1	32.3	32.7
31.7	30.4	31.4	32.7	31.4
30.1	32.5	30.8	31.2	31.8
31.6	30.3	32.8	30.7	31.9
32.1	31.3	31.9	31.7	33.0
33.3	32.1	31.4	31.4	31.5
31.3	32.5	32.4	32.2	31.6
31.0	31.8	31.0	31.5	30.6
32.0	30.5	29.8	31.7	32.3
32.4	30.5	31.1	30.7	31.4

represents a measurement in the data set. For instance, the first row in the display

$$29 \mid 8$$

tells us that the first two digits are 29 and that the last (tenth place) digit is 8—that is, this combination represents the mileage 29.8 mpg. Similarly, the last row

$$33 \mid 0\ 3$$

represents the mileages 33.0 mpg and 33.3 mpg.

The entire stem-and-leaf display portrays the overall distribution of the sample mileages. It groups the mileages into classes, and it graphically illustrates how many mileages are in each class, as well as how the mileages are distributed within each class. The first class corresponds to the stem 29 and consists of the mileages from 29.0 to 29.9. There is one mileage—29.8—in this class. The second class corresponds to the stem 30 and consists of the mileages from 30.0 to 30.9. There are 11 mileages in this class. Similarly, the third, fourth, and fifth classes correspond to the stems 31, 32, and 33 and contain, respectively, 22 mileages, 14 mileages, and 2 mileages. Moreover, the stem-and-leaf display shows that the distribution of mileages is quite symmetrical. To see this, imagine turning the stem-and-leaf display on its side so that the vertical line becomes a horizontal number line. We see that the display now resembles a symmetrically shaped histogram. However, *the stem-and-leaf display is advantageous because it allows us to actually see the measurements in the data set* in addition to the distribution's shape.

When constructing a stem-and-leaf display, there are no rules that dictate the number of stem values (rows) that should be used. If we feel that the display has collapsed the mileages too closely together, we can stretch the display by assigning each set of leading digits to two or more rows. This is called *splitting the stems*. For example, in the following stem-and-leaf display of the mileages the first (uppermost) stem value of 30 is used to represent mileages between 30.0 and 30.4. The second stem value of 30 is used to represent mileages between 30.5 and 30.9.

$$
\begin{array}{r|l}
29 & 8 \\
30 & 1\ 3\ 4 \\
30 & 5\ 5\ 6\ 7\ 7\ 8\ 8\ 8 \\
31 & 0\ 0\ 1\ 2\ 3\ 3\ 4\ 4\ 4\ 4\ 4 \\
31 & 5\ 5\ 6\ 6\ 7\ 7\ 7\ 8\ 8\ 9\ 9 \\
32 & 0\ 1\ 1\ 1\ 2\ 3\ 3\ 4\ 4 \\
32 & 5\ 5\ 7\ 7\ 8 \\
33 & 0\ 3 \\
\end{array}
$$

Notice that, in this particular case, splitting the stems produces a display that seems to more clearly reveal the symmetrical shape of the distribution of mileages.

Most statistical software packages can be used to construct stem-and-leaf displays. Figure 2.19 gives MINITAB and MegaStat outputs of a stem-and-leaf display of the 50 sample mileages. Each of these outputs has been obtained by splitting the stems—MINITAB produced this display

FIGURE 2.19   **MINITAB and MegaStat Outputs of a Stem-and-Leaf Display of the 50 Mileages**

(a) The MINITAB Output

Stem-and-Leaf Display: Mpg

Stem-and-leaf of Mpg   N = 50
Leaf unit = 0.10

```
 1     29   8
 4     30   134
12     30   55677888
23     31   00123344444
(11)   31   55667778899
16     32   011123344
 7     32   55778
 2     33   03
```

(b) The MegaStat Output

Stem-and-Leaf Plot for Mpg

Stem unit = 1
Leaf unit = 0.1

Frequency	Stem	Leaf
1	29	8
3	30	1 3 4
8	30	5 5 6 7 7 8 8 8
11	31	0 0 1 2 3 3 4 4 4 4 4
11	31	5 5 6 6 7 7 7 8 8 9 9
9	32	0 1 1 1 2 3 3 4 4
5	32	5 5 7 7 8
2	33	0 3
50		

automatically, while we requested that MegaStat split the stems. Each package provides an additional column of numbers (on the left) that provides information about how many mileages are in the various rows. For example, if we look at the MINITAB output, the 11 (in parentheses) tells us that there are 11 mileages between 31.5 mpg and 31.9 mpg. The 12 (no parentheses) tells us that a total of 12 mileages are at or below 30.9 mpg, while the 7 tells us that a total of 7 mileages are at or above 32.5 mpg. On the MegaStat output, the leftmost column of numbers tells us how many measurements are in each of the rows. For instance, 9 mileages are between 32.0 mpg and 32.4 mpg.

It is possible to construct a stem-and-leaf display from measurements containing any number of digits. To see how this can be done, consider the following data which consists of the number of DVD players sold by an electronics manufacturer for each of the last 12 months.

| 13,502 | 15,932 | 14,739 | 15,249 | 14,312 | 17,111 | ● DVDPlayers |
| 19,010 | 16,121 | 16,708 | 17,886 | 15,665 | 16,475 | |

To construct a stem-and-leaf display, we will use only the first three digits of each sales value, and we will define leaf values consisting of one digit. The stem will consist of the values 13, 14, 15, 16, 17, 18, and 19 (which represent thousands of units sold). Each leaf will represent the remaining three digits rounded to the nearest 100 units sold. For example, 13,502 will be represented by placing the leaf value 5 in the row corresponding to 13. To express the fact that the leaf 5 represents 500, we say that the **leaf unit** is 100. Using this procedure, we obtain the following stem-and-leaf display:

Leaf unit = 100

```
13 | 5
14 | 3 7
15 | 2 7 9
16 | 1 5 7
17 | 1 9
18 |
19 | 0
```

The standard practice of always using a single digit for each leaf allows us to construct a stem-and-leaf display for measurements having any number of digits as long as we appropriately define a leaf unit. However, it is not possible to recover the original measurements from such a display. If we do not have the original measurements, the best we can do is to approximate them by multiplying the digits in the display by the leaf unit. For instance, the measurements in the row corresponding to the stem value 17 can be approximated to be $171 \times (100) = 17,100$ and $179 \times (100) = 17,900$. In general, leaf units can be any power of 10 such as 0.1, 1, 10, 100, 1000, and so on. If no leaf unit is given for a stem-and-leaf display, we assume its value is 1.0.

We summarize how to set up a stem-and-leaf display in the following box:

Constructing a Stem-and-Leaf Display

1 Decide what units will be used for the stems and the leaves. Each leaf must be a single digit and the stem values will consist of appropriate leading digits. As a general rule, there should be between 5 and 20 stem values.

2 Place the stem values in a column to the left of a vertical line with the smallest value at the top of the column and the largest value at the bottom.

3 To the right of the vertical line, enter the leaf for each measurement into the row corresponding to the proper stem value. Each leaf should be a single digit—these can be rounded values that were originally more than one digit if we are using an appropriately defined leaf unit.

4 Rearrange the leaves so that they are in increasing order from left to right.

If we wish to compare two distributions, it is convenient to construct a **back-to-back stem-and-leaf display.** Figure 2.20 presents a back-to-back stem-and-leaf display for the previously discussed exam scores. The left side of the display summarizes the scores for the first exam. Remember, this exam was given before implementing a strict attendance policy. The right side of the display summarizes the scores for the second exam (which was given after imposing the attendance policy). Looking at the left side of the display, we see that for the first exam there are two

FIGURE 2.20   A Back-to-Back Stem-and-Leaf Display of the Exam Scores

	Exam 1			Exam 2
	2	3		
		3		
		4		
	5	4		
	0	5		
	8 6	5	5	
	4 4 3 1 1 0	6	2 3	
	9 9 8 7 7 6 5	6	6 7 7	
	2	7	1 3 4 4 4	
	8 6	7	5 6 7 7 8	
	3 3 1	8	0 2 3 4	
	9 8 7 7 6 5	8	5 6 6 7 7 8 9	
	4 3 3 2 2 1 0 0	9	0 1 1 2 3 3 4 4	
	8 6	9	5 7 9	

concentrations of scores—those in the 80s and 90s and those in the 60s. The right side of the display shows that the attendance policy eliminated the concentration of scores in the 60s and illustrates that the scores on exam 2 are quite single-peaked and somewhat skewed to the left.

Stem-and-leaf displays are useful for detecting **outliers,** which are unusually large or small observations that are well separated from the remaining observations. For example, the stem-and-leaf display for exam 1 indicates that the score 32 seems unusually low. How we handle an outlier depends on its cause. If the outlier results from a measurement error or an error in recording or processing the data, it should be corrected. If such an outlier cannot be corrected, it should be discarded. If an outlier is not the result of an error in measuring or recording the data, its cause may reveal important information. For example, the outlying exam score of 32 convinced the author that the student needed a tutor. After working with a tutor, the student showed considerable improvement on exam 2. A more precise way to detect outliers is presented in Section 3.3.

Exercises for Section 2.4

CONCEPTS

2.31 Explain the difference between a histogram and a stem-and-leaf display.

2.32 What are the advantages of using a stem-and-leaf display?

2.33 If a data set consists of 1,000 measurements, would you summarize the data set by using a stem-and-leaf display or a histogram? Explain.

connect

METHODS AND APPLICATIONS

2.34 The following data consist of the 2007 revenue growth rates (in percent) for a group of 20 firms. Construct a stem-and-leaf display for these data.   ● RevGrow2007

36	59	42	65	91	32	56	28	49	51
30	55	33	63	70	44	42	83	53	43

2.35 The following data consist of the 2007 profit margins (in percent) for a group of 20 firms. Construct a stem-and-leaf display for these data.   ● ProfitMar2007

25.2	16.1	22.2	15.2	14.1	15.2	14.4	15.9	10.4	14.0
16.4	13.9	10.4	13.8	14.9	16.1	15.8	13.2	16.8	12.6

2.36 The following data consist of the 2007 sales figures (in millions of dollars) for a group of 20 firms. Construct a stem-and-leaf display for these data. Use a leaf unit equal to 100.
● Sales2007

6835	1973	2820	5358	1233	3291	2707	3291	2675	3707
3517	1449	2384	1376	1725	6047	7903	4616	1541	4189

2.37 Figure 2.21 gives a stem-and-leaf display of the revenue growth rates (in percent) for the 30 fastest-growing companies as listed on March 16, 2005, on the *Fortune* magazine website.
   a Use the stem-and-leaf display to describe the distribution of revenue growth rates.
   b Write out the 30 observed revenue growth rates. That is, write out the original data.

FIGURE 2.21   Stem-and-Leaf Display of Revenue Growth Rates (in percent) (for Exercise 2.37)

```
Stem-and-leaf of revenue growth N = 30
Leaf unit = 1.0

    2    2   59
    5    3   0233
    9    3   5889
   13    4   0334
   (3)   4   689
   13    5   12
   11    5   9
   10    6   001
    7    6
    7    7   001
    4    7
    4    8
    4    8   77
    2    9   13
```

Source: Fortune.com (accessed March 16, 2005).

FIGURE 2.22   Stem-and-Leaf Display of the 40 Breaking Strengths (for Exercise 2.38)

Stem and leaf plot for strength
Stem unit = 1   Leaf unit = 0.1

Frequency	Stem	Leaf
1	46	8
0	47	
1	47	5
2	48	2 3
2	48	5 8
4	49	0 2 3 4
4	49	5 6 8 9
4	50	0 1 2 3
6	50	5 6 7 8 9 9
5	51	0 1 2 3 4
3	51	5 7 9
2	52	0 3
2	52	5 6
2	53	0 2
1	53	5
1	54	0
40		

TABLE 2.15   Mortgage Delinquency Rates for Each of the 50 States and the District of Columbia as Reported by USAToday.com on March 13, 2007 (for Exercise 2.40)   ● DelinqRate

Mississippi	10.6%	North Carolina	6.1%	Delaware	4.5%	Arizona	3.5%
Louisiana	9.1%	Arkansas	6.1%	Iowa	4.4%	Vermont	3.4%
Michigan	7.9%	Missouri	6.1%	New Hampshire	4.4%	Idaho	3.4%
Indiana	7.8%	Oklahoma	6.1%	Colorado	4.4%	California	3.3%
Georgia	7.5%	Illinois	5.4%	New Mexico	4.3%	Alaska	3.1%
West Virginia	7.4%	Kansas	5.1%	Connecticut	4.3%	Washington	2.9%
Texas	7.4%	Rhode Island	5.0%	Maryland	4.3%	South Dakota	2.9%
Tennessee	7.3%	Maine	4.9%	Wisconsin	4.1%	Wyoming	2.9%
Ohio	7.3%	Florida	4.9%	Nevada	4.1%	Montana	2.8%
Alabama	7.1%	New York	4.8%	Utah	4.0%	North Dakota	2.7%
Kentucky	6.3%	Nebraska	4.7%	Minnesota	4.0%	Oregon	2.6%
South Carolina	6.3%	Massachusetts	4.5%	Dist. of Columbia	3.7%	Hawaii	2.4%
Pennsylvania	6.3%	New Jersey	4.5%	Virginia	3.7%		

Source: Mortgage Bankers Association as reported by Noelle Knox, "Record Foreclosures Hit Mortgage Lenders," *USA Today,* March 13, 2007, http://www.usatoday.com/money/economy/housing/2007-03-13-foreclosures_N.htm.

2.38   THE TRASH BAG CASE   ● TrashBag

Figure 2.22 gives the MegaStat output of a stem-and-leaf display of the sample of 40 breaking strengths in the trash bag case.

a Use the stem-and-leaf display to describe the distribution of breaking strengths.

b Write out the 10 smallest breaking strengths as they would be expressed in the original data.

2.39 Babe Ruth's record of 60 home runs in a single year was broken by Roger Maris, who hit 61 home runs in 1961. The yearly home run totals for Ruth in his career as a New York Yankee are (arranged in increasing order) 22, 25, 34, 35, 41, 41, 46, 46, 46, 47, 49, 54, 54, 59, and 60. The yearly home run totals for Maris over his career in the American League are (arranged in increasing order) 8, 13, 14, 16, 23, 26, 28, 33, 39, and 61. Compare Ruth's and Maris's home run totals by constructing a back-to-back stem-and-leaf display. What would you conclude about Maris's record-breaking year?   ● HomeRuns

2.40 In March 2007 *USA Today* reported that more than 2.1 million Americans with a home missed at least one mortgage payment at the end of 2006. In addition, the rate of new foreclosures was reported to be at an all-time high. Table 2.15 gives the mortgage delinquency rates for each state and the District of Columbia as reported by USAToday.com on March 13, 2007.   ● DelinqRate

  a Construct a stem-and-leaf display of the mortgage delinquency rates and describe the distribution of these rates.

  b Do there appear to be any rates that are outliers? Can you suggest a reason for any possible outliers?

2.41 THE VIDEO GAME SATISFACTION RATING CASE   ● VideoGame

Recall that 65 purchasers have participated in a survey and have rated the XYZ-Box video game system. The composite ratings that have been obtained are as follows:

39	38	40	40	40	46	43	38	44	44	44
45	42	42	47	46	45	41	43	46	44	42
38	46	45	44	41	45	40	36	48	44	47
42	44	44	43	43	46	43	44	44	46	43
42	40	42	45	39	43	44	44	41	39	45
41	39	46	45	43	47	41	45	45	41	

  a Construct a stem-and-leaf display for the 65 composite ratings. Hint: Each whole number rating can be written with an "implied tenth place" of zero. For instance, 39 can be written as 39.0. Use the implied zeros as the leaf values and the whole numbers 36, 37, 38, 39, and so forth as the stem values.

  b Describe the distribution of composite ratings.

  c If we consider a purchaser to be "very satisfied" if his or her composite score is at least 42, can we say that almost all purchasers of the XYZ-Box video game system are "very satisfied"?

2.5 Crosstabulation Tables (Optional) ◔ ● ●

Previous sections in this chapter have presented methods for summarizing data for a single variable. Often, however, we wish to use statistics to study possible relationships between several variables. In this section we present a simple way to study the relationship between two variables. A **crosstabulation table** classifies data on two dimensions. Such a table consists of rows and columns—the rows classify the data according to one dimension and the columns classify the data according to a second dimension.

EXAMPLE 2.5 The Investor Satisfaction Case

An investment broker sells several kinds of investment products—a stock fund, a bond fund, and a tax-deferred annuity. The broker wishes to study whether client satisfaction with its products and services depends on the type of investment product purchased. To do this, 100 of the broker's clients are randomly selected from the population of clients who have purchased shares in exactly one of the funds. The broker records the fund type purchased by each client and has one of its investment counselors personally contact the client. When contacted, the client is asked to rate his or her level of satisfaction with the purchased fund as high, medium, or low. The resulting data are given in Table 2.16.

Looking at the raw data in Table 2.16, it is difficult to see whether the level of client satisfaction varies depending on the fund type. We can look at the data in an organized way by constructing a crosstabulation table. A crosstabulation of fund type versus level of client satisfaction is shown in Table 2.17. The classification categories for the two variables are defined along the left and top margins of the table. The three row labels—bond fund, stock fund, and tax-deferred annuity—define the three fund categories and are given in the left table margin. The three column labels—high, medium, and low—define the three levels of client satisfaction and are given along the top table margin. Each row and column combination (that is, each fund type and level of satisfaction combination) defines what we call a "cell" in the table. Because each of the randomly selected clients has invested in exactly one fund type and has reported exactly one level of satisfaction, each client can be placed in a particular cell in the crosstabulation table. For example, because client number 1 in Table 2.16 has invested in the bond fund and reports a high level of client satisfaction, client number 1 can be placed in the upper left cell of the table (the cell defined by the Bond Fund row and High Satisfaction column).

We fill in the cells in the table by moving through the 100 randomly selected clients and by tabulating the number of clients who can be placed in each cell. For instance, moving through the 100 clients results in placing 15 clients in the "bond fund—high" cell, 12 clients in the "bond fund—medium" cell, and so forth. The counts in the cells are called the **cell frequencies**.

TABLE 2.16   Results of a Customer Satisfaction Survey Given to 100 Randomly Selected Clients Who Invest in One of Three Fund Types—a Bond Fund, a Stock Fund, or a Tax-Deferred Annuity   ● Invest

Client	Fund Type	Level of Satisfaction	Client	Fund Type	Level of Satisfaction	Client	Fund Type	Level of Satisfaction
1	BOND	HIGH	35	STOCK	HIGH	69	BOND	MED
2	STOCK	HIGH	36	BOND	MED	70	TAXDEF	MED
3	TAXDEF	MED	37	TAXDEF	MED	71	TAXDEF	MED
4	TAXDEF	MED	38	TAXDEF	LOW	72	BOND	HIGH
5	STOCK	LOW	39	STOCK	HIGH	73	TAXDEF	MED
6	STOCK	HIGH	40	TAXDEF	MED	74	TAXDEF	LOW
7	STOCK	HIGH	41	BOND	HIGH	75	STOCK	HIGH
8	BOND	MED	42	BOND	HIGH	76	BOND	HIGH
9	TAXDEF	LOW	43	BOND	LOW	77	TAXDEF	LOW
10	TAXDEF	LOW	44	TAXDEF	LOW	78	BOND	MED
11	STOCK	MED	45	STOCK	HIGH	79	STOCK	HIGH
12	BOND	LOW	46	BOND	HIGH	80	STOCK	HIGH
13	STOCK	HIGH	47	BOND	MED	81	BOND	MED
14	TAXDEF	MED	48	STOCK	HIGH	82	TAXDEF	MED
15	TAXDEF	MED	49	TAXDEF	MED	83	BOND	HIGH
16	TAXDEF	LOW	50	TAXDEF	MED	84	STOCK	MED
17	STOCK	HIGH	51	STOCK	HIGH	85	STOCK	HIGH
18	BOND	HIGH	52	TAXDEF	MED	86	BOND	MED
19	BOND	MED	53	STOCK	HIGH	87	TAXDEF	MED
20	TAXDEF	MED	54	TAXDEF	MED	88	TAXDEF	LOW
21	TAXDEF	MED	55	STOCK	LOW	89	STOCK	HIGH
22	BOND	HIGH	56	BOND	HIGH	90	TAXDEF	MED
23	TAXDEF	MED	57	STOCK	HIGH	91	BOND	HIGH
24	TAXDEF	LOW	58	BOND	MED	92	TAXDEF	HIGH
25	STOCK	HIGH	59	TAXDEF	LOW	93	TAXDEF	LOW
26	BOND	HIGH	60	TAXDEF	LOW	94	TAXDEF	LOW
27	TAXDEF	LOW	61	STOCK	MED	95	STOCK	HIGH
28	BOND	MED	62	BOND	LOW	96	BOND	HIGH
29	STOCK	HIGH	63	STOCK	HIGH	97	BOND	MED
30	STOCK	HIGH	64	TAXDEF	MED	98	STOCK	HIGH
31	BOND	MED	65	TAXDEF	MED	99	TAXDEF	MED
32	TAXDEF	MED	66	TAXDEF	LOW	100	TAXDEF	MED
33	BOND	HIGH	67	STOCK	HIGH			
34	STOCK	MED	68	BOND	HIGH			

TABLE 2.17   A Crosstabulation Table of Fund Type versus Level of Client Satisfaction

Fund Type	Level of Satisfaction			Total
	High	Medium	Low	
Bond Fund	15	12	3	30
Stock Fund	24	4	2	30
Tax-Deferred Annuity	1	24	15	40
Total	40	40	20	100

In Table 2.17 these frequencies tell us that 15 clients invested in the bond fund and reported a high level of satisfaction, 4 clients invested in the stock fund and reported a medium level of satisfaction, and so forth.

The far right column in the table (labeled Total) is obtained by summing the cell frequencies across the rows. For instance, these totals tell us that $15 + 12 + 3 = 30$ clients invested in the bond fund, $24 + 4 + 2 = 30$ clients invested in the stock fund, and $1 + 24 + 15 = 40$ clients invested in the tax-deferred annuity. These **row totals** provide a frequency distribution for the different fund types. By dividing the row totals by the total of 100 clients surveyed, we can obtain relative frequencies; and by multiplying each relative frequency by 100, we can obtain percent frequencies. That is, we can obtain the frequency, relative frequency, and percent frequency distributions for fund type as follows:

Fund Type	Frequency	Relative Frequency	Percent Frequency
Bond fund	30	30/100 = .30	.30 (100) = 30%
Stock fund	30	30/100 = .30	.30 (100) = 30%
Tax-deferred annuity	40	40/100 = .40	.40 (100) = 40%
	100		

We see that 30 percent of the clients invested in the bond fund, 30 percent invested in the stock fund, and 40 percent invested in the tax-deferred annuity.

The bottom row in the table (labeled Total) is obtained by summing the cell frequencies down the columns. For instance, these totals tell us that $15 + 24 + 1 = 40$ clients reported a high level of satisfaction, $12 + 4 + 24 = 40$ clients reported a medium level of satisfaction, and $3 + 2 + 15 = 20$ clients reported a low level of satisfaction. These **column totals** provide a frequency distribution for the different satisfaction levels (see below). By dividing the column totals by the total of 100 clients surveyed, we can obtain relative frequencies, and by multiplying each relative frequency by 100, we can obtain percent frequencies. That is, we can obtain the frequency, relative frequency, and percent frequency distributions for level of satisfaction as follows:

Level of Satisfaction	Frequency	Relative Frequency	Percent Frequency
High	40	40/100 = .40	.40 (100) = 40%
Medium	40	40/100 = .40	.40 (100) = 40%
Low	20	20/100 = .20	.20 (100) = 20%
	100		

We see that 40 percent of all clients reported high satisfaction, 40 percent reported medium satisfaction, and 20 percent reported low satisfaction.

We have seen that the totals in the margins of the crosstabulation table give us frequency distributions that provide information about each of the variables *fund type* and *level of client satisfaction*. However, the main purpose of constructing the table is to investigate possible relationships *between* these variables. Looking at Table 2.17, we see that clients who have invested in the stock fund seem to be highly satisfied and that those who have invested in the bond fund seem to have a high to medium level of satisfaction. However, clients who have invested in the tax-deferred annuity seem to be less satisfied.

One good way to investigate relationships such as these is to compute **row percentages** and **column percentages.** We compute row percentages by dividing each cell's frequency by its corresponding row total and by expressing the resulting fraction as a percentage. For instance, the row percentage for the upper lefthand cell (bond fund and high level of satisfaction) in Table 2.17 is $(15/30) \times 100\% = 50\%$. Similarly, column percentages are computed by dividing each cell's frequency by its corresponding column total and by expressing the resulting fraction as a percentage. For example, the column percentage for the upper lefthand cell in Table 2.17 is $(15/40) \times 100\% = 37.5\%$. Table 2.18 summarizes all of the row percentages for the different fund types in Table 2.17. We see that each row in Table 2.18 gives a percentage frequency distribution of level of client satisfaction given a particular fund type.

For example, the first row in Table 2.18 gives a percent frequency distribution of client satisfaction for investors who have purchased shares in the bond fund. We see that 50 percent of

TABLE 2.18   **Row Percentages for Each Fund Type**

Fund Type	Level of Satisfaction			Total
	High	Medium	Low	
Bond Fund	50%	40%	10%	100%
Stock Fund	80%	13.33%	6.67%	100%
Tax-Deferred	2.5%	60%	37.5%	100%

FIGURE 2.23   Bar Charts Illustrating Percent Frequency Distributions of Client Satisfaction as Given by the
Row Percentages for the Three Fund Types in Table 2.18

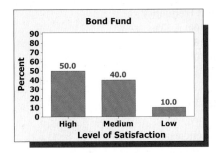

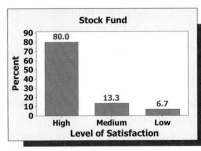

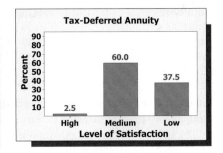

bond fund investors report high satisfaction, while 40 percent of these investors report medium satisfaction, and only 10 percent report low satisfaction. The other rows in Table 2.18 provide percent frequency distributions of client satisfaction for stock fund and annuity purchasers.

All three percent frequency distributions of client satisfaction—for the bond fund, the stock fund, and the tax-deferred annuity—are illustrated using bar charts in Figure 2.23. In this figure, the bar heights for each chart are the respective row percentages in Table 2.18. For example, these distributions tell us that 80 percent of stock fund investors report high satisfaction, while 97.5 percent of tax-deferred annuity purchasers report medium or low satisfaction. Looking at the entire table of row percentages (or the bar charts in Figure 2.23), we might conclude that stock fund investors are highly satisfied, that bond fund investors are quite satisfied (but somewhat less so than stock fund investors), and that tax-deferred annuity purchasers are less satisfied than either stock fund or bond fund investors. In general, row percentages and column percentages help us to quantify relationships such as these.

In the investment example, we have crosstabulated two qualitative variables. We can also crosstabulate a quantitative variable versus a qualitative variable or two quantitative variables against each other. If we are crosstabulating a quantitative variable, we often define categories by using appropriate ranges. For example, if we wished to crosstabulate level of education (grade school, high school, college, graduate school) versus income, we might define income classes $0–$50,000, $50,001–$100,000, $100,001–$150,000, and above $150,000.

Exercises for Section 2.5

CONCEPTS

connect

2.42 Explain the purpose behind constructing a crosstabulation table.

2.43 A crosstabulation table consists of several "cells." Explain how we fill the cells in the table.

2.44 Explain how to compute (1) the row percentages for a crosstabulation table (2) the column percentages. What information is provided by the row percentages in a particular row of the table? What information is provided by the column percentages in a particular column of the table?

METHODS AND APPLICATIONS

Exercises 2.45 through 2.47 are based on the following situation:

The marketing department at the Rola-Cola Bottling Company is investigating the attitudes and preferences of consumers towards Rola-Cola and a competing soft drink, Koka-Cola. Forty randomly selected shoppers are given a blind taste test and are asked to give their cola preferences. The results are given in Table 2.19—each shopper's preference, Rola-Cola or Koka-Cola, is revealed to the shopper only after he or she has tasted both brands without knowing which cola is which. In addition, each survey participant is asked to answer three more questions: (1) Have you previously purchased Rola-Cola: yes

TABLE 2.19 **Rola-Cola Bottling Company Survey Results** 🌐 ColaSurvey

Shopper	Cola Preference	Previously Purchased?	Sweetness Preference	Monthly Cola Consumption	Shopper	Cola Preference	Previously Purchased?	Sweetness Preference	Monthly Cola Consumption
1	Koka	No	Very sweet	4	21	Koka	No	Very sweet	4
2	Rola	Yes	Sweet	8	22	Rola	Yes	Not so sweet	9
3	Koka	No	Not so sweet	2	23	Rola	Yes	Not so sweet	3
4	Rola	Yes	Sweet	10	24	Koka	No	Not so sweet	2
5	Rola	No	Very sweet	7	25	Koka	No	Sweet	5
6	Rola	Yes	Not so sweet	6	26	Rola	Yes	Very sweet	7
7	Koka	No	Very sweet	4	27	Koka	No	Very sweet	7
8	Rola	No	Very sweet	3	28	Rola	Yes	Sweet	8
9	Koka	No	Sweet	3	29	Rola	Yes	Not so sweet	6
10	Rola	No	Very sweet	5	30	Koka	No	Not so sweet	3
11	Rola	Yes	Sweet	7	31	Koka	Yes	Sweet	10
12	Rola	Yes	Not so sweet	13	32	Rola	Yes	Very sweet	8
13	Rola	Yes	Very sweet	6	33	Koka	Yes	Sweet	4
14	Koka	No	Very sweet	2	34	Rola	No	Sweet	5
15	Koka	No	Not so sweet	7	35	Rola	Yes	Not so sweet	3
16	Rola	Yes	Sweet	9	36	Koka	No	Very sweet	11
17	Koka	No	Not so sweet	1	37	Rola	Yes	Not so sweet	9
18	Rola	Yes	Very sweet	5	38	Rola	No	Very sweet	6
19	Rola	No	Sweet	4	39	Koka	No	Not so sweet	2
20	Rola	No	Sweet	12	40	Rola	Yes	Sweet	5

or no? (2) What is your sweetness preference for cola drinks: very sweet, sweet, or not so sweet? (3) How many 12-packs of cola drinks does your family consume in a typical month? These responses are also given in Table 2.19.

2.45 Construct a crosstabulation table using cola preference (Rola or Koka) as the row variable and Rola-Cola purchase history (yes or no) as the column variable. Based on the table, answer the following:

a How many shoppers who preferred Rola-Cola in the blind taste test had previously purchased Rola-Cola?

b How many shoppers who preferred Koka-Cola in the blind taste test had not previously purchased Rola-Cola?

c What kind of relationship, if any, seems to exist between cola preference and Rola-Cola purchase history?

2.46 Construct a crosstabulation table using cola preference (Rola or Koka) as the row variable and sweetness preference (very sweet, sweet, or not so sweet) as the column variable. Based on the table, answer the following:

a How many shoppers who preferred Rola-Cola in the blind taste test said that they preferred a cola drink to be either very sweet or sweet?

b How many shoppers who preferred Koka-Cola in the blind taste test said that they preferred a cola drink to be not so sweet?

c What kind of relationship, if any, seems to exist between cola preference and sweetness preference?

2.47 Construct a crosstabulation table using cola preference (Rola or Koka) as the row variable and the number of 12-packs consumed in a typical month (categories 0 through 5, 6 through 10, and more than 10) as the column variable. Based on the table, answer the following:

a How many shoppers who preferred Rola-Cola in the blind taste test purchase 10 or fewer 12-packs of cola drinks in a typical month?

b How many shoppers who preferred Koka-Cola in the blind taste test purchase 6 or more 12-packs of cola drinks in a typical month?

c What kind of relationship, if any, seems to exist between cola preference and cola consumption in a typical month?

2.48 A marketing research firm wishes to study the relationship between wine consumption and whether a person likes to watch professional tennis on television. One hundred randomly selected people are asked whether they drink wine and whether they watch tennis. The following results are obtained: ● WineCons

	Watch Tennis	Do Not Watch Tennis	Total
Drink Wine	16	24	40
Do Not Drink Wine	4	56	60
Total	20	80	100

a What percentage of those surveyed both watch tennis and drink wine? What percentage of those surveyed do neither?

b Using the survey data, construct a table of row percentages.

c Using the survey data, construct a table of column percentages.

d What kind of relationship, if any, seems to exist between whether or not a person watches tennis and whether or not a person drinks wine?

e Illustrate your conclusion of part *d* by plotting bar charts of appropriate column percentages for people who watch tennis and for people who do not watch tennis.

2.49 In a survey of 1,000 randomly selected U.S. citizens aged 21 years or older, 721 believed that the amount of violent television programming had increased over the past 10 years, 454 believed that the overall quality of television programming had gotten worse over the past 10 years, and 362 believed both.

a Use this information to fill in the crosstabulation table below.

	TV Violence Increased	TV Violence Not Increased	Total
TV Quality Worse			
TV Quality Not Worse			
Total			

b Using the completed crosstabulation table, construct a table of row percentages.

c Using the completed crosstabulation table, construct a table of column percentages.

d What kind of relationship, if any, seems to exist between whether a person believed that TV violence had increased over the past 10 years and whether a person believed that the overall quality of TV programming had gotten worse over the past 10 years?

e Illustrate your answer to part *d* by constructing bar charts of appropriate row percentages.

In Exercises 2.50 and 2.51 we consider the results of a Gallup Lifestyle Poll about restaurant tipping habits as reported by the Gallup News Service on January 8, 2007. The poll asked Americans to recommend the percentage of a restaurant bill that should be left as a tip. As reported on galluppoll.com, Americans gave an overall (average) recommendation of 16.2 percent.

2.50 As part of its study, Gallup investigated a possible relationship between tipping attitudes and income. Using the poll results, the following row percentages can be obtained for three income ranges—less than $30,000; $30,000 through $74,999; and $75,000 or more.   ● RowPercents

Appropriate Tip Percent*

Income	Less Than 15%	15%	16–19%	20% or More	Total
Less Than $30,000	28.41%	42.04%	1.14%	28.41%	100%
$30,000 through $74,999	15.31%	42.86%	6.12%	35.71%	100%
$75,000 or More	8.16%	32.66%	9.18%	50.00%	100%

*Among those surveyed having an opinion.

a Construct a percentage bar chart of recommended tip percentage for each of the three income ranges.

b Using the bar charts, describe the relationship between recommended tip percentage and income level.

2.51 Gallup also asked survey participants if they have ever eaten at a restaurant and left no tip at all because of poor service. Almost half (46 percent) of those surveyed said they have done so. Because it seems that whether or not a person has left a restaurant without tipping might be related to a person's generosity in terms of recommended tip percentage, the survey investigated this possible relationship. Using the poll results, the column percentages at the top of page 81 can be obtained for each of the categories "Yes, have left without tipping" and "No, have not left without tipping."   ● ColPercents

	Tip Less Than 15%	Tip 15% through 19%	Tip 20% or More
Yes, have left without tipping	64%	50%	35%
No, have not left without tipping	36%	50%	65%
Total	100%	100%	100%

  a Construct a percentage bar chart of the categories "Yes, have left without tipping" and "No, have not left without tipping" for each of the tip categories "less than 15%," "15% through 19%," and "20% or more."

  b Using the bar charts, describe the relationship between whether or not a person has left without tipping and tipping generosity.

2.6 Scatter Plots (Optional) ◦ ● ●

We often study relationships between variables by using graphical methods. A simple graph that can be used to study the relationship between two variables is called a **scatter plot.** As an example, suppose that a marketing manager wishes to investigate the relationship between the sales volume (in thousands of units) of a product and the amount spent (in units of $10,000) on advertising the product. To do this, the marketing manager randomly selects 10 sales regions having equal sales potential. The manager assigns a different level of advertising expenditure for January 2008 to each sales region as shown in Table 2.20. At the end of the month, the sales volume for each region is recorded as also shown in Table 2.20.

A scatter plot of this data is given in Figure 2.24. To construct this plot, we place the variable advertising expenditure (denoted x) on the horizontal axis and we place the variable sales volume (denoted y) on the vertical axis. For the first sales region, advertising expenditure equals 5 and sales volume equals 89. We plot the point with coordinates $x = 5$ and $y = 89$ on the scatter plot to represent this sales region. Points for the other sales regions are plotted similarly. The scatter plot shows that there is a positive relationship between advertising expenditure and sales volume—that is, higher values of sales volume are associated with higher levels of advertising expenditure.

We have drawn a straight line through the plotted points of the scatter plot to represent the relationship between advertising expenditure and sales volume. We often do this when the relationship between two variables appears to be **straight line,** or **linear.** Of course, the relationship between x and y in Figure 2.24 is not perfectly linear—not all of the points in the scatter plot are exactly on the line. Nevertheless, because the relationship between x and y appears to be approximately linear, it seems reasonable to represent the general relationship between these variables using a straight line. In future chapters we will explain ways to quantify such a relationship—that is, describe such a relationship numerically. We will show that we can statistically express the strength of a linear relationship and that we can calculate the equation of the line that best fits the points of a scatter plot.

TABLE 2.20	Values of Advertising Expenditure (in $10,000s) and Sales Volume (in 1000s) for 10 Sales Regions ◐ SalesPlot

Sales Region	Advertising Expenditure, x	Sales Volume, y
1	5	89
2	6	87
3	7	98
4	8	110
5	9	103
6	10	114
7	11	116
8	12	110
9	13	126
10	14	130

FIGURE 2.24 A Scatter Plot of Sales Volume versus Advertising Expenditure

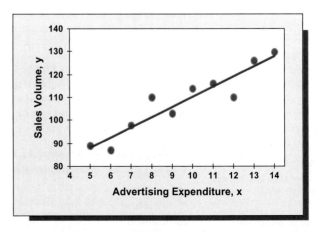

FIGURE 2.25 A Positive Linear Relationship	FIGURE 2.26 Little or No Linear Relationship	FIGURE 2.27 A Negative Linear Relationship
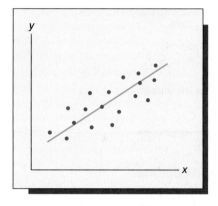	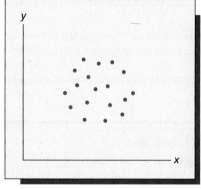	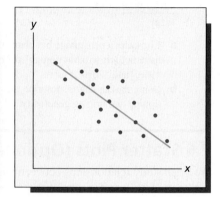

A scatter plot can reveal various kinds of relationships. For instance, Figures 2.25, 2.26, and 2.27 show several possible relationships between two variables x and y. Figure 2.25 shows a relationship similar to that of our advertising expenditure—sales volume example—here y has a tendency to increase as x increases. Figure 2.26 illustrates a situation in which x and y do not appear to have any linear relationship. Figure 2.27 illustrates a negative linear relationship—here y has a tendency to decrease as x increases. Finally, not all relationships are linear. In Exercise 14.43 we will consider how to represent and quantify curved relationships.

To conclude this section, recall from Chapter 1 that a runs plot—also called a **time series plot**—is a plot of individual process measurements versus time. This implies that a runs plot is a scatter plot, where values of a process variable are plotted on the vertical axis versus corresponding values of time on the horizontal axis.

Exercises for Section 2.6

CONCEPTS

2.52 Explain the purpose for constructing a scatter plot of y versus x.

2.53 Draw a scatter plot of y versus x in which y increases in a linear fashion as x increases.

2.54 Draw a scatter plot of y versus x in which y decreases in a linear fashion as x increases.

2.55 Draw a scatter plot of y versus x in which there is little or no linear relationship between y and x.

2.56 Discuss the relationship between a scatter plot and a runs plot.

METHODS AND APPLICATIONS

2.57 **THE REAL ESTATE SALES PRICE CASE**   ● RealEst

A real estate agency collects data concerning y = the sales price of a house (in thousands of dollars), and x = the home size (in hundreds of square feet). The data are given in Table 2.21. Construct a scatter plot of y versus x and interpret what the plot says.

2.58 **THE FUEL CONSUMPTION CASE**   ● FuelCon1

Table 2.22 gives the average hourly outdoor temperature (x) in a city during a week and the city's natural gas consumption (y) during the week for each of the previous eight weeks (the temperature readings are expressed in degrees Fahrenheit and the natural gas consumptions are expressed in millions of cubic feet of natural gas). The MINITAB output in Figure 2.28 gives a scatter plot of y versus x. Discuss the nature of the relationship between y and x.

TABLE 2.21
Real Estate Sales Price Data
● RealEst

Sales Price (y)	Home Size (x)
180	23
98.1	11
173.1	20
136.5	17
141	15
165.9	21
193.5	24
127.8	13
163.5	19
172.5	25

Source: Reprinted with permission from *The Real Estate Appraiser and Analyst* Spring 1986 issue. Copyright 1986 by the Appraisal Institute, Chicago, Illinois.

TABLE 2.22 **The Fuel Consumption Data** ● FuelCon1								
Week	1	2	3	4	5	6	7	8
Temperature, x	28.0	28.0	32.5	39.0	45.9	57.8	58.1	62.5
Natural Gas Consumption, y	12.4	11.7	12.4	10.8	9.4	9.5	8.0	7.5

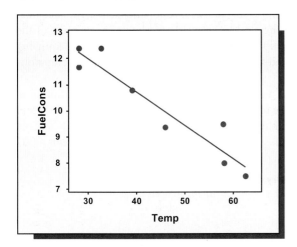

FIGURE 2.28   MINITAB Scatter Plot of the Fuel Consumption Data (for Exercise 2.58)

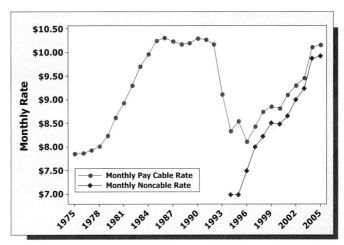

FIGURE 2.29   Runs Plots for Exercise 2.59   ● PayTVRates

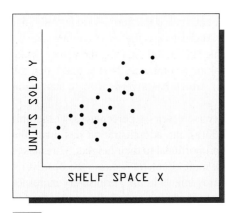

FIGURE 2.30   A Scatter Plot of Units Sold versus Shelf Space (for Exercise 2.60)

Source: W. R. Dillon, T. J. Madden, and N. H. Firtle, *Essentials of Marketing Research* (Burr Ridge, IL: Richard D. Irwin, Inc., 1993), p. 452. Copyright © 1993. Reprinted by permission of McGraw-Hill Companies, Inc.

FIGURE 2.31   Excel Output of the Mean Restaurant Ratings and a Scatter Plot of Mean Preference versus Mean Taste (for Exercise 2.61)   ● FastFood

	A	B	C	D	E	F
1	Restaurant	Meantaste	Meanconv	Meanfam	Meanprice	Meanpref
2	Borden Burger	3.5659	2.7005	2.5282	2.9372	4.2552
3	Hardee's	3.329	3.3483	2.7345	2.7513	4.0911
4	Burger King	2.4231	2.7377	2.3368	3.0761	3.0052
5	McDonald's	2.0895	1.938	1.4619	2.4884	2.2429
6	Wendy's	1.9661	2.892	2.3376	4.0814	2.5351
7	White Castle	3.8061	3.7242	2.6515	1.708	4.7812
8						
9						
10						
11						
12						
13						
14						
15						
16						
17						
18						
19						
20						
21						
22						

Source: The Ohio State University.

2.59   Figure 2.29 gives a runs plot of the average U.S. monthly pay cable TV rate (for premium services) for each year from 1975 to 2005. Figure 2.29 also gives a runs plot of the average monthly noncable (mostly satellite) TV rate (for premium services) for each year from 1994 to 2005.[7] Satellite TV became a serious competitor to cable TV in the early 1990s. Does it appear that the emergence of satellite TV had an influence on cable TV rates? What happened after satellite TV became more established in the marketplace?   ● PayTVRates

2.60   Figure 2.30 gives a scatter plot of the number of units sold, *y*, of 20 varieties of a canned soup versus the amount of shelf space, *x*, allocated to each variety. Do you think that sales are affected by the amount of allocated shelf space, or vice versa?

2.61   **THE FAST-FOOD RESTAURANT RATING CASE**   ● FastFood

Figure 2.31 presents the ratings given by 406 randomly selected individuals of six fast-food restaurants on the basis of taste, convenience, familiarity, and price. The data were collected by researchers of The Ohio State University in the early 1990s. Here, 1 is the best rating and 6 the worst. In addition, each individual ranked the restaurants from 1 through 6 on the basis of overall preference. Interpret the Excel scatter plot, and construct and interpret other relevant scatter plots.

[7]The time series data for this exercise is on the CD-ROM that accompanies this book.

2.7 Misleading Graphs and Charts (Optional) ● ● ●

The statistical analyst's goal should be to present the most accurate and truthful portrayal of a data set that is possible. Such a presentation allows managers using the analysis to make informed decisions. However, it is possible to construct statistical summaries that are misleading. Although we do not advocate using misleading statistics, you should be aware of some of the ways statistical graphs and charts can be manipulated in order to distort the truth. By knowing what to look for, you can avoid being misled by a (we hope) small number of unscrupulous practitioners.

As an example, suppose that the faculty at a major university will soon vote on a proposal to join a union. Both the union organizers and the university administration plan to distribute recent salary statistics to the entire faculty. Suppose that the mean faculty salary at the university and the mean salary increase at the university (expressed as a percentage) for each of the years 2004 through 2007 are as follows:

Year	Mean Salary (All Ranks)	Mean Salary Increase (Percent)
2004	$60,000	3.0%
2005	61,600	4.0
2006	63,500	4.5
2007	66,100	6.0

The university administration does not want the faculty to unionize and, therefore, hopes to convince the faculty that substantial progress has been made to increase salaries without a union. On the other hand, the union organizers wish to portray the salary increases as minimal so that the faculty will feel the need to unionize.

Figure 2.32 gives two bar charts of the mean salaries at the university for each year from 2004 to 2007. Notice that in Figure 2.32(a) the administration has started the vertical scale of the bar chart at a salary of $58,000 by using a *scale break* (⚡). Alternatively, the chart could be set up without the scale break by simply starting the vertical scale at $58,000. Starting the vertical scale at a value far above zero makes the salary increases look more dramatic. Notice that when the union organizers present the bar chart in Figure 2.32(b), which has a vertical scale starting at zero, the salary increases look far less impressive.

Figure 2.33 presents two bar charts of the mean salary increases (in percentages) at the university for each year from 2004 to 2007. In Figure 2.33(a), the administration has made the widths of the bars representing the percentage increases proportional to their heights. This makes the upward movement in the mean salary increases look more dramatic because the observer's eye tends to compare the areas of the bars, while the improvements in the mean salary increases are really only proportional to the heights of the bars. When the union organizers present the bar chart of Figure 2.33(b), the improvements in the mean salary increases look less impressive because each bar has the same width.

F I G U R E   2 . 3 2   **Two Bar Charts of the Mean Salaries at a Major University from 2004 to 2007**

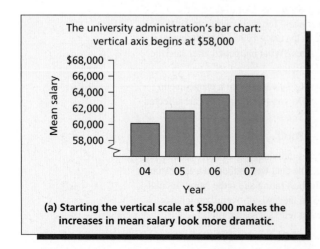

(a) Starting the vertical scale at $58,000 makes the increases in mean salary look more dramatic.

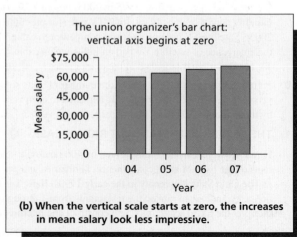

(b) When the vertical scale starts at zero, the increases in mean salary look less impressive.

FIGURE 2.33   **Two Bar Charts of the Mean Salary Increases at a Major University from 2004 to 2007**

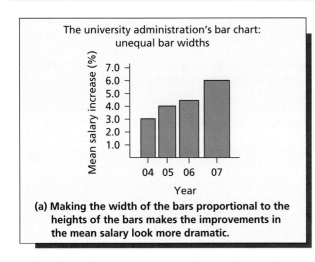

The university administration's bar chart: unequal bar widths

(a) Making the width of the bars proportional to the heights of the bars makes the improvements in the mean salary look more dramatic.

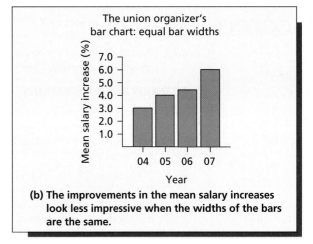

The union organizer's bar chart: equal bar widths

(b) The improvements in the mean salary increases look less impressive when the widths of the bars are the same.

FIGURE 2.34   **Two Time Series Plots of the Mean Salary Increases at a Major University from 2004 to 2007**

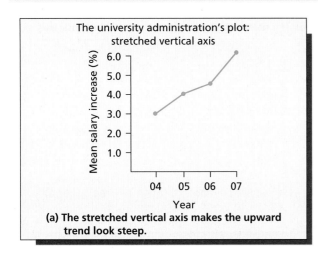

The university administration's plot: stretched vertical axis

(a) The stretched vertical axis makes the upward trend look steep.

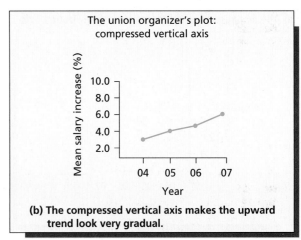

The union organizer's plot: compressed vertical axis

(b) The compressed vertical axis makes the upward trend look very gradual.

   Figure 2.34 gives two time series plots of the mean salary increases at the university from 2004 to 2007. In Figure 2.34(a) the administration has stretched the vertical axis of the graph. That is, the vertical axis is set up so that the distances between the percentages are large. This makes the upward trend of the mean salary increases appear to be steep. In Figure 2.34(b) the union organizers have compressed the vertical axis (that is, the distances between the percentages are small). This makes the upward trend of the mean salary increases appear to be gradual. As we will see in the exercises, stretching and compressing the horizontal axis in a time series plot can also greatly affect the impression given by the plot.

   It is also possible to create totally different interpretations of the same statistical summary by simply using different labeling or captions. For example, consider the bar chart of mean salary increases in Figure 2.33(b). To create a favorable interpretation, the university administration might use the caption "Salary Increase Is Higher for the Fourth Year in a Row." On the other hand, the union organizers might create a negative impression by using the caption "Salary Increase Fails to Reach 10% for Fourth Straight Year."

   In summary, we do not approve of using statistics to mislead and distort reality. Statistics should be used to present the most truthful and informative summary of the data that is possible. However, it is important to carefully study any statistical summary so that you will not be misled. Look for manipulations such as stretched or compressed axes on graphs, axes that do not begin at zero, and bar charts with bars of varying widths. Also, carefully think about assumptions, and make your own conclusions about the meaning of any statistical summary rather than relying on captions written by others. Doing these things will help you to see the truth and to make well-informed decisions.

Exercises for Section 2.7

CONCEPTS

2.62 When we construct a bar chart or graph, what is the effect of starting the vertical axis at a value that is far above zero? Explain.

2.63 Find an example of a misleading use of statistics in a newspaper, magazine, corporate annual report, or other source. Then explain why your example is misleading.

METHODS AND APPLICATIONS

2.64 Figure 2.35 gives two more time series plots of the previously discussed salary increases. In Figure 2.35(a) the administration has compressed the horizontal axis. In Figure 2.35(b) the union organizers have stretched the horizontal axis. Discuss the different impressions given by the two time series plots.

2.65 In the article "How to Display Data Badly" in the May 1984 issue of *The American Statistician*, Howard Wainer presents a *stacked bar chart* of the number of public and private elementary schools (1929–1970). This bar chart is given in Figure 2.36. Wainer also gives a line graph of the number of private elementary schools (1930–1970). This graph is shown in Figure 2.37.

FIGURE 2.35 Two Time Series Plots of the Mean Salary Increases at a Major University from 2004 to 2007 (for Exercise 2.64)

(a) The administration's plot: compressed horizontal axis

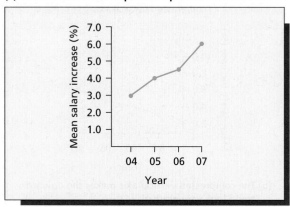

(b) The union organizer's plot: stretched horizontal axis

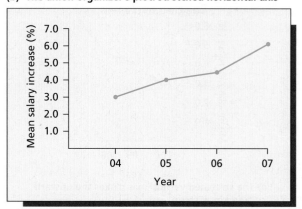

FIGURE 2.36 Wainer's Stacked Bar Chart (for Exercise 2.65)

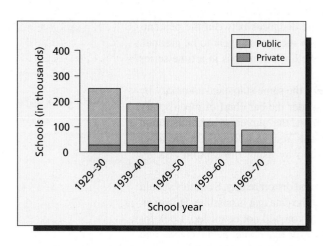

FIGURE 2.37 Wainer's Line Graph of Private Schools (for Exercise 2.65)

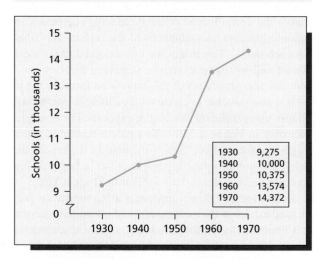

a Looking at the bar chart of Figure 2.36, does there appear to be an increasing trend in the number of private elementary schools from 1930 to 1970?

b Looking at the line graph of Figure 2.37, does there appear to be an increasing trend in the number of private elementary schools from 1930 to 1970?

c Which portrayal of the data do you think is more appropriate? Explain why.

d Is either portrayal of the data entirely appropriate? Explain.

Chapter Summary

We began this chapter by explaining how to summarize qualitative data. We learned that we often summarize this type of data in a table that is called a **frequency distribution.** Such a table gives the **frequency, relative frequency,** or **percent frequency** of items that are contained in each of several nonoverlapping classes or categories. We also learned that we can summarize qualitative data in graphical form by using **bar charts** and **pie charts** and that qualitative quality data is often summarized using a special bar chart called a **Pareto chart.** We continued in Section 2.2 by discussing how to graphically portray quantitative data. In particular, we explained how to summarize such data by using frequency distributions and histograms. We saw that a **histogram** can be constructed using frequencies, relative frequencies, or percentages, and that we often construct histograms using statistical software such as MINITAB, MegaStat, or the analysis toolpak in Excel. We used histograms to describe the shape of a distribution and we saw that distributions are sometimes **mound shaped and symmetrical,** but that a distribution can also be **skewed** (**to the right** or **to the left**). We also learned that a frequency distribution can be graphed by using a **frequency polygon** and that a graph of a **cumulative frequency distribution** is called an **ogive.** In Sections 2.3 and 2.4 we showed how to summarize relatively small data sets by using **dot plots** and **stem-and-leaf displays.** These graphics allow us to see all of the measurements in a data set and to (simultaneously) see the shape of the data set's distribution. Next, we learned about how to describe the relationship between two variables. First, in optional Section 2.5 we explained how to construct and interpret a **crosstabulation table** which classifies data on two dimensions using a table that consists of rows and columns. Then, in optional Section 2.6 we showed how to construct a **scatter plot.** Here, we plot numerical values of one variable on a horizontal axis versus numerical values of another variable on a vertical axis. We saw that we often use such a plot to look at possible straight-line relationships between the variables. Finally, in optional Section 2.7 we learned about misleading graphs and charts. In particular, we pointed out several graphical tricks to watch for. By careful analysis of a graph or chart, one can avoid being misled.

Glossary of Terms

bar chart: A graphical display of data in categories made up of vertical or horizontal bars. Each bar gives the frequency, relative frequency, or percentage frequency of items in its corresponding category. (page 50)

class midpoint: The point in a class that is halfway between the lower and upper class boundaries. (page 59)

crosstabulation table: A table consisting of rows and columns that is used to classify data on two dimensions. (page 75)

cumulative frequency distribution: A table that summarizes the number of measurements that are less than the upper class boundary of each class. (page 63)

cumulative percent frequency distribution: A table that summarizes the percentage of measurements that are less than the upper class boundary of each class. (page 64)

cumulative relative frequency distribution: A table that summarizes the fraction of measurements that are less than the upper class boundary of each class. (page 64)

dot plot: A graphical portrayal of a data set that shows the data set's distribution by plotting individual measurements above a horizontal axis. (page 68)

frequency distribution: A table that summarizes the number of items (or measurements) in each of several nonoverlapping classes. (page 49)

frequency polygon: A graphical display in which we plot points representing each class frequency (or relative frequency or percent frequency) above their corresponding class midpoints and connect the points with line segments. (page 62)

histogram: A graphical display of a frequency distribution, relative frequency distribution, or percentage frequency distribution. It divides measurements into classes and graphs the frequency, relative frequency, or percentage frequency for each class. (page 56)

ogive: A graph of a cumulative distribution (frequencies, relative frequencies, or percent frequencies may be used). (page 64)

outlier: An unusually large or small observation that is well separated from the remaining observations. (page 69)

Pareto chart: A bar chart of the frequencies or percentages for various types of defects. These are used to identify opportunities for improvement. (page 51)

percent frequency distribution: A table that summarizes the percentage of items (or measurements) in each of several nonoverlapping classes. (page 50)

pie chart: A graphical display of data in categories made up of "pie slices." Each pie slice represents the frequency, relative frequency, or percentage frequency of items in its corresponding category. (page 51)

relative frequency distribution: A table that summarizes the fraction of items (or measurements) in each of several nonoverlapping classes. (page 50)

scatter plot: A graph that is used to study the possible relationship between two variables y and x. The observed values of y are plotted on the vertical axis versus corresponding observed values of x on the horizontal axis. (page 81)

skewed to the left: A distribution shape having a long tail to left (page 61)

skewed to the right: A distribution shape having a long tail to the right. (page 61)

stem-and-leaf display: A graphical portrayal of a data set that shows the data set's distribution by using stems consisting of leading digits and leaves consisting of trailing digits. (page 70)

symmetrical distribution: A distribution shape having right and left sides that are "mirror images" of each other. (page 61)

Important Formulas and Graphics

Relative frequency: page 50

Percent frequency: page 50

Bar chart: page 50

Pie chart: page 51

Pareto chart: page 52

Frequency distribution: page 59

Histogram: page 59

Frequency polygon: page 62

Cumulative distribution: page 63

Ogive: page 64

Dot plot: page 68

Stem-and-leaf display: page 72

Crosstabulation table: page 75

Scatter plot: page 81

Time series plot: page 82

Supplementary Exercises

connect

2.66 A manufacturer produces a bulk chemical product. Customer requirements state that this product must have a specified viscosity when melted at a temperature of 300°F (viscosity measures how thick and gooey the product is when melted). Chemical XB-135 is used in the production of this chemical product, and the company's chemists feel that the amount of chemical XB-135 may be related to viscosity. In order to verify and quantify this relationship, 24 batches of the product are produced. The amount (x) of chemical XB-135 (in pounds) is varied from batch to batch and the viscosity (y) obtained for each batch is measured. Table 2.23 gives (in time order) the values of x and the corresponding values of y obtained for the 24 batches.   ◐ Viscosity

a Construct a scatter plot of viscosity (y) versus the amount (x) of chemical XB-135.

b Describe any apparent relationship between y and x.

c It might be tempting to conclude that changes in the amount of chemical XB-135 cause changes in viscosity. Under what circumstances might such a conclusion be reasonable?

TABLE 2.23 **Viscosity Data for 24 Batches of a Chemical Product Produced on August 1, 2007**   ◐ Viscosity

Batch	Pounds of Chemical XB-135 (x)	Viscosity (y)	Batch	Pounds of Chemical XB-135 (x)	Viscosity (y)
1	10.0	31.76	13	11.2	32.93
2	10.0	31.91	14	11.2	33.19
3	10.2	32.02	15	11.4	33.35
4	10.2	31.85	16	11.4	32.76
5	10.4	32.17	17	11.6	33.33
6	10.4	32.30	18	11.6	33.19
7	10.6	32.60	19	11.8	33.28
8	10.6	32.15	20	11.8	33.57
9	10.8	32.52	21	12.0	33.60
10	10.8	32.46	22	12.0	33.43
11	11.0	32.41	23	12.2	33.91
12	11.0	32.77	24	12.2	33.76

Exercises 2.67 through 2.74 are based on the data in Table 2.24. This table gives the results of the J.D. Power initial quality study of 2006 automobiles. Each model is rated on overall manufacturing quality and overall design quality on a scale from "among the best" to "the rest"—see the scoring legend at the bottom of the table.   ◐ JDPower

TABLE 2.24   Results of the J. D. Power Initial Quality Study of 2006 Automobiles   ● JDPower

Company	Country of Origin	Overall Quality Manufacturing	Overall Quality Design	Company	Country of Origin	Overall Quality Manufacturing	Overall Quality Design
Acura	Japan	●●●	●●●	Lexus	Japan	●●●●●	●●●●
Audi	Germany	●●●	●●●	Lincoln	United States	●●●	●●●
BMW	Germany	●●●●	●●	Mazda	Japan	●●	●●
Buick	United States	●●●●	●●	Mercedes-Benz	Germany	●●●	●●
Cadillac	United States	●●●●	●●●	Mercury	United States	●●●	●●
Chevrolet	United States	●●●	●●●	MINI	Great Britain	●●●	●●
Chrysler	United States	●●●●	●●●	Mitsubishi	Japan	●●	●●●
Dodge	United States	●●●	●●●	Nissan	Japan	●●●	●●●●
Ford	United States	●●●	●●●	Pontiac	United States	●●●	●●●
GMC	United States	●●●	●●●●	Porsche	Germany	●●●●	●●●●●
Honda	Japan	●●●	●●●●	Saab	Sweden	●●	●●●
HUMMER	United States	●●	●●	Saturn	United States	●●●	●●●
Hyundai	Korea	●●●●	●●●●	Scion	Japan	●●●	●●●
Infiniti	Japan	●●●	●●●	Subaru	Japan	●●●	●●●
Isuzu	Japan	●●	●●	Suzuki	Japan	●●	●●
Jaguar	Great Britain	●●●	●●●●	Toyota	Japan	●●●●	●●●
Jeep	United States	●●	●●●	Volkswagen	Germany	●●	●●
Kia	Korea	●●●	●●●	Volvo	Sweden	●●●	●●●
Land Rover	Great Britain	●●	●●				

Scoring Legend

●●●●● Among the best   ●●● About average

●●●● Better than most   ●● The rest

Source: http://www.jdpower.com/autos/brand-ratings/

2.67 Develop a frequency distribution of the overall manufacturing quality ratings. Describe the distribution.   ● JDPower

2.68 Develop a relative frequency distribution of the overall design quality ratings. Describe the distribution.   ● JDPower

2.69 Construct a percentage bar chart of the overall manufacturing quality ratings for each of the following: automobiles of United States origin; automobiles of Pacific Rim origin (Japan/Korea); and automobiles of European origin (Germany/Great Britain/Sweden). Compare the three distributions in a written report.   ● JDPower

2.70 Construct a percentage pie chart of the overall design quality ratings for each of the following: automobiles of United States origin; automobiles of Pacific Rim origin (Japan/Korea); and automobiles of European origin (Germany/Great Britain/Sweden). Compare the three distributions in a written report.   ● JDPower

2.71 Construct a crosstabulation table of automobile origin versus overall manufacturing quality rating. Set up rows corresponding to the United States, the Pacific Rim (Japan/Korea), and Europe (Germany/Great Britain/Sweden), and set up columns corresponding to the ratings "among the best" through "the rest." Describe any apparent relationship between origin and overall manufacturing quality rating.   ● JDPower

2.72 Develop a table of row percentages for the crosstabulation table you set up in Exercise 2.71. Using these row percentages, construct a percentage frequency distribution of overall manufacturing quality rating for each of the United States, the Pacific Rim, and Europe. Illustrate these three frequency distributions using percent bar charts and compare the distributions in a written report.   ● JDPower

2.73 Construct a crosstabulation table of automobile origin versus overall design quality rating. Set up rows corresponding to the United States, the Pacific Rim (Japan/Korea), and Europe (Germany/Great Britain/Sweden), and set up columns corresponding to the ratings "among the best" through "the rest." Describe any apparent relationship between origin and overall design quality.   ● JDPower

2.74 Develop a table of row percentages for the crosstabulation table you set up in Exercise 2.73. Using these row percentages, construct a percentage frequency distribution of overall design quality rating for each of the United States, the Pacific Rim, and Europe. Illustrate these three frequency distributions using percentage pie charts and compare the distributions in a written report.   ● JDPower

Exercises 2.75 through 2.78 are based on the following case.

THE CIGARETTE ADVERTISEMENT CASE   ● ModelAge

In an article in the *Journal of Marketing,* Mazis, Ringold, Perry, and Denman discuss the perceived ages of models in cigarette advertisements.[8] To quote the authors,

> Most relevant to our study is the Cigarette Advertiser's Code, initiated by the tobacco industry in 1964. The code contains nine advertising principles related to young people, including the following provision (*Advertising Age,* 1964): "Natural persons depicted as smokers in cigarette advertising shall be at least 25 years of age and shall not be dressed or otherwise made to appear to be less than 25 years of age."

Tobacco industry representatives have steadfastly maintained that code provisions are still being observed. A 1988 Tobacco Institute publication, "Three Decades of Initiatives by a Responsible Cigarette Industry," refers to the industry code as prohibiting advertising and promotion "directed at young people" and as "requiring that models in advertising must be, and must appear to be, at least 25 years old." John R. Nelson, Vice President of Corporate Affairs for Philip Morris, wrote, "We employ only adult models in our advertising who not only are but *look* over 25." However, industry critics have charged that current cigarette advertising campaigns use unusually young-looking models, thereby violating the voluntary industry code.

Suppose that a sample of 50 people is randomly selected at a shopping mall. Each person in the sample is shown a typical cigarette advertisement and is asked to estimate the age of the model in the ad. The 50 perceived age estimates so obtained are as follows:

26	30	23	27	27	32	28	19	25	29
31	28	24	26	29	27	28	17	28	21
30	28	25	31	22	29	18	27	29	23
28	26	24	30	27	25	26	28	20	24
29	32	27	17	30	27	21	29	26	28

2.75 Consider constructing a frequency distribution and histogram for the perceived age estimates.   ● ModelAge

  a How many classes should be used for the frequency distribution and histogram?

  b Develop a frequency distribution, a relative frequency distribution, and a percent frequency distribution for the perceived age estimates. Hint: Round the class length down to 2.

  c Draw a frequency histogram for the perceived age estimates.

  d Describe the shape of the distribution of perceived age estimates.

2.76 Construct a frequency polygon of the perceived age estimates. Hint: Round the class length down to 2.   ● ModelAge

2.77 Construct a dot plot of the perceived age estimates and describe the shape of the distribution. What percentage of the perceived ages are below the industry's code provision of 25 years old? Do you think that this percentage is too high?   ● ModelAge

2.78 Using the frequency distribution you developed in Exercise 2.75, develop   ● ModelAge

  a A cumulative frequency distribution.

  b A cumulative relative frequency distribution.

  c A cumulative percent frequency distribution.

  d A frequency ogive of the perceived age estimates.

  How many perceived age estimates are 28 or less? What percentage of perceived age estimates are 22 or less?

Exercises 2.79 through 2.84 are based on the data in Table 2.25. This table gives data concerning the 30 fastest-growing companies as listed on March 16, 2005, on the *Fortune* magazine website.   ● Fastgrow

2.79 Develop a stem-and-leaf display of the revenue growth percentages for the 30 fastest-growing companies and describe the shape of the distribution.   ● FastGrow

2.80 Develop a frequency distribution and a frequency histogram of the EPS (earnings per share) growth percentages. Then describe the shape of the distribution.   ● FastGrow

[8]Source: M. B. Mazis, D. J. Ringold, E. S. Perry, and D. W. Denman, "Perceived Age and Attractiveness of Models in Cigarette Advertisements," *Journal of Marketing* 56 (January 1992), pp. 22–37.

TABLE 2.25 Data Concerning the 30 Fastest-Growing Companies as Listed on March 16, 2005, on the *Fortune Magazine Website* ● FastGrow

Rank	Company	EPS Growth[*]	Revenue Growth[*]	Total Return[*]	Rank	Company	EPS Growth[*]	Revenue Growth[*]	Total Return[*]
1	InVision Technologies	222%	93%	135%	16	American Healthways	167%	48%	28%
2	eResearch Technology	256%	43%	218%	17	United PanAm Financial	65%	39%	62%
3	New Century Financial	85%	91%	89%	18	FTI Consulting	105%	61%	19%
4	Central European Distribution	98%	49%	135%	19	Jarden	99%	25%	109%
5	eBay	92%	70%	39%	20	Par Pharmaceutical	143%	87%	5%
6	National Medical Health Card Sys	85%	44%	107%	21	Capital Title Group	84%	87%	21%
7	Countrywide Financial	78%	71%	46%	22	Advanced Neuromodulation	128%	46%	24%
8	Neoware Systems	76%	70%	47%	23	Possis Medical	76%	38%	42%
9	Friedman Billing Ramsey Group	93%	52%	44%	24	Symantec	85%	30%	59%
10	Bradley Pharmaceuticals	59%	59%	76%	25	ASV	128%	33%	32%
11	Middleby	91%	33%	109%	26	Chicos FAS	47%	43%	66%
12	Hovnanian Enterprises	71%	40%	69%	27	Rewards Network	152%	29%	38%
13	Websense	162%	60%	23%	28	Fidelity National Financial	64%	38%	38%
14	Sanders Morris Harris Group	185%	35%	36%	29	NetBank	107%	60%	−1%
15	Career Education	66%	51%	45%	30	Electronic Arts	254%	32%	24%

[*]Three-year annual rate.

Source: "FORTUNE 100 Fastest Growing Companies," 30 companies excerpted, October 3, 2005 issue.

2.81 Construct a percent frequency polygon of the total return percentages and then describe the shape of the distribution. ● FastGrow

2.82 Construct cumulative frequency and cumulative relative frequency distributions of the EPS (earnings per share) growth percentages. Then construct a relative frequency ogive of these percentages. ● FastGrow

2.83 The price/earnings ratio of a firm is a multiplier applied to a firm's earnings per share (EPS) to determine the value of the firm's common stock. For instance, if a firm's earnings per share is $5, and if its price/earnings ratio (or P/E ratio) is 10, then the market value of each share of common stock is ($5)(10) = $50. To quote Stanley B. Block and Geoffrey A. Hirt in their book *Foundations of Financial Management,*[9]

> The P/E ratio indicates expectations about the future of a company. Firms expected to provide returns greater than those for the market in general with equal or less risk often have P/E ratios higher than the market P/E ratio.

In the figure below we give a dot plot of the P/E ratios for 29 of the 30 fastest-growing companies (the P/E ratio for one of the companies was not available to *Fortune*). Describe the distribution of P/E ratios. ● FastGrow

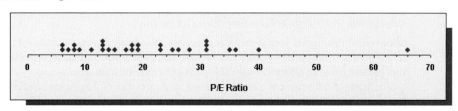

2.84 Construct a dot plot of the total return percentages for the 30 fastest-growing companies and describe the distribution of return percentages. ● FastGrow

2.85 In this exercise we consider how to deal with class lengths that are unequal (and with open-ended classes) when setting up histograms. Often data are published in this form and we wish to

[9]Source: Excerpt from S. B. Block and G. A. Hirt, *Foundations of Financial Management,* p. 28. © 1994 Richard D. Irwin. Reprinted with permission of McGraw-Hill Companies, Inc.

● ISO 9000

Annual Savings	Number of Companies
0 to $10K	162
$10K to 25K	62
$25K to 50K	53
$50K to 100K	60
$100K to 150K	24
$150K to 200K	19
$200K to 250K	22
$250K to 500K	21
(>$500K)	37

Note: (K = 1,000)

construct a histogram. An example is provided by data concerning the benefits of ISO 9000 registration published by CEEM Information Services. According to CEEM,[10]

> ISO 9000 is a series of international standards for quality assurance management systems. It establishes the organizational structure and processes for assuring that the production of goods or services meets a consistent and agreed-upon level of quality for a company's customers.

CEEM presents the results of a Quality Systems Update/Deloitte & Touche survey of ISO 9000–registered companies conducted in July 1993. Included in the results is a summary of the total annual savings associated with ISO 9000 implementation for surveyed companies. The findings (in the form of a frequency distribution of ISO 9000 savings) are given on the page margin. Notice that the classes in this distribution have unequal lengths and that there is an open-ended class (>$500K).

To construct a histogram for this data, we select one of the classes as a base. It is often convenient to choose the shortest class as the base (although it is not necessary to do so). Using this choice, the 0 to $10K class is the base. This means that we will draw a rectangle over the 0 to $10K class having a height equal to 162 (the frequency given for this class in the published data). Because the other classes are longer than the base, the heights of the rectangles above these classes will be adjusted. Remembering that the area of a rectangle positioned over a particular class should represent the relative proportion of measurements in the class, we proceed as follows. The length of the $10K to 25K class differs from the base class by a factor of $(25 - 10)/(10 - 0) = 3/2$, and, therefore, we make the height of the rectangle over the $10K to 25K class equal to $(2/3)(62) = 41.333$. Similarly, the length of the $25K to 50K class differs from the length of the base class by a factor of $(50 - 25)/(10 - 0) = 5/2$, and, therefore, we make the height of the rectangle over the $25K to 50K class equal to $(2/5)(53) = 21.2$.

a Use the procedure just outlined to find the heights of the rectangles drawn over all the other classes (with the exception of the open-ended class, >$500K).

b Draw the appropriate rectangles over the classes (except for >$500K). Note that the $250K to 500K class is a lot longer than the others. There is nothing wrong with this as long as we adjust its rectangle's height.

c We complete the histogram by placing a star (*) to the right of $500K on the scale of measurements and by noting "37" next to the * to indicate that 37 companies saved more than $500K. Complete the histogram by doing this.

2.86 A basketball player practices free throws by taking 25 shots each day, and he records the number of shots missed each day in order to track his progress. The numbers of shots missed on days 1 through 30 are, respectively, 17, 15, 16, 18, 14, 15, 13, 12, 10, 11, 11, 10, 9, 10, 9, 9, 9, 10, 8, 10, 6, 8, 9, 8, 7, 9, 8, 7, 5, 8. Construct a stem-and-leaf display and runs plot of the numbers of missed shots. Do you think that the stem-and-leaf display is representative of the numbers of shots that the player will miss on future days? Why or why not?   ● FreeThrw

2.87 Figure 2.38 was used in various Chevrolet magazine advertisements in 1997 to compare the overall resale values of Chevrolet, Dodge, and Ford trucks in the years from 1990 to 1997. What is somewhat misleading about this graph?

2.88 In the Fall 1993 issue of *VALIC Investment Digest,* the Variable Annuity Life Insurance Company used pie charts to illustrate an investment strategy called **rebalancing.** This strategy involves reviewing an investment portfolio annually to return the asset mix (stocks, bonds, Treasury bills, and so on) to a preselected allocation mix. VALIC describes rebalancing as follows (refer to the pie charts in Figure 2.39):

Rebalancing—A Strategy to Keep Your Allocation on Track

> Once you've established your ideal asset allocation mix, many experts recommend that you review your portfolio at least once a year to make sure your portfolio remains consistent with your preselected asset allocation mix. This practice is referred to as *rebalancing.*
>
> For example, let's assume a moderate asset allocation mix of 50 percent equities funds, 40 percent bond funds, and 10 percent cash equivalent funds. The chart [see Figure 2.39] based on data provided by Ibbotson, a major investment and consulting firm, illustrates how rebalancing works. Using the Standard & Poor's 500 Index, the Salomon Brothers Long-Term High-Grade Corporate Bond Index, and the U.S. 30-day Treasury bill average as a cash-equivalent rate, our hypothetical portfolio balance on 12/31/90 is $10,000. One year later the account had grown to $12,380. By the end of 1991, the allocation had changed to 52.7%/38.7%/8.5%. The third pie chart illustrates how the account was once again rebalanced to return to a 50%/40%/10% asset allocation mix.

FIGURE 2.38

A Graph Comparing the Resale Values of Chevy, Dodge, and Ford Trucks

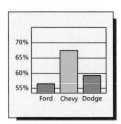

Source: Reprinted courtesy of General Motors Corporation.

[10]Source: CEEM Information Services, Fairfax, Virginia. *Is ISO 9000 for You?*

FIGURE 2.39   **Using Pie Charts to Illustrate Portfolio Rebalancing (for Exercise 2.88)**

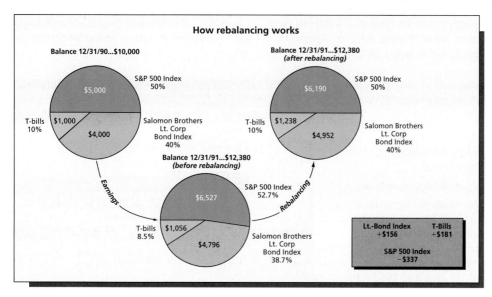

Source: The Variable Annuity Life Insurance Company, *VALIC* 6, no. 4 (Fall 1993).

Rebalancing has the potential for more than merely helping diversify your portfolio. By continually returning to your original asset allocation, it is possible to avoid exposure to more risk than you previously decided you were willing to assume.

a   Suppose you control a $100,000 portfolio and have decided to maintain an asset allocation mix of 60 percent stock funds, 30 percent bond funds, and 10 percent government securities. Draw a pie chart illustrating your portfolio (like the ones in Figure 2.39).

b   Over the next year your stock funds earn a return of 30 percent, your bond funds earn a return of 15 percent, and your government securities earn a return of 6 percent. Calculate the end-of-year values of your stock funds, bond funds, and government securities. After calculating the end-of-year value of your entire portfolio, determine the asset allocation mix (percent stock funds, percent bond funds, and percent government securities) of your portfolio before rebalancing. Finally, draw an end-of-year pie chart of your portfolio before rebalancing.

c   Rebalance your portfolio. That is, determine how much of the portfolio's end-of-year value must be invested in stock funds, bond funds, and government securities in order to restore your original asset allocation mix of 60 percent stock funds, 30 percent bond funds, and 10 percent government securities. Draw a pie chart of your portfolio after rebalancing.

2.89   Internet Exercise

The Gallup Organization provides market research and consulting services around the world. Gallup publishes the Gallup Poll, a widely recognized barometer of American and international opinion. The Gallup website provides access to many recent Gallup studies. Although a subscription is needed to access the entire site, many articles about recent Gallup Poll results can be accessed free of charge. To find poll results, go to the Gallup home page (http://www.gallup.com/) and click on the Gallup Poll icon or type the web address http://www.galluppoll.com/ directly into your web browser. The poll results are presented using a variety of statistical summaries and graphics that we have learned about in this chapter.

a   Go to the Gallup Organization website and access several of the articles presenting recent poll results.
Find and print examples of some of the statistical summaries and graphics that we studied in this chapter. Then write a summary describing which statistical methods and graphics seem to be used most frequently by Gallup when presenting poll results.

b   Read the results of a Gallup Poll that you find to be of particular interest and summarize (in your own words) its most important conclusions. Cite the statistical evidence in the article that you believe most clearly backs up each conclusion.

c   By searching the web, or by searching other sources (such as newspapers and magazines), find an example of a misleading statistical summary or graphic. Print or copy the misleading example and write a paragraph describing why you think the summary or graphic is misleading.

Appendix 2.1 ■ Tabular and Graphical Methods Using MINITAB

The instructions in this section begin by describing the entry of data into the MINITAB Data window. Alternatively, the data may be loaded directly from the data disk included with the text. The appropriate data file name is given at the top of each instruction block. Please refer to Appendix 1.1 for further information about entering data, saving data and printing results when using MINITAB.

Construct a frequency distribution of Jeep sales as in Table 2.2 on page 50 (data file: JeepSales.MTW):

- Enter the Jeep sales data in Table 2.1 on page 50 (C = Commander; G = Grand Cherokee; L = Liberty; W = Wrangler) into column C1 with label (variable name) Jeep Model.

- Select **Stat : Tables : Tally Individual Variables**

- In the Tally Individual Variables dialog box, enter the variable name 'Jeep Model' into the Variables window. Because this variable name consists of more than one word, we must enclose the name in single quotation marks—this defines both the words Jeep and Model to be parts of the same variable name.

- Place a checkmark in the Display "Counts" checkbox to obtain frequencies.

  We would check: "Percents" to obtain percent frequencies; "Cumulative counts" to obtain cumulative frequencies; and "Cumulative percents" to obtain cumulative percent frequencies.

- Click OK in the Tally Individual Variables dialog box.

- The frequency distribution is displayed in the Session window.

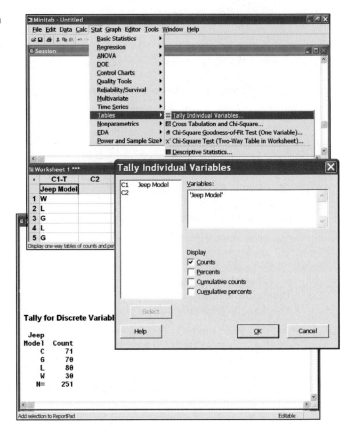

Construct a bar chart of the Jeep sales distribution from the raw sales data similar to Figure 2.1 on page 51 (data file: JeepSales.MTW):

- Enter the Jeep sales data in Table 2.1 on page 50 (C = Commander; G = Grand Cherokee; L = Liberty; W = Wrangler) into column C1 with label (variable name) Jeep Model.

- Select **Graph : Bar Chart...**

- In the Bar Charts dialog box, select "Counts of unique values" from the "Bars represent" pull-down menu.

- Select "Simple" from the gallery of bar chart types (this is the default selection, which is indicated by the reverse highlighting in black).

- Click OK in the Bar Charts dialog box.

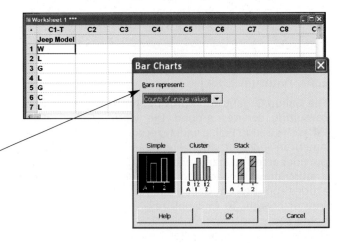

- In the "Bar Chart—Counts of unique values, Simple" dialog box, enter the variable name 'Jeep Model' into the "Categorical variables" window. Be sure to remember the single quotes around the name Jeep Model.

- To obtain **data labels** (numbers at the tops of the bars that indicate the heights of the bars—in this case, the frequencies), click on the Labels... button.

- In the "Bar Chart—Labels" dialog box, click on the Data Labels tab and select "Use y-value labels." This will produce data labels that are equal to the category frequencies.

- Click OK in the "Bar Chart—Labels" dialog box.

- Click OK in the "Bar Chart—Counts of unique values, Simple" dialog box.

- The bar chart will be displayed in a graphics window. The chart may be edited by right-clicking on various portions of the chart and by using the pop-up menus that appear—see Appendix 1.1 for more details.

- Here we have obtained a frequency bar chart. **To obtain a percent frequency bar chart,** click on the Chart Options... button and select "Show y as percent" in the "Bar Chart—Options" dialog box.

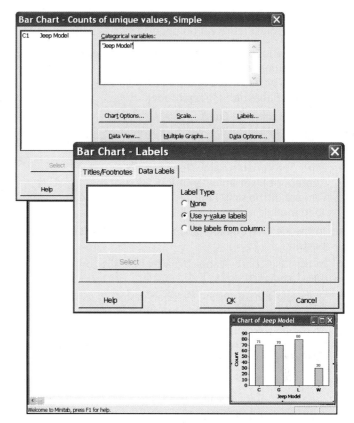

Construct a bar chart from the tabular frequency distribution of Jeep sales in Table 2.2 on page 50 (data file: JeepTable.MTW):

- Enter the Jeep sales distribution from Table 2.2 as shown in the screen with the four models in column C1 (with variable name Jeep Model) and with the associated frequencies in column C2 (with variable name Frequency).

- Select **Graph : Bar Chart**

- In the Bar Charts dialog box, select "Values from a table" in the "Bars represent" pull-down menu.

- Select "One column of values—Simple" from the gallery of bar chart types.

- Click OK in the Bar Charts dialog box.

- In the "Bar Chart—Values from a table, One column of values, Simple" dialog box, enter the variable name Frequency into the "Graph variables" window and enter the variable name 'Jeep Model' into the "Categorical variable" window. Be sure to remember the single quotes around the name Jeep Model.

- Click on the Labels... button and select "Use y-value labels" as shown previously.

- Click OK in the "Bar Chart—Labels" dialog box.

- Click OK in the "Bar Chart—Values from a table, One column of values, Simple" dialog box.

- The bar chart will be displayed in a graphics window.

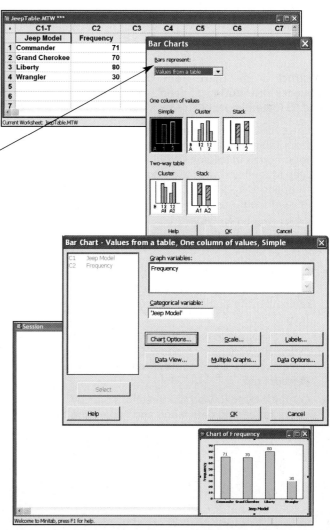

Construct a pie chart of Jeep sales percentages similar to that shown in Figure 2.3 on page 52:

- Enter the Jeep sales data in Table 2.1 on page 50 (C = Commander; G = Grand Cherokee; L = Liberty; W = Wrangler) into column C1 with label (variable name) Jeep Model.

- Select **Graph : Pie Chart**

- In the Pie Chart dialog box, select "Chart counts of unique values."

- Enter the variable name 'Jeep Model' into the "Categorical variables" window. Be sure to remember the single quotes around the name Jeep Model.

- In the Pie Chart dialog box, click on the Labels... button.

- In the "Pie Chart—Labels" dialog box, click on the Slice Labels tab.

- Place checkmarks in the Category name, Percent, and "Draw a line from label to slice" checkboxes.

  To obtain a frequency pie chart, select Frequency rather than Percent in this dialog box. Or, both Percent and Frequency can be selected.

- Click OK in the "Pie Chart—Labels" dialog box.

- Click OK in the Pie Chart dialog box.

- The pie chart will appear in a graphics window.

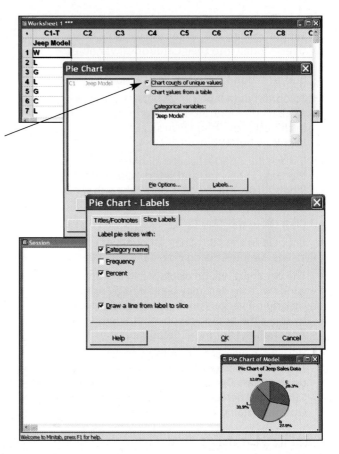

Construct a pie chart from the tabular percent frequency distribution of Jeep sales in Table 2.3 on page 50 (data file: JeepPercents.MTW):

- Enter the Jeep sales percent frequency distribution from Table 2.3 as shown in the screen with the four models in column C1 (with variable name Jeep Model) and with the associated percent frequencies in column C2 (with variable name Percent Freq).

- Select **Graph : Pie Chart**

- In the Pie Chart dialog box, select "Chart values from a table."

- Enter the variable name 'Jeep Model' into the "Categorical variable" window. Be sure to remember the single quotes around the name Jeep Model.

- Enter the variable name 'Percent Freq' into the "Summary variables" window. Be sure to remember the single quotes around the name Percent Freq.

- Continue by following the directions directly above for adding data labels and generating the pie chart.

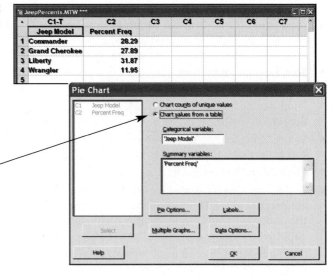

Construct a frequency histogram of the payment times in Figure 2.9 on page 60 (data file: PayTime .MTW):

- Enter the payment time data from Table 2.4 on page 56 into column C1 with variable name PayTime.

- Select **Graph : Histogram**

- In the Histograms dialog box, select Simple from the gallery of histogram types and click OK.

- In the "Histogram—Simple" dialog box, enter the variable name PayTime into the Graph Variables window and click on the Scale button.

- In the "Histogram—Scale" dialog box, click on the "Y- Scale Type" tab and select **Frequency** to obtain a frequency histogram. We would select **Percent** to request a percent frequency histogram. Then click OK in the "Histogram— Scale" dialog box.

- **Data labels** are requested in the same way as we have demonstrated for bar charts. Click on the Labels… button in the "Histogram— Simple" dialog box. In the "Histogram— Labels" dialog box, click on the Data Labels tab and select "Use y-value labels." Then click OK in the "Histogram—Labels" dialog box.

- To create the histogram, click OK in the "Histogram—Simple" dialog box.

- The histogram will appear in a graphics window and can be edited as described in Appendix 1.1.

- The histogram can be selected for printing or can be copied and pasted into a word processing document. (See Appendix 1.1.)

- Notice that MINITAB **automatically** defines classes for the histogram bars, and auto- matically provides labeled tick marks (here 12, 16, 20, 24, and 28) on the x-scale of the histogram. These automatic classes are not the same as those we formed in Example 2.2, summarized in Table 2.7, and illustrated in Figure 2.7 on page 58. However, we can edit the automatically constructed histogram to produce the histogram classes of Figure 2.7. This is sometimes called **"binning."**

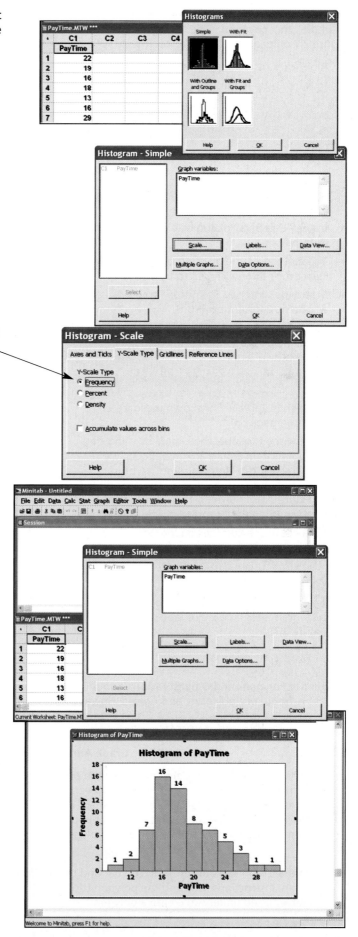

To obtain user-specified histogram classes—for example, the payment time histogram classes of Figure 2.7 on page 58 (data file: PayTime.MTW):

- Right-click inside any of the histogram bars.
- In the pop-up menu, select "Edit Bars."

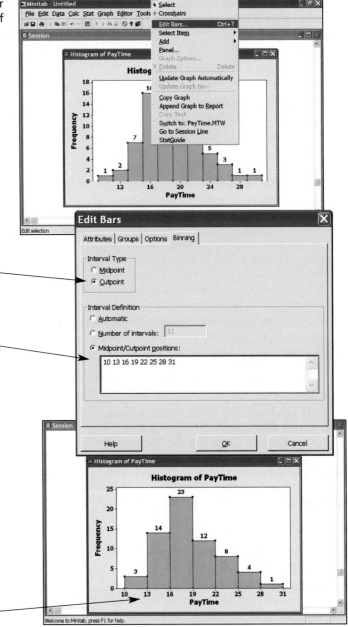

- In the "Edit Bars" dialog box, select the Binning tab.
- To label the x-scale by using class boundaries, select the "Interval Type" to be Cutpoint.
- Select the "Interval Definition" to be Midpoint/Cutpoint positions.
- In the Midpoint/Cutpoint positions window, enter the class boundaries (or cutpoints)

  10   13   16   19   22   25   28   31

  as given in Table 2.7 or shown in Figure 2.7 (both on page 58).

- If we wished to label the x-scale by using class midpoints as in Figure 2.8 on page 59, we would select the "Interval Type" to be Midpoint and we would enter the midpoints of Figure 2.8 (11.5, 14.5, 17.5, and so forth) into the Midpoint/Cutpoint positions window.
- Click OK in the Edit Bars dialog box.

- The histogram in the graphics window will be edited to produce the class boundaries, histogram bars, and x-axis labels shown in Figure 2.7.

Frequency Polygons and Ogives: MINITAB does not have automatic procedures for constructing frequency polygons and ogives. However, these graphics can be constructed quite easily by using the MINITAB Graph Annotation Tools. To access these tools and have them placed on the MINITAB toolbar, select

Tools : Toolbars : Graph Annotation Tools

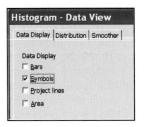

- **To construct a frequency polygon,** follow the preceding instructions for constructing a histogram. In addition, however, click on the Data View button, select the Data Display tab, place a checkmark in the Symbols checkbox (also uncheck the Bars checkbox). This will result in plotted points above the histogram classes—rather than bars. Now select the polygon tool

from the Graph Annotation Tools toolbar and draw connecting lines to form the polygon. Instructions for using the polygon tool can be found in the MINITAB help resources listed under "To create a polygon."

- **To construct an ogive,** follow the previous instructions for constructing a frequency polygon. In addition, however, click on the Scale button, select the "Y-Scale Type" tab, and place a checkmark in the "Accumulate values across bins" checkbox. This will result in a plot of cumulative frequencies—rather than histogram bars. Now select the polyline tool

from the Graph Annotation Tools toolbar and draw connecting lines to form the ogive. Instructions for using the polyline tool can be found in the MINITAB help resources listed under "To create a polyline."

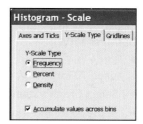

Construct a dot plot of the exam scores as in Figure 2.18(a) on page 69 (data file: FirstExam.MTW):

- Enter the scores for exam 1 in Table 2.8 on page 62 into column C1 with variable name 'Score on Exam 1.'

- Select **Graph : Dot Plot**

- In the Dotplots dialog box, select "One Y Simple" from the gallery of dot plots.

- Click OK in the Dotplots dialog box.

- In the "Dotplot—One Y, Simple" dialog box, enter the variable name 'Score on Exam 1' into the "Graph variables" window. Be sure to include the single quotes.

- Click OK in the "Dotplot—One Y, Simple" dialog box.

- The dotplot will be displayed in a graphics window.

- To change the *x*-axis labels (or **ticks**), right-click on any one of the existing labels (say, the 45, for instance) and select "Edit X Scale . . ." from the pop-up menu.

- In the Edit Scale dialog box, select the Scale tab and select "Position of ticks" as the "Major Ticks Positions" setting.

- Enter the desired ticks (30 40 50 60 70 80 90 100) into the "Position of ticks" window and click OK in the Edit Scale dialog box.

- The *x*-axis labels (ticks) will be changed and the new dot plot will be displayed in the graphics window.

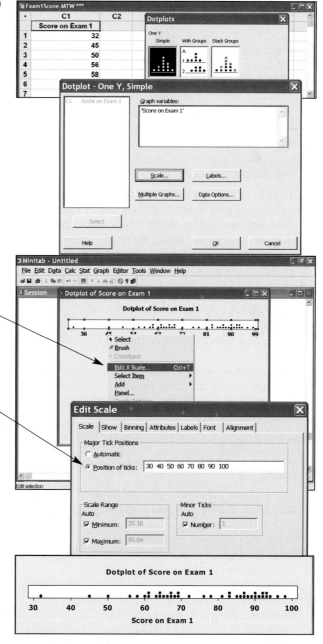

Construct a stem-and-leaf display of the gasoline mileages as in Figure 2.19(a) on page 71 (data file: GasMiles.MTW):

- Enter the mileage data from Table 2.14 on page 70 into column C1 with variable name Mpg.
- Select **Graph : Stem-and-Leaf**
- In the Stem-and-Leaf dialog box, enter the variable name Mpg into the "Graph Variables" window.
- Click OK in the Stem-and-Leaf dialog box.
- The stem-and-leaf display appears in the Session window and can be selected for printing or copied and pasted into a word processing document. (See Appendix 1.1.)

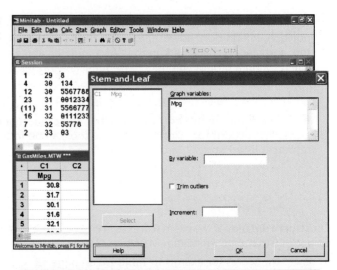

Construct a crosstabulation table of fund type versus level of client satisfaction as in Table 2.17 on page 76 (data file: Invest.MTW):

- Enter the client satisfaction data from Table 2.16 on page 76 with client number in column C1 having variable name Client, and with fund type and satisfaction rating in columns C2 and C3, respectively, having variable names 'Fund Type' and 'Satisfaction Level'.

The default ordering for the different levels of each categorical variable in the crosstabulation table will be alphabetical—that is, BOND, STOCK, TAXDEF for 'Fund Type' and HIGH, LOW, MED for 'Satisfaction Rating'. **To change the ordering to HIGH, MED, LOW** for 'Satisfaction Rating':

- Click on any cell in column C3 (Satisfaction Rating).
- Select **Editor : Column : Value order**
- In the "Value Order for C3 (Satisfaction Level)" dialog box, select the "User-specified order" option.
- In the "Define an order (one value per line)" window, specify the order HIGH, MED, LOW.
- Click OK in the "Value Order for C3 (Satisfaction Level)" dialog box.

To construct the cross tabulation table:

- Select **Stat : Tables : Cross Tabulation and Chi-Square**
- In the "Cross Tabulation and Chi-Square" dialog box, enter the variable name 'Fund Type' (including the single quotes) into the "Categorical variables: For rows" window.
- Enter the variable name 'Satisfaction Rating' (including the single quotes) into the "Categorical variables: For columns" window.
- Place a checkmark in the "Display Counts" checkbox. We would check "Display Row percents" to produce a table of row percentages and we would check "Display Column percents" to produce a table of column percentages.
- Click OK in the "Cross Tabulation and Chi-Square" dialog box to obtain results in the Session window.

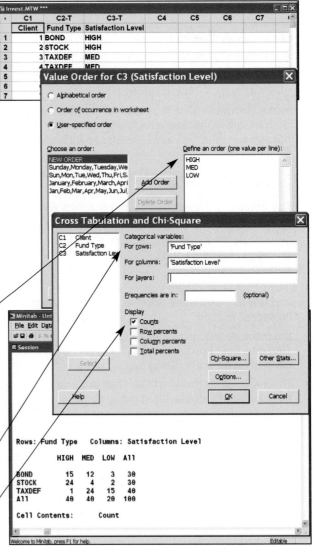

Construct a scatter plot of sales volume versus advertising expenditure as in Figure 2.24 on page 81 (data file: SalesPlot.MWT).

- Enter the sales and advertising data in Table 2.20 (on page 81)—sales region in column C1 (with variable name 'Sales Region'), advertising expenditure in column C2 (with variable name 'Adv Exp'), and sales volume in column C3 (with variable name 'Sales Vol').

- Select **Graph : Scatterplot**

- In the Scatterplots dialog box, select "With Regression" from the gallery of scatterplots in order to produce a scatterplot with a "best line" fitted to the data (see Chapter 13 for discussion of this "best line"). Select "Simple" if a fitted line is not desired.

- Click OK in the Scatterplots dialog box.

- In the "Scatterplot—With Regression" dialog box, enter the variable name 'Sales Vol' (including the single quotes) into row 1 of the "Y variables" window and enter the variable name 'Adv Exp' (including the single quotes) into row 1 of the "X variables" window.

- Click OK in the "Scatterplot—With Regression" dialog box.

- The scatterplot and fitted line will be displayed in a graphics window.

- Additional plots can be obtained by placing appropriate variable names in other rows in the "Y variables" and "X variables" windows.

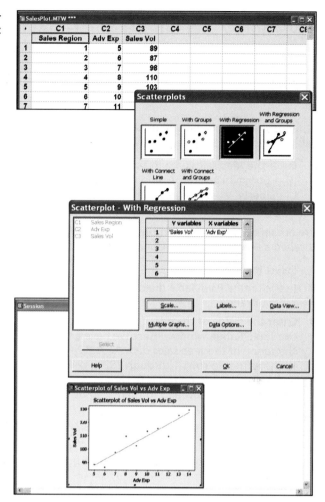

Appendix 2.2 ■ Tabular and Graphical Methods Using Excel

The instructions in this section begin by describing the entry of data into an Excel spreadsheet. Alternatively, the data may be loaded directly from the data disk included with the text. The appropriate data file name is given at the top of each instruction block. Please refer to Appendix 1.2 for further information about entering data, saving data, and printing results in Excel.

Construct a frequency distribution of Jeep sales as in Table 2.2 on page 50 (data file: JeepSales.xlsx):

- Enter the Jeep sales data in Table 2.1 on page 50 (C = Commander; G = Grand Cherokee; L = Liberty; W = Wrangler) into column A with label Jeep Model in cell A1.

We obtain the frequency distribution by forming what is called a **PivotTable.** This is done as follows:

- Select **Insert : PivotTable**
- In the Create PivotTable dialog box, click "Select a table or range."
- Enter the range of the data to be analyzed into the Table/Range window. Here we have entered the range of the Jeep sales data A1.A252—that is, the entries in rows 1 through 252 in column A. The easiest way to do this is to click in the Table/Range window and to then drag from cell A1 through cell A252 with the mouse.
- Select "New Worksheet" to have the PivotTable output displayed in a new worksheet.
- Click OK in the Create PivotTable dialog box

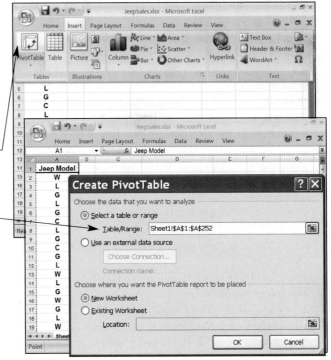

- In the **PivotTable Field List task pane,** drag the label "Jeep Model" and drop it into the Row Labels area.
- Also drag the label "Jeep Model" and drop it into the $\sum$ Values area. When this is done, the label will automatically change to "Count of Jeep Model" and the PivotTable will be displayed in the new worksheet.
- To calculate relative frequencies and percent frequencies of Jeep sales as in Table 2.3 on page 50, enter the cell formula =D3/D$7 into cell E3 and copy this cell formula down through all of the rows in the PivotTable (that is, through cell E7) to obtain a relative frequency for each row and the total relative frequency of 1.0000. Copy the cells containing the relative frequencies into cells F3 through F7, select them, right-click on them, and format the cells to represent percentages to the decimal place accuracy you desire.

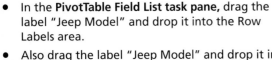

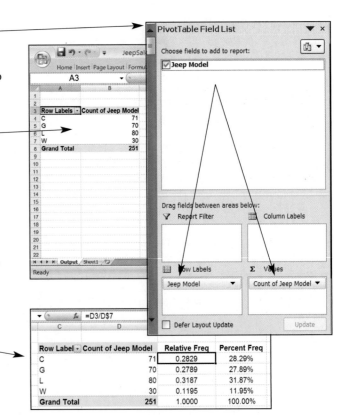

Row Label	Count of Jeep Model	Relative Freq	Percent Freq
C	71	0.2829	28.29%
G	70	0.2789	27.89%
L	80	0.3187	31.87%
W	30	0.1195	11.95%
Grand Total	251	1.0000	100.00%

After creating a tabular frequency distribution by using a PivotTable, it is easy to create **bar charts** and **pie charts**.

Construct a frequency bar chart of Jeep sales as in Figure 2.1 on page 51 (data file: JeepTable.xlsx):

- Enter the frequency distribution of Jeep sales in Table 2.2 on page 50 as shown in the screen with the various model identifiers in column A (with label Jeep Model) and with the corresponding frequencies in column B (with label Frequency).

- Click somewhere in the range of the data—here we have clicked on the label "Jeep Model," but anywhere in the range of the data would also work. Or, select the entire data set using the mouse.

- Select **Insert : Bar : All Chart Types**

- In the Insert Chart dialog box, select **Column** from the chart type list on the left, select **Clustered Column** from the gallery of charts on the right, and click OK.

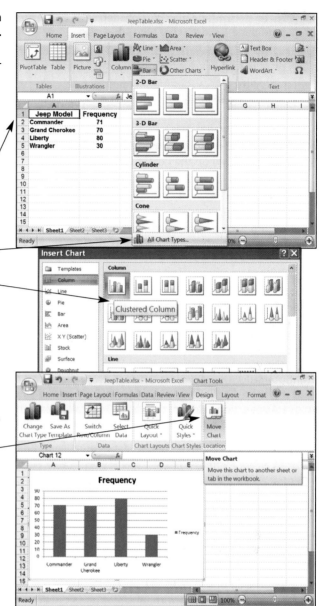

- The bar chart will be displayed in a graphics window.

- As demonstrated in Appendix 1.2, move the bar chart to a new worksheet before editing.

- In the new worksheet, the chart can be edited by selecting the **Layout** tab. By clicking on the Labels, Axes, Background, Analysis, and Properties groups, many of the chart characteristics can be edited, data labels (the numbers above the bars that give the bar heights) can be inserted, and so forth. Alternatively, the chart can be edited by right-clicking on various portions of the chart and by using the pop-up menus that are displayed.

- To construct a **relative frequency** or **percentage frequency bar chart,** simply replace the frequencies in the spreadsheet by their corresponding relative frequencies or percentage frequencies and follow the above instructions for constructing a frequency bar chart.

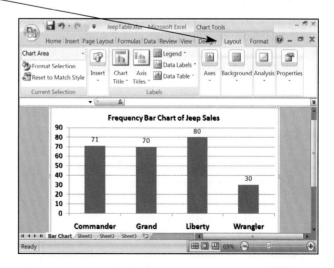

Construct a percentage pie chart of Jeep sales as in Figure 2.3 on page 52 (data file: JeepTable.xlsx):

- Enter the percent frequency distribution of Jeep sales in Table 2.3 on page 50 as shown in the screen with the various model identifiers in column A (with label Jeep Model) and with the corresponding percent frequencies in column B (with label Percent Freq).

- Click somewhere in the range of the data—here we have clicked on the label "Jeep Model." Or, select the entire data set using the mouse.

- Select **Insert : Pie : 2-D Pie : Pie**

- The pie chart is edited in the same way a bar chart is edited—see the instructions above related to editing bar charts.

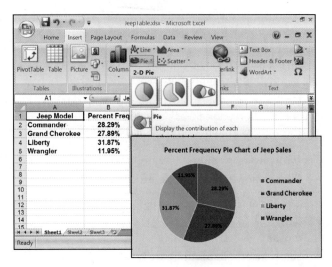

Constructing frequency distributions and histograms using the Analysis ToolPak: The Analysis ToolPak is an Excel add-in that is used for a variety of statistical analyses—including construction of frequency distributions and histograms from raw (that is, un-summarized) data. The ToolPak is available when Microsoft Office or Excel is installed. However, in order to use it, the ToolPak must first be loaded. To see if the Analysis ToolPak has been loaded on your computer, click the **Microsoft Office Button,** click **Excel Options,** and finally click **Add-Ins.** If the ToolPak has been loaded on your machine, it will be in the list of **Active Application Add-ins.** If Analysis ToolPak does not appear in this list, select **Excel Add-ins** in the **Manage** box and click **Go.** In the **Add-ins** box, place a checkmark in the **Analysis ToolPak** checkbox, and then click OK. Note that, if the Analysis ToolPak is not listed in the Add-Ins available box, click **Browse** to attempt to find it. If you get prompted that the Analysis ToolPak is not currently installed on your computer, click **Yes** to install it. In some cases, you might need to use your original MS Office or Excel CD/DVD to install and load the Analysis ToolPak by going through the setup process.

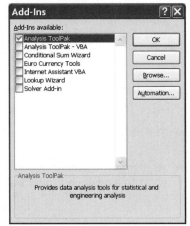

Constructing a frequency histogram of the bottle design ratings as in Figure 2.11 on page 61 (data file: Design.xlsx):

- Enter the 60 bottle design ratings in Table 1.3 on page 8 into Column A with label Rating in cell A1.

- Select **Data : Data Analysis**

- In the Data Analysis dialog box, select Histogram in the Analysis Tools window and click OK.

- In the Histogram dialog box, click in the Input Range window and select the range of the data A1.A61 into the Input Range window by dragging the mouse from cell A1 through cell A61.

- Place a checkmark in the Labels checkbox.

- Under "Output options," select "New Worksheet Ply."

- Enter a name for the new worksheet in the New Worksheet Ply window—here Histogram 1.

- Place a checkmark in the Chart Output checkbox.

- Click OK in the Histogram dialog box.

- **Notice that we are leaving the Bin Range window blank.** This will cause Excel to define **automatic classes** for the frequency distribution and histogram. However, because Excel's automatic classes are often not appropriate, we will revise these automatic classes below.

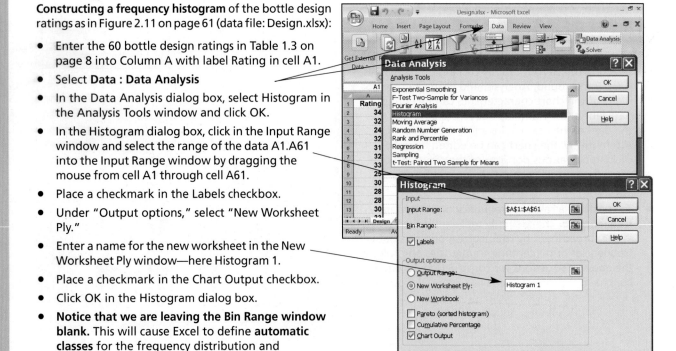

- The frequency distribution will be displayed in the new worksheet and the histogram will be displayed in a graphics window.

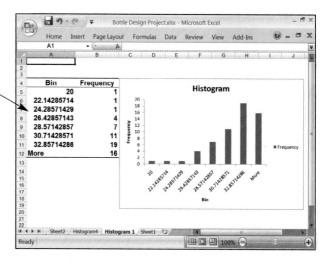

Notice that Excel defines what it calls **bins** when constructing the histogram. The **bins define the automatic classes** for the histogram. The bins that are automatically defined by Excel are often cumbersome—the bins in this example are certainly inconvenient for display purposes! Although one might be tempted to simply round the bin values, we have found that the rounded bin values can produce an unacceptable histogram with unequal class lengths (whether this happens depends on the particular bin values in a given situation).

To obtain more acceptable results, **we suggest that new bin values be defined that are roughly based on the automatic bin values.** We can do this as follows. First, we note that the smallest bin value is 20 and that this bin value is expressed using the same decimal place accuracy as the original data (recall that the bottle design ratings are all whole numbers). Remembering that Excel obtains a cell frequency by counting the number of measurements that are less than or equal to the upper class boundary and greater than the lower class boundary, the first class contains bottle design ratings less than or equal to 20. Based on the authors' experience, the first automatic bin value given by Excel is expressed to the same decimal place accuracy as the data being analyzed. However, if the smallest bin value were to be expressed using more decimal places than the original data, then **we suggest rounding it down to the decimal place accuracy of the original data being analyzed.** Frankly, the authors are not sure that this would ever need to be done—it was not necessary in any of the examples we have tried. Next, find the class length of the Excel automatic classes and round it to a convenient value. For the bottle design ratings, using the first and second bin values in the screen, the class length is 22.14285714 – 20 which equals 2.14285714. To obtain more convenient classes, we will round this value to 2. Starting at the first automatic bin value of 20, we now construct classes having length equal to 2. This gives us new bin values of 20, 22, 24, 26, and so on. We suggest continuing to define new bin values until a class containing the largest measurement in the data is found. Here, the largest bottle design rating is 35 (see Table 1.3 on page 8). Therefore, the last bin value is 36, which says that the last class will contain ratings greater than 34 and less than or equal to 36—that is, the ratings 35 and 36.

We suggest constructing classes in this way unless one or more measurements are unusually large compared to the rest of the data—we might call these unusually large measurements **outliers.** We will discuss outliers more thoroughly in Chapter 3 (and in later chapters). For now, if we (subjectively) believe that one or more outliers exist, we suggest placing these measurements in the "more" class and placing a histogram bar over this class having the same class length as the other bars. In such a situation, we must recognize that the Excel histogram will not be technically correct because **the area of the bar (or rectangle) above the "more" class will not necessarily equal the relative proportion of measurements in the class.** Nevertheless—given the way Excel constructs histogram classes—the approach we suggest seems reasonable. In the bottle design situation, the largest rating of 35 is not unusually large and, therefore, the "more" class will not contain any measurements.

To construct the revised histogram:

- Open a new worksheet, copy the bottle design ratings into column A and enter the new bin values into column B (with label Bin) as shown.

- Select **Data : Data Analysis : Histogram**

- Click OK in the Data Analysis dialog box.

- In the Histogram dialog box, select the range of the ratings data A1.A61 into the Input Range window.

- Click in the Bin Range window and enter the range of the bin values B1.B10.

- Place a checkmark in the Labels checkbox.

- Under "Output options," select "New Worksheet Ply" and enter a name for the new worksheet—here Histogram 2.

- Place a checkmark in the Chart Output checkbox.

- Click OK in the Histogram dialog box.

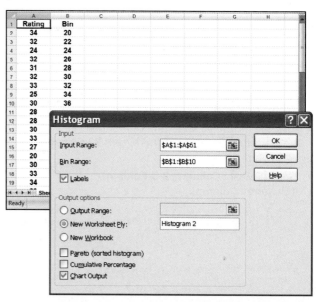

- The revised frequency distribution will be displayed in the new worksheet and the histogram will be displayed in a graphics window.

- Click in the graphics window and (as demonstrated in Appendix 1.2) move the histogram to a new worksheet for editing.

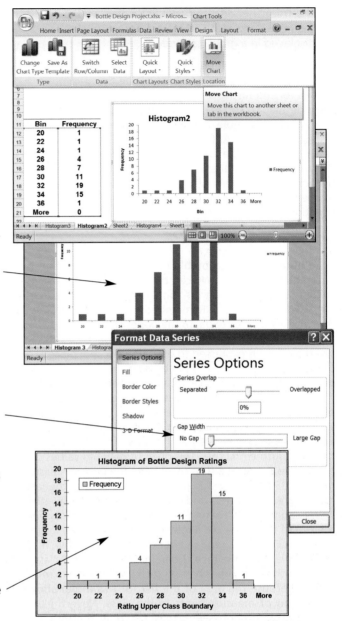

- The histogram will be displayed in the new chart sheet in a much larger format that makes it easier to carry out editing.

To remove the gaps between the histogram bars:

- Right click on one of the histogram bars and select Format Data Series from the pop-up window.

- Set the gap width to zero by moving the gap width slider to "No Gap" and click "Close" in the Format Data Series dialog box.

- By selecting the Chart Tools Layout tab, the histogram can be edited in many ways. This can also be done by right clicking on various portions of the histogram and by making desired pop-up menu selections.

- To obtain **data labels** (the numbers on the tops of the bars that indicate the bar heights), right click on one of the histogram bars and select "Add data labels" from the pop-up menu.

After final editing, the histogram might look like the one illustrated in Figure 2.11 on page 61.

Constructing a frequency histogram of bottle design ratings from summarized data:

- Enter the **midpoints** of the frequency distribution classes into column A with label Midpoint and enter the class frequencies into column B with label Frequency.

- Use the mouse to select the cell range that contains the frequencies (here, cells B2 through B10).

- Select **Insert : Column : 2-D Column (Clustered Column)**

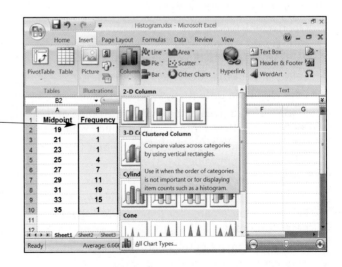

- Right-click on the chart that is displayed and click on Select Data in the pop-up menu.

- In the Select Data Source dialog box, click on the Edit button in the "Horizontal (Category) Axis Labels" window.

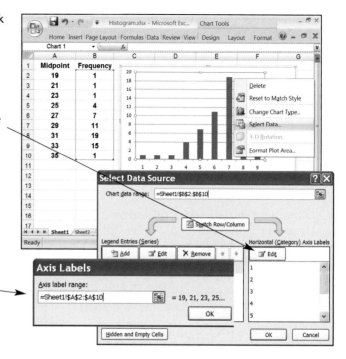

- In the Axis Labels dialog box, use the mouse to enter the cell range that contains the midpoints (here, A2.A10) into the "Axis label range" window.

- Click OK in the Axis Labels dialog box.
- Click OK in the Select Data Source dialog box.

- Move the chart that appears to a chart sheet, remove the gaps between the bars as previously shown, and edit the chart as desired.

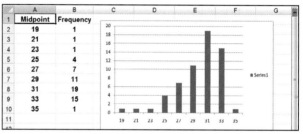

Relative frequency and percent frequency histograms would be constructed in the same way with the class midpoints in column A of the Excel spreadsheet and with the relative or percent frequencies in column B.

We now describe how to construct a **frequency polygon from summarized data.**

Note that, if the data are **not summarized,** first use the Histogram option in the Analysis ToolPak to develop a summarized frequency distribution.

- Enter the class midpoints and class frequencies as shown previously for summarized data.
- Use the mouse to select the cell range that contains the frequencies.
- Select **Insert : Line : Line with markers**
- Right-click on the chart that is displayed and click on Select Data in the pop-up menu.
- In the Select Data Source dialog box, click on the Edit button in the "Horizontal (Category) Axis Labels" window.
- In the Axis Labels dialog box, use the mouse to enter the cell range that contains the midpoints into the "Axis label range" window.
- Click OK in the Axis Labels dialog box.
- Click OK in the Select Data Source dialog box.
- Move the chart that appears to a chart sheet, and edit the chart as desired.

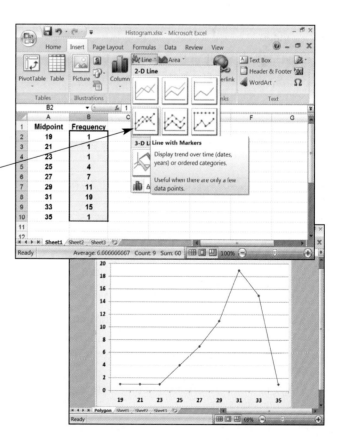

To construct **a percent frequency ogive for the bottle design rating distribution** (data file: Design.xlsx):

Follow the instructions for constructing a histogram by using the Analysis ToolPak with the following changes:

- In the Histogram dialog box, place a checkmark in the Cumulative Percentage checkbox.
- After moving the histogram to a chart sheet, right-click on any histogram bar.
- Select "Format Data Series" from the pop-up menu.
- In the "Format Data Series" dialog box, (1) select Fill from the list of "Series Options" and select "No fill" from the list of Fill options; (2) select Border Color from the list of "Series Options" and select "No line" from the list of Border Color options; (3) Click Close.
- Click on the chart to remove the histogram bars.

Construct a crosstabulation table of fund type versus level of client satisfaction as in Table 2.17 on page 76 (data file: Invest.xlsx):

- Enter the customer satisfaction data in Table 2.16 on page 76—fund types in column A with label "Fund Type" and satisfaction ratings in column B with label "Satisfaction Rating."
- Select **Insert : PivotTable**
- In the Create PivotTable dialog box, click "Select a table or range."
- By dragging with the mouse, enter the range of the data to be analyzed into the Table/Range window. Here we have entered the range of the client satisfaction data A1.B101.
- Select the New Worksheet option to place the PivotTable in a new worksheet.
- Click OK in the Create PivotTable dialog box.

- In the PivotTable Field List task pane, drag the label "Fund Type" and drop it into the Row Labels area.
- Also drag the label "Fund Type" and drop it into the $\sum$ Values area. When this is done, the label will automatically change to "Count of Fund Type."
- Drag the label "Satisfaction Rating" into the Column Labels area.

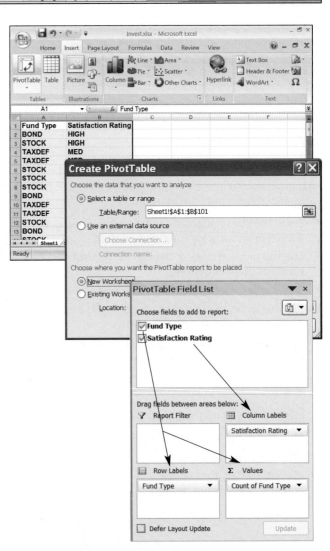

- The PivotTable will be created and placed in a new worksheet.

- Now right-click inside the PivotTable and select PivotTable Options from the pop-up menu.

- In the PivotTable Options dialog box, select the Totals & Filters tab and make sure that a checkmark has been placed in each of the "Show grand totals for rows" and the "Show grand totals for columns" checkboxes.

- Select the Layout & Format tab, place a checkmark in the "For empty cells show" checkbox and enter 0 (the number zero) into its corresponding window. (For the customer satisfaction data, none of the cell frequencies equal zero, but, in general, this setting should be made to prevent empty cells from being left blank in the crosstabulation table.)

- To change the order of the column labels from the default alphabetical ordering (High, Low, Medium) to the more logical ordering of High, Medium, Low, right-click on LOW, select Move from the pop-up menu, and select "Move LOW to End."

- The crosstabulation table is now complete.

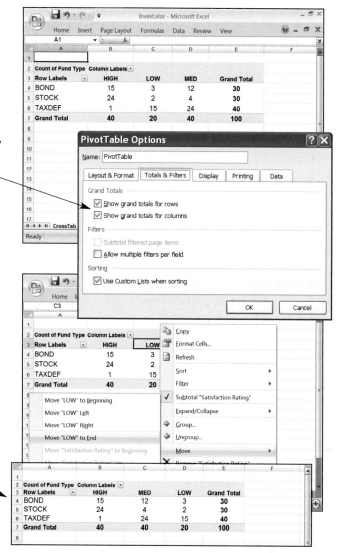

Construct a scatter plot of sales volume versus advertising expenditure as in Figure 2.24 on page 81 (data file: SalesPlot.xlsx):

- Enter the advertising and sales data in Table 2.20 on page 81 into columns A and B—advertising expenditures in column A with label "Ad Exp" and sales values in column B with label "Sales Vol." **Note: The variable to be graphed on the horizontal axis must be in the first column** (that is, the left-most column) and **the variable to be graphed on the vertical axis must be in the second column** (that is, the rightmost column).

- Click in the range of data to be graphed, or select the entire range of the data to be graphed.

- Select **Insert : Scatter : Scatter with only Markers**

- The scatter plot will be displayed in a graphics window. Move the plot to a chart sheet and edit appropriately.

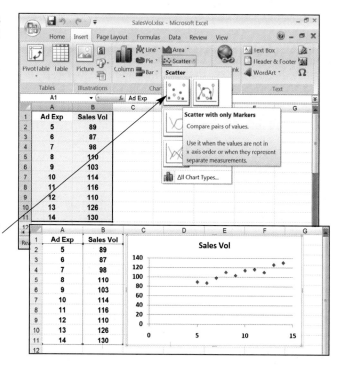

Appendix 2.3 ■ Tabular and Graphical Methods Using MegaStat

The instructions in this section begin by describing the entry of data into an Excel worksheet. Alternatively, the data may be loaded directly from the data disk included with the text. The appropriate data file name is given at the top of each instruction block. Please refer to Appendix 1.2 for further information about entering data, saving data, and printing results in Excel. Please refer to Appendix 1.3 for more information about MegaStat basics.

Construct a frequency distribution and bar chart of Jeep sales as in Table 2.2 on page 50 and Figure 2.2 on page 51 (data file: JeepSales.xlsx):

- Enter the Jeep sales data in Table 2.1 on page 50 (C = Commander; G = Grand Cherokee; L = Liberty; W = Wrangler) into column A with label Jeep Model in cell A1.

- Enter the categories for the qualitative variable (C, G, L, W) into the worksheet. Here we have placed them in cells B2 through B5—the location is arbitrary.

- Select **Add-Ins : MegaStat : Frequency Distributions : Qualitative**

- In the "Frequency Distributions—Qualitative" dialog box, use the AutoExpand feature to enter the range A1.A252 of the Jeep sales data into the Input Range window.

- Enter the cell range B2.B5 of the categories (C, G, L, W) into the "specification range" window.

- Place a checkmark in the "histogram" checkbox to obtain a bar chart.

- Click OK in the "Frequency Distributions—Qualitative" dialog box.

- The frequency distribution and bar chart will be placed in a new output sheet.

- The output can be edited in the output sheet. Alternatively, the bar chart can be moved to a chart sheet (see Appendix 1.2) for more convenient editing.

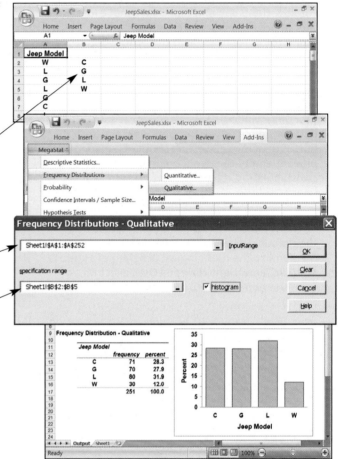

Construct a frequency distribution and percent frequency histogram of the gas mileages as in Figure 2.10 on page 60 (data file: GasMiles.xlsx):

- Enter the gasoline mileage data in Table 1.4 on page 10 into column A with the label Mpg in cell A1 and with the 50 gas mileages in cells A2 to A51.

- Select **Add-Ins : MegaStat : Frequency Distributions : Quantitative**

- In the "Frequency Distributions—Quantitative" dialog box, use the AutoExpand feature to enter the range A1.A51 of the gas mileages into the Input Range window.

- To obtain **automatic classes** for the histogram, leave the "interval width" and "lower boundary of first interval" windows blank.

- Place a checkmark in the Histogram checkbox.

- Click OK in the "Frequency Distributions—Quantitative" dialog box.

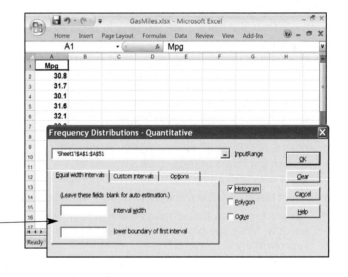

- The frequency distribution and histogram will be placed in a new output worksheet.
- The chart can be edited in the output worksheet, or you can move the chart to a chart sheet for editing.
- To obtain **data labels** (the numbers on the tops of the bars that indicate the bar heights), right-click on one of the histogram bars and select "Add data labels" from the pop-up menu.

To construct a **frequency polygon and a percent frequency ogive,** simply place checkmarks in the Polygon and Ogive checkboxes in the "Frequency Distributions—Quantitative" dialog box.

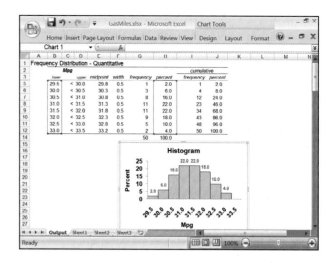

Construct a percent frequency histogram of the bottle design ratings similar to Figure 2.11 on page 61 with **user-specified classes** (data file: Design.xlsx):

- Enter the 60 bottle design ratings in Table 1.3 on page 8 into column A with label Rating in cell A1.
- Select **Add-Ins : MegaStat : Frequency Distributions : Quantitative**
- In the "Frequency Distributions—Quantitative" dialog box, use the AutoExpand feature to enter the input range A1.A61 of the bottle design ratings into the Input Range window.
- Enter the class width (in this case equal to 2) into the "interval width" window.
- Enter the lower boundary of the first—that is, leftmost—interval of the histogram (in this case equal to 20) into the "lower boundary of first interval" window.
- Make sure that the Histogram checkbox is checked.
- Click OK in the "Frequency Distributions— Quantitative" dialog box.
- We obtain a histogram with class boundaries 20, 22, 24, 26, 28, 30, 32, 34, and 36. Note that the appearance of this histogram is not exactly the same as that of the Excel histogram in Figure 2.11 on page 61 because we recall that MegaStat and Excel count frequencies differently.
- The histogram can be moved to a chart sheet for editing purposes.

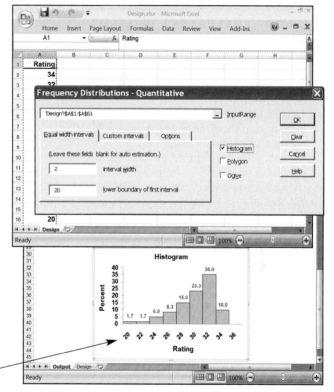

Construct a dot plot (as in Figure 2.18 on page 69) **and a stem-and-leaf display** (as in Figure 2.20 on page 73) of the scores on the first statistics exam as discussed in Example 2.3 on page 62 (data file: FirstExam.xlsx):

- Enter the 40 scores for exam 1 in Table 2.8 on page 62 into column A with label "Exam 1" in cell A1.
- Select **Add-Ins : MegaStat : Descriptive Statistics**
- In the "Descriptive Statistics" dialog box, use the AutoExpand feature to enter the range A1.A41 of the exam scores into the "Input range" window.
- Place a checkmark in the DotPlot checkbox to obtain a dot plot.
- Place a checkmark in the "Stem and Leaf Plot" checkbox to obtain a stem-and-leaf display.
- Place a checkmark in the "Split Stem" checkbox. (In general, whether or not this should be done depends on how you want the output to appear. You may wish to construct two plots—one with the Split Stem option and one without—and then choose the output you like best.) In the exam score situation, the Split Stem option is needed to obtain a display that looks like the one in Figure 2.20.
- Click OK in the "Descriptive Statistics" dialog box.
- The dot plot and stem-and-leaf display will be placed in an output sheet. Here, the stem-and-leaf display we have obtained for exam 1 is the "mirror image" of the plot shown in Figure 2.20 (because we have constructed a single display for exam 1, while Figure 2.20 shows back-to-back displays for both exams 1 and 2).
- The dot plot can be moved to a chart sheet for editing.

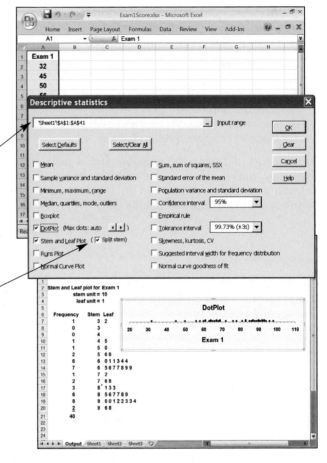

Construct a crosstabulation table of fund type versus level of client satisfaction as in Table 2.17 on page 76 (data file: Invest.xlsx):

- Enter the customer satisfaction data in Table 2.16 on page 76—fund types in column A with label FundType and satisfaction ratings in column B with label SRating.
- Enter the three labels (BOND; STOCK; TAXDEF) for the qualitative variable FundType into cells C2, C3, and C4 as shown in the screen.
- Enter the three labels (HIGH; MED; LOW) for the qualitative variable SRating into cells C6, C7, and C8 as shown in the screen.
- Select **Add-Ins : MegaStat : Chi-Square/CrossTab : Crosstabulation**
- In the Crosstabulation dialog box, use the AutoExpand feature to enter the range A1.A101 of the row variable FundType into the "Row variable Data range" window.
- Enter the range C2.C4 of the labels of the qualitative variable FundType into the "Row variable Specification range window."
- Use the AutoExpand feature to enter the range B1.B101 of the column variable SRating into the "Column variable Data range" window.
- Enter the range C6.C8 of the labels of the qualitative variable SRating into the "Column variable Specification range window."

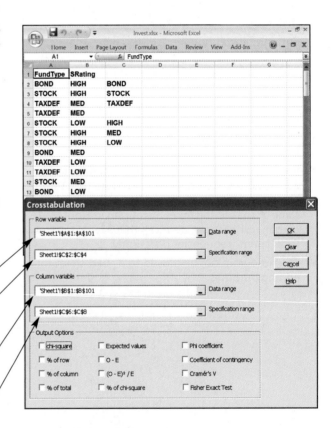

- Uncheck the "chi-square" checkbox.
- Click OK in the Crosstabulation dialog box.
- The crosstabulation table will be displayed in an output worksheet.
- **Row percentages and column percentages** can be obtained by simply placing checkmarks in the "% of row" and "% of column" checkboxes.

Construct a scatter plot of sales volume versus advertising expenditure as in Figure 2.24 on page 81 (data file: SalesPlot.xlsx):

- Enter the advertising and sales data in Table 2.20 on page 81 into columns A and B—advertising expenditures in column A with label "Ad Exp" and sales values in column B with label "Sales Vol."
- Select **Add-Ins : MegaStat : Correlation/Regression : Scatterplot**
- In the Scatterplot dialog box, use the AutoExpand feature to enter the range A1.A11 of the advertising expenditures into the "horizontal axis" window.
- Use the AutoExpand feature to enter the range B1.B11 of the sales volumes into the "vertical axis" window.
- Uncheck the "Plot linear regression line" checkbox.
- Under Display options, select Markers.
- Click OK in the Scatterplot dialog box.
- The scatter plot is displayed in an output worksheet and can be moved to a chart sheet for editing.

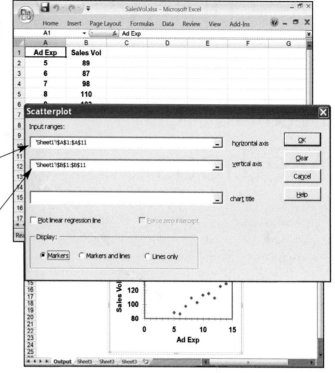

CHAPTER 3

Descriptive Statistics: Numerical Methods

Chapter Outline

3.1 Describing Central Tendency

3.2 Measures of Variation

3.3 Percentiles, Quartiles, and Box-and-Whiskers Displays

3.4 Covariance, Correlation, and the Least Squares Line (Optional)

3.5 Weighted Means and Grouped Data (Optional)

3.6 The Geometric Mean (Optional)

In this chapter we study numerical methods for describing the important aspects of a set of measurements. If the measurements are values of a quantitative variable, we often describe (1) what a typical measurement might be and (2) how the measurements vary, or differ, from each other. For example, in the car mileage case we might estimate (1) a typical EPA gas mileage for the new midsize model and (2) how the EPA mileages vary from car to car. Or, in the marketing research case, we might estimate (1) a typical bottle design rating and (2) how the bottle design ratings vary from consumer to consumer.

Taken together, the graphical displays of Chapter 2 and the numerical methods of this chapter give us a basic understanding of the important aspects of a set of measurements. We will illustrate this by continuing to analyze the car mileages, payment times, bottle design ratings, and cell phone usages introduced in Chapters 1 and 2.

3.1 Describing Central Tendency ● ● ●

CHAPTER 3

The mean, median, and mode   In addition to describing the shape of the distribution of a sample or population of measurements, we also describe the data set's **central tendency.** A measure of central tendency represents the *center* or *middle* of the data. Sometimes we think of a measure of central tendency as a *typical value.* However, as we will see, not all measures of central tendency are necessarily typical values.

One important measure of central tendency for a population of measurements is the **population mean.** We define it as follows:

The **population mean,** which is denoted μ and pronounced *mew*, is the average of the population measurements.

More precisely, the population mean is calculated by adding all the population measurements and then dividing the resulting sum by the number of population measurements. For instance, suppose that Chris is a college junior majoring in business. This semester Chris is taking five classes and the numbers of students enrolled in the classes (that is, the class sizes) are as follows:

Class	Class Size
Business Law	60
Finance	41
International Studies	15
Management	30
Marketing	34

The mean μ of this population of class sizes is

$$\mu = \frac{60 + 41 + 15 + 30 + 34}{5} = \frac{180}{5} = 36$$

Since this population of five class sizes is small, it is possible to compute the population mean. Often, however, a population is very large and we cannot obtain a measurement for each population unit. Therefore, we cannot compute the population mean. In such a case, we must estimate the population mean by using a sample of measurements.

In order to understand how to estimate a population mean, we must realize that the population mean is a **population parameter.**

A **population parameter** is a number calculated using the population measurements that describes some aspect of the population. That is, a population parameter is a descriptive measure of the population.

There are many population parameters, and we discuss several of them in this chapter. The simplest way to estimate a population parameter is to make a **point estimate,** which is a one-number estimate of the value of the population parameter. Although a point estimate is a guess of a population parameter's value, it should not be a *blind guess.* Rather, it should be an educated guess based on sample data. One sensible way to find a point estimate of a population parameter is to use a **sample statistic.**

> A **sample statistic** is a number calculated using the sample measurements that describes some aspect of the sample. That is, a sample statistic is a descriptive measure of the sample.

The sample statistic that we use to estimate the population mean is the **sample mean,** which is denoted as $\bar{x}$ (pronounced *x bar*) and is the average of the sample measurements.

In order to write a formula for the sample mean, we employ the letter n to represent the number of sample measurements, and we refer to n as the **sample size.** Furthermore, we denote the sample measurements as $x_1, x_2, \ldots, x_n$. Here x_1 is the first sample measurement, x_2 is the second sample measurement, and so forth. We denote the last sample measurement as x_n. Moreover, when we write formulas we often use *summation notation* for convenience. For instance, we write the sum of the sample measurements

$$x_1 + x_2 + \cdots + x_n$$

as $\sum_{i=1}^{n} x_i$. Here the symbol Σ simply tells us to add the terms that follow the symbol. The term x_i is a generic (or representative) observation in our data set, and the $i = 1$ and the n indicate where to start and stop summing. Thus

$$\sum_{i=1}^{n} x_i = x_1 + x_2 + \cdots + x_n$$

We define the sample mean as follows:

The **sample mean** $\bar{x}$ is defined to be

$$\bar{x} = \frac{\sum_{i=1}^{n} x_i}{n} = \frac{x_1 + x_2 + \cdots + x_n}{n}$$

and is the **point estimate of the population mean** μ.

EXAMPLE 3.1 The Car Mileage Case

In order to offer its tax credit, the federal government has decided to define the "typical" EPA combined city and highway mileage for a car model as the mean μ of the population of EPA combined mileages that would be obtained by all cars of this type. Here, using the mean to represent a typical value is probably reasonable. We know that some individual cars will get mileages that are lower than the mean and some will get mileages that are above it. However, because there will be many thousands of these cars on the road, the mean mileage obtained by these cars is probably a reasonable way to represent the model's overall fuel economy. Therefore, the government will offer its tax credit to any automaker selling a midsize model equipped with an automatic transmission that achieves a mean EPA combined mileage of at least 31 mpg.

To demonstrate that its new midsize model qualifies for the tax credit, the automaker in this case study wishes to use the sample of 50 mileages in Table 3.1 to estimate μ, the model's mean mileage. Before calculating the mean of the entire sample of 50 mileages, we will illustrate the formulas involved by calculating the mean of the first five of these mileages. Table 3.1 tells us that $x_1 = 30.8$, $x_2 = 31.7$, $x_3 = 30.1$, $x_4 = 31.6$, and $x_5 = 32.1$, so the sum of the first five mileages is

$$\sum_{i=1}^{5} x_i = x_1 + x_2 + x_3 + x_4 + x_5$$

$$= 30.8 + 31.7 + 30.1 + 31.6 + 32.1 = 156.3$$

Therefore, the mean of the first five mileages is

$$\bar{x} = \frac{\sum_{i=1}^{5} x_i}{5} = \frac{156.3}{5} = 31.26$$

TABLE 3.1   A Sample of 50 Mileages   ⬤ GasMiles

30.8	30.8	32.1	32.3	32.7
31.7	30.4	31.4	32.7	31.4
30.1	32.5	30.8	31.2	31.8
31.6	30.3	32.8	30.7	31.9
32.1	31.3	31.9	31.7	33.0
33.3	32.1	31.4	31.4	31.5
31.3	32.5	32.4	32.2	31.6
31.0	31.8	31.0	31.5	30.6
32.0	30.5	29.8	31.7	32.3
32.4	30.5	31.1	30.7	31.4

Of course, intuitively, we are likely to obtain a more accurate point estimate of the population mean by using all of the available sample information. The sum of all 50 mileages can be verified to be

$$\sum_{i=1}^{50} x_i = x_1 + x_2 + \cdots + x_{50} = 30.8 + 31.7 + \cdots + 31.4 = 1578$$

Therefore, the mean of the sample of 50 mileages is

$$\bar{x} = \frac{\sum_{i=1}^{50} x_i}{50} = \frac{1578}{50} = 31.56$$

This point estimate says we estimate that the mean mileage that would be obtained by all of the new midsize cars that will or could potentially be produced this year is 31.56 mpg. Unless we are extremely lucky, however, this sample mean will not exactly equal the average mileage that would be obtained by all cars. That is, the point estimate $\bar{x} = 31.56$ mpg, which is based on the sample of 50 randomly selected mileages, probably does not exactly equal the population mean μ. Therefore, although $\bar{x} = 31.56$ provides some evidence that μ is at least 31 and thus that the automaker should get the tax credit, it does not provide definitive evidence. In later chapters, we discuss how to assess the *reliability* of the sample mean and how to use a measure of reliability to decide whether sample information provides definitive evidence.

Another descriptive measure of the central tendency of a population or a sample of measurements is the **median.** Intuitively, the median divides a population or sample into two roughly equal parts. We calculate the median, which is denoted M_d, as follows:

> Consider a population or a sample of measurements, and arrange the measurements in increasing order. The **median,** M_d, is found as follows:
>
> **1** If the number of measurements is odd, the median is the middlemost measurement in the ordering.
>
> **2** If the number of measurements is even, the median is the average of the two middlemost measurements in the ordering.

For example, recall that Chris's five classes have sizes 60, 41, 15, 30, and 34. To find the median of the population of class sizes, we arrange the class sizes in increasing order as follows:

$$15 \quad 30 \quad \textcircled{34} \quad 41 \quad 60$$

Because the number of class sizes is odd, the median of the population of class sizes is the middlemost class size in the ordering. Therefore, the median is 34 students (it is circled).

As another example, suppose that in the middle of the semester Chris decides to take an additional class—a sprint class in individual exercise. If the individual exercise class has 30 students, then the sizes of Chris's six classes are (arranged in increasing order):

$$15 \quad 30 \quad \textcircled{30} \quad \textcircled{34} \quad 41 \quad 60$$

Because the number of classes is even, the median of the population of class sizes is the average of the two middlemost class sizes, which are circled. Therefore, the median is $(30 + 34)/2 = 32$ students. Note that, although two of Chris's classes have the same size, 30 students, each observation is listed separately (that is, 30 is listed twice) when we arrange the observations in increasing order.

As a third example, if we arrange the sample of 50 mileages in Table 3.1 in increasing order, we find that the two middlemost mileages—the 25th and 26th mileages—are 31.5 and 31.6. It follows that the median of the sample is 31.55. Therefore, we estimate that the median mileage that would be obtained by all of the new midsize cars that will or could potentially be produced this year is 31.55 mpg. The MegaStat output in Figure 3.1 shows this median mileage, as well as the previously calculated mean mileage of 31.56 mpg. Other quantities given on the MegaStat output will be discussed later in this chapter.

A third measure of the central tendency of a population or sample is the **mode,** which is denoted M_o.

> The **mode,** M_o, of a population or sample of measurements is the measurement that occurs most frequently.

For example, the mode of Chris's six class sizes is 30. This is because more classes (two) have a size of 30 than any other size. Sometimes the highest frequency occurs at more than one measurement. When this happens, two or more modes exist. When exactly two modes exist, we say the data are *bimodal*. When more than two modes exist, we say the data are *multimodal*. If data are presented in classes (such as in a frequency or percent histogram), the class having the highest frequency or percent is called the *modal class*. For example, the MegaStat output in Figure 3.2 shows a histogram of the car mileages that has two modal classes— the class from 31.0 mpg to 31.5 mpg and the class from 31.5 mpg to 32.0 mpg. Since the mileage 31.5 is in the middle of the modal classes, we might estimate that the population mode for the new midsize model is 31.5 mpg. Or, alternatively, since the MegaStat output in Figure 3.1 tells us that the mode of the sample of 50 mileages is 31.4 mpg (it can be verified that this mileage occurs five times in Table 3.1), we might estimate that the population mode is 31.4 mpg. Obviously, these two estimates are somewhat contradictory. In general, it can be difficult to define a reliable method for estimating the population mode. Therefore, although it can be informative to report the modal class or classes in a frequency or percent histogram, the mean or median is used more often than the mode when we wish to describe a data set's central tendency by using a single number. Finally, the mode is a useful descriptor of qualitative data. For example, we have seen in Chapter 2 that the most frequently sold Jeep model at the Cincinnati Jeep dealership was the Jeep Liberty, which accounted for 31.87 percent of Jeep sales.

FIGURE 3.1   **MegaStat Output of Statistics Describing the 50 Mileages**

Descriptive statistics

	Mpg
count	50
mean	31.560
sample variance	0.636
sample standard deviation	0.798
minimum	29.8
maximum	33.3
range	3.5
1st quartile	31.0
median	31.55
3rd quartile	32.1
interquartile range	1.1
mode	31.4

FIGURE 3.2   **MegaStat Output of a Percent Histogram Describing the 50 Mileages**

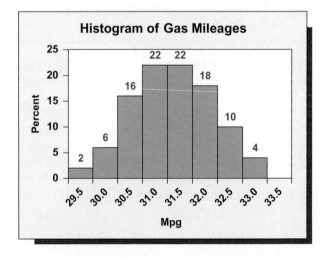

FIGURE 3.3   Relationships among the Mean μ, the Median M_d, and the Mode M_o

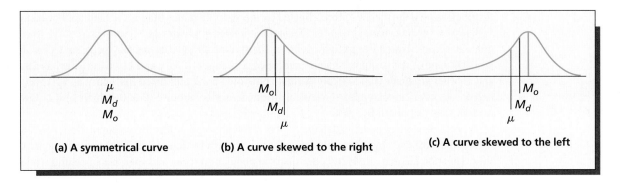

(a) A symmetrical curve   (b) A curve skewed to the right   (c) A curve skewed to the left

Comparing the mean, median, and mode   Often we construct a histogram for a sample to make inferences about the shape of the sampled population. When we do this, it can be useful to "smooth out" the histogram and use the resulting *relative frequency curve* to describe the shape of the population. Relative frequency curves can have many shapes. Three common shapes are illustrated in Figure 3.3. Part (a) of this figure depicts a population described by a symmetrical relative frequency curve. For such a population, the mean (μ), median (M_d), and mode (M_o) are all equal. Note that in this case all three of these quantities are located under the highest point of the curve. It follows that when the frequency distribution of a sample of measurements is approximately symmetrical, then the sample mean, median, and mode will be nearly the same. For instance, consider the sample of 50 mileages in Table 3.1. Because the histogram of these mileages in Figure 3.2 is approximately symmetrical, the mean—31.56—and the median—31.55—of the mileages are approximately equal to each other.

Figure 3.3(b) depicts a population that is skewed to the right. Here the population mean is larger than the population median, and the population median is larger than the population mode (the mode is located under the highest point of the relative frequency curve). In this case the population mean *averages in* the large values in the upper tail of the distribution. Thus the population mean is more affected by these large values than is the population median. To understand this, we consider the following example.

EXAMPLE 3.2 The Household Income Case   C

An economist wishes to study the distribution of household incomes in a midwestern city. To do this, the economist randomly selects a sample of $n = 12$ households from the city and determines last year's income for each household.[1] The resulting sample of 12 household incomes—arranged in increasing order—is as follows (the incomes are expressed in dollars):

7,524	11,070	18,211	26,817	36,551	(41,286)
(49,312)	57,283	72,814	90,416	135,540	190,250

◆ Incomes

Because the number of incomes is even, the median of the incomes is the average of the two middlemost incomes, which are enclosed in ovals. Therefore, the median is $(41,286 + 49,312)/2 = $45,299$. The mean of the incomes is the sum of the incomes, 737,076, divided by 12, or $61,423. Here, the mean has been affected by averaging in the large incomes $135,540 and $190,250 and thus is larger than the median. The median is said to be **resistant** to these large incomes because the value of the median is affected only by the position of these large incomes in the ordered list of incomes, not by the **exact sizes** of the incomes. For example, if the largest income were smaller—say $150,000—the median would remain the same but the mean would decrease. If the largest income were larger—say $300,000—the median would also remain the same but the mean would increase. Therefore, the median is resistant to large values but the mean is not. Similarly, the median is resistant to values that are much smaller than most of the measurements. In general, we say that **the median is resistant to extreme values.**

---

[1]Note that, realistically, an economist would sample many more than 12 incomes from a city. We have made the sample size in this case small so that we can simply illustrate various ideas throughout this chapter.

Figure 3.3(c) depicts a population that is skewed to the left. Here the population mean is smaller than the population median, and the population median is smaller than the population mode. In this case the population mean *averages in* the small values in the lower tail of the distribution, and the mean is more affected by these small values than is the median. For instance, in a survey several years ago of 20 Decision Sciences graduates at Miami University, 18 of the graduates had obtained employment in business consulting that paid a mean salary of about $43,000. One of the graduates had become a Christian missionary and listed his salary as $8,500, and another graduate was working for his hometown bank and listed his salary as $10,500. The two lower salaries decreased the overall mean salary to about $39,650, which was below the median salary of about $43,000.

When a population is skewed to the right or left with a very long tail, the population mean can be substantially affected by the extreme population values in the tail of the distribution. In such a case, the population median might be better than the population mean as a measure of central tendency. For example, the yearly incomes of all people in the United States are skewed to the right with a very long tail. Furthermore, the very large incomes in this tail cause the mean yearly income to be inflated above the typical income earned by most Americans. Because of this, the median income is more representative of a typical U.S. income. The following case illustrates that the choice of the mean or the median as a measure of central tendency can depend on the purpose of the study being conducted.

EXAMPLE 3.3 The Insurance Information Institute Case

In 1984 the Insurance Information Institute defended high liability insurance premiums by asserting that the mean reward in product liability cases exceeded one million dollars. Opponents of premium increases countered that the median award was only $271,000. The mean and median differed dramatically in this case because the mean was greatly inflated by a relatively few extremely large awards. From the point of view of reporting a *typical award* to the public, the median is probably superior. However, from the point of view of establishing premiums, the mean is probably superior. This is because the mean helps us determine the total amount that insurance companies paid out, which is the bottom line as far as the insurance industry is concerned. For example, if the mean award of one million dollars is based on 1,000 liability cases, then the insurance industry paid out a total of one billion dollars.

When a population is symmetrical or not highly skewed, then the population mean and the population median are either equal or roughly equal, and both provide a good measure of the population central tendency. In this situation, we usually make inferences about the population mean because much of statistical theory is based on the mean rather than the median.

EXAMPLE 3.4 The Marketing Research Case

The Excel output in Figure 3.4 tells us that the mean and the median of the sample of 60 bottle design ratings are 30.35 and 31, respectively. Because the histogram of the bottle design ratings in Figure 3.5 is not highly skewed to the left, the sample mean is not much less than the sample median. Therefore, using the mean as our measure of central tendency, we estimate that the mean rating of the new bottle design that would be given by all consumers is 30.35. This is considerably higher than the minimum standard of 25 for a successful bottle design.

EXAMPLE 3.5 The Payment Time Case

The MINITAB output in Figure 3.6 gives a histogram of the 65 payment times, and the MINITAB output in Figure 3.7 tells us that the mean and the median of the payment times are 18.108 days and 17 days, respectively. Because the histogram is not highly skewed to the right, the sample mean is not much greater than the sample median. Therefore, using the mean as our measure of central tendency, we estimate that the mean payment time of all bills using the new billing system is 18.108 days. This is substantially less than the typical payment time of 39 days that had been experienced using the old billing system.

FIGURE 3.4   Excel Output of Statistics Describing the 60 Bottle Design Ratings

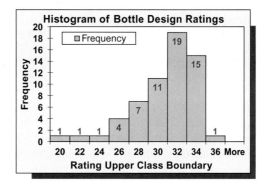

STATISTICS	
Mean	30.35
Standard Error	0.401146
Median	31
Mode	32
Standard Deviation	3.107263
Sample Variance	9.655085
Kurtosis	1.423397
Skewness	−1.17688
Range	15
Minimum	20
Maximum	35
Sum	1821
Count	60

FIGURE 3.5   Excel Frequency Histogram of the 60 Bottle Design Ratings

FIGURE 3.6   MINITAB Frequency Histogram of the 65 Payment Times

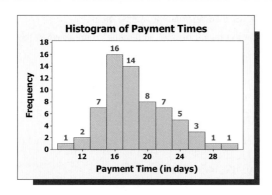

FIGURE 3.7   MINITAB Output of Statistics Describing the 65 Payment Times

Variable	Count	Mean	StDev	Variance		
PayTime	65	18.108	3.961	15.691		

Variable	Minimum	Q1	Median	Q3	Maximum	Range
PayTime	10.000	15.000	17.000	21.000	29.000	19.000

EXAMPLE 3.6 The Cell Phone Case

Remember that if the cellular cost per minute for the random sample of 100 bank employees is over 18 cents per minute, the bank will benefit from automated cellular management of its calling plans. Last month's cellular usages for the 100 randomly selected employees are given in Table 1.2 (page 7), and a dot plot of these usages is given in the page margin. If we add together the usages, we find that the 100 employees used a total of 46,652 minutes. Since each employee was on a 500-minute plan that costs $50, the base price of the cell phone plan for the 100 employees was 100($50) = $5,000. Furthermore, 51 of the employees used more than the 500 minutes allowed. The sum of the cellular usages for these 51 employees can be calculated to be 33,150 minutes, which implies that the total number of overage minutes is 33,150 − 51(500) = 7,650. Since

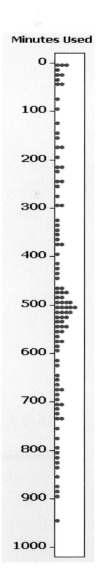

each overage minute is assessed a $.40 charge, the total overage charge is 7,650($.40) = $3,060. In addition, the 100 sampled employees were assessed $1,257 of long-distance and roaming charges. In summary, the 46,652 minutes used by the 100 sampled employees cost the bank a total of ($5,000 + $3,060 + $1,257) = $9,317. This works out to an average of $9,317/46,652 = $.1998, or 19.98 cents per minute. Because this average cellular cost per minute exceeds 18 cents per minute, the bank will hire the cellular management service to manage its calling plans.

To conclude this section, note that the mean and the median convey useful information about a population having a relative frequency curve with a sufficiently regular shape. For instance, the mean and median would be useful in describing the mound-shaped, or single-peaked, distributions in Figure 3.3. However, these measures of central tendency do not adequately describe a double-peaked distribution. For example, the mean and the median of the exam scores in the double-peaked distribution of Figure 2.12 (page 62) are 75.225 and 77. Looking at the distribution, neither the mean nor the median represents a *typical* exam score. This is because the exam scores really have *no central value*. In this case the most important message conveyed by the double-peaked distribution is that the exam scores fall into two distinct groups.

Exercises for Section 3.1

CONCEPTS

3.1 Explain the difference between each of the following:
a A population parameter and its point estimate.
b A population mean and a corresponding sample mean.

3.2 Explain how the population mean, median, and mode compare when the population's relative frequency curve is
a Symmetrical.
b Skewed with a tail to the left.
c Skewed with a tail to the right.

METHODS AND APPLICATIONS

3.3 Calculate the mean, median, and mode of each of the following populations of numbers:
a 9, 8, 10, 10, 12, 6, 11, 10, 12, 8
b 110, 120, 70, 90, 90, 100, 80, 130, 140

3.4 Calculate the mean, median, and mode for each of the following populations of numbers:
a 17, 23, 19, 20, 25, 18, 22, 15, 21, 20
b 505, 497, 501, 500, 507, 510, 501

3.5 **THE VIDEO GAME SATISFACTION RATING CASE** ⬤ VideoGame

Recall that Table 1.7 (page 14) presents the satisfaction ratings for the XYZ-Box game system that have been given by 65 randomly selected purchasers. Figures 3.8 and 3.11(a) give the MINITAB and MegaStat outputs of statistics describing the 65 satisfaction ratings.
a Find the sample mean on the outputs. Does the sample mean provide evidence that the mean of the population of all possible customer satisfaction ratings for the XYZ-Box is at least 42? (Recall that a "very satisfied" customer gives a rating that is at least 42.) Explain your answer.
b Find the sample median on the outputs. How do the mean and median compare? What does the histogram in Figure 2.15 (page 66) tell you about why they compare this way?

3.6 **THE BANK CUSTOMER WAITING TIME CASE** ⬤ WaitTime

Recall that Table 1.8 (page 14) presents the waiting times for teller service during peak business hours of 100 randomly selected bank customers. Figures 3.9 and 3.11(b) give the MINITAB and MegaStat outputs of statistics describing the 100 waiting times.

FIGURE 3.8   **MINITAB Output of Statistics Describing the 65 Satisfaction Ratings (for Exercise 3.5)**

Variable	Count	Mean	StDev	Variance		
Ratings	65	42.954	2.642	6.982		

Variable	Minimum	Q1	Median	Q3	Maximum	Range
Ratings	36.000	41.000	43.000	45.000	48.000	12.000

FIGURE 3.9 MINITAB Output of Statistics Describing the 100 Waiting Times (for Exercise 3.6)

Variable	Count	Mean	StDev	Variance			
WaitTime	100	5.460	2.475	6.128			

Variable	Minimum	Q1	Median	Q3	Maximum	Range
WaitTime	0.400	3.800	5.250	7.200	11.600	11.200

FIGURE 3.10 MINITAB Output of Statistics Describing the 40 Breaking Strengths (for Exercise 3.7)

Variable	Count	Mean	StDev	Variance
Strength	40	50.575	1.644	2.702

Variable	Minimum	Q1	Median	Q3	Maximum	Range
Strength	46.800	49.425	50.650	51.650	54.000	7.200

FIGURE 3.11 MegaStat Outputs of Statistics Describing Three Data Sets (for Exercises 3.5, 3.6, and 3.7)

(a) Satisfaction rating statistics

Descriptive statistics

	Rating
count	65
mean	42.95
median	43.00
sample variance	6.98
sample standard deviation	2.64
minimum	36
maximum	48
range	12
empirical rule	
mean − 1s	40.31
mean + 1s	45.60
percent in interval (68.26%)	63.1%
mean − 2s	37.67
mean + 2s	48.24
percent in interval (95.44%)	98.5%
mean − 3s	35.03
mean + 3s	50.88
percent in interval (99.73%)	100.0%

(b) Waiting time statistics

Descriptive statistics

	WaitTime
count	100
mean	5.460
median	5.250
sample variance	6.128
sample standard deviation	2.475
minimum	0.4
maximum	11.6
range	11.2
empirical rule	
mean − 1s	2.985
mean + 1s	7.935
percent in interval (68.26%)	66.0%
mean − 2s	0.509
mean + 2s	10.411
percent in interval (95.44%)	96.0%
mean − 3s	−1.966
mean + 3s	12.886
percent in interval (99.73%)	100.0%

(c) Breaking strength statistics

Descriptive statistics

	Strength
count	40
mean	50.575
median	50.650
sample variance	2.702
sample standard deviation	1.644
minimum	46.8
maximum	54
range	7.2
empirical rule	
mean − 1s	48.931
mean + 1s	52.219
percent in interval (68.26%)	67.5%
mean − 2s	47.287
mean + 2s	53.863
percent in interval (95.44%)	95.0%
mean − 3s	45.644
mean + 3s	55.506
percent in interval (99.73%)	100.0%

a Find the sample mean on the outputs. Does the sample mean provide evidence that the mean of the population of all possible customer waiting times during peak business hours is less than six minutes (as is desired by the bank manager)? Explain your answer.

b Find the sample median on the outputs. How do the mean and median compare? What does the histogram in Figure 2.16 (page 67) tell you about why they compare this way?

3.7 THE TRASH BAG CASE ● TrashBag

Consider the trash bag problem. Suppose that an independent laboratory has tested 30-gallon trash bags and has found that none of the 30-gallon bags currently on the market has a mean breaking strength of 50 pounds or more. On the basis of these results, the producer of the new, improved trash bag feels sure that its 30-gallon bag will be the strongest such bag on the market if the new trash bag's mean breaking strength can be shown to be at least 50 pounds. Recall that Table 1.9 (page 16) presents the breaking strengths of 40 trash bags of the new type that were selected during a 40-hour pilot production run. Figures 3.10 and 3.11(c) give the MINITAB and MegaStat outputs of statistics describing the 40 breaking strengths.

a Find the sample mean on the outputs. Does the sample mean provide evidence that the mean of the population of all possible trash bag breaking strengths is at least 50 pounds? Explain your answer.

b Find the sample median on the outputs. How do the mean and median compare? What does the histogram in Figure 2.17 (page 67) tell you about why they compare this way?

| TABLE 3.2 | Data Comparing Lifestyles in the United States and Eight Other Countries |

LifeStyle

| | Voters | Income Tax | | | | Religion |
	Percentage Who Voted in Last National Election	Highest Personal National Rate	Video Rentals Per Capita per Year	PCs Per 100 People		Percentage of Households Who Attend Services Regularly
United States	49.1%	40%	13.8	35.0		51.6%
Germany	82.2	56	2.1	17.0		20.0
France	68.9	54	0.9	16.0		N.A.
Britain	71.5	40	3.3	20.0		23.6
Netherlands	78.3	60	1.8	20.0		28.9
Sweden	78.6	55	2.1	18.0		10.0
Italy	85.0	46	0.7	11.5		55.8
Japan	58.8	50	7.5	14.0		N.A.
South Korea	63.9	44	N.A.	N.A.		N.A.

N.A.—Not available.

Source: "America vs. the New Europe: By the Numbers," FORTUNE, December 21, 1998, vol. 138, no. 12/U.S. Edition/1999 INVESTOR'S GUIDE.

TABLE 3.3
Top 10 Websites in December 2006 as Rated by comScore Media Metrix

WebVisit

	Unique Visitors (Millions)
Yahoo! sites	131
Time Warner Network	121
Microsoft sites	117
Google sites	113
eBay	84
Fox Interactive Media	73
Amazon sites	57
Ask Network	56
Wal-Mart	44
Viacom Digital	40

3.8   Lauren is a college sophomore majoring in business. This semester Lauren is taking courses in accounting, economics, management information systems, public speaking, and statistics. The sizes of these classes are, respectively, 350, 45, 35, 25, and 40. Find the mean and the median of the class sizes. What is a better measure of Lauren's typical class size—the mean or the median?

Exercises 3.9 through 3.13 refer to information in Table 3.2, which gives data concerning lifestyles in the United States and eight other countries. In each exercise (a) compute the appropriate mean and median; (b) compare the mean and median and explain what they say about skewness; (c) construct a dot plot and discuss what the dot plot says about skewness and whether this agrees with how the mean and median compare; (d) discuss how the United States compares to the mean and median.   LifeStyle

3.9   Analyze the data concerning voters in Table 3.2 as described above.   LifeStyle

3.10   Analyze the data concerning income tax rates in Table 3.2 as described above.   LifeStyle

3.11   Analyze the data concerning video rentals in Table 3.2 as described above.   LifeStyle

3.12   Analyze the data concerning PCs in Table 3.2 as described above.   LifeStyle

3.13   Analyze the data concerning religion in Table 3.2 as described above.   LifeStyle

3.14   Table 3.3 gives the number of unique visitors during December 2006 to the top 10 websites as rated by comScore Media Metrix, a division of comScore Networks, Inc. Compute the mean and median for the website data and compare them. What do they say about skewness?   WebVisit

3.15   In 1998 the National Basketball Association (NBA) experienced a labor dispute that canceled almost half of the professional basketball season. The NBA owners, who were worried about escalating salaries because several star players had recently signed huge contracts, locked out the players and demanded that a salary cap be established. This led to discussion in the media about excessive player salaries. On October 30, 1998, an article titled "What does average salary really mean in the NBA?" by Jonathan Sills appeared in his Behind the Numbers column on the ESPN.com website. The article discussed the validity of some media claims about NBA player salaries. Figure 3.12 shows a frequency distribution of NBA salaries as presented in the Sills article. Use the frequency distribution to do the following:

a   Compare the mean, median, and mode of the salaries and explain the relationship. Note that the minimum NBA salary at the time of the lockout was $272,500.

b   Noting that 411 NBA players were under contract, estimate the percentages of players who earned more than the mean salary and who earned more than the median salary.

c   Below we give three quotes from news stories cited by Sills in his article. Comment on the validity of each statement.

"Last year, the NBA middle class made an average of $2.6 million. On that scale, I'd take the NBA lower class."—*Houston Chronicle*

"The players make an obscene amount of money—the median salary is well over $2 million!"—*St. Louis Post Dispatch*

"The players want us to believe they literally can't 'survive' on $2.6 million a year, the average salary in the NBA."—*Washington Post*

FIGURE 3.12
1997–1998 NBA Salaries

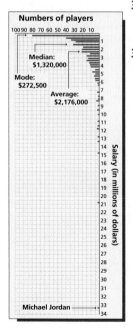

Source: Reprinted courtesy of ESPN.

3.2 Measures of Variation ● ● ●

Range, variance, and standard deviation   In addition to estimating a population's central tendency, it is important to estimate the **variation** of the population's individual values. For example, Figure 3.13 shows two histograms. Each portrays the distribution of 20 repair times (in days) for personal computers at a major service center. Because the mean (and median and mode) of each distribution equals four days, the measures of central tendency do not indicate any difference between the American and National Service Centers. However, the repair times for the American Service Center are clustered quite closely together, whereas the repair times for the National Service Center are spread farther apart (the repair time might be as little as one day, but it could also be as long as seven days). Therefore, we need measures of variation to express how the two distributions differ.

One way to measure the variation of a set of measurements is to calculate the *range*.

Consider a population or a sample of measurements. The **range** of the measurements is the largest measurement minus the smallest measurement.

In Figure 3.13, the smallest and largest repair times for the American Service Center are three days and five days; therefore, the range is $5 - 3 = 2$ days. On the other hand, the range for the National Service Center is $7 - 1 = 6$ days. The National Service Center's larger range indicates that this service center's repair times exhibit more variation.

In general, the range is not the best measure of a data set's variation. One reason is that it is based on only the smallest and largest measurements in the data set and therefore may reflect an extreme measurement that is not entirely representative of the data set's variation. For example, in the marketing research case, the smallest and largest ratings in the sample of 60 bottle design ratings are 20 and 35. However, to simply estimate that most bottle design ratings are between 20 and 35 misses the fact that 57, or 95 percent, of the 60 ratings are at least as large as the minimum rating of 25 for a successful bottle design. In general, to fully describe a population's variation, it is useful to estimate intervals that contain **different percentages** (for example, 70 percent, 95 percent, or almost 100 percent) of the individual population values. To estimate such intervals, we use the **population variance** and the **population standard deviation.**

The Population Variance and Standard Deviation

The **population variance** σ^2 (pronounced *sigma squared*) is the average of the squared deviations of the individual population measurements from the population mean μ.

The **population standard deviation** σ (pronounced *sigma*) is the positive square root of the population variance.

For example, consider again the population of Chris's class sizes this semester. These class sizes are 60, 41, 15, 30, and 34. To calculate the variance and standard deviation of these class sizes,

F I G U R E   3 . 1 3   **Repair Times for Personal Computers at Two Service Centers**

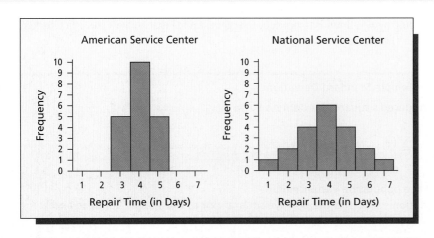

we first calculate the population mean to be

$$\mu = \frac{60 + 41 + 15 + 30 + 34}{5} = \frac{180}{5} = 36$$

Next, we calculate the deviations of the individual population measurements from the population mean $\mu = 36$ as follows:

$$(60 - 36) = 24 \quad (41 - 36) = 5 \quad (15 - 36) = -21 \quad (30 - 36) = -6 \quad (34 - 36) = -2$$

Then we compute the sum of the squares of these deviations:

$$(24)^2 + (5)^2 + (-21)^2 + (-6)^2 + (-2)^2 = 576 + 25 + 441 + 36 + 4 = 1082$$

Finally, we calculate the population variance σ^2, the average of the squared deviations, by dividing the sum of the squared deviations, 1,082, by the number of squared deviations, 5. That is, σ^2 equals $1,082/5 = 216.4$. Furthermore, this implies that the population standard deviation σ—the positive square root of σ^2—is $\sqrt{216.4} = 14.71$.

To see that the variance and standard deviation measure the variation, or spread, of the individual population measurements, suppose that the measurements are spread far apart. Then, many measurements will be far from the mean μ, many of the squared deviations from the mean will be large, and the sum of squared deviations will be large. It follows that the average of the squared deviations—the population variance—will be relatively large. On the other hand, if the population measurements are clustered close together, many measurements will be close to μ, many of the squared deviations from the mean will be small, and the average of the squared deviations—the population variance—will be small. Therefore, the more spread out the population measurements, the larger is the population variance, and the larger is the population standard deviation.

To further understand the population variance and standard deviation, note that one reason we square the deviations of the individual population measurements from the population mean is that the sum of the raw deviations themselves is zero. This is because the negative deviations cancel the positive deviations. For example, in the class size situation, the raw deviations are 24, 5, −21, −6, and −2, which sum to zero. Of course, we could make the deviations positive by finding their absolute values. We square the deviations instead because the resulting population variance and standard deviation have many important interpretations that we study throughout this book. Since the population variance is an average of squared deviations of the original population values, the variance is expressed in squared units of the original population values. On the other hand, the population standard deviation—the square root of the population variance—is expressed in the same units as the original population values. For example, the previously discussed class sizes are expressed in numbers of students. Therefore, the variance of these class sizes is $\sigma^2 = 216.4$ (students)^2, whereas the standard deviation is $\sigma = 14.71$ students. Since the population standard deviation is expressed in the same units as the population values, it is more often used to make practical interpretations about the variation of these values.

When a population is too large to measure all the population units, we estimate the population variance and the population standard deviation by the **sample variance** and the **sample standard deviation.** We calculate the sample variance by dividing the sum of the squared deviations of the sample measurements from the sample mean by $n - 1$, the sample size minus 1. Although we might intuitively think that we should divide by n rather than $n - 1$, it can be shown that dividing by n tends to produce an estimate of the population variance that is too small. On the other hand, dividing by $n - 1$ tends to produce a larger estimate that we will show in Chapter 7 is more appropriate. Therefore, we obtain:

The Sample Variance and the Sample Standard Deviation

The **sample variance** s^2 (pronounced *s squared*) is defined to be

$$s^2 = \frac{\sum_{i=1}^{n}(x_i - \bar{x})^2}{n - 1} = \frac{(x_1 - \bar{x})^2 + (x_2 - \bar{x})^2 + \cdots + (x_n - \bar{x})^2}{n - 1}$$

and is the **point estimate of the population variance** σ^2.

The **sample standard deviation** $s = \sqrt{s^2}$ is the positive square root of the sample variance and is the **point estimate of the population standard deviation** σ.

EXAMPLE 3.7 The Car Mileage Case   Ⓒ

To illustrate the calculation of the sample variance and standard deviation, we begin by considering the first five mileages in Table 3.1 (page 117): $x_1 = 30.8$, $x_2 = 31.7$, $x_3 = 30.1$, $x_4 = 31.6$, and $x_5 = 32.1$. Since the mean of these five mileages is $\bar{x} = 31.26$, it follows that

$$\sum_{i=1}^{5}(x_i - \bar{x})^2 = (x_1 - \bar{x})^2 + (x_2 - \bar{x})^2 + (x_3 - \bar{x})^2 + (x_4 - \bar{x})^2 + (x_5 - \bar{x})^2$$

$$= (30.8 - 31.26)^2 + (31.7 - 31.26)^2 + (30.1 - 31.26)^2$$
$$+ (31.6 - 31.26)^2 + (32.1 - 31.26)^2$$
$$= (-.46)^2 + (.44)^2 + (-1.16)^2 + (.34)^2 + (.84)^2$$
$$= 2.572$$

Therefore, the variance and the standard deviation of the sample of the first five mileages are

$$s^2 = \frac{2.572}{5-1} = .643 \quad \text{and} \quad s = \sqrt{.643} = .8019$$

Of course, intuitively, we are likely to obtain more accurate point estimates of the population variance and standard deviation by using all the available sample information. Recall that the mean of all 50 mileages is $\bar{x} = 31.56$. Using this sample mean, it can be verified that

$$\sum_{i=1}^{50}(x_i - \bar{x})^2 = (x_1 - \bar{x})^2 + (x_2 - \bar{x})^2 + \cdots + (x_{50} - \bar{x})^2$$

$$= (30.8 - 31.56)^2 + (31.7 - 31.56)^2 + \cdots + (31.4 - 31.56)^2$$
$$= (-.76)^2 + (.14)^2 + \cdots + (-.16)^2$$
$$= 31.18$$

Therefore, the variance and the standard deviation of the sample of 50 mileages are

$$s^2 = \frac{31.18}{50-1} = .6363 \quad \text{and} \quad s = \sqrt{.6363} = .7977$$

Notice that the MegaStat output in Figure 3.1 (page 118) gives these quantities rounded to three decimal places. Here $s^2 = .636$ and $s = .798$ are the point estimates of the variance, σ^2, and the standard deviation, σ, of the population of the mileages of all the cars that will be or could potentially be produced. Furthermore, the sample standard deviation is expressed in the same units as the sample values. Therefore $s = .798$ mpg.

Before explaining how we can use s^2 and s in a practical way, we present a formula that makes it easier to compute s^2. This formula is useful when we are using a handheld calculator that is not equipped with a statistics mode to compute s^2.

The **sample variance** can be calculated using the *computational formula*

$$s^2 = \frac{1}{n-1}\left[\sum_{i=1}^{n}x_i^2 - \frac{\left(\sum_{i=1}^{n}x_i\right)^2}{n}\right]$$

EXAMPLE 3.8 The Payment Time Case   Ⓒ

Consider the sample of 65 payment times in Table 2.4 (page 56). Using these data, it can be verified that

$$\sum_{i=1}^{65}x_i = x_1 + x_2 + \cdots + x_{65} = 22 + 19 + \cdots + 21 = 1,177 \quad \text{and}$$

$$\sum_{i=1}^{65}x_i^2 = x_1^2 + x_2^2 + \cdots + x_{65}^2 = (22)^2 + (19)^2 + \cdots + (21)^2 = 22,317$$

Therefore,

$$s^2 = \frac{1}{(65-1)}\left[22{,}317 - \frac{(1{,}177)^2}{65}\right] = \frac{1{,}004.2464}{64} = 15.69135$$

and $s = \sqrt{s^2} = \sqrt{15.69135} = 3.9612$ days (see the MINITAB output in Figure 3.7 on page 121).

A practical interpretation of the standard deviation: the Empirical Rule   One type of relative frequency curve describing a population is the *normal curve,* which is discussed in Chapter 6. The normal curve is a symmetrical, bell-shaped curve and is illustrated in Figure 3.14(a). If a population is described by a normal curve, we say that the population is normally distributed, and the following result can be shown to hold.

The Empirical Rule for a Normally Distributed Population

If a population has **mean μ** and **standard deviation σ** and is **described by a normal curve,** then, as illustrated in Figure 3.14(a),

1 68.26 percent of the population measurements are within (plus or minus) one standard deviation of the mean and thus lie in the interval $[\mu - \sigma, \mu + \sigma] = [\mu \pm \sigma]$

2 95.44 percent of the population measurements are within (plus or minus) two standard devi-

ations of the mean and thus lie in the interval $[\mu - 2\sigma, \mu + 2\sigma] = [\mu \pm 2\sigma]$

3 99.73 percent of the population measurements are within (plus or minus) three standard deviations of the mean and thus lie in the interval $[\mu - 3\sigma, \mu + 3\sigma] = [\mu \pm 3\sigma]$

FIGURE 3.14   **The Empirical Rule and Tolerance Intervals**

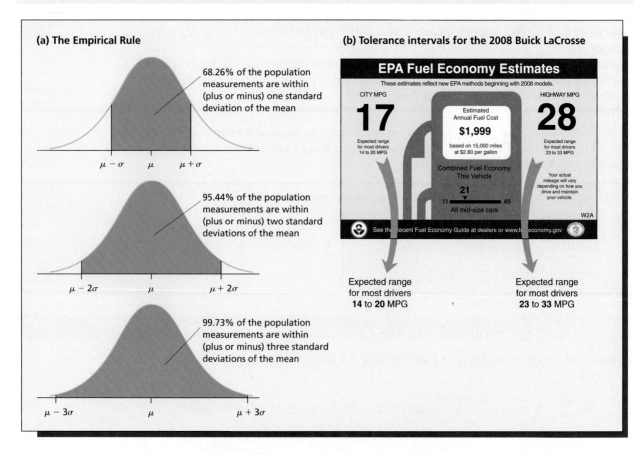

In general, an interval that contains a specified percentage of the individual measurements in a population is called a **tolerance interval.** It follows that the one, two, and three standard deviation intervals around μ given in (1), (2), and (3) are tolerance intervals containing, respectively, 68.26 percent, 95.44 percent, and 99.73 percent of the measurements in a normally distributed population. Often we interpret the *three-sigma interval* $[\mu \pm 3\sigma]$ to be a tolerance interval that contains *almost all* of the measurements in a normally distributed population. Of course, we usually do not know the true values of μ and σ. Therefore, we must estimate the tolerance intervals by replacing μ and σ in these intervals by the mean $\bar{x}$ and standard deviation s of a sample that has been randomly selected from the normally distributed population.

EXAMPLE 3.9 The Car Mileage Case

Again consider the sample of 50 mileages. We have seen that $\bar{x} = 31.56$ and $s = .798$ for this sample are the point estimates of the mean μ and the standard deviation σ of the population of all mileages. Furthermore, the MegaStat output in Figure 3.15 of a histogram of the 50 mileages suggests that the population of all mileages is normally distributed. To more simply illustrate the Empirical Rule, we will round $\bar{x}$ to 31.6 and s to .8. It follows that, using the interval

1   $[\bar{x} \pm s] = [31.6 \pm .8] = [31.6 - .8, 31.6 + .8] = [30.8, 32.4]$, we estimate that 68.26 percent of all individual cars will obtain mileages between 30.8 mpg and 32.4 mpg.

2   $[\bar{x} \pm 2s] = [31.6 \pm 2(.8)] = [31.6 \pm 1.6] = [30.0, 33.2]$, we estimate that 95.44 percent of all individual cars will obtain mileages between 30.0 mpg and 33.2 mpg.

3   $[\bar{x} \pm 3s] = [31.6 \pm 3(.8)] = [31.6 \pm 2.4] = [29.2, 34.0]$, we estimate that 99.73 percent of all individual cars will obtain mileages between 29.2 mpg and 34.0 mpg.

FIGURE 3.15   **Estimated Tolerance Intervals in the Car Mileage Case**

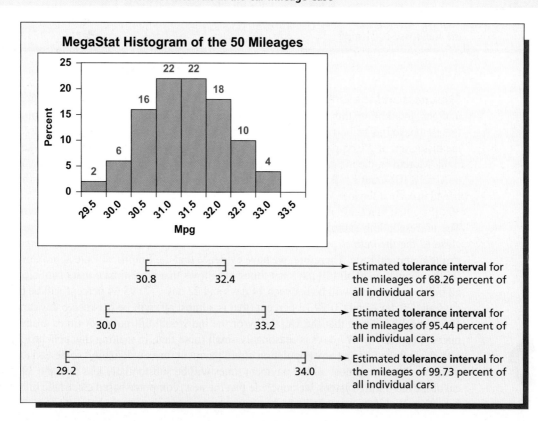

Figure 3.15 depicts these estimated tolerance intervals, which are shown below the MegaStat histogram. Since the difference between the upper and lower limits of each estimated tolerance interval is fairly small, we might conclude that the variability of the individual car mileages around the estimated mean mileage of 31.6 mpg is fairly small. Furthermore, the interval $[\bar{x} \pm 3s] = [29.2, 34.0]$ implies that almost any individual car that a customer might purchase this year will obtain a mileage between 29.2 mpg and 34.0 mpg.

Before continuing, recall that we have rounded $\bar{x}$ and s to one decimal point accuracy in order to simplify our initial example of the Empirical Rule. If, instead, we calculate the Empirical Rule intervals by using $\bar{x} = 31.56$ and $s = .798$ and then round the interval endpoints to one decimal place accuracy at the end of the calculations, we obtain the same intervals as obtained above. In general, however, rounding intermediate calculated results can lead to inaccurate final results. Because of this, throughout this book we will avoid greatly rounding intermediate results.

We next note that if we actually count the number of the 50 mileages in Table 3.1 that are contained in each of the intervals $[\bar{x} \pm s] = [30.8, 32.4]$, $[\bar{x} \pm 2s] = [30.0, 33.2]$, and $[\bar{x} \pm 3s] = [29.2, 34.0]$, we find that these intervals contain, respectively, 34, 48, and 50 of the 50 mileages. The corresponding sample percentages—68 percent, 96 percent, and 100 percent—are close to the theoretical percentages—68.26 percent, 95.44 percent, and 99.73 percent—that apply to a normally distributed population. This is further evidence that the population of all mileages is (approximately) normally distributed and thus that the Empirical Rule holds for this population.

To conclude this example, we note that the automaker has studied the combined city and highway mileages of the new model because the federal tax credit is based on these combined mileages. When reporting fuel economy estimates for a particular car model to the public, however, the EPA realizes that the proportions of city and highway driving vary from purchaser to purchaser. Therefore, the EPA reports both a combined mileage estimate and separate city and highway mileage estimates to the public. Figure 3.14(b) presents a window sticker that summarizes these estimates for the 2008 Buick LaCrosse equipped with a six-cylinder engine and an automatic transmission. The city mpg of 17 and the highway mpg of 28 given at the top of the sticker are point estimates of, respectively, the mean city mileage and the mean highway mileage that would be obtained by all such 2008 LaCrosses. The expected city range of 14 to 20 mpg says that most LaCrosses will get between 14 mpg and 20 mpg in city driving. The expected highway range of 23 to 33 mpg says that most LaCrosses will get between 23 mpg and 33 mpg in highway driving. The combined city and highway mileage estimate for the LaCrosse is 21 mpg.

Skewness and the Empirical Rule   The Empirical Rule holds for normally distributed populations. In addition, this rule also approximately holds for populations having **mound-shaped** (single-peaked) distributions that are not very skewed to the right or left. For example, note that the histogram of the 65 payment times in Figure 3.16 is somewhat but not highly skewed to the right. Moreover, the mean and the standard deviation of the payment times can be calculated to be $\bar{x} = 18.1077$ and $s = 3.9612$. If we actually count the number of payment times that are contained in each of the intervals $[\bar{x} \pm s] = [14.1, 22.1]$, $[\bar{x} \pm 2s] = [10.2, 26.0]$, and $[\bar{x} \pm 3s] = [6.2, 30.0]$, we find that these intervals contain, respectively, 45, 62, and 65 of the 65 payment times. The corresponding sample percentages—69.23 percent, 95.38 percent, and 100 percent—are close to the theoretical percentages—68.26 percent, 95.44 percent, and 99.73 percent—given by the Empirical Rule. Therefore, we have evidence that the Empirical Rule approximately holds for the population of all bill payment times. It follows that we estimate that (1) 68.26 percent of all bill payment times will be between 14 days and 22 days, (2) 95.44 percent will be between 10 days and 26 days, and (3) 99.73 percent (that is, almost all) will be between 6 days and 30 days. These results indicate that the variability of the individual bill payment times around the estimated mean of 18.1077 days is reasonably small (note that, in making this conclusion, we take into account the fact that any population of bill payment times will exhibit some variability). Furthermore, because almost all bill payment times will be substantially less than the 39 days typical of the old billing system, we conclude that the new, computer-based electronic billing system is a substantial improvement.

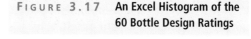

FIGURE 3.16   A MINITAB Histogram of
              the 65 Payment Times

FIGURE 3.17   An Excel Histogram of the
              60 Bottle Design Ratings

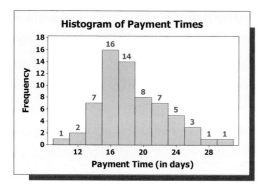

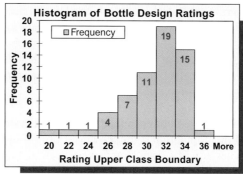

In some situations, the skewness of a mound-shaped distribution of population measurements can make it tricky to know whether to use the Empirical Rule. For example, we previously concluded that the histogram of the 60 bottle design ratings in Figure 3.17 is somewhat but not highly skewed to the left. The mean and the standard deviation of the 60 bottle design ratings are $\bar{x} = 30.35$ and $s = 3.1073$. If we actually count the number of ratings contained in each of the intervals $[\bar{x} \pm s] = [27.2, 33.5]$, $[\bar{x} \pm 2s] = [24.1, 36.6]$, and $[\bar{x} \pm 3s] = [21, 39.7]$, we find that these intervals contain, respectively, 44, 57, and 59 of the 60 ratings. The corresponding sample percentages—73.33 percent, 95 percent, and 98.33 percent—are, respectively, greater than, approximately equal to, and less than the theoretical percentages—68.26 percent, 95.44 percent, and 99.73 percent—given by the Empirical Rule. Specifically, the interval $[\bar{x} \pm s] = [27.2, 33.5]$ contains 5 percent more than the theoretical 68.26 percent of the ratings, and the interval $[\bar{x} \pm 3s] = [21, 39.7]$ contains less than the theoretical 99.73 percent of the ratings (it does not contain the lowest rating of 20). We conclude that the distribution of the ratings seems to be too skewed for the Empirical Rule to hold extremely well. In this situation it is probably best to describe the variation of the ratings by using **percentiles,** which are discussed in the next section.

Chebyshev's Theorem   If we fear that the Empirical Rule does not hold for a particular population, we can consider using **Chebyshev's Theorem** to find an interval that contains a specified percentage of the individual measurements in the population. Although Chebyshev's Theorem technically applies to any population, we will see that it is not as practically useful as we might hope.

Chebyshev's Theorem

Consider any population that has mean μ and standard deviation σ. Then, for any value of k greater than 1, at least $100(1 - 1/k^2)\%$ of the population measurements lie in the interval $[\mu \pm k\sigma]$.

For example, if we choose k equal to 2, then at least $100(1 - 1/2^2)\% = 100(3/4)\% = 75\%$ of the population measurements lie in the interval $[\mu \pm 2\sigma]$. As another example, if we choose k equal to 3, then at least $100(1 - 1/3^2)\% = 100(8/9)\% = 88.89\%$ of the population measurements lie in the interval $[\mu \pm 3\sigma]$. As yet a third example, suppose that we wish to find an interval containing at least 99.73 percent of all population measurements. Here we would set $100(1 - 1/k^2)\%$ equal to 99.73%, which implies that $(1 - 1/k^2) = .9973$. If we solve for k, we find that $k = 19.25$. This says that at least 99.73 percent of all population measurements lie in the interval $[\mu \pm 19.25\sigma]$. Unless σ is extremely small, this interval will be so long that it will tell us very little about where the population measurements lie. We conclude that Chebyshev's Theorem can help us find an interval that contains a reasonably high percentage (such as 75 percent or 88.89 percent) of all population measurements. However, unless σ is extremely small, Chebyshev's Theorem will not provide a useful interval that contains almost all (say, 99.73 percent) of the population measurements.

CHAPTER 3

Although Chebyshev's Theorem technically applies to any population, it is only of practical use when analyzing a **non-mound-shaped** (for example, a double-peaked) **population that is not *very* skewed to the right or left.** Why is this? First, **we would not use Chebyshev's Theorem to describe a mound-shaped population that is not very skewed because we can use the Empirical Rule** to do this. In fact, the Empirical Rule is better for such a population because it gives us a shorter interval that will contain a given percentage of measurements. For example, if the Empirical Rule can be used to describe a population, the interval $[\mu \pm 3\sigma]$ will contain 99.73 percent of all measurements. On the other hand, if we use Chebyshev's Theorem, the interval $[\mu \pm 19.25\sigma]$ is needed. As another example, the Empirical Rule tells us that 95.44 percent of all measurements lie in the interval $[\mu \pm 2\sigma]$, whereas Chebyshev's Theorem tells us only that at least 75 percent of all measurements lie in this interval.

It is also not appropriate to use Chebyshev's Theorem—or any other result making use of the population standard deviation σ—to describe a population that is very skewed. This is because, if a population is very skewed, the measurements in the long tail to the left or right will inflate σ. This implies that tolerance intervals calculated using σ will be so long that they are of little use. In this case, it is best to measure variation by using **percentiles,** which are discussed in the next section.

***z*-scores**   We can determine the relative location of any value in a population or sample by using the mean and standard deviation to compute the value's *z*-score. For any value x in a population or sample, the ***z*-score** corresponding to x is defined as follows:

---

z-score:

$$z = \frac{x - \text{mean}}{\text{standard deviation}}$$

The *z*-score, which is also called the *standardized value,* is the number of standard deviations that x is from the mean. A positive *z*-score says that x is above (greater than) the mean, while a negative *z*-score says that x is below (less than) the mean. For instance, a *z*-score equal to 2.3 says that x is 2.3 standard deviations above the mean. Similarly, a *z*-score equal to -1.68 says that x is 1.68 standard deviations below the mean. A *z*-score equal to zero says that x equals the mean.

A *z*-score indicates the relative location of a value within a population or sample. For example, below we calculate the *z*-scores for each of the profit margins for five of the best big companies in America as rated by *Forbes* magazine on its website on March 25, 2005.[2] For these five companies, the mean profit margin is 10% and the standard deviation is 3.406%.

Company	Profit Margin, x	x − mean	z-score
Black & Decker	8%	8 − 10 = −2	−2/3.406 = −.59
Washington Post	10	10 − 10 = 0	0/3.406 = 0
Texas Instruments	15	15 − 10 = 5	5/3.406 = 1.47
Clorox	12	12 − 10 = 2	2/3.406 = .59
Foot Locker	5	5 − 10 = −5	−5/3.406 = −1.47

These *z*-scores tell us that the profit margin for Texas Instruments is the farthest above the mean. More specifically, this profit margin is 1.47 standard deviations above the mean. The profit margin for Foot Locker is the farthest below the mean—it is 1.47 standard deviations below the mean. Since the *z*-score for the Washington Post equals zero, its profit margin equals the mean.

Values in two different populations or samples having the same *z*-score are the same number of standard deviations from their respective means and, therefore, have the same relative locations. For example, suppose that the mean score on the midterm exam for students in Section A of a statistics course is 65 and the standard deviation of the scores is 10. Meanwhile, the mean score on the same exam for students in Section B is 80 and the standard deviation is 5. A student in Section A who scores an 85 and a student in Section B who scores a 90 have the same relative locations within their respective sections because their *z*-scores, $(85 - 65)/10 = 2$ and $(90 - 80)/5 = 2$, are equal.

---

[2]Source: *Forbes*, 3/16/05. © 2005 Forbes, Inc. Reprinted with permission.

The coefficient of variation Sometimes we need to measure the size of the standard deviation of a population or sample relative to the size of the population or sample mean. The **coefficient of variation,** which makes this comparison, is defined for a population or sample as follows:

$$\text{coefficient of variation} = \frac{\text{standard deviation}}{\text{mean}} \times 100$$

The coefficient of variation compares populations or samples having different means and different standard deviations. For example, Morningstar.com[3] gives the mean and standard deviation[4] of the returns for each of the Morningstar Top 25 Large Growth Funds. As given on the Morningstar website, the mean return for the Strong Advisor Select A fund is 10.39 percent with a standard deviation of 16.18 percent, while the mean return for the Nations Marisco 21st Century fund is 17.7 percent with a standard deviation of 15.81 percent. It follows that the coefficient of variation for the Strong Advisor fund is $(16.18/10.39) \times 100 = 155.73$, and that the coefficient of variation for the Nations Marisco fund is $(15.81/17.7) \times 100 = 89.32$. This tells us that, for the Strong Advisor fund, the standard deviation is 155.73 percent of the value of its mean return. For the Nations Marisco fund, the standard deviation is 89.32 percent of the value of its mean return.

In the context of situations like the stock fund comparison, the coefficient of variation is often used as a measure of *risk* because it measures the variation of the returns (the standard deviation) relative to the size of the mean return. For instance, although the Strong Advisor fund and the Nations Marisco fund have comparable standard deviations (16.18 percent versus 15.81 percent), the Strong Advisor fund has a higher coefficient of variation than does the Nations Marisco fund (155.73 versus 89.32). This says that, *relative to the mean return,* the variation in returns for the Strong Advisor fund is higher. That is, we would conclude that investing in the Strong Advisor fund is riskier than investing in the Nations Marisco fund.

Exercises for Section 3.2

CONCEPTS

3.16 Define the range, variance, and standard deviation for a population.

3.17 Discuss how the variance and the standard deviation measure variation.

3.18 The Empirical Rule for a normally distributed population and Chebyshev's Theorem have the same basic purpose. In your own words, explain what this purpose is.

METHODS AND APPLICATIONS

3.19 Consider the following population of five numbers: 5, 8, 10, 12, 15. Calculate the range, variance, and standard deviation of this population.

3.20 Table 3.4 gives the percentage of homes sold during the fourth quarter of 2006 that a median income household could afford to purchase at the prevailing mortgage interest rate for six Texas metropolitan areas. The data were compiled by the National Association of Home Builders. Calculate the range, variance, and standard deviation of this population of affordability percentages. 🌑 HouseAff

3.21 Table 3.5 gives data concerning the top 10 U.S. airlines (ranked by revenue) as listed on the *Fortune* magazine website on April 27, 2007. 🌑 AirRev
   a Calculate the population range, variance, and standard deviation of the 10 revenues and of the 10 profits (note that negative values are losses rather than profits).
   b Using the population of profits, compute and interpret the *z*-score for each airline.

3.22 In order to control costs, a company wishes to study the amount of money its sales force spends entertaining clients. The following is a random sample of six entertainment expenses (dinner costs for four people) from expense reports submitted by members of the sales force. 🌑 DinnerCost

$157 $132 $109 $145 $125 $139

[3]Source: http://poweredby.morningstar.com/Selectors/AolTop25/AolTop25List.html, March 17, 2005.
[4]Annualized return based on the last 36 monthly returns.

TABLE 3.4	Housing Affordability in Texas ● HouseAff
Metro Area	**Percentage**
Austin–Round Rock	57.5
Dallas–Plano–Irving^^^	61.7
El Paso	32.5
Fort Worth–Arlington^^^	67.4
Houston–Sugar Land–Baytown	55.7
San Antonio	49.2

^^^ Indicate metropolitan divisions. All others are metropolitan statistical areas.

Data compiled by National Association of Home Builders, http//www.nabb.org/

TABLE 3.5	The Top 10 Airlines (Ranked by Revenue) in 2006 ● AirRev	
Airline	**Revenue ($ billions)**	**Profits ($ millions)**
American Airlines	22.6	231
United Airlines	19.3	22,876
Delta Air Lines	17.2	−6,203
Continental Airlines	13.1	343
Northwest Airlines	12.6	−2,835
US Airways Group	11.6	304
Southwest Airlines	9.1	499
Alaska Air Group	3.3	−53
SkyWest	3.1	146
Jetblue Airways	2.4	−1

Source: *Fortune* 500, April 27, 2007,
http://money.cnn.com/magazines/fortune500/2007/industries/Airlines/1.html

a Calculate $\bar{x}$, s^2, and s for the expense data. In addition, show that the two different formulas for calculating s^2 give the same result.

b Assuming that the distribution of entertainment expenses is approximately normally distributed, calculate estimates of tolerance intervals containing 68.26 percent, 95.44 percent, and 99.73 percent of all entertainment expenses by the sales force.

c If a member of the sales force submits an entertainment expense (dinner cost for four) of $190, should this expense be considered unusually high (and possibly worthy of investigation by the company)? Explain your answer.

d Compute and interpret the z-score for each of the six entertainment expenses.

3.23   THE TRASH BAG CASE   ● TrashBag

The mean and the standard deviation of the sample of 40 trash bag breaking strengths are $\bar{x} = 50.575$ and $s = 1.6438$.

a What does the histogram in Figure 2.17 (page 67) say about whether the Empirical Rule should be used to describe the trash bag breaking strengths?

b Use the Empirical Rule to calculate estimates of tolerance intervals containing 68.26 percent, 95.44 percent, and 99.73 percent of all possible trash bag breaking strengths.

c Does the estimate of a tolerance interval containing 99.73 percent of all breaking strengths provide evidence that almost any bag a customer might purchase will have a breaking strength that exceeds 45 pounds? Explain your answer.

d How do the percentages of the 40 breaking strengths in Table 1.9 (page 16) that actually fall into the intervals $[\bar{x} \pm s]$, $[\bar{x} \pm 2s]$, and $[\bar{x} \pm 3s]$ compare to those given by the Empirical Rule? Do these comparisons indicate that the statistical inferences you made in parts b and c are reasonably valid?

3.24   THE BANK CUSTOMER WAITING TIME CASE   ● WaitTime

The mean and the standard deviation of the sample of 100 bank customer waiting times are $\bar{x} = 5.46$ and $s = 2.475$.

a What does the histogram in Figure 2.16 (page 67) say about whether the Empirical Rule should be used to describe the bank customer waiting times?

b Use the Empirical Rule to calculate estimates of tolerance intervals containing 68.26 percent, 95.44 percent, and 99.73 percent of all possible bank customer waiting times.

c Does the estimate of a tolerance interval containing 68.26 percent of all waiting times provide evidence that at least two-thirds of all customers will have to wait less than eight minutes for service? Explain your answer.

d How do the percentages of the 100 waiting times in Table 1.8 (page 14) that actually fall into the intervals $[\bar{x} \pm s]$, $[\bar{x} \pm 2s]$, and $[\bar{x} \pm 3s]$ compare to those given by the Empirical Rule? Do these comparisons indicate that the statistical inferences you made in parts b and c are reasonably valid?

3.25   THE VIDEO GAME SATISFACTION RATING CASE   ● VideoGame

The mean and the standard deviation of the sample of 65 customer satisfaction ratings are $\bar{x} = 42.95$ and $s = 2.6424$.

a What does the histogram in Figure 2.15 (page 66) say about whether the Empirical Rule should be used to describe the satisfaction ratings?

b Use the Empirical Rule to calculate estimates of tolerance intervals containing 68.26 percent, 95.44 percent, and 99.73 percent of all possible satisfaction ratings.

c Does the estimate of a tolerance interval containing 99.73 percent of all satisfaction ratings provide evidence that 99.73 percent of all customers will give a satisfaction rating for the XYZ-Box game system that is at least 35 (the minimal rating of a "satisfied" customer)? Explain your answer.

d How do the percentages of the 65 customer satisfaction ratings in Table 1.7 (page 14) that actually fall into the intervals $[\bar{x} \pm s], [\bar{x} \pm 2s],$ and $[\bar{x} \pm 3s]$ compare to those given by the Empirical Rule? Do these comparisons indicate that the statistical inferences you made in parts b and c are reasonably valid?

3.26 Consider the 63 automatic teller machine (ATM) transaction times given in Table 3.6 below.

a Construct a histogram (or a stem-and-leaf display) for the 63 ATM transaction times. Describe the shape of the distribution of transaction times.   ● ATMTime

b When we compute the sample mean and sample standard deviation for the transaction times, we find that $\bar{x} = 36.56$ and $s = 4.475$. Compute each of the intervals $[\bar{x} \pm s], [\bar{x} \pm 2s],$ and $[\bar{x} \pm 3s]$. Then count the number of transaction times that actually fall into each interval and find the percentage of transaction times that actually fall into each interval.

c How do the percentages of transaction times that fall into the intervals $[\bar{x} \pm s], [\bar{x} \pm 2s],$ and $[\bar{x} \pm 3s]$ compare to those given by the Empirical Rule? How do the percentages of transaction times that fall into the intervals $[\bar{x} \pm 2s]$ and $[\bar{x} \pm 3s]$ compare to those given by Chebyshev's Theorem?

d Explain why the Empirical Rule does not describe the transaction times extremely well.

3.27 The Morningstar Top Fund lists at the Morningstar.com website give the mean yearly return and the standard deviation of the returns for each of the listed funds. As given by Morningstar.com on March 17, 2005, the RS Internet Age Fund has a mean yearly return of 10.93 percent with a standard deviation of 41.96 percent; the Franklin Income A fund has a mean yearly return of 13 percent with a standard deviation of 9.36 percent; the Jacob Internet fund has a mean yearly return of 34.45 percent with a standard deviation of 41.16 percent.

a For each mutual fund, find an interval in which you would expect 95.44 percent of all yearly returns to fall. Assume returns are normally distributed.

b Using the intervals you computed in part a, compare the three mutual funds with respect to average yearly returns and with respect to variability of returns.

c Calculate the coefficient of variation for each mutual fund, and use your results to compare the funds with respect to risk. Which fund is riskiest?

TABLE 3.6   **ATM Transaction Times (in Seconds) for 63 Withdrawals**   ● ATMTime

Transaction	Time	Transaction	Time	Transaction	Time
1	32	22	34	43	37
2	32	23	32	44	32
3	41	24	34	45	33
4	51	25	35	46	33
5	42	26	33	47	40
6	39	27	42	48	35
7	33	28	46	49	33
8	43	29	52	50	39
9	35	30	36	51	34
10	33	31	37	52	34
11	33	32	32	53	33
12	32	33	39	54	38
13	42	34	36	55	41
14	34	35	41	56	34
15	37	36	32	57	35
16	37	37	33	58	35
17	33	38	34	59	37
18	35	39	38	60	39
19	40	40	32	61	44
20	36	41	35	62	40
21	32	42	33	63	39

3.3 Percentiles, Quartiles, and Box-and-Whiskers Displays ● ● ●

Percentiles, quartiles, and five-number displays   In this section we consider **percentiles** and their applications. We begin by defining the **pth percentile.**

> For a set of measurements arranged in increasing order, the **pth percentile** is a value such that p percent of the measurements fall at or below the value, and $(100 - p)$ percent of the measurements fall at or above the value.

There are various procedures for calculating percentiles. **One procedure for calculating the pth percentile for a set of n measurements uses the following three steps:**

Step 1:   Arrange the measurements in increasing order.

Step 2:   Calculate the index

$$i = \left(\frac{p}{100}\right)n$$

Step 3:   (a) If i is not an integer, round up to obtain the next integer greater than i. This integer denotes the position of the pth percentile in the ordered arrangement.

          (b) If i is an integer, the pth percentile is the average of the measurements in positions i and $i + 1$ in the ordered arrangement.

To illustrate the calculation and interpretation of percentiles, recall in the household income case that an economist has randomly selected a sample of $n = 12$ households from a midwestern city and has determined last year's income for each household. In order to assess the variation of the population of household incomes in the city, we will calculate various percentiles for the sample of incomes. Specifically, we will calculate the 10th, 25th, 50th, 75th, and 90th percentiles of these incomes. The first step is to arrange the incomes in increasing order as follows:

7,524   11,070   18,211   26,817   36,551   41,286

49,312   57,283   72,814   90,416   135,540   190,250

To find the 10th percentile, we calculate (in step 2) the index

$$i = \left(\frac{p}{100}\right)n = \left(\frac{10}{100}\right)12 = 1.2$$

Because $i = 1.2$ is not an integer, step 3(a) says to round $i = 1.2$ up to 2. It follows that the 10th percentile is the income in position 2 in the ordered arrangement—that is, 11,070. To find the 25th percentile, we calculate the index

$$i = \left(\frac{p}{100}\right)n = \left(\frac{25}{100}\right)12 = 3$$

Because $i = 3$ is an integer, step 3(b) says that the 25th percentile is the average of the incomes in positions 3 and 4 in the ordered arrangement—that is, $(18{,}211 + 26{,}817)/2 = 22{,}514$. To find the 50th percentile, we calculate the index

$$i = \left(\frac{p}{100}\right)n = \left(\frac{50}{100}\right)12 = 6$$

Because $i = 6$ is an integer, step 3(b) says that the 50th percentile is the average of the incomes in positions 6 and 7 in the ordered arrangement—that is, $(41{,}286 + 49{,}312)/2 = 45{,}299$. To find the 75th percentile, we calculate the index

$$i = \left(\frac{p}{100}\right)n = \left(\frac{75}{100}\right)12 = 9$$

Because $i = 9$ is an integer, step 3(b) says that the 75th percentile is the average of the incomes in positions 9 and 10 in the ordered arrangement—that is, $(72{,}814 + 90{,}416)/2 = 81{,}615$. To find the 90th percentile, we calculate the index

$$i = \left(\frac{p}{100}\right)n = \left(\frac{90}{100}\right)12 = 10.8$$

Because $i = 10.8$ is not an integer, step 3(a) says to round $i = 10.8$ up to 11. It follows that the 90th percentile is the income in position 11 in the ordered arrangement—that is, 135,540.

One appealing way to describe the variation of a set of measurements is to divide the data into four parts, each containing approximately 25 percent of the measurements. This can be done by defining the *first, second,* and *third quartiles* as follows:

> The **first quartile,** denoted Q_1, is the **25th percentile.**
> The **second quartile** (or **median**), denoted M_d, is the **50th percentile.**
> The **third quartile,** denoted Q_3, is the **75th percentile.**

Note that the second quartile is simply another name for the median. Furthermore, the procedure we have described here that is used to find the 50th percentile (second quartile) will always give the same result as the previously described procedure (see Section 3.1) for finding the median. To illustrate how the quartiles divide a set of measurements into four parts, consider the following display of the sampled incomes, which shows the first quartile (the 25th percentile), $Q_1 = 22,514$, the median (the 50th percentile), $M_d = 45,299$, and the third quartile (the 75th percentile), $Q_3 = 81,615$:

$$7{,}524 \qquad 11{,}070 \qquad 18{,}211 \quad \Big| \quad 26{,}817 \qquad 36{,}511 \qquad 41{,}286 \quad \Big|$$

$$Q_1 = 22{,}514 \qquad\qquad\qquad\qquad M_d = 45{,}299$$

$$49{,}312 \qquad 57{,}283 \qquad 72{,}814 \quad \Big| \quad 90{,}416 \qquad 135{,}540 \qquad 190{,}250$$

$$Q_3 = 81{,}615$$

Using the quartiles, we estimate that for the household incomes in the midwestern city: (1) 25 percent of the incomes are less than or equal to \$22,514, (2) 25 percent of the incomes are between \$22,514 and \$45,299, (3) 25 percent of the incomes are between \$45,299 and \$81,615, and (4) 25 percent of the incomes are greater than or equal to \$81,615. In addition, to assess some of the lowest and highest incomes, the 10th percentile estimates than 10 percent of the incomes are less than or equal to \$11,070, and the 90th percentile estimates that 10 percent of the incomes are greater than or equal to \$135,540.

In general, unless percentiles correspond to very high or very low percentages, they are resistant (like the median) to extreme values. For example, the 75th percentile of the household incomes would remain \$81,615 even if the largest income—\$190,250—were, instead, \$7,000,000. On the other hand, the standard deviation in this situation would increase. In general, if a population is highly skewed to the right or left, the standard deviation is so large that using it to describe variation does not provide much useful information. For example, the standard deviation of the 12 household incomes is inflated by the large incomes \$135,540 and \$190,250 and can be calculated to be \$54,567. Because the mean of the 12 incomes is \$61,423, Chebyshev's Theorem says that we estimate that at least 75 percent of all household incomes in the city are in the interval $[\bar{x} \pm 2s] = [61{,}423 \pm 2(54{,}567)] = [-47{,}711, 170{,}557]$—that is, are \$170,557 or less. This is much less informative than using the 75th percentile, which estimates that 75 percent of all household incomes are less than or equal to \$81,615. In general, if a population is highly skewed to the right or left, it can be best to describe the variation of the population by using various percentiles. This is what we did when we estimated the variation of the household incomes in the city by using the 10th, 25th, 50th, 75th, and 90th percentiles of the 12 sampled incomes. Using other percentiles can also be informative. For example, the Bureau of the Census sometimes assesses the variation of all household incomes in the United States by using the 20th, 40th, 60th, and 80th percentiles of these incomes.

We sometimes describe a set of measurements by using a *five-number summary.* The summary consists of (1) the smallest measurement; (2) the first quartile, Q_1; (3) the median, M_d; (4) the third quartile, Q_3; and (5) the largest measurement. It is easy to graphically depict a five-number summary. For example, the MINITAB output in Figure 3.18 on the next page tells us that for the 65 payment times, the smallest payment time is 10, $Q_1 = 15$, $M_d = 17$, $Q_3 = 21$, and the largest payment time is 29. It follows that a graphical depiction of this five-number summary is as shown in the page margin. Notice that we have drawn a vertical line extending from the smallest payment time to the largest payment time. In addition, a rectangle is drawn that extends from Q_1 to Q_3, and

Payment Time Five-Number Summary

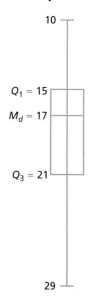

FIGURE 3.18   MINITAB Output of Statistics Describing the 65 Payment Times

Variable	Count	Mean	StDev	Variance
PayTime	65	18.108	3.961	15.691

Variable	Minimum	Q1	Median	Q3	Maximum	Range
PayTime	10.000	15.000	17.000	21.000	29.000	19.000

a horizontal line is drawn to indicate the location of the median. The summary divides the payment times into four parts, with the middle 50 percent of the payment times depicted by the rectangle. The summary indicates that the largest 25 percent of the payment times is more spread out than the smallest 25 percent of the payment times, and that the second-largest 25 percent of the payment times is more spread out than the second-smallest 25 percent of the payment times. Overall, the summary indicates that the payment times are somewhat skewed to the right.

Bottle Design Rating Five-Number Summary

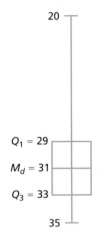

As another example, it can be shown that for the 60 bottle design ratings, the smallest rating is 20, $Q_1 = 29$, $M_d = 31$, $Q_3 = 33$, and the largest rating is 35. It follows that a graphical depiction of this five-number summary is also as shown in the page margin. The summary shows that the smallest 25 percent of the ratings is more spread out than any of the other quarters of the ratings, and that the other three quarters are equally spread out. Overall, the summary shows that the bottle design ratings are skewed to the left. In addition, it can be verified that the 5th percentile of the ratings is 25. This says that we estimate that 95 percent of all consumers would give the new bottle design ratings that are at least as large as the minimum rating of 25 for a successful bottle design.

Using the first and third quartiles, we define the **interquartile range** to be $IQR = Q_3 - Q_1$. This quantity can be interpreted as the length of the interval that contains the *middle 50 percent* of the measurements. For instance, the interquartile range of the 65 payment times is $Q_3 - Q_1 = 21 - 15 = 6$. This says that we estimate that the middle 50 percent of all payment times fall within a range that is six days long.

The procedure we have presented for calculating the first and third quartiles is not the only procedure for computing these quantities. In fact, several procedures exist, and, for example, different statistical computer packages use several somewhat different methods for computing the quartiles. These different procedures sometimes obtain different results, but the overall objective is always to divide the data into four equal parts.

Box-and-whiskers displays (box plots)   A more sophisticated modification of the graphical five-number summary is called a **box-and-whiskers display** (sometimes called a **box plot**). Such a display is constructed by using Q_1, M_d, Q_3, and the interquartile range. As an example, suppose that 20 randomly selected customers give the following satisfaction ratings (on a scale of 1 to 10) for a DVD recorder:

● DVDSat

CHAPTER 1

1   3   5   5   7   8   8   8   8   8   9   9   9   9   9   10   10   10   10

It can be shown that for these ratings $Q_1 = 7.5$, $M_d = 8$, $Q_3 = 9$, and $IQR = Q_3 - Q_1 = 9 - 7.5 = 1.5$. To construct a box-and-whiskers display, we first draw a box that extends from Q_1 to Q_3. As shown in Figure 3.19(a), for the satisfaction ratings data this box extends from $Q_1 = 7.5$ to $Q_3 = 9$. The box contains the middle 50 percent of the data set. Next a vertical line is drawn through the box at the value of the median M_d (sometimes a plus sign ($+$) is plotted at the median instead of a vertical line). This line divides the data set into two roughly equal parts. We next define what we call **inner** and **outer fences.** The **inner fences** are located $1.5 \times IQR$ below Q_1 and $1.5 \times IQR$ above Q_3. For the satisfaction ratings data, the inner fences are

$$Q_1 - 1.5(IQR) = 7.5 - 1.5(1.5) = 5.25 \quad \text{and} \quad Q_3 + 1.5(IQR) = 9 + 1.5(1.5) = 11.25$$

(again see Figure 3.19(a)). The **outer fences** are located $3 \times IQR$ below Q_1 and $3 \times IQR$ above Q_3. For the satisfaction ratings data, the outer fences are

$$Q_1 - 3(IQR) = 7.5 - 3(1.5) = 3.0 \quad \text{and} \quad Q_3 + 3(IQR) = 9 + 3(1.5) = 13.5$$

(these are also shown in Figure 3.19(a)). The inner and outer fences help us to draw the plot's **whiskers:** dashed lines extending below Q_1 and above Q_3 (as in Figure 3.19(a)). One whisker is

FIGURE 3.19   A Box-and-Whiskers Display of the Satisfaction Ratings

(a) Constructing the display

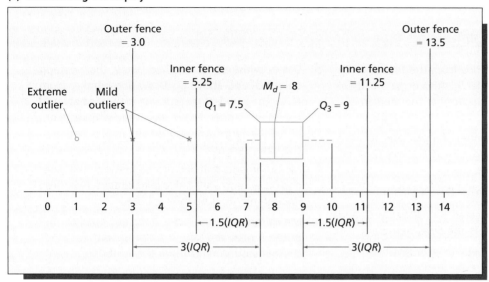

(b) MINITAB output

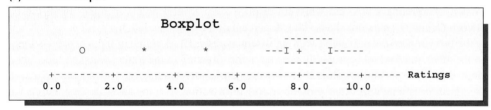

(c) MegaStat output

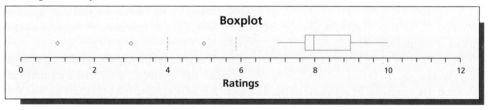

drawn from Q_1 to the smallest measurement between the inner fences. For the satisfaction ratings data, this whisker extends from $Q_1 = 7.5$ down to 7, because 7 is the smallest rating between the inner fences 5.25 and 11.25. The other whisker is drawn from Q_3 to the largest measurement between the inner fences. For the satisfaction ratings data, this whisker extends from $Q_3 = 9$ up to 10, because 10 is the largest rating between the inner fences 5.25 and 11.25. The inner and outer fences are also used to identify **outliers.** An **outlier** is a measurement that is separated from (that is, different from) most of the other measurements in the data set. Measurements that are located between the inner and outer fences are considered to be **mild outliers,** whereas measurements that are located outside the outer fences are considered to be **extreme outliers.** We indicate the locations of mild outliers by plotting these measurements with the symbol ∗, and we indicate the locations of extreme outliers by plotting these measurements with the symbol o. For the satisfaction ratings data, the ratings 3 and 5 are mild outliers (∗) because these ratings are between the inner fence of 5.25 and the outer fence of 3.0. The rating 1 is an extreme outlier (o) because this rating is outside the outer fence 3.0. These outliers are plotted in Figure 3.19(a). Parts (b) and (c) of Figure 3.19 give MINITAB and MegaStat outputs of the box-and-whiskers plot. Notice that MINITAB identifies the median by using a plus sign (+), while MegaStat uses a vertical line. In addition, MegaStat plots all outliers using the same symbol and marks the inner and outer fences using vertical dashed lines. Note here that MegaStat computes the quartiles Q_1 and Q_3 and the inner and outer fences using methods that differ slightly from the methods we have described. The MegaStat Help menus describe how the calculations are done. We now summarize how to construct a box-and-whiskers plot.

Constructing a Box-and-Whiskers Display (Box Plot)

1 Draw a **box** that extends from the first quartile Q_1 to the third quartile Q_3. Also draw a vertical line through the box located at the median M_d.

2 Determine the values of the **inner fences** and **outer fences**. The inner fences are located $1.5 \times IQR$ below Q_1 and $1.5 \times IQR$ above Q_3. That is, **the inner fences are**

$$Q_1 - 1.5(IQR) \quad \text{and} \quad Q_3 + 1.5(IQR)$$

The outer fences are located $3 \times IQR$ below Q_1 and $3 \times IQR$ above Q_3. That is, **the outer fences are**

$$Q_1 - 3(IQR) \quad \text{and} \quad Q_3 + 3(IQR)$$

3 Draw **whiskers** as dashed lines that extend below Q_1 and above Q_3. Draw one whisker from Q_1 to the *smallest* measurement that is between the inner fences. Draw the other whisker from Q_3 to the *largest* measurement that is between the inner fences.

4 Measurements that are located between the inner and outer fences are called **mild outliers.** Plot these measurements using the symbol *.

5 Measurements that are located outside the outer fences are called **extreme outliers.** Plot these measurements using the symbol o.

When interpreting a box-and-whiskers display, keep several points in mind. First, the box (between Q_1 and Q_3) contains the middle 50 percent of the data. Second, the median (which is inside the box) divides the data into two roughly equal parts. Third, if one of the whiskers is longer than the other, the data set is probably skewed in the direction of the longer whisker. Last, observations designated as outliers should be investigated. Understanding the root causes behind the outlying observations will often provide useful information. For instance, understanding why several of the satisfaction ratings in the box plot of Figure 3.19 are substantially lower than the great majority of the ratings may suggest actions that can improve the DVD recorder manufacturer's product and/or service. Outliers can also be caused by inaccurate measuring, reporting, or plotting of the data. Such possibilities should be investigated, and incorrect data should be adjusted or eliminated.

Generally, a box plot clearly depicts the central tendency, variability, and overall range of a set of measurements. A box plot also portrays whether the measurements are symmetrically distributed. However, the exact shape of the distribution is better portrayed by a stem-and-leaf display and/or a histogram. For instance, Figure 3.20 shows the MegaStat output of the stem-and-leaf

FIGURE 3.20   MegaStat Output of a Stem-and-Leaf Display and Box Plot of the Exam Scores

Stem and Leaf Plot for ExamScore

Stem unit = 10

Leaf unit = 1

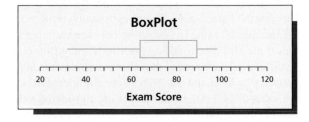

Frequency	Stem	Leaf
1	3	2
0	3	
0	4	
1	4	5
1	5	0
2	5	68
6	6	011344
7	6	5677899
1	7	2
2	7	68
3	8	133
6	8	567789
8	9	00122334
2	9	68
40		

FIGURE 3.21   Graphical Comparison of the Performance of Mutual Funds by Using Five-Number Summaries

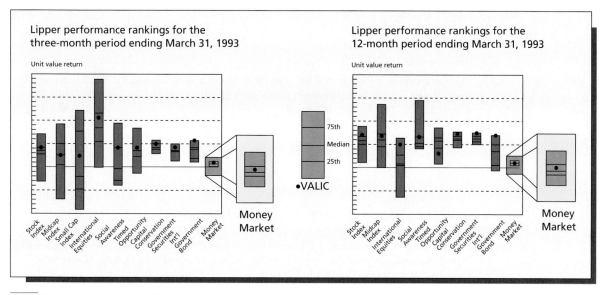

Source: Reprinted by permission of Lipper, Inc.

display and box plot of the scores on the 100-point statistics exam that was given before an attendance policy was begun (see Table 2.8 on page 62). We see that although the box plot in Figure 3.20 tells us that the exam scores are somewhat skewed with a tail to the left, it does not reveal the double-peaked nature of the exam score distribution. On the other hand, the stem-and-leaf display clearly shows that this distribution is double-peaked.

Graphical five-number summaries and box-and-whiskers displays are perhaps best used to compare different sets of measurements. We demonstrate this use of such displays in the following example.

EXAMPLE 3.10 The VALIC Case

In July of 1993, the Variable Annuity Life Insurance Company (VALIC) sent its investors an analysis of the performance of its variable account mutual fund options relative to other variable annuity fund options in various categories (stock index, money market, and so forth). VALIC used the graphical five-number summaries in Figure 3.21 to summarize and compare performances. The dot within each five-number summary represents the return of the VALIC mutual fund option for that category. In explaining the plots, VALIC said

> The data show that all of VALIC's mutual fund options ranked at or above their respective category median return for the three-month period ending March 31, 1993. Also, eight of VALIC's mutual fund options ranked above their respective category median return for the 12-month period ending March 31, 1993.

Notice that the lengths of the graphical five-number summaries indicate performance variability for the various funds. For example, while the median three-month returns for Midcap Index funds and Small Cap Index funds are similar, the returns for Small Cap funds are more variable. Also, in general, three-month returns for funds of all types are more variable than 12-month returns.

Exercises for Section 3.3

CONCEPTS

3.28   Explain each of the following in your own words: a percentile; the first quartile, Q_1; the third quartile, Q_3; and the interquartile range, *IQR*.

3.29   Discuss how a box-and-whiskers display is used to identify outliers.

connect

METHODS AND APPLICATIONS

3.30 Suppose that 20 randomly selected customers give the following satisfaction ratings (on a scale of 1 to 10) for a DVD recorder.

● DVDSat
$$1 \quad 3 \quad 5 \quad 5 \quad 7 \quad 8 \quad 8 \quad 8 \quad 8 \quad 8 \quad 8 \quad 9 \quad 9 \quad 9 \quad 9 \quad 9 \quad 10 \quad 10 \quad 10 \quad 10$$

Find the first quartile, the median, and the third quartile for these data. Construct a five-number summary. ● DVDSat

● DrSalary **3.31** Thirteen internists in the Midwest are randomly selected, and each internist is asked to report last year's income. The incomes obtained (in thousands of dollars) are 152, 144, 162, 154, 146, 241, 127, 141, 171, 177, 138, 132, 192. Find: ● DrSalary

   a The 90th percentile.

   b The median.

   c The first quartile.

   d The third quartile.

   e The 10th percentile.

   f The interquartile range.

   g Develop a five-number summary and a box-and-whiskers display.

3.32 In the book *Business Research Methods,* Donald R. Cooper and C. William Emory present box-and-whiskers plots comparing the net profits of firms in five different industry sectors. Each plot (for a sector) was constructed using net profit figures for a sample of firms from the *Forbes* 500s. Figure 3.22 gives the five box-and-whiskers plots.

   a Using the plots in Figure 3.22, write an analysis comparing net profits for the five sectors. Compare central tendency, variability, skewness, and outliers.

   b For which sectors are net profits most variable? Least variable?

   c Which sectors provide opportunities for the highest net profits?

3.33 On its website, the *Statesman Journal* newspaper (Salem, Oregon, 2005) reports mortgage loan interest rates for 30-year and 15-year fixed-rate mortgage loans for a number of Willamette Valley lending institutions. Of interest is whether there is any systematic difference between 30-year rates and 15-year rates (expressed as annual percentage rate or APR) and, if there is, what is the size of that difference. The table at the top of page 143 displays the 30-year rate and the 15-year rate for each of nine lending institutions. Also given is the difference between the 30-year rate and the 15-year rate for each lending institution. To the right of the table are given side-by-side MINITAB box-and-whiskers plots of the 30-year rates and the 15-year rates and a MINITAB box-and-whiskers plot of the differences between the rates. Use the box-and-whiskers plots to compare the 30-year rates and the 15-year rates. Also, calculate the average of the differences between the rates. ● Mortgage

---

FIGURE 3.22   Box-and-Whiskers Plots Comparing Net Profits for Five Industry Sectors (for Exercise 3.32)

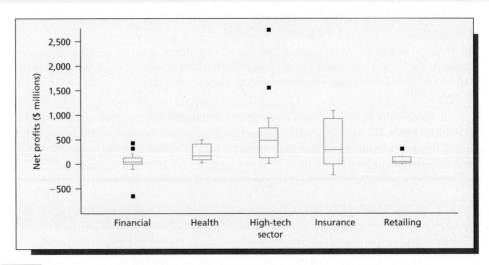

Data from: "The *Forbes* 500s Annual Directory," *Forbes,* April 30, 1990, pp. 221–434.

Source: D. R. Cooper and C. W. Emory, *Business Research Methods,* p. 409. Copyright © 1995. Reprinted by permission of McGraw-Hill Companies, Inc.

Lending Institution	30-Year	15-Year	Difference	● Mortgage
Blue Ribbon Home Mortgage	5.375	4.750	0.625	
Coast To Coast Mortgage Lending	5.250	4.750	0.500	
Community Mortgage Services Inc.	5.000	4.500	0.500	
Liberty Mortgage	5.375	4.875	0.500	
Jim Morrison's MBI	5.250	4.875	0.375	
Professional Valley Mortgage	5.250	5.000	0.250	
Mortgage First	5.750	5.250	0.500	
Professional Mortgage Corporation	5.500	5.125	0.375	
Resident Lending Group Inc.	5.625	5.250	0.375	

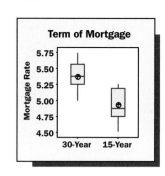

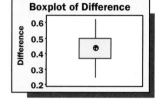

Source: http://online.statesmanjournal.com/mortrates.cfm

3.34 In this section we have presented a commonly accepted way to compute the first, second, and third quartiles. Some statisticians, however, advocate an alternative method for computing Q_1 and Q_3. This method defines the first quartile, Q_1, as what is called the *lower hinge* and defines the third quartile, Q_3, as the *upper hinge*. In order to calculate these quantities for a set of n measurements, we first arrange the measurements in increasing order. Then, if n is even, the *lower hinge* is the median of the smallest $n/2$ measurements, and the *upper hinge* is the median of the largest $n/2$ measurements. If n is odd, we insert M_d into the data set to obtain a set of $n + 1$ measurements. Then the *lower hinge* is the median of the smallest $(n + 1)/2$ measurements, and the *upper hinge* is the median of the largest $(n + 1)/2$ measurements.

a Consider the random sample of $n = 20$ customer satisfaction ratings:

$$\underbrace{1\ 3\ 5\ 5\ 7\ 8\ 8\ 8\ 8\ 8}_{\text{The smallest 10 ratings}}\ \underbrace{8\ 9\ 9\ 9\ 9\ 9\ 10\ 10\ 10\ 10}_{\text{The largest 10 ratings}}$$

Using the method presented on pages 136 and 137 of this section find Q_1 and Q_3. Then find the lower hinge and the upper hinge for the satisfaction ratings. How do your results compare? ● DVDSat

b Consider the following random sample of $n = 11$ doctors' salaries (in thousands of dollars):

    127   132   138   141   146   152   154   171   177   192   241   ● DrSalary2

Using the method presented on pages 136 and 137 of this section find Q_1 and Q_3. The median of the 11 salaries is $M_d = 152$. If we insert this median into the data set, we obtain the following set of $n + 1 = 12$ salaries:

$$\underbrace{127\ 132\ 138\ 141\ 146\ 152}_{\text{The smallest 6 salaries}}\ \underbrace{152\ 154\ 171\ 177\ 192\ 241}_{\text{The largest 6 salaries}}$$

Find the lower hinge and the upper hinge for the salaries. Compare your values of Q_1 and Q_3 with the lower and upper hinges.

c For the 11 doctors' salaries, which quantities (Q_1, M_d, and Q_3 as defined in on page 137 of this section or the lower hinge, M_d, and the upper hinge) in your opinion best divide the salaries into four parts?

3.35 Figure 3.23 gives seven pairs of five-number summaries presented in an article in the January 1995 issue of *Quality Progress*. In the article, authors Dale H. Myers and Jeffrey Heller discuss how AT&T has employed a quality award process (called the Chairman's Quality Award or CQA) to improve quality. To quote Myers and Heller:

> In 1989, AT&T began searching for a systematic process to achieve two major goals: aligning its business management systems more closely with customers' needs and integrating quality principles into every business practice. AT&T wanted this new process to be based on clear and quantifiable standards so that its key building blocks—the business units and divisions—could objectively assess the strengths and shortcomings of their operations.
>
> Within a year, AT&T took its first major step into the world of objective self-assessment. The New Jersey–based telecommunications giant created a Chairman's Quality Award (CQA) process modeled after the Malcolm Baldrige National Quality Award process.[5]
>
> Using clear and objective criteria, the CQA process helps units and divisions assess their business performance and share their most successful practices with each other. It also provides feedback that helps them identify their strengths and opportunities for improvement.

A business unit (department, division, etc.) that chooses to participate in the award program is examined and scored in seven categories—leadership, information and analysis, strategic quality planning, human resource development and management, management of process quality, quality and operational results, and customer focus and satisfaction.

---

[5]We discuss the Malcolm Baldrige National Quality Award process in Chapter 15 on the CD-ROM.

FIGURE 3.23   **Comparison of AT&T Chairman's Quality Award Scores from 1990 to 1993 for Eight Business Units (for Exercise 3.35)**

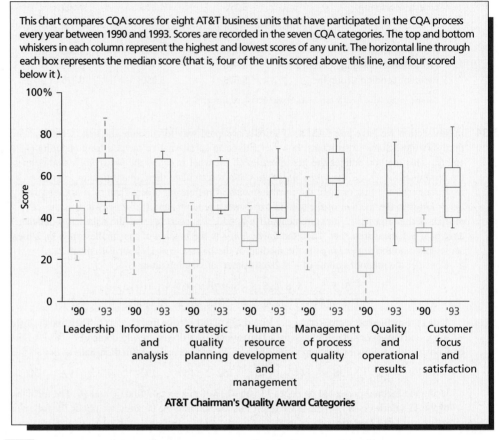

This chart compares CQA scores for eight AT&T business units that have participated in the CQA process every year between 1990 and 1993. Scores are recorded in the seven CQA categories. The top and bottom whiskers in each column represent the highest and lowest scores of any unit. The horizontal line through each box represents the median score (that is, four of the units scored above this line, and four scored below it).

Source: D. H. Myers and J. Heller, "The Dual Role of AT&T's Self-Assessment Process," *Quality Progress,* January 1995, pp. 79–83. Copyright © 1995. American Society for Quality Control. Used with permission.

In order to track AT&T's improvement from 1990 to 1993, the company identified eight business units that participated in the award process every year from 1990 to 1993. For each award category (leadership and so on), a five-number display of the eight business units' 1990 scores was compared to a five-number display of their 1993 scores. The two five-number displays (1990 and 1993) are given for all seven categories in Figure 3.23. Use this figure to answer the following:

a   Based on central tendency, which categories showed improvement from 1990 to 1993?
b   Based on central tendency, which categories showed the most improvement from 1990 to 1993? Which showed the least improvement?
c   In which categories did the variability of the CQA scores increase from 1990 to 1993? In which categories did the variability decrease? In which categories did the variability remain about the same from 1990 to 1993?
d   In which categories did the nature of the skewness of the CQA scores change from 1990 to 1993? Interpret these changes.

3.4 Covariance, Correlation, and the Least Squares Line (Optional) ● ● ●

In Section 2.6 we discussed how to use a scatter plot to explore the relationship between two variables x and y. To construct a scatter plot, a sample of n pairs of values of x and y—(x_1, y_1), (x_2, y_2), . . . , (x_n, y_n)—is collected. Then, each value of y is plotted against the corresponding value of x. If the plot points seem to fluctuate around a straight line, we say that there is a **linear relationship** between x and y. For example, suppose that 10 sales regions of equal sales potential for a company were randomly selected. The advertising expenditures (in units of $10,000) in these 10 sales regions were purposely set in July of last year at the values given in the second column of Figure 3.24(a). The sales volumes (in units of $10,000) were then recorded for the 10 sales regions and found to be as given in the third column of Figure 3.24(a). A scatter plot of sales volume, y, versus advertising expenditure, x, is given in Figure 3.24(b) and shows a linear relationship between x and y.

A measure of the **strength of the linear relationship** between x and y is the **covariance**. The **sample covariance** is calculated by using the sample of n pairs of observed values and x and y.

The **sample covariance** is denoted as s_{xy} and is defined as follows:

$$s_{xy} = \frac{\sum_{i=1}^{n}(x_i - \bar{x})(y_i - \bar{y})}{n - 1}$$

To use this formula, we first find the mean $\bar{x}$ of the n observed values of x and the mean $\bar{y}$ of the n observed values of y. For each observed (x_i, y_i) combination, we then multiply the deviation of x_i from $\bar{x}$ by the deviation of y_i from $\bar{y}$ to form the product $(x_i - \bar{x})(y_i - \bar{y})$. Finally, we add together the n products $(x_1 - \bar{x})(y_1 - \bar{y})$, $(x_2 - \bar{x})(y_2 - \bar{y})$, $\ldots$, $(x_n - \bar{x})(y_n - \bar{y})$ and divide the resulting sum by $n - 1$. For example, the mean of the 10 advertising expenditures in Figure 3.24(a) is $\bar{x} = 9.5$, and the mean of the 10 sales volumes in Figure 3.24(a) is $\bar{y} = 108.3$. It follows that the numerator of s_{xy} is the sum of the values of $(x_i - \bar{x})(y_i - \bar{y}) = (x_i - 9.5)(y_i - 108.3)$. Table 3.7 shows that this sum equals 365.50, which implies that the sample covariance is

$$s_{xy} = \frac{\sum(x_i - \bar{x})(y_i - \bar{y})}{n - 1} = \frac{365.50}{9} = 40.61111$$

FIGURE 3.24   The Sales Volume Data, and a Scatter Plot

(a) The sales volume data   ⬤ SalesPlot

Sales Region	Advertising Expenditure, x	Sales Volume, y
1	5	89
2	6	87
3	7	98
4	8	110
5	9	103
6	10	114
7	11	116
8	12	110
9	13	126
10	14	130

(b) A scatter plot of sales volume versus advertising expenditure

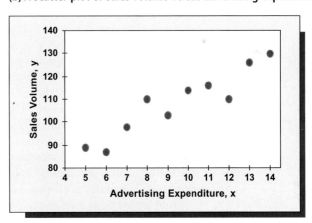

TABLE 3.7   The Calculation of the Numerator of s_{xy}

	x_i	y_i	$(x_i - 9.5)$	$(y_i - 108.3)$	$(x_i - 9.5)(y_i - 108.3)$
	5	89	−4.5	−19.3	86.85
	6	87	−3.5	−21.3	74.55
	7	98	−2.5	−10.3	25.75
	8	110	−1.5	1.7	−2.55
	9	103	−0.5	−5.3	2.65
	10	114	0.5	5.7	2.85
	11	116	1.5	7.7	11.55
	12	110	2.5	1.7	4.25
	13	126	3.5	17.7	61.95
	14	130	4.5	21.7	97.65
Totals	95	1,083	0	0	365.50

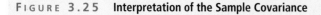

F I G U R E   3 . 2 5   **Interpretation of the Sample Covariance**

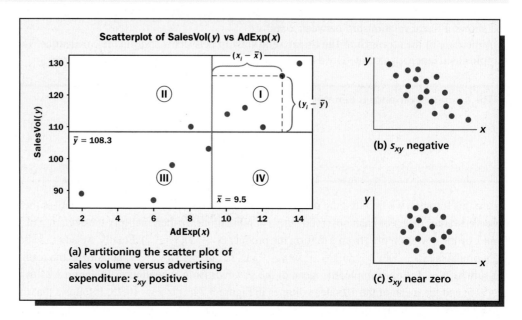

(a) Partitioning the scatter plot of sales volume versus advertising expenditure: s_{xy} positive

(b) s_{xy} negative

(c) s_{xy} near zero

To interpret the covariance, consider Figure 3.25(a). This figure shows the scatter plot of Figure 3.24(b) with a vertical blue line drawn at $\bar{x} = 9.5$ and a horizontal red line drawn at $\bar{y} = 108.3$. The lines divide the scatter plot into four quadrants. Points in quadrant I correspond to x_i greater than $\bar{x}$ and y_i greater than $\bar{y}$ and thus give a value of $(x_i - \bar{x})(y_i - \bar{y})$ greater than 0. Points in quadrant III correspond to x_i less than $\bar{x}$ and y_i less than $\bar{y}$ and thus also give a value of $(x_i - \bar{x})(y_i - \bar{y})$ greater than 0. It follows that if s_{xy} is positive, the points having the greatest influence on $\Sigma(x_i - \bar{x})(y_i - \bar{y})$ and thus on s_{xy} must be in quadrants I and III. Therefore, a positive value of s_{xy} (as in the sales volume example) indicates a positive linear relationship between x and y. That is, as x increases, y increases.

If we further consider Figure 3.25(a), we see that points in quadrant II correspond to x_i less than $\bar{x}$ and y_i greater than $\bar{y}$ and thus give a value of $(x_i - \bar{x})(y_i - \bar{y})$ less than 0. Points in quadrant IV correspond to x_i greater than $\bar{x}$ and y_i less than $\bar{y}$ and thus also give a value of $(x_i - \bar{x})(y_i - \bar{y})$ less than 0. It follows that if s_{xy} is negative, the points having the greatest influence on $\Sigma(x_i - \bar{x})(y_i - \bar{y})$ and thus on s_{xy} must be in quadrants II and IV. Therefore, a negative value of s_{xy} indicates a negative linear relationship between x and y. That is, as x increases, y decreases, as shown in Figure 3.25(b). For example, a negative linear relationship might exist between average hourly outdoor temperature (x) in a city during a week and the city's natural gas consumption (y) during the week. That is, as the average hourly outdoor temperature increases, the city's natural gas consumption would decrease. Finally, note that if s_{xy} is near zero, the (x_i, y_i) points would be fairly evenly distributed across all four quadrants. This would indicate little or no linear relationship between x and y, as shown in Figure 3.25(c).

From the previous discussion, it might seem that a large positive value for the covariance indicates that x and y have a strong positive linear relationship, and a large negative value for the covariance indicates that x and y have a strong negative linear relationship. However, one problem with using the covariance as a measure of the strength of the linear relationship between x and y is that the value of the covariance depends on the units in which x and y are measured. A measure of the strength of the linear relationship between x and y that does not depend on the units in which x and y are measured is the **correlation coefficient.**

The **sample correlation coefficient** is denoted as r and is defined as follows:

$$r = \frac{s_{xy}}{s_x s_y}$$

Here s_{xy} is the previously defined sample covariance, s_x is the sample standard deviation of the sample of x values, and s_y is the sample standard deviation of the sample of y values.

For the sales volume data:

$$s_x = \sqrt{\frac{\sum_{i=1}^{10}(x_i - \bar{x})^2}{9}} = 3.02765 \quad \text{and} \quad s_y = \sqrt{\frac{\sum_{i=1}^{10}(y_i - \bar{y})^2}{9}} = 14.30656$$

Therefore, the sample correlation coefficient is

$$r = \frac{s_{xy}}{s_x s_y} = \frac{40.61111}{(3.02765)(14.30656)} = .93757$$

It can be shown that the sample correlation coefficient r is always between -1 and 1. A value of r near 0 implies little linear relationship between x and y. A value of r close to 1 says that x and y have a strong tendency to move together in a straight-line fashion with a positive slope and, therefore, that x and y are highly related and **positively correlated.** A value of r close to -1 says that x and y have a strong tendency to move together in a straight-line fashion with a negative slope and, therefore, that x and y are highly related and **negatively correlated.** Note that if $r = 1$, the (x, y) points fall exactly on a positively sloped straight line, and, if $r = -1$, the (x, y) points fall exactly on a negatively sloped straight line. For example, since $r = .93757$ in the sales volume example, we conclude that advertising expenditure (x) and sales volume (y) have a strong tendency to move together in a straight-line fashion with a positive slope. That is, x and y have a strong positive linear relationship.

We next note that the sample covariance s_{xy} is the point estimate of the **population covariance,** which we denote as σ_{xy}, and the sample correlation coefficient r is the point estimate of the **population correlation coefficient,** which we denote as ρ. To define σ_{xy} and ρ, let μ_x and σ_x denote the mean and the standard deviation of the population of all possible x values, and let μ_y and σ_y denote the mean and the standard deviation of the population of all possible y values. Then, σ_{xy} is the average of all possible values of $(x - \mu_x)(y - \mu_y)$, and ρ equals $\sigma_{xy}/(\sigma_x \sigma_y)$. Similar to r, ρ is always between -1 and 1.

After establishing that a strong positive or a strong negative linear relationship exists between two variables x and y, we might wish to predict y on the basis of x. This can be done by drawing a straight line through a scatter plot of the observed data. Unfortunately, however, if different people *visually* drew lines through the scatter plot, their lines would probably differ from each other. What we need is the "best line" that can be drawn through the scatter plot. Although there are various definitions of what this best line is, one of the most useful best lines is the *least squares line*. The least squares line will be discussed in detail in Chapter 13. For now, we will say that, intuitively, the **least squares line** is the line that minimizes the sum of the squared vertical distances between the points on the scatter plot and the line.

It can be shown that the **slope b_1** (defined as rise/run) of the least squares line is given by the equation

$$b_1 = \frac{s_{xy}}{s_x^2}$$

In addition, the **y-intercept b_0** of the least squares line (where the line intercepts the y-axis when x equals 0) is given by the equation

$$b_0 = \bar{y} - b_1\bar{x}$$

For example, recall that for the sales volume data in Figure 3.24(a), $s_{xy} = 40.61111$, $s_x = 3.02765$, $\bar{x} = 9.5$, and $\bar{y} = 108.3$. It follows that the slope of the least squares line for these data is

$$b_1 = \frac{s_{xy}}{s_x^2} = \frac{40.61111}{(3.02765)^2} = 4.4303$$

F I G U R E   3 . 2 6   **The Least Squares Line for the Sales Volume Data**

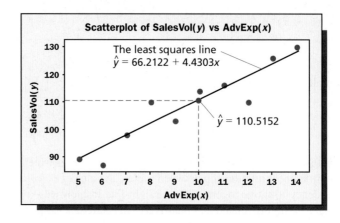

The y-intercept of the least squares line is

$$b_0 = \bar{y} - b_1\bar{x} = 108.3 - 4.4303(9.5) = 66.2122$$

Furthermore, we can write the equation of the least squares line as

$$\hat{y} = b_0 + b_1x$$
$$= 66.2122 + 4.4303x$$

Here, since we will use the line to predict y on the basis of x, we call $\hat{y}$ the predicted value of y when the advertising expenditure is x. For example, suppose that we will spend \$100,000 on advertising in a sales region in July of a future year. Because an advertising expenditure of \$100,000 corresponds to an x of 10, a prediction of sales volume in July of the future year is (see Figure 3.26):

$$\hat{y} = 66.2122 + 4.4303(10)$$
$$= 110.5152 \text{ (that is, \$1,105,152)}$$

Is this prediction likely to be accurate? If the least squares line developed from last July's data applies to the future July, then, since the sample correlation coefficient $r = .93757$ is fairly close to 1, we might hope that the prediction will be reasonably accurate. However, we will see in Chapter 13 that a sample correlation coefficient near 1 does not necessarily mean that the least squares line will predict accurately. We will also study (in Chapter 13) better ways to assess the potential accuracy of a prediction.

Exercises for Section 3.4

CONCEPTS

3.36 Discuss what the covariance and the correlation coefficient say about the linear relationship between two variables x and y.

3.37 Discuss how the least squares line is used to predict y on the basis of x.

METHODS AND APPLICATIONS

3.38 THE FUEL CONSUMPTION CASE   🔵 FuelCon1

On the next page we give the average hourly outdoor temperature (x) in a city during a week and the city's natural gas consumption (y) during the week for each of eight weeks (the temperature readings are expressed in degrees Fahrenheit and the natural gas consumptions are expressed in millions of cubic feet of natural gas—denoted MMcf). The output to the right of the data is obtained when MINITAB is used to fit a least squares line to the natural gas (fuel) consumption data.

connect

Week	Average Hourly Temperature, x (°F)	Weekly Fuel Consumption, y (MMcf)
1	28.0	12.4
2	28.0	11.7
3	32.5	12.4
4	39.0	10.8
5	45.9	9.4
6	57.8	9.5
7	58.1	8.0
8	62.5	7.5

● FuelCon1

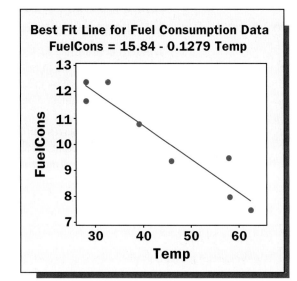

It can be shown that for the fuel consumption data:

$$\bar{x} = 43.98 \qquad \bar{y} = 10.2125 \qquad \sum_{i=1}^{8}(x_i - \bar{x})^2 = 1404.355$$

$$\sum_{i=1}^{8}(y_i - \bar{y})^2 = 25.549 \qquad \sum_{i=1}^{8}(x_i - \bar{x})(y_i - \bar{y}) = -179.6475$$

Calculate s_{xy}, s_x, s_y, and r. Show how the values $b_1 = -.1279$ and $b_0 = 15.84$ on the MINITAB output have been calculated. Find a prediction of the fuel consumption during a week when the average hourly temperature is 40° Fahrenheit.

3.39   THE SERVICE TIME CASE   ● SrvcTime

Accu-Copiers, Inc., sells and services the Accu-500 copying machine. As part of its standard service contract, the company agrees to perform routine service on this copier. To obtain information about the time it takes to perform routine service, Accu-Copiers has collected data for 11 service calls. The data are given on the left below, and the Excel output of a least squares line fit to these data is given on the right below.

Service Call	Number of Copiers Serviced, x	Number of Minutes Required, y
1	4	109
2	2	58
3	5	138
4	7	189
5	1	37
6	3	82
7	4	103
8	5	134
9	2	68
10	4	112
11	6	154

● SrvcTime

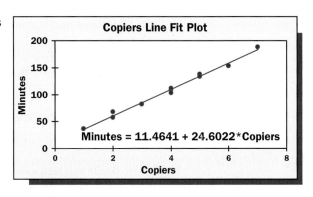

a   The sample correlation coefficient r can be calculated to equal .9952 for the service time data. What does this value of r say about the relationship between x and y?

b   Predict the service time for a future service call on which five copiers will be serviced.

3.5 Weighted Means and Grouped Data (Optional) ● ● ●

Weighted means   In Section 3.1 we studied the mean, which is an important measure of central tendency. In order to calculate a mean, we sum the population (or sample) measurements, and then divide this sum by the number of measurements in the population (or sample). When we do this, each measurement counts equally. That is, each measurement is given the same importance or weight.

Sometimes it makes sense to give different measurements unequal weights. In such a case, a measurement's weight reflects its importance, and the mean calculated using the unequal weights is called a **weighted mean.**

We calculate a weighted mean by multiplying each measurement by its weight, summing the resulting products, and dividing the resulting sum by the sum of the weights:

Weighted Mean

The weighted mean equals

$$\frac{\sum w_i x_i}{\sum w_i}$$

where
x_i = the value of the ith measurement
w_i = the weight applied to the ith measurement

Such a quantity can be computed for a population of measurements or for a sample of measurements.

In order to illustrate the need for a weighted mean and the required calculations, consider the June 2001 unemployment rates for various regions in the United States:[6]

● UnEmploy

Census Region	Civilian Labor Force (Millions)	Unemployment Rate
Northeast	26.9	4.1%
South	50.6	4.7%
Midwest	34.7	4.4%
West	32.5	5.0%

If we wish to compute a mean unemployment rate for the entire United States, we should use a weighted mean. This is because each of the four regional unemployment rates applies to a different number of workers in the labor force. For example, the 4.7 percent unemployed for the South applies to a labor force of 50.6 million workers and thus should count more heavily than the 5.0 percent unemployed for the West, which applies to a smaller labor force of 32.5 million workers.

The unemployment rate measurements are $x_1 = 4.1$ percent, $x_2 = 4.7$ percent, $x_3 = 4.4$ percent, and $x_4 = 5.0$ percent, and the weights applied to these measurements are $w_1 = 26.9$, $w_2 = 50.6$, $w_3 = 34.7$, and $w_4 = 32.5$. That is, we are weighting the unemployment rates by the regional labor force sizes. The weighted mean is computed as follows:

$$\mu = \frac{26.9(4.1) + 50.6(4.7) + 34.7(4.4) + 32.5(5.0)}{26.9 + 50.6 + 34.7 + 32.5}$$

$$= \frac{663.29}{144.7} = 4.58\%$$

In this case the unweighted mean of the four regional unemployment rates equals 4.55 percent. Therefore, the unweighted mean understates the U.S. unemployment rate by .03 percent (or understates U.S. unemployment by .0003(144.7 million) = 43,410 workers).

The weights chosen for calculating a weighted mean will vary depending on the situation. For example, in order to compute the mean percentage return for a portfolio of investments, the percentage returns for various investments might be weighted by the dollar amounts invested in

---

[6]Source: **U.S. Bureau of Labor Statistics,** http://stats.bls.gov/news.release/laus.t01.htm, **August 7, 2001.**

each. Or in order to compute a mean profit margin for a company consisting of several divisions, the profit margins for the different divisions might be weighted by the sales volumes of the divisions. Again, the idea is to choose weights that represent the relative importance of the measurements in the population or sample.

Descriptive statistics for grouped data We usually calculate measures of central tendency and variability using the individual measurements in a population or sample. However, sometimes the only data available are in the form of a frequency distribution or a histogram. For example, newspapers and magazines often summarize data using frequency distributions and histograms without giving the individual measurements in a data set. Data summarized in frequency distribution or histogram form are often called **grouped data.** In this section we show how to compute descriptive statistics for such data.

Suppose we are given a frequency distribution summarizing a sample of 65 customer satisfaction ratings for a consumer product.

Satisfaction Rating	Frequency
36–38	4
39–41	15
42–44	25
45–47	19
48–50	2

● SatRatings

Because we do not know each of the 65 individual satisfaction ratings, we cannot compute an exact value for the mean satisfaction rating. However, we can calculate an approximation of this mean. In order to do this, we use the midpoint of each class to represent the measurements in the class. When we do this, we are really assuming that the average of the measurements in each class equals the class midpoint. Letting M_i denote the midpoint of class i, and letting f_i denote the frequency of class i, we compute the mean by calculating a weighted mean of the class midpoints using the class frequencies as the weights. The logic here is that if f_i measurements are included in class i, then the midpoint of class i should count f_i times in the weighted mean. In this case, the sum of the weights equals the sum of the class frequencies, which equals the sample size. Therefore, we obtain the following equation for the sample mean of grouped data:

Sample Mean for Grouped Data

$$\bar{x} = \frac{\sum f_i M_i}{\sum f_i} = \frac{\sum f_i M_i}{n}$$

where
f_i = the frequency for class i
M_i = the midpoint for class i
$n = \sum f_i$ = the sample size

Table 3.8 summarizes the calculation of the mean satisfaction rating for the previously given frequency distribution of satisfaction ratings. Note that in this table each midpoint is halfway between its corresponding class limits. For example, for the first class $M_1 = (36 + 38)/2 = 37$. We find that the sample mean satisfaction rating is 43.

We can also compute an approximation of the sample variance for grouped data. Recall that when we compute the sample variance using individual measurements, we compute the squared deviation from the sample mean $(x_i - \bar{x})^2$ for each individual measurement x_i and then sum the squared deviations. For grouped data, we do not know each of the x_i values. Because of this, we again let the class midpoint M_i represent each measurement in class i. It follows that we compute the squared deviation $(M_i - \bar{x})^2$ for each class and then sum these squares, weighting each squared deviation by its corresponding class frequency f_i. That is, we approximate $\sum (x_i - \bar{x})^2$ by using $\sum f_i(M_i - \bar{x})^2$. Finally, we obtain the sample variance for the grouped

TABLE 3.8   Calculating the Sample Mean Satisfaction Rating

Satisfaction Rating	Frequency (f_i)	Class Midpoint (M_i)	f_iM_i
36–38	4	37	4(37) = 148
39–41	15	40	15(40) = 600
42–44	25	43	25(43) = 1,075
45–47	19	46	19(46) = 874
48–50	2	49	2(49) = 98
	$n = 65$		2,795

$$\bar{x} = \frac{\sum f_iM_i}{n} = \frac{2,795}{65} = 43$$

TABLE 3.9   Calculating the Sample Variance of the Satisfaction Ratings

Satisfaction Rating	Frequency f_i	Class Midpoint M_i	Deviation $(M_i - \bar{x})$	Squared Deviation $(M_i - \bar{x})^2$	$f_i(M_i - \bar{x})^2$
36–38	4	37	37 − 43 = −6	36	4(36) = 144
39–41	15	40	40 − 43 = −3	9	15(9) = 135
42–44	25	43	43 − 43 = 0	0	25(0) = 0
45–47	19	46	46 − 43 = 3	9	19(9) = 171
48–50	2	49	49 − 43 = 6	36	2(36) = 72
	65				$\sum f_i(M_i - \bar{x})^2 = 522$

$$s^2 = \text{sample variance} = \frac{\sum f_i(M_i - \bar{x})^2}{n - 1} = \frac{522}{65 - 1} = 8.15625$$

data by dividing this quantity by the sample size minus 1. We summarize this calculation in the following box:

Sample Variance for Grouped Data

$$s^2 = \frac{\sum f_i(M_i - \bar{x})^2}{n - 1}$$

where $\bar{x}$ is the sample mean for the grouped data.

Table 3.9 illustrates calculating the sample variance of the previously given frequency distribution of satisfaction ratings. We find that the sample variance is $s^2 = 8.15625$ and, therefore, that the sample standard deviation is $s = \sqrt{8.15625} = 2.8559$.

Finally, although we have illustrated calculating the mean and variance for grouped data in the context of a sample, similar calculations can be done for a population of measurements. If we let N be the size of the population, the grouped data formulas for the population mean and variance are given in the following box:

Population Mean for Grouped Data

$$\mu = \frac{\sum f_iM_i}{N}$$

Population Variance for Grouped Data

$$\sigma^2 = \frac{\sum f_i(M_i - \mu)^2}{N}$$

Exercises for Section 3.5

CONCEPTS

3.40 Consider calculating a student's grade point average using a scale where 4.0 represents an A and 0.0 represents an F. Explain why the grade point average is a weighted mean. What are the x_i values? What are the weights?

3.41 When we perform grouped data calculations, we represent the measurements in a class by using the midpoint of the class. Explain the assumption that is being made when we do this.

3.42 When we compute the mean, variance, and standard deviation using grouped data, the results obtained are approximations of the population (or sample) mean, variance, and standard deviation. Explain why this is true.

METHODS AND APPLICATIONS

3.43 According to the Morningstar.com website, the 2004 total return percentages for several popular funds were as follows: 🌐 FundReturns

Fund	2004 Total Return %
Vanguard 500 Index	10.7
Wasatch Core Growth	21.7
Fidelity Stock Selector	9.9
Fidelity Dividend Growth	5.8
Janus Worldwide	5.5

Source: http://quicktake.morningstar.com/Fund/TotalReturns.asp (accessed March 17, 2005).

Suppose that an investor had $100,000 invested in the Vanguard 500 Index fund, $500,000 invested in the Wasatch Core Growth fund, $500,000 invested in the Fidelity Stock Selector fund, $200,000 invested in the Fidelity Dividend Growth fund, and $50,000 invested in the Janus Worldwide fund.

a Compute a weighted mean that measures the 2004 average total return for the investor's portfolio.

b Compare your weighted mean with the unweighted mean of the five total return percentages. Explain why they differ.

3.44 The following are the January 2005 unemployment rates and civilian labor force sizes for five states in the Midwest: 🌐 UnEmpStates

State	Size of Civilian Labor Force (Millions)	Unemployment Rate (%)
Iowa	1.62	5.1
Michigan	5.09	7.1
Illinois	6.45	5.6
Indiana	3.18	5.4
Wisconsin	3.08	4.8

Source: U.S. Bureau of Labor Statistics, http://stats.bls.gov/ (accessed March 17, 2005).

a Using a weighted mean, compute an average unemployment rate for the five-state region.

b Calculate the unweighted mean for the five unemployment rates. Explain why the weighted and unweighted means differ.

3.45 The following frequency distribution summarizes the weights of 195 fish caught by anglers participating in a professional bass fishing tournament: 🌐 BassWeights

Weight (Pounds)	Frequency
1–3	53
4–6	118
7–9	21
10–12	3

a Calculate the (approximate) sample mean for these data.

b Calculate the (approximate) sample variance for these data.

3.46 The following is a frequency distribution summarizing earnings per share (EPS) growth data for the 30 fastest-growing firms as given on *Fortune* magazine's website on March 16, 2005:
● EPSGrowth

EPS Growth (Percent)	Frequency
0–49	1
50–99	17
100–149	5
150–199	4
200–249	1
250–299	2

Source: http://www.fortune.com (accessed March 16, 2005).

Calculate the (approximate) population mean, variance, and standard deviation for these data.

3.47 The Data and Story Library website (a website devoted to applications of statistics) gives a histogram of the ages of a sample of 60 CEOs taken in 1993. We present the data in the form of a frequency distribution below: ● CEOAges

Age (Years)	Frequency
28–32	1
33–37	3
38–42	3
43–47	13
48–52	14
53–57	12
58–62	9
63–67	1
68–72	3
73–77	1

Source: http://lib.stat.cmu.edu/DASL/Stories/ceo.html (accessed April 15, 2005).

Calculate the (approximate) sample mean, variance, and standard deviation of these data.

3.6 The Geometric Mean (Optional) ● ● ●

In Section 3.1 we defined the mean to be the average of a set of population or sample measurements. This mean is sometimes referred to as the arithmetic mean. While very useful, the arithmetic mean is not a good measure of the rate of change exhibited by a variable over time. To see this, consider the rate at which the value of an investment changes—its rate of return. Suppose that an initial investment of $10,000 increases in value to $20,000 at the end of one year and then decreases in value to its original $10,000 value after two years. The rate of return for the first year, R_1, is

$$R_1 = \left(\frac{20,000 - 10,000}{10,000} \right) \times 100\% = 100\%$$

and the rate of return for the second year, R_2, is

$$R_2 = \left(\frac{10,000 - 20,000}{20,000} \right) \times 100\% = -50\%$$

Although the value of the investment at the beginning and end of the two-year period is the same, the arithmetic mean of the yearly rates of return is $(R_1 + R_2)/2 = (100\% + (-50\%))/2 = 25\%$. This arithmetic mean does not communicate the fact that the value of the investment is unchanged at the end of the two years.

To remedy this situation, we define the **geometric mean** of the returns to be **the constant return R_g that yields the same wealth at the end of the investment period as do the actual returns.** In our example, this says that if we express R_g, R_1, and R_2 as decimal fractions (here $R_1 = 1$ and $R_2 = -.5$),

$$(1 + R_g)^2 \times 10{,}000 = (1 + R_1)(1 + R_2) \times 10{,}000$$

or

$$R_g = \sqrt{(1 + R_1)(1 + R_2)} - 1$$
$$= \sqrt{(1 + 1)(1 + (-.5))} - 1$$
$$= \sqrt{1} - 1 = 0$$

Therefore, the geometric mean R_g expresses the fact that the value of the investment is unchanged after two years.

In general, if $R_1, R_2, \ldots, R_n$ are returns (expressed in decimal form) over n time periods:

> The **geometric mean** of the returns $R_1, R_2, \ldots, R_n$ is
>
> $$R_g = \sqrt[n]{(1 + R_1)(1 + R_2) \cdots (1 + R_n)} - 1$$
>
> and the ending value of an initial investment I experiencing returns $R_1, R_2, \ldots, R_n$ is $I(1 + R_g)^n$.

As another example, suppose that in year 3 our investment's value increases to \$25,000, which says that the rate of return for year 3 (expressed as a percentage) is

$$R_3 = \left(\frac{25{,}000 - 10{,}000}{10{,}000}\right) \times 100\%$$
$$= 150\%$$

Since (expressed as decimals) $R_1 = 1$, $R_2 = -.5$, and $R_3 = 1.5$, the geometric mean return at the end of year 3 is

$$R_g = \sqrt[3]{(1 + 1)(1 + (-.5))(1 + 1.5)} - 1$$
$$= 1.3572 - 1$$
$$= .3572$$

and the value of the investment after three years is

$$10{,}000 (1 + .3572)^3 = \$25{,}000$$

Exercises for Section 3.6

CONCEPTS

3.48 In words, explain the interpretation of the geometric mean return for an investment.

connect

3.49 If we know the initial value of an investment and its geometric mean return over a period of years, can we compute the ending value of the investment? If so, how?

METHODS AND APPLICATIONS

3.50 Suppose that a company's sales were \$5,000,000 three years ago. Since that time sales have grown at annual rates of 10 percent, -10 percent, and 25 percent.
  a Find the geometric mean growth rate of sales over this three-year period.
  b Find the ending value of sales after this three-year period.

3.51 Suppose that a company's sales were \$1,000,000 four years ago and are \$4,000,000 at the end of the four years. Find the geometric mean growth rate of sales.

3.52 The Standard and Poor's 500 stock index is a commonly used measure of stock market performance in the United States. In the table below, we give the value of the S & P 500 index on the first day of market trading for each year from 2000 to 2005.   ● S&P500

Year	S&P 500 Index
2000	1,455.22
2001	1,283.27
2002	1,154.67
2003	909.03
2004	1,108.48
2005	1,211.92

Source: http://table.finance.yahoo.com.

a Show that the percentage changes (rates of return) for the S&P 500 index for the years from 2000 to 2001 and from 2001 to 2002 are, respectively, -11.8 percent and -10.0 percent (that is, $-.118$ and $-.100$ expressed as decimal fractions).

b Find the rates of return for the S&P 500 index for each of the years from 2002 to 2003; from 2003 to 2004; and from 2004 to 2005.

c Calculate the geometric mean return for the S&P 500 index over the period from 2000 to 2005.

d Suppose that an investment of \$1,000,000 is made in 2000 and that the portfolio performs with returns equal to those of the S&P 500 index. What is the investment portfolio worth in 2005?

3.53 According to the USA Statistics in Brief summary of U.S. census data, the amount of consumer credit outstanding (in billions of dollars) is as follows:[7]

1990 : \$789   1995 : \$1,096   2000 : \$1,534

a Find the geometric mean five-year rate of increase in consumer credit outstanding.

b Use the geometric mean rate of increase to project the amount of consumer credit outstanding in 2005.

Chapter Summary

We began this chapter by presenting and comparing several measures of **central tendency.** We defined the **population mean,** and we saw how to estimate the population mean by using a **sample mean.** We also defined the **median** and **mode,** and we compared the mean, median, and mode for symmetrical distributions and for distributions that are skewed to the right or left. We then studied measures of **variation** (or *spread*). We defined the **range, variance,** and **standard deviation,** and we saw how to estimate a population variance and standard deviation by using a sample. We learned that a good way to interpret the standard deviation when a population is (approximately) normally distributed is to use the **Empirical Rule,** and we studied **Chebyshev's Theorem,** which gives us intervals containing reasonably large fractions of

the population units no matter what the population's shape might be. We also saw that, when a data set is highly skewed, it is best to use **percentiles** and **quartiles** to measure variation, and we learned how to construct a **box-and-whiskers plot** by using the quartiles.

After learning how to measure and depict central tendency and variability, we presented several optional topics. First we discussed several numerical measures of the relationship between two variables. These included the **covariance,** the **correlation coefficient,** and the **least squares line.** We then introduced the concept of a **weighted mean** and also explained how to compute descriptive statistics for **grouped data.** Finally, we showed how to calculate the **geometric mean** and demonstrated its interpretation.

Glossary of Terms

box-and-whiskers display (box plot): A graphical portrayal of a data set that depicts both the central tendency and variability of the data. It is constructed using Q_1, M_d, and Q_3. (page 138)
central tendency: A term referring to the middle of a population or sample of measurements. (page 115)
Chebyshev's Theorem: A theorem that (for any population) allows us to find an interval that contains a specified percentage of the individual measurements in the population. (page 131)

coefficient of variation: A quantity that measures the variation of a population or sample relative to its mean. (page 133)
correlation coefficient: A numerical measure of the linear relationship between two variables that is between -1 and 1. (page 146)
covariance: A numerical measure of the linear relationship between two variables that depends upon the units in which the variables are measured. (page 145)

[7]Source: http://www.census.gov/statlab/www/part5.html.

Empirical Rule: For a normally distributed population, this rule tells us that 68.26 percent, 95.44 percent, and 99.73 percent, respectively, of the population measurements are within one, two, and three standard deviations of the population mean. (page 128)

extreme outlier (in a box-and-whiskers display): Measurements located outside the outer fences. (page 139)

first quartile (denoted Q_1): A value below which approximately 25 percent of the measurements lie; the 25th percentile. (page 137)

geometric mean: The constant return (or rate of change) that yields the same wealth at the end of several time periods as do actual returns. (page 155)

grouped data: Data presented in the form of a frequency distribution or a histogram. (page 151)

inner fences (in a box-and-whiskers display): Points located $1.5 \times IQR$ below Q_1 and $1.5 \times IQR$ above Q_3. (page 138)

interquartile range (denoted IQR): The difference between the third quartile and the first quartile (that is, $Q_3 - Q_1$). (page 138)

least squares line: The line y that minimizes the sum of the squared vertical differences between points on a scatter plot and the line. (page 147)

measure of variation: A descriptive measure of the spread of the values in a population or sample. (page 125)

median (denoted M_d): A measure of central tendency that divides a population or sample into two roughly equal parts. (page 117)

mild outlier (in a box-and-whiskers display): Measurements located between the inner and outer fences. (page 139)

mode (denoted M_o): The measurement in a sample or a population that occurs most frequently. (page 118)

mound-shaped: Description of a relative frequency curve that is "piled up in the middle." (page 130)

normal curve: A bell-shaped, symmetrical relative frequency curve. We will present the exact equation that gives this curve in Chapter 6. (page 128)

outer fences (in a box-and-whiskers display): Points located $3 \times IQR$ below Q_1 and $3 \times IQR$ above Q_3. (page 138)

percentile: The value such that a specified percentage of the measurements in a population or sample fall at or below it. (page 136)

point estimate: A one-number estimate for the value of a population parameter. (page 115)

population mean (denoted μ): The average of a population of measurements. (page 115)

population parameter: A descriptive measure of a population. It is calculated using the population measurements. (page 115)

population standard deviation (denoted σ): The positive square root of the population variance. It is a measure of the variation of the population measurements. (page 125)

population variance (denoted σ^2): The average of the squared deviations of the individual population measurements from the population mean. It is a measure of the variation of the population measurements. (page 125)

range: The difference between the largest and smallest measurements in a population or sample. It is a simple measure of variation. (page 125)

sample mean (denoted $\bar{x}$): The average of the measurements in a sample. It is the point estimate of the population mean. (page 116)

sample size (denoted n): The number of measurements in a sample. (page 116)

sample standard deviation (denoted s): The positive square root of the sample variance. It is the point estimate of the population standard deviation. (page 126)

sample statistic: A descriptive measure of a sample. It is calculated from the measurements in the sample. (page 116)

sample variance (denoted s^2): A measure of the variation of the sample measurements. It is the point estimate of the population variance. (page 126)

third quartile (denoted Q_3): A value below which approximately 75 percent of the measurements lie; the 75th percentile. (page 137)

tolerance interval: An interval of numbers that contains a specified percentage of the individual measurements in a population. (page 129)

weighted mean: A mean where different measurements are given different weights based on their importance. (page 150)

z-score (of a measurement): The number of standard deviations that a measurement is from the mean. This quantity indicates the relative location of a measurement within its distribution. (page 132)

Important Formulas

The population mean, μ: page 115

The sample mean, $\bar{x}$: page 116

The median: page 117

The mode: page 118

The population range: page 125

The population variance, σ^2: page 125

The population standard deviation, σ: page 125

The sample variance, s^2: pages 126 and 127

The sample standard deviation, s: page 126

Computational formula for s^2: page 127

The Empirical Rule: page 128

Chebyshev's Theorem: page 131

z-score: page 132

The coefficient of variation: page 133

The pth percentile: page 136

The quartiles: page 137

The sample covariance: page 145

The sample correlation coefficient: page 146

The least squares line: page 147

The weighted mean: page 150

Sample mean for grouped data: page 151

Sample variance for grouped data: page 152

Population mean for grouped data: page 152

Population variance for grouped data: page 152

The geometric mean: page 155

Supplementary Exercises

3.54 In the book *Modern Statistical Quality Control and Improvement,* Nicholas R. Farnum presents data concerning the elapsed times from the completion of medical lab tests until the results are recorded on patients' charts. Table 3.10 gives the times it took (in hours) to deliver and chart the results of 84 lab tests over one week. Use the techniques of this and the previous chapter to determine if there are some deliveries with excessively long waiting times. Which deliveries might be investigated in order to discover reasons behind unusually long delays?   ◐ LabTest

3.55 Figure 3.27 depicts data for a study of 80 software projects at NASA's Goddard Space Center. The figure shows the number of bugs per 1,000 lines of code from 1976 to 1990. Write a short paragraph describing how the reliability of the software has improved. Explain how the data indicate improvement.

3.56 **THE INVESTMENT CASE**   ◐ InvestRet

The Fall 1995 issue of *Investment Digest,* a publication of The Variable Annuity Life Insurance Company of Houston, Texas, discusses the importance of portfolio diversification for long-term investors. The article states:

> While it is true that investment experts generally advise long-term investors to invest in variable investments, they also agree that the key to any sound investment portfolio is diversification. That is, investing in a variety of investments with differing levels of historical return and risk.
>
>   Investment risk is often measured in terms of the volatility of an investment over time. When volatility, sometimes referred to as *standard deviation,* increases, so too does the level of return. Conversely, as risk (standard deviation) declines, so too do returns.

In order to explain the relationship between the return on an investment and its risk, *Investment Digest* presents a graph of mean return versus standard deviation (risk) for nine investment classes over the period from 1970 to 1994. This graph, which *Investment Digest* calls the "risk/return trade-off," is shown in Figure 3.28. The article says that this graph

> . . . illustrates the historical risk/return trade-off for a variety of investment classes over the 24-year period between 1970 and 1994.

TABLE 3.10	Elapsed Time (in Hours) for Completing and Delivering Medical Lab Tests ◐ LabTest		
6.1	8.7	1.1	4.0
2.1	3.9	2.2	5.0
2.1	7.1	4.3	8.8
3.5	1.2	3.2	1.3
1.3	9.3	4.2	7.3
5.7	6.5	4.4	16.2
1.3	1.3	3.0	2.7
15.7	4.9	2.0	5.2
3.9	13.9	1.8	2.2
8.4	5.2	11.9	3.0
24.0	24.5	24.8	24.0
1.7	4.4	2.5	16.2
17.8	2.9	4.0	6.7
5.3	8.3	2.8	5.2
17.5	1.1	3.0	8.3
1.2	1.1	4.5	4.4
5.0	2.6	12.7	5.7
4.7	5.1	2.6	1.6
3.4	8.1	2.4	16.7
4.8	1.7	1.9	12.1
9.1	5.6	13.0	6.4

Source: N. R. Farnum, *Modern Statistical Quality Control and Improvement,* p. 55. Reprinted by permission of Brooks/Cole, an imprint of the Wadsworth Group, a division of Thompson Learning. Fax 800-730-2215.

FIGURE 3.27   Software Performance at NASA's Goddard Space Center, 1976–1990 (for Exercise 3.55)

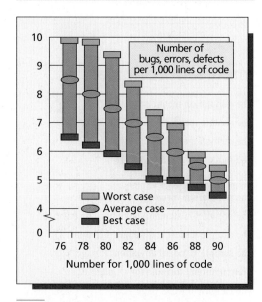

Source: Reprinted from the January 15, 1992, issue of *BusinessWeek* by special permission. Copyright © 1992 by The McGraw-Hill Companies.

FIGURE 3.28   **The Risk/Return Trade-Off (for Exercise 3.56)**

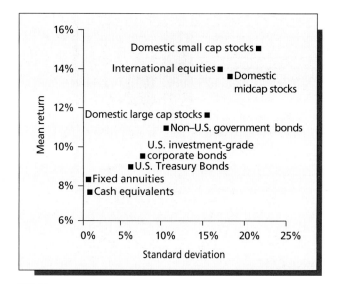

Source: The Variable Annuity Life Insurance Company, *VALIC* 9, (1995), no. 3.

TABLE 3.11   **Mean Return and Standard Deviation for Nine Investment Classes**   ● InvestRet

Investment Class	Mean Return	Standard Deviation
Fixed annuities	8.31%	.54%
Cash equivalents	7.73	.81
U.S. Treasury bonds	8.80	5.98
U.S. investment-grade corporate bonds	9.33	7.92
Non–U.S. government bonds	10.95	10.47
Domestic large cap stocks	11.71	15.30
International equities	14.02	17.16
Domestic midcap stocks	13.64	18.19
Domestic small cap stocks	14.93	21.82

In the chart, cash equivalents and fixed annuities, for instance, had a standard deviation of 0.81% and 0.54% respectively, while posting returns of just over 7.73% and 8.31%. At the other end of the spectrum, domestic small-company stocks were quite volatile—with a standard deviation of 21.82%—but compensated for that increased volatility with a return of 14.93%.

The answer seems to lie in asset allocation. Investment experts know the importance of asset allocation. In a nutshell, asset allocation is a method of creating a diversified portfolio of investments that minimize historical risk and maximize potential returns to help you meet your retirement goals and needs.

Suppose that, by reading off the graph of Figure 3.28, we obtain the mean return and standard deviation combinations for the various investment classes as shown in Table 3.11.

Further suppose that future returns in each investment class will behave as they have from 1970 to 1994. That is, for each investment class, regard the mean return and standard deviation in Table 3.11 as the population mean and the population standard deviation of all possible future returns. Then do the following:

a Assuming that future returns for the various investment classes are mound-shaped, for each investment class compute intervals that will contain approximately 68.26 percent and 99.73 percent of all future returns.

b Making no assumptions about the population shapes of future returns, for each investment class compute intervals that will contain at least 75 percent and 88.89 percent of all future returns.

c Assuming that future returns are mound-shaped, find

    (1) An estimate of the maximum return that might be realized for each investment class.

    (2) An estimate of the minimum return (or maximum loss) that might be realized for each investment class.

d Assuming that future returns are mound-shaped, which two investment classes have the highest estimated maximum returns? What are the estimated minimum returns (maximum losses) for these investment classes?

e Assuming that future returns are mound-shaped, which two investment classes have the smallest estimated maximum returns? What are the estimated minimum returns for these investment classes?

f Calculate the coefficient of variation for each investment class and compare the investment classes with respect to risk. Which class is riskiest? Least risky?

FIGURE 3.29   **1993 Insurance Expenditures of Households in the United Kingdom (for Exercise 3.57)**

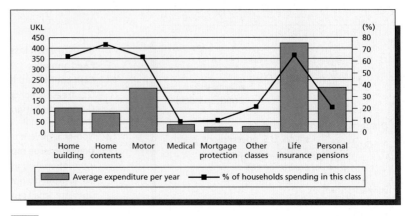

Source: CSO family expenditure survey.

3.57   THE UNITED KINGDOM INSURANCE CASE

Figure 3.29 summarizes information concerning insurance expenditures of households in the United Kingdom in 1993.

a Approximately what percentage of households spent money to buy life insurance?

b What is the approximate average expenditure (in UKL) per household on life insurance? Note: The averages given in Figure 3.29 are for households that spend in the class.

3.58   THE INTERNATIONAL BUSINESS TRAVEL EXPENSE CASE

Suppose that a large international corporation wishes to obtain its own benchmark for one-day travel expenses in Moscow. To do this, it records the one-day travel expenses for a random sample of 35 executives visiting Moscow. The mean and the standard deviation of these expenses are calculated to be $\bar{x} = \$538$ and $s = \$41$. Furthermore, a histogram shows that the expenses are approximately normally distributed.

a Find an interval that we estimate contains 99.73 percent of all one-day travel expenses in Moscow.

b If an executive submits an expense of $720 for a one-day stay in Moscow, should this expense be considered unusually high? Why or why not?

3.59   THE FLORIDA POOL HOME CASE   🌀 PoolHome

In Florida, real estate agents refer to homes having a swimming pool as *pool homes*. In this case, Sunshine Pools Inc. markets and installs pools throughout the state of Florida. The company wishes to estimate the percentage of a pool's cost that can be recouped by a buyer when he or she sells the home. For instance, if a homeowner buys a pool for which the current purchase price is $30,000 and then sells the home in the current real estate market for $20,000 more than the homeowner would get if the home did not have a pool, the homeowner has recouped $(20,000/30,000) \times 100\% = 66.67\%$ of the pool's cost. To make this estimate, the company randomly selects 80 homes from all of the homes sold in a Florida city (over the last six months) having a size between 2,000 and 3,500 square feet. For each sampled home, the following data are collected: selling price (in thousands of dollars); square footage; the number of bathrooms; a niceness rating (expressed as an integer from 1 to 7 and assigned by a real estate agent); and whether or not the home has a pool (1 = yes, 0 = no). The data are given in Table 3.12. Figure 3.30 gives descriptive statistics for the 43 homes having a pool and for the 37 homes that do not have a pool.

a Using Figure 3.30, compare the mean selling prices of the homes having a pool and the homes that do not have a pool. Using this data, and assuming that the average current purchase price of the pools in the sample is $32,500, estimate the percentage of a pool's cost that can be recouped when the home is sold.

b The comparison you made in part *a* could be misleading. Noting that different homes have different square footages, numbers of bathrooms, and niceness ratings, explain why.

TABLE 3.12 The Florida Pool Home Data ● PoolHome

Home	Price ($1000s)	Size (Sq Feet)	Number of Bathrooms	Niceness Rating	Pool? Yes=1; No=0	Home	Price ($1000s)	Size (Sq Feet)	Number of Bathrooms	Niceness Rating	Pool? Yes=1; No=0
1	260.9	2666	2 1/2	7	0	41	285.6	2761	3	6	1
2	337.3	3418	3 1/2	6	1	42	216.1	2880	2 1/2	2	0
3	268.4	2945	2	5	1	43	261.3	3426	3	1	1
4	242.2	2942	2 1/2	3	1	44	236.4	2895	2 1/2	2	1
5	255.2	2798	3	3	1	45	267.5	2726	3	7	0
6	205.7	2210	2 1/2	2	0	46	220.2	2930	2 1/2	2	0
7	249.5	2209	2	7	0	47	300.1	3013	2 1/2	6	1
8	193.6	2465	2 1/2	1	0	48	260.0	2675	2	6	0
9	242.7	2955	2	4	1	49	277.5	2874	3 1/2	6	1
10	244.5	2722	2 1/2	5	0	50	274.9	2765	2 1/2	4	1
11	184.2	2590	2 1/2	1	0	51	259.8	3020	3 1/2	2	1
12	325.7	3138	3 1/2	7	1	52	235.0	2887	2 1/2	1	1
13	266.1	2713	2	7	0	53	191.4	2032	2	3	0
14	166.0	2284	2 1/2	2	0	54	228.5	2698	2 1/2	4	0
15	330.7	3140	3 1/2	6	1	55	266.6	2847	3	2	1
16	289.1	3205	2 1/2	3	1	56	233.0	2639	3	3	0
17	268.8	2721	2 1/2	6	1	57	343.4	3431	4	5	1
18	276.7	3245	2 1/2	2	1	58	334.0	3485	3 1/2	5	1
19	222.4	2464	3	3	1	59	289.7	2991	2 1/2	6	1
20	241.5	2993	2 1/2	1	0	60	228.4	2482	2 1/2	2	0
21	307.9	2647	3 1/2	6	1	61	233.4	2712	2 1/2	1	1
22	223.5	2670	2 1/2	4	0	62	275.7	3103	2 1/2	2	1
23	231.1	2895	2 1/2	3	0	63	290.8	3124	2 1/2	3	1
24	216.5	2643	2 1/2	3	0	64	230.8	2906	2 1/2	2	0
25	205.5	2915	2	1	0	65	310.1	3398	4	4	1
26	258.3	2800	3 1/2	2	1	66	247.9	3028	3	4	0
27	227.6	2557	2 1/2	3	1	67	249.9	2761	2	5	0
28	255.4	2805	2	3	1	68	220.5	2842	3	3	0
29	235.7	2878	2 1/2	4	0	69	226.2	2666	2 1/2	6	0
30	285.1	2795	3	7	1	70	313.7	2744	2 1/2	7	1
31	284.8	2748	2 1/2	7	1	71	210.1	2508	2 1/2	4	0
32	193.7	2256	2 1/2	2	0	72	244.9	2480	2 1/2	5	0
33	247.5	2659	2 1/2	2	1	73	235.8	2986	2 1/2	4	0
34	274.8	3241	3 1/2	4	1	74	263.2	2753	2 1/2	7	0
35	264.4	3166	3	3	1	75	280.2	2522	2 1/2	6	1
36	204.1	2466	2	4	0	76	290.8	2808	2 1/2	7	1
37	273.9	2945	2 1/2	5	1	77	235.4	2616	2 1/2	3	0
38	238.5	2727	3	1	1	78	190.3	2603	2 1/2	2	0
39	274.4	3141	4	4	1	79	234.4	2804	2 1/2	4	0
40	259.6	2552	2	7	1	80	238.7	2851	2 1/2	5	0

FIGURE 3.30 Descriptive Statistics for Homes with and without Pools (for Exercise 3.59)

Descriptive Statistics (Homes with Pools)	Price	Descriptive Statistics (Homes without Pools)	Price
count	43	count	37
mean	276.056	mean	226.900
sample variance	937.821	sample variance	609.902
sample standard deviation	30.624	sample standard deviation	24.696
minimum	222.4	minimum	166
maximum	343.4	maximum	267.5
range	121	range	101.5

3.60   Internet Exercise

Overview: The Data and Story Library (DASL) houses a rich collection of data sets useful for teaching and learning statistics, from a variety of sources, contributed primarily by university faculty members. DASL can be reached through the BSC by clicking on the Data Bases button in the BSC home screen and by then clicking on the Data and Story Library link. The DASL can also be reached directly using the url http://lib.stat.cmu.edu/DASL/. The objective of this exercise is to retrieve a data set of chief executive officer salaries and to construct selected graphical and numerical statistical summaries of the data.

a From the McGraw-Hill/Irwin Business Statistics Center Data Bases page, go to the DASL website and select "List all topics." From the Stories by Topic page, select Economics, then CEO Salaries to reach the CEO Salaries story. From the CEO Salaries story page, select the Datafile Name: CEO Salaries to reach the data set page. The data set includes the ages and salaries (save for a single missing observation) for a sample of 60 CEOs. Capture these observations and copy them into an Excel or MINITAB worksheet. This data capture can be accomplished in a number of ways. One simple approach is to use simple copy and paste procedures from the DASL data set to Excel or MINITAB (data sets CEOSal.xlsx, CEOSal.MTW).

b Use your choice of statistical software to create graphical and numerical summaries of the CEO salary data and use these summaries to describe the data. In Excel, create a histogram of salaries and generate descriptive statistics. In MINITAB, create a histogram, stem-and-leaf display, box plot, and descriptive statistics. Offer your observations about typical salary level, the variation in salaries, and the shape of the distribution of CEO salaries.

Appendix 3.1 ■ Numerical Descriptive Statistics Using MINITAB

The instructions in this section begin by describing the entry of data into the MINITAB Data window. Alternatively, the data may be loaded directly from the data disk included with the text. The appropriate data file name is given at the top of each instruction block. Please refer to Appendix 1.1 for further information about entering data, saving data, and printing results when using MINITAB.

Numerical descriptive statistics in Figure 3.7 on page 121 (data file: PayTime.MTW):

- Enter the payment time data from Table 2.4 (page 56) into column C1 with variable name PayTime.

- Select **Stat : Basic Statistics : Display Descriptive Statistics.**

- In the Display Descriptive Statistics dialog box, select the variable Paytime into the Variables window.

- In the Display Descriptive Statistics dialog box, click on the Statistics button.

- In the "Descriptive Statistics—Statistics" dialog box, enter checkmarks in the checkboxes corresponding to the desired descriptive statistics. Here we have checked the mean, standard deviation, variance, first quartile, median, third quartile, minimum, maximum, range, and N total checkboxes.

- Click OK in the "Descriptive Statistics—Statistics" dialog box.

- Click OK in the Display Descriptive Statistics dialog box.

- The requested descriptive statistics are displayed in the Session window.

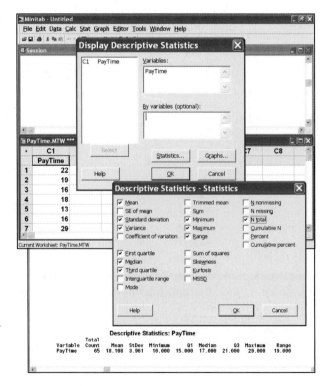

Box plot similar to Figure 3.19(b) on page 139 (data file: DVDSat.MTW):

- Enter the satisfaction rating data from page 138 into column C1 with variable name Ratings.

- Select **Graph : Boxplot**

- In the Boxplots dialog box, select "One Y Simple" and click OK.

- In the "Boxplot—One Y, Simple" dialog box, select Ratings into the "Graph variables" window.

- Click on the Scale button, select the Axes and Ticks tab, check "Transpose value and category scales" and click OK.

- Click OK in the "Boxplot—One Y, Simple" dialog box.

- The box plot is displayed in a graphics window.

- Note that the box plot produced by MINITAB is constructed using methods somewhat different from those presented in Section 3.3 of this book. Consult the MINITAB help menu for a precise description of the box plot construction method used. A box plot that is constructed using the methods of Section 3.3 can be displayed in the Session window—rather than in a graphics window. Instructions for constructing such a box plot—called a **character box plot**—can be found in the MINITAB help menu (see "Character graphs").

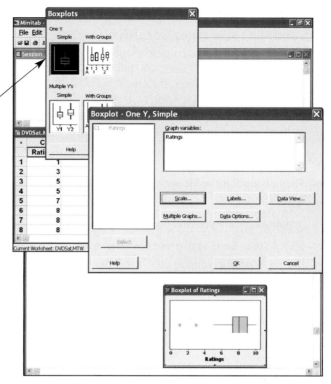

Least squares line, correlation, and covariance for the sales volume data in Section 3.4 (data file: SalesPlot.MTW):

To **compute the equation of the least squares line**:

- Enter the sales and advertising data in Figure 3.24(a) on page 145—advertising expenditure in column C1 with variable name 'Adv Exp' and sales volume in column C2 with variable name 'Sales Vol.'

- Select **Stat : Regression : Fitted Line Plot**

- In the Fitted Line Plot dialog box, enter the variable name 'Sales Vol' (including the single quotes) into the "Response (Y)" window.

- Enter the variable name 'Adv Exp' (including the single quotes) into the "Predictor (X)" window.

- Select Linear for the "Type of Regression Model."

- Click OK in the Fitted Line Plot dialog box.

- A scatter plot of sales volume versus advertising expenditure that includes the equation of the least squares line will be displayed in a graphics window.

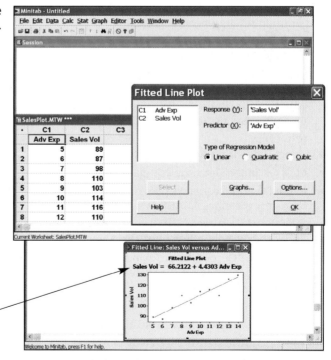

To compute the sample correlation coefficient:

- Select **Stat : Basic Statistics : Correlation**

- In the Correlation dialog box, enter the variable names 'Adv Exp' and 'Sales Vol' (including the single quotes) into the Variables window.

- Remove the checkmark from the "Display p-values" checkbox—or keep this checked as desired (we will learn about p-values in later chapters).

- Click OK in the Correlation dialog box.

- The correlation coefficient will be displayed in the Session window.

To compute the sample covariance:

- Select **Stat : Basic Statistics : Covariance**

- In the Covariance dialog box, enter the variable names 'Adv Exp' and 'Sales Vol' (including the single quotes) into the Variables window.

- Click OK in the Covariance dialog box.

- The covariance will be displayed in the Session window.

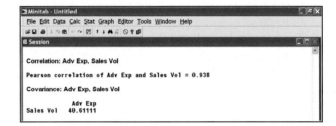

Appendix 3.2 ■ Numerical Descriptive Statistics Using Excel

The instructions in this section begin by describing the entry of data into an Excel worksheet. Alternatively, the data may be loaded directly from the data disk included with the text. The appropriate data file name is given at the top of each instruction block. Please refer to Appendix 1.2 for further information about entering data, saving data, and printing results when using Excel.

Numerical descriptive statistics for the bottle design ratings in Figure 3.4 on page 121 (data file: Design.xlsx):

- Enter the bottle design ratings data into column A with the label Rating in cell A1 and with the 60 design ratings from Table 1.3 on page 8 in cells A2 to A61.

- Select **Data : Data Analysis : Descriptive Statistics**

- Click OK in the Data Analysis dialog box.

- In the Descriptive Statistics dialog box, enter the range for the data, A1.A61, into the "Input Range" box.

- Check the "Labels in first row" checkbox.

- Click in the "Output Range" window and enter the desired cell location for the upper left corner of the output—say cell C1.

- Check the "Summary statistics" checkbox.

- Click OK in the Descriptive Statistics dialog box.

- The descriptive statistics summary will appear in cells C1.D15. Drag the column C border to reveal complete labels for all statistics.

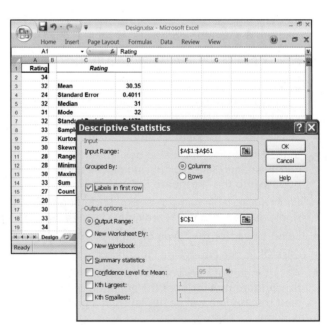

Least squares line, correlation, and covariance for the sales volume data in Figure 3.24(a) on page 145 (data file: SalesPlot.xlsx):

To **compute the equation of the least squares line:**

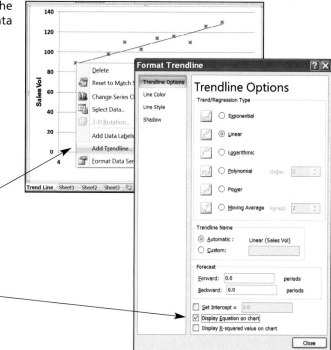

- Follow the directions in Appendix 2.2 for constructing a scatter plot of sales volume versus advertising expenditure.

- When the scatter plot is displayed in a graphics window, move the plot to a chart sheet.

- In the new chart sheet, right-click on any of the plotted points in the scatter plot (Excel refers to the plotted points as the **data series**) and select Add Trendline from the pop-up menu.

- In the Format Trendline dialog box, select Trendline Options.

- In the Trendline Options task pane, select Linear for the "Trend/Regression Type."

- Place a checkmark in the "Display Equation on chart" checkbox.

- Click the Close button in the Format Trendline dialog box.

- The trendline equation will be displayed in the scatter plot and the chart can be edited appropriately.

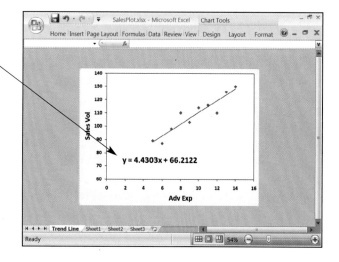

To compute the sample covariance between sales volume and advertising expenditure:

- Enter the advertising and sales data in Figure 3.24(a) on page 145 into columns A and B—advertising expenditures in column A with label "Ad Exp" and sales values in column B with label "Sales Vol."
- Select **Data : Data Analysis : Covariance**
- Click OK in the Data Analysis dialog box.
- In the Covariance dialog box, enter the range of the data, A1.B11 into the Input Range window.
- Select "Grouped By: Columns" if this is not already the selection.
- Place a checkmark in the "Labels in first row" checkbox.
- Under "Output options," select Output Range and enter the cell location for the upper left corner of the output, say A14, in the Output Range window.
- Click OK in the Covariance dialog box.

The Excel ToolPak Covariance routine calculates the population covariance. This quantity is the value in cell B16 (=36.55). To compute the sample covariance from this value, we multiply by $n/(n-1)$ where n is the sample size. In this situation, the sample size is 10. Therefore, we compute the sample covariance as follows:

- Type the label "Sample Covariance" in cell E15.
- In cell E16 write the cell formula =(10/9)*B16 and press Enter.
- The sample covariance (= 40.61111) is the result in cell E16.

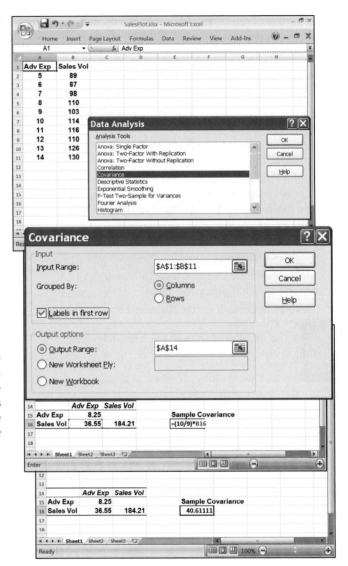

To compute the sample correlation coefficient between sales volume and advertising expenditure:

- Select **Data : Data Analysis : Correlation**
- In the Correlation dialog box, enter the range of the data, A1.B11 into the Input Range window.
- Select "Grouped By: Columns" if this is not already the selection.
- Place a checkmark in the "Labels in first row" checkbox.
- Under output options, select "New Worksheet Ply" to have the output placed in a new worksheet and enter the name Output for the new worksheet.
- Click OK in the Correlation dialog box.
- The sample correlation coefficient (=0.93757) is displayed in the Output worksheet.

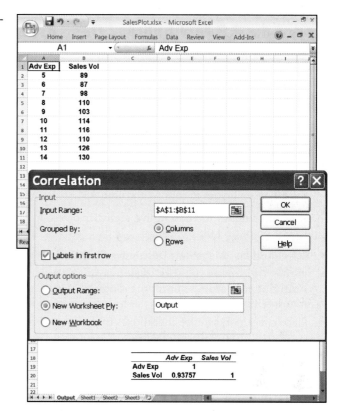

Appendix 3.3 ■ Numerical Descriptive Statistics Using MegaStat

The instructions in this section begin by describing the entry of data into an Excel worksheet. Alternatively, the data may be loaded directly from the data disk included with the text. The appropriate data file name is given at the top of each instruction block. Please refer to Appendix 1.2 for further information about entering data, saving data, and printing results in Excel. Please refer to Appendix 1.3 for more information about using MegaStat.

To analyze the gas mileage data in Table 3.1 on page 117 (data file: GasMiles.xlsx):

- Enter the mileage data from Table 3.1 into column A with the label Mpg in cell A1 and with the 50 gas mileages in cells A2 through A51.

In order to compute the **descriptive statistics** given in Figure 3.1 on page 118:

- Select **Add-Ins : MegaStat : Descriptive Statistics**
- In the "Descriptive statistics" dialog box, use the AutoExpand feature to enter the range A1.A51 into the Input range box.
- Place checkmarks in the checkboxes that correspond to the desired statistics. If tolerance intervals based on the Empirical Rule are desired, check the "Empirical rule" checkbox.
- Click OK in the "Descriptive statistics" dialog box.
- The output will be placed in an output worksheet.

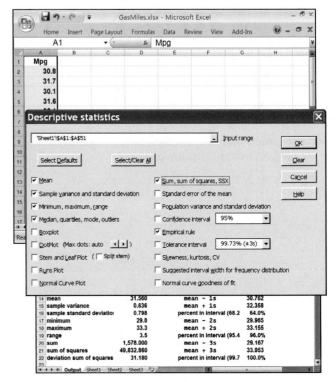

To construct the **box plot** of satisfaction ratings in Figure 3.19(c) on page 139 (data file: DVDSat.xlsx):

- Enter the satisfaction rating data on page 138 into column A with the label Ratings in cell A1 and with the 20 satisfaction ratings in cells A2 to A21.
- Select **Add-Ins : MegaStat : Descriptive Statistics**
- In the "Descriptive statistics" dialog box, use the AutoExpand feature to enter the input range A1.A21 into the Input range box.
- Place a checkmark in the Boxplot checkbox.
- Click OK in the "Descriptive statistics" dialog box.
- The box plot output will be placed in an output worksheet.
- Move the box plot to a chart sheet, and edit as desired.

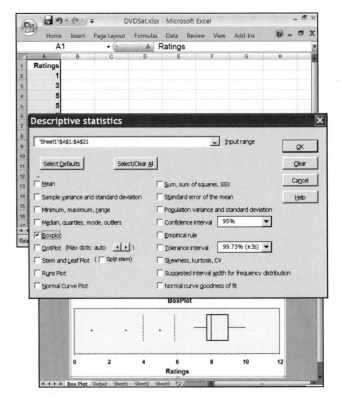

Least squares line and correlation for the sales volume data in Figure 3.24(a) on page 145 (data file: SalesPlot.xlsx):

To **compute the equation of the least squares line:**

- Enter the advertising and sales data in Figure 3.24(a) on page 145 into columns A and B—advertising expenditures in column A with label "Ad Exp" and sales values in column B with label "Sales Vol."

- Select **Add-Ins : MegaStat : Correlation / Regression : Scatterplot**

- In the Scatterplot dialog box, use the AutoExpand feature to enter the range of the values of advertising expenditure (x), A1.A11, into the "horizontal axis" window.

- Enter the range of the values of sales volume (y), B1.B11, into the "vertical axis" window.

- Place a checkmark in the "Plot linear regression line" checkbox.

- Select Markers as the Display option.

- Click OK in the Scatterplot dialog box.

- The equation of the least squares line is displayed in the scatter plot.

- Move the scatter plot to a chart sheet and edit the plot as desired.

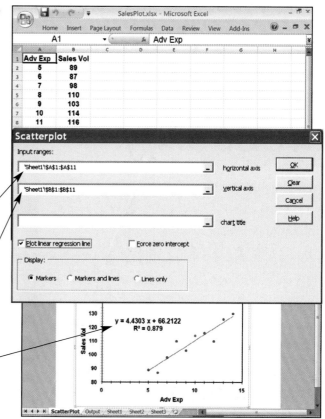

To **compute the sample correlation coefficient** between sales volume (y) and advertising expenditure (x):

- Select **Add-Ins : MegaStat : Correlation / Regression : Correlation Matrix**

- In the Correlation Matrix dialog box, use the mouse to select the range of the data A1.B11 into the Input window.

- Click OK in the Correlation Matrix dialog box.

- The sample correlation coefficient between advertising expenditure and sales volume is displayed in an output sheet.

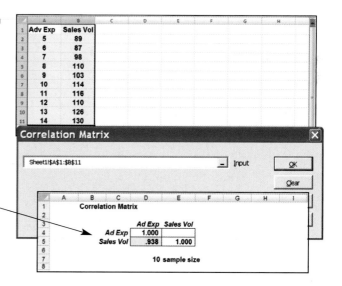

CHAPTER 4

Probability

Chapter Outline

4.1 The Concept of Probability

4.2 Sample Spaces and Events

4.3 Some Elementary Probability Rules

4.4 Conditional Probability and Independence

4.5 Bayes' Theorem (Optional)

I n Chapter 3 we explained how to use sample statistics as point estimates of population parameters. Starting in Chapter 7, we will focus on using sample statistics to make more sophisticated **statistical inferences** about population parameters. We will see that these statistical inferences are generalizations—based on calculating **probabilities**—about population parameters. In this chapter and in Chapters 5 and 6 we present the fundamental concepts about probability that are needed to understand how we make such statistical inferences. We begin our discussions in this chapter by considering rules for calculating probabilities.

In order to illustrate some of the concepts in this chapter, we will introduce a new case.

The AccuRatings Case: AccuRatings is a radio ratings service provided by Strategic Radio Research, a media research firm in Chicago, Illinois. AccuRatings clients include radio stations owned by CBS, Cap Cities/ABC, Group W, Tribune, and many other major broadcast groups across the United States and Canada. In addition, Strategic Radio Research is the primary research vendor for MTV/Music Television. Strategic has twice been named to the Inc. 500 list of fastest-growing privately held companies in America. Using portions of an AccuRatings report and the concepts of probability, we will analyze patterns of radio listenership in the Los Angeles market. We will also use Strategic Radio Research data and several *probability rules* to analyze the popularity of individual songs on a client's playlist.

4.1 The Concept of Probability ● ● ●

We use the concept of *probability* to deal with uncertainty. Intuitively, the probability of an event is a number that measures the chance, or likelihood, that the event will occur. For instance, the probability that your favorite football team will win its next game measures the likelihood of a victory. The probability of an event is always a number between 0 and 1. The closer an event's probability is to 1, the higher is the likelihood that the event will occur; the closer the event's probability is to 0, the smaller is the likelihood that the event will occur. For example, if you believe that the probability that your favorite football team will win its next game is .95, then you are almost sure that your team will win. However, if you believe that the probability of victory is only .10, then you have very little confidence that your team will win.

When performing statistical studies, we sometimes collect data by **performing a controlled experiment.** For instance, we might purposely vary the operating conditions of a manufacturing process in order to study the effects of these changes on the process output. Alternatively, we sometimes obtain data by **observing uncontrolled events.** For example, we might observe the closing price of a share of General Motors' stock every day for 30 trading days. In order to simplify our terminology, we will use the word *experiment* to refer to either method of data collection.

An **experiment** is any process of observation that has an uncertain outcome. The process must be defined so that on any single repetition of the experiment, *one and only one* of the possible outcomes will occur. The possible outcomes for an experiment are called **experimental outcomes.**

CHAPTER 2

For example, if the experiment consists of tossing a coin, the experimental outcomes are "head" and "tail." If the experiment consists of rolling a die, the experimental outcomes are 1, 2, 3, 4, 5, and 6. If the experiment consists of subjecting an automobile to a tailpipe emissions test, the experimental outcomes are pass and fail.

We often wish to assign probabilities to experimental outcomes. This can be done by several methods. Regardless of the method used, **probabilities must be assigned to the experimental outcomes so that two conditions are met:**

1 The probability assigned to each experimental outcome must be between 0 and 1. That is, if E represents an experimental outcome and if $P(E)$ represents the probability of this outcome, then $0 \leq P(E) \leq 1$.

2 The probabilities of all of the experimental outcomes must sum to 1.

Sometimes, when all of the experimental outcomes are equally likely, we can use logic to assign probabilities. This method, which is called the *classical method*, will be more fully discussed in the next section. As a simple example, consider the experiment of tossing a fair coin. Here, there are *two* equally likely experimental outcomes—head (H) and tail (T). Therefore, logic suggests that the probability of observing a head, denoted $P(H)$, is $1/2 = .5$, and that the probability of observing a tail, denoted $P(T)$, is also $1/2 = .5$. Notice that each probability is between 0 and 1. Furthermore, because H and T are all of the experimental outcomes, $P(H) + P(T) = 1$.

Probability is often interpreted to be a **long-run relative frequency.** As an example, consider repeatedly tossing a coin. If we get 6 heads in the first 10 tosses, then the relative frequency, or fraction, of heads is $6/10 = .6$. If we get 47 heads in the first 100 tosses, the relative frequency of heads is $47/100 = .47$. If we get 5,067 heads in the first 10,000 tosses, the relative frequency of heads is $5,067/10,000 = .5067$.[1] Since the relative frequency of heads is approaching (that is, getting closer to) .5, we might estimate that the probability of obtaining a head when tossing the coin is .5. When we say this, we mean that, if we tossed the coin an indefinitely large number of times (that is, a number of times *approaching infinity*), the relative frequency of heads obtained would approach .5. Of course, in actuality it is impossible to toss a coin (or perform any experiment) an indefinitely large number of times. Therefore, a relative frequency interpretation of probability is a mathematical idealization. To summarize, suppose that E is an experimental outcome that might occur when a particular experiment is performed. Then the probability that E will occur, $P(E)$, can be interpreted to be the number that would be approached by the relative frequency of E if we performed the experiment an indefinitely large number of times. It follows that we often think of a probability in terms of the percentage of the time the experimental outcome would occur in many repetitions of the experiment. For instance, when we say that the probability of obtaining a head when we toss a coin is .5, we are saying that, when we repeatedly toss the coin an indefinitely large number of times, we will obtain a head on 50 percent of the repetitions.

Sometimes it is either difficult or incorrect to use the classical method to assign probabilities. Since we can often make a relative frequency interpretation of probability, we can estimate a probability by performing the experiment in which an outcome might occur many times. Then, we estimate the probability of the experimental outcome to be the proportion of the time that the outcome occurs during the many repetitions of the experiment. For example, to estimate the probability that a randomly selected consumer prefers Coca-Cola to all other soft drinks, we perform an experiment in which we ask a randomly selected consumer for his or her preference. There are two possible experimental outcomes: "prefers Coca-Cola" and "does not prefer Coca-Cola." However, we have no reason to believe that these experimental outcomes are equally likely, so we cannot use the classical method. We might perform the experiment, say, 1,000 times by surveying 1,000 randomly selected consumers. Then, if 140 of those surveyed said that they prefer Coca-Cola, we would estimate the probability that a randomly selected consumer prefers Coca-Cola to all other soft drinks to be $140/1,000 = .14$. This is called the *relative frequency method* for assigning probability.

If we cannot perform the experiment many times, we might estimate the probability by using our previous experience with similar situations, intuition, or special expertise that we may possess. For example, a company president might estimate the probability of success for a one-time business venture to be .7. Here, on the basis of knowledge of the success of previous similar ventures, the opinions of company personnel, and other pertinent information, the president believes that there is a 70 percent chance the venture will be successful.

When we use experience, intuitive judgement, or expertise to assess a probability, we call this a **subjective probability.** Such a probability may or may not have a relative frequency interpretation. For instance, when the company president estimates that the probability of a successful business venture is .7, this may mean that, if business conditions similar to those that are about to be encountered could be repeated many times, then the business venture would be successful in 70 percent of the repetitions. Or, the president may not be thinking in relative frequency terms but rather may consider the venture a "one-shot" proposition. We will discuss some other

---

[1]The South African mathematician John Kerrich actually obtained this result when he tossed a coin 10,000 times while imprisoned by the Germans during World War II.

subjective probabilities later. However, the interpretations of statistical inferences we will explain in later chapters are based on the relative frequency interpretation of probability. For this reason, we will concentrate on this interpretation.

4.2 Sample Spaces and Events ● ● ●

CHAPTER 2

In order to calculate probabilities by using the classical method, it is important to understand and use the idea of a *sample space*.

> The **sample space** of an experiment is the set of all possible experimental outcomes. The experimental outcomes in the sample space are often called **sample space outcomes.**

EXAMPLE 4.1

A company is choosing a new chief executive officer (CEO). It has narrowed the list of candidates to four finalists (identified by last name only)—Adams, Chung, Hill, and Rankin. If we consider our experiment to be making a final choice of the company's CEO, then the experiment's sample space consists of the four possible experimental outcomes:

$A \equiv$ Adams is chosen as CEO.

$C \equiv$ Chung is chosen as CEO.

$H \equiv$ Hill is chosen as CEO.

$R \equiv$ Rankin is chosen as CEO.

Each of these outcomes is a sample space outcome, and the set of these sample space outcomes is the sample space.

  Next, suppose that industry analysts feel (subjectively) that the probabilities that Adams, Chung, Hill, and Rankin will be chosen as CEO are .1, .2, .5, and .2, respectively. That is, in probability notation

$$P(A) = .1 \quad P(C) = .2 \quad P(H) = .5 \quad \text{and} \quad P(R) = .2$$

Notice that each probability assigned to a sample space outcome is between 0 and 1 and that the sum of the probabilities equals 1.

EXAMPLE 4.2

A newly married couple plans to have two children. Naturally, they are curious about whether their children will be boys or girls. Therefore, we consider the experiment of having two children. In order to find the sample space of this experiment, we let B denote that a child is a boy and G denote that a child is a girl. Then, it is useful to construct the tree diagram shown in Figure 4.1. This diagram pictures the experiment as a two-step process—having the first child, which could be either a boy or a girl (B or G), and then having the second child, which could also be either a boy or a girl (B or G). Each branch of the tree leads to a sample space outcome. These outcomes are listed at the right ends of the branches. We see that there are four sample space outcomes. Therefore, the sample space (that is, the set of all the sample space outcomes) is

$$BB \quad BG \quad GB \quad GG$$

In order to consider the probabilities of these outcomes, suppose that boys and girls are equally likely each time a child is born. Intuitively, this says that each of the sample space outcomes is equally likely. That is, this implies that

$$P(BB) = P(BG) = P(GB) = P(GG) = \frac{1}{4}$$

This says that there is a 25 percent chance that each of these outcomes will occur. Again, notice that these probabilities sum to 1.

FIGURE 4.1   **A Tree Diagram of the Genders of Two Children**

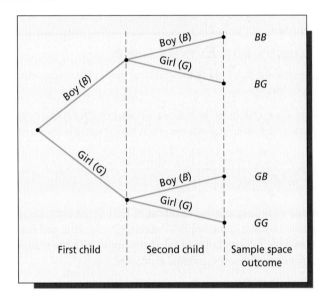

First child   Second child   Sample space outcome

EXAMPLE 4.3

A student takes a pop quiz that consists of three true–false questions. If we consider our experiment to be answering the three questions, each question can be answered correctly or incorrectly. We will let *C* denote answering a question correctly and *I* denote answering a question incorrectly. Then, Figure 4.2 depicts a tree diagram of the sample space outcomes for the experiment. The diagram portrays the experiment as a three-step process—answering the first question (correctly or incorrectly, that is, *C* or *I*), answering the second question, and answering the third question. The tree diagram has eight different branches, and the eight sample space outcomes are listed at the ends of the branches. We see that the sample space is

$$CCC \quad CCI \quad CIC \quad CII$$
$$ICC \quad ICI \quad IIC \quad III$$

Next, suppose that the student was totally unprepared for the quiz and had to blindly guess the answer to each question. That is, the student had a 50–50 chance (or .5 probability) of correctly answering each question. Intuitively, this would say that each of the eight sample space outcomes is equally likely to occur. That is,

$$P(CCC) = P(CCI) = \cdots = P(III) = \frac{1}{8}$$

Here, as in Examples 4.1 and 4.2, the sum of the probabilities of the sample space outcomes is equal to 1.

Events and finding probabilities by using sample spaces   At the beginning of this chapter, we informally talked about events. We now give the formal definition of an event.

An **event** is a set (or collection) of sample space outcomes.

For instance, if we consider the couple planning to have two children, the event "the couple will have at least one girl" consists of the sample space outcomes *BG*, *GB*, and *GG*. That is, the event "the couple will have at least one girl" will occur if and only if one of the sample

FIGURE 4.2   A Tree Diagram of Answering Three True–False Questions

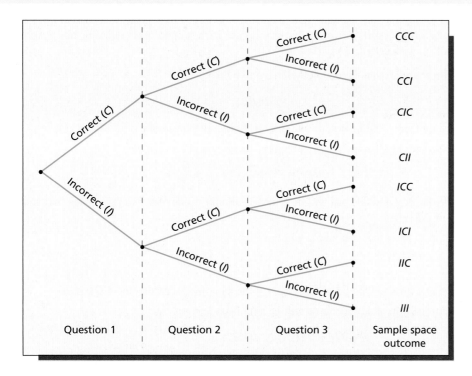

space outcomes *BG*, *GB*, or *GG* occurs. As another example, in the pop quiz situation, the event "the student will answer at least two out of three questions correctly" consists of the sample space outcomes *CCC*, *CCI*, *CIC*, and *ICC*, while the event "the student will answer all three questions correctly" consists of the sample space outcome *CCC*. In general, we see that the word description of an event determines the sample space outcomes that correspond to the event.

Suppose that we wish to find the probability that an event will occur. We can find such a probability as follows:

> The **probability of an event** is the **sum of the probabilities of the sample space outcomes** that correspond to the event.

As an example, in the CEO situation, suppose only Adams and Hill are internal candidates (they already work for the company). Letting *INT* denote the event that "an internal candidate is selected for the CEO position," then *INT* consists of the sample space outcomes *A* and *H* (that is, *INT* will occur if and only if either of the sample space outcomes *A* or *H* occurs). It follows that $P(INT) = P(A) + P(H) = .1 + .5 = .6$. This says that the probability that an internal candidate will be chosen to be CEO is .6.

In general, we have seen that the probability of any sample space outcome (experimental outcome) is a number between 0 and 1, and we have also seen that the probabilities of all the sample space outcomes sum to 1. It follows that **the probability of an event** (that is, the probability of a set of sample space outcomes) **is a number between 0 and 1.** That is,

> If *A* is an event, then $0 \leq P(A) \leq 1$.
>   Moreover:
>
> 1   If an event never occurs, then the probability of this event equals 0.
> 2   If an event is certain to occur, then the probability of this event equals 1.

EXAMPLE 4.4

Consider the couple that is planning to have two children, and suppose that each child is equally likely to be a boy or girl. Recalling that in this case each sample space outcome has a probability equal to 1/4, we see that:

1   The probability that the couple will have two boys is

$$P(BB) = \frac{1}{4}$$

since two boys will be born if and only if the sample space outcome *BB* occurs.

2   The probability that the couple will have one boy and one girl is

$$P(BG) + P(GB) = \frac{1}{4} + \frac{1}{4} = \frac{1}{2}$$

since one boy and one girl will be born if and only if one of the sample space outcomes *BG* or *GB* occurs.

3   The probability that the couple will have two girls is

$$P(GG) = \frac{1}{4}$$

since two girls will be born if and only if the sample space outcome *GG* occurs.

4   The probability that the couple will have at least one girl is

$$P(BG) + P(GB) + P(GG) = \frac{1}{4} + \frac{1}{4} + \frac{1}{4} = \frac{3}{4}$$

since at least one girl will be born if and only if one of the sample space outcomes *BG*, *GB*, or *GG* occurs.

EXAMPLE 4.5

Again consider the pop quiz consisting of three true–false questions, and suppose that the student blindly guesses the answers. Remembering that in this case each sample space outcome has a probability equal to 1/8, then:

1   The probability that the student will get all three questions correct is

$$P(CCC) = \frac{1}{8}$$

2   The probability that the student will get exactly two questions correct is

$$P(CCI) + P(CIC) + P(ICC) = \frac{1}{8} + \frac{1}{8} + \frac{1}{8} = \frac{3}{8}$$

since two questions will be answered correctly if and only if one of the sample space outcomes *CCI*, *CIC*, or *ICC* occurs.

3   The probability that the student will get exactly one question correct is

$$P(CII) + P(ICI) + P(IIC) = \frac{1}{8} + \frac{1}{8} + \frac{1}{8} = \frac{3}{8}$$

since one question will be answered correctly if and only if one of the sample space outcomes *CII*, *ICI*, or *IIC* occurs.

4   The probability that the student will get all three questions incorrect is

$$P(III) = \frac{1}{8}$$

5   The probability that the student will get at least two questions correct is

$$P(CCC) + P(CCI) + P(CIC) + P(ICC) = \frac{1}{8} + \frac{1}{8} + \frac{1}{8} + \frac{1}{8} = \frac{1}{2}$$

since the student will get at least two questions correct if and only if one of the sample space outcomes *CCC*, *CCI*, *CIC*, or *ICC* occurs.

Notice that in the true–false question situation we find that, for instance, the probability that the student will get exactly two questions correct equals the ratio

$$\frac{\text{the number of sample space outcomes resulting in two correct answers}}{\text{the total number of sample space outcomes}} = \frac{3}{8}$$

In general, when a sample space is finite we can use the following method for computing the probability of an event:

> *If all of the sample space outcomes are equally likely,* then the probability that an event will occur is equal to the ratio
>
> $$\frac{\text{the number of sample space outcomes that correspond to the event}}{\text{the total number of sample space outcomes}}$$

When we use this rule, we are using the *classical method* for computing probabilities. Furthermore, it is important to emphasize that we can use this rule only when all of the sample space outcomes are equally likely (as they are in the true–false question situation). For example, if we were to use this rule in the CEO situation, we would find that the probability of choosing an internal candidate as CEO is

$$P(INT) = \frac{\text{the number of internal candidates}}{\text{the total number of candidates}} = \frac{2}{4} = .5$$

This result is not equal to the correct value of $P(INT)$, which we previously found to be equal to .6. Here, this rule does not give us the correct answer because the sample space outcomes A, C, H, and R are not equally likely—recall that $P(A) = .1$, $P(C) = .2$, $P(H) = .5$, and $P(R) = .2$.

EXAMPLE 4.6

Suppose that 650,000 of the 1,000,000 households in an eastern U.S. city subscribe to a newspaper called the *Atlantic Journal,* and consider randomly selecting one of the households in this city. That is, consider selecting one household by giving each and every household in the city the same chance of being selected. Let A be the event that the randomly selected household subscribes to the *Atlantic Journal.* Then, because the sample space of this experiment consists of 1,000,000 equally likely sample space outcomes (households), it follows that

$$P(A) = \frac{\text{the number of households that subscribe to the \textit{Atlantic Journal}}}{\text{the total number of households in the city}}$$

$$= \frac{650,000}{1,000,000}$$

$$= .65$$

This says that the probability that the randomly selected household subscribes to the *Atlantic Journal* is .65.

EXAMPLE 4.7 The AccuRatings Case   Ⓒ

As discussed in the introduction to this chapter, AccuRatings is a radio ratings service provided by Strategic Radio Research, a media research firm in Chicago, Illinois. Figure 4.3 gives portions of an AccuRatings report on radio ratings in the Los Angeles market. This report, based on interviews with 5,528 randomly selected persons 12 years of age or older, gives estimates of the number and the percentage of Los Angeles residents who would name each of the top 10 radio stations in Los Angeles as the station they listen to most.

To better understand the estimates in Figure 4.3, we will consider how they were obtained. AccuRatings asked each of the 5,528 sampled residents to name which station (if any) he or

FIGURE 4.3   **Portions of an AccuRatings Report on Radio Ratings in the Los Angeles Market**

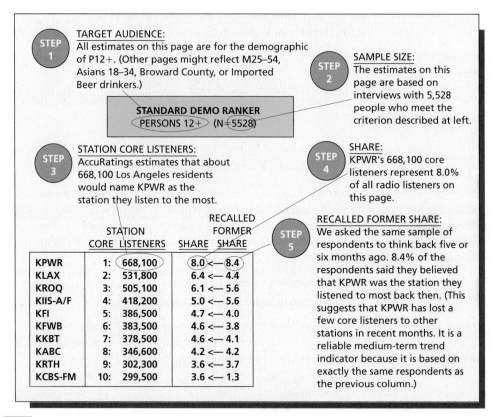

STEP 1 TARGET AUDIENCE:
All estimates on this page are for the demographic of P12+. (Other pages might reflect M25–54, Asians 18–34, Broward County, or Imported Beer drinkers.)

STANDARD DEMO RANKER
PERSONS 12+ (N=5528)

STEP 2 SAMPLE SIZE:
The estimates on this page are based on interviews with 5,528 people who meet the criterion described at left.

STEP 3 STATION CORE LISTENERS:
AccuRatings estimates that about 668,100 Los Angeles residents would name KPWR as the station they listen to the most.

STEP 4 SHARE:
KPWR's 668,100 core listeners represent 8.0% of all radio listeners on this page.

STEP 5 RECALLED FORMER SHARE:
We asked the same sample of respondents to think back five or six months ago. 8.4% of the respondents said they believed that KPWR was the station they listened to most back then. (This suggests that KPWR has lost a few core listeners to other stations in recent months. It is a reliable medium-term trend indicator because it is based on exactly the same respondents as the previous column.)

STATION		CORE LISTENERS	SHARE	RECALLED FORMER SHARE
KPWR	1:	668,100	8.0	<— 8.4
KLAX	2:	531,800	6.4	<— 4.4
KROQ	3:	505,100	6.1	<— 5.6
KIIS-A/F	4:	418,200	5.0	<— 5.6
KFI	5:	386,500	4.7	<— 4.0
KFWB	6:	383,500	4.6	<— 3.8
KKBT	7:	378,500	4.6	<— 4.1
KABC	8:	346,600	4.2	<— 4.2
KRTH	9:	302,300	3.6	<— 3.7
KCBS-FM	10:	299,500	3.6	<— 1.3

Source: Strategic Radio Research, *AccuRatings Introduction for Broadcasters.*

she listens to most. AccuRatings then used the responses of the sampled residents to calculate the proportion of these residents who favored each station. The sample proportion of the residents who favored a particular station is an estimate of the population proportion of all Los Angeles residents (12 years of age or older) who favor the station, or, equivalently, of the probability that a randomly selected Los Angeles resident would favor the station. For example, if 445 of the 5,528 sampled residents favored station KPWR, then $445/5{,}528 = .080499276$ is an estimate of $P(KPWR)$, the probability that a randomly selected Los Angeles resident would favor station KPWR. Furthermore, assuming that there are 8,300,000 Los Angeles residents 12 years of age or older, an estimate of the number of these residents who favor station KPWR is

$$(8{,}300{,}000) \times (.080499276) = 668{,}143.99$$

Now, if we

1 Round the estimated number of residents favoring station KPWR to 668,100, and

2 Express the estimated probability $P(KPWR)$ as the rounded percentage 8.0%,

we obtain what the AccuRatings report in Figure 4.3 states are (1) the estimated number of **core listeners** for station KPWR and (2) the estimated **share** of all listeners for station KPWR. These measures of listenership would be determined for other stations in a similar manner (see Figure 4.3).

To conclude this section, we note that in Appendix B on page 653 we discuss several *counting rules* that can be used to count the number of sample space outcomes in an experiment. These rules are particularly useful when there are so many sample space outcomes that the outcomes are tedious to list.

Exercises for Sections 4.1 and 4.2

CONCEPTS

4.1 Define the following terms: *experiment, event, probability, sample space.*

4.2 Explain the properties that must be satisfied by a probability.

METHODS AND APPLICATIONS

4.3 Two randomly selected grocery store patrons are each asked to take a blind taste test and to then state which of three diet colas (marked as *A*, *B*, or *C*) he or she prefers.
  a Draw a tree diagram depicting the sample space outcomes for the test results.
  b List the sample space outcomes that correspond to each of the following events:
    (1) Both patrons prefer diet cola *A*.
    (2) The two patrons prefer the same diet cola.
    (3) The two patrons prefer different diet colas.
    (4) Diet cola *A* is preferred by at least one of the two patrons.
    (5) Neither of the patrons prefers diet cola *C*.
  c Assuming that all sample space outcomes are equally likely, find the probability of each of the events given in part *b*.

4.4 Suppose that a couple will have three children. Letting *B* denote a boy and *G* denote a girl:
  a Draw a tree diagram depicting the sample space outcomes for this experiment.
  b List the sample space outcomes that correspond to each of the following events:
    (1) All three children will have the same gender.
    (2) Exactly two of the three children will be girls.
    (3) Exactly one of the three children will be a girl.
    (4) None of the three children will be a girl.
  c Assuming that all sample space outcomes are equally likely, find the probability of each of the events given in part *b*.

4.5 Four people will enter an automobile showroom, and each will either purchase a car (*P*) or not purchase a car (*N*).
  a Draw a tree diagram depicting the sample space of all possible purchase decisions that could potentially be made by the four people.
  b List the sample space outcomes that correspond to each of the following events:
    (1) Exactly three people will purchase a car.
    (2) Two or fewer people will purchase a car.
    (3) One or more people will purchase a car.
    (4) All four people will make the same purchase decision.
  c Assuming that all sample space outcomes are equally likely, find the probability of each of the events given in part *b*.

4.6 THE ACCURATINGS CASE

  Using the information given in the AccuRatings report of Figure 4.3 (page 178), find estimates of each of the following:
  a The probability that a randomly selected Los Angeles resident (12 years or older) would name station KLAX as the station that he or she listens to most.
  b The probability that a randomly selected Los Angeles resident (12 years or older) would name station KABC as the station that he or she listens to most.
  c The percentage of all Los Angeles residents (12 years or older) who would name KCBS-FM as the station that he or she listens to most.
  d The number of the 5,528 sampled residents who named station KFI as the station he or she listens to most.
  e The number of the 5,528 sampled residents who named station KROQ as the station he or she listens to most.

4.7 Let *A*, *B*, *C*, *D*, and *E* be sample space outcomes forming a sample space. Suppose that $P(A) = .2$, $P(B) = .15$, $P(C) = .3$, and $P(D) = .2$. What is $P(E)$? Explain how you got your answer.

4.3 Some Elementary Probability Rules ◉ ● ●

We can often calculate probabilities by using formulas called **probability rules.** We will begin by presenting the simplest probability rule: the *rule of complements.* To start, we define the complement of an event:

FIGURE 4.4
The Complement
of an Event (the
Shaded Region Is $\overline{A}$,
the Complement
of *A*)

> Given an event *A*, the **complement of *A*** is the event consisting of all sample space outcomes that do not correspond to the occurrence of *A*. The complement of *A* is denoted $\overline{A}$. Furthermore, $P(\overline{A})$ denotes **the probability that *A* will not occur.**

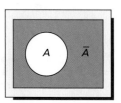

Figure 4.4 is a **Venn diagram** depicting the complement $\overline{A}$ of an event *A*. In any probability situation, either an event *A* or its complement $\overline{A}$ must occur. Therefore, we have

$$P(A) + P(\overline{A}) = 1$$

This implies the following result:

The Rule of Complements

Consider an event *A*. Then, **the probability that *A* will not occur** is

$$P(\overline{A}) = 1 - P(A)$$

EXAMPLE 4.8

Recall from Example 4.6 that the probability that a randomly selected household in an eastern U.S. city subscribes to the *Atlantic Journal* is .65. It follows that the probability of the complement of this event (that is, the probability that a randomly selected household in the eastern U.S. city does not subscribe to the *Atlantic Journal*) is $1 - .65 = .35$.

EXAMPLE 4.9

Consider Example 4.6, and recall that 650,000 of the 1,000,000 households in an eastern U.S. city subscribe to the *Atlantic Journal.* Also, suppose that 500,000 households in the city subscribe to a competing newspaper, the *Beacon News,* and further suppose that 250,000 households subscribe to both the *Atlantic Journal* and the *Beacon News.* As in Example 4.6, we consider randomly selecting one household in the city, and we define the following events:

   A ≡ the randomly selected household subscribes to the *Atlantic Journal.*
   $\overline{A}$ ≡ the randomly selected household does not subscribe to the *Atlantic Journal.*
   B ≡ the randomly selected household subscribes to the *Beacon News.*
   $\overline{B}$ ≡ the randomly selected household does not subscribe to the *Beacon News.*

Using the notation $A \cap B$ to denote *both A and B*, we also define

   $A \cap B$ ≡ the randomly selected household subscribes to both the *Atlantic Journal*
            and the *Beacon News.*

Since 650,000 of the 1,000,000 households subscribe to the *Atlantic Journal* (that is, correspond to the event *A* occurring), then 350,000 households do not subscribe to the *Atlantic Journal* (that is, correspond to the event $\overline{A}$ occurring). Similarly, 500,000 households subscribe to the *Beacon News* (*B*), so 500,000 households do not subscribe to the *Beacon News* ($\overline{B}$). We summarize this information, as well as the 250,000 households that correspond to the event $A \cap B$ occurring, in Table 4.1.

TABLE 4.1   A Summary of the Number of Households Corresponding to the Events A, $\bar{A}$, B, $\bar{B}$, and $A \cap B$

Events	Subscribes to Beacon News, B	Does Not Subscribe to Beacon News, $\bar{B}$	Total
Subscribes to *Atlantic Journal*, A	250,000		650,000
Does Not Subscribe to *Atlantic Journal*, $\bar{A}$			350,000
Total	500,000	500,000	1,000,000

Next, consider the events

$A \cap \bar{B} \equiv$ the randomly selected household subscribes to the *Atlantic Journal* and does not subscribe to the *Beacon News*.

$\bar{A} \cap B \equiv$ the randomly selected household does not subscribe to the *Atlantic Journal* and does subscribe to the *Beacon News*.

$\bar{A} \cap \bar{B} \equiv$ the randomly selected household does not subscribe to the *Atlantic Journal* and does not subscribe to the *Beacon News*.

Since 650,000 households subscribe to the *Atlantic Journal* (A) and 250,000 households subscribe to both the *Atlantic Journal* and the *Beacon News* ($A \cap B$), it follows that 650,000 − 250,000 = 400,000 households subscribe to the *Atlantic Journal* but do not subscribe to the *Beacon News* ($A \cap \bar{B}$). This subtraction is illustrated in Table 4.2(a). By similar logic, it also follows that:

1   As illustrated in Table 4.2(b), 500,000 − 250,000 = 250,000 households do not subscribe to the *Atlantic Journal* but do subscribe to the *Beacon News* ($\bar{A} \cap B$).

2   As illustrated in Table 4.2(c), 350,000 − 250,000 = 100,000 households do not subscribe to the *Atlantic Journal* and do not subscribe to the *Beacon News* ($\bar{A} \cap \bar{B}$).

TABLE 4.2   Subtracting to Find the Number of Households Corresponding to the Events $A \cap \bar{B}$, $\bar{A} \cap B$, and $\bar{A} \cap \bar{B}$

(a) The Number of Households Corresponding to (A and $\bar{B}$)

Events	Subscribes to Beacon News, B	Does Not Subscribe to Beacon News, $\bar{B}$	Total
Subscribes to *Atlantic Journal*, A	250,000	650,000 − 250,000 = 400,000	650,000
Does Not Subscribe to *Atlantic Journal*, $\bar{A}$			350,000
Total	500,000	500,000	1,000,000

(b) The Number of Households Corresponding to ($\bar{A}$ and B)

Events	Subscribes to Beacon News, B	Does Not Subscribe to Beacon News, $\bar{B}$	Total
Subscribes to *Atlantic Journal*, A	250,000	650,000 − 250,000 = 400,000	650,000
Does Not Subscribe to *Atlantic Journal*, $\bar{A}$	500,000 − 250,000 = 250,000		350,000
Total	500,000	500,000	1,000,000

TABLE 4.2 (*continued*)

(c) The Number of Households Corresponding to ($\overline{A}$ and $\overline{B}$)

Events	Subscribes to Beacon News, B	Does Not Subscribe to Beacon News, $\overline{B}$	Total
Subscribes to *Atlantic Journal, A*	250,000	650,000 − 250,000 = 400,000	650,000
Does Not Subscribe to *Atlantic Journal, $\overline{A}$*	500,000 − 250,000 = 250,000	350,000 − 250,000 = 100,000	350,000
Total	500,000	500,000	1,000,000

TABLE 4.3 A Contingency Table Summarizing Subscription Data for the *Atlantic Journal* and the *Beacon News*

Events	Subscribes to Beacon News, B	Does Not Subscribe to Beacon News, $\overline{B}$	Total
Subscribes to *Atlantic Journal, A*	250,000	400,000	650,000
Does Not Subscribe to *Atlantic Journal, $\overline{A}$*	250,000	100,000	350,000
Total	500,000	500,000	1,000,000

We summarize all of these results in Table 4.3, which is called a **contingency table.** Because we will randomly select one household (making all of the households equally likely to be chosen), the probability of any of the previously defined events is the ratio of the number of households corresponding to the event's occurrence to the total number of households in the city. Therefore, for example,

$$P(A) = \frac{650,000}{1,000,000} = .65 \qquad P(B) = \frac{500,000}{1,000,000} = .5$$

$$P(A \cap B) = \frac{250,000}{1,000,000} = .25$$

This last probability says that the probability that the randomly selected household subscribes to both the *Atlantic Journal* and the *Beacon News* is .25.

Next, letting $A \cup B$ denote *A* or *B* (or both), we consider finding the probability of the event

$A \cup B \equiv$ the randomly selected household subscribes to the *Atlantic Journal* or the *Beacon News* (or both)—that is, subscribes to at least one of the two newspapers.

Looking at Table 4.3, we see that the households subscribing to the *Atlantic Journal* or the *Beacon News* are (1) the 400,000 households that subscribe to only the *Atlantic Journal*, $A \cap \overline{B}$, (2) the 250,000 households that subscribe to only the *Beacon News*, $\overline{A} \cap B$, and (3) the 250,000 households that subscribe to both the *Atlantic Journal* and the *Beacon News*, $A \cap B$. Therefore, since a total of 900,000 households subscribe to the *Atlantic Journal* or the *Beacon News*, it follows that

$$P(A \cup B) = \frac{900,000}{1,000,000} = .9$$

This says that the probability that the randomly selected household subscribes to the *Atlantic Journal* or the *Beacon News* is .90. That is, 90 percent of the households in the city subscribe to the *Atlantic Journal* or the *Beacon News*. Notice that $P(A \cup B) = .90$ does not equal

$$P(A) + P(B) = .65 + .5 = 1.15$$

Logically, the reason for this is that both $P(A) = .65$ and $P(B) = .5$ count the 25 percent of the households that subscribe to both newspapers. Therefore, the sum of $P(A)$ and $P(B)$ counts this

25 percent of the households once too often. It follows that if we subtract $P(A \cap B) = .25$ from the sum of $P(A)$ and $P(B)$, then we will obtain $P(A \cup B)$. That is,

$$P(A \cup B) = P(A) + P(B) - P(A \cap B)$$
$$= .65 + .5 - .25 = .90$$

In order to generalize the ideas in the previous example, we make the following definitions:

The Intersection and Union of Two Events

Given two events A and B,

1 The **intersection of A and B** is the event consisting of the sample space outcomes belonging to both A and B. The intersection is denoted by $A \cap B$. Furthermore, $P(A \cap B)$ denotes **the probability that** *both A and B will simultaneously occur.*

2 The **union of A and B** is the event consisting of the sample space outcomes belonging to A or B (or both). The union is denoted $A \cup B$. Furthermore, $P(A \cup B)$ denotes **the probability that *A or B (or both) will occur.***

Noting that Figure 4.5 shows **Venn diagrams** depicting the events A, B, $A \cap B$, and $A \cup B$, we have the following general result:

The Addition Rule

Let A and B be events. Then, **the probability that *A or B (or both) will occur*** is

$$P(A \cup B) = P(A) + P(B) - P(A \cap B)$$

The reasoning behind this result has been illustrated at the end of Example 4.9. Similarly, the Venn diagrams in Figure 4.5 show that when we compute $P(A) + P(B)$, we are counting each of the sample space outcomes in $A \cap B$ twice. We correct for this by subtracting $P(A \cap B)$.

We next define the idea of *mutually exclusive events:*

Mutually Exclusive Events

Two events A and B are **mutually exclusive** if they have no sample space outcomes in common. In this case, the events A and B cannot occur simultaneously, and thus

$$P(A \cap B) = 0$$

Noting that Figure 4.6 is a Venn diagram depicting two mutually exclusive events, we consider the following example.

EXAMPLE 4.10

Consider randomly selecting a card from a standard deck of 52 playing cards. We define the following events:

$J \equiv$ the randomly selected card is a jack.

$Q \equiv$ the randomly selected card is a queen.

$R \equiv$ the randomly selected card is a red card (that is, a diamond or a heart).

Because there is no card that is both a jack and a queen, the events J and Q are mutually exclusive. On the other hand, there are two cards that are both jacks and red cards—the jack of diamonds and the jack of hearts—so the events J and R are not mutually exclusive.

FIGURE 4.5   **Venn Diagrams Depicting the Events *A*, *B*, *A* ∩ *B*, and *A* ∪ *B***

FIGURE 4.6
**Two Mutually
Exclusive Events**

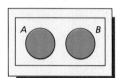

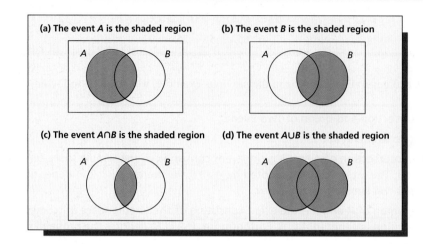

We have seen that for any two events *A* and *B*, the probability that *A* or *B* (or both) will occur is

$$P(A \cup B) = P(A) + P(B) - P(A \cap B)$$

Therefore, when calculating $P(A \cup B)$, we should always subtract $P(A \cap B)$ from the sum of $P(A)$ and $P(B)$. However, when *A* and *B* are mutually exclusive, $P(A \cap B)$ equals 0. Therefore, in this case—and only in this case—we have the following:

The Addition Rule for Two Mutually Exclusive Events

Let *A* and *B* be **mutually exclusive** events. Then, **the probability that *A* or *B* will occur** is

$$P(A \cup B) = P(A) + P(B)$$

EXAMPLE 4.11

Again consider randomly selecting a card from a standard deck of 52 playing cards, and define the events

  J ≡ the randomly selected card is a jack.

  Q ≡ the randomly selected card is a queen.

  R ≡ the randomly selected card is a red card (a diamond or a heart).

Since there are four jacks, four queens, and 26 red cards, we have $P(J) = \frac{4}{52}$, $P(Q) = \frac{4}{52}$, and $P(R) = \frac{26}{52}$. Furthermore, since there is no card that is both a jack and a queen, the events *J* and *Q* are mutually exclusive and thus $P(J \cap Q) = 0$. It follows that the probability that the randomly selected card is a jack or a queen is

$$P(J \cup Q) = P(J) + P(Q)$$
$$= \frac{4}{52} + \frac{4}{52} = \frac{8}{52} = \frac{2}{13}$$

Since there are two cards that are both jacks and red cards—the jack of diamonds and the jack of hearts—the events *J* and *R* are not mutually exclusive. Therefore, the probability that the randomly selected card is a jack or a red card is

$$P(J \cup R) = P(J) + P(R) - P(J \cap R)$$
$$= \frac{4}{52} + \frac{26}{52} - \frac{2}{52} = \frac{28}{52} = \frac{7}{13}$$

We now consider an arbitrary group of events—$A_1, A_2, \ldots, A_N$. We will denote the probability that A_1 or A_2 or $\cdots$ or A_N occurs (that is, the probability that at least one of the events occurs) as $P(A_1 \cup A_2 \cup \cdots \cup A_N)$. Although there is a formula for this probability, it is quite complicated and we will not present it in this book. However, sometimes we can use sample spaces to reason out such a probability. For instance, in the playing card situation of Example 4.11, there are four jacks, four queens, and 22 red cards that are not jacks or queens (the 26 red cards minus the two red jacks and the two red queens). Therefore, because there are a total of 30 cards corresponding to the event $J \cup Q \cup R$, it follows that

$$P(J \cup Q \cup R) = \frac{30}{52} = \frac{15}{26}$$

Because some cards are both jacks and red cards, and because some cards are both queens and red cards, we say that the events J, Q, and R are not mutually exclusive. When, however, a group of events is mutually exclusive, there is a simple formula for the probability that at least one of the events will occur:

The Addition Rule for *N* Mutually Exclusive Events

The events $A_1, A_2, \ldots, A_N$ are mutually exclusive if no two of the events have any sample space outcomes in common. In this case, no two of the events can occur simultaneously, and

$$P(A_1 \cup A_2 \cup \cdots \cup A_N) = P(A_1) + P(A_2) + \cdots + P(A_N)$$

As an example of using this formula, again consider the playing card situation and the events J and Q. If we define the event

$$K \equiv \text{the randomly selected card is a king}$$

then the events J, Q, and K are mutually exclusive. Therefore,

$$P(J \cup Q \cup K) = P(J) + P(Q) + P(K)$$
$$= \frac{4}{52} + \frac{4}{52} + \frac{4}{52} = \frac{12}{52} = \frac{3}{13}$$

EXAMPLE 4.12 The AccuRatings Case

Recall that Figure 4.3 (page 178) gives the AccuRatings estimates of the number and the percentage of Los Angeles residents who favor each of the 10 top radio stations in Los Angeles. We will let the call letters of each station denote the event that a randomly selected Los Angeles resident would favor the station. Since the AccuRatings survey asked each resident to name the *single* station (if any) that he or she listens to most, the 10 events

KPWR	KLAX	KROQ	KIIS–A/F		KFI
KFWB	KKBT	KABC	KRTH	and	KCBS–FM

are mutually exclusive. Therefore, for example, the probability that a randomly selected Los Angeles resident would favor a station that is rated among the top 10

$$P(\text{KPWR} \cup \text{KLAX} \cup \cdots \cup \text{KCBS–FM})$$

is the sum of the 10 individual station probabilities

$$P(\text{KPWR}) + P(\text{KLAX}) + \cdots + P(\text{KCBS–FM})$$

Since we can estimate each individual station probability by dividing the share for the station in Figure 4.3 by 100, we estimate that the probability that a randomly selected Los Angeles resident would favor a station that is rated among the top 10 is

$$.08 + .064 + .061 + .050 + .047 + .046 + .046 + .042 + .036 + .036 = .508$$

Note that these probabilities sum to less than 1 because there are far more than 10 stations in Los Angeles.

Exercises for Section 4.3

connect

CONCEPTS

4.8 Explain what it means for two events to be mutually exclusive; for N events.

4.9 If A and B are events, define $\bar{A}$, $A \cup B$, $A \cap B$, and $\bar{A} \cap \bar{B}$.

METHODS AND APPLICATIONS

4.10 Consider a standard deck of 52 playing cards, a randomly selected card from the deck, and the following events:

R = red B = black A = ace N = nine D = diamond C = club

a Describe the sample space outcomes that correspond to each of these events.

b For each of the following pairs of events, indicate whether the events are mutually exclusive. In each case, if you think the events are mutually exclusive, explain why the events have no common sample space outcomes. If you think the events are not mutually exclusive, list the sample space outcomes that are common to both events.

   (1) R and A **(3)** A and N **(5)** D and C

   (2) R and C **(4)** N and C

4.11 Of 10,000 students at a college, 2,500 have a MasterCard (M), 4,000 have a VISA (V), and 1,000 have both.

a Find the probability that a randomly selected student
   (1) Has a MasterCard.
   (2) Has a VISA.
   (3) Has both credit cards.

b Construct and fill in a contingency table summarizing the credit card data. Employ the following pairs of events: M and $\bar{M}$, V and $\bar{V}$.

c Use the contingency table to find the probability that a randomly selected student
   (1) Has a MasterCard or a VISA.
   (2) Has neither credit card.
   (3) Has exactly one of the two credit cards.

4.12 The card game of Euchre employs a deck that consists of all four of each of the aces, kings, queens, jacks, tens, and nines (one of each suit—clubs, diamonds, spades, and hearts). Find the probability that a randomly selected card from a Euchre deck is

a A jack (J).

b A spade (S).

c A jack or an ace (A).

d A jack or a spade.

e Are the events J and A mutually exclusive? J and S? Why or why not?

4.13 Each month a brokerage house studies various companies and rates each company's stock as being either "low risk" or "moderate to high risk." In a recent report, the brokerage house summarized its findings about 15 aerospace companies and 25 food retailers in the following table:

Company Type	Low Risk	Moderate to High Risk
Aerospace company	6	9
Food retailer	15	10

If we randomly select one of the total of 40 companies, find

a The probability that the company is a food retailer.

b The probability that the company's stock is "low risk."

c The probability that the company's stock is "moderate to high risk."

d The probability that the company is a food retailer and has a stock that is "low risk."

e The probability that the company is a food retailer or has a stock that is "low risk."

4.14 In the book *Essentials of Marketing Research,* William R. Dillon, Thomas J. Madden, and Neil H. Firtle present the results of a concept study for a new wine cooler. Three hundred consumers between 21 and 49 years old were randomly selected. After sampling the new beverage, each was asked to rate the appeal of the phrase

Not sweet like wine coolers, not filling like beer, and more refreshing than wine or mixed drinks

as it relates to the new wine cooler. The rating was made on a scale from 1 to 5, with 5 representing "extremely appealing" and with 1 representing "not at all appealing." The results obtained are given in Table 4.4. 🔵 WineCooler

Rating	Total	Gender		Age Group		
		Male	Female	21–24	25–34	35–49
Extremely appealing (5)	151	68	83	48	66	37
(4)	91	51	40	36	36	19
(3)	36	21	15	9	12	15
(2)	13	7	6	4	6	3
Not at all appealing (1)	9	3	6	4	3	2

T A B L E 4.4   **Results of a Concept Study for a New Wine Cooler**   ● WineCooler

Source: W. R. Dillon, T. J. Madden, and N. H. Firtle, *Essentials of Marketing Research* (Burr Ridge, IL: Richard D. Irwin, Inc., 1993), p. 390.

Based on these results, estimate the probability that a randomly selected 21- to 49-year-old consumer

a   Would give the phrase a rating of 5.

b   Would give the phrase a rating of 3 or higher.

c   Is in the 21–24 age group; the 25–34 age group; the 35–49 age group.

d   Is a male who gives the phrase a rating of 4.

e   Is a 35- to 49-year-old who gives the phrase a rating of 1.

4.15   THE ACCURATINGS CASE

Using the information in Figure 4.3 (page 178), find an estimate of the probability that a randomly selected Los Angeles resident (12 years or older) would

a   Name one of the top three rated stations (KPWR, KLAX, or KROQ) as the station that he or she listens to most.

b   Not name one of the top five rated stations as the station that he or she listens to most.

c   Name a station that is not rated among the top seven stations as the station that he or she listens to most.

d   Name a station that is neither rated among the top three stations nor rated lower than 10th as the station that he or she listens to most.

4.4 Conditional Probability and Independence ◉ ● ●

Conditional probability   In Table 4.5 we repeat the contingency table summarizing the subscription data for the *Atlantic Journal* and the *Beacon News*. Suppose that we randomly select a household, and that the chosen household reports that it subscribes to the *Beacon News*. Given this new information, we wish to find the probability that the household subscribes to the *Atlantic Journal*. This new probability is called a **conditional probability.**

> The **probability of the event** A, **given the condition that the event** B **has occurred,** is written as $P(A|B)$—pronounced "the probability of A given B." We often refer to such a probability as the **conditional probability of** A **given** B.

In order to find the conditional probability that a household subscribes to the *Atlantic Journal*, given that it subscribes to the *Beacon News*, notice that if we know that the randomly selected household subscribes to the *Beacon News*, we know that we are considering one of 500,000 households (see Table 4.5). That is, we are now considering what we might call a reduced sample space of 500,000 households. Since 250,000 of these 500,000 *Beacon News* subscribers also subscribe to the *Atlantic Journal*, we have

$$P(A|B) = \frac{250,000}{500,000} = .5$$

This says that the probability that the randomly selected household subscribes to the *Atlantic Journal*, given that the household subscribes to the *Beacon News*, is .5. That is, 50 percent of the *Beacon News* subscribers also subscribe to the *Atlantic Journal*.

Next, suppose that we randomly select another household from the community of 1,000,000 households, and suppose that this newly chosen household reports that it subscribes to the *Atlantic Journal*. We now wish to find the probability that this household subscribes to the

TABLE 4.5   A Contingency Table Summarizing Subscription Data for the *Atlantic Journal* and the *Beacon News*

Events	Subscribes to *Beacon News*, B	Does Not Subscribe to *Beacon News*, $\bar{B}$	Total
Subscribes to *Atlantic Journal, A*	250,000	400,000	650,000
Does Not Subscribe to *Atlantic Journal, $\bar{A}$*	250,000	100,000	350,000
Total	500,000	500,000	1,000,000

Beacon News. We write this new probability as $P(B|A)$. If we know that the randomly selected household subscribes to the *Atlantic Journal,* we know that we are considering a reduced sample space of 650,000 households (see Table 4.5). Since 250,000 of these 650,000 *Atlantic Journal* subscribers also subscribe to the *Beacon News,* we have

$$P(B|A) = \frac{250,000}{650,000} = .3846$$

This says that the probability that the randomly selected household subscribes to the *Beacon News,* given that the household subscribes to the *Atlantic Journal,* is .3846. That is, 38.46 percent of the *Atlantic Journal* subscribers also subscribe to the *Beacon News.*

If we divide both the numerator and denominator of each of the conditional probabilities $P(A \mid B)$ and $P(B \mid A)$ by 1,000,000, we obtain

$$P(A|B) = \frac{250,000}{500,000} = \frac{250,000/1,000,000}{500,000/1,000,000} = \frac{P(A \cap B)}{P(B)}$$

$$P(B|A) = \frac{250,000}{650,000} = \frac{250,000/1,000,000}{650,000/1,000,000} = \frac{P(A \cap B)}{P(A)}$$

We express these conditional probabilities in terms of $P(A)$, $P(B)$, and $P(A \cap B)$ in order to obtain a more general formula for a conditional probability. We need a more general formula because, although we can use the reduced sample space approach we have demonstrated to find conditional probabilities when all of the sample space outcomes are equally likely, this approach may not give correct results when the sample space outcomes are *not* equally likely. We now give expressions for conditional probability that are valid for any sample space.

Conditional Probability

1 The **conditional probability that A will occur given that B will occur** is written **P(A |B)** and is defined to be

$$P(A|B) = \frac{P(A \cap B)}{P(B)}$$

Here we assume that $P(B)$ is greater than 0.

2 The **conditional probability that B will occur given that A will occur** is written **P(B | A)** and is defined to be

$$P(B|A) = \frac{P(A \cap B)}{P(A)}$$

Here we assume that $P(A)$ is greater than 0.

If we multiply both sides of the equation

$$P(A|B) = \frac{P(A \cap B)}{P(B)}$$

by $P(B)$, we obtain the equation

$$P(A \cap B) = P(B)P(A \mid B)$$

Similarly, if we multiply both sides of the equation

$$P(B \mid A) = \frac{P(A \cap B)}{P(A)}$$

by $P(A)$, we obtain the equation

$$P(A \cap B) = P(A)P(B \mid A)$$

In summary, we now have two equations that can be used to calculate $P(A \cap B)$. These equations are often referred to as the **general multiplication rule** for probabilities.

The General Multiplication Rule—Two Ways to Calculate $P(A \cap B)$

Given any two events A and B,

$$P(A \cap B) = P(A)P(B \mid A)$$
$$= P(B)P(A \mid B)$$

EXAMPLE 4.13

In a soft drink taste test, each of 1,000 consumers chose between two colas—Cola 1 and Cola 2—and stated whether they preferred their cola drinks *sweet* or *very sweet*. Unfortunately, some of the survey information was lost. The following information remains:

1 68.3 percent of the consumers (that is, 683 consumers) preferred Cola 1 to Cola 2.

2 62 percent of the consumers (that is, 620 consumers) preferred their cola *sweet* (rather than *very sweet*).

3 85 percent of the consumers who said that they liked their cola *sweet* preferred Cola 1 to Cola 2.

To recover all of the lost survey information, consider randomly selecting one of the 1,000 survey participants, and define the following events:

$C1 \equiv$ the randomly selected consumer prefers Cola 1.

$C2 \equiv$ the randomly selected consumer prefers Cola 2.

$S \equiv$ the randomly selected consumer prefers *sweet* cola drinks.

$V \equiv$ the randomly selected consumer prefers *very sweet* cola drinks.

From the survey information that remains, (1) says that $P(C1) = .683$, (2) says that $P(S) = .62$, and (3) says that $P(C1 \mid S) = .85$.

We will see that we can recover all of the lost survey information if we can find $P(C1 \cap S)$. The general multiplication rule says that

$$P(C1 \cap S) = P(C1)P(S \mid C1) = P(S)P(C1 \mid S)$$

Although we know that $P(C1) = .683$, we do not know $P(S \mid C1)$. Therefore, we cannot calculate $P(C1 \cap S)$ as $P(C1)P(S \mid C1)$. However, because we know that $P(S) = .62$ and that $P(C1 \mid S) = .85$, we can calculate

$$P(C1 \cap S) = P(S)P(C1 \mid S) = (.62)(.85) = .527$$

This implies that 527 consumers preferred Cola 1 and preferred their cola *sweet*. Since 683 consumers preferred Cola 1, and 620 consumers preferred *sweet* cola drinks, we can summarize the numbers of consumers corresponding to the events $C1$, $C2$, S, V, and $C1 \cap S$ as shown in Table 4.6. Furthermore, by performing subtractions as shown in Table 4.7, the numbers of consumers corresponding to the events $C1 \cap V$, $C2 \cap S$, and $C2 \cap V$ can be obtained. We summarize all of our results in Table 4.8. We will use these results in the next subsection to investigate the relationship between cola preference and sweetness preference.

| TABLE 4.6 | A Summary of the Number of Consumers Corresponding to the Events C1, C2, S, V, and C1 ∩ S |

Events	S (Sweet)	V (Very Sweet)	Total
C1 (Cola 1)	527		683
C2 (Cola 2)			317
Total	620	380	1,000

| TABLE 4.7 | Subtractions to Obtain the Number of Consumers Corresponding to the Events C1 ∩ V, C2 ∩ S, and C2 ∩ V |

Events	S (Sweet)	V (Very Sweet)	Total
C1 (Cola 1)	527	683 − 527 = 156	683
C2 (Cola 2)	620 − 527 = 93	380 − 156 = 224	317
Total	620	380	1,000

TABLE 4.8   A Contingency Table Summarizing the Cola Brand and Sweetness Preferences

Events	S (Sweet)	V (Very Sweet)	Total
C1 (Cola 1)	527	156	683
C2 (Cola 2)	93	224	317
Total	620	380	1,000

Independence   We have seen in Example 4.13 that $P(C1) = .683$, while $P(C1 \mid S) = .85$. Because $P(C1 \mid S)$ is greater than $P(C1)$, the probability that a randomly selected consumer will prefer Cola 1 is higher if we know that the person prefers *sweet* cola than it is if we have no knowledge of the person's sweetness preference. Another way to see this is to use Table 4.8 to calculate

$$P(C1 \mid V) = \frac{P(C1 \cap V)}{P(V)} = \frac{156/1,000}{380/1,000} = .4105$$

Since $P(C1 \mid S) = .85$ is greater than $P(C1 \mid V) = .4105$, the probability that a randomly selected consumer will prefer Cola 1 is higher if the consumer prefers *sweet* colas than it is if the consumer prefers *very sweet* colas. Since the probability of the event $C1$ is influenced by whether the event S occurs, we say that the events $C1$ and S are **dependent.** If $P(C1 \mid S)$ were equal to $P(C1)$, then the probability of the event $C1$ would not be influenced by whether S occurs. In this case we would say that the events $C1$ and S are **independent.** This leads to the following definition of **independence:**

Independent Events

Two events A and B are **independent** if and only if

1 $P(A \mid B) = P(A)$ or, equivalently,

2 $P(B \mid A) = P(B)$

Here we assume that $P(A)$ and $P(B)$ are greater than 0.

When we say that conditions (1) and (2) are equivalent, we mean that condition (1) holds if and only if condition (2) holds. Although we will not prove this, we will demonstrate it in the next example.

EXAMPLE 4.14

In the soft drink taste test of Example 4.13, we have seen that $P(C1 \mid S) = .85$ does not equal $P(C1) = .683$. This implies that $P(S \mid C1)$ does not equal $P(S)$. To demonstrate this, note from Table 4.8 that

$$P(S \mid C1) = \frac{P(C1 \cap S)}{P(C1)} = \frac{527/1,000}{683/1,000} = .7716$$

This probability is larger than $P(S) = 620/1{,}000 = .62$. In summary:

1.   A comparison of $P(C1 \mid S) = .85$ and $P(C1) = .683$ says that a consumer is more likely to prefer Cola 1 if the consumer prefers *sweet* colas.

2.   A comparison of $P(S \mid C1) = .7716$ and $P(S) = .62$ says that a consumer is more likely to prefer *sweet* colas if the consumer prefers Cola 1.

This suggests, but does not prove, that one reason Cola 1 is preferred to Cola 2 is that Cola 1 is *sweet* (as opposed to *very sweet*).

If the occurrences of the events A and B have nothing to do with each other, then we know that A and B are independent events. This implies that $P(A \mid B)$ equals $P(A)$ and that $P(B \mid A)$ equals $P(B)$. Recall that the general multiplication rule tells us that, for any two events A and B, we can say that

$$P(A \cap B) = P(A)P(B \mid A)$$

Therefore, if $P(B \mid A)$ equals $P(B)$, it follows that

$$P(A \cap B) = P(A)P(B)$$

which is called the **multiplication rule for independent events.** To summarize:

The Multiplication Rule for Two Independent Events

If A and B are **independent events,** then

$$P(A \cap B) = P(A)P(B)$$

As a simple example, define the events C and P as follows:

$C \equiv$ your favorite college football team wins its first game next season.

$P \equiv$ your favorite professional football team wins its first game next season.

Suppose you believe that for next season $P(C) = .6$ and $P(P) = .6$. Then, because the outcomes of a college football game and a professional football game would probably have nothing to do with each other, it is reasonable to assume that C and P are independent events. It follows that

$$P(C \cap P) = P(C)P(P) = (.6)(.6) = .36$$

This probability might seem surprisingly low. That is, since you believe that each of your teams has a 60 percent chance of winning, you might feel reasonably confident that both your college and professional teams will win their first game. Yet, the chance of this happening is really only .36!

Next, consider a group of events $A_1, A_2, \ldots, A_N$. Intuitively, the events $A_1, A_2, \ldots, A_N$ are independent if the occurrences of these events have nothing to do with each other. Denoting the probability that A_1 and A_2 and $\ldots$ and A_N will simultaneously occur as $P(A_1 \cap A_2 \cap \cdots \cap A_N)$, we have the following:

The Multiplication Rule for N Independent Events

If $A_1, A_2, \ldots, A_N$ are independent events, then

$$P(A_1 \cap A_2 \cap \cdots \cap A_N) = P(A_1)P(A_2) \cdots P(A_N)$$

This says that the multiplication rule for two independent events can be extended to any number of independent events.

EXAMPLE 4.15

This example is based on a real situation encountered by a major producer and marketer of consumer products. The company assessed the service it provides by surveying the attitudes of its customers regarding 10 different aspects of customer service—order filled correctly, billing amount on invoice correct, delivery made on time, and so forth. When the survey results were analyzed, the company was dismayed to learn that only 59 percent of the survey participants indicated that they were satisfied with all 10 aspects of the company's service. Upon investigation, each of the 10 departments responsible for the aspects of service considered in the study insisted that it satisfied its customers 95 percent of the time. That is, each department claimed that its error rate was only 5 percent. Company executives were confused and felt that there was a substantial discrepancy between the survey results and the claims of the departments providing the services. However, a company statistician pointed out that there was no discrepancy. To understand this, consider randomly selecting a customer from among the survey participants, and define 10 events (corresponding to the 10 aspects of service studied):

$A_1 \equiv$ the customer is satisfied that the order is filled correctly (aspect 1).

$A_2 \equiv$ the customer is satisfied that the billing amount on the invoice is correct (aspect 2).

$\vdots$

$A_{10} \equiv$ the customer is satisfied that the delivery is made on time (aspect 10).

Also, define the event

$S \equiv$ the customer is satisfied with all 10 aspects of customer service.

Since 10 different departments are responsible for the 10 aspects of service being studied, it is reasonable to assume that all 10 aspects of service are independent of each other. For instance, billing amounts would be independent of delivery times. Therefore, $A_1, A_2, \ldots, A_{10}$ are independent events, and

$$P(S) = P(A_1 \cap A_2 \cap \cdots \cap A_{10})$$
$$= P(A_1)P(A_2) \cdots P(A_{10})$$

If, as the departments claim, each department satisfies its customers 95 percent of the time, then the probability that the customer is satisfied with all 10 aspects is

$$P(S) = (.95)(.95) \cdots (.95) = (.95)^{10} = .5987$$

This result is almost identical to the 59 percent satisfaction rate reported by the survey participants.

If the company wants to increase the percentage of its customers who are satisfied with all 10 aspects of service, it must improve the quality of service provided by the 10 departments. For example, to satisfy 95 percent of its customers with all 10 aspects of service, the company must require each department to raise the fraction of the time it satisfies its customers to x, where

$$(x)^{10} = .95$$

It follows that

$$x = (.95)^{\frac{1}{10}} = .9949$$

and that each department must satisfy its customers 99.49 percent of the time (rather than the current 95 percent of the time).

A real-world application of conditional probability, independence, and dependence

EXAMPLE 4.16 The AccuRatings Case: Estimating Radio Station Share by Daypart

In addition to asking each of the 5,528 sampled Los Angeles residents to name which station (if any) he or she listens to most on an overall basis, AccuRatings asked each resident to name which station (if any) he or she listens to most during various parts of the day. The various parts of the day considered by AccuRatings and the results of the survey are given in Figure 4.7. To explain these results, suppose that 2,827 of the 5,528 sampled residents said that they listen to the radio during

FIGURE 4.7 **Further Portions of an AccuRatings Report on Radio Ratings in the Los Angeles Market**

STATION CORE LISTENERS			SHARE	RECALLED FORMER SHARE	'SHARE OF CORE LISTENERSHIP' BY DAYPART				
					6–10A	10A–3P	3–7P	7P–12M	WKEND
KPWR	1:	668,100	8.0 ←	8.4	2: 6.9	1: 9.0	1: 10.0	1: 10.7	1: 10.4
KLAX	2:	531,800	6.4 ←	4.4	6: 5.1	3: 6.1	3: 5.9	5: 5.6	3: 7.1
KROQ	3:	505,100	6.1 ←	5.6	3: 5.4	4: 5.6	2: 6.8	2: 9.1	2: 7.5
KIIS-A/F	4:	418,200	5.0 ←	5.6	1: (7.1)	5: 4.9	4: 4.9	6: 3.5	5: 4.7
KFI	5:	386,500	4.7 ←	4.0	5: 5.2	2: (6.5)	6: 3.7	10: 2.7	13: 2.9
KFWB	6:	383,500	4.6 ←	3.8	etc.				
KKBT	7:	378,500	4.6 ←	4.1					
KABC	8:	346,600	4.2 ←	4.2					
KRTH	9:	302,300	3.6 ←	3.7					
KCBS-FM	10:	299,500	3.6 ←	1.3					

SHARE OF CORE LISTENERSHIP BY DAYPART:
KIIS's Rick Dees has the #1 morning show in the 6–10A daypart. Of people who listen to radio during that daypart, 7.1% say that their primary station during that daypart is KIIS.
  Similarly, KFI is the #2 station during middays (which includes Rush Limbaugh's shift), with 6.5% of midday listeners saying that KFI is the station they listen to most during that daypart.

Source: Strategic Radio Research, *AccuRatings Introduction for Broadcasters.*

some portion of the 6–10 A.M. daypart. Furthermore, suppose that 201 of these 2,827 residents named station KIIS as the station that they listen to most during that daypart. It follows that

$$\frac{201}{2,827} = .071100106$$

is an estimate of $P(\text{KIIS} \mid 6\text{–}10 \text{ A.M.})$, the probability that a randomly selected Los Angeles resident who listens to the radio during the 6–10 A.M. daypart would name KIIS as his or her primary station during that daypart. Said equivalently, station KIIS has an estimated share of 7.1 percent of the 6–10 A.M. radio listeners. In general, Figure 4.7 gives the estimated shares during the various dayparts for the five stations that are rated best overall (KPWR, KLAX, KROQ, KIIS, and KFI). Examination of this figure seems to reveal that a station's share depends somewhat on the daypart being considered. For example, note that Figure 4.7 tells us that the estimate of $P(\text{KIIS} \mid 6\text{–}10 \text{ A.M.})$ is .071, whereas the estimate of $P(\text{KIIS} \mid 3\text{–}7 \text{ P.M.})$ is .049. This says that station KIIS's estimated share of the 6–10 A.M. radio listeners is higher than its estimated share of the 3–7 P.M. radio listeners.

Estimating Probabilities of Radio Station Listenership

AccuRatings provides the sort of estimates given in Figures 4.3 and 4.7 not only for the Los Angeles market but for other markets as well. In addition, AccuRatings provides (for a given market) hour-by-hour estimates of the probabilities of different stations being listened to in the market. How this is done is an excellent real-world application of the general multiplication rule. As an example, consider how AccuRatings might find an estimate of "the probability that a randomly selected Los Angeles resident will be listening to station KIIS at an average moment from 7 to 8 A.M." To estimate this probability, AccuRatings estimates

1 The probability that a randomly selected Los Angeles resident will be listening to the radio at an average moment from 7 to 8 A.M.

and multiplies this estimate by an estimate of

2 The probability that a randomly selected Los Angeles resident who is listening to the radio at an average moment from 7 to 8 A.M. will be listening to station KIIS at that average moment.

Because the hour of 7 to 8 A.M. is in the 6–10 A.M. daypart, it is reasonable to estimate the probability in (2) by using an estimate of $P(\text{KIIS} \mid 6\text{–}10 \text{ A.M.})$, which Figure 4.7 tells us is .071. To find an estimate of the probability in (1), AccuRatings uses a 2,000-person national study. Here, each person is interviewed to obtain a detailed, minute-by-minute reconstruction of the times that the person listened to the radio on the previous day (with no attempt to identify the specific stations listened to). Then, for each minute of the day the proportion of the 2,000 people who listened to the radio during that minute is determined. The average of the 60 such proportions for a particular hour is the estimate of the probability that a randomly selected person will listen to the radio at an average moment during that hour. Using a national study is reasonable because the detailed reconstruction made by AccuRatings would be extremely time-consuming to construct for individual markets and because AccuRatings' studies show very consistent hour-by-hour patterns of radio usage across markets, across seasons, and across demographics. This implies that the national study applies to individual markets (such as the Los Angeles market). Suppose, then, that the national study estimate of the 7 to 8 A.M. radio listening probability in (1) is .242. Since (as previously discussed) an estimate of the station KIIS conditional listening probability in (2) is .071, it follows than an estimate of the desired probability is $.242 \times .071 = .017182 \approx .017$. This says that we estimate that 1.7 percent of all Los Angeles residents will be listening to station KIIS at an average moment from 7 to 8 A.M. Assuming that there are 8,300,000 Los Angeles residents, we estimate that

$$(8{,}300{,}000) \times (.017) = 141{,}000$$

of these residents will be listening to station KIIS at an average moment from 7 to 8 A.M. Finally, note that in making its hour-by-hour radio station listening estimates, AccuRatings makes a separate set of estimates for the hours on a weekday, for the hours on Saturday, and for the hours on Sunday. The above 7 to 8 A.M. estimate is for the 7 to 8 A.M. hour on a weekday.

Estimating Song Ratings

In addition to providing AccuRatings reports to radio stations, Strategic Radio Research does music research for clients such as MTV. Figure 4.8 gives a portion of a *title-by-title analysis* for the song "Gangsta's Paradise" by Coolio. Listeners are surveyed and are asked to rate the song on a 1 to 5 rating scale with 1 being the lowest possible rating and 5 being the highest. Figure 4.8 gives a histogram of these ratings; notice that *UNFAM* indicates that the listener was not familiar with this particular song. The percentages above the bars of the histogram give the percentages of listeners rating the song 5, 4, 3, 2, 1, and *UNFAM*, respectively. If we let the symbol denoting

FIGURE 4.8   A Portion of a Title-by-Title Analysis for the Song "Gangsta's Paradise" by Coolio

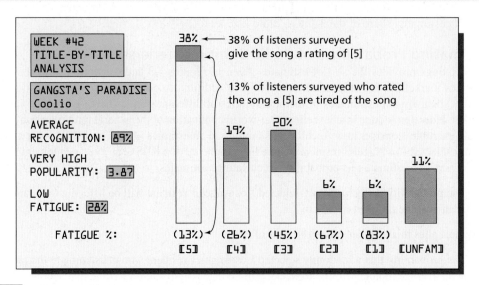

Source: Strategic Radio Research, Chicago, Illinois.

a particular rating also denote the event that a randomly selected listener would give the song the rating, it follows that we estimate that

$$P(5) = .38 \qquad P(4) = .19 \qquad P(3) = .20$$
$$P(2) = .06 \qquad P(1) = .06 \qquad P(UNFAM) = .11$$

The three boxes on the left of Figure 4.8 give *recognition, popularity,* and *fatigue* indexes for the song being analyzed. Although we will have to wait until Chapter 5 to learn the meaning of the popularity index, we now explain the meaning of the recognition and fatigue indexes. The recognition index estimates the probability that a randomly selected listener is familiar with the song. We have seen that the estimate of $P(UNFAM)$ is .11, so the recognition index is $1 - .11 = .89$, which is expressed as the 89 percent in Figure 4.8. This index says we estimate that 89 percent of all listeners are familiar with the song. The fatigue index, 28 percent, estimates the percentage of listeners who are tired of the song. That is, if T denotes the event that a randomly selected listener is tired of the song, we estimate that $P(T) = .28$. Finally, note that at the bottom of each histogram bar in Figure 4.8, and shaded in blue, is the fatigue percentage corresponding to the rating described by the bar. This percentage is an estimate of the conditional probability that a randomly selected listener giving the song that rating is tired of the song. Therefore, we estimate that $P(T \mid 1) = .83$, $P(T \mid 2) = .67$, $P(T \mid 3) = .45$, $P(T \mid 4) = .26$, and $P(T \mid 5) = .13$. From these conditional probabilities we might conclude that the higher the song is rated, the lower is its fatigue percentage.

Exercises for Section 4.4

CONCEPTS

4.16 Explain the concept of a conditional probability. Give an example of a conditional probability that would be of interest to a college student; to a business.

4.17 Explain what it means for two events to be independent.

METHODS AND APPLICATIONS

4.18 Recall from Exercise 4.11 (page 186) that of 10,000 students at a college, 2,500 have a MasterCard (M), 4,000 have a VISA (V), and 1,000 have both. Find
    a The proportion of MasterCard holders who have VISA cards. Interpret and write this proportion as a conditional probability.
    b The proportion of VISA cardholders who have MasterCards. Interpret and write this proportion as a conditional probability.
    c Are the events *having a MasterCard* and *having a VISA* independent? Justify your answer.

4.19 Recall from Exercise 4.13 (page 186) that each month a brokerage house studies various companies and rates each company's stock as being either "low risk" or "moderate to high risk." In a recent report, the brokerage house summarized its findings about 15 aerospace companies and 25 food retailers in the following table:

Company Type	Low Risk	Moderate to High Risk
Aerospace company	6	9
Food retailer	15	10

If we randomly select one of the total of 40 companies, find
    a The probability that the company's stock is moderate to high risk given that the firm is an aerospace company.
    b The probability that the company's stock is moderate to high risk given that the firm is a food retailer.
    c Determine if the *company type* is independent of the *level of risk* of the firm's stock.

4.20 John and Jane are married. The probability that John watches a certain television show is .4. The probability that Jane watches the show is .5. The probability that John watches the show, given that Jane does, is .7.
    a Find the probability that both John and Jane watch the show.
    b Find the probability that Jane watches the show, given that John does.
    c Do John and Jane watch the show independently of each other? Justify your answer.

4.21 In Exercise 4.20, find the probability that either John or Jane watches the show.

4.22   In the July 29, 2001, issue of *The Journal News* (Hamilton, Ohio), Lynn Elber of the Associated
Press reported that "while 40 percent of American families own a television set with a V-chip
installed to block designated programs with sex and violence, only 17 percent of those parents
use the device."[2]

    a   Use the report's results to find an estimate of the probability that a randomly selected American
family has used a V-chip to block programs containing sex and violence.

    b   According to the report, more than 50 percent of parents have used the TV rating system
(TV-14, etc.) to control their children's TV viewing. How does this compare to the percentage
using the V-chip?

4.23   According to the Associated Press report (in Exercise 4.22), 47 percent of parents who have
purchased TV sets after V-chips became standard equipment in January 2000 are aware that their
sets have V-chips, and of those who are aware of the option, 36 percent have programmed their
V-chips. Using these results, find an estimate of the probability that a randomly selected parent
who has bought a TV set since January 2000 has programmed the V-chip.

4.24   Fifteen percent of the employees in a company have managerial positions, and 25 percent of the
employees in the company have MBA degrees. Also, 60 percent of the managers have MBA
degrees. Using the probability formulas,

    a   Find the proportion of employees who are managers and have MBA degrees.

    b   Find the proportion of MBAs who are managers.

    c   Are the events *being a manager* and *having an MBA* independent? Justify your answer.

4.25   In Exercise 4.24, find the proportion of employees who either have MBAs or are managers.

4.26   Consider Exercise 4.14 (page 186). Using the results in Table 4.4 (page 187), estimate the
probability that a randomly selected 21- to 49-year-old consumer would

    a   Give the phrase a rating of 4 or 5 given that the consumer is male; give the phrase a rating of
4 or 5 given that the consumer is female. Based on these results, is the appeal of the phrase
among males much different from the appeal of the phrase among females? Explain.

    b   Give the phrase a rating of 4 or 5, given that the consumer is in the 21–24 age group; given that
the consumer is in the 25–34 age group; given that the consumer is in the 35–49 age group.
Based on these results, which age group finds the phrase most appealing? Least appealing?

4.27   In a survey of 100 insurance claims, 40 are fire claims (*FIRE*), 16 of which are fraudulent
(*FRAUD*). Also, there are a total of 40 fraudulent claims.

    a   Construct a contingency table summarizing the claims data. Use the pairs of events *FIRE* and
$\overline{FIRE}$, *FRAUD* and $\overline{FRAUD}$.

    b   What proportion of the fire claims are fraudulent?

    c   Are the events *a claim is fraudulent* and *a claim is a fire claim* independent? Use your
probability of part *b* to prove your answer.

4.28   Recall from Exercise 4.3 (page 179) that two randomly selected customers are each asked to take a
blind taste test and then to state which of three diet colas (marked as *A*, *B*, or *C*) he or she prefers.
Suppose that cola *A*'s distributor claims that 80 percent of all people prefer cola *A* and that each of
colas *B* and *C* is preferred by only 10 percent.

    a   Assuming that the distributor's claim is true and that the two taste test participants make
independent cola preference decisions, find the probability of each sample space outcome.

    b   Find the probability that neither taste test participant will prefer cola *A*.

    c   If, when the taste test is carried out, neither participant prefers cola *A*, use the probability you
computed in part *b* to decide whether the distributor's claim seems valid. Explain.

4.29   A sprinkler system inside an office building has two types of activation devices, *D*1 and *D*2, which
operate independently. When there is a fire, if either device operates correctly, the sprinkler system
is turned on. In case of fire, the probability that *D*1 operates correctly is .95, and the probability
that *D*2 operates correctly is .92. Find the probability that

    a   Both *D*1 and *D*2 will operate correctly.

    b   The sprinkler system will come on.

    c   The sprinkler system will fail.

4.30   A product is assembled using 10 different components, each of which must meet specifications for
five different quality characteristics. Suppose that there is a .9973 probability that each individual
specification will be met.

    a   Assuming that all 50 specifications are met independently, find the probability that the product
meets all 50 specifications.

---

[2]Source: *The Journal News* (Hamilton, Ohio), July 29, 2001, p. C5.

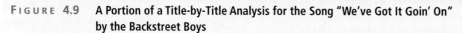

FIGURE 4.9   A Portion of a Title-by-Title Analysis for the Song "We've Got It Goin' On" by the Backstreet Boys

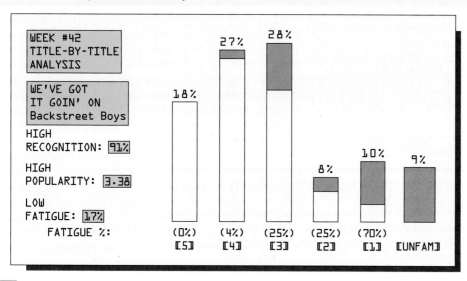

Source: Strategic Radio Research, Chicago, Illinois.

b   Suppose that we wish to have a 99.73 percent chance that all 50 specifications will be met. If each specification will have the same chance of being met, how large must we make the probability of meeting each individual specification?

4.31   THE ACCURATINGS CASE

Consider the share of core listenership by daypart information given in Figure 4.7 (page 193).

a   Find an estimate of $P(\text{KPWR} \mid 3\text{–}7 \text{ P.M.})$, the probability that a randomly selected Los Angeles resident who listens to the radio during the 3–7 P.M. daypart would name KPWR as his or her primary station during that daypart.

b   Find $P(\text{KLAX} \mid 3\text{–}7 \text{ P.M.})$, $P(\text{KROQ} \mid 3\text{–}7 \text{ P.M.})$, $P(\text{KIIS} \mid 3\text{–}7 \text{ P.M.})$, and $P(\text{KFI} \mid 3\text{–}7 \text{ P.M.})$.

c   Suppose that the AccuRatings national survey estimates that the probability that a randomly selected Los Angeles resident will be listening to the radio at an average moment between 5 and 6 P.M. is .256. Use this survey result and the estimate in part *a* to estimate the probability that a randomly selected Los Angeles resident will be listening to station KPWR at an average moment between 5 and 6 P.M.

d   Repeat part *c* for each of KLAX, KROQ, KIIS, and KFI.

e   Find an estimate of the probability that a randomly selected Los Angeles resident will be listening to one of the five most highly rated stations in the Los Angeles market (KPWR, KLAX, KROQ, KIIS, or KFI) at an average moment between 5 and 6 P.M.

4.32   THE ACCURATINGS CASE

Figure 4.9 gives a portion of a title-by-title analysis for the song "We've Got It Goin' On" by the Backstreet Boys. The ratings information given in this figure is the same type given in Figure 4.8 (page 194) and explained in Example 4.16 (pages 192–195). Using the ratings information:

a   Find an estimate of the probability that a randomly selected listener would give the song each of the ratings 5, 4, 3, 2, and 1.

b   Find an estimate of the probability that a randomly selected listener is (1) familiar with the song; (2) tired of the song.

c   Find estimates of each of $P(T \mid 5)$, $P(T \mid 4)$, $P(T \mid 3)$, $P(T \mid 2)$, and $P(T \mid 1)$, where T denotes the event that a listener is tired of the song.

4.33   In a murder trial in Los Angeles, the prosecution claims that the defendant was cut on the left middle finger at the murder scene, but the defendant claims the cut occurred in Chicago, the day after the murders had been committed. Because the defendant is a sports celebrity, many people noticed him before he reached Chicago. Twenty-two people saw him casually, one person on the plane to Chicago carefully studied his hands looking for a championship ring, and another person stood with him as he signed autographs and drove him from the airport to the hotel. None of these 24 people saw a cut on the defendant's finger. If in fact he was not cut at all, it would be extremely unlikely that he left blood at the murder scene.

a Since a person casually meeting the defendant would not be looking for a cut, assume that the probability is .9 that such a person would not have seen the cut, even if it was there. Furthermore, assume that the person who carefully looked at the defendant's hands had a .5 probability of not seeing the cut even if it was there and that the person who drove the defendant from the airport to the hotel had a .6 probability of not seeing the cut even if it was there. Given these assumptions, and also assuming that all 24 people looked at the defendant independently of each other, what is the probability that all 24 people would not have seen the cut, even if it was there?

b What is the probability that at least one of the 24 people would have seen the cut if it was there?

c Given the result of part *b* and given the fact that none of the 24 people saw a cut, do you think the defendant had a cut on his hand before he reached Chicago?

d How might we estimate what the assumed probabilities in *a* would actually be? (Note: This would not be easy.)

4.5 Bayes' Theorem (Optional) ● ● ●

Sometimes we have an initial or **prior probability** that an event will occur. Then, based on new information, we revise the prior probability to what is called a **posterior probability.** This revision can be done by using a theorem called **Bayes' theorem.**

EXAMPLE 4.17

HIV (Human Immunodeficiency Virus) is the virus that causes AIDS. Although many have proposed mandatory testing for HIV, statisticians have frequently spoken against such proposals. In this example, we use Bayes' theorem to see why.

Let *HIV* represent the event that a randomly selected American has the HIV virus, and let $\overline{HIV}$ represent the event that a randomly selected American does not have this virus. Since it is estimated that .6 percent of the American population has the HIV virus,

$$P(HIV) = .006 \quad \text{and} \quad P(\overline{HIV}) = .994$$

A diagnostic test is used to attempt to detect whether a person has HIV. According to historical data, 99.9 percent of people with HIV receive a positive (*POS*) result when this test is administered, while 1 percent of people who do not have HIV receive a positive result. That is,

$$P(POS\,|\,HIV) = .999 \quad \text{and} \quad P(POS\,|\,\overline{HIV}) = .01$$

If we administer the test to a randomly selected American (who may or may not have HIV) and the person receives a positive test result, what is the probability that the person actually has HIV? This probability is

$$P(HIV\,|\,POS) = \frac{P(HIV \cap POS)}{P(POS)}$$

The idea behind Bayes' theorem is that we can find $P(HIV\,|\,POS)$ by thinking as follows. A person will receive a positive result (*POS*) if the person receives a positive result and actually has HIV—that is, $(HIV \cap POS)$—or if the person receives a positive result and actually does not have HIV—that is, $(\overline{HIV} \cap POS)$. Therefore,

$$P(POS) = P(HIV \cap POS) + P(\overline{HIV} \cap POS)$$

This implies that

$$
\begin{aligned}
P(HIV\,|\,POS) &= \frac{P(HIV \cap POS)}{P(POS)} \\[2mm]
&= \frac{P(HIV \cap POS)}{P(HIV \cap POS) + P(\overline{HIV} \cap POS)} \\[2mm]
&= \frac{P(HIV)P(POS\,|\,HIV)}{P(HIV)P(POS\,|\,HIV) + P(\overline{HIV})P(POS\,|\,\overline{HIV})} \\[2mm]
&= \frac{.006(.999)}{.006(.999) + (.994)(.01)} = .38
\end{aligned}
$$

This probability says that, if all Americans were given a test for HIV, only 38 percent of the people who get a positive result would actually have HIV. That is, 62 percent of Americans identified as having HIV would actually be free of the virus! The reason for this rather surprising result is that, since so few people actually have HIV, the majority of people who test positive are people who are free of HIV and, therefore, erroneously test positive. This is why statisticians have spoken against proposals for mandatory HIV testing.

In the preceding example, there were two *states of nature—HIV* and $\overline{HIV}$—and two outcomes of the diagnostic test—*POS* and $\overline{POS}$. In general, there might be any number of states of nature and any number of experimental outcomes. This leads to a general statement of Bayes' theorem.

Bayes' Theorem

Let $S_1, S_2, \ldots, S_k$ be k mutually exclusive states of nature, one of which must be true, and suppose that $P(S_1)$, $P(S_2), \ldots, P(S_k)$ are the prior probabilities of these states of nature. Also, let E be a particular outcome of an experiment designed to help determine which state of nature is really true. Then, the **posterior probability** of a particular state of nature, say S_i, given the experimental outcome E, is

$$P(S_i \mid E) = \frac{P(S_i \cap E)}{P(E)} = \frac{P(S_i)P(E \mid S_i)}{P(E)}$$

where

$$P(E) = P(S_1 \cap E) + P(S_2 \cap E) + \cdots + P(S_k \cap E)$$
$$= P(S_1)P(E \mid S_1) + P(S_2)P(E \mid S_2) + \cdots + P(S_k)P(E \mid S_k)$$

Specifically, if there are two mutually exclusive states of nature, S_1 and S_2, one of which must be true, then

$$P(S_i \mid E) = \frac{P(S_i)P(E \mid S_i)}{P(S_1)P(E \mid S_1) + P(S_2)P(E \mid S_2)}$$

We have illustrated Bayes' theorem when there are two states of nature in Example 4.17. In the next example, we consider three states of nature.

EXAMPLE 4.18 The Oil Drilling Case   C

An oil company is attempting to decide whether to drill for oil on a particular site. There are three possible states of nature:

1   No oil (state of nature S_1, which we will denote as *none*).
2   Some oil (state of nature S_2, which we will denote as *some*).
3   Much oil (state of nature S_3, which we will denote as *much*).

Based on experience and knowledge concerning the site's geological characteristics, the oil company feels that the prior probabilities of these states of nature are as follows:

$$P(S_1 \equiv \text{none}) = .7 \qquad P(S_2 \equiv \text{some}) = .2 \qquad P(S_3 \equiv \text{much}) = .1$$

In order to obtain more information about the potential drilling site, the oil company can perform a seismic experiment, which has three readings—low, medium, and high. Moreover, information exists concerning the accuracy of the seismic experiment. The company's historical records tell us that

1   Of 100 past sites that were drilled and produced no oil, 4 sites gave a high reading. Therefore,

$$P(\text{high} \mid \text{none}) = \frac{4}{100} = .04$$

2   Of 400 past sites that were drilled and produced some oil, 8 sites gave a high reading. Therefore,

$$P(\text{high} \mid \text{some}) = \frac{8}{400} = .02$$

3   Of 300 past sites that were drilled and produced much oil, 288 sites gave a high reading. Therefore,

$$P(\text{high} \mid \text{much}) = \frac{288}{300} = .96$$

Intuitively, these conditional probabilities tell us that sites that produce no oil or some oil seldom give a high reading, while sites that produce much oil often give a high reading.

Now, suppose that when the company performs the seismic experiment on the site in question, it obtains a high reading. The previously given conditional probabilities suggest that, given this new information, the company might feel that the likelihood of much oil is higher than its prior probability $P(\text{much}) = .1$, and that the likelihoods of some oil and no oil are lower than the prior probabilities $P(\text{some}) = .2$ and $P(\text{none}) = .7$. To be more specific, we wish to *revise the prior probabilities* of no, some, and much oil to what we call *posterior probabilities*. We can do this by using Bayes' theorem as follows.

If we wish to compute $P(\text{none} \mid \text{high})$, we first calculate

$$P(\text{high}) = P(\text{none} \cap \text{high}) + P(\text{some} \cap \text{high}) + P(\text{much} \cap \text{high})$$

$$= P(\text{none})P(\text{high} \mid \text{none}) + P(\text{some})P(\text{high} \mid \text{some}) + P(\text{much})P(\text{high} \mid \text{much})$$

$$= (.7)(.04) + (.2)(.02) + (.1)(.96) = .128$$

Then Bayes' theorem says that

$$P(\text{none} \mid \text{high}) = \frac{P(\text{none} \cap \text{high})}{P(\text{high})} = \frac{P(\text{none})P(\text{high} \mid \text{none})}{P(\text{high})} = \frac{.7(.04)}{.128} = .21875$$

Similarly, we can compute $P(\text{some} \mid \text{high})$ and $P(\text{much} \mid \text{high})$ as follows:

$$P(\text{some} \mid \text{high}) = \frac{P(\text{some} \cap \text{high})}{P(\text{high})} = \frac{P(\text{some})P(\text{high} \mid \text{some})}{P(\text{high})} = \frac{.2(.02)}{.128} = .03125$$

$$P(\text{much} \mid \text{high}) = \frac{P(\text{much} \cap \text{high})}{P(\text{high})} = \frac{P(\text{much})P(\text{high} \mid \text{much})}{P(\text{high})} = \frac{.1(.96)}{.128} = .75$$

These revised probabilities tell us that, given that the seismic experiment gives a high reading, the revised probabilities of no, some, and much oil are .21875, .03125, and .75, respectively.

Since the posterior probability of much oil is .75, we might conclude that we should drill on the oil site. However, this decision should also be based on economic considerations. The science of **decision theory** provides various criteria for making such a decision. An introduction to decision theory can be found in Bowerman and O'Connell [2009].

In this section we have only introduced Bayes' theorem. There is an entire subject called **Bayesian statistics,** which uses Bayes' theorem to update prior belief about a probability or population parameter to posterior belief. The use of Bayesian statistics is controversial in the case where the prior belief is largely based on subjective considerations, because many statisticians do not believe that we should base decisions on subjective considerations. Realistically, however, we all do this in our daily lives. For example, how each of us viewed the evidence in the O. J. Simpson murder trial had a great deal to do with our prior beliefs about both O. J. Simpson and the police.

Exercises for Section 4.5

CONCEPTS

4.34 What is a prior probability? What is a posterior probability?

4.35 Explain the purpose behind using Bayes' theorem.

connect

METHODS AND APPLICATIONS

4.36 Suppose that A_1, A_2, and B are events where A_1 and A_2 are mutually exclusive and

$$P(A_1) = .8 \qquad P(B \mid A_1) = .1$$
$$P(A_2) = .2 \qquad P(B \mid A_2) = .3$$

Use this information to find $P(A_1 \mid B)$ and $P(A_2 \mid B)$.

4.37 Suppose that A_1, A_2, A_3, and B are events where A_1, A_2, and A_3 are mutually exclusive and

$$P(A_1) = .2 \qquad P(A_2) = .5 \qquad P(A_3) = .3$$
$$P(B \mid A_1) = .02 \qquad P(B \mid A_2) = .05 \qquad P(B \mid A_3) = .04$$

Use this information to find $P(A_1 \mid B)$, $P(A_2 \mid B)$, and $P(A_3 \mid B)$.

4.38 Again consider the diagnostic test for HIV discussed in Example 4.17 (page 198) and recall that $P(POS \mid HIV) = .999$ and $P(POS \mid \overline{HIV}) = .01$, where POS denotes a positive test result. Assuming that the percentage of people who have HIV is 1 percent, recalculate the probability that a randomly selected person has the HIV virus, given that his or her test result is positive.

4.39 A department store is considering a new credit policy to try to reduce the number of customers defaulting on payments. A suggestion is made to discontinue credit to any customer who has been one week or more late with his/her payment at least twice. Past records show 95 percent of defaults were late at least twice. Also, 3 percent of all customers default, and 30 percent of those who have not defaulted have had at least two late payments.

    a Find the probability that a customer with at least two late payments will default.

    b Based on part *a*, should the policy be adopted? Explain.

4.40 A company administers an "aptitude test for managers" to aid in selecting new management trainees. Prior experience suggests that 60 percent of all applicants for management trainee positions would be successful if they were hired. Furthermore, past experience with the aptitude test indicates that 85 percent of applicants who turn out to be successful managers pass the test and 90 percent of applicants who turn out not to be successful managers fail the test.

    a If an applicant passes the "aptitude test for managers," what is the probability that the applicant will succeed in a management position?

    b Based on your answer to part *a*, do you think that the "aptitude test for managers" is a valuable way to screen applicants for management trainee positions? Explain.

4.41 Three data entry specialists enter requisitions into a computer. Specialist 1 processes 30 percent of the requisitions, specialist 2 processes 45 percent, and specialist 3 processes 25 percent. The proportions of incorrectly entered requisitions by data entry specialists 1, 2, and 3 are .03, .05, and .02, respectively. Suppose that a random requisition is found to have been incorrectly entered. What is the probability that it was processed by data entry specialist 1? By data entry specialist 2? By data entry specialist 3?

4.42 A truth serum given to a suspect is known to be 90 percent reliable when the person is guilty and 99 percent reliable when the person is innocent. In other words, 10 percent of the guilty are judged innocent by the serum and 1 percent of the innocent are judged guilty. If the suspect was selected from a group of suspects of which only 5 percent are guilty of having committed a crime, and the serum indicates that the suspect is guilty of having committed a crime, what is the probability that the suspect is innocent?

Chapter Summary

In this chapter we studied **probability.** We began by defining an **event** to be an experimental outcome that may or may not occur and by defining the **probability of an event** to be a number that measures the likelihood that the event will occur. We learned that a probability is often interpreted as a **long-run relative frequency,** and we saw that probabilities can be found by examining **sample spaces** and by using **probability rules.** We learned several important probability rules—**addition rules, multiplication rules,** and **the rule of complements.** We also studied a special kind of probability called a **conditional probability,** which is the probability that one event will occur given that another event occurs, and we used probabilities to define **independent events.**

We concluded this chapter by studying **Bayes' theorem,** which can be used to update a **prior** probability to a **posterior** probability based on receiving new information.

Glossary of Terms

Bayes' theorem: A theorem (formula) that is used to compute posterior probabilities by revising prior probabilities. (page 198)

Bayesian statistics: An area of statistics that uses Bayes' theorem to update prior belief about a probability or population parameter to posterior belief. (page 200)

complement (of an event): If A is an event, the complement of A is the event that A will not occur. (page 180)

conditional probability: The probability that one event will occur given that we know that another event occurs. (page 187)

decision theory: An approach that helps decision makers to make intelligent choices. (page 200)

dependent events: When the probability of one event is influenced by whether another event occurs, the events are said to be dependent. (page 190)

event: A set of sample space outcomes. (page 174)

experiment: A process of observation that has an uncertain outcome. (page 171)

independent events: When the probability of one event is not influenced by whether another event occurs, the events are said to be independent. (page 190)

mutually exclusive events: Events that have no sample space outcomes in common, and, therefore, cannot occur simultaneously. (page 183)

prior probability: The initial probability that an event will occur. (page 198)

probability (of an event): A number that measures the chance, or likelihood, that an event will occur when an experiment is carried out. (page 175)

posterior probability: A revised probability obtained by updating a prior probability after receiving new information. (page 198)

sample space: The set of all possible experimental outcomes (sample space outcomes). (page 173)

sample space outcome: A distinct outcome of an experiment (that is, an element in the sample space). (page 173)

subjective probability: A probability assessment that is based on experience, intuitive judgment, or expertise. (page 172)

Important Formulas

Probabilities when all sample space outcomes are equally likely: page 177

The rule of complements: page 180

The addition rule for two events: page 183

The addition rule for two mutually exclusive events: page 184

The addition rule for N mutually exclusive events: page 185

Conditional probability: page 188

The general multiplication rule: page 189

Independence: page 190

The multiplication rule for two independent events: page 191

The multiplication rule for N independent events: page 191

Bayes' theorem: page 199

Supplementary Exercises

Exercises 4.43 through 4.46 are based on the following situation: An investor holds two stocks, each of which can rise (R), remain unchanged (U), or decline (D) on any particular day.

connect

4.43   Construct a tree diagram showing all possible combined movements for both stocks on a particular day (for instance, RR, RD, and so on, where the first letter denotes the movement of the first stock, and the second letter denotes the movement of the second stock).

4.44   If all outcomes are equally likely, find the probability that both stocks rise; that both stocks decline; that exactly one stock declines.

4.45   Find the probabilities you found in Exercise 4.44 by assuming that for each stock $P(R) = .6, P(U) = .1,$ and $P(D) = .3$, and assuming that the two stocks move independently.

4.46   Assume that for the first stock (on a particular day)

$$P(R) = .4, P(U) = .2, P(D) = .4$$

and that for the second stock (on a particular day)

$$P(R) = .8, P(U) = .1, P(D) = .1$$

Assuming that these stocks move independently, find the probability that both stocks decline; the probability that exactly one stock rises; the probability that exactly one stock is unchanged; the probability that both stocks rise.

4.47   A marketing major will interview for an internship with a major consumer products manufacturer/distributor. Before the interview, the marketing major feels that the chances of being offered an internship are 40 percent. Suppose that of the students who have been offered internships with this company, 90 percent had good interviews, and that of the students who have not been offered internships, 50 percent had good interviews. If the marketing major has a good interview, what is the probability that he or she will be offered an internship?

The Bureau of Labor Statistics reports on a variety of employment statistics. "College Enrollment and Work Activity of 2004 High School Graduates" provides information on high school graduates by gender, by race, and by labor force participation as of October 2004.[3] (All numbers are in thousands.) The following two tables provide information on the "Labor force status of persons 16 to 24 years old by educational attainment and gender, October 2004." Using the information contained in the tables, do Exercises 4.48 through 4.52.   ● LabForce

Women, age 16 to 24	Civilian labor force		Not in labor force	Row total	Men, age 16 to 24	Civilian labor force		Not in labor force	Row total
	Employed	Unemployed				Employed	Unemployed		
< High school	662	205	759	1626	< High school	1334	334	472	2140
HS degree	2050	334	881	3265	HS degree	3110	429	438	3977
Some college	1352	126	321	1799	Some college	1425	106	126	1657
Bachelor's degree or more	921	55	105	1081	Bachelor's degree or more	708	37	38	783
Column total	4985	720	2066	7771	Column total	6577	906	1074	8557

4.48 Find the probability that a randomly selected female aged 16 to 24 is in the civilian labor force, if she has a high school degree.   ● LabForce

4.49 Find the probability that a randomly selected female aged 16 to 24 is in the civilian labor force, if she has a bachelor's degree or more.   ● LabForce

4.50 Find the probability that a randomly selected female aged 16 to 24 is employed, if she is in the civilian labor force and has a high school degree.   ● LabForce

4.51 Find the probability that a randomly selected female aged 16 to 24 is employed, if she is in the civilian labor force and has a bachelor's degree or more.   ● LabForce

4.52 Repeat Exercises 4.48 through 4.51 for a randomly selected male aged 16 to 24. In general, do the above tables imply that labor force status and employment status depend upon educational attainment? Explain your answer.   ● LabForce

Suppose that in a survey of 1,000 U.S. residents, 721 residents believed that the amount of violent television programming had increased over the past 10 years, 454 residents believed that the overall quality of television programming had decreased over the past 10 years, and 362 residents believed both. Use this information to do Exercises 4.53 through 4.59.

4.53 What proportion of the 1,000 U.S. residents believed that the amount of violent programming had increased over the past 10 years?

4.54 What proportion of the 1,000 U.S. residents believed that the overall quality of programming had decreased over the past 10 years?

4.55 What proportion of the 1,000 U.S. residents believed that both the amount of violent programming had increased and the overall quality of programming had decreased over the past 10 years?

4.56 What proportion of the 1,000 U.S. residents believed that either the amount of violent programming had increased or the overall quality of programming had decreased over the past 10 years?

4.57 What proportion of the U.S. residents who believed that the amount of violent programming had increased believed that the overall quality of programming had decreased?

4.58 What proportion of the U.S. residents who believed that the overall quality of programming had decreased believed that the amount of violent programming had increased?

4.59 What sort of dependence seems to exist between whether U.S. residents believed that the amount of violent programming had increased and whether U.S. residents believed that the overall quality of programming had decreased? Explain your answer.

4.60 On any given day, the probability that the Ohio River at Cincinnati is polluted by a carbon tetrachloride spill is .10. Each day, a test is conducted to determine whether the river is polluted by carbon tetrachloride. This test has proved correct 80 percent of the time. Suppose that on a particular day the test indicates carbon tetrachloride pollution. What is the probability that such pollution actually exists?

[3]Source: www.bls.gov. *College Enrollment and Work Activity of 2004 High School Graduates,* Table 2. "Labor Force Status of Persons 16 to 24 Years Old by School Enrollment, Educational Attainment, Sex, Race, and Hispanic or Latino Ethnicity, October 2004."

4.61 Enterprise Industries has been running a television advertisement for Fresh liquid laundry detergent. When a survey was conducted, .21 of the individuals surveyed had purchased Fresh, .41 of the individuals surveyed had recalled seeing the advertisement, and .13 of the individuals surveyed had purchased Fresh and recalled seeing the advertisement.

     a What proportion of the individuals surveyed who recalled seeing the advertisement had purchased Fresh?

     b Based on your answer to part *a*, does the advertisement seem to have been effective? Explain.

4.62 A company employs 400 salespeople. Of these, 83 received a bonus last year, 100 attended a special sales training program at the beginning of last year, and 42 both attended the special sales training program and received a bonus. (Note: The bonus was based totally on sales performance.)

     a What proportion of the 400 salespeople received a bonus last year?

     b What proportion of the 400 salespeople attended the special sales training program at the beginning of last year?

     c What proportion of the 400 salespeople both attended the special sales training program and received a bonus?

     d What proportion of the salespeople who attended the special sales training program received a bonus?

     e Based on your answers to parts *a* and *d*, does the special sales training program seem to have been effective? Explain your answer.

Exercises 4.63, 4.64, and 4.65 extend Exercise 4.32 (page 197). Recall that Figure 4.9 (page 197) gives an AccuRatings analysis for the song "We've Got It Goin' On" by the Backstreet Boys. Also recall that

1 Estimates of the probabilities that a randomly selected listener would give the song the ratings 5, 4, 3, 2, and 1 are $P(5) = .18$, $P(4) = .27$, $P(3) = .28$, $P(2) = .08$, and $P(1) = .10$.

2 An estimate of the probability that a randomly selected listener is tired of the song is $P(T) = .17$.

3 We estimate that $P(T \mid 5) = 0$, $P(T \mid 4) = .04$, $P(T \mid 3) = .25$, $P(T \mid 2) = .25$, and $P(T \mid 1) = .70$.

4 We estimate that the probability that a randomly selected listener is familiar with the song is $P(FAM) = .91$.

4.63 Find estimates of $P(5 \mid T)$, $P(4 \mid T)$, $P(3 \mid T)$, $P(2 \mid T)$, and $P(1 \mid T)$.
Hint:

$$P(1 \mid T) = \frac{P(1 \cap T)}{P(T)} = \frac{P(1)P(T \mid 1)}{P(T)}$$

and the other probabilities are calculated similarly.

4.64 Let *NT* denote the event that a randomly selected listener is not tired of the song. Because we estimate that $P(T) = .17$ and $P(T \mid 1) = .70$, we estimate that

$$P(NT) = 1 - P(T) = .83 \quad \text{and} \quad P(NT \mid 1) = 1 - P(T \mid 1) = .30$$

     a Estimate $P(NT \mid 5)$, $P(NT \mid 4)$, $P(NT \mid 3)$, and $P(NT \mid 2)$.

     b Estimate $P(5 \mid NT)$, $P(4 \mid NT)$, $P(3 \mid NT)$, $P(2 \mid NT)$, and $P(1 \mid NT)$.
Hint:

$$P(1 \mid NT) = \frac{P(1 \cap NT)}{P(NT)} = \frac{P(1)P(NT \mid 1)}{P(NT)}$$

and the other probabilities are calculated similarly.

     c The reason that the probabilities in *b* do not sum to 1 (with rounding) is that, if a listener is not tired of the song, the listener could be unfamiliar (*UNFAM*) with the song. Using the facts that

$$P(UNFAM) = 1 - P(FAM) = .09 \quad \text{and} \quad P(NT \mid UNFAM) = 1$$

find $P(UNFAM \cap NT)$, $P(UNFAM \mid NT)$, and $P(UNFAM \cup NT)$.

4.65 In this exercise we estimate the proportions of listeners familiar with the song who would give the song each rating. Using the definition of conditional probability, we estimate that

$$P(5 \mid FAM) = \frac{P(5 \cap FAM)}{P(FAM)} = \frac{P(5)}{P(FAM)} = \frac{.18}{.91} = .1978$$

Note here that $P(5 \cap FAM)$ equals $P(5)$ because the event $5 \cap FAM$ and the event 5 are equivalent. That is, a randomly selected listener would give the song a rating of 5 if and only if the listener is familiar with the song and would give the song a rating of 5. By using similar reasoning, find $P(4 \mid FAM)$, $P(3 \mid FAM)$, $P(2 \mid FAM)$, and $P(1 \mid FAM)$.

4.66 Suppose that A and B are events and that $P(A)$ and $P(B)$ are both positive.

  a If A and B are mutually exclusive, what is $P(A \cap B)$?

  b If A and B are independent events, explain why $P(A \cap B)$ is positive.

  c Can two mutually exclusive events, each having a positive probability of occurrence, also be independent? Prove your answer using your answers to parts a and b.

4.67 Below we give two contingency tables of data from reports submitted by airlines to the U.S. Department of Transportation. The data concern the numbers of on-time and delayed flights for Alaska Airlines and America West Airlines at five major airports.   ● AirDelays

| | **Alaska Airlines** | | | | | **America West** | | |
	On Time	Delayed	Total			On Time	Delayed	Total
Los Angeles	497	62	559		Los Angeles	694	117	811
Phoenix	221	12	233		Phoenix	4,840	415	5,255
San Diego	212	20	232		San Diego	383	65	448
San Francisco	503	102	605		San Francisco	320	129	449
Seattle	1,841	305	2,146		Seattle	201	61	262
Total	3,274	501	3,775		**Total**	6,438	787	7,225

Source: A. Barnett, "How Numbers Can Trick You," *Technology Review,* October 1994, pp. 38–45. Copyright © 1994 MIT Technology Review. Reprinted by permission of the publisher via Copyright Clearance Center.

  a What percentage of all Alaska Airlines flights were delayed? That is, use the data to estimate the probability that an Alaska Airlines flight will be delayed. Do the same for America West Airlines. Which airline does best overall?

  b For Alaska Airlines find the percentage of delayed flights at each airport. That is, use the data to estimate each of the probabilities $P(\text{delayed} \mid \text{Los Angeles})$, $P(\text{delayed} \mid \text{Phoenix})$, and so on. Then do the same for America West Airlines. Which airline does best at each individual airport?

  c We find that America West Airlines does worse at every airport, yet America West does best overall. This seems impossible, but it is true! By looking carefully at the data, explain how this can happen. Hint: Consider the weather in Phoenix and Seattle. (This exercise is an example of what is called *Simpson's paradox.*)

4.68   Internet Exercise

What are the age, gender, and ethnic compositions of U.S. college students? As background for its 1995 study of college students and their risk behaviors, the Centers for Disease Control and Prevention collected selected demographic data—age, gender, and ethnicity—about college students. A report on the 1995 National Health Risk Behavior Survey can be found at the CDC website [http://www.cdc.gov: Data & Statistics: Youth Risk Behavior Surveillance System: Data Products: 1995 National College Health Risk Behavior Survey; or go directly to http://www.cdc.gov/nccdphp/dash/MMWRFile/ss4606.htm.] This report includes a large number of tables, the first of which summarizes the demographic information for the sample of $n = 4{,}609$ college students. An excerpt of Table 1 is given on the right.

  Using conditional probabilities, discuss (a) the dependence between age and gender and (b) the dependence between age and ethnicity for U.S. college students.
● CDCData

```
TABLE 1. Demographic Characteristics of
Undergraduate College Students Aged >=18
Years, by Age Group — United States, National
College Health Risk Behavior Survey, 1995
===============================================
                        Age Group (%)
                        ----------------------
Category    Total (%)   18-24 Years   >=25 Years
-----------------------------------------------
Total          --          63.6          36.4
Sex
  Female       55.5        52.0          61.8
  Male         44.5        48.0          38.2
Race/ethnicity
  White*       72.8        70.9          76.1
  Black*       10.3        10.5           9.6
  Hispanic      7.1         6.9           7.4
  Other         9.9        11.7           6.9
```

CHAPTER 5

Discrete Random Variables

Chapter Outline

5.1 Two Types of Random Variables

5.2 Discrete Probability Distributions

5.3 The Binomial Distribution

5.4 The Poisson Distribution (Optional)

e often use what we call **random variables** to describe the important aspects of the outcomes of experiments. In this chapter we introduce two important types of random variables—**discrete random variables** and **continuous** random variables—and learn how to find probabilities concerning discrete random variables. As one application, we will see in the AccuRatings case how Strategic Radio Research determines the popularity index of each song it rates.

5.1 Two Types of Random Variables ● ● ●

We begin with the definition of a random variable:

A **random variable** assumes numerical values that are determined by the outcome of an experiment, where one and only one numerical value is assigned to each experimental outcome.

Before an experiment is carried out, its outcome is uncertain. It follows that, since a random variable assigns a number to each experimental outcome, a random variable can be thought of as *representing an uncertain numerical outcome.*

To illustrate the idea of a random variable, suppose that Sound City sells and installs car stereo systems. One of Sound City's most popular stereo systems is the TrueSound-XL, a top-of-the-line stereo CD car radio. Consider (the experiment of) selling the TrueSound-XL radio at the Sound City store during a particular week. If we let x denote the number of radios sold during the week, then x is a random variable. That is, looked at before the week, the number of radios x that will be sold is uncertain, and, therefore, x is a random variable.

Notice that x, the number of TrueSound-XL radios sold in a week, might be 0 or 1 or 2 or 3, and so forth. In general, when the possible values of a random variable can be counted or listed, we say that the random variable is a **discrete random variable.** That is, either a discrete random variable may assume a finite number of possible values or the possible values may take the form of a *countable* sequence or list such as 0, 1, 2, 3, 4, . . . (a *countably infinite* list).

Some other examples of discrete random variables are

1   The number, x, of the next three customers entering a store who will make a purchase. Here x could be 0, 1, 2, or 3.

2   The number, x, of four patients taking a new antibiotic who experience gastrointestinal distress as a side effect. Here x could be 0, 1, 2, 3, or 4.

3   The number, x, of television sets in a sample of eight five-year-old television sets that have not needed a single repair. Here x could be any of the values 0, 1, 2, 3, 4, 5, 6, 7, or 8.

4   The rating, x, on a 1 through 5 scale given to a song by a listener in an AccuRatings music survey. Here x could be 1, 2, 3, 4, or 5.

5   The number, x, of major fires in a large city during the last two months. Here x could be 0, 1, 2, 3, and so forth (there is no definite maximum number of fires).

6   The number, x, of dirt specks in a one-square-yard sheet of plastic wrap. Here x could be 0, 1, 2, 3, and so forth (there is no definite maximum number of dirt specks).

The values of the random variables described in examples 1, 2, 3, and 4 are countable and finite. In contrast, the values of the random variables described in 5 and 6 are countable and infinite (or countably infinite lists). For example, in theory there is no limit to the number of major fires that could occur in a city in two months.

Not all random variables have values that are countable. When a random variable may assume any numerical value in one or more intervals on the real number line, then we say that the random variable is a **continuous random variable.**

EXAMPLE 5.1 The Car Mileage Case

Consider the car mileage situation that we have discussed in Chapters 1–3. The EPA combined city and highway mileage, x, of a randomly selected midsize car is a continuous random variable. This is because, although we have measured mileages to the nearest one-tenth of a mile per gallon, technically speaking, the potential mileages that might be obtained correspond (starting at, perhaps, 26 mpg) to an interval of numbers on the real line. We cannot count or list the numbers in such an interval because they are infinitesimally close together. That is, given any two numbers in an interval on the real line, there is always another number between them. To understand this, try listing the mileages starting with 26 mpg. Would the next mileage be 26.1 mpg? No, because we could obtain a mileage of 26.05 mpg. Would 26.05 mpg be the next mileage? No, because we could obtain a mileage of 26.025 mpg. We could continue this line of reasoning indefinitely. That is, whatever value we would try to list as the *next mileage,* there would always be another mileage between this *next mileage* and 26 mpg.

Some other examples of continuous random variables are

1   The temperature (in degrees Fahrenheit) of a cup of coffee served at a McDonald's restaurant.

2   The weight (in ounces) of strawberry preserves dispensed by an automatic filling machine into a 16-ounce jar.

3   The time (in minutes) that a customer in a store must wait to receive a credit card authorization.

4   The interest rate (in percent) charged for mortgage loans at a bank.

Exercises for Section 5.1

connect™

CONCEPTS

5.1   Explain the concept of a random variable.

5.2   Explain how the values of a discrete random variable differ from the values of a continuous random variable.

5.3   Classify each of the following random variables as discrete or continuous:
  a x = the number of girls born to a couple who will have three children.
  b x = the number of defects found on an automobile at final inspection.
  c x = the weight (in ounces) of the sandwich meat placed on a submarine sandwich.
  d x = the number of incorrect lab procedures conducted at a hospital during a particular week.
  e x = the number of customers served during a given day at a drive-through window.
  f x = the time needed by a clerk to complete a task.
  g x = the temperature of a pizza oven at a particular time.

5.2 Discrete Probability Distributions ● ● ●

The value assumed by a discrete random variable depends on the outcome of an experiment. Because the outcome of the experiment will be uncertain, the value assumed by the random variable will also be uncertain. However, it is often useful to know the probabilities that are associated with the different values that the random variable can take on. That is, we often wish to know the random variable's **probability distribution.**

> The **probability distribution** of a discrete random variable is a table, graph, or formula that gives the probability associated with each possible value that the random variable can assume.

We denote the probability distribution of the discrete random variable x as $p(x)$. As will be demonstrated in the following example, we can sometimes use the sample space of an experiment and probability rules to find the probability distribution of a random variable.

EXAMPLE 5.2

Consider the pop quiz consisting of three true–false questions. Remember that the sample space when a student takes such a quiz consists of the outcomes

$$CCC \quad CCI \quad CIC \quad ICC$$
$$CII \quad ICI \quad IIC \quad III$$

We now define the random variable x to be the number of questions that the student answers correctly. Here x can assume the values 0, 1, 2, or 3. That is, the student could answer anywhere between 0 and 3 questions correctly. In Examples 4.3 and 4.5 we assumed that the

TABLE 5.1 Finding the Probability Distribution of x = the Number of Questions Answered Correctly When the Student Studies and Has a 90 Percent Chance of Answering Each Question Correctly

Value of x = the Number of Correct Answers	Sample Space Outcomes Corresponding to Value of x	Probability of Sample Space Outcome	$p(x)$ = Probability of the Value of x
$x = 0$ (no correct answers)	III	$(.1)(.1)(.1) = .001$	$p(0) = .001$
$x = 1$ (one correct answer)	CII	$(.9)(.1)(.1) = .009$	$p(1) = .009 + .009 + .009 = .027$
	ICI	$(.1)(.9)(.1) = .009$	
	IIC	$(.1)(.1)(.9) = .009$	
$x = 2$ (two correct answers)	CCI	$(.9)(.9)(.1) = .081$	$p(2) = .081 + .081 + .081 = .243$
	CIC	$(.9)(.1)(.9) = .081$	
	ICC	$(.1)(.9)(.9) = .081$	
$x = 3$ (three correct answers)	CCC	$(.9)(.9)(.9) = .729$	$p(3) = .729$

student is totally unprepared for the quiz and thus has only a .5 probability of answering each question correctly. We now assume that the student studies and has a .9 probability of answering each question correctly. Table 5.1 summarizes finding the probabilities associated with each of the values of x (0, 1, 2, and 3). As an example of the calculations, consider finding the probability that x equals 2. Two questions will be answered correctly if and only if we obtain one of the sample space outcomes

$$CCI \qquad CIC \qquad ICC$$

Assuming that the three questions will be answered independently, these sample space outcomes have probabilities

$$P(CCI) = (.9)(.9)(.1) = .081$$

$$P(CIC) = (.9)(.1)(.9) = .081$$

$$P(ICC) = (.1)(.9)(.9) = .081$$

Therefore,

$$P(x = 2) = P(CCI) + P(CIC) + P(ICC)$$

$$= .081 + .081 + .081$$

$$= .243$$

Similarly, we can obtain probabilities associated with $x = 0$, $x = 1$, and $x = 3$. The probability distribution of x is summarized as follows:

x, Number of Questions Answered Correctly	$p(x)$, Probability of x
0	$p(0) = P(x = 0) = .001$
1	$p(1) = P(x = 1) = .027$
2	$p(2) = P(x = 2) = .243$
3	$p(3) = P(x = 3) = .729$

Notice that the probabilities in this probability distribution sum to $.001 + .027 + .243 + .729 = 1$.

To show the advantage of studying, note that the above probability distribution says that if the student has a .9 probability of answering each question correctly, then the probability that the student will answer all three questions correctly is .729. Furthermore, the probability that the student will answer *at least* two out of three questions correctly is (since the events $x = 2$ and $x = 3$ are mutually exclusive)

$$P(x \geq 2) = P(x = 2 \text{ or } x = 3)$$

$$= P(x = 2) + P(x = 3)$$

$$= .243 + .729$$

$$= .972$$

By contrast, we saw in Example 4.5 that if the student is totally unprepared and has only a .5 probability of answering each question correctly, then the probabilities that the student will answer zero, one, two, and three questions correctly are, respectively, 1/8, 3/8, 3/8, and 1/8. Therefore, the probability that the unprepared student will answer all three questions correctly is only 1/8, and the probability that this student will answer at least two out of three questions correctly is only $(3/8 + 1/8) = .5$.

In general, a discrete probability distribution $p(x)$ must satisfy two conditions:

Properties of a Discrete Probability Distribution $p(x)$

A **discrete probability distribution** $p(x)$ must be such that

1 $p(x) \geq 0$ for each value of x

2 $\sum\limits_{\text{All } x} p(x) = 1$

The first of these conditions says that each probability in a probability distribution must be zero or positive. The second condition says that the probabilities in a probability distribution must sum to 1. Looking at the probability distribution illustrated in Example 5.2, we can see that these properties are satisfied.

Often it is not possible to examine the entire sample space of an experiment. In such a case we sometimes collect data that will allow us to estimate the probabilities in a probability distribution.

EXAMPLE 5.3

Recall that Sound City sells the TrueSound-XL car radio, and define the random variable x to be the number of such radios sold in a particular week. In order to know the true probabilities of the various values of x, we would have to observe sales during all of the (potentially infinite number of) weeks in which the TrueSound-XL radio could be sold. That is, if we consider an experiment in which we randomly select a week and observe sales of the TrueSound-XL, the sample space would consist of a potentially infinite number of equally likely weeks. Obviously, it is not possible to examine this entire sample space.

Suppose, however, that Sound City has kept historical records of TrueSound-XL sales during the last 100 weeks. These records tell us that

1   No radios have been sold in 3 (that is, $3/100 = .03$) of the weeks.

2   One radio has been sold in 20 (that is, .20) of the weeks.

3   Two radios have been sold in 50 (that is, .50) of the weeks.

4   Three radios have been sold in 20 (that is, .20) of the weeks.

5   Four radios have been sold in 5 (that is, .05) of the weeks.

6   Five radios have been sold in 2 (that is, .02) of the weeks.

7   No more than five radios were sold in any of the past 100 weeks.

It follows that we might *estimate* that the probability distribution of x, the number of TrueSound-XL radios sold during a particular week at Sound City, is as shown in Table 5.2. A graph of this distribution is shown in Figure 5.1.

TABLE 5.2   **An Estimate (Based on 100 Weeks of Historical Data) of the Probability Distribution of x, the Number of TrueSound-XL Radios Sold at Sound City in a Week**

x, Number of Radios Sold	$p(x)$, the Probability of x
0	$p(0) = P(x = 0) = 3/100 = .03$
1	$p(1) = P(x = 1) = 20/100 = .20$
2	$p(2) = P(x = 2) = 50/100 = .50$
3	$p(3) = P(x = 3) = 20/100 = .20$
4	$p(4) = P(x = 4) = 5/100 = .05$
5	$p(5) = P(x = 5) = 2/100 = .02$

FIGURE 5.1   A Graph of the Probability Distribution of *x*, the Number of TrueSound-XL Radios Sold at Sound City in a Week

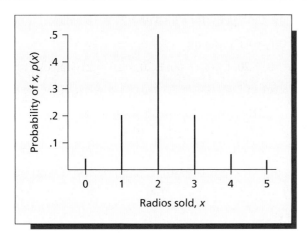

Finally, it is reasonable to use the historical sales data from the past 100 weeks to estimate the true probabilities associated with the various numbers of radios sold if the sales process remains stable over time and is not seasonal (that is, if radio sales are not higher at one time of the year than at others).

Suppose that the experiment described by a random variable *x* is repeated an indefinitely large number of times. If the values of the random variable *x* observed on the repetitions are recorded, we would obtain the population of all possible observed values of the random variable *x*. This population has a mean, which we denote as μ_x and which we sometimes call the **expected value of *x*.** In order to calculate μ_x, we multiply each value of *x* by its probability *p(x)* and then sum the resulting products over all possible values of *x*.

The Mean or Expected Value of a Discrete Random Variable

The **mean,** or **expected value,** of a discrete random variable *x* is

$$\mu_x = \sum_{\text{All } x} xp(x)$$

In the next example we illustrate how to calculate μ_x, and we reason that the calculation really does give the mean of all possible observed values of the random variable *x*.

EXAMPLE 5.4

Remember that Table 5.2 gives the probability distribution of *x*, the number of TrueSound-XL radios sold in a week at Sound City. Using this distribution, it follows that

$$\mu_x = \sum_{\text{All } x} xp(x)$$
$$= 0p(0) + 1p(1) + 2p(2) + 3p(3) + 4p(4) + 5p(5)$$
$$= 0(.03) + 1(.20) + 2(.50) + 3(.20) + 4(.05) + 5(.02)$$
$$= 2.1$$

To see that such a calculation gives the mean of all possible observed values of *x*, recall from Example 5.3 that the probability distribution in Table 5.2 was estimated from historical records of TrueSound-XL sales during the last 100 weeks. Also recall that these historical records tell us that during the last 100 weeks Sound City sold

1   Zero radios in 3 of the 100 weeks, for a total of 0(3) = 0 radios

2   One radio in 20 of the 100 weeks, for a total of 1(20) = 20 radios

3 Two radios in 50 of the 100 weeks, for a total of 2(50) = 100 radios

4 Three radios in 20 of the 100 weeks, for a total of 3(20) = 60 radios

5 Four radios in 5 of the 100 weeks, for a total of 4(5) = 20 radios

6 Five radios in 2 of the 100 weeks, for a total of 5(2) = 10 radios

In other words, Sound City sold a total of

$$0 + 20 + 100 + 60 + 20 + 10 = 210 \text{ radios}$$

in 100 weeks, or an average of $210/100 = 2.1$ radios per week. Now, the average

$$\frac{210}{100} = \frac{0 + 20 + 100 + 60 + 20 + 10}{100}$$

can be written as

$$\frac{0(3) + 1(20) + 2(50) + 3(20) + 4(5) + 5(2)}{100}$$

which can be rewritten as

$$0\left(\frac{3}{100}\right) + 1\left(\frac{20}{100}\right) + 2\left(\frac{50}{100}\right) + 3\left(\frac{20}{100}\right) + 4\left(\frac{5}{100}\right) + 5\left(\frac{2}{100}\right)$$
$$= 0(.03) + 1(.20) + 2(.50) + 3(.20) + 4(.05) + 5(.02)$$

which equals $\mu_x = 2.1$. That is, if observed sales values occur with relative frequencies equal to those specified by the probability distribution in Table 5.2, then the average number of radios sold per week is equal to the expected value of x.

Of course, if we observe radio sales for another 100 weeks, the relative frequencies of the observed sales values would not (unless we are very lucky) be exactly as specified by the estimated probabilities in Table 5.2. Rather, the observed relative frequencies would differ somewhat from the estimated probabilities in Table 5.2, and the average number of radios sold per week would not exactly equal $\mu_x = 2.1$ (although the average would likely be close). However, the point is this: If the probability distribution in Table 5.2 were the true probability distribution of weekly radio sales, and if we were to observe radio sales for an indefinitely large number of weeks, then we would observe sales values with relative frequencies that are exactly equal to those specified by the probabilities in Table 5.2. In this case, when we calculate the expected value of x to be $\mu_x = 2.1$, we are saying that *in the long run* (that is, over an indefinitely large number of weeks) Sound City would average selling 2.1 TrueSound-XL radios per week.

As another example, again consider Example 5.2, and let the random variable x denote the number of the three true–false questions that the student who studies answers correctly. Using the probability distribution shown in Table 5.1, the expected value of x is

$$\mu_x = 0(.001) + 1(.027) + 2(.243) + 3(.729)$$
$$= 2.7$$

This expected value says that if a student takes a large number of three-question true–false quizzes and has a .9 probability of answering any single question correctly, then the student will average approximately 2.7 correct answers per quiz.

EXAMPLE 5.5 The AccuRatings Case

In this example we will compute the *popularity* index for the song "Gangsta's Paradise" by Coolio. Recall from Example 4.16 (pages 192–195) that Strategic Radio Research had listeners rate this song as a 5, 4, 3, 2, 1, or *UNFAM*. Although not discussed in Example 4.16, Strategic Radio Research also estimated the proportions of listeners *familiar with the song* who would give the song ratings of 5, 4, 3, 2, and 1 to be, respectively, .43, .21, .22, .07, and .07. Now, it is reasonable to assign the numerical values 1 through 5 to the ratings 1 through 5 (this sort of thing is done when colleges assign the numerical values 4 through 0 to the grades A through F).

TABLE 5.3   An Estimate of the Probability Distribution of x, the Rating of the Song
            "Gangsta's Paradise" by a Randomly Selected Listener Who Is Familiar
            with This Song

x, Rating	$p(x)$, Probability of x
1	$p(1) = .07$
2	$p(2) = .07$
3	$p(3) = .22$
4	$p(4) = .21$
5	$p(5) = .43$

Therefore, we can regard the song's rating, x, by a randomly selected listener who is familiar with the song to be a discrete random variable having the estimated probability distribution shown in Table 5.3. It follows that the expected value of this estimated probability distribution is

$$\mu_x = 1(.07) + 2(.07) + 3(.22) + 4(.21) + 5(.43)$$
$$= 3.86$$

This estimated expected value is reported as the *popularity* index in Figure 4.8 (page 194) (the difference between the 3.86 calculated here and the 3.87 in Figure 4.8 is due to rounding). It says that Strategic Radio Research estimates that the mean rating of the song that would be given by all listeners who are familiar with the song is 3.86. As indicated in Figure 4.8, Strategic Radio Research reports that the song has a "very high popularity" index, which is the highest (#1) of all the songs rated for the week.

EXAMPLE 5.6

An insurance company sells a \$20,000 whole life insurance policy for an annual premium of \$300. Actuarial tables show that a person who would be sold such a policy with this premium has a .001 probability of death during a year. Let x be a random variable representing the insurance company's profit made on one of these policies during a year. The probability distribution of x is

x, Profit	$p(x)$, Probability of x
\$300 (if the policyholder lives)	.999
\$300 − \$20,000 = −\$19,700 (a \$19,700 loss if the policyholder dies)	.001

The expected value of x (expected profit per year) is

$$\mu_x = \$300(.999) + (-\$19,700)(.001)$$
$$= \$280$$

This says that if the insurance company sells a very large number of these policies, it will average a profit of \$280 per policy per year. Since insurance companies actually do sell large numbers of policies, it is reasonable for these companies to make profitability decisions based on expected values.

   Next, suppose that we wish to find the premium that the insurance company must charge for a \$20,000 policy if the company wishes the average profit per policy per year to be greater than \$0. If we let *prem* denote the premium the company will charge, then the probability distribution of the company's yearly profit x is

x, Profit	$p(x)$, Probability of x
prem (if policyholder lives)	.999
prem − \$20,000 (if policyholder dies)	.001

The expected value of x (expected profit per year) is

$$\mu_x = prem(.999) + (prem - 20{,}000)(.001)$$
$$= prem - 20$$

In order for this expected profit to be greater than zero, the premium must be greater than $20. If, as previously stated, the company charges $300 for such a policy, the $280 charged in excess of the needed $20 compensates the company for commissions paid to salespeople, administrative costs, dividends paid to investors, and other expenses.

In general, it is reasonable to base decisions on an expected value if we perform the experiment related to the decision (for example, if we sell the life insurance policy) many times. If we do not (for instance, if we perform the experiment only once), then it may not be a good idea to base decisions on the expected value. For example, it might not be wise for you—as an individual—to sell one person a $20,000 life insurance policy for a premium of $300. To see this, again consider the probability distribution of yearly profit:

x, Profit	p(x), Probability of x
$300 (if policyholder lives)	.999
$300 − $20,000 = −$19,700 (if policyholder dies)	.001

and recall that the expected profit per year is $280. However, since you are selling only one policy, you will not receive the $280. You will either gain $300 (with probability .999) or you will lose $19,700 (with probability .001). Although the decision is personal, and although the chance of losing $19,700 is very small, many people would not risk such a loss when the potential gain is only $300.

Just as the population of all possible observed values of a discrete random variable x has a mean μ_x, this population also has a variance σ_x^2 and a standard deviation σ_x. Recall that the variance of a population is the average of the squared deviations of the different population values from the population mean. To find σ_x^2, we calculate $(x - \mu_x)^2$ for each value of x, multiply $(x - \mu_x)^2$ by the probability $p(x)$, and sum the resulting products over all possible values of x.

The Variance and Standard Deviation of a Discrete Random Variable

The **variance** of a discrete random variable x is

$$\sigma_x^2 = \sum_{\text{All } x} (x - \mu_x)^2 p(x)$$

The **standard deviation** of x is the positive square root of the variance of x. That is,

$$\sigma_x = \sqrt{\sigma_x^2}$$

EXAMPLE 5.7

Table 5.2 gives the probability distribution of x, the number of TrueSound-XL radios sold in a week at Sound City. Remembering that we have calculated μ_x (in Example 5.4) to be 2.1, it follows that

$$\sigma_x^2 = \sum_{\text{All } x} (x - \mu_x)^2 p(x)$$

$$= (0 - 2.1)^2 p(0) + (1 - 2.1)^2 p(1) + (2 - 2.1)^2 p(2) + (3 - 2.1)^2 p(3)$$
$$+ (4 - 2.1)^2 p(4) + (5 - 2.1)^2 p(5)$$

$$= (4.41)(.03) + (1.21)(.20) + (.01)(.50) + (.81)(.20) + (3.61)(.05) + (8.41)(.02)$$

$$= .89$$

and that the standard deviation of x is $\sigma_x = \sqrt{.89} = .9434$.

The variance σ_x^2 and the standard deviation σ_x measure the spread of the population of all possible observed values of the random variable. To see how to use σ_x, remember that Chebyshev's

Theorem (see Chapter 3, page 131) tells us that, for any value of k that is greater than 1, at least $100(1 - 1/k^2)\%$ of all possible observed values of the random variable x lie in the interval $[\mu_x \pm k\sigma_x]$. Stated in terms of a probability, we have

$$P(x \text{ falls in the interval } [\mu_x \pm k\sigma_x]) \geq 1 - 1/k^2$$

For example, consider the probability distribution (in Table 5.2) of x, the number of TrueSound-XL radios sold in a week at Sound City. If we set k equal to 2, and if we use $\mu_x = 2.1$ and $\sigma_x = .9434$ to calculate the interval

$$[\mu_x \pm 2\sigma_x] = [2.1 \pm 2(.9434)]$$
$$= [.2132, \ 3.9868]$$

then Chebyshev's Theorem tells us that

$$P(x \text{ falls in the interval } [.2132, \ 3.9868]) \geq 1 - 1/2^2 = 3/4$$

This says that in at least 75 percent of all weeks, Sound City will sell between .2132 and 3.9868 TrueSound-XL radios. As illustrated in Figure 5.2, there are three values of x between .2132 and 3.9868—namely, $x = 1$, $x = 2$, and $x = 3$. Therefore, the exact probability that x will be in the interval $[\mu_x \pm 2\sigma_x]$ is

$$p(1) + p(2) + p(3) = .20 + .50 + .20 = .90$$

This illustrates that, although Chebyshev's Theorem guarantees us that at least $100(1 - 1/k^2)\%$ of all possible observed values of a random variable x fall in the interval $[\mu_x \pm k\sigma_x]$, often the percentage is considerably higher.

In some cases, the graph of the probability distribution of a discrete random variable has the symmetrical, bell-shaped appearance of a normal curve. For example, the graph in Figure 5.2 is roughly bell-shaped and symmetrical. In such a situation—and *under certain additional assumptions*—the probability distribution can sometimes be *approximated* by a normal curve. We will discuss the needed assumptions in Chapter 6. As an example of such assumptions, note that although the graph in Figure 5.2 is roughly bell-shaped and symmetrical, it can be shown that there are not enough values of x, and thus not enough probabilities $p(x)$, for us to approximate the probability distribution by using a normal curve. If, however, the probability distribution of a discrete random variable x can be approximated by a normal curve, then the **Empirical Rule** for normally distributed populations describes the population of all possible values of x. Specifically, we can say that approximately 68.26 percent, 95.44 percent, and 99.73 percent of all possible observed values of x fall in the intervals $[\mu_x \pm \sigma_x]$, $[\mu_x \pm 2\sigma_x]$, and $[\mu_x \pm 3\sigma_x]$.

FIGURE 5.2   **The Interval $[\mu_x \pm 2\sigma_x]$ for the Probability Distribution Describing TrueSound-XL Radio Sales (see Table 5.2)**

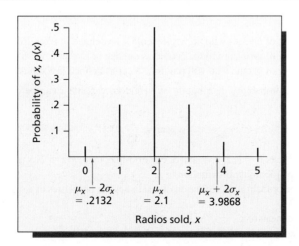

To summarize, the standard deviation σ_x of a discrete random variable measures the spread of the population of all possible observed values of x. When the probability distribution of x can be approximated by a normal curve, this spread can be characterized by the Empirical Rule. When this is not possible, we can use Chebyshev's Theorem to characterize the spread of x.

Exercises for Section 5.2

CONCEPTS

5.4   What is a discrete probability distribution? Explain in your own words.

5.5   What conditions must be satisfied by the probabilities in a discrete probability distribution? Explain what these conditions mean.

5.6   Describe how to compute the mean (or expected value) of a discrete random variable, and interpret what this quantity tells us about the observed values of the random variable.

5.7   Describe how to compute the standard deviation of a discrete random variable, and interpret what this quantity tells us about the observed values of the random variable.

METHODS AND APPLICATIONS

5.8   Explain whether each of the following is a valid probability distribution. If the probability distribution is valid, show why. Otherwise, show which condition(s) of a probability distribution are not satisfied.

a	x	p(x)	b	x	p(x)	c	x	p(x)	d	x	p(x)
	−1	.2		1/2	−1		2	.25		.1	2/7
	0	.6		3/4	0		4	.35		.7	4/7
	1	.2		1	2		6	.3		.9	1/7

5.9   Consider each of the following probability distributions:

a	x	p(x)	b	x	p(x)	c	x	p(x)
	0	.2		0	.25		−2	.1
	1	.8		1	.45		0	.3
				2	.2		2	.4
				3	.1		5	.2

Calculate μ_x and σ_x for each distribution. Then explain, using the probabilities, why μ_x is the mean of all possible observed values of x.

5.10 For each of the following, write out and graph the probability distribution of x. That is, list all the possible values of x and also list the corresponding probabilities. Then graph the distribution.
   a Refer to Exercise 4.3 (page 179), and let x equal the number of patrons who prefer diet cola A.
   b Refer to Exercise 4.4 (page 179), and let x equal the number of girls born to the couple.
   c Refer to Exercise 4.5 (page 179), and let x equal the number of people who will purchase a car.

5.11 For each of the following, find μ_x, σ_x^2, and σ_x. Then interpret in words the meaning of μ_x, and employ Chebyshev's Theorem to find intervals that contain at least 3/4 and 8/9 of the observed values of x.
   a x = the number of patrons who prefer diet cola A as defined in Exercise 5.10a.
   b x = the number of girls born to the couple as defined in Exercise 5.10b.
   c x = the number of people who will purchase a car as defined in Exercise 5.10c.

5.12 Suppose that the probability distribution of a random variable x can be described by the formula

$$p(x) = \frac{x}{15}$$

for each of the values x = 1, 2, 3, 4, and 5. For example, then, $P(x = 2) = p(2) = 2/15$.
   a Write out the probability distribution of x.
   b Show that the probability distribution of x satisfies the properties of a discrete probability distribution.
   c Calculate the mean of x.
   d Calculate the variance, σ_x^2, and the standard deviation, σ_x.

5.13 The following table summarizes investment outcomes and corresponding probabilities for a
particular oil well:

x = the outcome in $	p(x)
−$40,000 (no oil)	.25
10,000 (some oil)	.7
70,000 (much oil)	.05

a Graph $p(x)$; that is, graph the probability distribution of x.
b Find the expected monetary outcome. Mark this value on your graph of part a. Then interpret
this value.

5.14 In the book *Foundations of Financial Management* (7th ed.), Stanley B. Block and Geoffrey A.
Hirt discuss risk measurement for investments. Block and Hirt present an investment with the
possible outcomes and associated probabilities given in Table 5.4. The authors go on to say that the
probabilities

> may be based on past experience, industry ratios and trends, interviews with company execu-
> tives, and sophisticated simulation techniques. The probability values may be easy to deter-
> mine for the introduction of a mechanical stamping process in which the manufacturer has
> 10 years of past data, but difficult to assess for a new product in a foreign market.

a Use the probability distribution in Table 5.4 to calculate the expected value (mean) and the
standard deviation of the investment outcomes. Interpret the expected value.
b Block and Hirt interpret the standard deviation of the investment outcomes as follows:
"Generally, the larger the standard deviation (or spread of outcomes), the greater is the risk."
Explain why this makes sense. Use Chebyshev's Theorem to illustrate your point.
c Block and Hirt compare three investments having the following means and standard deviations
of the investment outcomes:

Investment 1	**Investment 2**	**Investment 3**
$\mu = \$600$	$\mu = \$600$	$\mu = \$600$
$\sigma = \$20$	$\sigma = \$190$	$\sigma = \$300$

Which of these investments involves the most risk? The least risk? Explain why by using
Chebyshev's Theorem to compute an interval for each investment that will contain at least 8/9
of the investment outcomes.
d Block and Hirt continue by comparing two more investments:

Investment A	**Investment B**
$\mu = \$6,000$	$\mu = \$600$
$\sigma = \$600$	$\sigma = \$190$

The authors explain that investment A

> appears to have a high standard deviation, but not when related to the expected value of
> the distribution. A standard deviation of $600 on an investment with an expected value of
> $6,000 may indicate less risk than a standard deviation of $190 on an investment with an
> expected value of only $600.
>
> We can eliminate the size difficulty by developing a third measure, the **coefficient of
> variation** (V). This term calls for nothing more difficult than dividing the standard devia-
> tion of an investment by the expected value. Generally, the larger the coefficient of varia-
> tion, the greater is the risk.

$$\text{Coefficient of variation } (V) = \frac{\sigma}{\mu}$$

TABLE 5.4   **Probability Distribution of Outcomes for an Investment**

Outcome	Probability of Outcome	Assumptions
$300	.2	Pessimistic
600	.6	Moderately successful
900	.2	Optimistic

Source: S. B. Block and G. A. Hirt, *Foundations of Financial Management,*
7th ed., p. 378. Copyright © 1994. Reprinted by permission of
McGraw-Hill Companies, Inc.

Calculate the coefficient of variation for investments A and B. Which investment carries the greater risk?

e Calculate the coefficient of variation for investments 1, 2, and 3 in part c. Based on the coefficient of variation, which investment involves the most risk? The least risk? Do we obtain the same results as we did by comparing standard deviations (in part c)? Why?

5.15 An insurance company will insure a $50,000 diamond for its full value against theft at a premium of $400 per year. Suppose that the probability that the diamond will be stolen is .005, and let x denote the insurance company's profit.

a Set up the probability distribution of the random variable x.

b Calculate the insurance company's expected profit.

c Find the premium that the insurance company should charge if it wants its expected profit to be $1,000.

5.16 In the book *Foundations of Financial Management* (7th ed.), Stanley B. Block and Geoffrey A. Hirt discuss a semiconductor firm that is considering two choices: (1) expanding the production of semiconductors for sale to end users or (2) entering the highly competitive home computer market. The cost of both projects is $60 million, but the net present value of the cash flows from sales and the risks are different.

Figure 5.3 gives a tree diagram of the project choices. The tree diagram gives a probability distribution of expected sales for each project. It also gives the present value of cash flows from sales and the net present value (NPV = present value of cash flow from sales minus initial cost) corresponding to each sales alternative. Note that figures in parentheses denote losses.

a For each project choice, calculate the expected net present value.

b For each project choice, calculate the variance and standard deviation of the net present value.

c Calculate the coefficient of variation for each project choice. See Exercise 5.14d for a discussion of the coefficient of variation.

d Which project has the higher expected net present value?

e Which project carries the least risk? Explain.

f In your opinion, which project should be undertaken? Justify your answer.

5.17 Five thousand raffle tickets are to be sold at $10 each to benefit a local community group. The prizes, the number of each prize to be given away, and the dollar value of winnings for each prize are as follows:

Prize	Number to Be Given Away	Dollar Value
Automobile	1	$20,000
Entertainment center	2	3,000 each
DVD recorder	5	400 each
Gift certificate	50	20 each

FIGURE 5.3   A Tree Diagram of Two Project Choices

		(1) Sales	(2) Probability	(3) Present Value of Cash Flow from Sales ($ millions)	(4) Initial Cost ($ millions)	(5) Net Present Value, NPV = (3) − (4) ($ millions)
Expand semiconductor capacity		High	.50	$100	$60	$40
		Moderate	.25	75	60	15
		Low	.25	40	60	(20)
A						
Start						
B						
Enter home computer market		High	.20	$200	$60	$140
		Moderate	.50	75	60	15
		Low	.30	25	60	(35)

Source: S. B. Block and G. A. Hirt, *Foundations of Financial Management,* 7th ed., p. 387. Copyright © 1994. Reprinted by permission of McGraw-Hill Companies, Inc.

TABLE 5.5 Return Distributions for Companies *A*, *B*, and *C* and for Two Possible Acquisitions

Economic Condition	Probability	Company *A* Returns	Company *B* Returns	Company *C* Returns	Company *A* + *B* Returns	Company *A* + *C* Returns
1	.2	17%	19%	13%	18%	15%
2	.2	15	17	11	16	13
3	.2	13	15	15	14	14
4	.2	11	13	17	12	14
5	.2	9	11	19	10	14

If you buy one ticket, calculate your expected winnings. (Form the probability distribution of x = your dollar winnings, and remember to subtract the cost of your ticket.)

5.18 Company *A* is considering the acquisition of two separate but large companies, Company *B* and Company *C*, having sales and assets equal to its own. Table 5.5 gives the probabilities of returns for each of the three companies under various economic conditions. The table also gives the probabilities of returns for each possible combination: Company *A* plus Company *B*, and Company *A* plus Company *C*.

  a For each of Companies *A*, *B*, and *C* find the mean return and the standard deviation of returns.

  b Find the mean return and the standard deviation of returns for the combination of Company *A* plus Company *B*.

  c Find the mean return and the standard deviation of returns for the combination of Company *A* plus Company *C*.

  d Compare the mean returns for each of the two possible combinations—Company *A* plus Company *B* and Company *A* plus Company *C*. Is either mean higher? How do they compare to Company *A*'s mean return?

  e Compare the standard deviations of the returns for each of the two possible combinations—Company *A* plus Company *B* and Company *A* plus Company *C*. Which standard deviation is smaller? Which possible combination involves less risk? How does the risk carried by this combination compare to the risk carried by Company *A* alone?

  f Which acquisition would you recommend—Company *A* plus Company *B* or Company *A* plus Company *C*?

5.19   THE ACCURATINGS CASE

Again consider Exercise 4.32 (page 197) and the title-by-title analysis of the song "We've Got It Goin' On" by the Backstreet Boys. Although not discussed in Exercise 4.32, Strategic Radio Research estimated the proportions of listeners *familiar with the song* who would give the song ratings of 5, 4, 3, 2, and 1 to be, respectively, .1978, .2967, .3077, .0879, and .1099. Assign the numerical values 1 through 5 to the ratings 1 through 5.

  a Find an estimate of the probability distribution of this song's rating, x, by a randomly selected listener who is familiar with the song.

  b Find the *popularity* index for the song "We've Got It Goin' On" that would be reported by Strategic Radio Research. That is, find an estimate of the mean rating of this song that would be given by all listeners who are familiar with this song.

5.3 The Binomial Distribution ◉ ● ●

In this section we discuss what is perhaps the most important discrete probability distribution— the binomial distribution. We begin with an example.

CHAPTER 4

EXAMPLE 5.8

Suppose that historical sales records indicate that 40 percent of all customers who enter a discount department store make a purchase. What is the probability that two of the next three customers will make a purchase?

In order to find this probability, we first note that the experiment of observing three customers making a purchase decision has several distinguishing characteristics:

1   The experiment consists of three identical *trials;* each trial consists of a customer making a purchase decision.

2   Two outcomes are possible on each trial: the customer makes a purchase (which we call a *success* and denote as S), or the customer does not make a purchase (which we call a *failure* and denote as F).

3   Since 40 percent of all customers make a purchase, it is reasonable to assume that $P(S)$, the probability that a customer makes a purchase, is .4 and is constant for all customers. This implies that $P(F)$, the probability that a customer does not make a purchase, is .6 and is constant for all customers.

4   We assume that customers make independent purchase decisions. That is, we assume that the outcomes of the three trials are independent of each other.

It follows that the sample space of the experiment consists of the following eight sample space outcomes:

$$
\begin{array}{cc}
SSS & FFS \\
SSF & FSF \\
SFS & SFF \\
FSS & FFF
\end{array}
$$

Here the sample space outcome SSS represents all three customers making purchases. On the other hand, the sample space outcome SFS represents the first customer making a purchase, the second customer not making a purchase, and the third customer making a purchase.

Two out of three customers make a purchase if one of the sample space outcomes SSF, SFS, or FSS occurs. Furthermore, since the trials (purchase decisions) are independent, we can simply multiply the probabilities associated with the different trial outcomes (each of which is S or F) to find the probability of a sequence of outcomes:

$$P(SSF) = P(S)P(S)P(F) = (.4)(.4)(.6) = (.4)^2(.6)$$
$$P(SFS) = P(S)P(F)P(S) = (.4)(.6)(.4) = (.4)^2(.6)$$
$$P(FSS) = P(F)P(S)P(S) = (.6)(.4)(.4) = (.4)^2(.6)$$

It follows that the probability that two out of the next three customers make a purchase is

$$
\begin{aligned}
&P(SSF) + P(SFS) + P(FSS) \\
&\quad = (.4)^2(.6) + (.4)^2(.6) + (.4)^2(.6) \\
&\quad = 3(.4)^2(.6) = .288
\end{aligned}
$$

We can now generalize the previous result and find the probability that x of the next n customers will make a purchase. Here we will assume that p is the probability that a customer makes a purchase, $q = 1 - p$ is the probability that a customer does not make a purchase, and purchase decisions (trials) are independent. To generalize the probability that two out of the next three customers make a purchase, which equals

$$3(.4)^2(.6)$$

we note that

1   The 3 in this expression is the number of sample space outcomes (SSF, SFS, and FSS) that correspond to the event "two out of the next three customers make a purchase." Note that this number equals the number of ways we can arrange two successes among the three trials.

2   The .4 is p, the probability that a customer makes a purchase.

3   The .6 is $q = 1 - p$, the probability that a customer does not make a purchase.

Therefore, the probability that two of the next three customers make a purchase is

$$\left(\begin{array}{c} \text{The number of ways} \\ \text{to arrange 2 successes} \\ \text{among 3 trials} \end{array} \right) p^2 q^1$$

Now, notice that, although each of the sample space outcomes *SSF*, *SFS*, and *FSS* represents a different arrangement of the two successes among the three trials, each of these sample space outcomes consists of two successes and one failure. For this reason, the probability of each of these sample space outcomes equals $(.4)^2(.6)^1 = p^2q^1$. It follows that p is raised to a power that equals the number of successes (2) in the three trials, and q is raised to a power that equals the number of failures (1) in the three trials.

In general, each sample space outcome describing the occurrence of x successes (purchases) in n trials represents a different arrangement of x successes in n trials. However, each outcome consists of x successes and $n - x$ failures. Therefore, the probability of each sample space outcome is p^xq^{n-x}. It follows by analogy that the probability that x of the next n trials are successes (purchases) is

$$\left(\begin{array}{c} \text{The number of ways} \\ \text{to arrange } x \text{ successes} \\ \text{among } n \text{ trials} \end{array} \right) p^xq^{n-x}$$

We can use the expression we have just arrived at to compute the probability of x successes in the next n trials if we can find a way to calculate the number of ways to arrange x successes among n trials. It can be shown that:

The number of ways to arrange x *successes among* n *trials* equals

$$\frac{n!}{x!\,(n - x)!}$$

where $n!$ is pronounced "n factorial" and is calculated as $n! = n(n - 1)(n - 2) \cdots (1)$ and where (by definition) $0! = 1$.

For instance, using this formula, we can see that the number of ways to arrange $x = 2$ successes among $n = 3$ trials equals

$$\frac{n!}{x!\,(n - x)!} = \frac{3!}{2!\,(3 - 2)!} = \frac{3!}{2!\,1!} = \frac{3 \cdot 2 \cdot 1}{2 \cdot 1 \cdot 1} = 3$$

Of course, we have previously seen that the three ways to arrange $x = 2$ successes among $n = 3$ trials are *SSF*, *SFS*, and *FSS*.

Using the preceding formula, we obtain the following general result:

The Binomial Distribution

A **binomial experiment** has the following characteristics:

1 The experiment consists of *n identical trials.*

2 Each trial results in a **success** or a **failure.**

3 The probability of a success on any trial is *p* and remains constant from trial to trial. This implies that the probability of failure, *q*, on any trial is $1 - p$ and remains constant from trial to trial.

4 The trials are **independent** (that is, the results of the trials have nothing to do with each other).

Furthermore, if we define the random variable

x = the total number of successes in *n* trials of a binomial experiment

then we call *x* a **binomial random variable,** and the probability of obtaining *x* successes in *n* trials is

$$p(x) = \frac{n!}{x!\,(n - x)!}\,p^xq^{n-x}$$

Noting that we sometimes refer to the formula for $p(x)$ as the **binomial formula,** we illustrate the use of this formula in the following example.

EXAMPLE 5.9

Consider the discount department store situation discussed in Example 5.8. In order to find the probability that three of the next five customers make purchases, we calculate

$$p(3) = \frac{5!}{3!\,(5-3)!}\,(.4)^3(.6)^{5-3} = \frac{5!}{3!\,2!}\,(.4)^3(.6)^2$$

$$= \frac{5 \cdot 4 \cdot 3 \cdot 2 \cdot 1}{(3 \cdot 2 \cdot 1)(2 \cdot 1)}\,(.4)^3(.6)^2$$

$$= 10(.064)(.36)$$

$$= .2304$$

Here we see that

1 $\frac{5!}{3!\,(5-3)!} = 10$ is the number of ways to arrange three successes among five trials. For instance, two ways to do this are described by the sample space outcomes *SSSFF* and *SFSSF.* There are eight other ways.

2 $(.4)^3(.6)^2$ is the probability of any sample space outcome consisting of three successes and two failures.

Thus far we have shown how to calculate binomial probabilities. We next give several examples that illustrate some practical applications of the binomial distribution. As we demonstrate in the first example, the term *success* does not necessarily refer to a *desirable* experimental outcome. Rather, it refers to an outcome that we wish to investigate.

EXAMPLE 5.10

Antibiotics occasionally cause nausea as a side effect. A major drug company has developed a new antibiotic called Phe-Mycin. The company claims that, at most, 10 percent of all patients treated with Phe-Mycin would experience nausea as a side effect of taking the drug. Suppose that we randomly select $n = 4$ patients and treat them with Phe-Mycin. Each patient will either experience nausea (which we arbitrarily call a success) or will not experience nausea (a failure). We will assume that p, the true probability that a patient will experience nausea as a side effect, is .10, the maximum value of p claimed by the drug company. Furthermore, it is reasonable to assume that patients' reactions to the drug would be independent of each other. Let x denote the number of patients among the four who will experience nausea as a side effect. It follows that x is a binomial random variable, which can take on any of the potential values 0, 1, 2, 3, or 4. That is, anywhere between none of the patients and all four of the patients could potentially experience nausea as a side effect. Furthermore, we can calculate the probability associated with each possible value of x as shown in Table 5.6. For instance, the probability that none of the four randomly selected patients experiences nausea is

$$p(0) = P(x = 0) = \frac{4!}{0!\,(4-0)!}\,(.1)^0(.9)^{4-0}$$

$$= \frac{4!}{0!\,4!}\,(.1)^0(.9)^4$$

$$= \frac{4!}{(1)(4!)}\,(1)(.9)^4$$

$$= (.9)^4 = .6561$$

Because Table 5.6 lists each possible value of x and also gives the probability of each value, we say that this table gives the **binomial probability distribution of x.**

The binomial probabilities given in Table 5.6 need not be hand calculated. MINITAB, Excel, and MegaStat can be used to calculate binomial probabilities. For instance, Figure 5.4(a) gives

TABLE 5.6 The Binomial Probability Distribution of x, the Number of Four Randomly Selected Patients Who Will Experience Nausea as a Side Effect of Being Treated with Phe-Mycin

x (Number Who Experience Nausea)	$p(x) = \dfrac{n!}{x!\,(n-x)!}\,p^{x}(1-p)^{n-x}$
0	$p(0) = P(x = 0) = \dfrac{4!}{0!\,(4-0)!}\,(.1)^{0}(.9)^{4-0} = .6561$
1	$p(1) = P(x = 1) = \dfrac{4!}{1!\,(4-1)!}\,(.1)^{1}(.9)^{4-1} = .2916$
2	$p(2) = P(x = 2) = \dfrac{4!}{2!\,(4-2)!}\,(.1)^{2}(.9)^{4-2} = .0486$
3	$p(3) = P(x = 3) = \dfrac{4!}{3!\,(4-3)!}\,(.1)^{3}(.9)^{4-3} = .0036$
4	$p(4) = P(x = 4) = \dfrac{4!}{4!\,(4-4)!}\,(.1)^{4}(.9)^{4-4} = .0001$

FIGURE 5.4 The Binomial Probability Distribution with $p = .10$ and $n = 4$

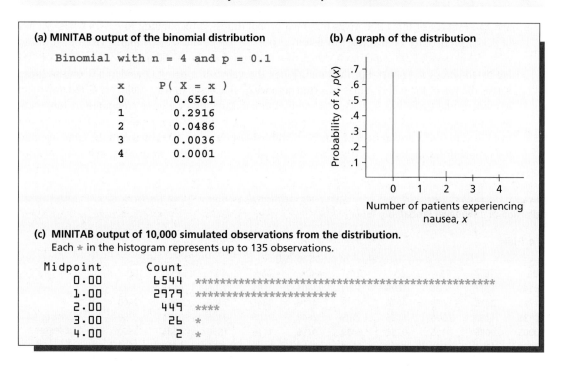

(a) MINITAB output of the binomial distribution

```
Binomial with n = 4 and p = 0.1

       x     P( X = x )
       0       0.6561
       1       0.2916
       2       0.0486
       3       0.0036
       4       0.0001
```

(b) A graph of the distribution

(c) MINITAB output of 10,000 simulated observations from the distribution.
Each * in the histogram represents up to 135 observations.

```
Midpoint       Count
   0.00         6544    **************************************************
   1.00         2979    ***********************
   2.00          449    ****
   3.00           26    *
   4.00            2    *
```

the MINITAB output of the binomial probability distribution listed in Table 5.6.[1] Figure 5.4(b) shows a graph of this distribution.

In order to interpret these binomial probabilities, consider administering the antibiotic Phe-Mycin to all possible samples of four randomly selected patients. Then, for example,

$$P(x = 0) = 0.6561$$

says that none of the four sampled patients would experience nausea in 65.61 percent of all possible samples. Furthermore, as another example,

$$P(x = 3) = 0.0036$$

says that three out of the four sampled patients would experience nausea in only .36 percent of all possible samples.

---

[1]As we will see in this chapter's appendixes, we can use Excel or MegaStat to obtain output of the binomial distribution that is essentially identical to the output given by MINITAB.

To better understand these interpretations, we can use MINITAB to *simulate* giving the antibiotic to a large number of samples of four randomly selected patients. That is, we can use MINITAB to randomly select a large number of observations from the binomial distribution of Table 5.6. The MINITAB output of a simulation of 10,000 samples of four randomly selected patients is given in Figure 5.4(c). In other words, this figure gives the results obtained when MINITAB has randomly selected 10,000 observations from the binomial distribution with $p = .10$ and $n = 4$. Each observation (or simulated sample of four patients) results in either 0, 1, 2, 3, or 4 patients experiencing nausea. The MINITAB output presents the results in the form of a histogram that shows the number of simulated samples in which 0, 1, 2, 3, or 4 patients experienced nausea. For instance, none of the four patients experienced nausea in 6,544 (that is, in 65.44 percent) of the 10,000 samples, whereas three out of four patients experienced nausea in 26 (or in .26 percent) of the 10,000 samples. These simulated results are quite close to the percentages given by the probabilities in Table 5.6. If we could use MINITAB to simulate an indefinitely large number of samples of four patients, then the simulated percentages would be exactly equal to the percentages given by the binomial probabilities. Note, of course, that we cannot do this—we can simulate only some large number of samples (say, 10,000 samples).

Another way to avoid hand calculating binomial probabilities is to use **binomial tables,** which have been constructed to give the probability of x successes in n trials. A table of binomial probabilities is given in Table A.1 (page 633). A portion of this table is reproduced in Table 5.7(a) and (b). Part (a) of this table gives binomial probabilities corresponding to $n = 4$ trials. Values of p, the probability of success, are listed across the top of the table (ranging from $p = .05$ to $p = .50$ in steps of .05), and more values of p (ranging from $p = .50$ to $p = .95$ in steps of .05) are listed across the bottom of the table. When the value of p being considered is one of those across the top of the table, values of x (the number of successes in four trials) are listed down the left side of the table. For instance, to find the probabilities that we have computed in Table 5.6, we look in part (a) of Table 5.7 ($n = 4$) and read down the column labeled .10. Remembering that the values of x are on the left side of the table because $p = .10$ is on top of the table, we find the probabilities in Table 5.6 (they are shaded). For example, the probability that none of four

---

TABLE 5.7   A Portion of a Binomial Probability Table

(a) A Table for $n = 4$ Trials

Values of p (.05 to .50)

	↓	.05	.10	.15	.20	.25	.30	.35	.40	.45	.50		
	0	.8145	.6561	.5220	.4096	.3164	.2401	.1785	.1296	.0915	.0625	4	
	1	.1715	.2916	.3685	.4096	.4219	.4116	.3845	.3456	.2995	.2500	3	
Number of	2	.0135	.0486	.0975	.1536	.2109	.2646	.3105	.3456	.3675	.3750	2	Number of
Successes	3	.0005	.0036	.0115	.0256	.0469	.0756	.1115	.1536	.2005	.2500	1	Successes
	4	.0000	.0001	.0005	.0016	.0039	.0081	.0150	.0256	.0410	.0625	0	
		.95	.90	.85	.80	.75	.70	.65	.60	.55	.50	↑	

Values of p (.50 to .95) ⟶

(b) A Table for $n = 8$ trials

Values of p (.05 to .50)

	↓	.05	.10	.15	.20	.25	.30	.35	.40	.45	.50		
	0	.6634	.4305	.2725	.1678	.1001	.0576	.0319	.0168	.0084	.0039	8	
	1	.2793	.3826	.3847	.3355	.2670	.1977	.1373	.0896	.0548	.0313	7	
	2	.0515	.1488	.2376	.2936	.3115	.2965	.2587	.2090	.1569	.1094	6	
Number of	3	.0054	.0331	.0839	.1468	.2076	.2541	.2786	.2787	.2568	.2188	5	Number of
Successes	4	.0004	.0046	.0185	.0459	.0865	.1361	.1875	.2322	.2627	.2734	4	Successes
	5	.0000	.0004	.0026	.0092	.0231	.0467	.0808	.1239	.1719	.2188	3	
	6	.0000	.0000	.0002	.0011	.0038	.0100	.0217	.0413	.0703	.1094	2	
	7	.0000	.0000	.0000	.0001	.0004	.0012	.0033	.0079	.0164	.0313	1	
	8	.0000	.0000	.0000	.0000	.0000	.0001	.0002	.0007	.0017	.0039	0	
		.95	.90	.85	.80	.75	.70	.65	.60	.55	.50	↑	

Values of p (.50 to .95) ⟶

patients experiences nausea is $p(0) = .6561$, the probability that one of the four patients experiences nausea is $p(1) = .2916$, and so forth. If the value of p is across the bottom of the table, then we read the values of x from the right side of the table. As an example, if p equals .60, then the probability of two successes in four trials is $p(2) = .3456$ (we have shaded this probability).

EXAMPLE 5.11

Suppose that we wish to investigate whether p, the probability that a patient will experience nausea as a side effect of taking Phe-Mycin, is greater than .10, the maximum value of p claimed by the drug company. This assessment will be made by assuming, for the sake of argument, that p equals .10, and by using sample information to weigh the evidence against this assumption and in favor of the conclusion that p is greater than .10. Suppose that when a sample of $n = 4$ randomly selected patients is treated with Phe-Mycin, three of the four patients experience nausea. Since the fraction of patients in the sample that experience nausea is $3/4 = .75$, which is far greater than .10, we have some evidence contradicting the assumption that p equals .10. To evaluate the strength of this evidence, we calculate the probability that at least three out of four randomly selected patients would experience nausea as a side effect if, in fact, p equals .10. Using the binomial probabilities in Table 5.7(a), and realizing that the events $x = 3$ and $x = 4$ are mutually exclusive, we have

$$
\begin{aligned}
P(x \geq 3) &= P(x = 3 \text{ or } x = 4) \\
&= P(x = 3) + P(x = 4) \\
&= .0036 + .0001 \\
&= .0037
\end{aligned}
$$

This probability says that, if p equals .10, then in only .37 percent of all possible samples of four randomly selected patients would at least three of the four patients experience nausea as a side effect. This implies that, if we are to believe that p equals .10, then we must believe that we have observed a sample result that is so rare that it can be described as a 37 in 10,000 chance. Because observing such a result is very unlikely, we have very strong evidence that p does not equal .10 and is, in fact, greater than .10.

Next suppose that we consider what our conclusion would have been if only one of the four randomly selected patients had experienced nausea. Since the sample fraction of patients who experienced nausea is $1/4 = .25$, which is greater than .10, we would have some evidence to contradict the assumption that p equals .10. To evaluate the strength of this evidence, we calculate the probability that at least one out of four randomly selected patients would experience nausea as a side effect of being treated with Phe-Mycin if, in fact, p equals .10. Using the binomial probabilities in Table 5.7(a), we have

$$
\begin{aligned}
P(x \geq 1) &= P(x = 1 \text{ or } x = 2 \text{ or } x = 3 \text{ or } x = 4) \\
&= P(x = 1) + P(x = 2) + P(x = 3) + P(x = 4) \\
&= .2916 + .0486 + .0036 + .0001 \\
&= .3439
\end{aligned}
$$

This probability says that, if p equals .10, then in 34.39 percent of all possible samples of four randomly selected patients, at least one of the four patients would experience nausea. Since it is not particularly difficult to believe that a 34.39 percent chance has occurred, we would not have much evidence against the claim that p equals .10.

Example 5.11 illustrates what is sometimes called the **rare event approach to making a statistical inference.** The idea of this approach is that if the probability of an observed sample result under a given assumption is *small,* then we have *strong evidence* that the assumption is false. Although there are no strict rules, many statisticians judge the probability of an observed sample result to be small if it is less than .05. The logic behind this will be explained more fully in Chapter 9.

EXAMPLE 5.12

The manufacturer of the ColorSmart-5000 television set claims that 95 percent of its sets last at least five years without requiring a single repair. Suppose that we contact $n = 8$ randomly selected ColorSmart-5000 purchasers five years after they purchased their sets. Each purchaser's set will have needed no repairs (a success) or will have been repaired at least once (a failure). We will assume that p, the true probability that a purchaser's television set will require no repairs within five years, is .95, as claimed by the manufacturer. Furthermore, it is reasonable to believe that the repair records of the purchasers' sets are independent of each other. Let x denote the number of the $n = 8$ randomly selected sets that have lasted at least five years without a single repair. Then x is a binomial random variable that can take on any of the potential values 0, 1, 2, 3, 4, 5, 6, 7, or 8. The binomial distribution of x is listed in Table 5.8. Here we have obtained these probabilities from Table 5.7(b). To use the table, we look at the column corresponding to $p = .95$. Because $p = .95$ is listed at the bottom of the table, we read the values of x and their corresponding probabilities from bottom to top (we have shaded the probabilities). Notice that the values of x are listed on the right side of the table.

Figure 5.5(a) gives the MINITAB output of the binomial distribution with $p = .95$ and $n = 8$ (that is, the binomial distribution of Table 5.8). This binomial distribution is graphed in

---

TABLE 5.8   **The Binomial Distribution of x, the Number of Eight ColorSmart-5000 Television Sets That Have Lasted at Least Five Years Without Needing a Single Repair, When p = .95**

x, Number of Sets That Require No Repairs	$p(x) = \dfrac{8!}{x!\,(8-x)!}(.95)^x(.05)^{8-x}$
0	$p(0) = .0000$
1	$p(1) = .0000$
2	$p(2) = .0000$
3	$p(3) = .0000$
4	$p(4) = .0004$
5	$p(5) = .0054$
6	$p(6) = .0515$
7	$p(7) = .2793$
8	$p(8) = .6634$

FIGURE 5.5   **The Binomial Probability Distribution with p = .95 and n = 8**

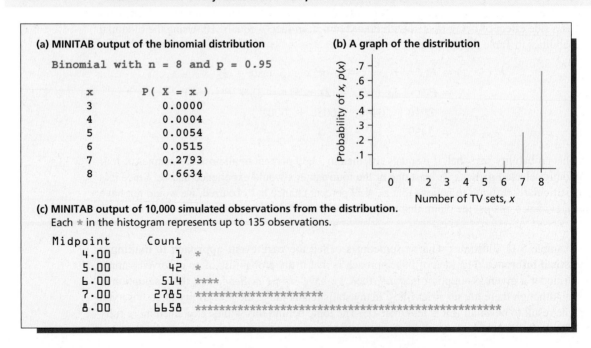

(a) MINITAB output of the binomial distribution

```
Binomial with n = 8 and p = 0.95

    x          P( X = x )
    3           0.0000
    4           0.0004
    5           0.0054
    6           0.0515
    7           0.2793
    8           0.6634
```

(b) A graph of the distribution

(c) MINITAB output of 10,000 simulated observations from the distribution.
Each * in the histogram represents up to 135 observations.

```
Midpoint        Count
   4.00             1    *
   5.00            42    *
   6.00           514    ****
   7.00          2785    *********************
   8.00          6658    ****************************************************
```

Figure 5.5(b), and Figure 5.5(c) gives the MINITAB output of 10,000 simulated observations from this distribution. Looking at Figure 5.5(c), we see that, for example, seven out of eight sets have lasted at least five years without a single repair in 2,785 (27.85 percent) of the 10,000 simulated samples. This result is very close to the percentage (27.93 percent) given by the binomial distribution (see Figure 5.5(a)).

Next, suppose that when we actually contact eight randomly selected purchasers, we find that five out of the eight television sets owned by these purchasers have lasted at least five years without a single repair. Since the sample fraction, $5/8 = .625$, of television sets needing no repairs is less than .95, we have some evidence contradicting the manufacturer's claim that p equals .95. To evaluate the strength of this evidence, we will calculate the probability that five or fewer of the eight randomly selected televisions would last five years without a single repair if, in fact, p equals .95. Using the binomial probabilities in Table 5.8, we have

$$P(x \le 5) = P(x = 5 \text{ or } x = 4 \text{ or } x = 3 \text{ or } x = 2 \text{ or } x = 1 \text{ or } x = 0)$$
$$= P(x = 5) + P(x = 4) + P(x = 3) + P(x = 2) + P(x = 1) + P(x = 0)$$
$$= .0054 + .0004 + .0000 + .0000 + .0000 + .0000$$
$$= .0058$$

This probability says that, if p equals .95, then in only .58 percent of all possible samples of eight randomly selected ColorSmart-5000 televisions would five or fewer of the eight televisions last five years without a single repair. Therefore, if we are to believe that p equals .95, we must believe that a 58 in 10,000 chance has occurred. Since it is difficult to believe that such a small chance has occurred, we have strong evidence that p does not equal .95, and is, in fact, less than .95.

In Examples 5.10 and 5.12 we have illustrated binomial distributions with different values of n and p. The values of n and p are often called the **parameters** of the binomial distribution. Figure 5.6 shows several different binomial distributions. We see that, depending on the parameters, a binomial distribution can be skewed to the right, skewed to the left, or symmetrical.

We next consider calculating the mean, variance, and standard deviation of a binomial random variable. If we place the binomial probability formula into the expressions (given in Section 5.2) for the mean and variance of a discrete random variable, we can derive formulas that allow us to

FIGURE 5.6   Several Binomial Distributions

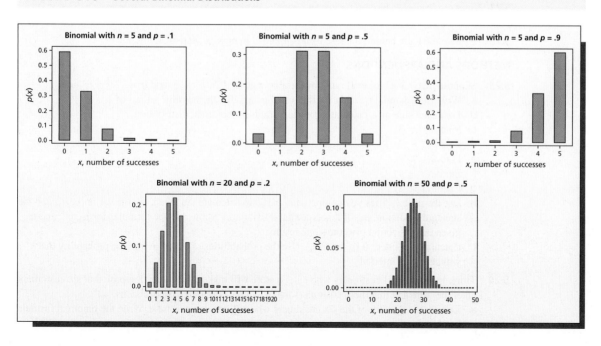

easily compute μ_x, σ_x^2, and σ_x for a binomial random variable. Omitting the details of the derivation, we have the following results:

The Mean, Variance, and Standard Deviation of a Binomial Random Variable

If x is a binomial random variable, then

$$\mu_x = np \qquad \sigma_x^2 = npq \qquad \sigma_x = \sqrt{npq}$$

where n is the number of trials, p is the probability of success on each trial, and $q = 1 - p$ is the probability of failure on each trial.

As a simple example, again consider the television manufacturer, and recall that x is the number of eight randomly selected ColorSmart-5000 televisions that last five years without a single repair. If the manufacturer's claim that p equals .95 is true (which implies that q equals $1 - p = 1 - .95 = .05$), it follows that

$$\mu_x = np = 8(.95) = 7.6$$
$$\sigma_x^2 = npq = 8(.95)(.05) = .38$$
$$\sigma_x = \sqrt{npq} = \sqrt{.38} = .6164$$

In order to interpret $\mu_x = 7.6$, suppose that we were to randomly select all possible samples of eight ColorSmart-5000 televisions and record the number of sets in each sample that last five years without a repair. If we averaged all of our results, we would find that the average number of sets per sample that last five years without a repair is equal to 7.6.

To conclude this section, note that in Appendix C on page 655 we discuss the **hypergeometric distribution.** This distribution is related to the binomial distribution. The main difference between the two distributions is that in the case of the hypergeometric distribution, the trials are not independent and the probabilities of success and failure change from trial to trial. This occurs when we sample without replacement from a finite population. However, when the finite population is large compared to the sample, the binomial distribution can be used to approximate the hypergeometric distribution. The details are explained in Appendix C.

Exercises for Section 5.3

connect™

CONCEPTS

5.20 List the four characteristics of a binomial experiment.

5.21 Suppose that x is a binomial random variable. Explain what the values of x represent. That is, how are the values of x defined?

5.22 Explain the logic behind the rare event approach to making statistical inferences.

METHODS AND APPLICATIONS

5.23 Suppose that x is a binomial random variable with $n = 5$, $p = .3$, and $q = .7$.
   a Write the binomial formula for this situation and list the possible values of x.
   b For each value of x, calculate $p(x)$, and graph the binomial distribution.
   c Find $P(x = 3)$.
   d Find $P(x \leq 3)$.
   e Find $P(x < 3)$.
   f Find $P(x \geq 4)$.
   g Find $P(x > 2)$.
   h Use the probabilities you computed in part b to calculate the mean, μ_x, the variance, σ_x^2, and the standard deviation, σ_x, of this binomial distribution. Show that the formulas for μ_x, σ_x^2, and σ_x given in this section give the same results.
   i Calculate the interval $[\mu_x \pm 2\sigma_x]$. Use the probabilities of part b to find the probability that x will be in this interval.

5.24 Thirty percent of all customers who enter a store will make a purchase. Suppose that six customers enter the store and that these customers make independent purchase decisions.
   a Let $x = $ the number of the six customers who will make a purchase. Write the binomial formula for this situation.

b Use the binomial formula to calculate
    (1) The probability that exactly five customers make a purchase.
    (2) The probability that at least three customers make a purchase.
    (3) The probability that two or fewer customers make a purchase.
    (4) The probability that at least one customer makes a purchase.

5.25 The customer service department for a wholesale electronics outlet claims that 90 percent of all customer complaints are resolved to the satisfaction of the customer. In order to test this claim, a random sample of 15 customers who have filed complaints is selected.

  a Let x = the number of sampled customers whose complaints were resolved to the customer's satisfaction. Assuming the claim is true, write the binomial formula for this situation.

  b Use the binomial tables (see Table A.1, page 633) to find each of the following if we assume that the claim is true:
    (1) $P(x \leq 13)$.
    (2) $P(x > 10)$.
    (3) $P(x \geq 14)$.
    (4) $P(9 \leq x \leq 12)$.
    (5) $P(x \leq 9)$.

  c Suppose that of the 15 customers selected, 9 have had their complaints resolved satisfactorily. Using part *b*, do you believe the claim of 90 percent satisfaction? Explain.

5.26 The United States Golf Association requires that the weight of a golf ball must not exceed 1.62 oz. The association periodically checks golf balls sold in the United States by sampling specific brands stocked by pro shops. Suppose that a manufacturer claims that no more than 1 percent of its brand of golf balls exceed 1.62 oz. in weight. Suppose that 24 of this manufacturer's golf balls are randomly selected, and let x denote the number of the 24 randomly selected golf balls that exceed 1.62 oz. Figure 5.7 gives part of a MegaStat output of the binomial distribution with $n = 24$, $p = .01$, and $q = .99$. (Note that, since $P(X = x) = .0000$ for values of x from 6 to 24, we omit these probabilities.) Use this output to

  a Find $P(x = 0)$—that is, find the probability that none of the randomly selected golf balls exceeds 1.62 oz. in weight.

  b Find the probability that at least one of the randomly selected golf balls exceeds 1.62 oz. in weight.

  c Find $P(x \leq 3)$.

  d Find $P(x \geq 2)$.

  e Suppose that 2 of the 24 randomly selected golf balls are found to exceed 1.62 oz. Using your result from part *d*, do you believe the claim that no more than 1 percent of this brand of golf balls exceed 1.62 oz. in weight?

5.27 An industry representative claims that 50 percent of all satellite dish owners subscribe to at least one premium movie channel. In an attempt to justify this claim, the representative will poll a randomly selected sample of dish owners.

  a Suppose that the representative's claim is true, and suppose that a sample of four dish owners is randomly selected. Assuming independence, use an appropriate formula to compute
    (1) The probability that none of the dish owners in the sample subscribes to at least one premium movie channel.
    (2) The probability that more than two dish owners in the sample subscribe to at least one premium movie channel.

  b Suppose that the representative's claim is true, and suppose that a sample of 20 dish owners is randomly selected. Assuming independence, what is the probability that
    (1) Nine or fewer dish owners in the sample subscribe to at least one premium movie channel?
    (2) More than 11 dish owners in the sample subscribe to at least one premium movie channel?
    (3) Fewer than five dish owners in the sample subscribe to at least one premium movie channel?

  c Suppose that, when we survey 20 randomly selected dish owners, we find that 4 of the dish owners actually subscribe to at least one premium movie channel. Using a probability you found in this exercise as the basis for your answer, do you believe the industry representative's claim? Explain.

5.28 For each of the following, calculate μ_x, σ_x^2, and σ_x by using the formulas given in this section. Then (1) interpret the meaning of μ_x, and (2) find the probability that x falls in the interval $[\mu_x \pm 2\sigma_x]$.

  a The situation of Exercise 5.24, where x = the number of the six customers who will make a purchase.

FIGURE 5.7

MegaStat Output of the Binomial Distribution with $n = 24$, $p = .01$, and $q = .99$

Binomial with
$n = 24$; $p = .01$

X	p(X)
0	0.78568
1	0.19047
2	0.02213
3	0.00164
4	0.00009
5	0.00000

  b The situation of Exercise 5.25, where x = the number of 15 sampled customers whose complaints were resolved to the customer's satisfaction.

  c The situation of Exercise 5.26, where x = the number of the 24 randomly selected golf balls that exceed 1.62 oz. in weight.

5.29 The January 1986 mission of the Space Shuttle Challenger was the 25th such shuttle mission. It was unsuccessful due to an explosion caused by an O-ring seal failure.

  a According to NASA, the probability of such a failure in a single mission was 1/60,000. Using this value of p and assuming all missions are independent, calculate the probability of no mission failures in 25 attempts. Then calculate the probability of at least one mission failure in 25 attempts.

  b According to a study conducted for the Air Force, the probability of such a failure in a single mission was 1/35. Recalculate the probability of no mission failures in 25 attempts and the probability of at least one mission failure in 25 attempts.

  c Based on your answers to parts *a* and *b*, which value of p seems more likely to be true? Explain.

  d How small must p be made in order to ensure that the probability of no mission failures in 25 attempts is .999?

5.4 The Poisson Distribution (Optional) ◦ ● ●

CHAPTER 4

We now discuss a discrete random variable that describes the number of occurrences of an event over a specified interval of time or space. For instance, we might wish to describe (1) the number of customers who arrive at the checkout counters of a grocery store in one hour, or (2) the number of major fires in a city during the last two months, or (3) the number of dirt specks found in one square yard of plastic wrap.

  Such a random variable can often be described by a **Poisson distribution.** We describe this distribution and give two assumptions needed for its use in the following box:

The Poisson Distribution

Consider the number of times an event occurs over an interval of time or space, and assume that

1 The probability of the event's occurrence is the same for any two intervals of equal length, and

2 Whether the event occurs in any interval is independent of whether the event occurs in any other nonoverlapping interval.

Then, the probability that the event will occur x times in a *specified interval* is

$$p(x) = \frac{e^{-\mu}\mu^x}{x!}$$

Here μ is the mean (or expected) number of occurrences of the event in the *specified interval,* and $e = 2.71828\ldots$ is the base of Napierian logarithms.

  In theory, there is no limit to how large x might be. That is, theoretically speaking, the event under consideration could occur an indefinitely large number of times during any specified interval. This says that a **Poisson random variable** might take on any of the values 0, 1, 2, 3, . . . and so forth. We will now look at an example.

EXAMPLE 5.13

In an article in the August 15, 1998, edition of *The Journal News* (Hamilton, Ohio),[2] the Associated Press reported that the Cleveland Air Route Traffic Control Center, the busiest in the nation for guiding planes on cross-country routes, had experienced an unusually high number of errors since the end of July. An error occurs when controllers direct flights either within five miles of each other horizontally, or within 2,000 feet vertically at a height of 18,000 feet or more (the standard is 1,000 feet vertically at heights less than 18,000 feet). The controllers' union blamed

---

[2]F. J. Frommer, "Errors on the Rise at Traffic Control Center in Ohio," *The Journal News,* August 15, 1998.

TABLE 5.9   A Portion of a Poisson Probability Table

x, Number of Occurrences	μ, Mean Number of Occurrences									
	.1	.2	.3	.4	.5	.6	.7	.8	.9	1.0
0	.9048	.8187	.7408	.6703	.6065	.5488	.4966	.4493	.4066	.3679
1	.0905	.1637	.2222	.2681	.3033	.3293	.3476	.3595	.3659	.3679
2	.0045	.0164	.0333	.0536	.0758	.0988	.1217	.1438	.1647	.1839
3	.0002	.0011	.0033	.0072	.0126	.0198	.0284	.0383	.0494	.0613
4	.0000	.0001	.0003	.0007	.0016	.0030	.0050	.0077	.0111	.0153
5	.0000	.0000	.0000	.0001	.0002	.0004	.0007	.0012	.0020	.0031
6	.0000	.0000	.0000	.0000	.0000	.0000	.0001	.0002	.0003	.0005

x, Number of Occurrences	μ, Mean Number of Occurrences									
	1.1	1.2	1.3	1.4	1.5	1.6	1.7	1.8	1.9	2.0
0	.3329	.3012	.2725	.2466	.2231	.2019	.1827	.1653	.1496	.1353
1	.3662	.3614	.3543	.3452	.3347	.3230	.3106	.2975	.2842	.2707
2	.2014	.2169	.2303	.2417	.2510	.2584	.2640	.2678	.2700	.2707
3	.0738	.0867	.0998	.1128	.1255	.1378	.1496	.1607	.1710	.1804
4	.0203	.0260	.0324	.0395	.0471	.0551	.0636	.0723	.0812	.0902
5	.0045	.0062	.0084	.0111	.0141	.0176	.0216	.0260	.0309	.0361
6	.0008	.0012	.0018	.0026	.0035	.0047	.0061	.0078	.0098	.0120
7	.0001	.0002	.0003	.0005	.0008	.0011	.0015	.0020	.0027	.0034
8	.0000	.0000	.0001	.0001	.0001	.0002	.0003	.0005	.0006	.0009

Source: From Brooks/Cole © 1991.

the errors on a staff shortage, whereas the Federal Aviation Administration (FAA) claimed that the cause was improved error reporting and an unusual number of thunderstorms.

Suppose that an air traffic control center has been averaging 20.8 errors per year and that the center experiences 3 errors in a week. The FAA must decide whether this occurrence is unusual enough to warrant an investigation as to the causes of the (possible) increase in errors. To investigate this possibility, we will find the probability distribution of x, the number of errors in a week, when we assume that the center is still averaging 20.8 errors per year.

Arbitrarily choosing a time unit of one week, the average (or expected) number of errors per week is $20.8/52 = .4$. Therefore, we can use the Poisson formula (note that the Poisson assumptions are probably satisfied) to calculate the probability of no errors in a week to be

$$p(0) = P(x = 0) = \frac{e^{-\mu}\mu^0}{0!} = \frac{e^{-.4}(.4)^0}{1} = .6703$$

Similarly, the probability of three errors in a week is

$$p(3) = P(x = 3) = \frac{e^{-.4}(.4)^3}{3!} = \frac{e^{-.4}(.4)^3}{3 \cdot 2 \cdot 1} = .0072$$

As with the binomial distribution, tables have been constructed that give Poisson probabilities. A table of these probabilities is given in Table A.2 (page 637). A portion of this table is reproduced in Table 5.9. In this table, values of the mean number of occurrences, μ, are listed across the top of the table, and values of x (the number of occurrences) are listed down the left side of the table. In order to use the table in the traffic control situation, we look at the column in Table 5.9 corresponding to .4, and we find the probabilities of 0, 1, 2, 3, 4, 5, and 6 errors (we have shaded these probabilities). For instance, the probability of one error in a week is .2681. Also, note that the probability of any number of errors greater than 6 is so small that it is not listed in the table. Table 5.10 summarizes the Poisson distribution of x, the number of errors in a week. This table also shows how the probabilities associated with the different values of x are calculated.

Poisson probabilities can also be calculated by using MINITAB, Excel, and MegaStat. For instance, Figure 5.8(a) gives the MINITAB output of the Poisson distribution presented in Table 5.10.[3] This Poisson distribution is graphed in Figure 5.8(b), and Figure 5.8(c) gives the

---

[3]As we will show in the appendixes to this chapter, we can use Excel and MegaStat to obtain output of the Poisson distribution that is essentially identical to the output given by MINITAB.

TABLE 5.10   The Poisson Distribution of x, the Number of Errors at an Air Traffic Control Center in a Week, When $\mu = .4$

x, the Number of Errors in a Week	$p(x) = \dfrac{e^{-\mu}\mu^x}{x!}$
0	$p(0) = \dfrac{e^{-.4}(.4)^0}{0!} = .6703$
1	$p(1) = \dfrac{e^{-.4}(.4)^1}{1!} = .2681$
2	$p(2) = \dfrac{e^{-.4}(.4)^2}{2!} = .0536$
3	$p(3) = \dfrac{e^{-.4}(.4)^3}{3!} = .0072$
4	$p(4) = \dfrac{e^{-.4}(.4)^4}{4!} = .0007$
5	$p(5) = \dfrac{e^{-.4}(.4)^5}{5!} = .0001$
6	$p(6) = \dfrac{e^{-.4}(.4)^6}{6!} = .0000$

FIGURE 5.8   The Poisson Probability Distribution with $\mu = .4$

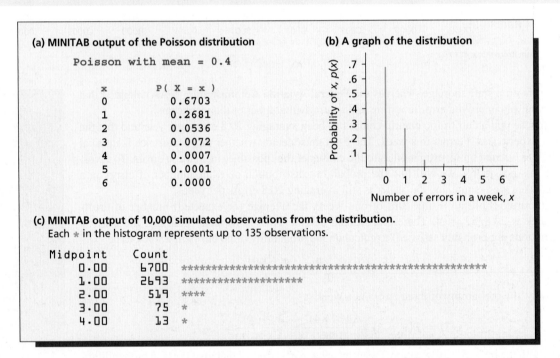

(a) MINITAB output of the Poisson distribution

```
Poisson with mean = 0.4

     x        P( X = x )
     0          0.6703
     1          0.2681
     2          0.0536
     3          0.0072
     4          0.0007
     5          0.0001
     6          0.0000
```

(b) A graph of the distribution

(c) MINITAB output of 10,000 simulated observations from the distribution. Each * in the histogram represents up to 135 observations.

```
Midpoint    Count
   0.00      6700    **************************************************
   1.00      2693    ********************
   2.00       519    ****
   3.00        75    *
   4.00        13    *
```

MINITAB output of a histogram of 10,000 simulated observations from this distribution. Looking at Figure 5.8(c), we see that, for example, three errors have occurred in 75 (.75 percent) of the 10,000 simulated weeks. This result is very close to the percentage (.72 percent) given by the Poisson distribution [see Figure 5.8(a)].

Next, recall that there have been three errors at the air traffic control center in the last week. This is considerably more errors than .4, the expected number of errors assuming the center is still averaging 20.8 errors per year. Therefore, we have some evidence to contradict this assumption. To evaluate the strength of this evidence, we calculate the probability that at least three errors will occur in a week if, in fact, μ equals .4. Using the Poisson probabilities in Table 5.10 (for $\mu = .4$), we obtain

$$P(x \geq 3) = p(3) + p(4) + p(5) + p(6) = .0072 + .0007 + .0001 + .0000 = .008$$

This probability says that, if the center is averaging 20.8 errors per year, then there would be three or more errors in a week in only .8 percent of all weeks. That is, if we are to believe that the control center is averaging 20.8 errors per year, then we must believe that an 8 in 1,000 chance has occurred. Since it is very difficult to believe that such a rare event has occurred, we have strong evidence that the average number of errors per week has increased. Therefore, an investigation by the FAA into the reasons for such an increase is probably justified.

EXAMPLE 5.14

In the book *Modern Statistical Quality Control and Improvement,* Nicholas R. Farnum (1994) presents an example dealing with the quality of computer software. In the example, Farnum measures software quality by monitoring the number of errors per 1,000 lines of computer code.

Suppose that the number of errors per 1,000 lines of computer code is described by a Poisson distribution with a mean of four errors per 1,000 lines of code. If we wish to find the probability of obtaining eight errors in 2,500 lines of computer code, we must adjust the mean of the Poisson distribution. To do this, we arbitrarily choose a *space unit* of one line of code, and we note that a mean of four errors per 1,000 lines of code is equivalent to $4/1,000$ of an error per line of code. Therefore, the mean number of errors per 2,500 lines of code is $(4/1,000)(2,500) = 10$. It follows that

$$p(8) = \frac{e^{-\mu}\mu^8}{8!} = \frac{e^{-10}10^8}{8!} = .1126$$

The mean, μ, is often called the *parameter* of the Poisson distribution. Figure 5.9 shows several Poisson distributions. We see that, depending on its parameter (mean), a Poisson distribution can be very skewed to the right or can be quite symmetrical.

Finally, if we place the Poisson probability formula into the general expressions (of Section 5.2) for μ_x, σ_x^2, and σ_x, we can derive formulas for calculating the mean, variance, and standard deviation of a Poisson distribution:

The Mean, Variance, and Standard Deviation of a Poisson Random Variable

Suppose that x is a **Poisson random variable.** If μ is the average number of occurrences of an event over the specified interval of time or space of interest, then

$$\mu_x = \mu \qquad \sigma_x^2 = \mu \qquad \sigma_x = \sqrt{\mu}$$

Here we see that both the mean and the variance of a Poisson random variable equal the average number of occurrences μ of the event of interest over the specified interval of time or space. For example, in the air traffic control situation, the Poisson distribution of x, the number of errors at the air traffic control center in a week, has a mean of $\mu_x = .4$ and a standard deviation of $\sigma_x = \sqrt{.4} = .6325$.

FIGURE 5.9 **Several Poisson Distributions**

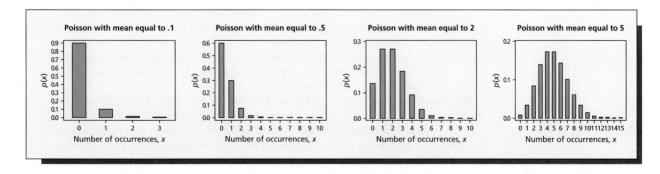

Exercises for Section 5.4

CONCEPTS

connect™

5.30 The values of a Poisson random variable are $x = 0, 1, 2, 3, \ldots$ Explain what these values represent.

5.31 Explain the assumptions that must be satisfied when a Poisson distribution adequately describes a random variable x.

METHODS AND APPLICATIONS

5.32 Suppose that x has a Poisson distribution with $\mu = 2$.
  a Write the Poisson formula and describe the possible values of x.
  b Starting with the smallest possible value of x, calculate $p(x)$ for each value of x until $p(x)$ becomes smaller than .001.
  c Graph the Poisson distribution using your results of b.
  d Find $P(x = 2)$.   **e** Find $P(x \leq 4)$.   **f** Find $P(x < 4)$.
  g Find $P(x \geq 1)$ and $P(x > 2)$.   **h** Find $P(1 \leq x \leq 4)$.
  i Find $P(2 < x < 5)$.   **j** Find $P(2 \leq x < 6)$.

5.33 Suppose that x has a Poisson distribution with $\mu = 2$.
  a Use the formulas given in this section to compute the mean, μ_x, variance, σ_x^2, and standard deviation, σ_x.
  b Calculate the intervals $[\mu_x \pm 2\sigma_x]$ and $[\mu_x \pm 3\sigma_x]$. Then use the probabilities you calculated in Exercise 5.32 to find the probability that x will be inside each of these intervals.

5.34 A bank manager wishes to provide prompt service for customers at the bank's drive-up window. The bank currently can serve up to 10 customers per 15-minute period without significant delay. The average arrival rate is 7 customers per 15-minute period. Let x denote the number of customers arriving per 15-minute period. Assuming x has a Poisson distribution:
  a Find the probability that 10 customers will arrive in a particular 15-minute period.
  b Find the probability that 10 or fewer customers will arrive in a particular 15-minute period.
  c Find the probability that there will be a significant delay at the drive-up window. That is, find the probability that more than 10 customers will arrive during a particular 15-minute period.

5.35 A telephone company's goal is to have no more than five monthly line failures on any 100 miles of line. The company currently experiences an average of two monthly line failures per 50 miles of line. Let x denote the number of monthly line failures per 100 miles of line. Assuming x has a Poisson distribution:
  a Find the probability that the company will meet its goal on a particular 100 miles of line.
  b Find the probability that the company will not meet its goal on a particular 100 miles of line.
  c Find the probability that the company will have no more than five monthly failures on a particular 200 miles of line.
  d Find the probability that the company will have more than 12 monthly failures on a particular 150 miles of line.

5.36 A local law enforcement agency claims that the number of times that a patrol car passes through a particular neighborhood follows a Poisson process with a mean of three times per nightly shift. Let x denote the number of times that a patrol car passes through the neighborhood during a nightly shift.
  a Calculate the probability that no patrol cars pass through the neighborhood during a nightly shift.
  b Suppose that during a randomly selected night shift no patrol cars pass through the neighborhood. Based on your answer in part a, do you believe the agency's claim? Explain.
  c Assuming that nightly shifts are independent and assuming that the agency's claim is correct, find the probability that exactly one patrol car will pass through the neighborhood on each of four consecutive nights.

5.37 When the number of trials, n, is large, binomial probability tables may not be available. Furthermore, if a computer is not available, hand calculations will be tedious. As an alternative, the Poisson distribution can be used to approximate the binomial distribution when n is large and p is small. Here the mean of the Poisson distribution is taken to be $\mu = np$. That is, when n is large and p is small, we can use the Poisson formula with $\mu = np$ to calculate binomial probabilities; we will obtain results close to those we would obtain by using the binomial formula. A common rule is to use this approximation when $n/p \geq 500$.

 To illustrate this approximation, in the movie *Coma,* a young female intern at a Boston hospital was very upset when her friend, a young nurse, went into a coma during routine anesthesia at the hospital. Upon investigation, she found that 10 of the last 30,000 healthy patients at the hospital had gone into comas during routine anesthesias. When she confronted the hospital administrator with this fact and the fact that the national average was 6 out of 100,000 healthy patients going into comas during routine anesthesias, the administrator replied that 10 out of 30,000 was still quite small and thus not that unusual.

    a Use the Poisson distribution to approximate the probability that 10 or more of 30,000 healthy patients would slip into comas during routine anesthesias, if in fact the true average at the hospital was 6 in 100,000. Hint: $\mu = np = 30,000(6/100,000) = 1.8$.

    b Given the hospital's record and part *a*, what conclusion would you draw about the hospital's medical practices regarding anesthesia?

    (Note: It turned out that the hospital administrator was part of a conspiracy to sell body parts and was purposely putting healthy adults into comas during routine anesthesias. If the intern had taken a statistics course, she could have avoided a great deal of danger.)

5.38   Suppose that an automobile parts wholesaler claims that .5 percent of the car batteries in a shipment are defective. A random sample of 200 batteries is taken, and four are found to be defective.

    a Use the Poisson approximation discussed in Exercise 5.37 to find the probability that four or more car batteries in a random sample of 200 such batteries would be found to be defective, if we assume that the wholesaler's claim is true.

    b Based on your answer to part *a*, do you believe the claim? Explain.

Chapter Summary

In this chapter we began our study of **random variables.** We learned that **a random variable represents an uncertain numerical outcome.** We also learned that a random variable whose values can be listed is called a **discrete random variable,** while the values of a **continuous random variable** correspond to one or more intervals on the real number line. We saw that a **probability distribution** of a discrete random variable is a table, graph, or formula that gives the probability associated with each of the random variable's possible values. We also discussed several descriptive measures of a discrete random variable—its **mean** (or **expected value**), its **variance,** and its **standard deviation.** We concluded this chapter by studying two important, commonly used discrete probability distributions—the **binomial distribution** and the **Poisson distribution**—and we demonstrated how these distributions can be used to make statistical inferences.

Glossary of Terms

binomial distribution: The probability distribution that describes a binomial random variable. (page 221)

binomial experiment: An experiment that consists of *n* independent, identical trials, each of which results in either a success or a failure and is such that the probability of success on any trial is the same. (page 221)

binomial random variable: A random variable that is defined to be the total number of successes in *n* trials of a binomial experiment. (page 221)

binomial tables: Tables in which we can look up binomial probabilities. (page 224)

continuous random variable: A random variable whose values correspond to one or more intervals of numbers on the real number line. (page 207)

discrete random variable: A random variable whose values can be counted or listed. (page 207)

expected value (of a random variable): The mean of the population of all possible observed values of a random variable. That is, the long-run average value obtained if values of a random variable are observed a (theoretically) infinite number of times. (page 211)

Poisson distribution: The probability distribution that describes a Poisson random variable. (page 230)

Poisson random variable: A discrete random variable that can often be used to describe the number of occurrences of an event over a specified interval of time or space. (page 230)

probability distribution (of a discrete random variable): A table, graph, or formula that gives the probability associated with each of the random variable's values. (page 208)

random variable: A variable that assumes numerical values that are determined by the outcome of an experiment. That is, a variable that represents an uncertain numerical outcome. (page 207)

standard deviation (of a random variable): The standard deviation of the population of all possible observed values of a random variable. It measures the spread of the population of all possible observed values of the random variable. (page 214)

variance (of a random variable): The variance of the population of all possible observed values of a random variable. It measures the spread of the population of all possible observed values of the random variable. (page 214)

Important Formulas

Properties of a discrete probability distribution: page 210

The mean (expected value) of a discrete random variable: page 211

Variance and standard deviation of a discrete random variable: page 214

Binomial probability formula: page 221

Mean, variance, and standard deviation of a binomial random variable: page 228

Poisson probability formula: page 230

Mean, variance, and standard deviation of a Poisson random variable: page 233

Supplementary Exercises

5.39 An investor holds two stocks, each of which can rise (R), remain unchanged (U), or decline (D) on any particular day. Let x equal the number of stocks that rise on a particular day.
  a Write the probability distribution of x assuming that all outcomes are equally likely.
  b Write the probability distribution of x assuming that for each stock $P(R) = .6$, $P(U) = .1$, and $P(D) = .3$ and assuming that movements of the two stocks are independent.
  c Write the probability distribution of x assuming that for the first stock

$$P(R) = .4, \quad P(U) = .2, \quad P(D) = .4$$

  and that for the second stock

$$P(R) = .8, \quad P(U) = .1, \quad P(D) = .1$$

  and assuming that movements of the two stocks are independent.

5.40 Repeat Exercise 5.39, letting x equal the number of stocks that decline on the particular day.

5.41 Consider Exercise 5.39, and let x equal the number of stocks that rise on the particular day. Find μ_x and σ_x for
  a The probability distribution of x in Exercise 5.39a.
  b The probability distribution of x in Exercise 5.39b.
  c The probability distribution of x in Exercise 5.39c.
  d In which case is μ_x the largest? Interpret what this means in words.
  e In which case is σ_x the largest? Interpret what this means in words.

5.42 Suppose that the probability distribution of a random variable x can be described by the formula

$$p(x) = \frac{(x - 3)^2}{55}$$

  for each of the values $x = -2, -1, 0, 1$, and 2.
  a Write the probability distribution of x.
  b Show that the probability distribution of x satisfies the properties of a discrete probability distribution.
  c Calculate the mean of x.
  d Calculate the variance and standard deviation of x.

5.43 A rock concert promoter has scheduled an outdoor concert on July 4th. If it does not rain, the promoter will make \$30,000. If it does rain, the promoter will lose \$15,000 in guarantees made to the band and other expenses. The probability of rain on the 4th is .4.
  a What is the promoter's expected profit? Is the expected profit a reasonable decision criterion? Explain.
  b How much should an insurance company charge to insure the promoter's full losses? Explain your answer.

5.44 The demand (in number of copies per day) for a city newspaper is listed below with corresponding probabilities:

$x =$ Demand	$p(x)$
50,000	.1
70,000	.25
90,000	.4
110,000	.2
130,000	.05

  a Graph the probability distribution of x.
  b Find the expected demand. Interpret this value, and label it on the graph of part a.
  c Using Chebyshev's Theorem, find the minimum percentage of all possible daily demand values that will fall in the interval $[\mu_x \pm 2\sigma_x]$.
  d Calculate the interval $[\mu_x \pm 2\sigma_x]$. Illustrate this interval on the graph of part a. According to the probability distribution of demand x previously given, what percentage of all possible daily demand values fall in the interval $[\mu_x \pm 2\sigma_x]$?

5.45 United Medicine, Inc., claims that a drug, Viro, significantly relieves the symptoms of a certain viral infection for 80 percent of all patients. Suppose that this drug is given to eight randomly selected patients who have been diagnosed with the viral infection.
  a Let x equal the number of the eight randomly selected patients whose symptoms are significantly relieved. What distribution describes the random variable x? Explain.
  b Assuming that the company's claim is correct, find $P(x \le 3)$.

c Suppose that of the eight randomly selected patients, three have had their symptoms significantly relieved by Viro. Based on the probability in part *b*, would you believe the claim of United Medicine, Inc.? Explain.

5.46 A consumer advocate claims that 80 percent of cable television subscribers are not satisfied with their cable service. In an attempt to justify this claim, a randomly selected sample of cable subscribers will be polled on this issue.

  a Suppose that the advocate's claim is true, and suppose that a random sample of five cable subscribers is selected. Assuming independence, use an appropriate formula to compute the probability that four or more subscribers in the sample are not satisfied with their service.

  b Suppose that the advocate's claim is true, and suppose that a random sample of 25 cable subscribers is selected. Assuming independence, find

  (1) The probability that 15 or fewer subscribers in the sample are not satisfied with their service.

  (2) The probability that more than 20 subscribers in the sample are not satisfied with their service.

  (3) The probability that between 20 and 24 (inclusive) subscribers in the sample are not satisfied with their service.

  (4) The probability that exactly 24 subscribers in the sample are not satisfied with their service.

  c Suppose that when we survey 25 randomly selected cable television subscribers, we find that 15 are actually not satisfied with their service. Using a probability you found in this exercise as the basis for your answer, do you believe the consumer advocate's claim? Explain.

5.47 A retail store has implemented procedures aimed at reducing the number of bad checks cashed by its cashiers. The store's goal is to cash no more than eight bad checks per week. The average number of bad checks cashed is three per week. Let x denote the number of bad checks cashed per week. Assuming that x has a Poisson distribution:

  a Find the probability that the store's cashiers will not cash any bad checks in a particular week.

  b Find the probability that the store will meet its goal during a particular week.

  c Find the probability that the store will not meet its goal during a particular week.

  d Find the probability that the store's cashiers will cash no more than 10 bad checks per two-week period.

  e Find the probability that the store's cashiers will cash no more than five bad checks per three-week period.

5.48 Suppose that the number of accidents occurring in an industrial plant is described by a Poisson process with an average of 1.5 accidents every three months. During the last three months, four accidents occurred.

  a Find the probability that no accidents will occur during the current three-month period.

  b Find the probability that fewer accidents will occur during the current three-month period than occurred during the last three-month period.

  c Find the probability that no more than 12 accidents will occur during a particular year.

  d Find the probability that no accidents will occur during a particular year.

5.49 A high-security government installation has installed four security systems to detect attempted break-ins. The four security systems operate independently of each other, and each has a .85 probability of detecting an attempted break-in. Assume an attempted break-in occurs. Use the binomial distribution to find the probability that at least one of the four security systems will detect it.

5.50 A new stain removal product claims to completely remove the stains on 90 percent of all stained garments. Assume that the product will be tested on 20 randomly selected stained garments, and let x denote the number of these garments from which the stains will be completely removed. Use the binomial distribution to find $P(x \leq 13)$ if the stain removal product's claim is correct. If x actually turns out to be 13, what do you think of the claim?

5.51 Consider Exercise 5.50, and find $P(x \leq 17)$ if the stain removal product's claim is correct. If x actually turns out to be 17, what do you think of the claim?

5.52 A state has averaged one small business failure per week over the past several years. Let x denote the number of small business failures in the next eight weeks. Use the Poisson distribution to find $P(x \geq 17)$ if the mean number of small business failures remains what it has been. If x actually turns out to be 17, what does this imply?

5.53 A candy company claims that its new chocolate almond bar averages 10 almonds per bar. Let x denote the number of almonds in the next bar that you buy. Use the Poisson distribution to find $P(x \leq 4)$ if the candy company's claim is correct. If x actually turns out to be 4, what do you think of the claim?

5.54 Consider Exercise 5.53, and find $P(x \leq 8)$ if the candy company's claim is true. If x actually turns out to be 8, what do you think of the claim?

Appendix 5.1 ■ Binomial and Poisson Probabilities Using MINITAB

Binomial probabilities in Figure 5.4(a) on page 223:

- In the Data window, enter the values 0 through 4 into column C1 and name the column x.
- Select **Calc : Probability Distributions : Binomial**
- In the Binomial Distribution dialog box, select the Probability option by clicking.
- In the "Number of trials" window, enter 4 for the value of n.
- In the "Event probability" window, enter 0.1 for the value of p.
- Select the "Input column" option and enter the variable name x into the "Input column" window.
- Click OK in the Binomial Distribution dialog box.
- The binomial probabilities will be displayed in the Session window.

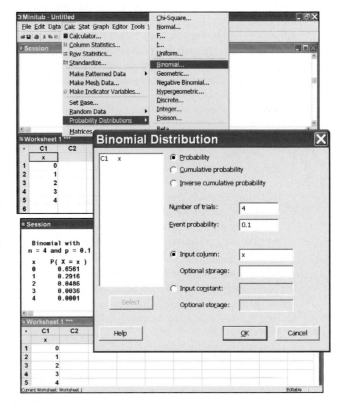

Poisson probabilities in Figure 5.8(a) on page 232:

- In the Data window, enter the values 0 through 6 into column C1 and name the column x.
- Select **Calc : Probability Distributions : Poisson**
- In the Poisson Distribution dialog box, select the Probability option by clicking.
- In the Mean window, enter 0.4.
- Select the "Input column" option and enter the variable name x into the "Input column" window.
- Click OK in the Poisson Distribution dialog box.
- The Poisson probabilities will be displayed in the Session window.

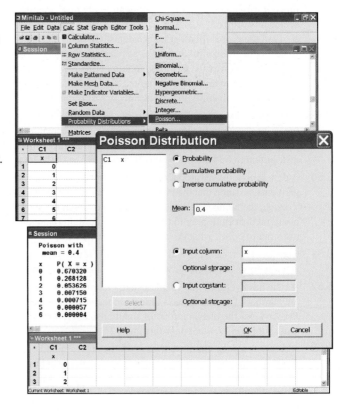

Appendix 5.2 ■ Binomial and Poisson Probabilities Using Excel

Binomial probabilities similar to Figure 5.4(a) on page 223:

- Enter the title "Binomial with n = 4 and p = 0.10" in the location in which you wish to place the binomial results. Here we have placed the title beginning in cell A15 (any other choice will do).

- In cell A16, enter the heading x.

- Enter the values 0 through 4 in cells A17 through A21.

- In cell B16, enter the heading P(X = x).

- Click in cell B17 (this is where the first binomial probability will be placed). Click on the Insert Function button f_x on the Excel toolbar.

- In the Insert Function dialog box, select Statistical from the "Or select a category:" menu; select BINOMDIST from the "Select a function:" menu; and click OK.

- In the BINOMDIST Function Arguments dialog box, enter the cell location A17 (this cell contains the value for which the first binomial probability will be calculated) in the "Number_s" box.

- Enter the value 4 in the Trials box.

- Enter the value 0.10 in the "Probability_s" box.

- Enter the value 0 in the Cumulative box.

- Click OK in the BINOMDIST Function Arguments dialog box.

- When you click OK, the calculated result (0.6561) will appear in cell B17. Double-click the drag handle (in the lower right corner) of cell B17 to automatically extend the cell formula to cells B18 through B21.

- The remaining probabilities will be placed in cells B18 through B21.

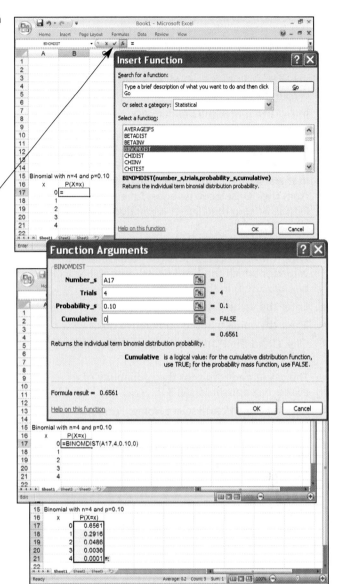

Poisson probabilities similar to Figure 5.8(a) on page 232:

- Enter the title "Poisson with mean = 0.40" in the location in which you wish to place the Poisson results. Here we have placed the title beginning in cell A13 (any other choice will do).

- In cell A14, enter the heading x.

- Enter the values 0 through 6 in cells A15 through A21.

- In cell B14, enter the heading P(X = x).

- Click in cell B15 (this is where the first Poisson probability will be placed). Click on the Insert Function button f_x on the Excel toolbar.

- In the Insert Function dialog box, select Statistical from the "Or select a category" menu; select POISSON from the "Select a function" menu; and click OK.

- In the POISSON Function Arguments dialog box, enter the cell location A15 (this cell contains the value for which the first Poisson probability will be calculated) in the "X" box.

- Enter the value 0.40 in the Mean box.

- Enter the value 0 in the Cumulative box.

- Click OK in the POISSON Function Arguments dialog box.

- The calculated result for the probability of 0 events will appear in cell B15.

- Click on cell B15 and select **Home: Format : Format Cells.**

- In the Format Cells dialog box, click on the Number tab, select Number from the Category menu, enter 4 in the Decimal places box, and click OK.

- Double-click the drag handle (in the lower right corner) of cell B15 to automatically extend the cell formula to cells B16 through B21.

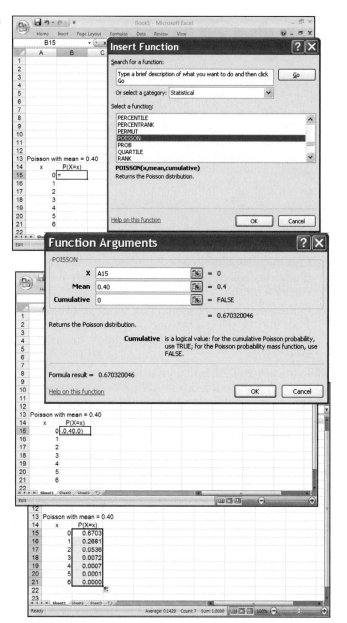

Appendix 5.3 ■ Binomial and Poisson Probabilities Using MegaStat

Binomial probabilities similar to those in Figure 5.7 on page 229:

- Select **Add-Ins : MegaStat : Probability : Discrete Probability Distributions**

- In the "Discrete Probability Distributions" dialog box, enter the number of trials (here equal to 24) and the probability of success p (here equal to .01) in the appropriate windows.

- Click the display graph checkbox if a plot of the distribution is desired.

- Click OK in the "Discrete Probability Distributions" dialog box.

The binomial output is placed in an output worksheet.

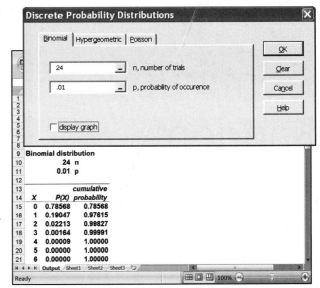

To calculate **Poisson probabilities**, click on the Poisson tab and enter the mean of the Poisson distribution. Then click OK.

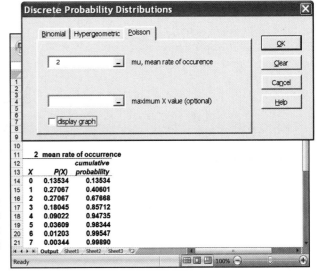

To calculate **hypergeometric probabilities** (discussed in Appendix C), click on the Hypergeometric tab. Then enter the population size, the number of successes in the population, and the sample size in the appropriate windows, and click OK.

CHAPTER 6

Continuous Random Variables

Chapter Outline

6.1 Continuous Probability Distributions

6.2 The Uniform Distribution

6.3 The Normal Probability Distribution

6.4 Approximating the Binomial Distribution by Using the Normal Distribution (Optional)

6.5 The Exponential Distribution (Optional)

6.6 The Normal Probability Plot (Optional)

I n Chapter 5 we defined discrete and continuous random variables. We also discussed discrete probability distributions, which are used to compute the probabilities of values of discrete random variables. In this chapter we discuss **continuous probability distributions.** These are used to find probabilities concerning continuous random variables. We begin by explaining the general idea behind a continuous probability distribution. Then we present three important continuous distributions—**the uniform, normal,** and **exponential distributions.** We also study when and how the normal distribution can be used to approximate the binomial distribution (which was discussed in Chapter 5).

In order to illustrate the concepts in this chapter, we continue one previously discussed case, and we also introduce two new cases:

The Car Mileage Case: A competitor claims that its midsize car gets better mileage than an automaker's new midsize model. The automaker uses sample information and a probability based on the normal distribution to provide strong evidence that the competitor's claim is false.

The Coffee Temperature Case: A fast-food restaurant uses the normal distribution to estimate the proportion of coffee it serves that has a temperature outside the range 153° to 167°, the customer requirement for best-tasting coffee.

The Cheese Spread Case: A food processing company markets a soft cheese spread that is sold

in a plastic container. The company has developed a new spout for the container. However, the new spout will be used only if fewer than 10 percent of all current purchasers would no longer buy the cheese spread if the new spout were used. The company uses sample information and a probability based on approximating the binomial distribution by the normal distribution to provide very strong evidence that fewer than 10 percent of all current purchasers would stop buying the spread if the new spout were used. This implies that the company can use the new spout without alienating its current customers.

6.1 Continuous Probability Distributions ● ● ●

Remember (from Section 5.1) that the values of a continuous random variable correspond to one or more intervals on the real number line. We often wish to compute probabilities about the range of values that a continuous random variable x might attain. We do this by assigning probabilities to **intervals of values** by using what we call a **continuous probability distribution.** To understand this idea, suppose that $f(x)$ is a continuous function of the numbers on the real line, and consider the continuous curve that results when $f(x)$ is graphed. Such a curve is illustrated in Figure 6.1. Then:

CHAPTER 3

Continuous Probability Distributions

The curve $f(x)$ is the **continuous probability distribution** of the random variable x if the probability that x will be in a specified interval of numbers is the area under the curve $f(x)$ corresponding to the interval. Sometimes we refer to a continuous probability distribution as a **probability curve** or as a **probability density function.**

An *area* under a continuous probability distribution (or probability curve) is a *probability*. For instance, consider the range of values on the number line from the number a to the number b—that is, the interval of numbers from a to b. If the continuous random variable x is described by the probability curve $f(x)$, then the area under $f(x)$ corresponding to the interval from a to b is the probability that x will attain a value between a and b. Such a probability is illustrated as the shaded area in Figure 6.1. We write this probability as $P(a \le x \le b)$. Since there is no area under a continuous curve at a single point, the probability that a continuous random variable x attains a single value is always equal to 0. It follows that in Figure 6.1 we have $P(x = a) = 0$ and $P(x = b) = 0$. Therefore, $P(a \le x \le b)$ equals $P(a < x < b)$ because each of the interval endpoints a and b has a probability that is equal to 0.

F I G U R E   6 . 1   **An Example of a Continuous Probability Distribution $f(x)$**

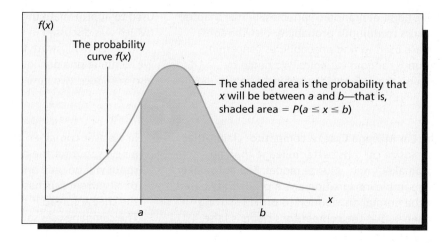

We know that any probability is 0 or positive, and we also know that the probability assigned to all possible values of x must be 1. It follows that, similar to the conditions required for a discrete probability distribution, a probability curve must satisfy the following properties:

Properties of a Continuous Probability Distribution

The **continuous probability distribution** (or **probability curve**) $f(x)$ of a random variable x must satisfy the following two conditions:

1 $f(x) \geq 0$ for any value of x.

2 The total area under the curve $f(x)$ is equal to 1.

Any continuous curve $f(x)$ that satisfies these conditions is a valid continuous probability distribution. Such probability curves can have a variety of shapes—bell-shaped and symmetrical, skewed to the right, skewed to the left, or any other shape. In a practical problem, the shape of a probability curve would be estimated by looking at a frequency (or relative frequency) histogram of observed data (as we have done in Chapter 2). Later in this chapter, we study probability curves having several different shapes. For example, in the next section we introduce the *uniform distribution*, which has a rectangular shape.

It is important to point out that *the height of a probability curve $f(x)$ at a particular point is not a probability. In order to calculate a probability concerning a continuous random variable, we must compute an appropriate area under the curve $f(x)$.* In theory, such areas are calculated by calculus methods and/or numerical techniques. Because these methods are difficult, needed areas under commonly used probability curves have been compiled in statistical tables. As we need them, we show how to use the required statistical tables.

Finally, we wish to emphasize that a continuous (or discrete) probability distribution is used to represent a population. That is, if $f(x)$ is a continuous probability distribution for a random variable x, then the area under the curve $f(x)$ between a and b—that is, $P(a \leq x \leq b)$—is *the proportion of values in the population of all possible values of x that are between a and b.* For instance, suppose that the probability curve $f(x)$ describes the random variable x = the mileage obtained by a midsize car model. Then the area under the curve $f(x)$ between 31 mpg and 33 mpg is the proportion of mileages in the population of all possible midsize car mileages that are between 31 mpg and 33 mpg.

6.2 The Uniform Distribution ● ● ●

Suppose that over a period of several days the manager of a large hotel has recorded the waiting times of 1,000 people waiting for an elevator in the lobby at dinnertime (5:00 P.M. to 7:00 P.M.). The observed waiting times range from zero to four minutes. Furthermore, when the waiting times are arranged into a histogram, the bars making up the histogram have approximately equal heights, giving the histogram a rectangular appearance. This implies that the relative frequencies of all waiting times from zero to four minutes are about the same. Therefore, it is reasonable to use the *uniform distribution* to describe the random variable x, the amount of time a randomly selected hotel patron spends waiting for the elevator. In general, the equation that describes the uniform distribution is given in the following box, and this equation is graphed in Figure 6.2(a).

The Uniform Distribution

If c and d are numbers on the real line, the probability curve describing the **uniform distribution** is

$$f(x) = \begin{cases} \dfrac{1}{d-c} & \text{for } c \leq x \leq d \\ 0 & \text{otherwise} \end{cases}$$

Furthermore, the mean and the standard deviation of the population of all possible observed values of a random variable x that has a uniform distribution are

$$\mu_x = \frac{c+d}{2} \qquad \text{and} \qquad \sigma_x = \frac{d-c}{\sqrt{12}}$$

FIGURE 6.2   **The Uniform Distribution**

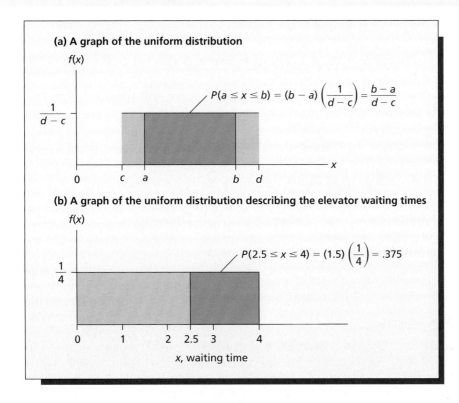

(a) A graph of the uniform distribution

$$P(a \leq x \leq b) = (b-a)\left(\frac{1}{d-c}\right) = \frac{b-a}{d-c}$$

(b) A graph of the uniform distribution describing the elevator waiting times

$$P(2.5 \leq x \leq 4) = (1.5)\left(\frac{1}{4}\right) = .375$$

x, waiting time

Notice that the total area under the uniform distribution is the area of a rectangle having a base equal to $(d - c)$ and a height equal to $1/(d - c)$. Therefore, the probability curve's total area is

$$\text{base} \times \text{height} = (d - c)\left(\frac{1}{d - c}\right) = 1$$

(remember that the total area under any continuous probability curve must equal 1). Furthermore, if a and b are numbers that are as illustrated in Figure 6.2(a), then the probability that x will be between a and b is the area of a rectangle with base $(b - a)$ and height $1/(d - c)$. That is,

$$P(a \leq x \leq b) = \text{base} \times \text{height}$$
$$= (b - a)\left(\frac{1}{d - c}\right)$$
$$= \frac{b - a}{d - c}$$

EXAMPLE 6.1

In the introduction to this section we have said that the amount of time, x, that a randomly selected hotel patron spends waiting for the elevator at dinnertime is uniformly distributed between zero and four minutes. In this case, $c = 0$ and $d = 4$. Therefore,

$$f(x) = \begin{cases} \dfrac{1}{d - c} = \dfrac{1}{4 - 0} = \dfrac{1}{4} & \text{for } 0 \leq x \leq 4 \\ 0 & \text{otherwise} \end{cases}$$

Noting that this equation is graphed in Figure 6.2(b), suppose that the hotel manager wishes to find the probability that a randomly selected patron will spend at least 2.5 minutes waiting for the elevator. This probability is the area under the curve $f(x)$ that corresponds to the interval [2.5, 4]. As shown in Figure 6.2(b), this probability is the area of a rectangle having a base equal to $4 - 2.5 = 1.5$ and a height equal to $1/4$. That is,

$$P(x \geq 2.5) = P(2.5 \leq x \leq 4) = \text{base} \times \text{height} = 1.5 \times \frac{1}{4} = .375$$

Similarly, the probability that a randomly selected patron will spend less than one minute waiting for the elevator is

$$P(x < 1) = P(0 \leq x \leq 1) = \text{base} \times \text{height} = 1 \times \frac{1}{4} = .25$$

We next note that the mean waiting time for the elevator at dinnertime is

$$\mu_x = \frac{c + d}{2} = \frac{0 + 4}{2} = 2 \text{ (minutes)}$$

and that the standard deviation of this waiting time is

$$\sigma_x = \frac{d - c}{\sqrt{12}} = \frac{4 - 0}{\sqrt{12}} = 1.1547 \text{ (minutes)}$$

Therefore, because

$$\mu_x - \sigma_x = 2 - 1.1547 = .8453$$

and

$$\mu_x + \sigma_x = 2 + 1.1547 = 3.1547$$

the probability that the waiting time of a randomly selected patron will be within (plus or minus) one standard deviation of the mean waiting time is

$$P(.8453 \le x \le 3.1547) = (3.1547 - .8453) \times \frac{1}{4}$$

$$= .57735$$

Exercises for Sections 6.1 and 6.2

CONCEPTS

6.1 A discrete probability distribution assigns probabilities to individual values. To what are probabilities assigned by a continuous probability distribution?

6.2 How do we use the continuous probability distribution (or probability curve) of a random variable x to find probabilities? Explain.

6.3 What two properties must be satisfied by a continuous probability distribution (or probability curve)?

6.4 Explain the meaning of the height of a probability curve over a given point.

6.5 When is it appropriate to use the uniform distribution to describe a random variable x?

METHODS AND APPLICATIONS

6.6 Suppose that the random variable x has a uniform distribution with $c = 2$ and $d = 8$.
   a Write the formula for the probability curve of x, and write an interval that gives the possible values of x.
   b Graph the probability curve of x.
   c Find $P(3 \le x \le 5)$.
   d Find $P(1.5 \le x \le 6.5)$.
   e Calculate the mean μ_x, variance σ_x^2, and standard deviation σ_x.
   f Calculate the interval $[\mu_x \pm 2\sigma_x]$. What is the probability that x will be in this interval?

6.7 Consider the figure given in the margin. Find the value h that makes the function $f(x)$ a valid continuous probability distribution.

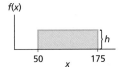

6.8 Assume that the waiting time x for an elevator is uniformly distributed between zero and six minutes.
   a Write the formula for the probability curve of x.
   b Graph the probability curve of x.
   c Find $P(2 \le x \le 4)$.
   d Find $P(3 \le x \le 6)$.
   e Find $P(\{0 \le x \le 2\}$ or $\{5 \le x \le 6\})$.

6.9 Refer to Exercise 6.8.
   a Calculate the mean, μ_x, the variance, σ_x^2, and the standard deviation, σ_x.
   b Find the probability that the waiting time of a randomly selected patron will be within one standard deviation of the mean.

6.10 Consider the figure given in the margin. Find the value k that makes the function $f(x)$ a valid continuous probability distribution.

6.11 Suppose that an airline quotes a flight time of 2 hours, 10 minutes between two cities. Furthermore, suppose that historical flight records indicate that the actual flight time between the two cities, x, is uniformly distributed between 2 hours and 2 hours, 20 minutes. Letting the time unit be one minute,
   a Write the formula for the probability curve of x.
   b Graph the probability curve of x.
   c Find $P(125 \le x \le 135)$
   d Find the probability that a randomly selected flight between the two cities will be at least five minutes late.

6.12 Refer to Exercise 6.11.
   a Calculate the mean flight time and the standard deviation of the flight time.
   b Find the probability that the flight time will be within one standard deviation of the mean.

6.13 Consider the figure given in the margin. Find the value c that makes the function $f(x)$ a valid continuous probability distribution.

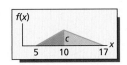

6.14 A weather forecaster predicts that the May rainfall in a local area will be between three and six inches but has no idea where within the interval the amount will be. Let x be the amount of May rainfall in the local area, and assume that x is uniformly distributed in the interval three to six inches.

   a Write the formula for the probability curve of x.

   b Graph the probability curve of x.

   c What is the probability that May rainfall will be at least four inches? At least five inches? At most 4.5 inches?

6.15 Refer to Exercise 6.14.

   a Calculate the expected May rainfall.

   b What is the probability that the observed May rainfall will fall within two standard deviations of the mean? Within one standard deviation of the mean?

CHAPTER 5

6.3 The Normal Probability Distribution ● ● ●

The normal curve The bell-shaped appearance of the normal probability distribution is illustrated in Figure 6.3. The equation that defines this normal curve is given in the following box:

The Normal Probability Distribution

The **normal probability distribution** is defined by the equation

$$f(x) = \frac{1}{\sigma\sqrt{2\pi}}\, e^{-\frac{1}{2}\left(\frac{x-\mu}{\sigma}\right)^2} \quad \text{for all values of } x \text{ on the real line}$$

Here μ and σ are the mean and standard deviation of the population of all possible observed values of the random variable x under consideration. Furthermore, $\pi = 3.14159\ldots$, and $e = 2.71828\ldots$ is the base of Napierian logarithms.

FIGURE 6.3
The Normal Probability Curve

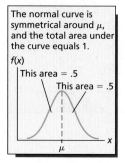

The normal curve is symmetrical around μ, and the total area under the curve equals 1.

$f(x)$

This area = .5

This area = .5

μ x

The normal probability distribution has several important properties:

1 There is an entire family of normal probability distributions; the specific shape of each normal distribution is determined by its mean μ and its standard deviation σ.

2 The highest point on the normal curve is located at the mean, which is also the median and the mode of the distribution.

3 The normal distribution is symmetrical: The curve's shape to the left of the mean is the mirror image of its shape to the right of the mean.

4 The tails of the normal curve extend to infinity in both directions and never touch the horizontal axis. However, the tails get close enough to the horizontal axis quickly enough to ensure that the total area under the normal curve equals 1.

5 Since the normal curve is symmetrical, the area under the normal curve to the right of the mean (μ) equals the area under the normal curve to the left of the mean, and each of these areas equals .5 (see Figure 6.3).

Intuitively, the mean μ positions the normal curve on the real line. This is illustrated in Figure 6.4(a). This figure shows two normal curves with different means μ_1 and μ_2 (where μ_1 is greater than μ_2) and with equal standard deviations. We see that the normal curve with mean μ_1 is centered farther to the right.

The variance σ^2 (and the standard deviation σ) measure the spread of the normal curve. This is illustrated in Figure 6.4(b), which shows two normal curves with the same mean and two different standard deviations σ_1 and σ_2. Because σ_1 is greater than σ_2, the normal curve with standard deviation σ_1 is more spread out (flatter) than the normal curve with standard deviation σ_2. In general, larger standard deviations result in normal curves that are flatter and more spread out, while smaller standard deviations result in normal curves that have higher peaks and are less spread out.

Suppose that a random variable x is normally distributed with mean μ and standard deviation σ. If a and b are numbers on the real line, we consider the probability that x will attain a value

FIGURE 6.4   How the Mean μ and Standard Deviation σ Affect the Position and Shape of a Normal Probability Curve

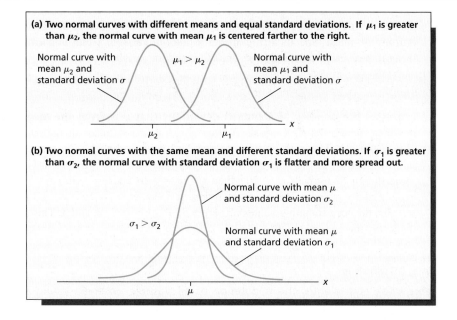

(a) Two normal curves with different means and equal standard deviations. If μ₁ is greater than μ₂, the normal curve with mean μ₁ is centered farther to the right.

Normal curve with mean μ₂ and standard deviation σ

$\mu_1 > \mu_2$

Normal curve with mean μ₁ and standard deviation σ

μ_2 μ_1 x

(b) Two normal curves with the same mean and different standard deviations. If σ₁ is greater than σ₂, the normal curve with standard deviation σ₁ is flatter and more spread out.

$\sigma_1 > \sigma_2$

Normal curve with mean μ and standard deviation σ₂

Normal curve with mean μ and standard deviation σ₁

μ x

FIGURE 6.5   An Area under a Normal Curve Corresponding to the Interval [a, b]

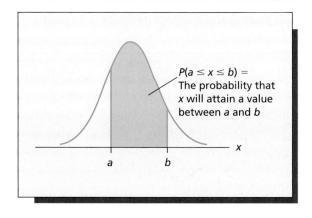

$P(a \leq x \leq b) =$ The probability that x will attain a value between a and b

a   b   x

FIGURE 6.6   Three Important Percentages Concerning a Normally Distributed Random Variable x with Mean μ and Standard Deviation σ

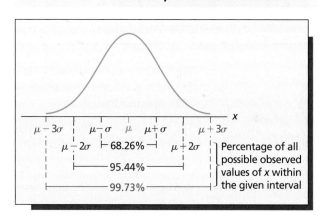

$\mu - 3\sigma$ $\mu - \sigma$ μ $\mu + \sigma$ $\mu + 3\sigma$ x

$\mu - 2\sigma$ ⊢ 68.26% ⊣ $\mu + 2\sigma$

95.44%

99.73%

Percentage of all possible observed values of x within the given interval

between *a* and *b*. That is, we consider

$$P(a \leq x \leq b)$$

which equals the area under the normal curve with mean μ and standard deviation σ corresponding to the interval [*a*, *b*]. Such an area is depicted in Figure 6.5. We soon explain how to find such areas using a statistical table called a **normal table.** For now, we emphasize three important areas under a normal curve. These areas form the basis for the **Empirical Rule** for a normally distributed population. Specifically, if *x* is normally distributed with mean μ and standard deviation σ, it can be shown (using a normal table) that, as illustrated in Figure 6.6:

Three Important Areas under the Normal Curve

1 $P(\mu - \sigma \leq x \leq \mu + \sigma) = .6826$

This means that 68.26 percent of all possible observed values of *x* are within (plus or minus) one standard deviation of μ.

2 $P(\mu - 2\sigma \leq x \leq \mu + 2\sigma) = .9544$

This means that 95.44 percent of all possible

observed values of *x* are within (plus or minus) two standard deviations of μ.

3 $P(\mu - 3\sigma \leq x \leq \mu + 3\sigma) = .9973$

This means that 99.73 percent of all possible observed values of *x* are within (plus or minus) three standard deviations of μ.

Finding normal curve areas   There is a unique normal curve for every combination of μ and σ. Since there are many (theoretically, an unlimited number of) such combinations, we would like to have one table of normal curve areas that applies to all normal curves. There is such a table, and we can use it by thinking in terms of how many standard deviations a value of interest is from the mean. Specifically, consider a random variable x that is normally distributed with mean μ and standard deviation σ. Then the random variable

$$z = \frac{x - \mu}{\sigma}$$

expresses the number of standard deviations that x is from the mean μ. To understand this idea, notice that if x equals μ (that is, x is zero standard deviations from μ), then $z = (\mu - \mu)/\sigma = 0$. However, if x is one standard deviation above the mean (that is, if x equals $\mu + \sigma$), then $x - \mu = \sigma$ and $z = \sigma/\sigma = 1$. Similarly, if x is two standard deviations below the mean (that is, if x equals $\mu - 2\sigma$), then $x - \mu = -2\sigma$ and $z = -2\sigma/\sigma = -2$. Figure 6.7 illustrates that for values of x of, respectively, $\mu - 3\sigma$, $\mu - 2\sigma$, $\mu - \sigma$, μ, $\mu + \sigma$, $\mu + 2\sigma$, and $\mu + 3\sigma$, the corresponding values of z are $-3, -2, -1, 0, 1, 2,$ and 3. This figure also illustrates the following general result:

The Standard Normal Distribution

If a random variable x (or, equivalently, the population of all possible observed values of x) is normally distributed with mean μ and standard deviation σ, then the random variable

$$z = \frac{x - \mu}{\sigma}$$

(or, equivalently, the population of all possible observed values of z) is normally distributed with mean 0 and standard deviation 1. A normal distribution (or curve) with mean 0 and standard deviation 1 is called a **standard normal distribution** (or **curve**).

Table A.3 (on pages 640 and 641) is a table of *cumulative* areas under the standard normal curve. This table is called a *cumulative normal table,* and it is reproduced as Table 6.1 (on pages 251 and 252). Specifically,

> The **cumulative normal table** gives, for many different values of z, the area under the standard normal curve to the left of z.

FIGURE 6.7   **If x Is Normally Distributed with Mean μ and Standard Deviation σ, Then $z = \dfrac{x - \mu}{\sigma}$ Is Normally Distributed with Mean 0 and Standard Deviation 1**

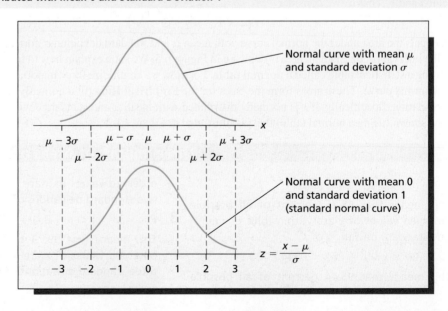

Two such areas are shown next to Table 6.1—one with a negative z value and one with a positive z value. The values of z in the cumulative normal table range from -3.99 to 3.99 in increments of .01. As can be seen from Table 6.1, values of z accurate to the nearest tenth are given in the far left column (headed z) of the table. Further graduations to the nearest hundredth (.00, .01, .02, . . . , .09) are given across the top of the table. The areas under the normal curve are given in the body of the table, accurate to four (or sometimes five) decimal places.

TABLE 6.1   Cumulative Areas under the Standard Normal Curve

z	0.00	0.01	0.02	0.03	0.04	0.05	0.06	0.07	0.08	0.09
−3.9	0.00005	0.00005	0.00004	0.00004	0.00004	0.00004	0.00004	0.00004	0.00003	0.00003
−3.8	0.00007	0.00007	0.00007	0.00006	0.00006	0.00006	0.00006	0.00005	0.00005	0.00005
−3.7	0.00011	0.00010	0.00010	0.00010	0.00009	0.00009	0.00008	0.00008	0.00008	0.00008
−3.6	0.00016	0.00015	0.00015	0.00014	0.00014	0.00013	0.00013	0.00012	0.00012	0.00011
−3.5	0.00023	0.00022	0.00022	0.00021	0.00020	0.00019	0.00019	0.00018	0.00017	0.00017
−3.4	0.00034	0.00032	0.00031	0.00030	0.00029	0.00028	0.00027	0.00026	0.00025	0.00024
−3.3	0.00048	0.00047	0.00045	0.00043	0.00042	0.00040	0.00039	0.00038	0.00036	0.00035
−3.2	0.00069	0.00066	0.00064	0.00062	0.00060	0.00058	0.00056	0.00054	0.00052	0.00050
−3.1	0.00097	0.00094	0.00090	0.00087	0.00084	0.00082	0.00079	0.00076	0.00074	0.00071
−3.0	0.00135	0.00131	0.00126	0.00122	0.00118	0.00114	0.00111	0.00107	0.00103	0.00100
−2.9	0.0019	0.0018	0.0018	0.0017	0.0016	0.0016	0.0015	0.0015	0.0014	0.0014
−2.8	0.0026	0.0025	0.0024	0.0023	0.0023	0.0022	0.0021	0.0021	0.0020	0.0019
−2.7	0.0035	0.0034	0.0033	0.0032	0.0031	0.0030	0.0029	0.0028	0.0027	0.0026
−2.6	0.0047	0.0045	0.0044	0.0043	0.0041	0.0040	0.0039	0.0038	0.0037	0.0036
−2.5	0.0062	0.0060	0.0059	0.0057	0.0055	0.0054	0.0052	0.0051	0.0049	0.0048
−2.4	0.0082	0.0080	0.0078	0.0075	0.0073	0.0071	0.0069	0.0068	0.0066	0.0064
−2.3	0.0107	0.0104	0.0102	0.0099	0.0096	0.0094	0.0091	0.0089	0.0087	0.0084
−2.2	0.0139	0.0136	0.0132	0.0129	0.0125	0.0122	0.0119	0.0116	0.0113	0.0110
−2.1	0.0179	0.0174	0.0170	0.0166	0.0162	0.0158	0.0154	0.0150	0.0146	0.0143
−2.0	0.0228	0.0222	0.0217	0.0212	0.0207	0.0202	0.0197	0.0192	0.0188	0.0183
−1.9	0.0287	0.0281	0.0274	0.0268	0.0262	0.0256	0.0250	0.0244	0.0239	0.0233
−1.8	0.0359	0.0351	0.0344	0.0336	0.0329	0.0322	0.0314	0.0307	0.0301	0.0294
−1.7	0.0446	0.0436	0.0427	0.0418	0.0409	0.0401	0.0392	0.0384	0.0375	0.0367
−1.6	0.0548	0.0537	0.0526	0.0516	0.0505	0.0495	0.0485	0.0475	0.0465	0.0455
−1.5	0.0668	0.0655	0.0643	0.0630	0.0618	0.0606	0.0594	0.0582	0.0571	0.0559
−1.4	0.0808	0.0793	0.0778	0.0764	0.0749	0.0735	0.0721	0.0708	0.0694	0.0681
−1.3	0.0968	0.0951	0.0934	0.0918	0.0901	0.0885	0.0869	0.0853	0.0838	0.0823
−1.2	0.1151	0.1131	0.1112	0.1093	0.1075	0.1056	0.1038	0.1020	0.1003	0.0985
−1.1	0.1357	0.1335	0.1314	0.1292	0.1271	0.1251	0.1230	0.1210	0.1190	0.1170
−1.0	0.1587	0.1562	0.1539	0.1515	0.1492	0.1469	0.1446	0.1423	0.1401	0.1379
−0.9	0.1841	0.1814	0.1788	0.1762	0.1736	0.1711	0.1685	0.1660	0.1635	0.1611
−0.8	0.2119	0.2090	0.2061	0.2033	0.2005	0.1977	0.1949	0.1922	0.1894	0.1867
−0.7	0.2420	0.2389	0.2358	0.2327	0.2296	0.2266	0.2236	0.2206	0.2177	0.2148
−0.6	0.2743	0.2709	0.2676	0.2643	0.2611	0.2578	0.2546	0.2514	0.2482	0.2451
−0.5	0.3085	0.3050	0.3015	0.2981	0.2946	0.2912	0.2877	0.2843	0.2810	0.2776
−0.4	0.3446	0.3409	0.3372	0.3336	0.3300	0.3264	0.3228	0.3192	0.3156	0.3121
−0.3	0.3821	0.3783	0.3745	0.3707	0.3669	0.3632	0.3594	0.3557	0.3520	0.3483
−0.2	0.4207	0.4168	0.4129	0.4090	0.4052	0.4013	0.3974	0.3936	0.3897	0.3859
−0.1	0.4602	0.4562	0.4522	0.4483	0.4443	0.4404	0.4364	0.4325	0.4286	0.4247
−0.0	0.5000	0.4960	0.4920	0.4880	0.4840	0.4801	0.4761	0.4721	0.4681	0.4641
0.0	0.5000	0.5040	0.5080	0.5120	0.5160	0.5199	0.5239	0.5279	0.5319	0.5359
0.1	0.5398	0.5438	0.5478	0.5517	0.5557	0.5596	0.5636	0.5675	0.5714	0.5753
0.2	0.5793	0.5832	0.5871	0.5910	0.5948	0.5987	0.6026	0.6064	0.6103	0.6141
0.3	0.6179	0.6217	0.6255	0.6293	0.6331	0.6368	0.6406	0.6443	0.6480	0.6517
0.4	0.6554	0.6591	0.6628	0.6664	0.6700	0.6736	0.6772	0.6808	0.6844	0.6879
0.5	0.6915	0.6950	0.6985	0.7019	0.7054	0.7088	0.7123	0.7157	0.7190	0.7224
0.6	0.7257	0.7291	0.7324	0.7357	0.7389	0.7422	0.7454	0.7486	0.7518	0.7549
0.7	0.7580	0.7611	0.7642	0.7673	0.7704	0.7734	0.7764	0.7794	0.7823	0.7852
0.8	0.7881	0.7910	0.7939	0.7967	0.7995	0.8023	0.8051	0.8078	0.8106	0.8133
0.9	0.8159	0.8186	0.8212	0.8238	0.8264	0.8289	0.8315	0.8340	0.8365	0.8389

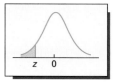

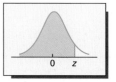

(Table continues)

TABLE 6.1   **Cumulative Areas under the Standard Normal Curve (*continued*)**

z	0.00	0.01	0.02	0.03	0.04	0.05	0.06	0.07	0.08	0.09
1.0	0.8413	0.8438	0.8461	0.8485	0.8508	0.8531	0.8554	0.8577	0.8599	0.8621
1.1	0.8643	0.8665	0.8686	0.8708	0.8729	0.8749	0.8770	0.8790	0.8810	0.8830
1.2	0.8849	0.8869	0.8888	0.8907	0.8925	0.8944	0.8962	0.8980	0.8997	0.9015
1.3	0.9032	0.9049	0.9066	0.9082	0.9099	0.9115	0.9131	0.9147	0.9162	0.9177
1.4	0.9192	0.9207	0.9222	0.9236	0.9251	0.9265	0.9279	0.9292	0.9306	0.9319
1.5	0.9332	0.9345	0.9357	0.9370	0.9382	0.9394	0.9406	0.9418	0.9429	0.9441
1.6	0.9452	0.9463	0.9474	0.9484	0.9495	0.9505	0.9515	0.9525	0.9535	0.9545
1.7	0.9554	0.9564	0.9573	0.9582	0.9591	0.9599	0.9608	0.9616	0.9625	0.9633
1.8	0.9641	0.9649	0.9656	0.9664	0.9671	0.9678	0.9686	0.9693	0.9699	0.9706
1.9	0.9713	0.9719	0.9726	0.9732	0.9738	0.9744	0.9750	0.9756	0.9761	0.9767
2.0	0.9772	0.9778	0.9783	0.9788	0.9793	0.9798	0.9803	0.9808	0.9812	0.9817
2.1	0.9821	0.9826	0.9830	0.9834	0.9838	0.9842	0.9846	0.9850	0.9854	0.9857
2.2	0.9861	0.9864	0.9868	0.9871	0.9875	0.9878	0.9881	0.9884	0.9887	0.9890
2.3	0.9893	0.9896	0.9898	0.9901	0.9904	0.9906	0.9909	0.9911	0.9913	0.9916
2.4	0.9918	0.9920	0.9922	0.9925	0.9927	0.9929	0.9931	0.9932	0.9934	0.9936
2.5	0.9938	0.9940	0.9941	0.9943	0.9945	0.9946	0.9948	0.9949	0.9951	0.9952
2.6	0.9953	0.9955	0.9956	0.9957	0.9959	0.9960	0.9961	0.9962	0.9963	0.9964
2.7	0.9965	0.9966	0.9967	0.9968	0.9969	0.9970	0.9971	0.9972	0.9973	0.9974
2.8	0.9974	0.9975	0.9976	0.9977	0.9977	0.9978	0.9979	0.9979	0.9980	0.9981
2.9	0.9981	0.9982	0.9982	0.9983	0.9984	0.9984	0.9985	0.9985	0.9986	0.9986
3.0	0.99865	0.99869	0.99874	0.99878	0.99882	0.99886	0.99889	0.99893	0.99897	0.99900
3.1	0.99903	0.99906	0.99910	0.99913	0.99916	0.99918	0.99921	0.99924	0.99926	0.99929
3.2	0.99931	0.99934	0.99936	0.99938	0.99940	0.99942	0.99944	0.99946	0.99948	0.99950
3.3	0.99952	0.99953	0.99955	0.99957	0.99958	0.99960	0.99961	0.99962	0.99964	0.99965
3.4	0.99966	0.99968	0.99969	0.99970	0.99971	0.99972	0.99973	0.99974	0.99975	0.99976
3.5	0.99977	0.99978	0.99978	0.99979	0.99980	0.99981	0.99981	0.99982	0.99983	0.99983
3.6	0.99984	0.99985	0.99985	0.99986	0.99986	0.99987	0.99987	0.99988	0.99988	0.99989
3.7	0.99989	0.99990	0.99990	0.99990	0.99991	0.99991	0.99992	0.99992	0.99992	0.99992
3.8	0.99993	0.99993	0.99993	0.99994	0.99994	0.99994	0.99994	0.99995	0.99995	0.99995
3.9	0.99995	0.99995	0.99996	0.99996	0.99996	0.99996	0.99996	0.99996	0.99997	0.99997

As an example, suppose that we wish to find the area under the standard normal curve to the left of a z value of 2.00. This area is illustrated in Figure 6.8. To find this area, we start at the top of the leftmost column in Table 6.1 (page 251) and scan down the column past the negative z values. We then scan through the positive z values (which continue on the top of this page) until we find the z value 2.0—see the red arrow above. We now scan across the row in the table corresponding to the z value 2.0 until we find the column corresponding to the heading .00. The desired area (which we have shaded blue) is in the row corresponding to the z value 2.0 and in the column headed .00. This area, which equals .9772, is the probability that the random variable z will be less than or equal to 2.00. That is, we have found that $P(z \leq 2) = .9772$. Note that, because there is no area under the normal curve at a single value of z, there is no difference between $P(z \leq 2)$ and $P(z < 2)$. As another example, the area under the standard normal curve to the left of the z value 1.25 is found in the row corresponding to 1.2 and in the column corresponding to .05. We find that this area (also shaded blue) is .8944. That is, $P(z \leq 1.25) = .8944$ (see Figure 6.9).

We now show how to use the cumulative normal table to find several other kinds of normal curve areas. First, suppose that we wish to find the area under the standard normal curve to the right of a z value of 2—that is, we wish to find $P(z \geq 2)$. This area is illustrated in Figure 6.10 and is called a **right-hand tail area.** Since the total area under the normal curve equals 1, the area under the curve to the right of 2 equals 1 minus the area under the curve to the left of 2. Because Table 6.1 tells us that the area under the standard normal curve to the left of 2 is .9772, the area under the standard normal curve to the right of 2 is $1 - .9772 = .0228$. Said in an equivalent fashion, because $P(z \leq 2) = .9772$, it follows that $P(z \geq 2) = 1 - P(z \leq 2) = 1 - .9772 = .0228$.

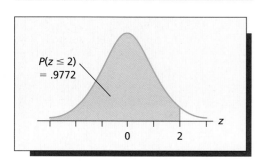

FIGURE 6.8   Finding $P(z \leq 2)$

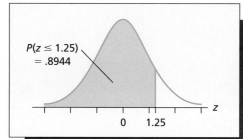

FIGURE 6.9   Finding $P(z \leq 1.25)$

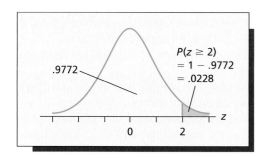

FIGURE 6.10   Finding $P(z \geq 2)$

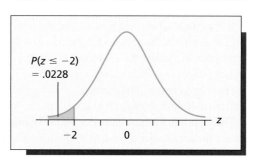

FIGURE 6.11   Finding $P(z \leq -2)$

Next, suppose that we wish to find the area under the standard normal curve to the left of a z value of -2. That is, we wish to find $P(z \leq -2)$. This area is illustrated in Figure 6.11 and is called a **left-hand tail area.** The needed area is found in the row of the cumulative normal table corresponding to -2.0 (on page 251) and in the column headed by .00. We find that $P(z \leq -2) = .0228$. Notice that the area under the standard normal curve to the left of -2 is equal to the area under this curve to the right of 2. This is true because of the symmetry of the normal curve.

Figure 6.12 illustrates how to find the area under the standard normal curve to the right of -2. Since the total area under the normal curve equals 1, the area under the curve to the right of -2 equals 1 minus the area under the curve to the left of -2. Because Table 6.1 tells us that the area under the standard normal curve to the left of -2 is .0228, the area under the standard normal curve to the right of -2 is $1 - .0228 = .9772$. That is, because $P(z \leq -2) = .0228$, it follows that $P(z \geq -2) = 1 - P(z \leq -2) = 1 - .0228 = .9772$.

The smallest z value in Table 6.1 is -3.99, and the table tells us that the area under the standard normal curve to the left of -3.99 is .00003 (see Figure 6.13). Therefore, if we wish to find the area under the standard normal curve to the left of any z value less than -3.99, the most we can say (without using a computer) is that this area is less than .00003. Similarly, the area under

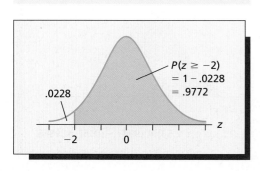

FIGURE 6.12   Finding $P(z \geq -2)$

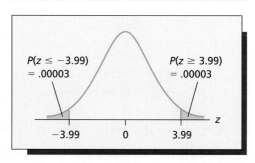

FIGURE 6.13   Finding $P(z \leq -3.99)$

FIGURE 6.14   Calculating $P(1 \leq z \leq 2)$

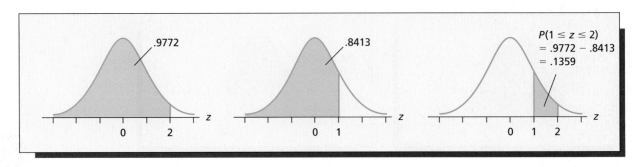

the standard normal curve to the right of any z value greater than 3.99 is also less than .00003 (see Figure 6.13).

Figure 6.14 illustrates how to find the area under the standard normal curve between 1 and 2. This area equals the area under the curve to the left of 2, which the normal table tells us is .9772, minus the area under the curve to the left of 1, which the normal table tells us is .8413. Therefore, $P(1 \leq z \leq 2) = .9772 - .8413 = .1359$.

To conclude our introduction to using the normal table, we will use this table to justify the Empirical Rule. Figure 6.15(a) illustrates the area under the standard normal curve between -1 and 1. This area equals the area under the curve to the left of 1, which the normal table tells us is .8413, minus the area under the curve to the left of -1, which the normal table tells us is .1587. Therefore, $P(-1 \leq z \leq 1) = .8413 - .1587 = .6826$. Now, suppose that a random variable x is normally distributed with mean μ and standard deviation σ, and remember that z is the number of standard deviations σ that x is from μ. It follows that when we say that $P(-1 \leq z \leq 1)$ equals .6826, we are saying that 68.26 percent of all possible observed values of x are between a point that is one standard deviation below μ (where z equals -1) and a point that is one standard deviation

FIGURE 6.15   Some Areas under the Standard Normal Curve

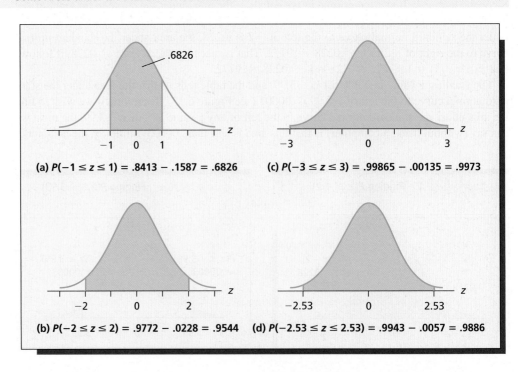

(a) $P(-1 \leq z \leq 1) = .8413 - .1587 = .6826$

(c) $P(-3 \leq z \leq 3) = .99865 - .00135 = .9973$

(b) $P(-2 \leq z \leq 2) = .9772 - .0228 = .9544$

(d) $P(-2.53 \leq z \leq 2.53) = .9943 - .0057 = .9886$

above μ (where z equals 1). That is, 68.26 percent of all possible observed values of x are within (plus or minus) one standard deviation of the mean μ.

Figure 6.15(b) illustrates the area under the standard normal curve between -2 and 2. This area equals the area under the curve to the left of 2, which the normal table tells us is .9772, minus the area under the curve to the left of -2, which the normal table tells us is .0228. Therefore, $P(-2 \leq z \leq 2) = .9772 - .0228 = .9544$. That is, 95.44 percent of all possible observed values of x are within (plus or minus) two standard deviations of the mean μ.

Figure 6.15(c) illustrates the area under the standard normal curve between -3 and 3. This area equals the area under the curve to the left of 3, which the normal table tells us is .99865, minus the area under the curve to the left of -3, which the normal table tells us is .00135. Therefore, $P(-3 \leq z \leq 3) = .99865 - .00135 = .9973$. That is, 99.73 percent of all possible observed values of x are within (plus or minus) three standard deviations of the mean μ.

Although the Empirical Rule gives the percentages of all possible values of a normally distributed random variable x that are within one, two, and three standard deviations of the mean μ, we can use the normal table to find the percentage of all possible values of x that are within any particular number of standard deviations of μ. For example, consider finding the percentage of all possible values of x that are within plus or minus 2.53 standard deviations of μ. (Note that there is nothing special about the number 2.53—it just represents an arbitrary number of standard deviations.) Figure 6.15(d) illustrates the area under the standard normal curve between -2.53 and 2.53. This area equals the area under the curve to the left of 2.53, which the normal table tells us is .9943, minus the area under the curve to the left of -2.53, which the table tells us is .0057. Therefore, $P(-2.53 \leq x \leq 2.53) = .9943 - .0057 = .9886$. That is, 98.86 percent of all possible values of x are within plus or minus 2.53 standard deviations of the mean μ.

Some practical applications   We have seen how to use z values and the normal table to find areas under the standard normal curve. However, most practical problems are not stated in such terms. We now consider an example in which we must restate the problem in terms of the standard normal random variable z before using the normal table.

EXAMPLE 6.2 The Car Mileage Case

Recall from previous chapters that an automaker has recently introduced a new midsize model and that we have used the sample of 50 mileages to estimate that the population of mileages of all cars of this type is normally distributed with a mean mileage equal to 31.56 mpg and a standard deviation equal to .798 mpg. Suppose that a competing automaker produces a midsize model that is somewhat smaller and less powerful than the new midsize model. The competitor claims, however, that its midsize model gets better mileages. Specifically, the competitor claims that the mileages of all its midsize cars are normally distributed with a mean mileage μ equal to 33 mpg and a standard deviation σ equal to .7 mpg. In the next example we consider one way to investigate the validity of this claim. In this example we assume that the claim is true, and we calculate the probability that the mileage, x, of a randomly selected competing midsize car will be between 32 mpg and 35 mpg. That is, we wish to find $P(32 \leq x \leq 35)$. As illustrated in Figure 6.16(a) on the next page, this probability is the area between 32 and 35 under the normal curve having mean $\mu = 33$ and standard deviation $\sigma = .7$. In order to use the normal table, we must restate the problem in terms of the standard normal random variable z. The z value corresponding to 32 is

$$z = \frac{x - \mu}{\sigma} = \frac{32 - 33}{.7} = \frac{-1}{.7} = -1.43$$

which says that the mileage 32 is 1.43 standard deviations below the mean $\mu = 33$. The z value corresponding to 35 is

$$z = \frac{x - \mu}{\sigma} = \frac{35 - 33}{.7} = \frac{2}{.7} = 2.86$$

FIGURE 6.16   **Illustrating the Results of Example 6.2**

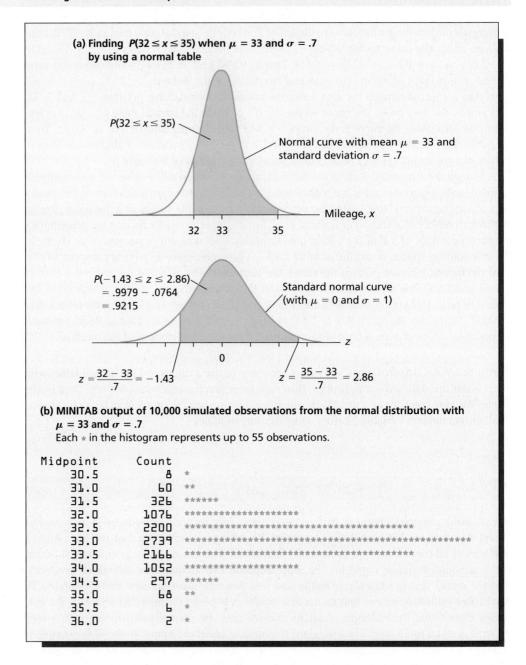

(a) Finding $P(32 \leq x \leq 35)$ **when** $\mu = 33$ **and** $\sigma = .7$ **by using a normal table**

$P(32 \leq x \leq 35)$

Normal curve with mean $\mu = 33$ and standard deviation $\sigma = .7$

Mileage, x

32   33   35

$P(-1.43 \leq z \leq 2.86)$
$= .9979 - .0764$
$= .9215$

Standard normal curve
(with $\mu = 0$ and $\sigma = 1$)

z

0

$z = \dfrac{32 - 33}{.7} = -1.43$ $z = \dfrac{35 - 33}{.7} = 2.86$

(b) MINITAB output of 10,000 simulated observations from the normal distribution with $\mu = 33$ **and** $\sigma = .7$
Each ∗ in the histogram represents up to 55 observations.

```
Midpoint       Count
   30.5            8    *
   31.0           60    **
   31.5          326    ******
   32.0         1076    *********************
   32.5         2200    *****************************************
   33.0         2739    ***************************************************
   33.5         2166    ****************************************
   34.0         1052    *********************
   34.5          297    ******
   35.0           68    **
   35.5            6    *
   36.0            2    *
```

which says that the mileage 35 is 2.86 standard deviations above the mean $\mu = 33$. Looking at Figure 6.16(a), we see that the area between 32 and 35 under the normal curve having mean $\mu = 33$ and standard deviation $\sigma = .7$ equals the area between -1.43 and 2.86 under the standard normal curve. This equals the area under the standard normal curve to the left of 2.86, which the normal table tells us is .9979, minus the area under the standard normal curve to the left of -1.43, which the normal table tells us is .0764. We summarize this result as follows:

$$P(32 \leq x \leq 35) = P\left(\frac{32 - 33}{.7} \leq \frac{x - \mu}{\sigma} \leq \frac{35 - 33}{.7}\right)$$

$$= P(-1.43 \leq z \leq 2.86) = .9979 - .0764 = .9215$$

This probability says that, if the competing automaker's claim is valid, then 92.15 percent of all of its midsize cars will get mileages between 32 mpg and 35 mpg.

In addition to using the normal table, we can find areas under the normal curve by using MINITAB, Excel, and MegaStat. We can also obtain simulated observations from a normal distribution. For instance, Figure 6.16(b) gives the MINITAB output of a histogram of 10,000 simulated mileages obtained from a normally distributed population of mileages having mean $\mu = 33$ mpg and standard deviation $\sigma = .7$ mpg. Looking at this figure, we see that, if we assume that 50 percent of the observed mileages in the class with midpoint 32.0 are above 32.0, and if we assume that 50 percent of the observed mileages in the class with midpoint 35.0 are below 35.0, then the fraction of simulated mileages between 32 mpg and 35 mpg is

$$(1{,}076/2 + 2{,}200 + 2{,}739 + 2{,}166 + 1{,}052 + 297 + 68/2) \div 10{,}000 = .9026$$

This fraction is quite close to the fraction (.9215) we calculated by using the normal table.

Example 6.2 illustrates the general procedure for finding a probability about a normally distributed random variable x. We summarize this procedure in the following box:

Finding Normal Probabilities

1 Formulate the problem in terms of the random variable x.

2 Calculate relevant z values and restate the problem in terms of the standard normal random variable

$$z = \frac{x - \mu}{\sigma}$$

3 Find the required area under the standard normal curve by using the normal table.

4 Note that it is always useful to draw a picture illustrating the needed area before using the normal table.

EXAMPLE 6.3 The Car Mileage Case

Recall from Example 6.2 that the competing automaker claims that the population of mileages of all its midsize cars is normally distributed with mean $\mu = 33$ and standard deviation $\sigma = .7$. Suppose that an independent testing agency randomly selects one of these cars and finds that it gets a mileage of 31.2 mpg when tested as prescribed by the EPA. Because the sample mileage of 31.2 mpg is *less than* the claimed mean $\mu = 33$, we have some evidence that contradicts the competing automaker's claim. To evaluate the strength of this evidence, we will calculate the probability that the mileage, x, of a randomly selected midsize car would be *less than or equal to* 31.2 if, in fact, the competing automaker's claim is true. To calculate $P(x \leq 31.2)$ under the assumption that the claim is true, we find the area to the left of 31.2 under the normal curve with mean $\mu = 33$ and standard deviation $\sigma = .7$ (see Figure 6.17 on the next page). In order to use the normal table, we must find the z value corresponding to 31.2. This z value is

$$z = \frac{x - \mu}{\sigma} = \frac{31.2 - 33}{.7} = -2.57$$

which says that the mileage 31.2 is 2.57 standard deviations below the mean mileage $\mu = 33$. Looking at Figure 6.17, we see that the area to the left of 31.2 under the normal curve having mean $\mu = 33$ and standard deviation $\sigma = .7$ equals the area to the left of -2.57 under the standard normal curve. The normal table tells us that the area under the standard normal curve to the left

FIGURE 6.17   Finding $P(x \le 31.2)$ When $\mu = 33$ and $\sigma = .7$ by Using a Normal Table

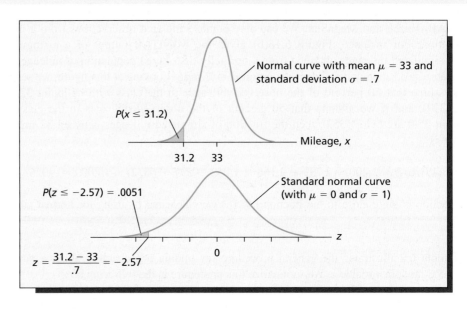

of -2.57 is .0051, as shown in Figure 6.17. It follows that we can summarize our calculations as follows:

$$P(x \le 31.2) = P\left(\frac{x - \mu}{\sigma} \le \frac{31.2 - 33}{.7}\right)$$

$$= P(z \le -2.57) = .0051$$

This probability says that, if the competing automaker's claim is valid, then only 51 in 10,000 cars would obtain a mileage of less than or equal to 31.2 mpg. Since it is very difficult to believe that a 51 in 10,000 chance has occurred, we have very strong evidence against the competing automaker's claim. It is probably true that μ is less than 33 and/or σ is greater than .7 and/or the population of all mileages is not normally distributed.

EXAMPLE 6.4 The Coffee Temperature Case

Marketing research done by a fast-food restaurant indicates that coffee tastes best if its temperature is between 153°(F) and 167°(F). The restaurant samples the coffee it serves and observes 24 temperature readings over a day. The temperature readings have a mean $\bar{x} = 160.0833$ and a standard deviation $s = 5.3724$ and are described by a bell-shaped histogram. Using $\bar{x}$ and s as point estimates of the mean μ and the standard deviation σ of the population of all possible coffee temperatures, we wish to calculate the probability that x, the temperature of a randomly selected cup of coffee, is outside the customer requirements for best-testing coffee (that is, less than 153° or greater than 167°). In order to compute the probability $P(x < 153 \text{ or } x > 167)$, we compute the z values:

$$z = \frac{153 - 160.0833}{5.3724} = -1.32 \quad \text{and} \quad z = \frac{167 - 160.0833}{5.3724} = 1.29$$

Because the events $\{x < 153\}$ and $\{x > 167\}$ are mutually exclusive, we have

$$P(x < 153 \text{ or } x > 167) = P(x < 153) + P(x > 167)$$

$$= P(z < -1.32) + P(z > 1.29)$$

$$= .0934 + .0985 = .1919$$

This calculation is illustrated in Figure 6.18. The probability of .1919 says that 19.19 percent of the coffee temperatures do not meet customer requirements. Therefore, if management believes that meeting this requirement is important, the coffeemaking process must be improved.

F I G U R E   6 . 1 8   **Finding $P(x < 153$ or $x > 167)$ in the Coffee Temperature Case**

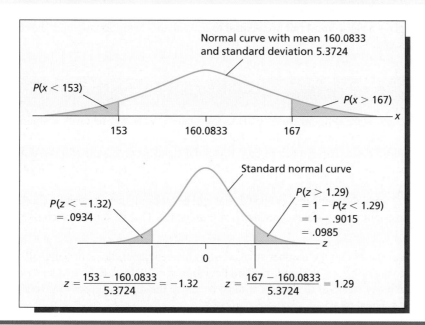

Finding a point on the horizontal axis under a normal curve   In order to use many of the formulas given in later chapters, we must be able to find the z value so that the tail area to the right of z under the standard normal curve is a particular value. For instance, we might need to find the z value so that the tail area to the right of z under the standard normal curve is .025. This z value is denoted $z_{.025}$, and we illustrate $z_{.025}$ in Figure 6.19(a). We refer to $z_{.025}$ as **the point on the horizontal axis under the standard normal curve that gives a right-hand tail area equal to .025.** It is easy to use the cumulative normal table to find such a point. For instance, in order to find $z_{.025}$, we note from Figure 6.19(b) that the area under the standard normal curve to the left of $z_{.025}$ equals .975. Remembering that areas under the standard normal curve to the left of z are the four-digit (or five-digit) numbers given in the body of Table 6.1, we scan the body of the table and find the area .9750. We have shaded this area in Table 6.1 on page 252, and we note that the area .9750 is in the row corresponding to a z of 1.9 and in the column headed by .06. It follows that the z value corresponding

F I G U R E   6 . 1 9   **The Point $z_{.025} = 1.96$**

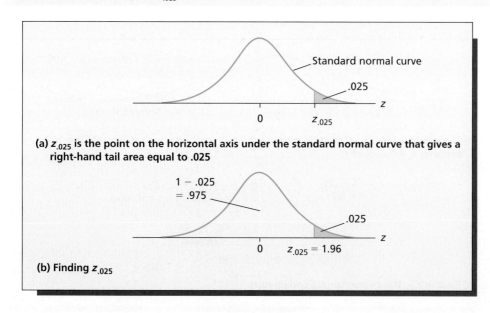

(a) $z_{.025}$ is the point on the horizontal axis under the standard normal curve that gives a right-hand tail area equal to .025

(b) Finding $z_{.025}$

to .9750 is 1.96. Because the z value 1.96 gives an area under the standard normal curve to its left that equals .975, it also gives a right-hand tail area equal to .025. Therefore, $z_{.025} = 1.96$.

In general, **we let z_α denote the point on the horizontal axis under the standard normal curve that gives a right-hand tail area equal to α.** With this definition in mind, we consider the following example.

EXAMPLE 6.5

A large discount store sells 50-packs of HX-150 blank DVDs and receives a shipment every Monday. Historical sales records indicate that the weekly demand, x, for HX-150 DVD 50-packs is normally distributed with a mean of $\mu = 100$ and a standard deviation of $\sigma = 10$. How many 50-packs should be stocked at the beginning of a week so that there is only a 5 percent chance that the store will run short during the week?

If we let st equal the number of 50-packs that will be stocked, then st must be chosen to allow only a .05 probability that weekly demand, x, will exceed st. That is, st must be chosen so that

$$P(x > st) = .05$$

Figure 6.20(a) shows that the number stocked, st, is located under the right-hand tail of the normal curve having mean $\mu = 100$ and standard deviation $\sigma = 10$. In order to find st, we need to determine how many standard deviations st must be above the mean in order to give a right-hand tail area that is equal to .05.

The z value corresponding to st is

$$z = \frac{st - \mu}{\sigma} = \frac{st - 100}{10}$$

and this z value is the number of standard deviations that st is from μ. This z value is illustrated in Figure 6.20(b), and it is the point on the horizontal axis under the standard normal curve that gives a right-hand tail area equal to .05. That is, the z value corresponding to st is $z_{.05}$. Since the area under the standard normal curve to the left of $z_{.05}$ is $1 - .05 = .95$—see Figure 6.20(b)—we look for .95 in the body of the normal table. In Table 6.1, we see that the areas closest to .95 are .9495, which has a corresponding z value of 1.64, and .9505, which has a corresponding z value of 1.65. Although it would probably be sufficient to use either of these z values, we will (because it is easy to do so) interpolate halfway between them and assume that $z_{.05}$ equals 1.645. To find st, we solve the equation

$$\frac{st - 100}{10} = 1.645$$

FIGURE 6.20   **Finding the Number of 50-Packs of DVDs Stocked, st, so That $P(x > st) = .05$ When $\mu = 100$ and $\sigma = 10$**

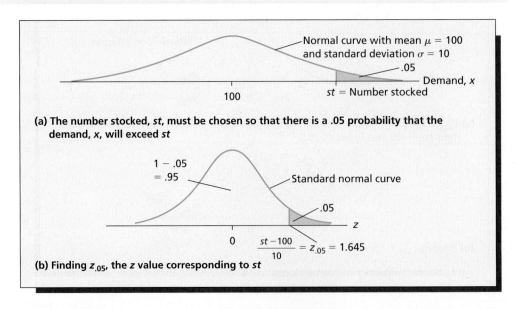

(a) The number stocked, st, must be chosen so that there is a .05 probability that the demand, x, will exceed st

(b) Finding $z_{.05}$, the z value corresponding to st

for *st*. Doing this yields

$$st - 100 = 1.645(10)$$

or

$$st = 100 + 1.645(10) = 116.45$$

This last equation says that *st* is 1.645 standard deviations ($\sigma = 10$) above the mean ($\mu = 100$). Rounding $st = 116.45$ up so that the store's chances of running short will be *no more* than 5 percent, the store should stock 117 of the 50-packs at the beginning of each week.

FIGURE 6.21   The *z* Value $-z_{.025} = -1.96$ Gives a Left-Hand Tail Area of .025 under the Standard Normal Curve

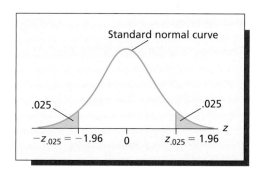

Sometimes we need to find the point on the horizontal axis under the standard normal curve that gives a particular **left-hand tail area** (say, for instance, an area of .025). Looking at Figure 6.21, it is easy to see that, if, for instance, we want a left-hand tail area of .025, the needed *z* value is $-z_{.025}$, where $z_{.025}$ gives a right-hand tail area equal to .025. To find $-z_{.025}$, we look for .025 in the body of the normal table and find that the *z* value corresponding to .025 is -1.96. Therefore, $-z_{.025} = -1.96$. In general, $-z_\alpha$ **is the point on the horizontal axis under the standard normal curve that gives a left-hand tail area equal to α.**

EXAMPLE 6.6

Extensive testing indicates that the lifetime of the Everlast automobile battery is normally distributed with a mean of $\mu = 60$ months and a standard deviation of $\sigma = 6$ months. The Everlast's manufacturer has decided to offer a free replacement battery to any purchaser whose Everlast battery does not last at least as long as the minimum lifetime specified in its guarantee. How can the manufacturer establish the guarantee period so that only 1 percent of the batteries will need to be replaced free of charge?

If the battery will be guaranteed to last *l* months, *l* must be chosen to allow only a .01 probability that the lifetime, *x*, of an Everlast battery will be less than *l*. That is, we must choose *l* so that

$$P(x < l) = .01$$

Figure 6.22(a) shows that the guarantee period, *l*, is located under the left-hand tail of the normal curve having mean $\mu = 60$ and standard deviation $\sigma = 6$. In order to find *l*, we need to determine how many standard deviations *l* must be below the mean in order to give a left-hand tail area that equals .01. The *z* value corresponding to *l* is

$$z = \frac{l - \mu}{\sigma} = \frac{l - 60}{6}$$

and this *z* value is the number of standard deviations that *l* is from μ. This *z* value is illustrated in Figure 6.22(b), and it is the point on the horizontal axis under the standard normal curve that gives a left-hand tail area equal to .01. That is, the *z* value corresponding to *l* is $-z_{.01}$. To find $-z_{.01}$, we look for .01 in the body of the normal table. Doing this, we see that the area closest to .01 is .0099, which has a corresponding *z* value of -2.33. Therefore, $-z_{.01}$ is (roughly) -2.33. To find *l*, we solve the equation

$$\frac{l - 60}{6} = -2.33$$

FIGURE 6.22   **Finding the Guarantee Period, *l*, so That *P(x < l) = .01* When *μ = 60* and *σ = 6*

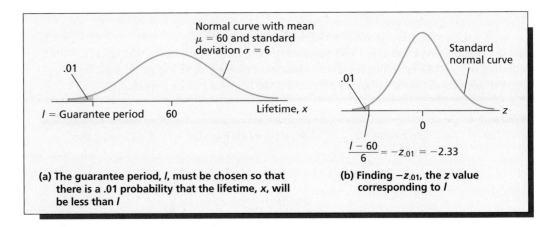

(a) The guarantee period, *l*, must be chosen so that
    there is a .01 probability that the lifetime, *x*, will
    be less than *l*

(b) Finding −*z*.01, the *z* value
    corresponding to *l*

for *l*. Doing this yields

$$l - 60 = -2.33(6)$$

or

$$l = 60 - 2.33(6) = 46.02$$

Note that this last equation says that *l* is 2.33 standard deviations ($\sigma = 6$) below the mean ($\mu = 60$). Rounding $l = 46.02$ down so that *no more* than 1 percent of the batteries will need to be replaced free of charge, it seems reasonable to guarantee the Everlast battery to last 46 months.

Earlier in this section we saw that the intervals $[\mu \pm \sigma]$, $[\mu \pm 2\sigma]$, and $[\mu \pm 3\sigma]$ are **tolerance intervals** containing, respectively, 68.26 percent, 95.44 percent, and 99.73 percent of the measurements in a normally distributed population having mean μ and standard deviation σ. In the following example we demonstrate how to use the normal table to find the value k so that the interval $[\mu \pm k\sigma]$ contains any desired percentage of the measurements in a normally distributed population.

EXAMPLE 6.7

Consider computing a tolerance interval $[\mu \pm k\sigma]$ that contains 99 percent of the measurements in a normally distributed population having mean μ and standard deviation σ. As illustrated in Figure 6.23, we must find the value k so that the area under the normal curve having mean μ and standard deviation σ between $(\mu - k\sigma)$ and $(\mu + k\sigma)$ is .99. Because the total area under this normal curve is 1, the area under the normal curve that is not between $(\mu - k\sigma)$ and $(\mu + k\sigma)$ is $1 - .99 = .01$. This implies, as illustrated in Figure 6.23, that the area under the normal curve to the left of $(\mu - k\sigma)$ is $.01/2 = .005$, and the area under the normal curve to the right of $(\mu + k\sigma)$ is also $.01/2 = .005$. This further implies, as illustrated in Figure 6.23, that the area under the normal curve to the left of $(\mu + k\sigma)$ is .995. Because the z value corresponding to a value of x tells us how many

FIGURE 6.23   **Finding a Tolerance Interval $[\mu \pm k\sigma]$ That Contains 99 Percent of the Measurements in a
Normally Distributed Population**

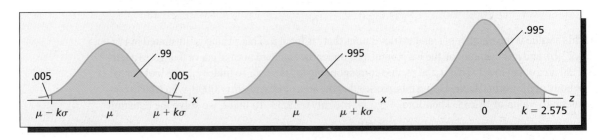

standard deviations x is from μ, the z value corresponding to $(\mu + k\sigma)$ is obviously k. It follows that k is the point on the horizontal axis under the standard normal curve so that the area to the left of k is .995. Looking up .995 in the body of the normal table, we find that the values closest to .995 are .9949, which has a corresponding z value of 2.57, and .9951, which has a corresponding z value of 2.58. Although it would be sufficient to use either of these z values, we will interpolate halfway between them, and we will assume that k equals 2.575. It follows that the interval $[\mu \pm 2.575\sigma]$ contains 99 percent of the measurements in a normally distributed population having mean μ and standard deviation σ.

Whenever we use a normal table to find a z point corresponding to a particular normal curve area, we will use the *halfway interpolation* procedure illustrated in Examples 6.5 and 6.7 if the area we are looking for is exactly halfway between two areas in the table. Otherwise, as illustrated in Example 6.6, we will use the z value corresponding to the area in the table that is closest to the desired area.

Exercises for Section 6.3

CONCEPTS

6.16 List five important properties of the normal probability curve.

6.17 Explain:
  a What the mean, μ, tells us about a normal curve.
  b What the standard deviation, σ, tells us about a normal curve.

6.18 If the random variable x is normally distributed, what percentage of all possible observed values of x will be
  a Within one standard deviation of the mean?
  b Within two standard deviations of the mean?
  c Within three standard deviations of the mean?

6.19 Explain how to compute the z value corresponding to a value of a normally distributed random variable. What does the z value tell us about the value of the random variable?

6.20 Explain how x relates to the mean μ if the z value corresponding to x
  a Equals zero.
  b Is positive.
  c Is negative.

6.21 Why do we compute z values when using the normal table? Explain.

METHODS AND APPLICATIONS

6.22 In each case, sketch the two specified normal curves on the same set of axes:
  a A normal curve with $\mu = 20$ and $\sigma = 3$, and a normal curve with $\mu = 20$ and $\sigma = 6$.
  b A normal curve with $\mu = 20$ and $\sigma = 3$, and a normal curve with $\mu = 30$ and $\sigma = 3$.
  c A normal curve with $\mu = 100$ and $\sigma = 10$, and a normal curve with $\mu = 200$ and $\sigma = 20$.

6.23 Let x be a normally distributed random variable having mean $\mu = 30$ and standard deviation $\sigma = 5$. Find the z value for each of the following observed values of x:
  a $x = 25$ **d** $x = 40$
  b $x = 15$ **e** $x = 50$
  c $x = 30$
  In each case, explain what the z value tells us about how the observed value of x compares to the mean, μ.

6.24 If the random variable z has a standard normal distribution, sketch and find each of the following probabilities:
  a $P(0 \le z \le 1.5)$ **d** $P(z \ge -1)$ **g** $P(-2.5 \le z \le .5)$
  b $P(z \ge 2)$ **e** $P(z \le -3)$ **h** $P(1.5 \le z \le 2)$
  c $P(z \le 1.5)$ **f** $P(-1 \le z \le 1)$ **i** $P(-2 \le z \le -.5)$

6.25 Suppose that the random variable z has a standard normal distribution. Sketch each of the following z points, and use the normal table to find each z point.
  a $z_{.01}$ **d** $-z_{.01}$
  b $z_{.05}$ **e** $-z_{.05}$
  c $z_{.02}$ **f** $-z_{.10}$

connect

6.26 Suppose that the random variable x is normally distributed with mean $\mu = 1,000$ and standard deviation $\sigma = 100$. Sketch and find each of the following probabilities:

    a $P(1,000 \leq x \leq 1,200)$ **e** $P(x \leq 700)$

    b $P(x > 1,257)$ **f** $P(812 \leq x \leq 913)$

    c $P(x < 1,035)$ **g** $P(x > 891)$

    d $P(857 \leq x \leq 1,183)$ **h** $P(1,050 \leq x \leq 1,250)$

6.27 Suppose that the random variable x is normally distributed with mean $\mu = 500$ and standard deviation $\sigma = 100$. For each of the following, use the normal table to find the needed value k. In each case, draw a sketch.

    a $P(x \geq k) = .025$ **d** $P(x \leq k) = .015$ **g** $P(x \leq k) = .975$

    b $P(x \geq k) = .05$ **e** $P(x < k) = .985$ **h** $P(x \geq k) = .0228$

    c $P(x < k) = .025$ **f** $P(x > k) = .95$ **i** $P(x > k) = .9772$

6.28 Stanford–Binet IQ Test scores are normally distributed with a mean score of 100 and a standard deviation of 16.

    a Sketch the distribution of Stanford–Binet IQ test scores.

    b Write the equation that gives the z score corresponding to a Stanford–Binet IQ test score. Sketch the distribution of such z scores.

    c Find the probability that a randomly selected person has an IQ test score

        (1) Over 140.

        (2) Under 88.

        (3) Between 72 and 128.

        (4) Within 1.5 standard deviations of the mean.

    d Suppose you take the Stanford–Binet IQ Test and receive a score of 136. What percentage of people would receive a score higher than yours?

6.29 Weekly demand at a grocery store for a brand of breakfast cereal is normally distributed with a mean of 800 boxes and a standard deviation of 75 boxes.

    a What is the probability that weekly demand is

        (1) 959 boxes or less?

        (2) More than 1,004 boxes?

        (3) Less than 650 boxes or greater than 950 boxes?

    b The store orders cereal from a distributor weekly. How many boxes should the store order for a week to have only a 2.5 percent chance of running short of this brand of cereal during the week?

6.30 The lifetimes of a particular brand of DVD player are normally distributed with a mean of eight years and a standard deviation of six months. Find each of the following probabilities where x denotes the lifetime in years. In each case, sketch the probability.

    a $P(7 \leq x \leq 9)$ **e** $P(x \leq 7)$

    b $P(8.5 \leq x \leq 9.5)$ **f** $P(x \geq 7)$

    c $P(6.5 \leq x \leq 7.5)$ **g** $P(x \leq 10)$

    d $P(x \geq 8)$ **h** $P(x > 10)$

6.31 United Motors claims that one of its cars, the Starbird 300, gets city driving mileages that are normally distributed with a mean of 30 mpg and a standard deviation of 1 mpg. Let x denote the city driving mileage of a randomly selected Starbird 300.

    a Assuming that United Motors' claim is correct, find $P(x \leq 27)$.

    b If you purchase (randomly select) a Starbird 300 and your car gets 27 mpg in city driving, what do you think of United Motors' claim? Explain your answer.

6.32 An investment broker reports that the yearly returns on common stocks are approximately normally distributed with a mean return of 12.4 percent and a standard deviation of 20.6 percent. On the other hand, the firm reports that the yearly returns on tax-free municipal bonds are approximately normally distributed with a mean return of 5.2 percent and a standard deviation of 8.6 percent. Find the probability that a randomly selected

    a Common stock will give a positive yearly return.

    b Tax-free municipal bond will give a positive yearly return.

    c Common stock will give more than a 10 percent return.

    d Tax-free municipal bond will give more than a 10 percent return.

    e Common stock will give a loss of at least 10 percent.

    f Tax-free municipal bond will give a loss of at least 10 percent.

6.33 A filling process is supposed to fill jars with 16 ounces of grape jelly. Specifications state that each jar must contain between 15.95 ounces and 16.05 ounces. A jar is selected from the process every half hour until a sample of 100 jars is obtained. When the fills of the jars are measured, it is found that $\bar{x} = 16.0024$ and $s = .02454$. Using $\bar{x}$ and s as point estimates of μ and σ, estimate the probability that a randomly selected jar will have a fill, x, that is out of specification. Assume that the process is in control and that the population of all jar fills is normally distributed.

6.34 A tire company has developed a new type of steel-belted radial tire. Extensive testing indicates the population of mileages obtained by all tires of this new type is normally distributed with a mean of 40,000 miles and a standard deviation of 4,000 miles. The company wishes to offer a guarantee providing a discount on a new set of tires if the original tires purchased do not exceed the mileage stated in the guarantee. What should the guaranteed mileage be if the tire company desires that no more than 2 percent of the tires will fail to meet the guaranteed mileage?

6.35 Recall from Exercise 6.32 that yearly returns on common stocks are normally distributed with a mean of 12.4 percent and a standard deviation of 20.6 percent.
     a What percentage of yearly returns are at or below the 10th percentile of the distribution of yearly returns? What percentage are at or above the 10th percentile? Find the 10th percentile of the distribution of yearly returns.
     b Find the first quartile, Q_1, and the third quartile, Q_3, of the distribution of yearly returns.

6.36 Two students take a college entrance exam known to have a normal distribution of scores. The students receive raw scores of 63 and 93, which correspond to z scores (often called the standardized scores) of -1 and 1.5, respectively. Find the mean and standard deviation of the distribution of raw exam scores.

6.37 THE TRASH BAG CASE   ● TrashBag

Suppose that a population of measurements is normally distributed with mean μ and standard deviation σ.
     a Write an expression (involving μ and σ) for a tolerance interval containing 98 percent of all the population measurements.
     b Estimate a tolerance interval containing 98 percent of all the trash bag breaking strengths by using the fact that a random sample of 40 breaking strengths has a mean of $\bar{x} = 50.575$ and a standard deviation of $s = 1.6438$.

6.38 Consider the situation of Exercise 6.32.
     a Use the investment broker's report to estimate the maximum yearly return that might be obtained by investing in tax-free municipal bonds.
     b Find the probability that the yearly return obtained by investing in common stocks will be higher than the maximum yearly return that might be obtained by investing in tax-free municipal bonds.

6.39 In the book *Advanced Managerial Accounting,* Robert P. Magee discusses monitoring cost variances. A *cost variance* is the difference between a budgeted cost and an actual cost. Magee describes the following situation:

> Michael Bitner has responsibility for control of two manufacturing processes. Every week he receives a cost variance report for each of the two processes, broken down by labor costs, materials costs, and so on. One of the two processes, which we'll call process A, involves a stable, easily controlled production process with a little fluctuation in variances. Process B involves more random events: the equipment is more sensitive and prone to breakdown, the raw material prices fluctuate more, and so on.
>
>   "It seems like I'm spending more of my time with process B than with process A," says Michael Bitner. "Yet I know that the probability of an inefficiency developing and the expected costs of inefficiencies are the same for the two processes. It's just the magnitude of random fluctuations that differs between the two, as you can see in the information below.
>
>   At present, I investigate variances if they exceed \$2,500, regardless of whether it was process A or B. I suspect that such a policy is not the most efficient. I should probably set a higher limit for process B."

The means and standard deviations of the cost variances of processes A and B, when these processes are in control, are as follows:

	Process A	Process B
Mean cost variance (in control)	$ 0	$ 0
Standard deviation of cost variance (in control)	$5,000	$10,000

Furthermore, the means and standard deviations of the cost variances of processes A and B, when these processes are out of control, are as follows:

	Process A	Process B
Mean cost variance (out of control)	$7,500	$ 7,500
Standard deviation of cost variance (out of control)	$5,000	$10,000

a Recall that the current policy is to investigate a cost variance if it exceeds $2,500 for either process. Assume that cost variances are normally distributed and that both process *A* and process *B* cost variances are in control. Find the probability that a cost variance for process *A* will be investigated. Find the probability that a cost variance for process *B* will be investigated. Which in-control process will be investigated more often?

b Assume that cost variances are normally distributed and that both process *A* and process *B* cost variances are out of control. Find the probability that a cost variance for process *A* will be investigated. Find the probability that a cost variance for process *B* will be investigated. Which out-of-control process will be investigated more often?

c If both processes *A* and *B* are almost always in control, which process will be investigated more often?

d Suppose that we wish to reduce the probability that process *B* will be investigated (when it is in control) to .3085. What cost variance investigation policy should be used? That is, how large a cost variance should trigger an investigation? Using this new policy, what is the probability that an out-of-control cost variance for process *B* will be investigated?

6.40 Suppose that yearly health care expenses for a family of four are normally distributed with a mean expense equal to $3,000 and a standard deviation of $500. An insurance company has decided to offer a health insurance premium reduction if a policyholder's health care expenses do not exceed a specified dollar amount. What dollar amount should be established if the insurance company wants families having the lowest 33 percent of yearly health care expenses to be eligible for the premium reduction?

6.41 Suppose that the 33rd percentile of a normal distribution is equal to 656 and that the 97.5th percentile of this normal distribution is 896. Find the mean μ and the standard deviation σ of the normal distribution. Hint: Sketch these percentiles.

6.4 Approximating the Binomial Distribution by Using the Normal Distribution (Optional) ● ● ●

Figure 6.24 illustrates several binomial distributions. In general, we can see that as *n* gets larger and as *p* gets closer to .5, the graph of a binomial distribution tends to have the symmetrical, bell-shaped appearance of a normal curve. It follows that, under conditions given in the following box, we can approximate the binomial distribution by using a normal distribution.

F I G U R E **6.24**   **Several Binomial Distributions**

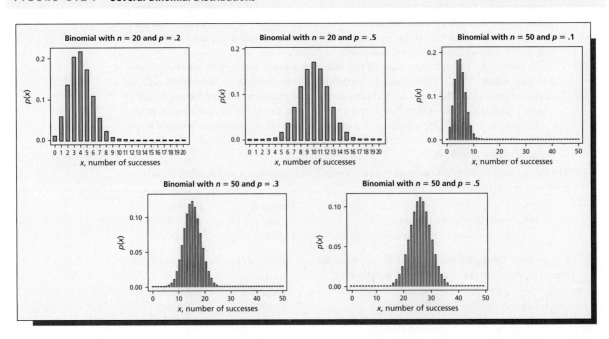

The Normal Approximation of the Binomial Distribution

Consider a binomial random variable x, where n is the number of trials performed and p is the probability of success on each trial. If n and p have values so that $np \geq 5$ and $n(1 - p) \geq 5$, then x is approximately normally distributed with mean $\mu = np$ and standard deviation $\sigma = \sqrt{npq}$, where $q = 1 - p$.

This approximation is often useful because binomial tables for large values of n are often unavailable. The conditions $np \geq 5$ and $n(1 - p) \geq 5$ must be met in order for the approximation to be appropriate. Note that if p is near 0 or near 1, then n must be larger for a good approximation, while if p is near .5, then n need not be as large.[1]

When we say that we can approximate the binomial distribution by using a normal distribution, we are saying that we can compute binomial probabilities by finding corresponding areas under a normal curve (rather than by using the binomial formula). We illustrate how to do this in the following example.

CHAPTER 4

EXAMPLE 6.8

Consider the binomial random variable x with $n = 50$ trials and probability of success $p = .5$. This binomial distribution is one of those illustrated in Figure 6.24. Suppose we want to use the normal approximation to this binomial distribution to compute the probability of 23 successes in the 50 trials. That is, we wish to compute $P(x = 23)$. Because $np = (50)(.5) = 25$ is at least 5, and $n(1 - p) = 50(1 - .5) = 25$ is also at least 5, we can appropriately use the approximation. Moreover, we can approximate the binomial distribution of x by using a normal distribution with mean $\mu = np = 50(.5) = 25$ and standard deviation $\sigma = \sqrt{npq} = \sqrt{50(.5)(1 - .5)} = 3.5355$.

In order to compute the needed probability, we must make a **continuity correction.** This is because a discrete distribution (the binomial) is being approximated by a continuous distribution (the normal). Because there is no area under a normal curve at the single point $x = 23$, we must assign an area under the normal curve to the binomial outcome $x = 23$. It is logical to assign the area corresponding to the interval from 22.5 to 23.5 to the integer outcome $x = 23$. That is, the area under the normal curve corresponding to all values within .5 units of the integer outcome $x = 23$ is assigned to the value $x = 23$. So we approximate the binomial probability $P(x = 23)$ by calculating the normal curve area $P(22.5 \leq x \leq 23.5)$. This area is illustrated in Figure 6.25. Calculating the z values

$$z = \frac{22.5 - 25}{3.5355} = -.71 \quad \text{and} \quad z = \frac{23.5 - 25}{3.5355} = -.42$$

we find that $P(22.5 \leq x \leq 23.5) = P(-.71 \leq z \leq -.42) = .3372 - .2389 = .0983$. Therefore, we estimate that the binomial probability $P(x = 23)$ is .0983.

FIGURE 6.25   **Approximating the Binomial Probability $P(x = 23)$ by Using the Normal Curve When $\mu = np = 25$ and $\sigma = \sqrt{npq} = 3.5355$**

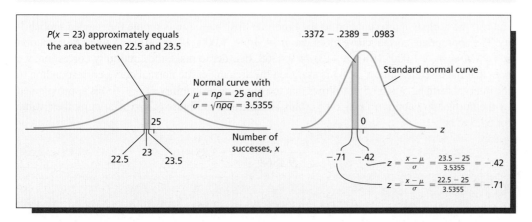

---

[1]As an alternative to the rule that both np and $n(1 - p)$ must be at least 5, some statisticians suggest using the more conservative rule that both np and $n(1 - p)$ must be at least 10.

TABLE 6.2	Several Examples of the Continuity Correction ($n = 50$)		
Binomial Probability	Numbers of Successes Included in Event	Normal Curve Area (with Continuity Correction)	
$P(25 < x \leq 30)$	26, 27, 28, 29, 30	$P(25.5 \leq x \leq 30.5)$	
$P(x \leq 27)$	0, 1, 2, . . . , 26, 27	$P(x \leq 27.5)$	
$P(x > 30)$	31, 32, 33, . . . , 50	$P(x \geq 30.5)$	
$P(27 < x < 31)$	28, 29, 30	$P(27.5 \leq x \leq 30.5)$	

Making the proper continuity correction can sometimes be tricky. A good way to approach this is to list the numbers of successes that are included in the event for which the binomial probability is being calculated. Then assign the appropriate area under the normal curve to each number of successes in the list. Putting these areas together gives the normal curve area that must be calculated. For example, again consider the binomial random variable x with $n = 50$ and $p = .5$. If we wish to find $P(27 \leq x \leq 29)$, then the event $27 \leq x \leq 29$ includes 27, 28, and 29 successes. Because we assign the areas under the normal curve corresponding to the intervals [26.5, 27.5], [27.5, 28.5], and [28.5, 29.5] to the values 27, 28, and 29, respectively, then the area to be found under the normal curve is $P(26.5 \leq x \leq 29.5)$. Table 6.2 gives several other examples.

EXAMPLE 6.9 The Cheese Spread Case

A food processing company markets a soft cheese spread that is sold in a plastic container with an "easy pour" spout. Although this spout works extremely well and is popular with consumers, it is expensive to produce. Because of the spout's high cost, the company has developed a new, less expensive spout. While the new, cheaper spout may alienate some purchasers, a company study shows that its introduction will increase profits if fewer than 10 percent of the cheese spread's current purchasers are lost. That is, if we let p be the true proportion of all current purchasers who would stop buying the cheese spread if the new spout were used, profits will increase as long as p is less than .10.

Suppose that (after trying the new spout) 63 of 1,000 randomly selected purchasers say that they would stop buying the cheese spread if the new spout were used. To assess whether p is less than .10, we will assume for the sake of argument that p equals .10, and we will use the sample information to weigh the evidence against this assumption and in favor of the conclusion that p is less than .10. Let the random variable x represent the number of the 1,000 purchasers who say they would stop buying the cheese spread. Assuming that p equals .10, then x is a binomial random variable with $n = 1,000$ and $p = .10$. Since the sample result of 63 is less than $\mu = np = 1,000(.1) = 100$, the expected value of x when p equals .10, we have some evidence to contradict the assumption that p equals .10. To evaluate the strength of this evidence, we calculate the probability that *63 or fewer* of the 1,000 randomly selected purchasers would say that they would stop buying the cheese spread if the new spout were used if, in fact, p equals .10.

Since both $np = 1,000(.10) = 100$ and $n(1 - p) = 1,000(1 - .10) = 900$ are at least 5, we can use the normal approximation to the binomial distribution to compute the needed probability. The appropriate normal curve has mean $\mu = np = 1,000(.10) = 100$ and standard deviation $\sigma = \sqrt{npq} = \sqrt{1,000(.10)(1 - .10)} = 9.4868$. In order to make the continuity correction, we note that the discrete value $x = 63$ is assigned the area under the normal curve corresponding to the interval from 62.5 to 63.5. It follows that the binomial probability $P(x \leq 63)$ is approximated by the normal probability $P(x \leq 63.5)$. This is illustrated in Figure 6.26. Calculating the z value for 63.5 to be

$$z = \frac{63.5 - 100}{9.4868} = -3.85$$

we find that

$$P(x \leq 63.5) = P(z \leq -3.85)$$

Using the normal table, we find that the area under the standard normal curve to the left of -3.85 is .00006. This says that, if p equals .10, then in only 6 in 100,000 of all possible random samples

F I G U R E   6 . 2 6   **Approximating the Binomial Probability $P(x \leq 63)$ by Using the Normal Curve When $\mu = np = 100$ and $\sigma = \sqrt{npq} = 9.4868$**

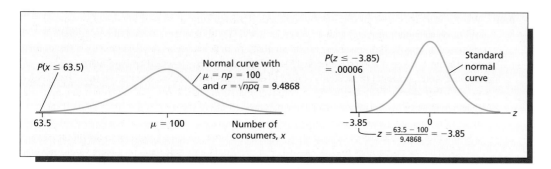

of 1,000 purchasers would 63 or fewer say they would stop buying the cheese spread if the new spout were used. Since it is very difficult to believe that such a small chance (a .00006 chance) has occurred, we have very strong evidence that p does not equal .10 and is, in fact, less than .10. Therefore, it seems that using the new spout will be profitable.

Exercises for Section 6.4

CONCEPTS

6.42   Explain why it might be convenient to approximate binomial probabilities by using areas under an appropriate normal curve.

6.43   Under what condition may we use the normal approximation to the binomial distribution?

6.44   Explain how we make a continuity correction. Why is a continuity correction needed when we approximate a binomial distribution by a normal distribution?

METHODS AND APPLICATIONS

6.45   Suppose that x has a binomial distribution with $n = 200$ and $p = .4$.
   a   Show that the normal approximation to the binomial can appropriately be used to calculate probabilities about x.
   b   Make continuity corrections for each of the following, and then use the normal approximation to the binomial to find each probability:
   (1) $P(x = 80)$
   (2) $P(x \leq 95)$
   (3) $P(x < 65)$
   (4) $P(x \geq 100)$
   (5) $P(x > 100)$

6.46   Repeat Exercise 6.45 with $n = 200$ and $p = .5$.

6.47   An advertising agency conducted an ad campaign aimed at making consumers in an Eastern state aware of a new product. Upon completion of the campaign, the agency claimed that 20 percent of consumers in the state had become aware of the product. The product's distributor surveyed 1,000 consumers in the state and found that 150 were aware of the product.
   a   Assuming that the ad agency's claim is true:
   (1)   Verify that we may use the normal approximation to the binomial.
   (2)   Calculate the mean, μ, and the standard deviation, σ, we should use in the normal approximation.
   (3)   Find the probability that 150 or fewer consumers in a random sample of 1,000 consumers would be aware of the product.
   b   Should the distributor believe the ad agency's claim? Explain.

6.48   In order to gain additional information about respondents, some marketing researchers have used ultraviolet ink to precode questionnaires that promise confidentiality to respondents. Of 205 randomly selected marketing researchers who participated in an actual survey, 117 said that they disapprove of this practice. Suppose that, before the survey was taken, a marketing manager claimed that at least 65 percent of all marketing researchers would disapprove of the practice.

   a   Assuming that the manager's claim is correct, calculate the probability that 117 or fewer of 205
           randomly selected marketing researchers would disapprove of the practice. Use the normal
           approximation to the binomial.

   b   Based on your result of part *a*, do you believe the marketing manager's claim? Explain.

6.49 When a store uses electronic article surveillance (EAS) to combat shoplifting, it places a small
          sensor on each item of merchandise. When an item is legitimately purchased, the sales clerk is
          supposed to remove the sensor to prevent an alarm from sounding as the customer exits the store.
          In an actual survey of 250 consumers, 40 said that if they were to set off an EAS alarm
          because store personnel (mistakenly) failed to deactivate merchandise leaving the store, then they
          would never shop at that store again. A company marketing the alarm system claimed that no more
          than 5 percent of all consumers would say that they would never shop at that store again if they
          were subjected to a false alarm.

   a   Assuming that the company's claim is valid, use the normal approximation to the binomial to
           calculate the probability that at least 40 of the 250 randomly selected consumers would say that
           they would never shop at that store again if they were subjected to a false alarm.

   b   Do you believe the company's claim based on your answer to part *a*? Explain.

6.50 A department store will place a sale item in a special display for a one-day sale. Previous
          experience suggests that 20 percent of all customers who pass such a special display will
          purchase the item. If 2,000 customers will pass the display on the day of the sale, and if a
          one-item-per-customer limit is placed on the sale item, how many units of the sale item
          should the store stock in order to have at most a 1 percent chance of running short of the
          item on the day of the sale? Assume here that customers make independent purchase decisions.

6.5 The Exponential Distribution (Optional) ◉ ● ●

Suppose that the number of times that a particular event occurs over an interval of time or space
has a Poisson distribution. Furthermore, consider an arbitrary time or space unit (for example,
minute, week, inch, square foot, or the like), and let x denote the number of time or space units
between successive occurrences of the event. Then, it can be shown that x is described by an
exponential distribution having parameter λ. Here, λ is the mean number of events that occur
per time or space unit. Furthermore, the mean value of x can be proven to be $1/\lambda$. In words, $1/\lambda$
is *the mean number of time or space units between successive occurrences of the event*. In general, we can describe the exponential distribution as follows:

The Exponential Distribution

If λ is a positive number, then the equation describing the exponential distribution is

$$f(x) = \begin{cases} \lambda e^{-\lambda x} & \text{for } x \geq 0 \\ 0 & \text{otherwise} \end{cases}$$

Using this probability curve, it can be shown that:

$$P(a \leq x \leq b) = e^{-\lambda a} - e^{-\lambda b}$$

In particular, since $e^0 = 1$ and $e^{-\infty} = 0$, this implies that

$$P(x \leq c) = 1 - e^{-\lambda c} \quad \text{and} \quad P(x \geq c) = e^{-\lambda c}$$

Furthermore, the mean and the standard deviation of the population of all possible observed values of a
random variable x that has an exponential distribution are

$$\mu_x = \frac{1}{\lambda} \quad \text{and} \quad \sigma_x = \frac{1}{\lambda}$$

The graph of the equation describing the exponential distribution and the probability $P(a \leq x \leq b)$
where x is described by this exponential distribution are illustrated in Figure 6.27.

We illustrate the use of the exponential distribution in the following examples.

FIGURE 6.27 A Graph of the Exponential Distribution $f(x) = \lambda e^{-\lambda x}$

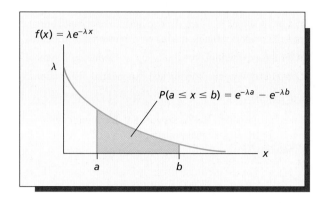

EXAMPLE 6.10

Recall from Example 5.13 (pages 230–233) that an air traffic control center is experiencing an average of 20.8 errors per year, and that it is reasonable to believe that the number of errors in a given time period is described by a Poisson distribution. If we consider x to be the number of weeks between successive errors, then x is described by an exponential distribution. Furthermore, since the air traffic control center is averaging 20.8 errors per year, it follows that λ, the average number of errors per week, is $20.8/52 = .4$. Therefore, the equation of the exponential distribution describing x is $f(x) = \lambda e^{-\lambda x} = .4e^{-.4x}$, and the mean number of weeks between successive errors is $1/\lambda = 1/.4 = 2.5$. For example, the probability that the time between successive errors will be between 1 and 2 weeks is

$$P(1 \le x \le 2) = e^{-\lambda a} - e^{-\lambda b} = e^{-\lambda(1)} - e^{-\lambda(2)}$$
$$= e^{-.4(1)} - e^{-.4(2)} = e^{-.4} - e^{-.8}$$
$$= .6703 - .4493 = .221$$

EXAMPLE 6.11

Suppose that the number of people who arrive at a hospital emergency room during a given time period has a Poisson distribution. It follows that the time, x, between successive arrivals of people to the emergency room has an exponential distribution. Furthermore, historical records indicate that the mean time between successive arrivals of people to the emergency room is seven minutes. Therefore, $\mu_x = 1/\lambda = 7$, which implies that $\lambda = 1/7 = .14286$. Noting that $\sigma_x = 1/\lambda = 7$, it follows that

$$\mu_x - \sigma_x = 7 - 7 = 0 \quad \text{and} \quad \mu_x + \sigma_x = 7 + 7 = 14$$

Therefore, the probability that the time between successive arrivals of people to the emergency room will be within (plus or minus) one standard deviation of the mean interarrival time is

$$P(0 \le x \le 14) = e^{-\lambda a} - e^{-\lambda b}$$
$$= e^{-(.14286)(0)} - e^{-(.14286)(14)}$$
$$= 1 - .1353$$
$$= .8647$$

To conclude this section we note that the exponential and related Poisson distributions are useful in analyzing waiting lines, or **queues.** In general, **queueing theory** attempts to determine the number of servers (for example, doctors in an emergency room) that strikes an optimal balance between the time customers wait for service and the cost of providing service. The reader is referred to any textbook on management science or operations research for a discussion of queueing theory.

Exercises for Section 6.5

CONCEPTS

6.51 Give two examples of situations in which the exponential distribution might appropriately be used. In each case, define the random variable having an exponential distribution.

6.52 State the formula for the exponential probability curve. Define each symbol in the formula.

6.53 Explain the relationship between the Poisson and exponential distributions.

METHODS AND APPLICATIONS

6.54 Suppose that the random variable x has an exponential distribution with $\lambda = 2$.
  a Write the formula for the exponential probability curve of x. What are the possible values of x?
  b Sketch the probability curve.
  c Find $P(x \leq 1)$.
  d Find $P(.25 \leq x \leq 1)$.
  e Find $P(x \geq 2)$.
  f Calculate the mean, μ_x, the variance, σ_x^2, and the standard deviation, σ_x, of the exponential distribution of x.
  g Find the probability that x will be in the interval $[\mu_x \pm 2\sigma_x]$.

6.55 Repeat Exercise 6.54 with $\lambda = 3$.

6.56 Recall in Exercise 5.34 (page 234) that the number of customer arrivals at a bank's drive-up window in a 15-minute period is Poisson distributed with a mean of seven customer arrivals per 15-minute period. Define the random variable x to be the time (in minutes) between successive customer arrivals at the bank's drive-up window.
  a Write the formula for the exponential probability curve of x.
  b Sketch the probability curve of x.
  c Find the probability that the time between arrivals is
    (1) Between one and two minutes.
    (2) Less than one minute.
    (3) More than three minutes.
    (4) Between $^1/_2$ and $3^1/_2$ minutes.
  d Calculate μ_x, σ_x^2, and σ_x.
  e Find the probability that the time between arrivals falls within one standard deviation of the mean; within two standard deviations of the mean.

6.57 The length of a particular telemarketing phone call, x, has an exponential distribution with mean equal to 1.5 minutes.
  a Write the formula for the exponential probability curve of x.
  b Sketch the probability curve of x.
  c Find the probability that the length of a randomly selected call will be
    (1) No more than three minutes.
    (2) Between one and two minutes.
    (3) More than four minutes.
    (4) Less than 30 seconds.

6.58 The maintenance department in a factory claims that the number of breakdowns of a particular machine follows a Poisson distribution with a mean of two breakdowns every 500 hours. Let x denote the time (in hours) between successive breakdowns.
  a Find λ and μ_x.
  b Write the formula for the exponential probability curve of x.
  c Sketch the probability curve.
  d Assuming that the maintenance department's claim is true, find the probability that the time between successive breakdowns is at most five hours.
  e Assuming that the maintenance department's claim is true, find the probability that the time between successive breakdowns is between 100 and 300 hours.
  f Suppose that the machine breaks down five hours after its most recent breakdown. Based on your answer to part d, do you believe the maintenance department's claim? Explain.

6.59 Suppose that the number of accidents occurring in an industrial plant is described by a Poisson distribution with an average of one accident per month. Let x denote the time (in months) between successive accidents.
  a Find the probability that the time between successive accidents is
    (1) More than two months.
    (2) Between one and two months.
    (3) Less than one week (1/4 of a month).

b Suppose that an accident occurs less than one week after the plant's most recent accident. Would you consider this event unusual enough to warrant special investigation? Explain.

6.6 The Normal Probability Plot (Optional) ● ● ●

The **normal probability plot** is a graphic that is used to visually check whether sample data come from a normal distribution. In order to illustrate the construction and interpretation of a normal probability plot, consider the payment time case and suppose that the trucking company operates in three regions of the country—the north, central, and south regions. In each region, 24 invoices are randomly selected and the payment time for each sampled invoice is found. The payment times obtained in each region are given in Table 6.3, along with MINITAB side-by-side box plots of the data. Examination of the data and box plots indicates that the payment times for the central region are skewed to the left, while the payment times for the south region are skewed to the right. The box plot of the payment times for the north region, along with the MegaStat dot plot of these payment times in Figure 6.28, indicate that the payment times for the north region are approximately normally distributed.

We will begin by constructing a normal probability plot for the payment times from the north region. We first arrange the payment times in order from smallest to largest. The ordered payment times are shown in column (1) of Table 6.4. Next, for each ordered payment time we compute the quantity $i/(n + 1)$, where i denotes the observation's position in the ordered list of data and n denotes the sample size. For instance, for the first and second ordered payment times, we compute $1/(24 + 1) = 1/25 = .04$ and $2/(24 + 1) = 2/25 = .08$. Similarly, for the last (24th) ordered payment time, we compute $24/(24 + 1) = 24/25 = .96$. The positions ($i$ values) of all 24 payment times are given in column (2) of Table 6.4, and the corresponding values of $i/(n + 1)$ are given in column (3) of this table. We continue by computing what is called the **standardized normal quantile value** for each ordered payment time. This value (denoted O_i) is the z value that

TABLE 6.3	Twenty-Four Randomly Selected Payment Times for Each of Three Geographical Regions in the United States		

North Region	Central Region	South Region	
26	26	28	
27	28	31	
21	21	21	
22	22	23	
22	23	23	
23	24	24	
27	27	29	
20	19	20	
22	22	22	
29	29	36	
18	15	19	
24	25	25	
28	28	33	
26	26	27	
21	20	21	
32	29	44	
23	24	24	
24	25	26	
25	25	27	
15	7	19	
17	12	19	
19	18	20	
34	29	50	
30	29	39	

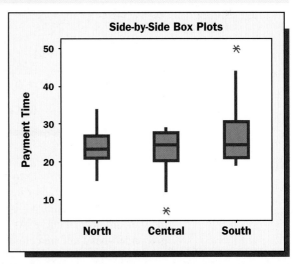

FIGURE 6.28	Dot Plot of the Payment Times for the North Region

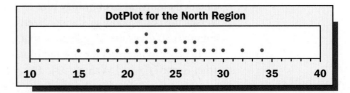

TABLE 6.4   Calculations for Normal Probability Plots in the Payment Time Example

Ordered North Region Payment Times Column (1)	Observation Number (i) Column (2)	Area i/(n + 1) Column (3)	z value O_i Column (4)	Ordered Central Region Payment Times Column (5)	Ordered South Region Payment Times Column (6)
15	1	0.04	−1.75	7	19
17	2	0.08	−1.41	12	19
18	3	0.12	−1.18	15	19
19	4	0.16	−0.99	18	20
20	5	0.2	−0.84	19	20
21	6	0.24	−0.71	20	21
21	7	0.28	−0.58	21	21
22	8	0.32	−0.47	22	22
22	9	0.36	−0.36	22	23
22	10	0.4	−0.25	23	23
23	11	0.44	−0.15	24	24
23	12	0.48	−0.05	24	24
24	13	0.52	0.05	25	25
24	14	0.56	0.15	25	26
25	15	0.6	0.25	25	27
26	16	0.64	0.36	26	27
26	17	0.68	0.47	26	28
27	18	0.72	0.58	27	29
27	19	0.76	0.71	28	31
28	20	0.8	0.84	28	33
29	21	0.84	0.99	29	36
30	22	0.88	1.18	29	39
32	23	0.92	1.41	29	44
34	24	0.96	1.75	29	50

FIGURE 6.29   Calculating Standardized Normal Quantile Values

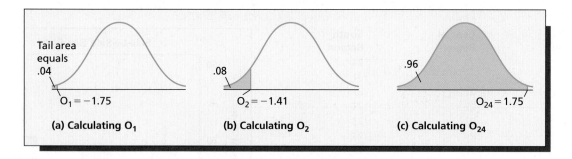

Tail area equals .04

$O_1 = -1.75$

(a) Calculating O_1

.08

$O_2 = -1.41$

(b) Calculating O_2

.96

$O_{24} = 1.75$

(c) Calculating O_{24}

gives an area of $i/(n + 1)$ to its left under the standard normal curve. Figure 6.29 illustrates finding O_1, O_2, and O_{24}. For instance, O_1—the standardized normal quantile value corresponding to the first ordered residual—is the z value that gives an area of $1/(24 + 1) = .04$ to its left under the standard normal curve. As shown in Figure 6.29(a), the z value (to two decimal places) that gives a left-hand tail area closest to .04 is $O_1 = -1.75$. Similarly, O_2 is the z value that gives an area of $2/(24 + 1) = .08$ to its left under the standard normal curve. As shown in Figure 6.29(b), the z value (to two decimal places) that gives a left-hand tail area closest to .08 is $O_2 = -1.41$. As a final example, Figure 6.29(c) shows that O_{24}, the z value that gives an area of $24/(24 + 1) = .96$ to its left under the standard normal curve, is 1.75. The standardized normal quantile values corresponding to the 24 ordered payment times are given in column (4) of Table 6.4. Finally, we obtain the **normal probability plot** by plotting the 24 ordered payment times on the vertical axis versus the corresponding standardized normal quantile values (O_i values) on the horizontal axis. Figure 6.30 gives the MegaStat output of this normal probability plot.

In order to interpret the normal plot, notice that, although the areas in column (3) of Table 6.4 (that is, the $i/(n + 1)$ values: .04, .08, .12, etc.) are equally spaced, the z values corresponding to

FIGURE 6.30   MegaStat Normal Probability Plot
               for the North Region: Approximate
               Normality

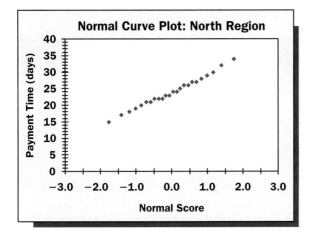

FIGURE 6.31   MegaStat Normal Probability Plot
               for the Central Region: Data
               Skewed to the Left

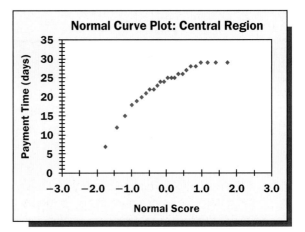

FIGURE 6.32   MegaStat Normal Probability Plot for the South Region: Data Skewed
               to the Right

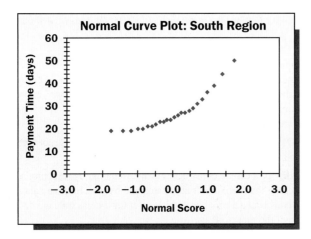

these areas are not equally spaced. Because of the mound-shaped nature of the standard normal curve, the negative z values get closer together as they get closer to the mean ($z = 0$) and the positive z values get farther apart as they get farther from the mean (more positive). If the distances between the payment times behave the same way as the distances between the z values—that is, if the distances between the payment times are proportional to the distances between the z values—then the normal probability plot will be a straight line. This would suggest that the payment times are normally distributed. Examining Figure 6.30, the normal probability plot for the payment times from the north region is approximately a straight line and, therefore, it is reasonable to assume that these payment times are approximately normally distributed.

Column (5) of Table 6.4 gives the ordered payment times for the central region, and Figure 6.31 plots these values versus the standardized normal quantile values in column (4). The resulting normal probability plot for the central region has a nonlinear appearance. The plot points rise more steeply at first and then continue to increase at a decreasing rate. This pattern indicates that the payment times for the central region are skewed to the left. Here the rapidly rising points at the beginning of the plot are due to the payment times being farther apart in the left tail of the distribution. Column (6) of Table 6.4 gives the ordered payment times for the south region, and Figure 6.32 gives the normal probability plot for this region. This plot also has a nonlinear appearance. The points rise slowly at first and then increase at an increasing rate. This pattern indicates that the payment times for the south region are skewed to the right. Here the rapidly rising points on the right side of the plot are due to the payment times being farther apart in the right tail of the distribution.

In the following box, we summarize how to construct and interpret a normal probability plot:

Normal Probability Plots

1 Order the values in the data from smallest to largest.

2 For each observation compute the area $i/(n + 1)$, where i denotes the position of the observation in the ordered listing and n is the number of observations.

3 Compute the standardized normal quantile value O_i for each observation. This is the z value that gives an area of $i/(n + 1)$ to its left under the standard normal curve.

4 Plot the ordered data values versus the standardized normal quantile values.

5 If the resulting normal probability plot has a straight-line appearance, it is reasonable to assume that the data come from a normal distribution.

Exercises for Section 6.6

CONCEPTS

6.60 Discuss how a normal probability plot is constructed.

6.61 If a normal probability plot has the appearance of a straight line, what should we conclude?

METHODS AND APPLICATIONS

6.62 Consider the sample of 12 incomes given in Example 3.2 (page 119).
   a Sort the income data from smallest to largest, and compute $i/(n + 1)$ for each observation.
   b Compute the standardized normal quantile value O_i for each observation.
   c Graph the normal probability plot for the salary data and interpret this plot. Does the plot indicate that the data are skewed? Explain.   Incomes

6.63 Consider the 20 DVD satisfaction ratings given on page 142. Construct a normal probability plot for these data and interpret the plot.   DVDSat

6.64 A normal probability plot can be constructed using MegaStat by selecting MegaStat: Descriptive Statistics, by checking the normal plot checkbox, and by selecting the data into the Input window. Use MegaStat to construct a normal probability plot for the gas mileage data in Table 3.1 (page 117). Interpret the plot.   GasMiles

Chapter Summary

In this chapter we have discussed **continuous probability distributions.** We began by learning that **a continuous probability distribution is described by a continuous probability curve** and that in this context **probabilities are areas under the probability curve.** We next studied several important continuous probability distributions—**the uniform distribution, the normal distribution,** and **the exponential distribution.** In particular, we concentrated on the normal distribution, which is the most important continuous probability distribution. We learned about the properties of the normal curve, and we saw how to use a **normal table** to find various areas under a normal curve. We also saw that the normal curve can be employed to approximate binomial probabilities, and we demonstrated how we can use a normal curve probability to make a statistical inference. We concluded this chapter with an optional section that covers the **normal probability plot.**

Glossary of Terms

continuous probability distribution (or **probability curve**): A curve that is defined so that the probability that a random variable will be in a specified interval of numbers is the area under the curve corresponding to the interval. (page 243)

cumulative normal table: A table in which we can look up areas under the standard normal curve. (pages 250–252)

exponential distribution: A probability distribution that describes the time or space between successive occurrences of an event when the number of times the event occurs over an interval of time or space is described by a Poisson distribution. (page 270)

normal probability distribution: The most important continuous probability distribution. Its probability curve is the *bell-shaped* normal curve. (page 248)

normal probability plot: A graphic used to visually check whether sample data come from a normal distribution. (page 273)

queueing theory: A methodology that attempts to determine the number of servers that strikes an optimal balance between the time customers wait for service and the cost of providing service. (page 271)

standard normal distribution (or curve): A normal distribution (or curve) having mean 0 and standard deviation 1. (page 250)

uniform distribution: A continuous probability distribution having a rectangular shape that says the probability is distributed evenly (or uniformly) over an interval of numbers. (page 245)

z_α **point:** The point on the horizontal axis under the standard normal curve that gives a right-hand tail area equal to α. (page 260)

$-z_\alpha$ **point:** The point on the horizontal axis under the standard normal curve that gives a left-hand tail area equal to α. (page 261)

z **value:** A value that tells us the number of standard deviations that a value x is from the mean of a normal curve. If the z value is positive, then x is above the mean. If the z value is negative, then x is below the mean. (page 250)

Important Formulas

The uniform probability curve: page 245

Mean and standard deviation of a uniform distribution: page 245

The normal probability curve: page 248

z values: page 250

Finding normal probabilities: page 257

Normal approximation to the binomial distribution: page 267

The exponential probability curve: page 270

Mean and standard deviation of an exponential distribution: page 270

Constructing a normal probability plot: page 276

Supplementary Exercises

6.65 In a bottle-filling process, the amount of drink injected into 16 oz bottles is normally distributed with a mean of 16 oz and a standard deviation of .02 oz. Bottles containing less than 15.95 oz do not meet the bottler's quality standard. What percentage of filled bottles do not meet the standard?

6.66 In a murder trial in Los Angeles, a shoe expert stated that the range of heights of men with a size 12 shoe is 71 inches to 76 inches. Suppose the heights of all men wearing size 12 shoes are normally distributed with a mean of 73.5 inches and a standard deviation of 1 inch. What is the probability that a randomly selected man who wears a size 12 shoe
  a Has a height outside the range 71 inches to 76 inches?
  b Is 74 inches or taller?
  c Is shorter than 70.5 inches?

6.67 In the movie *Forrest Gump,* the public school required an IQ of at least 80 for admittance.
  a If IQ test scores are normally distributed with mean 100 and standard deviation 16, what percentage of people would qualify for admittance to the school?
  b If the public school wishes 95 percent of all children to qualify for admittance, what minimum IQ test score should be required for admittance?

6.68 The amount of sales tax paid on a purchase is rounded to the nearest cent. Assume that the round-off error is uniformly distributed in the interval $-.5$ to $.5$ cents.
  a Write the formula for the probability curve describing the round-off error.
  b Graph the probability curve describing the round-off error.
  c What is the probability that the round-off error exceeds .3 cents or is less than $-.3$ cents?
  d What is the probability that the round-off error exceeds .1 cent or is less than $-.1$ cent?
  e Find the mean and the standard deviation of the round-off error.
  f Find the probability that the round-off error will be within one standard deviation of the mean.

6.69 A *consensus forecast* is the average of a large number of individual analysts' forecasts. Suppose the individual forecasts for a particular interest rate are normally distributed with a mean of 5.0 percent and a standard deviation of 1.2 percent. A single analyst is randomly selected. Find the probability that his/her forecast is
  a At least 3.5 percent.
  b At most 6 percent.
  c Between 3.5 percent and 6 percent.

connect

6.70 Recall from Exercise 6.69 that individual forecasts of a particular interest rate are normally distributed with a mean of 5 percent and a standard deviation of 1.2 percent.

   a What percentage of individual forecasts are at or below the 10th percentile of the distribution of forecasts? What percentage are at or above the 10th percentile? Find the 10th percentile of the distribution of individual forecasts.

   b Find the first quartile, Q_1, and the third quartile, Q_3, of the distribution of individual forecasts.

6.71 The scores on the entrance exam at a well-known, exclusive law school are normally distributed with a mean score of 200 and a standard deviation equal to 50. At what value should the lowest passing score be set if the school wishes only 2.5 percent of those taking the test to pass?

6.72 A machine is used to cut a metal automobile part to its desired length. The machine can be set so that the mean length of the part will be any value that is desired. The standard deviation of the lengths always runs at .02 inches. Where should the mean be set if we want only .4 percent of the parts cut by the machine to be shorter than 15 inches long?

6.73 A motel accepts 325 reservations for 300 rooms on July 1, expecting 10 percent no-shows on average from past records. Use the normal approximation to the binomial to find the probability that all guests who arrive on July 1 will receive a room.

6.74 Suppose a software company finds that the number of errors in its software per 1,000 lines of code is described by a Poisson distribution. Furthermore, it is found that there is an average of four errors per 1,000 lines of code. Letting x denote the number of lines of code between successive errors:

   a Find the probability that there will be at least 400 lines of code between successive errors in the company's software.

   b Find the probability that there will be no more than 100 lines of code between successive errors in the company's software.

6.75 **THE INVESTMENT CASE**   InvestRet

For each investment class in Table 3.11 (page 159), assume that future returns are normally distributed with the population mean and standard deviation given in Table 3.11. Based on this assumption:

   a For each investment class, find the probability of a return that is less than zero (that is, find the probability of a loss). Is your answer reasonable for all investment classes? Explain.

   b For each investment class, find the probability of a return that is

     (1) Greater than 5 percent.

     (2) Greater than 10 percent.

     (3) Greater than 20 percent.

     (4) Greater than 50 percent.

   c For which investment classes is the probability of a return greater than 50 percent essentially zero? For which investment classes is the probability of such a return greater than 1 percent? Greater than 5 percent?

   d For which investment classes is the probability of a loss essentially zero? For which investment classes is the probability of a loss greater than 1 percent? Greater than 10 percent? Greater than 20 percent?

6.76 The daily water consumption for an Ohio community is normally distributed with a mean consumption of 800,000 gallons and a standard deviation of 80,000 gallons. The community water system will experience a noticeable drop in water pressure when the daily water consumption exceeds 984,000 gallons. What is the probability of experiencing such a drop in water pressure?

6.77 Suppose the times required for a cable company to fix cable problems in its customers' homes are uniformly distributed between 10 minutes and 25 minutes. What is the probability that a randomly selected cable repair visit will take at least 15 minutes?

6.78 Suppose the waiting time to get food after placing an order at a fast-food restaurant is exponentially distributed with a mean of 60 seconds. If a randomly selected customer orders food at the restaurant, what is the probability that the customer will wait at least

   a One minute, 30 seconds?

   b Two minutes?

6.79 Net interest margin—often referred to as *spread*—is the difference between the rate banks pay on deposits and the rate they charge for loans. Suppose that the net interest margins for all U.S. banks are normally distributed with a mean of 4.15 percent and a standard deviation of .5 percent.

a Find the probability that a randomly selected U.S. bank will have a net interest margin that exceeds 5.40 percent.

b Find the probability that a randomly selected U.S. bank will have a net interest margin less than 4.40 percent.

c A bank wants its net interest margin to be less than the net interest margins of 95 percent of all U.S. banks. Where should the bank's net interest margin be set?

6.80 In an article in the November 11, 1991, issue of *Advertising Age,* Nancy Giges studies global spending patterns. Giges presents data concerning the percentage of adults in various countries who have purchased various consumer items (such as soft drinks, athletic footware, blue jeans, beer, and so on) in the past three months.

a Suppose we wish to justify the claim that fewer than 50 percent of adults in Germany have purchased blue jeans in the past three months. The survey reported by Giges found that 45 percent of the respondents in Germany had purchased blue jeans in the past three months.[2]

Assume that a random sample of 400 German adults was employed, and let p be the proportion of all German adults who have purchased blue jeans in the past three months. If, for the sake of argument, we assume that $p = .5$, use the normal approximation to the binomial distribution to calculate the probability that 45 percent or fewer of 400 randomly selected German adults would have purchased blue jeans in the past three months. Note: Because 45 percent of 400 is 180, you should calculate the probability that 180 or fewer of 400 randomly selected German adults would have purchased blue jeans in the past three months.

b Based on the probability you computed in part *a,* would you conclude that p is really less than .5? That is, would you conclude that fewer than 50 percent of adults in Germany have purchased blue jeans in the past three months? Explain.

6.81 Assume that the ages for first marriages are normally distributed with a mean of 26 years and a standard deviation of 4 years. What is the probability that a person getting married for the first time is in his or her twenties?

Appendix 6.1 ■ Normal Distribution Using MINITAB

Normal probability P(X ≤ 31.2) in Example 6.3 (pages 257–258):

- Select **Calc : Probability Distributions : Normal.**

- In the Normal Distribution dialog box, select the Cumulative probability option.

- In the Mean window, enter 33.

- In the Standard deviation window, enter 0.7.

- Click on the "Input constant" option and enter 31.2 in the "Input constant" window.

- Click OK in the Normal Distribution dialog box to see the desired probability in the Session window.

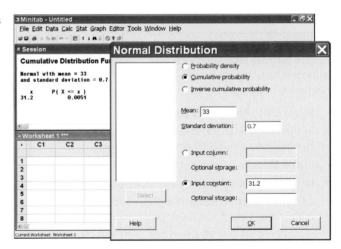

[2]Source: N. Giges, "Global Spending Patterns Emerge," *Advertising Age* (November 11, 1991), p. 64.

Normal probability P(X < 153 or X > 167) in Example 6.4 (page 258):

- In columns C1, C2, and C3, enter the variable names—x, P(X < x), and P(X > x).
- In column C1, enter the values 153 and 167.
- Select **Calc : Probability Distributions : Normal**
- In the Normal Distribution dialog box, select the Cumulative probability option.
- In the Mean window, enter 160.0833.
- In the Standard deviation window, enter 5.3724.
- Click the "Input column" option, enter x in the "Input column" window, and enter 'P(X < x)' in the "Optional storage" window.
- Click OK in the Normal Distribution dialog box.

- Select **Calc : Calculator**
- In the Calculator dialog box, enter 'P(X > x)' in the "Store result in variable" window.
- Enter 1 − 'P(X < x)' in the Expression window.
- Click OK in the Calculator dialog box.

The desired probability is the sum of the lower tail probability for 153 and the upper tail probability for 167 or 0.093675 + 0.098969 = 0.192644. This value differs slightly from the value in Example 6.4 since Minitab carries out probability calculations to higher precision than can be achieved using normal probability tables.

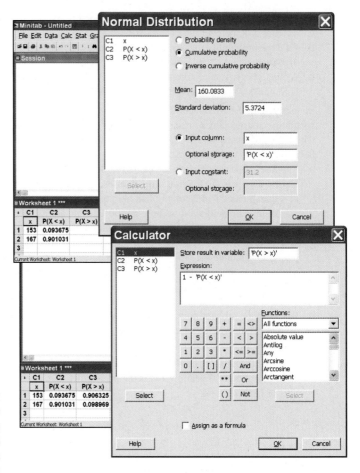

Inverse normal probability to find the number of units stocked, *st*, such that P(X > st) = 0.05 in Example 6.5 (pages 260–261):

- Select **Calc : Probability Distributions : Normal**
- In the Normal Distribution dialog box, select the Inverse cumulative probability option.
- In the Mean window, enter 100.
- In the Standard deviation window, enter 10.
- Click the "Input constant" option and enter 0.95 in the "Input constant" window. That is,

    P(X ≤ st) = 0.95 when P(X > st) = 0.05.

- Click OK in the Normal Distribution dialog box to see the desired value of *st* in the Session window.

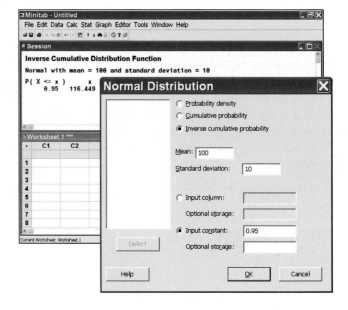

Appendix 6.2 ■ Normal Distribution Using Excel

Normal probability P(X ≤ 31.2) in Example 6.3 (pages 257–258):

- Click in the cell where you wish to place the answer. Here we have clicked in cell A15. Then select the Insert Function button f_x from the Excel toolbar.

- In the Insert Function dialog box, select Statistical from the "Or select a category:" menu, select NORMDIST from the "Select a function:" menu, and click OK.

- In the NORMDIST Function Arguments dialog box, enter the value 31.2 in the X window.

- Enter the value 33 in the Mean window.

- Enter the value 0.7 in the Standard_dev window.

- Enter the value 1 in the Cumulative window.

- Click OK in the NORMDIST Function Arguments dialog box.

- When you click OK in this dialog box, the answer will be placed in cell A15.

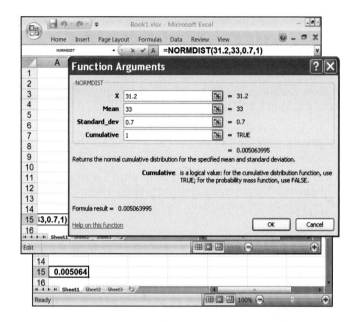

Normal probability P(X < 153 or X > 167) in Example 6.4 (page 258):

- Enter the headings—x, P(X < x), P(X > x) – in the spreadsheet where you wish the results to be placed. Here we will enter these headings in cells A16, B16, and C16. The calculated results will be placed below the headings.

- In cells A17 and A18, enter the values 153 and 167.

- Click in cell B17 and select the Insert Function button f_x from the Excel toolbar.

- In the Insert Function dialog box, select Statistical from the "Or select a category:" menu, select NORMDIST from the "Select a function:" menu, and click OK.

- In the NORMDIST Function Arguments dialog box, enter the cell location A17 in the X window.

- Enter the value 160.0833 in the Mean window.

- Enter the value 5.3724 in the Standard_dev window.

- Enter the value 1 in the Cumulative window.

- Click OK in the NORMDIST Function Arguments dialog box.

- When you click OK, the result for P(X < 153) will be placed in cell B17. Double-click the drag handle (in the lower right corner) of cell B17 to automatically extend the cell formula of B17 through cell B18.

- In cells C17 and C18, enter the formulas = 1 − B17 and = 1 − B18. The results for P(X > 153) and P(X > 167) will be placed in cells C17 and C18.

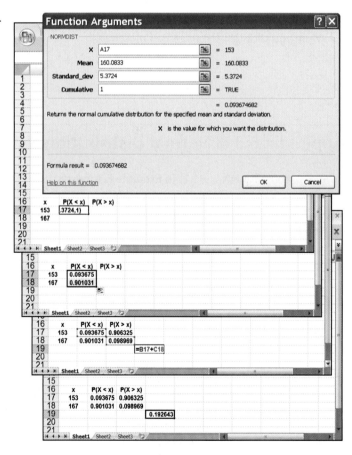

- In cell D19, enter the formula = B17 + C18.

The desired probability is in cell D19, the sum of the lower tail probability for 153 and the upper tail probability for 167. This value differs slightly from the value in Example 6.4 since Excel carries out probability calculations to higher precision than can be achieved using normal probability tables.

Inverse normal probability *st* such that $P(X > st) = 0.05$ in Example 6.5 (pages 260–261):

- Click in the cell where you wish the answer to be placed. Here we will click in cell A19. Select the Insert Function button f_x from the Excel toolbar.

- In the Insert Function dialog box, select Statistical from the "Or select a category:" menu, select NORMINV from the "Select a function:" menu, and click OK.

- In the NORMINV Function Arguments dialog box, enter the value 0.95 in the Probability window; that is,

    [$P(X \le st) = 0.95$ when $P(X > st) = 0.05$.]

- Enter the value 100 in the Mean window.
- Enter the value 10 in the Standard_dev window.
- Click OK in the NORMINV Function Arguments dialog box.
- When you click OK, the answer is placed in cell A19.

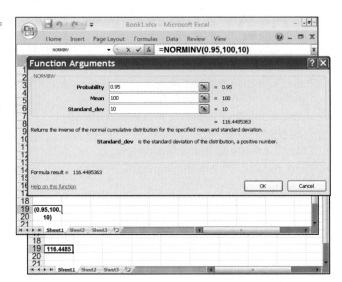

Appendix 6.3 ■ Normal Distribution Using MegaStat

Normal probability $P(X < 31.2)$ in Example 6.3 (pages 257–258):

- Select **Add-ins : MegaStat : Probability : Continuous Probability Distributions**

- In the "Continuous Probability Distributions" dialog box, select the normal distribution tab.

- Enter the distribution mean (here equal to 33) and the distribution standard deviation (here equal to 0.7) in the appropriate boxes.

- Enter the value of x (here equal to 31.2) into the "calculate p given x" window.

- Click OK in the "Continuous Probability Distributions" dialog box.

- The output includes **P(lower),** which is the area under the specified normal curve below the given value of x, and **P(upper),** which is the area under the specified normal curve above the given value of x. The value of z corresponding to the specified value of x is also included. In this case, $P(X < 31.2)$ equals P(lower) = .0051.

- (Optional) Click on the preview button to see the values of P(lower) and P(upper) before obtaining results in the output worksheet.

Note that if a **standard normal distribution** is specified—0 is entered in the mean box and 1 is entered in the standard deviation box—the "calculate P given X" box will read "calculate P given z." In this case, when we enter a value of z in the "calculate P given z" box, P(lower) and P(upper) are, respectively, the areas below and above the specified value of z under the standard normal curve.

Normal probability P(X < 153 or X > 167) in Example 6.4 on page 258:

- Enter 160.0833 into the mean box and enter 5.3724 into the standard deviation box.
- Find P(lower) corresponding to 153 and find P(upper) corresponding to 167.
- When these values are placed in the output worksheet, use a simple Excel cell formula to add them together.

Inverse normal probability *st* such that P(X > *st*) = 0.05 in Example 6.5 on pages 260–261:

- Select **Add-ins : MegaStat : Probability : Continuous Probability Distributions**
- Enter 100 into the mean box and enter 10 into the standard deviation box.
- Select the "calculate x given P" option.
- Enter 0.05 into the P box. This is the area under the normal curve we want to have above *st* (that is, above the desired value of x).
- Click OK in the "Continuous Probability Distributions" dialog box.
- The output includes P(lower) and P(upper)—as defined above—as well as the desired value of x (in this case x equals 116.45).

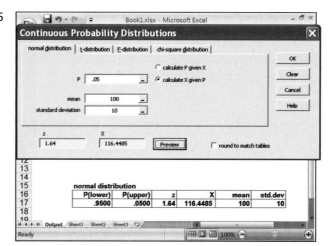

CHAPTER 7

Sampling Distributions

Chapter Outline

7.1 The Sampling Distribution of the Sample
Mean

7.2 The Sampling Distribution of the Sample
Proportion

W e have seen that the sample mean is the point estimate of the population mean and the sample proportion is the point estimate of the population proportion. In much of this book we use point estimates to make statistical inferences about populations and processes. As mentioned in Chapter 4, these inferences are based on calculating probabilities. To calculate these probabilities, we use a certain type of probability distribution called a **sampling distribution.**

In this chapter we discuss the properties of two important sampling distributions—the **sampling distribution of the sample mean** and the **sampling distribution of the sample proportion.** In order to help explain these sampling distributions, we consider three previously introduced cases:

The Car Mileage Case: The automaker uses the properties of the sampling distribution of the sample mean and its sample of 50 mileages to provide convincing evidence that the new midsize model's mean EPA combined city and highway mileage exceeds the tax credit standard of 31 mpg.

The Payment Time Case: The management consulting firm uses the properties of the sampling distribution of the sample mean and its sample of 65 payment times to provide strong evidence that the new electronic billing system has reduced the mean bill payment time by more than 50 percent.

The Cheese Spread Case: The food processing company uses the properties of the sampling distribution of the sample proportion and its survey results to provide extremely strong evidence that fewer than 10 percent of all current purchasers would stop buying the cheese spread if the new spout were used.

We also study a new case, **The Risk Analysis Case,** which introduces how to deal with risky situations in the contexts of game shows and investment strategy.

7.1 The Sampling Distribution of the Sample Mean ● ● ●

Introductory ideas and basic properties Suppose that we are about to randomly select a sample of n measurements from a population of measurements having mean μ and standard deviation σ. *Before* we actually select the sample, there are many different samples of n measurements that we might potentially obtain. Because different samples generally have different sample means, there are many different sample means that we might potentially obtain. It follows that, *before we draw the sample, the sample mean $\bar{x}$ is a random variable.*

The **sampling distribution of the sample mean $\bar{x}$** is the probability distribution of the population of all possible sample means obtained from all possible samples of the same size.

In order to illustrate the sampling distribution of the sample mean, we begin with an intuitive example.

EXAMPLE 7.1 The Risk Analysis Case: Game Shows and Stock Returns

Congratulations! You have just won the question-and-answer portion of a popular game show and will now be given an opportunity to select a grand prize. The game show host shows you a large revolving drum containing six identical white envelopes that have been thoroughly mixed in the drum. Each of the envelopes contains one of six checks made out for grand prizes of 10, 20, 30, 40, 50, and 60 thousand dollars. Usually, a contestant reaches into the drum, selects an envelope, and receives the grand prize in the envelope. Tonight, however, is a special night. You will be given the choice of either selecting one envelope or selecting two envelopes and receiving the average of the grand prizes in the two envelopes. What should you do?

If you select one envelope, you are randomly selecting one grand prize from the population of six grand prizes. The probability that you will receive any particular grand prize is 1/6, and therefore the probability distribution of the population of grand prizes is as shown in Table 7.1 on the next page. Furthermore, a graph of this probability distribution is as shown is Figure 7.1(a). If we calculate the mean μ of the population of grand prizes, we find that

$$\mu = \frac{10 + 20 + 30 + 40 + 50 + 60}{6} = \frac{210}{6} = 35 \text{ thousand dollars}$$

TABLE 7.1	A Probability Distribution Describing the Population of Six Individual Grand Prizes						
Grand Prize (thousands of dollars)		10	20	30	40	50	60
Probability		1/6	1/6	1/6	1/6	1/6	1/6

FIGURE 7.1   A Comparison of Individual Grand Prizes and Sample Mean Grand Prizes

(a) A graph of the probability distribution describing the population of six individual grand prizes

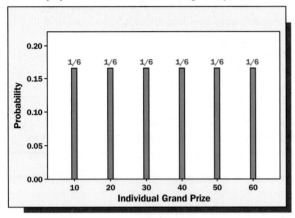

(b) A graph of the probability distribution describing the population of 15 sample mean grand prizes

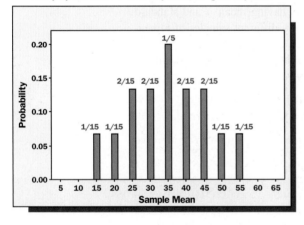

TABLE 7.2   The Population of Sample Means

(a) The population of the 15 samples of $n = 2$ grand prizes and corresponding sample means

Sample	Grand Prizes	Sample Mean
1	10, 20	15
2	10, 30	20
3	10, 40	25
4	10, 50	30
5	10, 60	35
6	20, 30	25
7	20, 40	30
8	20, 50	35
9	20, 60	40
10	30, 40	35
11	30, 50	40
12	30, 60	45
13	40, 50	45
14	40, 60	50
15	50, 60	55

(b) A probability distribution describing the population of 15 sample mean grand prizes: the sampling distribution of the sample mean

Sample Mean	Frequency	Probability
15	1	1/15
20	1	1/15
25	2	2/15
30	2	2/15
35	3	3/15
40	2	2/15
45	2	2/15
50	1	1/15
55	1	1/15

If, on the other hand, you select two envelopes, you are randomly selecting a sample of two grand prizes from the population of six grand prizes. The 15 samples of two grand prizes that you might obtain, as well as the means of these samples, are summarized in Table 7.2(a). For example, if you select an envelope containing 20 thousand dollars and an envelope containing 40 thousand dollars, you will receive a sample mean grand prize of

$$\bar{x} = \frac{20 + 40}{2} = 30 \text{ thousand dollars}$$

In order to find the probability distribution of the population of sample mean grand prizes, note that different sample mean grand prizes correspond to different numbers of samples. For example, since the sample mean grand prize of 30 thousand dollars corresponds to 2 out of 15 samples—the sample (10, 50) and the sample (20, 40)—the probability of obtaining the sample mean grand prize of 30 thousand dollars is 2/15. If we analyze all of the sample mean

FIGURE 7.2   **The New York Stock Exchange in 1987: A Comparison of Individual Stock Returns and Sample Mean Returns**

(a) The percent frequency histogram describing the population of individual stock returns

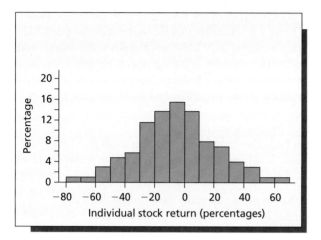

(b) The percent frequency histogram describing the population of all possible sample mean returns when n = 5

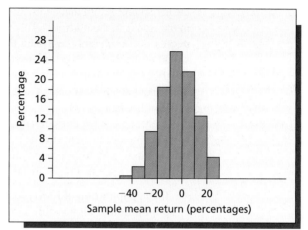

Source: Figure 7.2 is adapted with permission from *The American Association of Individual Investors Journal*, by John K. Ford, "A Method for Grading 1987 Stock Recommendations," March 1988, pp. 16–17.

grand prizes in a similar fashion, we find that the probability distribution of the population of sample mean grand prizes is as shown in Table 7.2(b). This distribution is the *sampling distribution of the sample mean*. A graph of this distribution is as shown in Figure 7.1(b).

We are now prepared to compare your two game show options. If we examine Figures 7.1(a) and (b), we see that, although the distribution of six individual grand prizes and the distribution of 15 sample mean grand prizes seem to be centered over the same mean of 35 thousand dollars, the distribution of sample mean grand prizes looks *more bell-shaped* and *less spread out* than the distribution of individual grand prizes. In particular, whereas the potential individual grand prizes range from 10 thousand dollars to 60 thousand dollars, the potential sample mean grand prizes range from 15 thousand dollars to 55 thousand dollars. It follows that if you wish to reduce the variability of your potential grand prize winnings, you should select two envelopes rather than one envelope. Doing this will, for example, guarantee a sample mean grand prize of at least 15 thousand dollars and give a 13/15 probability of a sample mean grand prize of at least 25 thousand dollars. On the other hand, whereas the probability of a sample mean grand prize of at least 50 thousand dollars is only 2/15, the probability of an individual grand prize of at least 50 thousand dollars is 2/6. Therefore, if you are willing to take on more risk and go for the larger grand prize winnings, you should select one envelope.

Although most of us will never participate in a game show, the game show example illustrates a useful principle. This principle, which is very important in financial investing, is that if you carefully diversify your financial opportunities, you can reduce the variability of your potential financial returns and thus reduce your risk. For example, the year 1987 featured extreme volatility in the stock market, including a loss of over 20 percent of the market's value on a single day. Figure 7.2(a) shows the percent frequency histogram of the percentage returns for the entire year 1987 for the population of all 1,815 stocks listed on the New York Stock Exchange. The mean of this population of percentage returns is −3.5 percent. Consider drawing a random sample of $n = 5$ stocks from the population of 1,815 stocks and calculating the mean return, $\bar{x}$, of the sampled stocks. If we use a computer, we can generate all the different samples of five stocks that can be obtained (there are trillions of such samples) and calculate the corresponding sample mean returns. For example, it can be verified that the five stocks in one sample gave 1987 percentage returns of −50 percent, −12 percent, −7 percent, 14 percent, and 30 percent. This implies that the sample mean return was

$$\bar{x} = \frac{(-50) + (-12) + (-7) + 14 + 30}{5} = \frac{-25}{5} = -5 \text{ percent}$$

A percent frequency histogram describing the population of all possible sample mean returns is given in Figure 7.2(b). Comparing Figures 7.2(a) and (b), we see that, although the histogram of individual stock returns and the histogram of sample mean returns are both bell-shaped and seem to be centered over the same mean of -3.5 percent, the histogram of sample mean returns looks considerably less spread out than the histogram of individual returns. In terms of investing in the stock market, a sample of five stocks is a portfolio of five stocks, and the sample mean return is the percentage return that an investor would realize if he or she invested equal amounts of money in the stocks in the portfolio. Therefore, Figure 7.2 illustrates that the variation among portfolio returns is considerably less than the variation among individual stock returns. Of course, one would probably not invest in the stock market by randomly selecting stocks. However, we have nevertheless illustrated an important conclusion reached by actual financial research: Careful investment diversification can reduce investment return variability and thus reduce the investor's exposure to risk.

Thus far we have considered a game show example and a stock return example. Together, these examples illustrate several important facts about randomly selecting a sample of n individual measurements from a population of individual measurements having mean μ and standard deviation σ. Specifically, it can be shown that

1. **If the population of individual measurements is normally distributed, then the population of all possible sample means is also normally distributed.** This is illustrated in Figures 7.2(a) and (b): Because the population of individual stock returns is (approximately) normally distributed, the population of all possible sample mean returns is also (approximately) normally distributed.

2. **Even if the population of individual measurements is not normally distributed, there are circumstances when the population of all possible sample means is approximately normally distributed.** This result is based on a theorem called the **Central Limit Theorem** and is discussed more fully in the next subsection. For now, note that the result is intuitively illustrated in Figures 7.1(a) and (b): Although the population of six individual grand prizes does not have a normal distribution (it has a uniform distribution), the population of 15 sample mean grand prizes has a distribution that looks somewhat like a normal distribution.

3. **The mean, $\mu_{\bar{x}}$, of the population of all possible sample means equals μ, the mean of the population of individual measurements.** This is illustrated in both Figures 7.1 and 7.2. That is, in each figure the distribution of individual population measurements and the distribution of all possible sample means are centered over the same mean μ. Note that μ equals 35 thousand dollars in Figure 7.1. In Figure 7.2 μ equals -3.5 percent.

4. **The standard deviation, $\sigma_{\bar{x}}$, of the population of all possible sample means is less than σ, the standard deviation of the population of individual measurements.** This is also illustrated in both Figures 7.1 and 7.2. That is, in each figure the distribution of all possible sample means is less spread out than the distribution of individual population measurements. Intuitively, $\sigma_{\bar{x}}$ is smaller than σ because each possible sample mean is an average of n measurements. Thus, **each sample mean *averages out* high and low sample measurements and can be expected to be closer to the population mean μ than many of the individual population measurements would be.** It follows that the different possible sample means are more closely clustered around μ than are the individual population measurements. (Note that we will see that $\sigma_{\bar{x}}$ is smaller than σ only if the sample size n is greater than 1.)

In the game show and stock return examples, the populations under consideration are small enough that we can calculate the population mean μ. Usually, however, the population under consideration is so large that it would be either impossible or impractical to calculate the population mean. That is, in most situations the population mean is unknown and our objective is to estimate this mean. To do this, we randomly select a sample of n observations from the population and use the sample mean $\bar{x}$ as the point estimate of the population mean. Furthermore, we can use theoretical properties about the probability distribution of the population of all possible sample means to make statistical inferences about the population mean. We have discussed some of these properties in the stock return case, and we will now explain how these properties relate to estimating the population mean.

To begin, unless we are extremely lucky, the sample mean $\bar{x}$ that we obtain will not equal the population mean μ. However, $\mu_{\bar{x}}$, the mean of the population of all possible sample means, is equal to μ. Therefore, we call the sample mean an **unbiased point estimate** of the population mean. This unbiasedness property says that, although most of the possible sample means that we might obtain are either above or below the population mean, there is no systematic tendency for the sample mean to overestimate or underestimate the population mean. That is, although we will randomly select only one sample, the unbiased sample mean is "correct on the average" in all possible samples.

In order to assess how close the different possible sample means are to the population mean, we consider $\sigma_{\bar{x}}$, the standard deviation of the population of all possible sample means. The following summary box gives a formula for $\sigma_{\bar{x}}$ and also summarizes other previously discussed facts about the probability distribution of the population of all possible sample means.

The Sampling Distribution of $\bar{x}$

Assume that the population from which we will randomly select a sample of n measurements has mean μ and standard deviation σ. Then, the population of all possible sample means

1   Has a normal distribution, if the sampled population has a normal distribution.

2   Has mean $\mu_{\bar{x}} = \mu$.

3   Has standard deviation $\sigma_{\bar{x}} = \dfrac{\sigma}{\sqrt{n}}$.

The formula for $\sigma_{\bar{x}}$ in (3) holds exactly if the sampled population is infinite. If the sampled population is finite, this formula holds approximately under conditions to be discussed later in this section.

Stated equivalently, the sampling distribution of $\bar{x}$ has mean $\mu_{\bar{x}} = \mu$, has standard deviation $\sigma_{\bar{x}} = \sigma/\sqrt{n}$ (if the sampled population is infinite), and is a normal distribution (if the sampled population has a normal distribution).

The third result in the summary box says that, if the sampled population is infinite, then

$$\sigma_{\bar{x}} = \frac{\sigma}{\sqrt{n}}$$

In words, $\sigma_{\bar{x}}$, the standard deviation of the population of all possible sample means, equals σ, the standard deviation of the sampled population, divided by the square root of the sample size n. Furthermore, in addition to showing that $\sigma_{\bar{x}}$ is smaller than σ (assuming that the sample size n is larger than 1), this formula for $\sigma_{\bar{x}}$ also says that $\sigma_{\bar{x}}$ decreases as n increases. That is, intuitively, as each possible sample averages more observations, the resulting different possible sample means will differ from each other by less and thus will become more closely clustered around the population mean. It follows that, if we take a larger sample, we are more likely to obtain a sample mean that is near the population mean.

We next use the car mileage case to illustrate the formula for $\sigma_{\bar{x}}$. In this and several other examples we will assume that, although we do not know the true value of the population mean μ, we do know the true value of the population standard deviation σ. Here, knowledge of σ might be based on theory or history related to the population under consideration. For example, because the automaker has been working to improve gas mileages, we cannot assume that we know the true value of the population mean mileage μ for the new midsize model. However, engineering data might indicate that the spread of individual car mileages for the automaker's midsize cars is the same from model to model and year to year. Therefore, if the mileages for previous models had a standard deviation equal to .8 mpg., it might be reasonable to assume that the standard deviation of the mileages for the new model will also equal .8 mpg. Such an assumption would, of course, be questionable, and in most real-world situations there would probably not be an actual basis for knowing σ. However, assuming that σ is known will help us to illustrate sampling distributions, and in later chapters we will see what to do when σ is unknown.

EXAMPLE 7.2 The Car Mileage Case

Part 1: Basic concepts   Consider the population of the mileages of all cars of the new mid-size model type. If we define this population to be the population of the mileages of all cars that could potentially be produced, then, since the automaker could always make "one more car," the population should be considered to be infinite. If we further assume that this infinite population is normally distributed with mean μ and standard deviation $\sigma = .8$ (see Figure 7.3(a)), and if the automaker will randomly select a sample of n cars and test them as prescribed by the EPA, then the population of all possible sample means is normally distributed with mean $\mu_{\bar{x}} = \mu$ and standard deviation $\sigma_{\bar{x}} = \sigma/\sqrt{n} = .8/\sqrt{n}$. In order to show that a larger sample is more likely to

FIGURE 7.3   **A Comparison of (1) the Population of All Individual Car Mileages, (2) the Sampling Distribution of the Sample Mean $\bar{x}$ When $n = 5$, and (3) the Sampling Distribution of the Sample Mean $\bar{x}$ When $n = 50$**

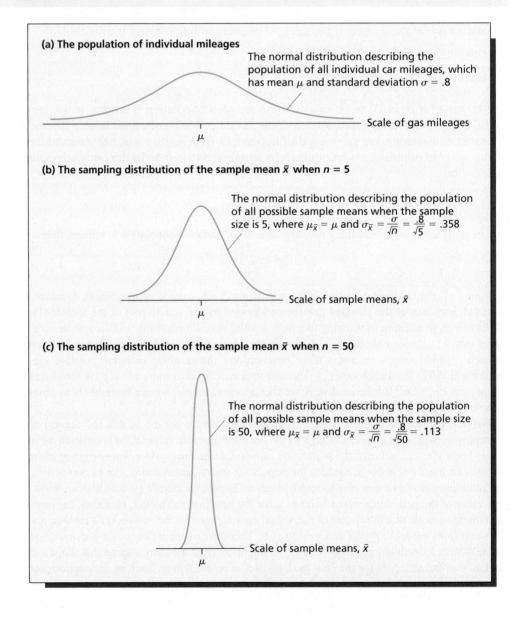

give a more accurate point estimate $\bar{x}$ of μ, compare taking a sample of size $n = 5$ with taking a sample of size $n = 50$. If $n = 5$, then

$$\sigma_{\bar{x}} = \frac{\sigma}{\sqrt{n}} = \frac{.8}{\sqrt{5}} = .358$$

and it follows (by the Empirical Rule) that 95.44 of all possible sample means are within plus or minus $2\sigma_{\bar{x}} = 2(.358) = .716$ mpg of the population mean μ. If $n = 50$, then

$$\sigma_{\bar{x}} = \frac{\sigma}{\sqrt{n}} = \frac{.8}{\sqrt{50}} = .113$$

and it follows that 95.44 of all possible sample means are within plus or minus $2\sigma_{\bar{x}} = 2(.113) = .226$ mpg of the population mean μ. Therefore, if $n = 50$, the different possible sample means that the automaker might obtain will be more closely clustered around μ than they will be if $n = 5$ (see Figures 7.3(b) and (c)). This implies that the larger sample of size $n = 50$ is more likely to give a sample mean $\bar{x}$ that is near μ.

Part 2: Statistical inference   Recall from Chapter 3 that the automaker has randomly selected a sample of $n = 50$ mileages, which has mean $\bar{x} = 31.56$. We now ask the following question: If the population mean mileage μ exactly equals 31 mpg (the minimum standard for the tax credit), what is the probability of observing a sample mean mileage that is greater than or equal to 31.56 mpg? To find this probability, recall from Chapter 2 that a histogram of the 50 mileages indicates that the population of all individual mileages is normally distributed. Assuming that the population standard deviation σ is known to equal .8 mpg, it follows that the sampling distribution of the sample mean $\bar{x}$ is a normal distribution, with mean $\mu_{\bar{x}} = \mu$ and standard deviation $\sigma_{\bar{x}} = \sigma/\sqrt{n} = .8/\sqrt{50} = .113$. Therefore,

$$P(\bar{x} \geq 31.56 \quad \text{if} \quad \mu = 31) = P\left(z \geq \frac{31.56 - \mu_{\bar{x}}}{\sigma_{\bar{x}}}\right) = P\left(z \geq \frac{31.56 - 31}{.113}\right)$$
$$= P(z \geq 4.96)$$

To find $P(z \geq 4.96)$, notice that the largest z value given in Table A.3 (page 641) is 3.99, which gives a right-hand tail area of .00003. Therefore, since $P(z \geq 3.99) = .00003$, it follows that $P(z \geq 4.96)$ is less than .00003 (see Figure 7.4). The fact that this probability is less than .00003

FIGURE 7.4   **The Probability That $\bar{x} \geq 31.56$ When $\mu = 31$ in the Car Mileage Case**

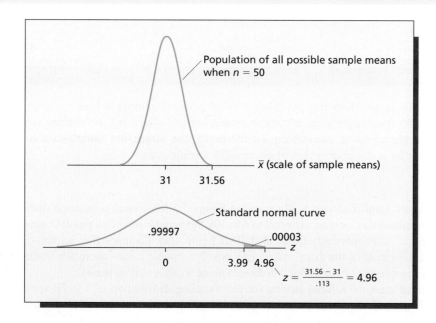

says that, if μ equals 31, then fewer than 3 in 100,000 of all possible sample means are at least as large as the sample mean $\bar{x} = 31.56$ that we have actually observed. Therefore, if we are to believe that μ equals 31, then we must believe that we have observed a sample mean that can be described as a smaller than 3 in 100,000 chance. Since it is extremely difficult to believe that such a small chance would occur, we have extremely strong evidence that μ does not equal 31 and that μ is, in fact, larger than 31. This evidence would probably convince the federal government that the midsize model's mean mileage μ exceeds 31 mpg and thus that the midsize model deserves the tax credit.

To conclude this subsection, it is important to make two comments. First, the formula $\sigma_{\bar{x}} = \sigma/\sqrt{n}$ follows, in theory, from the formula for $\sigma_{\bar{x}}^2$, the variance of the population of all possible sample means. The formula for $\sigma_{\bar{x}}^2$ is $\sigma_{\bar{x}}^2 = \sigma^2/n$. Second, in addition to holding exactly if the sampled population is infinite, **the formula $\sigma_{\bar{x}} = \sigma/\sqrt{n}$ holds approximately if the sampled population is finite and much larger than (say, at least 20 times) the size of the sample.** For example, if we define the population of mileages of all new midsize cars to be the population of mileages of all cars that will actually be produced this year, then the population is finite. However, the population would be very large—certainly at least as large as 20 times any reasonable sample size. For example, if the automaker produces 100,000 new midsize cars this year, and if we randomly select a sample of $n = 50$ of these cars, then the population size of 100,000 is larger than 20 times the sample size of 50 (which is 1,000). It follows that, even though the population is finite and thus the formula $\sigma_{\bar{x}} = \sigma/\sqrt{n}$ would not hold exactly, this formula would hold approximately. The exact formula for $\sigma_{\bar{x}}$ when the sampled population is finite is given in a technical note at the end of this section. It is important to use this exact formula if the sampled population is finite and less than 20 times the size of the sample. However, with the exception of the population considered in the technical note, all of the remaining populations to be considered in this book will be either infinite or finite and at least 20 times the size of the sample. Therefore, it will be appropriate to use the formula $\sigma_{\bar{x}} = \sigma/\sqrt{n}$.

Sampling a nonnormally distributed population: the Central Limit Theorem   We now consider what can be said about the sampling distribution of $\bar{x}$ when the sampled population is not normally distributed. First, as previously stated, the fact that $\mu_{\bar{x}} = \mu$ is still true. Second, as also previously stated, the formula $\sigma_{\bar{x}} = \sigma/\sqrt{n}$ is exactly correct if the sampled population is infinite and is approximately correct if the sampled population is finite and much larger than (say, at least 20 times as large as) the sample size. Third, an extremely important result called the **Central Limit Theorem** tells us that, **if the sample size n is large, then the sampling distribution of $\bar{x}$ is approximately normal, even if the sampled population is not normally distributed.**

The Central Limit Theorem

If the sample size n is sufficiently large, then the population of all possible sample means is approximately normally distributed (with mean $\mu_{\bar{x}} = \mu$ and standard deviation $\sigma_{\bar{x}} = \sigma/\sqrt{n}$), no matter what probability distribution describes the sampled population. Furthermore, the larger the sample size n is, the more nearly normally distributed is the population of all possible sample means.

CHAPTERS
7 AND 8

The Central Limit Theorem is illustrated in Figure 7.5 for several population shapes. Notice that as the sample size increases (from 2 to 6 to 30), the populations of all possible sample means become more nearly normally distributed. This figure also illustrates that, as the sample size increases, the spread of the distribution of all possible sample means decreases (remember that this spread is measured by $\sigma_{\bar{x}}$, which decreases as the sample size increases).

How large must the sample size be for the sampling distribution of $\bar{x}$ to be approximately normal? In general, the more skewed the probability distribution of the sampled population, the

FIGURE 7.5   **The Central Limit Theorem Says That the Larger the Sample Size Is, the More Nearly Normally Distributed Is the Population of All Possible Sample Means**

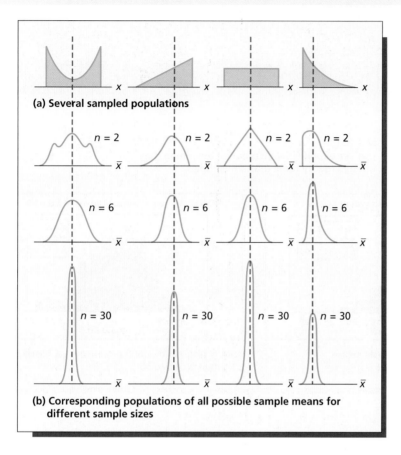

(a) Several sampled populations

(b) Corresponding populations of all possible sample means for different sample sizes

larger the sample size must be for the population of all possible sample means to be approximately normally distributed. For some sampled populations, particularly those described by symmetric distributions, the population of all possible sample means is approximately normally distributed for a fairly small sample size. In addition, studies indicate that, **if the sample size is at least 30, then for most sampled populations the population of all possible sample means is approximately normally distributed.** In this book, whenever the sample size n is at least 30, we will assume that the sampling distribution of $\bar{x}$ is approximately a normal distribution. Of course, if the sampled population is exactly normally distributed, the sampling distribution of $\bar{x}$ is exactly normal for any sample size.

We can see the shapes of sampling distributions such as those illustrated in Figure 7.5 by using computer simulation. Specifically, for a population having a particular probability distribution, we can have the computer draw a given number of samples of n observations, compute the mean of each sample, and arrange the sample means into a histogram. To illustrate this, consider Figure 7.6(a), which shows the exponential distribution describing the hospital emergency room interarrival times discussed in Example 6.11 (page 271). Figure 7.6(b) gives the results of a simulation in which MINITAB randomly selected 1,000 samples of five interarrival times from this exponential distribution, calculated the mean of each sample, and arranged the 1,000 sample means into a histogram. Figure 7.6(c) gives the results of a simulation in which MINITAB randomly selected 1,000 samples of 30 interarrival times from the exponential distribution, calculated the mean of each sample, and arranged the 1,000 sample means into a histogram. Note that, whereas the histogram in Figure 7.6(b) is somewhat skewed to the right, the histogram in Figure 7.6(c) appears approximately bell-shaped. Therefore, we might conclude that when we randomly select a sample of n observations from an exponential distribution, the sampling distribution of the sample mean is somewhat skewed to the right when $n = 5$ and is approximately normal when $n = 30$.

FIGURE 7.6   Simulating the Sampling Distribution of the Sample Mean When Sampling from an Exponential Distribution

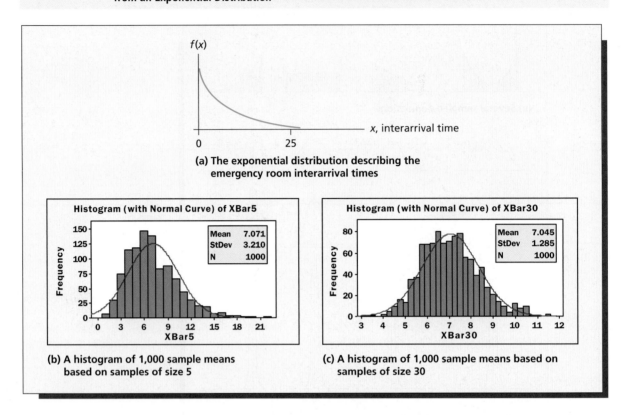

(a) The exponential distribution describing the emergency room interarrival times

Histogram (with Normal Curve) of XBar5

Mean	7.071
StDev	3.210
N	1000

(b) A histogram of 1,000 sample means based on samples of size 5

Histogram (with Normal Curve) of XBar30

Mean	7.045
StDev	1.285
N	1000

(c) A histogram of 1,000 sample means based on samples of size 30

EXAMPLE 7.3 The Payment Time Case

Recall that a management consulting firm has installed a new computer-based billing system in a Hamilton, Ohio, trucking company. Because of the previously discussed advantages of the new billing system, and because the trucking company's clients are receptive to using this system, the management consulting firm believes that the new system will reduce the mean bill payment time by more than 50 percent. The mean payment time using the old billing system was approximately equal to, but no less than, 39 days. Therefore, if μ denotes the new mean payment time, the consulting firm believes that μ will be less than 19.5 days. To assess whether μ is less than 19.5 days, the consulting firm has randomly selected a sample of $n = 65$ invoices processed using the new billing system and has determined the payment times for these invoices. The mean of the 65 payment times is $\bar{x} = 18.1077$ days, which is less than 19.5 days. Therefore, we ask the following question: If the population mean payment time is 19.5 days, what is the probability of observing a sample mean payment time that is less than or equal to 18.1077 days? To find this probability, recall from Chapter 2 that a histogram of the 65 payment times indicates that the population of all payment times is skewed with a tail to the right. However, the Central Limit Theorem tells us that, because the sample size $n = 65$ is large, the sampling distribution of $\bar{x}$ is approximately a normal distribution with mean $\mu_{\bar{x}} = \mu$ and standard deviation $\sigma_{\bar{x}} = \sigma/\sqrt{n}$. Assuming that the population standard deviation σ is known to be 4.2 days, $\sigma_{\bar{x}}$ equals $4.2/\sqrt{65} = .5209$. It follows that

$$P(\bar{x} \leq 18.1077 \text{ if } \mu = 19.5) = P\left(z \leq \frac{18.1077 - 19.5}{.5209}\right)$$

$$= P(z \leq -2.67)$$

which is the area under the standard normal curve to the left of -2.67. The normal table tells us that this area equals .0038. This probability says that, if μ equals 19.5, then only .0038 of all possible sample means are at least as small as the sample mean $\bar{x} = 18.1077$ that we have actually observed. Therefore, if we are to believe that μ equals 19.5, we must believe that we have observed a sample mean that can be described as a 38 in 10,000 chance. It is very difficult to believe that such a small chance would occur, so we have very strong evidence that μ does not equal 19.5 and is, in fact, less than 19.5. We conclude that the new billing system has reduced the mean bill payment time by more than 50 percent.

CHAPTERS
7 AND 8

Unbiasedness and minimum-variance estimates   Recall that a sample statistic is any descriptive measure of the sample measurements. For instance, the sample mean $\bar{x}$ is a statistic, and so are the sample median, the sample variance s^2, and the sample standard deviation s. Not only do different samples give different values of $\bar{x}$, different samples also give different values of the median, s^2, s, or any other statistic. It follows that, *before we draw the sample, any sample statistic is a random variable,* and

> The **sampling distribution of a sample statistic** is the probability distribution of the population of all possible values of the sample statistic.

In general, we wish to estimate a population parameter by using a sample statistic that is what we call an *unbiased point estimate* of the parameter.

> A sample statistic is an **unbiased point estimate** of a population parameter if the mean of the population of all possible values of the sample statistic equals the population parameter.

For example, we use the sample mean $\bar{x}$ as the point estimate of the population mean μ because $\bar{x}$ **is an unbiased point estimate of μ.** That is, $\mu_{\bar{x}} = \mu$. In words, the average of all the different possible sample means (that we could obtain from all the different possible samples) equals μ.

Although we want a sample statistic to be an unbiased point estimate of the population parameter of interest, we also want the statistic to have a small standard deviation (and variance). That is, we wish the different possible values of the sample statistic to be closely clustered around the population parameter. If this is the case, when we actually randomly select one sample and compute the sample statistic, its value is likely to be close to the value of the population parameter. Furthermore, some general results apply to estimating the mean μ of a normally distributed population. In this situation, it can be shown that both the sample mean and the sample median are unbiased point estimates of μ. In fact, there are many unbiased point estimates of μ. However, it can be shown that the variance of the population of all possible sample means is smaller than the variance of the population of all possible values of any other unbiased point estimate of μ. For this reason, **we call the sample mean a minimum-variance unbiased point estimate of μ.** When we use the sample mean as the point estimate of μ, we are more likely to obtain a point estimate close to μ than if we used any other unbiased sample statistic as the point estimate of μ. This is one reason why we use the sample mean as the point estimate of the population mean.

We next consider estimating the population variance σ^2. It can be shown that if the sampled population is infinite, then s^2 **is an unbiased point estimate of σ^2.** That is, the average of all the different possible sample variances that we could obtain (from all the different possible samples) is equal to σ^2. This is why we use a divisor equal to $n - 1$ rather than n when we estimate σ^2. It can be shown that, if we used n as the divisor when estimating σ^2, we would not obtain an unbiased point estimate of σ^2. When the population is finite, s^2 may be regarded as an approximately unbiased estimate of σ^2 as long as the population is fairly large (which is usually the case).

It would seem logical to think that, because s^2 is an unbiased point estimate of σ^2, s should be an unbiased point estimate of σ. This seems plausible, but it is not the case. There is no easy way to calculate an unbiased point estimate of σ. Because of this, the usual practice is to use s as the point estimate of σ (even though it is not an unbiased estimate).

This ends our discussion of the theory of point estimation. It suffices to say that in this book we estimate population parameters by using sample statistics that statisticians generally agree are best. Whenever possible, these sample statistics are unbiased point estimates and have small variances.

Technical note: If we randomly select a sample of size n without replacement from a finite population of size N, then it can be shown that $\sigma_{\bar{x}} = (\sigma/\sqrt{n})\sqrt{(N - n)/(N - 1)}$, where the quantity $\sqrt{(N - n)/(N - 1)}$ is called the *finite population multiplier.* If the size of the sampled population is at least 20 times the size of the sample (that is, if $N \geq 20n$), then the finite population multiplier is approximately equal to 1, and $\sigma_{\bar{x}}$ approximately equals $\sigma/\sqrt{n}$. However, if the population size N is smaller than 20 times the size of the sample, then the finite population multiplier is substantially less than 1, and we must include this multiplier in the calculation of $\sigma_{\bar{x}}$. For instance, in our initial game show example, where the standard deviation σ of the population of $N = 6$ grand prizes can be calculated to be 17.078, and where $N = 6$ is only three times the sample size $n = 2$, it follows that

$$\sigma_{\bar{x}} = \frac{\sigma}{\sqrt{n}}\sqrt{\frac{N-n}{N-1}} = \left(\frac{17.078}{\sqrt{2}}\right)\sqrt{\frac{6-2}{6-1}} = 12.076(.8944) = 10.8$$

Exercises for Section 7.1

CONCEPTS

7.1   Suppose that we will randomly select a sample of four measurements from a larger population of measurements. The sampling distribution of the sample mean $\bar{x}$ is the probability distribution of a population. In your own words, describe the units in this population.

7.2   Suppose that we will randomly select a sample of n measurements from a normally distributed population of measurements having mean μ and standard deviation σ. If we consider the sampling distribution of $\bar{x}$ (that is, if we consider the population of all possible sample means):
   a   Describe the shape of the population of all possible sample means.
   b   Write formulas that express the central tendency and the variability of the population of all possible sample means. Explain what these formulas say in your own words.

7.3   Explain how the central tendency of the population of all possible sample means compares to the central tendency of the individual measurements in the population from which the sample will be taken.

7.4   Explain how the variability of the population of all possible sample means compares to the variability of the individual measurements in the population from which the sample will be taken. Assume here that the sample size is greater than 1. Intuitively explain why this is true.

7.5   What does the Central Limit Theorem tell us about the sampling distribution of the sample mean?

7.6   In your own words, explain each of the following terms:
   a   Unbiased point estimate.   **b**   Minimum-variance unbiased point estimate.

METHODS AND APPLICATIONS

7.7   Suppose that we will take a random sample of size n from a population having mean μ and standard deviation σ. For each of the following situations, find the mean, variance, and standard deviation of the sampling distribution of the sample mean $\bar{x}$:
   a $\mu = 10$, $\sigma = 2$, $n = 25$ **c** $\mu = 3$, $\sigma = .1$, $n = 4$
   b $\mu = 500$, $\sigma = .5$, $n = 100$ **d** $\mu = 100$, $\sigma = 1$, $n = 1,600$

7.8   For each situation in Exercise 7.7, find an interval that contains (approximately or exactly) 99.73 percent of all the possible sample means. In which cases must we assume that the population is normally distributed? Why?

7.9   Suppose that we will randomly select a sample of 64 measurements from a population having a mean equal to 20 and a standard deviation equal to 4.
   a   Describe the shape of the sampling distribution of the sample mean $\bar{x}$. Do we need to make any assumptions about the shape of the population? Why or why not?
   b   Find the mean and the standard deviation of the sampling distribution of the sample mean $\bar{x}$.
   c   Calculate the probability that we will obtain a sample mean greater than 21; that is, calculate $P(\bar{x} > 21)$. Hint: Find the z value corresponding to 21 by using $\mu_{\bar{x}}$ and $\sigma_{\bar{x}}$ because we wish to calculate a probability about $\bar{x}$. Then sketch the sampling distribution and the probability.
   d   Calculate the probability that we will obtain a sample mean less than 19.385; that is, calculate $P(\bar{x} < 19.385)$.

7.10   Suppose that the percentage returns for a given year for all stocks listed on the New York Stock Exchange are approximately normally distributed with a mean of 12.4 percent and a standard deviation of 20.6 percent. Consider drawing a random sample of $n = 5$ stocks from the population of all stocks and calculating the mean return, $\bar{x}$, of the sampled stocks. Find the mean and the standard deviation of the sampling distribution of $\bar{x}$, and find an interval containing 95.44 percent of all possible sample mean returns.

7.11 THE BANK CUSTOMER WAITING TIME CASE ● WaitTime

Recall that the bank manager wants to show that the new system reduces typical customer waiting times to less than six minutes. One way to do this is to demonstrate that the mean of the population of all customer waiting times is less than 6. Letting this mean be μ, in this exercise we wish to investigate whether the sample of 100 waiting times provides evidence to support the claim that μ is less than 6.

For the sake of argument, we will begin by assuming that μ equals 6, and we will then attempt to use the sample to contradict this assumption in favor of the conclusion that μ is less than 6. Recall that the mean of the sample of 100 waiting times is $\bar{x} = 5.46$ and assume that σ, the standard deviation of the population of all customer waiting times, is known to be 2.47.

a Consider the population of all possible sample means obtained from random samples of 100 waiting times. What is the shape of this population of sample means? That is, what is the shape of the sampling distribution of $\bar{x}$? Why is this true?

b Find the mean and standard deviation of the population of all possible sample means when we assume that μ equals 6.

c The sample mean that we have actually observed is $\bar{x} = 5.46$. Assuming that μ equals 6, find the probability of observing a sample mean that is less than or equal to $\bar{x} = 5.46$.

d If μ equals 6, what percentage of all possible sample means are less than or equal to 5.46? Since we have actually observed a sample mean of $\bar{x} = 5.46$, is it more reasonable to believe that (1) μ equals 6 and we have observed one of the sample means that is less than or equal to 5.46 when μ equals 6, or (2) that we have observed a sample mean less than or equal to 5.46 because μ is less than 6? Explain. What do you conclude about whether the new system has reduced the typical customer waiting time to less than six minutes?

7.12 THE VIDEO GAME SATISFACTION RATING CASE ● VideoGame

Recall that a customer is considered to be very satisfied with his or her XYZ Box video game system if the customer's composite score on the survey instrument is at least 42. One way to show that customers are typically very satisfied is to show that the mean of the population of all satisfaction ratings is at least 42. Letting this mean be μ, in this exercise we wish to investigate whether the sample of 65 satisfaction ratings provides evidence to support the claim that μ exceeds 42 (and, therefore, is at least 42).

For the sake of argument, we begin by assuming that μ equals 42, and we then attempt to use the sample to contradict this assumption in favor of the conclusion that μ exceeds 42. Recall that the mean of the sample of 65 satisfaction ratings is $\bar{x} = 42.95$, and assume that σ, the standard deviation of the population of all satisfaction ratings, is known to be 2.64.

a Consider the sampling distribution of $\bar{x}$ for random samples of 65 customer satisfaction ratings. Use the properties of this sampling distribution to find the probability of observing a sample mean greater than or equal to 42.95 when we assume that μ equals 42.

b If μ equals 42, what percentage of all possible sample means are greater than or equal to 42.95? Since we have actually observed a sample mean of $\bar{x} = 42.95$, is it more reasonable to believe that (1) μ equals 42 and we have observed a sample mean that is greater than or equal to 42.95 when μ equals 42, or (2) that we have observed a sample mean that is greater than or equal to 42.95 because μ is greater than 42? Explain. What do you conclude about whether customers are typically very satisfied with the XYZ Box video game system?

7.13 In an article in the *Journal of Management*, Joseph Martocchio studied and estimated the costs of employee absences. Based on a sample of 176 blue-collar workers, Martocchio estimated that the mean amount of paid time lost during a three-month period was 1.4 days per employee with a standard deviation of 1.3 days. Martocchio also estimated that the mean amount of unpaid time lost during a three-month period was 1.0 day per employee with a standard deviation of 1.8 days.

Suppose we randomly select a sample of 100 blue-collar workers. Based on Martocchio's estimates:

a What is the probability that the average amount of paid time lost during a three-month period for the 100 blue-collar workers will exceed 1.5 days?

b What is the probability that the average amount of unpaid time lost during a three-month period for the 100 blue-collar workers will exceed 1.5 days?

c Suppose we randomly select a sample of 100 blue-collar workers, and suppose the sample mean amount of unpaid time lost during a three-month period actually exceeds 1.5 days. Would it be reasonable to conclude that the mean amount of unpaid time lost has increased above the previously estimated 1.0 days? Explain.

7.14 When a pizza restaurant's delivery process is operating effectively, pizzas are delivered in an average of 45 minutes with a standard deviation of 6 minutes. To monitor its delivery process, the restaurant randomly selects five pizzas each night and records their delivery times.

   a For the sake of argument, assume that the population of all delivery times on a given evening is normally distributed with a mean of $\mu = 45$ minutes and a standard deviation of $\sigma = 6$ minutes. (That is, we assume that the delivery process is operating effectively.)

   (1) Describe the shape of the population of all possible sample means. How do you know what the shape is?

   (2) Find the mean of the population of all possible sample means.

   (3) Find the standard deviation of the population of all possible sample means.

   (4) Calculate an interval containing 99.73 percent of all possible sample means.

   b Suppose that the mean of the five sampled delivery times on a particular evening is $\bar{x} = 55$ minutes. Using the interval that you calculated in $a(4)$, what would you conclude about whether the restaurant's delivery process is operating effectively? Why?

7.2 The Sampling Distribution of the Sample Proportion ● ● ●

A food processing company markets a soft cheese spread that is sold in a plastic container with an "easy pour" spout. Although this spout works extremely well and is popular with consumers, it is expensive to produce. Because of the spout's high cost, the company has developed a new, less expensive spout. While the new, cheaper spout may alienate some purchasers, a company study shows that its introduction will increase profits if fewer than 10 percent of the cheese spread's current purchasers are lost. That is, if we let p be the true proportion of all current purchasers who would stop buying the cheese spread if the new spout were used, profits will increase as long as p is less than .10.

Suppose that (after trying the new spout) 63 of 1,000 randomly selected purchasers say that they would stop buying the cheese spread if the new spout were used. The point estimate of the population proportion p is the sample proportion $\hat{p} = 63/1,000 = .063$. This sample proportion says that we estimate that 6.3 percent of all current purchasers would stop buying the cheese spread if the new spout were used. Since $\hat{p}$ equals .063, we have some evidence that the population proportion p is less than .10. In order to determine the strength of this evidence, we need to consider the sampling distribution of $\hat{p}$. In general, assume that we will randomly select a sample of n units from a population, and assume that a proportion p of all the units in the population fall into a particular category (for instance, the category of consumers who would stop buying the cheese spread). Before we actually select the sample, there are many different samples of n units that we might potentially obtain. The number of units that fall into the category in question will vary from sample to sample, so the sample proportion of units falling into the category will also vary from sample to sample. Therefore, we might potentially obtain many different sample proportions. It follows that, before we draw the sample, the sample proportion $\hat{p}$ is a random variable. In the following box we give the properties of the probability distribution of this random variable, which is called **the sampling distribution of the sample proportion $\hat{p}$.**

The Sampling Distribution of the Sample Proportion $\hat{p}$

The population of all possible sample proportions

1 Approximately has a normal distribution, if the sample size n is large.

2 Has mean $\mu_{\hat{p}} = p$.

3 Has standard deviation $\sigma_{\hat{p}} = \sqrt{\dfrac{p(1 - p)}{n}}$.

Stated equivalently, the sampling distribution of $\hat{p}$ has mean $\mu_{\hat{p}} = p$, has standard deviation $\sigma_{\hat{p}} = \sqrt{p(1 - p)/n}$, and is approximately a normal distribution (if the sample size n is large).

Property 1 in the box says that, if n is large, then the population of all possible sample proportions approximately has a normal distribution. Here, it can be shown that **n should be considered large if both np and $n(1 - p)$ are at least 5.**[1] Property 2, which says that $\mu_{\hat{p}} = p$, is valid for any sample size and tells us that $\hat{p}$ is an unbiased estimate of p. That is, although the sample proportion $\hat{p}$ that we calculate probably does not equal p, the average of all the different sample proportions that we could have calculated (from all the different possible samples) is equal to p. Property 3, which says that

$$\sigma_{\hat{p}} = \sqrt{\frac{p(1 - p)}{n}}$$

is exactly correct if the sampled population is infinite and is approximately correct if the sampled population is finite and much larger than (say, at least 20 times as large as) the sample size. Property 3 tells us that the standard deviation of the population of all possible sample proportions decreases as the sample size increases. That is, the larger n is, the more closely clustered are all the different sample proportions around the true population proportion. Finally, note that the formula for $\sigma_{\hat{p}}$ follows, in theory, from the formula for $\sigma_{\hat{p}}^2$, the variance of the population of all possible sample proportions. The formula for $\sigma_{\hat{p}}^2$ is $\sigma_{\hat{p}}^2 = p(1 - p)/n$.

EXAMPLE 7.4 The Cheese Spread Case

In the cheese spread situation, the food processing company must decide whether p, the proportion of all current purchasers who would stop buying the cheese spread if the new spout were used, is less than .10. In order to do this, remember that when 1,000 purchasers of the cheese spread are randomly selected, 63 of these purchasers say they would stop buying the cheese spread if the new spout were used. Noting that the sample proportion $\hat{p} = .063$ is less than .10, we ask the following question. If the true population proportion is .10, what is the probability of observing a sample proportion that is less than or equal to .063?

If p equals .10, we can assume that the sampling distribution of $\hat{p}$ is approximately a normal distribution, because both $np = 1,000(.10) = 100$ and $n(1 - p) = 1,000(1 - .10) = 900$ are at least 5. Furthermore, the mean and standard deviation of the sampling distribution of $\hat{p}$ are $\mu_{\hat{p}} = p = .10$ and

$$\sigma_{\hat{p}} = \sqrt{\frac{p(1 - p)}{n}} = \sqrt{\frac{(.10)(.90)}{1,000}} = .0094868$$

Therefore,

$$P(\hat{p} \leq .063 \text{ if } p = .10) = P\left(z \leq \frac{.063 - \mu_{\hat{p}}}{\sigma_{\hat{p}}}\right) = P\left(z \leq \frac{.063 - .10}{.0094868}\right)$$

$$= P(z \leq -3.90)$$

which is the area under the standard normal curve to the left of -3.90. The normal table tells us that this area equals .00005. This probability says that, if p equals .10, then only 5 in 100,000 of all possible sample proportions are at least as small as the sample proportion $\hat{p} = .063$ that we have actually observed. That is, if we are to believe that p equals .10, we must believe that we have observed a sample proportion that can be described as a 5 in 100,000 chance. It follows that we have extremely strong evidence that p does not equal .10 and is, in fact, less than .10. In other words, we have extremely strong evidence that fewer than 10 percent of current purchasers would stop buying the cheese spread if the new spout were used. It seems that introducing the new spout will be profitable.

---

[1]Some statisticians suggest using the more conservative rule that both np and $n(1 - p)$ must be at least 10.

Exercises for Section 7.2

CONCEPTS

connect™

7.15 What population is described by the sampling distribution of $\hat{p}$?

7.16 Suppose that we will randomly select a sample of n units from a population and that we will compute the sample proportion $\hat{p}$ of these units that fall into a category of interest. If we consider the sampling distribution of $\hat{p}$:

a If the sample size n is large, the sampling distribution of $\hat{p}$ is approximately a normal distribution. What condition must be satisfied to guarantee that n is large enough to say that $\hat{p}$ is normally distributed?

b Write formulas that express the central tendency and variability of the population of all possible sample proportions. Explain what each of these formulas means in your own words.

7.17 Describe the effect of increasing the sample size on the population of all possible sample proportions.

METHODS AND APPLICATIONS

7.18 In each of the following cases, determine whether the sample size n is large enough to say that the sampling distribution of $\hat{p}$ is a normal distribution:

a $p = .4$, $n = 100$ **d** $p = .8$, $n = 400$
b $p = .1$, $n = 10$ **e** $p = .98$, $n = 1{,}000$
c $p = .1$, $n = 50$ **f** $p = .99$, $n = 400$

7.19 In each of the following cases, find the mean, variance, and standard deviation of the sampling distribution of the sample proportion $\hat{p}$:

a $p = .5$, $n = 250$ **c** $p = .8$, $n = 400$
b $p = .1$, $n = 100$ **d** $p = .98$, $n = 1{,}000$

7.20 For each situation in Exercise 7.19, find an interval that contains approximately 95.44 percent of all the possible sample proportions.

7.21 Suppose that we will randomly select a sample of $n = 100$ units from a population and that we will compute the sample proportion $\hat{p}$ of these units that fall into a category of interest. If the true population proportion p equals .9:

a Describe the shape of the sampling distribution of $\hat{p}$. Why can we validly describe the shape?

b Find the mean and the standard deviation of the sampling distribution of $\hat{p}$.

c Calculate the following probabilities about the sample proportion $\hat{p}$. In each case sketch the sampling distribution and the probability.

(1) $P(\hat{p} \geq .96)$
(2) $P(.855 \leq \hat{p} \leq .945)$
(3) $P(\hat{p} \leq .915)$

7.22 In the July 29, 2001, issue of *The Journal News* (Hamilton, Ohio) Lynn Elber of the Associated Press reported on a study conducted by the Kaiser Family Foundation regarding parents' use of television set V-chips for controlling their children's TV viewing. The study asked parents who own TVs equipped with V-chips whether they use the devices to block programs with objectionable content.

a Suppose that we wish to use the study results to justify the claim that fewer than 20 percent of parents who own TV sets with V-chips use the devices. The study actually found that 17 percent of the parents polled used their V-chips.[2] If the poll surveyed 1,000 parents, and if for the sake of argument we assume that 20 percent of parents who own V-chips actually use the devices (that is, $p = .2$), calculate the probability of observing a sample proportion of .17 or less. That is, calculate $P(\hat{p} \leq .17)$.

b Based on the probability you computed in part a, would you conclude that fewer than 20 percent of parents who own TV sets equipped with V-chips actually use the devices? Explain.

7.23 On February 8, 2002, the Gallup Organization released the results of a poll concerning American attitudes toward the 19th Winter Olympic Games in Salt Lake City, Utah. The poll results were based on telephone interviews with a randomly selected national sample of 1,011 adults, 18 years and older, conducted February 4–6, 2002.

a Suppose we wish to use the poll's results to justify the claim that more than 30 percent of Americans (18 years or older) say that figure skating is their favorite Winter Olympic event. The poll actually found that 32 percent of respondents reported that figure skating was their favorite event.[3] If, for the sake of argument, we assume that 30 percent of Americans (18 years

---

[2]Source: L. Elber, "Study: Parents Make Scant Use of TV V-Chip," *The Journal News* (Hamilton, Ohio), July 29, 2001, p. c5.
[3]Source: http://www.gallup.com/poll/releases/, The Gallup Organization, February 13, 2002.

or older) say figure skating is their favorite event (that is, $p = .3$), calculate the probability of observing a sample proportion of .32 or more; that is, calculate $P(\hat{p} \geq .32)$.

b Based on the probability you computed in *a*, would you conclude that more than 30 percent of Americans (18 years or older) say that figure skating is their favorite Winter Olympic event?

7.24 *Quality Progress*, February 2005, reports on improvements in customer satisfaction and loyalty made by Bank of America. A key measure of customer satisfaction is the response (on a scale from 1 to 10) to the question: "Considering all the business you do with Bank of America, what is your overall satisfaction with Bank of America?" Here, a response of 9 or 10 represents "customer delight."

a Historically, the percentage of Bank of America customers expressing customer delight has been 48 percent. Suppose that we wish to use the results of a survey of 350 Bank of America customers to justify the claim that more than 48 percent of all current Bank of America customers would express customer delight. The survey finds that 189 of 350 randomly selected Bank of America customers express customer delight. If, for the sake of argument, we assume that the proportion of customer delight is $p = .48$, calculate the probability of observing a sample proportion greater than or equal to $189/350 = .54$. That is, calculate $P(\hat{p} \geq .54)$.

b Based on the probability you computed in part *a*, would you conclude that more than 48 percent of current Bank of America customers express customer delight? Explain.

7.25 Again consider the survey of 350 Bank of America customers discussed in Exercise 7.24, and assume that 48 percent of Bank of America customers would currently express customer delight. That is, assume $p = .48$. Find:

a The probability that the sample proportion obtained from the sample of 350 Bank of America customers would be within three percentage points of the population proportion. That is, find $P(.45 \leq \hat{p} \leq .51)$.

b The probability that the sample proportion obtained from the sample of 350 Bank of America customers would be within six percentage points of the population proportion. That is, find $P(.42 \leq \hat{p} \leq .54)$.

7.26 Based on your results in Exercise 7.25, would it be reasonable to state that the survey's "margin of error" is ± 3 percentage points? ± 6 percentage points? Explain.

7.27 A special advertising section in the July 20, 1998, issue of *Fortune* magazine discusses outsourcing. According to the article, outsourcing is "the assignment of critical, but noncore, business functions to outside specialists." This allows a company to immediately bring operations up to best-in-world standards while avoiding huge capital investments. The article includes the results of a poll of business executives addressing the benefits of outsourcing.

a Suppose we wish to use the poll's results to justify the claim that fewer than 26 percent of business executives feel that the benefits of outsourcing are either "less or much less than expected." The poll actually found that 15 percent of the respondents felt that the benefits of outsourcing were either "less or much less than expected."[4] If 1,000 randomly selected business executives were polled, and if for the sake of argument, we assume that 20 percent of all business executives feel that the benefits of outsourcing are either less or much less than expected (that is, $p = .20$), calculate the probability of observing a sample proportion of .15 or less. That is, calculate $P(\hat{p} \leq .15)$.

b Based on the probability you computed in part *a*, would you conclude that fewer than 20 percent of business executives feel that the benefits of outsourcing are either "less or much less than expected"? Explain.

7.28 The July 20, 1998, issue of *Fortune* magazine reported the results of a survey on executive training that was conducted by the Association of Executive Search Consultants. The survey showed that 75 percent of 300 polled CEOs believe that companies should have "fast-track training programs" for developing managerial talent.[5]

a Suppose we wish to use the results of this survey to justify the claim that more than 70 percent of CEOs believe that companies should have fast-track training programs. Assuming that the 300 surveyed CEOs were randomly selected, and assuming, for the sake of argument, that 70 percent of CEOs believe that companies should have fast-track training programs (that is, $p = .70$), calculate the probability of observing a sample proportion of .75 or more. That is, calculate $P(\hat{p} \geq .75)$.

b Based on the probability you computed in part *a*, would you conclude that more than 70 percent of CEOs believe that companies should have fast-track training programs? Explain.

[4]Source: M. R. Ozanne and M. F. Corbette, "Outsourcing 98," *Fortune* (July 20, 1998), p. 510.
[5]Source: E. P. Gunn, "The Fast Track Is Where to Be, If You Can Find It," *Fortune* (July 20, 1998), p. 152.

Chapter Summary

A **sampling distribution** is the probability distribution that describes the population of all possible values of a sample statistic. In this chapter we studied the properties of two important sampling distributions—the sampling distribution of the sample mean, $\bar{x}$, and the sampling distribution of the sample proportion, $\hat{p}$.

Because different samples that can be randomly selected from a population give different sample means, there is a population of sample means corresponding to a particular sample size. The probability distribution describing the population of all possible sample means is called the **sampling distribution of the sample mean, $\bar{x}$.** We studied the properties of this sampling distribution when the sampled population is and is not normally distributed. We found that, when the sampled population has a normal distribution, then the sampling distribution of the sample mean is a normal distribution. Furthermore, the **Central Limit Theorem** tells us that, if the sampled population is not normally distributed, then the sampling distribution of the sample mean is approximately a normal distribution when the sample size is large (at least 30). We also saw that the mean of the sampling distribution

of $\bar{x}$ always equals the mean of the sampled population, and we presented formulas for the variance and the standard deviation of this sampling distribution. Finally, we explained that the sample mean is a **minimum-variance unbiased point estimate** of the mean of a normally distributed population.

We also studied the properties of the **sampling distribution of the sample proportion $\hat{p}$.** We found that, if the sample size is large, then this sampling distribution is approximately a normal distribution, and we gave a rule for determining whether the sample size is large. We found that the mean of the sampling distribution of $\hat{p}$ is the population proportion p, and we gave formulas for the variance and the standard deviation of this sampling distribution.

Finally, we demonstrated that knowing the properties of sampling distributions can help us make statistical inferences about population parameters. In fact, we will see that the properties of various sampling distributions provide the foundation for most of the techniques to be discussed in future chapters.

Glossary of Terms

Central Limit Theorem: A theorem telling us that when the sample size n is sufficiently large, then the population of all possible sample means is approximately normally distributed no matter what probability distribution describes the sampled population. (page 292)

minimum-variance unbiased point estimate: An unbiased point estimate of a population parameter having a variance that is smaller than the variance of any other unbiased point estimate of the parameter. (page 295)

sampling distribution of a sample statistic: The probability distribution of the population of all possible values of the sample statistic. (page 295)

sampling distribution of the sample mean $\bar{x}$: The probability distribution of the population of all possible sample means obtained from samples of a particular size n. (page 285)
    when a population is normally distributed (page 289)
    Central Limit Theorem (page 292)

sampling distribution of the sample proportion $\hat{p}$: The probability distribution of the population of all possible sample proportions obtained from samples of a particular size n. (page 298)

unbiased point estimate: A sample statistic is an unbiased point estimate of a population parameter if the mean of the population of all possible values of the sample statistic equals the population parameter. (page 295)

Important Formulas

The sampling distribution of the sample mean: pages 289 and 292

The sampling distribution of the sample proportion: page 298

Supplementary Exercises

connect

7.29 A chain of audio/video equipment discount stores employs 36 salespeople. Daily dollar sales for individual sellers employed by the chain have a normal distribution with a mean of $2,000 and a standard deviation equal to $300.

    a Suppose that the chain's management decides to implement an incentive program that awards a daily bonus to any salesperson who achieves daily sales over $2,150. Calculate the probability that an individual salesperson will earn the bonus on any particular day.

    b Suppose that (as an alternative) the chain's management decides to award a daily bonus to the entire sales force if all 36 achieve an *average* daily sales figure that exceeds $2,150. Calculate the probability that average daily sales for the entire sales force will exceed $2,150 on any particular day.

c   Intuitively, do you think it would be more difficult for an individual salesperson to achieve a daily sales figure that exceeds $2,150 or for the entire sales force of 36 to achieve an *average* sales figure that exceeds $2,150? Are the probabilities you computed in parts *a* and *b* consistent with your intuition? Explain.

d   Sketch the distribution of individual daily sales figures and the probability you computed in part *a*. Place values that are three standard deviations above and below the mean in the tails of the distribution. Also sketch the distribution of all possible sample means (the sampling distribution of $\bar{x}$) and the probability you computed in part *b*. Place values that are three standard deviations of $\bar{x}$ above and below the mean in the tails of the sampling distribution. Compare the sketches. Do you see why the results in parts *a* and *b* turned out the way they did? Explain why.

7.30   In the book *Essentials of Marketing Research,* William R. Dillon, Thomas J. Madden, and Neil H. Firtle discuss an advertising study for a new suntan lotion. In this study, each respondent is assigned to a group whose members will evaluate an ad for the new lotion. Each respondent is asked to rate the ad on six items:

			Rating	Probability
High quality/low quality	Persuasive/nonpersuasive		1	0
Informative/uninformative	Artful/artless		2	.05
Good/bad	Refined/vulgar		3	.05
			4	.10
			5	.20
			6	.40
			7	.20

The rating for each item is made using a seven-point scale, where, for example, a rating of 1 on the informative/uninformative dimension indicates that the ad is extremely uninformative, and a rating of 7 says that the ad is extremely informative.

   Suppose experience shows that a "very informative" ad is typically rated by a large group of respondents according to the probability distribution given in the right page margin.

a   Calculate the mean, variance, and standard deviation of the ratings for a typical "very informative" ad.

b   Suppose that a group of 36 randomly selected respondents rates a typical "very informative" ad, and consider the sample mean $\bar{x}$ of the 36 ratings. Find the mean and standard deviation of the population of all possible sample means. What is the shape of the population of all possible sample means? How do you know?

c   Draw a sketch of the sampling distribution of the sample mean $\bar{x}$ and compare it to a sketch of the distribution of individual ratings.

d   Suppose that a randomly selected group of 36 respondents rates a typical "very informative" ad. Find the probability that the respondents give the ad a sample mean rating less than 5.

e   Suppose that 36 randomly selected respondents are exposed to a new ad in order to determine whether the ad is "very informative," and suppose that the sample mean rating is less than 5. In light of the probability you computed in part *d*, what would you conclude about whether the new ad is "very informative"? Explain.

7.31   The April 21, 2005, issue of *Sports Illustrated* reported the results of a poll of 757 Division I student athletes from 59 schools and all 36 NCAA championship sports. The athletes were asked 20 questions relating to college sports and college life. One of the questions asked was: "Have you ever received preferential treatment from a professor because of your status as an athlete?"

a   Suppose that we wish to justify the claim that more than 25 percent of Division I student athletes have received preferential treatment from a professor. The poll actually found that 29.7 percent of the 757 surveyed athletes had received preferential treatment from a professor. If, for the sake of argument, we assume that 25 percent of all Division I student athletes have received preferential treatment from a professor (that is, $p = .25$), and if we assume that the 757 sampled student athletes were randomly selected, calculate the probability of observing a sample proportion greater than or equal to .297. That is, calculate $P(\hat{p} \geq .297)$.

b   Based on the probability you computed in part *a*, would you conclude that more than 25 percent of Division I student athletes have received preferential treatment from a professor? Explain.

7.32   Suppose that we randomly select a sample of size 100.

a   What is the probability of obtaining a sample mean greater than 50.2 when the sampled population has mean 50 and standard deviation 1? Must we assume that the population is normally distributed in order to answer this question? Why or why not?

b   Rework part *a* of this exercise with a sample size of 225. Compare your answer here with that of part *a*. Why are they different?

7.33 Each day a manufacturing plant receives a large shipment of drums of Chemical ZX-900. These drums are supposed to have a mean fill of 50 gallons, while the fills have a standard deviation known to be .6 gallon.

   a Suppose that the mean fill for the shipment is actually 50 gallons. If we draw a random sample of 100 drums from the shipment, what is the probability that the average fill for the 100 drums is between 49.88 gallons and 50.12 gallons?

   b The plant manager is worried that the drums of Chemical ZX-900 are underfilled. Because of this, she decides to draw a sample of 100 drums from each daily shipment and will reject the shipment (send it back to the supplier) if the average fill for the 100 drums is less than 49.85 gallons. Suppose that a shipment that actually has a mean fill of 50 gallons is received. What is the probability that this shipment will be rejected and sent back to the supplier?

7.34 In its October 12, 1992, issue, *The Milwaukee Journal* published the results of an Ogilvy, Adams, and Rinehart poll of 1,250 American investors that was conducted in early October 1992. The poll investigated the stock market's appeal to investors five years after the market suffered its biggest one-day decline (in 1987).

   Assume that 50 percent of all American investors in 1992 found the stock market less attractive than it was in 1987 (that is, $p = .5$). Find the probability that the sample proportion obtained from the sample of 1,250 investors would be

   a Within 4 percentage points of the population proportion—that is, find $P(.46 \le \hat{p} \le .54)$.

   b Within 2 percentage points of the population proportion.

   c Within 1 percentage point of the population proportion.

   d Based on these probabilities, would it be reasonable to claim a ± 2 percentage point margin of error? A ± 1 percentage point margin of error? Explain.

7.35 Again consider the stock market poll discussed in Exercise 7.34.

   a Suppose we wish to use the poll's results to justify the claim that fewer than 50 percent of American investors in 1992 found the stock market less attractive than in 1987. The poll actually found that 41 percent of the respondents said the stock market was less attractive than in 1987. If, for the sake of argument, we assume that $p = .5$, calculate the probability of observing a sample proportion of .41 or less. That is, calculate $P(\hat{p} \le .41)$.

   b Based on the probability you computed in part *b*, would you conclude that fewer than 50 percent of American investors in 1992 found the stock market to be less attractive than in 1987? Explain.

7.36 Aamco Heating and Cooling, Inc., advertises that any customer buying an air conditioner during the first 16 days of July will receive a 25 percent discount if the average high temperature for this 16-day period is more than five degrees above normal.

   a If daily high temperatures in July are normally distributed with a mean of 84 degrees and a standard deviation of 8 degrees, what is the probability that Aamco Heating and Cooling will have to give its customers the 25 percent discount?

   b Based on the probability you computed in part *a*, do you think that Aamco's promotion is ethical? Write a paragraph justifying your opinion.

7.37 THE TRASH BAG CASE 🔵 TrashBag

   Recall that the trash bag manufacturer has concluded that its new 30-gallon bag will be the strongest such bag on the market if its mean breaking strength is at least 50 pounds. In order to provide statistical evidence that the mean breaking strength of the new bag is at least 50 pounds, the manufacturer randomly selects a sample of *n* bags and calculates the mean $\bar{x}$ of the breaking strengths of these bags. If the sample mean so obtained is at least 50 pounds, this provides some evidence that the mean breaking strength of all new bags is at least 50 pounds.

   Suppose that (unknown to the manufacturer) the breaking strengths of the new 30-gallon bag are normally distributed with a mean of $\mu = 50.6$ pounds and a standard deviation of $\sigma = 1.62$ pounds.

   a Find an interval containing 95.44 percent of all possible sample means if the sample size employed is $n = 5$.

   b Find an interval containing 95.44 percent of all possible sample means if the sample size employed is $n = 40$.

   c If the trash bag manufacturer hopes to obtain a sample mean that is at least 50 pounds (so that it can provide evidence that the population mean breaking strength of the new bags is at least 50), which sample size ($n = 5$ or $n = 40$) would be best? Explain why.

7.38   A computer supply house receives a large shipment of floppy disks each week. Past experience has shown that the number of flaws per disk can be described by the following probability distribution:

Number of Flaws per Floppy Disk	Probability
0	.65
1	.2
2	.1
3	.05

a   Calculate the mean and standard deviation of the number of flaws per floppy disk.

b   Suppose that we randomly select a sample of 100 floppy disks. Describe the shape of the sampling distribution of the sample mean $\bar{x}$. Then compute the mean and the standard deviation of the sampling distribution of $\bar{x}$.

c   Sketch the sampling distribution of the sample mean $\bar{x}$ and compare it to the distribution describing the number of flaws on a single floppy disk.

d   The supply house's managers are worried that the floppy disks being received have an excessive number of flaws. Because of this, a random sample of 100 disks is drawn from each shipment and the shipment is rejected (sent back to the supplier) if the average number of flaws per disk for the 100 sample disks is greater than .75. Suppose that the mean number of flaws per disk for this week's entire shipment is actually .55. What is the probability that this shipment will be rejected and sent back to the supplier?

7.39   On January 4, 2000, the Gallup Organization released the results of a poll concerning public skepticism about the extent of Y2K computer problems. The poll results were based on a randomly selected national sample of 622 adults, 18 years and older, conducted December 28, 1999. One question asked if the respondent felt that media warnings about possible Y2K computer problems were "necessary precautions."

a   Suppose that we want to justify the claim that a majority of U.S. adults believe that media warnings about possible Y2K computer problems were necessary precautions. The poll actually found that 59 percent of the respondents felt this way.[6] If, for the sake of argument, we assume that 50 percent of U.S. adults believe that the media warnings were necessary precautions (that is, $p = .5$), calculate the probability of observing a sample proportion of .59 or more. That is, calculate $P(\hat{p} \geq .59)$.

b   Based on the probability you computed in part a, would you conclude that a majority of U.S. adults believe that the media warnings were necessary precautions? Explain.

7.40   On January 7, 2000, the Gallup Organization released the results of a poll comparing lifestyles of today with those of yesteryear. The poll results were based on telephone interviews with a randomly selected national sample of 1,031 adults, 18 years and older, conducted December 20–21, 1999. One question asked if the respondent had vacationed for six days or longer within the last 12 months.

a   Suppose that we will attempt to use the poll's results to justify the claim that more than 40 percent of U.S. adults have vacationed for six days or longer within the last 12 months. The poll actually found that 42 percent of the respondents had done so.[7] If, for the sake of argument, we assume that 40 percent of U.S. adults have vacationed for six days or longer within the last 12 months (that is, $p = .4$), calculate the probability of observing a sample proportion of .42 or more; that is, calculate $P(\hat{p} \geq .42)$.

b   Based on the probability you computed in a, would you conclude that more than 40 percent of U.S. adults have vacationed for six days or longer within the last 12 months? Explain.

7.41   **THE INTERNATIONAL BUSINESS TRAVEL EXPENSE CASE**

Suppose that a large international corporation wants to assess whether the mean, μ, of all one-day travel expenses in Moscow exceeds $500. Recall that the mean of a random sample of 35 one-day travel expenses is $\bar{x} = \$538$, and assume that σ is known to equal $40.

a   Assuming that μ equals $500 and the sample size is 35, what is the probability of observing a sample mean that is greater than or equal to $538?

b   Based on your answer to a, do you think that the mean of all one-day travel expenses in Moscow exceeds $500? Explain.

---

[6]Source: http://www.gallup.com/poll/releases/, The Gallup Organization, January 4, 2000.

[7]Source: http://www.gallup.com/poll/releases/, The Gallup Organization, January 7, 2000.

7.42   THE UNITED KINGDOM INSURANCE CASE

Suppose that we wish to assess whether more than 60 percent of all United Kingdom households purchased life insurance in 1993. That is, we wish to assess whether the proportion, p, of all United Kingdom households that purchased life insurance in 1993 exceeds .60. Assume here that the U.K. insurance survey is based on 1,000 randomly selected households and that 640 of these households purchased life insurance in 1993.

a   Assuming that p equals .60 and the sample size is 1,000, what is the probability of observing a sample proportion that is at least .64?

b   Based on your answer in a, do you think more than 60 percent of all United Kingdom households purchased life insurance in 1993? Explain.

7.43   Internet Exercise

The best way to observe, firsthand, the concepts of sampling distributions is to conduct sampling experiments with real data. However, sampling experiments can be prohibitively time-consuming and tedious. An excellent alternative is to conduct computer-assisted sampling experiments or simulations. *Visual Statistics* by Doane, Mathieson, and Tracy (Irwin/McGraw-Hill) includes a simulation module to illustrate sampling distributions and the Central Limit Theorem. In this exercise, we will download and install the Central Limit Theorem demonstration module from *Visual Statistics* and use the software to demonstrate the Central Limit Theorem.

From the Irwin/McGraw-Hill Business Statistics Center (http://www.mhhe.com/business/opsci/bstat/), select in turn—"Visual Statistics and Other Data Visualization Tools" : "Visual Statistics by Doane" : "Free Stuff"—and download both the CLT module and the Worktext. When the download is complete, install the CLT module by double-clicking the installation file (vs_setup.exe). Study the overview and orientation sections of the Worktext, and work through the first four learning exercises on the "Width of Car Hood" example.

Appendix 7.1 ■ Simulating Sampling Distributions Using MINITAB

Histogram of sample means from an exponential distribution similar to Figure 7.6(b) on page 294:

In this example we construct a histogram of 1,000 sample means from exponential samples of size 5.

- Select **Calc : Random Data : Exponential**
- In the Exponential Distribution dialog box, enter 1000 into the "Number of rows of data to generate:" window.
- Enter C1-C5 in the "Store in column(s):" window to request 1,000 values per column in columns C1 to C5.
- Be sure that 0.0 is the entry in the Threshold window.
- Enter 7 in the Scale window. This specifies the mean of the exponential distribution when the threshold equals 0.
- Click OK in the Exponential Distribution dialog box. The 1,000 exponential samples of size 5 will be generated in rows 1 through 1,000.
- Select **Calc : Row Statistics**
- In the Row Statistics dialog box, under "Statistic" select the Mean option.
- Enter C1-C5 in the "Input variables" window.
- Enter XBar5 in the "Store result in" window.

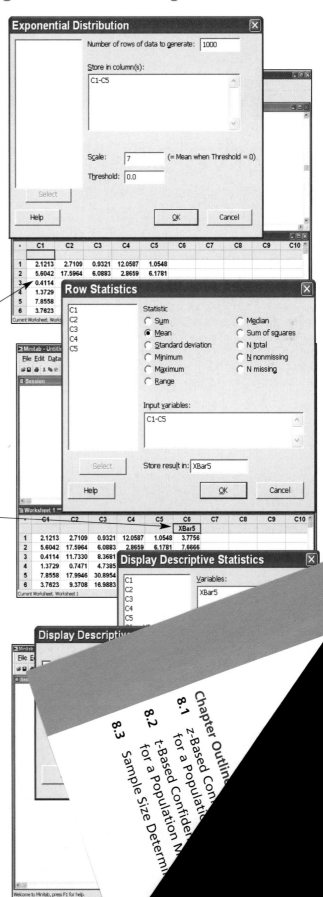

- Click OK in the Row Statistics dialog box to compute the means for the 1,000 samples of size 5.

- Select **Stat : Basic Statistics : Display Descriptive Statistics**
- In the Display Descriptive Statistics dialog box, enter XBar5 into the Variables window.
- Click on the Graphs... button.
- In the "Display Descriptive Statistics—Graphs" dialog box, check the "Histogram of data, with normal curve" checkbox.
- Click OK in the "Display Descriptive Statistics—Graphs" dialog box.
- Click OK in the Display Descriptive Statistics dialog box.

- The histogram will appear in a graphics window.

CHAPTER 8

Confidence Intervals

idence Intervals
on Mean: σ Known

ce Intervals
Mean: σ Unknown

nation

8.4 Confidence Intervals for a Population Proportion

8.5 A Comparison of Confidence Intervals and Tolerance Intervals (Optional)

We have seen that the sample mean is the point estimate of the population mean and the sample proportion is the point estimate of the population proportion. In general, although a point estimate is a reasonable one-number estimate of a population parameter (mean, proportion, or the like), the point estimate will not—unless we are extremely lucky—equal the true value of the population parameter.

In this chapter we study how to use a **confidence interval** to estimate a population parameter. A confidence interval for a population parameter is an interval, or range of numbers, constructed around the point estimate so that we are very sure, or confident, that the true value of the population parameter is inside the interval.

By computing such an interval, we estimate—with confidence—the possible values that a population parameter might equal. This, in turn, can help us to assess—with confidence—whether a particular business improvement has been made or is needed.

In order to illustrate confidence intervals, we revisit several cases introduced in earlier chapters and also introduce some new cases. Specifically:

In the **Car Mileage Case**, we use a confidence interval to provide strong evidence that the mean EPA combined city and highway mileage for the automaker's new midsize model meets the tax credit standard of 31 mpg.

In the **Payment Time Case**, we use a confidence interval to more completely assess the reduction in mean payment time that was achieved by the new billing system.

In the **Marketing Research Case**, we use a confidence interval to provide strong evidence that the mean rating of the new bottle design exceeds the minimum standard for a successful design.

In the **Cheese Spread Case**, we use a confidence interval to provide strong evidence that fewer than 10 percent of all current purchasers will stop buying the cheese spread if the new spout is used, and, therefore, that it is reasonable to use the new spout.

In the **Marketing Ethics Case**, we use a confidence interval to provide strong evidence that more than half of all marketing researchers disapprove of the actions taken in an "ultraviolet ink scenario."

Sections 8.1 through 8.4 present confidence intervals for population means and proportions. These intervals are appropriate when the sampled population is either infinite or finite and *much* *larger* than (say, at least 20 times as large as) the size of the sample. Optional Section 8.5 compares confidence intervals and tolerance intervals.

8.1 *z*-Based Confidence Intervals for a Population Mean: σ Known ● ● ●

An introduction to confidence intervals for a population mean We have seen that we use the sample mean as the point estimate of the population mean. A **confidence interval** for the population mean is an interval constructed around the sample mean so that we are very sure, or confident, that this interval contains the population mean. In order to illustrate a confidence interval, we consider the following intuitive example.

EXAMPLE 8.1 The Car Mileage Case

Recall that an automaker has introduced a new midsize model and wishes to estimate the mean EPA combined city and highway mileage, μ, that would be obtained by all cars of this type. If the automaker can show that the population mean μ is at least 31 mpg, the government will give the automaker a tax credit. In order to estimate μ, the automaker has conducted EPA mileage tests on a random sample of 50 of its new midsize cars and has obtained the sample of mileages in Table 1.4 (page 10). The mean of this sample of mileages, which is $\bar{x} = 31.56$ mpg, is the point estimate of μ. However, a sample mean will not—unless we are extremely lucky—equal the true value of a population mean. Therefore, although $\bar{x} = 31.56$ mpg suggests that μ is at least 31 mpg, it does not make us *confident* that μ is at least 31 mpg. Later in this section we will find that a *confidence interval for μ*

is [31.34 mpg, 31.78 mpg]. This interval says that we are confident that the true mean mileage μ for the new midsize model is between 31.34 mpg and 31.78 mpg. Furthermore, since this interval estimates that the smallest μ might be is 31.34 mpg, we can be confident that μ exceeds 31 mpg, the minimum standard for the tax credit. As we will see later, the federal government might regard this confidence interval as convincing evidence that the midsize model deserves the tax credit.

When we find a confidence interval for a population mean, we base this interval on what is called a **confidence level.** This confidence level is a percentage (for example, 95 percent or 99 percent) that, intuitively, expresses *how* confident we are that the confidence interval contains the population mean. The exact meaning of a confidence level—as well as the confidence level for the interval of the previous example—will be discussed later in this section. First, however, we need to explain how a confidence level is used to find a confidence interval. To do this, we will begin in the car mileage example by showing how a confidence level based on a familiar percentage—95.44 percent— can be used to find a confidence interval. Then, we will generalize our discussions and show how any particular confidence level can be used to find a confidence interval. In addition, since it is simpler to present our initial discussions in terms of a smaller sample size, we will begin by considering a random sample of $n = 5$ car mileages, and we will then consider using any sample size.

Assume, therefore, that we will randomly select a sample of $n = 5$ new midsize cars and calculate the mean $\bar{x}$ of the mileages that the cars obtain when tested as prescribed by the EPA. Also, assume that the population of all individual car mileages is normally distributed and that, although we do not know the true value of the population mean mileage μ, we do know that the true value of the population standard deviation σ is .8 mpg (as discussed on pages 289 and 290 of Chapter 7). A confidence interval for the population mean μ is based on the sampling distribution of the sample mean $\bar{x}$. We have seen in Chapter 7 that the sampling distribution of $\bar{x}$ is the probability distribution of the population of all possible sample means that would be obtained from all possible samples of $n = 5$ car mileages. We have also seen that, if the assumptions discussed above hold, then the sampling distribution of $\bar{x}$ is a normal distribution, centered at the unknown population mean μ (because $\mu_{\bar{x}} = \mu$) and having standard deviation

$$\sigma_{\bar{x}} = \frac{\sigma}{\sqrt{n}} = \frac{.8}{\sqrt{5}} = .358$$

We now reason as follows:

1 The Empirical Rule for a normally distributed population implies that the probability is .9544 that the sample mean $\bar{x}$ will be within plus or minus $2\sigma_{\bar{x}} = 2(.358) \approx .7$ of the population mean μ. (Note that, although it is generally best to carry more decimal places in intermediate calculations, we have rounded $2\sigma_{\bar{x}}$ to one decimal place to make it easier to understand the logic to follow.)

2 Saying

> $\bar{x}$ will be within plus or minus .7 of μ.

is the same as saying

> $\bar{x}$ will be such that the interval $[\bar{x} \pm .7]$ contains μ.

To see this, consider Table 8.1, which gives three samples and the means of these samples. Also, assume that (unknown to any human being) the true value of the population mean μ is 31.5. Then, as illustrated in Figure 8.1, because the sample mean $\bar{x} = 31.3$ is within .7 of $\mu = 31.5$, the interval $[31.3 \pm .7] = [30.6, 32.0]$ contains μ. Similarly, since the sample mean $\bar{x} = 31.7$ is within .7 of $\mu = 31.5$, the interval $[31.7 \pm .7] = [31.0, 32.4]$ contains μ. However, because the sample mean $\bar{x} = 32.5$ is not within .7 of $\mu = 31.5$, the interval $[32.5 \pm .7] = [31.8, 33.2]$ does not contain μ.

3 Combining 1 and 2, we have the probability is .9544 that the sample mean $\bar{x}$ will be such that the interval $[\bar{x} \pm .7]$ contains the population mean μ.

Statement 3 says that, **before we randomly select the sample,** there is a .9544 probability that we will obtain an interval $[\bar{x} \pm .7]$ that contains μ. In other words, 95.44 percent of all intervals that we might obtain contain μ, and 4.56 percent of these intervals do not contain μ. For this reason, we call the interval $[\bar{x} \pm .7]$ a **95.44 percent confidence interval for μ.** To better

TABLE 8.1	Three Samples of Five Mileages	
Sample	**Sample**	**Sample**
$x_1 = 30.7$	$x_1 = 32.3$	$x_1 = 32.7$
$x_2 = 31.9$	$x_2 = 30.8$	$x_2 = 31.6$
$x_3 = 30.3$	$x_3 = 31.9$	$x_3 = 33.3$
$x_4 = 32.0$	$x_4 = 31.5$	$x_4 = 32.3$
$x_5 = 31.6$	$x_5 = 32.0$	$x_5 = 32.6$
$\bar{x} = 31.3$	$\bar{x} = 31.7$	$\bar{x} = 32.5$

FIGURE 8.1   Three 95.44 Percent Confidence Intervals for μ

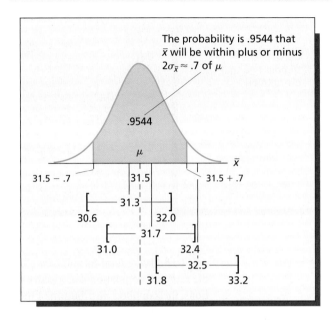

understand this interval, we must realize that, **when we actually select the sample,** we will observe one particular sample from the extremely large number of possible samples. Therefore, we will obtain one particular confidence interval from the extremely large number of possible confidence intervals. For example, suppose that when we actually select the sample of five cars and record their mileages, we obtain the leftmost sample of mileages in Table 8.1. Since the mean of our sample is $\bar{x} = 31.3$, the 95.44 percent confidence interval for μ that it gives is

$$[\bar{x} \pm .7] = [31.3 \pm .7]$$
$$= [30.6, 32.0]$$

Because we do not know the true value of μ, we do not know for sure whether μ is contained in our interval. However, we are 95.44 percent confident that μ is contained in this interval. What we mean by this is that we hope that the interval [30.6, 32.0] is one of the 95.44 percent of all intervals that contain μ and not one of the 4.56 percent of all intervals that do not contain μ. Here we say that 95.44 percent is the *confidence level* associated with the confidence interval.

To practically interpret the confidence interval [30.6, 32.0], this interval says that we are 95.44 percent confident that μ is between 30.6 mpg and 32.0 mpg. Furthermore, since this interval estimates that μ could be as small as 30.6 mpg, the interval (based on a small sample of five mileages) does not make us 95.44 percent confident that μ is at least 31 mpg, the minimum standard for the tax credit. As described in Example 8.1, we will soon see that a confidence interval based on the sample of 50 mileages in Table 1.4 (page 10) makes us confident that μ is at least 31 mpg. In addition, we will see that we need not base a confidence interval on a 95.44 percent confidence level. Rather, we can base a confidence interval on any confidence level less than 100 percent.

A general confidence interval formula   We will now present a general formula for finding a confidence interval for a population mean. To do this, recall from the previous example that, before we randomly select the sample, the probability that the confidence interval

$$[\bar{x} \pm .7]$$

will contain the population mean is .9544. It follows that the probability that this confidence interval will not contain the population mean is .0456. In general, we denote the probability that a confidence interval for a population mean will *not* contain the population mean by the symbol α (pronounced alpha). This implies that $(1 - \alpha)$, which we call the **confidence coefficient,** is the probability that the confidence interval will contain the population mean. We can base a confidence interval for a population mean on any confidence coefficient $(1 - \alpha)$ less than 1. However, in practice, we usually use two decimal place confidence coefficients, such as .95 or

FIGURE 8.2 The Point $z_{\alpha/2}$

FIGURE 8.2 **The Point $z_{\alpha/2}$**

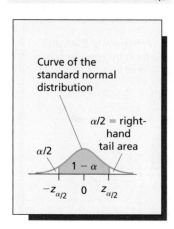

FIGURE 8.3 **The Point $z_{.025}$**

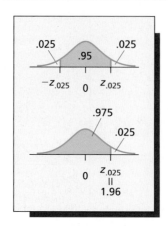

FIGURE 8.4 **The Point $z_{.005}$**

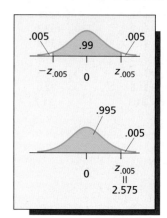

.99. To find a general formula for a confidence interval for a population mean μ, we assume that the sampled population is normally distributed, or the sample size n is large. Under these conditions, the sampling distribution of the sample mean $\bar{x}$ is exactly (or approximately, by the Central Limit Theorem) a normal distribution with mean $\mu_{\bar{x}} = \mu$ and standard deviation $\sigma_{\bar{x}} = \sigma/\sqrt{n}$. Then, in order to obtain a confidence interval that has a $(1 - \alpha)$ probability of containing μ, we find the normal point $z_{\alpha/2}$ that gives a right-hand tail area under the standard normal curve equal to $\alpha/2$, and we find the normal point $-z_{\alpha/2}$ that gives a left-hand tail area under this curve equal to $\alpha/2$ (see Figure 8.2). Noting from Figure 8.2 that the area under the standard normal curve between $-z_{\alpha/2}$ and $z_{\alpha/2}$ is $(1 - \alpha)$, it can be shown that the probability is $(1 - \alpha)$ that the sample mean $\bar{x}$ will be within plus or minus $z_{\alpha/2}\sigma_{\bar{x}}$ units of the population mean μ. The quantity $z_{\alpha/2}\sigma_{\bar{x}}$ is called the **margin of error** when estimating μ by $\bar{x}$. If this margin of error is added to and subtracted from $\bar{x}$ to form the interval

$$[\bar{x} \pm z_{\alpha/2}\sigma_{\bar{x}}] = \left[\bar{x} \pm z_{\alpha/2}\frac{\sigma}{\sqrt{n}} \right]$$

then this interval will contain the population mean with probability $(1 - \alpha)$. In other words, this interval is a confidence interval for μ based on a confidence coefficient of $(1 - \alpha)$, and hence we call this interval a **$100(1 - \alpha)$ percent confidence interval for the population mean.** Here, **$100(1 - \alpha)$ percent** is called the **confidence level** associated with the confidence interval. This confidence level is the percentage of the time that the confidence interval would contain the population mean if all possible samples were used to calculate this interval. (Note that we will formally justify the confidence interval formula at the end of this section.)

For example, suppose we wish to find a 95 percent confidence interval for the population mean. Since the confidence level is 95 percent, we have $100(1 - \alpha) = 95$. This implies that the confidence coefficient is $(1 - \alpha) = .95$, which implies that $\alpha = .05$ and $\alpha/2 = .025$. Therefore, we need to find the normal point $z_{.025}$. As shown in Figure 8.3, the area under the standard normal curve between $-z_{.025}$ and $z_{.025}$ is .95, and the area under this curve to the left of $z_{.025}$ is .975. Looking up the area .975 in Table A.3 (page 641), we find that $z_{.025} = 1.96$. It follows that the interval

$$[\bar{x} \pm z_{.025}\sigma_{\bar{x}}] = \left[\bar{x} \pm 1.96\frac{\sigma}{\sqrt{n}} \right]$$

is a 95 percent confidence interval for the population mean μ. This means that if all possible samples were used to calculate this interval, 95 percent of the resulting intervals would contain μ.

As another example, consider a 99 percent confidence interval for the population mean. Because the confidence level is 99 percent, we have $100(1 - \alpha) = 99$, and the confidence coefficient is $(1 - \alpha) = .99$. This implies that $\alpha = .01$ and $\alpha/2 = .005$. Therefore, we need to find the normal point $z_{.005}$. As shown in Figure 8.4, the area under the standard normal curve between

TABLE 8.2 **The Normal Point $z_{\alpha/2}$ for Various Levels of Confidence**

100(1 − α) percent	α	α/2	Normal Point $z_{\alpha/2}$
90% = 100(1 − .10)%	.10	.05	$z_{.05} = 1.645$
95% = 100(1 − .05)%	.05	.025	$z_{.025} = 1.96$
98% = 100(1 − .02)%	.02	.01	$z_{.01} = 2.33$
99% = 100(1 − .01)%	.01	.005	$z_{.005} = 2.575$

$-z_{.005}$ and $z_{.005}$ is .99, and the area under this curve to the left of $z_{.005}$ is .995. Looking up the area .995 in Table A.3, we find that $z_{.005} = 2.575$. It follows that the interval

$$[\bar{x} \pm z_{.005}\sigma_{\bar{x}}] = \left[\bar{x} \pm 2.575 \frac{\sigma}{\sqrt{n}} \right]$$

is a 99 percent confidence interval for the population mean μ. This means that if all possible samples were used to calculate this interval, 99 percent of the resulting intervals would contain μ.

To compare the 95 percent and 99 percent confidence intervals, notice that the margin of error $2.575(\sigma/\sqrt{n})$ used to compute the 99 percent interval is larger than the margin of error $1.96(\sigma/\sqrt{n})$ used to compute the 95 percent interval. Therefore, the 99 percent interval is the longer of these intervals. In general, increasing the confidence level (1) has the advantage of making us more confident that μ is contained in the confidence interval, but (2) has the disadvantage of increasing the margin of error and thus providing a less precise estimate of the true value of μ. Frequently, 95 percent confidence intervals are used to make conclusions. If conclusions based on stronger evidence are desired, 99 percent intervals are sometimes used.

Table 8.2 shows the confidence levels 95 percent and 99 percent, as well as two other confidence levels—90 percent and 98 percent—that are sometimes used to calculate confidence intervals. In addition, this table gives the values of α, $\alpha/2$, and $z_{\alpha/2}$ that correspond to these confidence levels. The following box summarizes the formula used in calculating a $100(1 - \alpha)$ percent confidence interval for a population mean μ.

A Confidence Interval for a Population Mean μ: σ Known

Suppose that the sampled population is normally distributed. Then a **100(1 − α) percent confidence interval for μ** is

$$\left[\bar{x} \pm z_{\alpha/2} \frac{\sigma}{\sqrt{n}} \right] = \left[\bar{x} - z_{\alpha/2} \frac{\sigma}{\sqrt{n}}, \bar{x} + z_{\alpha/2} \frac{\sigma}{\sqrt{n}} \right]$$

This interval is also approximately correct for non-normal populations if the sample size is large (at least 30).

The confidence interval in the summary box is based on the normal distribution and assumes that the true value of the population standard deviation σ is known. Therefore, in the examples to follow we will assume that we know—through theory or history related to the population under consideration—the true value of σ. Of course, in most real-world situations, there would not be a basis for knowing σ. In the next section we will discuss a confidence interval based on the t distribution that does not assume that σ is known. Furthermore, we will revisit the examples of this section assuming that σ is unknown.

EXAMPLE 8.2 The Car Mileage Case

Recall that the federal government will give a tax credit to any automaker selling a midsize model equipped with an automatic transmission that has an EPA combined city and highway mileage estimate of at least 31 mpg. Furthermore, to ensure that it does not overestimate a car model's mileage, the EPA will obtain the model's mileage estimate by rounding down—to the nearest mile per gallon—the lower limit of a 95 percent confidence interval for the model's mean mileage μ. That is, the model's mileage estimate is an estimate of the smallest that μ might reasonably be. Suppose an automaker conducts mileage tests on a sample of 50 of its new midsize cars and obtains the sample of 50 mileages in Table 1.4, which has mean $\bar{x} = 31.56$. As illustrated in Figure 8.3, in order to compute a 95 percent confidence interval, we use the normal point $z_{\alpha/2} = z_{.05/2} = z_{.025} = 1.96$. Assuming that σ is known to equal .8, it follows that the 95 percent confidence interval for μ is

$$\left[\bar{x} \pm z_{.025}\frac{\sigma}{\sqrt{n}}\right] = \left[31.56 \pm 1.96\frac{.8}{\sqrt{50}}\right]$$
$$= [31.56 \pm .222]$$
$$= [31.34, 31.78]$$

This interval says we are 95 percent confident that the model's mean mileage μ is between 31.34 mpg and 31.78 mpg. Based on this interval, the model's EPA mileage estimate is 31 mpg, and the automaker will receive the tax credit.

If we wish to compute a 99 percent confidence interval for μ, then, as illustrated in Figure 8.4, we use the normal point $z_{\alpha/2} = z_{.01/2} = z_{.005} = 2.575$. We therefore obtain the interval

$$\left[\bar{x} \pm z_{.005}\frac{\sigma}{\sqrt{n}}\right] = \left[31.56 \pm 2.575\frac{.8}{\sqrt{50}}\right]$$
$$= [31.56 \pm .291]$$
$$= [31.27, 31.85]$$

This interval says we are 99 percent confident that the model's mean mileage μ is between 31.27 mpg and 31.85 mpg. Note that increasing the level of confidence to 99 percent has increased the margin of error from .222 to .291, which makes the 99 percent interval longer than the 95 percent interval.

EXAMPLE 8.3 The Payment Time Case

Recall that a management consulting firm has installed a new computer-based, electronic billing system at a Hamilton, Ohio, trucking company. The mean payment time using the trucking company's old billing system was approximately equal to, but no less than, 39 days. In order to assess whether the mean payment time, μ, using the new billing system is substantially less than 39 days, the consulting firm will use the sample of $n = 65$ payment times in Table 2.4 to find a 95 percent confidence interval for μ. The mean of the 65 payment times is $\bar{x} = 18.1077$. Using the normal point $z_{\alpha/2} = z_{.025} = 1.96$, and assuming that σ is known to equal 4.2, it follows that the 95 percent confidence interval for μ is

$$\left[\bar{x} \pm z_{.025}\frac{\sigma}{\sqrt{n}}\right] = \left[18.1077 \pm 1.96\frac{4.2}{\sqrt{65}}\right]$$
$$= [18.1077 \pm 1.021]$$
$$= [17.1, 19.1]$$

Recalling that the mean payment time using the old billing system is 39 days, this interval says that we are 95 percent confident that the mean payment time using the new billing system is between 17.1 days and 19.1 days. Therefore, we are 95 percent confident that the new billing system reduces the mean payment time by at most 21.9 days and by at least 19.9 days.

Justifying the confidence interval formula   To show why the interval

$$\left[\bar{x} \pm z_{\alpha/2}\frac{\sigma}{\sqrt{n}}\right]$$

is a $100(1 - \alpha)$ percent confidence interval for μ, recall that if the sampled population is normally distributed or the sample size n is large, then the sampling distribution of $\bar{x}$ is (exactly or approximately) a normal distribution with mean $\mu_{\bar{x}} = \mu$ and standard deviation $\sigma_{\bar{x}} = \sigma/\sqrt{n}$. It follows that the sampling distribution of

$$z = \frac{\bar{x} - \mu}{\sigma/\sqrt{n}}$$

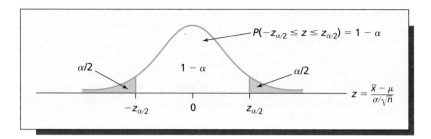

FIGURE 8.5   **A Probability for Deriving a Confidence Interval for the Population Mean**

is (exactly or approximately) a standard normal distribution. Therefore, the probability that we will obtain a sample mean $\bar{x}$ such that z is between $-z_{\alpha/2}$ and $z_{\alpha/2}$ is $1 - \alpha$ (see Figure 8.5). That is, we can say that the probability that

$$-z_{\alpha/2} \leq \frac{\bar{x} - \mu}{\sigma/\sqrt{n}} \leq z_{\alpha/2}$$

equals $1 - \alpha$. Using some algebraic manipulations, we can show that this is equivalent to saying that the probability that

$$\bar{x} - z_{\alpha/2}\frac{\sigma}{\sqrt{n}} \leq \mu \leq \bar{x} + z_{\alpha/2}\frac{\sigma}{\sqrt{n}}$$

equals $1 - \alpha$. This probability statement says that the probability is $1 - \alpha$ (for example, .95) that we will obtain a sample mean $\bar{x}$ such that the interval

$$\left[\bar{x} \pm z_{\alpha/2}\frac{\sigma}{\sqrt{n}}\right]$$

contains μ. In other words, this interval is a $100(1 - \alpha)$ percent confidence interval for μ.

Exercises for Section 8.1

CONCEPTS

8.1   Explain why it is important to calculate a confidence interval in addition to calculating a point estimate of a population parameter.

8.2   Write a paragraph explaining exactly what the term "95 percent confidence" means in the context of calculating a 95 percent confidence interval for a population mean.

8.3   For each of the following changes, indicate whether a confidence interval for μ will have a larger or smaller margin of error:
   a   An increase in the level of confidence.
   b   An increase in the sample size.
   c   A decrease in the level of confidence.
   d   A decrease in the sample size.

METHODS AND APPLICATIONS

8.4   For each of the following confidence levels, $100(1 - \alpha)$ percent, find the $z_{\alpha/2}$ point needed to compute a confidence interval for μ:
   a   95%   **c**   99.73%   **e**   97%
   b   99%   **d**   80%   **f**   92%

8.5   Suppose that, for a sample of size $n = 100$ measurements, we find that $\bar{x} = 50$. Assuming that σ equals 2, calculate confidence intervals for the population mean μ with the following confidence levels:
   a   95%   **b**   99%   **c**   97%   **d**   80%   **e**   99.73%

8.6   **THE TRASH BAG CASE**   ⬤ TrashBag

Consider the trash bag problem. Suppose that an independent laboratory has tested trash bags and has found that no 30-gallon bags that are currently on the market have a mean breaking strength of 50 pounds or more. On the basis of these results, the producer of the new, improved trash bag feels sure that its 30-gallon bag will be the strongest such bag on the market if the new trash bag's mean breaking strength can be shown to be at least 50 pounds. The mean of the sample of 40 trash bag breaking strengths in Table 1.9 is $\bar{x} = 50.575$. If we let μ denote the mean of the breaking strengths of all possible trash bags of the new type and assume that σ equals 1.65:

a Calculate 95 percent and 99 percent confidence intervals for μ.

b Using the 95 percent confidence interval, can we be 95 percent confident that μ is at least 50 pounds? Explain.

c Using the 99 percent confidence interval, can we be 99 percent confident that μ is at least 50 pounds? Explain.

d Based on your answers to parts *b* and *c*, how convinced are you that the new 30-gallon trash bag is the strongest such bag on the market?

8.7 **THE BANK CUSTOMER WAITING TIME CASE**   ● WaitTime

Recall that a bank manager has developed a new system to reduce the time customers spend waiting to be served by tellers during peak business hours. The mean waiting time during peak business hours under the current system is roughly 9 to 10 minutes. The bank manager hopes that the new system will have a mean waiting time that is less than six minutes. The mean of the sample of 100 bank customer waiting times in Table 1.8 is $\bar{x} = 5.46$. If we let μ denote the mean of all possible bank customer waiting times using the new system and assume that σ equals 2.47:

a Calculate 95 percent and 99 percent confidence intervals for μ.

b Using the 95 percent confidence interval, can the bank manager be 95 percent confident that μ is less than six minutes? Explain.

c Using the 99 percent confidence interval, can the bank manager be 99 percent confident that μ is less than six minutes? Explain.

d Based on your answers to parts *b* and *c*, how convinced are you that the new mean waiting time is less than six minutes?

8.8 **THE VIDEO GAME SATISFACTION RATING CASE**   ● VideoGame

The mean of the sample of 65 customer satisfaction ratings in Table 1.7 is $\bar{x} = 42.95$. If we let μ denote the mean of all possible customer satisfaction ratings for the XYZ-Box video game system, and assume that σ equals 2.64:

a Calculate 95 percent and 99 percent confidence intervals for μ.

b Using the 95 percent confidence interval, can we be 95 percent confident that μ is at least 42 (recall that a very satisfied customer gives a rating of at least 42)? Explain.

c Using the 99 percent confidence interval, can we be 99 percent confident that μ is at least 42? Explain.

d Based on your answers to parts *b* and *c*, how convinced are you that the mean satisfaction rating is at least 42?

8.9 In an article in the *Journal of Management,* Morris, Avila, and Allen studied innovation by surveying firms to find (among other things) the number of new products introduced by the firms. Suppose a random sample of 100 California-based firms is selected and each firm is asked to report the number of new products it has introduced during the last year. The sample mean is found to be $\bar{x} = 5.68$. Assuming σ equals 8.70:

a Calculate a 98 percent confidence interval for the population mean number of new products introduced in the last year.

b Based on your confidence interval, find a reasonable estimate for the smallest value that the mean number of new products might be. Explain.

8.10 In an article in *Marketing Science,* Silk and Berndt investigate the output of advertising agencies. They describe ad agency output by finding the shares of dollar billing volume coming from various media categories such as network television, spot television, newspapers, radio, and so forth.

a Suppose that a random sample of 400 U.S. advertising agencies gives an average percentage share of billing volume from network television equal to 7.46 percent, and assume that σ equals 1.42 percent. Calculate a 95 percent confidence interval for the mean percentage share of billing volume from network television for the population of all U.S. advertising agencies.

b Suppose that a random sample of 400 U.S. advertising agencies gives an average percentage share of billing volume from spot television commercials equal to 12.44 percent, and assume that σ equals 1.55 percent. Calculate a 95 percent confidence interval for the mean percentage share of billing volume from spot television commercials for the population of all U.S. advertising agencies.

c Compare the confidence intervals in parts *a* and *b*. Does it appear that the mean percentage share of billing volume from spot television commercials for U.S. advertising agencies is greater than the mean percentage share of billing volume from network television? Explain.

8.11   In an article in *Accounting and Business Research,* Carslaw and Kaplan investigate factors that influence "audit delay" for firms in New Zealand. Audit delay, which is defined to be the length of time (in days) from a company's financial year-end to the date of the auditor's report, has been found to affect the market reaction to the report. This is because late reports seem to often be associated with lower returns and early reports seem to often be associated with higher returns.

Carslaw and Kaplan investigated audit delay for two kinds of public companies—owner-controlled and manager-controlled companies. Here a company is considered to be owner-controlled if 30 percent or more of the common stock is controlled by a single outside investor (an investor not part of the management group or board of directors). Otherwise, a company is considered to be manager-controlled. It was felt that the type of control influences audit delay. To quote Carslaw and Kaplan:

> Large external investors, having an acute need for timely information, may be expected to pressure the company and auditor to start and to complete the audit as rapidly as practicable.

   a   Suppose that a random sample of 100 public owner-controlled companies in New Zealand is found to give a mean audit delay of $\bar{x} = 82.6$ days, and assume that σ equals 33 days. Calculate a 95 percent confidence interval for the population mean audit delay for all public owner-controlled companies in New Zealand.

   b   Suppose that a random sample of 100 public manager-controlled companies in New Zealand is found to give a mean audit delay of $\bar{x} = 93$ days, and assume that σ equals 37 days. Calculate a 95 percent confidence interval for the population mean audit delay for all public manager-controlled companies in New Zealand.

   c   Use the confidence intervals you computed in parts *a* and *b* to compare the mean audit delay for all public owner-controlled companies versus that of all public manager-controlled companies. How do the means compare? Explain.

8.12   In an article in the *Journal of Marketing,* Bayus studied the differences between "early replacement buyers" and "late replacement buyers" in making consumer durable good replacement purchases. Early replacement buyers are consumers who replace a product during the early part of its lifetime, while late replacement buyers make replacement purchases late in the product's lifetime. In particular, Bayus studied automobile replacement purchases. Consumers who traded in cars with ages of zero to three years and mileages of no more than 35,000 miles were classified as early replacement buyers. Consumers who traded in cars with ages of seven or more years and mileages of more than 73,000 miles were classified as late replacement buyers. Bayus compared the two groups of buyers with respect to demographic variables such as income, education, age, and so forth. He also compared the two groups with respect to the amount of search activity in the replacement purchase process. Variables compared included the number of dealers visited, the time spent gathering information, and the time spent visiting dealers.

   a   Suppose that a random sample of 800 early replacement buyers yields a mean number of dealers visited of $\bar{x} = 3.3$, and assume that σ equals .71. Calculate a 99 percent confidence interval for the population mean number of dealers visited by early replacement buyers.

   b   Suppose that a random sample of 500 late replacement buyers yields a mean number of dealers visited of $\bar{x} = 4.3$, and assume that σ equals .66. Calculate a 99 percent confidence interval for the population mean number of dealers visited by late replacement buyers.

   c   Use the confidence intervals you computed in parts *a* and *b* to compare the mean number of dealers visited by early replacement buyers with the mean number of dealers visited by late replacement buyers. How do the means compare? Explain.

8.2 *t*-Based Confidence Intervals
for a Population Mean: σ Unknown ● ● ●

If we do not know σ (which is usually the case), we can use the sample standard deviation s to help construct a confidence interval for μ. The interval is based on the sampling distribution of

$$t = \frac{\bar{x} - \mu}{s/\sqrt{n}}$$

If the sampled population is normally distributed, then for any sample size n this sampling distribution is what is called a *t* **distribution.**

The curve of the *t* distribution has a shape similar to that of the standard normal curve. Two *t* curves and a standard normal curve are illustrated in Figure 8.6. A *t* curve is symmetrical about zero, which is the mean of any *t* distribution. However, the *t* distribution is more spread out, or variable, than the standard normal distribution. Since the above *t* statistic is a function of two random

CHAPTER 5

FIGURE 8.6   As the Number of Degrees of Freedom Increases, the Spread of the *t* Distribution Decreases and the *t* Curve Approaches the Standard Normal Curve

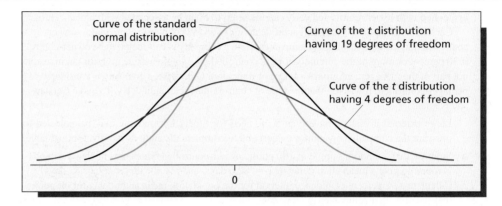

FIGURE 8.7   An Example of a *t* Point Giving a Specified Right-Hand Tail Area (This *t* Point Gives a Right-Hand Tail Area Equal to *α*)

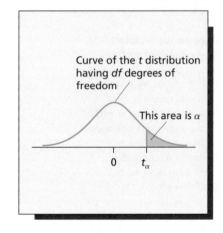

FIGURE 8.8   The *t* Point Giving a Right-Hand Tail Area of .025 under the *t* Curve Having 14 Degrees of Freedom: $t_{.025} = 2.145$

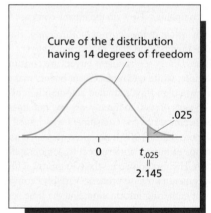

variables, $\bar{x}$ and s, it is logical that the sampling distribution of this statistic is more variable than the sampling distribution of the z statistic, which is a function of only one random variable, $\bar{x}$. The exact spread, or standard deviation, of the t distribution depends on a parameter that is called the **number of degrees of freedom (denoted *df*).** The degrees of freedom df varies depending on the problem. In the present situation the sampling distribution of t has a number of degrees of freedom that equals the sample size minus 1. We say that this sampling distribution is a **t distribution with $n - 1$ degrees of freedom.** As the sample size n (and thus the number of degrees of freedom) increases, the spread of the t distribution decreases (see Figure 8.6). Furthermore, as the number of degrees of freedom approaches infinity, the curve of the t distribution approaches (that is, becomes shaped more and more like) the curve of the standard normal distribution.

In order to use the t distribution, we employ a **t point that is denoted t_α.** As illustrated in Figure 8.7, **t_α is the point on the horizontal axis under the curve of the t distribution that gives a right-hand tail area equal to α.** The value of t_α in a particular situation depends upon the right-hand tail area α and the number of degrees of freedom of the t distribution. Values of t_α are tabulated in a **t table.** Such a table is given in Table A.4 of Appendix A (pages 642 and 643), and a portion of Table A.4 is reproduced in this chapter as Table 8.3. In this t table, the rows correspond to the different numbers of degrees of freedom (which are denoted as df). The values of df are listed down the left side of the table, while the columns designate the right-hand tail area α. For example, suppose we wish to find the t point that gives a right-hand tail area of .025 under a t curve having $df = 14$ degrees of freedom. To do this, we look in Table 8.3 at the row labeled 14 and the column labeled $t_{.025}$. We find that this $t_{.025}$ point is 2.145 (also see Figure 8.8).

TABLE 8.3   A *t* Table

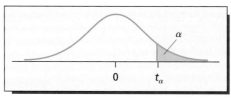

df	$t_{.100}$	$t_{.050}$	$t_{.025}$	$t_{.01}$	$t_{.005}$	$t_{.001}$	$t_{.0005}$
1	3.078	6.314	12.706	31.821	63.657	318.31	636.62
2	1.886	2.920	4.303	6.965	9.925	22.326	31.598
3	1.638	2.353	3.182	4.541	5.841	10.213	12.924
4	1.533	2.132	2.776	3.747	4.604	7.173	8.610
5	1.476	2.015	2.571	3.365	4.032	5.893	6.869
6	1.440	1.943	2.447	3.143	3.707	5.208	5.959
7	1.415	1.895	2.365	2.998	3.499	4.785	5.408
8	1.397	1.860	2.306	2.896	3.355	4.501	5.041
9	1.383	1.833	2.262	2.821	3.250	4.297	4.781
10	1.372	1.812	2.228	2.764	3.169	4.144	4.587
11	1.363	1.796	2.201	2.718	3.106	4.025	4.437
12	1.356	1.782	2.179	2.681	3.055	3.930	4.318
13	1.350	1.771	2.160	2.650	3.012	3.852	4.221
14	1.345	1.761	2.145	2.624	2.977	3.787	4.140
15	1.341	1.753	2.131	2.602	2.947	3.733	4.073
16	1.337	1.746	2.120	2.583	2.921	3.686	4.015
17	1.333	1.740	2.110	2.567	2.898	3.646	3.965
18	1.330	1.734	2.101	2.552	2.878	3.610	3.922
19	1.328	1.729	2.093	2.539	2.861	3.579	3.883
20	1.325	1.725	2.086	2.528	2.845	3.552	3.850
21	1.323	1.721	2.080	2.518	2.831	3.527	3.819
22	1.321	1.717	2.074	2.508	2.819	3.505	3.792
23	1.319	1.714	2.069	2.500	2.807	3.485	3.767
24	1.318	1.711	2.064	2.492	2.797	3.467	3.745
25	1.316	1.708	2.060	2.485	2.787	3.450	3.725
26	1.315	1.706	2.056	2.479	2.779	3.435	3.707
27	1.314	1.703	2.052	2.473	2.771	3.421	3.690
28	1.313	1.701	2.048	2.467	2.763	3.408	3.674
29	1.311	1.699	2.045	2.462	2.756	3.396	3.659
30	1.310	1.697	2.042	2.457	2.750	3.385	3.646
40	1.303	1.684	2.021	2.423	2.704	3.307	3.551
60	1.296	1.671	2.000	2.390	2.660	3.232	3.460
120	1.289	1.658	1.980	2.358	2.617	3.160	3.373
∞	1.282	1.645	1.960	2.326	2.576	3.090	3.291

Similarly, when there are $df = 14$ degrees of freedom, we find that $t_{.005} = 2.977$ (see Table 8.3 and Figure 8.9).

Table 8.3 gives *t* points for degrees of freedom *df* from 1 to 30. The table also gives *t* points for 40, 60, 120, and an infinite number of degrees of freedom. Looking at this table, it is useful to realize that the normal points giving the various right-hand tail areas are listed in the row of the *t* table corresponding to an infinite (∞) number of degrees of freedom. Looking at the row corresponding to ∞, we see that, for example, $z_{.025} = 1.96$. Therefore, we can use this row in the *t* table as an alternative to using the normal table when we need to find normal points (such as $z_{\alpha/2}$ in Section 8.1).

Table A.4 of Appendix A (pages 642 and 643) gives *t* points for values of *df* from 1 to 100. We can use a computer to find *t* points based on values of *df* greater than 100. Alternatively, because a *t* curve based on more than 100 degrees of freedom is approximately the shape of the standard normal curve, *t* points based on values of *df* greater than 100 can be approximated by their

FIGURE 8.9   **The *t* Point Giving a Right-Hand Tail Area of .005 under the *t* Curve Having 14 Degrees of Freedom: $t_{.005} = 2.977$**

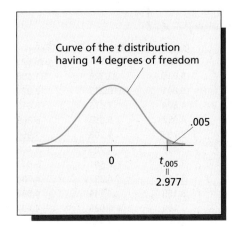

FIGURE 8.10   **The Point $t_{\alpha/2}$ with *n* − 1 Degrees of Freedom**

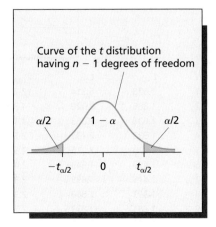

corresponding *z* points. That is, when performing hand calculations, it is reasonable to approximate values of t_α by z_α when *df* is greater than 100.

We now present the formula for a $100(1 - \alpha)$ percent confidence interval for a population mean μ based on the *t* distribution.

A *t*-Based Confidence Interval for a Population Mean μ: σ Unknown

If the sampled population is normally distributed with mean μ, then a **$100(1 - \alpha)$ percent confidence interval for μ** is

$$\left[\bar{x} \pm t_{\alpha/2} \frac{s}{\sqrt{n}} \right]$$

Here *s* is the sample standard deviation, $t_{\alpha/2}$ is the *t* point giving a right-hand tail area of $\alpha/2$ under the *t* curve having *n* − 1 degrees of freedom, and *n* is the sample size.

CHAPTER 9

Before presenting an example, we need to make a few comments. First, it has been shown that this confidence interval is approximately valid for many populations that are not exactly normally distributed. In particular, this interval is approximately valid for a mound-shaped, or single-peaked, population, even if the population is somewhat skewed to the right or left. Second, this interval employs the point $t_{\alpha/2}$, which as shown in Figure 8.10, gives a right-hand tail area equal to $\alpha/2$ under the *t* curve having *n* − 1 degrees of freedom. Here $\alpha/2$ is determined from the desired confidence level $100(1 - \alpha)$ percent.

EXAMPLE 8.4

One measure of a company's financial health is its *debt-to-equity ratio*. This quantity is defined to be the ratio of the company's corporate debt to the company's equity. If this ratio is too high, it is one indication of financial instability. For obvious reasons, banks often monitor the financial health of companies to which they have extended commercial loans. Suppose that, in order to reduce risk, a large bank has decided to initiate a policy limiting the mean debt-to-equity ratio for its portfolio of commercial loans to 1.5. In order to estimate the mean debt-to-equity ratio of its loan portfolio, the bank randomly selects a sample of 15 of its commercial loan accounts. Audits of these companies result in the following debt-to-equity ratios:

1.31	1.05	1.45	1.21	1.19
1.78	1.37	1.41	1.22	1.11
1.46	1.33	1.29	1.32	1.65

A stem-and-leaf display of these ratios is given on the page margin, and a box plot of the ratios is given below. The stem-and-leaf display looks reasonably mound-shaped, and both the stem-and-leaf display and the box plot look reasonably symmetrical. Furthermore, the sample mean and standard deviation of the ratios can be calculated to be $\bar{x} = 1.3433$ and $s = .1921$.

```
1.0 | 5
1.1 | 1 9
1.2 | 1 2 9
1.3 | 1 2 3 7
1.4 | 1 5 6
1.5 |
1.6 | 5
1.7 | 8
```

● DebtEq

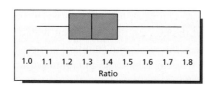

Suppose the bank wishes to calculate a 95 percent confidence interval for the loan portfolio's mean debt-to-equity ratio, μ. Because the bank has taken a sample of size $n = 15$, we have $n - 1 = 15 - 1 = 14$ degrees of freedom, and the level of confidence $100(1 - \alpha)\% = 95\%$ implies that $\alpha = .05$. Therefore, we use the *t* point $t_{\alpha/2} = t_{.05/2} = t_{.025} = 2.145$ (see Table 8.3). It follows that the 95 percent confidence interval for μ is

$$\left[\bar{x} \pm t_{.025} \frac{s}{\sqrt{n}} \right] = \left[1.3433 \pm 2.145 \frac{.1921}{\sqrt{15}} \right]$$

$$= [1.3433 \pm 0.1064]$$

$$= [1.2369, 1.4497]$$

This interval says the bank is 95 percent confident that the mean debt-to-equity ratio for its portfolio of commercial loan accounts is between 1.2369 and 1.4497. Based on this interval, the bank has strong evidence that the portfolio's mean ratio is less than 1.5 (or that the bank is in compliance with its new policy).

BI

Recall that in the two cases discussed in Section 8.1 we calculated *z*-based confidence intervals for μ by assuming that the population standard deviation σ is known. If σ is actually not known (which would probably be true), we should compute *t*-based confidence intervals. Furthermore, recall that in each of these cases the sample size is large (at least 30). In general, it can be shown that if the sample size is large, the *t*-based confidence interval for μ is approximately valid even if the sampled population is not normally distributed (or mound-shaped). Therefore, consider the car mileage case and the sample of 50 mileages in Table 1.4, which has mean $\bar{x} = 31.56$ and standard deviation $s = .798$. The 95 percent *t*-based confidence interval for the population mean mileage μ of the new midsize model is

$$\left[\bar{x} \pm t_{.025} \frac{s}{\sqrt{n}} \right] = \left[31.56 \pm 2.010 \frac{.798}{\sqrt{50}} \right] = [31.33, 31.79]$$

where $t_{.025} = 2.010$ is based on $n - 1 = 50 - 1 = 49$ degrees of freedom—see Table A.4 (page 643). This interval says we are 95 percent confident that the model's mean mileage μ is between 31.33 mpg and 31.78 mpg. Based on this interval, the model's EPA mileage estimate is 31 mpg, and the automaker will receive the tax credit.

BI

As another example, the sample of 65 payment times in Table 2.4 has mean $\bar{x} = 18.1077$ and standard deviation $s = 3.9612$. The 95 percent *t*-based confidence interval for the population mean payment time using the new electronic billing system is

$$\left[\bar{x} \pm t_{.025} \frac{s}{\sqrt{n}} \right] = \left[18.1077 \pm 1.998 \frac{3.9612}{\sqrt{65}} \right] = [17.1, 19.1]$$

where $t_{.025} = 1.998$ is based on $n - 1 = 65 - 1 = 64$ degrees of freedom—see Table A.4 (page 643). Recalling that the mean payment time using the old billing system is 39 days, the interval says that we are 95 percent confident that the mean payment time using the new billing system is between 17.1 days and 19.1 days. Therefore, we are 95 percent confident that the new billing system reduces the mean payment time by at most 21.9 days and by at least 19.9 days.

EXAMPLE 8.5 The Marketing Research Case

Recall that a brand group is considering a new bottle design for a popular soft drink and that Table 1.3 (page 8) gives a random sample of $n = 60$ consumer ratings of this new bottle design. Let μ denote the mean rating of the new bottle design that would be given by all consumers. In order to assess whether μ exceeds the minimum standard composite score of 25 for a successful bottle design, the brand group will calculate a 95 percent confidence interval for μ. The mean and the standard deviation of the 60 bottle design ratings are $\bar{x} = 30.35$ and $s = 3.1073$. It follows that a 95 percent confidence interval for μ is

$$\left[\bar{x} \pm t_{.025}\frac{s}{\sqrt{n}} \right] = \left[30.35 \pm 2.001\frac{3.1073}{\sqrt{60}} \right] = [29.5, 31.2]$$

where $t_{.025} = 2.001$ is based on $n - 1 = 60 - 1 = 59$ degrees of freedom—see Table A.4. Since the interval says we are 95 percent confident that the mean rating of the new bottle design is between 29.5 and 31.2, we are 95 percent confident that this mean rating exceeds the minimum standard of 25 by at least 4.5 points and by at most 6.2 points.

Confidence intervals for μ can be computed using MINITAB, Excel, and MegaStat. For example, the MINITAB output in Figure 8.11 tells us that the t-based 95 percent confidence interval for the mean debt-to-equity ratio is [1.2370, 1.4497]. This result is, within rounding, the same interval calculated in Example 8.4. The MINITAB output also gives the sample mean $\bar{x} = 1.3433$, as well as the sample standard deviation $s = .1921$ and the quantity $s/\sqrt{n} = .0496$, which is called the **standard error of the estimate** $\bar{x}$ and is denoted "SE Mean" on the MINITAB output. Finally, the MINITAB output gives a box plot of the sample of 15 debt-to-equity ratios and graphically illustrates under the box plot the 95 percent confidence interval for the mean debt-to-equity ratio. Figure 8.12(a) gives the MegaStat output of the 95 percent confidence interval for the mean debt-to-equity ratio, and Figure 8.12(b) gives the Excel output of the information needed to calculate this interval. If we consider the Excel output, we note that $\bar{x} = 1.3433$ (see "Mean"), $s = .1921$ (see "Standard Deviation"), $s/\sqrt{n} = .0496$ (see "Standard Error"), and $t_{.025}(s/\sqrt{n}) = .1064$ [see "Confidence Level (95.0%)"]. The interval, which must be hand calculated, is $[1.3433 \pm .1064] = [1.2369, 1.4497]$.

To conclude this section, we note that if the sample size n is small and the sampled population is not mound-shaped or is highly skewed, then the t-based confidence interval for the population mean might not be valid. In this case we can use a **nonparametric method**—a method that

FIGURE 8.11   **MINITAB Output of a t-Based 95 Percent Confidence Interval for the Mean Debt-to-Equity Ratio**

Variable	N	Mean	StDev	SE Mean	95% CI
Ratio	15	1.3433	0.1921	0.0496	(1.2370, 1.4497)

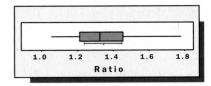

FIGURE 8.12   MegaStat and Excel Outputs for the Debt-to-Equity Ratio Example

(a) The MegaStat output

Confidence interval - mean

| 1.3433 mean | 15 n | **1.4497 upper confidence limit** |
| 0.1921 std. dev | 2.145 t (df = 14) | **1.2369 lower confidence limit** |

(b) The Excel output

STATISTICS	
Mean	1.343333
Standard Error	0.049595
Median	1.32
Mode	#N/A
Standard Deviation	0.192081
Sample Variance	0.036895
Kurtosis	0.833414
Skewness	0.805013
Range	0.73
Minimum	1.05
Maximum	1.78
Sum	20.15
Count	15
Confidence Level(95.0%)	0.106371

makes no assumption about the shape of the sampled population and is valid for any sample size. Nonparametric methods are discussed in Bowerman, O'Connell, and Murphree (2008).

Exercises for Section 8.2

CONCEPTS

8.13 Explain how each of the following changes as *the number of degrees of freedom* describing a *t* curve *increases:*

a The standard deviation of the *t* curve.   **b** The points t_α and $t_{\alpha/2}$.

8.14 Discuss when it is appropriate to use the *t*-based confidence interval for μ.

METHODS AND APPLICATIONS

8.15 Using Table 8.3, find $t_{.10}$, $t_{.025}$, and $t_{.001}$ based on 11 degrees of freedom. Also, find these *t* points based on 6 degrees of freedom.

8.16 Suppose that for a sample of $n = 11$ measurements, we find that $\bar{x} = 72$ and $s = 5$. Assuming normality, compute confidence intervals for the population mean μ with the following levels of confidence:

a 95%   **b** 99%   **c** 80%   **d** 90%   **e** 98%   **f** 99.8%

8.17 The *bad debt ratio* for a financial institution is defined to be the dollar value of loans defaulted divided by the total dollar value of all loans made. Suppose a random sample of seven Ohio banks is selected and that the bad debt ratios (written as percentages) for these banks are 7 percent, 4 percent, 6 percent, 7 percent, 5 percent, 4 percent, and 9 percent. Assuming the bad debt ratios are approximately normally distributed, the MINITAB output of a 95 percent confidence interval for the mean bad debt ratio of all Ohio banks is as follows: ● BadDebt

```
Variable   N     Mean     StDev    SE Mean        95% CI
D-Ratio    7   6.00000   1.82574   0.69007   (4.31147, 7.68853)
```

a Using the $\bar{x}$ and *s* on the MINITAB output, verify the calculation of the 95 percent confidence interval, and calculate a 99 percent confidence interval for the mean debt-to-equity ratio.

b Banking officials claim that the mean bad debt ratio for all banks in the Midwest region is 3.5 percent and that the mean bad debt ratio for Ohio banks is higher. Using the 95 percent confidence interval, can we be 95 percent confident that this claim is true? Using the 99 percent confidence interval, can we be 99 percent confident that this claim is true?

8.18 In an article in *Quality Progress,* Blauw and During study how long it takes Dutch companies to complete five stages in the adoption of total quality control (TQC). According to Blauw and During, the adoption of TQC can be divided into five stages as follows: ● TQC

1   Knowledge: the organization has heard of TQC.

2   Attitude formation: the organization seeks information and compares advantages and disadvantages.

3   Decision making: the organization decides to implement TQC.

4   Implementation: the organization implements TQC.

5   Confirmation: the organization decides to apply TQC as a normal business activity.

Suppose a random sample of five Dutch firms that have adopted TQC is selected. Each firm is asked to report how long it took to complete the implementation stage. The firms report the following durations (in years) for this stage: 2.5, 1.5, 1.25, 3.5, and 1.25. Assuming that the durations are approximately normally distributed, the MegaStat output of a 95 percent confidence interval for the mean duration of the implementation stage for Dutch firms is as follows:

Confidence interval - mean

2 mean	5 n	3.222 upper confidence limit
0.984 std. dev.	2.776 t (df = 4)	0.778 lower confidence limit

Based on the 95 percent confidence interval, is there conclusive evidence that the mean duration of the implementation stage exceeds one year? Explain. What is one possible reason for the lack of conclusive evidence?

8.19   THE AIR TRAFFIC CONTROL CASE   ◐ AlertTime

Air traffic controllers have the crucial task of ensuring that aircraft don't collide. To do this, they must quickly discern when two planes are about to enter the same air space at the same time. They are aided by video display panels that track the aircraft in their sector and alert the controller when two flight paths are about to converge. The display panel currently in use has a mean "alert time" of 15 seconds. (The alert time is the time elapsing between the instant when two aircraft enter into a collision course and when a controller initiates a call to reroute the planes.) According to Ralph Rudd, a supervisor of air traffic controllers at the Greater Cincinnati International Airport, a new display panel has been developed that uses artificial intelligence to project a plane's current flight path into the future. This new panel provides air traffic controllers with an earlier warning that a collision is likely. It is hoped that the mean "alert time," μ, for the new panel is less than 8 seconds. In order to test the new panel, 15 randomly selected air traffic controllers are trained to use the panel and their alert times for a simulated collision course are recorded. The sample alert times (in seconds) are: 7.2, 7.5, 8.0, 6.8, 7.2, 8.4, 5.3, 7.3, 7.6, 7.1, 9.4, 6.4, 7.9, 6.2, 8.7.

a   Using the fact that $\bar{x} = 7.4$ and $s = 1.026$, find a 95 percent confidence interval for the mean alert time, μ, for the new panel.

b   Can we be 95 percent confident that μ is less than 8 seconds?

8.20   Whole Foods is an all-natural grocery chain that has 50,000-square-foot stores, up from the industry average of 34,000 square feet. Sales per square foot of supermarkets average just under $400 per square foot, as reported by *USA Today* in an article titled "A whole new ballgame in grocery shopping." Suppose that sales per square foot in the most recent fiscal year are recorded for a random sample of 10 Whole Foods supermarkets. The data (sales dollars per square foot) are as follows: 854, 858, 801, 892, 849, 807, 894, 863, 829, 815. Using the fact that $\bar{x} = 846.2$ and $s = 32.866$, find a 95 percent confidence interval for the true mean sales dollars per square foot for all Whole Foods supermarkets during the most recent fiscal year. Are we 95 percent confident that this mean is greater than $800, the historical average for Whole Foods?   ◐ WholeFoods

8.21   A production supervisor at a major chemical company wishes to determine whether a new catalyst, catalyst XA-100, increases the mean hourly yield of a chemical process beyond the current mean hourly yield, which is known to be roughly equal to, but no more than, 750 pounds per hour. To test the new catalyst, five trial runs using catalyst XA-100 are made. The resulting yields for the trial runs (in pounds per hour) are 801, 814, 784, 836, and 820. Assuming that all factors affecting yields of the process have been held as constant as possible during the test runs, it is reasonable to regard the five yields obtained using the new catalyst as a random sample from the population of all possible yields that would be obtained by using the new catalyst. Furthermore, we will assume that this population is approximately normally distributed.   ◐ ChemYield

a   Using the Excel output in Figure 8.13, find a 95 percent confidence interval for the mean of all possible yields obtained using catalyst XA-100.

b   Based on the confidence interval, can we be 95 percent confident that the mean yield using catalyst XA-100 exceeds 750 pounds per hour? Explain.

8.22   THE TRASH BAG CASE   ◐ TrashBag

The mean and the standard deviation of the sample of 40 trash bag breaking strengths in Table 1.9 are $\bar{x} = 50.575$ and $s = 1.6438$. Calculate a *t*-based 95 percent confidence interval for μ, the mean of the breaking strengths of all possible trash bags of the new type. Also, find this interval using the Excel output in Figure 8.14. Are we 95 percent confident that μ is at least 50 pounds?

FIGURE 8.13   Excel Output for Exercise 8.21

FIGURE 8.13   Excel Output for Exercise 8.21

STATISTICS	
Mean	811
Standard Error	8.786353
Median	814
Mode	#N/A
Standard Deviation	19.64688
Sample Variance	386
Kurtosis	−0.12472
Skewness	−0.23636
Range	52
Minimum	784
Maximum	836
Sum	4055
Count	5
Confidence Level(95.0%)	24.39488

FIGURE 8.14   Excel Output for Exercise 8.22

STATISTICS	
Mean	50.575
Standard Error	0.2599
Median	50.65
Mode	50.9
Standard Deviation	1.643753
Sample Variance	2.701923
Kurtosis	−0.2151
Skewness	−0.05493
Range	7.2
Minimum	46.8
Maximum	54
Sum	2023
Count	40
Confidence Level(95.0%)	0.525697

8.23   THE BANK CUSTOMER WAITING TIME CASE   ◕ WaitTime

The mean and the standard deviation of the sample of 100 bank customer waiting times in Table 1.8 are $\bar{x} = 5.46$ and $s = 2.475$. Calculate a t-based 95 percent confidence interval for μ, the mean of all possible bank customer waiting times using the new system. Are we 95 percent confident that μ is less than six minutes?

8.24   THE VIDEO GAME SATISFACTION RATING CASE   ◕ VideoGame

The mean and the standard deviation of the sample of $n = 65$ customer satisfaction ratings in Table 1.7 are $\bar{x} = 42.95$ and $s = 2.6424$. Calculate a t-based 95 percent confidence interval for μ, the mean of all possible customer satisfaction ratings for the XYZ-Box video game system. Are we 95 percent confident that μ is at least 42, the minimal rating given by a very satisfied customer?

8.3 Sample Size Determination ◦ ● ●

In Example 8.2 we used a sample of 50 mileages to construct a 95 percent confidence interval for the midsize model's mean mileage μ. The size of this sample was not arbitrary—it was planned. To understand this, suppose that before the automaker selected the random sample of 50 mileages, it randomly selected the small sample of five mileages that is shown as the leftmost sample in Table 8.1. This sample consists of the mileages

$$30.7 \quad 31.9 \quad 30.3 \quad 32.0 \quad 31.6$$

and has mean $\bar{x} = 31.3$. Assuming that the population of all mileages is normally distributed and that the population standard deviation σ is known to equal .8, it follows that a 95 percent confidence interval for μ is

$$\left[\bar{x} \pm z_{.025} \frac{\sigma}{\sqrt{n}} \right] = \left[31.3 \pm 1.96 \frac{.8}{\sqrt{5}} \right]$$
$$= [31.3 \pm .701]$$
$$= [30.6, 32.0]$$

Although the sample mean $\bar{x} = 31.3$ is at least 31, the lower limit of the 95 percent confidence interval for μ is less than 31. Therefore, the midsize model's EPA mileage estimate would be 30 mpg, and the automaker would not receive its tax credit. One reason that the lower limit of this 95 percent interval is less than 31 is that the sample size of 5 is not large enough to make the interval's margin of error

$$z_{.025} \frac{\sigma}{\sqrt{n}} = 1.96 \frac{.8}{\sqrt{5}} = .701$$

small enough. We can attempt to make the margin of error in the interval smaller by increasing the sample size. If we feel that the mean $\bar{x}$ of the larger sample will be at least 31.3 mpg (the mean of the small sample we have already taken), then the lower limit of a $100(1 - \alpha)$ percent confidence interval for μ will be at least 31 if the margin of error is .3 or less.

We will now explain how to find the size of the sample that will be needed to make the margin of error in a confidence interval for μ as small as we wish. In order to develop a formula for the needed sample size, we will initially assume that we know σ. Then, if the population is normally distributed or the sample size is large, the z-based $100(1 - \alpha)$ percent confidence interval for μ is

$$\left[\bar{x} \pm z_{\alpha/2} \frac{\sigma}{\sqrt{n}} \right]$$

To find the needed sample size, we set $z_{\alpha/2}(\sigma/\sqrt{n})$ equal to the desired margin of error and solve for n. Letting E denote the desired margin of error, we obtain

$$z_{\alpha/2} \frac{\sigma}{\sqrt{n}} = E$$

Multiplying both sides of this equation by $\sqrt{n}$ and dividing both sides by E, we obtain

$$\sqrt{n} = \frac{z_{\alpha/2}\sigma}{E}$$

Squaring both sides of this result gives us the formula for n.

Determining the Sample Size for a Confidence Interval for μ: σ Known

A sample of size

$$n = \left(\frac{z_{\alpha/2}\sigma}{E} \right)^2$$

makes the margin of error in a $100(1 - \alpha)$ percent confidence interval for μ equal to E. That is, this sample size makes us $100(1 - \alpha)$ percent confident that $\bar{x}$ is within E units of μ. If the calculated value of n is not a whole number, round this value up to the next whole number (so that the margin of error is at least as small as desired).

If we consider the formula for the sample size n, it intuitively follows that the value E is the farthest that the user is willing to allow $\bar{x}$ to be from μ at a given level of confidence, and the normal point $z_{\alpha/2}$ follows directly from the given level of confidence. Furthermore, because the population standard deviation σ is in the numerator of the formula for n, it follows that the more variable that the individual population measurements are, the larger is the sample size needed to estimate μ with a specified accuracy.

In order to use this formula for n, we must either know σ (which is unlikely) or we must compute an estimate of σ. We first consider the case where we know σ. For example, suppose in the car mileage situation we wish to find the sample size that is needed to make the margin of error in a 95 percent confidence interval for μ equal to .3. Assuming that σ is known to equal .8, and using $z_{.025} = 1.96$, the appropriate sample size is

$$n = \left(\frac{z_{.025}\,\sigma}{E} \right)^2 = \left(\frac{1.96(.8)}{.3} \right)^2 = 27.32$$

Rounding up, we would employ a sample of size 28.

In most real situations, of course, we do not know the true value of σ. If σ is not known, we often estimate σ by using a preliminary sample. In this case we modify the above formula for n by replacing σ by the standard deviation s of the preliminary sample and by replacing $z_{\alpha/2}$ by $t_{\alpha/2}$.

Thus we obtain

$$n = \left(\frac{t_{\alpha/2}\, s}{E}\right)^2$$

where the number of degrees of freedom for the $t_{\alpha/2}$ point is the size of the preliminary sample minus 1. Intuitively, using $t_{\alpha/2}$ compensates for the fact that the preliminary sample's value of s might underestimate σ.

EXAMPLE 8.6 The Car Mileage Case

Suppose that in the car mileage situation we wish to find the sample size that is needed to make the margin of error in a 95 percent confidence interval for μ equal to .3. Assuming we do not know σ, we regard the previously discussed sample of five mileages (see page 325) as a preliminary sample. Therefore, we replace σ by the standard deviation of the preliminary sample, which can be calculated to be $s = .7583$, and we replace $z_{\alpha/2} = z_{.025} = 1.96$ by $t_{.025} = 2.776$, which is based on $n - 1 = 4$ degrees of freedom. We find that the appropriate sample size is

$$n = \left(\frac{t_{.025}\, s}{E}\right)^2 = \left(\frac{2.776(.7583)}{.3}\right)^2 = 49.24$$

Rounding up, we employ a sample of size 50.

When we make the margin of error in our 95 percent confidence interval for μ equal to .3, we can say we are 95 percent confident that the sample mean $\bar{x}$ is within .3 of μ. To understand this, suppose the true value of μ is 31.5. Recalling that the mean of the sample of 50 mileages is $\bar{x} = 31.56$, we see that this sample mean is within .3 of μ (in fact, it is $31.56 - 31.5 = .06$ mpg from $\mu = 31.5$). Other samples of 50 mileages would give different sample means that would be different distances from μ. When we say that our sample of 50 mileages makes us 95 percent confident that $\bar{x}$ is within .3 of μ, we mean that **95 percent of all possible sample means based on 50 mileages are within .3 of μ** and 5 percent of such sample means are not. Therefore, when we randomly select one sample of size 50 and compute its sample mean $\bar{x} = 31.56$, we can be 95 percent confident that this sample mean is within .3 of μ.

In general, the purpose behind replacing $z_{\alpha/2}$ by $t_{\alpha/2}$ (when we are using a preliminary sample to obtain an estimate of σ) is to be **conservative,** so that we compute a sample size that is **at least as large as needed.** Because of this, as we illustrate in the next example, we often obtain a margin of error that is even smaller than we have requested.

EXAMPLE 8.7 The Car Mileage Case

To see that the sample of 50 mileages has actually produced a 95 percent confidence interval with a margin of error that is as small as we requested, recall that the 50 mileages have mean $\bar{x} = 31.56$ and standard deviation $s = .798$. Therefore, the t-based 95 percent confidence interval for μ is

$$\left[\bar{x} \pm t_{.025}\frac{s}{\sqrt{n}}\right] = \left[31.56 \pm 2.010\frac{.798}{\sqrt{50}}\right]$$
$$= [31.56 \pm .227]$$
$$= [31.33, 31.79]$$

where $t_{.025} = 2.010$ is based on $n - 1 = 50 - 1 = 49$ degrees of freedom—see Table A.4 (page 643). We see that the margin of error in this interval is .227, which is smaller than the .3 we asked for. Furthermore, as the automaker had hoped, the sample mean $\bar{x} = 31.56$ of the sample of 50 mileages turned out to be at least 31.3. Therefore, since the margin of error is less than .3, the lower limit of the 95 percent confidence interval is higher than 31 mpg, and the midsize model's EPA mileage estimate is 31 mpg. Because of this, the automaker will receive its tax credit.

Finally, sometimes we do not know σ and we do not have a preliminary sample that can be used to estimate σ. In this case it can be shown that, if we can make a reasonable guess of the range of the population being studied, then a conservatively large estimate of σ is this estimated range divided by 4. For example, if the automaker's design engineers feel that almost all of its midsize cars should get mileages within a range of 5 mpg, then a conservatively large estimate of σ is $5/4 = 1.25$ mpg. When employing such an estimate of σ, it is sufficient to use the z-based sample size formula $n = (z_{\alpha/2}\sigma/E)^2$, because a conservatively large estimate of σ will give us a conservatively large sample size.

Exercises for Section 8.3

CONCEPTS

connect

8.25 Explain what is meant by the margin of error for a confidence interval. What error are we talking about in the context of an interval for μ?

8.26 Explain exactly what we mean when we say that a sample of size n makes us 99 percent confident that $\bar{x}$ is within E units of μ.

8.27 Why do we often need to take a preliminary sample when determining the size of the sample needed to make the margin of error of a confidence interval equal to E?

METHODS AND APPLICATIONS

8.28 Consider a population having a standard deviation equal to 10. We wish to estimate the mean of this population.
  a How large a random sample is needed to construct a 95 percent confidence interval for the mean of this population with a margin of error equal to 1?
  b Suppose that we now take a random sample of the size we have determined in part a. If we obtain a sample mean equal to 295, calculate the 95 percent confidence interval for the population mean. What is the interval's margin of error?

8.29 Referring to Exercise 8.11a, assume that σ equals 33. How large a random sample of public owner-controlled companies is needed to make us
  a 95 percent confident that $\bar{x}$, the sample mean audit delay, is within a margin of error of four days of μ, the true mean audit delay?
  b 99 percent confident that $\bar{x}$ is within a margin of error of four days of μ?

8.30 Referring to Exercise 8.12b, assume that σ equals .66. How large a sample of late replacement buyers is needed to make us
  a 99 percent confident that $\bar{x}$, the sample mean number of dealers visited, is within a margin of error of .04 of μ, the true mean number of dealers visited?
  b 99.73 percent confident that $\bar{x}$ is within a margin of error of .05 of μ?

8.31 Referring to Exercise 8.21, regard the sample of five trial runs for which $s = 19.65$ as a preliminary sample. Determine the number of trial runs of the chemical process needed to make us
  a 95 percent confident that $\bar{x}$, the sample mean hourly yield, is within a margin of error of eight pounds of the true mean hourly yield μ when catalyst XA-100 is used.
  b 99 percent confident that $\bar{x}$ is within a margin of error of five pounds of μ.   ChemYield

8.32 Referring to Exercise 8.20, regard the sample of 10 sales figures for which $s = 32.866$ as a preliminary sample. How large a sample of sales figures is needed to make us 95 percent confident that $\bar{x}$, the sample mean sales dollars per square foot, is within a margin of error of $10 of μ, the true mean sales dollars per square foot for all Whole Foods supermarkets?   WholeFoods

8.33 THE AIR TRAFFIC CONTROL CASE   AlertTime

Referring to Exercise 8.19, regard the sample of 15 alert times for which $s = 1.026$ as a preliminary sample. Determine the sample size needed to make us 95 percent confident that $\bar{x}$, the sample mean alert time, is within a margin of error of .3 seconds of μ, the true mean alert time using the new display panel.

8.4 Confidence Intervals for a Population Proportion ● ● ●

In Chapter 7, the soft cheese spread producer decided to replace its current spout with the new spout if p, the true proportion of all current purchasers who would stop buying the cheese spread if the new spout were used, is less than .10. Suppose that when 1,000 current purchasers are randomly selected and are asked to try the new spout, 63 say they would stop buying the spread if the new spout were used. The point estimate of the population proportion p is the sample proportion $\hat{p} = 63/1,000 = .063$. This sample proportion says we estimate that 6.3 percent of all current purchasers would stop buying the cheese spread if the new spout were used. Since $\hat{p}$ equals .063, we have some evidence that p is less than .10.

In order to see if there is strong evidence that p is less than .10, we can calculate a confidence interval for p. As explained in Chapter 7, if the sample size n is large, then the sampling distribution of the sample proportion $\hat{p}$ is approximately a normal distribution with mean $\mu_{\hat{p}} = p$ and standard deviation $\sigma_{\hat{p}} = \sqrt{p(1 - p)/n}$. By using the same logic we used in developing confidence intervals for μ, it follows that a $100(1 - \alpha)$ percent confidence interval for p is

$$\left[\hat{p} \pm z_{\alpha/2} \sqrt{\frac{p(1 - p)}{n}} \right]$$

Estimating $p(1 - p)$ by $\hat{p}(1 - \hat{p})$, it follows that a $100(1 - \alpha)$ percent confidence interval for p can be calculated as summarized below.

A Large Sample Confidence Interval for a Population Proportion p

I f the sample size n is large, a $100(1 - \alpha)$ percent confidence interval for the population proportion p is

$$\left[\hat{p} \pm z_{\alpha/2} \sqrt{\frac{\hat{p}(1 - \hat{p})}{n}} \right]$$

Here n should be considered large if both $n\hat{p}$ and $n(1 - \hat{p})$ are at least 5.[1]

EXAMPLE 8.8 The Cheese Spread Case   C

In the cheese spread situation, consider calculating a confidence interval for p, the population proportion of purchasers who would stop buying the cheese spread if the new spout were used. In order to see whether the sample size $n = 1,000$ is large enough to enable us to use the confidence interval formula just given, recall that the point estimate of p is $\hat{p} = 63/1,000 = .063$. Therefore, because $n\hat{p} = 1,000(.063) = 63$ and $n(1 - \hat{p}) = 1,000(.937) = 937$ are both greater than 5, we can use the confidence interval formula. For example, a 95 percent confidence interval for p is

$$\left[\hat{p} \pm z_{.025} \sqrt{\frac{\hat{p}(1 - \hat{p})}{n}} \right] = \left[.063 \pm 1.96 \sqrt{\frac{(.063)(.937)}{1,000}} \right]$$
$$= [.063 \pm .0151]$$
$$= [.0479, .0781]$$

This interval says that we are 95 percent confident that between 4.79 percent and 7.81 percent of all current purchasers would stop buying the cheese spread if the new spout were used. Below we give the MegaStat output of this interval.

Confidence interval - proportion

1000 n	95% confidence level	**0.078 upper confidence limit**
1.960 z	0.063 proportion	**0.048 lower confidence limit**

[1]Some statisticians suggest using the more conservative rule that both $n\hat{p}$ and $n(1 - \hat{p})$ must be at least 10. Furthermore, because $\hat{p}(1 - \hat{p})/(n - 1)$ is an unbiased point estimate of $p(1 - p)/n$, a more correct $100(1 - \alpha)$ percent confidence interval for p is $[\hat{p} \pm z_{\alpha/2} \sqrt{\hat{p}(1 - \hat{p})/(n - 1)}]$. However, because n is large, there is little difference between intervals obtained by using this formula and those obtained by using the formula in the above box.

A 99 percent confidence interval for p is

$$\left[\hat{p} \pm z_{.005}\sqrt{\frac{\hat{p}(1 - \hat{p})}{n}}\right] = \left[.063 \pm 2.575\sqrt{\frac{(.063)(.937)}{1,000}}\right]$$
$$= [.063 \pm .0198]$$
$$= [.0432, .0828]$$

The upper limits of both the 95 percent and 99 percent intervals are less than .10. Therefore, we have very strong evidence that the true proportion p of all current purchasers who would stop buying the cheese spread is less than .10. Based on this result, it seems reasonable to use the new spout.

In the cheese spread example, a sample of 1,000 purchasers gives us a 95 percent confidence interval for p—[.063 ± .0151]—with a reasonably small margin of error of .0151. Generally speaking, quite a large sample is needed in order to make the margin of error in a confidence interval for p reasonably small. The next two examples demonstrate that a sample size of 200, which most people would consider quite large, does not necessarily give a 95 percent confidence interval for p with a small margin of error.

EXAMPLE 8.9

Antibiotics occasionally cause nausea as a side effect. Scientists working for a major drug company have developed a new antibiotic called Phe-Mycin. The company wishes to estimate p, the proportion of all patients who would experience nausea as a side effect when being treated with Phe-Mycin. Suppose that a sample of 200 patients is randomly selected. When these patients are treated with Phe-Mycin, 35 patients experience nausea. The point estimate of the population proportion p is the sample proportion $\hat{p} = 35/200 = .175$. This sample proportion says that we estimate that 17.5 percent of all patients would experience nausea as a side effect of taking Phe-Mycin. Furthermore, because $n\hat{p} = 200(.175) = 35$ and $n(1 - \hat{p}) = 200(.825) = 165$ are both at least 5, we can use the previously given formula to calculate a confidence interval for p. Doing this, we find that a 95 percent confidence interval for p is

$$\left[\hat{p} \pm z_{.025}\sqrt{\frac{\hat{p}(1 - \hat{p})}{n}}\right] = \left[.175 \pm 1.96\sqrt{\frac{(.175)(.825)}{200}}\right]$$
$$= [.175 \pm .053]$$
$$= [.122, .228]$$

This interval says we are 95 percent confident that between 12.2 percent and 22.8 percent of all patients would experience nausea as a side effect of taking Phe-Mycin. Notice that the margin of error (.053) in this interval is rather large. Therefore, this interval is fairly long, and it does not provide a very precise estimate of p.

EXAMPLE 8.10 The Marketing Ethics Case: Estimating Marketing Researchers' Disapproval Rates

In the book *Essentials of Marketing Research,* William R. Dillon, Thomas J. Madden, and Neil H. Firtle discuss a survey of marketing professionals, the results of which were originally published by Ishmael P. Akoah and Edward A. Riordan in the *Journal of Marketing Research.* In the study, randomly selected marketing researchers were presented with various scenarios involving ethical issues such as confidentiality, conflict of interest, and social acceptability. The marketing researchers were asked to indicate whether they approved or disapproved of the actions described in each scenario. For instance, one scenario that involved the issue of confidentiality was described as follows:

> **Use of ultraviolet ink**   A project director went to the marketing research director's office and requested permission to use an ultraviolet ink to precode a questionnaire for a mail survey. The project director pointed out that although the cover letter promised confidentiality, respondent identification was needed to permit adequate cross-tabulations of the data. The marketing research director gave approval.

Of the 205 marketing researchers who participated in the survey, 117 said they disapproved of the actions taken in the scenario. It follows that a point estimate of p, the proportion of all marketing researchers who disapprove of the actions taken in the scenario, is $\hat{p} = 117/205 = .5707$. Furthermore, because $n\hat{p} = 205(.5707) = 117$ and $n(1 - \hat{p}) = 205(.4293) = 88$ are both at least 5, a 95 percent confidence interval for p is

$$\left[\hat{p} \pm z_{.025}\sqrt{\frac{\hat{p}(1 - \hat{p})}{n}} \right] = \left[.5707 \pm 1.96\sqrt{\frac{(.5707)(.4293)}{205}} \right]$$

$$= [.5707 \pm .0678]$$

$$= [.5029, .6385]$$

This interval says we are 95 percent confident that between 50.29 percent and 63.85 percent of all marketing researchers disapprove of the actions taken in the ultraviolet ink scenario. Notice that since the margin of error (.0678) in this interval is rather large, this interval does not provide a very precise estimate of p. Below we show the MINITAB output of this interval.

CI for One Proportion

X	N	Sample p	95% CI
117	205	0.570732	(0.502975, 0.638488)

In order to find the size of the sample needed to estimate a population proportion, we consider the theoretically correct interval

$$\left[\hat{p} \pm z_{\alpha/2}\sqrt{\frac{p(1 - p)}{n}} \right]$$

To obtain the sample size needed to make the margin of error in this interval equal to E, we set

$$z_{\alpha/2}\sqrt{\frac{p(1 - p)}{n}} = E$$

and solve for n. When we do this, we get the following result:

Determining the Sample Size for a Confidence Interval for p

A sample of size

$$n = p(1 - p)\left(\frac{z_{\alpha/2}}{E}\right)^2$$

makes the margin of error in a $100(1 - \alpha)$ percent confidence interval for p equal to E. That is, this sample size makes us $100(1 - \alpha)$ percent confident that $\hat{p}$ is within E units of p. If the calculated value of n is not a whole number, round this value up to the next whole number.

Looking at this formula, we see that, the larger $p(1 - p)$ is, the larger n will be. To make sure n is large enough, consider Figure 8.15, which is a graph of $p(1 - p)$ versus p. This figure shows that $p(1 - p)$ equals .25 when p equals .5. Furthermore, $p(1 - p)$ is never larger than .25. Therefore, if the true value of p could be near .5, we should set $p(1 - p)$ equal to .25. This will ensure that n is as large as needed to make the margin of error as small as desired. For example, suppose

FIGURE 8.15   The Graph of $p(1 - p)$ versus p

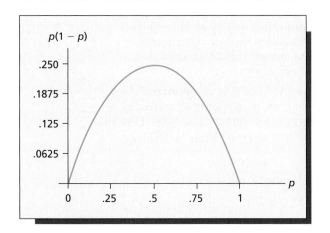

FIGURE 8.16   MegaStat Output of a Sample Size Calculation

Sample size - proportion
0.02 E, error tolerance
0.5 estimated population proportion
95% confidence level
1.960 z
2400.905 sample size
2401 rounded up

we wish to estimate the proportion p of all registered voters who currently favor a particular candidate for president of the United States. If this candidate is the nominee of a major political party, or if the candidate enjoys broad popularity for some other reason, then p could be near .5. Furthermore, suppose we wish to make the margin of error in a 95 percent confidence interval for p equal to .02. If the sample to be taken is random, it should consist of

$$n = p(1 - p)\left(\frac{z_{\alpha/2}}{E}\right)^2 = .25\left(\frac{1.96}{.02}\right)^2 = 2{,}401$$

registered voters. The MegaStat output of the results of this calculation is shown in Figure 8.16. In reality, a list of all registered voters in the United States is not available to polling organizations. Therefore, it is not feasible to take a (technically correct) random sample of registered voters. For this reason, polling organizations actually employ other (more complicated) kinds of samples. We have explained some of the basic ideas behind these more complex samples in optional Section 1.4. For now, we consider the samples taken by polling organizations to be approximately random. Suppose, then, that when the sample of voters is actually taken, the proportion $\hat{p}$ of sampled voters who favor the candidate turns out to be greater than .52. It follows, because the sample is large enough to make the margin of error in a 95 percent confidence interval for p equal to .02, that the lower limit of such an interval is greater than .50. This says we have strong evidence that a majority of all registered voters favor the candidate. For instance, if the sample proportion $\hat{p}$ equals .53, we are 95 percent confident that the proportion of all registered voters who favor the candidate is between .51 and .55.

Major polling organizations conduct public opinion polls concerning many kinds of issues. Whereas making the margin of error in a 95 percent confidence interval for p equal to .02 requires a sample size of 2,401, making the margin of error in such an interval equal to .03 requires a sample size of only

$$n = p(1 - p)\left(\frac{z_{\alpha/2}}{E}\right)^2 = .25\left(\frac{1.96}{.03}\right)^2 = 1{,}067.1$$

or 1,068 (rounding up). Of course, these calculations assume that the proportion p being estimated could be near .5. However, for any value of p, increasing the margin of error from .02 to .03 substantially decreases the needed sample size and thus saves considerable time and money. For this reason, although the most accurate public opinion polls use a margin of error of .02, the vast majority of public opinion polls use a margin of error of .03 or larger.

When the news media report the results of a public opinion poll, they express the margin of error in a 95 percent confidence interval for p **in percentage points.** For instance, if the margin of error is .03, the media would say the poll's margin of error is 3 percentage points. The media seldom report the level of confidence, but almost all polling results are based on 95 percent confidence. Sometimes the media make a vague reference to the level of confidence. For instance, if the margin of error is 3 percentage points, the media might say that "the sample result will be within

FIGURE 8.17 As *p* Gets Closer to .5, *p*(1 − *p*) Increases

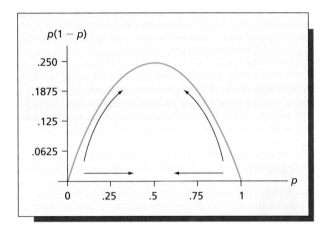

3 percentage points of the population value in 19 out of 20 samples." Here the "19 out of 20 samples" is a reference to the level of confidence, which is $100(19/20) = 100(.95) = 95$ percent.

As an example, suppose a news report says a recent poll finds that 34 percent of the public favors military intervention in an international crisis, and suppose the poll's margin of error is reported to be 3 percentage points. This means the sample taken is large enough to make us 95 percent confident that the sample proportion $\hat{p} = .34$ is within .03 (that is, 3 percentage points) of the true proportion p of the entire public that favors military intervention. That is, we are 95 percent confident that p is between .31 and .37.

If the population proportion we are estimating is substantially different from .5, setting p equal to .5 will give a sample size that is much larger than is needed. In this case, we should use our intuition or previous sample information—along with Figure 8.17—to determine the largest reasonable value for $p(1 - p)$. Figure 8.17 implies that as p gets closer to .5, $p(1 - p)$ increases. It follows that $p(1 - p)$ is maximized by the reasonable value of p that is closest to .5. Therefore, **when we are estimating a proportion that is substantially different from .5, we use the reasonable value of p that is closest to .5 to calculate the sample size needed to obtain a specified margin of error.**

EXAMPLE 8.11

Again consider estimating the proportion of all patients who would experience nausea as a side effect of taking the new antibiotic Phe-Mycin. Suppose the drug company wishes to find the size of the random sample that is needed in order to obtain a 2 percent margin of error with 95 percent confidence. In Example 8.9 we employed a sample of 200 patients to compute a 95 percent confidence interval for p. This interval, which is [.122, .228], makes us very confident that p is between .122 and .228. Because .228 is the reasonable value of p that is closest to .5, the largest reasonable value of $p(1 - p)$ is $.228(1 - .228) = .1760$, and thus the drug company should take a sample of

$$n = p(1 - p)\left(\frac{z_{\alpha/2}}{E}\right)^2 = .1760\left(\frac{1.96}{.02}\right)^2 = 1{,}691 \text{ (rounded up)}$$

patients.

Finally, as a last example of choosing p for sample size calculations, suppose that experience indicates that a population proportion p is at least .75. Then, .75 is the reasonable value of p that is closest to .5, and we would use the largest reasonable value of $p(1 - p)$, which is $.75(1 - .75) = .1875$.

Exercises for Section 8.4

CONCEPTS

connect™

8.34 **a** What does a population proportion tell us about the population?
    b Explain the difference between p and $\hat{p}$.
    c What is meant when a public opinion poll's *margin of error* is 3 percent?

8.35 Suppose we are using the sample size formula in the box on page 331 to find the sample size needed to make the margin of error in a confidence interval for p equal to E. In each of the following situations, explain what value of p would be used in the formula for finding n:
    a We have no idea what value p is—it could be any value between 0 and 1.
    b Past experience tells us that p is no more than .3.
    c Past experience tells us that p is at least .8.

METHODS AND APPLICATIONS

8.36 In each of the following cases, determine whether the sample size n is large enough to use the large sample formula presented in the box on page 329 to compute a confidence interval for p.
    a $\hat{p} = .1$, $n = 30$ **d** $\hat{p} = .8$, $n = 400$
    b $\hat{p} = .1$, $n = 100$ **e** $\hat{p} = .9$, $n = 30$
    c $\hat{p} = .5$, $n = 50$ **f** $\hat{p} = .99$, $n = 200$

8.37 In each of the following cases, compute 95 percent, 98 percent, and 99 percent confidence intervals for the population proportion p.
    a $\hat{p} = .4$ and $n = 100$ **c** $\hat{p} = .9$ and $n = 100$
    b $\hat{p} = .1$ and $n = 300$ **d** $\hat{p} = .6$ and $n = 50$

8.38 *Quality Progress,* February 2005, reports on the results achieved by Bank of America in improving customer satisfaction and customer loyalty by listening to the "voice of the customer." A key measure of customer satisfaction is the response on a scale from 1 to 10 to the question: "Considering all the business you do with Bank of America, what is your overall satisfaction with Bank of America?"[2] Suppose that a random sample of 350 current customers results in 195 customers with a response of 9 or 10 representing "customer delight." Find a 95 percent confidence interval for the true proportion of all current Bank of America customers who would respond with a 9 or 10. Are we 95 percent confident that this proportion exceeds .48, the historical proportion of customer delight for Bank of America?

8.39 **THE MARKETING ETHICS CASE: CONFLICT OF INTEREST**

    Consider the marketing ethics case described in Example 8.10. One of the scenarios presented to the 205 marketing researchers is as follows:

> A marketing testing firm to which X company gives most of its business recently went public. The marketing research director of X company had been looking for a good investment and proceeded to buy some $20,000 of their stock. The firm continues as X company's leading supplier for testing.

a Of the 205 marketing researchers who participated in the ethics survey, 111 said that they disapproved of the actions taken in the scenario. Use this sample result to show that the 95 percent confidence interval for the proportion of all marketing researchers who disapprove of the actions taken in the conflict of interest scenario is as given in the MINITAB output below. Interpret this interval.

CI for One Proportion

```
   X     N      Sample p          95% CI
  111   205     0.541463     (0.473254, 0.609673)
```

b On the basis of this interval, is there convincing evidence that a majority of all marketing researchers disapprove of the actions taken in the conflict of interest scenario? Explain.

8.40 In a news story distributed by the *Washington Post,* Lew Sichelman reports that a substantial fraction of mortgage loans that go into default within the first year of the mortgage were approved on the basis of falsified applications. For instance, loan applicants often exaggerate their income or fail to declare debts. Suppose that a random sample of 1,000 mortgage loans that were defaulted within the first year reveals that 410 of these loans were approved on the basis of falsified applications.
    a Find a point estimate of and a 95 percent confidence interval for p, the proportion of all first-year defaults that are approved on the basis of falsified applications.
    b Based on your interval, what is a reasonable estimate of the minimum percentage of first-year defaults that are approved on the basis of falsified applications?

───────
[2]Source: "Driving Organic Growth at Bank of America" *Quality Progress* (February 2005), pp. 23–27.

8.41　On January 7, 2000, the Gallup Organization released the results of a poll comparing the lifestyles of today with yesteryear. The survey results were based on telephone interviews with a randomly selected national sample of 1,031 adults,18 years and older, conducted December 20–21, 1999.[3]

  a　The Gallup poll found that 42 percent of the respondents said that they spend less than three hours watching TV on an average weekday. Based on this finding, calculate a 99 percent confidence interval for the proportion of U.S. adults who say that they spend less than three hours watching TV on an average weekday. Based on this interval, is it reasonable to conclude that more than 40 percent of U.S. adults say they spend less than three hours watching TV on an average weekday?

  b　The Gallup poll found that 60 percent of the respondents said they took part in some form of daily activity (outside of work, including housework) to keep physically fit. Based on this finding, find a 95 percent confidence interval for the proportion of U.S. adults who say they take part in some form of daily activity to keep physically fit. Based on this interval, is it reasonable to conclude that more than 50 percent of U.S. adults say they take part in some form of daily activity to keep physically fit?

  c　In explaining its survey methods, Gallup states the following: "For results based on this sample, one can say with 95 percent confidence that the maximum error attributable to sampling and other random effects is plus or minus 3 percentage points." Explain how your calculations for part *b* verify that this statement is true.

8.42　In an article in the *Journal of Advertising,* Weinberger and Spotts compare the use of humor in television ads in the United States and the United Kingdom. They found that a substantially greater percentage of U.K. ads use humor.

  a　Suppose that a random sample of 400 television ads in the United Kingdom reveals that 142 of these ads use humor. Show that the point estimate and 95 percent confidence interval for the proportion of all U.K. television ads that use humor are as given in the MegaStat output below.

  Confidence interval—proportion

400 n	95% confidence level	0.402 upper confidence limit
1.960 z	0.355 proportion	0.308 lower confidence limit

  b　Suppose a random sample of 500 television ads in the United States reveals that 122 of these ads use humor. Find a point estimate of and a 95 percent confidence interval for the proportion of all U.S. television ads that use humor.

  c　Do the confidence intervals you computed in parts *a* and *b* suggest that a greater percentage of U.K. ads use humor? Explain. How might an ad agency use this information?

8.43　In an article in *CA Magazine,* Neil Fitzgerald surveyed Scottish business customers concerning their satisfaction with aspects of their banking relationships. Fitzgerald reported that, in 418 telephone interviews conducted by George Street Research, 67 percent of the respondents gave their banks a high rating for overall satisfaction.

  a　Assuming that the sample was randomly selected, calculate a 99 percent confidence interval for the proportion of Scottish business customers who give their banks a high rating for overall satisfaction.

  b　Based on this interval, can we be 99 percent confident that more than 60 percent of Scottish business customers give their banks a high rating for overall satisfaction?

8.44　In the March 16, 1998, issue of *Fortune* magazine, the results of a survey of 2,221 MBA students from across the United States conducted by the Stockholm-based academic consulting firm Universum showed that only 20 percent of MBA students expect to stay at their first job five years or more.[4] Assuming that a random sample was employed, find a 95 percent confidence interval for the proportion of all U.S. MBA students who expect to stay at their first job five years or more. Based on this interval, is there strong evidence that fewer than one-fourth of all U.S. MBA students expect to stay?

8.45　*Consumer Reports* (January 2005) indicates that profit margins on extended warranties are much greater than on the purchase of most products.[5] In this exercise we consider a major electronics retailer that wishes to increase the proportion of customers who buy extended warranties on digital cameras. Historically, 20 percent of digital camera customers have purchased the retailer's extended warranty. To increase this percentage, the retailer has decided to offer a new warranty

[3]Source: http://www.gallup.com/poll/releases/, The Gallup Organization, January 7, 2000.
[4]Source: Shelly Branch, "MBAs: What Do They Really Want?" *Fortune* (March 16, 1998), p. 167.
[5]*Consumer Reports,* January 2005, p. 51.

that is less expensive and more comprehensive. Suppose that three months after starting to offer the new warranty, a random sample of 500 customer sales invoices shows that 152 out of 500 digital camera customers purchased the new warranty. Find a 95 percent confidence interval for the proportion of all digital camera customers who have purchased the new warranty. Are we 95 percent confident that this proportion exceeds .20?

8.46   The manufacturer of the ColorSmart-5000 television set claims 95 percent of its sets last at least five years without needing a single repair. In order to test this claim, a consumer group randomly selects 400 consumers who have owned a ColorSmart-5000 television set for five years. Of these 400 consumers, 316 say their ColorSmart-5000 television sets did not need a repair, whereas 84 say their ColorSmart-5000 television sets did need at least one repair.

   a   Find a 99 percent confidence interval for the proportion of all ColorSmart-5000 television sets that have lasted at least five years without needing a single repair.

   b   Does this confidence interval provide strong evidence that the percentage of ColorSmart-5000 television sets that last at least five years without a single repair is less than the 95 percent claimed by the manufacturer? Explain.

8.47   In the book *Cases in Finance,* Nunnally and Plath present a case in which the estimated percentage of uncollectible accounts varies with the age of the account. Here the age of an unpaid account is the number of days elapsed since the invoice date.

   Suppose an accountant believes the percentage of accounts that will be uncollectible increases as the ages of the accounts increase. To test this theory, the accountant randomly selects 500 accounts with ages between 31 and 60 days from the accounts receivable ledger dated one year ago. The accountant also randomly selects 500 accounts with ages between 61 and 90 days from the accounts receivable ledger dated one year ago.

   a   If 10 of the 500 accounts with ages between 31 and 60 days were eventually classified as uncollectible, find a point estimate of and a 95 percent confidence interval for the proportion of all accounts with ages between 31 and 60 days that will be uncollectible.

   b   If 27 of the 500 accounts with ages between 61 and 90 days were eventually classified as uncollectible, find a point estimate of and a 95 percent confidence interval for the proportion of all accounts with ages between 61 and 90 days that will be uncollectible.

   c   Based on these intervals, is there strong evidence that the percentage of accounts aged between 61 and 90 days that will be uncollectible is higher than the percentage of accounts aged between 31 and 60 days that will be uncollectible? Explain.

8.48   Consider Exercise 8.41b and suppose we wish to find the sample size n needed in order to be 95 percent confident that $\hat{p}$, the sample proportion of respondents who said they took part in some sort of daily activity to keep physically fit, is within a margin of error of .02 of p, the true proportion of all U.S. adults who say that they take part in such activity. In order to find an appropriate value for $p(1 - p)$, note that the 95 percent confidence interval for p that you calculated in Exercise 8.41b was [.57, .63]. This indicates that the reasonable value for p that is closest to .5 is .57, and thus the largest reasonable value for $p(1 - p)$ is .57(1 − .57) = .2451. Calculate the required sample size n.

8.49   Referring to Exercise 8.46, determine the sample size needed in order to be 99 percent confident that $\hat{p}$, the sample proportion of ColorSmart-5000 television sets that last at least five years without a single repair, is within a margin of error of .03 of p, the true proportion of sets that last at least five years without a single repair.

8.50   Suppose we conduct a poll to estimate the proportion of voters who favor a major presidential candidate. Assuming that 50 percent of the electorate could be in favor of the candidate, determine the sample size needed so that we are 95 percent confident that $\hat{p}$, the sample proportion of voters who favor the candidate, is within a margin of error of .01 of p, the true proportion of all voters who are in favor of the candidate.

8.5 A Comparison of Confidence Intervals and Tolerance Intervals (Optional) ● ● ●

In this section we compare confidence intervals with tolerance intervals. We saw in Chapter 3 that a tolerance interval is an interval that is meant to contain a specified percentage (often 68.26 percent, 95.44 percent, or 99.73 percent) of the **individual** population measurements. By contrast, a confidence interval for the population mean μ is an interval that is meant to contain one thing—the population mean μ—and the confidence level associated with the confidence interval expresses how sure we are that this interval contains μ. Often we choose the confidence level to be 95 percent or 99 percent because such a confidence level is usually considered high enough to provide convincing evidence about the true value of μ.

EXAMPLE 8.12 The Car Mileage Case

Recall in the car mileage case that the mean and the standard deviation of the sample of 50 mileages are $\bar{x} = 31.56$ and $s = .798$. Also, recall that we have concluded in Example 3.9 (page 129) that the estimated tolerance intervals $[\bar{x} \pm s] = [30.8, 32.4]$, $[\bar{x} \pm 2s] = [30.0, 33.2]$, and $[\bar{x} \pm 3s] = [29.2, 34.0]$ imply that approximately (1) 68.26 percent of all individual cars will obtain mileages between 30.8 mpg and 32.4 mpg; (2) 95.44 percent of all individual cars will obtain mileages between 30.0 mpg and 33.2 mpg; and (3) 99.73 percent of all individual cars will obtain mileages between 29.2 mpg and 34.0 mpg. By contrast, we have seen in Section 8.2 (page 321) that a 95 percent t-based confidence interval for the mean, μ, of the mileages of all individual cars is $[\bar{x} \pm 2.010 \, (s/\sqrt{50})] = [31.33, 31.79]$. This interval says that we are 95 percent confident that μ is between 31.33 mpg and 31.79 mpg. Figure 8.18 graphically depicts the three estimated tolerance intervals and the 95 percent confidence interval, which are shown below a MegaStat histogram of the 50 mileages. Note that the estimated tolerance intervals, which are meant to contain the *many* mileages that comprise specified percentages of all individual cars, are longer than the 95 percent confidence interval, which is meant to contain the *single* population mean μ.

FIGURE 8.18   A Comparison of Confidence Intervals and Tolerance Intervals

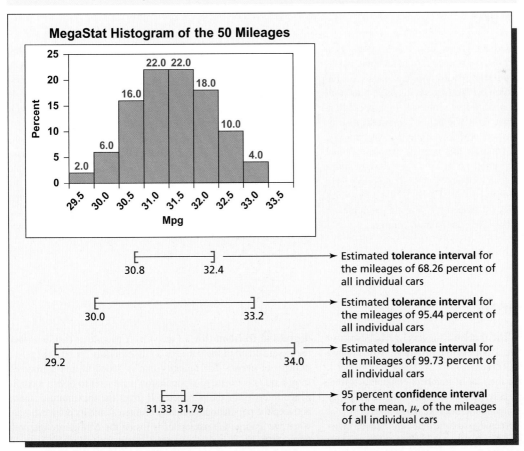

Exercises for Section 8.5

CONCEPTS

8.51   What is a tolerance interval meant to contain?

8.52   What is a confidence interval for the population mean meant to contain?

8.53   Intuitively, why is a tolerance interval longer than a corresponding confidence interval?

METHODS AND APPLICATIONS

In Exercises 8.54 through 8.56 we give the mean and the standard deviation of a sample that has been randomly selected from a population. For each exercise, find estimated tolerance intervals that contain approximately 68.26 percent, 95.44 percent, and 99.73 percent of the individual population measurements. Also, find a 95 percent confidence interval for the population mean. Interpret the estimated tolerance intervals and the confidence interval in the context of the situation related to the exercise.

8.54   THE TRASH BAG CASE   ● TrashBag

The mean and the standard deviation of the sample of 40 trash bag breaking strengths are $\bar{x} = 50.575$ and $s = 1.6438$.

8.55   THE BANK CUSTOMER WAITING TIME CASE   ● WaitTime

The mean and the standard deviation of the sample of 100 bank customer waiting times are $\bar{x} = 5.46$ and $s = 2.475$.

8.56   THE VIDEO GAME SATISFACTION RATING CASE   ● VideoGame

The mean and the standard deviation of the sample of 65 customer satisfaction ratings are $\bar{x} = 42.95$ and $s = 2.6424$.

Chapter Summary

In this chapter we discussed **confidence intervals** for population **means** and **proportions**. First, we studied how to compute a confidence interval for a **population mean.** We saw that when the population standard deviation σ is known, we can use the **normal distribution** to compute a confidence interval for a population mean. When σ is not known, if the population is normally distributed (or at least mound-shaped) or if the sample size n is large, we use the t **distribution** to compute this interval. We also studied how to find the size of the sample needed if we wish to compute a confidence interval for a mean with a prespecified *confidence level* and with a prespecified *margin of error.* Figure 8.19 is a flowchart summarizing our discussions concerning how to compute an appropriate confidence interval for a population mean.

Next we saw that we are often interested in estimating the proportion of population units falling into a category of interest. We showed how to compute a large sample confidence interval for a **population proportion,** and we saw how to find the sample size needed to estimate a population proportion with a prespecified *confidence level* and with a prespecified *margin of error.*

In optional Section 8.5 we concluded this chapter by comparing confidence intervals for μ with tolerance intervals. We emphasized that a tolerance interval is meant to contain a specified percentage of the individual population measurements, while the confidence interval is meant to contain only one number—the population mean.

Glossary of Terms

confidence coefficient: The (before sampling) probability that a confidence interval for a population parameter will contain the population parameter. (page 311)

confidence interval: An interval of numbers computed so that we can be very confident (say, 95 percent confident) that a population parameter is contained in the interval. (page 309)

confidence level: The percentage of time that a confidence interval would contain a population parameter if all possible samples were used to calculate the interval. (pages 310 and 312)

degrees of freedom (for a t curve): A parameter that describes the exact spread of the curve of a t distribution. (page 318)

margin of error: The quantity that is added to and subtracted from a point estimate of a population parameter to obtain a confidence interval for the parameter. It gives the maximum distance between the population parameter of interest and its point estimate when we assume the parameter is inside the confidence interval. (page 312)

FIGURE 8.19   Computing an Appropriate Confidence Interval for a Population Mean

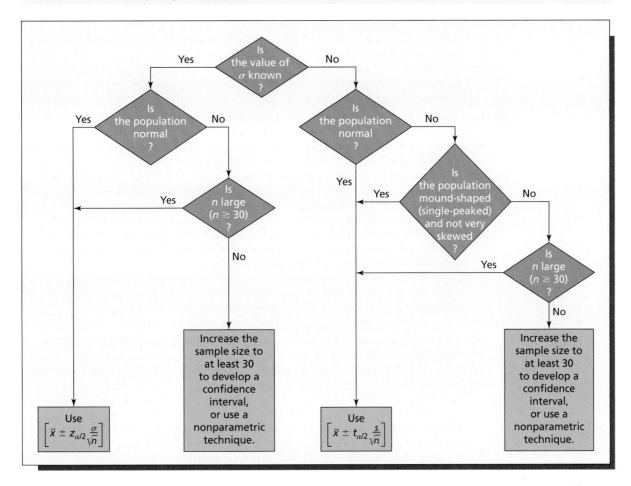

standard error of the estimate $\bar{x}$**:** The point estimate of $\sigma_{\bar{x}}$. (page 322)

t distribution: A commonly used continuous probability distribution that is described by a distribution curve similar to a normal curve. The t curve is symmetrical about zero and is more spread out than a standard normal curve. (pages 317 and 318)

t point, t_{α}: The point on the horizontal axis under a t curve that gives a right-hand tail area equal to α. (page 318)

t table: A table of t point values listed according to the area in the tail of the t curve and according to values of the degrees of freedom. (pages 318–319)

Important Formulas

A z-based confidence interval for a population mean μ with σ known: page 313

A t-based confidence interval for a population mean μ with σ unknown: page 320

Sample size when estimating μ: page 326

A large sample confidence interval for a population proportion p: page 329

Sample size when estimating p: page 331

Supplementary Exercises

8.57   In an article in the *Journal of Accounting Research,* Ashton, Willingham, and Elliott studied audit delay (the length of time from a company's fiscal year-end to the date of the auditor's report) for industrial and financial companies. In the study, a random sample of 250 industrial companies yielded a mean audit delay of 68.04 days with a standard deviation of 35.72 days, while a random

sample of 238 financial companies yielded a mean audit delay of 56.74 days with a standard deviation of 34.87 days. Use these sample results to do the following:

a Calculate a 95 percent confidence interval for the mean audit delay for all industrial companies. Note: $t_{.025} = 1.97$ when $df = 249$.

b Calculate a 95 percent confidence interval for the mean audit delay for all financial companies. Note: $t_{.025} = 1.97$ when $df = 237$.

c By comparing the 95 percent confidence intervals you calculated in parts *a* and *b*, is there strong evidence that the mean audit delay for financial companies is shorter than the mean audit delay for industrial companies? Explain.

8.58 In an article in *Accounting and Business Research,* Beattie and Jones investigate the use and abuse of graphic presentations in the annual reports of United Kingdom firms. The authors found that 65 percent of the sampled companies graph at least one key financial variable, but that 30 percent of the graphics are materially distorted (nonzero vertical axis, exaggerated trend, or the like). Results for U.S. firms have been found to be similar.

a Suppose that in a random sample of 465 graphics from the annual reports of United Kingdom firms, 142 of the graphics are found to be distorted. Find a point estimate of and a 95 percent confidence interval for the proportion of U.K. annual report graphics that are distorted.

b Based on this interval, can we be 95 percent confident that more than 25 percent of all graphics appearing in the annual reports of U.K. firms are distorted? Explain. Does this suggest that auditors should understand proper graphing methods?

c Determine the sample size needed in order to be 95 percent confident that $\hat{p}$, the sample proportion of U.K. annual report graphics that are distorted, is within a margin of error of .03 of p, the true proportion of U.K. annual report graphics that are distorted.

8.59 On January 4, 2000, the Gallup Organization released the results of a poll dealing with the likelihood of computer-related Y2K problems and the possibility of terrorist attacks during the New Year's holiday at the turn of the century.[6] The survey results were based on telephone interviews with a randomly selected national sample of 622 adults, 18 years and older, conducted December 28, 1999.

a The Gallup poll found that 61 percent of the respondents believed that one or more terrorist attacks were likely to happen on the New Year's holiday. Based on this finding, calculate a 95 percent confidence interval for the proportion of all U.S. adults who believed that one or more terrorist attacks were likely to happen on the 2000 New Year's holiday. Based on this interval, is it reasonable to conclude that fewer than two-thirds of all U.S. adults believed that one or more terrorist attacks were likely?

b In explaining its survey methods, Gallup stated the following: "For results based on this sample, one can say with 95 percent confidence that the maximum error attributable to sampling and other random effects is plus or minus 4 percentage points." Explain how your calculations for part *a* verify that this statement is true.

8.60 The manager of a chain of discount department stores wishes to estimate the total number of erroneous discounts allowed by sales clerks during the last month. A random sample of 200 of the chain's 57,532 transactions for the last month reveals that erroneous discounts were allowed on eight of the transactions. Use this sample information to find a point estimate of and a 95 percent confidence interval for the total number of erroneous discounts allowed during the last month.

8.61 **THE DISK BRAKE CASE**

National Motors has equipped the ZX-900 with a new disk brake system. We define the stopping distance for a ZX-900 to be the distance (in feet) required to bring the automobile to a complete stop from a speed of 35 mph under normal driving conditions using this new brake system. In addition, we define μ to be the mean stopping distance of all ZX-900s. One of the ZX-900's major competitors is advertised to achieve a mean stopping distance of 60 feet. National Motors would like to claim in a new advertising campaign that the ZX-900 achieves a shorter mean stopping distance.

Suppose that National Motors randomly selects a sample of $n = 81$ ZX-900s. The company records the stopping distance of each automobile and calculates the mean and standard deviation of the sample of $n = 81$ stopping distances to be $\bar{x} = 57.8$ ft and $s = 6.02$ ft.

a Calculate a 95 percent confidence interval for μ. Can National Motors be 95 percent confident that μ is less than 60 ft? Explain.

b Using the sample of $n = 81$ stopping distances as a preliminary sample, find the sample size necessary to make National Motors 95 percent confident that $\bar{x}$ is within a margin of error of one foot of μ.

[6]Source: http://www.gallup.com/poll/releases/, **The Gallup Organization, January 4, 2000.**

8.62 In an article in the *Journal of Retailing,* J. G. Blodgett, D. H. Granbois, and R. G. Walters investigated negative word-of-mouth consumer behavior. In a random sample of 201 consumers, 150 reported that they engaged in negative word-of-mouth behavior (for instance, they vowed never to patronize a retailer again). In addition, the 150 respondents who engaged in such behavior, on average, told 4.88 people about their dissatisfying experience (with a standard deviation equal to 6.11).

a Use these sample results to compute a 95 percent confidence interval for the proportion of all consumers who engage in negative word-of-mouth behavior. On the basis of this interval, would it be reasonable to claim that more than 70 percent of all consumers engage in such behavior? Explain.

b Use the sample results to compute a 95 percent confidence interval for the mean number of people who are told about a dissatisfying experience by consumers who engage in negative word-of-mouth behavior. On the basis of this interval, would it be reasonable to claim that these dissatisfied consumers tell, on average, at least three people about their bad experience? Explain. Note: $t_{.025} = 1.98$ when $df = 149$.

8.63 THE CIGARETTE ADVERTISEMENT CASE ModelAge

A random sample of 50 perceived age estimates for a model in a cigarette advertisement showed that $\bar{x} = 26.22$ years and that $s = 3.7432$ years.

a Use this sample to calculate a 95 percent confidence interval for the population mean age estimate for all viewers of the ad.

b Remembering that the cigarette industry requires that models must appear at least 25 years old, does the confidence interval make us 95 percent confident that the mean perceived age estimate is at least 25? Is the mean perceived age estimate much more than 25? Explain.

8.64 In an article in the *Journal of Management Information Systems,* Mahmood and Mann investigate how information technology (IT) investment relates to company performance. In particular, Mahmood and Mann obtain sample data concerning IT investment for companies that effectively use information systems. Among the variables studied are the company's IT budget as a percentage of company revenue, percentages of the IT budget spent on staff and training, and number of PCs and terminals as a percentage of total employees.

a Suppose a random sample of 15 companies considered to effectively use information systems yields a sample mean IT budget as a percentage of company revenue of $\bar{x} = 2.73$ with a standard deviation of $s = 1.64$. Assuming that IT budget percentages are approximately normally distributed, calculate a 99 percent confidence interval for the mean IT budget as a percentage of company revenue for all firms that effectively use information systems. Does this interval provide evidence that a firm can successfully use information systems with an IT budget that is less than 5 percent of company revenue? Explain.

b Suppose a random sample of 15 companies considered to effectively use information systems yields a sample mean number of PCs and terminals as a percentage of total employees of $\bar{x} = 34.76$ with a standard deviation of $s = 25.37$. Assuming approximate normality, calculate a 99 percent confidence interval for the mean number of PCs and terminals as a percentage of total employees for all firms that effectively use information systems. Why is this interval so wide? What can we do to obtain a narrower (more useful) confidence interval?

8.65 THE INVESTMENT CASE InvestRet

Suppose that random samples of 50 returns for each of the following investment classes give the indicated sample mean and sample standard deviation:

Fixed annuities: $\bar{x} = 7.83\%$, $s = .51\%$

Domestic large cap stocks: $\bar{x} = 13.42\%$, $s = 15.17\%$

Domestic midcap stocks: $\bar{x} = 15.03\%$, $s = 18.44\%$

Domestic small cap stocks: $\bar{x} = 22.51\%$, $s = 21.75\%$

a For each investment class, compute a 95 percent confidence interval for the population mean return.

b Do these intervals suggest that the current mean return for each investment class differs from the historical (1970 to 1994) mean return given in Table 3.11 (page 159)? Explain.

8.66 THE INTERNATIONAL BUSINESS TRAVEL EXPENSE CASE

Recall that the mean and the standard deviation of a random sample of 35 one-day travel expenses in Moscow are $\bar{x} = \$538$ and $s = \$41$. Find a 95 percent confidence interval for the mean, μ, of all one-day travel expenses in Moscow.

8.67   THE UNITED KINGDOM INSURANCE CASE

Assume that the U.K. insurance survey is based on 1,000 randomly selected U.K. households and that 640 of these households spent money for life insurance in 1993. Find a 95 percent confidence interval for the proportion, p, of all U.K. households that spent money for life insurance in 1993.

8.68   How safe are child car seats? *Consumer Reports* (May 2005) tested the safety of child car seats in 30 mph crashes. They found "slim safety margins" for some child car seats. Suppose that *Consumer Reports* simulates the safety of the market-leading child car seat. Their test consists of placing the maximum claimed weight in the car seat and simulating crashes at higher and higher miles per hour until a problem occurs. The following data identifies the speed at which a problem with the car seat first appeared, such as the strap breaking, seat shell cracking, strap adjuster breaking, seat detaching from the base, and so on: 31.0, 29.4, 30.4, 28.9, 29.7, 30.1, 32.3, 31.7, 35.4, 29.1, 31.2, 30.2. Using the fact that $\bar{x} = 30.7833$ and $s = 1.7862$, find a 95 percent confidence interval for the true mean speed at which a problem with the car seat first appears. Are we 95 percent confident that this mean is at least 30 mph?   ● CarSeat

8.69   In Exercise 2.85 (pages 91–92), we briefly described a series of international quality standards called ISO 9000. In the results of a Quality Systems Update/Deloitte & Touche survey of ISO 9000–registered companies published by CEEM Information Systems, 515 of 620 companies surveyed reported that they are encouraging their suppliers to pursue ISO 9000 registration.[7]

a   Using these survey results, compute a 95.44 percent confidence interval for the proportion of all ISO 9000–registered companies that encourage their suppliers to pursue ISO 9000 registration. Assume here that the survey participants have been randomly selected.

b   Based on this interval, is there conclusive evidence that more than 75 percent of all ISO 9000–registered companies encourage their suppliers to pursue ISO 9000 registration?

8.70   Internet Exercise

What is the average selling price of a home? The Data and Story Library (DASL) contains data, including the sale price, for a random sample of 117 homes sold in Albuquerque, New Mexico. Go to the DASL website (http://lib.stat.cmu.edu/DASL/) and retrieve the home price data set (http://lib.stat.cmu.edu/DASL/Datafiles/homedat.html.) Use MINITAB, Excel, or MegaStat to produce appropriate graphical (histogram, stem-and-leaf, box plot) and numerical summaries of the price data. Identify, from your numerical summaries, the sample mean and standard deviation. Use these summaries to construct a 99 percent confidence interval for μ, the mean sale price. Use statistical software (MINITAB, Excel,

or MegaStat) to compute a 99 percent confidence interval for μ. Do the results of your hand calculations agree with those from your statistical software?

Technical note: There are many ways to capture the home price data from the DASL site. One simple way is to select just the rows containing the data values (and not the labels), copy, paste directly into an Excel or MINITAB worksheet, add your own variable labels, and save the resulting worksheet. It is possible to copy the variable labels from DASL as well, but the differences in alignment and the intervening blank line add to the difficulty.   ● AlbHome

Appendix 8.1 ■ Confidence Intervals Using MINITAB

The instruction blocks in this section each begin by describing the entry of data into the MINITAB Data window. Alternatively, the data may be loaded directly from the data disk included with the text. The appropriate data file name is given at the top of each instruction block. Please refer to Appendix 1.1 for further information about entering data, saving data, and printing results when using MINITAB.

Confidence interval for a population mean in Figure 8.11 on page 322 (data file: Ratio.MTW):

- In the Data window, enter the debt-to-equity ratio data from Example 8.4 (page 321) into a single column with variable name Ratio.

- Select **Stat : Basic Statistics : 1-Sample t**

- In the "1-Sample t (Test and Confidence Interval)" dialog box, select "Samples in columns."

- Select the variable name Ratio into the "Samples in columns" window.

- Click the Options... button.

- In the "1-Sample t—Options" dialog box, enter the desired level of confidence (here 95.0) into the "Confidence level" window.

- Select "not equal" from the Alternative drop-down menu, and click OK in the "1-Sample t—Options" dialog box.

- To produce a box plot of the data with a graphical representation of the confidence interval, click the Graphs . . . button, check the "Boxplot of data" checkbox, and click OK in the "1-Sample t—Graphs" dialog box.

- Click OK in the "1-Sample t (Test and Confidence Interval)" dialog box.

- The confidence interval is given in the Session window, and the box plot appears in a graphics window.

A "1-Sample Z" interval is also available in MINITAB under Basic Statistics. It requires a user-specified value of the population standard deviation, which is rarely known.

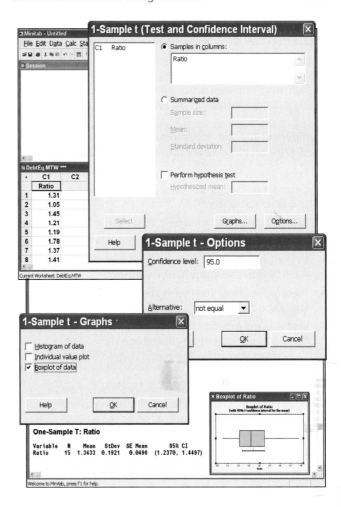

Confidence interval for a population proportion in the marketing ethics situation of Example 8.10 on pages 330 and 331:

- Select **Stat : Basic Statistics : 1 Proportion**

- In the "1 Proportion (Test and Confidence Interval)" dialog box, select "Summarized data."

- Enter the number of trials (here equal to 205) and the number of successes—or events—(here equal to 117) into the appropriate windows.

- Click on the Options . . . button.

- In the "1 Proportion—Options" dialog box, enter the desired level of confidence (here 95.0) into the "Confidence level" window.

- Select "not equal" from the Alternative drop-down menu.

- Check the "Use test and interval based on normal distribution" checkbox.

- Click OK in the "1 Proportion—Options" dialog box.

- Click OK in the "1 Proportion (Test and Confidence Interval)" dialog box.

- The confidence interval will be displayed in the Session window.

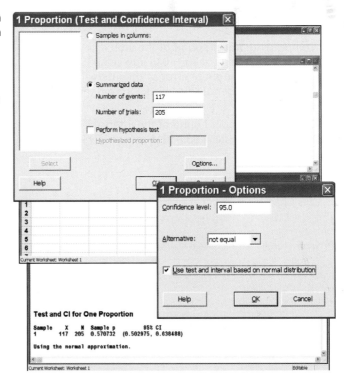

Appendix 8.2 ■ Confidence Intervals Using Excel

The instruction block in this section begins by describing the entry of data into an Excel spreadsheet. Alternatively, the data may be loaded directly from the data disk included with the text. The appropriate data file name is given at the top of the instruction block. Please refer to Appendix 1.2 for further information about entering data, saving data, and printing results when using Excel.

Confidence interval for a population mean in Figure 8.12(b) on page 323 (data file: DebtEq.xlsx):

- Enter the debt-to-equity ratio data from Example 8.4 (page 321) into cells A2 to A16 with the label Ratio in cell A1.

- Select **Data : Data Analysis : Descriptive Statistics.**

- Click OK in the Data Analysis dialog box.

- In the Descriptive Statistics dialog box, enter A1.A16 into the Input Range window.

- Place a checkmark in the "Labels in first row" checkbox.

- Under output options, select "New Worksheet Ply" to have the output placed in a new worksheet and enter the name Output for the new worksheet.

- Place checkmarks in the Summary Statistics and "Confidence Level for Mean" checkboxes. This produces a *t*-based margin of error for a confidence interval.

- Type 95 in the "Confidence Level for Mean" box.

- Click OK in the Descriptive Statistics dialog box.

- A descriptive statistics summary will be displayed in cells A3 through B16 in the Output worksheet. Drag the column borders to reveal complete labels for all of the descriptive statistics.

- Type the heading "95% Confidence Interval" into cells D13 to E13.

- Compute the lower bound of the interval by typing the formula = B3 − B16 into cell D15. This subtracts the margin of error of the interval (labeled "Confidence Level (95%)") from the sample mean.

- Compute the upper bound of the interval by typing the formula = B3 + B16 into cell E15.

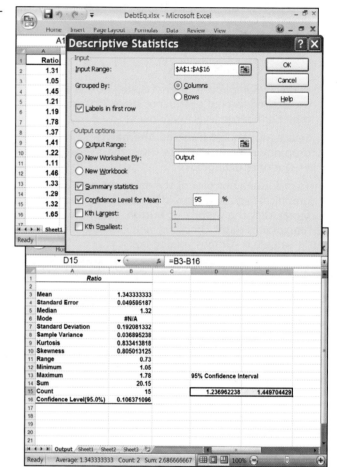

Appendix 8.3 ■ Confidence Intervals Using MegaStat

Confidence interval for the population mean debt-to-equity ratio in Figure 8.12(a) on page 323:

- Select **Add-Ins : MegaStat : Confidence Intervals / Sample Size**

- In the "Confidence Intervals / Sample Size" dialog box, click on the "Confidence Interval—mean" tab.

- Enter the sample mean (here equal to 1.3433) into the Mean window.

- Enter the sample standard deviation (here equal to .1921) into the "Std Dev" window.

- Enter the sample size (here equal to 15) into the "n" window.

- Select a level of confidence from the pull-down menu or type a desired percentage.

- Select a t-based or z-based interval by clicking on "t" or "z." Here we request a t-based interval.

- Click OK in the "Confidence Intervals / Sample Size" dialog box.

Confidence interval for a population proportion in the cheese spread situation of Example 8.8 on page 329:

- In the "Confidence Intervals / Sample Size" dialog box, click on the "Confidence interval—p" tab.

- Enter the sample proportion (here equal to .063) into the "p" window.

- Enter the sample size (here equal to 1000) into the "n" window.

- Select a level of confidence from the pull-down menu or type a desired percentage.

- Click OK in the "Confidence Intervals / Sample Size" dialog box.

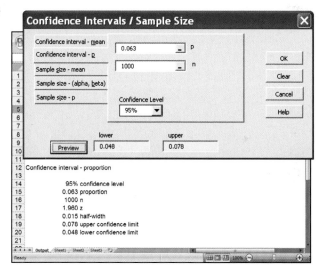

Sample size determination for a proportion problem in Figure 8.16 on page 332:

- In the "Confidence Intervals / Sample Size" dialog box, click on the "Sample size—p" tab.

- Enter the desired margin of error (here equal to 0.02) into the "E" window and enter an estimate of the population proportion into the "p" window.

- Select a level of confidence from the pull-down menu or type a desired percentage.

- Click OK in the "Confidence Intervals / Sample Size" dialog box.

Sample size determination for a population mean problem is done by clicking on the "Sample Size—mean" tab. Then enter a desired margin of error, an estimate of the population standard deviation, and the desired level of confidence. Click OK.

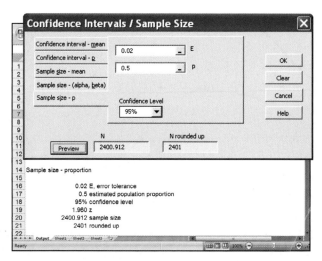

Hypothesis Testing

Chapter Outline

9.1 The Null and Alternative Hypotheses and Errors in Hypothesis Testing

9.2 z Tests about a Population Mean: σ Known

9.3 t Tests about a Population Mean: σ Unknown

9.4 z Tests about a Population Proportion

9.5 Type II Error Probabilities and Sample Size Determination (Optional)

9.6 The Chi-Square Distribution (Optional)

9.7 Statistical Inference for a Population Variance (Optional)

Hypothesis testing is a statistical procedure used to provide evidence in favor of some statement (called a *hypothesis*). For instance, hypothesis testing might be used to assess whether a population parameter, such as a population mean, differs from a specified standard or previous value. In this chapter we discuss testing hypotheses about population means, proportions, and variances.

In order to illustrate how hypothesis testing works, we revisit several cases introduced in previous chapters and also introduce some new cases:

The Payment Time Case: The consulting firm uses hypothesis testing to provide strong evidence that the new electronic billing system has reduced the mean payment time by more than 50 percent.

The Cheese Spread Case: The cheese spread producer uses hypothesis testing to supply extremely strong evidence that fewer than 10 percent of all current purchasers would stop buying the cheese spread if the new spout were used.

The Electronic Article Surveillance Case: A company that sells and installs EAS systems claims that at most 5 percent of all consumers would never shop in a store again if the store subjected them to a false EAS alarm. A store considering the purchase

of such a system uses hypothesis testing to provide extremely strong evidence that this claim is not true.

The Trash Bag Case: A marketer of trash bags uses hypothesis testing to support its claim that the mean breaking strength of its new trash bag is greater than 50 pounds. As a result, a television network approves use of this claim in a commercial.

The Valentine's Day Chocolate Case: A candy company projects that this year's sales of its special valentine box of assorted chocolates will be 10 percent higher than last year. The candy company uses hypothesis testing to assess whether it is reasonable to plan for a 10 percent increase in sales of the valentine box.

9.1 The Null and Alternative Hypotheses and Errors in Hypothesis Testing ● ● ●

One of the authors' former students is employed by a major television network in the standards and practices division. One of the division's responsibilities is to reduce the chances that advertisers will make false claims in commercials run on the network. Our former student reports that the network uses a statistical methodology called **hypothesis testing** to do this.

To see how this might be done, suppose that a company wishes to advertise a claim, and suppose that the network has reason to doubt that this claim is true. The network assumes for the sake of argument that **the claim is not valid.** This assumption is called the **null hypothesis.** The statement that **the claim is valid** is called the **alternative,** or **research, hypothesis.** The network will run the commercial only if the company making the claim provides **sufficient sample evidence** to reject the null hypothesis that the claim is not valid in favor of the alternative hypothesis that the claim is valid. Explaining the exact meaning of *sufficient sample evidence* is quite involved and will be discussed in the next section.

The Null Hypothesis and the Alternative Hypothesis

| n hypothesis testing

1 The **null hypothesis,** denoted H_0, is the statement being tested. Usually this statement represents the *status quo* and is not rejected unless there is convincing sample evidence that it is false.

2 The **alternative,** or **research, hypothesis,** denoted H_a, is a statement that will be accepted only if there is convincing sample evidence that it is true.

Setting up the null and alternative hypotheses in a practical situation can be tricky. In some situations there is a condition for which we need to attempt to find supportive evidence. We then formulate (1) the alternative hypothesis to be the statement that this condition exists and (2) the null hypothesis to be the statement that this condition does not exist. To illustrate this, we consider the following case studies.

EXAMPLE 9.1 The Trash Bag Case[1]

A leading manufacturer of trash bags produces the strongest trash bags on the market. The company has developed a new 30-gallon bag using a specially formulated plastic that is stronger and more biodegradable than other plastics. This plastic's increased strength allows the bag's thickness to be reduced, and the resulting cost savings will enable the company to lower its bag price by 25 percent. The company also believes the new bag is stronger than its current 30-gallon bag.

The manufacturer wants to advertise the new bag on a major television network. In addition to promoting its price reduction, the company also wants to claim the new bag is better for the environment and stronger than its current bag. The network is convinced of the bag's environmental advantages on scientific grounds. However, the network questions the company's claim of increased strength and requires statistical evidence to justify this claim. Although there are various measures of bag strength, the manufacturer and the network agree to employ "breaking strength." A bag's breaking strength is the amount of a representative trash mix (in pounds) that, when loaded into a bag suspended in the air, will cause the bag to rip or tear. Tests show that the current bag has a mean breaking strength that is very close to (but does not exceed) 50 pounds. The new bag's mean breaking strength μ is unknown and in question. The alternative hypothesis H_a is the statement for which we wish to find supportive evidence. Because we hope the new bags are stronger than the current bags, H_a says that μ is greater than 50. The null hypothesis states that H_a is false. Therefore, H_0 says that μ is less than or equal to 50. We summarize these hypotheses by stating that we are testing

$$H_0: \mu \le 50 \quad \text{versus} \quad H_a: \mu > 50$$

The network will run the manufacturer's commercial if a random sample of n new bags provides sufficient evidence to reject $H_0: \mu \le 50$ in favor of $H_a: \mu > 50$.

EXAMPLE 9.2 The Payment Time Case

Recall that a management consulting firm has installed a new computer-based, electronic billing system for a Hamilton, Ohio, trucking company. Because of the system's advantages, and because the trucking company's clients are receptive to using this system, the management consulting firm believes that the new system will reduce the mean bill payment time by more than 50 percent. The mean payment time using the old billing system was approximately equal to, but no less than, 39 days. Therefore, if μ denotes the mean payment time using the new system, the consulting firm believes that μ will be less than 19.5 days. Because it is hoped that the new billing system *reduces* mean payment time, we formulate the alternative hypothesis as $H_a: \mu < 19.5$ and the null hypothesis as $H_0: \mu \ge 19.5$. The consulting firm will randomly select a sample of n invoices and determine if their payment times provide sufficient evidence to reject $H_0: \mu \ge 19.5$ in favor of $H_a: \mu < 19.5$. If such evidence exists, the consulting firm will conclude that the new electronic billing system has reduced the Hamilton trucking company's mean bill payment time by more than 50 percent. This conclusion will be used to help demonstrate the benefits of the new billing system both to the Hamilton company and to other trucking companies that are considering using such a system.

EXAMPLE 9.3 The Valentine's Day Chocolate Case[2]

A candy company annually markets a special 18-ounce box of assorted chocolates to large retail stores for Valentine's Day. This year the candy company has designed an extremely attractive

---

[1]This case is based on conversations by the authors with several employees working for a leading producer of trash bags. For purposes of confidentiality, we have agreed to withhold the company's name.
[2]Thanks to Krogers of Oxford, Ohio, for helpful discussions concerning this case.

new valentine box and will fill the box with an especially appealing assortment of chocolates. For this reason, the candy company subjectively projects—based on past experience and knowledge of the candy market—that sales of its valentine box will be 10 percent higher than last year. However, since the candy company must decide how many valentine boxes to produce, the company needs to assess whether it is reasonable to plan for a 10 percent increase in sales.

Before the beginning of each Valentine's Day sales season, the candy company sends large retail stores information about its newest valentine box of assorted chocolates. This information includes a description of the box of chocolates, as well as a preview of advertising displays that the candy company will provide to help retail stores sell the chocolates. Each retail store then places a single (nonreturnable) order of valentine boxes to satisfy its anticipated customer demand for the Valentine's Day sales season. Last year the mean order quantity of large retail stores was 300 boxes per store. If the projected 10 percent sales increase will occur, the mean order quantity, μ, of large retail stores this year will be 330 boxes per store. Therefore, the candy company wishes to test the null hypothesis $H_0: \mu = 330$ versus the alternative hypothesis $H_a: \mu \neq 330$.

To perform the hypothesis test, the candy company will randomly select a sample of n large retail stores and will make an early mailing to these stores promoting this year's valentine box. The candy company will then ask each retail store to report how many valentine boxes it anticipates ordering. If the sample data do not provide sufficient evidence to reject $H_0: \mu = 330$ in favor of $H_a: \mu \neq 330$, the candy company will base its production on the projected 10 percent sales increase. On the other hand, if there is sufficient evidence to reject $H_0: \mu = 330$, the candy company will change its production plans.

We next summarize the sets of null and alternative hypotheses that we have thus far considered.

$$H_0: \mu \leq 50 \qquad\qquad H_0: \mu \geq 19.5 \qquad\qquad H_0: \mu = 330$$
$$\text{versus} \qquad\qquad\qquad \text{versus} \qquad\qquad\qquad \text{versus}$$
$$H_a: \mu > 50 \qquad\qquad H_a: \mu < 19.5 \qquad\qquad H_a: \mu \neq 330$$

The alternative hypothesis $H_a: \mu > 50$ is called a **one-sided, greater than alternative** hypothesis, whereas $H_a: \mu < 19.5$ is called a **one-sided, less than alternative** hypothesis, and $H_a: \mu \neq 330$ is called a **two-sided, not equal to alternative** hypothesis. Many of the alternative hypotheses we consider in this book are one of these three types. Also, note that each null hypothesis we have considered involves an **equality.** For example, the null hypothesis $H_0: \mu \leq 50$ says that μ is either less than or **equal to** 50. We will see that, in general, the approach we use to test a null hypothesis versus an alternative hypothesis requires that the null hypothesis involve an equality.

The idea of a test statistic   Suppose that in the trash bag case the manufacturer randomly selects a sample of $n = 40$ new trash bags. Each of these bags is tested for breaking strength, and the sample mean $\bar{x}$ of the 40 breaking strengths is calculated. In order to test $H_0: \mu \leq 50$ versus $H_a: \mu > 50$, we utilize the **test statistic**

$$z = \frac{\bar{x} - 50}{\sigma_{\bar{x}}} = \frac{\bar{x} - 50}{\sigma/\sqrt{n}}$$

The test statistic z measures the distance between $\bar{x}$ and 50. The division by $\sigma_{\bar{x}}$ says that this distance is measured in units of the standard deviation of all possible sample means. For example, a value of z equal to, say, 2.4 would tell us that $\bar{x}$ is 2.4 such standard deviations above 50. In general, a value of the test statistic that is less than or equal to zero results when $\bar{x}$ is less than or equal to 50. This provides no evidence to support rejecting H_0 in favor of H_a because the point estimate $\bar{x}$ indicates that μ is probably less than or equal to 50. However, a value of the test statistic that is greater than zero results when $\bar{x}$ is greater than 50. This provides evidence to support rejecting H_0 in favor of H_a because the point estimate $\bar{x}$ indicates that μ might be greater than 50. Furthermore, the farther the value of the test statistic is above zero (the farther $\bar{x}$ is above 50), the stronger is the evidence to support rejecting H_0 in favor of H_a.

TABLE 9.1   Type I and Type II Errors

	State of Nature	
Decision	H_0 True	H_0 False
Reject H_0	Type I error	Correct decision
Do not reject H_0	Correct decision	Type II error

TABLE 9.2   The Implications of Type I and Type II Errors in the Trash Bag Example

	State of Nature	
Decision	Claim False	Claim True
Advertise the claim	Advertise a false claim	Advertise a true claim
Do not advertise the claim	Do not advertise a false claim	Do not advertise a true claim

Hypothesis testing and the legal system   If the value of the test statistic z is far enough above zero, we reject H_0 in favor of H_a. To see how large z must be in order to reject H_0, we must understand that **a hypothesis test rejects a null hypothesis H_0 only if there is strong statistical evidence against H_0.** This is similar to our legal system, which rejects the innocence of the accused only if evidence of guilt is beyond a reasonable doubt. For instance, the network will reject H_0: $\mu \le 50$ and run the trash bag commercial only if the test statistic z is far enough above zero to show beyond a reasonable doubt that H_0: $\mu \le 50$ is false and H_a: $\mu > 50$ is true. A test statistic that is only slightly greater than zero might not be convincing enough. However, because such a test statistic would result from a sample mean $\bar{x}$ that is slightly greater than 50, it would provide some evidence to support rejecting H_0: $\mu \le 50$, and it certainly would not provide strong evidence supporting H_0: $\mu \le 50$. Therefore, if the value of the test statistic is not large enough to convince us to reject H_0, **we do not say that we accept H_0. Rather we say that we do not reject H_0** because the evidence against H_0 is not strong enough. Again, this is similar to our legal system, where the lack of evidence of guilt beyond a reasonable doubt results in a verdict of **not guilty,** but does not prove that the accused is innocent.

Type I and Type II errors and their probabilities   To determine exactly how much statistical evidence is required to reject H_0, we consider the errors and the correct decisions that can be made in hypothesis testing. These errors and correct decisions, as well as their implications in the trash bag advertising example, are summarized in Tables 9.1 and 9.2. Across the top of each table are listed the two possible "states of nature." Either H_0: $\mu \le 50$ is true, which says the manufacturer's claim that μ is greater than 50 is false, or H_0 is false, which says the claim is true. Down the left side of each table are listed the two possible decisions we can make in the hypothesis test. Using the sample data, we will either reject H_0: $\mu \le 50$, which implies that the claim will be advertised, or we will not reject H_0, which implies that the claim will not be advertised.

In general, the two types of errors that can be made in hypothesis testing are defined here:

Type I and Type II Errors

If we reject H_0 when it is true, this is a **Type I error.**
If we do not reject H_0 when it is false, this is a **Type II error.**

As can be seen by comparing Tables 9.1 and 9.2, if we commit a Type I error, we will advertise a false claim. If we commit a Type II error, we will fail to advertise a true claim.

We now let the symbol α (pronounced **alpha**) **denote the probability of a Type I error,** and we let β (pronounced **beta**) **denote the probability of a Type II error.** Obviously, we would like both α and β to be small. A common (but not the only) procedure is to base a hypothesis test on taking a sample of a fixed size (for example, $n = 40$ trash bags) and on setting α equal to a small prespecified value. Setting α low means there is only a small chance of rejecting H_0 when it is true. This implies that we are requiring strong evidence against H_0 before we reject it.

We sometimes choose α as high as .10, but we usually choose α between .05 and .01. A frequent choice for α is .05. In fact, our former student tells us that the network often tests advertising claims by setting the probability of a Type I error equal to .05. That is, the network will run a commercial making a claim if the sample evidence allows it to reject a null hypothesis that says the claim is not valid in favor of an alternative hypothesis that says the claim is valid with α set equal to .05. Since a Type I error is deciding that the claim is valid when it is not, the policy of setting α equal to .05 says that, in the long run, the network will advertise only 5 percent of all invalid claims made by advertisers.

One might wonder why the network does not set α lower—say at .01. One reason is that **it can be shown that, for a fixed sample size, the lower we set α, the higher is β, and the higher we set α, the lower is β.** Setting α at .05 means that β, the probability of failing to advertise a true claim (a Type II error), will be smaller than it would be if α were set at .01. As long as (1) the claim to be advertised is plausible and (2) the consequences of advertising the claim even if it is false are not terribly serious, then it is reasonable to set α equal to .05. However, if either (1) or (2) is not true, then we might set α lower than .05. For example, suppose a pharmaceutical company wishes to advertise that it has developed an effective treatment for a disease that has formerly been very resistant to treatment. Such a claim is (perhaps) difficult to believe. Moreover, if the claim is false, patients suffering from the disease would be subjected to false hope and needless expense. In such a case, it might be reasonable for the network to set α at .01 because this would lower the chance of advertising the claim if it is false. We usually do not set α lower than .01 because doing so often leads to an unacceptably large value of β. We explain some methods for computing the probability of a Type II error in optional Section 9.5. However, β can be difficult or impossible to calculate in many situations, and we often must rely on our intuition when deciding how to set α.

Exercises for Section 9.1

CONCEPTS

connect

9.1   Which hypothesis (the null hypothesis, H_0, or the alternative hypothesis, H_a) is the "status quo" hypothesis (that is, the hypothesis that states that things are remaining "as is")? Which hypothesis is the hypothesis that says that a "hoped for" or "suspected" condition exists?

9.2   Which hypothesis (H_0 or H_a) is not rejected unless there is convincing sample evidence that it is false? Which hypothesis (H_0 or H_a) will be accepted only if there is convincing sample evidence that it is true?

9.3   Define each of the following:
   a Type I error   **b** Type II error
   c α **d** β

9.4   For each of the following situations, indicate whether an error has occurred and, if so, indicate what kind of error (Type I or Type II) has occurred.
   a We do not reject H_0 and H_0 is true.
   b We reject H_0 and H_0 is true.
   c We do not reject H_0 and H_0 is false.
   d We reject H_0 and H_0 is false.

9.5   If we reject H_0, what is the only type of error that we could be making? Explain.

9.6   If we do not reject H_0, what is the only type of error that we could be making? Explain.

9.7   When testing a hypothesis, why don't we set the probability of a Type I error to be extremely small? Explain.

METHODS AND APPLICATIONS

9.8 THE VIDEO GAME SATISFACTION RATING CASE ● VideoGame

Recall that "very satisfied" customers give the XYZ-Box video game system a rating that is at least 42. Suppose that the manufacturer of the XYZ-Box wishes to use the random sample of 65 satisfaction ratings to provide evidence supporting the claim that the mean composite satisfaction rating for the XYZ-Box exceeds 42.

a Letting μ represent the mean composite satisfaction rating for the XYZ-Box, set up the null and alternative hypotheses needed if we wish to attempt to provide evidence supporting the claim that μ exceeds 42.

b In the context of this situation, interpret making a Type I error; interpret making a Type II error.

9.9 THE BANK CUSTOMER WAITING TIME CASE ● WaitTime

Recall that a bank manager has developed a new system to reduce the time customers spend waiting for teller service during peak hours. The manager hopes the new system will reduce waiting times from the current 9 to 10 minutes to less than 6 minutes.

Suppose the manager wishes to use the random sample of 100 waiting times to support the claim that the mean waiting time under the new system is shorter than six minutes.

a Letting μ represent the mean waiting time under the new system, set up the null and alternative hypotheses needed if we wish to attempt to provide evidence supporting the claim that μ is shorter than six minutes.

b In the context of this situation, interpret making a Type I error; interpret making a Type II error.

9.10 An automobile parts supplier owns a machine that produces a cylindrical engine part. This part is supposed to have an outside diameter of three inches. Parts with diameters that are too small or too large do not meet customer requirements and must be rejected. Lately, the company has experienced problems meeting customer requirements. The technical staff feels that the mean diameter produced by the machine is off target. In order to verify this, a special study will randomly sample 100 parts produced by the machine. The 100 sampled parts will be measured, and if the results obtained cast a substantial amount of doubt on the hypothesis that the mean diameter equals the target value of three inches, the company will assign a problem-solving team to intensively search for the causes of the problem.

a The parts supplier wishes to set up a hypothesis test so that the problem-solving team will be assigned when the null hypothesis is rejected. Set up the null and alternative hypotheses for this situation.

b In the context of this situation, interpret making a Type I error; interpret making a Type II error.

c Suppose it costs the company $3,000 a day to assign the problem-solving team to a project. Is this $3,000 figure the daily cost of a Type I error or a Type II error? Explain.

9.11 The Crown Bottling Company has just installed a new bottling process that will fill 16-ounce bottles of the popular Crown Classic Cola soft drink. Both overfilling and underfilling bottles are undesirable: Underfilling leads to customer complaints and overfilling costs the company considerable money. In order to verify that the filler is set up correctly, the company wishes to see whether the mean bottle fill, μ, is close to the target fill of 16 ounces. To this end, a random sample of 36 filled bottles is selected from the output of a test filler run. If the sample results cast a substantial amount of doubt on the hypothesis that the mean bottle fill is the desired 16 ounces, then the filler's initial setup will be readjusted.

a The bottling company wants to set up a hypothesis test so that the filler will be readjusted if the null hypothesis is rejected. Set up the null and alternative hypotheses for this hypothesis test.

b In the context of this situation, interpret making a Type I error; interpret making a Type II error.

9.12 Consolidated Power, a large electric power utility, has just built a modern nuclear power plant. This plant discharges waste water that is allowed to flow into the Atlantic Ocean. The Environmental Protection Agency (EPA) has ordered that the waste water may not be excessively warm so that thermal pollution of the marine environment near the plant can be avoided. Because of this order, the waste water is allowed to cool in specially constructed ponds and is then released into the ocean. This cooling system works properly if the mean temperature of waste water discharged is 60°F or cooler. Consolidated Power is required to monitor the temperature of the waste water. A sample of 100 temperature readings will be obtained each day, and if the sample results cast a substantial amount of doubt on the hypothesis that the cooling system is working properly (the mean temperature of waste water discharged is 60°F or cooler), then the plant must be shut down and appropriate actions must be taken to correct the problem.

    a Consolidated Power wishes to set up a hypothesis test so that the power plant will be shut down when the null hypothesis is rejected. Set up the null and alternative hypotheses that should be used.

    b In the context of this situation, interpret making a Type I error; interpret making a Type II error.

    c The EPA periodically conducts spot checks to determine whether the waste water being discharged is too warm. Suppose the EPA has the power to impose very severe penalties (for example, very heavy fines) when the waste water is excessively warm. Other things being equal, should Consolidated Power set the probability of a Type I error equal to $\alpha = .01$ or $\alpha = .05$? Explain.

9.13 Consider Exercise 9.12, and suppose that Consolidated Power has been experiencing technical problems with the cooling system. Because the system has been unreliable, the company feels it must take precautions to avoid failing to shut down the plant when its waste water is too warm. Other things being equal, should Consolidated Power set the probability of a Type I error equal to $\alpha = .01$ or $\alpha = .05$? Explain.

9.2 *z* Tests about a Population Mean: σ Known ● ● ●

CHAPTER 9

In this section we discuss hypothesis tests about a population mean that are *based on the normal distribution*. These tests are called *z* **tests,** and they require that the *true value of the population standard deviation σ is known*. Of course, in most real-world situations the true value of σ is not known. However, the concepts and calculations of hypothesis testing are most easily illustrated using the normal distribution. Therefore, in this section we will assume that—through theory or history related to the population under consideration—we know σ. When σ is unknown, we test hypotheses about a population mean by using the *t distribution*. In Section 9.3 we study *t* **tests,** and we will revisit the examples of this section assuming that σ is unknown.

Testing a "greater than" alternative hypothesis by using a critical value rule In Section 9.1 we explained how to set up appropriate null and alternative hypotheses. We also discussed how to specify a value for α, the probability of a Type I error (also called the **level of significance**) of the hypothesis test, and we introduced the idea of a test statistic. We can use these concepts to begin developing a seven-step hypothesis testing procedure. We will introduce these steps in the context of the trash bag case and testing a "greater than" alternative hypothesis.

Step 1: State the null hypothesis H_0 and the alternative hypothesis H_a. In the trash bag case, we will test H_0: $\mu \le 50$ versus H_a: $\mu > 50$. Here, μ is the mean breaking strength of the new trash bag.

Step 2: Specify the level of significance α. The television network will run the commercial stating that the new trash bag is stronger than the former bag if we can reject H_0: $\mu \le 50$ in favor of H_a: $\mu > 50$ by setting α equal to .05.

Step 3: Select the test statistic. In order to test H_0: $\mu \le 50$ versus H_a: $\mu > 50$, we will test the modified null hypothesis H_0: $\mu = 50$ versus H_a: $\mu > 50$. The idea here is that if there is sufficient evidence to reject the hypothesis that μ equals 50 in favor of $\mu > 50$, then there is certainly also sufficient evidence to reject the hypothesis that μ is less than or equal to 50. In order to test H_0: $\mu = 50$ versus H_a: $\mu > 50$, we will randomly select a sample of $n = 40$ new trash bags and calculate the mean $\bar{x}$ of the breaking strengths of these bags. We will then utilize the **test statistic**

$$z = \frac{\bar{x} - 50}{\sigma_{\bar{x}}} = \frac{\bar{x} - 50}{\sigma/\sqrt{n}}$$

A positive value of this test statistic results from an $\bar{x}$ that is greater than 50 and thus provides evidence against H_0: $\mu = 50$ and in favor of H_a: $\mu > 50$.

Step 4: Determine the critical value rule for deciding whether to reject H_0. To decide how large the test statistic z must be to reject H_0 in favor of H_a by setting the probability of a Type I error equal to α, we note that different samples would give different sample means and thus different values of z. Because the sample size $n = 40$ is large, the Central Limit Theorem tells us that the sampling distribution of z is (approximately) a standard normal distribution if the null

FIGURE 9.1   **The Critical Value for Testing H_0: $\mu = 50$ versus H_a: $\mu > 50$ by Setting $\alpha = .05$**

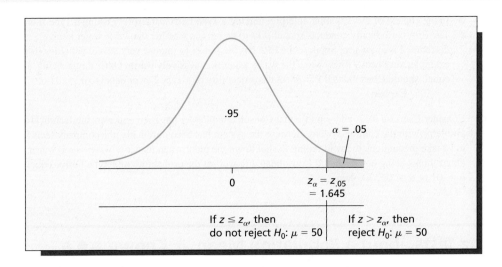

hypothesis H_0: $\mu = 50$ is true. Therefore, we do the following:

- Place the probability of a Type I error, α, in the right-hand tail of the standard normal curve and use the normal table (see Table A.3, page 640) to find the normal point z_α. Here z_α, which we call a **critical value,** is the point on the horizontal axis under the standard normal curve that gives a right-hand tail area equal to α.

- **Reject H_0: $\mu = 50$ in favor of H_a: $\mu > 50$ if and only if the test statistic z is greater than the critical value z_α.** (This is the **critical value rule.**)

Figure 9.1 illustrates that since we have set α equal to .05, we should use the critical value $z_\alpha = z_{.05} = 1.645$ (see Table A.3). This says that we should reject H_0 if $z > 1.645$ and we should not reject H_0 if $z \leq 1.645$.

To better understand the critical value rule, consider the standard normal curve in Figure 9.1. The area of .05 in the right-hand tail of this curve implies that values of the test statistic z that are greater than 1.645 are unlikely to occur if the null hypothesis H_0: $\mu = 50$ is true. There is a 5 percent chance of observing one of these values—and thus wrongly rejecting H_0—if H_0 is true. However, we are more likely to observe a value of z greater than 1.645—and thus correctly reject H_0—if H_0 is false. Therefore, it is intuitively reasonable to reject H_0 if the value of the test statistic z is greater than 1.645.

Step 5: Collect the sample data and compute the value of the test statistic. When the sample of $n = 40$ new trash bags is randomly selected, the mean of the breaking strengths is calculated to be $\bar{x} = 50.575$. Assuming that σ is known to equal 1.65, the value of the test statistic is

$$z = \frac{\bar{x} - 50}{\sigma/\sqrt{n}} = \frac{50.575 - 50}{1.65/\sqrt{40}} = 2.20$$

Step 6: Decide whether to reject H_0 by using the test statistic value and the critical value rule. Since the test statistic value $z = 2.20$ is greater than the critical value $z_{.05} = 1.645$, we can reject H_0: $\mu = 50$ in favor of H_a: $\mu > 50$ by setting α equal to .05. Furthermore, we can be intuitively confident that H_0: $\mu = 50$ is false and H_a: $\mu > 50$ is true. This is because, since we have rejected H_0 by setting α equal to .05, we have rejected H_0 by using a test that allows only a 5 percent chance of wrongly rejecting H_0. In general, if we can reject a null hypothesis in favor of an alternative hypothesis by setting the probability of a Type I error equal to α, we say that we have **statistical significance at the α level.**

Step 7: Interpret the statistical results in managerial (real-world) terms and assess their practical importance. Since we have rejected H_0: $\mu = 50$ in favor of H_a: $\mu > 50$ by setting α equal to .05, we conclude (at an α of .05) that the mean breaking strength of the new trash bag exceeds 50 pounds. Furthermore, this conclusion has practical importance to the trash bag manufacturer because it means that the television network will approve running commercials

FIGURE 9.2   **The Critical Values for Testing H_0: $\mu = 50$ versus H_a: $\mu > 50$ by Setting $\alpha = .05$ and .01**

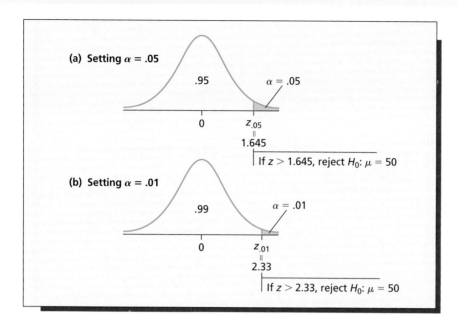

claiming that the new trash bag is stronger than the former bag. Note, however, that the point estimate of μ, $\bar{x} = 50.575$, indicates that μ is not much larger than 50. Therefore, the trash bag manufacturer can claim only that its new bag is slightly stronger than its former bag. Of course, this might be practically important to consumers who feel that, because the new bag is 25 percent less expensive and is more environmentally sound, it is definitely worth purchasing if it has any strength advantage. However, to customers who are looking only for a substantial increase in bag strength, the statistical results would not be practically important. This illustrates that, in general, a finding of statistical significance (that is, concluding that the alternative hypothesis is true) can be practically important to some people but not to others. Notice that the point estimate of the parameter involved in a hypothesis test can help us to assess practical importance. We can also use confidence intervals to help assess practical importance.

Considerations in setting α   We have reasoned in Section 9.1 that the television network has set α equal to .05 rather than .01 because doing so means that β, the probability of failing to advertise a true claim (a Type II error), will be smaller than it would be if α were set at .01. It is informative, however, to see what would have happened if the network had set α equal to .01. Figure 9.2 illustrates that as we decrease α from .05 to .01, the critical value z_α increases from $z_{.05} = 1.645$ to $z_{.01} = 2.33$. Because the test statistic value $z = 2.20$ is less than $z_{.01} = 2.33$, we cannot reject H_0: $\mu = 50$ in favor of H_a: $\mu > 50$ by setting α equal to .01. This illustrates the point that, the smaller we set α, the larger is the critical value, and thus the stronger is the statistical evidence that we are requiring to reject the null hypothesis H_0. Some statisticians have concluded (somewhat subjectively) that (1) **if we set α equal to .05, then we are requiring strong evidence to reject H_0;** and (2) **if we set α equal to .01, then we are requiring very strong evidence to reject H_0.**

A *p*-value for testing a "greater than" alternative hypothesis   To decide whether to reject the null hypothesis H_0 at level of significance α, steps 4, 5, and 6 of the seven-step hypothesis testing procedure compare the test statistic value with a critical value. Another way to make this decision is to calculate a ***p*-value,** which measures the likelihood of the sample results if the null hypothesis H_0 is true. Sample results that are not likely if H_0 is true are evidence that H_0 is not true. To test H_0 by using a *p*-value, we use the following steps 4, 5, and 6:

Step 4: Collect the sample data and compute the value of the test statistic. In the trash bag case, we have computed the value of the test statistic to be $z = 2.20$.

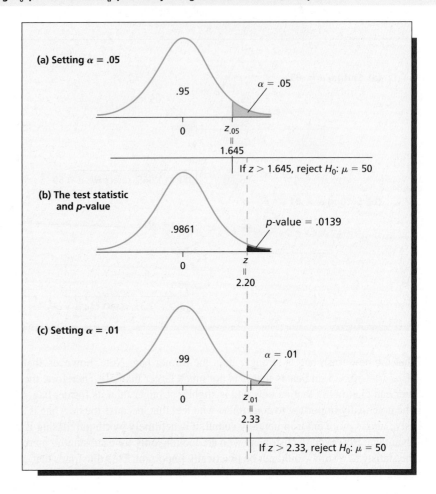

Step 5: Calculate the p-value by using the test statistic value. The p-value for testing H_0: $\mu = 50$ versus H_a: $\mu > 50$ in the trash bag case is the area under the standard normal curve to the right of the test statistic value $z = 2.20$. As illustrated in Figure 9.3(b), this area is $1 - .9861 = .0139$. The p-value is the probability, computed assuming that H_0: $\mu = 50$ is true, of observing a value of the test statistic that is greater than or equal to the value $z = 2.20$ that we have actually computed from the sample data. The p-value of .0139 says that, if H_0: $\mu = 50$ is true, then only 139 in 10,000 of all possible test statistic values are at least as large, or extreme, as the value $z = 2.20$. That is, if we are to believe that H_0 is true, we must believe that we have observed a test statistic value that can be described as a 139 in 10,000 chance. Because it is difficult to believe that we have observed a 139 in 10,000 chance, we intuitively have strong evidence that H_0: $\mu = 50$ is false and H_a: $\mu > 50$ is true.

Step 6: Reject H_0 if the p-value is less than α. Recall that the television network has set α equal to .05. **The p-value of .0139 is less than the α of .05.** Comparing the two normal curves in Figures 9.3(a) and (b), we see that this implies that the test statistic value $z = 2.20$ is greater than the critical value $z_{.05} = 1.645$. Therefore, **we can reject H_0 by setting α equal to .05.** As another example, suppose that the television network had set α equal to .01. **The p-value of .0139 is greater than the α of .01.** Comparing the two normal curves in Figures 9.3(b) and (c), we see that this implies that the test statistic value $z = 2.20$ is less than the critical value $z_{.01} = 2.33$. Therefore, **we cannot reject H_0 by setting α equal to .01.** Generalizing these examples, we conclude that the value of the test statistic z will be greater than the critical value z_α if and only if the p-value is less than α. **That is, we can reject H_0 in favor of H_a at level of significance α if and only if the p-value is less than α.**

Comparing the critical value and *p*-value methods Thus far we have considered two methods for testing H_0: $\mu = 50$ versus H_a: $\mu > 50$ at the .05 and .01 values of α. Using the first method, we determine if the test statistic value $z = 2.20$ is greater than the critical values $z_{.05} = 1.645$ and $z_{.01} = 2.33$. Using the second method, we determine if the *p*-value of .0139 is less than .05 and .01. Whereas the critical value method requires that we look up a different critical value for each different α value, the *p*-value method requires only that we calculate a single *p*-value and compare it directly with the different α values. *It follows that the p-value method is the most efficient way to test a hypothesis at different α values.* This can be useful when there are different decision makers who might use different α values. For example, television networks do not always evaluate advertising claims by setting α equal to .05. The reason is that the consequences of a Type I error (advertising a false claim) are more serious for some claims than for others. For example, the consequences of a Type I error would be fairly serious for a claim about the effectiveness of a drug or for the superiority of one product over another. However, these consequences might not be as serious for a noncomparative claim about an inexpensive and safe product, such as a cosmetic. Networks sometimes use α values between .01 and .04 for claims having more serious Type I error consequences, and they sometimes use α values between .06 and .10 for claims having less serious Type I error consequences. Furthermore, one network's policies for setting α can differ somewhat from those of another. As a result, reporting an advertising claim's *p*-value to each network is the most efficient way to tell the network whether to allow the claim to be advertised. For example, most networks would evaluate the trash bag claim by choosing an α value between .025 and .10. Since the *p*-value of .0139 is less than all these α values, most networks would allow the trash bag claim to be advertised.

Note: This logo appears on an NBC advertising standards booklet. This booklet, along with other information provided by NBC and CBS, forms the basis for much of the discussion in the adjacent paragraph.

A summary of the seven steps of hypothesis testing For almost every hypothesis test discussed in this book, statisticians have developed both a critical value rule and a *p*-value that can be used to perform the hypothesis test. Furthermore, it can be shown that for each hypothesis test the *p*-value has been defined so that **we can reject the null hypothesis at level of significance α if and only if the *p*-value is less than α.** We now summarize a seven-step procedure for performing a hypothesis test.

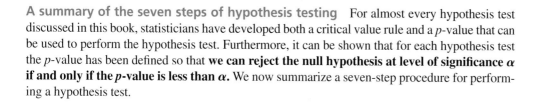

The Seven Steps of Hypothesis Testing

1 State the null hypothesis H_0 and the alternative hypothesis H_a.

2 Specify the level of significance α.

3 Select the test statistic.

Using a critical value rule:

4 Determine the critical value rule for deciding whether to reject H_0. Use the specified value of α to find the critical value in the critical value rule.

5 Collect the sample data and compute the value of the test statistic.

6 Decide whether to reject H_0 by using the test statistic value and the critical value rule.

Using a *p*-value:

4 Collect the sample data and compute the value of the test statistic.

5 Calculate the *p*-value by using the test statistic value.

6 Reject H_0 at level of significance α if the *p*-value is less than α.

7 Interpret your statistical results in managerial (real-world) terms and assess their practical importance.

In the real world both critical value rules and *p*-values are used to carry out hypothesis tests. For example, NBC uses critical value rules, whereas CBS uses *p*-values, to statistically verify the validity of advertising claims. Throughout this book we will continue to present both the critical value and the *p*-value approaches to hypothesis testing.

Testing a "less than" alternative hypothesis   We next consider the payment time case and testing a "less than" alternative hypothesis:

Step 1: In order to study whether the new electronic billing system reduces the mean bill payment time by more than 50 percent, the management consulting firm will test $H_0: \mu \geq 19.5$ versus $H_a: \mu < 19.5$.

Step 2: The management consulting firm wishes to make sure that it truthfully describes the benefits of the new system both to the Hamilton, Ohio, trucking company and to other companies that are considering installing such a system. Therefore, the firm will require very strong evidence to conclude that μ is less than 19.5, which implies that it will test $H_0: \mu \geq 19.5$ versus $H_a: \mu < 19.5$ by setting α equal to .01.

Step 3: In order to test $H_0: \mu \geq 19.5$ versus $H_a: \mu < 19.5$, we will test the modified null hypothesis $H_0: \mu = 19.5$ versus $H_a: \mu < 19.5$. The idea here is that if there is sufficient evidence to reject the hypothesis that μ equals 19.5 in favor of $\mu < 19.5$, then there is certainly also sufficient evidence to reject the hypothesis that μ is greater than or equal to 19.5. In order to test $H_0: \mu = 19.5$ versus $H_a: \mu < 19.5$, we will randomly select a sample of $n = 65$ invoices paid using the billing system and calculate the mean $\bar{x}$ of the payment times of these invoices. Since the sample size is large, the Central Limit Theorem applies, and we will utilize the test statistic

$$z = \frac{\bar{x} - 19.5}{\sigma/\sqrt{n}}$$

A value of the test statistic z that is less than zero results when $\bar{x}$ is less than 19.5. This provides evidence to support rejecting H_0 in favor of H_a because the point estimate $\bar{x}$ indicates that μ might be less than 19.5.

Step 4: To decide how much less than zero the test statistic must be to reject H_0 in favor of H_a by setting the probability of a Type I error equal to α, we do the following:

- Place the probability of a Type I error, α, in the left-hand tail of the standard normal curve and use the normal table to find the critical value $-z_\alpha$. Here $-z_\alpha$ is the negative of the normal point z_α. That is, $-z_\alpha$ is the point on the horizontal axis under the standard normal curve that gives a left-hand tail area equal to α.

- **Reject $H_0: \mu = 19.5$ in favor of $H_a: \mu < 19.5$ if and only if the test statistic z is less than the critical value $-z_\alpha$.** Because α equals .01, the critical value $-z_\alpha$ is $-z_{.01} = -2.33$ [see Fig. 9.4(a)].

Step 5: When the sample of $n = 65$ invoices is randomly selected, the mean of the payment times of these invoices is calculated to be $\bar{x} = 18.1077$. Assuming that σ is known to equal 4.2, the value of the test statistic is

$$z = \frac{\bar{x} - 19.5}{\sigma/\sqrt{n}} = \frac{18.1077 - 19.5}{4.2/\sqrt{65}} = -2.67$$

Step 6: Since the test statistic value $z = -2.67$ is less than the critical value $-z_{.01} = -2.33$, we can reject $H_0: \mu = 19.5$ in favor of $H_a: \mu < 19.5$ by setting α equal to .01.

Step 7: We conclude (at an α of .01) that the mean payment time for the new electronic billing system is less than 19.5 days. This, along with the fact that the sample mean $\bar{x} = 18.1077$ is slightly less than 19.5, implies that it is reasonable for the management consulting firm to conclude that the new electronic billing system has reduced the mean payment time by slightly more than 50 percent (a substantial improvement over the old system).

A p-value for testing a "less than" alternative hypothesis   To test $H_0: \mu = 19.5$ versus $H_a: \mu < 19.5$ in the payment time case by using a p-value, we use the following steps 4, 5, and 6:

Step 4: We have computed the value of the test statistic in the payment time case to be $z = -2.67$.

Step 5: The p-value for testing $H_0: \mu = 19.5$ versus $H_a: \mu < 19.5$ is the area under the standard normal curve to the left of the test statistic value $z = -2.67$. As illustrated in Figure 9.4(b), this area is .0038. The p-value is the probability, computed assuming that $H_0: \mu = 19.5$ is true, of observing a value of the test statistic that is less than or equal to the value $z = -2.67$ that we have actually

F I G U R E   9 . 4   **Testing H_0: $\mu = 19.5$ versus H_a: $\mu < 19.5$ by Using Critical Values and the *p*-Value**

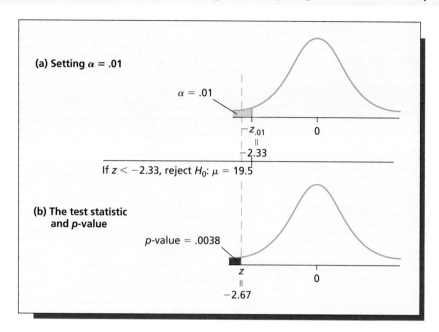

(a) Setting $\alpha = .01$

$\alpha = .01$

$-z_{.01}$ = -2.33 0

If $z < -2.33$, reject H_0: $\mu = 19.5$

(b) The test statistic and *p*-value

p-value = .0038

z = -2.67 0

computed from the sample data. The *p*-value of .0038 says that, if H_0: $\mu = 19.5$ is true, then only 38 in 10,000 of all possible test statistic values are at least as negative, or extreme, as the value $z = -2.67$. That is, if we are to believe that H_0 is true, we must believe that we have observed a test statistic value that can be described as a 38 in 10,000 chance.

Step 6: The management consulting firm has set α equal to .01. **The *p*-value of .0038 is less than the α of .01. Therefore, we can reject H_0 by setting α equal to .01.**

Testing a "not equal to" alternative hypothesis   We next consider the Valentine's Day chocolate case and testing a "not equal to" alternative hypothesis.

Step 1: To assess whether this year's sales of its valentine box of assorted chocolates will be 10 percent higher than last year's, the candy company will test H_0: $\mu = 330$ versus H_a: $\mu \neq 330$. Here, μ is the mean order quantity of this year's valentine box by large retail stores.

Step 2: If the candy company does not reject H_0: $\mu = 330$ and H_0: $\mu = 330$ is false—a Type II error—the candy company will base its production of valentine boxes on a 10 percent projected sales increase that is not correct. Since the candy company wishes to have a reasonably small probability of making this Type II error, the company will set α equal to .05. Setting α equal to .05 rather than .01 makes the probability of a Type II error smaller than it would be if α were set at .01. Note that in optional Section 9.5 we will verify that the probability of a Type II error in this situation is reasonably small. Therefore, if the candy company ends up not rejecting H_0: $\mu = 330$ and therefore decides to base its production of valentine boxes on the 10 percent projected sales increase, the company can be intuitively confident that it has made the right decision.

Step 3: The candy company will randomly select $n = 100$ large retail stores and will make an early mailing to these stores promoting this year's valentine box of assorted chocolates. The candy company will then ask each sampled retail store to report its anticipated order quantity of valentine boxes and will calculate the mean $\bar{x}$ of the reported order quantities. Since the sample size is large, the Central Limit Theorem applies, and we will utilize the test statistic

$$z = \frac{\bar{x} - 330}{\sigma/\sqrt{n}}$$

A value of the test statistic that is greater than zero results when $\bar{x}$ is greater than 330. This provides evidence to support rejecting H_0 in favor of H_a because the point estimate $\bar{x}$ indicates that μ might be greater than 330. Similarly, a value of the test statistic that is less than zero results when $\bar{x}$ is less than 330. This also provides evidence to support rejecting H_0 in favor of H_a because the point estimate $\bar{x}$ indicates that μ might be less than 330.

FIGURE 9.5   **Testing H_0: $\mu = 330$ versus H_a: $\mu \neq 330$ by Using Critical Values and the p-Value**

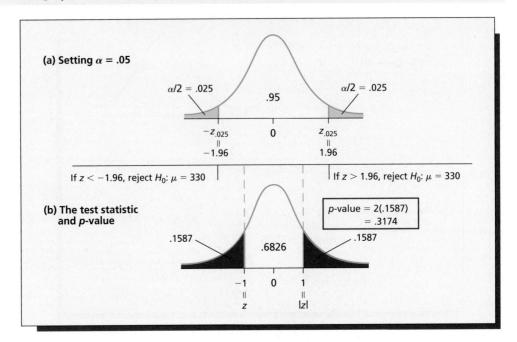

Step 4: To decide how different from zero (positive or negative) the test statistic must be in order to reject H_0 in favor of H_a by setting the probability of a Type I error equal to α, we do the following:

- Divide the probability of a Type I error, α, into two equal parts, and place the area $\alpha/2$ in the right-hand tail of the standard normal curve and the area $\alpha/2$ in the left-hand tail of the standard normal curve. Then use the normal table to find the critical values $z_{\alpha/2}$ and $-z_{\alpha/2}$. Here $z_{\alpha/2}$ is the point on the horizontal axis under the standard normal curve that gives a right-hand tail area equal to $\alpha/2$, and $-z_{\alpha/2}$ is the point giving a left-hand tail area equal to $\alpha/2$.

- **Reject H_0: $\mu = 330$ in favor of H_a: $\mu \neq 330$ if and only if the test statistic z is greater than the critical value $z_{\alpha/2}$ or less than the critical value $-z_{\alpha/2}$.** Note that this is equivalent to saying that we should **reject H_0 if and only if the absolute value of the test statistic, $|z|$, is greater than the critical value $z_{\alpha/2}$.** Because α equals .05, the critical values are [see Figure 9.5(a)]

$$z_{\alpha/2} = z_{.05/2} = z_{.025} = 1.96 \qquad \text{and} \qquad -z_{\alpha/2} = -z_{.025} = -1.96$$

Step 5: When the sample of $n = 100$ large retail stores is randomly selected, the mean of their reported order quantities is calculated to be $\bar{x} = 326$. Assuming that σ is known to equal 40, the value of the test statistic is

$$z = \frac{\bar{x} - 330}{\sigma/\sqrt{n}} = \frac{326 - 330}{40/\sqrt{100}} = -1$$

Step 6: Since the test statistic value $z = -1$ is greater than $-z_{.025} = -1.96$ (or equivalently, since $|z| = 1$ is less than $z_{.025} = 1.96$), we cannot reject H_0: $\mu = 330$ in favor of H_a: $\mu \neq 330$ by setting α equal to .05.

Step 7: We cannot conclude (at an α of .05) that the mean order quantity of this year's valentine box by large retail stores will differ from 330 boxes. Therefore, the candy company will base its production of valentine boxes on the 10 percent projected sales increase.

A p-value for testing a "not equal to" alternative hypothesis   To test H_0: $\mu = 330$ versus H_a: $\mu \neq 330$ in the Valentine's Day chocolate case by using a p-value, we use the following steps 4, 5, and 6:

Step 4: We have computed the value of the test statistic in the Valentine's Day chocolate case to be $z = -1$.

Step 5: Note from Figure 9.5(b) that the area under the standard normal curve to the right of $|z| = 1$ is .1587. Twice this area—that is, $2(.1587) = .3174$—is the p-value for testing $H_0: \mu = 330$ versus $H_a: \mu \neq 330$. To interpret the p-value as a probability, note that the symmetry of the standard normal curve implies that twice the area under the curve to the right of $|z| = 1$ equals the area under this curve to the right of 1 plus the area under the curve to the left of -1 [see Figure 9.5(b)]. Also, note that since both positive and negative test statistic values count against $H_0: \mu = 330$, a test statistic value that is either greater than or equal to 1 or less than or equal to -1 is at least as extreme as the observed test statistic value $z = -1$. It follows that the p-value of .3174 says that, if $H_0: \mu = 330$ is true, then 31.74 percent of all possible test statistic values are at least as extreme as $z = -1$. That is, if we are to believe that H_0 is true, we must believe that we have observed a test statistic value that can be described as a 31.74 percent chance.

Step 6: The candy company has set α equal to .05. **The p-value of .3174 is greater than the α of .05. Therefore, we cannot reject H_0 by setting α equal to .05.**

A general procedure for testing a hypothesis about a population mean   In the trash bag case we have tested $H_0: \mu \leq 50$ versus $H_a: \mu > 50$ by testing $H_0: \mu = 50$ versus $H_a: \mu > 50$. In the payment time case we have tested $H_0: \mu \geq 19.5$ versus $H_a: \mu < 19.5$ by testing $H_0: \mu = 19.5$ versus $H_a: \mu < 19.5$. In general, the usual procedure for testing a "less than or equal to" null hypothesis or a "greater than or equal to" null hypothesis is to change the null hypothesis to an equality. We then test the "equal to" null hypothesis versus the alternative hypothesis. Furthermore, the critical value and p-value procedures for testing a null hypothesis versus an alternative hypothesis depend on whether the alternative hypothesis is a "greater than," a "less than," or a "not equal to" alternative hypothesis. The following summary box gives the appropriate procedures. Specifically, letting μ_0 be a particular number, the summary box shows how to test $H_0: \mu = \mu_0$ versus $H_a: \mu > \mu_0$, $H_a: \mu < \mu_0$, or $H_a: \mu \neq \mu_0$:

Testing a Hypothesis about a Population Mean When σ Is Known

Define the test statistic

$$z = \frac{\bar{x} - \mu_0}{\sigma/\sqrt{n}}$$

and assume that the population sampled is normally distributed or that the sample size n is large. We can test $H_0: \mu = \mu_0$ versus a particular alternative hypothesis at level of significance α by using the appropriate critical value rule, or equivalently, the corresponding p-value.

Alternative Hypothesis	Critical Value Rule: Reject H_0 If	p-Value (Reject H_0 If p-Value $< \alpha$)
$H_a: \mu > \mu_0$	$z > z_\alpha$	The area under the standard normal curve to the right of z
$H_a: \mu < \mu_0$	$z < -z_\alpha$	The area under the standard normal curve to the left of z
$H_a: \mu \neq \mu_0$	$\|z\| > z_{\alpha/2}$—that is, $z > z_{\alpha/2}$ or $z < -z_{\alpha/2}$	Twice the area under the standard normal curve to the right of $\|z\|$

Using confidence intervals to test hypotheses   Confidence intervals can be used to test hypotheses. Specifically, it can be proven that we can reject $H_0: \mu = \mu_0$ in favor of $H_a: \mu \neq \mu_0$ by setting the probability of a Type I error equal to α if and only if the $100(1 - \alpha)$ percent confidence interval for μ does not contain μ_0. For example, consider the Valentine's Day chocolate case and testing $H_0: \mu = 330$ versus $H_a: \mu \neq 330$ by setting α equal to .05. To do this, we use the mean $\bar{x} = 326$ of the sample of $n = 100$ reported order quantities to calculate the 95 percent confidence interval for μ to be

$$\left[\bar{x} \pm z_{\alpha/2}\, \frac{\sigma}{\sqrt{n}} \right] = \left[326 \pm 1.96\, \frac{40}{\sqrt{100}} \right] = [318.2, 333.8]$$

Because this interval does contain 330, we cannot reject $H_0: \mu = 330$ in favor of $H_a: \mu \neq 330$ by setting α equal to .05.

Whereas we can use **two-sided** confidence intervals to test "not equal to" alternative hypotheses, we must use **one-sided** confidence intervals to test "greater than" or "less than" alternative hypotheses. We will not study one-sided confidence intervals in this book. However, it should be emphasized that we do not need to use confidence intervals (one-sided or two-sided) to test hypotheses. We can test hypotheses by using test statistics and critical values or p-values, and these are the approaches that we will feature throughout this book.

Measuring the weight of evidence against the null hypothesis   We have seen that in some situations the decision to take an action is based solely on whether a null hypothesis can be rejected in favor of an alternative hypothesis by setting α equal to a single, prespecified value. For example, in the trash bag case the television network decided to run the trash bag commercial because $H_0: \mu = 50$ was rejected in favor of $H_a: \mu > 50$ by setting α equal to .05. Also, in the payment time case the management consulting firm decided to claim that the new electronic billing system has reduced the Hamilton trucking company's mean payment time by more than 50 percent because $H_0: \mu = 19.5$ was rejected in favor of $H_a: \mu < 19.5$ by setting α equal to .01. Furthermore, in the Valentine's Day chocolate case, the candy company decided to base its production of valentine boxes on the 10 percent projected sales increase because $H_0: \mu = 330$ could not be rejected in favor of $H_a: \mu \neq 330$ by setting α equal to .05.

Although hypothesis testing at a fixed α level is sometimes used as the sole basis for deciding whether to take an action, this is not always the case. For example, consider again the payment time case. The reason that the management consulting firm wishes to make the claim about the new electronic billing system is to demonstrate the benefits of the new system both to the Hamilton company and to other trucking companies that are considering using such a system. Note, however, that a potential user will decide whether to install the new system by considering factors beyond the results of the hypothesis test. For example, the cost of the new billing system and the receptiveness of the company's clients to using the new system are among other factors that must be considered. In complex business and industrial situations such as this, hypothesis testing is used to accumulate knowledge about and understand the problem at hand. The ultimate decision (such as whether to adopt the new billing system) is made on the basis of nonstatistical considerations, intuition, and the results of one or more hypothesis tests. Therefore, it is important to know all the information—called the **weight of evidence**—that a hypothesis test provides against the null hypothesis and in favor of the alternative hypothesis. Furthermore, even when hypothesis testing at a fixed α level is used as the sole basis for deciding whether to take an action, it is useful to evaluate the weight of evidence. For example, the trash bag manufacturer would almost certainly wish to know *how much* evidence there is that its new bag is stronger than its former bag.

The most informative way to measure the weight of evidence is to use the p-value. For every hypothesis test considered in this book we can interpret the p-value to be the **probability, computed assuming that the null hypothesis H_0 is true, of observing a value of the test statistic that is at least as extreme as the value actually computed from the sample data. The smaller the p-value is, the less likely are the sample results if the null hypothesis H_0 is true. Therefore, the stronger is the evidence that H_0 is false and that the alternative hypothesis H_a is true.** Experience with hypothesis testing has resulted in statisticians making the following (somewhat subjective) conclusions:

Interpreting the Weight of Evidence against the Null Hypothesis

If the p-value for testing H_0 is less than

- .10, we have **some evidence** that H_0 is false.
- .05, we have **strong evidence** that H_0 is false.

- .01, we have **very strong evidence** that H_0 is false.
- .001, we have **extremely strong evidence** that H_0 is false.

We will frequently use these conclusions in future examples. Understand, however, that there are really no sharp borders between different weights of evidence. Rather, there is really only increasingly strong evidence against the null hypothesis as the p-value decreases.

For example, recall that the p-value for testing $H_0: \mu = 50$ versus $H_a: \mu > 50$ in the trash bag case is .0139. This p-value is less than .05 but not less than .01. Therefore, we have strong evidence, but not very strong evidence, that $H_0: \mu = 50$ is false and $H_a: \mu > 50$ is true. That is, we have strong evidence that the mean breaking strength of the new trash bag exceeds 50 pounds. As another example, the p-value for testing $H_0: \mu = 19.5$ versus $H_a: \mu < 19.5$ in the payment time case is .0038.

This p-value is less than .01 but not less than .001. Therefore, we have very strong evidence, but not extremely strong evidence, that H_0: $\mu = 19.5$ is false and H_a: $\mu < 19.5$ is true. That is, we have very strong evidence that the new billing system has reduced the mean payment time by more than 50 percent. Finally, the p-value for testing H_0: $\mu = 330$ versus H_a: $\mu \neq 330$ in the Valentine's Day chocolate case is .3174. This p-value is greater than .10. Therefore, we have little evidence that H_0: $\mu = 330$ is false and H_a: $\mu \neq 330$ is true. That is, we have little evidence that the increase in the mean order quantity of the valentine box by large retail stores will differ from 10 percent.

Exercises for Section 9.2

CONCEPTS

connect™

9.14 Explain what a critical value is, and explain how it is used to test a hypothesis.

9.15 Explain what a p-value is, and explain how it is used to test a hypothesis.

METHODS AND APPLICATIONS

In Exercises 9.16 through 9.22 we consider using a random sample of 100 measurements to test H_0: $\mu = 80$ versus H_a: $\mu > 80$. If $\bar{x} = 85$ and $\sigma = 20$:

9.16 Calculate the value of the test statistic z.

9.17 Use a critical value to test H_0 versus H_a by setting α equal to .10.

9.18 Use a critical value to test H_0 versus H_a by setting α equal to .05.

9.19 Use a critical value to test H_0 versus H_a by setting α equal to .01.

9.20 Use a critical value to test H_0 versus H_a by setting α equal to .001.

9.21 Calculate the p-value and use it to test H_0 versus H_a at each of $\alpha = .10, .05, .01,$ and .001.

9.22 How much evidence is there that H_0: $\mu = 80$ is false and H_a: $\mu > 80$ is true?

In Exercises 9.23 through 9.29 we consider using a random sample of 49 measurements to test H_0: $\mu = 20$ versus H_a: $\mu < 20$. If $\bar{x} = 18$ and $\sigma = 7$:

9.23 Calculate the value of the test statistic z.

9.24 Use a critical value to test H_0 versus H_a by setting α equal to .10.

9.25 Use a critical value to test H_0 versus H_a by setting α equal to .05.

9.26 Use a critical value to test H_0 versus H_a by setting α equal to .01.

9.27 Use a critical value to test H_0 versus H_a by setting α equal to .001.

9.28 Calculate the p-value and use it to test H_0 versus H_a at each of $\alpha = .10, .05, .01,$ and .001.

9.29 How much evidence is there that H_0: $\mu = 20$ is false and H_a: $\mu < 20$ is true?

In Exercises 9.30 through 9.36 we consider using a random sample of $n = 81$ measurements to test H_0: $\mu = 40$ versus H_a: $\mu \neq 40$. If $\bar{x} = 34$ and $\sigma = 18$:

9.30 Calculate the value of the test statistic z.

9.31 Use critical values to test H_0 versus H_a by setting α equal to .10.

9.32 Use critical values to test H_0 versus H_a by setting α equal to .05.

9.33 Use critical values to test H_0 versus H_a by setting α equal to .01.

9.34 Use critical values to test H_0 versus H_a by setting α equal to .001.

9.35 Calculate the p-value and use it to test H_0 versus H_a at each of $\alpha = .10, .05, .01,$ and .001.

9.36 How much evidence is there that H_0: $\mu = 40$ is false and H_a: $\mu \neq 40$ is true?

9.37 **THE VIDEO GAME SATISFACTION RATING CASE** ◆ VideoGame

Recall that "very satisfied" customers give the XYZ-Box video game system a rating that is at least 42. Suppose that the manufacturer of the XYZ-Box wishes to use the random sample of 65 satisfaction ratings to provide evidence supporting the claim that the mean composite satisfaction rating for the XYZ-Box exceeds 42.

a Letting μ represent the mean composite satisfaction rating for the XYZ-Box, set up the null hypothesis H_0 and the alternative hypothesis H_a needed if we wish to attempt to provide evidence supporting the claim that μ exceeds 42.

b The random sample of 65 satisfaction ratings yields a sample mean of $\bar{x} = 42.954$. Assuming that σ equals 2.64, use critical values to test H_0 versus H_a at each of $\alpha = .10, .05, .01,$ and .001.

c Using the information in part *b*, calculate the *p*-value and use it to test H_0 versus H_a at each of $\alpha = .10, .05, .01,$ and $.001$.

d How much evidence is there that the mean composite satisfaction rating exceeds 42?

9.38   **THE BANK CUSTOMER WAITING TIME CASE**   ⬤ WaitTime

Letting μ be the mean waiting time under the new system, we found in Exercise 9.9 that we should test $H_0: \mu \geq 6$ versus $H_a: \mu < 6$ in order to attempt to provide evidence that μ is less than six minutes. The random sample of 100 waiting times yields a sample mean of $\bar{x} = 5.46$ minutes. Moreover, Figure 9.6 gives the MINITAB output obtained when we use the waiting time data to test $H_0: \mu = 6$ versus $H_a: \mu < 6$. On this output the label "SE Mean," which stands for "the standard error of the mean," denotes the quantity $\sigma/\sqrt{n}$, and the label "Z" denotes the calculated test statistic. Assuming that σ equals 2.47:

a Use critical values to test H_0 versus H_a at each of $\alpha = .10, .05, .01,$ and $.001$.

b Calculate the *p*-value and verify that it equals .014, as shown on the MINITAB output. Use the *p*-value to test H_0 versus H_a at each of $\alpha = .10, .05, .01,$ and $.001$.

c How much evidence is there that the new system has reduced the mean waiting time to below six minutes?

9.39   Again consider the audit delay situation of Exercise 8.11. Letting μ be the mean audit delay for all public owner-controlled companies in New Zealand, formulate the null hypothesis H_0 and the alternative hypothesis H_a that would be used to attempt to provide evidence supporting the claim that μ is less than 90 days. Suppose that a random sample of 100 public owner-controlled companies in New Zealand is found to give a mean audit delay of $\bar{x} = 86.6$ days. Assuming that σ equals 32.83, calculate the *p*-value for testing H_0 versus H_a and determine how much evidence there is that the mean audit delay for all public owner-controlled companies in New Zealand is less than 90 days.

9.40   Consolidated Power, a large electric power utility, has just built a modern nuclear power plant. This plant discharges waste water that is allowed to flow into the Atlantic Ocean. The Environmental Protection Agency (EPA) has ordered that the waste water may not be excessively warm so that thermal pollution of the marine environment near the plant can be avoided. Because of this order, the waste water is allowed to cool in specially constructed ponds and is then released into the ocean. This cooling system works properly if the mean temperature of waste water discharged is 60°F or cooler. Consolidated Power is required to monitor the temperature of the waste water. A sample of 100 temperature readings will be obtained each day, and if the sample results cast a substantial amount of doubt on the hypothesis that the cooling system is working properly (the mean temperature of waste water discharged is 60°F or cooler), then the plant must be shut down and appropriate actions must be taken to correct the problem.

a Consolidated Power wishes to set up a hypothesis test so that the power plant will be shut down when the null hypothesis is rejected. Set up the null hypothesis H_0 and the alternative hypothesis H_a that should be used.

b Suppose that Consolidated Power decides to use a level of significance of $\alpha = .05$, and suppose a random sample of 100 temperature readings is obtained. If the sample mean of the 100 temperature readings is $\bar{x} = 60.482$, test H_0 versus H_a and determine whether the power plant should be shut down and the cooling system repaired. Perform the hypothesis test by using a critical value and a *p*-value. Assume $\sigma = 2$.

9.41   Do part *b* of Exercise 9.40 if $\bar{x} = 60.262$.

9.42   Do part *b* of Exercise 9.40 if $\bar{x} = 60.618$.

9.43   An automobile parts supplier owns a machine that produces a cylindrical engine part. This part is supposed to have an outside diameter of three inches. Parts with diameters that are too small or too large do not meet customer requirements and must be rejected. Lately, the company has experienced problems meeting customer requirements. The technical staff feels that the mean diameter produced by the machine is off target. In order to verify this, a special study will

---

FIGURE 9.6   **MINITAB Output of the Test of $H_0: \mu = 6$ versus $H_a: \mu < 6$ in the Bank Customer Waiting Time Case**

```
Test of mu = 6 vs < 6.   The assumed standard deviation = 2.47

Variable    N     Mean    StDev   SE Mean      Z      P
WaitTime   100  5.46000  2.47546  0.24700   -2.19  0.014
```

Note: Because the test statistic *z* has a denominator $\sigma/\sqrt{n}$ that uses the population standard deviation σ, MINITAB makes the user specify an assumed value for σ.

randomly sample 100 parts produced by the machine. The 100 sampled parts will be measured, and if the results obtained cast a substantial amount of doubt on the hypothesis that the mean diameter equals the target value of three inches, the company will assign a problem-solving team to intensively search for the causes of the problem.

  a The parts supplier wishes to set up a hypothesis test so that the problem-solving team will be assigned when the null hypothesis is rejected. Set up the null and alternative hypotheses for this situation.

  b A sample of 40 parts yields a sample mean diameter of $\bar{x} = 3.006$ inches. Assuming σ equals .016, use a critical value and a p-value to test H_0 versus H_a by setting α equal to .05. Should the problem-solving team be assigned?

9.44 The Crown Bottling Company has just installed a new bottling process that will fill 16-ounce bottles of the popular Crown Classic Cola soft drink. Both overfilling and underfilling bottles are undesirable: Underfilling leads to customer complaints and overfilling costs the company considerable money. In order to verify that the filler is set up correctly, the company wishes to see whether the mean bottle fill, μ, is close to the target fill of 16 ounces. To this end, a random sample of 36 filled bottles is selected from the output of a test filler run. If the sample results cast a substantial amount of doubt on the hypothesis that the mean bottle fill is the desired 16 ounces, then the filler's initial setup will be readjusted.

  a The bottling company wants to set up a hypothesis test so that the filler will be readjusted if the null hypothesis is rejected. Set up the null and alternative hypotheses for this hypothesis test.

  b Suppose that Crown Bottling Company decides to use a level of significance of $\alpha = .01$, and suppose a random sample of 36 bottle fills is obtained from a test run of the filler. For each of the following three sample means, determine whether the filler's initial setup should be readjusted. In each case, use a critical value and a p-value, and assume that σ equals .1.

$$\text{First sample mean:} \quad \bar{x} = 16.05$$
$$\text{Second sample mean:} \quad \bar{x} = 15.96$$
$$\text{Third sample mean:} \quad \bar{x} = 16.02$$

9.45 Use the first sample mean in Exercise 9.44 and a confidence interval to perform the hypothesis test by setting α equal to .05. What considerations would help you to decide whether the result has practical importance?

9.46 THE DISK BRAKE CASE

National Motors has equipped the ZX-900 with a new disk brake system. We define the stopping distance for a ZX-900 as the distance (in feet) required to bring the automobile to a complete stop from a speed of 35 mph under normal driving conditions using this new brake system. In addition, we define μ to be the mean stopping distance of all ZX-900s. One of the ZX-900's major competitors is advertised to achieve a mean stopping distance of 60 ft. National Motors would like to claim in a new television commercial that the ZX-900 achieves a shorter mean stopping distance.

  a Set up the null hypothesis H_0 and the alternative hypothesis H_a that would be used to attempt to provide evidence supporting the claim that μ is less than 60.

  b A television network will permit National Motors to claim that the ZX-900 achieves a shorter mean stopping distance than the competitor if H_0 can be rejected in favor of H_a by setting α equal to .05. If the stopping distances of a random sample of $n = 81$ ZX-900s have a mean of $\bar{x} = 57.8$ ft, will National Motors be allowed to run the commercial? Perform the hypothesis test by using a critical value and a p-value. Assume here that $\sigma = 6.02$.

9.47 Consider part b of Exercise 9.46, and calculate a 95 percent confidence interval for μ. Do the point estimate of μ and confidence interval for μ indicate that μ might be far enough below 60 feet to suggest that we have a practically important result?

9.48 Recall from Exercise 8.12 that Bayus (1991) studied the mean numbers of auto dealers visited by early and late replacement buyers.

  a Letting μ be the mean number of dealers visited by early replacement buyers, suppose that we wish to test $H_0: \mu = 4$ versus $H_a: \mu \neq 4$. A random sample of 800 early replacement buyers yields a mean number of dealers visited of $\bar{x} = 3.3$. Assuming σ equals .71, calculate the p-value and test H_0 versus H_a. Do we estimate that μ is less than 4 or greater than 4?

  b Letting μ be the mean number of dealers visited by late replacement buyers, suppose that we wish to test $H_0: \mu = 4$ versus $H_a: \mu \neq 4$. A random sample of 500 late replacement buyers yields a mean number of dealers visited of $\bar{x} = 4.3$. Assuming σ equals .66, calculate the p-value and test H_0 versus H_a. Do we estimate that μ is less than 4 or greater than 4?

9.3 *t* Tests about a Population Mean: σ Unknown ● ● ●

If we do not know σ (which is usually the case), we can base a hypothesis test about μ on the sampling distribution of

$$\frac{\bar{x} - \mu}{s/\sqrt{n}}$$

If the sampled population is normally distributed, then this sampling distribution is a *t* **distribution having** $n - 1$ **degrees of freedom.** This leads to the following results:

A *t* Test about a Population Mean: σ Unknown

Define the test statistic

$$t = \frac{\bar{x} - \mu_0}{s/\sqrt{n}}$$

and assume that the population sampled is normally distributed. We can test H_0: $\mu = \mu_0$ versus a particular alternative hypothesis at level of significance α by using the appropriate critical value rule, or, equivalently, the corresponding *p*-value.

Alternative Hypothesis	Critical Value Rule: Reject H_0 If	*p*-Value (Reject H_0 If *p*-Value $< \alpha$)
H_a: $\mu > \mu_0$	$t > t_\alpha$	The area under the *t* distribution curve to the right of *t*
H_a: $\mu < \mu_0$	$t < -t_\alpha$	The area under the *t* distribution curve to the left of *t*
H_a: $\mu \neq \mu_0$	$|t| > t_{\alpha/2}$—that is, $t > t_{\alpha/2}$ or $t < -t_{\alpha/2}$	Twice the area under the *t* distribution curve to the right of $|t|$

Here t_α, $t_{\alpha/2}$, and the *p*-values are based on $n - 1$ degrees of freedom.

In the rest of this chapter and in Chapter 10 we will present most of the hypothesis testing examples by using hypothesis testing summary boxes and the seven hypothesis testing steps given in the previous section. However, to be concise, we will not formally number each hypothesis testing step. Rather, for each of the first six steps, we will set out in boldface font a key phrase that indicates that the step is being carried out. Then, we will highlight the seventh step—the business improvement conclusion—as we highlight all business improvement conclusions in this book. After Chapter 10, we will continue to use hypothesis testing summary boxes, and we will more informally use the seven steps.

As illustrated in the following example, we will often first use a critical value rule to test the hypotheses under consideration at a fixed value of α and then use a *p*-value to assess the weight of evidence against the null hypothesis.

EXAMPLE 9.4

In 1991 the average interest rate charged by U.S. credit card issuers was 18.8 percent. Since that time, there has been a proliferation of new credit cards affiliated with retail stores, oil companies, alumni associations, professional sports teams, and so on. A financial officer wishes to study whether the increased competition in the credit card business has reduced interest rates. To do this, the officer will test a hypothesis about the current mean interest rate, μ, charged by U.S. credit card issuers. **The null hypothesis to be tested is H_0: $\mu = 18.8\%$, and the alternative hypothesis is H_a: $\mu < 18.8\%$.** If H_0 can be rejected in favor of H_a at the **.05 level of significance,** the officer will conclude that the current mean interest rate is less than the 18.8 percent mean interest rate charged in 1991. To perform the hypothesis test, suppose that we randomly select $n = 15$ credit cards and determine their current interest rates. The interest rates for the 15 sampled cards are given in Table 9.3. A stem-and-leaf display and MINITAB box plot are given in Figure 9.7. The stem-and-leaf display looks reasonably mound-shaped, and both the stem-and-leaf display and the box plot look reasonably symmetrical. It follows that it is appropriate to calculate the value of the **test statistic *t* in the summary box.** Furthermore, since H_a: $\mu < 18.8\%$ is of the form H_a: $\mu < \mu_0$, we should **reject H_0: $\mu = 18.8\%$ if the value of *t* is less than the critical value $-t_\alpha = -t_{.05} = -1.761$.** Here, $-t_{.05} = -1.761$ is based on $n - 1 = 15 - 1 = 14$ degrees of freedom and this critical value is

TABLE 9.3	Interest Rates Charged by 15 Randomly Selected Credit Cards ● CreditCd		
15.6%	15.3%	19.2%
17.8	16.4	15.8
14.6	18.4	18.1
17.3	17.6	16.6
18.7	14.0	17.0

FIGURE 9.7   Stem-and-Leaf Display and Box Plot of the Interest Rates

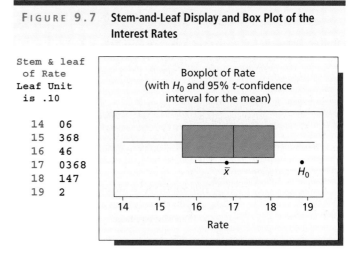

```
Stem & leaf
 of Rate
Leaf Unit
 is .10

   14   06
   15   368
   16   46
   17   0368
   18   147
   19   2
```

FIGURE 9.8   Testing H_0: $\mu = 18.8\%$ versus H_a: $\mu < 18.8\%$ by Using a Critical Value and a p-Value

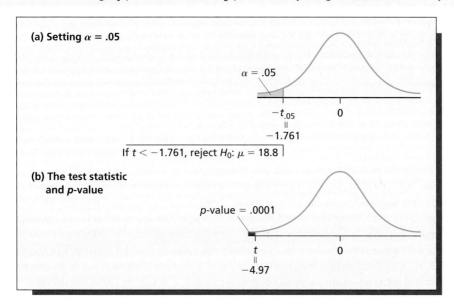

(a) Setting $\alpha = .05$

$\alpha = .05$

$-t_{.05}$
=
-1.761

0

If $t < -1.761$, reject H_0: $\mu = 18.8$

(b) The test statistic and p-value

p-value = .0001

t
=
-4.97

0

illustrated in Figure 9.8(a). The mean and the standard deviation of the $n = 15$ interest rates in Table 9.3 are $\bar{x} = 16.827$ and $s = 1.538$. This implies that the **value of the test statistic** is

$$t = \frac{\bar{x} - 18.8}{s/\sqrt{n}} = \frac{16.827 - 18.8}{1.538/\sqrt{15}} = -4.97$$

Since $t = -4.97$ is less than $-t_{.05} = -1.761$, we reject H_0: $\mu = 18.8\%$ in favor of H_a: $\mu < 18.8\%$. That is, we conclude (at an α of .05) that the current mean credit card interest rate is lower than 18.8 percent, the mean interest rate in 1991. Furthermore, the sample mean $\bar{x} = 16.827$ says that we estimate the mean interest rate is $18.8\% - 16.827\% = 1.973\%$ lower than it was in 1991.

The p-value for testing H_0: $\mu = 18.8\%$ versus H_a: $\mu < 18.8\%$ is the area under the curve of the t distribution having 14 degrees of freedom to the left of $t = -4.97$. Tables of t points (such as Table A.4, page 642) are not complete enough to give such areas for most t statistic values, so we use computer software packages to calculate p-values that are based on the t distribution. For example, the MINITAB output in Figure 9.9(a) and the MegaStat output in Figure 9.10 tell us that the p-value for testing H_0: $\mu = 18.8\%$ versus H_a: $\mu < 18.8\%$ is .0001. Notice that both MINITAB and MegaStat round p-values to three or four decimal places. The Excel output in Figure 9.9(b) gives the slightly more accurate value of 0.000103 for the p-value. Because this p-value is less than .05, .01, and .001, we can reject H_0 at the .05, .01, and .001 levels of significance. Also note that the p-value of .0001 on the MegaStat output is shaded dark yellow. This indicates that we can reject H_0 at the .01 level of significance (light yellow shading would indicate

FIGURE 9.9   The MINITAB and Excel Outputs for Testing H_0: $\mu = 18.8\%$ versus H_a: $\mu < 18.8\%$

(a) The MINITAB output   **(b) The Excel output**

```
Test of mu = 18.8 vs < 18.8

Variable    N     Mean    StDev    SE Mean       T        P
Rate       15   16.8267  1.5378   0.3971     -4.97    0.000
```

t-statistic
−4.97

p-value
0.000103

FIGURE 9.10   The MegaStat Output for Testing H_0: $\mu = 18.8\%$ versus H_a: $\mu < 18.8\%$

Hypothesis Test: Mean vs. Hypothesized Value

18.8000 hypothesized value	1.5378 std. dev.	15 n	−4.97 t
16.8267 mean Rate	0.3971 std. error	14 df	.0001 p-value (one-tailed, lower)

= Significant at .05 level   = Significant at .01 level

significance at the .05 level, but not at the .01 level). As a probability, the p-value of .0001 says that if we are to believe that H_0: $\mu = 18.8\%$ is true, we must believe that we have observed a t statistic value ($t = -4.97$) that can be described as a 1 in 10,000 chance. In summary, we have extremely strong evidence that H_0: $\mu = 18.8\%$ is false and H_a: $\mu < 18.8\%$ is true. That is, we have extremely strong evidence that the current mean credit card interest rate is less than 18.8 percent.

Recall that in three cases discussed in Section 9.2 we tested hypotheses by assuming that the population standard deviation σ is known and by using z tests. If σ is actually not known in these cases (which would probably be true), we should test the hypotheses under consideration by using t tests. Furthermore, recall that in each case the sample size is large (at least 30). In general, it can be shown that if the sample size is large, the t test is approximately valid even if the sampled population is not normally distributed (or mound-shaped). Therefore, consider the Valentine's Day chocolate case and testing **H_0: $\mu = 330$ versus H_a: $\mu \neq 330$ at the .05 level of significance.** To perform the hypothesis test, assume that we will randomly select $n = 100$ large retail stores and use their anticipated order quantities to calculate the value of the **test statistic t in the summary box.** Then, since the alternative hypothesis H_a: $\mu \neq 330$ is of the form H_a: $\mu \neq \mu_0$, we will **reject H_0: $\mu = 330$ if the absolute value of t is greater than $t_{\alpha/2} = t_{.025} = 1.984$ (based on $n - 1 = 99$ degrees of freedom).** Suppose that when the sample is randomly selected, the mean and the standard deviation of the $n = 100$ reported order quantities are calculated to be $\bar{x} = 326$ and $s = 39.1$. The **value of the test statistic** is

$$t = \frac{\bar{x} - 330}{s/\sqrt{n}} = \frac{326 - 330}{39.1/\sqrt{100}} = -1.023$$

Since $|t| = 1.023$ is less than $t_{.025} = 1.984$, we cannot reject H_0: $\mu = 330$ by setting α equal to .05. It follows that we cannot conclude (at an α of .05) that this year's mean order quantity of the valentine box by large retail stores will differ from 330 boxes. Therefore, the candy company will base its production of valentine boxes on the 10 percent projected sales increase. The p-value for the hypothesis test is twice the area under the t distribution curve having 99 degrees of freedom to the right of $|t| = 1.023$. Using a computer, we find that this p-value is .3088, which provides little evidence against H_0: $\mu = 330$ and in favor of H_a: $\mu \neq 330$.

As another example, consider the trash bag case and note that the sample of $n = 40$ trash bag breaking strengths has mean $\bar{x} = 50.575$ and standard deviation $s = 1.6438$. The p-value for testing H_0: $\mu = 50$ versus H_a: $\mu > 50$ is the area under the t distribution curve having $n - 1 = 39$ degrees of freedom to the right of

$$t = \frac{\bar{x} - 50}{s/\sqrt{n}} = \frac{50.575 - 50}{1.6438/\sqrt{40}} = 2.2123$$

Using a computer, we find that this *p*-value is .0164, which provides strong evidence against H_0: $\mu = 50$ and in favor of H_a: $\mu > 50$. In particular, recall that most television networks would evaluate the claim that the new trash bag has a mean breaking strength that exceeds 50 pounds by choosing an α value between .025 and .10. It follows, since the *p*-value of .0164 is less than all these α values, that most networks would allow the trash bag claim to be advertised.

As a third example, consider the payment time case and note that the sample of $n = 65$ payment times has mean $\bar{x} = 18.1077$ and standard deviation $s = 3.9612$. The *p*-value for testing H_0: $\mu = 19.5$ versus H_a: $\mu < 19.5$ is the area under the *t* distribution curve having $n - 1 = 64$ degrees of freedom to the left of

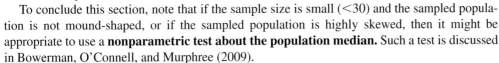

$$t = \frac{\bar{x} - 19.5}{s/\sqrt{n}} = \frac{18.1077 - 19.5}{3.9612/\sqrt{65}} = -2.8338$$

Using a computer, we find that this *p*-value is .0031, which is less than the management consulting firm's α value of .01. It follows that the consulting firm will claim that the new electronic billing system has reduced the Hamilton, Ohio, trucking company's mean bill payment time by more than 50 percent.

To conclude this section, note that if the sample size is small (<30) and the sampled population is not mound-shaped, or if the sampled population is highly skewed, then it might be appropriate to use a **nonparametric test about the population median.** Such a test is discussed in Bowerman, O'Connell, and Murphree (2009).

Exercises for Section 9.3

CONCEPTS

9.49 What assumptions must be met in order to carry out the test about a population mean based on the *t* distribution?

9.50 How do we decide whether to use a *z* test or a *t* test when testing a hypothesis about a population mean?

METHODS AND APPLICATIONS

9.51 Suppose that a random sample of 16 measurements from a normally distributed population gives a sample mean of $\bar{x} = 13.5$ and a sample standard deviation of $s = 6$. Use critical values to test H_0: $\mu \le 10$ versus H_a: $\mu > 10$ using levels of significance $\alpha = .10$, $\alpha = .05$, $\alpha = .01$, and $\alpha = .001$. What do you conclude at each value of α?

9.52 Suppose that a random sample of nine measurements from a normally distributed population gives a sample mean of $\bar{x} = 2.57$ and a sample standard deviation of $s = .3$. Use critical values to test H_0: $\mu = 3$ versus H_a: $\mu \ne 3$ using levels of significance $\alpha = .10$, $\alpha = .05$, $\alpha = .01$, and $\alpha = .001$. What do you conclude at each value of α?

9.53 **THE AIR TRAFFIC CONTROL CASE**   🌐 AlertTime

Recall that it is hoped that the mean alert time, μ, using the new display panel is less than eight seconds. Formulate the null hypothesis H_0 and the alternative hypothesis H_a that would be used to attempt to provide evidence that μ is less than eight seconds. The mean and the standard deviation of the sample of $n = 15$ alert times are $\bar{x} = 7.4$ and $s = 1.0261$. Perform a *t* test of H_0 versus H_a by setting α equal to .05 and using a critical value. Interpret the results of the test.

9.54 **THE AIR TRAFFIC CONTROL CASE**   🌐 AlertTime

The *p*-value for the hypothesis test of Exercise 9.53 can be computer calculated to be .0200. How much evidence is there that μ is less than eight seconds?

9.55 The *bad debt ratio* for a financial institution is defined to be the dollar value of loans defaulted divided by the total dollar value of all loans made. Suppose that a random sample of seven Ohio banks is selected and that the bad debt ratios (written as percentages) for these banks are 7%, 4%, 6%, 7%, 5%, 4%, and 9%.   🌐 BadDebt

a Banking officials claim that the mean bad debt ratio for all Midwestern banks is 3.5 percent and that the mean bad debt ratio for Ohio banks is higher. Set up the null and alternative hypotheses needed to attempt to provide evidence supporting the claim that the mean bad debt ratio for Ohio banks exceeds 3.5 percent.

b Assuming that bad debt ratios for Ohio banks are approximately normally distributed, use critical values and the given sample information to test the hypotheses you set up in part *a* by setting α

equal to .10, .05, .01, and .001. How much evidence is there that the mean bad debt ratio for Ohio banks exceeds 3.5 percent? What does this say about the banking official's claim?

c Are you qualified to decide whether we have a practically important result? Who would be? How might practical importance be defined in this situation?

d The p-value for the hypothesis test of part b can be computer calculated to be .006. What does this p-value say about whether the mean bad debt ratio for Ohio banks exceeds 3.5 percent?

9.56 In the book *Business Research Methods,* Donald R. Cooper and C. William Emory (1995) discuss using hypothesis testing to study receivables outstanding. To quote Cooper and Emory:

> . . . the controller of a large retail chain may be concerned about a possible slowdown in payments by the company's customers. She measures the rate of payment in terms of the average number of days receivables outstanding. Generally, the company has maintained an average of about 50 days with a standard deviation of 10 days. Since it would be too expensive to analyze all of a company's receivables frequently, we normally resort to sampling.

a Set up the null and alternative hypotheses needed to attempt to show that there has been a slowdown in payments by the company's customers (there has been a slowdown if the average days outstanding exceeds 50).

b Assume approximate normality and suppose that a random sample of 25 accounts gives an average days outstanding of $\bar{x} = 54$ with a standard deviation of $s = 8$. Use critical values to test the hypotheses you set up in part a at levels of significance $\alpha = .10$, $\alpha = .05$, $\alpha = .01$, and $\alpha = .001$. How much evidence is there of a slowdown in payments?

c Are you qualified to decide whether this result has practical importance? Who would be?

9.57 Consider a chemical company that wishes to determine whether a new catalyst, catalyst XA-100, changes the mean hourly yield of its chemical process from the historical process mean of 750 pounds per hour. When five trial runs are made using the new catalyst, the following yields (in pounds per hour) are recorded: 801, 814, 784, 836, and 820.   ChemYield

a Let μ be the mean of all possible yields using the new catalyst. Assuming that chemical yields are approximately normally distributed, the MegaStat output of the test statistic and p-value, and the Excel output of the p-value, for testing $H_0: \mu = 750$ versus $H_a: \mu \neq 750$ are as follows:

Hypothesis Test: Mean vs. Hypothesized Value

750.000 hypothesized value	19.647 std. dev.	5 n	**6.94 t**
811.000 mean Hourly Yield	8.786 std. error	4 df	**.0023** p-value (two-tailed)

t-statistic
6.942585
p-value
0.002261

(Here we had Excel calculate twice the area under the t distribution curve having 4 degrees of freedom to the right of 6.942585.) Use the sample data to verify that the values of $\bar{x}$, s, and t given on the output are correct.

b Use the test statistic and critical values to test H_0 versus H_a by setting α equal to .10, .05, .01, and .001.

9.58 Consider Exercise 9.57. Use the p-value to test $H_0: \mu = 750$ versus $H_a: \mu \neq 750$ by setting α equal to .10, .05, .01, and .001. How much evidence is there that the new catalyst changes the mean hourly yield?

9.59 Whole Foods is an all-natural grocery chain that has 50,000-square-foot stores, up from the industry average of 34,000 square feet. Sales per square foot of supermarkets average just under $400 per square foot, as reported by *USA Today* in an article titled "A Whole New Ballgame in Grocery Shopping." Suppose that sales per square foot in the most recent fiscal year are recorded for a random sample of 10 Whole Foods supermarkets. The data (sales dollars per square foot) are as follows: 854, 858, 801, 892, 849, 807, 894, 863, 829, 815. Let μ denote the mean sales dollars per square foot for all Whole Foods supermarkets during the most recent fiscal year, and note that the historical mean sales dollars per square foot for Whole Foods supermarkets in previous years has been $800. Below we present the MINITAB output obtained by using the sample data to test $H_0: \mu = 800$ versus $H_a: \mu > 800$.   WholeFoods

```
Test of mu = 800 vs > 800

Variable    N    Mean    StDev   SE Mean    T      P
SqFtSales  10  846.200  32.866   10.393   4.45  0.001
```

a Use the p-value to test H_0 versus H_a by setting α equal to .10, .05, and .01.

b How much evidence is there that μ exceeds $800?

9.60 Consider Exercise 9.59. Do you think that the difference between the sample mean of $846.20 and the historical average of $800 has practical importance?

9.61   THE VIDEO GAME SATISFACTION RATING CASE   🔵 VideoGame

The mean and the standard deviation of the sample of $n = 65$ customer satisfaction ratings are $\bar{x} = 42.95$ and $s = 2.6424$. Let μ denote the mean of all possible customer satisfaction ratings for the XYZ-Box video game system, and consider testing $H_0: \mu = 42$ versus $H_a: \mu > 42$. Perform a t test of these hypotheses by setting α equal to .05 and using a critical value. Also, interpret the p-value of .0025 for the hypothesis test.

9.62   THE BANK CUSTOMER WAITING TIME CASE   🔵 WaitTime

The mean and the standard deviation of the sample of 100 bank customer waiting times are $\bar{x} = 5.46$ and $s = 2.475$. Let μ denote the mean of all possible bank customer waiting times using the new system and consider testing $H_0: \mu = 6$ versus $H_a: \mu < 6$. Perform a t test of these hypotheses by setting α equal to .05 and using a critical value. Also, interpret the p-value of .0158 for the hypothesis test.

9.4 z Tests about a Population Proportion ⚫ ⚫ ●

In this section we study a large sample hypothesis test about a population proportion (that is, about the fraction of population units that possess some characteristic). We begin with an example.

EXAMPLE 9.5 The Cheese Spread Case   C

Recall that the soft cheese spread producer has decided that replacing the current spout with the new spout is profitable only if p, the true proportion of all current purchasers who would stop buying the cheese spread if the new spout were used, is less than .10. The producer feels that it is unwise to change the spout unless it has very strong evidence that p is less than .10. Therefore, the spout will be changed if and only if the null hypothesis $H_0: p = .10$ can be rejected in favor of the alternative hypothesis $H_a: p < .10$ at the .01 level of significance.

In order to see how to test this kind of hypothesis, remember that when n is large, the sampling distribution of

$$\frac{\hat{p} - p}{\sqrt{\dfrac{p(1 - p)}{n}}}$$

is approximately a standard normal distribution. Let p_0 denote a specified value between 0 and 1 (its exact value will depend on the problem), and consider testing the null hypothesis $H_0: p = p_0$. We then have the following result:

A Large Sample Test about a Population Proportion

D efine the test statistic

$$z = \frac{\hat{p} - p_0}{\sqrt{\dfrac{p_0(1 - p_0)}{n}}}$$

If the sample size n is large, we can test $H_0: p = p_0$ versus a particular alternative hypothesis at level of significance α by using the appropriate critical value rule, or, equivalently, the corresponding p-value.

Alternative Hypothesis	Critical Value Rule: Reject H_0 If	p-Value (Reject H_0 If p-Value $< \alpha$)
$H_a: p > p_0$	$z > z_\alpha$	The area under the standard normal curve to the right of z
$H_a: p < p_0$	$z < -z_\alpha$	The area under the standard normal curve to the left of z
$H_a: p \neq p_0$	$\lvert z \rvert > z_{\alpha/2}$—that is, $z > z_{\alpha/2}$ or $z < -z_{\alpha/2}$	Twice the area under the standard normal curve to the right of $\lvert z \rvert$

Here n should be considered large if both np_0 and $n(1 - p_0)$ are at least 5.[3]

---

[3]Some statisticians suggest using the more conservative rule that both np_0 and $n(1 - p_0)$ must be at least 10.

EXAMPLE 9.6 The Cheese Spread Case

We have seen that the cheese spread producer wishes to test H_0: $p = .10$ versus H_a: $p < .10$, where p is the proportion of all current purchasers who would stop buying the cheese spread if the new spout were used. The producer will use the new spout if H_0 can be rejected in favor of H_a at the **.01 level of significance.** To perform the hypothesis test, we will randomly select $n =$ 1,000 current purchasers of the cheese spread, find the proportion ($\hat{p}$) of these purchasers who would stop buying the cheese spread if the new spout were used, and calculate the value of the **test statistic z in the summary box.** Then, since the alternative hypothesis H_a: $p < .10$ is of the form H_a: $p < p_0$, we will **reject H_0: $p = .10$ if the value of z is less than $-z_\alpha = -z_{.01} = -2.33$.** (Note that using this procedure is valid because $np_0 = 1,000(.10) = 100$ and $n(1 - p_0) = 1,000(1 - .10) = 900$ are both at least 5.) Suppose that when the sample is randomly selected, we find that 63 of the 1,000 current purchasers say they would stop buying the cheese spread if the new spout were used. Since $\hat{p} = 63/1,000 = .063$, the **value of the test statistic** is

$$z = \frac{\hat{p} - p_0}{\sqrt{\dfrac{p_0(1 - p_0)}{n}}} = \frac{.063 - .10}{\sqrt{\dfrac{.10(1 - .10)}{1,000}}} = -3.90$$

Because $z = -3.90$ is less than $-z_{.01} = -2.33$, we reject H_0: $p = .10$ in favor of H_a: $p < .10$. That is, we conclude (at an α of .01) that the proportion of current purchasers who would stop buying the cheese spread if the new spout were used is less than .10. It follows that the company will use the new spout. Furthermore, the point estimate $\hat{p} = .063$ says we estimate that 6.3 percent of all current customers would stop buying the cheese spread if the new spout were used.

Although the cheese spread producer has made its decision by setting α equal to a single, pre-chosen value (.01), it would probably also wish to know the weight of evidence against H_0 and in favor of H_a. The p-value is the area under the standard normal curve to the left of $z = -3.90$. Table A.3 (page 640) tells us that this area is .00005. Because this p-value is less than .001, we have extremely strong evidence that H_a: $p < .10$ is true. That is, we have extremely strong evidence that fewer than 10 percent of current purchasers would stop buying the cheese spread if the new spout were used.

EXAMPLE 9.7

Recent medical research has sought to develop drugs that lessen the severity and duration of viral infections. Virol, a relatively new drug, has been shown to provide relief for 70 percent of all patients suffering from viral upper respiratory infections. A major drug company is developing a competing drug called Phantol. The drug company wishes to investigate whether Phantol is more effective than Virol. To do this, the drug company will test a hypothesis about the true proportion, p, of all patients whose symptoms would be relieved by Phantol. **The null hypothesis to be tested is H_0: $p = .70$, and the alternative hypothesis is H_a: $p > .70$.** If H_0 can be rejected in favor of H_a at the **.05 level of significance,** the drug company will conclude that Phantol helps more than the 70 percent of patients helped by Virol. To perform the hypothesis test, we will randomly select $n = 300$ patients having viral upper respiratory infections, find the proportion ($\hat{p}$) of these patients whose symptoms are relieved by Phantol and calculate the value of the **test statistic z in the summary box.** Then, since the alternative hypothesis H_a: $p > .70$ is of the form H_a: $p > p_0$, we will **reject H_0: $p = .70$ if the value of z is greater than $z_\alpha = z_{.05} = 1.645$.** (Note that using this procedure is valid because $np_0 = 300(.70) = 210$ and $n(1 - p_0) = 300(1 - .70) = 90$ are both at least 5.) Suppose that when the sample is randomly selected, we find that Phantol provides relief for 231 of the 300 patients. Since $\hat{p} = 231/300 = .77$, the **value of the test statistic** is

$$z = \frac{\hat{p} - p_0}{\sqrt{\dfrac{p_0(1 - p_0)}{n}}} = \frac{.77 - .70}{\sqrt{\dfrac{(.70)(1 - .70)}{300}}} = 2.65$$

Because $z = 2.65$ is greater than $z_{.05} = 1.645$, we reject $H_0: p = .70$ in favor of $H_a: p > .70$. That is, we conclude (at an α of .05) that Phantol will provide relief for more than 70 percent of all patients suffering from viral upper respiratory infections. More specifically, the point estimate $\hat{p} = .77$ of p says that we estimate that Phantol will provide relief for 77 percent of all such patients. Comparing this estimate to the 70 percent of patients whose symptoms are relieved by Virol, we conclude that Phantol is somewhat more effective.

The p-value for testing $H_0: p = .70$ versus $H_a: p > .70$ is the area under the standard normal curve to the right of $z = 2.65$. This p-value is $(1.0 - .9960) = .004$ (see Table A.3, page 641), and it provides very strong evidence against $H_0: p = .70$ and in favor of $H_a: p > .70$. That is, we have very strong evidence that Phantol will provide relief for more than 70 percent of all patients suffering from viral upper respiratory infections.

EXAMPLE 9.8 The Electronic Article Surveillance Case

Suppose that a company selling electronic article surveillance devices claims that the proportion, p, of all consumers who would never shop in a store again if the store subjected them to a false alarm is no more than .05. A store considering installing such a device is concerned that p is greater than .05 and wishes to test $H_0: p = .05$ versus $H_a: p > .05$. To perform the hypothesis test, the store will calculate a p-value and use it to measure the **weight of evidence** against H_0 and in favor of H_a. In an actual systematic sample, 40 out of 250 consumers said they would never shop in a store again if the store subjected them to a false alarm. Therefore, the sample proportion of lost consumers is $\hat{p} = 40/250 = .16$. Since $np_0 = 250(.05) = 12.5$ and $n(1 - p_0) = 250(1 - .05) = 237.5$ are both at least 5, we can use the **test statistic z in the summary box.** The **value of the test statistic** is

$$z = \frac{\hat{p} - p_0}{\sqrt{\dfrac{p_0(1 - p_0)}{n}}} = \frac{.16 - .05}{\sqrt{\dfrac{(.05)(.95)}{250}}} = 7.98$$

Noting that $H_a: p > .05$ is of the form $H_a: p > p_0$, **the p-value is the area under the standard normal curve to the right of $z = 7.98$. The normal table tells us that the area under the standard normal curve to the right of 3.99 is $(1.0 - .99997) = .00003$. Therefore, the p-value is less than .00003** and provides **extremely strong evidence against $H_0: p = .05$ and in favor of $H_a: p > .05$.** That is, we have extremely strong evidence that the proportion of all consumers who say they would never shop in a store again if the store subjected them to a false alarm is greater than .05. Furthermore, the point estimate $\hat{p} = .16$ says we estimate that the percentage of such consumers is 11 percent more than the 5 percent maximum claimed by the company selling the electronic article surveillance devices. A 95 percent confidence interval for p is

$$\left[\hat{p} \pm z_{.025} \sqrt{\frac{\hat{p}(1 - \hat{p})}{n}} \right] = \left[.16 \pm 1.96 \sqrt{\frac{(.16)(.84)}{250}} \right]$$

$$= [.1146, .2054]$$

This interval says we are 95 percent confident that the percentage of consumers who would never shop in a store again if the store subjected them to a false alarm is between 6.46 percent and 15.54 percent more than the 5 percent maximum claimed by the company selling the electronic article surveillance devices. The rather large increases over the claimed 5 percent maximum implied by the point estimate and the confidence interval would mean substantially more lost customers and thus are practically important. Figure 9.11 gives the MegaStat output for testing $H_0: p = .05$ versus $H_a: p > .05$. Note that this output includes a 95 percent confidence interval for p. Also notice that MegaStat expresses the p-value for this test in scientific notation. In general, when a p-value is less than .0001, MegaStat (and also Excel) express the p-value in scientific notation. Here the p-value of 7.77 E-16 says that we must move the decimal point 16 places to the left to obtain the decimal equivalent. That is, the p-value is .0000000000000000777.

F I G U R E   9 . 1 1   **The MegaStat Output for Testing $H_0: p = .05$ versus $H_a: p > .05$**

Hypothesis Test for Proportion vs Hypothesized Value

Observed	Hypothesized		
0.16	0.05 p (as decimal)	0.0138 std. error	0.1146 confidence interval 95.% lower
40/250	13/250 p (as fraction)	7.98 z	0.2054 confidence interval 95.% upper
40.	12.5 X	7.77E-16 p-value	0.0454 half-width
250	250 n	(one-tailed upper)	

Exercises for Section 9.4

CONCEPTS

connect

9.63   If we test a hypothesis to provide evidence supporting the claim that a majority of voters prefer a political candidate, explain the difference between p and $\hat{p}$.

9.64   If we test a hypothesis to provide evidence supporting the claim that more than 30 percent of all consumers prefer a particular brand of beer, explain the difference between p and $\hat{p}$.

9.65   If we test a hypothesis to provide evidence supporting the claim that fewer than 5 percent of the units produced by a process are defective, explain the difference between p and $\hat{p}$.

9.66   What condition must be satisfied in order to appropriately use the methods of this section?

METHODS AND APPLICATIONS

9.67   For each of the following sample sizes and hypothesized values of the population proportion p, determine whether the sample size is large enough to use the large sample test about p given in this section:

    a $n = 400$ and $p_0 = .5$.   **e** $n = 256$ and $p_0 = .7$.
    b $n = 100$ and $p_0 = .01$.   **f** $n = 200$ and $p_0 = .98$.
    c $n = 10,000$ and $p_0 = .01$.   **g** $n = 1,000$ and $p_0 = .98$.
    d $n = 100$ and $p_0 = .2$.   **h** $n = 25$ and $p_0 = .4$.

9.68   Suppose we wish to test $H_0: p \leq .8$ versus $H_a: p > .8$ and that a random sample of $n = 400$ gives a sample proportion $\hat{p} = .86$.

    a   Test H_0 versus H_a at the .05 level of significance by using a critical value. What do you conclude?
    b   Find the p-value for this test.
    c   Use the p-value to test H_0 versus H_a by setting α equal to .10, .05, .01, and .001. What do you conclude at each value of α?

9.69   Suppose we test $H_0: p = .3$ versus $H_a: p \neq .3$ and that a random sample of $n = 100$ gives a sample proportion $\hat{p} = .20$.

    a   Test H_0 versus H_a at the .01 level of significance by using a critical value. What do you conclude?
    b   Find the p-value for this test.
    c   Use the p-value to test H_0 versus H_a by setting α equal to .10, .05, .01, and .001. What do you conclude at each value of α?

9.70   Suppose we are testing $H_0: p \leq .5$ versus $H_a: p > .5$, where p is the proportion of all beer drinkers who have tried at least one brand of "cold-filtered beer." If a random sample of 500 beer drinkers has been taken and if $\hat{p}$ equals .57, how many beer drinkers in the sample have tried at least one brand of "cold-filtered beer"?

9.71   **THE MARKETING ETHICS CASE: CONFLICT OF INTEREST**

Recall that a conflict of interest scenario was presented to a sample of 205 marketing researchers and that 111 of these researchers disapproved of the actions taken.

    a   Let p be the proportion of all marketing researchers who disapprove of the actions taken in the conflict of interest scenario. Set up the null and alternative hypotheses needed to attempt to provide evidence supporting the claim that a majority (more than 50 percent) of all marketing researchers disapprove of the actions taken.
    b   Assuming that the sample of 205 marketing researchers has been randomly selected, use critical values and the previously given sample information to test the hypotheses you set up in part a at the .10, .05, .01, and .001 levels of significance. How much evidence is there that a majority of all marketing researchers disapprove of the actions taken?

c Suppose a random sample of 1,000 marketing researchers reveals that 540 of the researchers disapprove of the actions taken in the conflict of interest scenario. Use critical values to determine how much evidence there is that a majority of all marketing researchers disapprove of the actions taken.

d Note that in parts *b* and *c* the sample proportion $\hat{p}$ is (essentially) the same. Explain why the results of the hypothesis tests in parts *b* and *c* differ.

9.72 Last year, television station WXYZ's share of the 11 P.M. news audience was approximately equal to, but no greater than, 25 percent. The station's management believes that the current audience share is higher than last year's 25 percent share. In an attempt to substantiate this belief, the station surveyed a random sample of 400 11 P.M. news viewers and found that 146 watched WXYZ.

a Let *p* be the current proportion of all 11 P.M. news viewers who watch WXYZ. Set up the null and alternative hypotheses needed to attempt to provide evidence supporting the claim that the current audience share for WXYZ is higher than last year's 25 percent share.

b Use critical values and the following MINITAB output to test the hypotheses you set up in part *a* at the .10, .05, .01, and .001 levels of significance. How much evidence is there that the current audience share is higher than last year's 25 percent share?

```
Test of p = 0.25 vs p > 0.25

Sample     X      N      Sample p     Z-Value     P-Value
1         146    400     0.365000       5.31        0.000
```

c Find the *p*-value for the hypothesis test in part *b*. Use the *p*-value to carry out the test by setting α equal to .10, .05, .01, and .001. Interpret your results.

d Do you think that the result of the station's survey has practical importance? Why or why not?

9.73 In the book *Essentials of Marketing Research,* William R. Dillon, Thomas J. Madden, and Neil H. Firtle discuss a marketing research proposal to study day-after recall for a brand of mouthwash. To quote the authors:

> The ad agency has developed a TV ad for the introduction of the mouthwash. The objective of the ad is to create awareness of the brand. The objective of this research is to evaluate the awareness generated by the ad measured by aided- and unaided-recall scores.
>
> A minimum of 200 respondents who claim to have watched the TV show in which the ad was aired the night before will be contacted by telephone in 20 cities.
>
> The study will provide information on the incidence of unaided and aided recall.

Suppose a random sample of 200 respondents shows that 46 of the people interviewed were able to recall the commercial without any prompting (unaided recall).

a In order for the ad to be considered successful, the percentage of unaided recall must be above the category norm for a TV commercial for the product class. If this norm is 18 percent, set up the null and alternative hypotheses needed to attempt to provide evidence that the ad is successful.

b Use the previously given sample information to compute the *p*-value for the hypothesis test you set up in part *a*. Use the *p*-value to carry out the test by setting α equal to .10, .05, .01, and .001. How much evidence is there that the TV commercial is successful?

c Do you think the result of the ad agency's survey has practical importance? Explain your opinion.

9.74 *Quality Progress,* February 2005, reports on the results achieved by Bank of America in improving customer satisfaction and customer loyalty by listening to the "voice of the customer." A key measure of customer satisfaction is the response on a scale from 1 to 10 to the question "Considering all the business you do with Bank of America, what is your overall satisfaction with Bank of America?"[4] Suppose that a random sample of 350 current customers results in 195 customers with a response of 9 or 10 representing "customer delight."

a Let *p* denote the true proportion of all current Bank of America customers who would respond with a 9 or 10, and note that the historical proportion of customer delight for Bank of America has been .48. Calculate the *p*-value for testing H_0: $p = .48$ versus H_a: $p > .48$. How much evidence is there that *p* exceeds .48?

b Bank of America has a base of nearly 30 million customers. Do you think that the sample results have practical importance? Explain your opinion.

9.75 The manufacturer of the ColorSmart-5000 television set claims that 95 percent of its sets last at least five years without needing a single repair. In order to test this claim, a consumer group randomly selects 400 consumers who have owned a ColorSmart-5000 television set for five years. Of

[4]Source: "Driving Organic Growth at Bank of America," *Quality Progress* (February 2005), pp. 23–27.

these 400 consumers, 316 say that their ColorSmart-5000 television sets did not need repair, while 84 say that their ColorSmart-5000 television sets did need at least one repair.

a Letting p be the proportion of ColorSmart-5000 television sets that last five years without a single repair, set up the null and alternative hypotheses that the consumer group should use to attempt to show that the manufacturer's claim is false.

b Use critical values and the previously given sample information to test the hypotheses you set up in part a by setting α equal to .10, .05, .01, and .001. How much evidence is there that the manufacturer's claim is false?

c Do you think the results of the consumer group's survey have practical importance? Explain your opinion.

9.5 Type II Error Probabilities and Sample Size Determination (Optional) ● ● ●

CHAPTERS
9 AND 11

As we have seen, we usually take action (for example, advertise a claim) on the basis of having rejected the null hypothesis. In this case, we know the chances that the action has been taken erroneously because we have prespecified α, the probability of rejecting a true null hypothesis. However, sometimes we must act (for example, use a day's production of camshafts to make V6 engines) on the basis of *not* rejecting the null hypothesis. If we must do this, it is best to know the probability of not rejecting a false null hypothesis (a Type II error). If this probability is not small enough, we may change the hypothesis testing procedure. In order to discuss this further, we must first see how to compute the probability of a Type II error.

As an example, the Federal Trade Commission (FTC) often tests claims that companies make about their products. Suppose coffee is being sold in cans that are labeled as containing three pounds, and also suppose that the FTC wishes to determine if the mean amount of coffee μ in all such cans is at least three pounds. To do this, the FTC tests $H_0: \mu \geq 3$ (or $\mu = 3$) versus $H_a: \mu < 3$ by setting $\alpha = .05$. Suppose that a sample of 35 coffee cans yields $\bar{x} = 2.9973$. Assuming that σ equals .0147, we see that because

$$z = \frac{2.9973 - 3}{.0147/\sqrt{35}} = -1.08$$

is not less than $-z_{.05} = -1.645$, we cannot reject $H_0: \mu \geq 3$ by setting $\alpha = .05$. Since we cannot reject H_0, we cannot have committed a Type I error, which is the error of rejecting a true H_0. However, we might have committed a Type II error, which is the error of not rejecting a false H_0. Therefore, before we make a final conclusion about μ, we should calculate the probability of a Type II error.

A Type II error is not rejecting $H_0: \mu \geq 3$ when H_0 is false. Because any value of μ that is less than 3 makes H_0 false, there is a different Type II error (and, therefore, a different Type II error probability) associated with each value of μ that is less than 3. In order to demonstrate how to calculate these probabilities, we will calculate the probability of not rejecting $H_0: \mu \geq 3$ when in fact μ equals 2.995. This is the probability of failing to detect an average underfill of .005 pounds. For a fixed sample size (for example, $n = 35$ coffee can fills), the value of β, the probability of a Type II error, depends upon how we set α, the probability of a Type I error. Since we have set $\alpha = .05$, we reject H_0 if

$$\frac{\bar{x} - 3}{\sigma/\sqrt{n}} < -z_{.05}$$

or, equivalently, if

$$\bar{x} < 3 - z_{.05}\frac{\sigma}{\sqrt{n}} = 3 - 1.645\frac{.0147}{\sqrt{35}} = 2.9959126$$

Therefore, we do not reject H_0 if $\bar{x} \geq 2.9959126$. It follows that β, the probability of not rejecting $H_0: \mu \geq 3$ when μ equals 2.995, is

$$\beta = P(\bar{x} \geq 2.9959126 \text{ when } \mu = 2.995)$$

$$= P\left(z \geq \frac{2.9959126 - 2.995}{.0147/\sqrt{35}}\right)$$

$$= P(z \geq .37) = 1 - .6443 = .3557$$

FIGURE 9.12   Calculating β When μ Equals 2.995

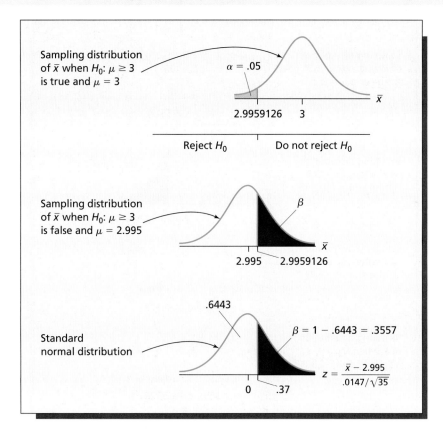

This calculation is illustrated in Figure 9.12. Similarly, it follows that β, the probability of not rejecting H_0: $\mu \geq 3$ when μ equals 2.99, is

$$\beta = P(\bar{x} \geq 2.9959126 \text{ when } \mu = 2.99)$$

$$= P\left(z \geq \frac{2.9959126 - 2.99}{.0147/\sqrt{35}}\right)$$

$$= P(z \geq 2.38) = 1 - .9913 = .0087$$

It also follows that β, the probability of not rejecting H_0: $\mu \geq 3$ when μ equals 2.985, is

$$\beta = P(\bar{x} \geq 2.9959126 \text{ when } \mu = 2.985)$$

$$= P\left(z \geq \frac{2.9959126 - 2.985}{.0147/\sqrt{35}}\right)$$

$$= P(z \geq 4.39)$$

This probability is less than .00003 (because z is greater than 3.99).

In Figure 9.13 we illustrate the values of β that we have calculated. Notice that the closer an alternative value of μ is to 3 (the value specified by H_0: $\mu = 3$), the larger is the associated value of β. Although alternative values of μ that are closer to 3 have larger associated probabilities of Type II errors, these values of μ have associated Type II errors with less serious consequences. For example, we are more likely to not reject H_0: $\mu = 3$ when $\mu = 2.995$ ($\beta = .3557$) than we are to not reject H_0: $\mu = 3$ when $\mu = 2.99$ ($\beta = .0087$). However, not rejecting H_0: $\mu = 3$ when $\mu = 2.995$, which means that we are failing to detect an average underfill of .005 pounds, is less serious than not rejecting H_0: $\mu = 3$ when $\mu = 2.99$, which means that we are failing to detect a larger average underfill of .01 pounds. In order to decide whether a particular hypothesis test adequately controls the probability of a Type II error, we must determine which Type II errors are serious, and then we must decide whether the probabilities of these errors are small enough. For

FIGURE 9.13   **How β Changes as the Alternative Value of μ Changes**

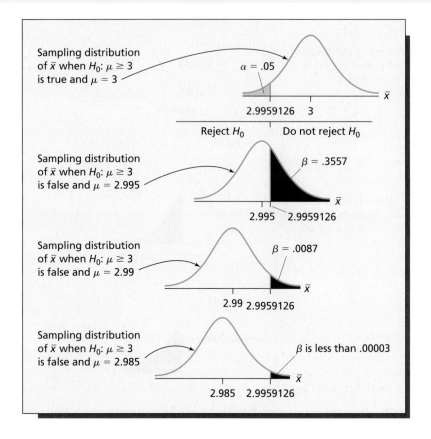

example, suppose that the FTC and the coffee producer agree that failing to reject H_0: $\mu = 3$ when μ equals 2.99 is a serious error, but that failing to reject H_0: $\mu = 3$ when μ equals 2.995 is not a particularly serious error. Then, since the probability of not rejecting H_0: $\mu = 3$ when μ equals 2.99, which is .0087, is quite small, we might decide that the hypothesis test adequately controls the probability of a Type II error. To understand the implication of this, recall that the sample of 35 coffee cans, which has $\bar{x} = 2.9973$, does not provide enough evidence to reject H_0: $\mu \geq 3$ by setting $\alpha = .05$. We have just shown that the probability that we have failed to detect a serious underfill is quite small (.0087), so the FTC might decide that no action should be taken against the coffee producer. Of course, this decision should also be based on the variability of the fills of the individual cans. Because $\bar{x} = 2.9973$ and $\sigma = .0147$, we estimate that 99.73 percent of all individual coffee can fills are contained in the interval $[\bar{x} \pm 3\sigma] = [2.9973 \pm 3(.0147)] = [2.9532, 3.0414]$. If the FTC believes it is reasonable to accept fills as low as (but no lower than) 2.9532 pounds, this evidence also suggests that no action against the coffee producer is needed.

Suppose, instead, that the FTC and the coffee producer had agreed that failing to reject H_0: $\mu \geq 3$ when μ equals 2.995 is a serious mistake. The probability of this Type II error, which is .3557, is large. Therefore, we might conclude that the hypothesis test is not adequately controlling the probability of a serious Type II error. In this case, we have two possible courses of action. First, we have previously said that, for a fixed sample size, the lower we set α, the higher is β, and the higher we set α, the lower is β. Therefore, if we keep the sample size fixed at $n = 35$ coffee cans, we can reduce β by increasing α. To demonstrate this, suppose we increase α to .10. In this case we reject H_0 if

$$\frac{\bar{x} - 3}{\sigma/\sqrt{n}} < -z_{.10}$$

or, equivalently, if

$$\bar{x} < 3 - z_{.10}\frac{\sigma}{\sqrt{n}} = 3 - 1.282\frac{.0147}{\sqrt{35}} = 2.9968145$$

Therefore, we do not reject H_0 if $\bar{x} \geq 2.9968145$. It follows that β, the probability of not rejecting $H_0 : \mu \geq 3$ when μ equals 2.995, is

$$\beta = P(\bar{x} \geq 2.9968145 \text{ when } \mu = 2.995)$$

$$= P\left(z \geq \frac{2.9968145 - 2.995}{.0147/\sqrt{35}}\right)$$

$$= P(z \geq .73) = 1 - .7673 = .2327$$

We thus see that increasing α from .05 to .10 reduces β from .3557 to .2327. However, β is still too large, and, besides, we might not be comfortable making α larger than .05. Therefore, if we wish to decrease β and maintain α at .05, we must increase the sample size. We will soon present a formula we can use to find the sample size needed to make both α and β as small as we wish.

Once we have computed β, we can calculate what we call the *power* of the test.

> The **power** of a statistical test is the probability of rejecting the null hypothesis when it is false.

Just as β depends upon the alternative value of μ, so does the power of a test. In general, **the power associated with a particular alternative value of μ equals $1 - \beta$,** where β is the probability of a Type II error associated with the same alternative value of μ. For example, we have seen that, when we set $\alpha = .05$, the probability of not rejecting $H_0 : \mu \geq 3$ when μ equals 2.99 is .0087. Therefore, the power of the test associated with the alternative value 2.99 (that is, the probability of rejecting $H_0 : \mu \geq 3$ when μ equals 2.99) is $1 - .0087 = .9913$.

Thus far we have demonstrated how to calculate β when testing a *less than* alternative hypothesis. In the following box we present (without proof) a method for calculating the probability of a Type II error when testing a *less than*, a *greater than*, or a *not equal to* alternative hypothesis:

Calculating the Probability of a Type II Error

Assume that the sampled population is normally distributed, or that a large sample will be taken. Consider testing $H_0 : \mu = \mu_0$ versus one of $H_a : \mu > \mu_0$, $H_a : \mu < \mu_0$, or $H_a : \mu \neq \mu_0$. Then, if we set the probability of a Type I error equal to α and randomly select a sample of size n, the probability, β, of a Type II error corresponding to the alternative value μ_a of μ is (exactly or approximately) equal to the area under the standard normal curve to the left of

$$z^* - \frac{|\mu_0 - \mu_a|}{\sigma/\sqrt{n}}$$

Here z^* equals z_α if the alternative hypothesis is one-sided ($\mu > \mu_0$ or $\mu < \mu_0$), in which case the method for calculating β is exact. Furthermore, z^* equals $z_{\alpha/2}$ if the alternative hypothesis is two-sided ($\mu \neq \mu_0$), in which case the method for calculating β is approximate.

EXAMPLE 9.9 The Valentine's Day Chocolate Case

In the Valentine's Day chocolate case we are testing $H_0 : \mu = 330$ versus $H_a : \mu \neq 330$ by setting $\alpha = .05$. We have seen that the mean of the reported order quantities of a random sample of $n = 100$ large retail stores is $\bar{x} = 326$. Assuming that σ equals 40, it follows that because

$$z = \frac{326 - 330}{40/\sqrt{100}} = -1$$

is between $-z_{.025} = -1.96$ and $z_{.025} = 1.96$, we cannot reject $H_0 : \mu = 330$ by setting $\alpha = .05$. Since we cannot reject H_0, we might have committed a Type II error. Suppose that the candy company decides that failing to reject $H_0 : \mu = 330$ when μ differs from 330 by as many as 15 valentine boxes (that is, when μ is 315 or 345) is a serious Type II error. Because we have set α

equal to .05, β for the alternative value $\mu_a = 315$ (that is, the probability of not rejecting H_0: $\mu = 330$ when μ equals 315) is the area under the standard normal curve to the left of

$$z^* - \frac{|\mu_0 - \mu_a|}{\sigma/\sqrt{n}} = z_{.025} - \frac{|\mu_0 - \mu_a|}{\sigma/\sqrt{n}}$$

$$= 1.96 - \frac{|330 - 315|}{40/\sqrt{100}}$$

$$= -1.79$$

Here $z^* = z_{\alpha/2} = z_{.05/2} = z_{.025}$ since the alternative hypothesis ($\mu \neq 330$) is two-sided. The area under the standard normal curve to the left of -1.79 is $1 - .9633 = .0377$. Therefore, β for the alternative value $\mu_a = 315$ is .0377. Similarly, it can be verified that β for the alternative value $\mu_a = 345$ is .0377. It follows, because we cannot reject H_0: $\mu = 330$ by setting $\alpha = .05$, and because we have just shown that there is a reasonably small (.0377) probability that we have failed to detect a serious (that is, a 15 valentine box) deviation of μ from 330, that it is reasonable for the candy company to base this year's production of valentine boxes on the projected mean order quantity of 330 boxes per large retail store.

In the following box we present (without proof) a formula that tells us the sample size needed to make both the probability of a Type I error and the probability of a Type II error as small as we wish:

Calculating the Sample Size Needed to Achieve Specified Values of α and β

Assume that the sampled population is normally distributed, or that a large sample will be taken. Consider testing H_0: $\mu = \mu_0$ versus one of H_a: $\mu > \mu_0$, H_a: $\mu < \mu_0$, or H_a: $\mu \neq \mu_0$. Then, in order to make the probability of a Type I error equal to α and the probability of a Type II error corresponding to the alternative value μ_a of μ equal to β, we should take a sample of size

$$n = \frac{(z^* + z_\beta)^2 \sigma^2}{(\mu_0 - \mu_a)^2}$$

Here z^* equals z_α if the alternative hypothesis is one-sided ($\mu > \mu_0$ or $\mu < \mu_0$), and z^* equals $z_{\alpha/2}$ if the alternative hypothesis is two-sided ($\mu \neq \mu_0$). Also, z_β is the point on the scale of the standard normal curve that gives a right-hand tail area equal to β.

EXAMPLE 9.10

Again consider the coffee fill example and suppose we wish to test H_0: $\mu \geq 3$ (or $\mu = 3$) versus H_a: $\mu < 3$. If we wish α to be .05 and β for the alternative value $\mu_a = 2.995$ of μ to be .05, we should take a sample of size

$$n = \frac{(z^* + z_\beta)^2 \sigma^2}{(\mu_0 - \mu_a)^2} = \frac{(z_\alpha + z_\beta)^2 \sigma^2}{(\mu_0 - \mu_a)^2}$$

$$= \frac{(z_{.05} + z_{.05})^2 \sigma^2}{(\mu_0 - \mu_a)^2}$$

$$= \frac{(1.645 + 1.645)^2 (.0147)^2}{(3 - 2.995)^2}$$

$$= 93.5592 = 94 \text{ (rounding up)}$$

Here, $z^* = z_\alpha = z_{.05} = 1.645$ because the alternative hypothesis ($\mu < 3$) is one-sided, and $z_\beta = z_{.05} = 1.645$.

Although we have set both α and β equal to the same value in the coffee fill situation, it is not necessary for α and β to be equal. As an example, again consider the Valentine's Day chocolate case, in which we are testing H_0: $\mu = 330$ versus H_a: $\mu \neq 330$. Suppose that the candy company decides that failing to reject H_0: $\mu = 330$ when μ differs from 330 by as many as 15 valentine boxes (that is, when μ is 315 or 345) is a serious Type II error. Furthermore, suppose that it is also decided that this Type II error is more serious than a Type I error. Therefore, α will be set equal to .05 and β for the alternative value $\mu_a = 315$ (or $\mu_a = 345$) of μ will be set equal to .01. It follows that the candy company should take a sample of size

$$n = \frac{(z^* + z_\beta)^2 \sigma^2}{(\mu_0 - \mu_a)^2} = \frac{(z_{\alpha/2} + z_\beta)^2 \sigma^2}{(\mu_0 - \mu_a)^2}$$

$$= \frac{(z_{.025} + z_{.01})^2 \sigma^2}{(\mu_0 - \mu_a)^2}$$

$$= \frac{(1.96 + 2.326)^2 (40)^2}{(330 - 315)^2}$$

$$= 130.62 = 131 \text{ (rounding up)}$$

Here, $z^* = z_{\alpha/2} = z_{.05/2} = z_{.025} = 1.96$ because the alternative hypothesis ($\mu \neq 330$) is two-sided, and $z_\beta = z_{.01} = 2.326$ (see the bottom row of the t table on page 643).

To conclude this section, we point out that the methods we have presented for calculating the probability of a Type II error and determining sample size can be extended to other hypothesis tests that utilize the normal distribution. We will not, however, present the extensions in this book.

Exercises for Section 9.5

CONCEPTS

9.76 We usually take action on the basis of having rejected the null hypothesis. When we do this, we know the chances that the action has been taken erroneously because we have prespecified α, the probability of rejecting a true null hypothesis. Here, it is obviously important to know (prespecify) α, the probability of a Type I error. When is it important to know the probability of a Type II error? Explain why.

connect

9.77 Explain why we are able to compute many different values of β, the probability of a Type II error, for a single hypothesis test.

9.78 Explain what is meant by
  a A serious Type II error.
  b The power of a statistical test.

9.79 In general, do we want the power corresponding to a serious Type II error to be near 0 or near 1? Explain.

METHODS AND APPLICATIONS

9.80 Again consider the Consolidated Power waste water situation. Remember that the power plant will be shut down and corrective action will be taken on the cooling system if the null hypothesis H_0: $\mu \leq 60$ is rejected in favor of H_a: $\mu > 60$. In this exercise we calculate probabilities of various Type II errors in the context of this situation.
  a Recall that Consolidated Power's hypothesis test is based on a sample of $n = 100$ temperature readings and assume that σ equals 2. If the power company sets $\alpha = .025$, calculate the probability of a Type II error for each of the following alternative values of μ: 60.1, 60.2, 60.3, 60.4, 60.5, 60.6, 60.7, 60.8, 60.9, 61.
  b If we want the probability of making a Type II error when μ equals 60.5 to be very small, is Consolidated Power's hypothesis test adequate? Explain why or why not. If not, and if we wish to maintain the value of α at .025, what must be done?
  c The **power curve** for a statistical test is a plot of the power $= 1 - \beta$ on the vertical axis versus values of μ that make the null hypothesis false on the horizontal axis. Plot the power curve for Consolidated Power's test of H_0: $\mu \leq 60$ versus H_a: $\mu > 60$ by plotting power $= 1 - \beta$ for each of the alternative values of μ in part a. What happens to the power of the test as the alternative value of μ moves away from 60?

9.81 Again consider the automobile parts supplier situation. Remember that a problem-solving team will be assigned to rectify the process producing the cylindrical engine parts if the null hypothesis H_0: $\mu = 3$ is rejected in favor of H_a: $\mu \neq 3$. In this exercise we calculate probabilities of various Type II errors in the context of this situation.

a Suppose that the parts supplier's hypothesis test is based on a sample of $n = 100$ diameters and that σ equals .023. If the parts supplier sets $\alpha = .05$, calculate the probability of a Type II error for each of the following alternative values of μ: 2.990, 2.995, 3.005, 3.010.

b If we want the probabilities of making a Type II error when μ equals 2.995 and when μ equals 3.005 to both be very small, is the parts supplier's hypothesis test adequate? Explain why or why not. If not, and if we wish to maintain the value of α at .05, what must be done?

c Plot the power of the test versus the alternative values of μ in part *a*. What happens to the power of the test as the alternative value of μ moves away from 3?

9.82 In the Consolidated Power hypothesis test of H_0: $\mu \leq 60$ versus H_a: $\mu > 60$ (as discussed in Exercise 9.80) find the sample size needed to make the probability of a Type I error equal to .025 and the probability of a Type II error corresponding to the alternative value $\mu_a = 60.5$ equal to .025. Here, assume σ equals 2.

9.83 In the automobile parts supplier's hypothesis test of H_0: $\mu = 3$ versus H_a: $\mu \neq 3$ (as discussed in Exercise 9.81) find the sample size needed to make the probability of a Type I error equal to .05 and the probability of a Type II error corresponding to the alternative value $\mu_a = 3.005$ equal to .05. Here, assume σ equals .023.

9.6 The Chi-Square Distribution (Optional)

CHAPTER 5

Sometimes we can make statistical inferences by using the **chi-square distribution.** The probability curve of the χ^2 (pronounced *chi-square*) distribution is skewed to the right. Moreover, the exact shape of this probability curve depends on a parameter that is called the **number of degrees of freedom** (denoted *df*). Figure 9.14 illustrates chi-square distributions having 2, 5, and 10 degrees of freedom.

In order to use the chi-square distribution, we employ a **chi-square point,** which is denoted χ^2_α. As illustrated in the upper portion of Figure 9.15, χ^2_α is the point on the horizontal axis under the curve of the chi-square distribution that gives a right-hand tail area equal to α. The value of χ^2_α in a particular situation depends on the right-hand tail area α and the number of degrees of freedom (*df*) of the chi-square distribution. Values of χ^2_α are tabulated in a **chi-square table.** Such a table is given in Table A.10 of Appendix A (page 651); a portion of this table is reproduced as Table 9.4. Looking at the chi-square table, the rows correspond to the appropriate number of degrees of freedom (values of which are listed down the left side of the table), while the columns designate the right-hand tail area α. For example, suppose we wish to find the chi-square point

FIGURE 9.14 Chi-Square Distributions with 2, 5, and 10 Degrees of Freedom

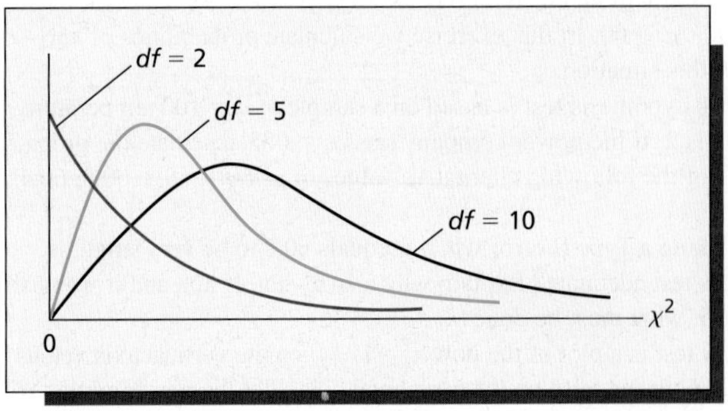

FIGURE 9.15 Chi-Square Points

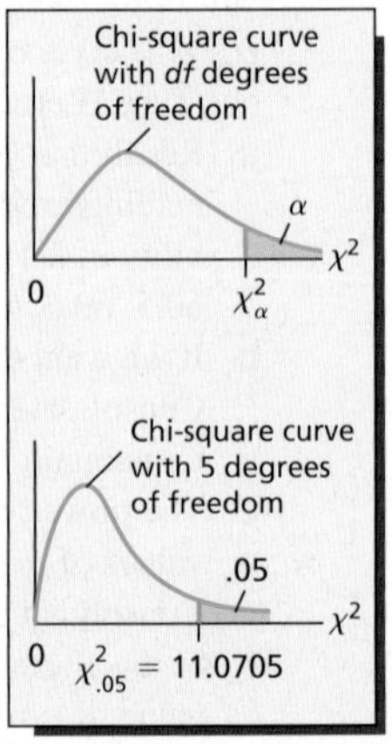

TABLE 9.4   A Portion of the Chi-Square Table

Degrees of Freedom (df)	$\chi^2_{.10}$	$\chi^2_{.05}$	$\chi^2_{.025}$	$\chi^2_{.01}$	$\chi^2_{.005}$
1	2.70554	3.84146	5.02389	6.63490	7.87944
2	4.60517	5.99147	7.37776	9.21034	10.5966
3	6.25139	7.81473	9.34840	11.3449	12.8381
4	7.77944	9.48773	11.1433	13.2767	14.8602
5	9.23635	11.0705	12.8325	15.0863	16.7496
6	10.6446	12.5916	14.4494	16.8119	18.5476
7	12.0170	14.0671	16.0123	18.4753	20.2777
8	13.3616	15.5073	17.5346	20.0902	21.9550
9	14.6837	16.9190	19.0228	21.6660	23.5893
10	15.9871	18.3070	20.4831	23.2093	25.1882

that gives a right-hand tail area of .05 under a chi-square curve having 5 degrees of freedom. To do this, we look in Table 9.4 at the row labeled 5 and the column labeled $\chi^2_{.05}$. We find that this $\chi^2_{.05}$ point is 11.0705 (see the lower portion of Figure 9.15).

9.7 Statistical Inference for a Population Variance (Optional) ● ● ●

A vital part of a V6 automobile engine is the engine camshaft. As the camshaft turns, parts of the camshaft make repeated contact with *engine lifters* and thus must have the appropriate hardness to wear properly. To harden the camshaft, a heat treatment process is used, and a hardened layer is produced on the surface of the camshaft. The depth of the layer is called the **hardness depth** of the camshaft. Suppose that an automaker knows that the mean and the variance of the camshaft hardness depths produced by its current heat treatment process are, respectively, 4.5 mm and .2209 mm. To reduce the variance of the camshaft hardness depths, a new heat treatment process is designed, and a random sample of $n = 30$ camshaft hardness depths produced by using the new process has a mean of $\bar{x} = 4.50$ and a variance of $s^2 = .0885$. In order to attempt to show that the variance, σ^2, of the population of all camshaft hardness depths that would be produced by using the new process is less than .2209, we can use the following result:

CHAPTER 9

Statistical Inference for a Population Variance

Suppose that s^2 is the variance of a sample of n measurements randomly selected from a normally distributed population having variance σ^2. The sampling distribution of the statistic $(n - 1)s^2/\sigma^2$ is a chi-square distribution having $n - 1$ degrees of freedom. This implies that

1 A $100(1 - \alpha)$ percent confidence interval for σ^2 is

$$\left[\frac{(n - 1)s^2}{\chi^2_{\alpha/2}}, \frac{(n - 1)s^2}{\chi^2_{1-(\alpha/2)}} \right]$$

Here $\chi^2_{\alpha/2}$ and $\chi^2_{1-(\alpha/2)}$ are the points under the curve of the chi-square distribution having $n - 1$ degrees of freedom that give right-hand tail areas of, respectively, $\alpha/2$ and $1 - (\alpha/2)$.

2 We can test $H_0: \sigma^2 = \sigma_0^2$ by using the test statistic

$$\chi^2 = \frac{(n - 1)s^2}{\sigma_0^2}$$

Specifically, if we set the probability of a Type I error equal to α, then we can reject H_0 in favor of

  a $H_a: \sigma^2 > \sigma_0^2$ if $\chi^2 > \chi^2_\alpha$

  b $H_a: \sigma^2 < \sigma_0^2$ if $\chi^2 < \chi^2_{1-\alpha}$

  c $H_a: \sigma^2 \neq \sigma_0^2$ if $\chi^2 > \chi^2_{\alpha/2}$ or $\chi^2 < \chi^2_{1-(\alpha/2)}$

Here χ^2_α, $\chi^2_{1-\alpha}$, $\chi^2_{\alpha/2}$, and $\chi^2_{1-(\alpha/2)}$ are based on $n - 1$ degrees of freedom.

FIGURE 9.16   The Chi-Square Points $\chi^2_{.025}$ and $\chi^2_{.975}$

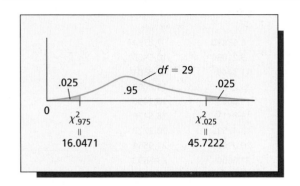

FIGURE 9.17   Testing H_0: $\sigma^2 = .2209$ versus H_a: $\sigma^2 <$ .2209 by Setting $\alpha = .05$

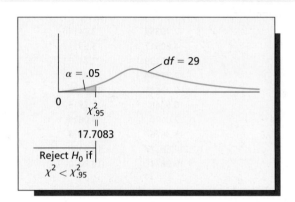

The assumption that the sampled population is normally distributed must hold fairly closely for the statistical inferences just given about σ^2 to be valid. When we check this assumption in the camshaft situation, we find that a histogram (not given here) of the sample of $n = 30$ hardness depths is bell-shaped and symmetrical. In order to compute a 95 percent confidence interval for σ^2, we note that $\chi^2_{\alpha/2}$ is $\chi^2_{.025}$ and $\chi^2_{1-(\alpha/2)}$ is $\chi^2_{.975}$. Table A.10 (page 651) tells us that these points—based on $n - 1 = 29$ degrees of freedom—are $\chi^2_{.025} = 45.7222$ and $\chi^2_{.975} = 16.0471$ (see Figure 9.16). It follows that a 95 percent confidence interval for σ^2 is

$$\left[\frac{(n - 1)s^2}{\chi^2_{\alpha/2}}, \frac{(n - 1)s^2}{\chi^2_{1-(\alpha/2)}} \right] = \left[\frac{(29)(.0885)}{45.7222}, \frac{(29)(.0885)}{16.0471} \right]$$

$$= [.0561, .1599]$$

This interval provides strong evidence that σ^2 is less than .2209.

If we wish to use a hypothesis test, we test **the null hypothesis H_0: $\sigma^2 = .2209$ versus the alternative hypothesis H_a: $\sigma^2 < .2209$. If H_0 can be rejected in favor of H_a at the .05 level of significance,** we will conclude that the new process has reduced the variance of the camshaft hardness depths. Since the histogram of the sample of $n = 30$ hardness depths is bell-shaped and symmetrical, **the appropriate test statistic is given in the summary box.** Furthermore, since H_a: $\sigma^2 < .2209$ is of the form H_a: $\sigma^2 < \sigma_0^2$, we should **reject H_0: $\sigma^2 = .2209$ if the value of χ^2 is less than the critical value $\chi^2_{1-\alpha} = \chi^2_{.95} = 17.7083$.** Here $\chi^2_{.95} = 17.7083$ is based on $n - 1 = 30 - 1 = 29$ degrees of freedom, and this critical value is illustrated in Figure 9.17. Since the sample variance is $s^2 = .0885$, the **value of the test statistic** is

$$\chi^2 = \frac{(n - 1)s^2}{\sigma_0^2} = \frac{(29)(.0885)}{.2209} = 11.6184$$

Since $\chi^2 = 11.6184$ is less than $\chi^2_{.95} = 17.7083$, we reject H_0: $\sigma^2 = .2209$ in favor of H_a: $\sigma^2 < .2209$. That is, we conclude (at an α of .05) that the new process has reduced the variance of the camshaft hardness depths.

Exercises for Sections 9.6 and 9.7

CONCEPTS

9.84   What assumption must hold to use the chi-square distribution to make statistical inferences about a population variance?

9.85   Define the meaning of the chi-square points $\chi^2_{\alpha/2}$ and $\chi^2_{1-(\alpha/2)}$. Hint: Draw a picture.

9.86   Give an example of a situation in which we might wish to compute a confidence interval for σ^2.

METHODS AND APPLICATIONS

Exercises 9.87 through 9.90 relate to the following situation: Consider an engine parts supplier and suppose the supplier has determined that the variance of the population of all cylindrical engine part outside diameters produced by the current machine is approximately equal to, but no less than, .0005. To reduce this variance, a new machine is designed, and a random sample of $n = 25$ outside diameters produced by this new machine has a mean of $\bar{x} = 3$ and a variance of $s^2 = .00014$. Assume the population of all cylindrical engine part outside diameters that would be produced by the new machine is normally distributed, and let σ^2 denote the variance of this population.

9.87 Find a 95 percent confidence interval for σ^2.

9.88 Test H_0: $\sigma^2 = .0005$ versus H_a: $\sigma^2 < .0005$ by setting $\alpha = .05$.

9.89 Find a 99 percent confidence interval for σ^2.

9.90 Test H_0: $\sigma^2 = .0005$ versus H_a: $\sigma^2 \neq .0005$ by setting $\alpha = .01$.

Chapter Summary

We began this chapter by learning about the two hypotheses that make up the structure of a hypothesis test. The **null hypothesis** is the statement being tested. Usually it represents the *status quo* and it is not rejected unless there is convincing sample evidence that it is false. The **alternative, or, research, hypothesis** is a statement that is accepted only if there is convincing sample evidence that it is true and that the null hypothesis is false. In some situations, the alternative hypothesis is a condition for which we need to attempt to find supportive evidence. We also learned that two types of errors can be made in a hypothesis test. A **Type I error** occurs when we reject a true null hypothesis, and a **Type II error** occurs when we do not reject a false null hypothesis.

We studied two commonly used ways to conduct a hypothesis test. The first involves comparing the value of a test statistic with what is called a **critical value**, and the second employs what is called a **p-value**. The *p*-value measures the weight of evidence against the null hypothesis. The smaller the *p*-value, the more we doubt the null hypothesis. We learned that, if we can reject the null hypothesis with the probability of a Type I error equal to α, then we say that the test result has **statistical significance at the α level**. However, we also learned that, even if the result of a

hypothesis test tells us that statistical significance exists, we must carefully assess whether the result is practically important. One good way to do this is to use a point estimate and confidence interval for the parameter of interest.

The specific hypothesis tests we covered in this chapter all dealt with a hypothesis about one population parameter. First, we studied a test about a **population mean** that is based on the assumption that the population standard deviation σ **is known**. This test employs the **normal distribution**. Second, we studied a test about a population mean that assumes that σ **is unknown**. We learned that this test is based on the **t distribution**. Figure 9.18 presents a flowchart summarizing how to select an appropriate test statistic to test a hypothesis about a population mean. Then we presented a test about a **population proportion** that is based on the **normal distribution**. Next (in optional Section 9.5) we studied Type II error probabilities, and we showed how we can find the sample size needed to make both the probability of a Type I error and the probability of a serious Type II error as small as we wish. We concluded this chapter by discussing (in optional Sections 9.6 and 9.7) the **chi-square distribution** and its use in making statistical inferences about a **population variance**.

Glossary of Terms

alternative (research) hypothesis: A statement that will be accepted only if there is convincing sample evidence that it is true. Sometimes it is a condition for which we need to attempt to find supportive evidence. (page 347)

chi-square distribution: A useful continuous probability distribution. Its probability curve is skewed to the right, and the exact shape of the probability curve depends on the number of degrees of freedom associated with the curve. (page 382)

critical value: The value of the test statistic is compared with a critical value in order to decide whether the null hypothesis can be rejected. (pages 354, 358, 360)

greater than alternative: An alternative hypothesis that is stated as a *greater than* ($>$) inequality. (page 349)

less than alternative: An alternative hypothesis that is stated as a *less than* ($<$) inequality. (page 349)

not equal to alternative: An alternative hypothesis that is stated as a *not equal to* ($\neq$) inequality. (page 349)

null hypothesis: The statement being tested in a hypothesis test. It usually represents the status quo and it is not rejected

unless there is convincing sample evidence that it is false. (page 347)

one-sided alternative hypothesis: An alternative hypothesis that is stated as either a *greater than* ($>$) or a *less than* ($<$) inequality. (page 349)

power (of a statistical test): The probability of rejecting the null hypothesis when it is false. (page 379)

p-value (probability value): The probability, computed assuming that the null hypothesis is true, of observing a value of the test statistic that is at least as extreme as the value actually computed from the sample data. The *p*-value measures how much doubt is cast on the null hypothesis by the sample data. The smaller the *p*-value, the more we doubt the null hypothesis. (pages 355, 358, 360, 362)

statistical significance at the α level: When we can reject the null hypothesis by setting the probability of a Type I error equal to α. (page 354)

test statistic: A statistic computed from sample data in a hypothesis test. It is either compared with a critical value or used to compute a *p*-value. (page 349)

FIGURE 9.18   Selecting an Appropriate Test Statistic to Test a Hypothesis about a Population Mean

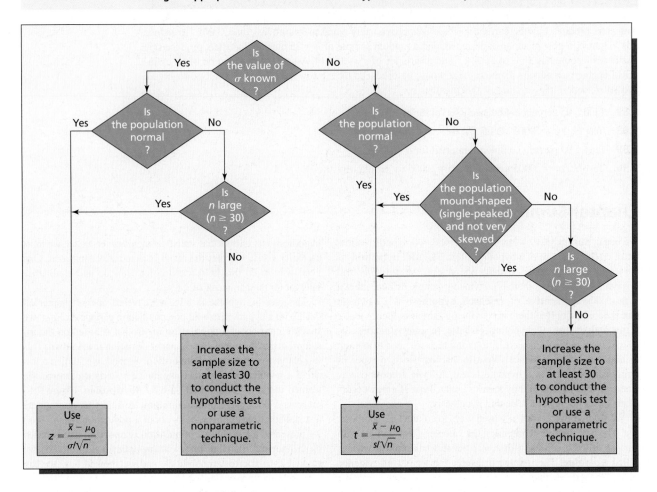

two-sided alternative hypothesis: An alternative hypothesis that is stated as a *not equal to* (≠) inequality. (page 349)

Type I error: Rejecting a true null hypothesis. (page 350)
Type II error: Failing to reject a false null hypothesis. (page 350)

Important Formulas and Tests

Hypothesis testing steps: page 357

A hypothesis test about a population mean (σ known): page 361

A *t* test about a population mean (σ unknown): page 366

A large sample hypothesis test about a population proportion: page 371

Calculating the probability of a Type II error: page 379

Sample size determination to achieve specified values of α and β: page 380

Statistical inference about a population variance: page 383

Supplementary Exercises

connect

9.91   The auditor for a large corporation routinely monitors cash disbursements. As part of this process, the auditor examines check request forms to determine whether they have been properly approved. Improper approval can occur in several ways. For instance, the check may have no approval, the check request might be missing, the approval might be written by an unauthorized person, or the dollar limit of the authorizing person might be exceeded.

   a   Last year the corporation experienced a 5 percent improper check request approval rate. Since this was considered unacceptable, efforts were made to reduce the rate of improper approvals. Letting *p* be the proportion of all checks that are now improperly approved, set up the null and alternative hypotheses needed to attempt to demonstrate that the current rate of improper approvals is lower than last year's rate of 5 percent.

b Suppose that the auditor selects a random sample of 625 checks that have been approved in the last month. The auditor finds that 18 of these 625 checks have been improperly approved. Use critical values and this sample information to test the hypotheses you set up in part *a* at the .10, .05, .01, and .001 levels of significance. How much evidence is there that the rate of improper approvals has been reduced below last year's 5 percent rate?

c Find the *p*-value for the test of part *b*. Use the *p*-value to carry out the test by setting α equal to .10, .05, .01, and .001. Interpret your results.

d Suppose the corporation incurs a $10 cost to detect and correct an improperly approved check. If the corporation disburses at least 2 million checks per year, does the observed reduction of the rate of improper approvals seem to have practical importance? Explain your opinion.

9.92 THE CIGARETTE ADVERTISEMENT CASE ● ModelAge

Recall that the cigarette industry requires that models in cigarette ads must appear to be at least 25 years old. Also recall that a sample of 50 people is randomly selected at a shopping mall. Each person in the sample is shown a "typical cigarette ad" and is asked to estimate the age of the model in the ad.

a Let μ be the mean perceived age estimate for all viewers of the ad, and suppose we consider the industry requirement to be met if μ is at least 25. Set up the null and alternative hypotheses needed to attempt to show that the industry requirement is not being met.

b Suppose that a random sample of 50 perceived age estimates gives a mean of $\bar{x} = 23.663$ years and a standard deviation of $s = 3.596$ years. Use these sample data and critical values to test the hypotheses of part *a* at the .10, .05, .01, and .001 levels of significance.

c How much evidence do we have that the industry requirement is not being met?

d Do you think that this result has practical importance? Explain your opinion.

9.93 THE CIGARETTE ADVERTISEMENT CASE ● ModelAge

Consider the cigarette ad situation discussed in Exercise 9.92. Using the sample information given in that exercise, the *p*-value for testing H_0 versus H_a can be calculated to be .0057.

a Determine whether H_0 would be rejected at each of $\alpha = .10$, $\alpha = .05$, $\alpha = .01$, and $\alpha = .001$.

b Describe how much evidence we have that the industry requirement is not being met.

9.94 In an article in the *Journal of Retailing,* Kumar, Kerwin, and Pereira study factors affecting merger and acquisition activity in retailing. As part of the study, the authors compare the characteristics of "target firms" (firms targeted for acquisition) and "bidder firms" (firms attempting to make acquisitions). Among the variables studied in the comparison were earnings per share, debt-to-equity ratio, growth rate of sales, market share, and extent of diversification.

a Let μ be the mean growth rate of sales for all target firms (firms that have been targeted for acquisition in the last five years and that have not bid on other firms), and assume growth rates are approximately normally distributed. Furthermore, suppose a random sample of 25 target firms yields a sample mean sales growth rate of $\bar{x} = 0.16$ with a standard deviation of $s = 0.12$. Use critical values and this sample information to test $H_0: \mu \leq .10$ versus $H_a: \mu > .10$ by setting α equal to .10, .05, .01, and .001. How much evidence is there that the mean growth rate of sales for target firms exceeds .10 (that is, exceeds 10 percent)?

b Now let μ be the mean growth rate of sales for all firms that are bidders (firms that have bid to acquire at least one other firm in the last five years), and again assume growth rates are approximately normally distributed. Furthermore, suppose a random sample of 25 bidders yields a sample mean sales growth rate of $\bar{x} = 0.12$ with a standard deviation of $s = 0.09$. Use critical values and this sample information to test $H_0: \mu \leq .10$ versus $H_a: \mu > .10$ by setting α equal to .10, .05, .01, and .001. How much evidence is there that the mean growth rate of sales for bidders exceeds .10 (that is, exceeds 10 percent)?

9.95 A consumer electronics firm has developed a new type of remote control button that is designed to operate longer before becoming intermittent. A random sample of 35 of the new buttons is selected and each is tested in continuous operation until becoming intermittent. The resulting lifetimes are found to have a sample mean of $\bar{x} = 1{,}241.2$ hours and a sample standard deviation of $s = 110.8$.

a Independent tests reveal that the mean lifetime (in continuous operation) of the best remote control button on the market is 1,200 hours. Letting μ be the mean lifetime of the population of all new remote control buttons that will or could potentially be produced, set up the null and alternative hypotheses needed to attempt to provide evidence that the new button's mean lifetime exceeds the mean lifetime of the best remote button currently on the market.

b Using the previously given sample results, use critical values to test the hypotheses you set up in part *a* by setting α equal to .10, .05, .01, and .001. What do you conclude for each value of α?

c Suppose that $\bar{x} = 1{,}241.2$ and $s = 110.8$ had been obtained by testing a sample of 100 buttons. Use critical values to test the hypotheses you set up in part *a* by setting α equal to .10, .05, .01, and .001. Which sample (the sample of 35 or the sample of 100) gives a more statistically significant result? That is, which sample provides stronger evidence that H_a is true?

d If we define practical importance to mean that μ exceeds 1,200 by an amount that would be clearly noticeable to most consumers, do you think that the result has practical importance? Explain why the samples of 35 and 100 both indicate the same degree of practical importance.

e Suppose that further research and development effort improves the new remote control button and that a random sample of 35 buttons gives $\bar{x} = 1,524.6$ hours and $s = 102.8$ hours. Test your hypotheses of part *a* by setting α equal to .10, .05, .01, and .001.

  (1) Do we have a highly statistically significant result? Explain.

  (2) Do you think we have a practically important result? Explain.

9.96 Again consider the remote control button lifetime situation discussed in Exercise 9.95. Using the sample information given in the introduction to Exercise 9.95, the *p*-value for testing H_0 versus H_a can be calculated to be .0174.

a Determine whether H_0 would be rejected at each of $\alpha = .10$, $\alpha = .05$, $\alpha = .01$, and $\alpha = .001$.

b Describe how much evidence we have that the new button's mean lifetime exceeds the mean lifetime of the best remote button currently on the market.

9.97 Calculate and use an appropriate 95 percent confidence interval to help evaluate practical importance as it relates to the hypothesis test in each of the following situations discussed in previous review exercises. Explain what you think each confidence interval says about practical importance.

a The check approval situation of Exercise 9.91.

b The cigarette ad situation of Exercise 9.92.

c The remote control button situation of Exercise 9.95*a*, *c*, and *e*.

9.98 Several industries located along the Ohio River discharge a toxic substance called carbon tetrachloride into the river. The state Environmental Protection Agency monitors the amount of carbon tetrachloride pollution in the river. Specifically, the agency requires that the carbon tetrachloride contamination must average no more than 10 parts per million. In order to monitor the carbon tetrachloride contamination in the river, the agency takes a daily sample of 100 pollution readings at a specified location. If the mean carbon tetrachloride reading for this sample casts substantial doubt on the hypothesis that the average amount of carbon tetrachloride contamination in the river is at most 10 parts per million, the agency must issue a shutdown order. In the event of such a shutdown order, industrial plants along the river must be closed until the carbon tetrachloride contamination is reduced to a more acceptable level. Assume that the state Environmental Protection Agency decides to issue a shutdown order if a sample of 100 pollution readings implies that $H_0: \mu \leq 10$ can be rejected in favor of $H_a: \mu > 10$ by setting $\alpha = .01$. If σ equals 2, calculate the probability of a Type II error for each of the following alternative values of μ: 10.1, 10.2, 10.3, 10.4, 10.5, 10.6, 10.7, 10.8, 10.9, and 11.0.

9.99 **THE INVESTMENT CASE** ◐ InvestRet

Suppose that random samples of 50 returns for each of the following investment classes give the indicated sample means and sample standard deviations:

Fixed annuities: $\bar{x} = 7.83\%$, $s = .51\%$
Domestic large-cap stocks: $\bar{x} = 13.42\%$, $s = 15.17\%$
Domestic midcap stocks: $\bar{x} = 15.03\%$, $s = 18.44\%$
Domestic small-cap stocks: $\bar{x} = 22.51\%$, $s = 21.75\%$

a For each investment class, set up the null and alternative hypotheses needed to test whether the current mean return differs from the historical (1970 to 1994) mean return given in Table 3.11 (page 159).

b Test each hypothesis you set up in part *a* at the .05 level of significance. What do you conclude? For which investment classes does the current mean return differ from the historical mean?

9.100 **THE UNITED KINGDOM INSURANCE CASE**

Assume that the U.K. insurance survey is based on 1,000 randomly selected United Kingdom households and that 640 of these households purchased life insurance in 1993.

a If *p* denotes the proportion of all U.K. households that purchased life insurance in 1993, set up the null and alternative hypotheses needed to attempt to justify the claim that more than 60 percent of U.K. households purchased life insurance in 1993.

b Test the hypotheses you set up in part *a* by setting $\alpha = .10, .05, .01$, and .001. How much evidence is there that more than 60 percent of U.K. households purchased life insurance in 1993?

9.101 How safe are child car seats? *Consumer Reports* (May 2005) tested the safety of child car seats in 30 mph crashes. They found "slim safety margins" for some child car seats. Suppose that *Consumer Reports* simulates the safety of the market-leading child car seat. Their test consists of placing the maximum claimed weight in the car seat and simulating crashes at higher and higher miles per hour until a problem occurs. The following data identify the speed at which a problem with the car seat first appeared, such as the strap breaking, seat shell cracking, strap adjuster breaking, the seat detaching from the base, and so on: 31.0, 29.4, 30.4, 28.9, 29.7, 30.1, 32.3, 31.7, 35.4, 29.1, 31.2, 30.2. Let μ denote the true mean speed at which a problem with the car seat first appears. The following MINITAB output gives the results of using the sample data to test $H_0: \mu = 30$ versus $H_a: \mu > 30$.   💿 CarSeat

```
Test of mu = 30 vs > 30

Variable   N     Mean   StDev   SE Mean    T      P
mph       12   30.7833  1.7862  0.5156    1.52  0.078
```

How much evidence is there that μ exceeds 30 mph?

9.102 *Consumer Reports* (January 2005) indicates that profit margins on extended warranties are much greater than on the purchase of most products.[5] In this exercise we consider a major electronics retailer that wishes to increase the proportion of customers who buy extended warranties on digital cameras. Historically, 20 percent of digital camera customers have purchased the retailer's extended warranty. To increase this percentage, the retailer has decided to offer a new warranty that is less expensive and more comprehensive. Suppose that three months after starting to offer the new warranty, a random sample of 500 customer sales invoices shows that 152 out of 500 digital camera customers purchased the new warranty. Letting p denote the proportion of all digital camera customers who have purchased the new warranty, calculate the p-value for testing $H_0: p = .20$ versus $H_a: p > .20$. How much evidence is there that p exceeds .20? Does the difference between $\hat{p}$ and .2 seem to be practically important? Explain your opinion.

9.103 *Fortune* magazine has periodically reported on the rise of fees and expenses charged by stock funds.

   a Suppose that 10 years ago the average annual expense for stock funds was 1.19 percent. Let μ be the current mean annual expense for all stock funds, and assume that stock fund annual expenses are approximately normally distributed. If a random sample of 12 stock funds gives a sample mean annual expense of $\bar{x} = 1.63\%$ with a standard deviation of $s = .31\%$, use critical values and this sample information to test $H_0: \mu \leq 1.19\%$ versus $H_a: \mu > 1.19\%$ by setting α equal to .10, .05, .01, and .001. How much evidence is there that the current mean annual expense for stock funds exceeds the average of 10 years ago?

   b Do you think that the result in part *a* has practical importance? Explain your opinion.

9.104   Internet Exercise

Are American consumers comfortable using their credit cards to make purchases over the Internet? Suppose that a noted authority suggests that credit cards will be firmly established on the Internet once the 80 percent barrier is broken—that is, as soon as more than 80 percent of those who make purchases over the Internet are willing to use a credit card to pay for their transactions. A recent Gallup Poll (story, survey results, and analysis can be found at http://www.gallup.com/poll/releases/pr000223.asp) found that, out of $n = 302$ Internet purchasers surveyed, 267 have paid for Internet purchases using a credit card. Based on the results of the Gallup survey, is there sufficient evidence to conclude that the proportion of Internet purchasers willing to use a credit card now exceeds 0.80? Set up the appropriate null and alternative hypotheses, test at the 0.05 and 0.01 levels of significance, and calculate a p-value for your test.

Go to the Gallup Organization website (http://www.gallup.com) and find the index of recent poll results (http://www.gallup.com/poll/index.asp). Select an interesting current poll and prepare a brief written summary of the poll or some aspect thereof. Include a statistical test for the significance of a proportion (you may have to make up your own value for the hypothesized proportion p_0) as part of your report. For example, you might select a political poll and test whether a particular candidate is preferred by a majority of voters ($p > 0.50$).

Appendix 9.1 ■ One-Sample Hypothesis Testing Using MINITAB

The first instruction block in this section begins by describing the entry of data into the MINITAB Data window. Alternatively, the data may be loaded directly from the data disk included with the text. The appropriate data file name is given at the top of the instruction block. Please refer to Appendix 1.1 for further information about entering data, saving data, and printing results when using MINITAB.

---

[5]*Consumer Reports,* January 2005, page 51.

Hypothesis test for a population mean in Figure 9.9(a) on page 368 (data file: CreditCd.MTW):

- In the Data window, enter the interest rate data from Table 9.3 (page 367) into a single column with variable name Rate.
- Select **Stat : Basic Statistics : 1-Sample t**
- In the "1-Sample t (Test and Confidence Interval)" dialog box, select the "Samples in columns" option.
- Select the variable name Rate into the "Samples in columns" window.
- Place a checkmark in the "Perform hypothesis test" checkbox.
- Enter the hypothesized mean (here 18.8) into the "Hypothesized mean" window.
- Click the Options... button, select the desired alternative (in this case "less than") from the Alternative drop-down menu, and click OK in the "1-Sample t-Options" dialog box.
- To produce a box plot of the data with a graphical representation of the hypothesis test, click the Graphs... button in the "1-Sample t (Test and Confidence Interval)" dialog box, check the "Boxplot of data" checkbox, and click OK in the "1-Sample t—Graphs" dialog box.
- Click OK in the "1-Sample t (Test and Confidence Interval)" dialog box.
- The confidence interval is given in the Session window, and the box plot is displayed in a graphics window.

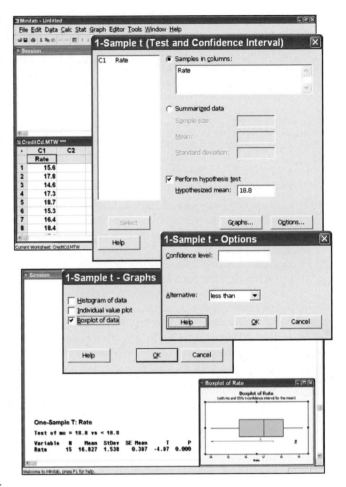

A "1-Sample Z" test is also available in MINITAB under Basic Statistics. It requires a user-specified value of the population standard deviation, which is rarely known.

Hypothesis test for a population proportion in Exercise 9.72 on page 375:

- Select **Stat : Basic Statistics : 1 Proportion**
- In the "1 Proportion (Test and Confidence Interval)" dialog box, select the "Summarized data" option.
- Enter the sample number of successes (here equal to 146) into the "Number of events" window.
- Enter the sample size (here equal to 400) into the "Number of trials" window.
- Place a checkmark in the "Perform hypothesis test" checkbox.
- Enter the hypothesized proportion (here equal to 0.25) into the "Hypothesized proportion" window.
- Click on the Options... button.
- In the "1 Proportion—Options" dialog box, select the desired alternative (in this case "greater than") from the Alternative drop-down menu.
- Place a checkmark in the "Use test and interval based on normal distribution" checkbox.
- Click OK in the "1 Proportion—Options" dialog box, and click OK in the "1 Proportion (Test and Confidence Interval)" dialog box.
- The hypothesis test results are given in the Session window.

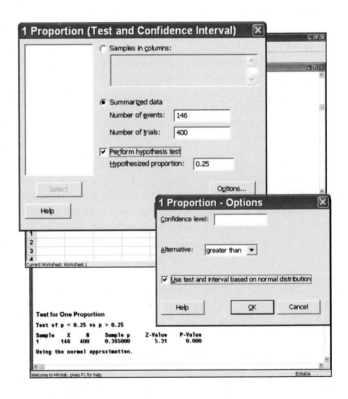

Appendix 9.2 ■ One-Sample Hypothesis Testing Using Excel

The instruction block in this section begins by describing the entry of data into an Excel spreadsheet. Alternatively, the data may be loaded directly from the data disk included with the text. The appropriate data file name is given at the top of the instruction block. Please refer to Appendix 1.2 for further information about entering data, saving data, and printing results.

Hypothesis test for a population mean in Figure 9.9(b) on page 368 (data file: CreditCd.xlsx):

The Data Analysis ToolPak in Excel does not explicitly provide for one-sample tests of hypotheses. A one-sample test can be conducted using the Descriptive Statistics component of the Analysis ToolPak and a few additional computations using Excel.

Descriptive statistics:

- Enter the interest rate data from Table 9.3 (page 367) into cells A2.A16 with the label Rate in cell A1.

- Select **Data : Data Analysis : Descriptive Statistics**

- Click OK in the Data Analysis dialog box.

- In the Descriptive Statistics dialog box, enter A1.A16 into the Input Range box.

- Place a checkmark in the "Labels in first row" checkbox.

- Under output options, select "New Worksheet Ply" to have the output placed in a new worksheet and enter the name Output for the new worksheet.

- Place a checkmark in the Summary statistics checkbox.

- Click OK in the Descriptive Statistics dialog box.

The resulting block of descriptive statistics is displayed in the Output worksheet and the entries needed to carry out the test computations have been entered into the range D3.E6.

Computation of the test statistic and *p*-value:

- In cell E7, use the formula

  = (E3 − E4)/(E5/SQRT(E6))

  to compute the test statistic *t* (= −4.970).

- Click on cell E8 and then select the Insert Function button f_x on the Excel toolbar.

- In the Insert Function dialog box, select Statistical from the "Or select a category:" menu, select TDIST from the "Select a function:" menu, and click OK in the Insert Function dialog box.

- In the TDIST Function Arguments dialog box, enter abs(E7) in the X window.

- Enter 14 in the Deg_freedom window.

- Enter 1 in the Tails window to select a one-tailed test.

- Click OK in the TDIST Function Arguments dialog box.

- The *p*-value related to the test will be placed in cell E8.

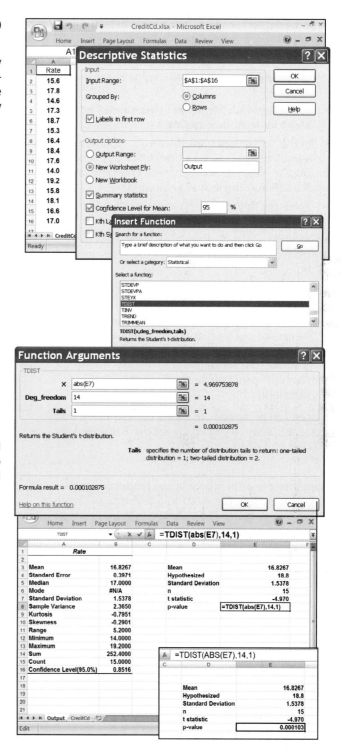

Appendix 9.3 ■ One-Sample Hypothesis Testing Using MegaStat

The instructions in this section begin by describing the entry of data into an Excel worksheet. Alternatively, the data may be loaded directly from the data disk included with the text. The appropriate data file name is given at the top of each instruction block. Please refer to Appendix 1.2 for further information about entering data and saving and printing results in Excel. Please refer to Appendix 1.3 for more information about using MegaStat.

Hypothesis test for a population mean in Figure 9.10 on page 368 (data file: CreditCd.xlsx):

- Enter the interest rate data from Table 9.3 (page 367) into cells A2.A16 with the label Rate in cell A1.

- Select **Add-Ins : MegaStat : Hypothesis Tests : Mean vs. Hypothesized Value**

- In the "Hypothesis Test: Mean vs. Hypothesized Value" dialog box, click on "data input" and use the AutoExpand feature to enter the range A1.A16 into the Input Range window.

- Enter the hypothesized value (here equal to 18.8) into the Hypothesized mean window.

- Select the desired alternative (here "less than") from the drop-down menu in the Alternative box.

- Click on t-test and click OK in the "Hypothesis Test: Mean vs. Hypothesized Value" dialog box.

- A hypothesis test employing summary data can be carried out by clicking on "summary input" and by entering a range into the Input Range window that contains the following—label; sample mean; sample standard deviation; sample size *n*.

A *z* test can be carried out (in the unlikely event that the population standard deviation is known) by clicking on "z-test."

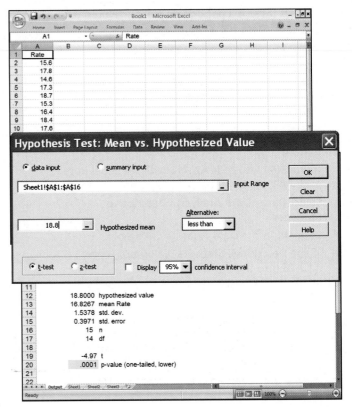

Hypothesis test for a population proportion shown in Figure 9.11 in the electronic article surveillance situation on pages 373 and 374:

- Select **Add-Ins : MegaStat : Hypothesis Tests : Proportion vs. Hypothesized Value**

- In the "Hypothesis Test: Proportion vs. Hypothesized Value" dialog box, enter the hypothesized value (here equal to 0.05) into the "Hypothesized p" window.

- Enter the observed sample proportion (here equal to 0.16) into the "Observed p" window.

- Enter the sample size (here equal to 250) into the "n" window.

- Select the desired alternative (here "greater than") from the drop-down menu in the Alternative box.

- Check the "Display confidence interval" checkbox (if desired), and select or type the appropriate level of confidence.

- Click OK in the "Hypothesis Test: Proportion vs. Hypothesized Value" dialog box.

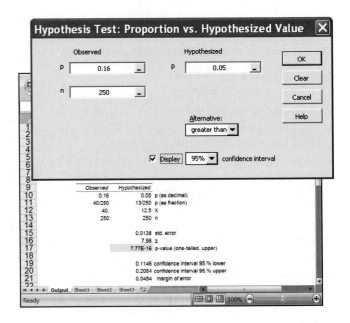

Hypothesis test for a population variance in the camshaft situation of Section 9.7 on pages 383 and 384:

- Enter a label (in this case Depth) into cell A1, the sample variance (here equal to .0885) into cell A2, and the sample size (here equal to 30) into cell A3.

- Select **Add-Ins : MegaStat : Hypothesis Tests : Chi-square Variance Test**

- Click on "summary input."

- Enter the range A1.A3 into the Input Range window—that is, enter the range containing the data label, the sample variance, and the sample size.

- Enter the hypothesized value (here equal to 0.2209) into the "Hypothesized variance" window.

- Select the desired alternative (in this case "less than") from the drop-down menu in the Alternative box.

- Check the "Display confidence interval" checkbox (if desired) and select or type the appropriate level of confidence.

- Click OK in the "Chi-square Variance Test" dialog box.

- A chi-square variance test may be carried out using **data input** by entering the observed sample values into a column in the Excel worksheet, and by then using the AutoExpand feature to enter the range containing the label and sample values into the Input Range window.

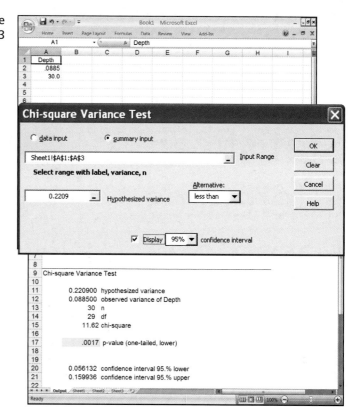

Statistical Inferences Based on Two Samples

Chapter Outline

10.1 Comparing Two Population Means by Using Independent Samples: Variances Known

10.2 Comparing Two Population Means by Using Independent Samples: Variances Unknown

10.3 Paired Difference Experiments

10.4 Comparing Two Population Proportions by Using Large, Independent Samples

10.5 Comparing Two Population Variances by Using Independent Samples

usiness improvement often requires making comparisons. For example, to increase consumer awareness of a product or service, it might be necessary to compare different types of advertising campaigns. Or to offer more profitable investments to its customers, an investment firm might compare the profitability of different investment portfolios. As a third example, a manufacturer might compare different production methods in order to minimize or eliminate out-of-specification product.

In this chapter we discuss using confidence intervals and hypothesis tests to **compare two populations.** Specifically, we compare two population means, two population variances, and two population proportions. We make these comparisons by studying **differences** and **ratios.** For instance, to compare two population means, say μ_1 and μ_2, we consider the difference between these means, $\mu_1 - \mu_2$. If, for example, we use a confidence interval or hypothesis test to conclude that $\mu_1 - \mu_2$ is a positive number, then we conclude that μ_1 is greater than μ_2. On the other hand, if a confidence interval or hypothesis test shows that $\mu_1 - \mu_2$ is a negative number, then we conclude that μ_1 is less than μ_2. As another example, if we compare two population variances, say σ_1^2 and σ_2^2, we might consider the ratio σ_1^2/σ_2^2. If a hypothesis test shows that this ratio exceeds 1, then we can conclude that σ_1^2 is greater than σ_2^2.

We explain many of this chapter's methods in the context of three new cases:

The Catalyst Comparison Case: The production supervisor at a chemical plant uses confidence intervals and hypothesis tests for the difference between two population means to determine which of two catalysts maximizes the hourly yield of a chemical process. By maximizing yield, the plant increases its productivity and improves its profitability.

The Repair Cost Comparison Case: In order to reduce the costs of automobile accident claims, an insurance company uses confidence intervals and hypothesis tests for the difference between two population means to compare repair cost estimates for damaged cars at two different garages.

The Advertising Media Case: An advertising agency is test marketing a new product by using one advertising campaign in Des Moines, Iowa, and a different campaign in Toledo, Ohio. The agency uses confidence intervals and hypothesis tests for the difference between two population proportions to compare the effectiveness of the two advertising campaigns.

10.1 Comparing Two Population Means by Using Independent Samples: Variances Known ● ● ●

A bank manager has developed a new system to reduce the time customers spend waiting to be served by tellers during peak business hours. We let μ_1 denote the mean customer waiting time during peak business hours under the current system. To estimate μ_1, the manager randomly selects $n_1 = 100$ customers and records the length of time each customer spends waiting for service. The manager finds that the sample mean waiting time for these 100 customers is $\bar{x}_1 = 8.79$ minutes. We let μ_2 denote the mean customer waiting time during peak business hours for the new system. During a trial run, the manager finds that the mean waiting time for a random sample of $n_2 = 100$ customers is $\bar{x}_2 = 5.14$ minutes.

In order to compare μ_1 and μ_2, the manager estimates $\mu_1 - \mu_2$, the difference between μ_1 and μ_2. Intuitively, a logical point estimate of $\mu_1 - \mu_2$ is the difference between the sample means

$$\bar{x}_1 - \bar{x}_2 = 8.79 - 5.14 = 3.65 \text{ minutes}$$

This says we estimate that the current mean waiting time is 3.65 minutes longer than the mean waiting time under the new system. That is, we estimate that the new system reduces the mean waiting time by 3.65 minutes.

To compute a confidence interval for $\mu_1 - \mu_2$ (or to test a hypothesis about $\mu_1 - \mu_2$), we need to know the properties of the sampling distribution of $\bar{x}_1 - \bar{x}_2$. To understand this sampling distribution, consider randomly selecting a sample[1] of n_1 measurements from a population having mean μ_1 and variance σ_1^2. Let $\bar{x}_1$ be the mean of this sample. Also consider randomly selecting a

---

[1]Each sample in this chapter is a *random* sample. As has been our practice throughout this book, for brevity we sometimes refer to "random samples" as "samples."

FIGURE 10.1   **The Sampling Distribution of $\bar{x}_1 - \bar{x}_2$ Has Mean $\mu_1 - \mu_2$ and Standard Deviation $\sigma_{\bar{x}_1 - \bar{x}_2}$**

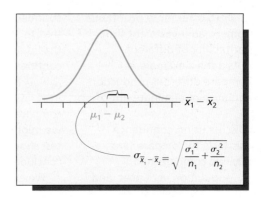

sample of n_2 measurements from another population having mean μ_2 and variance σ_2^2. Let $\bar{x}_2$ be the mean of this sample. Different samples from the first population would give different values of $\bar{x}_1$, and different samples from the second population would give different values of $\bar{x}_2$—so different pairs of samples from the two populations would give different values of $\bar{x}_1 - \bar{x}_2$. In the following box we describe the **sampling distribution of $\bar{x}_1 - \bar{x}_2$**, which is the probability distribution of all possible values of $\bar{x}_1 - \bar{x}_2$:

The Sampling Distribution of $\bar{x}_1 - \bar{x}_2$

If the randomly selected samples are **independent** of each other,[2] then the population of all possible values of $\bar{x}_1 - \bar{x}_2$

1   Has a normal distribution if each sampled population has a normal distribution, or has approximately a normal distribution if the sampled populations are not normally distributed and each of the sample sizes n_1 and n_2 is large.

2   Has mean $\mu_{\bar{x}_1 - \bar{x}_2} = \mu_1 - \mu_2$

3   Has standard deviation $\sigma_{\bar{x}_1 - \bar{x}_2} = \sqrt{\dfrac{\sigma_1^2}{n_1} + \dfrac{\sigma_2^2}{n_2}}$

Figure 10.1 illustrates the sampling distribution of $\bar{x}_1 - \bar{x}_2$. Using this sampling distribution, we can find a confidence interval for and test a hypothesis about $\mu_1 - \mu_2$. Although the interval and test assume that the true values of the population variances σ_1^2 and σ_2^2 are known, we believe that they are worth presenting because they provide a simple introduction to the basic idea of comparing two population means. Readers who wish to proceed more quickly to the more practical t-based procedures of the next section may skip the rest of this section without loss of continuity.

A *z*-Based Confidence Interval for the Difference between Two Population Means When σ_1 and σ_2 Are Known

Let $\bar{x}_1$ be the mean of a sample of size n_1 that has been randomly selected from a population with mean μ_1 and standard deviation σ_1, and let $\bar{x}_2$ be the mean of a sample of size n_2 that has been randomly selected from a population with mean μ_2 and standard deviation σ_2. Furthermore, suppose that each sampled population is normally distributed, or that each of the sample sizes n_1 and n_2 is large. Then, if the samples are independent of each other, a **100(1 − α) percent confidence interval for $\mu_1 - \mu_2$** is

$$\left[(\bar{x}_1 - \bar{x}_2) \pm z_{\alpha/2} \sqrt{\frac{\sigma_1^2}{n_1} + \frac{\sigma_2^2}{n_2}} \right]$$

[2]This means that there is no relationship between the measurements in one sample and the measurements in the other sample.

EXAMPLE 10.1 The Bank Customer Waiting Time Case

Suppose the random sample of $n_1 = 100$ waiting times observed under the current system gives a sample mean $\bar{x}_1 = 8.79$ and the random sample of $n_2 = 100$ waiting times observed during the trial run of the new system yields a sample mean $\bar{x}_2 = 5.14$. Assuming that σ_1^2 is known to equal 4.7 and σ_2^2 is known to equal 1.9, and noting that each sample is large, a 95 percent confidence interval for $\mu_1 - \mu_2$ is

$$\left[(\bar{x}_1 - \bar{x}_2) \pm z_{.025}\sqrt{\frac{\sigma_1^2}{n_1} + \frac{\sigma_2^2}{n_2}} \right] = \left[(8.79 - 5.14) \pm 1.96\sqrt{\frac{4.7}{100} + \frac{1.9}{100}} \right]$$

$$= [3.65 \pm .5035]$$

$$= [3.15, \ 4.15]$$

This interval says we are 95 percent confident that the new system reduces the mean waiting time by between 3.15 minutes and 4.15 minutes.

Suppose we wish to test a hypothesis about $\mu_1 - \mu_2$. In the following box we describe how this can be done. Here we test the null hypothesis $H_0: \mu_1 - \mu_2 = D_0$, where D_0 is a number whose value varies depending on the situation.

A *z* Test about the Difference between Two Population Means When σ_1 and σ_2 Are Known

Let all notation be as defined in the preceding box, and define the test statistic

$$z = \frac{(\bar{x}_1 - \bar{x}_2) - D_0}{\sqrt{\dfrac{\sigma_1^2}{n_1} + \dfrac{\sigma_2^2}{n_2}}}$$

Assume that each sampled population is normally distributed, or that each of the sample sizes n_1 and n_2 is large. Then, if the samples are independent of each other, we can test $H_0: \mu_1 - \mu_2 = D_0$ versus a particular alternative hypothesis at level of significance α by using the appropriate critical value rule, or, equivalently, the corresponding *p*-value.

Alternative Hypothesis	Critical Value Rule: Reject H_0 If	*p*-Value (Reject H_0 If *p*-Value $< \alpha$)
$H_a: \mu_1 - \mu_2 > D_0$	$z > z_\alpha$	The area under the standard normal curve to the right of z
$H_a: \mu_1 - \mu_2 < D_0$	$z < -z_\alpha$	The area under the standard normal curve to the left of z
$H_a: \mu_1 - \mu_2 \neq D_0$	$\|z\| > z_{\alpha/2}$—that is, $z > z_{\alpha/2}$ or $z < -z_{\alpha/2}$	Twice the area under the standard normal curve to the right of $\|z\|$

Often D_0 will be the number 0. In such a case, the null hypothesis $H_0: \mu_1 - \mu_2 = 0$ says there is **no difference** between the population means μ_1 and μ_2. For example, in the bank customer waiting time situation, the null hypothesis $H_0: \mu_1 - \mu_2 = 0$ says there is no difference between the mean customer waiting times under the current and new systems. When D_0 is 0, each alternative hypothesis in the box implies that the population means μ_1 and μ_2 differ. For instance, in the bank waiting time situation, the alternative hypothesis $H_a: \mu_1 - \mu_2 > 0$ says that the current mean customer waiting time is longer than the new mean customer waiting time. That is, this alternative hypothesis says that the new system reduces the mean customer waiting time.

EXAMPLE 10.2 The Bank Customer Waiting Time Case

To attempt to provide evidence supporting the claim that the new system reduces the mean bank customer waiting time, we will test $H_0: \mu_1 - \mu_2 = 0$ versus $H_a: \mu_1 - \mu_2 > 0$ at the **.05 level of significance.** To perform the hypothesis test, we will use the sample information in Example 10.1 to calculate the value of the **test statistic z in the summary box.** Then, since $H_a: \mu_1 - \mu_2 > 0$ is of the form $H_a: \mu_1 - \mu_2 > D_0$, we will **reject $H_0: \mu_1 - \mu_2 = 0$ if the value of z is greater than** $z_\alpha = z_{.05} = 1.645$. Assuming that $\sigma_1^2 = 4.7$ and $\sigma_2^2 = 1.9$, the **value of the test statistic is**

$$z = \frac{(\bar{x}_1 - \bar{x}_2) - D_0}{\sqrt{\dfrac{\sigma_1^2}{n_1} + \dfrac{\sigma_2^2}{n_2}}} = \frac{(8.79 - 5.14) - 0}{\sqrt{\dfrac{4.7}{100} + \dfrac{1.9}{100}}} = \frac{3.65}{.2569} = 14.21$$

Because $z = 14.21$ is greater than $z_{.05} = 1.645$, we reject $H_0: \mu_1 - \mu_2 = 0$ in favor of H_a: $\mu_1 - \mu_2 > 0$. We conclude (at an α of .05) that $\mu_1 - \mu_2$ is greater than zero and, therefore, that the new system reduces the mean customer waiting time. Furthermore, the point estimate $\bar{x}_1 - \bar{x}_2 = 3.65$ says we estimate that the new system reduces mean waiting time by 3.65 minutes. The *p*-value for the test is the area under the standard normal curve to the right of $z = 14.21$. Because this *p*-value is less than .00003, it provides extremely strong evidence that H_0 is false and that H_a is true. That is, we have extremely strong evidence that $\mu_1 - \mu_2$ is greater than zero and, therefore, that the new system reduces the mean customer waiting time.

Next, suppose that because of cost considerations, the bank manager wants to implement the new system only if it reduces mean waiting time by more than three minutes. In order to demonstrate that $\mu_1 - \mu_2$ is greater than 3, the manager (setting D_0 equal to 3) will attempt to reject the null hypothesis $H_0: \mu_1 - \mu_2 = 3$ in favor of the alternative hypothesis $H_a: \mu_1 - \mu_2 > 3$ at the .05 level of significance. To perform the hypothesis test, we compute

$$z = \frac{(\bar{x}_1 - \bar{x}_2) - 3}{\sqrt{\dfrac{\sigma_1^2}{n_1} + \dfrac{\sigma_2^2}{n_2}}} = \frac{(8.79 - 5.14) - 3}{\sqrt{\dfrac{4.7}{100} + \dfrac{1.9}{100}}} = \frac{.65}{.2569} = 2.53$$

Because $z = 2.53$ is greater than $z_{.05} = 1.645$, we can reject $H_0: \mu_1 - \mu_2 = 3$ in favor of H_a: $\mu_1 - \mu_2 > 3$. The *p*-value for the test is the area under the standard normal curve to the right of $z = 2.53$. Table A.3 (page 641) tells us that this area is $1 - .9943 = .0057$. Therefore, we have very strong evidence against $H_0: \mu_1 - \mu_2 = 3$ and in favor of $H_a: \mu_1 - \mu_2 > 3$. In other words, we have very strong evidence that the new system reduces mean waiting time by more than three minutes.

Exercises for Section 10.1

CONCEPTS

connect

10.1 Suppose we compare two population means, μ_1 and μ_2, and consider the difference $\mu_1 - \mu_2$. In each case, indicate how μ_1 relates to μ_2. (That is, is μ_1 greater than, less than, equal to, or not equal to μ_2?)

    a $\mu_1 - \mu_2 < 0$ **d** $\mu_1 - \mu_2 > 0$

    b $\mu_1 - \mu_2 = 0$ **e** $\mu_1 - \mu_2 > 20$

    c $\mu_1 - \mu_2 < -10$ **f** $\mu_1 - \mu_2 \neq 0$

10.2 Suppose we compute a 95 percent confidence interval for $\mu_1 - \mu_2$. If the interval is

    a [3, 5], can we be 95 percent confident that μ_1 is greater than μ_2? Why or why not?

    b [3, 5], can we be 95 percent confident that μ_1 is not equal to μ_2? Why or why not?

    c [−20, −10], can we be 95 percent confident that μ_1 is not equal to μ_2? Why or why not?

    d [−20, −10], can we be 95 percent confident that μ_1 is greater than μ_2? Why or why not?

    e [−3, 2], can we be 95 percent confident that μ_1 is not equal to μ_2? Why or why not?

    f [−10, 10], can we be 95 percent confident that μ_1 is less than μ_2? Why or why not?

    g [−10, 10], can we be 95 percent confident that μ_1 is greater than μ_2? Why or why not?

10.3   In order to employ the formulas and tests of this section, the samples that have been randomly selected from the populations being compared must be independent of each other. In such a case, we say that we are performing an **independent samples experiment.** In your own words, explain what it means when we say that samples are independent of each other.

10.4   Describe the assumptions that must be met in order to validly use the methods of Section 10.1.

METHODS AND APPLICATIONS

10.5   Suppose we randomly select two independent samples from populations having means μ_1 and μ_2. If $\bar{x}_1 = 25$, $\bar{x}_2 = 20$, $\sigma_1 = 3$, $\sigma_2 = 4$, $n_1 = 100$, and $n_2 = 100$:

    a   Calculate a 95 percent confidence interval for $\mu_1 - \mu_2$. Can we be 95 percent confident that μ_1 is greater than μ_2? Explain.

    b   Test the null hypothesis H_0: $\mu_1 - \mu_2 = 0$ versus H_a: $\mu_1 - \mu_2 > 0$ by setting $\alpha = .05$. What do you conclude about how μ_1 compares to μ_2?

    c   Find the p-value for testing H_0: $\mu_1 - \mu_2 = 4$ versus H_a: $\mu_1 - \mu_2 > 4$. Use the p-value to test these hypotheses by setting α equal to .10, .05, .01, and .001.

10.6   Suppose we select two independent random samples from populations having means μ_1 and μ_2. If $\bar{x}_1 = 151$, $\bar{x}_2 = 162$, $\sigma_1 = 6$, $\sigma_2 = 8$, $n_1 = 625$, and $n_2 = 625$:

    a   Calculate a 95 percent confidence interval for $\mu_1 - \mu_2$. Can we be 95 percent confident that μ_2 is greater than μ_1? By how much? Explain.

    b   Test the null hypothesis H_0: $\mu_1 - \mu_2 = -10$ versus H_a: $\mu_1 - \mu_2 < -10$ by setting $\alpha = .05$. What do you conclude?

    c   Test the null hypothesis H_0: $\mu_1 - \mu_2 = -10$ versus H_a: $\mu_1 - \mu_2 \neq -10$ by setting α equal to .01. What do you conclude?

    d   Find the p-value for testing H_0: $\mu_1 - \mu_2 = -10$ versus H_a: $\mu_1 - \mu_2 \neq -10$. Use the p-value to test these hypotheses by setting α equal to .10, .05, .01, and .001.

10.7   In an article in *Accounting and Business Research,* Carslaw and Kaplan study the effect of control (owner versus manager control) on audit delay (the length of time from a company's financial year-end to the date of the auditor's report) for public companies in New Zealand. Suppose a random sample of 100 public owner-controlled companies in New Zealand gives a mean audit delay of $\bar{x}_1 = 82.6$ days, while a random sample of 100 public manager-controlled companies in New Zealand gives a mean audit delay of $\bar{x}_2 = 93$ days. Assuming the samples are independent and that $\sigma_1 = 32.83$ and $\sigma_2 = 37.18$:

    a   Let μ_1 be the mean audit delay for all public owner-controlled companies in New Zealand, and let μ_2 be the mean audit delay for all public manager-controlled companies in New Zealand. Calculate a 95 percent confidence interval for $\mu_1 - \mu_2$. Based on this interval, can we be 95 percent confident that the mean audit delay for all public owner-controlled companies in New Zealand is less than that for all public manager-controlled companies in New Zealand? If so, by how much?

    b   Consider testing the null hypothesis H_0: $\mu_1 - \mu_2 = 0$ versus H_a: $\mu_1 - \mu_2 < 0$. Interpret (in writing) the meaning (in practical terms) of each of H_0 and H_a.

    c   Use a critical value to test the null hypothesis H_0: $\mu_1 - \mu_2 = 0$ versus H_a: $\mu_1 - \mu_2 < 0$ at the .05 level of significance. Based on this test, what do you conclude about how μ_1 and μ_2 compare? Write your conclusion in practical terms.

    d   Find the p-value for testing H_0: $\mu_1 - \mu_2 = 0$ versus H_a: $\mu_1 - \mu_2 < 0$. Use the p-value to test H_0 versus H_a by setting α equal to .10, .05, .025, .01, and .001. How much evidence is there that μ_1 is less than μ_2?

10.8   In an article in the *Journal of Management,* Wright and Bonett study the relationship between voluntary organizational turnover and such factors as work performance, work satisfaction, and company tenure. As part of the study, the authors compare work performance ratings for "stayers" (employees who stay in their organization) and "leavers" (employees who voluntarily quit their jobs). Suppose that a random sample of 175 stayers has a mean performance rating (on a 20-point scale) of $\bar{x}_1 = 12.8$, and that a random sample of 140 leavers has a mean performance rating of $\bar{x}_2 = 14.7$. Assuming these random samples are independent and that $\sigma_1 = 3.7$ and $\sigma_2 = 4.5$:

    a   Let μ_1 be the mean performance rating for stayers, and let μ_2 be the mean performance rating for leavers. Use the sample information to calculate a 99 percent confidence interval for $\mu_1 - \mu_2$. Based on this interval, can we be 99 percent confident that the mean performance rating for leavers is greater than the mean performance rating for stayers? What are the managerial implications of this result?

    b   Set up the null and alternative hypotheses needed to try to establish that the mean performance rating for leavers is higher than the mean performance rating for stayers.

    c Use critical values to test the hypotheses you set up in part *b* by setting α equal to .10, .05, .01, and .001. How much evidence is there that leavers have a higher mean performance rating than do stayers?

10.9 An Ohio university wishes to demonstrate that car ownership is detrimental to academic achievement. A random sample of 100 students who do not own cars had a mean grade point average (GPA) of 2.68, while a random sample of 100 students who own cars had a mean GPA of 2.55.

    a Assuming that the independence assumption holds, and letting μ_1 = the mean GPA for all students who do not own cars, and μ_2 = the mean GPA for all students who own cars, use the above data to compute a 95 percent confidence interval for $\mu_1 - \mu_2$. Assume here that σ_1 = .7 and σ_2 = .6.

    b On the basis of the interval calculated in part *a*, can the university claim that car ownership is associated with decreased academic achievement? That is, can the university justify that μ_1 is greater than μ_2? Explain.

    c Set up the null and alternative hypotheses that should be used to attempt to justify that the mean GPA for non–car owners is higher than the mean GPA for car owners.

    d Test the hypotheses that you set up in part *c* with α = .05. Again assume that σ_1 = .7 and σ_2 = .6. Interpret the results of this test. That is, what do your results say about whether car ownership is associated with decreased academic achievement?

10.10 In the *Journal of Marketing,* Bayus studied differences between "early replacement buyers" and "late replacement buyers." Suppose that a random sample of 800 early replacement buyers yields a mean number of dealers visited of $\bar{x}_1$ = 3.3, and that a random sample of 500 late replacement buyers yields a mean number of dealers visited of $\bar{x}_2$ = 4.5. Assuming that these samples are independent:

    a Let μ_1 be the mean number of dealers visited by early replacement buyers, and let μ_2 be the mean number of dealers visited by late replacement buyers. Calculate a 95 percent confidence interval for $\mu_2 - \mu_1$. Assume here that σ_1 = .71 and σ_2 = .66. Based on this interval, can we be 95 percent confident that on average late replacement buyers visit more dealers than do early replacement buyers?

    b Set up the null and alternative hypotheses needed to attempt to show that the mean number of dealers visited by late replacement buyers exceeds the mean number of dealers visited by early replacement buyers by more than 1.

    c Test the hypotheses you set up in part *b* by using critical values and by setting α equal to .10, .05, .01, and .001. How much evidence is there that H_0 should be rejected?

    d Find the *p*-value for testing the hypotheses you set up in part *b*. Use the *p*-value to test these hypotheses with α equal to .10, .05, .01, and .001. How much evidence is there that H_0 should be rejected? Explain your conclusion in practical terms.

    e Do you think that the results of the hypothesis tests in parts *c* and *d* have practical significance? Explain and justify your answer.

10.11 In the book *Essentials of Marketing Research,* William R. Dillon, Thomas J. Madden, and Neil H. Firtle discuss a corporate image study designed to find out whether perceptions of technical support services vary depending on the position of the respondent in the organization. The management of a company that supplies telephone cable to telephone companies commissioned a media campaign primarily designed to

> (1) increase awareness of the company and (2) create favorable perceptions of the company's technical support. The campaign was targeted to purchasing managers and technical managers at independent telephone companies with greater than 10,000 trunk lines.

> Perceptual ratings were measured with a nine-point agree–disagree scale. Suppose the results of a telephone survey of 175 technical managers and 125 purchasing managers reveal that the mean perception score for technical managers is 7.3 and that the mean perception score for purchasing managers is 8.2.

    a Let μ_1 be the mean perception score for all purchasing managers, and let μ_2 be the mean perception score for all technical managers. Set up the null and alternative hypotheses needed to establish whether the mean perception scores for purchasing managers and technical managers differ. Hint: If μ_1 and μ_2 do not differ, what does $\mu_1 - \mu_2$ equal?

    b Assuming that the samples of 175 technical managers and 125 purchasing managers are independent random samples, test the hypotheses you set up in part *a* by using a critical value with α = .05. Assume here that σ_1 = 1.6 and σ_2 = 1.4. What do you conclude about whether the mean perception scores for purchasing managers and technical managers differ?

    c Find the *p*-value for testing the hypotheses you set up in part *a*. Use the *p*-value to test these hypotheses by setting α equal to .10, .05, .01, and .001. How much evidence is there that the mean perception scores for purchasing managers and technical managers differ?

    d Calculate a 99 percent confidence interval for $\mu_1 - \mu_2$. Interpret this interval.

10.2 Comparing Two Population Means by Using Independent Samples: Variances Unknown ●●●

CHAPTER 10

Suppose that (as is usually the case) the true values of the population variances σ_1^2 and σ_2^2 are not known. We then estimate σ_1^2 and σ_2^2 by using s_1^2 and s_2^2, the variances of the samples randomly selected from the populations being compared. There are two approaches to doing this. The first approach assumes that the population variances σ_1^2 and σ_2^2 are equal. Denoting the common value of these variances as σ^2, it follows that

$$\sigma_{\bar{x}_1 - \bar{x}_2} = \sqrt{\frac{\sigma_1^2}{n_1} + \frac{\sigma_2^2}{n_2}} = \sqrt{\frac{\sigma^2}{n_1} + \frac{\sigma^2}{n_2}} = \sqrt{\sigma^2 \left(\frac{1}{n_1} + \frac{1}{n_2} \right)}$$

Because we are assuming that $\sigma_1^2 = \sigma_2^2 = \sigma^2$, we do not need separate estimates of σ_1^2 and σ_2^2. Instead, we combine the results of the two independent random samples to compute a single estimate of σ^2. This estimate is called the **pooled estimate** of σ^2, and it is a weighted average of the two sample variances s_1^2 and s_2^2. Denoting the pooled estimate as s_p^2, it is computed using the formula

$$s_p^2 = \frac{(n_1 - 1)s_1^2 + (n_2 - 1)s_2^2}{n_1 + n_2 - 2}$$

Using s_p^2, the estimate of $\sigma_{\bar{x}_1 - \bar{x}_2}$ is

$$\sqrt{s_p^2 \left(\frac{1}{n_1} + \frac{1}{n_2} \right)}$$

and we form the statistic

$$\frac{(\bar{x}_1 - \bar{x}_2) - (\mu_1 - \mu_2)}{\sqrt{s_p^2 \left(\frac{1}{n_1} + \frac{1}{n_2} \right)}}$$

It can be shown that, if we have randomly selected independent samples from two normally distributed populations having equal variances, then the sampling distribution of this statistic is a t distribution having $(n_1 + n_2 - 2)$ degrees of freedom. Therefore, we can obtain the following confidence interval for $\mu_1 - \mu_2$:

A t-Based Confidence Interval for the Difference between Two Population Means: Equal Variances

Suppose we have randomly selected independent samples from two normally distributed populations having equal variances. Then, a **100(1 − α) percent confidence interval for $\mu_1 - \mu_2$** is

$$\left[(\bar{x}_1 - \bar{x}_2) \pm t_{\alpha/2} \sqrt{s_p^2 \left(\frac{1}{n_1} + \frac{1}{n_2} \right)} \right] \quad \text{where} \quad s_p^2 = \frac{(n_1 - 1)s_1^2 + (n_2 - 1)s_2^2}{n_1 + n_2 - 2}$$

and $t_{\alpha/2}$ is based on $(n_1 + n_2 - 2)$ degrees of freedom.

EXAMPLE 10.3 The Catalyst Comparison Case Ⓒ

A production supervisor at a major chemical company must determine which of two catalysts, catalyst XA-100 or catalyst ZB-200, maximizes the hourly yield of a chemical process. In order to compare the mean hourly yields obtained by using the two catalysts, the supervisor runs the process using each catalyst for five one-hour periods. The resulting yields (in pounds per hour)

TABLE 10.1   Yields of a Chemical Process Obtained Using Two Catalysts   ◐ Catalyst

Catalyst XA-100	Catalyst ZB-200
801	752
814	718
784	776
836	742
820	763
$\bar{x}_1 = 811$	$\bar{x}_2 = 750.2$
$s_1^2 = 386$	$s_2^2 = 484.2$

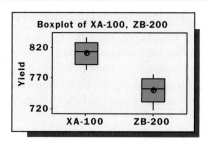

for each catalyst, along with the means, variances, and box plots[3] of the yields, are given in Table 10.1. Assuming that all other factors affecting yields of the process have been held as constant as possible during the test runs, it seems reasonable to regard the five observed yields for each catalyst as a random sample from the population of all possible hourly yields for the catalyst. Furthermore, since the sample variances $s_1^2 = 386$ and $s_2^2 = 484.2$ do not differ substantially (notice that $s_1 = 19.65$ and $s_2 = 22.00$ differ by even less), it might be reasonable to conclude that the population variances are approximately equal.[4] It follows that the pooled estimate

$$s_p^2 = \frac{(n_1 - 1)s_1^2 + (n_2 - 1)s_2^2}{n_1 + n_2 - 2}$$

$$= \frac{(5 - 1)(386) + (5 - 1)(484.2)}{5 + 5 - 2} = 435.1$$

is a point estimate of the common variance σ^2.

We define μ_1 as the mean hourly yield obtained by using catalyst XA-100, and we define μ_2 as the mean hourly yield obtained by using catalyst ZB-200. If the populations of all possible hourly yields for the catalysts are normally distributed, then a 95 percent confidence interval for $\mu_1 - \mu_2$ is

$$\left[(\bar{x}_1 - \bar{x}_2) \pm t_{.025}\sqrt{s_p^2\left(\frac{1}{n_1} + \frac{1}{n_2}\right)} \right]$$

$$= \left[(811 - 750.2) \pm 2.306\sqrt{435.1\left(\frac{1}{5} + \frac{1}{5}\right)} \right]$$

$$= [60.8 \pm 30.4217]$$

$$= [30.38, \ 91.22]$$

Here $t_{.025} = 2.306$ is based on $n_1 + n_2 - 2 = 5 + 5 - 2 = 8$ degrees of freedom. This interval tells us that we are 95 percent confident that the mean hourly yield obtained by using catalyst XA-100 is between 30.38 and 91.22 pounds higher than the mean hourly yield obtained by using catalyst ZB-200.

Suppose we wish to test a hypothesis about $\mu_1 - \mu_2$. In the following box we describe how this can be done. Here we test the null hypothesis $H_0: \mu_1 - \mu_2 = D_0$, where D_0 is a number whose value varies depending on the situation. Often D_0 will be the number 0. In such a case, the null hypothesis $H_0: \mu_1 - \mu_2 = 0$ says there is **no difference** between the population means μ_1 and μ_2. In this case, each alternative hypothesis in the box implies that the population means μ_1 and μ_2 differ in a particular way.

---

[3]All of the box plots presented in this chapter and in Chapter 11 have been obtained using MINITAB.
[4]We describe how to test the equality of two variances in Section 10.5 (although, as we will explain, this test has drawbacks).

A t Test about the Difference between Two Population Means: Equal Variances

Define the test statistic

$$t = \frac{(\bar{x}_1 - \bar{x}_2) - D_0}{\sqrt{s_p^2\left(\dfrac{1}{n_1} + \dfrac{1}{n_2}\right)}}$$

and assume that the sampled populations are normally distributed with equal variances. Then, if the samples are independent of each other, we can test $H_0: \mu_1 - \mu_2 = D_0$ versus a particular alternative hypothesis at level of significance α by using the appropriate critical value rule, or, equivalently, the corresponding p-value.

Alternative Hypothesis	Critical Value Rule: Reject H_0 If	p-Value (Reject H_0 If p-Value $< \alpha$)
$H_a: \mu_1 - \mu_2 > D_0$	$t > t_\alpha$	The area under the t distribution curve to the right of t
$H_a: \mu_1 - \mu_2 < D_0$	$t < -t_\alpha$	The area under the t distribution curve to the left of t
$H_a: \mu_1 - \mu_2 \neq D_0$	$|t| > t_{\alpha/2}$—that is, $t > t_{\alpha/2}$ or $t < -t_{\alpha/2}$	Twice the area under the t distribution curve to the right of $|t|$.

Here t_α, $t_{\alpha/2}$, and the p-values are based on $n_1 + n_2 - 2$ degrees of freedom.

EXAMPLE 10.4 The Catalyst Comparison Case

In order to compare the mean hourly yields obtained by using catalysts XA-100 and ZB-200, we will test $H_0: \mu_1 - \mu_2 = 0$ versus $H_a: \mu_1 - \mu_2 \neq 0$ at the **.05 level of significance.** To perform the hypothesis test, we will use the sample information in Table 10.1 to calculate the value of the **test statistic t in the summary box.** Then, because $H_a: \mu_1 - \mu_2 \neq 0$ is of the form $H_a: \mu_1 - \mu_2 \neq D_0$, we will **reject $H_0: \mu_1 - \mu_2 = 0$ if the absolute value of t is greater than $t_{\alpha/2} = t_{.025} = 2.306$.** Here the $t_{\alpha/2}$ point is based on $n_1 + n_2 - 2 = 5 + 5 - 2 = 8$ degrees of freedom. Using the data in Table 10.1, the **value of the test statistic is**

$$t = \frac{(\bar{x}_1 - \bar{x}_2) - D_0}{\sqrt{s_p^2\left(\dfrac{1}{n_1} + \dfrac{1}{n_2}\right)}} = \frac{(811 - 750.2) - 0}{\sqrt{435.1\left(\dfrac{1}{5} + \dfrac{1}{5}\right)}} = 4.6087$$

Because $|t| = 4.6087$ is greater than $t_{.025} = 2.306$, we can reject $H_0: \mu_1 - \mu_2 = 0$ in favor of $H_a: \mu_1 - \mu_2 \neq 0$. We conclude (at an α of .05) that the mean hourly yields obtained by using the two catalysts differ. Furthermore, the point estimate $\bar{x}_1 - \bar{x}_2 = 811 - 750.2 = 60.8$ says we estimate that the mean hourly yield obtained by using catalyst XA-100 is 60.8 pounds higher than the mean hourly yield obtained by using catalyst ZB-200.

Figures 10.2(a) and (b) give the MegaStat and Excel outputs for testing H_0 versus H_a. The outputs tell us that $t = 4.61$ and that the associated p-value is .001736 (rounded to .0017 on the MegaStat output). The very small p-value tells us that we have very strong evidence against $H_0: \mu_1 - \mu_2 = 0$ and in favor of $H_a: \mu_1 - \mu_2 \neq 0$. In other words, we have very strong evidence that the mean hourly yields obtained by using the two catalysts differ. Finally, notice that the MegaStat output gives the 95 percent confidence interval for $\mu_1 - \mu_2$, which is [30.378, 91.222].

FIGURE 10.2   **MegaStat and Excel Outputs for Testing the Equality of Means in the Catalyst Comparison Case Assuming Equal Variances**

(a) The MegaStat Output

Hypothesis Test: Independent Groups
(t-test, pooled variance)

XA-100	ZB-200			
811.00	750.20	mean	4.61	t
19.65	22.00	std. dev.	.0017	p-value (two-tailed)
5	5	n	30.378	confidence interval 95% lower
			91.222	confidence interval 95% upper

8	df		
60.800	difference (XA-100 - ZB-200)	**F-test for equality of variance**	
435.100	pooled variance	484.20	variance: ZB-200
20.859	pooled std. dev.	386.00	variance: XA-100
13.192	standard error of difference	1.25	F
0	hypothesized difference	.8314	p-value

(b) The Excel Output

t-Test: Two-Sample Assuming Equal Variances

	XA-100	ZB-200
Mean	811	750.2
Variance	386	484.2
Observations	5	5
Pooled Variance	435.1	
Hypothesized Mean Diff	0	
df	8	
t Stat	4.608706	
P(T<=t) one-tail	0.000868	
t Critical one-tail	1.859548	
P(T<=t) two-tail	0.001736	
t Critical two-tail	2.306004	

When the sampled populations are normally distributed and the population variances σ_1^2 and σ_2^2 differ, the following can be shown.

t-Based Confidence Intervals for $\mu_1 - \mu_2$, and t Tests about $\mu_1 - \mu_2$: Unequal Variances

1 When the sample sizes n_1 and n_2 are equal, the "equal variances" t-based confidence interval and hypothesis test given in the preceding two boxes are approximately valid even if the population variances σ_1^2 and σ_2^2 differ substantially. As a rough rule of thumb, if the larger sample variance is not more than three times the smaller sample variance when the sample sizes are equal, we can use the equal variances interval and test.

2 Suppose that the larger sample variance is more than three times the smaller sample variance when the sample sizes are equal or, suppose that both the sample sizes and the sample variances differ substantially. Then, we can use an approximate procedure that is sometimes called an "unequal variances" procedure. This procedure says that an **approximate 100$(1 - \alpha)$ percent confidence interval for $\mu_1 - \mu_2$** is

$$\left[(\bar{x}_1 - \bar{x}_2) \pm t_{\alpha/2} \sqrt{\frac{s_1^2}{n_1} + \frac{s_2^2}{n_2}} \right]$$

Furthermore, we can test $H_0: \mu_1 - \mu_2 = D_0$ by using the test statistic

$$t = \frac{(\bar{x}_1 - \bar{x}_2) - D_0}{\sqrt{\dfrac{s_1^2}{n_1} + \dfrac{s_2^2}{n_2}}}$$

and by using the previously given critical value and p-value conditions.

For both the interval and the test, the degrees of freedom are equal to

$$df = \frac{(s_1^2/n_1 + s_2^2/n_2)^2}{\dfrac{(s_1^2/n_1)^2}{n_1 - 1} + \dfrac{(s_2^2/n_2)^2}{n_2 - 1}}$$

Here, if df is not a whole number, we can round df down to the next smallest whole number.

In general, both the "equal variances" and the "unequal variances" procedures have been shown to be approximately valid when the sampled populations are only approximately normally distributed (say, if they are mound-shaped). Furthermore, although the above summary box might seem to imply that we should use the unequal variances procedure only if we cannot use the equal variances procedure, this is not necessarily true. In fact, since the unequal variances procedure can be shown to be a very accurate approximation whether or not the population variances are equal and for most sample sizes (here, both n_1 and n_2 should be at least 5), **many statisticians believe that it is best to use the unequal variances procedure in almost every situation.** If each of n_1 and n_2 is large (at least 30), both the equal variances procedure and the unequal variances procedure are approximately valid, no matter what probability distributions describe the sampled populations.

To illustrate the unequal variances procedure, consider the bank customer waiting time situation, and recall that $\mu_1 - \mu_2$ is the difference between the mean customer waiting time under the current system and the mean customer waiting time under the new system. Because of cost considerations, the bank manager wants to implement the new system only if it reduces the mean waiting time by more than three minutes. Therefore, the manager will test the **null hypothesis H_0: $\mu_1 - \mu_2 = 3$ versus the alternative hypothesis H_a: $\mu_1 - \mu_2 > 3$.** If H_0 can be rejected in favor of H_a at the **.05 level of significance,** the manager will implement the new system. Suppose that a random sample of $n_1 = 100$ waiting times observed under the current system gives a sample mean $\bar{x}_1 = 8.79$ and a sample variance $s_1^2 = 4.8237$. Further, suppose a random sample of $n_2 = 100$ waiting times observed during the trial run of the new system yields a sample mean $\bar{x}_2 = 5.14$ and a sample variance $s_2^2 = 1.7927$. Since each sample is large, we can use the **unequal variances test statistic t in the summary box.** The degrees of freedom for this statistic are

$$
df = \frac{(s_1^2/n_1 + s_2^2/n_2)^2}{\dfrac{(s_1^2/n_1)^2}{n_1 - 1} + \dfrac{(s_2^2/n_2)^2}{n_2 - 1}}
$$

$$
= \frac{[(4.8237/100) + (1.7927/100)]^2}{\dfrac{(4.8237/100)^2}{99} + \dfrac{(1.7927/100)^2}{99}}
$$

$$
= 163.657
$$

which we will round down to 163. Therefore, because H_a: $\mu_1 - \mu_2 > 3$ is of the form H_a: $\mu_1 - \mu_2 > D_0$, we will **reject H_0: $\mu_1 - \mu_2 = 3$ if the value of the test statistic t is greater than $t_\alpha = t_{.05} = 1.65$** (which is based on 163 degrees of freedom and has been found using a computer). Using the sample data, the **value of the test statistic** is

$$
t = \frac{(\bar{x}_1 - \bar{x}_2) - 3}{\sqrt{\dfrac{s_1^2}{n_1} + \dfrac{s_2^2}{n_2}}} = \frac{(8.79 - 5.14) - 3}{\sqrt{\dfrac{4.8237}{100} + \dfrac{1.7927}{100}}} = \frac{.65}{.25722} = 2.53
$$

Because $t = 2.53$ is greater than $t_{.05} = 1.65$, we reject H_0: $\mu_1 - \mu_2 = 3$ in favor of H_a: $\mu_1 - \mu_2 > 3$. We conclude (at an α of .05) that $\mu_1 - \mu_2$ is greater than 3 and, therefore, that the new system reduces the mean customer waiting time by more than 3 minutes. Therefore, the bank manager will implement the new system. Furthermore, the point estimate $\bar{x}_1 - \bar{x}_2 = 3.65$ says that we estimate that the new system reduces mean waiting time by 3.65 minutes.

Figure 10.3 gives the MegaStat output of using the unequal variances procedure to test H_0: $\mu_1 - \mu_2 = 3$ versus H_a: $\mu_1 - \mu_2 > 3$. The output tells us that $t = 2.53$ and that the associated p-value is .0062. The very small p-value tells us that we have very strong evidence against H_0: $\mu_1 - \mu_2 = 3$ and in favor of H_a: $\mu_1 - \mu_2 > 3$. That is, we have very strong evidence that $\mu_1 - \mu_2$ is greater than 3 and, therefore, that the new system reduces the mean customer waiting time by more than 3 minutes. To find a 95 percent confidence interval for $\mu_1 - \mu_2$, note that we can use a computer to find that $t_{.025}$ based on 163 degrees of freedom is 1.97. It follows that the 95 percent confidence interval for $\mu_1 - \mu_2$ is

$$
\left[(\bar{x}_1 - \bar{x}_2) \pm t_{.025}\sqrt{\frac{s_1^2}{n_1} + \frac{s_2^2}{n_2}} \right] = \left[(8.79 - 5.14) \pm 1.97\sqrt{\frac{4.8237}{100} + \frac{1.7927}{100}} \right]
$$

$$
= [3.65 \pm .50792]
$$

$$
= [3.14, 4.16]
$$

This interval is given on the MegaStat output and says that we are 95 percent confident that the new system reduces the mean customer waiting time by between 3.14 minutes and 4.16 minutes.

FIGURE 10.3	MegaStat Output of the Unequal Variances Procedure for the Bank Customer Waiting Time Situation

Hypothesis Test: Independent Groups (t-test, unequal variance)

Current	New			
8.79	5.14	mean	163	df
2.1963	1.3389	std. dev.	3.65000	difference (Current - New)
100	100	n	0.25722	standard error of difference
			3	hypothesized difference
			2.53	t

F-test for equality of variance

		.0062	p-value (one-tailed, upper)
2.69	F	3.14208	confidence interval 95.% lower
1.46E-06	p-value	4.15792	confidence interval 95.% upper
		0.50792	half-width

FIGURE 10.4	MINITAB Output of the Unequal Variances Procedure for the Catalyst Comparison Case

Two-Sample T-Test and CI: XA-100, ZB-200

```
            N     Mean    StDev   SE Mean
XA-100      5     811.0    19.6      8.8
ZB-200      5     750.2    22.0      9.8

Difference = mu (XA-100) - mu (ZB-200)
Estimate for difference:   60.8000
95% CI for difference:  (29.6049, 91.9951)
T-Test of difference = 0 (vs not =):
   T-Value = 4.61      P-Value = 0.002   DF = 7
```

In general, the degrees of freedom for the unequal variances procedure will always be less than or equal to $n_1 + n_2 - 2$, the degrees of freedom for the equal variances procedure. For example, if we use the unequal variances procedure to analyze the catalyst comparison data in Table 10.1, we can calculate df to be 7.9. This is slightly less than $n_1 + n_2 - 2 = 5 + 5 - 2 = 8$, the degrees of freedom for the equal variances procedure. Figure 10.4 gives the MINITAB output of the unequal variances analysis of the catalyst comparison data. Note that MINITAB rounds df down to 7 and finds that a 95 percent confidence interval for $\mu_1 - \mu_2$ is [29.6049, 91.9951]. MINITAB also finds that the test statistic for testing $H_0: \mu_1 - \mu_2 = 0$ versus $H_a: \mu_1 - \mu_2 \neq 0$ is $t = 4.61$ and that the associated p-value is .002. These results do not differ by much from the results given by the equal variances procedure (see Figure 10.2).

To conclude this section, it is important to point out that if the sample sizes n_1 and n_2 are not large (at least 30), and if we fear that the sampled populations might be far from normally distributed, we can use a **nonparametric method.** One nonparametric method for comparing populations when using independent samples is the **Wilcoxon rank sum test.** This test is discussed in Bowerman, O'Connell, and Murphree (2009).

Exercises for Section 10.2

CONCEPTS

connect™

For each of the formulas described below, list all of the assumptions that must be satisfied in order to validly use the formula.

10.12 The confidence interval formula in the formula box on page 401.

10.13 The confidence interval formula in the formula box on page 404.

10.14 The hypothesis test described in the formula box on page 403.

10.15 The hypothesis test described in the formula box on page 404.

METHODS AND APPLICATIONS

Suppose we have taken independent, random samples of sizes $n_1 = 7$ and $n_2 = 7$ from two normally distributed populations having means μ_1 and μ_2, and suppose we obtain $\bar{x}_1 = 240$, $\bar{x}_2 = 210$, $s_1 = 5$, and $s_2 = 6$. Using the equal variances procedure, do Exercises 10.16, 10.17, and 10.18.

10.16 Calculate a 95 percent confidence interval for $\mu_1 - \mu_2$. Can we be 95 percent confident that $\mu_1 - \mu_2$ is greater than 20? Explain why we can use the equal variances procedure here.

10.17 Use critical values to test the null hypothesis $H_0: \mu_1 - \mu_2 \leq 20$ versus the alternative hypothesis $H_a: \mu_1 - \mu_2 > 20$ by setting α equal to .10, .05, .01, and .001. How much evidence is there that the difference between μ_1 and μ_2 exceeds 20?

10.18 Use critical values to test the null hypothesis $H_0: \mu_1 - \mu_2 = 20$ versus the alternative hypothesis $H_a: \mu_1 - \mu_2 \neq 20$ by setting α equal to .10, .05, .01, and .001. How much evidence is there that the difference between μ_1 and μ_2 is not equal to 20?

10.19 Repeat Exercises 10.16 through 10.18 using the unequal variances procedure. Compare your results to those obtained using the equal variances procedure.

10.20 The October 7, 1991, issue of *Fortune* magazine reported on the rapid rise of fees and expenses charged by mutual funds. Assuming that stock fund expenses and municipal bond fund expenses are each approximately normally distributed, suppose a random sample of 12 stock funds gives a mean annual expense of 1.63 percent with a standard deviation of .31 percent, and an independent random sample of 12 municipal bond funds gives a mean annual expense of 0.89 percent with a standard deviation of .23 percent. Let μ_1 be the mean annual expense for stock funds, and let μ_2 be the mean annual expense for municipal bond funds. Do parts *a*, *b*, and *c* by using the equal variances procedure. Then repeat *a*, *b*, and *c* using the unequal variances procedure. Compare your results.

a Set up the null and alternative hypotheses needed to attempt to establish that the mean annual expense for stock funds is larger than the mean annual expense for municipal bond funds. Test these hypotheses at the .05 level of significance. What do you conclude?

b Set up the null and alternative hypotheses needed to attempt to establish that the mean annual expense for stock funds exceeds the mean annual expense for municipal bond funds by more than .5 percent. Test these hypotheses at the .05 level of significance. What do you conclude?

c Calculate a 95 percent confidence interval for the difference between the mean annual expenses for stock funds and municipal bond funds. Can we be 95 percent confident that the mean annual expense for stock funds exceeds that for municipal bond funds by more than .5 percent? Explain.

10.21 In the book *Business Research Methods,* Donald R. Cooper and C. William Emory (1995) discuss a manager who wishes to compare the effectiveness of two methods for training new salespeople. The authors describe the situation as follows:

> The company selects 22 sales trainees who are randomly divided into two experimental groups—one receives type *A* and the other type *B* training. The salespeople are then assigned and managed without regard to the training they have received. At the year's end, the manager reviews the performances of salespeople in these groups and finds the following results:

	A Group	B Group
Average Weekly Sales	$\bar{x}_1 = \$1,500$	$\bar{x}_2 = \$1,300$
Standard Deviation	$s_1 = 225$	$s_2 = 251$

a Set up the null and alternative hypotheses needed to attempt to establish that type *A* training results in higher mean weekly sales than does type *B* training.

b Because different sales trainees are assigned to the two experimental groups, it is reasonable to believe that the two samples are independent. Assuming that the normality assumption holds, and using the equal variances procedure, test the hypotheses you set up in part *a* at levels of significance .10, .05, .01, and .001. How much evidence is there that type *A* training produces results that are superior to those of type *B*?

c Use the equal variances procedure to calculate a 95 percent confidence interval for the difference between the mean weekly sales obtained when type *A* training is used and the mean weekly sales obtained when type *B* training is used. Interpret this interval.

10.22 A marketing research firm wishes to compare the prices charged by two supermarket chains—Miller's and Albert's. The research firm, using a standardized one-week shopping plan (grocery list), makes identical purchases at 10 of each chain's stores. The stores for each chain are randomly selected, and all purchases are made during a single week.

The shopping expenses obtained at the two chains, along with box plots of the expenses, are as follows: ● ShopExp

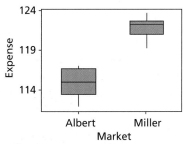

Miller's

$119.25 $121.32 $122.34 $120.14 $122.19
$123.71 $121.72 $122.42 $123.63 $122.44

Albert's

$111.99 $114.88 $115.11 $117.02 $116.89
$116.62 $115.38 $114.40 $113.91 $111.87

Because the stores in each sample are different stores in different chains, it is reasonable to assume that the samples are independent, and we assume that weekly expenses at each chain are normally distributed.

a Letting μ_M be the mean weekly expense for the shopping plan at Miller's, and letting μ_A be the mean weekly expense for the shopping plan at Albert's, Figure 10.5 gives the MINITAB output of the test of H_0: $\mu_M - \mu_A = 0$ (that is, there is no difference between μ_M and μ_A) versus H_a: $\mu_M - \mu_A \neq 0$ (that is, μ_M and μ_A differ). Note that MINITAB has employed the

FIGURE 10.5   MINITAB Output of Testing the Equality of Mean Weekly Expenses at Miller's and
               Albert's Supermarket Chains (for Exercise 10.22)

```
Two-sample T for Millers vs Alberts

              N      Mean    StDev    SE Mean
Millers      10    121.92    1.40      0.44
Alberts      10    114.81    1.84      0.58

Difference = mu(Millers)- mu(Alberts)    Estimate for difference: 7.10900
95% CI for difference: (5.57350, 8.64450)
T-Test of diff = 0 (vs not =): T-Value = 9.73    P-Value = 0.000   DF = 18
Both use Pooled StDev = 1.6343
```

     equal variances procedure. Use the sample data to show that $\bar{x}_M = 121.92$, $s_M = 1.40$,
     $\bar{x}_A = 114.81$, $s_A = 1.84$, and $t = 9.73$.

b Using the t statistic given on the output and critical values, test H_0 versus H_a by setting α
     equal to .10, .05, .01, and .001. How much evidence is there that the mean weekly expenses at
     Miller's and Albert's differ?

c Figure 10.5 gives the p-value for testing H_0: $\mu_M - \mu_A = 0$ versus H_a: $\mu_M - \mu_A \neq 0$. Use the
     p-value to test H_0 versus H_a by setting α equal to .10, .05, .01, and .001. How much evidence
     is there that the mean weekly expenses at Miller's and Albert's differ?

d Figure 10.5 gives a 95 percent confidence interval for $\mu_M - \mu_A$. Use this confidence interval to
     describe the size of the difference between the mean weekly expenses at Miller's and Albert's.
     Do you think that these means differ in a practically important way?

e Set up the null and alternative hypotheses needed to attempt to establish that the mean weekly
     expense for the shopping plan at Miller's exceeds the mean weekly expense at Albert's by
     more than $5. Test the hypotheses at the .10, .05, .01, and .001 levels of significance. How
     much evidence is there that the mean weekly expense at Miller's exceeds that at Albert's by
     more than $5?

10.23 A large discount chain compares the performance of its credit managers in Ohio and Illinois by
     comparing the mean dollar amounts owed by customers with delinquent charge accounts in these
     two states. Here a small mean dollar amount owed is desirable because it indicates that bad credit
     risks are not being extended large amounts of credit. Two independent, random samples of
     delinquent accounts are selected from the populations of delinquent accounts in Ohio and Illinois,
     respectively. The first sample, which consists of 10 randomly selected delinquent accounts in
     Ohio, gives a mean dollar amount of $524 with a standard deviation of $68. The second sample,
     which consists of 20 randomly selected delinquent accounts in Illinois, gives a mean dollar
     amount of $473 with a standard deviation of $22.

a Set up the null and alternative hypotheses needed to test whether there is a difference between
     the population mean dollar amounts owed by customers with delinquent charge accounts in
     Ohio and Illinois.

b Figure 10.6 gives the MegaStat output of using the unequal variances procedure to test the
     equality of mean dollar amounts owed by customers with delinquent charge accounts in Ohio
     and Illinois. Assuming that the normality assumption holds, test the hypotheses you set up in
     part a by setting α equal to .10, .05, .01, and .001. How much evidence is there that the mean
     dollar amounts owed in Ohio and Illinois differ?

c Assuming that the normality assumption holds, calculate a 95 percent confidence interval for
     the difference between the mean dollar amounts owed in Ohio and Illinois. Based on this
     interval, do you think that these mean dollar amounts differ in a practically important way?

10.24 A loan officer compares the interest rates for 48-month fixed-rate auto loans and 48-month
     variable-rate auto loans. Two independent, random samples of auto loan rates are selected. A
     sample of eight 48-month fixed-rate auto loans had the following loan rates: ● AutoLoan

        8.29%   7.75%   7.50%   7.99%   7.75%   7.99%   9.40%   8.00%

     while a sample of five 48-month variable-rate auto loans had loan rates as follows:

        7.59%   6.75%   6.99%   6.50%   7.00%

a Set up the null and alternative hypotheses needed to determine whether the mean rates for
     48-month fixed-rate and variable-rate auto loans differ.

b Figure 10.7 gives the MegaStat output of using the equal variances procedure to test the
     hypotheses you set up in part a. Assuming that the normality and equal variances assumptions
     hold, use the MegaStat output and critical values to test these hypotheses by setting α equal to

FIGURE 10.6	MegaStat Output of Testing the Equality of Mean Dollar Amounts Owed for Ohio and Illinois (for Exercise 10.23)

Hypothesis Test: Independent Groups (t-test, unequal variance)

	Ohio	Illinois	
	524	473	mean
	68	22	std. dev.
	10	20	n

9 df
51.000 difference (Ohio - Illinois)
22.059 standard error of difference
0 hypothesized difference
2.31 t
.0461 p-value (two-tailed)

FIGURE 10.7	MegaStat Output of Testing the Equality of Mean Loan Rates for Fixed and Variable 48-Month Auto Loans (for Exercise 10.24)

Hypothesis Test: Independent Groups (t-test, pooled variance)

Fixed	Variable			
8.0838	6.9660	mean	11	df
0.5810	0.4046	std. dev.	1.11775	difference (Fixed - Variable)
8	5	n	0.27437	pooled variance

F-test for equality of variance

0.3376 variance: Fixed   0.52381 pooled std. dev.
0.1637 variance: Variable   0.29862 standard error of difference
2.06 F   0 hypothesized difference
.5052 p-value   3.74 t
                                          .0032 p-value (two-tailed)

.10, .05, .01, and .001. How much evidence is there that the mean rates for 48-month fixed- and variable-rate auto loans differ?

c Figure 10.7 gives the p-value for testing the hypotheses you set up in part a. Use the p-value to test these hypotheses by setting α equal to .10, .05, .01, and .001. How much evidence is there that the mean rates for 48-month fixed- and variable-rate auto loans differ?

d Calculate a 95 percent confidence interval for the difference between the mean rates for fixed- and variable-rate 48-month auto loans. Can we be 95 percent confident that the difference between these means is .4 percent or more? Explain.

e Use a hypothesis test to establish that the difference between the mean rates for fixed- and variable-rate 48-month auto loans exceeds .4 percent. Use α equal to .05.

10.3 Paired Difference Experiments ● ● ●

EXAMPLE 10.5 The Repair Cost Comparison Case

Home State Casualty, specializing in automobile insurance, wishes to compare the repair costs of moderately damaged cars (repair costs between $700 and $1,400) at two garages. One way to study these costs would be to take two independent samples (here we arbitrarily assume that each sample is of size $n = 7$). First we would randomly select seven moderately damaged cars that have recently been in accidents. Each of these cars would be taken to the first garage (garage 1), and repair cost estimates would be obtained. Then we would randomly select seven *different* moderately damaged cars, and repair cost estimates for these cars would be obtained at the second garage (garage 2). This sampling procedure would give us independent samples because the cars taken to garage 1 differ from those taken to garage 2. However, because the repair costs for moderately damaged cars can range from $700 to $1,400, there can be substantial differences in damages to moderately damaged cars. These differences might tend to conceal any real differences between repair costs at the two garages. For example, suppose the repair cost estimates for the cars taken to garage 1 are higher than those for the cars taken to garage 2. This difference might exist because garage 1 charges customers more for repair work than does garage 2. However, the difference could also arise because the cars taken to garage 1 are more severely damaged than the cars taken to garage 2.

To overcome this difficulty, we can perform a **paired difference experiment.** Here we could randomly select one sample of $n = 7$ moderately damaged cars. The cars in this sample would be taken to both garages, and a repair cost estimate for each car would be obtained at each garage. The advantage of the paired difference experiment is that the repair cost estimates at the two garages are obtained for the same cars. Thus, any true differences in the repair cost estimates would not be concealed by possible differences in the severity of damages to the cars.

Suppose that when we perform the paired difference experiment, we obtain the repair cost estimates in Table 10.2 (these estimates are given in units of $100). To analyze these data, we

TABLE 10.2 A Sample of $n = 7$ Paired Differences of the Repair Cost Estimates at Garages 1 and 2 (Cost Estimates in Hundreds of Dollars) ● Repair

Sample of $n = 7$ Damaged Cars	Repair Cost Estimates at Garage 1	Repair Cost Estimates at Garage 2	Sample of $n = 7$ Paired Differences
Car 1	$ 7.1	$ 7.9	$d_1 = -.8$
Car 2	9.0	10.1	$d_2 = -1.1$
Car 3	11.0	12.2	$d_3 = -1.2$
Car 4	8.9	8.8	$d_4 = .1$
Car 5	9.9	10.4	$d_5 = -.5$
Car 6	9.1	9.8	$d_6 = -.7$
Car 7	10.3	11.7	$d_7 = -1.4$
	$\bar{x}_1 = 9.329$	$\bar{x}_2 = 10.129$	$\bar{d} = -.8 = \bar{x}_1 - \bar{x}_2$
			$s_d^2 = .2533$
			$s_d = .5033$

calculate the difference between the repair cost estimates at the two garages for each car. The resulting **paired differences** are given in the last column of Table 10.2. The mean of the sample of $n = 7$ paired differences is

$$\bar{d} = \frac{-.8 + (-1.1) + (-1.2) + \cdots + (-1.4)}{7} = -.8$$

which equals the difference between the sample means of the repair cost estimates at the two garages

$$\bar{x}_1 - \bar{x}_2 = 9.329 - 10.129 = -.8$$

Furthermore, $\bar{d} = -.8$ (that is, $-\$80$) is the point estimate of

$$\mu_d = \mu_1 - \mu_2$$

the mean of the population of all possible paired differences of the repair cost estimates (for all possible moderately damaged cars) at garages 1 and 2—which is equivalent to μ_1, the mean of all possible repair cost estimates at garage 1, minus μ_2, the mean of all possible repair cost estimates at garage 2. This says we estimate that the mean of all possible repair cost estimates at garage 1 is $\$80$ less than the mean of all possible repair cost estimates at garage 2.

In addition, the variance and standard deviation of the sample of $n = 7$ paired differences

$$s_d^2 = \frac{\sum_{i=1}^{7}(d_i - \bar{d})^2}{7 - 1} = .2533$$

and

$$s_d = \sqrt{.2533} = .5033$$

are the point estimates of σ_d^2 and σ_d, the variance and standard deviation of the population of all possible paired differences.

In general, suppose we wish to compare two population means, μ_1 and μ_2. Also suppose that we have obtained two different measurements (for example, repair cost estimates) on the same n units (for example, cars), and suppose we have calculated the n paired differences between these measurements. Let $\bar{d}$ and s_d be the mean and the standard deviation of these n paired differences. If it is reasonable to assume that the paired differences have been randomly selected from a normally distributed (or at least mound-shaped) population of paired differences with mean μ_d and standard deviation σ_d, then the sampling distribution of

$$\frac{\bar{d} - \mu_d}{s_d/\sqrt{n}}$$

is a t distribution having $n - 1$ degrees of freedom. This implies that we have the following confidence interval for μ_d:

A Confidence Interval for the Mean, μ_d, of a Population of Paired Differences

Let μ_d be the mean of a **normally distributed population of paired differences**, and let $\bar{d}$ and s_d be the mean and standard deviation of a sample of n paired differences that have been randomly selected from the population. Then, a **100(1 − α) percent** confidence interval for $\mu_d = \mu_1 - \mu_2$ is

$$\left[\bar{d} \pm t_{\alpha/2} \frac{s_d}{\sqrt{n}} \right]$$

Here $t_{\alpha/2}$ is based on $(n-1)$ degrees of freedom.

EXAMPLE 10.6 The Repair Cost Comparison Case

Using the data in Table 10.2, and assuming that the population of paired repair cost differences is normally distributed, a 95 percent confidence interval for $\mu_d = \mu_1 - \mu_2$ is

$$\left[\bar{d} \pm t_{.025} \frac{s_d}{\sqrt{n}} \right] = \left[-.8 \pm 2.447 \frac{.5033}{\sqrt{7}} \right]$$

$$= [-.8 \pm .4654]$$

$$= [-1.2654, -.3346]$$

Here $t_{.025} = 2.447$ is based on $n - 1 = 7 - 1 = 6$ degrees of freedom. This interval says that Home State Casualty can be 95 percent confident that μ_d, the mean of all possible paired differences of the repair cost estimates at garages 1 and 2, is between −$126.54 and −$33.46. That is, we are 95 percent confident that μ_1, the mean of all possible repair cost estimates at garage 1, is between $126.54 and $33.46 less than μ_2, the mean of all possible repair cost estimates at garage 2.

We can also test a hypothesis about μ_d, the mean of a population of paired differences. We show how to test the null hypothesis

$$H_0: \mu_d = D_0$$

in the following box. Here the value of the constant D_0 depends on the particular problem. Often D_0 equals 0, and the null hypothesis $H_0: \mu_d = 0$ says that μ_1 and μ_2 do not differ.

Testing a Hypothesis about the Mean, μ_d, of a Population of Paired Differences

Let μ_d, $\bar{d}$, and s_d be defined as in the preceding box. Also, assume that the population of paired differences is normally distributed, and consider testing

$$H_0: \mu_d = D_0$$

by using the test statistic

$$t = \frac{\bar{d} - D_0}{s_d/\sqrt{n}}$$

We can test $H_0: \mu_d = D_0$ versus a particular alternative hypothesis at level of significance α by using the appropriate critical value rule, or, equivalently, the corresponding p-value.

Alternative Hypothesis	Critical Value Rule: Reject H_0 If	p-Value (Reject H_0 If p-Value $< \alpha$)
$H_a: \mu_d > D_0$	$t > t_\alpha$	The area under the t distribution curve to the right of t
$H_a: \mu_d < D_0$	$t < -t_\alpha$	The area under the t distribution curve to the left of t
$H_a: \mu_d \neq D_0$	$\|t\| > t_{\alpha/2}$—that is, $t > t_{\alpha/2}$ or $t < -t_{\alpha/2}$	Twice the area under the t distribution curve to the right of $\|t\|$

Here t_α, $t_{\alpha/2}$, and the p-values are based on $n - 1$ degrees of freedom.

EXAMPLE 10.7 The Repair Cost Comparison Case

Home State Casualty currently contracts to have moderately damaged cars repaired at garage 2. However, a local insurance agent suggests that garage 1 provides less expensive repair service that is of equal quality. Because it has done business with garage 2 for years, Home State has decided to give some of its repair business to garage 1 only if it has very strong evidence that μ_1, the mean repair cost estimate at garage 1, is smaller than μ_2, the mean repair cost estimate at garage 2—that is, if $\mu_d = \mu_1 - \mu_2$ is less than zero. Therefore, we will test $H_0: \mu_d = 0$ or, equivalently, $H_0: \mu_1 - \mu_2 = 0$, versus $H_a: \mu_d < 0$ or, equivalently, $H_a: \mu_1 - \mu_2 < 0$, at the **.01 level of significance.** To perform the hypothesis test, we will use the sample data in Table 10.2 to calculate the value of the **test statistic t in the summary box.** Because $H_a: \mu_d < 0$ is of the form $H_a: \mu_d < D_0$, we will **reject** $H_0: \mu_d = 0$ if the value of t is less than $-t_\alpha = -t_{.01} = -3.143$. Here the t_α point is based on $n - 1 = 7 - 1 = 6$ degrees of freedom. Using the data in Table 10.2, the **value of the test statistic is**

$$t = \frac{\bar{d} - D_0}{s_d/\sqrt{n}} = \frac{-.8 - 0}{.5033/\sqrt{7}} = -4.2053$$

Because $t = -4.2053$ is less than $-t_{.01} = -3.143$, we can reject $H_0: \mu_d = 0$ in favor of $H_a: \mu_d < 0$. We conclude (at an α of .01) that μ_1, the mean repair cost estimate at garage 1, is less than μ_2, the mean repair cost estimate at garage 2. As a result, Home State will give some of its repair business to garage 1. Furthermore, Figure 10.8(a), which gives the MINITAB output of this hypothesis test, shows us that the p-value for the test is .003. Since this p-value is very small, we have very strong evidence that H_0 should be rejected and that μ_1 is less than μ_2.

To demonstrate testing a "not equal to" alternative hypothesis, Figure 10.8(b) gives the MegaStat output of testing $H_0: \mu_d = 0$ versus $H_a: \mu_d \neq 0$. The output shows that the p-value for this two-tailed test is .0057. MegaStat will, of course, also perform the test of $H_0: \mu_d = 0$ versus $H_a: \mu_d < 0$. For this test (output not shown), MegaStat finds that the p-value is .0028 (or .003

FIGURE 10.8   MINITAB and MegaStat Outputs of Testing $H_0: \mu_d = 0$

(a) MINITAB output of testing $H_0: \mu_d = 0$ versus $H_a: \mu_d < 0$

```
Paired T for Garage1 - Garage2

              N       Mean       StDev     SE Mean
Garage1       7     9.3286      1.2500      0.4724
Garage2       7    10.1286      1.5097      0.5706
Difference    7   -0.800000    0.503322    0.190238

T-Test of mean difference = 0 (vs < 0):
                  T-Value = -4.21     P-Value = 0.003
```

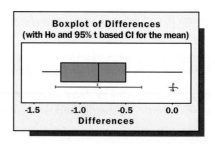

(b) MegaStat output of testing $H_0: \mu_d = 0$ versus $H_a: \mu_d \neq 0$

Hypothesis Test: Paired Observations

0.0000	hypothesized value
9.3286	mean Garage1
10.1286	mean Garage2
−0.8000	mean difference (Garage1 - Garage2)
0.5033	std. dev.
0.1902	std. error
7	n
6	df
−4.21	t
.0057	p-value (two-tailed)

FIGURE 10.9   Excel Output of Testing $H_0: \mu_d = 0$

t-Test: Paired Two Sample for Means

	Garage1	Garage2
Mean	9.328571	10.12857
Variance	1.562381	2.279048
Observations	7	7
Pearson Correlation	0.950744	
Hypothesized Mean	0	
df	6	
t Stat	−4.20526	
P(T<=t) one-tail	0.002826	
t Critical one-tail	1.943181	
P(T<=t) two-tail	0.005653	
t Critical two-tail	2.446914	

rounded). Finally, Figure 10.9 gives the Excel output of both the one- and two-tailed tests. The small p-value related to the one-tailed test tells us that Home State has very strong evidence that the mean repair cost at garage 1 is less than the mean repair cost at garage 2.

In general, an experiment in which we have obtained two different measurements on the same n units is called a **paired difference experiment.** The idea of this type of experiment is to remove the variability due to the variable (for example, the amount of damage to a car) on which the observations are paired. In many situations, a paired difference experiment will provide more information than an independent samples experiment. As another example, suppose that we wish to assess which of two different machines produces a higher hourly output. If we randomly select 10 machine operators and randomly assign 5 of these operators to test machine 1 and the others to test machine 2, we would be performing an independent samples experiment. This is because different machine operators test machines 1 and 2. However, any difference in machine outputs could be obscured by differences in the abilities of the machine operators. For instance, if the observed hourly outputs are higher for machine 1 than for machine 2, we might not be able to tell whether this is due to (1) the superiority of machine 1 or (2) the possible higher skill level of the operators who tested machine 1. Because of this, it might be better to randomly select five machine operators, thoroughly train each operator to use both machines, and have each operator test both machines. We would then be **pairing on the machine operator,** and this would remove the variability due to the differing abilities of the operators.

The formulas we have given for analyzing a paired difference experiment are based on the t distribution. These formulas assume that the population of all possible paired differences is normally distributed (or at least mound-shaped). If the sample size is large (say, at least 30), the t based interval and tests of this section are approximately valid no matter what the shape of the population of all possible paired differences. If the sample size is small, and if we fear that the population of all paired differences might be far from normally distributed, we can use a nonparametric method. One nonparametric method for comparing two populations when using a paired difference experiment is the **Wilcoxon signed ranks test.** This test is discussed in Bowerman, O'Connell, and Murphree (2009).

Exercises for Section 10.3

CONCEPTS

connect™

10.25 Explain how a paired difference experiment differs from an independent samples experiment in terms of how the data for these experiments are collected.

10.26 Why is a paired difference experiment sometimes more informative than an independent samples experiment? Give an example of a situation in which a paired difference experiment might be advantageous.

10.27 What assumptions must be satisfied to appropriately carry out a paired difference experiment? When can we carry out a paired difference experiment no matter what the shape of the population of all paired differences might be?

10.28 Suppose a company wishes to compare the hourly output of its employees before and after vacations. Explain how you would collect data for a paired difference experiment to make this comparison.

METHODS AND APPLICATIONS

10.29 Suppose a sample of 11 paired differences that has been randomly selected from a normally distributed population of paired differences yields a sample mean of $\bar{d} = 103.5$ and a sample standard deviation of $s_d = 5$.
    a Calculate 95 percent and 99 percent confidence intervals for $\mu_d = \mu_1 - \mu_2$. Can we be 95 percent confident that the difference between μ_1 and μ_2 exceeds 100? Can we be 99 percent confident?
    b Test the null hypothesis $H_0: \mu_d \leq 100$ versus $H_a: \mu_d > 100$ by setting α equal to .05 and .01. How much evidence is there that $\mu_d = \mu_1 - \mu_2$ exceeds 100?
    c Test the null hypothesis $H_0: \mu_d \geq 110$ versus $H_a: \mu_d < 110$ by setting α equal to .05 and .01. How much evidence is there that $\mu_d = \mu_1 - \mu_2$ is less than 110?

10.30 Suppose a sample of 49 paired differences that have been randomly selected from a normally distributed population of paired differences yields a sample mean of $\bar{d} = 5$ and a sample standard deviation of $s_d = 7$.

    a Calculate a 95 percent confidence interval for $\mu_d = \mu_1 - \mu_2$. Can we be 95 percent confident that the difference between μ_1 and μ_2 is greater than zero?

    b Test the null hypothesis $H_0: \mu_d = 0$ versus the alternative hypothesis $H_a: \mu_d \neq 0$ by setting α equal to .10, .05, .01, and .001. How much evidence is there that μ_d differs from zero? What does this say about how μ_1 and μ_2 compare?

    c The p-value for testing $H_0: \mu_d \leq 3$ versus $H_a: \mu_d > 3$ equals .0256. Use the p-value to test these hypotheses with α equal to .10, .05, .01, and .001. How much evidence is there that μ_d exceeds 3? What does this say about the size of the difference between μ_1 and μ_2?

10.31 On its website, the *Statesman Journal* newspaper (Salem, Oregon, 1999) reports mortgage loan interest rates for 30-year and 15-year fixed-rate mortgage loans for a number of Willamette Valley lending institutions. Of interest is whether there is any systematic difference between 30-year rates and 15-year rates (expressed as annual percentage rate or APR) and, if there is, what is the size of that difference. Table 10.3 displays mortgage loan rates and the difference between 30-year and 15-year rates for nine randomly selected lending institutions. Assuming that the population of paired differences is normally distributed: 🌐 Mortgage99

    a Set up the null and alternative hypotheses needed to determine whether there is a difference between mean 30-year rates and mean 15-year rates.

    b Figure 10.10 gives the MINITAB output for testing the hypotheses that you set up in part *a*. Use the output and critical values to test these hypotheses by setting α equal to .10, .05, .01, and .001. How much evidence is there that mean mortgage loan rates for 30-year and 15-year terms differ?

TABLE 10.3 **1999 Mortgage Loan Interest Rates for Nine Randomly Selected Willamette Valley Lending Institutions** 🌐 Mortgage99

Lending Institution	Annual Percentage Rate		
	30-Year	**15-Year**	**Difference**
American Mortgage N.W. Inc.	6.715	6.599	0.116
City and Country Mortgage	6.648	6.367	0.281
Commercial Bank	6.740	6.550	0.190
Landmark Mortgage Co.	6.597	6.362	0.235
Liberty Mortgage, Inc.	6.425	6.162	0.263
MaPS Credit Union	6.880	6.583	0.297
Mortgage Brokers, Inc.	6.900	6.800	0.100
Mortgage First Corp.	6.675	6.394	0.281
Silver Eagle Mortgage	6.790	6.540	0.250

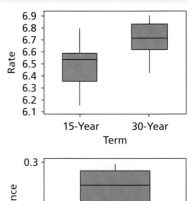

Source: Salem Homeplace Mortgage Rates Directory, http://www.salemhomeplace.com/pages/finance/, *Statesman Journal Newspaper*, Salem, Oregon, January 4, 1999.

FIGURE 10.10 **MINITAB Paired Difference *t* Test of the Mortgage Loan Rate Data (for Exercise 10.31)**

```
Paired T for 30-Year - 15-Year

             N       Mean        StDev       SE Mean
30-Year      9       6.70778     0.14635     0.04878
15-Year      9       6.48411     0.18396     0.06132
Difference   9       0.223667    0.072750    0.024250

95% CI for mean difference: (0.167746, 0.279587)
T-Test of mean difference = 0 (vs not = 0):
                         T-Value = 9.22   P-Value = 0.000
```

   c Figure 10.10 gives the *p*-value for testing the hypotheses that you set up in part *a*. Use the *p*-value to test these hypotheses by setting α equal to .10, .05, .01, and .001. How much evidence is there that mean mortgage loan rates for 30-year and 15-year terms differ?

   d Calculate a 95 percent confidence interval for the difference between mean mortgage loan rates for 30-year rates versus 15-year rates. Interpret this interval.

10.32 In the book *Essentials of Marketing Research,* William R. Dillon, Thomas J. Madden, and Neil H. Firtle (1993) present preexposure and postexposure attitude scores from an advertising study involving 10 respondents. The data for the experiment are given in Table 10.4. Assuming that the differences between pairs of postexposure and preexposure scores are normally distributed: ● AdStudy

   a Set up the null and alternative hypotheses needed to attempt to establish that the advertisement increases the mean attitude score (that is, that the mean postexposure attitude score is higher than the mean preexposure attitude score).

   b Test the hypotheses you set up in part *a* at the .10, .05, .01, and .001 levels of significance. How much evidence is there that the advertisement increases the mean attitude score?

   c Estimate the minimum difference between the mean postexposure attitude score and the mean preexposure attitude score. Justify your answer.

10.33 National Paper Company must purchase a new machine for producing cardboard boxes. The company must choose between two machines. The machines produce boxes of equal quality, so the company will choose the machine that produces (on average) the most boxes. It is known that there are substantial differences in the abilities of the company's machine operators. Therefore National Paper has decided to compare the machines using a paired difference experiment. Suppose that eight randomly selected machine operators produce boxes for one hour using machine 1 and for one hour using machine 2, with the following results: ● BoxYield

Machine Operator

	1	2	3	4	5	6	7	8
Machine 1	53	60	58	48	46	54	62	49
Machine 2	50	55	56	44	45	50	57	47

   a Assuming normality, perform a hypothesis test to determine whether there is a difference between the mean hourly outputs of the two machines. Use $\alpha = .05$.

   b Estimate the minimum and maximum differences between the mean outputs of the two machines. Justify your answer.

10.34 During 2004 a company implemented a number of policies aimed at reducing the ages of its customers' accounts. In order to assess the effectiveness of these measures, the company randomly selects 10 customer accounts. The average age of each account is determined for the years 2003 and 2004. These data are given in Table 10.5. Assuming that the population of paired differences between the average ages in 2004 and 2003 is normally distributed: ● AcctAge

   a Set up the null and alternative hypotheses needed to establish that the mean average account age has been reduced by the company's new policies.

TABLE 10.4   **Preexposure and Postexposure Attitude Scores (for Exercise 10.32)**   ● AdStudy

Subject	Preexposure Attitudes (A_1)	Postexposure Attitudes (A_2)	Attitude Change (d_i)
1	50	53	3
2	25	27	2
3	30	38	8
4	50	55	5
5	60	61	1
6	80	85	5
7	45	45	0
8	30	31	1
9	65	72	7
10	70	78	8

Source: W. R. Dillon, T. J. Madden, and N. H. Firtle, *Essentials of Marketing Research* (Burr Ridge, IL: Richard D. Irwin, 1993), p. 435. Copyright © 1993. Reprinted by permission of McGraw-Hill Companies, Inc.

TABLE 10.5   **Average Account Ages in 2003 and 2004 for 10 Randomly Selected Accounts (for Exercise 10.34)**   ● AcctAge

Account	Average Age of Account in 2004 (Days)	Average Age of Account in 2003 (Days)
1	27	35
2	19	24
3	40	47
4	30	28
5	33	41
6	25	33
7	31	35
8	29	51
9	15	18
10	21	28

FIGURE 10.11   **MegaStat and Excel Outputs of a Paired Difference Analysis of the Account Age Data (for Exercise 10.34)**

(a) The MegaStat Output

Hypothesis Test: Paired Observations

0.000	hypothesized value
27.000	mean Average age of account in 2004 (days)
34.000	mean Average age of account in 2003 (days)
−7.000	mean difference (2004 Average - 2003 Average)
6.128	std. dev.
1.938	std. error
10	n
9	df
−3.61	t
.0028	p-value (one-tailed, lower)

(b) The Excel Output

t-Test: Paired Two Sample for Means

	04 Age	03 Age
Mean	27	34
Variance	53.55556	104.2222
Observations	10	10
Pearson Correlation	0.804586	
Hypothesized Mean	0	
df	9	
t Stat	−3.61211	
P(T<=t) one-tail	0.00282	
t Critical one-tail	1.833114	
P(T<=t) Two-tail	0.005641	
t Critical two-tail	2.262159	

TABLE 10.6   **Weekly Study Time Data for Students Who Perform Well on the Midterm**   ⬤ StudyTime

Students	1	2	3	4	5	6	7	8
Before	15	14	17	17	19	14	13	16
After	9	9	11	10	19	10	14	10

b Figure 10.11 gives the MegaStat and Excel outputs needed to test the hypotheses of part *a*. Use critical values to test these hypotheses by setting α equal to .10, .05, .01, and .001. How much evidence is there that the mean average account age has been reduced?

c Figure 10.11 gives the *p*-value for testing the hypotheses of part *a*. Use the *p*-value to test these hypotheses by setting α equal to .10, .05, .01, and .001. How much evidence is there that the mean average account age has been reduced?

d Calculate a 95 percent confidence interval for the mean difference in the average account ages between 2004 and 2003. Estimate the minimum reduction in the mean average account ages from 2003 to 2004.

10.35 Do students reduce study time in classes where they achieve a higher midterm score? In a *Journal of Economic Education* article (Winter 2005), Gregory Krohn and Catherine O'Connor studied student effort and performance in a class over a semester. In an intermediate macroeconomics course, they found that "students respond to higher midterm scores by reducing the number of hours they subsequently allocate to studying for the course."[5] Suppose that a random sample of $n = 8$ students who performed well on the midterm exam was taken, and weekly study times before and after the exam were compared. The resulting data are given in Table 10.6. Assume that the population of all possible paired differences is normally distributed.

a Set up the null and alternative hypotheses to test whether there is a difference in the true mean study time before and after the midterm exam.

b Below we present the MINITAB output for the paired differences test. Use the output and critical values to test the hypotheses at the .10, .05 and .01 levels of significance. Has the true mean study time changed?

Paired T-Test and CI: StudyBefore, StudyAfter

```
Paired T for StudyBefore - StudyAfter
             N     Mean    StDev    SE Mean
StudyBefore  8   15.6250   1.9955   0.7055
StudyAfter   8   11.5000   3.4226   1.2101
Difference   8    4.12500  2.99702  1.05961

95% CI for mean difference: (1.61943, 6.63057)
T-Test of mean difference = 0 (vs not = 0): T-Value = 3.89   P-Value = 0.006
```

c Use the *p*-value to test the hypotheses at the .10, .05, and .01 levels of significance. How much evidence is there against the null hypothesis?

[5]Source: "Student Effort and Performance over the Semester," *Journal of Economic Education,* Winter 2005, pages 3–28.

10.4 Comparing Two Population Proportions by Using Large, Independent Samples ● ● ●

EXAMPLE 10.8 The Advertising Media Case   C

Suppose a new product was test marketed in the Des Moines, Iowa, and Toledo, Ohio, metropolitan areas. Equal amounts of money were spent on advertising in the two areas. However, different advertising media were employed in the two areas. Advertising in the Des Moines area was done entirely on television, while advertising in the Toledo area consisted of a mixture of television, radio, newspaper, and magazine ads. Two months after the advertising campaigns commenced, surveys are taken to estimate consumer awareness of the product. In the Des Moines area, 631 out of 1,000 randomly selected consumers are aware of the product, whereas in the Toledo area 798 out of 1,000 randomly selected consumers are aware of the product. We define p_1 to be the true proportion of consumers in the Des Moines area who are aware of the product and p_2 to be the true proportion of consumers in the Toledo area who are aware of the product. It follows that, since the sample proportions of consumers who are aware of the product in the Des Moines and Toledo areas are

$$\hat{p}_1 = \frac{631}{1,000} = .631$$

and

$$\hat{p}_2 = \frac{798}{1,000} = .798$$

then a point estimate of $p_1 - p_2$ is

$$\hat{p}_1 - \hat{p}_2 = .631 - .798 = -.167$$

This says we estimate that p_1 is .167 less than p_2. That is, we estimate that the percentage of consumers who are aware of the product in the Toledo area is 16.7 percentage points higher than the percentage in the Des Moines area.

In order to find a confidence interval for and to carry out a hypothesis test about $p_1 - p_2$, we need to know the properties of the sampling distribution of $\hat{p}_1 - \hat{p}_2$. In general, therefore, consider randomly selecting n_1 units from a population, and assume that a proportion p_1 of all the units in the population fall into a particular category. Let $\hat{p}_1$ denote the proportion of units in the sample that fall into the category. Also, consider randomly selecting a sample of n_2 units from a second population, and assume that a proportion p_2 of all the units in this population fall into the particular category. Let $\hat{p}_2$ denote the proportion of units in the second sample that fall into the category.

The Sampling Distribution of $\hat{p}_1 - \hat{p}_2$

If the randomly selected samples are independent of each other, then the population of all possible values of $\hat{p}_1 - \hat{p}_2$:

1   Approximately has a normal distribution if each of the sample sizes n_1 and n_2 is large. Here n_1 and n_2 are large enough if $n_1 p_1$, $n_1(1 - p_1)$, $n_2 p_2$, and $n_2(1 - p_2)$ are all at least 5.

2   Has mean $\mu_{\hat{p}_1 - \hat{p}_2} = p_1 - p_2$

3   Has standard deviation $\sigma_{\hat{p}_1 - \hat{p}_2} = \sqrt{\dfrac{p_1(1 - p_1)}{n_1} + \dfrac{p_2(1 - p_2)}{n_2}}$

If we estimate p_1 by $\hat{p}_1$ and p_2 by $\hat{p}_2$ in the expression for $\sigma_{\hat{p}_1 - \hat{p}_2}$, then the sampling distribution of $\hat{p}_1 - \hat{p}_2$ implies the following $100(1 - \alpha)$ percent confidence interval for $p_1 - p_2$.

A Large Sample Confidence Interval for the Difference between Two Population Proportions[6]

Suppose we randomly select a sample of size n_1 from a population, and let $\hat{p}_1$ denote the proportion of units in this sample that fall into a category of interest. Also suppose we randomly select a sample of size n_2 from another population, and let $\hat{p}_2$ denote the proportion of units in this second sample that fall into the category of interest. Then, if each of the sample sizes n_1 and n_2 is large ($n_1\hat{p}_1$, $n_1(1 - \hat{p}_1)$, $n_2\hat{p}_2$, and $n_2(1 - \hat{p}_2)$ must all be at least 5), and if the random samples are independent of each other, a **100(1 − α) percent confidence interval for $p_1 - p_2$** is

$$\left[(\hat{p}_1 - \hat{p}_2) \pm z_{\alpha/2} \sqrt{\frac{\hat{p}_1(1 - \hat{p}_1)}{n_1} + \frac{\hat{p}_2(1 - \hat{p}_2)}{n_2}} \right]$$

EXAMPLE 10.9 The Advertising Media Case   C

Recall that in the advertising media situation described at the beginning of this section, 631 of 1,000 randomly selected consumers in Des Moines are aware of the new product, while 798 of 1,000 randomly selected consumers in Toledo are aware of the new product. Also recall that

$$\hat{p}_1 = \frac{631}{1{,}000} = .631$$

and

$$\hat{p}_2 = \frac{798}{1{,}000} = .798$$

Because $n_1\hat{p}_1 = 1{,}000(.631) = 631$, $n_1(1 - \hat{p}_1) = 1{,}000(1 - .631) = 369$, $n_2\hat{p}_2 = 1{,}000(.798) = 798$, and $n_2(1 - \hat{p}_2) = 1{,}000(1 - .798) = 202$ are all at least 5, both n_1 and n_2 can be considered large. It follows that a 95 percent confidence interval for $p_1 - p_2$ is

$$\left[(\hat{p}_1 - \hat{p}_2) \pm z_{.025} \sqrt{\frac{\hat{p}_1(1 - \hat{p}_1)}{n_1} + \frac{\hat{p}_2(1 - \hat{p}_2)}{n_2}} \right]$$

$$= \left[(.631 - .798) \pm 1.96 \sqrt{\frac{(.631)(.369)}{1{,}000} + \frac{(.798)(.202)}{1{,}000}} \right]$$

$$= [-.167 \pm .0389]$$

$$= [-.2059, \ -.1281]$$

This interval says we are 95 percent confident that p_1, the proportion of all consumers in the Des Moines area who are aware of the product, is between .2059 and .1281 less than p_2, the proportion of all consumers in the Toledo area who are aware of the product. Thus, we have substantial evidence that advertising the new product by using a mixture of television, radio, newspaper, and magazine ads (as in Toledo) is more effective than spending an equal amount of money on television commercials only.

---

[6]More correctly, because $\hat{p}_1(1 - \hat{p}_1)/(n_1 - 1)$ and $\hat{p}_2(1 - \hat{p}_2)/(n_2 - 1)$ are unbiased point estimates of $p_1(1 - p_1)/n_1$ and $p_2(1 - p_2)/n_2$, a point estimate of $\sigma_{\hat{p}_1 - \hat{p}_2}$ is

$$s_{\hat{p}_1 - \hat{p}_2} = \sqrt{\frac{\hat{p}_1(1 - \hat{p}_1)}{n_1 - 1} + \frac{\hat{p}_2(1 - \hat{p}_2)}{n_2 - 1}}$$

and a 100(1 − α) percent confidence interval for $p_1 - p_2$ is $[(\hat{p}_1 - \hat{p}_2) \pm z_{\alpha/2} s_{\hat{p}_1 - \hat{p}_2}]$. Because both n_1 and n_2 are large, there is little difference between the interval obtained by using this formula and those obtained by using the formula in the box above.

To test the null hypothesis H_0: $p_1 - p_2 = D_0$, we use the test statistic

$$z = \frac{(\hat{p}_1 - \hat{p}_2) - D_0}{\sigma_{\hat{p}_1 - \hat{p}_2}}$$

A commonly employed special case of this hypothesis test is obtained by setting D_0 equal to zero. In this case, the null hypothesis H_0: $p_1 - p_2 = 0$ says there is **no difference** between the population proportions p_1 and p_2. When $D_0 = 0$, the best estimate of the common population proportion $p = p_1 = p_2$ is obtained by computing

$$\hat{p} = \frac{\text{the total number of units in the two samples that fall into the category of interest}}{\text{the total number of units in the two samples}}$$

Therefore, the point estimate of $\sigma_{\hat{p}_1 - \hat{p}_2}$ is

$$s_{\hat{p}_1 - \hat{p}_2} = \sqrt{\frac{\hat{p}(1 - \hat{p})}{n_1} + \frac{\hat{p}(1 - \hat{p})}{n_2}}$$

$$= \sqrt{\hat{p}(1 - \hat{p})\left(\frac{1}{n_1} + \frac{1}{n_2}\right)}$$

For the case where $D_0 \neq 0$, the point estimate of $\sigma_{\hat{p}_1 - \hat{p}_2}$ is obtained by estimating p_1 by $\hat{p}_1$ and p_2 by $\hat{p}_2$. With these facts in mind, we present the following procedure for testing H_0: $p_1 - p_2 = D_0$:

A Hypothesis Test about the Difference between Two Population Proportions

Let $\hat{p}$ be as just defined, and let $\hat{p}_1$, $\hat{p}_2$, n_1, and n_2 be as defined in the preceding box. Furthermore, define the test statistic

$$z = \frac{(\hat{p}_1 - \hat{p}_2) - D_0}{\sigma_{\hat{p}_1 - \hat{p}_2}}$$

and assume that each of the sample sizes n_1 and n_2 is large. Then, if the samples are independent of each other, we can test H_0: $p_1 - p_2 = D_0$ versus a particular alternative hypothesis at level of significance α by using the appropriate critical value rule, or, equivalently, the corresponding p-value.

Alternative Hypothesis	Critical Value Rule: Reject H_0 If	p-Value (Reject H_0 If p-Value $< \alpha$)
H_a: $p_1 - p_2 > D_0$	$z > z_\alpha$	The area under the standard normal curve to the right of z
H_a: $p_1 - p_2 < D_0$	$z < -z_\alpha$	The area under the standard normal curve to the left of z
H_a: $p_1 - p_2 \neq D_0$	$\lvert z \rvert > z_{\alpha/2}$—that is, $z > z_{\alpha/2}$ or $z < -z_{\alpha/2}$	Twice the area under the standard normal curve to the right of $\lvert z \rvert$

Note:

1   If $D_0 = 0$, we estimate $\sigma_{\hat{p}_1 - \hat{p}_2}$ by

$$s_{\hat{p}_1 - \hat{p}_2} = \sqrt{\hat{p}(1 - \hat{p})\left(\frac{1}{n_1} + \frac{1}{n_2}\right)}$$

2   If $D_0 \neq 0$, we estimate $\sigma_{\hat{p}_1 - \hat{p}_2}$ by

$$s_{\hat{p}_1 - \hat{p}_2} = \sqrt{\frac{\hat{p}_1(1 - \hat{p}_1)}{n_1} + \frac{\hat{p}_2(1 - \hat{p}_2)}{n_2}}$$

EXAMPLE 10.10 The Advertising Media Case

Recall that p_1 is the proportion of all consumers in the Des Moines area who are aware of the new product and that p_2 is the proportion of all consumers in the Toledo area who are aware of the new product. To test for the equality of these proportions, we will test H_0: $p_1 - p_2 = 0$ versus H_a: $p_1 - p_2 \neq 0$ at the .05 level of significance. Because both of the Des Moines and Toledo samples are large (see Example 10.9), we will calculate the value of the **test statistic z in the summary box** (where $D_0 = 0$). Since H_a: $p_1 - p_2 \neq 0$ is of the form H_a: $p_1 - p_2 \neq D_0$, we will **reject H_0: $p_1 - p_2 = 0$ if the absolute value of z is greater than $z_{\alpha/2} = z_{.05/2} = z_{.025} = 1.96$.** Because 631 out of 1,000 randomly selected Des Moines residents were aware of the product and 798 out of 1,000 randomly selected Toledo residents were aware of the product, the estimate of $p = p_1 = p_2$ is

$$\hat{p} = \frac{631 + 798}{1,000 + 1,000} = \frac{1,429}{2,000} = .7145$$

and the **value of the test statistic is**

$$z = \frac{(\hat{p}_1 - \hat{p}_2) - D_0}{\sqrt{\hat{p}(1 - \hat{p})(\frac{1}{n_1} + \frac{1}{n_2})}} = \frac{(.631 - .798) - 0}{\sqrt{(.7145)(.2855)(\frac{1}{1,000} + \frac{1}{1,000})}} = \frac{-.167}{.0202} = -8.2673$$

Because |z| = 8.2673 is greater than 1.96, we can reject H_0: $p_1 - p_2 = 0$ in favor of H_a: $p_1 - p_2 \neq 0$. We conclude (at an α of .05) that the proportions of consumers who are aware of the product in Des Moines and Toledo differ. Furthermore, the point estimate $\hat{p}_1 - \hat{p}_2 = .631 - .798 = -.167$ says we estimate that the percentage of consumers who are aware of the product in Toledo is 16.7 percentage points higher than the percentage of consumers who are aware of the product in Des Moines. The p-value for this test is twice the area under the standard normal curve to the right of $|z| = 8.2673$. Since the area under the standard normal curve to the right of 3.99 is .00003, the p-value for testing H_0 is less than 2(.00003) = .00006. It follows that we have extremely strong evidence that H_0: $p_1 - p_2 = 0$ should be rejected in favor of H_a: $p_1 - p_2 \neq 0$. That is, this small p-value provides extremely strong evidence that p_1 and p_2 differ. Figure 10.12 presents the MegaStat output of the hypothesis test of H_0: $p_1 - p_2 = 0$ versus H_a: $p_1 - p_2 \neq 0$ and of a 95 percent confidence interval for $p_1 - p_2$. A MINITAB output of the test and confidence interval is given in Appendix 10.1 on pages 435–436.

FIGURE 10.12   MegaStat Output of Statistical Inference in the Advertising Media Case

(a) Testing H_0: $p_1 - p_2 = 0$ versus H_a: $p_1 - p_2 \neq 0$

Hypothesis test for two independent proportions

p1	p2	pc		
0.631	0.798	0.7145	−0.167	difference
631/1000	798/1000	1429/2000	0.	hypothesized difference
631.	798.	1429. X	0.0202	std. error
1000	1000	2000 n	−8.27	z
			0.00E+00	p-value (two-tailed)

(b) 95 percent confidence interval for $p_1 - p_2$

Confidence Interval for $p_1 - p_2$

−0.2059	confidence interval 95.% lower
−0.1281	confidence interval 95.% upper
0.0389	half-width

Exercises for Section 10.4

CONCEPTS

10.36 Explain what population is described by the sampling distribution of $\hat{p}_1 - \hat{p}_2$.

10.37 What assumptions must be satisfied in order to use the methods presented in this section?

METHODS AND APPLICATIONS

In Exercises 10.38 through 10.40 we assume that we have selected two independent random samples from populations having proportions p_1 and p_2 and that $\hat{p}_1 = 800/1,000 = .8$ and $\hat{p}_2 = 950/1,000 = .95$.

10.38 Calculate a 95 percent confidence interval for $p_1 - p_2$. Interpret this interval. Can we be 95 percent confident that $p_1 - p_2$ is less than zero? That is, can we be 95 percent confident that p_1 is less than p_2? Explain.

10.39 Test H_0: $p_1 - p_2 = 0$ versus H_a: $p_1 - p_2 \neq 0$ by using critical values and by setting α equal to .10, .05, .01, and .001. How much evidence is there that p_1 and p_2 differ? Explain. Hint: $z_{.0005} = 3.29$.

10.40 Test H_0: $p_1 - p_2 \geq -.12$ versus H_a: $p_1 - p_2 < -.12$ by using a p-value and by setting α equal to .10, .05, .01, and .001. How much evidence is there that p_2 exceeds p_1 by more than .12? Explain.

10.41 In an article in the *Journal of Advertising,* Weinberger and Spotts compare the use of humor in television ads in the United States and in the United Kingdom. Suppose that independent random samples of television ads are taken in the two countries. A random sample of 400 television ads in the United Kingdom reveals that 142 use humor, while a random sample of 500 television ads in the United States reveals that 122 use humor.

  a Set up the null and alternative hypotheses needed to determine whether the proportion of ads using humor in the United Kingdom differs from the proportion of ads using humor in the United States.

  b Test the hypotheses you set up in part *a* by using critical values and by setting α equal to .10, .05, .01, and .001. How much evidence is there that the proportions of U.K. and U.S. ads using humor are different?

  c Set up the hypotheses needed to attempt to establish that the difference between the proportions of U.K. and U.S. ads using humor is more than .05 (five percentage points). Test these hypotheses by using a p-value and by setting α equal to .10, .05, .01, and .001. How much evidence is there that the difference between the proportions exceeds .05?

  d Calculate a 95 percent confidence interval for the difference between the proportion of U.K. ads using humor and the proportion of U.S. ads using humor. Interpret this interval. Can we be 95 percent confident that the proportion of U.K. ads using humor is greater than the proportion of U.S. ads using humor?

10.42 In the book *Essentials of Marketing Research,* William R. Dillon, Thomas J. Madden, and Neil H. Firtle discuss a research proposal in which a telephone company wants to determine whether the appeal of a new security system varies between homeowners and renters. Independent samples of 140 homeowners and 60 renters are randomly selected. Each respondent views a TV pilot in which a test ad for the new security system is embedded twice. Afterward, each respondent is interviewed to find out whether he or she would purchase the security system.

  Results show that 25 out of the 140 homeowners definitely would buy the security system, while 9 out of the 60 renters definitely would buy the system.

  a Letting p_1 be the proportion of homeowners who would buy the security system, and letting p_2 be the proportion of renters who would buy the security system, set up the null and alternative hypotheses needed to determine whether the proportion of homeowners who would buy the security system differs from the proportion of renters who would buy the security system.

  b Find the test statistic z and the p-value for testing the hypotheses of part *a*. Use the p-value to test the hypotheses with α equal to .10, .05, .01, and .001. How much evidence is there that the proportions of homeowners and renters differ?

  c Calculate a 95 percent confidence interval for the difference between the proportions of homeowners and renters who would buy the security system. On the basis of this interval, can we be 95 percent confident that these proportions differ? Explain.

  Note: A MegaStat output of the hypothesis test and confidence interval in parts *b* and *c* is given in Appendix 10.3 on page 439.

10.43 In the book *Cases in Finance,* Nunnally and Plath (1995) present a case in which the estimated percentage of uncollectible accounts varies with the age of the account. Here the age of an unpaid account is the number of days elapsed since the invoice date.

  An accountant believes that the percentage of accounts that will be uncollectible increases as the ages of the accounts increase. To test this theory, the accountant randomly selects independent samples of 500 accounts with ages between 31 and 60 days and 500 accounts with ages between 61 and 90 days from the accounts receivable ledger dated one year ago. When the sampled accounts are examined, it is found that 10 of the 500 accounts with ages between 31 and 60 days were eventually classified as uncollectible, while 27 of the 500 accounts with ages between 61 and 90 days were eventually classified as uncollectible. Let p_1 be the proportion of accounts with ages between 31 and 60 days that will be uncollectible, and let p_2 be the proportion of accounts with ages between 61 and 90 days that will be uncollectible. Use the MINITAB output below to determine how much evidence there is that we should reject H_0: $p_1 - p_2 = 0$ in favor of H_a: $p_1 - p_2 \neq 0$. Also, identify a 95 percent confidence interval for $p_1 - p_2$, and estimate the smallest that the difference between p_1 and p_2 might be.

Test and CI for Two Proportions

```
Sample                    X    N     Sample p
1 (31 to 60 days)        10   500    0.020000      Difference = p(1) - p(2)
2 (61 to 90 days         27   500    0.054000      Estimate for difference:  -0.034

95% CI for difference:   (-0.0573036, -0.0106964)
Test for difference = 0 (vs not = 0):  Z = -2.85    P-Value = 0.004
```

10.44   On January 7, 2000, the Gallup Organization released the results of a poll comparing the lifestyles of today with yesteryear. The survey results were based on telephone interviews with a randomly selected national sample of 1,031 adults, 18 years and older, conducted December 20–21, 1999. The poll asked several questions and compared the 1999 responses with the responses given in polls taken in previous years. Below we summarize some of the poll's results.[7]
Percentage of respondents who

1	Had taken a vacation lasting six days or more within the last 12 months:	**December 1999** 42%	**December 1968** 62%
2	Took part in some sort of daily activity to keep physically fit:	**December 1999** 60%	**September 1977** 48%
3	Watched TV more than four hours on an average weekday:	**December 1999** 28%	**April 1981** 25%
4	Drove a car or truck to work:	**December 1999** 87%	**April 1971** 81%

Assuming that each poll was based on a randomly selected national sample of 1,031 adults and that the samples in different years are independent:

a   Let p_1 be the December 1999 population proportion of U.S. adults who had taken a vacation lasting six days or more within the last 12 months, and let p_2 be the December 1968 population proportion who had taken such a vacation. Calculate a 99 percent confidence interval for the difference between p_1 and p_2. Interpret what this interval says about how these population proportions differ.

b   Let p_1 be the December 1999 population proportion of U.S. adults who took part in some sort of daily activity to keep physically fit, and let p_2 be the September 1977 population proportion who did the same. Carry out a hypothesis test to attempt to justify that the proportion who took part in such daily activity increased from September 1977 to December 1999. Use $\alpha = .05$ and explain your result.

c   Let p_1 be the December 1999 population proportion of U.S. adults who watched TV more than four hours on an average weekday, and let p_2 be the April 1981 population proportion who did the same. Carry out a hypothesis test to determine whether these population proportions differ. Use $\alpha = .05$ and interpret the result of your test.

d   Let p_1 be the December 1999 population proportion of U.S. adults who drove a car or truck to work, and let p_2 be the April 1971 population proportion who did the same. Calculate a 95 percent confidence interval for the difference between p_1 and p_2. On the basis of this interval, can it be concluded that the 1999 and 1971 population proportions differ?

10.45   In the book *International Marketing*, Philip R. Cateora reports the results of an MTV-commissioned study of the lifestyles and spending habits of the 14–34 age group in six countries. The survey results are given in Table 10.7.   ◐ PurchPct

a   As shown in Table 10.7, 96 percent of the 14- to 34-year-olds surveyed in the United States had purchased soft drinks in the last three months, while 90 percent of the 14- to 34-year-olds surveyed in Australia had done the same. Assuming that these results were obtained from

[7]Source: http://www.gallup.com/poll/releases/, PR991230.ASP. The Gallup Poll, December 30, 1999. © 1999 The Gallup Organization. All rights reserved.

TABLE 10.7   Results of an MTV-Commissioned Survey of the Lifestyles and Spending Habits of the 14–34 Age Group in Six Countries   ● PurchPct

Which of the Following Have You Purchased in the Past Three Months?

Product	Percentage in United States	Percentage in Australia	Percentage in Brazil	Percentage in Germany	Percentage in Japan	Percentage in United Kingdom
Soft drinks	96%	90%	93%	83%	91%	94%
Fast food	94	94	91	70	86	85
Athletic footwear	59	40	54	33	30	49
Blue jeans	56	39	62	45	42	44
Beer*	46	50	60	46	57	57
Cigarettes*	24	33	30	38	39	40

*Among adults 18+. Source: Yankelovich Clancy Shulman.

Source: Philip R. Cateora, *International Marketing*, 9th ed. (Burr Ridge, IL: Richard D. Irwin, 1993), p. 262. Copyright © 1993. Reprinted by permission of McGraw-Hill Companies, Inc.

independent random samples of 500 respondents in each country, carry out a hypothesis test that tests the equality of the population proportions of 14- to 34-year-olds in the United States and in Australia who have purchased soft drinks in the last three months. Also, calculate a 95 percent confidence interval for the difference between these two population proportions, and use this interval to estimate the largest and smallest values that the difference between these proportions might be. Based on your confidence interval, do you feel that this result has practical importance?

b Again as shown in Table 10.7, 40 percent of the 14- to 34-year-olds surveyed in Australia had purchased athletic footwear in the last three months, while 54 percent of the 14- to 34-year-olds surveyed in Brazil had done the same. Assuming that these results were obtained from independent random samples of 500 respondents in each country, carry out a hypothesis test that tests the equality of the population proportions of 14- to 34-year-olds in Australia and in Brazil who have purchased athletic footwear in the last three months. Also, calculate a 95 percent confidence interval for the difference between these two population proportions, and use this interval to estimate the largest and smallest values that the difference between these proportions might be. Based on your confidence interval, do you feel that this result has practical importance?

10.5 Comparing Two Population Variances by Using Independent Samples ● ● ●

We have seen (in Sections 10.1 and 10.2) that we often wish to compare two population means. In addition, it is often useful to compare two population variances. For example, in the bank waiting time situation of Example 10.1, we might compare the variance of the waiting times experienced under the current and new systems. Or, as another example, we might wish to compare the variance of the chemical yields obtained when using Catalyst XA-100 with those obtained when using Catalyst ZB-200. Here the catalyst that produces yields with the smaller variance is giving more consistent (or predictable) results.

If σ_1^2 and σ_2^2 are the population variances that we wish to compare, one approach is to test the null hypothesis

$$H_0: \ \sigma_1^2 = \sigma_2^2$$

We might test H_0 versus an alternative hypothesis of, for instance,

$$H_a: \ \sigma_1^2 > \sigma_2^2$$

Dividing by σ_2^2, we see that testing these hypotheses is equivalent to testing

$$H_0: \ \frac{\sigma_1^2}{\sigma_2^2} = 1 \qquad \text{versus} \qquad H_a: \ \frac{\sigma_1^2}{\sigma_2^2} > 1$$

CHAPTER 10

FIGURE 10.13 *F Distribution Curves and F Points*

(a) The point F_α corresponding to df_1 and df_2 degrees of freedom

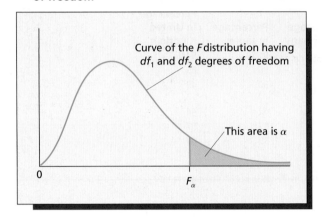

(b) The point $F_{.05}$ corresponding to 4 and 7 degrees of freedom

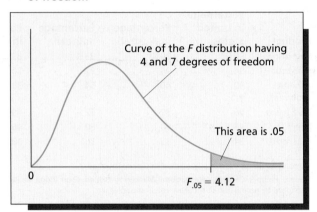

Intuitively, we would reject H_0 in favor of H_a if s_1^2/s_2^2 is significantly larger than 1. Here s_1^2 is the variance of a random sample of n_1 observations from the population with variance σ_1^2, and s_2^2 is the variance of a random sample of n_2 observations from the population with variance σ_2^2. To decide exactly how large s_1^2/s_2^2 must be in order to reject H_0, we need to consider the sampling distribution of s_1^2/s_2^2.[8]

It can be shown that, if the null hypothesis H_0: $\sigma_1^2/\sigma_2^2 = 1$ is true, then the population of all possible values of s_1^2/s_2^2 is described by what is called an **F distribution.** In general, as illustrated in Figure 10.13, the curve of the F distribution is skewed to the right. Moreover, the exact shape of this curve depends on two parameters that are called the **numerator degrees of freedom (denoted df_1)** and the **denominator degrees of freedom (denoted df_2).** The values of df_1 and df_2 that describe the sampling distribution of s_1^2/s_2^2 are given in the following result:

The Sampling Distribution of s_1^2/s_2^2

Suppose we randomly select independent samples from two normally distributed populations having variances σ_1^2 and σ_2^2. Then, if the null hypothesis H_0: $\sigma_1^2/\sigma_2^2 = 1$ is true, the population of all possible values of s_1^2/s_2^2 has an **F distribution** with $df_1 = (n_1 - 1)$ **numerator degrees of freedom** and with $df_2 = (n_2 - 1)$ **denominator degrees of freedom.**

In order to use the F distribution, we employ an **F point,** which is denoted F_α. As illustrated in Figure 10.13(a), **F_α is the point on the horizontal axis under the curve of the F distribution that gives a right-hand tail area equal to α.** The value of F_α in a particular situation depends on the size of the right-hand tail area (the size of α) and on the numerator degrees of freedom (df_1) and the denominator degrees of freedom (df_2). Values of F_α are given in an **F table.** Tables A.5, A.6, A.7, and A.8 (pages 644–647) give values of $F_{.10}$, $F_{.05}$, $F_{.025}$, and $F_{.01}$, respectively. Each table tabulates values of F_α according to the appropriate numerator degrees of freedom (values listed across the top of the table) and the appropriate denominator degrees of freedom (values listed down the left side of the table). A portion of Table A.6, which gives values of $F_{.05}$, is reproduced in this chapter as Table 10.8. For instance, suppose we wish to find the F point that gives a right-hand tail area of .05 under the curve of the F distribution having 4 numerator and

---

[8]Note that we divide by σ_2^2 to form a null hypothesis of the form H_0: $\frac{\sigma_1^2}{\sigma_2^2} = 1$ rather than subtracting σ_2^2 to form a null hypothesis of the form H_0: $\sigma_1^2 - \sigma_2^2 = 0$. This is because the population of all possible values of $s_1^2 - s_2^2$ has no known sampling distribution.

TABLE 10.8   A Portion of an *F* Table: Values of *F*.05

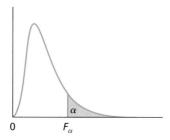

df_1 df_2	Numerator Degrees of Freedom, df_1								
	1	2	3	4	5	6	7	8	9
1	161.4	199.5	215.7	224.6	230.2	234.0	236.8	238.9	240.5
2	18.51	19.00	19.16	19.25	19.30	19.33	19.35	19.37	19.38
3	10.13	9.55	9.28	9.12	9.01	8.94	8.89	8.85	8.81
4	7.71	6.94	6.59	6.39	6.26	6.16	6.09	6.04	6.00
5	6.61	5.79	5.41	5.19	5.05	4.95	4.88	4.82	4.77
6	5.99	5.14	4.76	4.53	4.39	4.28	4.21	4.15	4.10
7	5.59	4.71	4.25	4.12	3.97	3.87	3.79	3.73	3.68
8	5.32	4.46	4.07	3.84	3.69	3.58	3.50	3.44	3.39
9	5.12	4.26	3.86	3.63	3.48	3.37	3.29	3.23	3.18
10	4.96	4.10	3.71	3.48	3.33	3.22	3.14	3.07	3.02
11	4.84	3.98	3.59	3.36	3.20	3.09	3.01	2.95	2.90
12	4.75	3.89	3.49	3.26	3.11	3.00	2.91	2.85	2.80
13	4.67	3.81	3.41	3.18	3.03	2.92	2.83	2.77	2.71
14	4.60	3.74	3.34	3.11	2.96	2.85	2.76	2.70	2.65
15	4.54	3.68	3.29	3.06	2.90	2.79	2.71	2.64	2.59
16	4.49	3.63	3.24	3.01	2.85	2.74	2.66	2.59	2.54
17	4.45	3.59	3.20	2.96	2.81	2.70	2.61	2.55	2.49
18	4.41	3.55	3.16	2.93	2.77	2.66	2.58	2.51	2.46
19	4.38	3.52	3.13	2.90	2.74	2.63	2.54	2.48	2.42
20	4.35	3.49	3.10	2.87	2.71	2.60	2.51	2.45	2.39
21	4.32	3.47	3.07	2.84	2.68	2.57	2.49	2.42	2.37
22	4.30	3.44	3.05	2.82	2.66	2.55	2.46	2.40	2.34
23	4.28	3.42	3.03	2.80	2.64	2.53	2.44	2.37	2.32
24	4.26	3.40	3.01	2.78	2.62	2.51	2.42	2.36	2.30
25	4.24	3.39	2.99	2.76	2.60	2.49	2.40	2.34	2.28
26	4.23	3.37	2.98	2.74	2.59	2.47	2.39	2.32	2.27
27	4.21	3.35	2.96	2.73	2.57	2.46	2.37	2.31	2.25
28	4.20	3.34	2.95	2.71	2.56	2.45	2.36	2.29	2.24
29	4.18	3.33	2.93	2.70	2.55	2.43	2.35	2.28	2.22
30	4.17	3.32	2.92	2.69	2.53	2.42	2.33	2.27	2.21
40	4.08	3.23	2.84	2.61	2.45	2.34	2.25	2.18	2.12
60	4.00	3.15	2.76	2.53	2.37	2.25	2.17	2.10	2.04
120	3.92	3.07	2.68	2.45	2.29	2.17	2.09	2.02	1.96
∞	3.84	3.00	2.60	2.37	2.21	2.10	2.01	1.94	1.88

Denominator Degrees of Freedom, df_2

Source: M. Merrington and C. M. Thompson, "Tables of Percentage Points of the Inverted Beta (*F*) Distribution," *Biometrika,* Vol. 33 (1943), pp. 73–88. Reproduced by permission of Oxford University Press and *Biometrika* trustees.

7 denominator degrees of freedom. To do this, we scan across the top of Table 10.8 until we find the column corresponding to 4 numerator degrees of freedom, and we scan down the left side of the table until we find the row corresponding to 7 denominator degrees of freedom. The table entry in this column and row is the desired F point. We find that the $F_{.05}$ point is 4.12 [see Figure 10.13(b)].

We now present the procedure for testing the equality of two population variances when the alternative hypothesis is one-tailed.

Testing the Equality of Population Variances versus a One-Tailed Alternative Hypothesis

Suppose we randomly select independent samples from two normally distributed populations—populations 1 and 2. Let s_1^2 be the variance of the random sample of n_1 observations from population 1, and let s_2^2 be the variance of the random sample of n_2 observations from population 2.

1 In order to test $H_0: \sigma_1^2 = \sigma_2^2$ versus $H_a: \sigma_1^2 > \sigma_2^2$, define the test statistic

$$F = \frac{s_1^2}{s_2^2}$$

and define the corresponding p-value to be the area to the right of F under the curve of the F distribution having $df_1 = n_1 - 1$ numerator degrees of freedom and $df_2 = n_2 - 1$ denominator degrees of freedom. We can reject H_0 at level of significance α if and only if

a $F > F_\alpha$ or, equivalently,

b p-value $< \alpha$.

Here F_α is based on $df_1 = n_1 - 1$ and $df_2 = n_2 - 1$ degrees of freedom.

2 In order to test $H_0: \sigma_1^2 = \sigma_2^2$ versus $H_a: \sigma_1^2 < \sigma_2^2$, define the test statistic

$$F = \frac{s_2^2}{s_1^2}$$

and define the corresponding p-value to be the area to the right of F under the curve of the F distribution having $df_1 = n_2 - 1$ numerator degrees of freedom and $df_2 = n_1 - 1$ denominator degrees of freedom. We can reject H_0 at level of significance α if and only if

a $F > F_\alpha$ or, equivalently,

b p-value $< \alpha$.

Here F_α is based on $df_1 = n_2 - 1$ and $df_2 = n_1 - 1$ degrees of freedom.

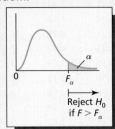

EXAMPLE 10.11 The Catalyst Comparison Case

Again consider the catalyst comparison situation of Example 10.3, and suppose the production supervisor wishes to use the sample data in Table 10.1 to determine whether σ_1^2, the variance of the chemical yields obtained by using Catalyst XA-100, is smaller than σ_2^2, the variance of the chemical yields obtained by using Catalyst ZB-200. To do this, the supervisor will test the null hypothesis

$$H_0: \sigma_1^2 = \sigma_2^2$$

which says the catalysts produce yields having the same amount of variability, versus the alternative hypothesis

$$H_a: \sigma_1^2 < \sigma_2^2 \qquad \text{or, equivalently,} \qquad H_a: \sigma_2^2 > \sigma_1^2$$

which says Catalyst XA-100 produces yields that are less variable (that is, more consistent) than the yields produced by Catalyst ZB-200. Recall from Table 10.1 that $n_1 = n_2 = 5$, $s_1^2 = 386$, and $s_2^2 = 484.2$. In order to test H_0 versus H_a, we compute the test statistic

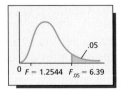

$$F = \frac{s_2^2}{s_1^2} = \frac{484.2}{386} = 1.2544$$

and we compare this value with F_α based on $df_1 = n_2 - 1 = 5 - 1 = 4$ numerator degrees of freedom and $df_2 = n_1 - 1 = 5 - 1 = 4$ denominator degrees of freedom. If we test H_0 versus H_a at the .05 level of significance, then Table 10.8 tells us that when $df_1 = 4$ and $df_2 = 4$, we have $F_{.05} = 6.39$. Because $F = 1.2544$ is not greater than $F_{.05} = 6.39$, we cannot reject H_0 at the .05 level of significance. That is, at the .05 level of significance we cannot conclude that σ_1^2 is less than σ_2^2. This says that there is little evidence that Catalyst XA-100 produces yields that are more consistent than the yields produced by Catalyst ZB-200.

FIGURE 10.14 Excel and MINITAB Outputs for Testing $H_0: \sigma_1^2 = \sigma_2^2$ in the Catalyst Comparison Case

(a) Excel output of testing $H_0: \sigma_1^2 = \sigma_2^2$ versus $H_a: \sigma_1^2 < \sigma_2^2$

F-Test Two-Sample for Variances

	ZB-200	XA-100
Mean	750.2	811
Variance	484.2	386
Observations	5	5
df	4	4
F	1.254404	
P(F<=f) one-tail	0.415724	
F Critical one-tail	6.388234	

(b) MINITAB output of testing $H_0: \sigma_1^2 = \sigma_2^2$ versus $H_a: \sigma_1^2 \neq \sigma_2^2$

```
           F-Test
   Test Statistic: 0.797
   P-Value       : 0.831
```

The *p*-value for testing H_0 versus H_a is the area to the right of $F = 1.2544$ under the curve of the F distribution having 4 numerator degrees of freedom and 4 denominator degrees of freedom. The Excel output in Figure 10.14(a) tells us that this *p*-value equals 0.415724. Since this *p*-value is large, we have little evidence to support rejecting H_0 in favor of H_a. That is, there is little evidence that Catalyst XA-100 produces yields that are more consistent than the yields produced by Catalyst ZB-200.

Again considering the catalyst comparison case, suppose we wish to test

$$H_0: \sigma_1^2 = \sigma_2^2 \quad \text{versus} \quad H_a: \sigma_1^2 \neq \sigma_2^2$$

One way to carry out this test is to compute

$$F = \frac{s_1^2}{s_2^2} = \frac{386}{484.2} = .797$$

As illustrated in Figure 10.15, if we set $\alpha = .10$, we compare F with the critical values $F_{.95}$ and $F_{.05}$ under the curve of the F distribution having $n_1 - 1 = 4$ numerator and $n_2 - 1 = 4$ denominator degrees of freedom. We see that we can easily find the appropriate upper-tail critical value to be $F_{.05} = 6.39$. In order to find the lower-tail critical value, $F_{.95}$, we use the following relationship:

$$F_{(1-\alpha)} \text{ with } df_1 \text{ numerator and } df_2 \text{ denominator degrees of freedom}$$

$$= \frac{1}{F_\alpha \text{ with } df_2 \text{ numerator and } df_1 \text{ denominator degrees of freedom}}$$

FIGURE 10.15 Critical Values for Testing $H_0: \sigma_1^2 = \sigma_2^2$ versus $H_a: \sigma_1^2 \neq \sigma_2^2$ with $\alpha = .10$

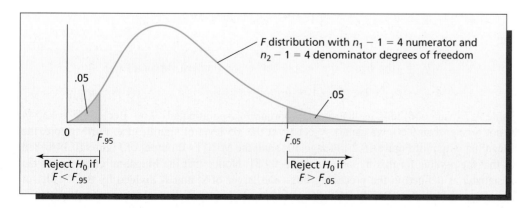

This says that for the F curve with 4 numerator and 4 denominator degrees of freedom, $F_{(1-.05)} = F_{.95} = 1/F_{.05} = 1/6.39 = .1565$. Therefore, because $F = .797$ is not greater than $F_{.05} = 6.39$ and since $F = .797$ is not less than $F_{.95} = .1565$, we cannot reject H_0 in favor of H_a at the .10 level of significance.

Although we can calculate the lower-tail rejection point for this hypothesis test as just illustrated, it is common practice to compute the test statistic F so that its value is always greater than 1. This means that we will always compare F with the upper-tail rejection point when carrying out the test. This can be done by always calculating F to be the larger of s_1^2 and s_2^2 divided by the smaller of s_1^2 and s_2^2. We obtain the following result:

Testing the Equality of Population Variances (Two-Tailed Alternative)

Suppose we randomly select independent samples from two normally distributed populations and define all notation as in the previous box. Then, in order to test H_0: $\sigma_1^2 = \sigma_2^2$ versus H_a: $\sigma_1^2 \neq \sigma_2^2$, define the test statistic

$$F = \frac{\text{the larger of } s_1^2 \text{ and } s_2^2}{\text{the smaller of } s_1^2 \text{ and } s_2^2}$$

and let

$df_1 = \{$the size of the sample having the largest variance$\} - 1$

$df_2 = \{$the size of the sample having the smallest variance$\} - 1$

Also, define the corresponding p-value to be twice the area to the right of F under the curve of the F distribution having df_1 numerator degrees of freedom and df_2 denominator degrees of freedom. We can reject H_0 at level of significance α if and only if

1 $F > F_{\alpha/2}$ or, equivalently,

2 p-value $< \alpha$.

Here $F_{\alpha/2}$ is based on df_1 and df_2 degrees of freedom.

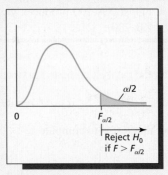

EXAMPLE 10.12 The Catalyst Comparison Case

In the catalyst comparison situation, we can reject H_0: $\sigma_1^2 = \sigma_2^2$ in favor of H_a: $\sigma_1^2 \neq \sigma_2^2$ at the .05 level of significance if

$$F = \frac{\text{the larger of } s_1^2 \text{ and } s_2^2}{\text{the smaller of } s_1^2 \text{ and } s_2^2} = \frac{484.2}{386} = 1.2544$$

is greater than $F_{\alpha/2} = F_{.05/2} = F_{.025}$. Here the degrees of freedom are

$$df_1 = \{\text{the size of the sample having the largest variance}\} - 1$$

$$= n_2 - 1 = 5 - 1 = 4$$

and

$$df_2 = \{\text{the size of the sample having the smallest variance}\} - 1$$

$$= n_1 - 1 = 5 - 1 = 4$$

Table A.7 (page 646) tells us that the appropriate $F_{.025}$ point equals 9.60. Because $F = 1.2544$ is not greater than 9.60, we cannot reject H_0 at the .05 level of significance. Furthermore, the MegaStat output of Figure 10.2(a) (page 404) and the MINITAB output of Figure 10.14(b) tell us that the p-value for this hypothesis test is 0.831. Notice that the MegaStat output gives the F statistic as defined in the preceding box—the larger of s_1^2 and s_2^2 divided by the smaller of s_1^2 and s_2^2, whereas the MINITAB output gives the reciprocal of this value (as we calculated on

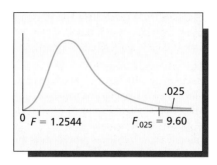

page 427). Since the p-value is large, we have little evidence that the consistencies of the yields produced by Catalysts XA-100 and ZB-200 differ.

It has been suggested that the F test of H_0: $\sigma_1^2 = \sigma_2^2$ be used to choose between the equal variances and unequal variances t based procedures when comparing two means (as described in Section 10.2). Certainly the F test is one approach to making this choice. However, studies have shown that the validity of the F test is very sensitive to violations of the normality assumption—much more sensitive, in fact, than the equal variances procedure is to violations of the equal variances assumption. While opinions vary, some statisticians believe that this is a serious problem and that the F test should never be used to choose between the equal variances and unequal variances procedures. Others feel that performing the test for this purpose is reasonable if the test's limitations are kept in mind.

As an example for those who believe that using the F test is reasonable, we found in Example 10.12 that we do not reject H_0: $\sigma_1^2 = \sigma_2^2$ at the .05 level of significance in the context of the catalyst comparison situation. Further, the p-value related to the F test, which equals 0.831, tells us that there is little evidence to suggest that the population variances differ. It follows that it might be reasonable to compare the mean yields of the catalysts by using the equal variances procedures (as we have done in Examples 10.3 and 10.4).

Exercises for Section 10.5

CONCEPTS

10.46   Explain what population is described by the sampling distribution of s_1^2/s_2^2.

10.47   Intuitively explain why a value of s_1^2/s_2^2 that is substantially greater than 1 provides evidence that σ_1^2 is not equal to σ_2^2.

connect™

METHODS AND APPLICATIONS

10.48   Use Table 10.8 to find the $F_{.05}$ point for each of the following:
  a $df_1 = 3$ numerator degrees of freedom and $df_2 = 14$ denominator degrees of freedom.
  b $df_1 = 6$ and $df_2 = 10$.
  c $df_1 = 2$ and $df_2 = 22$.
  d $df_1 = 7$ and $df_2 = 5$.

10.49   Use Tables A.5, A.6, A.7, and A.8 (pages 644–647) to find the following F_α points:
  a $F_{.10}$ with $df_1 = 4$ numerator degrees of freedom and $df_2 = 7$ denominator degrees of freedom.
  b $F_{.01}$ with $df_1 = 3$ and $df_2 = 25$.
  c $F_{.025}$ with $df_1 = 7$ and $df_2 = 17$.
  d $F_{.05}$ with $df_1 = 9$ and $df_2 = 3$.

10.50   Suppose two independent random samples of sizes $n_1 = 9$ and $n_2 = 7$ that have been taken from two normally distributed populations having variances σ_1^2 and σ_2^2 give sample variances of $s_1^2 = 100$ and $s_2^2 = 20$.
  a   Test H_0: $\sigma_1^2 = \sigma_2^2$ versus H_a: $\sigma_1^2 \neq \sigma_2^2$ with $\alpha = .05$. What do you conclude?
  b   Test H_0: $\sigma_1^2 \leq \sigma_2^2$ versus H_a: $\sigma_1^2 > \sigma_2^2$ with $\alpha = .05$. What do you conclude?

10.51   Suppose two independent random samples of sizes $n_1 = 5$ and $n_2 = 16$ that have been taken from two normally distributed populations having variances σ_1^2 and σ_2^2 give sample standard deviations of $s_1 = 5$ and $s_2 = 9$.
  a   Test H_0: $\sigma_1^2 = \sigma_2^2$ versus H_a: $\sigma_1^2 \neq \sigma_2^2$ with $\alpha = .05$. What do you conclude?
  b   Test H_0: $\sigma_1^2 \geq \sigma_2^2$ versus H_a: $\sigma_1^2 < \sigma_2^2$ with $\alpha = .01$. What do you conclude?

10.52 Consider the situation of Exercise 10.23 (page 408). Use the sample information to test $H_0\colon \sigma_1^2 = \sigma_2^2$ versus $H_a\colon \sigma_1^2 \neq \sigma_2^2$ with $\alpha = .05$. Based on this test, does it make sense to believe that the unequal variances procedure is appropriate? Explain.

10.53 Consider the situation of Exercise 10.24 (page 408). ● AutoLoan
  a Use the MegaStat output in Figure 10.7 (page 409) and a critical value to test $H_0\colon \sigma_1^2 = \sigma_2^2$ versus $H_a\colon \sigma_1^2 \neq \sigma_2^2$ with $\alpha = .05$. What do you conclude?
  b Use a p-value on the MegaStat output in Figure 10.7 to test $H_0\colon \sigma_1^2 = \sigma_2^2$ versus $H_a\colon \sigma_1^2 \neq \sigma_2^2$ with $\alpha = .05$. What do you conclude?
  c Does it make sense to use the equal variances procedure in this situation?
  d Hand calculate the value of the F statistic for testing $H_0\colon \sigma_1^2 = \sigma_2^2$. Show that your result turns out to be the same as the F statistic given in Figure 10.7.

Chapter Summary

This chapter has explained **how to compare two populations** by using confidence intervals and hypothesis tests. First we discussed how to compare **two population means** by using **independent samples.** Here the measurements in one sample are not related to the measurements in the other sample. We saw that in the unlikely event that the population variances are known, a *z*-**based** inference can be made. When these variances are unknown, *t*-**based** inferences are appropriate if the populations are normally distributed or the sample sizes are large. Both **equal variances and unequal variances *t*-based procedures** exist. We learned that, because it can be difficult to compare the population variances, many statisticians believe that it is almost always best to use the unequal variances procedure.

Sometimes samples are not independent. We learned that one such case is what is called a **paired difference experiment.** Here we obtain two different measurements on the same sample units, and we can compare two population means by using a confidence interval or by conducting a hypothesis test that employs the differences between the pairs of measurements. We next explained how to compare **two population proportions** by using **large, independent samples.** Finally, we concluded this chapter by discussing how to compare **two population variances** by using independent samples, and we learned that this comparison is done by using a test based on the ***F* distribution.**

Glossary of Terms

***F* distribution:** A continuous probability curve having a shape that depends on two parameters—the numerator degrees of freedom, df_1, and the denominator degrees of freedom, df_2. (pages 424–425)
independent samples experiment: An experiment in which there is no relationship between the measurements in the different samples. (page 396)
paired difference experiment: An experiment in which two different measurements are taken on the same units and inferences are made using the differences between the pairs of measurements. (page 413)
sampling distribution of $\hat{p}_1 - \hat{p}_2$: The probability distribution that describes the population of all possible values of $\hat{p}_1 - \hat{p}_2$, where $\hat{p}_1$ is the sample proportion for a random sample taken

from one population and $\hat{p}_2$ is the sample proportion for a random sample taken from a second population. (page 417)
sampling distribution of s_1^2/s_2^2: The probability distribution that describes the population of all possible values of s_1^2/s_2^2, where s_1^2 is the sample variance of a random sample taken from one population and s_2^2 is the sample variance of a random sample taken from a second population. (page 424)
sampling distribution of $\bar{x}_1 - \bar{x}_2$: The probability distribution that describes the population of all possible values of $\bar{x}_1 - \bar{x}_2$, where $\bar{x}_1$ is the sample mean of a random sample taken from one population and $\bar{x}_2$ is the sample mean of a random sample taken from a second population. (page 396)

Important Formulas and Tests

Sampling distribution of $\bar{x}_1 - \bar{x}_2$ (independent random samples): page 396

z-based confidence interval for $\mu_1 - \mu_2$: page 396

z test about $\mu_1 - \mu_2$: page 397

t-based confidence interval for $\mu_1 - \mu_2$ when $\sigma_1^2 = \sigma_2^2$: page 401

t test about $\mu_1 - \mu_2$ when $\sigma_1^2 = \sigma_2^2$: page 403

t-based confidence interval for $\mu_1 - \mu_2$ when $\sigma_1^2 \neq \sigma_2^2$: page 404

t test about $\mu_1 - \mu_2$ when $\sigma_1^2 \neq \sigma_2^2$: page 404

Confidence interval for μ_d: page 411

A hypothesis test about μ_d: page 411

Sampling distribution of $\hat{p}_1 - \hat{p}_2$ (independent random samples): page 417

Large sample confidence interval for $p_1 - p_2$: page 418

Large sample hypothesis test about $p_1 - p_2$: page 419

Sampling distribution of s_1^2/s_2^2 (independent random samples): page 424

A hypothesis test about the equality of σ_1^2 and σ_2^2: pages 426 and 428

Supplementary Exercises

10.54   In its February 2, 1998, issue, *Fortune* magazine published the results of a Yankelovich Partners survey of 600 adults that investigated their ideas about marriage, divorce, and the contributions of the corporate wife. The survey results are shown in Figure 10.16. For each statement in the figure, the proportions of men and women who agreed with the statement are given. Assuming that the survey results were obtained from independent random samples of 300 men and 300 women:

   a   For each statement, carry out a hypothesis test that tests the equality of the population proportions of men and women who agree with the statement. Use α equal to .10, .05, .01, and .001. How much evidence is there that the population proportions of men and women who agree with each statement differ?

   b   For each statement, calculate a 95 percent confidence interval for the difference between the population proportion of men who agree with the statement and the population proportion of women who agree with the statement. Use the interval to help assess whether you feel that the difference between population proportions has practical significance.

Exercises 10.55 and 10.56 deal with the following situation:

   In an article in the *Journal of Retailing,* Kumar, Kerwin, and Pereira study factors affecting merger and acquisition activity in retailing by comparing "target firms" and "bidder firms" with respect to several financial and marketing-related variables. If we consider two of the financial variables included in the study, suppose a random sample of 36 "target firms" gives a mean earnings per share of $1.52 with a standard deviation of $0.92, and that this sample gives a mean debt-to-equity ratio of 1.66 with a standard deviation of 0.82. Furthermore, an independent random sample of 36 "bidder firms" gives a mean earnings per share of $1.20 with a standard deviation of $0.84, and this sample gives a mean debt-to-equity ratio of 1.58 with a standard deviation of 0.81.

10.55   **a**   Set up the null and alternative hypotheses needed to test whether the mean earnings per share for all "target firms" differs from the mean earnings per share for all "bidder firms." Test these hypotheses at the .10, .05, .01, and .001 levels of significance. How much evidence is there that these means differ? Explain.

   b   Calculate a 95 percent confidence interval for the difference between the mean earnings per share for "target firms" and "bidder firms." Interpret the interval.

F I G U R E   1 0 . 1 6   **The Results of a Yankelovich Partners Survey of 600 Adults on Marriage, Divorce, and the Contributions of the Corporate Wife (All Respondents with Income $50,000 or More)**

People were magnanimous on the general proposition:

- In a divorce in a long-term marriage where the husband works outside the home and the wife is not employed for pay, the wife should be entitled to half the assets accumulated during the marriage.
  93% of women agree
  85% of men agree

But when we got to the goodies, a gender gap began to appear . . .

- The pension accumulated during the marriage should be split evenly.
  80% of women agree
  68% of men agree
- Stock options granted during the marriage should be split evenly.
  77% of women agree
  62% of men agree

. . . and turned into a chasm over the issue of how important a stay-at-home wife is to a husband's success.

- Managing the household and child rearing are extremely important to a husband's success.
  57% of women agree
  41% of men agree
- A corporate wife who also must travel, entertain, and act as a sounding board is extremely important to the success of a high-level business executive.
  51% of women agree
  28% of men agree
- The lifestyle of a corporate wife is more of a job than a luxury.
  73% of women agree
  57% of men agree

Source: Reprinted from the February 2, 1998, issue of *Fortune.* Copyright 1998 Time, Inc. Reprinted by permission.

10.56 **a** Set up the null and alternative hypotheses needed to test whether the mean debt-to-equity ratio for all "target firms" differs from the mean debt-to-equity ratio for all "bidder firms." Test these hypotheses at the .10, .05, .01, and .001 levels of significance. How much evidence is there that these means differ? Explain.

b Calculate a 95 percent confidence interval for the difference between the mean debt-to-equity ratios for "target firms" and "bidder firms." Interpret the interval.

c Based on the results of this exercise and Exercise 10.55, does a firm's earnings per share or the firm's debt-to-equity ratio seem to have the most influence on whether a firm will be a "target" or a "bidder"? Explain.

10.57 What impact did the September 11, 2001, terrorist attacks have on U.S. airline demand? An analysis was conducted by Ito and Lee, "Assessing the Impact of the September 11 Terrorist Attacks on U.S. Airline Demand," in the *Journal of Economics and Business* (January–February 2005). They found a negative short-term effect of over 30 percent and an ongoing negative impact of over 7 percent. Suppose that we wish to test the impact by taking a random sample of 12 airline routes before and after 9/11. Passenger miles (millions of passenger miles) for the same routes were tracked for the 12 months prior to and the 12 months immediately following 9/11. Assume that the population of all possible paired differences is normally distributed.

a Set up the null and alternative hypotheses needed to determine whether there was a reduction in mean airline passenger demand.

b Below we present the MINITAB output for the paired differences test. Use the output and critical values to test the hypotheses at the .10, .05, and .01 levels of significance. Has the true mean airline demand been reduced?

Paired T-Test and CI: Before911, After911

```
Paired T for Before911 - After911
              N     Mean     StDev   SE Mean
Before911     12   117.333   26.976   7.787
After911      12    87.583   25.518   7.366
Difference    12    29.7500  10.3056  2.9750

T-Test of mean difference = 0 (vs > 0): T-Value = 10.00   P-Value = 0.000
```

c Use the *p*-value to test the hypotheses at the .10, .05, and .01 levels of significance. How much evidence is there against the null hypothesis?

10.58 In the book *Essentials of Marketing Research,* William R. Dillon, Thomas J. Madden, and Neil H. Firtle discuss evaluating the effectiveness of a test coupon. Samples of 500 test coupons and 500 control coupons were randomly delivered to shoppers. The results indicated that 35 of the 500 control coupons were redeemed, while 50 of the 500 test coupons were redeemed.

a In order to consider the test coupon for use, the marketing research organization required that the proportion of all shoppers who would redeem the test coupon be statistically shown to be greater than the proportion of all shoppers who would redeem the control coupon. Assuming that the two samples of shoppers are independent, carry out a hypothesis test at the .01 level of significance that will show whether this requirement is met by the test coupon. Explain your conclusion.

b Use the sample data to find a point estimate and a 95 percent interval estimate of the difference between the proportions of all shoppers who would redeem the test coupon and the control coupon. What does this interval say about whether the test coupon should be considered for use? Explain.

c Carry out the test of part *a* at the .10 level of significance. What do you conclude? Is your result statistically significant? Compute a 90 percent interval estimate instead of the 95 percent interval estimate of part *b*. Based on the interval estimate, do you feel that this result is practically important? Explain.

10.59 A marketing manager wishes to compare the mean prices charged for two brands of CD players. The manager conducts a random survey of retail outlets and obtains independent random samples of prices with the following results:

	Onkyo	JVC
Sample mean, $\bar{x}$	$189	$145
Sample standard deviation, s	$ 12	$ 10
Sample size	6	12

Assuming normality and equal variances:

a   Use an appropriate hypothesis test to determine whether the mean prices for the two brands differ. How much evidence is there that the mean prices differ?

b   Use an appropriate 95 percent confidence interval to estimate the difference between the mean prices of the two brands of CD players. Do you think that the difference has practical importance?

c   Use an appropriate hypothesis test to provide evidence supporting the claim that the mean price of the Onkyo CD player is more than $30 higher than the mean price for the JVC CD player. Set α equal to .05.

10.60   Consider the situation of Exercise 10.59. Use the sample information to test H_0: $\sigma_1^2 = \sigma_2^2$ versus H_a: $\sigma_1^2 \neq \sigma_2^2$ with $\alpha = .05$. Based on this test, does it make sense to use the equal variances procedure? Explain.

10.61   Internet Exercise

a   A prominent issue of the 2000 U.S. presidential campaign was campaign finance reform. A *Washington Post*/ABC News poll (reported April 4, 2000) found that 63 percent of 1,083 American adults surveyed believed that stricter campaign finance laws would be effective (a lot or somewhat) in reducing the influence of money in politics. Was this view uniformly held or did it vary by gender, race, or political party affiliation? A summary of survey responses, broken down by gender, is given in the table below.

Summary of Responses	Male	Female	All
Believe reduce influence, *p*	59%	66%	63%
Number surveyed, *n*	520	563	1,083

[Source: *Washington Post* website: http://www.washingtonpost.com/wp-srv/politics/polls/vault/vault.htm. Click on the data link under *Gore Seen More Able to Reform Education, April 4, 2000,* then click again on the date link, *04/04/2000,* to the right of the campaign finance question. For a gender breakdown, select *sex* in the *Results By:* box and click *Go.* Note that the survey report does not include numbers of males and females questioned. These values were estimated using 1990 U.S. Census figures showing that males made up 48 percent of the U.S. adult population.]

Is there sufficient evidence in this survey to conclude that the proportion of individuals who believed that campaign finance laws can reduce the influence of money in politics differs between females and males? Set up the appropriate null and alternative hypotheses. Conduct your test at the .05 and .01 levels of significance and calculate the *p*-value for your test. Make sure your conclusion is clearly stated.

b   Search the World Wide Web for an interesting recent political poll dealing with an issue or political candidates, where responses are broken down by gender or some other two-category classification. (A list of high-potential websites is given below.) Use a difference in proportions test to determine whether political preference differs by gender or other two-level grouping.

Political polls on the World Wide Web:

ABC News:	http://www.abcnews.go.com/sections/politics/PollVault/PollVault.html
Washington Post:	http://www.washingtonpost.com/wp-srv/politics/polls/vault/vault.htm
Gallup:	http://www.gallup.com/poll/index.asp
L. A. Times:	http://www.latimes.com/news/timespoll/
CBS News:	http://cbsnews.cbs.com/now/section/0,1636,215-412,00.shtml
Newsweek:	http://www.newsweek.com/nw-srv/web/special/campaign2000/pollsurveys_front.htm
Polling report:	http://www.pollingreport.com/

Appendix 10.1 ■ Two-Sample Hypothesis Testing Using MINITAB

The instruction blocks in this section each begin by describing the entry of data into the Minitab Data window. Alternatively, the data may be loaded directly from the data disk included with the text. The appropriate data file name is given at the top of each instruction block. Please refer to Appendix 1.1 for further information about entering data, saving data, and printing results when using MINITAB.

Test for the difference between means, unequal variances, in Figure 10.4 on page 406 (data file: Catalyst.MTW):

- In the Data window, enter the data from Table 10.1 (page 402) into two columns with variable names XA-100 and ZB-200.

- Select **Stat : Basic Statistics : 2-Sample t**

- In the "2-Sample t (Test and Confidence Interval)" dialog box, select the "Samples in different columns" option.

- Select the XA-100 variable into the First window.

- Select the ZB-200 variable into the Second window.

- Click on the Options... button, enter the desired level of confidence (here, 95.0) in the "Confidence level" window, enter 0.0 in the "Test difference" window, and select "not equal" from the Alternative pull-down menu. Click OK in the "2-Sample t—Options" dialog box.

- To produce yield by catalyst type box plots, click the Graphs... button, check the "Boxplots of data" checkbox, and click OK in the "2-Sample t—Graphs" dialog box.

- Click OK in the "2-Sample t (Test and Confidence Interval)" dialog box.

- The results of the two-sample *t* test (including the *t* statistic and *p*-value) and the confidence interval for the difference between means appear in the Session window, while the box plots will be displayed in a graphics window.

- A test for the difference between two means when the **variances are equal** can be performed by placing a checkmark in the "Assume equal variances" checkbox in the "2-Sample t (Test and Confidence Interval)" dialog box.

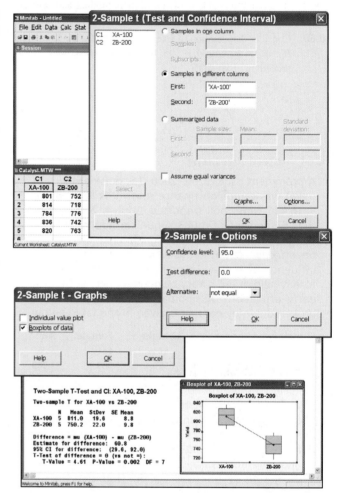

Test for paired differences in Figure 10.8(a) on page 412 (data file: Repair.MTW):

- In the Data window, enter the data from Table 10.2 (page 410) into two columns with variable names Garage1 and Garage2.

- Select **Stat : Basic Statistics : Paired t**

- In the "Paired t (Test and Confidence Interval)" dialog box, select the "Samples in columns" option.

- Select Garage1 into the "First sample" window and Garage2 into the "Second sample" window.

- Click the Options… button.

- In the "Paired t—Options" dialog box, enter the desired level of confidence (here, 95.0) in the "Confidence level" window, enter 0.0 in the "Test mean" window, select "less than" from the Alternative pull-down menu, and click OK.

- To produce a box plot of differences with a graphical summary of the test, click the Graphs… button, check the "Boxplot of differences" checkbox, and click OK in the "Paired t—Graphs" dialog box.

- Click OK in the "Paired t (Test and Confidence Interval)" dialog box.

The results of the paired *t* test are given in the Session window, and graphical output is displayed in a graphics window.

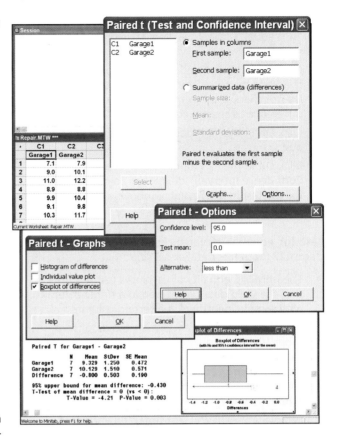

Hypothesis test and confidence interval for two independent proportions in the advertising media situation of Examples 10.9 and 10.10 on pages 418 to 420:

- Select **Stat : Basic Statistics : 2 Proportions**

- In the "2 Proportions (Test and Confidence Interval)" dialog box, select the "Summarized data" option.

- Enter the sample size for Des Moines (equal to 1000) into the "First—Trials" window, and enter the number of successes for Des Moines (equal to 631) into the "First—Events" window.

- Enter the sample size for Toledo (equal to 1000) into the "Second—Trials" window, and enter the number of successes for Toledo (equal to 798) into the "Second—Events" window.

- Click on the Options… button.

- In the "2 Proportions—Options" dialog box, enter the desired level of confidence (here 95.0) in the "Confidence level" window.

- Enter 0.0 into the "Test difference" window because we are testing that the difference between the two proportions equals zero.

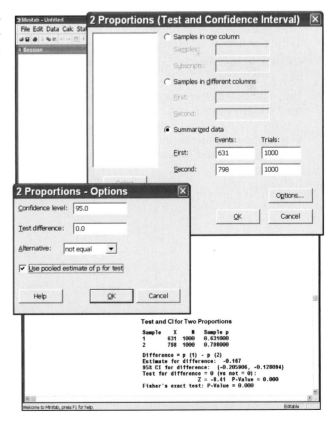

- Select the desired alternative hypothesis (here "not equal") from the Alternative drop-down menu.

- Check the "Use pooled estimate of p for test" checkbox because "Test difference" equals zero. Do not check this box in cases where "Test difference" does not equal zero.

- Click OK in the "2 Proportions—Options" dialog box.

- Click OK in the "2 Proportions (Test and Confidence Interval)" dialog box to obtain results for the test in the Session window.

Test for equality of variances in Figure 10.14(b) on page 427 (data file: Catalyst.MTW):

- The MINITAB equality of variances test requires that the yield data be entered in a single column with sample identifiers in a second column.

- In the Data window, enter the yield data from Table 10.1 (page 402) into a single column with variable name Yield. In a second column with variable name Catalyst, enter the corresponding identifying tag, XA-100 or ZB-200, for each yield figure.

- Select **Stat : ANOVA : Test for Equal Variances**

- In the "Test for Equal Variances" dialog box, select the Yield variable into the Response window.

- Select the Catalyst variable into the Factors window.

- Enter the desired level of confidence (here, 95.0) in the Confidence level window.

- Click OK in the "Test for Equal Variances" dialog box.

- The reciprocal of the F statistic (as described in the text) and the p-value will be displayed in the Session window (along with additional output that we do not describe in this book). A graphical summary of the test is shown in a graphics window.

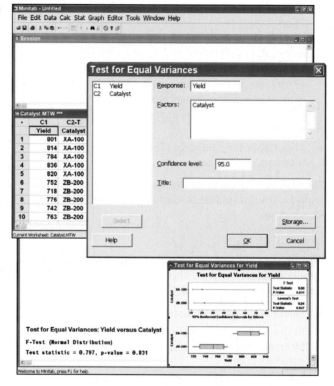

Appendix 10.2 ■ Two-Sample Hypothesis Testing Using Excel

The instruction blocks in this section each begin by describing the entry of data into an Excel spreadsheet. Alternatively, the data may be loaded directly from the data disk included with the text. The appropriate data file name is given at the top of each instruction block. Please refer to Appendix 1.2 for further information about entering data, saving data, and printing results when using Excel.

Test for the difference between means, equal variances, in Figure 10.2(b) on page 404 (data file: Catalyst.xlsx):

- Enter the data from Table 10.1 (page 402) into two columns: yields for catalyst XA-100 in column A and yields for catalyst ZB-200 in column B, with labels XA-100 and ZB-200.

- Select **Data : Data Analysis : t-Test: Two-Sample Assuming Equal Variances** and click OK in the Data Analysis dialog box.

- In the t-Test dialog box, enter A1.A6 in the "Variable 1 Range" window.

- Enter B1.B6 in the "Variable 2 Range" window.

- Enter 0 (zero) in the "Hypothesized Mean Difference" box.

- Place a checkmark in the Labels checkbox.

- Enter 0.05 into the Alpha box.

- Under output options, select "New Worksheet Ply" to have the output placed in a new worksheet and enter the name Output for the new worksheet.

- Click OK in the t-Test dialog box.

- The output will be displayed in a new worksheet.

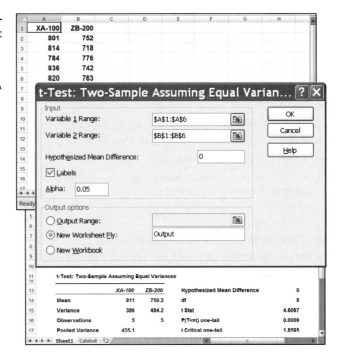

Test for equality of variances similar to Figure 10.14(a) on page 427 (data file: Catalyst.xlsx):

- Enter the data from Table 10.1 (page 402) into two columns: yields for catalyst XA-100 in column A and yields for catalyst ZB-200 in column B, with labels XA-100 and ZB-200.

- Select **Data : Data Analysis : F-Test Two-Sample for Variances** and click OK in the Data Analysis dialog box.

- In the F-Test dialog box, enter A1.A6 in the "Variable 1 Range" window.

- Enter B1.B6 in the "Variable 2 Range" window.

- Place a checkmark in the Labels checkbox.

- Enter 0.05 into the Alpha box.

- Under output options, select "New Worksheet Ply" to have the output placed in a new worksheet and enter the name Output for the new worksheet.

- Click OK in the F-Test dialog box.

- The output will be displayed in a new worksheet.

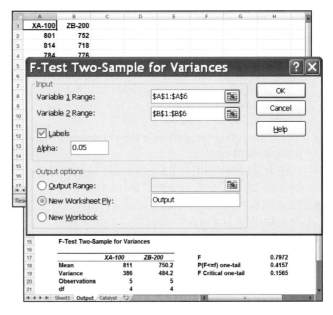

Test for paired differences in Figure 10.9 on page 412 (data file: Repair.xls):

- Enter the data from Table 10.2 (page 410) into two columns: costs for garage 1 in column A and costs for garage 2 in column B, with labels Garage 1 and Garage 2.

- Select **Data : Data Analysis : t-Test: Paired Two Sample for Means** and click OK in the Data Analysis dialog box.

- In the t-Test dialog box, enter A1.A8 into the "Variable 1 Range" window.

- Enter B1.B8 into the "Variable 2 Range" window.

- Enter 0 (zero) in the "Hypothesized Mean Difference" box.

- Place a checkmark in the Labels checkbox.

- Enter 0.05 into the Alpha box.

- Under output options, select "New Worksheet Ply" to have the output placed in a new worksheet and enter the name Output for the new worksheet.

- Click OK in the t-Test dialog box.

- The output will be displayed in a new worksheet.

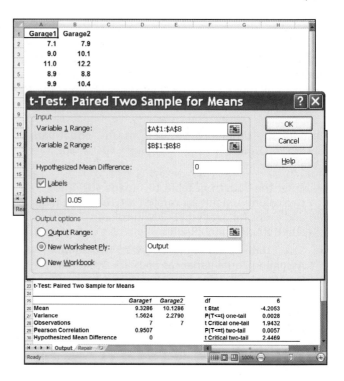

Appendix 10.3 ■ Two-Sample Hypothesis Testing Using MegaStat

The instructions in this section begin by describing the entry of data into an Excel worksheet. Alternatively, the data may be loaded directly from the data disk included with the text. The appropriate data file name is given at the top of each instruction block. Please refer to Appendix 1.2 for further information about entering data and saving and printing results in Excel. Please refer to Appendix 1.3 for more information about using MegaStat.

Test for the difference between means, equal variances, in Figure 10.2(a) on page 404 (data file: Catalyst.xlsx):

- Enter the data from Table 10.1 (page 402) into two columns: yields for catalyst XA-100 in column A and yields for catalyst ZB-200 in column B, with labels XA-100 and ZB-200.

- Select **MegaStat : Hypothesis Tests : Compare Two Independent Groups**

- In the "Hypothesis Test: Compare Two Independent Groups" dialog box, click on "data input."

- Click in the Group 1 window and use the AutoExpand feature to enter the range A1.A6.

- Click in the Group 2 window and use the AutoExpand feature to enter the range B1.B6.

- Enter the Hypothesized difference (here equal to 0) into the so-labeled window.

- Select an Alternative (here "not equal") from the drop-down menu in the Alternative box.

- Click on "t-test (pooled variance)" to request the equal variances test described on page 403.

- Check the "Display confidence interval" checkbox, and select or type a desired level of confidence.

- Check the "Test for equality of variances" checkbox to request the *F* test described on page 428.
- Click OK in the "Hypothesis Test: Compare Two Independent Groups" dialog box.
- The *t* test assuming unequal variances described on page 404 can be done by clicking "t-test (unequal variances)".

Test for paired differences in Figure 10.8(b) on page 412 (data file: Repair.xlsx):

- Enter the data from Table 10.2 (page 410) into two columns: costs for garage 1 in column A and costs for garage 2 in column B, with labels Garage1 and Garage2.

- Select **Add-Ins : MegaStat : Hypothesis Tests : Paired Observations**

- In the "Hypothesis Test: Paired Observations" dialog box, click on "data input."

- Click in the Group 1 window, and use the AutoExpand feature to enter the range A1.A8.

- Click in the Group 2 window, and use the AutoExpand feature to enter the range B1.B8.

- Enter the Hypothesized difference (here equal to 0) into the so-labeled window.

- Select an Alternative (here "not equal") from the drop-down menu in the Alternative box.

- Click on "t-test."

- Click OK in the "Hypothesis Test: Paired Observations" dialog box.

- If the sample sizes are large, a test based on the normal distribution can be done by clicking on "z-test."

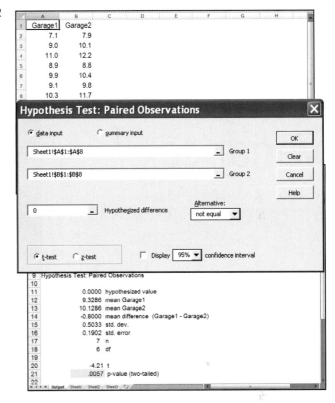

Hypothesis Test and Confidence Interval for Two Independent Proportions in Exercise 10.42 on page 421:

- Select **Add-Ins : MegaStat : Hypothesis Tests: Compare Two Independent Proportions**

- In the "Hypothesis Test: Compare Two Proportions" dialog box, enter the number of successes *x* (here equal to 25) and the sample size *n* (here equal to 140) for homeowners in the "x" and "n" Group 1 windows.

- Enter the number of successes *x* (here equal to 9) and the sample size *n* (here equal to 60) for renters in the "x" and "n" Group 2 windows.

- Enter the Hypothesized difference (here equal to 0) into the so-labeled window.

- Select an Alternative (here "not equal") from the drop-down menu in the Alternative box.

- Check the "Display confidence interval" checkbox, and select or type a desired level of confidence (here equal to 95%).

- Click OK in the "Hypothesis Test: Compare Two Proportions" dialog box.

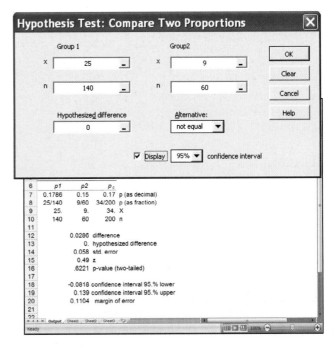

CHAPTER 11

Experimental Design and Analysis of Variance

Chapter Outline

11.1 Basic Concepts of Experimental Design

11.2 One-Way Analysis of Variance

11.3 The Randomized Block Design

Note: Two-Way Analysis of Variance is discussed in Appendix D, which is included on this book's Website.

n Chapter 10 we learned that business improvement often involves making **comparisons.** In that chapter we presented several confidence intervals and several hypothesis testing procedures for comparing two population means. However, business improvement often requires that we compare more than two population means. For instance, we might compare the mean sales obtained by using three different advertising campaigns in order to improve a company's marketing process. Or, we might compare the mean production output obtained by using four different manufacturing process designs to improve productivity.

In this chapter we extend the methods presented in Chapter 10 by considering statistical procedures for **comparing two or more population means.** Each of the methods we discuss is called an **analysis of variance (ANOVA)** procedure. We also present some basic concepts of **experimental design,** which involves deciding how to collect data in a way that allows us to most effectively compare population means.

We explain the methods of this chapter in the context of three cases:

The Gasoline Mileage Case: An oil company wishes to develop a reasonably priced gasoline that will deliver improved mileages. The company uses **one-way analysis of variance** to compare the effects of three types of gasoline on mileage in order to find the gasoline type that delivers the highest mean mileage.

The Commercial Response Case: Firms that run commercials on television want to make the best use of their advertising dollars. In this case, researchers use **one-way analysis of variance** to compare the effects of varying program content on a viewer's ability to recall brand names after watching TV commercials.

The Defective Cardboard Box Case: A paper company performs an experiment to investigate the effects of four production methods on the number of defective cardboard boxes produced in an hour. The company uses a **randomized block ANOVA** to determine which production method yields the smallest mean number of defective boxes.

11.1 Basic Concepts of Experimental Design ● ● ●

In many statistical studies a variable of interest, called the **response variable** (or **dependent variable**), is identified. Then data are collected that tell us about how one or more **factors** (or **independent variables**) influence the variable of interest. If we cannot control the factor(s) being studied, we say that the data obtained are **observational.** For example, suppose that in order to study how the size of a home relates to the sales price of the home, a real estate agent randomly selects 50 recently sold homes and records the square footages and sales prices of these homes. Because the real estate agent cannot control the sizes of the randomly selected homes, we say that the data are observational.

If we can control the factors being studied, we say that the data are **experimental.** Furthermore, in this case the values, or **levels,** of the factor (or combination of factors) are called **treatments.** The purpose of most experiments is **to compare and estimate the effects of the different treatments on the response variable.** For example, suppose that an oil company wishes to study how three different gasoline types (A, B, and C) affect the mileage obtained by a popular midsize automobile model. Here the response variable is gasoline mileage, and the company will study a single factor—gasoline type. Since the oil company can control which gasoline type is used in the midsize automobile, the data that the oil company will collect are experimental. Furthermore, the treatments—the levels of the factor gasoline type—are gasoline types A, B, and C.

In order to collect data in an experiment, the different treatments are assigned to objects (people, cars, animals, or the like) that are called **experimental units.** For example, in the gasoline mileage situation, gasoline types A, B, and C will be compared by conducting mileage tests using a midsize automobile. The automobiles used in the tests are the experimental units.

In general, when a treatment is applied to more than one experimental unit, it is said to be **replicated.** Furthermore, when the analyst controls the treatments employed and how they are applied to the experimental units, a **designed experiment** is being carried out. A commonly used, simple experimental design is called the **completely randomized experimental design.**

> In a **completely randomized experimental design,** independent random samples of experimental units are assigned to the treatments.

Suppose we assign three experimental units to each of five treatments. We can achieve a completely randomized experimental design by assigning experimental units to treatments as follows. First, randomly select three experimental units and assign them to the first treatment. Next, randomly select three *different* experimental units from those remaining and assign them to the second treatment. That is, select these units from those not assigned to the first treatment. Third, randomly select three *different* experimental units from those not assigned to either the first or second treatment. Assign these experimental units to the third treatment. Continue this procedure until the required number of experimental units have been assigned to each treatment.

Once experimental units have been assigned to treatments, a value of the response variable is observed for each experimental unit. Thus we obtain a **sample** of values of the response variable for each treatment. When we employ a completely randomized experimental design, we assume that each sample has been randomly selected from the population of all values of the response variable that could potentially be observed when using its particular treatment. We also assume that the different samples of response variable values are **independent** of each other. This is usually reasonable because the completely randomized design ensures that each different sample results from **different measurements** being taken on **different experimental units.** Thus we sometimes say that we are conducting an **independent samples experiment.**

EXAMPLE 11.1 The Gasoline Mileage Case

North American Oil Company is attempting to develop a reasonably priced gasoline that will deliver improved gasoline mileages. As part of its development process, the company would like to compare the effects of three types of gasoline (*A*, *B*, and *C*) on gasoline mileage. For testing purposes, North American Oil will compare the effects of gasoline types *A*, *B*, and *C* on the gasoline mileage obtained by a popular midsize model called the Fire-Hawk. Suppose the company has access to 1,000 Fire-Hawks that are representative of the population of all Fire-Hawks, and suppose the company will utilize a completely randomized experimental design that employs samples of size 5. In order to accomplish this, 5 Fire-Hawks will be randomly selected from the 1,000 available Fire-Hawks. These autos will be assigned to gasoline type *A*. Next, 5 *different* Fire-Hawks will be randomly selected from the remaining 995 available Fire-Hawks. These autos will be assigned to gasoline type *B*. Finally, 5 *different* Fire-Hawks will be randomly selected from the remaining 990 available Fire-Hawks. These autos will be assigned to gasoline type *C*.

Each randomly selected Fire-Hawk is test-driven using the appropriate gasoline type (treatment) under normal conditions for a specified distance, and the gasoline mileage for each test-drive is measured. We let x_{ij} denote the jth mileage obtained when using gasoline type i. The mileage data obtained are given in Table 11.1. Here we assume that the set of gasoline mileage observations obtained by using a particular gasoline type is a sample randomly selected from the infinite population of all Fire-Hawk mileages that could be obtained using that gasoline type. Examining the box plots shown next to the mileage data, we see some evidence that gasoline type *B* yields the highest gasoline mileages.[1]

TABLE 11.1   The Gasoline Mileage Data   🌢 GasMile2

Gasoline Type *A*	Gasoline Type *B*	Gasoline Type *C*
$x_{A1} = 34.0$	$x_{B1} = 35.3$	$x_{C1} = 33.3$
$x_{A2} = 35.0$	$x_{B2} = 36.5$	$x_{C2} = 34.0$
$x_{A3} = 34.3$	$x_{B3} = 36.4$	$x_{C3} = 34.7$
$x_{A4} = 35.5$	$x_{B4} = 37.0$	$x_{C4} = 33.0$
$x_{A5} = 35.8$	$x_{B5} = 37.6$	$x_{C5} = 34.9$

[1]All of the box plots presented in this chapter have been obtained using MINITAB.

EXAMPLE 11.2 The Shelf Display Case

The Tastee Bakery Company supplies a bakery product to many supermarkets in a metropolitan area. The company wishes to study the effect of the shelf display height employed by the supermarkets on monthly sales (measured in cases of 10 units each) for this product. Shelf display height, the factor to be studied, has three levels—bottom (*B*), middle (*M*), and top (*T*)—which are the treatments. To compare these treatments, the bakery uses a completely randomized experimental design. For each shelf height, six supermarkets (the experimental units) of equal sales potential are randomly selected, and each supermarket displays the product using its assigned shelf height for a month. At the end of the month, sales of the bakery product (the response variable) at the 18 participating stores are recorded, giving the data in Table 11.2. Here we assume that the set of sales amounts for each display height is a sample randomly selected from the population of all sales amounts that could be obtained (at supermarkets of the given sales potential) at that display height. Examining the box plots that are shown next to the sales data, we seem to have evidence that a middle display height gives the highest bakery product sales.

TABLE 11.2   The Bakery Product Sales Data 🌑 BakeSale

Bottom (*B*)	Shelf Display Height Middle (*M*)	Top (*T*)
58.2	73.0	52.4
53.7	78.1	49.7
55.8	75.4	50.9
55.7	76.2	54.0
52.5	78.4	52.1
58.9	82.1	49.9

EXAMPLE 11.3 The Commercial Response Case

Advertising research indicates that when a television program is involving (such as the 2002 Super Bowl between the St. Louis Rams and New England Patriots, which was very exciting), individuals exposed to commercials tend to have difficulty recalling the names of the products advertised. Therefore, in order for companies to make the best use of their advertising dollars, it is important to show their most original and memorable commercials during involving programs.

In an article in the *Journal of Advertising Research*, Soldow and Principe (1981) studied the effect of program content on the response to commercials. Program content, the factor studied, has three levels—more involving programs, less involving programs, and no program (that is, commercials only)—which are the treatments. To compare these treatments, Soldow and Principe employed a completely randomized experimental design. For each program content level, 29 subjects were randomly selected and exposed to commercials in that program content level. Then a brand recall score (measured on a continuous scale) was obtained for each subject. The 29 brand recall scores for each program content level are assumed to be a sample randomly selected from the population of all brand recall scores for that program content level. Although we do not give the results in this example, the reader will analyze summary statistics describing these results in the exercises of Section 11.2.

Exercises for Section 11.1

CONCEPTS

11.1   Define the meaning of the terms *response variable, factor, treatments,* and *experimental units.*

11.2   What is a completely randomized experimental design?

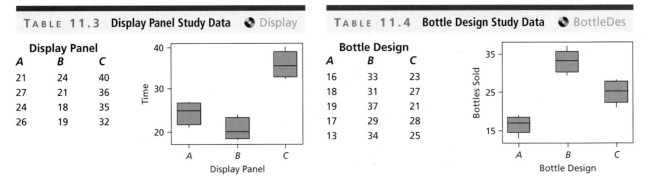

TABLE 11.3 Display Panel Study Data ● Display

Display Panel		
A	B	C
21	24	40
27	21	36
24	18	35
26	19	32

TABLE 11.4 Bottle Design Study Data ● BottleDes

Bottle Design		
A	B	C
16	33	23
18	31	27
19	37	21
17	29	28
13	34	25

METHODS AND APPLICATIONS

11.3   A study compared three different display panels for use by air traffic controllers. Each display panel was tested in a simulated emergency condition; 12 highly trained air traffic controllers took part in the study. Four controllers were randomly assigned to each display panel. The time (in seconds) needed to stabilize the emergency condition was recorded. The results of the study are given in Table 11.3. For this situation, identify the response variable, factor of interest, treatments, and experimental units.   ● Display

11.4   A consumer preference study compares the effects of three different bottle designs (*A*, *B*, and *C*) on sales of a popular fabric softener. A completely randomized design is employed. Specifically, 15 supermarkets of equal sales potential are selected, and 5 of these supermarkets are randomly assigned to each bottle design. The number of bottles sold in 24 hours at each supermarket is recorded. The data obtained are displayed in Table 11.4. For this situation, identify the response variable, factor of interest, treatments, and experimental units.   ● BottleDes

CHAPTER 12

11.2 One-Way Analysis of Variance ● ● ●

Suppose we wish to study the effects of p **treatments** (treatments 1, 2, . . . , p) on a **response variable.** For any particular treatment, say treatment i, we define μ_i and σ_i to be the mean and standard deviation of the population of all possible values of the response variable that could potentially be observed when using treatment i. Here we refer to μ_i as **treatment mean i.** The goal of **one-way analysis of variance** (often called **one-way ANOVA**) is to estimate and compare the effects of the different treatments on the response variable. We do this by **estimating and comparing the treatment means** $\mu_1, \mu_2, . . . , \mu_p$. Here we assume that a sample has been randomly selected for each of the p treatments by employing a completely randomized experimental design. We let n_i denote the size of the sample that has been randomly selected for treatment i, and we let x_{ij} denote the jth value of the response variable that is observed when using treatment i. It then follows that the point estimate of μ_i is $\bar{x}_i$, the average of the sample of n_i values of the response variable observed when using treatment i. It further follows that the point estimate of σ_i is s_i, the standard deviation of the sample of n_i values of the response variable observed when using treatment i.

EXAMPLE 11.4 The Gasoline Mileage Case

Consider the gasoline mileage situation. We let μ_A, μ_B, and μ_C denote the means and σ_A, σ_B, and σ_C denote the standard deviations of the populations of all possible gasoline mileages using gasoline types A, B, and C. To estimate these means and standard deviations, North American Oil has employed a completely randomized experimental design and has obtained the samples of mileages in Table 11.1. The means of these samples—$\bar{x}_A = 34.92$, $\bar{x}_B = 36.56$, and $\bar{x}_C = 33.98$—are the point estimates of μ_A, μ_B, and μ_C. The standard deviations of these samples—$s_A = .7662$, $s_B = .8503$, and $s_C = .8349$—are the point estimates of σ_A, σ_B, and σ_C. Using these point estimates, we will (later in this section) test to see whether there are any statistically significant differences between the treatment means μ_A, μ_B, and μ_C. If such differences exist, we will estimate the magnitudes of these differences. This will allow North American Oil to judge whether these differences have practical importance.

The one-way ANOVA formulas allow us to test for significant differences between treatment means and allow us to estimate differences between treatment means. The validity of these formulas requires that the following assumptions hold:

Assumptions for One-Way Analysis of Variance

1   **Constant variance**—the p populations of values of the response variable associated with the treatments have equal variances.

2   **Normality**—the p populations of values of the response variable associated with the treatments all have normal distributions.

3   **Independence**—the samples of experimental units associated with the treatments are randomly selected, independent samples.

The one-way ANOVA results are not very sensitive to violations of the equal variances assumption. Studies have shown that this is particularly true when the sample sizes employed are equal (or nearly equal). Therefore, a good way to make sure that unequal variances will not be a problem is to take samples that are the same size. In addition, it is useful to compare the sample standard deviations $s_1, s_2, \ldots, s_p$ to see if they are reasonably equal. As a general rule, *the one-way ANOVA results will be approximately correct if the largest sample standard deviation is no more than twice the smallest sample standard deviation.* The variations of the samples can also be compared by constructing a box plot for each sample (as we have done for the gasoline mileage data in Table 11.1). Several statistical texts also employ the sample variances to test the equality of the population variances [see Bowerman and O'Connell (1990) for two of these tests]. However, these tests have some drawbacks—in particular, their results are very sensitive to violations of the normality assumption. Because of this, there is controversy as to whether these tests should be performed.

The normality assumption says that each of the p populations is normally distributed. This assumption is not crucial. It has been shown that the one-way ANOVA results are approximately valid for mound-shaped distributions. It is useful to construct a box plot and/or a stem-and-leaf display for each sample. If the distributions are reasonably symmetric, and if there are no outliers, the ANOVA results can be trusted for sample sizes as small as 4 or 5. As an example, consider the gasoline mileage study of Examples 11.1 and 11.4. The box plots of Table 11.1 suggest that the variability of the mileages in each of the three samples is roughly the same. Furthermore, the sample standard deviations $s_A = .7662$, $s_B = .8503$, and $s_C = .8349$ are reasonably equal (the largest is not even close to twice the smallest). Therefore, it is reasonable to believe that the constant variance assumption is satisfied. Moreover, because the sample sizes are the same, unequal variances would probably not be a serious problem anyway. Many small, independent factors influence gasoline mileage, so the distributions of mileages for gasoline types A, B, and C are probably mound-shaped. In addition, the box plots of Table 11.1 indicate that each distribution is roughly symmetric with no outliers. Thus, the normality assumption probably approximately holds. Finally, because North American Oil has employed a completely randomized design, the independence assumption probably holds. This is because the gasoline mileages in the different samples were obtained for *different* Fire-Hawks.

Testing for significant differences between treatment means   As a preliminary step in one-way ANOVA, we wish to determine whether there are any statistically significant differences between the treatment means $\mu_1, \mu_2, \ldots, \mu_p$. To do this, we test the null hypothesis

$$H_0: \mu_1 = \mu_2 = \cdots = \mu_p$$

This hypothesis says that all the treatments have the same effect on the mean response. We test H_0 versus the alternative hypothesis

$$H_a: \text{At least two of } \mu_1, \mu_2, \ldots, \mu_p \text{ differ}$$

This alternative says that at least two treatments have different effects on the mean response.

FIGURE 11.1   **Comparing Between-Treatment Variability and Within-Treatment Variability**

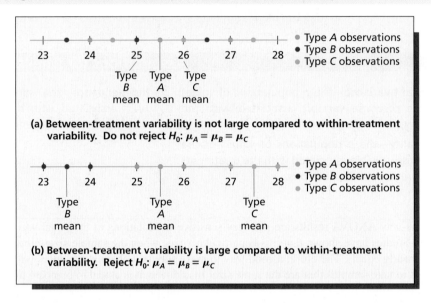

To carry out such a test, we compare what we call the **between-treatment variability** to the **within-treatment variability.** For instance, suppose we wish to study the effects of three gasoline types (A, B, and C) on mean gasoline mileage, and consider Figure 11.1(a). This figure depicts three independent random samples of gasoline mileages obtained using gasoline types A, B, and C. Observations obtained using gasoline type A are plotted as blue dots (•), observations obtained using gasoline type B are plotted as red dots (•), and observations obtained using gasoline type C are plotted as green dots (•). Furthermore, the sample treatment means are labeled as "type A mean," "type B mean," and "type C mean." We see that the variability of the sample treatment means—that is, the **between-treatment variability**—is not large compared to the variability within each sample (the **within-treatment variability**). In this case, the differences between the sample treatment means could quite easily be the result of sampling variation. Thus we would not have sufficient evidence to reject

$$H_0: \mu_A = \mu_B = \mu_C$$

Next look at Figure 11.1(b), which depicts a different set of three independent random samples of gasoline mileages. Here the variability of the sample treatment means (the between-treatment variability) is large compared to the variability within each sample. This would probably provide enough evidence to tell us to reject

$$H_0: \mu_A = \mu_B = \mu_C$$

in favor of

$$H_a: \text{At least two of } \mu_A, \mu_B, \text{ and } \mu_C \text{ differ}$$

We would conclude that at least two of gasoline types A, B, and C have different effects on mean mileage.

In order to numerically compare the between-treatment and within-treatment variability, we can define several **sums of squares** and **mean squares.** To begin, we define n to be the total number of experimental units employed in the one-way ANOVA, and we define $\bar{x}$ to be the overall mean of all observed values of the response variable. Then we define the following:

The **treatment sum of squares** is

$$SST = \sum_{i=1}^{p} n_i (\bar{x}_i - \bar{x})^2$$

In order to compute SST, we calculate the difference between each sample treatment mean $\bar{x}_i$ and the overall mean $\bar{x}$, we square each of these differences, we multiply each squared difference by the number of observations for that treatment, and we sum over all treatments. The SST

measures the variability of the sample treatment means. For instance, if all the sample treatment means ($\bar{x}_i$ values) were equal, then the treatment sum of squares would be equal to zero. The more the $\bar{x}_i$ values vary, the larger will be SST. In other words, the **treatment sum of squares** measures the amount of **between-treatment variability.**

As an example, consider the gasoline mileage data in Table 11.1. In this experiment we employ a total of

$$n = n_A + n_B + n_C = 5 + 5 + 5 = 15$$

experimental units. Furthermore, the overall mean of the 15 observed gasoline mileages is

$$\bar{x} = \frac{34.0 + 35.0 + \cdots + 34.9}{15} = \frac{527.3}{15} = 35.153$$

Then

$$
\begin{aligned}
SST &= \sum_{i = A,B,C} n_i(\bar{x}_i - \bar{x})^2 \\
&= n_A(\bar{x}_A - \bar{x})^2 + n_B(\bar{x}_B - \bar{x})^2 + n_C(\bar{x}_C - \bar{x})^2 \\
&= 5(34.92 - 35.153)^2 + 5(36.56 - 35.153)^2 + 5(33.98 - 35.153)^2 \\
&= 17.0493
\end{aligned}
$$

In order to measure the within-treatment variability, we define the following quantity:

The **error sum of squares** is

$$SSE = \sum_{j=1}^{n_1}(x_{1j} - \bar{x}_1)^2 + \sum_{j=1}^{n_2}(x_{2j} - \bar{x}_2)^2 + \cdots + \sum_{j=1}^{n_p}(x_{pj} - \bar{x}_p)^2$$

Here x_{1j} is the jth observed value of the response in the first sample, x_{2j} is the jth observed value of the response in the second sample, and so forth. The formula above says that we compute SSE by calculating the squared difference between each observed value of the response and its corresponding treatment mean and by summing these squared differences over all the observations in the experiment.

The SSE measures the variability of the observed values of the response variable around their respective treatment means. For example, if there were no variability within each sample, the error sum of squares would be equal to zero. The more the values within the samples vary, the larger will be SSE.

As an example, in the gasoline mileage study, the sample treatment means are $\bar{x}_A = 34.92$, $\bar{x}_B = 36.56$, and $\bar{x}_C = 33.98$. It follows that

$$
\begin{aligned}
SSE &= \sum_{j=1}^{n_A}(x_{Aj} - \bar{x}_A)^2 + \sum_{j=1}^{n_B}(x_{Bj} - \bar{x}_B)^2 + \sum_{j=1}^{n_C}(x_{Cj} - \bar{x}_C)^2 \\
&= [(34.0 - 34.92)^2 + (35.0 - 34.92)^2 + (34.3 - 34.92)^2 + (35.5 - 34.92)^2 + (35.8 - 34.92)^2] \\
&\quad + [(35.3 - 36.56)^2 + (36.5 - 36.56)^2 + (36.4 - 36.56)^2 + (37.0 - 36.56)^2 + (37.6 - 36.56)^2] \\
&\quad + [(33.3 - 33.98)^2 + (34.0 - 33.98)^2 + (34.7 - 33.98)^2 + (33.0 - 33.98)^2 + (34.9 - 33.98)^2] \\
&= 8.028
\end{aligned}
$$

Finally, we define a sum of squares that measures the total amount of variability in the observed values of the response:

The **total sum of squares** is

$$SSTO = SST + SSE$$

The variability in the observed values of the response must come from one of two sources—the between-treatment variability or the within-treatment variability. It follows that the total sum of squares equals the sum of the treatment sum of squares and the error sum of squares. Therefore, the **SST and SSE are said to partition the total sum of squares.**

In the gasoline mileage study, we see that

$$SSTO = SST + SSE = 17.0493 + 8.028 = 25.0773$$

Using the treatment and error sums of squares, we next define two **mean squares:**

The **treatment mean square** is

$$MST = \frac{SST}{p - 1}$$

The **error mean square** is

$$MSE = \frac{SSE}{n - p}$$

In order to decide whether there are any statistically significant differences between the treatment means, it makes sense to compare the amount of between-treatment variability to the amount of within-treatment variability. This comparison suggests the following F test:

An F Test for Differences between Treatment Means

Suppose that we wish to compare p treatment means $\mu_1, \mu_2, \ldots, \mu_p$ and consider testing

$H_0: \mu_1 = \mu_2 = \cdots = \mu_p$ versus H_a: At least two of $\mu_1, \mu_2, \ldots, \mu_p$ differ
       (all treatment means are equal)   (at least two treatment means differ)

Define the F statistic

$$F = \frac{MST}{MSE} = \frac{SST/(p - 1)}{SSE/(n - p)}$$

and its p-value to be the area under the F curve with $p - 1$ and $n - p$ degrees of freedom to the right of F. We can reject H_0 in favor of H_a at level of significance α if either of the following equivalent conditions holds:

1 $F > F_\alpha$ **2** p-value $< \alpha$

Here the F_α point is based on $p - 1$ numerator and $n - p$ denominator degrees of freedom.

A large value of F results when SST, which measures the between-treatment variability, is large compared to SSE, which measures the within-treatment variability. If F is large enough, this implies that H_0 should be rejected. The critical value F_α tells us when F is large enough to allow us to reject H_0 at level of significance α. When F is large, the associated p-value is small. If this p-value is less than α, we can reject H_0 at level of significance α.

EXAMPLE 11.5 The Gasoline Mileage Case

Consider the North American Oil Company data in Table 11.1. The company wishes to determine whether any of gasoline types A, B, and C have different effects on mean Fire-Hawk gasoline mileage. That is, we wish to see whether there are any statistically significant differences between μ_A, μ_B, and μ_C. To do this, we test the null hypothesis

$$H_0: \mu_A = \mu_B = \mu_C$$

which says that gasoline types A, B, and C have the same effects on mean gasoline mileage. We test H_0 versus the alternative

$$H_a: \text{At least two of } \mu_A, \mu_B, \text{ and } \mu_C \text{ differ}$$

which says that at least two of gasoline types A, B, and C have different effects on mean gasoline mileage.

Since we have previously computed SST to be 17.0493 and SSE to be 8.028, and because we are comparing $p = 3$ treatment means, we have

$$MST = \frac{SST}{p - 1} = \frac{17.0493}{3 - 1} = 8.525$$

Figure 11.2   MINITAB and Excel Output of an Analysis of Variance of the Gasoline Mileage Data in Table 11.1

(a) The MINITAB output

```
One-way   ANOVA:   Type A,    Type B,    Type C              Tukey 95% Simultaneous
Source    DF         SS         MS        F        P          Confidence Intervals
Gas Type   2 [1]   17.049 [4]  8.525 [7]  12.74 [9]  0.001 [10]
Error     12 [2]    8.028 [5]  0.669 [8]                    Type A subtracted from:
Total     14 [3]   25.077 [6]                                           Lower    Center   Upper
                               Individual 95%              Type B    0.2610   1.6400   3.0190
                               CIs For Mean Based on Pooled StDev   Type C   -2.3190  -0.9400   0.439
Level    N    Mean        StDev  ---+---------+---------+---------+------
Type A   5   34.920 [11]  0.766         (------*------)          Type B subtracted from:
Type B   5   36.560 [12]  0.850                   (------*-----)            Lower    Center   Upper
Type C   5   33.980 [13]  0.835 (-----*------)                  Type C   -3.9590  -2.5800  -1.2010
                                ---+---------+---------+---------+------
Pooled StDev = 0.818               33.6      34.8     36.0     37.2
```

(b) The Excel output

SUMMARY

Groups	Count	Sum	Average	Variance
Type A	5	174.6	34.92 [11]	0.587
Type B	5	182.8	36.56 [12]	0.723
Type C	5	169.9	33.98 [13]	0.697

ANOVA

Source of Variation	SS	df	MS	F	P-value	F crit
Between Groups	17.0493 [4]	2 [1]	8.5247 [7]	12.7424 [9]	0.0011 [10]	3.8853 [14]
Within Groups	8.0280 [5]	12 [2]	0.6690 [8]			
Total	25.0773 [6]	14 [3]				

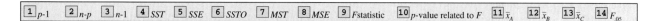

| [1] p-1 | [2] n-p | [3] n-1 | [4] SST | [5] SSE | [6] $SSTO$ | [7] MST | [8] MSE | [9] Fstatistic | [10] p-value related to F | [11] $\bar{x}_A$ | [12] $\bar{x}_B$ | [13] $\bar{x}_C$ | [14] $F_{.05}$ |

and

$$MSE = \frac{SSE}{n - p} = \frac{8.028}{15 - 3} = 0.669$$

It follows that

$$F = \frac{MST}{MSE} = \frac{8.525}{0.669} = 12.74$$

In order to test H_0 at the .05 level of significance, we use $F_{.05}$ with $p - 1 = 3 - 1 = 2$ numerator and $n - p = 15 - 3 = 12$ denominator degrees of freedom. Table A.6 (page 645) tells us that this F point equals 3.89, so we have

$$F = 12.74 > F_{.05} = 3.89$$

Therefore, we reject H_0 at the .05 level of significance. This says we have strong evidence that at least two of the treatment means $\mu_A, \mu_B,$ and μ_C differ. In other words, we conclude that at least two of gasoline types A, B, and C have different effects on mean gasoline mileage.

Figure 11.2 gives the MINITAB and Excel output of an analysis of variance of the gasoline mileage data. Note that each output gives the value $F = 12.74$ and the related p-value, which equals .001 (rounded). Since this p-value is less than .05, we reject H_0 at the .05 level of significance.

The results of an analysis of variance are often summarized in what is called an **analysis of variance table.** This table gives the sums of squares (*SST, SSE, SSTO*), the mean squares (*MST* and *MSE*), and the F statistic and its related p-value for the ANOVA. The table also gives the degrees of freedom associated with each source of variation—treatments, error, and total. Table 11.5 gives the ANOVA table for the gasoline mileage problem. Notice that in the column labeled "Sums of Squares," the values of *SST* and *SSE* sum to *SSTO*. Also notice that the upper portion of the MINITAB output and the lower portion of the Excel output give the ANOVA table of Table 11.5.

TABLE 11.5   Analysis of Variance Table for Testing $H_0 : \mu_A = \mu_B = \mu_C$ in the Gasoline Mileage Problem ($p = 3$ Gasoline Types, $n = 15$ Observations)

Source	Degrees of Freedom	Sums of Squares	Mean Squares	F Statistic	p-Value
Treatments	$p - 1 = 3 - 1$ $= 2$	$SST = 17.0493$	$MST = \dfrac{SST}{p - 1}$ $= \dfrac{17.0493}{3 - 1}$ $= 8.525$	$F = \dfrac{MST}{MSE}$ $= \dfrac{8.525}{0.669}$ $= 12.74$	0.001
Error	$n - p = 15 - 3$ $= 12$	$SSE = 8.028$	$MSE = \dfrac{SSE}{n - p}$ $= \dfrac{8.028}{15 - 3}$ $= 0.669$		
Total	$n - 1 = 15 - 1$ $= 14$	$SSTO = 25.0773$			

Before continuing, note that if we use the ANOVA F statistic to test the equality of two population means, it can be shown that

1   F equals t^2, where t is the equal variances t statistic discussed in Section 10.2 (page 403) used to test the equality of the two population means and

2   The critical value F_α, which is based on $p - 1 = 2 - 1 = 1$ and $n - p = n_1 + n_2 - 2$ degrees of freedom, equals $t_{\alpha/2}^2$, where $t_{\alpha/2}$ is the critical value for the equal variances t test and is based on $n_1 + n_2 - 2$ degrees of freedom.

Hence, the rejection conditions

$$F > F_\alpha \qquad \text{and} \qquad |t| > t_{\alpha/2}$$

are equivalent. It can also be shown that in this case the p-value related to F equals the p-value related to t. Therefore, the ANOVA F test of the equality of p treatment means can be regarded as a generalization of the equal variances t test of the equality of two treatment means.

Pairwise comparisons   If the one-way ANOVA F test says that at least two treatment means differ, then we investigate which treatment means differ and we estimate how large the differences are. We do this by making what we call **pairwise comparisons** (that is, we compare treatment means **two at a time**). One way to make these comparisons is to compute point estimates of and confidence intervals for **pairwise differences.** For example, in the gasoline mileage case we might estimate the pairwise differences $\mu_A - \mu_B$, $\mu_A - \mu_C$, and $\mu_B - \mu_C$. Here, for instance, the pairwise difference $\mu_A - \mu_B$ can be interpreted as the change in mean mileage achieved by changing from using gasoline type B to using gasoline type A.

There are two approaches to calculating confidence intervals for pairwise differences. The first involves computing the usual, or **individual,** confidence interval for each pairwise difference. Here, if we are computing $100(1 - \alpha)$ percent confidence intervals, we are $100(1 - \alpha)$ percent confident that each individual pairwise difference is contained in its respective interval. That is, the confidence level associated with each (individual) comparison is $100(1 - \alpha)$ percent, and we refer to α as the **comparisonwise error rate.** However, we are less than $100(1 - \alpha)$ percent confident that all of the pairwise differences are simultaneously contained in their respective intervals. A more conservative approach is to compute **simultaneous** confidence intervals. Such intervals make us $100(1 - \alpha)$ percent confident that all of the pairwise differences are simultaneously contained in their respective intervals. That is, when we compute simultaneous intervals, the overall confidence level associated with all the comparisons being made in the experiment is $100(1 - \alpha)$ percent, and we refer to α as the **experimentwise error rate.**

Several kinds of simultaneous confidence intervals can be computed. In this book we present what is called the **Tukey formula** for simultaneous intervals. We do this because, *if we are interested in studying all pairwise differences between treatment means, the Tukey formula yields the most precise (shortest) simultaneous confidence intervals.* In general, a Tukey simultaneous $100(1 - \alpha)$ percent confidence interval is longer than the corresponding individual $100(1 - \alpha)$

percent confidence interval. Thus, intuitively, we are paying a penalty for simultaneous confidence by obtaining longer intervals. One pragmatic approach to comparing treatment means is to first determine if we can use the more conservative Tukey intervals to make meaningful pairwise comparisons. If we cannot, then we might see what the individual intervals tell us. In the following box we present both individual and Tukey simultaneous confidence intervals for pairwise differences. We also present the formula for a confidence interval for a single treatment mean, which we might use after we have used pairwise comparisons to determine the "best" treatment.

Estimation in One-Way ANOVA

1 Consider the **pairwise difference** $\mu_i - \mu_h$, which can be interpreted to be the change in the mean value of the response variable associated with changing from using treatment h to using treatment i. Then, a **point estimate of the difference** $\mu_i - \mu_h$ is $\bar{x}_i - \bar{x}_h$, where $\bar{x}_i$ and $\bar{x}_h$ are the sample treatment means associated with treatments i and h.

2 An **individual** $100(1 - \alpha)$ **percent confidence interval** for $\mu_i - \mu_h$ is

$$\left[(\bar{x}_i - \bar{x}_h) \pm t_{\alpha/2} \sqrt{MSE \left(\frac{1}{n_i} + \frac{1}{n_h} \right)} \right]$$

Here the $t_{\alpha/2}$ point is based on $n - p$ degrees of freedom, and MSE is the previously defined error mean square found in the ANOVA table.

3 A **Tukey simultaneous** $100(1 - \alpha)$ **percent confidence interval** for $\mu_i - \mu_h$ is

$$\left[(\bar{x}_i - \bar{x}_h) \pm q_\alpha \sqrt{\frac{MSE}{m}} \right]$$

Here the value q_α is obtained from Table A.9 (pages 648–650), which is a **table of percentage points of the studentized range**. In this table q_α is listed corresponding to values of p and $n - p$. Furthermore, we assume that the sample sizes n_i and n_h are equal to the same value, which we denote as m. If n_i and n_h are not equal, we replace $q_\alpha \sqrt{MSE/m}$ by $(q_\alpha/\sqrt{2})\sqrt{MSE[(1/n_i) + (1/n_h)]}$.

4 A **point estimate of the treatment mean** μ_i is $\bar{x}_i$ and an **individual** $100(1 - \alpha)$ **percent confidence interval** for μ_i is

$$\left[\bar{x}_i \pm t_{\alpha/2} \sqrt{\frac{MSE}{n_i}} \right]$$

Here the $t_{\alpha/2}$ point is based on $n - p$ degrees of freedom.

EXAMPLE 11.6 The Gasoline Mileage Case　　Ⓒ

In the gasoline mileage study, we are comparing $p = 3$ treatment means (μ_A, μ_B, and μ_C). Furthermore, each sample is of size $m = 5$, there are a total of $n = 15$ observed gas mileages, and the MSE found in Table 11.5 is .669. Because $q_{.05} = 3.77$ is the entry found in Table A.9 (page 649) corresponding to $p = 3$ and $n - p = 12$, a Tukey simultaneous 95 percent confidence interval for $\mu_B - \mu_A$ is

$$\left[(\bar{x}_B - \bar{x}_A) \pm q_{.05} \sqrt{\frac{MSE}{m}} \right] = \left[(36.56 - 34.92) \pm 3.77 \sqrt{\frac{.669}{5}} \right]$$
$$= [1.64 \pm 1.379]$$
$$= [.261, 3.019]$$

Similarly, Tukey simultaneous 95 percent confidence intervals for $\mu_A - \mu_C$ and $\mu_B - \mu_C$ are, respectively,

$$[(\bar{x}_A - \bar{x}_C) \pm 1.379] \qquad \text{and} \qquad [(\bar{x}_B - \bar{x}_C) \pm 1.379]$$
$$= [(34.92 - 33.98) \pm 1.379] \qquad\qquad = [(36.56 - 33.98) \pm 1.379]$$
$$= [-0.439, 2.319] \qquad\qquad\qquad = [1.201, 3.959]$$

These intervals make us simultaneously 95 percent confident that (1) changing from gasoline type A to gasoline type B increases mean mileage by between .261 and 3.019 mpg, (2) changing from gasoline type C to gasoline type A might decrease mean mileage by as much as .439 mpg or might increase mean mileage by as much as 2.319 mpg, *and* (3) changing from gasoline type C to gasoline type B increases mean mileage by between 1.201 and 3.959 mpg. The first and third of these intervals make us 95 percent confident that μ_B is at least .261 mpg greater than μ_A and at least 1.201 mpg greater than μ_C. Therefore, we have strong evidence that gasoline type B yields the highest mean mileage of the gasoline types tested. Furthermore, noting that $t_{.025}$ based on $n - p = 12$ degrees of freedom is 2.179, it follows that an individual 95 percent confidence interval for μ_B is

$$\left[\bar{x}_B \pm t_{.025}\sqrt{\frac{MSE}{n_B}} \right] = \left[36.56 \pm 2.179\sqrt{\frac{.669}{5}} \right]$$
$$= [35.763, 37.357]$$

This interval says we can be 95 percent confident that the mean mileage obtained by using gasoline type B is between 35.763 and 37.357 mpg. Notice that this confidence interval is graphed on the MINITAB output of Figure 11.2. This output also shows the 95 percent confidence intervals for μ_A and μ_C and gives Tukey simultaneous 95 percent intervals. For example, consider finding the Tukey interval for $\mu_B - \mu_A$ on the MINITAB output. To do this, we look in the table corresponding to "Type A subtracted from" and find the row in this table labeled "Type B." This row gives the interval for "Type A subtracted from Type B"—that is, the interval for $\mu_B - \mu_A$. This interval is [.261, 3.019], as calculated above. Finally, note that the half-length of the individual 95 percent confidence interval for a pairwise comparison is (because $n_A = n_B = n_C = 5$)

$$t_{.025}\sqrt{MSE\left(\frac{1}{n_i} + \frac{1}{n_h}\right)} = 2.179\sqrt{.669\left(\frac{1}{5} + \frac{1}{5}\right)} = 1.127$$

This half-length implies that the individual intervals are shorter than the previously constructed Tukey intervals, which have a half-length of 1.379. Recall, however, that the Tukey intervals are short enough to allow us to conclude with 95 percent confidence that μ_B is greater than μ_A and μ_C.

We next consider testing $H_0: \mu_i - \mu_h = 0$ versus $H_a: \mu_i - \mu_h \neq 0$. The test statistic t for performing this test is calculated by dividing $\bar{x}_i - \bar{x}_h$ by $\sqrt{MSE\,[(1/n_i) + (1/n_h)]}$. For example, consider testing $H_0: \mu_B - \mu_A = 0$ versus $H_a: \mu_B - \mu_A \neq 0$. Since $\bar{x}_B - \bar{x}_A = 36.56 - 34.92 = 1.64$ and $\sqrt{MSE\,[(1/n_B) + (1/n_A)]} = \sqrt{.669[(1/5) + (1/5)]} = .5173$, the test statistic t equals $1.64/.5173 = 3.17$. This test statistic value is given in the leftmost table of the following MegaStat output, as is the test statistic value for testing $H_0: \mu_B - \mu_C = 0$ $(t = 4.99)$ and the test statistic value for testing $H_0: \mu_A - \mu_C = 0$ $(t = 1.82)$:

Tukey simultaneous comparison t-values (d.f. = 12)

		Type C 33.98	Type A 34.92	Type B 36.56
Type C	33.98			
Type A	34.92	1.82		
Type B	36.56	4.99	3.17	

critical values for experimentwise error rate:

0.05	2.67
0.01	3.56

p-values for pairwise t-tests

		Type C 33.98	Type A 34.92	Type B 36.56
Type C	33.98			
Type A	34.92	.0942		
Type B	36.56	.0003	.0081	

☐ = Significant at .05 level
☐ = Significant at .01 level
☐ = Significant at .01 level

If we wish to use the Tukey simultaneous comparison procedure having an experimentwise error rate of α, we reject $H_0: \mu_i - \mu_h = 0$ in favor of $H_a: \mu_i - \mu_h \neq 0$ if the absolute value of t is greater than the rejection point $q_\alpha/\sqrt{2}$. Table A.9 tells us that $q_{.05}$ is 3.77 and $q_{.01}$ is 5.04. Therefore, the rejection points for experimentwise error rates of .05 and .01 are, respectively, $3.77/\sqrt{2} = 2.67$ and $5.04/\sqrt{2} = 3.56$ (see the MegaStat output). Suppose we set α equal to .05. Then, since the test statistic value for testing $H_0: \mu_B - \mu_A = 0$ $(t = 3.17)$ and the test statistic value for testing $H_0: \mu_B - \mu_C = 0$ $(t = 4.99)$ are greater than the rejection point 2.67, we reject both null hypotheses. This, along with the fact that $\bar{x}_B = 36.56$ is greater than $\bar{x}_A = 34.92$ and $\bar{x}_C = 33.98$, leads us to conclude that gasoline type B yields the highest mean mileage of the gasoline types tested (note that the MegaStat output conveniently arranges the sample means in increasing order). Finally, note that the rightmost table of the MegaStat output gives the p-values for individual (rather than simultaneous) pairwise hypothesis tests. For example, the individual p-value for testing $H_0: \mu_B - \mu_C = 0$ is .0003, and the individual p-value for testing $H_0: \mu_B - \mu_A = 0$ is .0081.

In general, when we use a completely randomized experimental design, it is important to compare the treatments by using experimental units that are essentially the same with respect to the characteristic under study. For example, in the gasoline mileage case we have used cars of the same type (Fire-Hawks) to compare the different gasoline types, and in the shelf display case we have used grocery stores of the same sales potential for the bakery product to compare the shelf display heights (the reader will analyze the data for this case in the exercises). Sometimes, however, it is not possible to use experimental units that are essentially the same with respect to the characteristic under study. For example, suppose a chain of stores that sells audio and video equipment wishes to compare the effects of street, mall, and downtown locations on the sales volume of its stores. The experimental units in this situation are the areas where the stores are located, but these areas are not of the same sales potential because each area is populated by a different number of households. In such a situation we must explicitly account for the differences in the experimental units. One way to do this is to use **regression analysis,** which is discussed in Chapters 13–15. When we use regression analysis to explicitly account for a variable (such as the number of households in the store's area) that causes differences in the experimental units, we call the variable a **covariate.** Furthermore, we say that we are performing an **analysis of covariance.** Finally, another way to deal with differing experimental units is to employ a **randomized block design.** This experimental design is discussed in Section 11.3.

To conclude this section, we note that if we fear that the normality and/or equal variances assumptions for one-way analysis of variance do not hold, we can use a nonparametric approach to compare several populations. One such approach is the Kruskal–Wallis H test, which is discussed in Bowerman, O'Connell, and Murphree (2009).

Exercises for Section 11.2

CONCEPTS

11.5   Explain the assumptions that must be satisfied in order to validly use the one-way ANOVA formulas.

11.6   Explain the difference between the between-treatment variability and the within-treatment variability when performing a one-way ANOVA.

11.7   Explain why we conduct pairwise comparisons of treatment means.

11.8   Explain the difference between individual and simultaneous confidence intervals for a set of several pairwise differences.

METHODS AND APPLICATIONS

11.9   **THE SHELF DISPLAY CASE**   BakeSale

Consider Example 11.2, and let μ_B, μ_M, and μ_T represent the mean monthly sales when using the bottom, middle, and top shelf display heights, respectively. Figure 11.3 gives the MINITAB output of a one-way ANOVA of the bakery sales study data in Table 11.2 (page 443).

a   Test the null hypothesis that μ_B, μ_M, and μ_T are equal by setting $\alpha = .05$. On the basis of this test, can we conclude that the bottom, middle, and top shelf display heights have different effects on mean monthly sales?

b   Consider the pairwise differences $\mu_M - \mu_B$, $\mu_T - \mu_B$, and $\mu_T - \mu_M$. Find a point estimate of and a Tukey simultaneous 95 percent confidence interval for each pairwise difference. Interpret the meaning of each interval in practical terms. Which display height maximizes mean sales?

c   Find an individual 95 percent confidence interval for each pairwise difference in part *b*. Interpret each interval.

d   Find 95 percent confidence intervals for μ_B, μ_M, and μ_T. Interpret each interval.

11.10   Consider the display panel situation in Exercise 11.3, and let μ_A, μ_B, and μ_C represent the mean times to stabilize the emergency condition when using display panels A, B, and C, respectively. Figure 11.4 gives the MINITAB output of a one-way ANOVA of the display panel data in Table 11.3 (page 444).   Display

a   Test the null hypothesis that μ_A, μ_B, and μ_C are equal by setting $\alpha = .05$. On the basis of this test, can we conclude that display panels A, B, and C have different effects on the mean time to stabilize the emergency condition?

b   Consider the pairwise differences $\mu_B - \mu_A$, $\mu_C - \mu_A$, and $\mu_C - \mu_B$. Find a point estimate of and a Tukey simultaneous 95 percent confidence interval for each pairwise difference. Interpret the results by describing the effects of changing from using each display panel to

FIGURE 11.3   MINITAB Output of a One-Way ANOVA of the Bakery Sales Study Data in Table 11.2

```
One-way ANOVA: Bakery Sales versus Display Height

Source           DF       SS      MS       F       P
Display Height    2  2273.88 1136.94  184.57   0.000
Error            15    92.40    6.16
Total            17  2366.28
                                  Individual 95%
                                  CIs For Mean Based on Pooled StDev
Level    N    Mean  StDev  --------+---------+---------+---------+-
Bottom   6  55.800  2.477          (--*-)
Middle   6  77.200  3.103                              (--*-)
Top      6  51.500  1.648  (-*--)
                          --------+---------+---------+---------+-
  Pooled StDev = 2.482        56.0      64.0      72.0      80.0
```

```
Tukey 95% Simultaneous
  Confidence Intervals

Bottom subtracted from:
            Lower    Center   Upper
Middle    17.681    21.400  25.119
Top       -8.019    -4.300  -0.581

Middle subtracted from:
            Lower    Center   Upper
Top      -29.419   -25.700 -21.981
```

FIGURE 11.4   MINITAB Output of a One-Way ANOVA of the Display Panel Study Data in Table 11.3

```
One-way ANOVA: Time versus Display

Source   DF      SS      MS       F       P
Display   2  500.17  250.08   30.11   0.000
Error     9   74.75    8.31
Total    11  574.92
                                  Individual 95%
                                  CIs For Mean Based on Pooled StDev
Level   N    Mean  StDev  -+---------+---------+---------+---------
A       4  24.500  2.646            (-----*----)
B       4  20.500  2.646   (----*-----)
C       4  35.750  3.304                         (-----*----)
                          -+---------+---------+---------+---------
  Pooled StDev = 2.882    18.0      24.0      30.0      36.0
```

```
Tukey 95% Simultaneous
  Confidence Intervals

A subtracted from:
          Lower    Center   Upper
B        -9.692    -4.000   1.692
C         5.558    11.250  16.942

B subtracted from:
          Lower    Center   Upper
C         9.558    15.250  20.942
```

FIGURE 11.5   Excel Output of a One-Way ANOVA of the Bottle Design Study Data in Table 11.4

SUMMARY

Groups	Count	Sum	Average	Variance
DESIGN A	5	83	16.6	5.3
DESIGN B	5	164	32.8	9.2
DESIGN C	5	124	24.8	8.2

ANOVA

Source of Variation	SS	df	MS	F	P-Value	F crit
Between Groups	656.1333	2	328.0667	43.35683	3.23E-06	3.88529
Within Groups	90.8	12	7.566667			
Total	746.9333	14				

using each of the other panels. Which display panel(s) minimize the time required to stabilize the emergency condition?

c Find an individual 95 percent confidence interval for each pairwise difference in part b. Interpret the results.

11.11 Consider the bottle design study situation in Exercise 11.4, and let μ_A, μ_B, and μ_C represent mean daily sales using bottle designs A, B, and C, respectively. Figure 11.5 gives the Excel output of a one-way ANOVA of the bottle design study data in Table 11.4 (page 444).   ◆ BottleDes

a Test the null hypothesis that μ_A, μ_B, and μ_C are equal by setting $\alpha = .05$. That is, test for statistically significant differences between these treatment means at the .05 level of significance. Based on this test, can we conclude that bottle designs A, B, and C have different effects on mean daily sales?

b Consider the pairwise differences $\mu_B - \mu_A$, $\mu_C - \mu_A$, and $\mu_C - \mu_B$. Find a point estimate of and a Tukey simultaneous 95 percent confidence interval for each pairwise difference. Interpret the results in practical terms. Which bottle design maximizes mean daily sales?

c Find an individual 95 percent confidence interval for each pairwise difference in part b. Interpret the results in practical terms.

d Find a 95 percent confidence interval for each of the treatment means μ_A, μ_B, and μ_C. Interpret these intervals.

11.12 In order to compare the durability of four different brands of golf balls (ALPHA, BEST, CENTURY, and DIVOT), the National Golf Association randomly selects five balls of each brand

TABLE 11.6 Golf Ball Durability Test Results and a MegaStat Plot of the Results GolfBall

Brand			
Alpha	Best	Century	Divot
281	270	218	364
220	334	244	302
274	307	225	325
242	290	273	337
251	331	249	355

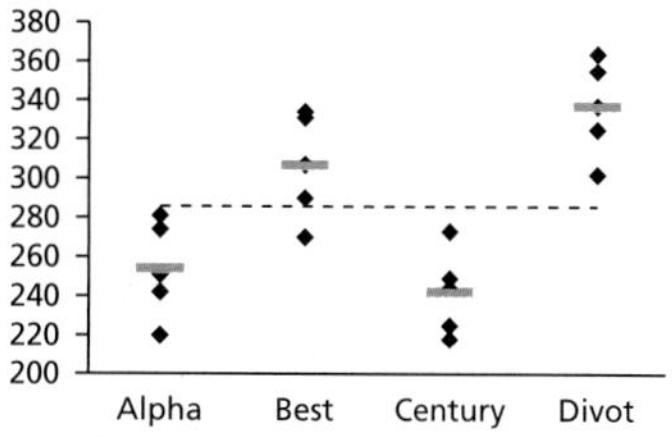

FIGURE 11.6 MegaStat Output of a One-Way ANOVA of the Golf Ball Durability Data

ANOVA table

Source	SS	df	MS	F [6]	p-value [7]
Treatment	29,860.40 [1]	3	9,953.467 [4]	16.42	3.85E-05
Error	9,698.40 [2]	16	606.150 [5]		
Total	39,558.80 [3]	19			

Mean	n	Std. Dev	
253.6	5	24.68	Alpha
306.4	5	27.21	Best
241.8	5	21.67	Century
336.6	5	24.60	Divot
284.6	20	45.63	Total

Tukey simultaneous comparison t-values (d.f. = 16)

		Century 241.8	Alpha 253.6	Best 306.4	Divot 336.6
Century	241.8				
Alpha	253.6	0.76			
Best	306.4	4.15	3.39		
Divot	336.6	6.09	5.33	1.94	

p-values for pairwise t-tests

		Century 241.8	Alpha 253.6	Best 306.4	Divot 336.6
Century	241.8				
Alpha	253.6	.4596			
Best	306.4	.0008	.0037		
Divot	336.6	1.57E-05	.0001	.0703	

Critical values for experimentwise error rate:

0.05	2.86
0.01	3.67

[1] SST [2] SSE [3] SSTO [4] MST [5] MSE [6] F [7] p-value for F

and places each ball into a machine that exerts the force produced by a 250-yard drive. The number of simulated drives needed to crack or chip each ball is recorded. The results are given in Table 11.6. The MegaStat output of a one-way ANOVA of this data is shown in Figure 11.6. Test for statistically significant differences between the treatment means μ_{ALPHA}, μ_{BEST}, μ_{CENTURY}, and μ_{DIVOT}. Set $\alpha = .05$. GolfBall

11.13 Perform pairwise comparisons of the treatment means in Exercise 11.12. Which brand(s) are most durable? Find a 95 percent confidence interval for each of the treatment means.

11.14 THE COMMERCIAL RESPONSE CASE

Recall from Example 11.3 that (1) 29 randomly selected subjects were exposed to commercials shown in more involving programs, (2) 29 randomly selected subjects were exposed to commercials shown in less involving programs, and (3) 29 randomly selected subjects watched commercials only (note: this is called the **control group**). The mean brand recall scores for these three groups were, respectively, $\bar{x}_1 = 1.21$, $\bar{x}_2 = 2.24$, and $\bar{x}_3 = 2.28$. Furthermore, a one-way ANOVA of the data shows that $SST = 21.40$ and $SSE = 85.56$.

a Define appropriate treatment means μ_1, μ_2, and μ_3. Then test for statistically significant differences between these treatment means. Set $\alpha = .05$.

b Perform pairwise comparisons of the treatment means by computing a Tukey simultaneous 95 percent confidence interval for each of the pairwise differences $\mu_1 - \mu_2$, $\mu_1 - \mu_3$, and $\mu_2 - \mu_3$. Which type of program content results in the worst mean brand recall score?

11.3 The Randomized Block Design

Not all experiments employ a completely randomized design. For instance, suppose that when we employ a completely randomized design, we fail to reject the null hypothesis of equality of treatment means because the within-treatment variability (which is measured by the SSE) is large. This could happen because differences between the experimental units are concealing true differences between the treatments. We can often remedy this by using what is called a **randomized block design.**

EXAMPLE 11.7 The Defective Cardboard Box Case

The Universal Paper Company manufactures cardboard boxes. The company wishes to investigate the effects of four production methods (methods 1, 2, 3, and 4) on the number of defective boxes produced in an hour. To compare the methods, the company could utilize a completely randomized design. For each of the four production methods, the company would select several (say, as an example, three) machine operators, train each operator to use the production method to which he or she has been assigned, have each operator produce boxes for one hour, and record the number of defective boxes produced. The three operators using any one production method would be *different* from those using any other production method. That is, the completely randomized design would utilize a total of 12 machine operators. However, the abilities of the machine operators could differ substantially. These differences might tend to conceal any real differences between the production methods. To overcome this disadvantage, the company will employ a **randomized block experimental design.** This involves randomly selecting three machine operators and training each operator thoroughly to use all four production methods. Then each operator will produce boxes for one hour using each of the four production methods. The order in which each operator uses the four methods should be random. We record the number of defective boxes produced by each operator using each method. The advantage of the randomized block design is that the defective rates obtained by using the four methods result from employing the *same* three operators. Thus any true differences in the effectiveness of the methods would not be concealed by differences in the operators' abilities.

When Universal Paper employs the randomized block design, it obtains the 12 defective box counts in Table 11.7. We let x_{ij} denote the number of defective boxes produced by machine operator j using production method i. For example, $x_{32} = 5$ says that 5 defective boxes were produced by machine operator 2 using production method 3 (see Table 11.7). In addition to the 12 defective box counts, Table 11.7 gives the sample mean of these 12 observations, which is $\bar{x} = 7.5833$, and also gives **sample treatment means** and **sample block means.** The sample treatment means are the average defective box counts obtained when using production methods 1, 2, 3, and 4. Denoting these sample treatment means as $\bar{x}_{1\cdot}, \bar{x}_{2\cdot}, \bar{x}_{3\cdot}$, and $\bar{x}_{4\cdot}$, we see from Table 11.7 that $\bar{x}_{1\cdot} = 10.3333$, $\bar{x}_{2\cdot} = 10.3333, \bar{x}_{3\cdot} = 5.0$, and $\bar{x}_{4\cdot} = 4.6667$. Because $\bar{x}_{3\cdot}$ and $\bar{x}_{4\cdot}$ are less than $\bar{x}_{1\cdot}$ and $\bar{x}_{2\cdot}$, we estimate that the mean number of defective boxes produced per hour by production method 3 or 4 is less than the mean number of defective boxes produced per hour by production method 1 or 2. The sample block means are the average defective box counts obtained by machine operators 1, 2, and 3. Denoting these sample block means as $\bar{x}_{\cdot 1}, \bar{x}_{\cdot 2}$, and $\bar{x}_{\cdot 3}$, we see from Table 11.7 that $\bar{x}_{\cdot 1} = 6.0$, $\bar{x}_{\cdot 2} = 7.75$, and $\bar{x}_{\cdot 3} = 9.0$. Because $\bar{x}_{\cdot 1}, \bar{x}_{\cdot 2}$, and $\bar{x}_{\cdot 3}$ differ, we have evidence that the abilities of the machine operators differ and thus that using the machine operators as blocks is reasonable.

TABLE 11.7   **Numbers of Defective Cardboard Boxes Obtained by Production Methods 1, 2, 3, and 4 and Machine Operators 1, 2, and 3**   ● CardBox

Treatment (Production Method)	Block (Machine Operator) 1	2	3	Sample Treatment Mean
1	9	10	12	10.3333
2	8	11	12	10.3333
3	3	5	7	5.0
4	4	5	5	4.6667
Sample Block Mean	6.0	7.75	9.0	$\bar{x} = 7.5833$

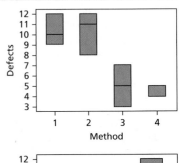

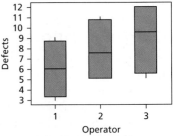

In general, a **randomized block design** compares p treatments (for example, production methods) by using b blocks (for example, machine operators). Each block is used exactly once to measure the effect of each and every treatment. The advantage of the randomized block design over the completely randomized design is that we are comparing the treatments by using the *same* experimental units. Thus any true differences in the treatments will not be concealed by differences in the experimental units.

In some experiments a block consists of **similar or matched sets of experimental units.** For example, suppose we wish to compare the performance of business majors, science majors, and fine arts majors on a graduate school admissions test. Here the blocks might be matched sets of students. Each matched set (block) would consist of a business major, a science major, and a fine arts major selected so that each is in his or her senior year, attends the same university, and has the same grade point average. By selecting blocks in this fashion, any true differences between majors would not be concealed by differences between college classes, universities, or grade point averages.

In order to analyze the data obtained in a randomized block design, we define

x_{ij} = the value of the response variable observed when block j uses treatment i

$\bar{x}_{i\bullet}$ = the mean of the b values of the response variable observed when using treatment i

$\bar{x}_{\bullet j}$ = the mean of the p values of the response variable observed when using block j

$\bar{x}$ = the mean of the total of the bp values of the response variable that we have observed in the experiment

The ANOVA procedure for a randomized block design partitions the **total sum of squares (SSTO)** into three components: the **treatment sum of squares (SST)**, the **block sum of squares (SSB)**, and the **error sum of squares (SSE).** The formula for this partitioning is

$$SSTO = SST + SSB + SSE$$

The steps for calculating these sums of squares, as well as what is measured by the sums of squares, can be summarized as follows:

Step 1: Calculate *SST*, which measures the amount of between-treatment variability:

$$SST = b \sum_{i=1}^{p} (\bar{x}_{i\bullet} - \bar{x})^2$$

Step 2: Calculate *SSB*, which measures the amount of variability due to the blocks:

$$SSB = p \sum_{j=1}^{b} (\bar{x}_{\bullet j} - \bar{x})^2$$

Step 3: Calculate *SSTO*, which measures the total amount of variability:

$$SSTO = \sum_{i=1}^{p} \sum_{j=1}^{b} (x_{ij} - \bar{x})^2$$

Step 4: Calculate *SSE*, which measures the amount of variability due to the error:

$$SSE = SSTO - SST - SSB$$

These sums of squares are shown in Table 11.8, which is the ANOVA table for a randomized block design. This table also gives the degrees of freedom associated with each source of variation—treatments, blocks, error, and total—as well as the mean squares and F statistics used to test the hypotheses of interest in a randomized block experiment.

Before discussing these hypotheses, we will illustrate how the entries in the ANOVA table are calculated. The sums of squares in the defective cardboard box case are calculated as follows (note that $p = 4$ and $b = 3$):

Step 1: $SST = 3[(\bar{x}_{1\bullet} - \bar{x})^2 + (\bar{x}_{2\bullet} - \bar{x})^2 + (\bar{x}_{3\bullet} - \bar{x})^2 + (\bar{x}_{4\bullet} - \bar{x})^2]$

  $= 3[(10.3333 - 7.5833)^2 + (10.3333 - 7.5833)^2$

  $+ (5.0 - 7.5833)^2 + (4.6667 - 7.5833)^2]$

  $= 90.9167$

TABLE 11.8   ANOVA Table for the Randomized Block Design with p Treatments and b Blocks

Source of Variation	Degrees of Freedom	Sum of Squares	Mean Square	F
Treatments	$p - 1$	SST	$MST = \dfrac{SST}{p - 1}$	$F(\text{treatments}) = \dfrac{MST}{MSE}$
Blocks	$b - 1$	SSB	$MSB = \dfrac{SSB}{b - 1}$	$F(\text{blocks}) = \dfrac{MSB}{MSE}$
Error	$(p - 1)(b - 1)$	SSE	$MSE = \dfrac{SSE}{(p - 1)(b - 1)}$	
Total	$pb - 1$	SSTO		

Step 2:
$$SSB = 4[(\bar{x}_{\bullet 1} - \bar{x})^2 + (\bar{x}_{\bullet 2} - \bar{x})^2 + (\bar{x}_{\bullet 3} - \bar{x})^2]$$
$$= 4[(6.0 - 7.5833)^2 + (7.75 - 7.5833)^2 + (9.0 - 7.5833)^2]$$
$$= 18.1667$$

Step 3:
$$SSTO = (9 - 7.5833)^2 + (10 - 7.5833)^2 + (12 - 7.5833)^2$$
$$+ (8 - 7.5833)^2 + (11 - 7.5833)^2 + (12 - 7.5833)^2$$
$$+ (3 - 7.5833)^2 + (5 - 7.5833)^2 + (7 - 7.5833)^2$$
$$+ (4 - 7.5833)^2 + (5 - 7.5833)^2 + (5 - 7.5833)^2$$
$$= 112.9167$$

Step 4:
$$SSE = SSTO - SST - SSB$$
$$= 112.9167 - 90.9167 - 18.1667$$
$$= 3.8333$$

Figure 11.7 gives the MINITAB output of a randomized block ANOVA of the defective box data. This figure shows the above calculated sums of squares, as well as the degrees of freedom (recall that $p = 4$ and $b = 3$), the mean squares, and the F statistics (and associated p-values) used to test the hypotheses of interest.

Of main interest is the test of the null hypothesis H_0 that **no differences exist between the treatment effects** on the mean value of the response variable versus the alternative hypothesis H_a that **at least two treatment effects differ.** We can reject H_0 in favor of H_a at level of

FIGURE 11.7   MINITAB Output of a Randomized Block ANOVA of the Defective Box Data

```
       Rows: Method   Columns: Operator
                    1          2          3        All
         1      9.000     10.000     12.000     10.333
         2      8.000     11.000     12.000     10.333
         3      3.000      5.000      7.000      5.000
         4      4.000      5.000      5.000      4.667
       All      6.000      7.750      9.000      7.583

    Two-way ANOVA: Rejects versus Method, Operator

    Source      DF         SS              MS           F            P
    Method       3     90.917 [1]     30.3056 [5]   47.43 [8]   0.000 [9]
    Operator     2     18.167 [2]      9.0833 [6]   14.22 [10]  0.005 [11]
    Error        6      3.833 [3]      0.6389 [7]
    Total       11    112.917 [4]

    Method    Mean              Operator   Mean
      1     10.3333 [12]           1       6.00 [16]
      2     10.3333 [13]           2       7.75 [17]
      3      5.0000 [14]           3       9.00 [18]
      4      4.6667 [15]
```

[1] SST [2] SSB [3] SSE [4] SSTO [5] MST [6] MSB [7] MSE [8] F(treatments) [9] p-value for F(treatments)
[10] F(blocks) [11] p-value for F(blocks) [12] $\bar{x}_{1\bullet}$ [13] $\bar{x}_{2\bullet}$ [14] $\bar{x}_{3\bullet}$ [15] $\bar{x}_{4\bullet}$ [16] $\bar{x}_{\bullet 1}$ [17] $\bar{x}_{\bullet 2}$ [18] $\bar{x}_{\bullet 3}$

significance α if

$$F(\text{treatments}) = \frac{MST}{MSE}$$

is greater than the F_α point based on $p - 1$ numerator and $(p - 1)(b - 1)$ denominator degrees of freedom. In the defective cardboard box case, $F_{.05}$ based on $p - 1 = 3$ numerator and $(p - 1)(b - 1) = 6$ denominator degrees of freedom is 4.76 (see Table A.6, page 645). Because

$$F(\text{treatments}) = \frac{MST}{MSE} = \frac{30.306}{.639} = 47.43$$

is greater than $F_{.05} = 4.76$, we reject H_0 at the .05 level of significance. Therefore, we have strong evidence that at least two production methods have different effects on the mean number of defective boxes produced per hour. Alternatively, we can reject H_0 in favor of H_a at level of significance α if the p-value is less than α. Here the p-value is the area under the curve of the F distribution [having $p - 1$ and $(p - 1)(b - 1)$ degrees of freedom] to the right of $F(\text{treatments})$. The MINITAB output in Figure 11.7 tells us that this p-value is 0.000 (that is, less than .001) for the defective box data. Therefore, we have extremely strong evidence that at least two production methods have different effects on the mean number of defective boxes produced per hour.

It is also of interest to test the null hypothesis H_0 that **no differences exist between the block effects** on the mean value of the response variable versus the alternative hypothesis H_a that **at least two block effects differ.** We can reject H_0 in favor of H_a at level of significance α if

$$F(\text{blocks}) = \frac{MSB}{MSE}$$

is greater than the F_α point based on $b - 1$ numerator and $(p - 1)(b - 1)$ denominator degrees of freedom. In the defective cardboard box case, $F_{.05}$ based on $b - 1 = 2$ numerator and $(p - 1)(b - 1) = 6$ denominator degrees of freedom is 5.14 (see Table A.6, page 645). Because

$$F(\text{blocks}) = \frac{MSB}{MSE} = \frac{9.083}{.639} = 14.22$$

is greater than $F_{.05} = 5.14$, we reject H_0 at the .05 level of significance. Therefore, we have strong evidence that at least two machine operators have different effects on the mean number of defective boxes produced per hour. Alternatively, we can reject H_0 in favor of H_a at level of significance α if the p-value is less than α. Here the p-value is the area under the curve of the F distribution [having $b - 1$ and $(p - 1)(b - 1)$ degrees of freedom] to the right of $F(\text{blocks})$. The MINITAB output tells us that this p-value is .005 for the defective box data. Therefore, we have very strong evidence that at least two machine operators have different effects on the mean number of defective boxes produced per hour. This implies that using the machine operators as blocks is reasonable.

If, in a randomized block design, we conclude that at least two treatment effects differ, we can perform pairwise comparisons to determine how they differ.

Point Estimates and Confidence Intervals in a Randomized Block ANOVA

Consider the **difference between the effects of treatments i and h on the mean value of the response variable.** Then:

1 A **point estimate** of this difference is $\bar{x}_{i\cdot} - \bar{x}_{h\cdot}$.

2 An **individual $100(1 - \alpha)$ percent confidence interval** for this difference is

$$\left[(\bar{x}_{i\cdot} - \bar{x}_{h\cdot}) \pm t_{\alpha/2}\, s \sqrt{\frac{2}{b}} \right]$$

Here $t_{\alpha/2}$ is based on $(p - 1)(b - 1)$ degrees of freedom, and s is the square root of the MSE found in the randomized block ANOVA table.

3 A **Tukey simultaneous $100(1 - \alpha)$ percent confidence interval** for this difference is

$$\left[(\bar{x}_{i\cdot} - \bar{x}_{h\cdot}) \pm q_\alpha \frac{s}{\sqrt{b}} \right]$$

Here the value q_α is obtained from Table A.9 (pages 648–650), which is a table of percentage points of the studentized range. In this table q_α is listed corresponding to values of p and $(p - 1)(b - 1)$.

EXAMPLE 11.8 The Defective Cardboard Box Case

We have previously concluded that we have extremely strong evidence that at least two production methods have different effects on the mean number of defective boxes produced per hour. We have also seen that the sample treatment means are $\bar{x}_{1\cdot} = 10.3333$, $\bar{x}_{2\cdot} = 10.3333$, $\bar{x}_{3\cdot} = 5.0$, and $\bar{x}_{4\cdot} = 4.6667$. Since $\bar{x}_{4\cdot}$ is the smallest sample treatment mean, we will use Tukey simultaneous 95 percent confidence intervals to compare the effect of production method 4 with the effects of production methods 1, 2, and 3. To compute these intervals, we first note that $q_{.05} = 4.90$ is the entry in Table A.9 (page 649) corresponding to $p = 4$ and $(p - 1)(b - 1) = 6$. Also, note that the *MSE* found in the randomized block ANOVA table is .639 (see Figure 11.7), which implies that $s = \sqrt{.639} = .7994$. It follows that a Tukey simultaneous 95 percent confidence interval for the difference between the effects of production methods 4 and 1 on the mean number of defective boxes produced per hour is

$$\left[(\bar{x}_{4\cdot} - \bar{x}_{1\cdot}) \pm q_{.05}\frac{s}{\sqrt{b}} \right] = \left[(4.6667 - 10.3333) \pm 4.90\left(\frac{.7994}{\sqrt{3}}\right) \right]$$
$$= [-5.6666 \pm 2.2615]$$
$$= [-7.9281, -3.4051]$$

Furthermore, it can be verified that a Tukey simultaneous 95 percent confidence interval for the difference between the effects of production methods 4 and 2 on the mean number of defective boxes produced per hour is also $[-7.9281, -3.4051]$. Therefore, we can be 95 percent confident that changing from production method 1 or 2 to production method 4 decreases the mean number of defective boxes produced per hour by a machine operator by between 3.4051 and 7.9281 boxes. A Tukey simultaneous 95 percent confidence interval for the difference between the effects of production methods 4 and 3 on the mean number of defective boxes produced per hour is

$$[(\bar{x}_{4\cdot} - \bar{x}_{3\cdot}) \pm 2.2615] = [(4.6667 - 5) \pm 2.2615]$$
$$= [-2.5948, 1.9282]$$

This interval tells us (with 95 percent confidence) that changing from production method 3 to production method 4 might decrease the mean number of defective boxes produced per hour by as many as 2.5948 boxes or might increase this mean by as many as 1.9282 boxes. In other words, because this interval contains 0, we cannot conclude that the effects of production methods 4 and 3 differ.

Exercises for Section 11.3

CONCEPTS

11.15   In your own words, explain why we sometimes employ the randomized block design.

11.16   How can we test to determine if the blocks we have chosen are reasonable?

METHODS AND APPLICATIONS

11.17   A marketing organization wishes to study the effects of four sales methods on weekly sales of a product. The organization employs a randomized block design in which three salesman use each sales method. The results obtained are given in Table 11.9. Figure 11.8 gives the Excel output of a randomized block ANOVA of the sales method data.   ● SaleMeth

T A B L E   1 1 . 9   Results of a Sales Method Experiment Employing a Randomized Block Design   ● SaleMeth

Sales Method, *i*	Salesman, *j*		
	A	B	C
1	32	29	30
2	32	30	28
3	28	25	23
4	25	24	23

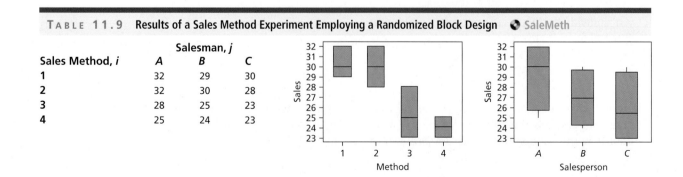

FIGURE 11.10   MegaStat Output of an ANOVA of the Cholesterol Reduction Data

ANOVA table

Source	SS	df	MS	F	p-value
Treatment	2,152.11	2	1,076.056	40.79	8.59E-07
Error	395.67	15	26.378		
Total	2,547.78	17			

Mean	n	Std. Dev	
23.7	6	4.97	X
39.2	6	4.92	Y
12.5	6	5.50	Z
25.1	18	12.24	Total

Post hoc analysis

Tukey simultaneous comparison t-values (d.f. = 15)

		Z	X	Y
		12.5	23.7	39.2
Z	12.5			
X	23.7	3.77		
Y	39.2	8.99	5.23	

critical values for experimentwise error rate:

0.05	2.60
0.01	3.42

TABLE 11.13   Results of a Loan Evaluation Experiment ● LoanEval

	Loan Evaluation Method		
Loan Officer	B	F	D
1	8	5	4
2	6	4	3
3	5	2	1
4	4	1	0

TABLE 11.14   Results of an Execution Speed Experiment for Three Compilers (Seconds) ● ExecSpd

	Compiler		
Computer	1	2	3
Model 235	9.9	8.0	7.1
Model 335	12.5	10.6	9.1
Model 435	10.8	9.0	7.8

auditor groups have different effects on the mean additional time allocated to investigating the accounts receivable audit program?

b Perform pairwise comparisons of the treatment means by computing a Tukey simultaneous 95 percent confidence interval for each of the pairwise differences $\mu_1 - \mu_2$, $\mu_1 - \mu_3$, and $\mu_2 - \mu_3$. Interpret the results. What do your results imply about the objectivity of auditors? What are the practical implications of this result?

11.24 The loan officers at a large bank can use three different methods for evaluating loan applications. Loan decisions can be based on (1) the applicant's balance sheet (B), (2) examination of key financial ratios (F), or (3) use of a new decision support system (D). In order to compare these three methods, four of the bank's loan officers are randomly selected. Each officer employs each of the evaluation methods for one month (the methods are employed in randomly selected orders). After a year has passed, the percentage of bad loans for each loan officer and evaluation method is determined. The data obtained by using this randomized block design are given in Table 11.13. Completely analyze the data using a randomized block ANOVA. ● LoanEval

11.25 An information systems manager wishes to compare the execution speed (in seconds) for a standard statistical software package using three different compilers. The manager tests each compiler using three different computer models, and the data in Table 11.14 are obtained. Completely analyze the data (using a computer package if you wish). In particular, test for compiler effects and computer model effects, and also perform pairwise comparisons. ● ExecSpd

11.26   Internet Exercise

In an article from the *Journal of Statistics Education*, Robin Lock describes a rich set of interesting data on selected attributes for a sample of 1993-model new cars. These data support a wide range of analyses. Indeed, the analysis possibilities are the subject of Lock's article. Here our interest is in comparing mean highway gas mileage figures among the six identified vehicle types— compact, small, midsize, large, sporty, and van.

Go to the *Journal of Statistics Education* Web archive and retrieve the 1993-cars data set and related documentation: http://www.amstat.org/publications/jse/

archive.htm. Click on *93cars.dat* for data, *93cars.txt* for documentation, and *article associated with this data set* for a full text of the article. Excel and MINITAB data files are also included on the CD-ROM (● 93Cars). Construct box plots of *Highway MPG* by *Vehicle Type* (if MINITAB or other suitable statistical software is available). Describe any apparent differences in gas mileage by vehicle type. Conduct an analysis of variance to test for differences in mean gas mileage by vehicle type. Prepare a brief report of your analysis and conclusions.

Appendix 11.1 ■ Experimental Design and Analysis of Variance Using MINITAB

The instruction blocks in this section each begin by describing the entry of data into the MINITAB Data window. Alternatively, the data may be loaded directly from the data disk included with the text. The appropriate data file name is given at the top of each instruction block. Please refer to Appendix 1.1 for further information about entering data, saving data, and printing results when using MINITAB.

One-way ANOVA in Figure 11.2(a) on page 449 (data file: GasMile2.MTW):

- In the Data window, enter the data from Table 11.1 (page 442) into three columns with variable names Type A, Type B, and Type C.

- Select **Stat : ANOVA : One-way (Unstacked)**

- In the "One-Way Analysis of Variance" dialog box, select 'Type A' 'Type B' 'Type C' into the "Responses (in separate columns)" window. (The single quotes are necessary because of the blank spaces in the variable names. The quotes will be added automatically if the names are selected from the variable list or if they are selected by double-clicking.)

- Click OK in the "One-Way Analysis of Variance" dialog box.

To produce mileage by gasoline type box plots similar to those shown in Table 11.1 (page 442):

- Click the Graphs... button in the "One-Way Analysis of Variance" dialog box.

- Check the "Boxplots of data" checkbox and click OK in the "One-Way Analysis of Variance—Graphs" dialog box.

- Click OK in the "One-Way Analysis of Variance" dialog box.

To produce Tukey pairwise comparisons:

- Click on the Comparisons... button in the "One-Way Analysis of Variance" dialog box.

- Check the "Tukey's family error rate" checkbox.

- In the "Tukey's family error rate" box, enter the desired experimentwise error rate (here we have entered 5, which denotes 5%— alternatively, we could enter the decimal fraction .05).

- Click OK in the "One-Way Multiple Comparisons" dialog box.

- Click OK in the "One-Way Analysis of Variance" dialog box.

- The one-way ANOVA output and the Tukey multiple comparisons will be given in the Session window, and the box plots will appear in a graphics window.

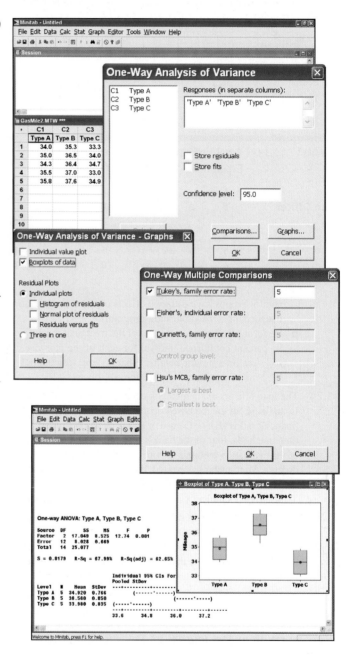

Randomized Block ANOVA in Figure 11.7 on page 458 (data File: CardBox.MTW):

- In the Data window, enter the observed number of defective boxes from Table 11.7 into column C1 with variable name Rejects; enter the corresponding production method (1,2,3,or 4) into column C2 with variable name Method; and enter the corresponding machine operator (1,2,or 3) into column C3 with variable name Operator.

- Select **Stat : ANOVA : Two-way**

- In the "Two-Way Analysis of Variance" dialog box, select Rejects into the Response window.

- Select Method into the Row factor window and check the "Display means" checkbox.

- Select Operator into the Column factor window and check the "Display means" checkbox.

- Check the "Fit additive model" checkbox.

- Click OK in the "Two-Way Analysis of Variance" dialog box to display the randomized block ANOVA in the Session window.

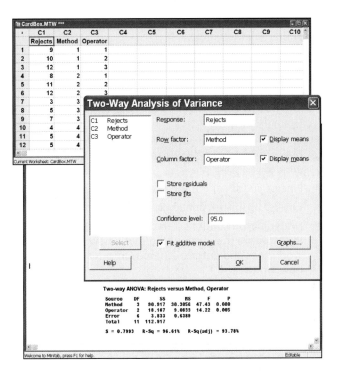

Appendix 11.2 ■ Experimental Design and Analysis of Variance Using Excel

The instruction blocks in this section each begin by describing the entry of data into an Excel spreadsheet. Alternatively, the data may be loaded directly from the data disk included with the text. The appropriate data file name is given at the top of each instruction block. Please refer to Appendix 1.2 for further information about entering data, saving data, and printing results when using Excel.

One-way ANOVA in Figure 11.2(b) on page 449 (data file: GasMile2.xlsx):

- Enter the gasoline mileage data from Table 11.1 (page 442) as follows: type the label "Type A" in cell A1 with its five mileage values in cells A2 to A6; type the label "Type B" in cell B1 with its five mileage values in cells B2 to B6; type the label "Type C" in cell C1 with its five mileage values in cells C2 to C6.

- Select **Data : Data Analysis : Anova : Single Factor** and click OK in the Data Analysis dialog box.

- In the "Anova: Single Factor" dialog box, enter A1.C6 into the "Input Range" window.

- Select the "Grouped By: Columns" option.

- Place a checkmark in the "Labels in First Row" checkbox.

- Enter 0.05 into the Alpha box.

- Under Output options, select "New Worksheet Ply" to have the output placed in a new worksheet and enter the name Output for the new worksheet.

- Click OK in the "Anova: Single Factor" dialog box.

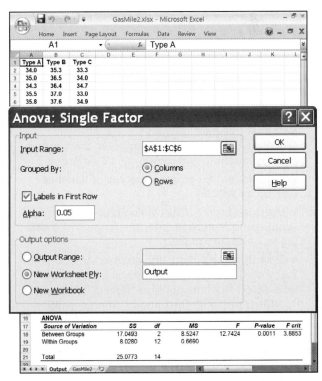

Randomized block ANOVA in Figure 11.8 on page 461 (data file: SaleMeth.xlsx):

- Enter the sales methods data from Table 11.9 (page 460) as shown in the screen.

- Select **Data : Data Analysis : Anova: Two-Factor Without Replication** and click OK in the Data Analysis dialog box.

- In the "Anova: Two-Factor Without Replication" dialog box, enter A1.D5 into the "Input Range" window.

- Place a checkmark in the "Labels" checkbox.

- Enter 0.05 in the Alpha box.

- Under Output options, select "New Worksheet Ply" to have the output placed in a new worksheet and enter the name Output for the new worksheet.

- Click OK in the "Anova: Two-Factor Without Replication" dialog box.

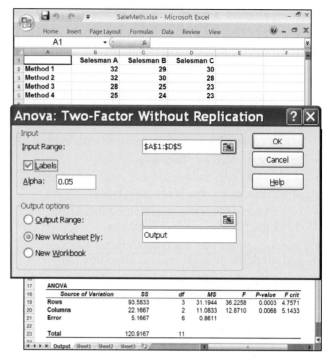

Appendix 11.3 ■ Experimental Design and Analysis of Variance Using MegaStat

The instructions in this section begin by describing the entry of data into an Excel worksheet. Alternatively, the data may be loaded directly from the data disk included with the text. The appropriate data file name is given at the top of each instruction block. Please refer to Appendix 1.2 for further information about entering data, saving data, and printing results in Excel. Please refer to Appendix 1.3 for more information about using MegaStat.

One-way ANOVA similar to Figure 11.2(b) on page 449 (data file: GasMile2.xlsx):

- Enter the gas mileage data in Table 11.1 (page 442) into columns A, B, and C—Type A mileages in column A (with label Type A), Type B mileages in column B (with label Type B), and Type C mileages in column C (with label Type C). Note that the input columns for the different groups must be side by side. However, the number of observations in each group can be different.

- Select **Add-Ins : MegaStat : Analysis of Variance : One-Factor ANOVA**

- In the One-Factor ANOVA dialog box, use the AutoExpand feature to enter the range A1.C6 into the Input range window.

- If desired, request "Post-Hoc Analysis" to obtain Tukey simultaneous comparisons and pairwise t tests. Select from the options: "Never," "Always," or "When $p < .05$." The option "When $p < .05$" gives post-hoc analysis when the p-value for the F statistic is less than .05.

- Check the Plot Data checkbox to obtain a plot comparing the groups.

- Click OK in the One-Factor ANOVA dialog box.

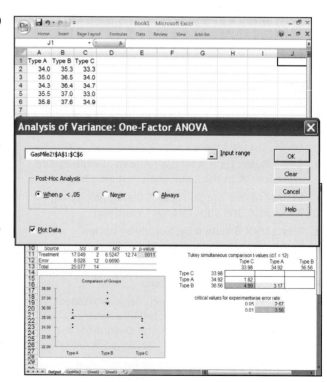

Randomized block ANOVA similar to Figure 11.7 on page 458 (data file: CardBox.xlsx):

- Enter the cardboard box data in Table 11.7 (page 456) in the arrangement shown in the screen. Here each column corresponds to a **treatment** (in this case, a production method) and each row corresponds to a **block** (in this case, a machine operator). Identify the production methods using the labels Method 1, Method 2, Method 3, and Method 4 in cells B1, C1, D1, and E1. Identify the blocks using the labels Operator 1, Operator 2, and Operator 3 in cells A2, A3, and A4.

- Select **Add-Ins : MegaStat : Analysis of Variance : Randomized Blocks ANOVA**

- In the Randomized Blocks ANOVA dialog box, click in the Input range window and enter the range A1.E4.

- If desired, request "Post-Hoc Analysis" to obtain Tukey simultaneous comparisons and pairwise t tests. Select from the options: "Never," "Always," or "When $p < .05$." The option "When $p < .05$" gives post-hoc analysis when the p-value related to the F statistic for the treatments is less than .05.

- Check the Plot Data checkbox to obtain a plot comparing the treatments.

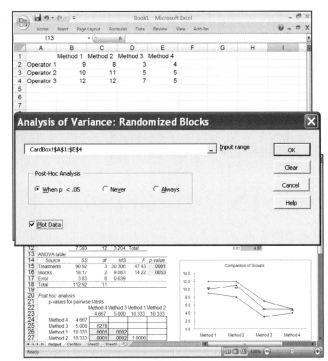

Chi-Square Tests

Chapter Outline

12.1 Chi-Square Goodness of Fit Tests

12.2 A Chi-Square Test for Independence

n this chapter we present two useful hypothesis tests based on the **chi-square distribution** (we have discussed the chi-square distribution in Section 9.6). First, we consider the **chi-square test of goodness of fit.** This test evaluates whether data falling into several categories do so with a hypothesized set of probabilities. Second, we discuss the **chi-square test for independence.** Here data are classified on two dimensions and are summarized in a **contingency table.** The test for independence then evaluates whether the cross-classified variables are independent of each other. If we conclude that the variables are not independent, then we have established that the variables in question are related, and we must then investigate the nature of the relationship.

12.1 Chi-Square Goodness of Fit Tests ● ● ●

Multinomial probabilities Sometimes we collect count data in order to study how the counts are distributed among several **categories** or **cells.** As an example, we might study consumer preferences for four different brands of a product. To do this, we select a random sample of consumers, and we ask each survey participant to indicate a brand preference. We then count the number of consumers who prefer each of the four brands. Here we have four categories (brands), and we study the distribution of the counts in each category in order to see which brands are preferred.

We often use categorical data to carry out a statistical inference. For instance, suppose that a major wholesaler in Cleveland, Ohio, carries four different brands of microwave ovens. Historically, consumer behavior in Cleveland has resulted in the market shares shown in Table 12.1. The wholesaler plans to begin doing business in a new territory—Milwaukee, Wisconsin. To study whether its policies for stocking the four brands of ovens in Cleveland can also be used in Milwaukee, the wholesaler compares consumer preferences for the four ovens in Milwaukee with the historical market shares observed in Cleveland. A random sample of 400 consumers in Milwaukee gives the preferences shown in Table 12.2.

To compare consumer preferences in Cleveland and Milwaukee, we must consider a **multinomial experiment.** This is similar to the binomial experiment. However, a binomial experiment concerns count data that can be classified into two categories, while a multinomial experiment concerns count data that are classified into more than two categories. Specifically, the assumptions for the multinomial experiment are as follows:

The Multinomial Experiment

1 We perform an experiment in which we carry out n identical trials and in which there are k possible outcomes on each trial.

2 The probabilities of the k outcomes are denoted $p_1, p_2, \ldots, p_k$ where $p_1 + p_2 + \cdots + p_k = 1$. These probabilities stay the same from trial to trial.

3 The trials in the experiment are independent.

4 The results of the experiment are observed frequencies (counts) of the number of trials that result in each of the k possible outcomes. The frequencies are denoted $f_1, f_2, \ldots, f_k$. That is, f_1 is the number of trials resulting in the first possible outcome, f_2 is the number of trials resulting in the second possible outcome, and so forth.

TABLE 12.1 **Market Shares for Four Microwave Oven Brands in Cleveland, Ohio** ◐ MicroWav

Brand	Market Share
1	20%
2	35%
3	30%
4	15%

TABLE 12.2 **Brand Preferences for Four Microwave Ovens in Milwaukee, Wisconsin** ◐ MicroWav

Brand	Observed Frequency (Number of Consumers Sampled Who Prefer the Brand)
1	102
2	121
3	120
4	57

Notice that the scenario that defines a multinomial experiment is similar to that which defines a binomial experiment. In fact, a binomial experiment is simply a multinomial experiment where k equals 2 (there are two possible outcomes on each trial).

In general, the probabilities $p_1, p_2, \ldots, p_k$ are unknown, and we estimate their values. Or, we compare estimates of these probabilities with a set of specified values. We now look at such an example.

EXAMPLE 12.1 The Microwave Oven Preference Case

Suppose the microwave oven wholesaler wishes to compare consumer preferences in Milwaukee with the historical market shares in Cleveland. If the consumer preferences in Milwaukee are substantially different, the wholesaler will consider changing its policies for stocking the ovens. Here we will define

$p_1 =$ the proportion of Milwaukee consumers who prefer brand 1

$p_2 =$ the proportion of Milwaukee consumers who prefer brand 2

$p_3 =$ the proportion of Milwaukee consumers who prefer brand 3

$p_4 =$ the proportion of Milwaukee consumers who prefer brand 4

Remembering that the historical market shares for brands 1, 2, 3, and 4 in Cleveland are 20 percent, 35 percent, 30 percent, and 15 percent, we test the null hypothesis

$$H_0: p_1 = .20, \quad p_2 = .35, \quad p_3 = .30, \quad \text{and} \quad p_4 = .15$$

which says that consumer preferences in Milwaukee are consistent with the historical market shares in Cleveland. We test H_0 versus

$$H_a: \text{the previously stated null hypothesis is not true}$$

To test H_0 we must compare the "observed frequencies" given in Table 12.2 with the "expected frequencies" for the brands calculated on the assumption that H_0 is true. For instance, if H_0 is true, we would expect $400(.20) = 80$ of the 400 Milwaukee consumers surveyed to prefer brand 1. Denoting this expected frequency for brand 1 as E_1, the expected frequencies for brands 2, 3, and 4 when H_0 is true are $E_2 = 400(.35) = 140$, $E_3 = 400(.30) = 120$, and $E_4 = 400(.15) = 60$. Recalling that Table 12.2 gives the observed frequency for each brand, we have $f_1 = 102$, $f_2 = 121$, $f_3 = 120$, and $f_4 = 57$. We now compare the observed and expected frequencies by computing a **chi-square statistic** as follows:

$$\chi^2 = \sum_{i=1}^{k=4} \frac{(f_i - E_i)^2}{E_i}$$

$$= \frac{(102 - 80)^2}{80} + \frac{(121 - 140)^2}{140} + \frac{(120 - 120)^2}{120} + \frac{(57 - 60)^2}{60}$$

$$= \frac{484}{80} + \frac{361}{140} + \frac{0}{120} + \frac{9}{60} = 8.7786$$

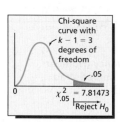

Chi-square curve with $k - 1 = 3$ degrees of freedom

$\chi_{.05}^2 = 7.81473$

Reject H_0

Clearly, the more the observed frequencies differ from the expected frequencies, the larger χ^2 will be and the more doubt will be cast on the null hypothesis. If the chi-square statistic is large enough (beyond a critical value), then we reject H_0.

To find an appropriate critical value, it can be shown that, when the null hypothesis is true, the sampling distribution of χ^2 is approximately a χ^2 distribution with $k - 1 = 4 - 1 = 3$ degrees of freedom. If we wish to test H_0 at the .05 level of significance, we reject H_0 if and only if

$$\chi^2 > \chi_{.05}^2$$

F I G U R E   1 2 . 1   **Output of a MINITAB Session That Computes the Chi-Square Statistic and Its Related *p*-Value for the Oven Wholesaler Example**

	C1	C2	C3	C4	C5	C6	C7	C8	
	Frequency	MarketShr	Expected	ChiSq	PValue				
1	102	0.20	80	6.05000	0.0323845				
2	121	0.35	140	2.57857					
3	120	0.30	120	0.00000					
4	57	0.15	60	0.15000					
5									
6									

Sum of ChiSq

Sum of ChiSq = 8.77857

Data Display

PValue
     0.0323845

Since Table A.10 (page 651) tells us that the $\chi^2_{.05}$ point corresponding to $k - 1 = 3$ degrees of freedom equals 7.81473, we find that

$$\chi^2 = 8.7786 > \chi^2_{.05} = 7.81473$$

and we reject H_0 at the .05 level of significance. Alternatively, the *p*-value for this hypothesis test is the area under the curve of the chi-square distribution having 3 degrees of freedom to the right of $\chi^2 = 8.7786$. This *p*-value can be calculated to be .0323845. Since this *p*-value is less than .05, we can reject H_0 at the .05 level of significance. Although there is no single MINITAB dialog box that produces a chi-square goodness of fit test, Figure 12.1 shows the output of a MINITAB session that computes the chi-square statistic and its related *p*-value for the oven wholesaler problem.

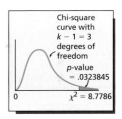

We conclude that consumer preferences in Milwaukee for the four brands of ovens are not consistent with the historical market shares in Cleveland. Based on this conclusion, the wholesaler should consider changing its stocking policies for microwave ovens when it enters the Milwaukee market. To study how to change its policies, the wholesaler might compute a 95 percent confidence interval for, say, the proportion of consumers in Milwaukee who prefer brand 2. Since $\hat{p}_2 = 121/400 = .3025$, this interval is (see Section 8.4, page 329)

$$\left[\hat{p}_2 \pm z_{.025} \sqrt{\frac{\hat{p}_2(1 - \hat{p}_2)}{n_2}} \right] = \left[.3025 \pm 1.96 \sqrt{\frac{.3025(1 - .3025)}{400}} \right]$$

$$= [.2575, .3475]$$

Since this entire interval is below .35, it suggests that (1) the market share for brand 2 ovens in Milwaukee will be smaller than the 35 percent market share that this brand commands in Cleveland, and (2) fewer brand 2 ovens (on a percentage basis) should be stocked in Milwaukee. Notice here that by restricting our attention to one particular brand (brand 2), we are essentially combining the other brands into a single group. It follows that we now have two possible outcomes—"brand 2" and "all other brands." Therefore, we have a binomial experiment, and we can employ the methods of Section 8.4, which are based on the binomial distribution.

In the following box we give a general chi-square goodness of fit test for multinomial probabilities:

A Goodness of Fit Test for Multinomial Probabilities

Consider a **multinomial experiment** in which each of n randomly selected items is classified into one of k groups. We let

f_i = the number of items classified into group i (that is, the ith observed frequency)

$E_i = np_i$

= the expected number of items that would be classified into group i if p_i is the probability of a randomly selected item being classified into group i (that is, the ith expected frequency)

If we wish to test

H_0: the values of the multinomial probabilities are $p_1, p_2, \ldots, p_k$—that is, the probability of a randomly selected item being classified into group 1 is p_1, the probability of a randomly selected item being classified into group 2 is p_2, and so forth

versus

H_a: at least one of the multinomial probabilities is not equal to the value stated in H_0

we define the **chi-square goodness of fit statistic** to be

$$\chi^2 = \sum_{i=1}^{k} \frac{(f_i - E_i)^2}{E_i}$$

Also, define the p-value related to χ^2 to be the area under the curve of the chi-square distribution having $k - 1$ degrees of freedom to the right of χ^2.

Then, we can reject H_0 in favor of H_a at level of significance α if either of the following equivalent conditions holds:

1 $\chi^2 > \chi_\alpha^2$

2 p-value $< \alpha$

Here the χ_α^2 point is based on $k - 1$ degrees of freedom.

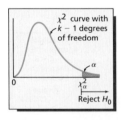

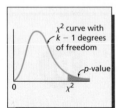

This test is based on the fact that it can be shown that, when H_0 is true, the sampling distribution of χ^2 is approximately a chi-square distribution with $k - 1$ degrees of freedom, if the sample size n is large. **It is generally agreed that n should be considered large if all of the "expected cell frequencies" (E_i values) are at least 5.** Furthermore, recent research implies that this condition on the E_i values can be somewhat relaxed. For example, Moore and McCabe (1993) indicate that **it is reasonable to use the chi-square approximation if the number of groups (k) exceeds 4, the average of the E_i values is at least 5, and the smallest E_i value is at least 1.** Notice that in Example 12.1 all of the E_i values are much larger than 5. Therefore, the chi-square test is valid.

A special version of the chi-square goodness of fit test for multinomial probabilities is called a **test for homogeneity.** This involves testing the null hypothesis that all of the multinomial probabilities are equal. For instance, in the microwave oven situation we would test

$$H_0: p_1 = p_2 = p_3 = p_4 = .25$$

which would say that no single brand of microwave oven is preferred to any of the other brands (equal preferences). If this null hypothesis is rejected in favor of

$$H_a: \text{At least one of } p_1, p_2, p_3, \text{ and } p_4 \text{ exceeds .25}$$

we would conclude that there is a preference for one or more of the brands. Here each of the expected cell frequencies equals $.25(400) = 100$. Remembering that the observed cell frequencies are $f_1 = 102, f_2 = 121, f_3 = 120,$ and $f_4 = 57$, the chi-square statistic is

$$\chi^2 = \sum_{i=1}^{4} \frac{(f_i - E_i)^2}{E_i}$$

$$= \frac{(102 - 100)^2}{100} + \frac{(121 - 100)^2}{100} + \frac{(120 - 100)^2}{100} + \frac{(57 - 100)^2}{100}$$

$$= .04 + 4.41 + 4 + 18.49 = 26.94$$

Since $\chi^2 = 26.94$ is greater than $\chi_{.05}^2 = 7.81473$ (see Table A.10 on page 651 with $k - 1 = 4 - 1 = 3$ degrees of freedom), we reject H_0 at level of significance .05. We conclude that preferences for the four brands are not equal and that at least one brand is preferred to the others.

Normal distributions We have seen that many statistical methods are based on the assumption that a random sample has been selected from a normally distributed population. We can check the validity of the normality assumption by using frequency distributions, stem-and-leaf displays, histograms, and normal plots. Another approach is to use a chi-square goodness of fit test to check the normality assumption. We show how this can be done in the following example.

EXAMPLE 12.2 The Car Mileage Case   C

Consider the sample of 50 gas mileages given in Table 1.4 (page 10). A histogram of these mileages (see Figure 2.10, page 60) is symmetrical and bell-shaped. This suggests that the sample of mileages has been randomly selected from a normally distributed population. In this example we use a chi-square goodness of fit test to check the normality of the mileages.

To perform this test, we first divide the number line into intervals (or categories). One way to do this is to use the class boundaries of the histogram in Figure 2.10. Table 12.3 gives these intervals and also gives observed frequencies (counts of the number of mileages in each interval), which have been obtained from the histogram of Figure 2.10. The chi-square test is done by comparing these observed frequencies with the expected frequencies in the rightmost column of Table 12.3. To explain how the expected frequencies are calculated, we first use the sample mean $\bar{x} = 31.56$ and the sample standard deviation $s = .798$ of the 50 mileages as point estimates of the population mean μ and population standard deviation σ. Then, for example, consider p_1, the probability that a randomly selected mileage will be in the first interval (less than 30.0) in Table 12.3, if the population of all mileages is normally distributed. We estimate p_1 to be

$$p_1 = P(\text{mileage} < 30.0) = P\left(z < \frac{30.0 - 31.56}{.798}\right)$$
$$= P(z < -1.95) = .0256$$

It follows that $E_1 = 50p_1 = 50(.0256) = 1.28$ is the expected frequency for the first interval under the normality assumption. Next, if we consider p_2, the probability that a randomly selected mileage will be in the second interval in Table 12.3 if the population of all mileages is normally distributed, we estimate p_2 to be

$$p_2 = P(30.0 \leq \text{mileage} < 30.5) = P\left(\frac{30.0 - 31.56}{.798} \leq z < \frac{30.5 - 31.56}{.798}\right)$$
$$= P(-1.95 \leq z < -1.33) = .0918 - .0256 = .0662$$

It follows that $E_2 = 50p_2 = 50(.0662) = 3.31$ is the expected frequency for the second interval under the normality assumption. The other expected frequencies are computed similarly. In general, p_i is the probability that a randomly selected mileage will be in interval i if the population of all possible mileages is normally distributed with mean 31.56 and standard deviation .798, and E_i is the expected number of the 50 mileages that would be in interval i if the population of all possible mileages has this normal distribution.

It seems reasonable to reject the null hypothesis

H_0: the population of all mileages is normally distributed

in favor of the alternative hypothesis

H_a: the population of all mileages is not normally distributed

---

TABLE 12.3   **Observed and Expected Cell Frequencies for a Chi-Square Goodness of Fit Test for Testing the Normality of the 50 Gasoline Mileages in Table 1.4**   🔵 GasMiles

Interval	Observed Frequency (f_i)	p_i If the Population of Mileages Is Normally Distributed	Expected Frequency, $E_i = np_i = 50p_i$
Less than 30.0	1	$p_1 = P(\text{mileage} < 30.0) = .0256$	$E_1 = 50(.0256) = 1.28$
$30.0 < 30.5$	3	$p_2 = P(30.0 \leq \text{mileage} < 30.5) = .0662$	$E_2 = 50(.0662) = 3.31$
$30.5 < 31.0$	8	$p_3 = P(30.5 \leq \text{mileage} < 31.0) = .1502$	$E_3 = 50(.1502) = 7.51$
$31.0 < 31.5$	11	$p_4 = P(31.0 \leq \text{mileage} < 31.5) = .2261$	$E_4 = 50(.2261) = 11.305$
$31.5 < 32.0$	11	$p_5 = P(31.5 \leq \text{mileage} < 32.0) = .2407$	$E_5 = 50(.2407) = 12.035$
$32.0 < 32.5$	9	$p_6 = P(32.0 \leq \text{mileage} < 32.5) = .1722$	$E_6 = 50(.1722) = 8.61$
$32.5 < 33.0$	5	$p_7 = P(32.5 \leq \text{mileage} < 33.0) = .0831$	$E_7 = 50(.0831) = 4.155$
Greater than 33.0	2	$p_8 = P(\text{mileage} > 33.0) = .0359$	$E_8 = 50(.0359) = 1.795$

if the observed frequencies in Table 12.3 differ substantially from the corresponding expected frequencies in Table 12.3. We compare the observed frequencies with the expected frequencies under the normality assumption by computing the chi-square statistic

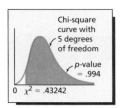

$$\chi^2 = \sum_{i=1}^{8} \frac{(f_i - E_i)^2}{E_i}$$

$$= \frac{(1 - 1.28)^2}{1.28} + \frac{(3 - 3.31)^2}{3.31} + \frac{(8 - 7.51)^2}{7.51} + \frac{(11 - 11.305)^2}{11.305}$$

$$+ \frac{(11 - 12.035)^2}{12.035} + \frac{(9 - 8.61)^2}{8.61} + \frac{(5 - 4.155)^2}{4.155} + \frac{(2 - 1.795)^2}{1.795}$$

$$= .43242$$

Since we have estimated $m = 2$ parameters (μ and σ) in computing the expected frequencies (E_i values), it can be shown that the sampling distribution of χ^2 is approximately a chi-square distribution with $k - 1 - m = 8 - 1 - 2 = 5$ degrees of freedom. Therefore, we can reject H_0 at level of significance α if

$$\chi^2 > \chi_\alpha^2$$

where the χ_α^2 point is based on $k - 1 - m = 8 - 1 - 2 = 5$ degrees of freedom. If we wish to test H_0 at the .05 level of significance, Table A.10 tells us that $\chi_{.05}^2 = 11.0705$. Therefore, since

$$\chi^2 = .43242 < \chi_{.05}^2 = 11.0705$$

we cannot reject H_0 at the .05 level of significance, and we cannot reject the hypothesis that the population of all mileages is normally distributed. Therefore, for practical purposes it is probably reasonable to assume that the population of all mileages is approximately normally distributed and that inferences based on this assumption are valid. Finally, the p-value for this test, which is the area under the chi-square curve having 5 degrees of freedom to the right of $\chi^2 = .43242$, can be shown to equal .994. Since this p-value is large (much greater than .05), we have little evidence to support rejecting the null hypothesis (normality).

Note that although some of the expected cell frequencies in Table 12.3 are not at least 5, the number of classes (groups) is 8 (which exceeds 4), the average of the expected cell frequencies is at least 5, and the smallest expected cell frequency is at least 1. Therefore, it is probably reasonable to consider the result of this chi-square test valid. If we choose to base the chi-square test on the more restrictive assumption that all of the expected cell frequencies are at least 5, then we can combine adjacent cell frequencies as follows:

Original f_i Values	Original p_i Values	Original E_i Values	Combined E_i Values	Combined p_i Values	Combined f_i Values
1	.0256	1.28			
3	.0662	3.31	12.1	.2420	12
8	.1502	7.51			
11	.2261	11.305	11.305	.2261	11
11	.2407	12.035	12.035	.2407	11
9	.1722	8.61	8.61	.1722	9
5	.0831	4.155			
2	.0359	1.795	5.95	.1190	7

When we use these combined cell frequencies, the chi-square approximation is based on $k - 1 - m = 5 - 1 - 2 = 2$ degrees of freedom. We find that $\chi^2 = .30102$ and that p-value $= .860$. Since this p-value is much greater than .05, we cannot reject the hypothesis of normality at the .05 level of significance.

In Example 12.2 we based the intervals employed in the chi-square goodness of fit test on the class boundaries of a histogram for the observed mileages. Another way to establish intervals for such a test is to compute the sample mean $\bar{x}$ and the sample standard deviation s and to use intervals based on the Empirical Rule as follows:

Interval 1: less than $\bar{x} - 2s$

Interval 2: $\bar{x} - 2s < \bar{x} - s$

Interval 3: $\bar{x} - s < \bar{x}$

Interval 4: $\bar{x} < \bar{x} + s$

Interval 5: $\bar{x} + s < \bar{x} + 2s$

Interval 6: greater than $\bar{x} + 2s$

However, care must be taken to ensure that each of the expected frequencies is large enough (using the previously discussed criteria).

No matter how the intervals are established, we use $\bar{x}$ as an estimate of the population mean μ and we use s as an estimate of the population standard deviation σ when we calculate the expected frequencies (E_i values). Since we are estimating $m = 2$ population parameters, the critical value χ^2_α is based on $k - 1 - m = k - 1 - 2 = k - 3$ degrees of freedom, where k is the number of intervals employed.

In the following box we summarize how to carry out this chi-square test:

A Goodness of Fit Test for a Normal Distribution

1 We will test the following null and alternative hypotheses:

H_0: the population has a normal distribution

H_a: the population does not have a normal distribution

2 Select a random sample of size n and compute the sample mean $\bar{x}$ and sample standard deviation s.

3 Define k intervals for the test. Two reasonable ways to do this are to use the classes of a histogram of the data or to use intervals based on the Empirical Rule.

4 Record the observed frequency (f_i) for each interval.

5 Calculate the expected frequency (E_i) for each interval under the normality assumption. Do this by computing the probability that a normal variable having mean $\bar{x}$ and standard deviation s

is within the interval and by multiplying this probability by n. Make sure that each expected frequency is large enough. If necessary, combine intervals to make the expected frequencies large enough.

6 Calculate the chi-square statistic

$$\chi^2 = \sum_{i=1}^{k} \frac{(f_i - E_i)^2}{E_i}$$

and define the p-value for the test to be the area under the curve of the chi-square distribution having $k - 3$ degrees of freedom to the right of χ^2.

7 Reject H_0 in favor of H_a at level of significance α if either of the following equivalent conditions holds:

a $\chi^2 > \chi^2_\alpha$ **b** p-value $< \alpha$

Here the χ^2_α point is based on $k - 3$ degrees of freedom.

While chi-square goodness of fit tests are often used to verify that it is reasonable to assume that a random sample has been selected from a normally distributed population, such tests can also check other distribution forms. For instance, we might verify that it is reasonable to assume that a random sample has been selected from a Poisson distribution. In general, **the number of degrees of freedom for the chi-square goodness of fit test will equal $k - 1 - m$,** where k is the number of intervals or categories employed in the test and m is the number of population parameters that must be estimated to calculate the needed expected frequencies.

Exercises for Section 12.1

CONCEPTS

12.1 Describe the characteristics that define a multinomial experiment.

12.2 Give the conditions that the expected cell frequencies must meet in order to validly carry out a chi-square goodness of fit test.

12.3 Explain the purpose of a goodness of fit test.

12.4 When performing a chi-square goodness of fit test, explain why a large value of the chi-square statistic provides evidence that H_0 should be rejected.

12.5 Explain two ways to obtain intervals for a goodness of fit test of normality.

connect

METHODS AND APPLICATIONS

12.6 The shares of the U.S. automobile market held in 1990 by General Motors, Japanese manufacturers, Ford, Chrysler, and other manufacturers were, respectively, 36%, 26%, 21%, 9%, and 8%. Suppose that a new survey of 1,000 new-car buyers shows the following purchase frequencies:

GM	Japanese	Ford	Chrysler	Other
391	202	275	53	79

a Show that it is appropriate to carry out a chi-square test using these data. ● AutoMkt

b Test to determine whether the current market shares differ from those of 1990. Use $\alpha = .05$.

12.7 Last rating period, the percentages of viewers watching several channels between 11 P.M. and 11:30 P.M. in a major TV market were as follows: ● TVRate

WDUX (News)	WWTY (News)	WACO (*Cheers* Reruns)	WTJW (News)	Others
15%	19%	22%	16%	28%

Suppose that in the current rating period, a survey of 2,000 viewers gives the following frequencies:

WDUX (News)	WWTY (News)	WACO (*Cheers* Reruns)	WTJW (News)	Others
182	536	354	151	777

a Show that it is appropriate to carry out a chi-square test using these data.

b Test to determine whether the viewing shares in the current rating period differ from those in the last rating period at the .10 level of significance. What do you conclude?

12.8 In the *Journal of Marketing Research* (November 1996), Gupta studied the extent to which the purchase behavior of **scanner panels** is representative of overall brand preferences. A scanner panel is a sample of households whose purchase data are recorded when a magnetic identification card is presented at a store checkout. The table below gives peanut butter purchase data collected by the A. C. Nielson Company using a panel of 2,500 households in Sioux Falls, South Dakota. The data were collected over 102 weeks. The table also gives the market shares obtained by recording all peanut butter purchases at the same stores during the same period. ● ScanPan

a Show that it is appropriate to carry out a chi-square test.

b Test to determine whether the purchase behavior of the panel of 2,500 households is consistent with the purchase behavior of the population of all peanut butter purchasers. Assume here that purchase decisions by panel members are reasonably independent, and set $\alpha = .05$.

Brand	Size	Number of Purchases by Household Panel	Market Shares
Jif	18 oz.	3,165	20.10%
Jif	28	1,892	10.10
Jif	40	726	5.42
Peter Pan	10	4,079	16.01
Skippy	18	6,206	28.56
Skippy	28	1,627	12.33
Skippy	40	1,420	7.48
Total		19,115	

Goodness of Fit Test

obs	expected	O − E	(O − E)²/E	% of chisq
3165	3842.115	−677.115	119.331	13.56
1892	1930.615	−38.615	0.772	0.09
726	1036.033	−310.033	92.777	10.54
4079	3060.312	1018.689	339.092	38.52
6206	5459.244	746.756	102.147	11.60
1627	2356.880	−729.880	226.029	25.68
1420	1429.802	−9.802	0.067	0.01
19115	19115.000	0.000	880.216	100.00

880.22 chisquare   6 df   7.10E-187   p-value

Source: Reprinted with permission from *The Journal of Marketing Research*, published by the American Marketing Association, S. Gupta et al., Vol. 33, "Do Household Scanner Data Provide Representative Inferences from Brand Choices? A Comparison with Store Data," p. 393 (Table 6).

12.9 The purchase frequencies for six different brands of videotape are observed at a video store over one month: ● VidTape

Brand	Memorex	Scotch	Kodak	TDK	BASF	Sony
Purchase Frequency	131	273	119	301	176	200

a Carry out a test of homogeneity for this data with $\alpha = .025$.

b Interpret the result of your test.

12.10 A wholesaler has recently developed a computerized sales invoicing system. Prior to implementing this system, a manual system was used. The distribution of the number of errors per invoice for the manual system is as follows: ◑ Invoice2

Errors per Invoice	0	1	2	3	More Than 3
Percentage of Invoices	87%	8%	3%	1%	1%

After implementation of the computerized system, a random sample of 500 invoices gives the following error distribution:

Errors per Invoice	0	1	2	3	More Than 3
Number of Invoices	479	10	8	2	1

   a Show that it is appropriate to carry out a chi-square test using these data.
   b Use the following Excel output to determine whether the error percentages for the computerized system differ from those for the manual system at the .05 level of significance. What do you conclude?

```
    pi      Ei      fi     (f-E)^2/E
  0.87     435     479      4.4506
  0.08      40      10     22.5000
  0.03      15       8      3.2667
  0.01       5       2      1.8000
  0.01       5       1      3.2000
                  Chi-     35.21724   p-value 0.0000001096
                  Square
```

12.11 Consider the sample of 65 payment times given in Table 2.4 (page 56). Use these data to carry out a chi-square goodness of fit test to test whether the population of all payment times is normally distributed by doing the following: ◑ PayTime
   a It can be shown that $\bar{x} = 18.1077$ and that $s = 3.9612$ for the payment time data. Use these values to compute the intervals
      (1) Less than $\bar{x} - 2s$
      (2) $\bar{x} - 2s < \bar{x} - s$
      (3) $\bar{x} - s < \bar{x}$
      (4) $\bar{x} < \bar{x} + s$
      (5) $\bar{x} + s < \bar{x} + 2s$
      (6) Greater than $\bar{x} + 2s$
   b Assuming that the population of all payment times is normally distributed, find the probability that a randomly selected payment time will be contained in each of the intervals found in part a. Use these probabilities to compute the expected frequency under the normality assumption for each interval.
   c Verify that the average of the expected frequencies is at least 5 and that the smallest expected frequency is at least 1. What does this tell us?
   d Formulate the null and alternative hypotheses for the chi-square test of normality.
   e For each interval given in part a, find the observed frequency. Then calculate the chi-square statistic needed for the chi-square test of normality.
   f Use the chi-square statistic to test normality at the .05 level of significance. What do you conclude?

12.12 Consider the sample of 60 bottle design ratings given in Table 1.3 (page 8). Use these data to carry out a chi-square goodness of fit test to determine whether the population of all bottle design ratings is normally distributed. Use $\alpha = .05$, and note that $\bar{x} = 30.35$ and $s = 3.1073$ for the 60 bottle design ratings. ◑ Design

12.13 **THE BANK CUSTOMER WAITING TIME CASE**

Consider the sample of 100 waiting times given in Table 1.8 (page 14). Use these data to carry out a chi-square goodness of fit test to determine whether the population of all waiting times is normally distributed. Use $\alpha = .10$, and note that $\bar{x} = 5.46$ and $s = 2.475$ for the 100 waiting times. ◑ WaitTime

12.14 The table on the next page gives a frequency distribution describing the number of errors found in 30 1,000-line samples of computer code. Suppose that we wish to determine whether the number of errors can be described by a Poisson distribution with mean $\mu = 4.5$. Using the Poisson probability tables, fill in the table. Then perform an appropriate chi-square goodness of fit test at the .05 level of significance. What do you conclude about whether the number of errors can be described by a Poisson distribution with $\mu = 4.5$? Explain. ● CodeErr

Number of Errors	Observed Frequency	Probability Assuming Errors Are Poisson Distributed with $\mu = 4.5$	Expected Frequency
0–1	6		
2–3	5		
4–5	7		
6–7	8		
8 or more	4		

12.2 A Chi-Square Test for Independence ● ● ●

We have spent considerable time in previous chapters studying relationships between variables. One way to study the relationship between two variables is to classify multinomial count data on two scales (or dimensions) by setting up a *contingency table*.

EXAMPLE 12.3 The Client Satisfaction Case

A financial institution sells several kinds of investment products—a stock fund, a bond fund, and a tax-deferred annuity. The company is examining whether customer satisfaction depends on the type of investment product purchased. To do this, 100 clients are randomly selected from the population of clients who have purchased shares in exactly one of the funds. The company records the fund type purchased by these clients and asks each sampled client to rate his or her level of satisfaction with the fund as high, medium, or low. Table 12.4 on page 482 gives the survey results.

We can look at the data in Table 12.4 in an organized way by constructing a **contingency table** (also called a **two-way cross-classification table**). Such a table classifies the data on two dimensions—type of fund and degree of client satisfaction. Figure 12.2 gives MegaStat and MINITAB output of a contingency table of fund type versus level of satisfaction. This table consists of a row for each fund type and a column for each level of satisfaction. Together, the rows and columns form a "cell" for each fund type–satisfaction level combination. That is, there is a cell for each "contingency" with respect to fund type and satisfaction level. Both the MegaStat and MINITAB output give a **cell frequency** for each cell, which is the top number given in the cell. This is a count (observed frequency) of the number of surveyed clients with the cell's fund type–satisfaction level combination. For instance, 15 of the surveyed clients invest in the bond fund and report high satisfaction, while 24 of the surveyed clients invest in the tax-deferred annuity and report medium satisfaction. In addition to the cell frequencies, each output also gives

Row totals (at the far right of each table): These are counts of the numbers of clients who invest in each fund type. These row totals tell us that

1 30 clients invest in the bond fund.
2 30 clients invest in the stock fund.
3 40 clients invest in the tax-deferred annuity.

Column totals (at the bottom of each table): These are counts of the numbers of clients who report high, medium, and low satisfaction. These column totals tell us that

1 40 clients report high satisfaction.
2 40 clients report medium satisfaction.
3 20 clients report low satisfaction.

Overall total (the bottom-right entry in each table): This tells us that a total of 100 clients were surveyed.

Besides the row and column totals, both outputs give **row and column percentages** (directly below the row and column totals). For example, 30.00 percent of the surveyed clients invest in the bond fund, and 20.00 percent of the surveyed clients report low satisfaction. Furthermore, in addition to a cell frequency, the MegaStat output gives a **row percentage**, a **column percentage**, and a **cell percentage** for each cell (these are below the cell frequency in each cell). For instance,

FIGURE 12.2 MegaStat and MINITAB Output of a Contingency Table of Fund Type versus Level of Client Satisfaction (See the Survey Results in Table 12.4) Invest

(a) The MegaStat output

Crosstabulation

Fund Type		Satisfaction Rating: HIGH	MED	LOW	Total
BOND	**Observed**	15	12	3	30
	% of row	50.0%	40.0%	10.0%	100.5%
	% of column	37.5%	30.0%	15.0%	30.0%
	% of total	15.0%	12.0%	3.0%	30.0%
STOCK	**Observed**	24	4	2	30
	% of row	80.0%	13.3%	6.7%	100.0%
	% of column	60.0%	10.0%	10.0%	30.0%
	% of total	24.0%	4.0%	2.0%	30.0%
TAXDEF	**Observed**	1	24	15	40
	% of row	2.5%	60.0%	37.5%	100.0%
	% of column	2.5%	60.0%	75.0%	40.0%
	% of total	1.0%	24.0%	15.0%	40.0%
Total	**Observed**	40	40	20	100
	% of row	40.0%	40.0%	20.0%	100.0%
	% of column	100.0%	100.0%	100.0%	100.0%
	% of total	40.0%	40.0%	20.0%	100.0%

46.44[a] chi-square
4 df
2.00E-09[b] p-value

[a]Chi-square statistic.
[b]p-value for chi-square.

(b) The MINITAB output

```
Rows: FundType    Columns: SatRating

            High     Med     Low     All

Bond          15      12       3      30
           50.00   40.00   10.00  100.00
           37.50   30.00   15.00   30.00
              12      12       6      30

Stock         24       4       2      30
           80.00   13.33    6.67  100.00
           60.00   10.00   10.00   30.00
              12      12       6      30

TaxDef         1      24      15      40
            2.50   60.00   37.50  100.00
            2.50   60.00   75.00   40.00
              16      16       8      40

All           40      40      20     100
           40.00   40.00   20.00  100.00
          100.00  100.00  100.00  100.00
              40      40      20     100

Pearson Chi-Square = 46.438, DF = 4
   P-Value = 0.000

Cell Contents:     Count
                   % of Row
                   % of Column
                   Expected count
```

looking at the "bond fund–high satisfaction cell," we see that the 15 clients in this cell make up 50.0 percent of the 30 clients who invest in the bond fund, and they make up 37.5 percent of the 40 clients who report high satisfaction. In addition, these 15 clients make up 15.0 percent of the 100 clients surveyed. The MINITAB output gives a row percentage and a column percentage, but not a cell percentage, for each cell. We will explain the last number that appears in each cell of the MINITAB output later in this section.

Looking at the contingency tables, it appears that the level of client satisfaction may be related to the fund type. We see that higher satisfaction ratings seem to be reported by stock and bond fund investors, while holders of tax-deferred annuities report lower satisfaction ratings. To carry out a formal statistical test we can test the null hypothesis

H_0: fund type and level of client satisfaction are independent

versus

H_a: fund type and level of client satisfaction are dependent

In order to perform this test, we compare the counts (or **observed cell frequencies**) in the contingency table with the counts that would appear in the contingency table if we assume that fund type and level of satisfaction are independent. Because these latter counts are computed by assuming independence, we call them the **expected cell frequencies under the independence assumption.** We illustrate how to calculate these expected cell frequencies by considering the cell corresponding to the bond fund and high client satisfaction. We first use the data in the contingency table to compute an estimate of the probability that a randomly selected client invests in the bond fund. Denoting this probability as p_B, we estimate p_B by dividing the row total for the bond fund by the total number of clients surveyed. That is, denoting the row total for the bond fund as r_B and letting n denote the total number of clients surveyed, the estimate of p_B is $r_B/n = 30/100 = .3$. Next we compute an estimate of the probability that a randomly selected client will report high satisfaction. Denoting this probability as p_H, we estimate p_H by dividing the column

TABLE 12.4   Results of a Customer Satisfaction Survey Given to 100 Randomly Selected Clients Who Invest
             in One of Three Fund Types—a Bond Fund, a Stock Fund, or a Tax-Deferred Annuity   ● Invest

Client	Fund Type	Level of Satisfaction	Client	Fund Type	Level of Satisfaction	Client	Fund Type	Level of Satisfaction
1	BOND	HIGH	35	STOCK	HIGH	69	BOND	MED
2	STOCK	HIGH	36	BOND	MED	70	TAXDEF	MED
3	TAXDEF	MED	37	TAXDEF	MED	71	TAXDEF	MED
4	TAXDEF	MED	38	TAXDEF	LOW	72	BOND	HIGH
5	STOCK	LOW	39	STOCK	HIGH	73	TAXDEF	MED
6	STOCK	HIGH	40	TAXDEF	MED	74	TAXDEF	LOW
7	STOCK	HIGH	41	BOND	HIGH	75	STOCK	HIGH
8	BOND	MED	42	BOND	HIGH	76	BOND	HIGH
9	TAXDEF	LOW	43	BOND	LOW	77	TAXDEF	LOW
10	TAXDEF	LOW	44	TAXDEF	LOW	78	BOND	MED
11	STOCK	MED	45	STOCK	HIGH	79	STOCK	HIGH
12	BOND	LOW	46	BOND	HIGH	80	STOCK	HIGH
13	STOCK	HIGH	47	BOND	MED	81	BOND	MED
14	TAXDEF	MED	48	STOCK	HIGH	82	TAXDEF	MED
15	TAXDEF	MED	49	TAXDEF	MED	83	BOND	HIGH
16	TAXDEF	LOW	50	TAXDEF	MED	84	STOCK	MED
17	STOCK	HIGH	51	STOCK	HIGH	85	STOCK	HIGH
18	BOND	HIGH	52	TAXDEF	MED	86	BOND	MED
19	BOND	MED	53	STOCK	HIGH	87	TAXDEF	MED
20	TAXDEF	MED	54	TAXDEF	MED	88	TAXDEF	LOW
21	TAXDEF	MED	55	STOCK	LOW	89	STOCK	HIGH
22	BOND	HIGH	56	BOND	HIGH	90	TAXDEF	MED
23	TAXDEF	MED	57	STOCK	HIGH	91	BOND	HIGH
24	TAXDEF	LOW	58	BOND	MED	92	TAXDEF	HIGH
25	STOCK	HIGH	59	TAXDEF	LOW	93	TAXDEF	LOW
26	BOND	HIGH	60	TAXDEF	LOW	94	TAXDEF	LOW
27	TAXDEF	LOW	61	STOCK	MED	95	STOCK	HIGH
28	BOND	MED	62	BOND	LOW	96	BOND	HIGH
29	STOCK	HIGH	63	STOCK	HIGH	97	BOND	MED
30	STOCK	HIGH	64	TAXDEF	MED	98	STOCK	HIGH
31	BOND	MED	65	TAXDEF	MED	99	TAXDEF	MED
32	TAXDEF	MED	66	TAXDEF	LOW	100	TAXDEF	MED
33	BOND	HIGH	67	STOCK	HIGH			
34	STOCK	MED	68	BOND	HIGH			

total for high satisfaction by the total number of clients surveyed. That is, denoting the column total for high satisfaction as c_H, the estimate of p_H is $c_H/n = 40/100 = .4$. Next, assuming that investing in the bond fund and reporting high satisfaction are **independent,** we compute an estimate of the probability that a randomly selected client invests in the bond fund and reports high satisfaction. Denoting this probability as p_{BH}, we can compute its estimate by recalling from Section 4.4 that if two events A and B are statistically independent, then $P(A \cap B)$ equals $P(A)P(B)$. It follows that, if we assume that investing in the bond fund and reporting high satisfaction are independent, we can compute an estimate of p_{BH} by multiplying the estimate of p_B by the estimate of p_H. That is, the estimate of p_{BH} is $(r_B/n)(c_H/n) = (.3)(.4) = .12$. Finally, we compute an estimate of the expected cell frequency under the independence assumption. Denoting the expected cell frequency as E_{BH}, the estimate of E_{BH} is

$$\hat{E}_{BH} = n \left(\frac{r_B}{n}\right)\left(\frac{c_H}{n}\right) = 100(.3)(.4) = 12$$

This estimated expected cell frequency is given in the MINITAB output of Figure 12.2(b) as the last number under the observed cell frequency for the bond fund–high satisfaction cell.

Noting that the expression for $\hat{E}_{BH}$ can be written as

$$\hat{E}_{BH} = n\left(\frac{r_B}{n}\right)\left(\frac{c_H}{n}\right) = \frac{r_B c_H}{n}$$

we can generalize to obtain a formula for the estimated expected cell frequency for any cell in the contingency table. Letting $\hat{E}_{ij}$ denote the estimated expected cell frequency corresponding to row i and column j in the contingency table, we see that

$$\hat{E}_{ij} = \frac{r_i c_j}{n}$$

where r_i is the row total for row i and c_j is the column total for column j. For example, for the fund type–satisfaction level contingency table, we obtain

$$\hat{E}_{SL} = \frac{r_S c_L}{n} = \frac{30(20)}{100} = \frac{600}{100} = 6$$

and

$$\hat{E}_{TM} = \frac{r_T c_M}{n} = \frac{40(40)}{100} = \frac{1{,}600}{100} = 16$$

These (and the other estimated expected cell frequencies under the independence assumption) are the last numbers below the observed cell frequencies in the MINITAB output of Figure 12.2(b). Intuitively, these estimated expected cell frequencies tell us what the contingency table looks like if fund type and level of client satisfaction are independent.

To test the null hypothesis of independence, we will compute a chi-square statistic that compares the observed cell frequencies with the estimated expected cell frequencies calculated assuming independence. Letting f_{ij} denote the observed cell frequency for cell ij, we compute

$$\chi^2 = \sum_{\text{all cells}} \frac{(f_{ij} - \hat{E}_{ij})^2}{\hat{E}_{ij}}$$

$$= \frac{(f_{BH} - \hat{E}_{BH})^2}{\hat{E}_{BH}} + \frac{(f_{BM} - \hat{E}_{BM})^2}{\hat{E}_{BM}} + \cdots + \frac{(f_{TL} - \hat{E}_{TL})^2}{\hat{E}_{TL}}$$

$$= \frac{(15 - 12)^2}{12} + \frac{(12 - 12)^2}{12} + \frac{(3 - 6)^2}{6} + \frac{(24 - 12)^2}{12} + \frac{(4 - 12)^2}{12}$$

$$+ \frac{(2 - 6)^2}{6} + \frac{(1 - 16)^2}{16} + \frac{(24 - 16)^2}{16} + \frac{(15 - 8)^2}{8}$$

$$= 46.4375$$

If the value of the chi-square statistic is large, this indicates that the observed cell frequencies differ substantially from the expected cell frequencies calculated by assuming independence. Therefore, the larger the value of chi-square, the more doubt is cast on the null hypothesis of independence.

To find an appropriate critical value, we let r denote the number of rows in the contingency table and we let c denote the number of columns. Then, it can be shown that, when the null hypothesis of independence is true, the sampling distribution of χ^2 is approximately a χ^2 distribution with $(r - 1)(c - 1) = (3 - 1)(3 - 1) = 4$ degrees of freedom. If we test H_0 at the .05 level of significance, we reject H_0 if and only if

$$\chi^2 > \chi^2_{.05}$$

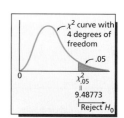

Since Table A.10 (page 651) tells us that the $\chi^2_{.05}$ point corresponding to $(r - 1)(c - 1) = 4$ degrees of freedom equals 9.48773, we have

$$\chi^2 = 46.4375 > \chi^2_{.05} = 9.48773$$

and we reject H_0 at the .05 level of significance. We conclude that fund type and level of client satisfaction are not independent.

In the following box we summarize how to carry out a chi-square test for independence:

A Chi-Square Test for Independence

Suppose that each of n randomly selected elements is classified on two dimensions, and suppose that the result of the two-way classification is a **contingency table having r rows and c columns**. Let

f_{ij} = the cell frequency corresponding to row i and column j of the contingency table (that is, the number of elements classified in row i and column j)

r_i = the row total for row i in the contingency table

c_j = the column total for column j in the contingency table

$$\hat{E}_{ij} = \frac{r_i c_j}{n}$$

= the estimated expected number of elements that would be classified in row i and column j of the contingency table if the two classifications are statistically independent

If we wish to test

H_0: the two classifications are statistically independent

versus

H_a: the two classifications are statistically dependent

we define the test statistic

$$\chi^2 = \sum_{\text{all cells}} \frac{(f_{ij} - \hat{E}_{ij})^2}{\hat{E}_{ij}}$$

Also, define the p-value related to χ^2 to be the area under the curve of the chi-square distribution having $(r-1)(c-1)$ degrees of freedom to the right of χ^2.

Then, we can reject H_0 in favor of H_a at level of significance α if either of the following equivalent conditions holds:

1 $\chi^2 > \chi^2_\alpha$

2 p-value $< \alpha$

Here the χ^2_α point is based on $(r-1)(c-1)$ degrees of freedom.

This test is based on the fact that it can be shown that, when the null hypothesis of independence is true, the sampling distribution of χ^2 is approximately a chi-square distribution with $(r-1)(c-1)$ degrees of freedom, if the sample size n is large. **It is generally agreed that n should be considered large if all of the estimated expected cell frequencies ($\hat{E}_{ij}$ values) are at least 5.** Moore and McCabe (1993) indicate that **it is reasonable to use the chi-square approximation if the number of cells (rc) exceeds 4, the average of the $\hat{E}_{ij}$ values is at least 5, and the smallest $\hat{E}_{ij}$ value is at least 1.** Notice that in Figure 12.2(b) all of the estimated expected cell frequencies are greater than 5.

EXAMPLE 12.4 The Client Satisfaction Case

Again consider the MegaStat and MINITAB outputs of Figure 12.2, which give the contingency table of fund type versus level of client satisfaction. Both outputs give the chi-square statistic ($= 46.438$) for testing the null hypothesis of independence, as well as the related p-value. We see that this p-value is less than .001. It follows, therefore, that we can reject

H_0: fund type and level of client satisfaction are independent

at the .05 level of significance, since the p-value is less than .05.

In order to study the nature of the dependency between the classifications in a contingency table, it is often useful to plot the row and/or column percentages. As an example, Figure 12.3 gives plots of the row percentages in the contingency table of Figure 12.2(a). For instance, looking at the column in this contingency table corresponding to a high level of satisfaction, the contingency table tells us that 40.00 percent of the surveyed clients report a high level of satisfaction. If fund type and level of satisfaction really are independent, then we would expect roughly 40 percent of the clients in each of the three categories—bond fund participants, stock fund participants, and tax-deferred annuity holders—to report a high level of satisfaction. That is, we would expect the row percentages in the "high satisfaction" column to be roughly 40 percent in each row.

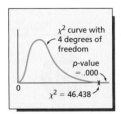

χ^2 curve with 4 degrees of freedom

p-value = .000

0

$\chi^2 = 46.438$

F I G U R E   1 2 . 3   **Plots of Row Percentages versus Investment Type for the Contingency Table in Figure 12.2(a)**

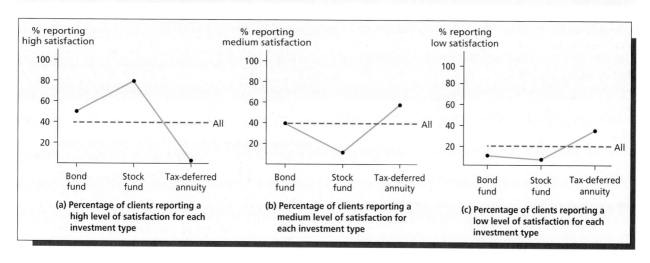

(a) Percentage of clients reporting a high level of satisfaction for each investment type

(b) Percentage of clients reporting a medium level of satisfaction for each investment type

(c) Percentage of clients reporting a low level of satisfaction for each investment type

However, Figure 12.3(a) gives a plot of the percentages of clients reporting a high level of satisfaction for each investment type (that is, the figure plots the three row percentages in the column corresponding to "high satisfaction"). We see that these percentages vary considerably. Noting that the dashed line in the figure is the 40 percent reporting a high level of satisfaction for the overall group, we see that the percentage of stock fund participants reporting high satisfaction is 80 percent. This is far above the 40 percent we would expect if independence exists. On the other hand, the percentage of tax-deferred annuity holders reporting high satisfaction is only 2.5 percent—way below the expected 40 percent if independence exists. In a similar fashion, Figures 12.3(b) and (c) plot the row percentages for the medium and low satisfaction columns in the contingency table. These plots indicate that stock fund participants report medium and low levels of satisfaction less frequently than the overall group of clients, and that tax-deferred annuity participants report medium and low levels of satisfaction more frequently than the overall group of clients.

To conclude this section, we note that the chi-square test for independence can be used to test the equality of several population proportions. We will show how this is done in Exercise 12.21.

Exercises for Section 12.2

CONCEPTS

12.15   What is the purpose behind summarizing data in the form of a two-way contingency table?

12.16   When performing a chi-square test for independence, explain how the "cell frequencies under the independence assumption" are calculated. For what purpose are these frequencies calculated?

METHODS AND APPLICATIONS

12.17   A marketing research firm wishes to study the relationship between wine consumption and whether a person likes to watch professional tennis on television. One hundred randomly selected people are asked whether they drink wine and whether they watch tennis. The following results are obtained: ◑ WineCons

	Watch Tennis	Do Not Watch Tennis	Totals
Drink Wine	16	24	40
Do Not Drink Wine	4	56	60
Totals	20	80	100

a   For each row and column total, calculate the corresponding row or column percentage.
b   For each cell, calculate the corresponding cell, row, and column percentages.

TABLE 12.5   Depreciation Methods Used by a Sample of 78 Firms   ⬤ DeprMeth

Depreciation Methods	France	Germany	UK	Total
A. Straight line (S)	15	0	25	40
B. Declining Bal (D)	1	1	1	3
C. (D & S)	10	25	0	35
Total companies	26	26	26	78

Source: E. N. Emenyonu and S. J. Gray, "EC Accounting Harmonisation: An Empirical Study of Measurement Practices in France, Germany, and the UK," *Accounting and Business Research* 23, no. 89 (1992), pp. 49–58. Reprinted by permission of the author.

Chi-Square Test for Independence

	France	Germany	UK	Total
A. Straight line (S)	15	0	25	40
B. Declining Bal (D)	1	1	1	3
C. (D & S)	10	25	0	35
Total	26	26	26	78

50.89 chisquare   4 df   2.35E-10   p-value

TABLE 12.6   A Contingency Table of the Results of the Accidents Study   ⬤ Accident

	On-the-Job Accident		
Smoker	Yes	No	Row Total
Heavy	12	4	16
Moderate	9	6	15
Nonsmoker	13	22	35
Column total	34	32	66

Source: D. R. Cooper and C. W. Emory, *Business Research Methods* (5th ed.) (Burr Ridge, IL: Richard D. Irwin, 1995), p. 451.

FIGURE 12.4   MINITAB Output of a Chi-Square Test for Independence in the Accident Study

```
Expected counts are below observed counts

              Accident   No Accident   Total
Heavy             12             4        16
                8.24          7.76

Moderate           9             6        15
                7.73          7.27

Nonsmoker         13            22        35
               18.03         16.97

Total             34            32        66

Chi-Sq = 6.860, DF = 2, P-Value = 0.032
```

   c   Test the hypothesis that whether people drink wine is independent of whether people watch tennis. Set $\alpha = .05$.

   d   Given the results of the chi-square test, does it make sense to advertise wine during a televised tennis match (assuming that the ratings for the tennis match are high enough)? Explain.

12.18   In recent years major efforts have been made to standardize accounting practices in different countries; this is called *harmonization*. In an article in *Accounting and Business Research,* Emmanuel N. Emenyonu and Sidney J. Gray (1992) studied the extent to which accounting practices in France, Germany, and the United Kingdom are harmonized.   ⬤ DeprMeth

   a   Depreciation method is one of the accounting practices studied by Emenyonu and Gray. Three methods were considered—the straight-line method (*S*), the declining balance method (*D*), and a combination of *D* & *S* (sometimes European firms start with the declining balance method and then switch over to the straight-line method when the figure derived from straight line exceeds that from declining balance). The data in Table 12.5 summarize the depreciation methods used by a sample of 78 French, German, and U.K. firms. Use these data and the MegaStat output to test the hypothesis that depreciation method is independent of a firm's location (country) at the .05 level of significance.

   b   Perform a graphical analysis to study the relationship between depreciation method and country. What conclusions can be made about the nature of the relationship?

12.19   In the book *Business Research Methods* (5th ed.), Donald R. Cooper and C. William Emory discuss studying the relationship between on-the-job accidents and smoking. Cooper and Emory describe the study as follows: ⬤ Accident

> Suppose a manager implementing a smoke-free workplace policy is interested in whether smoking affects worker accidents. Since the company has complete reports of on-the-job accidents, she draws a sample of names of workers who were involved in accidents during the last year. A similar sample from among workers who had no reported accidents in the last year is drawn. She interviews members of both groups to determine if they are smokers or not.

The sample results are given in Table 12.6.

   a   For each row and column total in Table 12.6, find the corresponding row/column percentage.

   b   For each cell in Table 12.6, find the corresponding cell, row, and column percentages.

TABLE 12.7 A Contingency Table Relating Delivery Time and Computer-Assisted Ordering ● DelTime

Computer-Assisted Ordering	Below Industry Average	Delivery Time Equal to Industry Average	Above Industry Average	Row Total
No	4	12	8	24
Yes	10	4	2	16
Column total	14	16	10	40

TABLE 12.8 A Summary of the Results of a TV Viewership Study ● TVView

Watch 11 P.M. News?	18 or Less	Age Group 19 to 35	36 to 54	55 or Older	Total
Yes	37	48	56	73	214
No	213	202	194	177	786
Total	250	250	250	250	1,000

    c Use the MINITAB output in Figure 12.4 to test the hypothesis that the incidence of on-the-job accidents is independent of smoking habits. Set $\alpha = .01$.

    d Is there a difference in on-the-job accident occurrences between smokers and nonsmokers? Explain.

12.20 In the book *Essentials of Marketing Research,* William R. Dillon, Thomas J. Madden, and Neil A. Firtle discuss the relationship between delivery time and computer-assisted ordering. A sample of 40 firms shows that 16 use computer-assisted ordering, while 24 do not. Furthermore, past data are used to categorize each firm's delivery times as below the industry average, equal to the industry average, or above the industry average. The results obtained are given in Table 12.7.

    a Test the hypothesis that delivery time performance is independent of whether computer-assisted ordering is used. What do you conclude by setting $\alpha = .05$? ● DelTime

    b Verify that a chi-square test is appropriate.

    c Is there a difference between delivery-time performance between firms using computer-assisted ordering and those not using computer-assisted ordering?

    d Carry out graphical analysis to investigate the relationship between delivery-time performance and computer-assisted ordering. Describe the relationship.

12.21 A television station wishes to study the relationship between viewership of its 11 P.M. news program and viewer age (18 years or less, 19 to 35, 36 to 54, 55 or older). A sample of 250 television viewers in each age group is randomly selected, and the number who watch the station's 11 P.M. news is found for each sample. The results are given in Table 12.8. ● TVView

    a Let p_1, p_2, p_3, and p_4 be the proportions of all viewers in each age group who watch the station's 11 P.M. news. If these proportions are equal, then whether a viewer watches the station's 11 P.M. news is independent of the viewer's age group. Therefore, we can test the null hypothesis H_0 that p_1, p_2, p_3, and p_4 are equal by carrying out a chi-square test for independence. Perform this test by setting $\alpha = .05$.

    b Compute a 95 percent confidence interval for the difference between p_1 and p_4.

Chapter Summary

In this chapter we presented two hypothesis tests that employ the **chi-square distribution.** In Section 12.1 we discussed a **chi-square test of goodness of fit.** Here we considered a situation in which we study how count data are distributed among various categories. In particular, we considered a **multinomial experiment** in which randomly selected items are classified into several groups, and we saw how to perform a goodness of fit test for the multinomial probabilities associated with these groups. We also explained how to perform a goodness of fit test for normality. In

Section 12.2 we presented a **chi-square test for independence.** Here we classify count data on two dimensions, and we summarize the cross-classification in the form of a **contingency table.** We use the cross-classified data to test whether the two classifications are **statistically independent,** which is really a way to see whether the classifications are related. We also learned that we can use graphical analysis to investigate the nature of the relationship between the classifications.

Glossary of Terms

chi-square test for independence: A test to determine whether two classifications are independent. (page 484)
contingency table: A table that summarizes data that have been classified on two dimensions or scales. (page 480)
goodness of fit test for multinomial probabilities: A test to determine whether multinomial probabilities are equal to a specific set of values. (page 474)

goodness of fit test for normality: A test to determine if a sample has been randomly selected from a normally distributed population. (page 477)
homogeneity (test for): A test of the null hypothesis that all multinomial probabilities are equal. (page 474)
multinomial experiment: An experiment that concerns count data that are classified into more than two categories. (page 471)

Important Formulas and Tests

A goodness of fit test for multinomial probabilities: page 474
A test for homogeneity: page 474

A goodness of fit test for a normal distribution: page 477
A chi-square test for independence: page 484

Supplementary Exercises

connect

12.22 A large supermarket conducted a consumer preference study by recording the brand of wheat bread purchased by customers in its stores. The supermarket carries four brands of wheat bread, and the brand preferences of a random sample of 200 purchasers are given in the following table: ● BreadPref

		Brand		
A	**B**	**C**	**D**
51	82	27	40

Test the null hypothesis that the four brands are equally preferred by setting α equal to .05. Find a 95 percent confidence interval for the proportion of all purchasers who prefer Brand *B*.

12.23 An occupant traffic study was carried out to aid in the remodeling of a large building on a university campus. The building has five entrances, and the choice of entrance was recorded for a random sample of 300 persons entering the building. The results obtained are given in the following table: ● EntrPref

		Entrance		
I	**II**	**III**	**IV**	**V**
30	91	97	40	42

Test the null hypothesis that the five entrances are equally used by setting α equal to .05. Find a 95 percent confidence interval for the proportion of all people who use Entrance III.

12.24 In a 1993 article in *Accounting and Business Research,* Meier, Alam, and Pearson studied auditor lobbying on several proposed U.S. accounting standards that affect banks and savings and loan associations. As part of this study, the authors investigated auditors' positions regarding proposed changes in accounting standards that would increase client firms' reported earnings. It was hypothesized that auditors would favor such proposed changes because their clients' managers would receive higher compensation (salary, bonuses, and so on) when client earnings were reported to be higher. Table 12.9 summarizes auditor and client positions (in favor or opposed) regarding proposed changes in accounting standards that would increase client firms' reported earnings. Here the auditor and client positions are cross-classified versus the size of the client firm.   ● AuditPos

  a Test to determine whether auditor positions regarding earnings-increasing changes in accounting standards depend on the size of the client firm. Use $\alpha = .05$.
  b Test to determine whether client positions regarding earnings-increasing changes in accounting standards depend on the size of the client firm. Use $\alpha = .05$.
  c Carry out a graphical analysis to investigate a possible relationship between (1) auditor positions and the size of the client firm and (2) client positions and the size of the client firm.

TABLE 12.9   Auditor and Client Positions Regarding Earnings-Increasing Changes in Accounting Standards 🔵 AuditPos

(a) Auditor Positions

	Large Firms	Small Firms	Total
In Favor	13	130	143
Opposed	10	24	34
Total	23	154	177

(b) Client Positions

	Large Firms	Small Firms	Total
In Favor	12	120	132
Opposed	11	34	45
Total	23	154	177

Source: Heidi Hylton Meier, Pervaiz Alam, and Michael A. Pearson, "Auditor Lobbying for Accounting Standards: The Case of Banks and Savings and Loan Associations," *Accounting and Business Research* 23, no. 92 (1993), pp. 477–487.

TABLE 12.10   Auditor Positions Regarding Earnings-Decreasing Changes in Accounting Standards 🔵 AuditPos2

	Large Firms	Small Firms	Total
In Favor	27	152	179
Opposed	29	154	183
Total	56	306	362

Source: Heidi Hylton Meier, Pervaiz Alam, and Michael A. Pearson, "Auditor Lobbying for Accounting Standards: The Case of Banks and Savings and Loan Associations," *Accounting and Business Research* 23, no. 92 (1993), pp. 477–487.

TABLE 12.11   Results of the Coupon Redemption Study 🔵 Coupon

Coupon Redemption Level	Midtown	Store Location North Side	South Side	Total
High	69	97	52	218
Medium	101	93	76	270
Low	30	10	72	112
Total	200	200	200	600

d Does the relationship between position and the size of the client firm seem to be similar for both auditors and clients? Explain.

12.25 In the book *Business Research Methods* (5th ed.), Donald R. Cooper and C. William Emory discuss a market researcher for an automaker who is studying consumer preferences for styling features of larger sedans. Buyers, who were classified as "first-time" buyers or "repeat" buyers, were asked to express their preference for one of two types of styling—European styling or Japanese styling. Of 40 first-time buyers, 8 preferred European styling and 32 preferred Japanese styling. Of 60 repeat buyers, 40 preferred European styling, and 20 preferred Japanese styling.
 a Set up a contingency table for these data.
 b Test the hypothesis that buyer status (repeat versus first-time) and styling preference are independent at the .05 level of significance. What do you conclude?
 c Carry out a graphical analysis to investigate the nature of any relationship between buyer status and styling preference. Describe the relationship.

12.26 Again consider the situation of Exercise 12.24. Table 12.10 summarizes auditor positions regarding proposed changes in accounting standards that would decrease client firms' reported earnings. Determine whether the relationship between auditor position and the size of the client firm is the same for earnings-decreasing changes in accounting standards as it is for earnings-increasing changes in accounting standards. Justify your answer using both a statistical test and a graphical analysis. 🔵 AuditPos2

12.27 The manager of a chain of three discount drugstores wishes to investigate the level of discount coupon redemption at its stores. All three stores have the same sales volume. Therefore, the manager will randomly sample 200 customers at each store with regard to coupon usage. The survey results are given in Table 12.11. Test the hypothesis that redemption level and location are independent with $\alpha = .01$. Use the MINITAB output in Figure 12.5. 🔵 Coupon

12.28 THE VIDEO GAME SATISFACTION RATING CASE

Consider the sample of 65 customer satisfaction ratings given in Table 12.12. Carry out a chi-square goodness of fit test of normality for the population of all customer satisfaction ratings. Recall that we previously calculated $\bar{x} = 42.95$ and $s = 2.6424$ for the 65 ratings. 🔵 VideoGame

FIGURE 12.5	MINITAB Output of a Chi-Square Test for Independence in the Coupon Redemption Study

Expected counts are below observed counts

	Midtown	North	South	Total
High	69	97	52	218
	72.67	72.67	72.67	
Medium	101	93	76	270
	90.00	90.00	90.00	
Low	30	10	72	112
	37.33	37.33	37.33	
Total	200	200	200	600

Chi-Sq = **71.476**, DF = **4**, P-Value = **0.000**

TABLE 12.12	A Sample of 65 Customer Satisfaction Ratings
	● VideoGame

39	46	42	40	45	44	44	44	45
45	44	46	46	46	41	46	46	
38	40	40	41	43	38	48	39	
42	39	47	43	47	43	44	41	
42	40	44	39	43	36	41	44	
41	42	43	43	41	44	45	42	
38	45	45	46	40	44	44	47	
42	44	45	45	43	45	44	43	

12.29   Internet Exercise

A report on the 1995 National Health Risk Behavior Survey, conducted by the Centers for Disease Control and Prevention, can be found at the CDC website [http://www.cdc.gov: Data & Statistics : Youth Risk Behavior Surveillance System : Data Products : 1995 National College Health Risk Behavior Survey or, directly, go to http://www.cdc.gov/nocdphp/dash/MMWRFile/ss4606.htm]. Among the issues addressed in the survey was whether the subjects had, in the prior 30 days, ridden with a driver who had been drinking alcohol. Does the proportion of students exhibiting this selected risk behavior vary by ethnic group? The report includes tables summarizing the "Ridden Drinking" risk behavior by ethnic group (Table 3) and the ethnic composition (Table 1) for a sample of $n = 4,609$ college students. The "Ridden Drinking" and ethnic group information is extracted from Tables 1 and 3 and is displayed as proportions or probabilities in the leftmost panel of the table below. Note that the values in the body of the leftmost panel are given as conditional probabilities, the probabilities of exhibiting the "Ridden Drinking" risk behavior, given ethnic group.

These conditional probabilities can be multiplied by the appropriate marginal probabilities to compute the joint probabilities for all the risk behavior by ethnic group combinations to obtain the summaries in the center panel. Finally, the joint probabilities are multiplied by the sample size to obtain projected counts for the number of students in each "Ridden Drinking" by ethnic group combination. The "Other" ethnic group was omitted from the Table 3 summaries and is thus not included in this analysis.

Is there sufficient evidence to conclude that the proportion of college students exhibiting the "Ridden Drinking" behavior varies by ethnic group? Conduct a chi-square test for independence using the projected count data provided in the rightmost panel of the summary table. (Data are available in MINITAB and Excel files, YouthRisk.mtw and YouthRisk.xls.) Test at the 0.01 level of significance and report an approximate p-value for your test. Be sure to clearly state your hypotheses and conclusion.   ● YouthRisk

	Conditional Probabilities [Table 3: P(R|E). Table 1: P(E)]			Joint Probabilities [P(ER) = P(R|E)P(E)]			Projected Counts [n = 4609] [n(ER) = P(ER) × 4609]		
	Ridden Drinking?			Ridden Drinking?			Ridden Drinking?		
Ethnic	%Y|Eth	%N|Eth	% Ethnic	Yes	No	Total	Yes	No	Total
White	0.383	0.617	0.728	0.2788	0.4492	0.7280	1,285	2,070	3,355
Black	0.275	0.725	0.103	0.0283	0.0747	0.1030	131	344	475
Hispanic	0.307	0.693	0.071	0.0218	0.0492	0.0710	100	227	327

Appendix 12.1 ■ Chi-Square Tests Using MINITAB

The instruction blocks in this section each begin by describing the entry of data into the MINITAB Data window. Alternatively, the data may be loaded directly from the data disk included with the text. The appropriate data file name is given at the top of each instruction block. Please refer to Appendix 1.1 for further information about entering data, saving data, and printing results when using MINITAB.

Chi-square test for goodness of fit in Figure 12.1 on page 473 (data file: MicroWav.MTW):

- Enter the microwave oven data from Tables 12.1 and 12.2 on page 471—observed frequencies in column C1 with variable name Frequency and market shares (entered as decimal fractions) in column C2 with variable name MarketShr.

To compute the chi-square statistic:

- Select **Calc : Calculator**
- In the Calculator dialog box, enter Expected into the "Store result in variable" box.
- In the Expression window, enter 400*MarketShr and click OK to compute the expected values.
- Select **Calc : Calculator**
- Enter ChiSq into the "Store result in variable" box.
- In the Expression window enter the formula (Frequency—Expected)**2/Expected and click OK to compute the cell Chi-square contributions.
- Select **Calc : Column Statistics**
- In the Column Statistics dialog box, click on Sum.
- Enter ChiSq in the "Input variable" box.
- Enter k1 in the "Store result in" box and click OK to compute the Chi-square statistic and to store it as the constant k1.
- The chi-square statistic will be displayed in the Session window.

To compute the _p_-value for the test:

We first compute the probability of obtaining a value of the chi-square statistic that is less than or equal to the computed value (=8.77857):

- Select **Calc : Probability Distributions : Chi-Square**
- In the Chi-Square Distribution dialog box, click on "Cumulative probability."
- Enter 3 in the "Degrees of freedom" box.
- Click the "Input constant" option and enter k1 into the corresponding box.
- Enter k2 into the "Optional storage" box.
- Click OK in the Chi-Square Distribution dialog box. This computes the needed probability and stores its value as a constant k2.

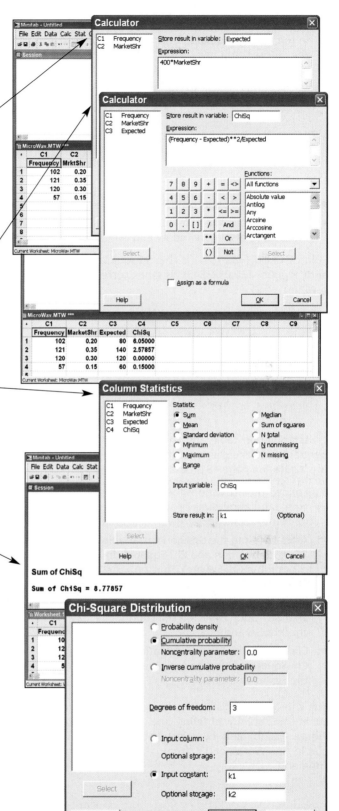

- Select **Calc : Calculator**
- In the Calculator dialog box, enter PValue into the "Store result in variable" box.
- In the Expression window, enter the formula $1 - k2$, and click OK to compute the *p*-value related to the chi-square statistic.

To display the *p*-value:

- Select **Data : Display Data**
- Enter PValue in the "Columns, constants, and matrices to display" window and click OK.

Sum of ChiSq (=8.77857) is the chi-square statistic, and PValue (=0.0323845) is the corresponding *p*-value.

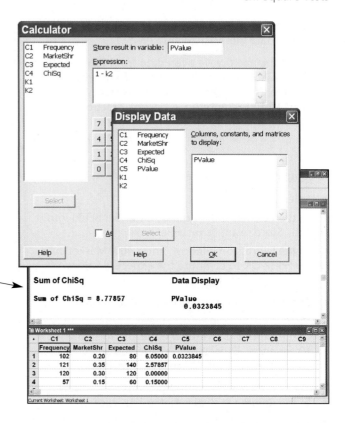

Crosstabulation table and chi-square test of independence for the client satisfaction data as in Figure 12.2(b) on page 481 (data file: Invest.MTW):

- Follow the instructions for constructing a cross-tabulation table of fund type versus level of client satisfaction as given in Appendix 2.1.
- After entering the categorical variables into the "Cross Tabulation and Chi-Square" dialog box, click on the Chi-Square... button.
- In the "Cross Tabulation—Chi-Square" dialog box, place checkmarks in the "Chi-Square analysis" and "Expected cell counts" checkboxes and click OK.
- Click OK in the "Cross Tabulation and Chi-Square" dialog box to obtain results in the Session window.

The chi-square statistic can also be calculated from summary data by entering the cell counts from Figure 12.2(b) and by selecting "Chi-Square Test (Table in Worksheet)" from the Stat : Tables submenu.

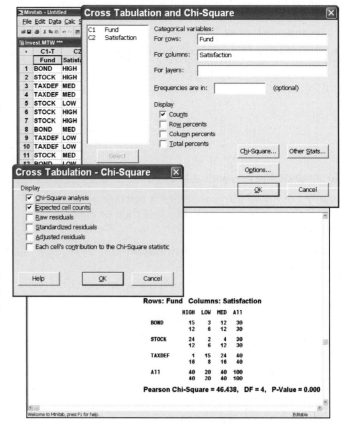

Appendix 12.2 ■ Chi-Square Tests Using Excel

The instruction blocks in this section each begin by describing the entry of data into an Excel spreadsheet. Alternatively, the data may be loaded directly from the data disk included with the text. The appropriate data file name is given at the top of each instruction block. Please refer to Appendix 1.2 for further information about entering data, saving data, and printing results when using Excel.

Chi-square goodness of fit test in Exercise 12.10 on page 479 (data file: Invoice2.xlsx):

- In the first row of the spreadsheet, enter the following column headings in order—Percent, Expected, Number, and ChiSqContribution.

- Beginning in cell A2, enter the percentage of invoice figures from Exercise 12.10 as decimal fractions into column A.

- Compute expected values. Enter the formula =500*A2 into cell B2 and press Enter. Copy this formula through cell B6 by double-clicking the drag handle (in the lower right corner) of cell B2.

- Enter the number of invoice figures from Exercise 12.10 into cells C2 through C6.

- Compute cell chi-square contributions. In cell D2, enter the formula =(C2 − B2)^2/B2 and press Enter. Copy this formula through cell D6 by double-clicking the drag handle (in the lower right corner) of cell D2.

- Compute the chi-square statistic in cell D8. Use the mouse to select the range of cells D2.D8 and click the Σ button on the Excel ribbon.

- Click on an empty cell, say cell A15, and select the Insert Function button f_x on the Excel ribbon.

- In the Insert Function dialog box, select Statistical from the "Or select a category:" menu, select CHIDIST from the "Select a function:" menu, and click OK.

- In the "CHIDIST Function Arguments" dialog box, enter D8 into the "X" box and 3 into the "Deg_freedom" box.

- Click OK in the "CHIDIST Function Arguments" dialog box to produce the p-value related to the chi-square statistic in cell A15.

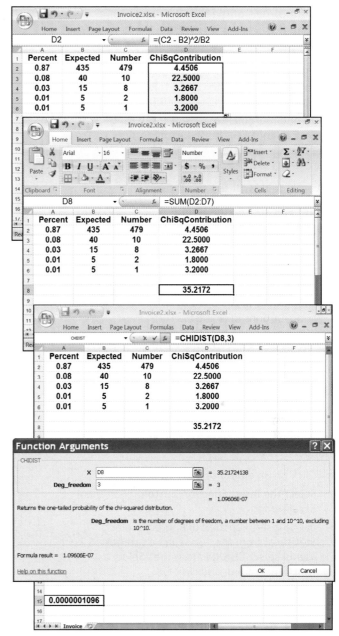

Contingency table and chi-square test of independence similar to Figure 12.2(b) on page 481 (data file: Invest.xlsx):

- Follow the instructions given in Appendix 2.2 for using a PivotTable to construct a cross-tabulation table of fund type versus level of customer satisfaction and place the table in a new worksheet.

To compute a table of expected values:

- In cell B9, type the formula =$E4*B$7/$E$7 (be very careful to include the $ in all the correct places) and press the Enter key (to obtain the expected value 12 in cell B9).

- Click on cell B9 and use the mouse to point the cursor to the drag handle (in the lower right corner) of the cell. The cursor will change to a black cross. Using the black cross, drag the handle right to cell D9 and release the mouse button to fill cells C9.D9. With B9.D9 still selected, use the black cross to drag the handle down to cell D11. Release the mouse button to fill cells B10.D11.

- To add marginal totals, select the range B9.E12 and click the Σ button on the Excel ribbon.

To compute the chi-square statistic:

- In cell B15, type the formula = (B4 – B9)^2/B9 and press the Enter key to obtain the cell contribution 0.75 in cell B15.

- Click on cell B15 and (using the procedure described above) use the black cross cursor to drag the cell handle right to cell D15 and then down to cell D17 (obtaining the cell contributions in cells B15.D17).

- To add marginal totals, select the range B15.E18 and click the Σ button on the Excel ribbon.

- The chi-square statistic is in cell E18 (=46.4375).

To compute the _p_-value for the chi-square test of independence:

- Click on an empty cell, say E20.

- Select the Insert Function button f_x on the Excel ribbon.

- In the Insert Function dialog box, select Statistical from the "Or select a category:" menu, select CHIDIST from the "Select a function:" menu, and click OK.

- In the "CHIDIST Function Arguments" dialog box, enter E18 (the cell location of the chi-square statistic) into the "X" window and 4 into the "Deg_freedom" window.

- Click OK in the "CHIDIST Function Arguments" dialog box to produce the _p_-value related to the chi-square statistic in cell E20.

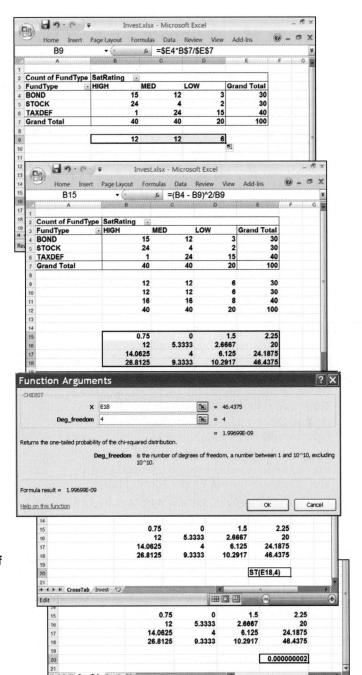

Appendix 12.3 ■ Chi-Square Tests Using MegaStat

The instructions in this section begin by describing the entry of data into an Excel worksheet. Alternatively, the data may be loaded directly from the data disk included with the text. The appropriate data file name is given at the top of each instruction block. Please refer to Appendix 1.2 for further information about entering data, saving data, and printing results in Excel. Please refer to Appendix 1.3 for more information about using MegaStat.

Contingency table and chi-square test of independence in Figure 12.2(a) on page 481 (data file: Invest. xlsx):

- Follow the instructions given in Appendix 2.3 for using MegaStat to construct a crosstabulation table of fund type versus level of customer satisfaction.

- After having made entries to specify the row and column variables for the table, in the list of Output Options place a checkmark in the "chi-square" checkbox.

- If desired, row, column, and cell percentages can be obtained by placing checkmarks in the "% of row," "% of column," and "% of total" checkboxes in the list of Output Options. Here we have elected to not request these percentages.

- Click OK in the Crosstabulation dialog box.

- The value of the chi-square statistic (=46.44) and its related *p*-value (=0.000000002) are given below the crosstabulation table.

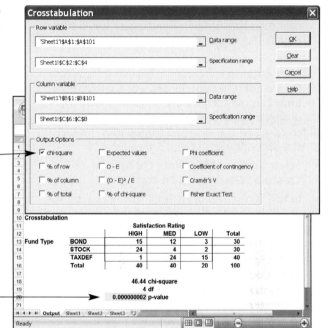

Chi-square goodness of fit test for the scanner panel data in Exercise 12.8 on page 478 (data file: ScanPan.xlsx):

- Enter the scanner panel data in Exercise 12.8 (page 478) as shown in the screen with the number of purchases for each brand in column C and with the market share for each brand (expressed as a percentage) in column D. Note that the total number of purchases for all brands equals 19,115 (which is in cell C11).

- In cell E4, type the cell formula =D4*19115 and press Enter to compute the expected frequency for the Jiff—18 ounce brand/size combination. Copy this cell formula (by double-clicking the drag handle in the lower right corner of cell E4) to compute the expected frequencies for each of the other brands in cells E5 through E10.

- Select **Add-Ins : MegaStat : Chi-square/ Crosstab : Goodness of Fit Test**

- In the "Goodness of Fit Test" dialog box, click in the "Observed values Input range" window and enter the range C4.C10. Enter this range by dragging with the mouse—the AutoExpand feature cannot be used in the "Goodness of Fit Test" dialog box.

- Click in the "Expected values Input range" window, and enter the range E4.E10. Again, enter this range by dragging with the mouse.

- Click OK in the "Goodness of Fit Test" dialog box.

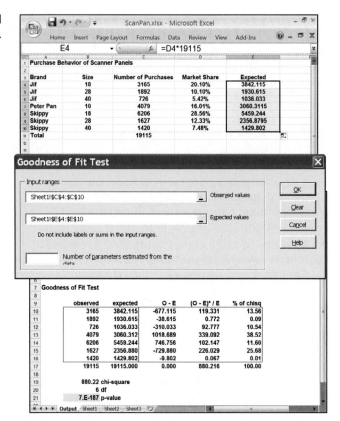

Chi-square test for independence with contingency table input data in the depreciation situation of Exercise 12.18 on page 486 (data file: DeprMeth.xlsx):

- Enter the depreciation method contingency table data in Table 12.5 on page 486 as shown in the screen—depreciation methods in rows and countries in columns.

- Select **Add-Ins : MegaStat : Chi-square/ Crosstab : Contingency Table**

- In the "Contingency Table Test for Independence" dialog box, click in the Input range window and (by dragging the mouse) enter the range A4.D7. Note that the entered range may contain row and column labels, but the range should not include the total row or total column.

- In the list of Output Options, check the chi-square checkbox to obtain the results of the chi-square test for independence.

- If desired, row, column, and cell percentages can be obtained by placing checkmarks in the "% of row," "% of column," and "% of total" checkboxes in the list of Output Options. Here we have elected to not request these percentages.

- Click OK in the "Contingency Table Test for Independence" dialog box.

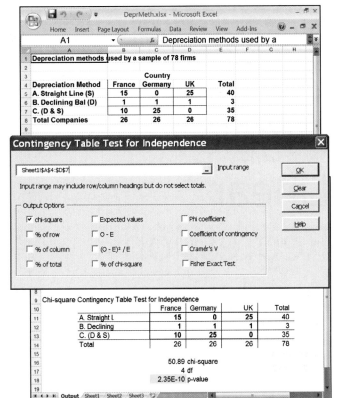

CHAPTER 13

Simple Linear Regression Analysis

Chapter Outline

13.1 The Simple Linear Regression Model and the Least Squares Point Estimates

13.2 Model Assumptions and the Standard Error

13.3 Testing the Significance of the Slope and *y*-Intercept

13.4 Confidence and Prediction Intervals

13.5 Simple Coefficients of Determination and Correlation (This section may be read anytime after reading Section 13.1.)

13.6 Testing the Significance of the Population Correlation Coefficient (Optional)

13.7 An *F* Test for the Model

13.8 Residual Analysis (Optional)

13.9 Some Shortcut Formulas (Optional)

anagers often make decisions by studying the relationships between variables, and process improvements can often be made by understanding how changes in one or more variables affect the process output. **Regression analysis** is a statistical technique in which we use observed data to relate a variable of interest, which is called the **dependent** (or **response**) **variable,** to one or more **independent** (or **predictor**) **variables.** The objective is to build a **regression model,** or **prediction equation,** that can be used to **describe, predict,** and **control** the dependent variable on the basis of the independent variables. For example, a company might wish to improve its marketing process. After collecting data concerning the demand for a product, the product's price, and the advertising

expenditures made to promote the product, the company might use regression analysis to develop an equation to predict demand on the basis of price and advertising expenditure. Predictions of demand for various price–advertising expenditure combinations can then be used to evaluate potential changes in the company's marketing strategies.

In the next two chapters we give a thorough presentation of regression analysis. We begin in this chapter by presenting **simple linear regression** analysis. Using this technique is appropriate when we are relating a dependent variable to a single independent variable and when *a straight-line model* describes the relationship between these two variables. We explain many of the methods of this chapter in the context of two new cases:

The Fuel Consumption Case: A management consulting firm uses simple linear regression analysis to predict the weekly amount of fuel (in millions of cubic feet of natural gas) that will be required to heat the homes and businesses in a small city on the basis of the week's average hourly temperature. A natural gas company uses these predictions to improve its gas ordering process. One of the gas company's objectives is to reduce the fines imposed by its pipeline transmission system when the

company places inaccurate natural gas orders.

The QHIC Case: The marketing department at Quality Home Improvement Center (QHIC) uses simple linear regression analysis to predict home upkeep expenditure on the basis of home value. Predictions of home upkeep expenditures are used to help determine which homes should be sent advertising brochures promoting QHIC's products and services.

13.1 The Simple Linear Regression Model and the Least Squares Point Estimates ● ● ●

The simple linear regression model   The **simple linear regression model** assumes that the relationship between the **dependent variable, which is denoted y,** and the **independent variable, denoted x,** can be approximated by a straight line. We can tentatively decide whether there is an approximate straight-line relationship between y and x by making a **scatter diagram,** or **scatter plot,** of y versus x. First, data concerning the two variables are observed in pairs. To construct the scatter plot, each value of y is plotted against its corresponding value of x. If the y values tend to increase or decrease in a straight-line fashion as the x values increase, and if there is a scattering of the (x, y) points around the straight line, then it is reasonable to describe the relationship between y and x by using the simple linear regression model. We illustrate this in the following case study, which shows how regression analysis can help a natural gas company improve its ordering process.

EXAMPLE 13.1 The Fuel Consumption Case: Reducing Natural Gas Transmission Fines   FuelCon1

Part 1: The natural gas transmission problem   When the natural gas industry was deregulated in 1993, natural gas companies became responsible for acquiring the natural gas needed to heat the homes and businesses in the cities they serve. To do this, natural gas companies purchase natural gas from marketers (usually through long-term contracts) and periodically (perhaps daily, weekly, or monthly) place orders for natural gas to be transmitted by pipeline transmission systems to their cities. There are hundreds of pipeline transmission systems in the United States, and many of these systems supply a large number of cities. For instance, the map in Figure 13.1 illustrates the pipelines of and the cities served by the Columbia Gas System.

FIGURE 13.1   **The Columbia Gas System**

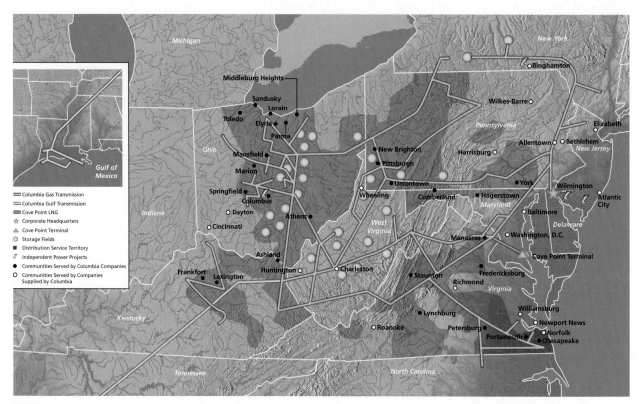

Source: Columbia Gas System 1995 Annual Report.   © Reprinted courtesy of Columbia Gas System.

To place an order (called a *nomination*) for an amount of natural gas to be transmitted to its city over a period of time (day, week, month), a natural gas company makes its best prediction of the city's natural gas needs for that period. The natural gas company then instructs its marketer(s) to deliver this amount of gas to its pipeline transmission system. If most of the natural gas companies being supplied by the transmission system can predict their cities' natural gas needs with reasonable accuracy, then the overnominations of some companies will tend to cancel the undernominations of other companies. As a result, the transmission system will probably have enough natural gas to efficiently meet the needs of the cities it supplies.

In order to encourage natural gas companies to make accurate transmission nominations and to help control costs, pipeline transmission systems charge, in addition to their usual fees, transmission fines. A natural gas company is charged a transmission fine if it substantially undernominates natural gas, which can lead to an excessive number of unplanned transmissions, or if it substantially overnominates natural gas, which can lead to excessive storage of unused gas. Typically, pipeline transmission systems allow a certain percentage nomination error before they impose a fine. For example, some systems do not impose a fine unless the actual amount of natural gas used by a city differs from the nomination by more than 10 percent. Beyond the allowed percentage nomination error, fines are charged on a sliding scale—the larger the nomination error, the larger the transmission fine.

Part 2: The fuel consumption data   Suppose we are analysts in a management consulting firm. The natural gas company serving a small city has hired the consulting firm to develop an accurate way to predict the amount of fuel (in millions of cubic feet—MMcf—of natural gas) that will be required to heat the city. Because the pipeline transmission system supplying the city evaluates nomination errors and assesses fines weekly, the natural gas company wants predictions of future weekly fuel consumptions. Moreover, since the pipeline transmission system allows a 10 percent nomination error before assessing a fine, the natural gas company would like the actual and predicted weekly fuel consumptions to differ by no more than 10 percent. Our experience suggests that weekly fuel consumption substantially depends on the average hourly temperature (in degrees Fahrenheit) measured in the city during the week. Therefore, we will try to predict

	T ABLE 13.1	**The Fuel Consumption Data** ● FuelCon1

Week	Average Hourly Temperature, x (°F)	Weekly Fuel Consumption, y (MMcf)
1	28.0	12.4
2	28.0	11.7
3	32.5	12.4
4	39.0	10.8
5	45.9	9.4
6	57.8	9.5
7	58.1	8.0
8	62.5	7.5

F IGURE 13.2   Excel Output of a Scatter Plot of y versus x

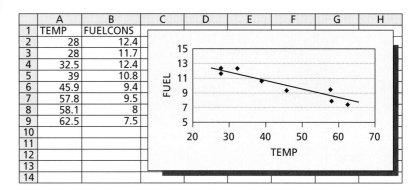

the **dependent (response) variable** weekly fuel consumption (y) on the basis of the **independent (predictor) variable** average hourly temperature (x) during the week. To this end, we observe values of y and x for eight weeks. The data are given in Table 13.1. In Figure 13.2 we give an Excel output of a scatter plot of y versus x. This plot shows (1) a tendency for the fuel consumptions to decrease in a straight-line fashion as the temperatures increase and (2) a scattering of points around the straight line. A **regression model** describing the relationship between y and x must represent these two characteristics. We now develop such a model.[1]

Part 3: The simple linear regression model   To begin, suppose that there is an exact straight-line relationship between y (weekly fuel consumption) and x (average hourly temperature). Specifically, suppose we know that when the average hourly temperature is 0°F, weekly fuel consumption is 15.5 MMcf of natural gas. Also suppose we know that, for each one-degree increase in average hourly temperature, weekly fuel consumption decreases by .1 MMcf of natural gas. In this case, the straight line relating y to x would have y-intercept 15.5 and slope $-.1$ and would be given by the equation

$$y = 15.5 - .1x$$

For example, if we know that the average hourly temperature in a future week will be 40°F, then it would follow that fuel consumption in the future week will be

$$y = 15.5 - .1(40) = 11.5 \text{ MMcf of natural gas}$$

In reality, Figure 13.2 shows that the relationship between y and x is not exactly a straight line. However, we can use a modified straight-line equation—called the **simple linear regression model**—to relate y to x. The simple linear regression model employs a y-*intercept* β_0, a *slope* β_1, and an *error term* ε (the meanings of which will soon be discussed) and is expressed as follows:

$$y = \beta_0 + \beta_1 x + \varepsilon$$

This model says that the values of y can be represented by a *mean level*—$\beta_0 + \beta_1 x$—that changes in a straight-line fashion as x changes, combined with random fluctuations—described by the error term ε—that cause the values of y to deviate from the mean level. Here:

1   The **mean level** $\beta_0 + \beta_1 x$, which we denote as μ_y, is the mean of the fuel consumptions (y) that would be observed in all weeks having an average hourly temperature of x. Furthermore, when we say that the mean level changes in a straight-line fashion as x changes, we mean that different mean fuel consumptions corresponding to different values of x form a straight line. This line, which we call the **line of means,** is defined by the equation $\mu_y = \beta_0 + \beta_1 x$. The line of means has y-intercept β_0 and slope β_1, and the values of β_0 and β_1 determine the values of μ_y for different values of x. For example, Table 13.1 tells us that the average hourly temperature in week 1 was 28°F and the average hourly temperature in week 5 was 45.9°F.

[1]Generally, the larger the sample size is—that is, the more combinations of values of y and x that we have observed—the more accurately we can describe the relationship between y and x. Therefore, as the natural gas company observes values of y and x in future weeks, the new data should be added to the data in Table 13.1.

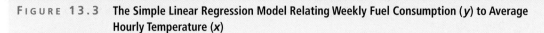

FIGURE 13.3   The Simple Linear Regression Model Relating Weekly Fuel Consumption (*y*) to Average Hourly Temperature (*x*)

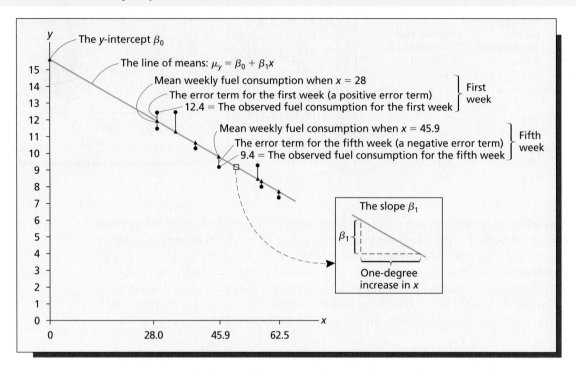

It follows that the mean fuel consumption for all weeks that have an average hourly temperature of 28°F is $\beta_0 + \beta_1(28)$. Similarly, the mean fuel consumption for all weeks that have an average hourly temperature of 45.9°F is $\beta_0 + \beta_1(45.9)$. Because we do not know the true values of β_0 and β_1, we cannot actually calculate these mean fuel consumptions. However, when we learn (in the next subsection) how to estimate β_0 and β_1, we will be able to estimate these means. For now, note that these means are explicitly identified in Figure 13.3, which illustrates the line of means. These means—and the mean fuel consumptions that correspond to the other average hourly temperatures in Table 13.1—are depicted as triangles that lie on the line of means.

2   The **y-intercept** β_0 of the line of means can be understood by considering Figure 13.3. As illustrated in this figure, the y-intercept β_0 is the mean fuel consumption for all weeks that have an average hourly temperature of 0°F. However, since we have not observed any temperatures near 0°F, we do not have any data to tell us whether the line of means describes mean fuel consumption when the average hourly temperature is 0°F. Therefore, although β_0 is an important component of the line of means, its interpretation is of dubious practical value. More will be said about this later.

3   The **slope** β_1 of the line of means can also be understood by considering Figure 13.3. As illustrated in this figure, the slope β_1 is the change in mean weekly fuel consumption that is associated with a one-degree increase in average hourly temperature.

4   The **error term** ε of the simple linear regression model describes the effect on weekly fuel consumption of all factors other than the average hourly temperature. Such factors would include the average hourly wind velocity and the amount of cloud cover in the city. For example, Figure 13.3 shows that the error term for the first week is positive. Therefore, the observed fuel consumption $y = 12.4$ in the first week is above the corresponding mean fuel consumption for all weeks when $x = 28$. As another example, Figure 13.3 also shows that the error term for the fifth week is negative. Therefore, the observed fuel consumption $y = 9.4$ in the fifth week is below the corresponding mean fuel consumption for all weeks when $x = 45.9$. Of course, since we do not know the true values of β_0 and β_1, the relative positions of the quantities pictured in Figure 13.3 are only hypothetical.

FIGURE 13.4   **The Simple Linear Regression Model (Here the Slope β_1 Is Positive)**

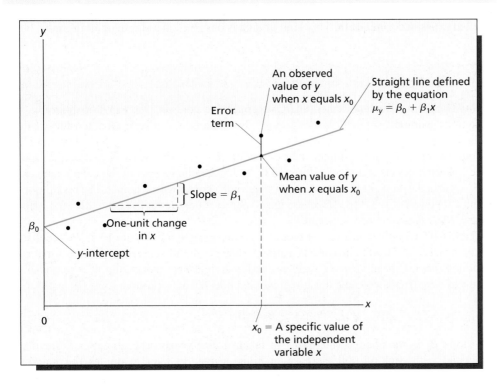

With the fuel consumption example as background, we are ready to define the **simple linear regression model relating the dependent variable y to the independent variable x.** We suppose that we have gathered n observations—each observation consists of an observed value of x and its corresponding value of y. Then:

The Simple Linear Regression Model

The **simple linear (or straight-line) regression model** is: $y = \beta_0 + \beta_1 x + \varepsilon$. Here

1 $\mu_y = \beta_0 + \beta_1 x$ is the **mean value** of the dependent variable y when the value of the independent variable is x.

2 β_0 is the **y-intercept**. β_0 is the mean value of y when x equals zero.[2]

3 β_1 is the **slope**. β_1 is the change (amount of increase or decrease) in the mean value of y associated with a one-unit increase in x. If β_1 is positive, the mean value of y increases as x increases. If β_1 is negative, the mean value of y decreases as x increases.

4 ε is an **error term** that describes the effects on y of all factors other than the value of the independent variable x.

This model is illustrated in Figure 13.4 (note that x_0 in this figure denotes a specific value of the independent variable x). The y-intercept β_0 and the slope β_1 are called **regression parameters.** Because we do not know the true values of these parameters, we must use the sample data to estimate these values. We see how this is done in the next subsection. In later sections we show how to use these estimates to predict y.

---

[2]As implied by the discussion of Example 13.1, if we have not observed any values of x near 0, this interpretation is of dubious practical value.

The fuel consumption data in Table 13.1 were observed sequentially over time (in eight consecutive weeks). When data are observed in time sequence, the data are called **time series data.** Many applications of regression utilize such data. Another frequently used type of data is called **cross-sectional data.** This kind of data is observed at a single point in time.

EXAMPLE 13.2 The QHIC Case ⬙ QHIC

Quality Home Improvement Center (QHIC) operates five stores in a large metropolitan area. The marketing department at QHIC wishes to study the relationship between x, home value (in thousands of dollars), and y, yearly expenditure on home upkeep (in dollars). A random sample of 40 homeowners is asked to estimate their expenditures during the previous year on the types of home upkeep products and services offered by QHIC. Public records of the county auditor are used to obtain the previous year's assessed values of the homeowners' homes. The resulting x and y values are given in Table 13.2. Because the 40 observations are for the same year (for different homes), *these data are cross-sectional.*

The MINITAB output of a scatter plot of y versus x is given in Figure 13.5. We see that the observed values of y tend to increase in a straight-line (or slightly curved) fashion as x increases. Assuming that the mean value of y given x has a straight-line relationship, it is reasonable to relate y to x by using the simple linear regression model having a positive slope ($\beta_1 > 0$)

$$y = \beta_0 + \beta_1 x + \varepsilon$$

The slope β_1 is the change (increase) in mean dollar yearly upkeep expenditure that is associated with each \$1,000 increase in home value. In later examples the marketing department at QHIC will use predictions given by this simple linear regression model to help determine which homes should be sent advertising brochures promoting QHIC's products and services.

We have interpreted the slope β_1 of the simple linear regression model to be the change in the mean value of y associated with a one-unit increase in x. We sometimes refer to this change as *the effect of the independent variable x on the dependent variable y.* However, we cannot prove that

TABLE 13.2   The QHIC Upkeep Expenditure Data ⬙ QHIC

Home	Value of Home, x (Thousands of Dollars)	Upkeep Expenditure, y (Dollars)	Home	Value of Home, x (Thousands of Dollars)	Upkeep Expenditure, y (Dollars)
1	237.00	1,412.08	21	153.04	849.14
2	153.08	797.20	22	232.18	1,313.84
3	184.86	872.48	23	125.44	602.06
4	222.06	1,003.42	24	169.82	642.14
5	160.68	852.90	25	177.28	1,038.80
6	99.68	288.48	26	162.82	697.00
7	229.04	1,288.46	27	120.44	324.34
8	101.78	423.08	28	191.10	965.10
9	257.86	1,351.74	29	158.78	920.14
10	96.28	378.04	30	178.50	950.90
11	171.00	918.08	31	272.20	1,670.32
12	231.02	1,627.24	32	48.90	125.40
13	228.32	1,204.76	33	104.56	479.78
14	205.90	857.04	34	286.18	2,010.64
15	185.72	775.00	35	83.72	368.36
16	168.78	869.26	36	86.20	425.60
17	247.06	1,396.00	37	133.58	626.90
18	155.54	711.50	38	212.86	1,316.94
19	224.20	1,475.18	39	122.02	390.16
20	202.04	1,413.32	40	198.02	1,090.84

F I G U R E **13.5** **MINITAB Plot of Upkeep Expenditure versus Value of Home**	F I G U R E **13.6** **An Estimated Regression Line Drawn through the Fuel Consumption Scatter Plot**

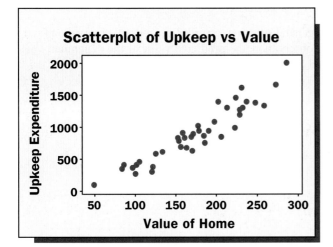

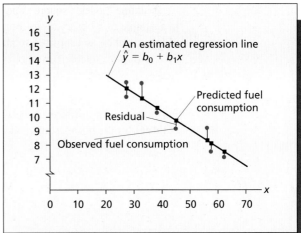

a *change in an independent variable causes a change in the dependent variable.* Rather, regression can be used only to establish that the two variables move together and that the independent variable contributes information for predicting the dependent variable. For instance, regression analysis might be used to establish that as liquor sales have increased over the years, college professors' salaries have also increased. However, this does not prove that increases in liquor sales cause increases in college professors' salaries. Rather, both variables are influenced by a third variable—long-run growth in the national economy.

The least squares point estimates   Suppose that we have gathered n observations (x_1, y_1), $(x_2, y_2), \ldots, (x_n, y_n)$, where each observation consists of a value of an independent variable x and a corresponding value of a dependent variable y. Also, suppose that a scatter plot of the n observations indicates that the simple linear regression model relates y to x. In order to estimate the y-intercept β_0 and the slope β_1 of the line of means of this model, we could visually draw a line—called an **estimated regression line**—through the scatter plot. Then, we could read the y-intercept and slope off the estimated regression line and use these values as the point estimates of β_0 and β_1. Unfortunately, if different people visually drew lines through the scatter plot, their lines would probably differ from each other. What we need is the "best line" that can be drawn through the scatter plot. Although there are various definitions of what this best line is, one of the most useful best lines is the *least squares line*.

To understand the least squares line, we let

$$\hat{y} = b_0 + b_1 x$$

denote the general equation of an estimated regression line drawn through a scatter plot. Here, since we will use this line to predict y on the basis of x, we call $\hat{y}$ *the predicted value of y* when the value of the independent variable is x. In addition, b_0 is the y-intercept and b_1 is the slope of the estimated regression line. When we determine numerical values for b_0 and b_1, these values will be the point estimates of the y-intercept β_0 and the slope β_1 of the line of means. To explain which estimated regression line is the least squares line, we begin with the fuel consumption situation. Figure 13.6 shows an estimated regression line drawn through a scatter plot of the fuel consumption data. In this figure the red dots represent the eight observed fuel consumptions and the black squares represent the eight predicted fuel consumptions given by the estimated regression line. Furthermore, the line segments drawn between the red dots and black squares represent *residuals,* which are the differences between the observed and predicted fuel consumptions. Intuitively, if a particular estimated regression line provides a good "fit" to the fuel consumption

FuelCon1

data, it will make the predicted fuel consumptions "close" to the observed fuel consumptions, and thus the residuals given by the line will be small. The *least squares line* is the line that minimizes the sum of squared residuals. That is, the least squares line is the line positioned on the scatter plot so as to minimize the sum of the squared vertical distances between the observed and predicted fuel consumptions.

To define the least squares line in a general situation, consider an arbitrary observation (x_i, y_i) in a sample of n observations. For this observation, the **predicted value of the dependent variable y** given by an estimated regression line is

$$\hat{y}_i = b_0 + b_1 x_i$$

Furthermore, the difference between the observed and predicted values of y, $y_i - \hat{y}_i$, is the **residual** for the observation, and the **sum of squared residuals** for all n observations is

$$SSE = \sum_{i=1}^{n} (y_i - \hat{y}_i)^2$$

The **least squares line** is the line that minimizes SSE. To find this line, we find the values of the y-intercept b_0 and slope b_1 that give values of $\hat{y}_i = b_0 + b_1 x_i$ that minimize SSE. These values of b_0 and b_1 are called the **least squares point estimates** of β_0 and β_1. Using calculus, it can be shown that these estimates are calculated as follows:[3]

The Least Squares Point Estimates

For the simple linear regression model:

1 The **least squares point estimate of the slope β_1** is $b_1 = \dfrac{SS_{xy}}{SS_{xx}}$ where

$$SS_{xy} = \sum (x_i - \bar{x})(y_i - \bar{y}) = \sum x_i y_i - \frac{\left(\sum x_i\right)\left(\sum y_i\right)}{n} \quad \text{and} \quad SS_{xx} = \sum (x_i - \bar{x})^2 = \sum x_i^2 - \frac{\left(\sum x_i\right)^2}{n}$$

2 The **least squares point estimate of the y-intercept β_0** is $b_0 = \bar{y} - b_1 \bar{x}$ where

$$\bar{y} = \frac{\sum y_i}{n} \quad \text{and} \quad \bar{x} = \frac{\sum x_i}{n}$$

Here n is the number of observations (an observation is an observed value of x and its corresponding value of y).

The following example illustrates how to calculate these point estimates and how to use these point estimates to estimate mean values and predict individual values of the dependent variable. Note that the quantities SS_{xy} and SS_{xx} used to calculate the least squares point estimates are also used throughout this chapter to perform other important calculations.

---

[3]In order to simplify notation, we will often drop the limits on summations in this and subsequent chapters. That is, instead of using the summation $\sum_{i=1}^{n}$ we will simply write $\sum$.

EXAMPLE 13.3 The Fuel Consumption Case ● FuelCon1

Part 1: Calculating the least squares point estimates Again consider the fuel consumption problem. To compute the least squares point estimates of the regression parameters β_0 and β_1 we first calculate the following preliminary summations:

y_i	x_i	x_i^2	$x_i y_i$
12.4	28.0	$(28.0)^2 = 784$	$(28.0)(12.4) = 347.2$
11.7	28.0	$(28.0)^2 = 784$	$(28.0)(11.7) = 327.6$
12.4	32.5	$(32.5)^2 = 1{,}056.25$	$(32.5)(12.4) = 403$
10.8	39.0	$(39.0)^2 = 1{,}521$	$(39.0)(10.8) = 421.2$
9.4	45.9	$(45.9)^2 = 2{,}106.81$	$(45.9)(9.4) = 431.46$
9.5	57.8	$(57.8)^2 = 3{,}340.84$	$(57.8)(9.5) = 549.1$
8.0	58.1	$(58.1)^2 = 3{,}375.61$	$(58.1)(8.0) = 464.8$
7.5	62.5	$(62.5)^2 = 3{,}906.25$	$(62.5)(7.5) = 468.75$
$\sum y_i = 81.7$	$\sum x_i = 351.8$	$\sum x_i^2 = 16{,}874.76$	$\sum x_i y_i = 3{,}413.11$

Using these summations, we calculate SS_{xy} and SS_{xx} as follows.

$$SS_{xy} = \sum x_i y_i - \frac{\left(\sum x_i\right)\left(\sum y_i\right)}{n}$$

$$= 3{,}413.11 - \frac{(351.8)(81.7)}{8}$$

$$= -179.6475$$

$$SS_{xx} = \sum x_i^2 - \frac{\left(\sum x_i\right)^2}{n}$$

$$= 16{,}874.76 - \frac{(351.8)^2}{8}$$

$$= 1{,}404.355$$

It follows that the least squares point estimate of the slope β_1 is

$$b_1 = \frac{SS_{xy}}{SS_{xx}} = \frac{-179.6475}{1{,}404.355} = -.1279$$

Furthermore, because

$$\bar{y} = \frac{\sum y_i}{8} = \frac{81.7}{8} = 10.2125 \quad \text{and} \quad \bar{x} = \frac{\sum x_i}{8} = \frac{351.8}{8} = 43.98$$

the least squares point estimate of the y-intercept β_0 is

$$b_0 = \bar{y} - b_1\bar{x} = 10.2125 - (-.1279)(43.98) = 15.84$$

Since $b_1 = -.1279$, we estimate that mean weekly fuel consumption decreases (since b_1 is negative) by .1279 MMcf of natural gas when average hourly temperature increases by one degree. Since $b_0 = 15.84$, we estimate that the mean weekly fuel consumption is 15.84 MMcf of natural gas when the average hourly temperature is 0°F. However, we have not observed any weeks with temperatures near 0°F, so making this interpretation of b_0 might be dangerous. We discuss this point more fully after this example.

The least squares line

$$\hat{y} = b_0 + b_1 x = 15.84 - .1279x$$

is sometimes called the *least squares prediction equation*. In Table 13.3 (on the next page) we summarize using this prediction equation to calculate the predicted fuel consumptions and the

TABLE 13.3   Calculation of *SSE* Obtained by Using the Least Squares Point Estimates

y_i	x_i	$\hat{y}_i = 15.84 - .1279x_i$	$y_i - \hat{y}_i =$ residual
12.4	28.0	$15.84 - .1279(28.0) = 12.2588$	$12.4 - 12.2588 = .1412$
11.7	28.0	$15.84 - .1279(28.0) = 12.2588$	$11.7 - 12.2588 = -.5588$
12.4	32.5	$15.84 - .1279(32.5) = 11.68325$	$12.4 - 11.68325 = .71675$
10.8	39.0	$15.84 - .1279(39.0) = 10.8519$	$10.8 - 10.8519 = -.0519$
9.4	45.9	$15.84 - .1279(45.9) = 9.96939$	$9.4 - 9.96939 = -.56939$
9.5	57.8	$15.84 - .1279(57.8) = 8.44738$	$9.5 - 8.44738 = 1.05262$
8.0	58.1	$15.84 - .1279(58.1) = 8.40901$	$8.0 - 8.40901 = -.40901$
7.5	62.5	$15.84 - .1279(62.5) = 7.84625$	$7.5 - 7.84625 = -.34625$

$$SSE = \sum (y_i - \hat{y}_i)^2 = (.1412)^2 + (-.5588)^2 + \cdots + (-.34625)^2 = 2.568$$

FIGURE 13.7   The MINITAB Output of the Least Squares Line

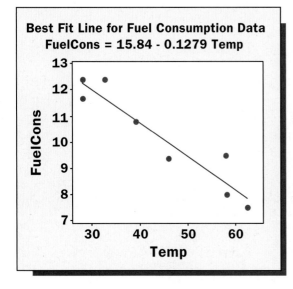

FIGURE 13.8   Point Estimation and Point Prediction in the Fuel Consumption Case

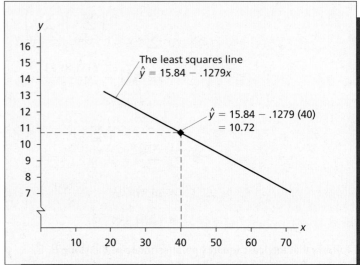

residuals for the eight weeks of fuel consumption data. For example, since in week 1 the average hourly temperature was 28°F, the predicted fuel consumption for week 1 is

$$\hat{y}_1 = 15.84 - .1279(28) = 12.2588$$

It follows, since the observed fuel consumption in week 1 was $y_1 = 12.4$, that the residual for week 1 is

$$y_1 - \hat{y}_1 = 12.4 - 12.2588 = .1412$$

If we consider all of the residuals in Table 13.3 and add their squared values, we find that *SSE*, the sum of squared residuals, is 2.568. This *SSE* value will be used throughout this chapter. Figure 13.7 gives the MINITAB output of the least squares line. Note that this output gives the least squares estimates $b_0 = 15.84$ and $b_1 = -0.1279$. In general, we will rely on MINITAB, Excel, and MegaStat to compute the least squares estimates (and to perform many other regression calculations).

Part 2: Estimating a mean fuel consumption and predicting an individual fuel consumption   We define the **experimental region** to be the range of the previously observed values of the average hourly temperature x. Referring to Table 13.3, we see that the experimental region consists of the range of average hourly temperatures from 28°F to 62.5°F. The simple linear regression model relates weekly fuel consumption y to average hourly temperature x for

FIGURE 13.9   The Danger of Extrapolation Outside the Experimental Region

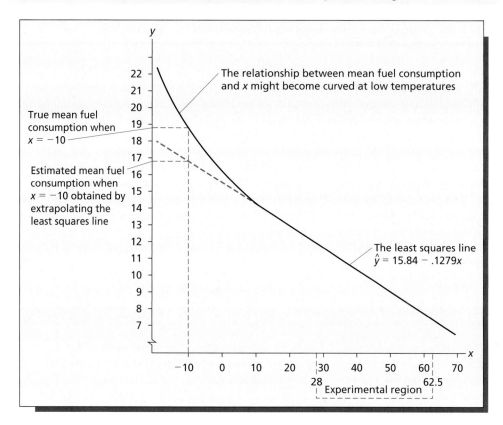

values of x that are in the experimental region. For such values of x, the least squares line is the estimate of the line of means. It follows that the point on the least squares line corresponding to an average hourly temperature of x

$$\hat{y} = b_0 + b_1 x$$

is the point estimate of $\beta_0 + \beta_1 x$, the mean fuel consumption for all weeks that have an average hourly temperature of x. In addition, we predict the error term ε to be zero. Therefore, $\hat{y}$ is also the *point prediction* of an *individual value* $y = \beta_0 + \beta_1 x + \varepsilon$, which is the amount of fuel consumed in a single week that has an average hourly temperature of x. Note that the reason we predict the error term ε to be zero is that, because of several *regression assumptions* to be discussed in the next section, ε has a 50 percent chance of being positive and a 50 percent chance of being negative.

For example, suppose a weather forecasting service predicts that the average hourly temperature in the next week will be 40°F. Because 40°F is in the experimental region

$$\hat{y} = 15.84 - .1279(40)$$

$$= 10.72 \text{ MMcf of natural gas}$$

is

1   The point estimate of the mean fuel consumption for all weeks that have an average hourly temperature of 40°F.

2   The point prediction of the amount of fuel consumed in a single week that has an average hourly temperature of 40°F.

Figure 13.8 illustrates $\hat{y} = 10.72$ as a square on the least squares line.

To conclude this example, note that Figure 13.9 illustrates the potential danger of using the least squares line to predict outside the experimental region. In the figure, we extrapolate the least squares line far beyond the experimental region to obtain a prediction for a temperature of −10°F. As shown in Figure 13.7 for values of x in the experimental region the observed values of y tend to decrease in a straight-line fashion as the values of x increase. However, for temperatures lower than 28°F the relationship between y and x might become curved. If it does, extrapolating the straight-line prediction equation to obtain a prediction for $x = -10$ might badly underestimate mean weekly fuel consumption (see Figure 13.9).

The previous example illustrates that when we are using a least squares regression line, we should not estimate a mean value or predict an individual value unless the corresponding value of x is in the **experimental region**—the range of the previously observed values of x. Often the value $x = 0$ is not in the experimental region. In such a situation, it would not be appropriate to interpret the y-intercept b_0 as the estimate of the mean value of y when x equals zero. For example, consider the fuel consumption problem. Figure 13.9 illustrates that the average hourly temperature 0°F is not in the experimental region. Therefore, it would not be appropriate to use $b_0 = 15.84$ as the point estimate of the mean weekly fuel consumption when the average hourly temperature is 0°F. Because it is not meaningful to interpret the y-intercept in many regression situations, we often omit such interpretations.

We now present a general procedure for estimating a mean value and predicting an individual value:

Point Estimation and Point Prediction in Simple Linear Regression

Let b_0 and b_1 be the least squares point estimates of the y-intercept β_0 and the slope β_1 in the simple linear regression model, and suppose that x_0, a specified value of the independent variable x, is inside the experimental region. Then

$$\hat{y} = b_0 + b_1 x_0$$

1 is the **point estimate** of the **mean value of the dependent variable** when the value of the independent variable is x_0.

2 is the **point prediction** of an **individual value of the dependent variable** when the value of the independent variable is x_0. Here we predict the error term to be zero.

EXAMPLE 13.4 The QHIC Case ◇ QHIC

Consider the simple linear regression model relating yearly home upkeep expenditure, y, to home value, x. Using the data in Table 13.2 (page 504), we can calculate the least squares point estimates of the y-intercept β_0 and the slope β_1 to be $b_0 = -348.3921$ and $b_1 = 7.2583$. Since $b_1 = 7.2583$, we estimate that mean yearly upkeep expenditure increases by \$7.26 for each additional \$1,000 increase in home value. Consider a home worth \$220,000, and note that $x_0 = 220$ is in the range of previously observed values of x: 48.9 to 286.18 (see Table 13.2 on page 504). It follows that

$$\hat{y} = b_0 + b_1 x_0$$
$$= -348.3921 + 7.2583(220)$$
$$= 1{,}248.43 \text{ (or } \$1{,}248.43)$$

is the point estimate of the mean yearly upkeep expenditure for all homes worth \$220,000 and is the point prediction of a yearly upkeep expenditure for an individual home worth \$220,000.

The marketing department at QHIC wishes to determine which homes should be sent advertising brochures promoting QHIC's products and services. If the marketing department has decided to send an advertising brochure to any home that has a predicted yearly upkeep expenditure of at least \$500, then a home worth \$220,000 would be sent an advertising brochure. This is because the predicted yearly upkeep expenditure for such a home is (as calculated above) \$1,248.43. Other homes can be evaluated in a similar fashion.

Exercises for Section 13.1

CONCEPTS

13.1   When does the scatter plot of the values of a dependent variable y versus the values of an independent variable x suggest that the simple linear regression model

$$y = \beta_0 + \beta_1 x + \varepsilon$$

might appropriately relate y to x?

13.2   What is the least squares regression line, and what are the least squares point estimates?

13.3   How do we obtain a point estimate of the mean value of the dependent variable and a point prediction of an individual value of the dependent variable?

13.4   Why is it dangerous to extrapolate outside the experimental region?

METHODS AND APPLICATIONS

In Exercises 13.5 through 13.9 we present five data sets involving a dependent variable y and an independent variable x. For each data set, assume that the simple linear regression model

$$y = \beta_0 + \beta_1 x + \varepsilon$$

relates y to x.

13.5   THE STARTING SALARY CASE   ● StartSal

The chairman of the marketing department at a large state university undertakes a study to relate starting salary (y) after graduation for marketing majors to grade point average (GPA) in major courses. To do this, records of seven recent marketing graduates are randomly selected, and the data shown below on the left are obtained. The MINITAB output obtained by fitting a least squares regression line to the data is below on the right.

Marketing Graduate	GPA, x	Starting Salary, y (Thousands of Dollars)
1	3.26	33.8
2	2.60	29.8
3	3.35	33.5
4	2.86	30.4
5	3.82	36.4
6	2.21	27.6
7	3.47	35.3

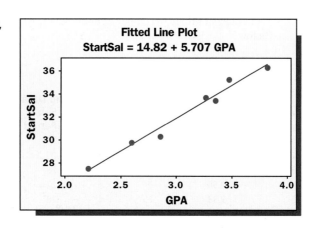

a   Find the least squares point estimates b_0 and b_1 on the computer output and report their values. Interpret b_0 and b_1. Does the interpretation of b_0 make practical sense?

b   Use the least squares line to compute a point estimate of the mean starting salary for all marketing graduates having a grade point average of 3.25 and a point prediction of the starting salary for an individual marketing graduate having a grade point average of 3.25.

13.6   THE SERVICE TIME CASE   ● SrvcTime

Accu-Copiers, Inc., sells and services the Accu-500 copying machine. As part of its standard service contract, the company agrees to perform routine service on this copier. To obtain information about the time it takes to perform routine service, Accu-Copiers has collected data for 11 service calls. The data and Excel output from fitting a least squares regression line to the data follow on the next page.

a   Find the least squares point estimates b_0 and b_1 on the computer output and report their values. Interpret b_0 and b_1. Does the interpretation of b_0 make practical sense?

b   Use the least squares line to compute a point estimate of the mean time to service four copiers and a point prediction of the time to service four copiers on a single call.

Service Call	Number of Copiers Serviced, x	Number of Minutes Required, y
1	4	109
2	2	58
3	5	138
4	7	189
5	1	37
6	3	82
7	4	103
8	5	134
9	2	68
10	4	112
11	6	154

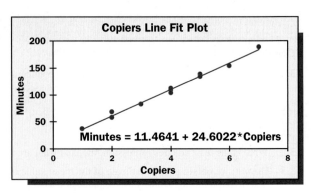

13.7 THE FRESH DETERGENT CASE   ◑ Fresh

Enterprise Industries produces Fresh, a brand of liquid laundry detergent. In order to study the relationship between price and demand for the large bottle of Fresh, the company has gathered data concerning demand for Fresh over the last 30 sales periods (each sales period is four weeks). Here, for each sales period,

y = demand for the large bottle of Fresh (in hundreds of thousands of bottles) in the sales period, and

x = the difference between the average industry price (in dollars) of competitors' similar detergents and the price (in dollars) of Fresh as offered by Enterprise Industries in the sales period.

The data and MINITAB output from fitting a least squares regression line to the data follow below.

Fresh Detergent Demand Data

Sales Period	y	x	Sales Period	y	x
1	7.38	−.05	24	8.50	.10
2	8.51	.25	25	8.75	.50
3	9.52	.60	26	9.21	.60
4	7.50	0	27	8.27	−.05
5	9.33	.25	28	7.67	0
6	8.28	.20	29	7.93	.05
7	8.75	.15	30	9.26	.55
8	7.87	.05			
9	7.10	−.15			
10	8.00	.15			
11	7.89	.20			
12	8.15	.10			
13	9.10	.40			
14	8.86	.45			
15	8.90	.35			
16	8.87	.30			
17	9.26	.50			
18	9.00	.50			
19	8.75	.40			
20	7.95	−.05			
21	7.65	−.05			
22	7.27	−.10			
23	8.00	.20			

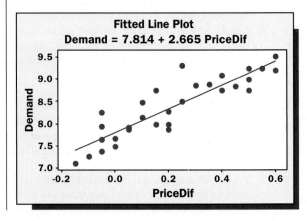

a Find the least squares point estimates b_0 and b_1 on the computer output and report their values. Interpret b_0 and b_1. Does the interpretation of b_0 make practical sense?

b Use the least squares line to compute a point estimate of the mean demand in all sales periods when the price difference is .10 and a point prediction of the actual demand in an individual sales period when the price difference is .10.

13.8 THE DIRECT LABOR COST CASE   ● DirLab

An accountant wishes to predict direct labor cost (y) on the basis of the batch size (x) of a product produced in a job shop. Data for 12 production runs are given in the table below, along with the Excel output from fitting a least squares regression line to the data.

Direct Labor Cost Data   ● DirLab

Direct Labor Cost, y ($100s)	Batch Size, x
71	5
663	62
381	35
138	12
861	83
145	14
493	46
548	52
251	23
1024	100
435	41
772	75

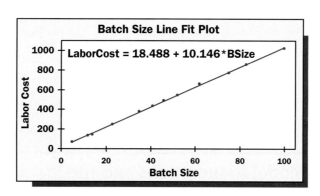

Batch Size Line Fit Plot

LaborCost = 18.488 + 10.146*BSize

a By using the formulas illustrated in Example 13.3 (see page 507) and the data provided, verify that (within rounding) $b_0 = 18.488$ and $b_1 = 10.146$, as shown on the Excel output.

b Interpret the meanings of b_0 and b_1. Does the interpretation of b_0 make practical sense?

c Write the least squares prediction equation.

d Use the least squares line to obtain a point estimate of the mean direct labor cost for all batches of size 60 and a point prediction of the direct labor cost for an individual batch of size 60.

13.9 THE REAL ESTATE SALES PRICE CASE   ● RealEst

A real estate agency collects data concerning $y =$ the sales price of a house (in thousands of dollars), and $x =$ the home size (in hundreds of square feet). The data are given in the table below. The MINITAB output from fitting a least squares regression line to the data is on the next page.

Real Estate Sales Price Data   ● RealEst

Sales Price (y)	Home Size (x)	Sales Price (y)	Home Size (x)
180	23	165.9	21
98.1	11	193.5	24
173.1	20	127.8	13
136.5	17	163.5	19
141	15	172.5	25

Source: Reprinted with permission from *The Real Estate Appraiser and Analyst* Spring 1986 issue. Copyright 1986 by the Appraisal Institute, Chicago, Illinois.

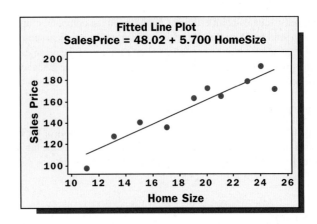

Fitted Line Plot
SalesPrice = 48.02 + 5.700 HomeSize

a By using the formulas illustrated in Example 13.3 (see page 507) and the data provided, verify that (within rounding) $b_0 = 48.02$ and $b_1 = 5.700$, as shown on the MINITAB output.

b Interpret the meanings of b_0 and b_1. Does the interpretation of b_0 make practical sense?

c Write the least squares prediction equation.

d Use the least squares line to obtain a point estimate of the mean sales price of all houses having 2,000 square feet and a point prediction of the sales price of an individual house having 2,000 square feet.

13.2 Model Assumptions and the Standard Error ● ● ●

Model assumptions   In order to perform hypothesis tests and set up various types of intervals when using the simple linear regression model

$$y = \mu_y + \varepsilon$$
$$= \beta_0 + \beta_1 x + \varepsilon$$

we need to make certain assumptions about the error term ε. At any given value of x, there is a population of error term values that could potentially occur. These error term values describe the different potential effects on y of all factors other than the value of x. Therefore, these error term values explain the variation in the y values that could be observed when the independent variable is x. Our statement of the simple linear regression model assumes that μ_y, the mean of the population of all y values that could be observed when the independent variable is x, is $\beta_0 + \beta_1 x$. This model also implies that $\varepsilon = y - (\beta_0 + \beta_1 x)$, so this is equivalent to assuming that the mean of the corresponding population of potential error term values is zero. In total, we make four assumptions—called the **regression assumptions**—about the simple linear regression model. These assumptions can be stated in terms of potential y values or, equivalently, in terms of potential error term values. Following tradition, we begin by stating these assumptions in terms of potential error term values:

The Regression Assumptions

1 At any given value of x, the population of potential error term values has a **mean equal to zero.**

2 Constant Variance Assumption
At any given value of x, the population of potential error term values has a variance that does not depend on the value of x. That is, the different populations of potential error term values corresponding to different values of x have **equal variances.** We denote the **constant variance** as σ^2.

3 Normality Assumption
At any given value of x, the population of potential error term values has a **normal distribution.**

4 Independence Assumption
Any one value of the error term ε is **statistically independent** of any other value of ε. That is, the value of the error term ε corresponding to an observed value of y is statistically independent of the value of the error term corresponding to any other observed value of y.

FIGURE 13.10   An Illustration of the Model Assumptions

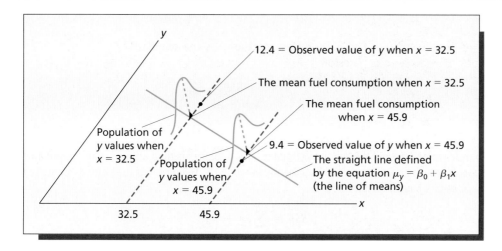

Taken together, the first three assumptions say that, at any given value of x, the population of potential error term values is **normally distributed** with **mean zero** and a **variance σ^2 that does not depend on the value of x.** Because the potential error term values cause the variation in the potential y values, these assumptions imply that the population of all y values that could be observed when the independent variable is x is **normally distributed** with **mean $\beta_0 + \beta_1 x$** and **a variance σ^2 that does not depend on x.** These three assumptions are illustrated in Figure 13.10 in the context of the fuel consumption problem. Specifically, this figure depicts the populations of weekly fuel consumptions corresponding to two values of average hourly temperature—32.5 and 45.9. Note that these populations are shown to be normally distributed with different means (each of which is on the line of means) and with the same variance (or spread).

FuelCon1

The independence assumption is most likely to be violated when time series data are being utilized in a regression study. Intuitively, this assumption says that there is no pattern of positive error terms being followed (in time) by other positive error terms, and there is no pattern of positive error terms being followed by negative error terms. That is, there is no pattern of higher-than-average y values being followed by other higher-than-average y values, and there is no pattern of higher-than-average y values being followed by lower-than-average y values.

It is important to point out that the regression assumptions very seldom, if ever, hold exactly in any practical regression problem. However, it has been found that regression results are not extremely sensitive to mild departures from these assumptions. In practice, only pronounced departures from these assumptions require attention. In optional Section 13.8 we show how to check the regression assumptions. Prior to doing this, we will suppose that the assumptions are valid in our examples.

In Section 13.1 we stated that, when we predict an individual value of the dependent variable, we predict the error term to be zero. To see why we do this, note that the regression assumptions state that, at any given value of the independent variable, the population of all error term values that can potentially occur is normally distributed with a mean equal to zero. Since we also assume that successive error terms (observed over time) are statistically independent, each error term has a 50 percent chance of being positive and a 50 percent chance of being negative. Therefore, it is reasonable to predict any particular error term value to be zero.

The mean square error and the standard error   To present statistical inference formulas in later sections, we need to be able to compute point estimates of σ^2 and σ, the constant variance and standard deviation of the error term populations. The point estimate of σ^2 is called the **mean square error** and the point estimate of σ is called the **standard error.** In the following box, we show how to compute these estimates:

The Mean Square Error and the Standard Error

If the regression assumptions are satisfied and SSE is the sum of squared residuals,

1 The point estimate of σ^2 is the **mean square error**

$$s^2 = \frac{SSE}{n-2}$$

2 The point estimate of σ is the **standard error**

$$s = \sqrt{\frac{SSE}{n-2}}$$

In order to understand these point estimates, recall that σ^2 is the variance of the population of y values (for a given value of x) around the mean value μ_y. Because $\hat{y}$ is the point estimate of this mean, it seems natural to use

$$SSE = \sum (y_i - \hat{y}_i)^2$$

to help construct a point estimate of σ^2. We divide SSE by $n - 2$ because it can be proven that doing so makes the resulting s^2 an unbiased point estimate of σ^2. Here we call $n - 2$ the **number of degrees of freedom** associated with SSE.

EXAMPLE 13.5 The Fuel Consumption Case   ● FuelCon1

Consider the fuel consumption situation, and recall that in Table 13.3 (page 508) we have calculated the sum of squared residuals to be $SSE = 2.568$. It follows, because we have observed $n = 8$ fuel consumptions, that the point estimate of σ^2 is the mean square error

$$s^2 = \frac{SSE}{n-2} = \frac{2.568}{8-2} = .428$$

This implies that the point estimate of σ is the standard error

$$s = \sqrt{s^2} = \sqrt{.428} = .6542$$

● QHIC   As another example, it can be verified that the standard error for the simple linear regression model describing the QHIC data is $s = 146.8970$.

To conclude this section, note that in optional Section 13.9 we present a shortcut formula for calculating SSE. The reader may study Section 13.9 now or at any later point.

Exercises for Section 13.2

CONCEPTS

13.10 What four assumptions do we make about the simple linear regression model?

13.11 What is estimated by the mean square error, and what is estimated by the standard error?

METHODS AND APPLICATIONS

13.12 THE STARTING SALARY CASE   ● StartSal

When a least squares line is fit to the seven observations in the starting salary data, we obtain $SSE = 1.438$. Calculate s^2 and s.

13.13 THE SERVICE TIME CASE   ● SrvcTime

When a least squares line is fit to the 11 observations in the service time data, we obtain $SSE = 191.7017$. Calculate s^2 and s.

13.14 THE FRESH DETERGENT CASE   ● Fresh

When a least squares line is fit to the 30 observations in the Fresh detergent data, we obtain $SSE = 2.806$. Calculate s^2 and s.

13.15   THE DIRECT LABOR COST CASE   ◑ DirLab

When a least squares line is fit to the 12 observations in the labor cost data, we obtain $SSE = 746.7624$. Calculate s^2 and s.

13.16   THE REAL ESTATE SALES PRICE CASE   ◑ RealEst

When a least squares line is fit to the 10 observations in the real estate sales price data, we obtain $SSE = 896.8$. Calculate s^2 and s.

13.17   Ten sales regions of equal sales potential for a company were randomly selected. The advertising expenditures (in units of \$10,000) in these 10 sales regions were purposely set during July of last year at, respectively, 5, 6, 7, 8, 9, 10, 11, 12, 13 and 14. The sales volumes (in units of \$10,000) were then recorded for the 10 sales regions and found to be, respectively, 89, 87, 98, 110, 103, 114, 116, 110, 126, and 130. Assuming that the simple linear regression model is appropriate, it can be shown that $b_0 = 66.2121$, $b_1 = 4.4303$, and $SSE = 222.8242$. Calculate s^2 and s.   ◑ SalesVol

---

13.3 Testing the Significance of the Slope and y-Intercept ● ● ●

Testing the significance of the slope   A simple linear regression model is not likely to be useful unless there is a **significant relationship between y and x.** In order to judge the significance of the relationship between y and x, we test the null hypothesis

$$H_0: \beta_1 = 0$$

which says that there is no change in the mean value of y associated with an increase in x, versus the alternative hypothesis

$$H_a: \beta_1 \neq 0$$

which says that there is a (positive or negative) change in the mean value of y associated with an increase in x. It would be reasonable to conclude that x is significantly related to y if we can be quite certain that we should reject H_0 in favor of H_a.

In order to test these hypotheses, recall that we compute the least squares point estimate b_1 of the true slope β_1 by using a sample of n observed values of the dependent variable y. Different samples of n observed y values would yield different values of the least squares point estimate b_1. It can be shown that, if the regression assumptions hold, then the population of all possible values of b_1 is normally distributed with a mean of β_1 and with a standard deviation of

$$\sigma_{b_1} = \frac{\sigma}{\sqrt{SS_{xx}}}$$

The standard error s is the point estimate of σ, so it follows that a point estimate of σ_{b_1} is

$$s_{b_1} = \frac{s}{\sqrt{SS_{xx}}}$$

which is called the **standard error of the estimate b_1.** Furthermore, if the regression assumptions hold, then the population of all values of

$$\frac{b_1 - \beta_1}{s_{b_1}}$$

has a t distribution with $n - 2$ degrees of freedom. It follows that, if the null hypothesis $H_0: \beta_1 = 0$ is true, then the population of all possible values of the test statistic

$$t = \frac{b_1}{s_{b_1}}$$

has a t distribution with $n - 2$ degrees of freedom. Therefore, we can test the significance of the regression relationship as follows:

Testing the Significance of the Regression Relationship: Testing the Significance of the Slope

D efine the test statistic

$$t = \frac{b_1}{s_{b_1}} \quad \text{where} \quad s_{b_1} = \frac{s}{\sqrt{SS_{xx}}}$$

and suppose that the regression assumptions hold. Then we can test H_0: $\beta_1 = 0$ versus a particular alternative hypothesis at significance level α (that is, by setting the probability of a Type I error equal to α) by using the appropriate critical value rule, or, equivalently, the corresponding p-value.

Alternative Hypothesis	Critical Value Rule: Reject H_0 If	p-Value (Reject H_0 If p-Value $< \alpha$)
H_a: $\beta_1 \neq 0$	$|t| > t_{\alpha/2}$	Twice the area under the t curve to the right of $|t|$
H_a: $\beta_1 > 0$	$t > t_\alpha$	The area under the t curve to the right of t
H_a: $\beta_1 < 0$	$t < -t_\alpha$	The area under the t curve to the left of t

Here $t_{\alpha/2}$, t_α, and all p-values are based on $n - 2$ degrees of freedom. **If we can reject H_0: $\beta_1 = 0$ at a given value of α, then we conclude that the slope (or, equivalently, the regression relationship) is significant at the α level.**

We usually use the two-sided alternative H_a: $\beta_1 \neq 0$ for this test of significance. However, sometimes a one-sided alternative is appropriate. For example, in the fuel consumption problem we can say that if the slope β_1 is not zero, then it must be negative. A negative β_1 would say that mean fuel consumption decreases as temperature x increases. Because of this, it would be appropriate to decide that x is significantly related to y if we can reject H_0: $\beta_1 = 0$ in favor of the one-sided alternative H_a: $\beta_1 < 0$. Although this test would be slightly more effective than the usual two-sided test, there is little practical difference between using the one-sided or two-sided alternative. Furthermore, computer packages (such as MINITAB and Excel) present results for testing a two-sided alternative hypothesis. For these reasons we will emphasize the two-sided test.

It should also be noted that

1   **If we can decide that the slope is significant at the .05 significance level,** then we have concluded that x is significantly related to y by using a test that allows only a .05 probability of concluding that x is significantly related to y when it is not. **This is usually regarded as strong evidence that the regression relationship is significant.**

2   **If we can decide that the slope is significant at the .01 significance level, this is usually regarded as very strong evidence that the regression relationship is significant.**

3   The smaller the significance level α at which H_0 can be rejected, the stronger is the evidence that the regression relationship is significant.

EXAMPLE 13.6 The Fuel Consumption Case   FuelCon1

Again consider the fuel consumption model

$$y = \beta_0 + \beta_1 x + \varepsilon$$

For this model $SS_{xx} = 1,404.355$, $b_1 = -.1279$, and $s = .6542$ [see Examples 13.3 (page 507) and 13.5 (page 516)]. Therefore

$$s_{b_1} = \frac{s}{\sqrt{SS_{xx}}} = \frac{.6542}{\sqrt{1,404.355}} = .01746$$

and

$$t = \frac{b_1}{s_{b_1}} = \frac{-.1279}{.01746} = -7.33$$

FIGURE 13.11   MINITAB and Excel Output of a Simple Linear Regression Analysis
                of the Fuel Consumption Data

(a) The MINITAB Output

```
The regression equation is
FuelCons = 15.8 - 0.128 Temp

Predictor           Coef        SE Coef             T          P 7
Constant         15.8379 1      0.8018 3       19.75 5      0.000
Temp            -0.12792 2      0.01746 4       -7.33 6      0.000

S = 0.654209 8      R-Sq = 89.9% 9       R-Sq(adj) = 88.3%

Analysis of Variance
Source              DF          SS            MS           F           P
Regression          1       22.981 10      22.981      53.69 13    0.000 14
Residual Error      6        2.568 11       0.428
Total               7       25.549 12

Values of Predictors for New Obs    Predicted Values for New Observations
New Obs  Temp                       New Obs    Fit 15 SE Fit 16    95% CI 17          95% PI 18
     1   40.0                            1   10.721    0.241   (10.130, 11.312)   (9.015, 12.427)
```

(b) The Excel Output

Regression Statistics

Multiple R	0.9484
R Square	0.8995 9
Adjusted R Square	0.8827
Standard Error	0.6542 8
Observations	8

ANOVA

	df	SS	MS	F	Significance F
Regression	1	22.9808 10	22.9808	53.6949 13	0.0003 14
Residual	6	2.5679 11	0.4280		
Total	7	25.5488 12			

	Coefficients	Standard Error	t Stat	P-value 7	Lower 95%	Upper 95%
Intercept	15.8379 1	0.8018 3	19.7535 5	1.09E-06	13.8760	17.7997
TEMP	-0.1279 2	0.0175 4	-7.3277 6	0.0003	-0.1706 19	-0.0852 19

---

1 b_0 = point estimate of the y-intercept 2 b_1 = point estimate of the slope 3 s_{b_0} = standard error of the estimate b_0 4 s_{b_1} = standard error of the estimate b_1
5 t for testing significance of the y-intercept 6 t for testing significance of the slope 7 p-values for t statistics 8 s = standard error 9 r^2 10 Explained variation
11 SSE = Unexplained variation 12 Total variation 13 F(model) statistic 14 p-value for F(model) 15 $\hat{y}$ = point prediction when x = 40 16 $s_{\hat{y}}$ = standard error
of the estimate $\hat{y}$ 17 95% confidence interval when x = 40 18 95% prediction interval when x = 40 19 95% confidence interval for the slope β_1

To test the significance of the slope we compare $|t|$ with $t_{\alpha/2}$ based on $n - 2 = 8 - 2 = 6$ degrees of freedom. Because

$$|t| = 7.33 > t_{.025} = 2.447$$

we can reject H_0: $\beta_1 = 0$ in favor of H_a: $\beta_1 \neq 0$ and conclude that the slope (regression relationship) is significant at the .05 level.

The p-value for testing H_0 versus H_a is twice the area to the right of $|t| = 7.33$ under the curve of the t distribution having $n - 2 = 6$ degrees of freedom. Since this p-value can be shown to be .0003, we can reject H_0 in favor of H_a at level of significance .05, .01, or .001. We therefore have extremely strong evidence that x is significantly related to y and that the regression relationship is significant.

Figure 13.11 presents the MINITAB and Excel output of a simple linear regression analysis of the fuel consumption data. Note that b_0 (labeled as 1 on the outputs), b_1 (labeled 2), s (labeled 8), s_{b_1} (labeled 4), and t (labeled 6) are given on each output. Also note that each output gives the p-value related to $t = -7.33$ (labeled 7). Excel tells us that this p-value equals 0.0003, while MINITAB has rounded this p-value to 0.000 (which means less than .001). Other quantities on the MINITAB and Excel output will be discussed later.

In addition to testing the significance of the slope, it is often useful to calculate a confidence interval for β_1. We show how this is done in the following box:

A Confidence Interval for the Slope

If the regression assumptions hold, a **100(1 − α) percent confidence interval for the true slope β_1** is $[b_1 \pm t_{\alpha/2}s_{b_1}]$. Here $t_{\alpha/2}$ is based on $n − 2$ degrees of freedom.

EXAMPLE 13.7 The Fuel Consumption Case ● FuelCon1

The MINITAB output in Figure 13.11(a) tells us that $b_1 = -.12792$ and $s_{b_1} = .01746$. Thus, for instance, because $t_{.025}$ based on $n − 2 = 8 − 2 = 6$ degrees of freedom equals 2.447, a 95 percent confidence interval for β_1 is

$$[b_1 \pm t_{.025}s_{b_1}] = [-.12792 \pm 2.447(.01746)]$$
$$= [-.1706, -.0852]$$

This interval says we are 95 percent confident that, if average hourly temperature increases by one degree, then mean weekly fuel consumption will decrease (because both the lower bound and the upper bound of the interval are negative) by at least .0852 MMcf of natural gas and by at most .1706 MMcf of natural gas. Also, because the 95 percent confidence interval for β_1 does not contain zero, we can reject H_0: $\beta_1 = 0$ in favor of H_a: $\beta_1 \neq 0$ at level of significance .05. Note that the 95 percent confidence interval for β_1 is given on the Excel output but not on the MINITAB output (see Figure 13.11).

EXAMPLE 13.8 The QHIC Case ● QHIC

Figure 13.12 presents the MegaStat output of a simple linear regression analysis of the QHIC data. We summarize some important quantities from the output as follows (we discuss the other quantities later): $b_0 = -348.3921$, $b_1 = 7.2583$, $s = 146.897$, $s_{b_1} = .4156$, and $t = b_1/s_{b_1} = 17.466$. Since the p-value related to $t = 17.466$ is less than .001 (see the MegaStat output), we can reject H_0: $\beta_1 = 0$ in favor of H_a: $\beta_1 \neq 0$ at the .001 level of significance. It follows that we have extremely strong evidence that the regression relationship is significant. The MegaStat output also tells us that a 95 percent confidence interval for the true slope β_1 is [6.4170, 8.0995]. This interval says we are 95 percent confident that mean yearly upkeep expenditure increases by between $6.42 and $8.10 for each additional $1,000 increase in home value.

Testing the significance of the y-intercept We can also test the significance of the y-intercept β_0. We do this by testing the null hypothesis H_0: $\beta_0 = 0$ versus the alternative hypothesis H_a: $\beta_0 \neq 0$. **If we can reject H_0 in favor of H_a by setting the probability of a Type I error equal to α, we conclude that the intercept β_0 is significant at the α level.** To carry out the hypothesis test, we use the test statistic

$$t = \frac{b_0}{s_{b_0}} \quad \text{where} \quad s_{b_0} = s\sqrt{\frac{1}{n} + \frac{\bar{x}^2}{SS_{xx}}}$$

Here the critical value and p-value conditions for rejecting H_0 are the same as those given previously for testing the significance of the slope, except that t is calculated as b_0/s_{b_0}. For example, if we consider the fuel consumption problem and the MINITAB output in Figure 13.11, we see that $b_0 = 15.8379$, $s_{b_0} = .8018$, $t = 19.75$, and the p-value = .000. Because $t = 19.75 > t_{.025} = 2.447$ and the p-value < .05, we can reject H_0: $\beta_0 = 0$ in favor of H_a: $\beta_0 \neq 0$ at the .05 level of significance. In fact, since the p-value < .001, we can also reject H_0 at the .001 level of significance. This

● FuelCon1

FIGURE 13.12   MegaStat Output of a Simple Linear Regression Analysis of the QHIC Data

Regression		r^2 0.889 [9]			n 40	
Analysis		r 0.943			k 1	
		Std. Error 146.897 [8]			Dep. Var. Upkeep	

ANOVA table

Source	SS	df	MS	F[13]	p-value[14]
Regression	6,582,759.6972 [10]	1	6,582,759.6972	305.06	9.49E-20
Residual	819,995.5427 [11]	38	21,578.8301		
Total	7,402,755.2399 [12]	39			

Regression output

variables	coefficients	std. error	t (df=38)	p-value[7]	confidence interval 95% lower	95% upper
Intercept	-348.3921 [1]	76.1410 [3]	-4.576 [5]	4.95E-05	-502.5314	-194.2527
Value	7.2583 [2]	0.4156 [4]	17.466 [6]	9.49E-20	6.4170 [19]	8.0995 [19]

Predicted values for: Upkeep

Value	Predicted[15]	95% Confidence Interval [16] lower	upper	95% Prediction Interval [17] lower	upper	Leverage[18]
220	1,248.42597	1,187.78944	1,309.06251	944.92879	1,551.92315	0.042

> [1] b_0 = point estimate of the *y*-intercept [2] b_1 = point estimate of the slope [3] s_{b_0} = standard error of the estimate b_0 [4] s_{b_1} = standard error of the estimate b_1
> [5] *t* for testing significance of the *y*-intercept [6] *t* for testing significance of the slope [7] *p*-values for *t* statistics [8] *s* = standard error [9] r^2 [10] Explained variation
> [11] SSE = Unexplained variation [12] Total variation [13] *F*(model) statistic [14] *p*-value for *F*(model) [15] $\hat{y}$ = point prediction when *x* = 220 [16] 95% confidence
> interval when *x* = 220 [17] 95% prediction interval when *x* = 220 [18] distance value [19] 95% confidence interval for the slope β_1

provides extremely strong evidence that the *y*-intercept β_0 does not equal zero and thus is significant. Therefore, we should include β_0 in the fuel consumption model.

In general, if we fail to conclude that the intercept is significant at a level of significance of .05, it might be reasonable to drop the *y*-intercept from the model. However, remember that β_0 equals the mean value of *y* when *x* equals zero. If, logically speaking, the mean value of *y* would not equal zero when *x* equals zero (for example, in the fuel consumption problem, mean fuel consumption would not equal zero when the average hourly temperature is zero), it is common practice to include the *y*-intercept whether or not H_0: $\beta_0 = 0$ is rejected. In fact, experience suggests that it is definitely safest, when in doubt, to include the intercept β_0.

Exercises for Section 13.3

CONCEPTS

13.18 What do we conclude if we can reject H_0: $\beta_1 = 0$ in favor of H_a: $\beta_1 \neq 0$ by setting
    a α equal to .05?   **b** α equal to .01?

connect™

13.19 Give an example of a practical application of the confidence interval for β_1.

METHODS AND APPLICATIONS

In Exercises 13.20 through 13.24, we refer to MINITAB, MegaStat, and Excel output of simple linear regression analyses of the data sets related to the five case studies introduced in the exercises for Section 13.1. Using the appropriate output for each case study,
a Find the least squares point estimates b_0 and b_1 of β_0 and β_1 on the output and report their values.
b Find *SSE* and *s* on the computer output and report their values.
c Find s_{b_1} and the *t* statistic for testing the significance of the slope on the output and report their values. Show how *t* has been calculated by using b_1 and s_{b_1} from the computer output.
d Using the *t* statistic and appropriate critical value, test H_0: $\beta_1 = 0$ versus H_a: $\beta_1 \neq 0$ by setting α equal to .05. Is the slope (regression relationship) significant at the .05 level?
e Using the *t* statistic and appropriate critical value, test H_0: $\beta_1 = 0$ versus H_a: $\beta_1 \neq 0$ by setting α equal to .01. Is the slope (regression relationship) significant at the .01 level?
f Find the *p*-value for testing H_0: $\beta_1 = 0$ versus H_a: $\beta_1 \neq 0$ on the output and report its value. Using the *p*-value, determine whether we can reject H_0 by setting α equal to .10, .05, .01, and .001. How much evidence is there that the slope (regression relationship) is significant?
g Calculate the 95 percent confidence interval for β_1 using numbers on the output. Interpret the interval.

h Calculate the 99 percent confidence interval for β_1 using numbers on the output.

i Find s_{b_0} and the t statistic for testing the significance of the y-intercept on the output and report their values. Show how t has been calculated by using b_0 and s_{b_0} from the computer output.

j Find the p-value for testing $H_0: \beta_0 = 0$ versus $H_a: \beta_0 \neq 0$. Using the p-value, determine whether we can reject H_0 by setting α equal to .10, .05, .01, and .001. What do you conclude about the significance of the y-intercept?

k Using the appropriate data set and s from the computer output, hand calculate SS_{xx}, s_{b_0}, and s_{b_1}.

13.20 THE STARTING SALARY CASE ● StartSal

The MINITAB output of a simple linear regression analysis of the data set for this case (see Exercise 13.5 on page 511) is given in Figure 13.13. Recall that a labeled MINITAB regression output is on page 519.

13.21 THE SERVICE TIME CASE ● SrvcTime

The MegaStat output of a simple linear regression analysis of the data set for this case (see Exercise 13.6 on pages 511 and 512) is given in Figure 13.14. Recall that a labeled MegaStat regression output is on page 521.

FIGURE 13.13 MINITAB Output of a Simple Linear Regression Analysis of the Starting Salary Data

```
The regression equation is
StartSal = 14.8 + 5.71 GPA

Predictor    Coef   SE Coef      T      P
Constant   14.816     1.235  12.00  0.000
GPA         5.7066    0.3953  14.44  0.000

S = 0.536321    R-Sq = 97.7%    R-Sq(adj) = 97.2%

Analysis of Variance
Source          DF       SS      MS       F      P
Regression       1   59.942  59.942  208.39  0.000
Residual Error   5    1.438   0.288
Total            6   61.380

Values of Predictors for New Obs   Predicted Values for New Observations
New Obs    GPA                      New Obs    Fit   SE Fit      95% CI              95% PI
    1     3.25                          1   33.362   0.213  (32.813, 33.911)   (31.878, 34.846)
```

FIGURE 13.14 MegaStat Output of a Simple Linear Regression Analysis of the Service Time Data

Regression Analysis	r^2 0.990		n 11		
	r 0.995		k 1		
	Std. Error 4.615		Dep. Var. **Minutes (y)**		

ANOVA table

Source	SS	df	MS	F	p-value
Regression	19,918.8438	1	19,918.8438	935.15	2.09E-10
Residual	191.7017	9	21.3002		
Total	20,110.5455	10			

Regression output

variables	coefficients	std. error	t (df=9)	p-value	confidence interval 95% lower	95% upper
Intercept	11.4641	3.4390	3.334	0.0087	3.6845	19.2437
Copiers (x)	24.6022	0.8045	30.580	2.09E-10	22.7823	26.4221

Predicted values for: Minutes (y)

Copiers (x)	Predicted	95% Confidence Intervals lower	upper	95% Prediction Intervals lower	upper	Leverage
1	36.066	29.907	42.226	23.944	48.188	0.348
2	60.669	55.980	65.357	49.224	72.113	0.202
3	85.271	81.715	88.827	74.241	96.300	0.116
4	109.873	106.721	113.025	98.967	120.779	0.091
5	134.475	130.753	138.197	123.391	145.559	0.127
6	159.077	154.139	164.016	147.528	170.627	0.224
7	183.680	177.233	190.126	171.410	195.950	0.381

FIGURE 13.15   **MINITAB Output of a Simple Linear Regression Analysis of the Fresh Detergent Demand Data**

```
The regression equation is
Demand = 7.81 + 2.67 PriceDif

Predictor      Coef    SE Coef      T       P
Constant    7.81409    0.07988   97.82   0.000
PriceDif     2.6652     0.2585   10.31   0.000

S = 0.316561    R-Sq = 79.2%    R-Sq(adj) = 78.4%

Analysis of Variance
Source          DF      SS       MS       F       P
Regression       1   10.653   10.653   106.30   0.000
Residual Error  28    2.806    0.100
Total           29   13.459

Values of Predictors for New Obs     Predicted Values for New Observations
New Obs   PriceDif                   New Obs    Fit   SE Fit      95% CI            95% PI
      1      0.100                         1  8.0806  0.0648  (7.9479, 8.2133)  (7.4187, 8.7425)
      2      0.250                         2  8.4804  0.0586  (8.3604, 8.6004)  (7.8209, 9.1398)
```

FIGURE 13.16   **Excel and MegaStat Output of a Simple Linear Regression Analysis of the Direct Labor Cost Data**

(a) The Excel Output

Regression Statistics

Multiple R	0.9996
R Square	0.9993
Adjusted R Square	0.9992
Standard Error	8.6415
Observations	12

ANOVA	df	SS	MS	F	Significance F
Regression	1	1024592.9043	1024592.9043	13720.4677	5.04E-17
Residual	10	746.7624	74.6762		
Total	11	1025339.6667			

	Coefficients	Standard Error	t Stat	P-value	Lower 95%	Upper 95%
Intercept	18.4875	4.6766	3.9532	0.0027	8.0674	28.9076
BatchSize (x)	10.1463	0.0866	117.1344	5.04E-17	9.9533	10.3393

(b) Prediction Using MegaStat

Predicted values for: LaborCost (y)

BatchSize (x)	Predicted	95% Confidence Interval lower	95% Confidence Interval upper	95% Prediction Interval lower	95% Prediction Interval upper	Leverage
60	627.263	621.054	633.472	607.032	647.494	0.104

13.22   THE FRESH DETERGENT CASE   ● Fresh

The MINITAB output of a simple linear regression analysis of the data set for this case (see Exercise 13.7 on page 512) is given in Figure 13.15. Recall that a labeled MINITAB regression output is on page 519.

13.23   THE DIRECT LABOR COST CASE   ● DirLab

The Excel and MegaStat output of a simple linear regression analysis of the data set for this case (see Exercise 13.8 on page 513) is given in Figure 13.16. Recall that labeled Excel and MegaStat regression outputs are on pages 519 and 521.

13.24   THE REAL ESTATE SALES PRICE CASE   ● RealEst

The MINITAB output of a simple linear regression analysis of the data set for this case (see Exercise 13.9 on page 513) is given in Figure 13.17 on page 524. Recall that a labeled MINITAB regression output is on page 519.

13.25   Find and interpret a 95 percent confidence interval for the slope β_1 of the simple linear regression model describing the sales volume data in Exercise 13.17 (page 517).   ● SalesVol

FIGURE 13.17   MINITAB Output of a Simple Linear Regression Analysis of the Real Estate
Sales Price Data

```
The regression equation is
SPrice = 48.0 + 5.70 HomeSize

Predictor    Coef   SE Coef    T      P
Constant    48.02    14.41   3.33   0.010
HomeSize    5.7003   0.7457  7.64   0.000

S = 10.5880     R-Sq = 88.0%     R-Sq(adj) = 86.5%

Analysis of Variance
Source             DF      SS      MS      F      P
Regression          1   6550.7  6550.7  58.43  0.000
Residual Error      8    896.8   112.1
Total               9   7447.5

Values of Predictors for New Obs    Predicted Values for New Observations
New Obs  HomeSize                   New Obs    Fit   SE Fit      95% CI            95% PI
      1     20.0                          1  162.03   3.47  (154.04, 170.02)  (136.34, 187.72)
```

FIGURE 13.18   Excel Output of a Simple Linear Regression Analysis of the Fast-Food
Restaurant Rating Data

Regression Statistics	
Multiple R	0.9873
R Square	0.9747
Adjusted R Square	0.9684
Standard Error	0.1833
Observations	6

ANOVA	df	SS	MS	F	Significance F
Regression	1	5.1817	5.1817	154.2792	0.0002
Residual	4	0.1343	0.0336		
Total	5	5.3160			

	Coefficients	Standard Error	t Stat	P-value	Lower 95%	Upper 95%
Intercept	-0.1602	0.3029	-0.5289	0.6248	-1.0011	0.6807
MeanTaste (x)	1.2731	0.1025	12.4209	0.0002	0.9885	1.5577

13.26 THE FAST-FOOD RESTAURANT RATING CASE   ● FastFood

In the early 1990s researchers at The Ohio State University studied consumer ratings of six
fast-food restaurants: Borden Burger, Hardee's, Burger King, McDonald's, Wendy's, and White
Castle. Each of 406 randomly selected individuals gave each restaurant a rating of 1, 2, 3, 4, 5, or
6 on the basis of taste, and then ranked the restaurants from 1 through 6 on the basis of overall
preference. In each case, 1 is the best rating and 6 the worst. The mean ratings given by the
406 individuals are given in the following table:

Restaurant	Mean Taste	Mean Preference
Borden Burger	3.5659	4.2552
Hardee's	3.329	4.0911
Burger King	2.4231	3.0052
McDonald's	2.0895	2.2429
Wendy's	1.9661	2.5351
White Castle	3.8061	4.7812

Figure 13.18 gives the Excel output of a simple linear regression analysis of this data. Here, mean
preference is the dependent variable and mean taste is the independent variable. Recall that a
labeled Excel regression output is given on page 519.

a   Find the least squares point estimate b_1 of β_1 on the computer output. Report and interpret this
estimate.

b   Find the 95 percent confidence interval for β_1 on the output. Report and interpret the interval.

13.4 Confidence and Prediction Intervals ● ● ●

We have seen that

$$\hat{y} = b_0 + b_1 x_0$$

is the **point estimate of the mean value of y** when the value of the independent variable x is x_0. We have also seen that $\hat{y}$ is the **point prediction of an individual value of y** when the value of the independent variable x is x_0. In this section we will assess the accuracy of $\hat{y}$ as both a point estimate and a point prediction. To do this, we will find a **confidence interval for the mean value of y** and a **prediction interval for an individual value of y**.

Because each possible sample of n values of the dependent variable gives values of b_0 and b_1 that differ from the values given by other samples, different samples give different values of $\hat{y} = b_0 + b_1 x_0$. A confidence interval for the mean value of y is based on the estimated standard deviation of the population of all possible values of $\hat{y}$. This estimated standard deviation is called the **standard error of $\hat{y}$** and is denoted $s_{\hat{y}}$. If the regression assumptions hold, the formula for $s_{\hat{y}}$ is

$$s_{\hat{y}} = s\sqrt{\frac{1}{n} + \frac{(x_0 - \bar{x})^2}{SS_{xx}}}$$

Here, s is the standard error (see Section 13.2), $\bar{x}$ is the average of the n previously observed values of x, and $SS_{xx} = \Sigma x_i^2 - (\Sigma x_i)^2/n$.

As explained above, a confidence interval for the mean value of y is based on the standard error $s_{\hat{y}}$. A prediction interval for an individual value of y is based on a more complex standard error: the estimated standard deviation of the population of all possible values of $y - \hat{y}$, the prediction error obtained when predicting y by $\hat{y}$. We refer to this estimated standard deviation as the **standard error of $\hat{y} - \hat{y}$** and denote it as $s_{(y-\hat{y})}$. If the regression assumptions hold, the formula for $s_{(y-\hat{y})}$ is

$$s_{(y-\hat{y})} = s\sqrt{1 + \frac{1}{n} + \frac{(x_0 - \bar{x})^2}{SS_{xx}}}$$

Intuitively, the "extra 1" under the radical in the formula for $s_{(y-\hat{y})}$ accounts for the fact that there is more uncertainty in predicting an individual value $y = \beta_0 + \beta_1 x_0 + \varepsilon$ than in estimating the mean value $\beta_0 + \beta_1 x_0$ (because we must predict the error term ε when predicting an individual value). Therefore, as shown in the following summary box, the prediction interval for an individual value of y is longer than the confidence interval for the mean value of y.

A Confidence Interval and a Prediction Interval

If the regression assumptions hold,

1 A 100$(1 - \alpha)$ percent confidence interval for the mean value of y when x equals x_0 is

$$\left[\hat{y} \pm t_{\alpha/2} s\sqrt{\frac{1}{n} + \frac{(x_0 - \bar{x})^2}{SS_{xx}}} \right]$$

2 A 100$(1 - \alpha)$ percent prediction interval for an individual value of y when x equals x_0 is

$$\left[\hat{y} \pm t_{\alpha/2} s\sqrt{1 + \frac{1}{n} + \frac{(x_0 - \bar{x})^2}{SS_{xx}}} \right]$$

Here, $t_{\alpha/2}$ is based on $(n - 2)$ degrees of freedom.

The summary box tells us that both the formula for the confidence interval and the formula for the prediction interval use the quantity $1/n + (x_0 - \bar{x})^2/SS_{xx}$. We will call this quantity the **distance**

value, because it is a measure of the distance between x_0, the value of x for which we will make a point estimate or a point prediction, and $\bar{x}$, the average of the previously observed values of x. The farther that x_0 is from $\bar{x}$, which represents the center of the experimental region, the larger is the distance value, and thus the longer are both the confidence interval $[\hat{y} \pm t_{\alpha/2}s\sqrt{\text{distance value}}]$ and the prediction interval $[\hat{y} \pm t_{\alpha/2}s\sqrt{1 + \text{distance value}}]$. Said another way, when x_0 is farther from the center of the data, $\hat{y} = b_0 + b_1x_0$ is likely to be less accurate as both a point estimate and a point prediction.

EXAMPLE 13.9 The Fuel Consumption Case ◆ FuelCon1

In the fuel consumption problem, recall that a weather forecasting service has predicted that in the next week the average hourly temperature will be $x_0 = 40°F$. Also, recall that

$$\hat{y} = b_0 + b_1x_0$$

$$= 15.84 - .1279(40)$$

$$= 10.72 \text{ MMcf of natural gas}$$

is the point estimate of the mean fuel consumption for all weeks that have an average hourly temperature of 40°F and is the point prediction of the fuel consumption in a single week that has an average hourly temperature of 40°F. Using the information in Example 13.3 (page 507), we compute

$$\text{distance value} = \frac{1}{n} + \frac{(x_0 - \bar{x})^2}{SS_{xx}}$$

$$= \frac{1}{8} + \frac{(40 - 43.98)^2}{1,404.355}$$

$$= .1363$$

Since $s = .6542$ (see Example 13.5 on page 516) and since $t_{\alpha/2} = t_{.025}$ based on $n - 2 = 8 - 2 = 6$ degrees of freedom equals 2.447, it follows that a 95 percent confidence interval for the mean fuel consumption when x equals 40°F is

$$[\hat{y} \pm t_{\alpha/2}s\sqrt{\text{distance value}}]$$

$$= [10.72 \pm 2.447(.6542)\sqrt{.1363}]$$

$$= [10.72 \pm .59]$$

$$= [10.13, 11.31]$$

This interval says we are 95 percent confident that the mean fuel consumption for all weeks that have an average hourly temperature of 40°F is between 10.13 MMcf of natural gas and 11.31 MMcf of natural gas.

If the natural gas company bases its transmission nomination for next week on the point prediction $\hat{y} = 10.72$, it will order 10.72 MMcf of natural gas. To evaluate the accuracy of the point prediction $\hat{y} = 10.72$, we can calculate the following 95 percent prediction interval for the fuel consumption in a single week that has an average hourly temperature of 40°F:

$$[\hat{y} \pm t_{\alpha/2}s\sqrt{1 + \text{distance value}}]$$

$$= [10.72 \pm 2.447(.6542)\sqrt{1.1363}]$$

$$= [10.72 \pm 1.71]$$

$$= [9.01, 12.43]$$

This interval says that we are 95 percent confident that the fuel consumption in a single week that has an average hourly temperature of 40°F will be between 9.01 MMcf of natural gas and

FIGURE 13.19 **MINITAB Output of 95 Percent Confidence and Prediction Intervals for the Fuel Consumption Case**

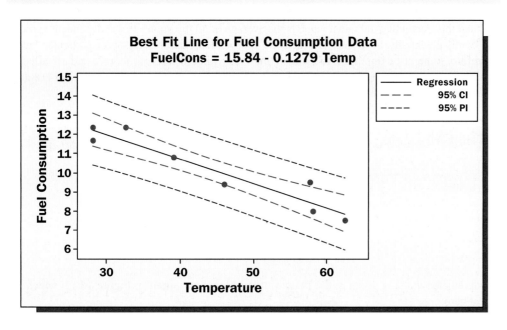

12.43 MMcf of natural gas. Furthermore, note that the half-length of the 95 percent prediction interval is $(12.43 - 9.01)/2 = 1.71$, which is $(1.71/10.72)100\% = 15.91\%$ of the transmission nomination 10.72. It follows that we are 95 percent confident that the actual amount of natural gas that will be used by the city next week will differ from the natural gas company's transmission nomination by no more than 15.91 percent. That is, we are 95 percent confident that the natural gas company's percentage nomination error will be less than or equal to 15.91 percent. Although this does not imply that the natural gas company is likely to make a terribly inaccurate nomination, we are not confident that the company's percentage nomination error will be within the 10 percent allowance granted by the pipeline transmission system. Therefore, the natural gas company may be assessed a transmission fine. In Chapter 14 we use a *multiple regression model* to substantially reduce the natural gas company's percentage nomination errors.

Below we repeat the bottom of the MINITAB output in Figure 13.11(a) on page 519. This output gives the point estimate and prediction $\hat{y} = 10.72$, the 95 percent confidence interval for the mean value of y when x equals 40, and the 95 percent prediction interval for an individual value of y when x equals 40.

```
Predicted Values for New Observations
New Obs    Fit    SE Fit      95% CI              95% PI
      1   10.721   0.241   (10.130, 11.312)   (9.015, 12.427)
```

Although the MINITAB output does not directly give the distance value, it does give $s_{\hat{y}} = s\sqrt{\text{distance value}}$ under the heading "SE Fit." A little algebra shows that this implies that the distance value equals $(s_{\hat{y}}/s)^2$. Specifically, because $s_{\hat{y}} = .241$ and $s = .6542$, the distance value equals $(.241/.6542)^2 = .1357$. This distance value is (within rounding) equal to the distance value that we hand calculated earlier.

To conclude this example, note that Figure 13.19 illustrates the MINITAB output of the 95 percent confidence and prediction intervals corresponding to all values of x in the experimental region. Here $\bar{x} = 43.98$ can be regarded as the center of the experimental region. Notice that the farther x_0 is from $\bar{x} = 43.98$, the larger is the distance value and, therefore, the longer are the 95 percent confidence and prediction intervals. These longer intervals are undesirable because they give us less information about mean and individual values of y.

In general, the prediction interval is useful if, as in the fuel consumption problem, it is important to predict an individual value of the dependent variable. A confidence interval is useful if it is important to estimate the mean value. Although it is not important to estimate a mean value in the fuel consumption problem, it is important to estimate a mean value in other situations. To understand this, recall that the mean value is the average of all the values of the dependent variable that could potentially be observed when the independent variable equals a particular value. Therefore, it might be important to estimate the mean value if we will observe and are affected by a very large number of values of the dependent variable when the independent variable equals a particular value. We illustrate this in the following example.

EXAMPLE 13.10 The QHIC Case ◆ QHIC

Consider a home worth $220,000. We have seen that the predicted yearly upkeep expenditure for such a home is

$$\hat{y} = b_0 + b_1 x_0$$
$$= -348.3921 + 7.2583(220)$$
$$= 1{,}248.43 \text{ (that is, } \$1{,}248.43)$$

This predicted value is given at the bottom of the MegaStat output in Figure 13.12, which we repeat here:

Predicted values for: Upkeep

Value	Predicted	95% Confidence Interval		95% Prediction Interval		Leverage
		lower	upper	lower	upper	
220	1,248.42597	1,187.78944	1,309.06251	944.92879	1,551.92315	0.042

In addition to giving $\hat{y} = 1{,}248.43$, the MegaStat output also tells us that the distance value, which is given under the heading "Leverage" on the output, equals .042. Therefore, since s equals 146.897 (see Figure 13.12 on page 521), it follows that a 95 percent prediction interval for the yearly upkeep expenditure of an individual home worth $220,000 is calculated as follows:

$$[\hat{y} \pm t_{.025} s \sqrt{1 + \text{distance value}}]$$
$$= [1{,}248.43 \pm 2.024(146.897)\sqrt{1.042}]$$
$$= [944.93, 1551.93]$$

Here $t_{.025}$ is based on $n - 2 = 40 - 2 = 38$ degrees of freedom. Note that this interval is given on the MegaStat output.

Because there are many homes worth roughly $220,000 in the metropolitan area, QHIC is more interested in the mean upkeep expenditure for all such homes than in the individual upkeep expenditure for one such home. The MegaStat output tells us that a 95 percent confidence interval for this mean upkeep expenditure is [1,187.79, 1,309.06]. This interval says that QHIC is 95 percent confident that the mean upkeep expenditure for all homes worth $220,000 is at least $1,187.79 and is no more than $1,309.06. Furthermore, suppose that a special, more expensive advertising brochure will be sent only to homes that QHIC is very sure have a mean yearly upkeep expenditure that exceeds $1,000. Because the lower end of the 95 percent confidence interval for $220,000 homes is above $1,000, the special brochure will be sent to homes worth $220,000.

Exercises for Section 13.4

CONCEPTS

13.27   What is the difference between a confidence interval and a prediction interval?

13.28   What does the distance value measure? How does the distance value affect a confidence or prediction interval?

METHODS AND APPLICATIONS

13.29 THE STARTING SALARY CASE   🌐 StartSal

The following partial MINITAB regression output for the starting salary data relates to predicting the starting salary of a marketing graduate having a grade point average of 3.25:

```
Predicted Values for New Observations
New Obs     Fit   SE Fit      95% CI             95% PI
      1   33.362   0.213   (32.813, 33.911)   (31.878, 34.846)
```

a Report (as shown on the computer output) a point estimate of and a 95 percent confidence interval for the mean starting salary of all marketing graduates having a grade point average of 3.25.

b Report (as shown on the computer output) a point prediction of and a 95 percent prediction interval for the starting salary of an individual marketing graduate having a grade point average of 3.25.

c Remembering that $s = .536321$ and that the distance value equals $(s_{\hat{y}}/s)^2$, use $s_{\hat{y}}$ from the computer output to hand calculate the distance value when $x = 3.25$.

d Remembering that for the starting salary data $n = 7$, $b_0 = 14.816$, and $b_1 = 5.7066$, hand calculate (within rounding) the confidence interval of part a and the prediction interval of part b.

13.30 THE SERVICE TIME CASE   🌐 SrvcTime

The following partial MegaStat regression output for the service time data relates to predicting service times for 1, 2, 3, 4, 5, 6, and 7 copiers.

Predicted values for: Minutes (y)

Copiers (x)	Predicted	95% Confidence Intervals		95% Prediction Intervals		Leverage
		lower	upper	lower	upper	
1	36.066	29.907	42.226	23.944	48.188	0.348
2	60.669	55.980	65.357	49.224	72.113	0.202
3	85.271	81.715	88.827	74.241	96.300	0.116
4	109.873	106.721	113.025	98.967	120.779	0.091
5	134.475	130.753	138.197	123.391	145.559	0.127
6	159.077	154.139	164.016	147.528	170.627	0.224
7	183.680	177.233	190.126	171.410	195.950	0.381

a Report (as shown on the computer output) a point estimate of and a 95 percent confidence interval for the mean time to service four copiers.

b Report (as shown on the computer output) a point prediction of and a 95 percent prediction interval for the time to service four copiers on a single call.

c For this case: $n = 11$, $b_0 = 11.4641$, $b_1 = 24.6022$, and $s = 4.615$. Using this information and a distance value from the MegaStat output, hand calculate (within rounding) the confidence interval of part a and the prediction interval of part b.

d If we examine the service time data, we see that there was at least one call on which Accu-Copiers serviced each of 1, 2, 3, 4, 5, 6, and 7 copiers. The 95 percent confidence intervals for the mean service times on these calls might be used to schedule future service calls. To understand this, note that a person making service calls will (in, say, a year or more) make a very large number of service calls. Some of the person's individual service times will be below, and some will be above, the corresponding mean service times. However, since the very large number of individual service times will average out to the mean service times, it seems fair to both the efficiency of the company and to the person making service calls to schedule service calls by using estimates of the mean service times. Therefore, suppose we wish to schedule a call to service five copiers. Examining the MegaStat output, we see that a 95 percent confidence interval for the mean time to service five copiers is [130.753, 138.197]. Since the mean time might be 138.197 minutes, it would seem fair to allow 138 minutes to make the service call. Now suppose we wish to schedule a call to service four copiers. Determine how many minutes to allow for the service call.

13.31 THE FRESH DETERGENT CASE   🌐 Fresh

The following partial MINITAB regression output for the Fresh detergent data relates to predicting demand for future sales periods in which the price difference will be .10 (see New

Obs 1) and .25 (see New Obs2).

```
Predicted Values for New Observations
New Obs    Fit   SE Fit        95% CI              95% PI
      1  8.0806  0.0648   (7.9479, 8.2133)    (7.4187, 8.7425)
      2  8.4804  0.0586   (8.3604, 8.6004)    (7.8209, 9.1398)
```

a Report (as shown on the computer output) a point estimate of and a 95 percent confidence interval for the mean demand for Fresh in all sales periods when the price difference is .10.

b Report (as shown on the computer output) a point prediction of and a 95 percent prediction interval for the actual demand for Fresh in an individual sales period when the price difference is .10.

c Remembering that $s = .316561$ and that the distance value equals $(s_{\hat{y}}/s)^2$, use $s_{\hat{y}}$ from the computer output to hand calculate the distance value when $x = .10$.

d For this case: $n = 30$, $b_0 = 7.81409$, $b_1 = 2.6652$, and $s = .316561$. Using this information, and your result from part c, find 99 percent confidence and prediction intervals for mean and - individual demands when $x = .10$.

e Repeat parts a, b, c, and d when $x = .25$.

13.32   THE DIRECT LABOR COST CASE   ● DirLab

The following partial MegaStat regression output for the direct labor cost data relates to predicting direct labor cost when the batch size is 60.

Predicted values for: LaborCost (y)

| BatchSize (x) | Predicted | 95% Confidence Interval | | 95% Prediction Interval | | Leverage |
		lower	upper	lower	upper	
60	627.263	621.054	633.472	607.032	647.494	0.104

a Report (as shown on the MegaStat output) a point estimate of and a 95 percent confidence interval for the mean direct labor cost of all batches of size 60.

b Report (as shown on the MegaStat output) a point prediction of and a 95 percent prediction interval for the actual direct labor cost of an individual batch of size 60.

c For this case: $n = 12$, $b_0 = 18.4875$, $b_1 = 10.1463$, and $s = 8.6415$. Use this information and the distance value from the MegaStat output to compute 99 percent confidence and prediction intervals for the mean and individual labor costs when $x = 60$.

13.33   THE REAL ESTATE SALES PRICE CASE   ● RealEst

The following partial MINITAB regression output for the real estate sales price data relates to predicting the sales price of a home having 2,000 square feet.

```
Predicted Values for New Observations
New Obs    Fit   SE Fit        95% CI              95% PI
      1  162.03   3.47   (154.04, 170.02)   (136.34, 187.72)
```

a Report (as shown on the MINITAB output) a point estimate of and a 95 percent confidence interval for the mean sales price of all houses having 2,000 square feet.

b Report (as shown on the MINITAB output) a point prediction of and a 95 percent prediction interval for the sales price of an individual house having 2,000 square feet.

c If you were purchasing a home having 2,000 square feet, which of the above intervals would you find to be most useful? Explain.

13.5 Simple Coefficients of Determination and Correlation ◉ ● ●

The simple coefficient of determination   The **simple coefficient of determination** is a measure of the usefulness of a simple linear regression model. To introduce this quantity, which is denoted r^2 (pronounced **r squared**), suppose we have observed n values of the dependent variable y. However, we choose to predict y without using a predictor (independent) variable x. In such a case the only reasonable prediction of a specific value of y, say y_i, would be $\bar{y}$, which is simply the average of the n observed values $y_1, y_2, \ldots, y_n$. Here the error of prediction in

FIGURE 13.20   **The Reduction in the Prediction Errors Accomplished by Employing the Predictor Variable x**

(a) Prediction errors for the fuel consumption problem when we do not use the information contributed by x

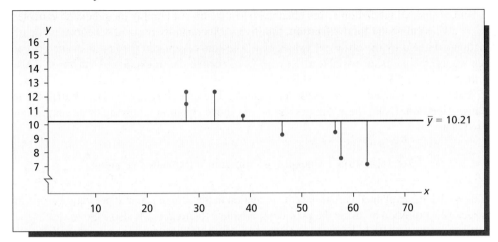

(b) Prediction errors for the fuel consumption problem when we use the information contributed by x by using the least squares line

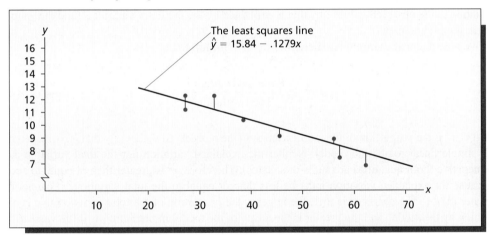

predicting y_i would be $y_i - \bar{y}$. For example, Figure 13.20(a) illustrates the prediction errors obtained for the fuel consumption data when we do not use the information provided by the independent variable x, average hourly temperature.

● FuelCon1

Next, suppose we decide to employ the predictor variable x and observe the values $x_1, x_2, \ldots, x_n$ corresponding to the observed values of y. In this case the prediction of y_i is

$$\hat{y}_i = b_0 + b_1 x_i$$

and the error of prediction is $y_i - \hat{y}_i$. For example, Figure 13.20(b) illustrates the prediction errors obtained in the fuel consumption problem when we use the predictor variable x. Together, Figures 13.20(a) and (b) show the reduction in the prediction errors accomplished by employing the predictor variable x (and the least squares line).

Using the predictor variable x decreases the prediction error in predicting y_i from $(y_i - \bar{y})$ to $(y_i - \hat{y}_i)$, or by an amount equal to

$$(y_i - \bar{y}) - (y_i - \hat{y}_i) = (\hat{y}_i - \bar{y})$$

It can be shown that in general

$$\sum (y_i - \bar{y})^2 - \sum (y_i - \hat{y}_i)^2 = \sum (\hat{y}_i - \bar{y})^2$$

The sum of squared prediction errors obtained when we do not employ the predictor variable x, $\sum (y_i - \bar{y})^2$, is called the **total variation.** Intuitively, this quantity measures the total amount of variation exhibited by the observed values of y. The sum of squared prediction errors obtained when we use the predictor variable x, $\sum (y_i - \hat{y}_i)^2$, is called the **unexplained variation (this is another name for *SSE*).** Intuitively, this quantity measures the amount of variation in the values of y that is not explained by the predictor variable. The quantity $\sum (\hat{y}_i - \bar{y})^2$ is called the **explained variation.** Using these definitions and the above equation involving these summations, we see that

Total variation − Unexplained variation = Explained variation

It follows that the explained variation is the reduction in the sum of squared prediction errors that has been accomplished by using the predictor variable x to predict y. It also follows that

Total variation = Explained variation + Unexplained variation

Intuitively, this equation implies that the explained variation represents the amount of the total variation in the observed values of y that is explained by the predictor variable x (and the simple linear regression model).

We now define the **simple coefficient of determination** to be

$$r^2 = \frac{\text{Explained variation}}{\text{Total variation}}$$

That is, r^2 is the proportion of the total variation in the n observed values of y that is explained by the simple linear regression model. Neither the explained variation nor the total variation can be negative (both quantities are sums of squares). Therefore, r^2 is greater than or equal to zero. Because the explained variation must be less than or equal to the total variation, r^2 cannot be greater than 1. The nearer r^2 is to 1, the larger is the proportion of the total variation that is explained by the model, and the greater is the utility of the model in predicting y. If the value of r^2 is not reasonably close to 1, the independent variable in the model does not provide accurate predictions of y. In such a case, a different predictor variable must be found in order to accurately predict y. It is also possible that no regression model employing a single predictor variable will accurately predict y. In this case the model must be improved by including more than one independent variable. We see how to do this in Chapter 14.

In the following box we summarize the results of this section:

The Simple Coefficient of Determination, r^2

For the simple linear regression model

1 Total variation $= \sum (y_i - \bar{y})^2$

2 Explained variation $= \sum (\hat{y}_i - \bar{y})^2$

3 Unexplained variation $= \sum (y_i - \hat{y}_i)^2$

4 Total variation = Explained variation + Unexplained variation

5 The simple coefficient of determination is

$$r^2 = \frac{\text{Explained variation}}{\text{Total variation}}$$

6 r^2 is the proportion of the total variation in the n observed values of the dependent variable that is explained by the simple linear regression model.

EXAMPLE 13.11 The Fuel Consumption Case   ✪ FuelCon1

For the fuel consumption data (see Table 13.1 on page 501) we have seen that $\bar{y} = (12.4 + 11.7 + \cdots + 7.5)/8 = 81.7/8 = 10.2125$. It follows that the total variation is

$$\sum (y_i - \bar{y})^2 = (12.4 - 10.2125)^2 + (11.7 - 10.2125)^2 + \cdots + (7.5 - 10.2125)^2$$

$$= 25.549$$

Furthermore, we found in Table 13.3 (page 508) that the unexplained variation is $SSE = 2.568$. Therefore, we can compute the explained variation and r^2 as follows:

$$\text{Explained variation} = \text{Total variation} - \text{Unexplained variation}$$

$$= 25.549 - 2.568 = 22.981$$

$$r^2 = \frac{\text{Explained variation}}{\text{Total variation}} = \frac{22.981}{25.549} = .899$$

This value of r^2 says that the regression model explains 89.9 percent of the total variation in the eight observed fuel consumptions.

EXAMPLE 13.12 The QHIC Case   ✪ QHIC

In the QHIC case, it can be shown that total variation = 7,402,755.2399; explained variation = 6,582,759.6972; SSE = unexplained variation = 819,995.5427; and

$$r^2 = \frac{\text{Explained variation}}{\text{Total variation}} = \frac{6,582,759.6972}{7,402,755.2399} = 0.889$$

This value of r^2 says that the simple linear regression model that employs home value as a predictor variable explains 88.9 percent of the total variation in the 40 observed home upkeep expenditures.

In optional Section 13.9 we present some shortcut formulas for calculating the total, explained, and unexplained variations. Finally, for those who have already read Section 13.3, r^2, the explained variation, the unexplained variation, and the total variation are calculated by MINITAB, Excel, and MegaStat. These quantities are identified on the MINITAB and Excel outputs of Figure 13.11 (page 519) and on the MegaStat output of Figure 13.12 (page 521) by, respectively, the labels 9, 10, 11, and 12. These outputs also give an "adjusted r^2." We explain the meaning of this quantity in Chapter 14.

The simple correlation coefficient, r   People often claim that two variables are correlated. For example, a college admissions officer might feel that the academic performance of college students (measured by grade point average) is correlated with the students' scores on a standardized college entrance examination. This means that college students' grade point averages are related to their college entrance exam scores. One measure of the relationship between two variables y and x is the **simple correlation coefficient.** We define this quantity as follows:

The Simple Correlation Coefficient

The **simple correlation coefficient between y and x,** denoted by r, is

$$r = +\sqrt{r^2} \quad \text{if } b_1 \text{ is positive} \qquad \text{and} \qquad r = -\sqrt{r^2} \quad \text{if } b_1 \text{ is negative}$$

where b_1 is the slope of the least squares line relating y to x. This correlation coefficient **measures the strength of the linear relationship between y and x.**

FIGURE 13.21   An Illustration of Different Values of the Simple Correlation Coefficient

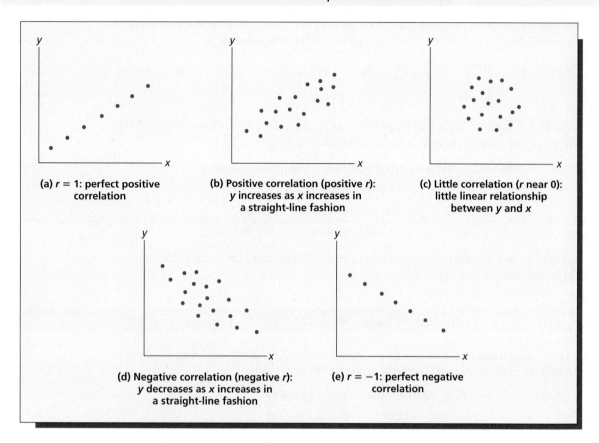

(a) $r = 1$: perfect positive correlation

(b) Positive correlation (positive r): y increases as x increases in a straight-line fashion

(c) Little correlation (r near 0): little linear relationship between y and x

(d) Negative correlation (negative r): y decreases as x increases in a straight-line fashion

(e) $r = -1$: perfect negative correlation

Because r^2 is always between 0 and 1, the correlation coefficient r is between -1 and 1. A value of r near 0 implies little linear relationship between y and x. A value of r close to 1 says that y and x have a strong tendency to move together in a straight-line fashion with a positive slope and, therefore, that y and x are highly related and **positively correlated.** A value of r close to -1 says that y and x have a strong tendency to move together in a straight-line fashion with a negative slope and, therefore, that y and x are highly related and **negatively correlated.** Figure 13.21 illustrates these relationships. Notice that when $r = 1$, y and x have a perfect linear relationship with a positive slope, whereas when $r = -1$, y and x have a perfect linear relationship with a negative slope.

EXAMPLE 13.13 The Fuel Consumption Case   ● FuelCon1

In the fuel consumption problem we have previously found that $b_1 = -.1279$ and $r^2 = .899$. It follows that the simple correlation coefficient between y (weekly fuel consumption) and x (average hourly temperature) is

$$r = -\sqrt{r^2} = -\sqrt{.899} = -.948$$

This simple correlation coefficient says that x and y have a strong tendency to move together in a linear fashion with a negative slope. We have seen this tendency in Figure 13.2 (page 501), which indicates that y and x are negatively correlated.

If we have computed the least squares slope b_1 and r^2, the method given in the previous box provides the easiest way to calculate r. The simple correlation coefficient can also be calculated using the formula

$$r = \frac{SS_{xy}}{\sqrt{SS_{xx} SS_{yy}}}$$

Here SS_{xy} and SS_{xx} have been defined in Section 13.1 on page 506, and SS_{yy} denotes the total variation, which has been defined in this section. Furthermore, this formula for r automatically gives r the correct ($+$ or $-$) sign. For instance, in the fuel consumption problem, $SS_{xy} = -179.6475$, $SS_{xx} = 1,404.355$, and $SS_{yy} = 25.549$ (see Examples 13.3 on page 507 and 13.11 on page 533). Therefore

$$r = \frac{SS_{xy}}{\sqrt{SS_{xx}SS_{yy}}} = \frac{-179.6475}{\sqrt{(1,404.355)(25.549)}} = -.948$$

It is important to make two points. First, **the value of the simple correlation coefficient is not the slope of the least squares line.** If we wish to find this slope, we should use the previously given formula for b_1.[4] Second, **high correlation does not imply that a cause-and-effect relationship exists.** When r indicates that y and x are highly correlated, this says that y and x have a strong tendency to move together in a straight-line fashion. The correlation does not mean that changes in x cause changes in y. Instead, some other variable (or variables) could be causing the apparent relationship between y and x. For example, suppose that college students' grade point averages and college entrance exam scores are highly positively correlated. This does not mean that earning a high score on a college entrance exam causes students to receive a high grade point average. Rather, other factors such as intellectual ability, study habits, and attitude probably determine both a student's score on a college entrance exam and a student's college grade point average. In general, while the simple correlation coefficient can show that variables tend to move together in a straight-line fashion, scientific theory must be used to establish cause-and-effect relationships.

Exercises for Section 13.5

CONCEPTS

13.34 Discuss the meanings of the total variation, the unexplained variation, and the explained variation.

13.35 What does the simple coefficient of determination measure?

METHODS AND APPLICATIONS

In Exercises 13.36 through 13.40, we give the total variation, the unexplained variation (SSE), and the least squares point estimate b_1 that are obtained when simple linear regression is used to analyze the data set related to each of five previously discussed case studies. Using the information given in each exercise, find the explained variation, the simple coefficient of determination (r^2), and the simple correlation coefficient (r). Interpret r^2.

13.36 THE STARTING SALARY CASE   StartSal

Total variation = 61.380; $SSE = 1.438$; $b_1 = 5.7066$.

13.37 THE SERVICE TIME CASE   SrvcTime

Total variation = 20,110.5455; $SSE = 191.7017$; $b_1 = 24.6022$.

13.38 THE FRESH DETERGENT CASE   Fresh

Total variation = 13.459; $SSE = 2.806$; $b_1 = 2.6652$.

13.39 THE DIRECT LABOR COST CASE   DirLab

Total variation = 1,025,339.6667; $SSE = 746.7624$; $b_1 = 10.1463$.

13.40 THE REAL ESTATE SALES PRICE CASE   RealEst

Total variation = 7447.5; $SSE = 896.8$; $b_1 = 5.7003$.

13.41 THE FAST-FOOD RESTAURANT RATING CASE   FastFood

Note: This exercise is only for those who have previously read Section 13.3. Use the Excel output of Figure 13.18 (page 524) to find and report each of the following: explained variation, unexplained variation, total variation, r^2. Interpret r^2.

---

[4]Essentially, the difference between r and b_1 is a change of scale. It can be shown that b_1 and r are related by the equation $b_1 = (SS_{yy}/SS_{xx})^{1/2}\, r$.

13.6 Testing the Significance of the Population Correlation Coefficient (Optional) ● ● ●

We have seen that the simple correlation coefficient measures the linear relationship between the observed values of x and the observed values of y that make up the sample. A similar coefficient of linear correlation can be defined for the population of *all possible combinations of observed values of x and y.* We call this coefficient the **population correlation coefficient** and denote it by the symbol ρ (pronounced **rho**). We use r as the point estimate of ρ. In addition, we can carry out a hypothesis test. Here we test the null hypothesis $H_0: \rho = 0$, **which says there is no linear relationship between x and y,** against the alternative $H_a: \rho \neq 0$, **which says there is a positive or negative linear relationship between x and y.** This test employs the test statistic

$$t = \frac{r\sqrt{n-2}}{\sqrt{1-r^2}}$$

and is based on the assumption that the population of all possible observed combinations of values of x and y has a **bivariate normal probability distribution.** See Wonnacott and Wonnacott (1981) for a discussion of this distribution. It can be shown that the preceding test statistic t and the p-value used to test $H_0: \rho = 0$ versus $H_a: \rho \neq 0$ are equal to, respectively, the test statistic $t = b_1/s_{b_1}$ and the p-value used to test $H_0: \beta_1 = 0$ versus $H_a: \beta_1 \neq 0$, where β_1 is the slope in the simple linear regression model. Keep in mind, however, that although the mechanics involved in these hypothesis tests are the same, these tests are based on different assumptions (remember that the test for significance of the slope is based on the regression assumptions). If the bivariate normal distribution assumption for the test concerning ρ is badly violated, we can use a nonparametric approach to correlation. One such approach is **Spearman's rank correlation coefficient.** This approach is discussed in Bowerman, O'Connell, and Murphree (2009).

EXAMPLE 13.14 The Fuel Consumption Case 🔹 FuelCon1

Again consider testing the significance of the slope in the fuel consumption problem. Recall that in Example 13.6 (page 518) we found that $t = -7.33$ and that the p-value related to this t statistic is .0003. We therefore (if the regression assumptions hold) can reject $H_0: \beta_1 = 0$ at level of significance .05, .01, or .001, and we have extremely strong evidence that x is significantly related to y. This also implies (if the population of all possible observed combinations of x and y has a bivariate normal probability distribution) that we can reject $H_0: \rho = 0$ in favor of $H_a: \rho \neq 0$ at level of significance .05, .01, or .001. It follows that we have extremely strong evidence of a linear relationship, or correlation, between x and y. Furthermore, because we have previously calculated r to be $-.9482$, we estimate that x and y are negatively correlated.

Exercises for Section 13.6

CONCEPTS

13.42   Explain what is meant by the population correlation coefficient ρ.

13.43   Explain how we test $H_0: \rho = 0$ versus $H_a: \rho \neq 0$. What do we conclude if we reject $H_0: \rho = 0$?

METHODS AND APPLICATIONS

13.44   THE STARTING SALARY CASE 🔹 StartSal

Consider testing $H_0: \beta_1 = 0$ versus $H_a: \beta_1 \neq 0$. Figure 13.13 (page 522) tells us that $t = 14.44$ and that the related p-value is less than .001. Assuming that the bivariate normal probability distribution assumption holds, test $H_0: \rho = 0$ versus $H_a: \rho \neq 0$ by setting α equal to .05, .01, and .001. What do you conclude about how x and y are related?

13.45   THE SERVICE TIME CASE 🔹 SrvcTime

Consider testing $H_0: \beta_1 = 0$ versus $H_a: \beta_1 \neq 0$. Figure 13.14 (page 522) tells us that $t = 30.580$ and that the related p-value is less than .001. Assuming that the bivariate normal probability distribution assumption holds, test $H_0: \rho = 0$ versus $H_a: \rho \neq 0$ by setting α equal to .05, .01, and .001. What do you conclude about how x and y are related?

13.7 An *F* Test for the Model ● ● ●

In this section we discuss an *F* test that can be used to test the significance of the regression relationship between *x* and *y*. Sometimes people refer to this as testing the significance of the simple linear regression model. For simple linear regression, this test is another way to test the null hypothesis $H_0: \beta_1 = 0$ (the relationship between *x* and *y* is not significant) versus $H_a: \beta_1 \neq 0$ (the relationship between *x* and *y* is significant). If we can reject H_0 at level of significance α, we often say that **the simple linear regression model is significant at level of significance α.**

An *F* Test for the Simple Linear Regression Model

Suppose that the regression assumptions hold, and define the **overall *F* statistic** to be

$$F(\text{model}) = \frac{\text{Explained variation}}{(\text{Unexplained variation})/(n - 2)}$$

Also define the *p*-value related to $F(\text{model})$ to be the area under the curve of the *F* distribution (having 1 numerator and $n - 2$ denominator degrees of freedom) to the right of $F(\text{model})$—see Figure 13.22(b).

We can reject $H_0: \beta_1 = 0$ in favor of $H_a: \beta_1 \neq 0$ at level of significance α if either of the following equivalent conditions holds:

1 $F(\text{model}) > F_{\alpha}$

2   *p*-value $< \alpha$

Here the point F_{α} is based on 1 numerator and $n - 2$ denominator degrees of freedom.

The first condition in the box says we should reject $H_0: \beta_1 = 0$ (and conclude that the relationship between *x* and *y* is significant) when $F(\text{model})$ is large. This is intuitive because a large overall *F* statistic would be obtained when the explained variation is large compared to the unexplained variation. This would occur if *x* is significantly related to *y*, which would imply that the slope β_1 is not equal to zero. Figure 13.22(a) illustrates that we reject H_0 when $F(\text{model})$ is greater

FIGURE 13.22   **An *F* Test for the Simple Linear Regression Model**

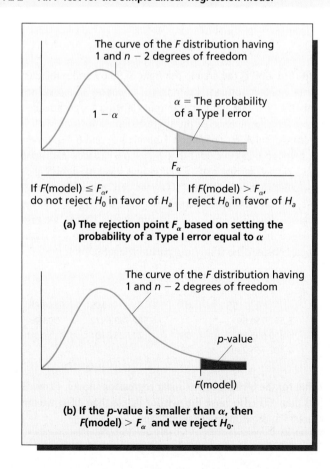

than F_α. As can be seen in Figure 13.22(b), when $F(\text{model})$ is large, the related p-value is small. When the p-value is small enough [resulting from an $F(\text{model})$ statistic that is large enough], we reject H_0. Figure 13.22(b) illustrates that the second condition in the box (p-value $< \alpha$) is an equivalent way to carry out this test.

EXAMPLE 13.15 The Fuel Consumption Case   ♦ FuelCon1

Consider the fuel consumption problem and the following partial MINITAB output of the simple linear regression analysis relating weekly fuel consumption y to average hourly temperature x:

```
Analysis of Variance
Source            DF              SS              MS              F              P
Regression         1          22.981          22.981          53.69          0.000
Residual Error     6           2.568           0.428
Total              7          25.549
```

Looking at this output, we see that the explained variation is 22.981 and the unexplained variation is 2.568. It follows that

$$F(\text{model}) = \frac{\text{Explained variation}}{(\text{Unexplained variation})/(n-2)}$$

$$= \frac{22.981}{2.568/(8-2)} = \frac{22.981}{.428}$$

$$= 53.69$$

Note that this overall F statistic is given on the MINITAB output and is also given on the following partial Excel output:

ANOVA	df	SS	MS	F	Significance F
Regression	1	22.9808	22.9808	53.6949	0.0003
Residual	6	2.5679	0.4280		
Total	7	25.5488			

The p-value related to $F(\text{model})$ is the area to the right of 53.69 under the curve of the F distribution having 1 numerator and 6 denominator degrees of freedom. This p-value is given on both the MINITAB output (labeled "p") and the Excel output (labeled "Significance F") and is less than .001. If we wish to test the significance of the regression relationship with level of significance $\alpha = .05$, we use the critical value $F_{.05}$ based on 1 numerator and 6 denominator degrees of freedom. Using Table A.6 (page 645), we find that $F_{.05} = 5.99$. Since $F(\text{model}) = 53.69 > F_{.05} = 5.99$, we can reject H_0: $\beta_1 = 0$ in favor of H_a: $\beta_1 \neq 0$ at level of significance .05. Alternatively, since the p-value is smaller than .05, .01, and .001, we can reject H_0 at level of significance .05, .01, or .001. Therefore, we have extremely strong evidence that H_0: $\beta_1 = 0$ should be rejected and that the regression relationship between x and y is significant. That is, we might say that we have extremely strong evidence that the simple linear model relating y to x is significant.

♦ QHIC   As another example, consider the following partial MegaStat output:

ANOVA table					
Source	SS	df	MS	F	p-value
Regression	6,582,759.6972	1	6,582,759.6972	305.06	9.49E-20
Residual	819,995.5427	38	21,578.8301		
Total	7,402,755.2399	39			

This output tells us that for the QHIC simple linear regression model, $F(\text{model})$ is 305.06 and the related p-value is less than .001. Because the p-value is less than .001, we have extremely strong evidence that the regression relationship is significant.

Testing the significance of the regression relationship between y and x by using the overall F statistic and its related p-value is equivalent to doing this test by using the t statistic and its related p-value. Specifically, it can be shown that $(t)^2 = F(\text{model})$ and that $(t_{\alpha/2})^2$ based on $n - 2$ degrees of freedom equals F_α based on 1 numerator and $n - 2$ denominator degrees of freedom. It follows that the critical value conditions

$$|t| > t_{\alpha/2} \quad \text{and} \quad F(\text{model}) > F_\alpha$$

are equivalent. Furthermore, the p-values related to t and $F(\text{model})$ can be shown to be equal. Because these tests are equivalent, it would be logical to ask why we have presented the F test. There are two reasons. First, most standard regression computer packages include the results of the F test as a part of the regression output. Second, the F test has a useful generalization in multiple regression analysis (where we employ more than one predictor variable). The F test in multiple regression is not equivalent to a t test. This is further explained in Chapter 14.

Exercises for Section 13.7

CONCEPTS

13.46 What are the null and alternative hypotheses for the F test in simple linear regression?

13.47 The F test in simple linear regression is equivalent to what other test?

connect™

METHODS AND APPLICATIONS

In Exercises 13.48 through 13.53, we give MINITAB, MegaStat, and Excel outputs of simple linear regression analyses of the data sets related to six previously discussed case studies. Using the appropriate computer output,

a Use the explained variation and the unexplained variation as given on the computer output to calculate the $F(\text{model})$ statistic.

b Utilize the $F(\text{model})$ statistic and the appropriate critical value to test $H_0: \beta_1 = 0$ versus $H_a: \beta_1 \neq 0$ by setting α equal to .05. What do you conclude about the regression relationship between y and x?

c Utilize the $F(\text{model})$ statistic and the appropriate critical value to test $H_0: \beta_1 = 0$ versus $H_a: \beta_1 \neq 0$ by setting α equal to .01. What do you conclude about the regression relationship between y and x?

d Find the p-value related to $F(\text{model})$ on the computer output and report its value. Using the p-value, test the significance of the regression model at the .10, .05, .01, and .001 levels of significance. What do you conclude?

e Show that the $F(\text{model})$ statistic is (within rounding) the square of the t statistic for testing $H_0: \beta_1 = 0$ versus $H_a: \beta_1 \neq 0$. Also, show that the $F_{.05}$ critical value is the square of the $t_{.025}$ critical value.

Note that in the lower right hand corner of each output we give (in parentheses) the number of observations, n, used to perform the regression analysis and the t statistic for testing $H_0: \beta_1 = 0$ versus $H_a: \beta_1 \neq 0$.

13.48 **THE STARTING SALARY CASE** ● StartSal

```
Analysis of Variance
Source            DF      SS       MS        F       P
Regression         1   59.942   59.942   208.39   0.000
Residual Error     5    1.438    0.288
Total              6   61.380            (n=7;  t=14.44)
```

13.49 **THE SERVICE TIME CASE** ● SrvcTime

| ANOVA table | | | | | |
Source	SS	df	MS	F	p-value
Regression	19,918.8438	1	19,918.8438	935.15	2.09E-10
Residual	191.7017	9	21.3002		
Total	20,110.5455	10		(n=11; t=30.580)	

13.50   THE FRESH DETERGENT CASE   ● Fresh

```
Analysis of Variance
Source          DF      SS       MS       F       P
Regression       1    10.653   10.653  106.30  0.000
Residual Error  28     2.806    0.100
Total           29    13.459          (n=30; t=10.31)
```

13.51   THE DIRECT LABOR COST CASE   ● DirLab

ANOVA	df	SS	MS	F	Significance F
Regression	1	1024592.9043	1024592.9043	13720.4677	5.04E-17
Residual	10	746.7624	74.6762		
Total	11	1025339.6667		(n=12; t=117.1344)	

13.52   THE REAL ESTATE SALES PRICE CASE   ● RealEst

```
Analysis of Variance
Source          DF     SS      MS      F      P
Regression       1   6550.7  6550.7  58.43  0.000
Residual Error   8    896.8   112.1
Total            9   7447.5        (n=10; t=7.64)
```

13.53   THE FAST-FOOD RESTAURANT RATING CASE   ● FastFood

ANOVA	df	SS	MS	F	Significance F
Regression	1	5.1817	5.1817	154.2792	0.0002
Residual	4	0.1343	0.0336		
Total	5	5.3160		(n=6; t=12.4209)	

13.8 Residual Analysis (Optional) ● ● ●

CHAPTER 16

In this section we explain how to check the validity of the regression assumptions. The required checks are carried out by analyzing the **regression residuals.** The residuals are defined as follows:

For any particular observed value of y, the corresponding **residual** is

$$e = y - \hat{y} = (\text{observed value of } y - \text{predicted value of } y)$$

where the predicted value of y is calculated using the **least squares prediction equation**

$$\hat{y} = b_0 + b_1 x$$

The linear regression model $y = \beta_0 + \beta_1 x + \varepsilon$ implies that the error term ε is given by the equation $\varepsilon = y - (\beta_0 + \beta_1 x)$. Since $\hat{y}$ in the previous box is clearly the point estimate of $\beta_0 + \beta_1 x$, we see that the residual $e = y - \hat{y}$ is the point estimate of the error term ε. If the regression assumptions are valid, then, for any given value of the independent variable, the population of potential error term values will be normally distributed with mean zero and variance σ^2 (see the regression assumptions in Section 13.2 on page 514). Furthermore, the different error terms will be statistically independent. Because the residuals provide point estimates of the error terms, it follows that

If the regression assumptions hold, the residuals should look like they have been randomly and independently selected from normally distributed populations having mean zero and variance σ^2.

In any real regression problem, the regression assumptions will not hold exactly. In fact, it is important to point out that mild departures from the regression assumptions do not seriously hinder our ability to use a regression model to make statistical inferences. Therefore, we are looking for pronounced, rather than subtle, departures from the regression assumptions. Because of this, we will require that the residuals only approximately fit the description just given.

FIGURE 13.23　The QHIC Upkeep Expenditure Data and a Scatter Plot of the Data　● QHIC

Home	Value of Home, x (Thousands of Dollars)	Upkeep Expenditure, y (Dollars)	Home	Value of Home, x (Thousands of Dollars)	Upkeep Expenditure, y (Dollars)
1	237.00	1,412.08	21	153.04	849.14
2	153.08	797.20	22	232.18	1,313.84
3	184.86	872.48	23	125.44	602.06
4	222.06	1,003.42	24	169.82	642.14
5	160.68	852.90	25	177.28	1,038.80
6	99.68	288.48	26	162.82	697.00
7	229.04	1,288.46	27	120.44	324.34
8	101.78	423.08	28	191.10	965.10
9	257.86	1,351.74	29	158.78	920.14
10	96.28	378.04	30	178.50	950.90
11	171.00	918.08	31	272.20	1,670.32
12	231.02	1,627.24	32	48.90	125.40
13	228.32	1,204.76	33	104.56	479.78
14	205.90	857.04	34	286.18	2,010.64
15	185.72	775.00	35	83.72	368.36
16	168.78	869.26	36	86.20	425.60
17	247.06	1,396.00	37	133.58	626.90
18	155.54	711.50	38	212.86	1,316.94
19	224.20	1,475.18	39	122.02	390.16
20	202.04	1,413.32	40	198.02	1,090.84

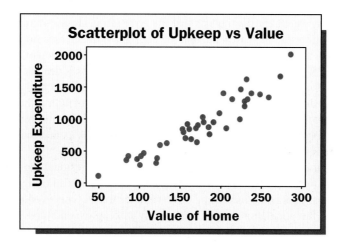

Residual plots　One useful way to analyze residuals is to plot them versus various criteria. The resulting plots are called **residual plots.** To construct a residual plot, we compute the residual for each observed y value. The calculated residuals are then plotted versus some criterion. To validate the regression assumptions, we make residual plots against (1) values of the independent variable x; (2) values of $\hat{y}$, the predicted value of the dependent variable; and (3) the time order in which the data have been observed (if the regression data are time series data).

We next look at an example of constructing residual plots. Then we explain how to use these plots to check the regression assumptions.

EXAMPLE 13.16 The QHIC Case　● QHIC

Figure 13.23 gives the QHIC upkeep expenditure data and a scatter plot of the data. If we use a simple linear regression model to describe the QHIC data, we find that the least squares point estimates of β_0 and β_1 are $b_0 = -348.3921$ and $b_1 = 7.2583$. The MegaStat output in Figure 13.24(a) presents the predicted home upkeep expenditures and residuals that are given by the simple linear regression model. Here each residual is computed as

$$e = y - \hat{y} = y - (b_0 + b_1 x) = y - (-348.3921 + 7.2583x)$$

For instance, for the first observation (home) when $y = 1{,}412.08$ and $x = 237.00$ (see Figure 13.23), the residual is

$$e = 1{,}412.08 - (-348.3921 + 7.2583(237))$$
$$= 1{,}412.08 - 1{,}371.816 = 40.264$$

The MINITAB output in Figure 13.24(b) and (c) gives plots of the residuals for the QHIC simple linear regression model against values of x and $\hat{y}$. To understand how these plots are constructed, recall that for the first observation (home) $y = 1{,}412.08$, $x = 237.00$, $\hat{y} = 1{,}371.816$, and the residual is 40.264. It follows that the point plotted in Figure 13.24(b) corresponding to the first observation has a horizontal axis coordinate of the x value 237.00 and a vertical axis coordinate of the residual 40.264. It also follows that the point plotted in Figure 13.24(c) corresponding to the first observation has a horizontal axis coordinate of the $\hat{y}$ value 1,371.816, and a vertical axis coordinate of the residual 40.264. Finally, note that the QHIC data are cross-sectional data, not time series data. Therefore, we cannot make a residual plot versus time.

The constant variance assumption   To check the validity of the constant variance assumption, we examine plots of the residuals against values of x, $\hat{y}$, and time (if the regression data are time series data). When we look at these plots, the pattern of the residuals' fluctuation around zero tells us about the validity of the constant variance assumption. A residual plot that "fans out" [as in Figure 13.25(a)] suggests that the error terms are becoming more spread out as the horizontal plot value increases and that the constant variance assumption is violated. Here we would say that an **increasing error variance** exists. A residual plot that "funnels in" [as in Figure 13.25(b)] suggests that the spread of the error terms is decreasing as the horizontal plot value increases and that again the constant variance assumption is violated. In this case we would say that a **decreasing error variance** exists. A residual plot with a "horizontal band appearance" [as in Figure 13.25(c)] suggests that the spread of the error terms around zero is not changing much as the horizontal plot value increases. Such a plot tells us that the constant variance assumption (approximately) holds.

● QHIC   As an example, consider the QHIC case and the residual plot in Figure 13.24(b). This plot appears to fan out as x increases, indicating that the spread of the error terms is increasing as x increases. That is, an increasing error variance exists. This is equivalent to saying that the variance of the population of potential yearly upkeep expenditures for houses worth x (thousand dollars) appears to increase as x increases. The reason is that the model $y = \beta_0 + \beta_1 x + \varepsilon$ says that the variation of y is the same as the variation of ε. For example, the variance of the population of potential yearly upkeep expenditures for houses worth \$200,000 would be larger than the variance of the population of potential yearly upkeep expenditures for houses worth \$100,000. Increasing variance makes some intuitive sense because people with more expensive homes generally have more discretionary income. These people can choose to spend either a substantial amount or a much smaller amount on home upkeep, thus causing a relatively large variation in upkeep expenditures.

Another residual plot showing the increasing error variance in the QHIC case is Figure 13.24(c). This plot tells us that the residuals appear to fan out as $\hat{y}$ (predicted y) increases, which is logical because $\hat{y}$ is an increasing function of x. Also, note that the scatter plot of y versus x in Figure 13.23 shows the increasing error variance—the y values appear to fan out as x increases. In fact, one might ask why we need to consider residual plots when we can simply look at scatter plots of y versus x. One answer is that, in general, because of possible differences in scaling between residual plots and scatter plots of y versus x, one of these types of plots might be more informative in a particular situation. Therefore, we should always consider both types of plots.

When the constant variance assumption is violated, we cannot use the formulas of this chapter to make statistical inferences. Later in this section we discuss how we can make statistical inferences when a nonconstant error variance exists.

FIGURE 13.24   MegaStat and MINITAB Output of the Residuals and Residual Plots for
                     the QHIC Simple Linear Regression Model

(a) MegaStat output of the residuals

Observation	Upkeep	Predicted	Residual	Observation	Upkeep	Predicted	Residual
1	1,412.080	1,371.816	40.264	21	849.140	762.413	86.727
2	797.200	762.703	34.497	22	1,313.840	1,336.832	−22.992
3	872.480	993.371	−120.891	23	602.060	562.085	39.975
4	1,003.420	1,263.378	−259.958	24	642.140	884.206	−242.066
5	852.900	817.866	35.034	25	1,038.800	938.353	100.447
6	288.480	375.112	−86.632	26	697.000	833.398	−136.398
7	1,288.460	1,314.041	−25.581	27	324.340	525.793	−201.453
8	423.080	390.354	32.726	28	965.100	1,038.662	−73.562
9	1,351.740	1,523.224	−171.484	29	920.140	804.075	116.065
10	378.040	350.434	27.606	30	950.900	947.208	3.692
11	918.080	892.771	25.309	31	1,670.320	1,627.307	43.013
12	1,627.240	1,328.412	298.828	32	125.400	6.537	118.863
13	1,204.760	1,308.815	−104.055	33	479.780	410.532	69.248
14	857.040	1,146.084	−289.044	34	2,010.640	1,728.778	281.862
15	775.000	999.613	−224.613	35	368.360	259.270	109.090
16	869.260	876.658	−7.398	36	425.600	277.270	148.330
17	1,396.000	1,444.835	−48.835	37	626.900	621.167	5.733
18	711.500	780.558	−69.058	38	1,316.940	1,196.602	120.338
19	1,475.180	1,278.911	196.269	39	390.160	537.261	−147.101
20	1,413.320	1,118.068	295.252	40	1,090.840	1,088.889	1.951

(b) MINITAB output of residual plot versus x

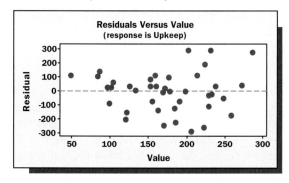

(c) MINITAB output of residual plot versus $\hat{y}$

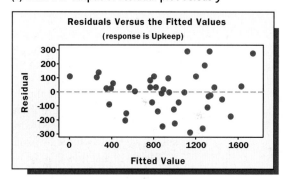

FIGURE 13.25   Residual Plots and the Constant Variance Assumption

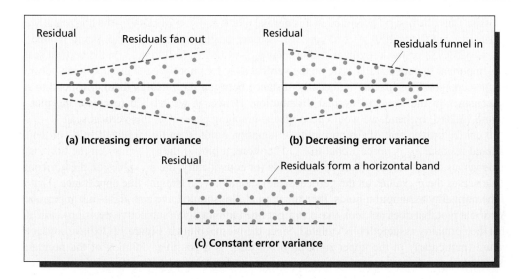

The assumption of correct functional form If the functional form of a regression model is incorrect, the residual plots constructed by using the model often display a pattern suggesting the form of a more appropriate model. For instance, if we use a simple linear regression model when the true relationship between y and x is curved, the residual plot will have a curved appearance. For example, the scatter plot of upkeep expenditure, y, versus home value, x, in Figure 13.23 (page 541) has either a straight-line or slightly curved appearance. We used a simple linear regression model to describe the relationship between y and x, but note that there is a "dip," or slightly curved appearance, in the upper left portion of each residual plot in Figure 13.24. Therefore, both the scatter plot and residual plots indicate that there might be a slightly curved relationship between y and x. Later in this section we discuss one way to model curved relationships.

The normality assumption If the normality assumption holds, a histogram and/or stem-and-leaf display of the residuals should look reasonably bell-shaped and reasonably symmetric about zero. Figure 13.26(a) gives the MINITAB output of a stem-and-leaf display of the residuals from the simple linear regression model describing the QHIC data. The stem-and-leaf display looks fairly bell-shaped and symmetric about zero. However, the tails of the display look somewhat long and "heavy" or "thick," indicating a possible violation of the normality assumption.

Another way to check the normality assumption is to construct a **normal plot** of the residuals. To make a normal plot, we first arrange the residuals in order from smallest to largest. Letting the ordered residuals be denoted as $e_{(1)}, e_{(2)}, \ldots, e_{(n)}$ we denote the ith residual in the ordered listing as $e_{(i)}$. We plot $e_{(i)}$ on the vertical axis against a point called $z_{(i)}$ on the horizontal axis. Here $z_{(i)}$ is defined to be the point on the horizontal axis under the standard normal curve so that the area under this curve to the left of $z_{(i)}$ is $(3i - 1)/(3n + 1)$. For example, recall in the QHIC case that there are $n = 40$ residuals given in Figure 13.24(a). It follows that, when $i = 1$, then

$$\frac{3i - 1}{3n + 1} = \frac{3(1) - 1}{3(40) + 1} = \frac{2}{121} = .0165$$

Therefore, $z_{(1)}$ is the normal point having an area of .0165 under the standard normal curve to its left. Thus, as illustrated in Figure 13.26(b), $z_{(1)}$ equals -2.13. Because the smallest residual in Figure 13.24(a) is -289.044, the first point plotted is $e_{(1)} = -289.044$ on the vertical scale versus $z_{(1)} = -2.13$ on the horizontal scale. When $i = 2$, it can be verified that $(3i - 1)/(3n + 1)$ equals .0413 and thus that $z_{(2)} = -1.74$. Therefore, because the second-smallest residual in Figure 13.24(a) is -259.958, the second point plotted is $e_{(2)} = -259.958$ on the vertical scale versus $z_{(2)} = -1.74$ on the horizontal scale. This process is continued until the entire normal plot is constructed. The MegaStat output of this plot is given in Figure 13.26(c).

An equivalent plot is shown in Figure 13.26(d), which is a MINITAB output. In this figure, we plot the percentage $p_{(i)}$ of the area under the standard normal curve to the left of $z_{(i)}$ on the vertical axis. Thus, the first point plotted in this normal plot is $e_{(1)} = -289.044$ on the horizontal scale versus $p_{(1)} = (.0165)(100) = 1.65$ on the vertical scale, and the second point plotted is $e_{(2)} = -259.958$ on the horizontal scale versus $p_{(2)} = (.0413)(100) = 4.13$ on the vertical scale. It is important to note that the scale on the vertical axis does not have the usual spacing between the percentages. The spacing reflects the distance between the z-scores that correspond to the percentages in the standard normal distribution. Hence, if we wished to create the plot in Figure 13.26(d) by hand, we would need special graphing paper with this vertical scale.

It can be proven that, if the normality assumption holds, then the expected value of the ith ordered residual $e_{(i)}$ is proportional to $z_{(i)}$. Therefore, a plot of the $e_{(i)}$ values on the horizontal scale versus the $z_{(i)}$ values on the vertical scale (or equivalently, the $e_{(i)}$ values on the horizontal scale versus the $p_{(i)}$ values on the vertical scale) should have a straight-line appearance. That is, if the normality assumption holds, then the normal plot should have a straight-line appearance. A normal plot that does not look like a straight line (admittedly, a subjective decision) indicates that the normality assumption is violated. Since the normal plots in Figure 13.26 have some curvature (particularly in the upper right portion), there is a possible violation of the normality assumption.

FIGURE 13.26   **Stem-and-Leaf Display and Normal Plots of the Residuals from the Simple Linear Regression Model Describing the QHIC Data**

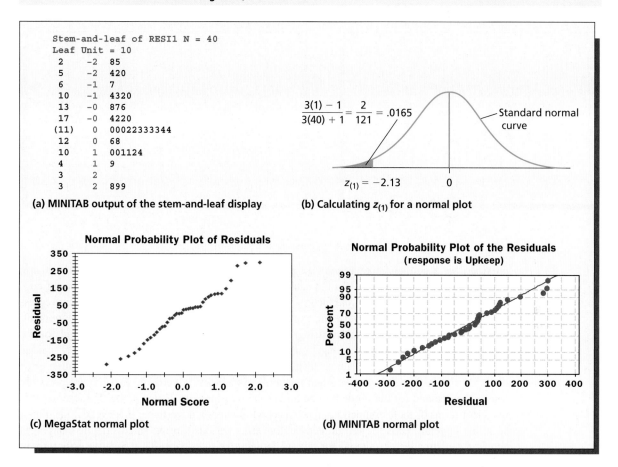

(a) MINITAB output of the stem-and-leaf display

(b) Calculating $z_{(1)}$ for a normal plot

(c) MegaStat normal plot

(d) MINITAB normal plot

It is important to realize that violations of the constant variance and correct functional form assumptions can often cause a histogram and/or stem-and-leaf display of the residuals to look nonnormal and can cause the normal plot to have a curved appearance. Because of this, it is usually a good idea to use residual plots to check for nonconstant variance and incorrect functional form before making any final conclusions about the normality assumption. Later in this section we discuss a procedure that sometimes remedies simultaneous violations of the constant variance, correct functional form, and normality assumptions.

The independence assumption   The independence assumption is most likely to be violated when the regression data are **time series data**—that is, data that have been collected in a time sequence. For such data the time-ordered error terms can be **autocorrelated.** Intuitively, we say that error terms occurring over time have **positive autocorrelation** if a positive error term in time period i tends to produce, or be followed by, another positive error term in time period $i + k$ (some later time period) and if a negative error term in time period i tends to produce, or be followed by, another negative error term in time period $i + k$. In other words, positive autocorrelation exists when positive error terms tend to be followed over time by positive error terms and when negative error terms tend to be followed over time by negative error terms. Positive autocorrelation in the error terms is depicted in Figure 13.27(a), which illustrates that **positive autocorrelation can produce a cyclical error term pattern over time.** The simple linear regression model implies that a positive error term produces a greater-than-average value of y and a negative error term produces a smaller-than-average value of y. It follows that positive autocorrelation in the error terms means that greater-than-average values of y tend to be followed by greater-than-average values of y, and smaller-than-average values of y tend to be followed by smaller-than-average values of y. An example of positive autocorrelation could hypothetically be

FIGURE 13.27   Positive and Negative Autocorrelation

(a) Positive Autocorrelation in the Error Terms: Cyclical Pattern

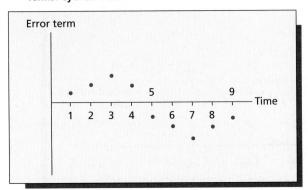

(b) Negative Autocorrelation in the Error Terms: Alternating Pattern

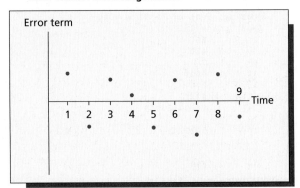

provided by a simple linear regression model relating demand for a product to advertising expenditure. Here we assume that the data are time series data observed over a number of consecutive sales periods. One of the factors included in the error term of the simple linear regression model is competitors' advertising expenditure for their similar products. If, for the moment, we assume that competitors' advertising expenditure significantly affects the demand for the product, then a higher-than-average competitors' advertising expenditure probably causes demand for the product to be lower than average and hence probably causes a negative error term. On the other hand, a lower-than-average competitors' advertising expenditure probably causes the demand for the product to be higher than average and hence probably causes a positive error term. If, then, competitors tend to spend money on advertising in a cyclical fashion—spending large amounts for several consecutive sales periods (during an advertising campaign) and then spending lesser amounts for several consecutive sales periods—a negative error term in one sales period will tend to be followed by a negative error term in the next sales period, and a positive error term in one sales period will tend to be followed by a positive error term in the next sales period. In this case the error terms would display positive autocorrelation, and thus these error terms would not be statistically independent.

Intuitively, error terms occurring over time have **negative autocorrelation** if a positive error term in time period i tends to produce, or be followed by, a negative error term in time period $i + k$ and if a negative error term in time period i tends to produce, or be followed by, a positive error term in time period $i + k$. In other words, negative autocorrelation exists when positive error terms tend to be followed over time by negative error terms and negative error terms tend to be followed over time by positive error terms. An example of negative autocorrelation in the error terms is depicted in Figure 13.27(b), which illustrates that **negative autocorrelation in the error terms can produce an alternating pattern over time.** It follows that negative autocorrelation in the error terms means that greater-than-average values of y tend to be followed by smaller-than-average values of y and smaller-than-average values of y tend to be followed by greater-than-average values of y. An example of negative autocorrelation might be provided by a retailer's weekly stock orders. Here a larger-than-average stock order one week might result in an oversupply and hence a smaller-than-average order the next week.

The **independence assumption** basically says that the time-ordered error terms display no positive or negative autocorrelation. This says that **the error terms occur in a random pattern over time.** Such a random pattern would imply that the error terms (and their corresponding y values) are statistically independent.

Because the residuals are point estimates of the error terms, a residual plot versus time is used to check the independence assumption. If a residual plot versus the data's time sequence has a cyclical appearance, the error terms are positively autocorrelated, and the independence assumption is violated. If a plot of the time-ordered residuals has an alternating pattern, the error terms are negatively autocorrelated, and again the independence assumption is violated.

However, if a plot of the time-ordered residuals displays a random pattern, the error terms have little or no autocorrelation. In such a case, it is reasonable to conclude that the independence assumption holds.

EXAMPLE 13.17

Figure 13.28(a) presents data concerning weekly sales at Pages' Bookstore (Sales), Pages' weekly advertising expenditure (Adver), and the weekly advertising expenditure of Pages' main competitor (Compadv). Here the sales values are expressed in thousands of dollars, and the advertising expenditure values are expressed in hundreds of dollars. Figure 13.28(a) also gives the residuals that are obtained when MegaStat is used to perform a simple linear regression analysis relating Pages' sales to Pages' advertising expenditure. These residuals are plotted versus time in Figure 13.28(b). We see that the residual plot has a cyclical pattern. This tells us that the error terms for the model are positively autocorrelated and the independence assumption is violated. Furthermore, there tend to be positive residuals when the competitor's advertising expenditure is lower (in weeks 1 through 8 and weeks 14, 15, and 16) and negative residuals when the competitor's advertising expenditure is higher (in weeks 9 through 13). Therefore, the competitor's advertising expenditure seems to be causing the positive autocorrelation.

FIGURE 13.28   Pages' Bookstore Sales and Advertising Data, and Residual Analysis

(a) The data and the MegaStat output of the residuals from a simple linear regression relating Pages' sales to Pages' advertising expenditure   ● BookSales

Observation	Adver	Compadv	Sales	Predicted	Residual
1	18	10	22	18.7	3.3
2	20	10	27	23.0	4.0
3	20	15	23	23.0	−0.0
4	25	15	31	33.9	−2.9
5	28	15	45	40.4	4.6
6	29	20	47	42.6	4.4
7	29	20	45	42.6	2.4
8	28	25	42	40.4	1.6
9	30	35	37	44.7	−7.7
10	31	35	39	46.9	−7.9
11	34	35	45	53.4	−8.4
12	35	30	52	55.6	−3.6
13	36	30	57	57.8	−0.8
14	38	25	62	62.1	−0.1
15	41	20	73	68.6	4.4
16	45	20	84	77.3	6.7

Durbin-Watson = 0.65

(b) MegaStat output of a plot of the residuals in
     Figure 13.28(a) versus time

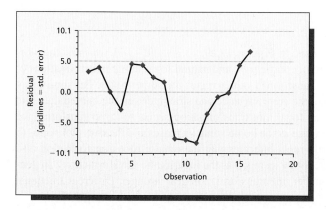

To conclude this example, note that the simple linear regression model relating Pages' sales to Pages' advertising expenditure has a standard error, s, of 5.038. The MegaStat residual plot in Figure 13.28(b) includes grid lines that are placed one and two standard errors above and below the residual mean of 0. All MegaStat residual plots use such grid lines to help better diagnose potential violations of the regression assumptions.

When the independence assumption is violated, various remedies can be employed. One approach is to identify which independent variable left in the error term (for example, competitors' advertising expenditure) is causing the error terms to be autocorrelated. We can then remove this independent variable from the error term and insert it directly into the regression model, forming a **multiple regression model.** (Multiple regression models are discussed in Chapter 14.)

Transforming the dependent variable: A possible remedy for violations of the constant variance, correct functional form, and normality assumptions   In general, if a data or residual plot indicates that the error variance of a regression model increases as an independent variable or the predicted value of the dependent variable increases, then we can sometimes remedy the situation by transforming the dependent variable. One transformation that works well is to take each y value to a fractional power. As an example, we might use a transformation in which we take the square root (or one-half power) of each y value. Letting y^* denote the value obtained when the transformation is applied to y, we would write the **square root transformation** as

$$y^* = \sqrt{y} = y^{.5}$$

Another commonly used transformation is the **quartic root transformation.** Here we take each y value to the one-fourth power. That is,

$$y^* = y^{.25}$$

If we consider a transformation that takes each y value to a fractional power (such as .5, .25, or the like), as the power approaches zero, the transformed value y^* approaches the natural logarithm of y (commonly written lny). In fact, we sometimes use the **logarithmic transformation**

$$y^* = lny$$

which takes the natural logarithm of each y value. In general, when we take a fractional power (including the natural logarithm) of the dependent variable, the transformation not only tends to equalize the error variance but also tends to "straighten out" certain types of nonlinear data plots. Specifically, if a data plot indicates that the dependent variable is increasing at an increasing rate (as in Figure 13.23 on page 541), then a fractional power transformation tends to straighten out the data plot. A fractional power transformation can also help to remedy a violation of the normality assumption. Because we cannot know which fractional power to use before we actually take the transformation, we recommend taking all of the square root, quartic root, and natural logarithm transformations and seeing which one best equalizes the error variance and (possibly) straightens out a nonlinear data plot.

EXAMPLE 13.18 The QHIC Case   ✎ QHIC   **C**

Consider the QHIC upkeep expenditures. In Figures 13.29, 13.30, and 13.31 we show the plots that result when we take the square root, quartic root, and natural logarithmic transformations of the upkeep expenditures and plot the transformed values versus the home values. The square root transformation seems to best equalize the error variance and straighten out the curved data plot in Figure 13.23. Note that the natural logarithm transformation seems to "overtransform" the data—the error variance tends to decrease as the home value increases and the data plot seems to "bend down." The plot of the quartic roots indicates that the quartic root transformation also seems to overtransform the data (but not by as much as the logarithmic transformation). In general, as the fractional power gets smaller, the transformation gets stronger. Different fractional powers are best in different situations.

FIGURE 13.29   MINITAB Plot of the Square Roots of the Upkeep Expenditures versus the Home Values

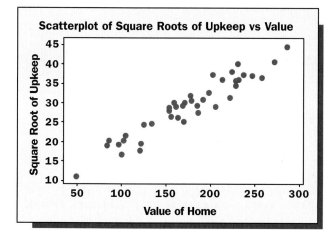

FIGURE 13.30   MINITAB Plot of the Quartic Roots of the Upkeep Expenditures versus the Home Values

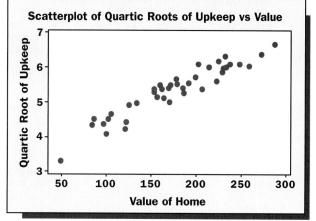

FIGURE 13.31   MINITAB Plot of the Natural Logarithms of the Upkeep Expenditures versus the Home Values

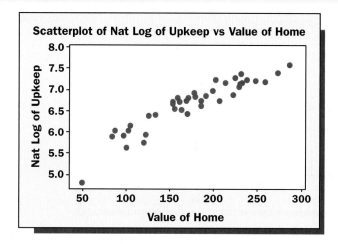

Since the plot in Figure 13.29 of the square roots of the upkeep expenditures versus the home values has a straight-line appearance, we consider the model

$$y^* = \beta_0 + \beta_1 x + \varepsilon \quad \text{where } y^* = y^{.5}$$

The MINITAB output of a regression analysis using this transformed model is given in Figure 13.32, and the MINITAB output of an analysis of the model's residuals is given in Figure 13.33. Note that the residual plot versus x for the transformed model in Figure 13.33(a) has a horizontal band appearance. It can also be verified that the transformed model's residual plot versus $\hat{y}$, which we do not give here, has a similar horizontal band appearance. Therefore, we conclude that the constant variance and the correct functional form assumptions approximately hold for the transformed model. Next, note that the histogram of the transformed model's residuals in Figure 13.33(b) looks reasonably bell-shaped and symmetric, and note that the normal plot of these residuals in Figure 13.33(c) looks straighter than the normal plots for the untransformed model (see Figure 13.26 on page 545). Therefore, we also conclude that the normality assumption approximately holds for the transformed model.

Because the regression assumptions approximately hold for the transformed regression model, we can use this model to make statistical inferences. Consider a home worth $220,000.

FIGURE 13.32   MINITAB Output of a Regression Analysis of the Upkeep Expenditure
                  Data by Using the Model $y^* = \beta_0 + \beta_1 x + \varepsilon$ where $y^* = y^{.5}$

```
The regression equation is
SqRtUpkeep = 7.20 + 0.127 Value

Predictor       Coef    SE Coef        T       P
Constant       7.201      1.205     5.98   0.000
Value       0.127047   0.006577    19.32   0.000

S = 2.32479    R-Sq = 90.8%    R-Sq(adj) = 90.5%

Analysis of Variance
Source            DF        SS       MS        F       P
Regression         1    2016.8   2016.8   373.17   0.000
Residual Error    38     205.4      5.4
Total             39    2222.2

Values of Predictors for New Obs    Predicted Values for New Observations
New Obs   Value                      New Obs      Fit   SE Fit        95% CI              95% PI
      1     220                            1   35.151    0.474   (34.191, 36.111)   (30.348, 39.954)
```

FIGURE 13.33   MINITAB Output of Residual Analysis for the Upkeep Expenditure Model
                  $y^* = \beta_0 + \beta_1 x + \varepsilon$ where $y^* = y^{.5}$

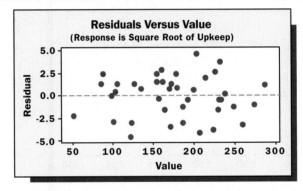

(a) Residual plot versus x

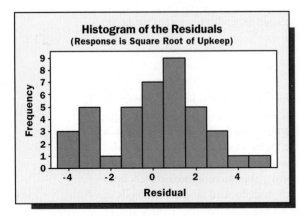

(b) Histogram of the residuals

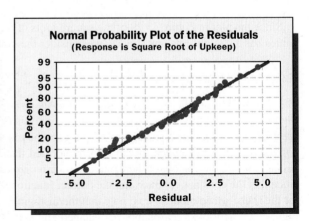

(c) Normal plot of the residuals

Using the least squares point estimates on the MINITAB output in Figure 13.32, it follows that a point prediction of y^* for such a home is

$$\hat{y}^* = 7.201 + .127047(220)$$
$$= 35.151$$

This point prediction is given at the bottom of the MINITAB output, as is the 95 percent prediction interval for y^*, which is [30.348, 39.954]. It follows that a point prediction of the upkeep expenditure for a home worth \$220,000 is $(35.151)^2 = \$1,235.59$ and that a 95 percent prediction interval for this upkeep expenditure is $[(30.348)^2, (39.954)^2] = [\$921.00, \$1,596.32]$. Suppose that QHIC wishes to send an advertising brochure to any home that has a predicted upkeep expenditure of at least \$500. Solving the prediction equation $\hat{y}^* = b_0 + b_1 x$ for x, and noting that a predicted upkeep expenditure of \$500 corresponds to a $\hat{y}^*$ of $\sqrt{500} = 22.36068$, it follows that QHIC should send the advertising brochure to any home that has a value of at least

$$x = \frac{\hat{y}^* - b_0}{b_1} = \frac{22.36068 - 7.201}{.127047} = 119.3234 \text{ (or } \$119,323)$$

Recall that because there are many homes of a particular value in the metropolitan area, QHIC is interested in estimating the mean upkeep expenditure corresponding to this value. Consider all homes worth, for example, \$220,000. The MINITAB output in Figure 13.32 tells us that a point estimate of the mean of the square roots of the upkeep expenditures for all such homes is 35.151 and that a 95 percent confidence interval for this mean is [34.191, 36.111]. Unfortunately, because it can be shown that the mean of the square root is not the square root of the mean, we cannot transform the results for the mean of the square roots back into a result for the mean of the original upkeep expenditures. This is a major drawback to transforming the dependent variable and one reason why many statisticians avoid transforming the dependent variable unless the regression assumptions are badly violated. Furthermore, if we reconsider the residual analysis of the original, untransformed QHIC model in Figures 13.24 (page 543) and 13.26 (page 545), we might conclude that the regression assumptions are not badly violated for the untransformed model. Also, note that the point prediction and 95 percent prediction interval obtained here using the transformed model are not very different from the results obtained in Example 13.10 (page 528) using the untransformed model. This implies that it might be reasonable to rely on the results obtained using the untransformed model, or to at least rely on the results for the mean upkeep expenditures obtained using the untransformed model.

In this section we have concentrated on analyzing the residuals for the QHIC simple linear regression model. If we analyze the residuals in Table 13.3 (page 508) for the fuel consumption simple linear regression model (recall that the fuel consumption data are time series data), we conclude that the regression assumptions approximately hold for this model.

Exercises for Section 13.8

CONCEPTS

13.54 In a regression analysis, what variables should the residuals be plotted against? What types of patterns in residual plots indicate violations of the regression assumptions?

13.55 In regression analysis, how do we check the normality assumption?

13.56 What is one possible remedy for violations of the constant variance, correct functional form, and normality assumptions?

METHODS AND APPLICATIONS

13.57 THE FUEL CONSUMPTION CASE   FuelCon1

Recall that Table 13.3 gives the residuals from the simple linear regression model relating weekly fuel consumption to average hourly temperature. Figure 13.34(a) gives the Excel output of a plot

FIGURE 13.34   Residual Diagnostics for Exercises 13.57 and 13.58

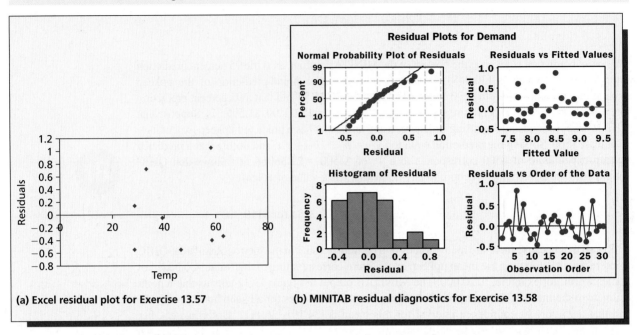

(a) Excel residual plot for Exercise 13.57   (b) MINITAB residual diagnostics for Exercise 13.58

FIGURE 13.35   MegaStat Output of the Residuals for the Service Time Model

Observation	Minutes	Predicted	Residual
1	109.0	109.9	−0.9
2	58.0	60.7	−2.7
3	138.0	134.5	3.5
4	189.0	183.7	5.3
5	37.0	36.1	0.9
6	82.0	85.3	−3.3
7	103.0	109.9	−6.9
8	134.0	134.5	−0.5
9	68.0	60.7	7.3
10	112.0	109.9	2.1
11	154.0	159.1	−5.1

TABLE 13.4   Ordered Residuals and Normal Plot Calculations

i	Ordered Residual, $e_{(i)}$	$\dfrac{3i-1}{3n+1}$	$z_{(i)}$
1	−6.9	.0588	−1.565
2	−5.1	.1470	−1.05
3	−3.3	.2353	−.72
4	−2.7	.3235	−.46
5	−0.9	.4118	−.22
6	−0.5	.5000	0
7	0.9	.5882	.22
8	2.1	.6765	.46
9	3.5	.7647	.72
10	5.3	.8529	1.05
11	7.3	.9412	1.565

of these residuals versus average hourly temperature. Describe the appearance of this plot. Does the plot indicate any violations of the regression assumptions?

13.58   THE FRESH DETERGENT CASE   ● Fresh

Figure 13.34(b) gives the MINITAB output of residual diagnostics that are obtained when the simple linear regression model is fit to the Fresh detergent demand data. Interpret the diagnostics and determine if they indicate any violations of the regression assumptions.

13.59   THE SERVICE TIME CASE   ● SrvcTime

The MegaStat output of the residuals given by the service time model is given in Figure 13.35, and MegaStat output of residual plots versus x and $\hat{y}$ is given in Figure 13.36(a) and (b). Do the plots indicate any violations of the regression assumptions?

13.60   THE SERVICE TIME CASE   ● SrvcTime

Figure 13.35 gives the MegaStat output of the residuals from the simple linear regression model describing the service time data.

a In this exercise we construct a normal plot of the residuals from the simple linear regression model. To construct this plot, we must first arrange the residuals in order from smallest to

FIGURE 13.36 MegaStat Residual Plots for the Service Time Model

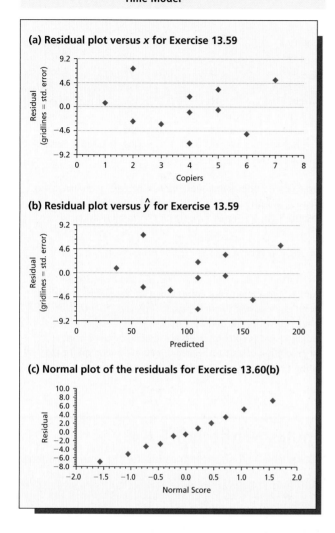

(a) Residual plot versus x for Exercise 13.59

(b) Residual plot versus $\hat{y}$ for Exercise 13.59

(c) Normal plot of the residuals for Exercise 13.60(b)

TABLE 13.5 Sales and Advertising Data for Exercise 13.61 ● SalesAdv

Month	Monthly Total Sales, y	Advertising Expenditures, x
1	202.66	116.44
2	232.91	119.58
3	272.07	125.74
4	290.97	124.55
5	299.09	122.35
6	296.95	120.44
7	279.49	123.24
8	255.75	127.55
9	242.78	121.19
10	255.34	118.00
11	271.58	121.81
12	268.27	126.54
13	260.51	129.85
14	266.34	122.65
15	281.24	121.64
16	286.19	127.24
17	271.97	132.35
18	265.01	130.86
19	274.44	122.90
20	291.81	117.15
21	290.91	109.47
22	264.95	114.34
23	228.40	123.72
24	209.33	130.33

Source: *Forecasting Methods and Applications,* "Sales and Advertising Data," by S. Makridakis, S. C. Wheelwright, and V. E. McGee, *Forecasting: Methods and Applications* (copyright © 1983 John Wiley & Sons, Inc.). Reprinted by permission of John Wiley & Sons, Inc.

FIGURE 13.37 Residual Plot for Exercise 13.61

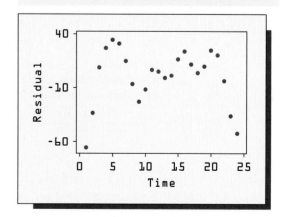

largest. These ordered residuals are given in Table 13.4. Denoting the ith ordered residual as $e_{(i)}$ ($i = 1, 2, \ldots, 11$), we next compute for each value of i the point $z_{(i)}$. These computations are summarized in Table 13.4. Show how $z_{(4)} = -.46$ and $z_{(10)} = 1.05$ have been obtained.

b The ordered residuals ($e_{(i)}$) are plotted against the $z_{(i)}$ values on the MegaStat output of Figure 13.36(c). Does this figure indicate a violation of the normality assumption?

13.61 A simple linear regression model is employed to analyze the 24 monthly observations given in Table 13.5. Residuals are computed and are plotted versus time. The resulting residual plot is shown in Figure 13.37. Discuss why the residual plot suggests the existence of positive autocorrelation. ● SalesAdv

13.62   Western Steakhouses, a fast-food chain, opened 15 years ago. Each year since then the number of steakhouses in operation, y_t, was recorded. An analyst for the firm wishes to use these data to predict the number of steakhouses that will be in operation next year. The data are as follows: ● WestStk

Year (t)	y_t	$\ln(y_t)$	Year (t)	y_t	$\ln(y_t)$
0	11	2.398	8	82	4.407
1	14	2.639	9	99	4.595
2	16	2.773	10	119	4.779
3	22	3.091	11	156	5.050
4	28	3.332	12	257	5.549
5	36	3.584	13	284	5.649
6	46	3.829	14	403	5.999
7	67	4.205			

A plot of the steakhouse values versus time (t) shows that these values increase at an increasing rate over time and also exhibit increasing variation. A plot of the natural logarithms of the steakhouse values has an approximate straight-line appearance with constant variation. If we consider the model

$$\ln y_t = \beta_0 + \beta_1 t + \varepsilon_t$$

we find that the least squares point estimates of β_0 and β_1 are $b_0 = 2.327$ and $b_1 = .256880$. We also find that a point prediction of and a 95 percent prediction interval for the natural logarithm of the number of steakhouses in operation next year (year 15) are 6.1802 and [5.9945, 6.3659].

a   Use the least squares point estimates to verify the point prediction.

b   By exponentiating the point prediction and prediction interval—that is, by calculating $e^{6.1802}$ and [$e^{5.9945}$, $e^{6.3659}$]—find a point prediction of and a 95 percent prediction interval for the number of steakhouses in operation next year.

13.9 Some Shortcut Formulas (Optional) ● ● ●

Calculating the sum of squared residuals   A shortcut formula for the sum of squared residuals is

$$SSE = SS_{yy} - \frac{SS_{xy}^2}{SS_{xx}} \quad \text{where} \quad SS_{yy} = \sum (y_i - \bar{y})^2 = \sum y_i^2 - \frac{\left(\sum y_i\right)^2}{n}$$

For example, consider the fuel consumption case. If we square each of the eight observed fuel consumptions in Table 13.1 (page 501) and add up the resulting squared values, we find that $\sum y_i^2 = 859.91$. We have also found in Example 13.3 (page 507) that $\sum y_i = 81.7$, $SS_{xy} = -179.6475$, and $SS_{xx} = 1,404.355$. It follows that

$$SS_{yy} = \sum y_i^2 - \frac{\left(\sum y_i\right)^2}{n} = 859.91 - \frac{(81.7)^2}{8} = 25.549$$

and

$$SSE = SS_{yy} - \frac{SS_{xy}^2}{SS_{xx}} = 25.549 - \frac{(-179.6475)^2}{1,404.355}$$

$$= 25.549 - 22.981 = 2.568$$

Finally, note that SS_{xy}^2/SS_{xx} equals $b_1 SS_{xy}$. However, we recommend using the first of these expressions, because doing so usually gives less round-off error.

Calculating the total, explained, and unexplained variations   The **unexplained variation** is SSE, and thus the shortcut formula for SSE is a shortcut formula for the unexplained variation. The quantity SS_{yy} defined on page 554 is the **total variation,** and thus the shortcut formula for SS_{yy} is a shortcut formula for the total variation. Lastly, it can be shown that the expression SS_{xy}^2/SS_{xx} equals the **explained variation** and thus is a shortcut formula for this quantity.

Chapter Summary

This chapter has discussed **simple linear regression analysis,** which relates a **dependent variable** to a single **independent** (predictor) **variable.** We began by considering the **simple linear regression model,** which employs two parameters: the **slope** and **y intercept.** We next discussed how to compute the **least squares point estimates** of these parameters and how to use these estimates to calculate a **point estimate of the mean value of the dependent variable** and a **point prediction of an individual value** of the dependent variable. Then, after considering the assumptions behind the simple linear regression model, we discussed **testing the significance of the regression relationship** **(slope),** calculating a **confidence interval** for the mean value of the dependent variable, and calculating a **prediction interval** for an individual value of the dependent variable. We next explained several measures of the utility of the simple linear regression model. These include the **simple coefficient of determination** and an **F test for the simple linear model.** We concluded this chapter by giving an optional discussion of using **residual analysis** to detect violations of the regression assumptions. We learned that we can sometimes remedy violations of these assumptions by **transforming** the dependent variable.

Glossary of Terms

cross-sectional data: Data that are observed at a single point in time. (page 504)

dependent variable: The variable that is being described, predicted, or controlled. (page 499)

distance value: A measure of the distance between a particular value x_0 of the independent variable x and $\bar{x}$, the average of the previously observed values of x (the center of the experimental region). (pages 525–526)

error term: The difference between an individual value of the dependent variable and the corresponding mean value of the dependent variable. (page 502)

experimental region: The range of the previously observed values of the independent variable. (page 508)

independent variable: A variable used to describe, predict, and control the dependent variable. (page 499)

least squares point estimates: The point estimates of the slope and y-intercept of the simple linear regression model that minimize the sum of squared residuals. (page 506)

negative autocorrelation: The situation in which positive error terms tend to be followed over time by negative error terms and negative error terms tend to be followed over time by positive error terms. (page 546)

normal plot: A residual plot that is used to check the normality assumption. (page 544)

positive autocorrelation: The situation in which positive error terms tend to be followed over time by positive error terms and

negative error terms tend to be followed over time by negative error terms. (page 545)

residual: The difference between the observed value of the dependent variable and the corresponding predicted value of the dependent variable. (pages 506, 540)

residual plot: A plot of the residuals against some criterion. The plot is used to check the validity of one or more regression assumptions. (page 541)

simple coefficient of determination: The proportion of the total variation in the observed values of the dependent variable that is explained by the simple linear regression model. (page 532)

simple correlation coefficient: A measure of the linear association between two variables. (page 533)

simple linear regression model: An equation that describes the straight-line relationship between a dependent variable and an independent variable. (page 503)

slope (of the simple linear regression model): The change in the mean value of the dependent variable that is associated with a one-unit increase in the value of the independent variable. (page 502)

time series data: Data that are observed in time sequence. (page 504)

y-intercept (of the simple linear regression model): The mean value of the dependent variable when the value of the independent variable is zero. (page 502)

Important Formulas and Tests

Simple linear regression model: page 503

Least squares point estimates of β_0 and β_1: pages 506–507

Least squares line (prediction equation): page 506

The predicted value of y: page 506

The residual: pages 506 and 540

Sum of squared residuals: pages 506 and 554

Point estimate of a mean value of y: page 510

Point prediction of an individual value of y: page 510

Mean square error: page 516

Standard error: page 516

Sampling distribution of b_1: page 517

Standard error of the estimate b_1: page 517

Testing the significance of the slope: page 518

Confidence interval for the slope: page 520

Testing the significance of the y-intercept: page 520
Sampling distribution of $\hat{y}$: page 525
Standard error of $\hat{y}$: page 525
Distance value for simple linear regression: pages 525–526
Confidence interval for a mean value of y: page 525
Prediction interval for y: page 525
Explained variation: page 532
Unexplained variation: page 532

Total variation: page 532
Simple coefficient of determination: page 532
Simple correlation coefficient: page 533
Testing the significance of the population correlation coefficient: page 536
An F test for the simple linear regression model: page 537
Constructing a normal plot: page 544

Supplementary Exercises

connect

13.63 Consider the following data concerning the demand (y) and price (x) of a consumer product. ● Demand

Demand, y	252	244	241	234	230	223
Price, x	$2.00	$2.20	$2.40	$2.60	$2.80	$3.00

a Plot y versus x. Does it seem reasonable to use the simple linear regression model to relate y to x?
b Calculate the least squares point estimates of the parameters in the simple linear regression model.
c Write the least squares prediction equation. Graph this equation on the plot of y versus x.
d Test the significance of the regression relationship between y and x.
e Find a point prediction of and a 95 percent prediction interval for the demand corresponding to each of the prices $2.10, $2.75, and $3.10.

13.64 In an article in *Public Roads* (1983), Bissell, Pilkington, Mason, and Woods study bridge safety (measured in accident rates per 100 million vehicles) and the **difference** between the width of the bridge and the width of the roadway approach (road plus shoulder):[5] ● AutoAcc

WidthDiff.	−6	−4	−2	0	2	4	6	8	10	12
Accident	120	103	87	72	58	44	31	20	12	7

The MINITAB output of a simple linear regression analysis relating accident rate to width difference is as follows:

```
The regression equation is
Accident Rate = 74.7 - 6.44 WidthDif

Predictor        Coef      SE Coef         T          P
Constant       74.727        1.904     39.25      0.000
WidthDif      -6.4424        0.2938    -21.93      0.000

S = 5.33627    R-Sq = 98.4%    R-Sq(adj) = 98.2%

Analysis of Variance
Source            DF         SS        MS         F          P
Regression         1      13697     13697    480.99      0.000
Residual Error     8        228        28
Total              9      13924
```

Using the MINITAB output
a Identify and interpret the least squares point estimate of the slope of the simple linear regression model.
b Identify and interpret the p-value for testing $H_0: \beta_1 = 0$ versus $H_a: \beta_1 \neq 0$.
c Identify and interpret r^2.

13.65 The data in Table 13.6 concerning the relationship between smoking and lung cancer deaths are presented in a course of The Open University, *Statistics in Society,* Unit C4, The Open University Press, Milton Keynes, England, 1983. The original source of the data is *Occupational Mortality: The Registrar General's Decennial Supplement for England and Wales, 1970–1972,* Her Majesty's Stationery Office, London, 1978. In the table, a smoking index greater (less) than 100 indicates that men in the occupational group smoke more (less) than average when compared to all men of the same age. Similarly, a lung cancer death index greater (less) than 100 indicates that men in the occupational group have a greater (less) than average lung cancer death rate when compared to all men of the same age. In Figure 13.38 we present a portion of a MINITAB output of a simple linear regression analysis relating the lung cancer death index to the smoking index. In Figure 13.39 we present a plot of the lung cancer death index versus the smoking index. ● Smoking

---
[5]Source: H. H. Bissell, G. B. Pilkington II, J. M. Mason, and D. L. Woods, "Roadway Cross Section and Alignment," *Public Roads* 46 (March 1983), pp. 132–41.

TABLE 13.6   The Smoking and Lung Cancer Death Data   ◐ Smoking

Occupational Group	Smoking Index	Lung Cancer Death Index
Farmers, foresters, and fisherman	77	84
Miners and quarrymen	137	116
Gas, coke, and chemical makers	117	123
Glass and ceramics makers	94	128
Furnace, forge, foundry, and rolling mill workers	116	155
Electrical and electronics workers	102	101
Engineering and allied trades	111	118
Woodworkers	93	113
Leather workers	88	104
Textile workers	102	88
Clothing workers	91	104
Food, drink, and tobacco workers	104	129
Paper and printing workers	107	86
Makers of other products	112	96
Construction workers	113	144
Painters and decorators	110	139
Drivers of stationary engines, cranes, etc.	125	113
Laborers not included elsewhere	133	146
Transport and communications workers	115	128
Warehousemen, storekeepers, packers, and bottlers	105	115
Clerical workers	87	79
Sales workers	91	85
Service, sport, and recreation workers	100	120
Administrators and managers	76	60
Professionals, technical workers, and artists	66	51

FIGURE 13.38   MINITAB Output of a Simple Linear Regression Analysis of
the Data in Table 13.6

```
The regression equation is
Death Index = - 2.9 + 1.09 Smoking Index

Predictor          Coef       SE Coef            T          P
Constant          -2.89         23.03        -0.13      0.901
Smoking Index     1.0875        0.2209         4.92       0.00

S = 18.6154    R-Sq = 51.3%    R-Sq(adj) = 49.2%
```

FIGURE 13.39   A Plot of the Lung Cancer Death Index versus the Smoking Index

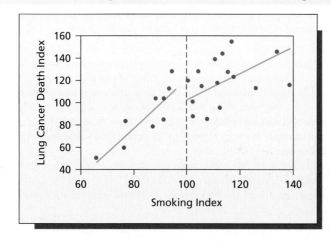

FIGURE 13.40   **A Data Plot Based on Seven Launches**   FIGURE 13.41   **A Data Plot Based on All 24 Launches**

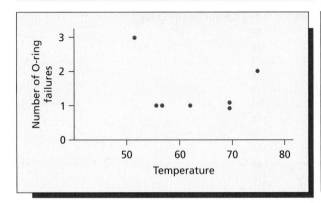 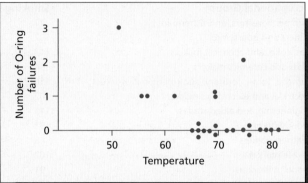

a Although the data do not prove that smoking increases your chance of getting lung cancer, can you think of a third factor that would cause the two indexes to move together?

b Does the slope of the hypothetical line relating the two indexes when the smoking index is less than 100 seem to equal the slope of the hypothetical line relating the two indexes when the smoking index is greater than 100? If you wish, use simple linear regression to make a more precise determination. What practical conclusion might you make?

13.66 On January 28, 1986, the space shuttle *Challenger* exploded soon after takeoff, killing all eight astronauts aboard. The temperature at the Kennedy Space Center at liftoff was 31°F. Before the launch, several scientists argued that the launch should be delayed because the shuttle's O-rings might harden in the cold and leak. Other scientists used the data plot in Figure 13.40 to argue that there was no relationship between temperature and O-ring failure. On the basis of this figure and other considerations, *Challenger* was launched to its disastrous, last flight.

Scientists using the data plot in Figure 13.40 made a horrible mistake. They relied on a data plot that was created by using only the seven previous launches where there was at least one O-ring failure. A plot based on all 24 previous launches—17 of which had no O-ring failures—is given in Figure 13.41.

a Intuitively, do you think that Figure 13.41 indicates that there is a relationship between temperature and O-ring failure? Use simple linear regression to justify your answer.

b Even though the figure using only seven launches is incomplete, what about it should have cautioned the scientists not to make the launch?

13.67 In an article in the *Journal of Accounting Research,* Benzion Barlev and Haim Levy consider relating accounting rates on stocks and market returns. Fifty-four companies were selected. For each company the authors recorded values of *x*, the mean yearly accounting rate for the period 1959 to 1974, and *y*, the mean yearly market return rate for the period 1959 to 1974. The data in Table 13.7 were obtained. Here the accounting rate can be interpreted to represent input into investment and therefore is a logical predictor of market return. Use the simple linear regression model and a computer to   ⬤ AcctRet

a Find a point estimate of and a 95 percent confidence interval for the mean market return rate of all stocks having an accounting rate of 15.00.

b Find a point prediction of and a 95 percent prediction interval for the market return rate of an individual stock having an accounting rate of 15.00.

TABLE 13.7 **Accounting Rates on Stocks and Market Returns for 54 Companies** ● AcctRet

Company	Market Rate	Accounting Rate	Company	Market Rate	Accounting Rate
McDonnell Douglas	17.73	17.96	FMC	5.71	13.30
NCR	4.54	8.11	Caterpillar Tractor	13.38	17.66
Honeywell	3.96	12.46	Georgia Pacific	13.43	14.59
TRW	8.12	14.70	Minnesota Mining & Manufacturing	10.00	20.94
Raytheon	6.78	11.90	Standard Oil (Ohio)	16.66	9.62
W. R. Grace	9.69	9.67	American Brands	9.40	16.32
Ford Motors	12.37	13.35	Aluminum Company of America	.24	8.19
Textron	15.88	16.11	General Electric	4.37	15.74
Lockheed Aircraft	−1.34	6.78	General Tire	3.11	12.02
Getty Oil	18.09	9.41	Borden	6.63	11.44
Atlantic Richfield	17.17	8.96	American Home Products	14.73	32.58
Radio Corporation of America	6.78	14.17	Standard Oil (California)	6.15	11.89
Westinghouse Electric	4.74	9.12	International Paper	5.96	10.06
Johnson & Johnson	23.02	14.23	National Steel	6.30	9.60
Champion International	7.68	10.43	Republic Steel	.68	7.41
R. J. Reynolds	14.32	19.74	Warner Lambert	12.22	19.88
General Dynamics	−1.63	6.42	U.S. Steel	.90	6.97
Colgate-Palmolive	16.51	12.16	Bethlehem Steel	2.35	7.90
Coca-Cola	17.53	23.19	Armco Steel	5.03	9.34
International Business Machines	12.69	19.20	Texaco	6.13	15.40
Allied Chemical	4.66	10.76	Shell Oil	6.58	11.95
Uniroyal	3.67	8.49	Standard Oil (Indiana)	14.26	9.56
Greyhound	10.49	17.70	Owens Illinois	2.60	10.05
Cities Service	10.00	9.10	Gulf Oil	4.97	12.11
Philip Morris	21.90	17.47	Tenneco	6.65	11.53
General Motors	5.86	18.45	Inland Steel	4.25	9.92
Philips Petroleum	10.81	10.06	Kraft	7.30	12.27

Source: Reprinted by permission from Benzion Barlev and Haim Levy, "On the Variability of Accounting Income Numbers," *Journal of Accounting Research* (Autumn 1979), pp. 305–315. Copyright © 1979. Used with permission of Blackwell Publishers.

TABLE 13.8   The New Jersey Bank Data
● NJBank

County	Percentage of Minority Population, x	Number of Residents Per Bank Branch, y
Atlantic	23.3	3,073
Bergen	13.0	2,095
Burlington	17.8	2,905
Camden	23.4	3,330
Cape May	7.3	1,321
Cumberland	26.5	2,557
Essex	48.8	3,474
Gloucester	10.7	3,068
Hudson	33.2	3,683
Hunterdon	3.7	1,998
Mercer	24.9	2,607
Middlesex	18.1	3,154
Monmouth	12.6	2,609
Morris	8.2	2,253
Ocean	4.7	2,317
Passaic	28.1	3,307
Salem	16.7	2,511
Somerset	12.0	2,333
Sussex	2.4	2,568
Union	25.6	3,048
Warren	2.8	2,349

Source: P. D'Ambrosio and S. Chambers, "No Checks and Balances," *Asbury Park Press*, September 10, 1995. Copyright © 1995 Asbury Park Press. Used with permission.

FIGURE 13.42   Excel Output of a Simple Linear Regression Analysis of the New Jersey Bank Data

Regression Statistics

Multiple R	0.7256
R Square	0.5265
Adjusted R Square	0.5016
Standard Error	400.2546
Observations	21

ANOVA	df	SS	MS	F	Significance F
Regression	1	3385090.234	3385090	21.1299	0.0002
Residual	19	3043870.432	160203.7		
Total	20	6428960.667			

	Coefficients	Standard Error	t Stat	P-value	Lower 95%	Upper 95%
Intercept	2082.0153	159.1070	13.0856	5.92E-11	1749.0005	2415.0301
% Minority Pop (x)	35.2877	7.6767	4.5967	0.0002	19.2202	51.3553

13.68 In New Jersey, banks have been charged with withdrawing from counties having a high percentage of minorities. To substantiate this charge, P. D'Ambrosio and S. Chambers (1995) present the data in Table 13.8 concerning the percentage, x, of minority population and the number of county residents, y, per bank branch in each of New Jersey's 21 counties. If we use Excel to perform a simple linear regression analysis of this data, we obtain the output given in Figure 13.42.   ● NJBank

   a Determine if there is a significant relationship between x and y.

   b Describe the exact nature of any relationship that exists between x and y. (Hint: Estimate β_1 by a point estimate and a confidence interval.)

13.69 In analyzing the stock market, we sometimes use the model $y = \beta_0 + \beta_1 x + \varepsilon$ to relate y, the rate of return on a particular stock, to x, the rate of return on the overall stock market. When using the preceding model, we can interpret β_1 to be the percentage point change in the mean (or expected) rate of return on the particular stock that is associated with an increase of one percentage point in the rate of return on the overall stock market.

If regression analysis can be used to conclude (at a high level of confidence) that β_1 is greater than 1 (for example, if the 95 percent confidence interval for β_1 were [1.1826, 1.4723]), this indicates that the mean rate of return on the particular stock changes more quickly than the rate of return on the overall stock market. Such a stock is called an *aggressive stock* because gains for such a stock tend to be greater than overall market gains (which occur when the market is bullish). However, losses for such a stock tend to be greater than overall market losses (which occur when the market is bearish). Aggressive stocks should be purchased if you expect the market to rise and avoided if you expect the market to fall.

If regression analysis can be used to conclude (at a high level of confidence) that β_1 is less than 1 (for example, if the 95 percent confidence interval for β_1 were [.4729, .7861]), this indicates that the mean rate of return on the particular stock changes more slowly than the rate of return on the overall stock market. Such a stock is called a *defensive stock*. Losses for such a stock tend to be less than overall market losses, whereas gains for such a stock tend to be less than overall market gains. Defensive stocks should be held if you expect the market to fall and sold off if you expect the market to rise.

If the least squares point estimate b_1 of β_1 is nearly equal to 1, and if the 95 percent confidence interval for β_1 contains 1, this might indicate that the mean rate of return on the particular stock changes at roughly the same rate as the rate of return on the overall stock market. Such a stock is called a *neutral stock*.

In a 1984 article in *Financial Analysts Journal,* Haim Levy considers how a stock's value of β_1 depends on the length of time for which the rate of return is calculated. Levy calculated estimated values of β_1 for return length times varying from 1 to 30 months for each of 38 aggressive stocks, 38 defensive stocks, and 68 neutral stocks. Each estimated value was based on data from 1946 to 1975. In the following table we present the average estimate of β_1 for each stock type for different return length times:

Average Estimate of β_1 ● Beta

Return Length Time	Aggressive Stocks	Defensive Stocks	Neutral Stocks
1	1.37	.50	.98
3	1.42	.44	.95
6	1.53	.41	.94
9	1.69	.39	1.00
12	1.83	.40	.98
15	1.67	.38	1.00
18	1.78	.39	1.02
24	1.86	.35	1.14
30	1.83	.33	1.22

Source: Reprinted by permission from H. Levy, "Measuring Risk and Performance over Alternative Investment Horizons," *Financial Analysts Journal* (March–April 1984), pp. 61–68. Copyright © 1984, CFA Institute. Reproduced and modified from Financial Analysts Journal with permission of CFA Institute.

Let y = average estimate of β_1 and x = return length time, and consider relating y to x for each stock type by using the simple linear regression model

$$y = \beta_0^* + \beta_1^* x + \varepsilon$$

Here β_0^* and β_1^* are regression parameters relating y to x. We use the asterisks to indicate that these regression parameters are different from β_0 and β_1. Calculate a 95 percent confidence interval for β_1^* for each stock type. Carefully interpret the meaning of each interval.

13.70 The State Department of Taxation wishes to investigate the effect of experience, x, on the amount of time, y, required to fill out Form ST 1040AVG, the state income-averaging form. In order to do this, nine people whose financial status makes income averaging advantageous are chosen at random. Each is asked to fill out Form ST 1040AVG and to report (1) the time y (in hours) required to complete the form and (2) the number of times x (including this one) that he or she has filled out this form. The following data are obtained: ● TaxTime

FIGURE 13.43   **Plot of y versus x in Exercise 13.70**

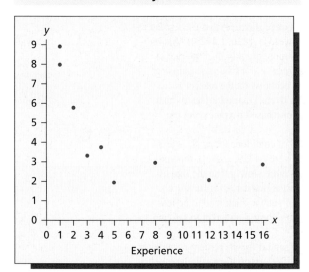

FIGURE 13.44   **Plot of y versus 1/x in Exercise 13.70**

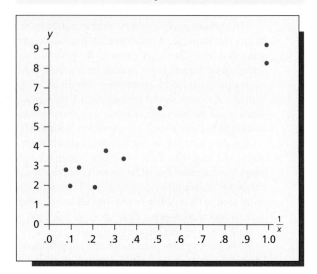

Completion time, y (in Hours)	8.0	4.7	3.7	2.8	8.9	5.8	2.0	1.9	3.3
Experience, x	1	8	4	16	1	2	12	5	3

A plot of these data is given in Figure 13.43 and indicates that the model

$$y = \mu_y + \varepsilon = \beta_0 + \beta_1\left(\frac{1}{x}\right) + \varepsilon$$

might appropriately relate y to x. To understand this model, note that as x increases, $1/x$ decreases and thus μ_y decreases. This seems to be what the data plot indicates is happening. To further understand this model, note that a plot of the values of y versus the values of $1/x$ in Figure 13.44 has a straight-line appearance. This indicates that a simple linear regression model having y as the dependent variable and $1/x$ as the independent variable—that is, the model we are considering—might be appropriate. Using the formulas of simple linear regression analysis, the least squares point estimates of β_0 and β_1 can be calculated to be $b_0 = 2.0572$ and $b_1 = 6.3545$. Furthermore, consider the completion time of an individual filling out the form for the fifth time (that is, $x = 5$). Then, it can be verified that a point prediction of and a 95 percent prediction interval for this completion time are, respectively, 3.3281 and [.7225, 5.9337]. Show how the point prediction has been calculated.

13.71   Internet Exercise   ◆ US News

Graduate business schools use a variety of factors to guide the selection of applicants for admission to MBA programs. Among the key indicators are undergraduate GPA and Graduate Management Admissions Test (GMAT) score. Is there a statistically significant relationship between the average GMAT score and the average undergraduate GPA for admitted MBA program applicants? Can we develop a statistical model describing the relationship? How reliable are the predictions of the model? The U.S. News website ranks the top MBA programs and provides some interesting data on these questions—the average undergraduate GPA and the average GMAT score of admitted applicants for its 50 top-ranked MBA programs. Note that the data are somewhat limited in scope in that they reflect only the experience of top 50 programs.

Go to the U.S. News website and retrieve the data for the 50 top-ranked MBA programs, http://www.usnews. com. Click on (in turn) .edu : Business : Top Business Schools

or go directly to http://www.usnews.com/usnews/edu/ beyond/gradrank/mba/gdmbat1.htm. To capture the data—select the entire data table, copy and paste it into Excel or MINITAB, add your own variable labels, and clean up the data as necessary. Excel and MINITAB data files are also included on the CD-ROM (USNews.xls and USNews.mtw). Construct a scatter plot of *GMAT* versus *GPA*. Describe any apparent relationship between the two variables. Develop a simple linear regression model expressing *GMAT* as a linear function of *GPA*. Identify and interpret the key summary measures—R^2, the standard error, and the *F*-statistic from the ANOVA table. Identify and interpret the estimated regression coefficients. Suppose that the average undergraduate GPA for a particular program is 3.50. Use your regression model to predict the average GMAT score for the program. Prepare a brief report summarizing your analysis and conclusions.

Appendix 13.1 ■ Simple Linear Regression Analysis Using MINITAB

The instruction blocks in this section each begin by describing the entry of data into the MINITAB Data window. Alternatively, the data may be loaded directly from the data disk included with the text. The appropriate data file name is given at the top of each instruction block. Please refer to Appendix 1.1 for further information about entering data, saving data, and printing results when using MINITAB.

Simple linear regression of the fuel consumption data in Figure 13.11(a) on page 519 (data file: FuelCon1. MTW):

- In the Data window, enter the fuel consumption data from Table 13.1 on page 501—average hourly temperatures in column C1 with variable name Temp and weekly fuel consumptions in column C2 with variable name FuelCons.
- Select **Stat : Regression : Regression**
- In the Regression dialog box, select FuelCons into the Response window.
- Select Temp into the Predictors window.

To compute a **prediction** for fuel consumption when temperature is 40° F:

- In the Regression dialog box, click on the Options... button.
- In the "Regression—Options" dialog box, type 40 in the "Prediction intervals for new observations" window.
- Click OK in the "Regression—Options" dialog box.

To produce **residual analysis** similar to Figure 13.34 on page 552:

- In the Regression dialog box, click on the Graphs... button.
- In the "Regression—Graphs" dialog box, select the "Residuals for Plots: Regular" option.
- To obtain a histogram and normal plot of the residuals, a plot of the residuals versus the fitted values, and a plot of the residuals versus time order, select "Four in one" in the list of options under Residual Plots. (Note that the plot versus time order is generally informative only if the data are in time sequence order.)
- Enter Temp in the "Residuals versus the variables" window to obtain a plot of the residuals versus the values of average hourly temperature.
- Click OK in the "Regression—Graphs" dialog box.
- To see the regression results in the Session window and high-resolution graphs in two graphics windows, click OK in the Regression dialog box.

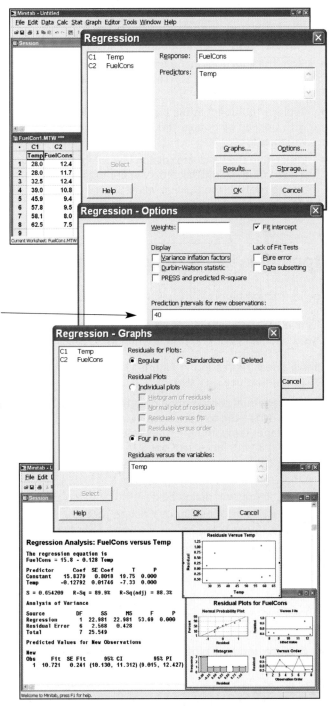

Simple linear regression with a transformed response in Figure 13.32 on page 550 (data file: QHIC.MTW):

- In the Data window, enter the QHIC upkeep expenditure data from Figure 13.23 (page 541)—home values in column C1 with variable name Value and upkeep expenditures in column C2 with variable name Upkeep.

- Select **Calc : Calculator**

- In the Calculator dialog box, enter SqRtUpkeep into the "Store result in variable" window.

- From the Functions menu list, double-click on "Square root" giving SQRT(number) in the Expression window.

- Replace "number" in the Expression window with Upkeep by double-clicking Upkeep in the variables list.

- Click OK in the Calculator dialog box to obtain a new column, SqRtUpkeep, containing the square roots of the Upkeep values.

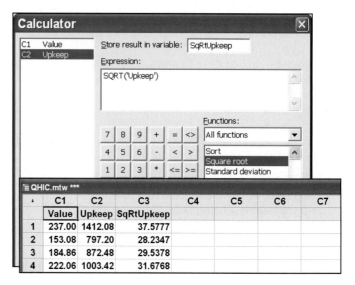

- Follow the steps for **simple linear regression** on page 563 using SqRtUpkeep as the response and Value as the predictor.

Appendix 13.2 ■ Simple Linear Regression Analysis Using Excel

The instruction blocks in this section each begin by describing the entry of data into an Excel spreadsheet. Alternatively, the data may be loaded directly from the data disk included with the text. The appropriate data file name is given at the top of each instruction block. Please refer to Appendix 1.2 for further information about entering data, saving data, and printing results when using Excel.

Simple linear regression in Figure 13.11(b) on page 519 (data file: FuelCon1.xlsx):

- Enter the fuel consumption data from Table 13.1 (page 501)—the temperatures in column A with label Temp and the fuel consumptions in column B with label FuelCons.

- Select **Data : Data Analysis : Regression** and click OK in the Data Analysis dialog box.

- In the Regression dialog box:
  Enter B1.B9 into the "Input Y Range" box.
  Enter A1.A9 into the "Input X Range" box.

- Place a checkmark in the Labels checkbox.

- Be sure that the "Constant is Zero" checkbox is NOT checked.

- Select the "New Worksheet Ply" option.

- Click OK in the Regression dialog box to obtain the regression results in a new worksheet.

To produce residual plots similar to Figures 13.24 (page 543) and 13.26 (page 545):

- In the Regression dialog box, place a checkmark in the Residuals checkbox to request predicted values and residuals.

- Place a checkmark in the Residual Plots checkbox.

- Place a checkmark in the Normal Probability Plots checkbox.

- Click OK in the Regression dialog box.

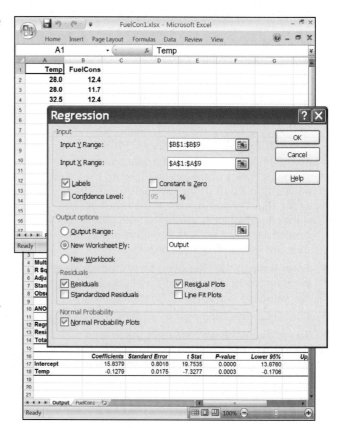

- Move the plots to chart sheets to format them for effective viewing. Additional residual plots—residuals versus predicted values and residuals versus time—can be produced using the Excel charting features.

To compute a point prediction for fuel consumption when temperature is 40°F (data file: FuelCon1.xlsx):

- The Excel Analysis ToolPak does not provide an option for computing point or interval predictions. A point prediction can be computed from the regression results using Excel cell formulas.

- In the regression output, the estimated intercept and slope parameters from cells A17.B18 have been copied to cells D2.E3 and the predictor value 40 has been placed in cell E5.

- In cell E6, enter the Excel formula = E2 + E3*E5(= 10.7210) to compute the prediction.

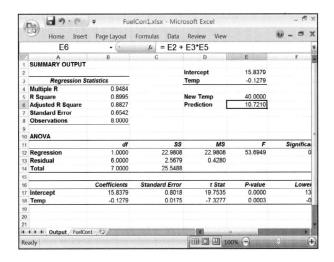

Simple linear regression with a transformed response similar to Figure 13.32 on page 550 (data file: QHIC.xlsx):

- Enter the QHIC upkeep expenditure data from Figure 13.23 (page 541). Enter the label Value in cell A1 with the home values in cells A2 to A41 and enter the label Upkeep in cell B1 with the upkeep expenditures in cells B2 to B41.

- Enter the label SqUpkeep in cell C1.

- Click on cell C2 and then select the Insert Function button f_x on the Excel ribbon.

- Select **Math & Trig** from the "Or select a category:" menu, select **SQRT** from the "Select a function:" menu, and click OK in the Insert Function dialog box.

- In the "SQRT Function Arguments" dialog box, enter B2 in the Number box and click OK to compute the square root of the value in B2.

- Copy the cell formula of C2 through cell C41 by double-clicking the drag handle (in the lower right corner) of cell C2 to compute the square roots of the remaining upkeep values.

- Follow the steps for **simple linear regression** (on page 564) using cells C1.C41 as the response (Input Y Range) and cells A1.A41 as the predictor (Input X Range).

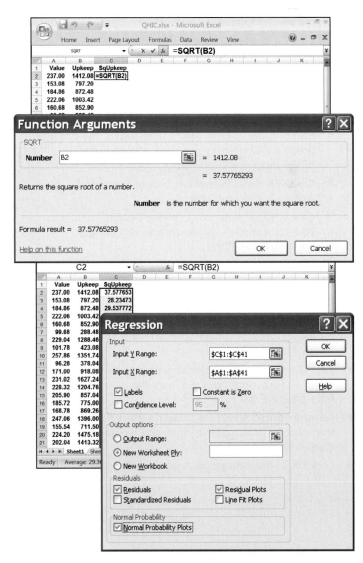

Appendix 13.3 ■ Simple Linear Regression Analysis Using MegaStat

The instructions in this section begin by describing the entry of data into an Excel worksheet. Alternatively, the data may be loaded directly from the data disk included with the text. The appropriate data file name is given at the top of each instruction block. Please refer to Appendix 1.2 for further information about entering data, saving data, and printing results in Excel. Please refer to Appendix 1.3 for more information about using MegaStat.

Simple linear regression for the service time data in Figure 13.14 on page 522 (data file: SrvcTime.xlsx):

- Enter the service time data (page 512)—the numbers of copiers serviced in column A with label Copiers and with the service times in column B with label Minutes.

- Select **Add-Ins : MegaStat : Correlation/ Regression : Regression Analysis**

- In the Regression Analysis dialog box, click in the Independent variables window and use the AutoExpand feature to enter the range A1.A12.

- Click in the Dependent variable window and use the AutoExpand feature to enter the range B1.B12.

- Check the appropriate Options and Residuals checkboxes as follows:

  1 Check "Test Intercept" to include a y-intercept and to test its significance.

  2 Check "Output Residuals" to obtain a list of the model residuals.

  3 Check "Plot Residuals by Observation" and "Plot Residuals by Predicted Y and X" to obtain residual plots versus time, versus the predicted values of y, and versus the values of the independent variable.

  4 Check "Normal Probability Plot of Residuals" to obtain a normal plot.

  5 Check "Durbin-Watson" for the Durbin-Watson statistic—see Bowerman, O'Connell, and Murphree (2009).

To obtain a **point prediction** of y when four computers will be serviced (as well as a confidence interval and prediction interval):

- Click on the drop-down menu above the predictor values window and select "Type in predictor values."

- Type the value of the independent variable for which a prediction is desired (here equal to 4) into the predictor values window.

- Select a desired level of confidence (here 95%) from the Confidence Level drop-down menu or type in a value.

- Click OK in the Regression Analysis dialog box.

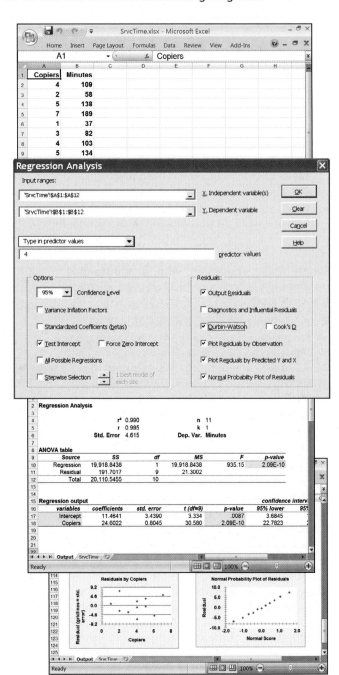

To compute several point predictions of *y*—say, when 1, 2, 3, and 4 computers will be serviced—(and to compute corresponding confidence and prediction intervals):

- Enter the values of *x* for which predictions are desired into a column in the spreadsheet—these values can be in any column. Here we have entered the values 1, 2, 3, and 4 into cells E1 through E4.
- Click on the drop-down menu above the predictor values box and select "Predictor values from spreadsheet cells."
- Enter the range E1.E4 into the predictor values box.
- Click OK in the Regression Analysis dialog box.

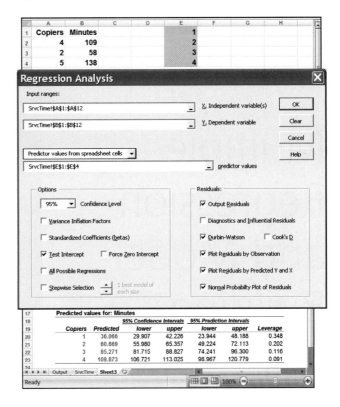

Simple linear regression with a transformed response similar to Figure 13.32 on page 550 (data file: QHIC.xlsx):

- Enter the QHIC data from Figure 13.23 (page 541)— the home values in column A (with label Value) and the upkeep expenditures in column B (with label Upkeep).
- Follow the instructions on page 565 in Appendix 13.2 to calculate the square roots of the upkeep expenditures in column C (with label SRUpkeep).
- Select **Add-Ins : MegaStat : Correlation/ Regression : Regression Analysis**
- In the Regression Analysis dialog box, click in the Independent variables window, and use the AutoExpand feature to enter the range A1.A41.
- Click in the Dependent variable window and use the AutoExpand feature to enter the range C1.C41.
- Check the "Test Intercept" checkbox to include a *y*-intercept and test its significance.

To compute a **point prediction of the square root of y** (as well as a confidence interval and prediction interval) for a house having a value of $220,000:

- Select "Type in predictor values" from the drop-down menu above the predictor values window.
- Type 220 into the predictor values window.
- Select a desired level of confidence (here 95%) from the drop-down menu in the Confidence Level box or type in a value.
- Click OK in the Regression Analysis dialog box.

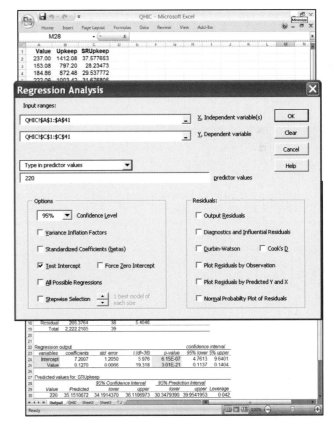

CHAPTER 14

Multiple Regression and Model Building

Chapter Outline

14.1 The Multiple Regression Model and the Least Squares Point Estimates

14.2 Model Assumptions and the Standard Error

14.3 R^2 and Adjusted R^2 (This section can be read anytime after reading Section 14.1.)

14.4 The Overall F Test

14.5 Testing the Significance of an Independent Variable

14.6 Confidence and Prediction Intervals

14.7 Using Dummy Variables to Model Qualitative Independent Variables

14.8 Model Building and the Effects of Multicollinearity

14.9 Residual Analysis in Multiple Regression

ften we can more accurately describe, predict, and control a dependent variable by using a regression model that employs more than one independent variable. Such a model is called a **multiple regression model,** which is the subject of this chapter.

In order to explain the ideas of this chapter, we consider the following cases:

The Fuel Consumption Case: The management consulting firm more accurately predicts the city's future weekly fuel consumptions by using a multiple regression model that employs as independent variables the average hourly temperature and the "chill index." The chill index measures weather-related factors such as the wind velocity and the cloud cover. The more accurate predictions given by the multiple regression model are likely to produce percentage nomination errors within the 10 percent allowance granted by the pipeline transmission system.

The Sales Territory Performance Case: A sales manager evaluates the performance of sales representatives by using a multiple regression model that predicts sales performance on the basis of five independent variables. Salespeople whose actual performance is far worse than predicted performance will get extra training to help improve their sales techniques.

14.1 The Multiple Regression Model and the Least Squares Point Estimates ●●●

Regression models that employ more than one independent variable are called **multiple regression models.** We begin our study of these models by considering the following example.

EXAMPLE 14.1 The Fuel Consumption Case ● FuelCon2

Part 1: The data and a regression model Consider the fuel consumption problem in which the natural gas company wishes to predict weekly fuel consumption for its city. In Chapter 13 we used the single predictor variable x, average hourly temperature, to predict y, weekly fuel consumption. We now consider predicting y on the basis of average hourly temperature and a second predictor variable—the chill index. The chill index for a given average hourly temperature expresses the combined effects of all other major weather-related factors that influence fuel consumption, such as wind velocity, cloud cover, and the passage of weather fronts. The chill index is expressed as a whole number between 0 and 30. A weekly chill index near 0 indicates that, given the average hourly temperature during the week, all other major weather-related factors will only slightly increase weekly fuel consumption. A weekly chill index near 30 indicates that, given the average hourly temperature during the week, other weather-related factors will greatly increase weekly fuel consumption.

CHAPTER 17

The company has collected data concerning weekly fuel consumption (y), average hourly temperature (x_1), and the chill index (x_2) for the last eight weeks. These data are given in Table 14.1.

TABLE 14.1 **Fuel Consumption Data** ● FuelCon2

Week	Average Hourly Temperature, x_1 (°F)	Chill Index, x_2	Fuel Consumption, y (MMcf)
1	28.0	18	12.4
2	28.0	14	11.7
3	32.5	24	12.4
4	39.0	22	10.8
5	45.9	8	9.4
6	57.8	16	9.5
7	58.1	1	8.0
8	62.5	0	7.5

FIGURE 14.1   Plot of *y* (Weekly Fuel Consumption) versus x_1 (Average Hourly Temperature)

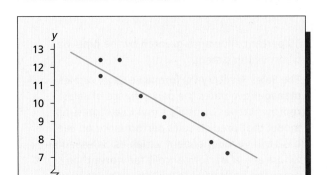

FIGURE 14.2   Plot of *y* (Weekly Fuel Consumption) versus x_2 (the Chill Index)

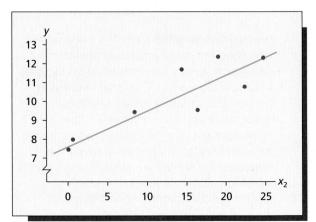

Figure 14.1 presents a scatter plot of *y* versus x_1. This plot shows that *y* tends to decrease in a straight-line fashion as x_1 increases. Figure 14.2 shows a scatter plot of *y* versus x_2. This plot shows that *y* tends to increase in a straight-line fashion as x_2 increases. Together, the scatter plots in Figures 14.1 and 14.2 imply that a reasonable multiple regression model relating *y* (weekly fuel consumption) to x_1 (average hourly temperature) and x_2 (the chill index) is

$$y = \beta_0 + \beta_1 x_1 + \beta_2 x_2 + \varepsilon$$

This model says that the values of *y* can be represented by a **mean level**—$\beta_0 + \beta_1 x_1 + \beta_2 x_2$—that changes as x_1 and x_2 change, combined with random fluctuations—described by the **error term** ε—that cause the values of *y* to deviate from the mean level. Here:

1   The mean level $\beta_0 + \beta_1 x_1 + \beta_2 x_2$, which we denote as μ_y, is the mean of the fuel consumptions (*y*) that would be observed in all weeks that have an average hourly temperature of x_1 and a chill index of x_2. Furthermore, the equation

$$\mu_y = \beta_0 + \beta_1 x_1 + \beta_2 x_2$$

is the equation of a plane—called the **plane of means**—in three-dimensional space. The plane of means is illustrated in Figure 14.3. It is the dark blue plane that is positioned between the red dots. These red dots represent the eight observed fuel consumptions in Table 14.1. In addition, there are eight black triangles located on the plane of means. These triangles represent the mean fuel consumptions that correspond to the observed temperature–chill index combinations in Table 14.1. For example, in week 1 the average hourly temperature (x_1) was 28 and the chill index (x_2) was 18. It follows that

$$\beta_0 + \beta_1 (28) + \beta_2 (18)$$

is the mean fuel consumption for all weeks that have an average hourly temperature of 28 and a chill index of 18.

2   β_0, β_1, and β_2 are (unknown) regression parameters that relate mean weekly fuel consumption to x_1 and x_2. Specifically:

• β_0—the *intercept of the model*—is the mean fuel consumption for all weeks that have an average hourly temperature of 0 and a chill index of 0. This interpretation, however, is of dubious practical value, because we have not observed any weeks that have an average hourly temperature of 0 and a chill index of 0.

FIGURE 14.3   A Geometrical Interpretation of the Regression Model Relating *y* to *x*$_1$ and *x*$_2$

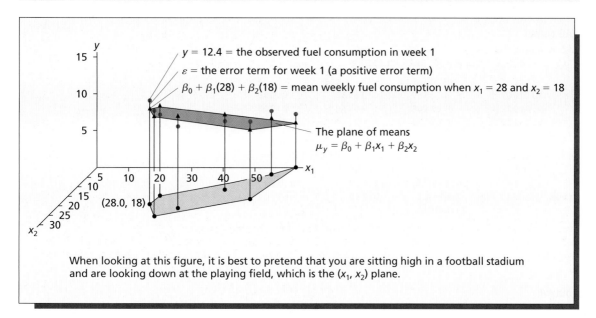

When looking at this figure, it is best to pretend that you are sitting high in a football stadium and are looking down at the playing field, which is the (x_1, x_2) plane.

- β_1—the **regression parameter for the variable** x_1—is the change in mean weekly fuel consumption that is associated with a one-degree increase in the average hourly temperature (x_1) when the chill index (x_2) does not change. Intuitively, β_1 is the slope of the plane of means in the x_1 direction.

- β_2—the **regression parameter for the variable** x_2—is the change in mean weekly fuel consumption that is associated with a one-unit increase in the chill index (x_2) when the average hourly temperature (x_1) does not change. Intuitively, β_2 is the slope of the plane of means in the x_2 direction.

3   ε is an error term that describes the effect on *y* of all factors other than x_1 and x_2. One such factor is the average thermostat setting in the city during the week. For example, Figure 14.3 shows that the error term for week 1 is positive. This implies that the observed fuel consumption in week 1, *y* = 12.4, is greater than the mean fuel consumption for all weeks that have an average hourly temperature of 28 and a chill index of 18. In general, positive error terms cause their respective observed fuel consumptions to be greater than the corresponding mean fuel consumptions. On the other hand, negative error terms cause their respective observed fuel consumptions to be less than the corresponding mean fuel consumptions.

Part 2: The least squares point estimates   If b_0, b_1, and b_2 denote point estimates of β_0, β_1, and β_2, then the point prediction of an observed fuel consumption $y = \beta_0 + \beta_1 x_1 + \beta_2 x_2 + \varepsilon$ is

$$\hat{y} = b_0 + b_1 x_1 + b_2 x_2$$

which we call a *predicted fuel consumption*. Here, since the regression assumptions (to be discussed in Section 14.2) imply that the error term ε has a 50 percent chance of being positive and a 50 percent chance of being negative, we predict ε to be zero. Now, consider the eight weeks of fuel consumption data in Table 14.1. If any particular values of b_0, b_1, and b_2 are good point estimates, they will make the predicted fuel consumption for each week fairly close to the observed fuel consumption for the week. This will make the week's *residual*—the difference between the week's observed and predicted fuel consumptions—fairly small (in magnitude). We define the **least squares point estimates** to be the values of b_0, b_1, and b_2 that minimize *SSE*, the sum of squared residuals for the eight weeks.

FIGURE 14.4   MINITAB and Excel Output of a Regression Analysis of the Fuel Consumption Data in Table 14.1 Using the Model $y = \beta_0 + \beta_1 x_1 + \beta_2 x_2 + \varepsilon$

(a) The MINITAB output

```
The regression equation is
FuelCons = 13.1 - 0.0900 Temp + 0.0825 Chill
```

Predictor	Coef	SE Coef [4]	T [5]	P [6]
Constant	13.1087 [1]	0.8557	15.32	0.000
Temp	-0.09001 [2]	0.01408	-6.39	0.001
Chill	0.08249 [3]	0.02200	3.75	0.013

s = 0.367078 [7]   R-Sq = 97.4% [8]   R-Sq(adj) = 96.3% [9]

Analysis of Variance

Source	DF	SS	MS	F	P
Regression	2	24.875 [10]	12.438	92.30 [13]	0.000 [14]
Residual Error	5	0.674 [11]	0.135		
Total	7	25.549 [12]			

Values of Predictors for New Obs   Predicted Values for New Observations

New Obs	Temp	Chill		New Obs	Fit [15]	SE Fit [16]	95% CI [17]	95% PI [18]
1	40.0	10.0		1	10.333	0.170	(9.895, 10.771)	(9.293, 11.374)

(b) The Excel output

Regression Statistics

Multiple R	0.9867
R Square	0.9736 [8]
Adjusted R Square	0.9631 [9]
Standard Error	0.3671 [7]
Observations	8

ANOVA

	df	SS	MS	F	Significance F
Regression	2	24.8750 [10]	12.4375	92.3031 [13]	0.0001 [14]
Residual	5	0.6737 [11]	0.1347		
Total	7	25.5488 [12]			

	Coefficients	Standard Error [4]	t Stat [5]	P-value [6]	Lower 95% [19]	Upper 95% [19]
Intercept	13.1087 [1]	0.8557	15.3193	2.15E-05	10.9091	15.3084
TEMP	-0.0900 [2]	0.0141	-6.3942	0.0014	-0.1262	-0.0538
CHILL	0.0825 [3]	0.0220	3.7493	0.0133	0.0259	0.1391

[1] b_0 [2] b_1 [3] b_2 [4] s_{b_j} = standard error of the estimate b_j [5] t statistics [6] p-values for t statistics [7] s = standard error			
[8] R^2 [9] Adjusted R^2 [10] Explained variation [11] SSE = Unexplained variation [12] Total variation [13] F(model) statistic			
[14] p-value for F(model) [15] $\hat{y}$ = point prediction when $x_1 = 40$ and $x_2 = 10$ [16] $s_{\hat{y}}$ = standard error of the estimate $\hat{y}$			
[17] 95% confidence interval when $x_1 = 40$ and $x_2 = 10$ [18] 95% prediction interval when $x_1 = 40$ and $x_2 = 10$ [19] 95% confidence interval for β_j			

The formula for the least squares point estimates of the parameters in a multiple regression model is expressed using a branch of mathematics called **matrix algebra.** This formula is presented in Appendix G of the CD-ROM included with this book. In the main body of the book, we will rely on MINITAB, Excel, and MegaStat to compute the needed estimates. For example, consider the MINITAB and Excel output in Figure 14.4. This output tells us that the least squares point estimates of β_0, β_1, and β_2 in the fuel consumption model are $b_0 = 13.1087$, $b_1 = -.09001$, and $b_2 = .08249$ (see [1], [2], and [3])—note that these estimates are slightly rounded on the Excel output. The point estimate $b_1 = -.09001$ of β_1 says we estimate that mean weekly fuel consumption decreases (since b_1 is negative) by .09001 MMcf of natural gas when average hourly temperature increases by one degree and the chill index does not change. The point estimate $b_2 = .08249$ of β_2 says we estimate that mean weekly fuel consumption increases (since b_2 is positive) by .08249 MMcf of natural gas when there is a one-unit increase in the chill index and average hourly temperature does not change.

TABLE 14.2   The Point Predictions and Residuals Using the Least Squares Point Estimates, $b_0 = 13.1087$, $b_1 = -.09001$, and $b_2 = .08249$

Week	Average Hourly Temperature, x_1 (°F)	Chill Index, x_2	Observed Fuel Consumption, y (MMcf)	Predicted Fuel Consumption $\hat{y} = 13.1087 - .09001x_1$ $+ .08249x_2$	Residual, $y - \hat{y}$
1	28.0	18	12.4	12.0733	.3267
2	28.0	14	11.7	11.7433	−.0433
3	32.5	24	12.4	12.1632	.2368
4	39.0	22	10.8	11.4131	−.6131
5	45.9	8	9.4	9.6371	−.2371
6	57.8	16	9.5	9.2259	.2741
7	58.1	1	8.0	7.9614	.0386
8	62.5	0	7.5	7.4829	.0171

$$SSE = (.3267)^2 + (-.0433)^2 + \cdots + (.0171)^2 = .674$$

The equation

$$\hat{y} = b_0 + b_1x_1 + b_2x_2$$
$$= 13.1087 - 0.09001x_1 + 0.08249x_2$$

is called the **least squares prediction equation.** In Table 14.2 we summarize using this prediction equation to calculate the predicted fuel consumptions and the residuals for the eight weeks of fuel consumption data. For example, since in week 1 the average hourly temperature was 28 and the chill index was 18, the predicted fuel consumption for week 1 is

$$\hat{y} = 13.1087 - 0.09001(28.0) + 0.08249(18)$$
$$= 12.0733$$

It follows, since the observed fuel consumption in week 1 was $y = 12.4$, that the residual for week 1 is

$$y - \hat{y} = 12.4 - 12.0733 = .3267$$

If we consider all of the residuals in Table 14.2 and add their squared values, we find that SSE, the sum of squared residuals, is .674. This SSE value is given on the MINITAB and Excel outputs in Figure 14.4 (see [11]) and will be used throughout this chapter.

Part 3: Estimating means and predicting individual values   The least squares prediction equation is the equation of a plane—called the **least squares plane**—in three-dimensional space. The least squares plane is the estimate of the plane of means. It follows that the point on the least squares plane corresponding to the average hourly temperature x_1 and the chill index x_2

$$\hat{y} = b_0 + b_1x_1 + b_2x_2$$
$$= 13.1087 - .09001x_1 + .08249x_2$$

is the point estimate of $\beta_0 + \beta_1x_1 + \beta_2x_2$, the mean fuel consumption for all weeks that have an average hourly temperature of x_1 and a chill index of x_2. In addition, since we predict the error term to be zero, $\hat{y}$ is also the point prediction of $y = \beta_0 + \beta_1x_1 + \beta_2x_2 + \varepsilon$, the amount of fuel consumed in a single week that has an average hourly temperature of x_1 and a chill index of x_2.

For example, suppose a weather forecasting service predicts that in the next week the average hourly temperature will be 40 and the chill index will be 10. It follows that

$$\hat{y} = 13.1087 - .09001(40) + .08249(10)$$
$$= 10.333 \text{ MMcf of natural gas}$$

is

1   The **point estimate** of the mean fuel consumption for all weeks that have an average hourly temperature of 40 and a chill index of 10.

2   The **point prediction** of the amount of fuel consumed in a single week that has an average hourly temperature of 40 and a chill index of 10.

Notice that $\hat{y} = 10.333$ is given at the bottom of the MINITAB output in Figure 14.4 (see ⟨15⟩).

The fuel consumption model expresses the dependent variable as a function of two independent variables. In general, we can use a multiple regression model to express a dependent variable as a function of any number of independent variables. For example, the Cincinnati Gas and Electric Company predicts daily natural gas consumption as a function of four independent variables—average temperature, average wind velocity, average sunlight, and change in average temperature from the previous day. The general form of a multiple regression model expresses the dependent variable y as a function of k independent variables $x_1, x_2, \ldots, x_k$. We express this general form in the following box.

The Multiple Regression Model

The **multiple regression model relating y to $x_1, x_2, \ldots, x_k$ is**

$$y = \beta_0 + \beta_1 x_1 + \beta_2 x_2 + \cdots + \beta_k x_k + \varepsilon$$

Here

1   $\mu_y = \beta_0 + \beta_1 x_1 + \beta_2 x_2 + \cdots + \beta_k x_k$ is the mean value of the dependent variable y when the values of the independent variables are $x_1, x_2, \ldots, x_k$.

2   $\beta_0, \beta_1, \beta_2, \ldots, \beta_k$ are (unknown) **regression parameters** relating the mean value of y to $x_1, x_2, \ldots, x_k$.

3   ε is an **error term** that describes the effects on y of all factors other than the values of the independent variables $x_1, x_2, \ldots, x_k$.

If $b_0, b_1, b_2, \ldots, b_k$ denote point estimates of $\beta_0, \beta_1, \beta_2, \ldots, \beta_k$, then

$$\hat{y} = b_0 + b_1 x_1 + b_2 x_2 + \cdots + b_k x_k$$

is the point estimate of the mean value of the dependent variable when the values of the independent variables are $x_1, x_2, \ldots, x_k$. In addition, since we predict the error term ε to be zero, $\hat{y}$ is also the point prediction of an individual value of the dependent variable when the values of the independent variables are $x_1, x_2, \ldots, x_k$. Now, assume that we have obtained n observations, where each observation consists of an observed value of the dependent variable y and corresponding observed values of the independent variables $x_1, x_2, \ldots, x_k$. For the ith observation, let y_i and $\hat{y}_i$ denote the observed and predicted values of the dependent variable, and define the residual to be $e_i = y_i - \hat{y}_i$. It then follows that the **least squares point estimates** are the values of $b_0, b_1, b_2, \ldots, b_k$ that minimize the sum of squared residuals:

$$SSE = \sum_{i=1}^{n} (y_i - \hat{y}_i)^2$$

As illustrated in Example 14.1, we use MINITAB, Excel, and MegaStat to find the least squares point estimates.

EXAMPLE 14.2 The Sales Territory Performance Case   ◆ SalePerf

Suppose the sales manager of a company wishes to evaluate the performance of the company's sales representatives. Each sales representative is solely responsible for one sales territory, and the manager decides that it is reasonable to measure the performance, y, of a sales representative

TABLE 14.3   **Sales Territory Performance Study Data**   ◐ SalePerf

	Sales, y	Time with Company, x_1	Market Potential, x_2	Advertising, x_3	Market Share, x_4	Market Share Change, x_5
Sales ∕ *Time*	3,669.88	43.10	74,065.11	4,582.88	2.51	0.34
	3,473.95	108.13	58,117.30	5,539.78	5.51	0.15
	2,295.10	13.82	21,118.49	2,950.38	10.91	−0.72
Sales ∕ *MktPoten*	4,675.56	186.18	68,521.27	2,243.07	8.27	0.17
	6,125.96	161.79	57,805.11	7,747.08	9.15	0.50
	2,134.94	8.94	37,806.94	402.44	5.51	0.15
Sales ∕ *Adver*	5,031.66	365.04	50,935.26	3,140.62	8.54	0.55
	3,367.45	220.32	35,602.08	2,086.16	7.07	−0.49
	6,519.45	127.64	46,176.77	8,846.25	12.54	1.24
	4,876.37	105.69	42,053.24	5,673.11	8.85	0.31
	2,468.27	57.72	36,829.71	2,761.76	5.38	0.37
Sales ∕ *MktShare*	2,533.31	23.58	33,612.67	1,991.85	5.43	−0.65
	2,408.11	13.82	21,412.79	1,971.52	8.48	0.64
	2,337.38	13.82	20,416.87	1,737.38	7.80	1.01
	4,586.95	86.99	36,272.00	10,694.20	10.34	0.11
Sales ∕ *Change*	2,729.24	165.85	23,093.26	8,618.61	5.15	0.04
	3,289.40	116.26	26,878.59	7,747.89	6.64	0.68
	2,800.78	42.28	39,571.96	4,565.81	5.45	0.66
	3,264.20	52.84	51,866.15	6,022.70	6.31	−0.10
	3,453.62	165.04	58,749.82	3,721.10	6.35	−0.03
	1,741.45	10.57	23,990.82	860.97	7.37	−1.63
	2,035.75	13.82	25,694.86	3,571.51	8.39	−0.43
	1,578.00	8.13	23,736.35	2,845.50	5.15	0.04
	4,167.44	58.54	34,314.29	5,060.11	12.88	0.22
	2,799.97	21.14	22,809.53	3,552.00	9.14	−0.74

Source: This data set is from a research study published in "An Analytical Approach for Evaluation of Sales Territory Performance," *Journal of Marketing,* January 1972, 31–37 (authors are David W. Cravens, Robert B. Woodruff, and Joseph C. Stamper). We have updated the situation in our case study to be more modern.

by using the yearly sales of the company's product in the representative's sales territory. The manager feels that sales performance y substantially depends on five independent variables:

x_1 = number of months the representative has been employed by the company

x_2 = sales of the company's product and competing products in the sales territory

x_3 = dollar advertising expenditure in the territory

x_4 = weighted average of the company's market share in the territory for the previous four years

x_5 = change in the company's market share in the territory over the previous four years

In Table 14.3 we present values of y and x_1 through x_5 for 25 randomly selected sales representatives. To understand the values of y and x_2 in the table, note that sales of the company's product or any competing product are measured in hundreds of units of the product sold. Therefore, for example, the first sales figure of 3,669.88 in Table 14.3 means that the first randomly selected sales representative sold 366,988 units of the company's product during the year.

Plots of y versus x_1 through x_5 are given on the page margin next to Table 14.3. Since each plot has an approximate straight-line appearance, it is reasonable to relate y to x_1 through x_5 by using the regression model

$$y = \beta_0 + \beta_1 x_1 + \beta_2 x_2 + \beta_3 x_3 + \beta_4 x_4 + \beta_5 x_5 + \varepsilon$$

Here, $\beta_0 + \beta_1 x_1 + \beta_2 x_2 + \beta_3 x_3 + \beta_4 x_4 + \beta_5 x_5$ is, intuitively, the mean sales in all sales territories where the values of the previously described five independent variables are x_1, x_2, x_3, x_4, and x_5. Furthermore, for example, the parameter β_3 equals the increase in mean sales that is associated

FIGURE 14.5   **MegaStat Output of a Regression Analysis of the Sales Territory Performance Data Using the Model** $y = \beta_0 + \beta_1 x_1 + \beta_2 x_2 + \beta_3 x_3 + \beta_4 x_4 + \beta_5 x_5 + \varepsilon$

Regression Analysis

R^2	0.915 [6]	n	25	▨ = significant at .05 level
Adjusted R^2	0.893 [7]	k	5	▨ = significant at .01 level
R	0.957			
Std. Error	430.232 [8]	Dep. Var.	**Sales**	

ANOVA table

Source	SS	df	MS	F	p-value
Regression	37,862,658.9002 [1]	5	7,572,531.7800	40.91 [4]	1.59E-09 [5]
Residual	3,516,890.0266 [2]	19	185,099.4751		
Total	41,379,548.9269 [3]	24			

Regression output

					confidence interval [17]	
variables	coefficients [9]	std. error [10]	t(df=19) [11]	p-value [12]	95% lower	95% upper
Intercept	-1,113.7879	419.8869	-2.653	0.0157	-1,992.6213	-234.9545
Time	3.6121	1.1817	3.057	0.0065	1.1388	6.0854
MktPoten	0.0421	0.0067	6.253	5.27E-06	0.0280	0.0562
Adver	0.1289	0.0370	3.479	0.0025	0.0513	0.2064
MktShare	256.9555	39.1361	6.566	2.76E-06	175.0428	338.8683
Change	324.5334	157.2831	2.063	0.0530	-4.6638	653.7307

Predicted values for: Sales

	95% Confidence Interval [14]		95% Prediction Interval [15]		
Predicted [13]	lower	upper	lower	upper	Leverage [16]
4,181.74333	3,884.90651	4,478.58015	3,233.59431	5,129.89235	0.109

[1] Explained variation	[2] SSE = Unexplained variation	[3] Total variation	[4] F(model)	[5] p-value for F(model)
[6] R^2 [7] Adjusted R^2	[8] s = standard error	[9] b_j = least squares estimate of β_j	[10] s_{b_j} = standard error of the estimate b_j	
[11] t statistics for testing significance of independent variables	[12] p-values for t statistics	[13] $\hat{y}$ = point prediction		
[14] 95% confidence interval	[15] 95% prediction interval	[16] distance value	[17] 95% confidence interval for β_j	

with a \$1 increase in advertising expenditure (x_3) when the other four independent variables do not change. The main objective of the regression analysis is to help the sales manager evaluate sales performance by comparing actual performance to predicted performance. The manager has randomly selected the 25 representatives from all the representatives the company considers to be effective and wishes to use a regression model based on effective representatives to evaluate questionable representatives.

Figure 14.5 gives the MegaStat output of a regression analysis of the sales territory performance data using the five independent variable model. The output tells us that the least squares point estimates of the model parameters are $b_0 = -1,113.7879$, $b_1 = 3.6121$, $b_2 = .0421$, $b_3 = .1289$, $b_4 = 256.9555$, and $b_5 = 324.5334$. Recalling that the sales values in Table 14.3 are measured in hundreds of units of the product sold, the point estimate $b_3 = .1289$ says we estimate that mean sales increase by .1289 hundreds of units—that is, by 12.89 units—for each dollar increase in advertising expenditure when the other four independent variables do not change. If the company sells each unit for \$1.10, this implies that we estimate that mean sales revenue increases by (\$1.10)(12.89) = \$14.18 for each dollar increase in advertising expenditure when the other four independent variables do not change. The other β values in the model can be interpreted similarly.

Consider a questionable sales representative for whom Time = 85.42, MktPoten = 35,182.73, Adver = 7,281.65, MktShare = 9.64, and Change = .28. The point prediction of the sales corresponding to this combination of values of the independent variables is

$$\hat{y} = -1,113.7879 + 3.6121(85.42) + .0421(35,182.73)$$
$$+ .1289(7,281.65) + 256.9555(9.64) + 324.5334(.28)$$
$$= 4,181.74 \text{ (that is, } 418,174 \text{ units)}$$

which is given on the MegaStat output. The actual sales for the questionable sales representative were 3,087.52. This sales figure is 1,094.22 less than the point prediction $\hat{y} = 4,181.74$. However, we will have to wait until we study prediction intervals in multiple regression (see Section 14.6) to determine whether there is strong evidence that this sales figure is unusually low.

To conclude this section, consider an arbitrary independent variable, which we will denote as x_j, in a multiple regression model. We can then interpret the parameter β_j to be the change in the mean value of the dependent variable that is associated with a one-unit increase in x_j when the other independent variables in the model do not change. This interpretation is based, however, on the assumption that x_j can increase by one unit without the other independent variables in the model changing. In some situations (as we will see) this assumption is not true.

Exercises for Section 14.1

CONCEPTS

14.1   In the multiple regression model, what sum of squared deviations do the least squares point estimates minimize?

14.2   When using the multiple regression model, how do we obtain a point estimate of the mean value of the dependent variable and a point prediction of an individual value of the dependent variable?

METHODS AND APPLICATIONS

14.3   **THE REAL ESTATE SALES PRICE CASE**   RealEst2

A real estate agency collects the data in Table 14.4 concerning

y = sales price of a house (in thousands of dollars)

x_1 = home size (in hundreds of square feet)

x_2 = rating (an overall "niceness rating" for the house expressed on a scale from 1 [worst] to 10 [best], and provided by the real estate agency)

The agency wishes to develop a regression model that can be used to predict the sales prices of future houses it will list. Figures 14.6 and 14.7 on the next page give the MINITAB and Excel output of a regression analysis of the real estate sales price data in Table 14.4 using the model

$$y = \beta_0 + \beta_1 x_1 + \beta_2 x_2 + \varepsilon$$

a   Using the MINITAB or Excel output, identify and interpret b_1 and b_2, the least squares point estimates of β_1 and β_2.

b   Calculate a point estimate of the mean sales price of all houses having 2,000 square feet and a rating of 8, and a point prediction of the sales price of an individual house having 2,000 square feet and a rating of 8. Find this point estimate (prediction), which is given at the bottom of the MINITAB output.

14.4   **THE FRESH DETERGENT CASE**   Fresh2

Enterprise Industries produces Fresh, a brand of liquid laundry detergent. In order to manage its inventory more effectively and make revenue projections, the company would like to better predict demand for Fresh. To develop a prediction model, the company has gathered data concerning demand for Fresh over the last 30 sales periods (each sales period is defined to be a four-week period). The demand data are presented in Table 14.5. Here, for each sales period,

y = the demand for the large size bottle of Fresh (in hundreds of thousands of bottles) in the sales period

x_1 = the price (in dollars) of Fresh as offered by Enterprise Industries in the sales period

x_2 = the average industry price (in dollars) of competitors' similar detergents in the sales period

x_3 = Enterprise Industries' advertising expenditure (in hundreds of thousands of dollars) to promote Fresh in the sales period

TABLE 14.4

The Real Estate Sales Price Data   RealEst2

Sales Price (y)	Home Size (x_1)	Rating (x_2)
180	23	5
98.1	11	2
173.1	20	9
136.5	17	3
141	15	8
165.9	21	4
193.5	24	7
127.8	13	6
163.5	19	7
172.5	25	2

Source: R. L. Andrews and J. T. Ferguson, "Integrating Judgement with a Regression Appraisal," *The Real Estate Appraiser and Analyst* 52, no. 2 (1986). Reprinted by permission.

```
The regression equation is
SalesPrice = 29.3 + 5.61 HomeSize + 3.83 Rating

Predictor     Coef   SE Coef      T       P
Constant    29.347     4.891    6.00   0.001
HomeSize    5.6128    0.2285   24.56   0.000
Rating      3.8344    0.4332    8.85   0.000

S = 3.24164   R-Sq = 99.0%   R-Sq(adj) = 98.7%

Analysis of Variance
Source          DF        SS       MS       F       P
Regression       2    7374.0   3687.0  350.87   0.000
Residual Error   7      73.6     10.5
Total            9    7447.5

Values of Predictors for New Obs    Predicted Values for New Observations
New Obs   HomeSize   Rating        New Obs      Fit   SE Fit       95% CI              95% PI
      1       20.0     8.00              1   172.28     1.57  (168.56, 175.99)  (163.76, 180.80)
```

Regression Statistics

Multiple R	0.9950
R Square	0.9901
Adjusted R Square	0.9873
Standard Error	3.2416
Observations	10

ANOVA	df	SS	MS	F	Significance F
Regression	2	7373.9516	3686.9758	350.8665	9.58E-08
Residual	7	73.5574	10.5082		
Total	9	7447.5090			

	Coefficients	Standard Error	t Stat	P-value	Lower 95%	Upper 95%
Intercept	29.3468	4.8914	5.9996	0.0005	17.7804	40.9132
Home Size (x1)	5.6128	0.2285	24.5615	4.73E-08	5.0724	6.1532
Rating (x2)	3.8344	0.4332	8.8514	4.75E-05	2.8101	4.8588

Figure 14.8 gives the MegaStat output of a regression analysis of the Fresh Detergent demand data in Table 14.5 using the model

$$y = \beta_0 + \beta_1 x_1 + \beta_2 x_2 + \beta_3 x_3 + \varepsilon$$

a Find (on the output) and report the values of b_1, b_2, and b_3, the least squares point estimates of β_1, β_2, and β_3. Interpret b_1, b_2, and b_3.

b Consider the demand for Fresh Detergent in a future sales period when Enterprise Industries' price for Fresh will be $x_1 = 3.70$, the average price of competitors' similar detergents will be $x_2 = 3.90$ and Enterprise Industries' advertising expenditure for Fresh will be $x_3 = 6.50$. The point prediction of this demand is given at the bottom of the MegaStat output. Report this point prediction and show how it has been calculated.

TABLE 14.5   Historical Data Concerning Demand for Fresh Detergent   ● Fresh2

Sales Period	Price for Fresh, x_1	Average Industry Price, x_2	Advertising Expenditure for Fresh, x_3	Demand for Fresh, y	Sales Period	Price for Fresh, x_1	Average Industry Price, x_2	Advertising Expenditure for Fresh, x_3	Demand for Fresh, y
1	3.85	3.80	5.50	7.38	16	3.80	4.10	6.80	8.87
2	3.75	4.00	6.75	8.51	17	3.70	4.20	7.10	9.26
3	3.70	4.30	7.25	9.52	18	3.80	4.30	7.00	9.00
4	3.70	3.70	5.50	7.50	19	3.70	4.10	6.80	8.75
5	3.60	3.85	7.00	9.33	20	3.80	3.75	6.50	7.95
6	3.60	3.80	6.50	8.28	21	3.80	3.75	6.25	7.65
7	3.60	3.75	6.75	8.75	22	3.75	3.65	6.00	7.27
8	3.80	3.85	5.25	7.87	23	3.70	3.90	6.50	8.00
9	3.80	3.65	5.25	7.10	24	3.55	3.65	7.00	8.50
10	3.85	4.00	6.00	8.00	25	3.60	4.10	6.80	8.75
11	3.90	4.10	6.50	7.89	26	3.65	4.25	6.80	9.21
12	3.90	4.00	6.25	8.15	27	3.70	3.65	6.50	8.27
13	3.70	4.10	7.00	9.10	28	3.75	3.75	5.75	7.67
14	3.75	4.20	6.90	8.86	29	3.80	3.85	5.80	7.93
15	3.75	4.10	6.80	8.90	30	3.70	4.25	6.80	9.26

FIGURE 14.8   MegaStat Output of a Regression Analysis of the Fresh Detergent Demand Data Using the Model $y = \beta_0 + \beta_1 x_1 + \beta_2 x_2 + \beta_3 x_3 + \varepsilon$

Regression Analysis

R^2	0.894		
Adjusted R^2	0.881	n	30
R	0.945	k	3
Std. Error	0.235	Dep. Var.	**Demand (y)**

ANOVA table

Source	SS	df	MS	F	p-value
Regression	12.0268	3	4.0089	72.80	8.88E-13
Residual	1.4318	26	0.0551		
Total	13.4586	29			

Regression output

variables	coefficients	std. error	t (df = 26)	p-value	confidence interval 95% lower	95% upper
Intercept	7.5891	2.4450	3.104	0.0046	2.5633	12.6149
Price (x1)	-2.3577	0.6379	-3.696	0.0010	-3.6690	-1.0464
IndPrice (x2)	1.6122	0.2954	5.459	1.01E-05	1.0051	2.2193
AdvExp (x3)	0.5012	0.1259	3.981	0.0005	0.2424	0.7599

Predicted values for: Demand (y)

Price (x1)	IndPrice (x2)	AdvExp (x3)	Predicted	95% Confidence Interval lower	upper	95% Prediction Interval lower	upper	Leverage
3.7	3.9	6.5	8.4107	8.3143	8.5070	7.9188	8.9025	0.040

14.5 THE HOSPITAL LABOR NEEDS CASE   ● HospLab

Table 14.6 presents data concerning the need for labor in 16 U.S. Navy hospitals. Here, y = monthly labor hours required; x_1 = monthly X-ray exposures; x_2 = monthly occupied bed days (a hospital has one occupied bed day if one bed is occupied for an entire day); and x_3 = average length of patients' stay (in days). Figure 14.9 gives the Excel and MegaStat output of a

TABLE 14.6   Hospital Labor Needs Data   ● HospLab

Hospital	Monthly X-Ray Exposures, x_1	Monthly Occupied Bed Days, x_2	Average Length of Stay, x_3	Monthly Labor Hours Required, y
1	2,463	472.92	4.45	566.52
2	2,048	1,339.75	6.92	696.82
3	3,940	620.25	4.28	1,033.15
4	6,505	568.33	3.90	1,603.62
5	5,723	1,497.60	5.50	1,611.37
6	11,520	1,365.83	4.60	1,613.27
7	5,779	1,687.00	5.62	1,854.17
8	5,969	1,639.92	5.15	2,160.55
9	8,461	2,872.33	6.18	2,305.58
10	20,106	3,655.08	6.15	3,503.93
11	13,313	2,912.00	5.88	3,571.89
12	10,771	3,921.00	4.88	3,741.40
13	15,543	3,865.67	5.50	4,026.52
14	34,703	12,446.33	10.78	11,732.17
15	39,204	14,098.40	7.05	15,414.94
16	86,533	15,524.00	6.35	18,854.45

Source: *Procedures and Analysis for Staffing Standards Development Regression Analysis Handbook* (San Diego, CA: Navy Manpower and Material Analysis Center, 1979).

FIGURE 14.9   Excel and MegaStat Output of a Regression Analysis of the Hospital Labor Needs Data Using the Model $y = \beta_0 + \beta_1 x_1 + \beta_2 x_2 + \beta_3 x_3 + \varepsilon$

(a) The Excel output

Regression Statistics

Multiple R	0.9981
R Square	0.9961
Adjusted R Square	0.9952
Standard Error	387.1598
Observations	16

ANOVA	df	SS	MS	F	Significance F
Regression	3	462327889.4	154109296.5	1028.1309	9.92E-15
Residual	12	1798712.2	149892.7		
Total	15	464126601.6			

	Coefficients	Standard Error	t Stat	P-value	Lower 95%	Upper 95%
Intercept	1946.8020	504.1819	3.8613	0.0023	848.2840	3045.3201
XRay (x1)	0.0386	0.0130	2.9579	0.0120	0.0102	0.0670
BedDays (x2)	1.0394	0.0676	15.3857	2.91E-09	0.8922	1.1866
LengthStay (x3)	-413.7578	98.5983	-4.1964	0.0012	-628.5850	-198.9306

(b) Prediction Using MegaStat

Predicted values for: LaborHours

XRay (x1)	BedDays (x2)	LengthStay (x3)	Predicted	95% Confidence Interval lower	upper	95% Prediction Interval lower	upper	Leverage
56194	14077.88	6.89	15,896.2473	15,378.0313	16,414.4632	14,906.2361	16,886.2584	0.3774

regression analysis of the data using the model

$$y = \beta_0 + \beta_1 x_1 + \beta_2 x_2 + \beta_3 x_3 + \varepsilon$$

Note that the variables x_1, x_2, and x_3 are denoted as XRay, BedDays, and LengthStay on the output.

a Find (on the output) and interpret b_1, b_2, and b_3, the least squares point estimates of β_1, β_2, and β_3.

b Consider a questionable hospital for which XRay = 56,194, BedDays = 14,077.88, and LengthStay = 6.89. A point prediction of the labor hours corresponding to this combination of values of the independent variables is given on the MegaStat output. Report this point prediction and show how it has been calculated.

c If the actual number of labor hours used by the questionable hospital was $y = 17,207.31$, how does this y value compare with the point prediction?

14.2 Model Assumptions and the Standard Error ●●●

Model assumptions   In order to perform hypothesis tests and set up various types of intervals when using the multiple regression model

$$y = \beta_0 + \beta_1 x_1 + \beta_2 x_2 + \cdots + \beta_k x_k + \varepsilon$$

CHAPTER 17

we need to make certain assumptions about the error term ε. At any given combination of values of $x_1, x_2, \ldots, x_k$, there is a population of error term values that could potentially occur. These error term values describe the different potential effects on y of all factors other than the combination of values of $x_1, x_2, \ldots, x_k$. Therefore, these error term values explain the variation in the y values that could be observed at the combination of values of $x_1, x_2, \ldots, x_k$. We make the following four assumptions about the potential error term values:

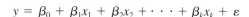

Assumptions for the Multiple Regression Model

1 At any given combination of values of x_1, $x_2, \ldots, x_k$, the population of potential error term values has a mean equal to zero.

2 **Constant variance assumption:** At any given combination of values of $x_1, x_2, \ldots, x_k$, the population of potential error term values has a variance that does not depend on the combination of values of $x_1, x_2, \ldots, x_k$. That is, the different populations of potential error term values corresponding to different combinations of values of $x_1, x_2, \ldots, x_k$ have equal variances. We denote the constant variance as σ^2.

3 **Normality assumption:** At any given combination of values of $x_1, x_2, \ldots, x_k$, the population of potential error term values has a **normal distribution**.

4 **Independence assumption:** Any one value of the error term ε is **statistically independent** of any other value of ε. That is, the value of the error term ε corresponding to an observed value of y is statistically independent of the error term corresponding to any other observed value of y.

Taken together, the first three assumptions say that, at any given combination of values of x_1, $x_2, \ldots, x_k$, the population of potential error term values is normally distributed with mean zero and a variance σ^2 that does not depend on the combination of values of $x_1, x_2, \ldots, x_k$. Because the potential error term values cause the variation in the potential y values, the first three assumptions imply that, at any given combination of values of $x_1, x_2, \ldots, x_k$, the population of y values that could be observed is normally distributed with mean $\beta_0 + \beta_1 x_1 + \beta_2 x_2 + \cdots + \beta_k x_k$ and a variance σ^2 that does not depend on the combination of values of $x_1, x_2, \ldots, x_k$. Furthermore, the independence assumption says that, when time series data are utilized in a regression study, there are no patterns in the error term values. In Section 14.9 we show how to check the validity of the regression assumptions. That section can be read at any time after Section 14.6. As in simple linear regression, only pronounced departures from the assumptions must be remedied.

The mean square error and the standard error   To present statistical inference formulas in later sections, we need to be able to compute point estimates of σ^2 and σ (the constant variance and standard deviation of the different error term populations). We show how to do this in the following box:

The Mean Square Error and the Standard Error

Suppose that the multiple regression model

$$y = \beta_0 + \beta_1 x_1 + \beta_2 x_2 + \cdots + \beta_k x_k + \varepsilon$$

utilizes k independent variables and thus has $(k + 1)$ parameters $\beta_0, \beta_1, \beta_2, \ldots, \beta_k$. Then, if the regression assumptions are satisfied, and if SSE denotes the sum of squared residuals for the model:

1 A point estimate of σ^2 is the **mean square error**

$$s^2 = \frac{SSE}{n - (k + 1)}$$

2 A point estimate of σ is the **standard error**

$$s = \sqrt{\frac{SSE}{n - (k + 1)}}$$

In order to explain these point estimates, recall that σ^2 is the variance of the population of y values (for given values of $x_1, x_2, \ldots, x_k$) around the mean value μ_y. Since $\hat{y}$ is the point estimate of this mean, it seems natural to use $SSE = \Sigma(y_i - \hat{y}_i)^2$ to help construct a point estimate of σ^2. We divide SSE by $n - (k + 1)$ because it can be proven that doing so makes the resulting s^2 an unbiased point estimate of σ^2. We call $n - (k + 1)$ the **number of degrees of freedom** associated with SSE.

We will see in Section 14.6 that if a particular regression model gives a small standard error, then the model will give short prediction intervals and thus accurate predictions of individual y

● FuelCon2   values. For example, Table 14.2 (page 573) shows that SSE for the fuel consumption model

$$y = \beta_0 + \beta_1 x_1 + \beta_2 x_2 + \varepsilon$$

is .674. Since this model utilizes $k = 2$ independent variables and thus has $k + 1 = 3$ parameters (β_0, β_1, and β_2), a point estimate of σ^2 is the mean square error

$$s^2 = \frac{SSE}{n - (k + 1)} = \frac{.674}{8 - 3} = \frac{.674}{5} = .1348$$

and a point estimate of σ is the standard error $s = \sqrt{.1348} = .3671$. Note that $SSE = .674$, $s^2 = .1348 \approx .135$, and $s = .3671$ are given on the MINITAB and Excel outputs in Figure 14.4 (page 572). Also note that the s of .3671 for the two independent variable model is less than the s of .6542 for the simple linear regression model that uses only the average hourly temperature to predict weekly fuel consumption (see Example 13.5, page 516).

● SalePerf   As another example, the SSE for the sales territory performance model

$$y = \beta_0 + \beta_1 x_1 + \beta_2 x_2 + \beta_3 x_3 + \beta_4 x_4 + \beta_5 x_5 + \varepsilon$$

is 3,516,890.0266. Since this model utilizes $k = 5$ independent variables and thus has $k + 1 = 6$ parameters, a point estimate of σ^2 is the mean square error

$$s^2 = \frac{SSE}{n - (k + 1)} = \frac{3,516,890.0266}{25 - 6} = 185,099.4751$$

and a point estimate of σ is the standard error $s = \sqrt{185,099.4751} = 430.232$. Note that these values of SSE, s^2, and s are given on the MegaStat output in Figure 14.5 (page 576).

14.3 R^2 and Adjusted R^2 ◦●●

The multiple coefficient of determination, R^2   In this section we discuss several ways to assess the utility of a multiple regression model. We first discuss a quantity called the **multiple coefficient of determination,** which is denoted **R^2**. The formulas for R^2 and several other related quantities are given in the following box:

The Multiple Coefficient of Determination, R^2

For the multiple regression model:

1. **Total variation** $= \sum (y_i - \bar{y})^2$
2. **Explained variation** $= \sum (\hat{y}_i - \bar{y})^2$
3. **Unexplained variation** $= \sum (y_i - \hat{y}_i)^2$
4. **Total variation = Explained variation + Unexplained variation**

5. The **multiple coefficient of determination** is

$$R^2 = \frac{\text{Explained variation}}{\text{Total variation}}$$

6. R^2 is the proportion of the total variation in the n observed values of the dependent variable that is explained by the overall regression model.

7. **Multiple correlation coefficient** $= R = \sqrt{R^2}$

As an example, consider the fuel consumption model   ● FuelCon2

$$y = \beta_0 + \beta_1 x_1 + \beta_2 x_2 + \varepsilon$$

and the following MINITAB output:

```
S = 0.367078    R-Sq = 97.4%    R-Sq(adj) = 96.3%

Analysis of Variance
Source           DF      SS       MS       F       P
Regression        2   24.875   12.438   92.30   0.000
Residual Error    5    0.674    0.135
Total             7   25.549
```

This output tells us that the total variation (SS Total), explained variation (SS Regression), and unexplained variation (SS Residual Error) for the model are, respectively, 25.549, 24.875, and .674. The output also tells us that the multiple coefficient of determination is

$$R^2 = \frac{\text{Explained variation}}{\text{Total variation}} = \frac{24.875}{25.549} = .974 \quad (97.4\% \text{ on the output})$$

which implies that the multiple correlation coefficient is $R = \sqrt{.974} = .9869$. The value of $R^2 = .974$ says that the two independent variable fuel consumption model explains 97.4 percent of the total variation in the eight observed fuel consumptions. Note this R^2 value is larger than the r^2 of .899 for the simple linear regression model that uses only the average hourly temperature to predict weekly fuel consumption. Also note that the quantities given on the MINITAB output are given on the following Excel output.

Regression Statistics

Multiple R	0.9867
R Square	0.9736
Adjusted R Square	0.9631
Standard Error	0.3671
Observations	8

ANOVA	df	SS	MS	F	Significance F
Regression	2	24.8750	12.4375	92.3031	0.0001
Residual	5	0.6737	0.1347		
Total	7	25.5488			

● SalePerf   As another example, consider the sales territory performance model

$$y = \beta_0 + \beta_1 x_1 + \beta_2 x_2 + \beta_3 x_3 + \beta_4 x_4 + \beta_5 x_5 + \varepsilon$$

and the following MegaStat output

Regression Analysis

R^2	0.915		
Adjusted R^2	0.893	n	25
R	0.957	k	5
Std. Error	430.232	Dep. Var.	**Sales**

ANOVA table

Source	SS	df	MS	F	p-value
Regression	37,862,658.9002	5	7,572,531.7800	40.91	1.59E-09
Residual	3,516,890.0266	19	185,099.4751		
Total	41,379,548.9269	24			

This output tells us that the total, explained, and unexplained variations for the model are, respectively, 41,379,548.9269, 37,862,658.9002, and 3,516,890.0266. The MegaStat output also tells us that R^2 equals .915.

Adjusted R^2   Even if the independent variables in a regression model are unrelated to the dependent variable, they will make R^2 somewhat greater than zero. To avoid overestimating the importance of the independent variables, many analysts recommend calculating an *adjusted* multiple coefficient of determination.

Adjusted R^2

The **adjusted multiple coefficient of determination (adjusted R^2)** is

$$\overline{R}^2 = \left(R^2 - \frac{k}{n-1} \right)\left(\frac{n-1}{n-(k+1)} \right)$$

where R^2 is the multiple coefficient of determination, n is the number of observations, and k is the number of independent variables in the model under consideration.

To briefly explain this formula, note that it can be shown that subtracting $k/(n-1)$ from R^2 helps avoid overestimating the importance of the k independent variables. Furthermore, multiplying $[R^2 - (k/(n-1))]$ by $(n-1)/(n-(k+1))$ makes $\overline{R}^2$ equal to 1 when R^2 equals 1.

● FuelCon2   As an example, consider the fuel consumption model

$$y = \beta_0 + \beta_1 x_1 + \beta_2 x_2 + \varepsilon$$

Since we have seen that $R^2 = .974$, it follows that

$$\overline{R}^2 = \left(R^2 - \frac{k}{n-1} \right)\left(\frac{n-1}{n-(k+1)} \right)$$

$$= \left(.974 - \frac{2}{8-1} \right)\left(\frac{8-1}{8-(2+1)} \right)$$

$$= .963$$

which is given on the MINITAB and Excel output. Similarly, in addition to telling us that $R^2 = .915$ for the five independent variable sales territory performance model, the MegaStat output tells us that $\overline{R}^2 = .893$ for this model.

If R^2 is less than $k/(n-1)$ (which can happen), then $\overline{R}^2$ will be negative. In this case, statistical software systems set $\overline{R}^2$ equal to 0. Historically, R^2 and $\overline{R}^2$ have been popular measures of model utility—possibly because they are unitless and between 0 and 1. In general, we desire R^2 and $\overline{R}^2$ to be near 1. However, sometimes even if a regression model has an R^2 and an $\overline{R}^2$ that are near 1, the model is still not able to predict accurately. We will discuss assessing a model's ability to predict accurately, as well as using R^2 and $\overline{R}^2$ to help choose a regression model, as we proceed through this chapter.

14.4 The Overall *F* Test ●●●

Another way to assess the utility of a regression model is to test the significance of the regression relationship between y and $x_1, x_2, \ldots, x_k$. For the multiple regression model, we test the null hypothesis $H_0: \beta_1 = \beta_2 = \cdots = \beta_k = 0$, which says that **none of the independent variables x_1, $x_2, \ldots, x_k$ is significantly related to y (the regression relationship is not significant),** versus the alternative hypothesis H_a: At least one of $\beta_1, \beta_2, \ldots, \beta_k$ does not equal zero, which says that **at least one of the independent variables is significantly related to y (the regression relationship is significant).** If we can reject H_0 at level of significance α, we say that **the multiple regression model is significant at level of significance α.** We carry out the test as follows:

An *F* Test for the Multiple Regression Model

Suppose that the regression assumptions hold and that the multiple regression model has $(k + 1)$ parameters, and consider testing

$$H_0: \beta_1 = \beta_2 = \cdots = \beta_k = 0$$

versus

H_a: At least one of $\beta_1, \beta_2, \ldots, \beta_k$ does not equal zero.

We define the **overall *F* statistic** to be

$$F(\text{model}) = \frac{(\text{Explained variation})/k}{(\text{Unexplained variation})/[n - (k + 1)]}$$

Also define the *p*-value related to $F(\text{model})$ to be the area under the curve of the *F* distribution (having k and $[n - (k + 1)]$ degrees of freedom) to the right of $F(\text{model})$. Then, we can reject H_0 in favor of H_a at level of significance α if either of the following equivalent conditions holds:

1 $F(\text{model}) > F_\alpha$

2 *p*-value $< \alpha$

Here the point F_α is based on k numerator and $n - (k + 1)$ denominator degrees of freedom.

Condition 1 is intuitively reasonable because a large value of $F(\text{model})$ would be caused by an explained variation that is large relative to the unexplained variation. This would occur if at least one independent variable in the regression model significantly affects y, which would imply that H_0 is false and H_a is true.

EXAMPLE 14.3 The Fuel Consumption Case ● FuelCon2

Consider the fuel consumption model

$$y = \beta_0 + \beta_1 x_1 + \beta_2 x_2 + \varepsilon$$

and the following MINITAB output.

```
Analysis of Variance
Source          DF       SS       MS       F       P
Regression       2   24.875   12.438   92.30   0.000
Residual Error   5    0.674    0.135
Total            7   25.549
```

This output tells us that the explained and unexplained variations for this model are, respectively, 24.875 and .674. It follows, since there are $k = 2$ independent variables, that

$$F(\text{model}) = \frac{(\text{Explained variation})/k}{(\text{Unexplained variation})/[n - (k + 1)]}$$

$$= \frac{24.875/2}{.674/[8 - (2 + 1)]} = \frac{12.438}{.135}$$

$$= 92.30$$

Note that this overall F statistic is given on the MINITAB output and is also given on the following Excel output:

ANOVA	df	SS	MS	F	Significance F
Regression	2	24.8750	12.4375	92.3031	0.0001
Residual	5	0.6737	0.1347		
Total	7	25.5488			

The p-value related to F(model) is the area to the right of 92.30 under the curve of the F distribution having $k = 2$ numerator and $n - (k + 1) = 8 - 3 = 5$ denominator degrees of freedom. Both the MINITAB and Excel output say this p-value is less than .001.

If we wish to test the significance of the regression model at level of significance $\alpha = .05$, we use the critical value $F_{.05}$ based on 2 numerator and 5 denominator degrees of freedom. Using Table A.6 (page 645), we find that $F_{.05} = 5.79$. Since F(model) $= 92.30 > F_{.05} = 5.79$, we can reject H_0 in favor of H_a at level of significance .05. Alternatively, since the p-value is smaller than .05, .01, and .001, we can reject H_0 at level of significance .05, .01, and .001. Therefore, we have extremely strong evidence that the fuel consumption model is significant. That is, we have extremely strong evidence that at least one of the independent variables x_1 and x_2 in the model is significantly related to y.

SalePerf   Similarly, consider the following MegaStat output:

ANOVA table					
Source	SS	df	MS	F	p-value
Regression	37,862,658.9002	5	7,572,531.7800	40.91	1.59E-09
Residual	3,516,890.0266	19	185,099.4751		
Total	41,379,548.9269	24			

This output tells us that F(model) $= 40.91$ for the five independent variable sales territory performance model. Furthermore, since the MegaStat output also tells us that the p-value related to F(model) is less than .001, we have extremely strong evidence that at least one of the five independent variables in this model is significantly related to sales territory performance.

If the overall F test tells us that at least one independent variable in a regression model is significant, we next attempt to decide which independent variables are significant. In the next section we discuss one way to do this.

Exercises for Sections 14.2, 14.3, and 14.4

CONCEPTS

connect™

14.6 What is estimated by the mean square error, and what is estimated by the standard error?

14.7 **a** What do R^2 and $\overline{R}^2$ measure?   **b** How do R^2 and $\overline{R}^2$ differ?

14.8 What is the purpose of the overall F test?

METHODS AND APPLICATIONS

In Exercises 14.9 to 14.11 we give MINITAB, MegaStat, and Excel output of regression analyses of the data sets related to three case studies introduced in Section 14.1. Above each output we give the regression model and the number of observations, n, used to perform the regression analysis under consideration. Using the appropriate model, sample size n, and output:

a   Report SSE, s^2, and s as shown on the output. Calculate s^2 from SSE and other numbers.

b   Report the total variation, unexplained variation, and explained variation as shown on the output.

c   Report R^2 and $\overline{R}^2$ as shown on the output. Interpret R^2 and $\overline{R}^2$. Show how $\overline{R}^2$ has been calculated from R^2 and other numbers.

d   Calculate the F(model) statistic by using the explained variation, the unexplained variation, and other relevant quantities. Find F(model) on the output to check your answer (within rounding).

e   Use the F(model) statistic and the appropriate critical value to test the significance of the linear regression model under consideration by setting α equal to .05.

f   Use the F(model) statistic and the appropriate critical value to test the significance of the linear regression model under consideration by setting α equal to .01.

g   Find the p-value related to F(model) on the output. Using the p-value, test the significance of the linear regression model by setting $\alpha = .10, .05, .01$, and $.001$. What do you conclude?

14.9   THE REAL ESTATE SALES PRICE CASE   ● RealEst2

Model: $y = \beta_0 + \beta_1 x_1 + \beta_2 x_2 + \varepsilon$ Sample size: $n = 10$

```
S = 3.24164    R-Sq = 99.0%    R-Sq(adj) = 98.7%


Analysis of Variance
Source           DF      SS       MS       F       P
Regression        2   7374.0   3687.0   350.87   0.000
Residual Error    7     73.6     10.5
Total             9   7447.5
```

14.10   THE FRESH DETERGENT CASE   ● Fresh2

Model: $y = \beta_0 + \beta_1 x_1 + \beta_2 x_2 + \beta_3 x_3 + \varepsilon$ Sample size: $n = 30$

Regression Analysis

R^2	0.894			
Adjusted R^2	0.881		n	30
R	0.945		k	3
Std. Error	0.235		Dep. Var.	**Demand (y)**

ANOVA table

Source	SS	df	MS	F	p-value
Regression	12.0268	3	4.0089	72.80	8.88E-13
Residual	1.4318	26	0.0551		
Total	13.4586	29			

14.11   THE HOSPITAL LABOR NEEDS CASE   ● HospLab

Model: $y = \beta_0 + \beta_1 x_1 + \beta_2 x_2 + \beta_3 x_3 + \varepsilon$ Sample size: $n = 16$

Regression Statistics

Multiple R	0.9981
R Square	0.9961
Adjusted R Square	0.9952
Standard Error	387.1598
Observations	16

ANOVA	df	SS	MS	F	Significance F
Regression	3	462327889.4	154109296.5	1028.1309	9.92E-15
Residual	12	1798712.2	149892.7		
Total	15	464126601.6			

14.5 Testing the Significance of an Independent Variable ◦●●

Consider the multiple regression model

$$y = \beta_0 + \beta_1 x_1 + \beta_2 x_2 + \cdots + \beta_k x_k + \varepsilon$$

In order to gain information about which independent variables significantly affect y, we can test the significance of a single independent variable. We arbitrarily refer to this variable as x_j and assume that it is multiplied by the parameter β_j. For example, if $j = 1$, we are testing the significance of x_1, which is multiplied by β_1; if $j = 2$, we are testing the significance of x_2, which is

CHAPTER 17

multiplied by β_2. To test the significance of x_j, we test the null hypothesis H_0: $\beta_j = 0$. We usually test H_0 versus the alternative hypothesis H_a: $\beta_j \neq 0$. **It is reasonable to conclude that x_j is significantly related to y in the regression model under consideration if H_0 can be rejected in favor of H_a at a small level of significance.** Here the phrase *in the regression model under consideration* is very important. This is because it can be shown that whether x_j is significantly related to y in a particular regression model can depend on what other independent variables are included in the model. This issue will be discussed in detail in Section 14.8.

Testing the significance of x_j in a multiple regression model is similar to testing the significance of the slope in the simple linear regression model (recall we test H_0: $\beta_1 = 0$ in simple regression). It can be proved that, if the regression assumptions hold, the population of all possible values of the least squares point estimate b_j is normally distributed with mean β_j and standard deviation σ_{b_j}. The point estimate of σ_{b_j} is called the **standard error of the estimate b_j** and is denoted s_{b_j}. The formula for s_{b_j} involves matrix algebra and is discussed in Appendix G of the CD-ROM included with this book. In our discussion here, we will rely on MINITAB, MegaStat, and Excel to compute s_{b_j}. It can be shown that, if the regression assumptions hold, then the population of all possible values of

$$\frac{b_j - \beta_j}{s_{b_j}}$$

has a t distribution with $n - (k + 1)$ degrees of freedom. It follows that, if the null hypothesis H_0: $\beta_j = 0$ is true, then the population of all possible values of the test statistic

$$t = \frac{b_j}{s_{b_j}}$$

has a t distribution with $n - (k + 1)$ degrees of freedom. Therefore, we can test the significance of x_j as follows:

Testing the Significance of the Independent Variable x_j

Define the test statistic

$$t = \frac{b_j}{s_{b_j}}$$

and suppose that the regression assumptions hold. Then we can test H_0: $\beta_j = 0$ versus a particular alternative hypothesis at significance level α by using the appropriate critical value rule, or, equivalently, the corresponding p-value.

Alternative Hypothesis	Critical Value Rule: Reject H_0 If	p-Value (Reject H_0 If p-Value $< \alpha$)
H_a: $\beta_j \neq 0$	$\lvert t \rvert > t_{\alpha/2}$	Twice the area under the t curve to the right of $\lvert t \rvert$
H_a: $\beta_j > 0$	$t > t_\alpha$	The area under the t curve to the right of t
H_a: $\beta_j < 0$	$t < -t_\alpha$	The area under the t curve to the left of t

Here $t_{\alpha/2}$, t_α, and all p-values are based on $n - (k + 1)$ degrees of freedom.

As in testing H_0: $\beta_1 = 0$ in simple linear regression, we usually use the two-sided alternative hypothesis H_a: $\beta_j \neq 0$ unless we have theoretical reasons to believe that β_j has a particular (plus or minus) sign. Moreover, MINITAB, MegaStat, and Excel present the results for the two-sided test.

It is customary to test the significance of each and every independent variable in a regression model. Generally speaking,

1   If we can reject H_0: $\beta_j = 0$ at the .05 level of significance, we have strong evidence that the independent variable x_j is significantly related to y in the regression model.

2   If we can reject H_0: $\beta_j = 0$ at the .01 level of significance, we have very strong evidence that x_j is significantly related to y in the regression model.

3   The smaller the significance level α at which H_0 can be rejected, the stronger is the evidence that x_j is significantly related to y in the regression model.

TABLE 14.7 *t* Statistics and *p*-Values for Testing the Significance of the Intercept, x_1, and x_2 in the Fuel Consumption Model $y = \beta_0 + \beta_1 x_1 + \beta_2 x_2 + \varepsilon$

(a) Calculation of the *t* statistics

Independent Variable	Null Hypothesis	b_j	s_{b_j}	$t = \dfrac{b_j}{s_{b_j}}$	*p*-Value
Intercept	$H_0: \beta_0 = 0$	$b_0 = 13.1087$	$s_{b_0} = .8557$	$t = \dfrac{b_0}{s_{b_0}} = \dfrac{13.1087}{.8557} = 15.32$	.000
x_1	$H_0: \beta_1 = 0$	$b_1 = -0.09001$	$s_{b_1} = .01408$	$t = \dfrac{b_1}{s_{b_1}} = \dfrac{-.09001}{.01408} = -6.39$	.001
x_2	$H_0: \beta_2 = 0$	$b_2 = 0.08249$	$s_{b_2} = .02200$	$t = \dfrac{b_2}{s_{b_2}} = \dfrac{.08249}{.02200} = 3.75$	.013

(b) The MINITAB output

```
Predictor      Coef  SE Coef       T       P
Constant    13.1087   0.8557   15.32   0.000
Temp       -0.09001   0.01408  -6.39   0.001
Chill       0.08249   0.02200   3.75   0.013
```

(c) The Excel output

	Coefficients	Standard Error	t Stat	P-value	Lower 95%	Upper 95%
Intercept	13.1087	0.8557	15.3193	2.15E-05	10.9091	15.3084
TEMP	-0.0900	0.0141	-6.3942	0.0014	-0.1262	-0.0538
CHILL	0.0825	0.0220	3.7493	0.0133	0.0259	0.1391

EXAMPLE 14.4 The Fuel Consumption Case ✔ FuelCon2

Again consider the fuel consumption model

$$y = \beta_0 + \beta_1 x_1 + \beta_2 x_2 + \varepsilon$$

Table 14.7(a) summarizes the calculation of the *t* statistics and related *p*-values for testing the significance of the intercept and each of the independent variables x_1 and x_2. Here the values of b_j, s_{b_j}, *t*, and the *p*-value have been obtained from the MINITAB and Excel outputs of Table 14.7(b) and (c). If we wish to carry out tests at the .05 level of significance, we use the critical value $t_{.05/2} = t_{.025} = 2.571$, which is based on $n - (k + 1) = 8 - 3 = 5$ degrees of freedom. Looking at Table 14.7 (a), we see that

1 For the intercept, $|t| = 15.32 > 2.571$.
2 For x_1, $|t| = 6.39 > 2.571$.
3 For x_2, $|t| = 3.75 > 2.571$.

Since in each case $|t| > t_{.025}$, we reject each of the null hypotheses in Table 14.7(a) at the .05 level of significance. Furthermore, since the *p*-values related to the intercept and x_1 are each less than .01, we can reject $H_0: \beta_0 = 0$ and $H_0: \beta_1 = 0$ at the .01 level of significance. Since the *p*-value related to x_2 is less than .05 but not less than .01, we can reject $H_0: \beta_2 = 0$ at the .05 level of significance, but not at the .01 level of significance. On the basis of these results, we have very strong evidence that in the above model the intercept β_0 is significant and x_1 (average hourly temperature) is significantly related to y. We also have strong evidence that in this model x_2 (the chill index) is significantly related to y.

EXAMPLE 14.5 The Sales Territory Performance Case ✔ SalePerf

Consider the sales territory performance model

$$y = \beta_0 + \beta_1 x_1 + \beta_2 x_2 + \beta_3 x_3 + \beta_4 x_4 + \beta_5 x_5 + \varepsilon$$

Since the MegaStat output in Figure 14.10 tells us that the *p*-values associated with Time, MktPoten, Adver, and MktShare are all less than .01, we have very strong evidence that these

FIGURE 14.10　MegaStat Output of *t* Statistics and *p*-Values for the Sales Territory Performance Model

Regression output variables	coefficients	std. error	t (df=19)	p-value	confidence interval 95% lower	95% upper
Intercept	-1,113.7879	419.8869	-2.653	0.0157	-1,992.6213	-234.9545
Time	3.6121	1.1817	3.057	0.0065	1.1388	6.0854
MktPoten	0.0421	0.0067	6.253	5.27E-06	0.0280	0.0562
Adver	0.1289	0.0370	3.479	0.0025	0.0513	0.2064
MktShare	256.9555	39.1361	6.566	2.76E-06	175.0428	338.8683
Change	324.5334	157.2831	2.063	0.0530	-4.6638	653.7307

variables are significantly related to y and, thus, are important in this model. Since the p-value associated with Change is .0530, we have close to strong evidence that this variable is also important.

We next consider how to calculate a confidence interval for a regression parameter.

A Confidence Interval for the Regression Parameter β_j

If the regression assumptions hold, a **100(1 − α) percent confidence interval for β_j** is

$$[b_j \pm t_{\alpha/2}s_{b_j}]$$

Here $t_{\alpha/2}$ is based on $n - (k + 1)$ degrees of freedom.

EXAMPLE 14.6 The Fuel Consumption Case ◆ FuelCon2　　Ⓒ

Consider the fuel consumption model

$$y = \beta_0 + \beta_1 x_1 + \beta_2 x_2 + \varepsilon$$

The MINITAB and Excel output in Table 14.7 tells us that $b_1 = -.09001$ and $s_{b_1} = .01408$. It follows, since $t_{.025}$ based on $n - (k + 1) = 8 - 3 = 5$ degrees of freedom equals 2.571, that a 95 percent confidence interval for β_1 is (see the Excel output)

$$[b_1 \pm t_{.025}s_{b_1}] = [-.09001 \pm 2.571(.01408)]$$
$$= [-.1262, -.0538]$$

This interval says we are 95 percent confident that, if average hourly temperature increases by one degree and the chill index does not change, then mean weekly fuel consumption will decrease by at least .0538 MMcf of natural gas and by at most .1262 MMcf of natural gas. Furthermore, since this 95 percent confidence interval does not contain 0, we can reject H_0: $\beta_1 = 0$ in favor of H_a: $\beta_1 \neq 0$ at the .05 level of significance.

Exercises for Section 14.5

CONCEPTS

14.12 What do we conclude about x_j if we can reject H_0: $\beta_j = 0$ in favor of H_a: $\beta_j \neq 0$ by setting
　　a　α equal to .05?
　　b　α equal to .01?

14.13 Give an example of a practical application of the confidence interval for β_j.

METHODS AND APPLICATIONS

In Exercises 14.14 through 14.16 we refer to MINITAB, MegaStat, and Excel outputs of regression analyses of the data sets related to three case studies introduced in Section 14.1. The outputs are given in Figure 14.11. Using the appropriate output, do the following for **each parameter** β_j in the model under consideration:

FIGURE 14.11   *t* Statistics and *p*-Values for Three Case Studies

(a) MINITAB output for the real estate sales price case (sample size: *n* = 10)

Predictor	Coef	SE Coef	T	P
Constant	29.347	4.891	6.00	0.001
HomeSize	5.6128	0.2285	24.56	0.000
Rating	3.8344	0.4332	8.85	0.000

(b) MegaStat output for the Fresh detergent case (sample size: *n* = 30)

Regression output					confidence interval	
variables	coefficients	std. error	t (df=26)	p-value	95% lower	95% upper
Intercept	7.5891	2.4450	3.104	0.0046	2.5633	12.6149
Price (x1)	-2.3577	0.6379	-3.696	0.0010	-3.6690	-1.0464
IndPrice (x2)	1.6122	0.2954	5.459	1.01E-05	1.0051	2.2193
AdvExp (x3)	0.5012	0.1259	3.981	0.0005	0.2424	0.7599

(c) Excel output for the hospital labor needs case (sample size: *n* = 16)

	Coefficients	Standard Error	t Stat	P-value	Lower 95%	Upper 95%
Intercept	1946.8020	504.1819	3.8613	0.0023	848.2840	3045.3201
XRay (x1)	0.0386	0.0130	2.9579	0.0120	0.0102	0.0670
BedDays (x2)	1.0394	0.0676	15.3857	2.91E-09	0.8922	1.1866
LengthStay (x3)	-413.7578	98.5983	-4.1964	0.0012	-628.5850	-198.9306

a   Find b_j, s_{b_j}, and the *t* statistic for testing $H_0: \beta_j = 0$ on the output and report their values. Show how *t* has been calculated by using b_j and s_{b_j}.

b   Using the *t* statistic and appropriate critical values, test $H_0: \beta_j = 0$ versus $H_a: \beta_j \neq 0$ by setting α equal to .05. Which independent variables are significantly related to *y* in the model with $\alpha = .05$?

c   Using the *t* statistic and appropriate critical values, test $H_0: \beta_j = 0$ versus $H_a: \beta_j \neq 0$ by setting α equal to .01. Which independent variables are significantly related to *y* in the model with $\alpha = .01$?

d   Find the *p*-value for testing $H_0: \beta_j = 0$ versus $H_a: \beta_j \neq 0$ on the output. Using the *p*-value, determine whether we can reject H_0 by setting α equal to .10, .05, .01, and .001. What do you conclude about the significance of the independent variables in the model?

e   Calculate the 95 percent confidence interval for β_j. Discuss one practical application of this interval.

f   Calculate the 99 percent confidence interval for β_j.

14.14   THE REAL ESTATE SALES PRICE CASE ◔ RealEst2

Use the MINITAB output in Figure 14.11(a) to do *a* through *f* for each of β_0, β_1, and β_2.

14.15   THE FRESH DETERGENT CASE ◔ Fresh2

Use the MegaStat output in Figure 14.11(b) to do *a* through *f* for each of β_0, β_1, β_2, and β_3.

14.16   THE HOSPITAL LABOR NEEDS CASE ◔ HospLab

Use the Excel output in Figure 14.11(c) to do *a* through *f* for each of β_0, β_1, β_2, and β_3.

14.6 Confidence and Prediction Intervals ●●●

In this section we show how to use the multiple regression model to find a **confidence interval for a mean value of *y*** and a **prediction interval for an individual value of *y*.** We first present two examples of these intervals, and we then discuss (in an optional technical note) the formulas used to compute the intervals.

EXAMPLE 14.7 The Fuel Consumption Case ◔ FuelCon2

In the fuel consumption problem, recall that the weather forecasting service has predicted that in the next week the average hourly temperature will be 40°F and the chill index will be 10. Also

recall from Example 14.1 that

$$\hat{y} = 13.1087 - .09001x_1 + .08249x_2$$
$$= 13.1087 - .09001(40) + .08249(10)$$
$$= 10.333 \text{ MMcf of natural gas}$$

is the point estimate of mean weekly fuel consumption when x_1 equals 40 and x_2 equals 10, and is the point prediction of fuel consumption in a single week when x_1 equals 40 and x_2 equals 10. This point estimate and prediction are given at the bottom of the MINITAB output in Figure 14.4, which we repeat here as follows:

```
New Obs     Fit   SE Fit        95% CI             95% PI
    1     10.333   0.170   (9.895, 10.771)   (9.293, 11.374)
```

In addition to giving $\hat{y} = 10.333$, the MINITAB output also gives a 95 percent confidence interval and a 95 percent prediction interval. The 95 percent confidence interval—[9.895, 10.771]—says that we are 95 percent confident that the mean fuel consumption for all weeks that have an average hourly temperature of 40°F and a chill index of 10 is between 9.895 MMcf and 10.771 MMcf of natural gas. The 95 percent prediction interval—[9.293, 11.374]—says that we are 95 percent confident that the fuel consumption in a single week that has an average hourly temperature of 40°F and a chill index of 10 will be between 9.293 MMcf and 11.374 MMcf of natural gas.

If the natural gas company bases its transmission nomination for next week on the point prediction $\hat{y} = 10.333$, it will order 10.333 MMcf of natural gas to be transmitted to its city next week. The point prediction $\hat{y} = 10.333$ is the midpoint of the 95 percent prediction interval, [9.293, 11.374], for next week's fuel consumption. The half-length of this interval is $(11.374 - 9.293)/2 = 1.041$, which implies that the interval can be expressed as [10.333 ± 1.041]. Therefore, since 1.041 is $(1.041/10.333)100\% = 10.07\%$ of the transmission nomination of 10.333, the model makes us 95 percent confident that the actual amount of natural gas that will be used by the city next week will differ from the natural gas company's transmission nomination by no more than 10.07 percent. That is, we are 95 percent confident that the natural gas company's percentage nomination error will be less than or equal to 10.07 percent. Therefore, this error will probably be within the 10 percent allowance granted by the pipeline transmission system, and it is unlikely that the natural gas company will be required to pay a transmission fine.

EXAMPLE 14.8 The Sales Territory Performance Case ◔ SalePerf

Consider a questionable sales representative for whom Time = 85.42, MktPoten = 35,182.73, Adver = 7,281.65, MktShare = 9.64, and Change = .28. We have seen in Example 14.2 that the point prediction of the sales corresponding to this combination of values of the independent variables is

$$\hat{y} = -1,113.7879 + 3.6121(85.42) + .0421(35,182.73)$$
$$+ .1289(7,281.65) + 256.9555(9.64) + 324.5334(.28)$$
$$= 4,181.74 \text{ (that is, 418,174 units)}$$

This point prediction is given at the bottom of the MegaStat output in Figure 14.5, which we repeat here:

Predicted values for: Sales

	95% Confidence Interval		95% Prediction Interval		
Predicted	lower	upper	lower	upper	Leverage
4,181.74333	3,884.90651	4,478.58015	3,233.59431	5,129.89235	0.109

In addition to giving $\hat{y} = 4,181.74$, the MegaStat output tells us that a 95 percent prediction interval for y is [3233.59, 5129.89]. Furthermore, the actual sales y for the questionable representative were 3,087.52. This actual sales figure is less than the point prediction $\hat{y} = 4,181.74$ and is less than the lower bound of the 95 percent prediction interval for y, [3233.59, 5129.89]. Therefore, we conclude that there is strong evidence that the actual performance of the questionable representative is less than predicted performance. We should investigate the reason for this. Perhaps the questionable representative needs special training.

A technical note (optional)   In general

$$\hat{y} = b_0 + b_1x_1 + b_2x_2 + \cdots + b_kx_k$$

is the **point estimate of the mean value of the dependent variable y** when the values of the independent variables are $x_1, x_2, \ldots, x_k$ and is the **point prediction of an individual value of the dependent variable y** when the values of the independent variables are $x_1, x_2, \ldots, x_k$. Furthermore:

A Confidence Interval and a Prediction Interval

If the regression assumptions hold,

1 A 100(1 − α) percent confidence interval for the mean value of y when the values of the independent variables are $x_1, x_2, \ldots, x_k$ is

$$[\hat{y} \pm t_{\alpha/2}s\sqrt{\text{distance value}}]$$

2 A 100(1 − α) percent prediction interval for an individual value of y when the values of the independent variables are $x_1, x_2, \ldots, x_k$ is

$$[\hat{y} \pm t_{\alpha/2}s\sqrt{1 + \text{distance value}}]$$

Here $t_{\alpha/2}$ is based on $n - (k + 1)$ degrees of freedom and s is the standard error (see Section 14.2). Furthermore, the formula for the distance value involves matrix algebra and is given in Bowerman, O'Connell, and Murphree (2009). In practice, we can obtain the distance value from the outputs of statistical software packages (such as MINITAB and MegaStat).

Intuitively, the **distance value** is a measure of the distance of the combination of values $x_1, x_2, \ldots, x_k$ from the center of the observed data. The farther that this combination is from the center of the observed data, the larger is the distance value, and thus the longer are both the confidence interval and the prediction interval.

MINITAB gives $s_{\hat{y}} = s\sqrt{\text{distance value}}$ under the heading "SE Fit." Since the MINITAB output also gives s, the distance value can be found by calculating $(s_{\hat{y}}/s)^2$. For example, the MINITAB output in Example 14.7 tells us that $\hat{y} = 10.333$ (see "Fit") and $s_{\hat{y}} = .170$ (see "SE Fit"). Therefore, since s for the two variable fuel consumption model equals .3671 (see Figure 14.4, page 572), the distance value equals $(.170/.3671)^2 = .2144515$. It follows that the 95 percent confidence and prediction intervals given on the MINITAB output of Example 14.7 have been calculated as follows: ● FuelCon2

$[\hat{y} \pm t_{.025}s\sqrt{\text{distance value}}]$ $[\hat{y} \pm t_{.025}s\sqrt{1 + \text{distance value}}]$

$= [10.333 \pm 2.571(.3671)\sqrt{.2144515}]$ $= [10.333 \pm 2.571(.3671)\sqrt{1 + .2144515}]$

$= [10.333 \pm .438]$ $= [10.333 \pm 1.041]$

$= [9.895, 10.771]$ $= [9.292, 11.374]$

Here $t_{\alpha/2} = t_{.025} = 2.571$ is based on $n - (k + 1) = 8 - 3 = 5$ degrees of freedom.

As another example, the MegaStat output in Example 14.8 tells us that $\hat{y} = 4{,}181.74$. This output also tells us that the distance value, which is given under the heading "Leverage" on the output, equals .109. Therefore, since s for the five variable sales territory performance model equals 430.232 (see Figure 14.5, page 576), it follows that the 95 percent prediction interval given on the MegaStat output of Example 14.8 has been calculated as follows: ● SalePerf

$$[\hat{y} \pm t_{.025}s\sqrt{1 + \text{distance value}}]$$
$$= [4{,}181.74 \pm 2.093(430.232)\sqrt{1 + .109}]$$
$$= [3233.59, 5129.89]$$

Here $t_{.025} = 2.093$ is based on $n - (k + 1) = 25 - 6 = 19$ degrees of freedom.

Exercises for Section 14.6

CONCEPTS

14.17 What is the difference between a confidence interval and a prediction interval?

14.18 How do we compute and interpret the midpoint of a confidence interval and a prediction interval?

METHODS AND APPLICATIONS

14.19 THE REAL ESTATE SALES PRICE CASE ● RealEst2

The following MINITAB output relates to a house having 2,000 square feet and a rating of 8.

```
New Obs    Fit    SE Fit      95% CI              95% PI
  1      172.28    1.57    (168.56, 175.99)    (163.76, 180.80)
```

a Report (as shown on the output) a point estimate of and a 95 percent confidence interval for the mean sales price of all houses having 2,000 square feet and a rating of 8.

b Report (as shown on the output) a point prediction of and a 95 percent prediction interval for the actual sales price of an individual house having 2,000 square feet and a rating of 8.

c Find 99 percent confidence and prediction intervals for the mean and actual sales prices referred to in parts *a* and *b*. Hint: $n = 10$ and $s = 3.24164$. Technical note needed.

14.20 THE FRESH DETERGENT CASE ● Fresh2

Consider the demand for Fresh Detergent in a future sales period when Enterprise Industries' price for Fresh will be $x_1 = 3.70$, the average price of competitors' similar detergents will be $x_2 = 3.90$, and Enterprise Industries' advertising expenditure for Fresh will be $x_3 = 6.50$. A 95 percent prediction interval for this demand is given on the following MegaStat output:

	95% Confidence Interval		95% Prediction Interval		
Predicted	lower	upper	lower	upper	Leverage
8.4107	8.3143	8.5070	7.9188	8.9025	0.040

a Find and report the 95 percent prediction interval on the output. If Enterprise Industries plans to have in inventory the number of bottles implied by the upper limit of this interval, it can be very confident that it will have enough bottles to meet demand for Fresh in the future sales period. How many bottles is this? If we multiply the number of bottles implied by the lower limit of the prediction interval by the price of Fresh ($3.70), we can be very confident that the resulting dollar amount will be the minimal revenue from Fresh in the future sales period. What is this dollar amount?

b Calculate a 99 percent prediction interval for the demand for Fresh in the future sales period. Hint: $n = 30$ and $s = .235$. Technical note needed.

14.21 THE HOSPITAL LABOR NEEDS CASE ● HospLab

Consider a questionable hospital for which XRay = 56,194, BedDays = 14,077.88, and LengthStay = 6.89. A 95 percent prediction interval for the labor hours corresponding to this combination of values of the independent variables is given on the following MegaStat output:

	95% Confidence Interval		95% Prediction Interval		
Predicted	lower	upper	lower	upper	Leverage
15,896.2473	15,378.0313	16,414.4632	14,906.2361	16,886.2584	0.3774

Find and report the prediction interval on the output. Then, use this interval to determine if the actual number of labor hours used by the questionable hospital ($y = 17,207.31$) is unusually low or high.

14.7 Using Dummy Variables to Model Qualitative Independent Variables ◐●●

While the levels (or values) of a quantitative independent variable are numerical, the levels of a **qualitative** independent variable are defined by describing them. For instance, the type of sales technique used by a door-to-door salesperson is a qualitative independent variable. Here we might define three different levels—high pressure, medium pressure, and low pressure.

TABLE 14.8   The Electronics World Sales Volume Data
 Electronics1

Store	Number of Households, x	Location	Sales Volume, y
1	161	Street	157.27
2	99	Street	93.28
3	135	Street	136.81
4	120	Street	123.79
5	164	Street	153.51
6	221	Mall	241.74
7	179	Mall	201.54
8	204	Mall	206.71
9	214	Mall	229.78
10	101	Mall	135.22

FIGURE 14.12   Plot of the Sales Volume Data and a Geometrical Interpretation of the Model $y = \beta_0 + \beta_1 x + \beta_2 D_M + \varepsilon$

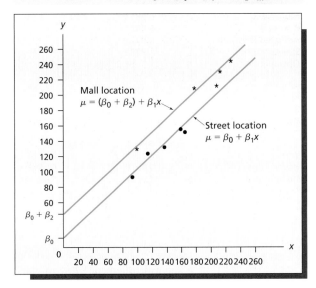

We can model the effects of the different levels of a qualitative independent variable by using what we call **dummy variables** (also called **indicator variables**). Such variables are usually defined so that they take on two values—either 0 or 1. To see how we use dummy variables, we begin with an example.

CHAPTER 19

EXAMPLE 14.9

Part 1: The data and data plots   Suppose that Electronics World, a chain of stores that sells audio and video equipment, has gathered the data in Table 14.8. These data concern store sales volume in July of last year (y, measured in thousands of dollars), the number of households in the store's area (x, measured in thousands), and the location of the store (on a suburban street or in a suburban shopping mall—a qualitative independent variable). Figure 14.12 gives a data plot of y versus x. Stores having a street location are plotted as solid dots, while stores having a mall location are plotted as asterisks. Notice that the line relating y to x for mall locations has a higher y-intercept than does the line relating y to x for street locations.

Part 2: A dummy variable model   In order to model the effects of the street and shopping mall locations, we define a dummy variable denoted D_M as follows:

$$D_M = \begin{cases} 1 & \text{if a store is in a mall location} \\ 0 & \text{otherwise} \end{cases}$$

Using this dummy variable, we consider the regression model

$$y = \beta_0 + \beta_1 x + \beta_2 D_M + \varepsilon$$

This model and the definition of D_M imply that

1   For a street location, mean sales volume equals

$$\beta_0 + \beta_1 x + \beta_2 D_M = \beta_0 + \beta_1 x + \beta_2(0)$$
$$= \beta_0 + \beta_1 x$$

2   For a mall location, mean sales volume equals

$$\beta_0 + \beta_1 x + \beta_2 D_M = \beta_0 + \beta_1 x + \beta_2(1)$$
$$= (\beta_0 + \beta_2) + \beta_1 x$$

FIGURE 14.13   **Excel Output of a Regression Analysis of the Sales Volume Data Using the Model**
$y = \beta_0 + \beta_1 x + \beta_2 D_M + \varepsilon$

Regression Statistics

Multiple R	0.9913
R Square	0.9827
Adjusted R Square	0.9778
Standard Error	7.3288
Observations	10

ANOVA	df	SS	MS	F	Significance F
Regression	2	21411.7977	10705.8989	199.3216	6.75E-07
Residual	7	375.9817	53.7117		
Total	9	21787.7795			

	Coefficients	Standard Error	t Stat	P-value	Lower 95%	Upper 95%
Intercept	17.3598	9.4470	1.8376	0.1087	-4.9788	39.6985
Households (x)	0.8510	0.0652	13.0439	3.63E-06	0.6968	1.0053
DummyMall	29.2157	5.5940	5.2227	0.0012	15.9881	42.4434

Thus the dummy variable allows us to model the situation illustrated in Figure 14.12. Here, the lines relating mean sales volume to x for street and mall locations have different y-intercepts—β_0 and $(\beta_0 + \beta_2)$—and the same slope β_1. Note that β_2 is the difference between the mean monthly sales volume for stores in mall locations and the mean monthly sales volume for stores in street locations, when all these stores have the same number of households in their areas. That is, we can say that β_2 represents the effect on mean sales of a mall location compared to a street location. The Excel output in Figure 14.13 tells us that the least squares point estimate of β_2 is $b_2 = 29.2157$. This says that for any given number of households in a store's area, we estimate that the mean monthly sales volume in a mall location is \$29,215.70 greater than the mean monthly sales volume in a street location.

Part 3: A dummy variable model for comparing three locations   In addition to the data concerning street and mall locations in Table 14.8, Electronics World has also collected data concerning downtown locations. The complete data set is given in Table 14.9 and plotted in Figure 14.14. Here stores having a downtown location are plotted as open circles. A model describing these data is

$$y = \beta_0 + \beta_1 x + \beta_2 D_M + \beta_3 D_D + \varepsilon$$

Here the dummy variable D_M is as previously defined and the dummy variable D_D is defined as follows

$$D_D = \begin{cases} 1 & \text{if a store is in a downtown location} \\ 0 & \text{otherwise} \end{cases}$$

It follows that

1   For a street location, mean sales volume equals

$$\beta_0 + \beta_1 x + \beta_2 D_M + \beta_3 D_D = \beta_0 + \beta_1 x + \beta_2(0) + \beta_3(0)$$
$$= \beta_0 + \beta_1 x$$

2   For a mall location, mean sales volume equals

$$\beta_0 + \beta_1 x + \beta_2 D_M + \beta_3 D_D = \beta_0 + \beta_1 x + \beta_2(1) + \beta_3(0)$$
$$= (\beta_0 + \beta_2) + \beta_1 x$$

TABLE 14.9	The Complete Electronics World Sales Volume Data

🔵 Electronics2

Store	Number of Households, x	Location	Sales Volume, y
1	161	Street	157.27
2	99	Street	93.28
3	135	Street	136.81
4	120	Street	123.79
5	164	Street	153.51
6	221	Mall	241.74
7	179	Mall	201.54
8	204	Mall	206.71
9	214	Mall	229.78
10	101	Mall	135.22
11	231	Downtown	224.71
12	206	Downtown	195.29
13	248	Downtown	242.16
14	107	Downtown	115.21
15	205	Downtown	197.82

FIGURE 14.14 Plot of the Complete Electronics World Sales Volume Data and a Geometrical Interpretation of the Model

$$y = \beta_0 + \beta_1 x + \beta_2 D_M + \beta_3 D_D + \varepsilon$$

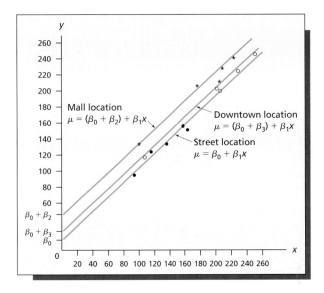

3　For a downtown location, mean sales volume equals

$$\beta_0 + \beta_1 x + \beta_2 D_M + \beta_3 D_D = \beta_0 + \beta_1 x + \beta_2(0) + \beta_3(1)$$
$$= (\beta_0 + \beta_3) + \beta_1 x$$

Thus the dummy variables allow us to model the situation illustrated in Figure 14.14. Here the lines relating mean sales volume to x for street, mall, and downtown locations have different y-intercepts—β_0, $(\beta_0 + \beta_2)$, and $(\beta_0 + \beta_3)$—and the same slope β_1. Note that β_2 represents the effect on mean sales of a mall location compared to a street location, and β_3 represents the effect on mean sales of a downtown location compared to a street location. Furthermore, the difference between β_2 and β_3, $\beta_2 - \beta_3$, represents the effect on mean sales of a mall location compared to a downtown location.

Part 4: Comparing the three locations　Figure 14.15 gives the MINITAB and Excel output of a regression analysis of the sales volume data using the dummy variable model. The output tells us that the least squares point estimate of β_2 is $b_2 = 28.374$. This says that for any given number of households in a store's area, we estimate that the mean monthly sales volume in a mall location is \$28,374 greater than the mean monthly sales volume in a street location. Furthermore, since the Excel output tells us that a 95 percent confidence interval for β_2 is [18.5545, 38.193], we are 95 percent confident that for any given number of households in a store's area, the mean monthly sales volume in a mall location is between \$18,554.50 and \$38,193 greater than the mean monthly sales volume in a street location. The MINITAB and Excel output also shows that the t statistic for testing H_0: $\beta_2 = 0$ versus H_a: $\beta_2 \neq 0$ equals 6.36 and that the related p-value is less than .001. Therefore, we have very strong evidence that there is a difference between the mean monthly sales volumes in mall and street locations.

We next note that the output in Figure 14.15 shows that the least squares point estimate of β_3 is $b_3 = 6.864$. Therefore, we estimate that for any given number of households in a store's area, the mean monthly sales volume in a downtown location is \$6,864 greater than the mean monthly sales volume in a street location. Furthermore, the Excel output shows that a 95 percent confidence interval for β_3 is [−3.636, 17.3635]. This says we are 95 percent confident that for any given number of households in a store's area, the mean monthly sales volume in a downtown

FIGURE 14.15 MINITAB and Excel Output of a Regression Analysis of the Sales Volume Data Using the Model $y = \beta_0 + \beta_1 x + \beta_2 D_M + \beta_3 D_D + \varepsilon$

(a) The MINITAB output

```
The regression equation is
Sales = 15.0 + 0.869 Households + 28.4 DMall + 6.86 DDowntown

Predictor      Coef  SE Coef      T      P
Constant     14.978    6.188   2.42  0.034
Households  0.86859  0.04049  21.45  0.000
DMall        28.374    4.461   6.36  0.000
DDowntown     6.864    4.770   1.44  0.178

S = 6.34941   R-Sq = 98.7%   R-Sq(adj) = 98.3%

Analysis of Variance
Source          DF     SS     MS       F      P
Regression       3  33269  11090  275.07  0.000
Residual Error  11    443     40
Total           14  33712

Values of Predictors for New Obs     Predicted Values for New Observations
New Obs  Households  DMall DDowntown   New Obs     Fit  SE Fit       95% CI            95% PI
      1         200      1         0         1  217.07    2.91  (210.65, 223.48)  (201.69, 232.45)
```

(b) The Excel output

Regression Statistics

Multiple R	0.9934
R Square	0.9868
Adjusted R Square	0.9833
Standard Error	6.3494
Observations	15

ANOVA

	df	SS	MS	F	Significance F
Regression	3	33268.6953	11089.5651	275.0729	1.27E-10
Residual	11	443.4650	40.3150		
Total	14	33712.1603			

	Coefficients	Standard Error	t Stat	P-value	Lower 95%	Upper 95%
Intercept	14.9777	6.1884	2.4203	0.0340	1.3570	28.5984
Households (x)	0.8686	0.0405	21.4520	2.52E-10	0.7795	0.9577
DummyMall	28.3738	4.4613	6.3600	5.37E-05	18.5545	38.1930
DummyDtown	6.8638	4.7705	1.4388	0.1780	-3.6360	17.3635

location is between \$3,636 less than and \$17,363.50 greater than the mean monthly sales volume in a street location. The MINITAB and Excel output also shows that the t statistic and p-value for testing $H_0: \beta_3 = 0$ versus $H_a: \beta_3 \neq 0$ are $t = 1.44$ and p-value $= .178$. Therefore, we do not have strong evidence that there is a difference between the mean monthly sales volumes in downtown and street locations.

Finally, note that, since $b_2 = 28.374$ and $b_3 = 6.864$, the point estimate of $\beta_2 - \beta_3$ is $b_2 - b_3 = 28.374 - 6.864 = 21.51$. Therefore, we estimate that mean monthly sales volume in a mall location is \$21,510 higher than mean monthly sales volume in a downtown location. Near the end of this section we show how to compare the mall and downtown locations by using a confidence interval and a hypothesis test. We will find that there is very strong evidence that the mean monthly sales volume in a mall location is higher than the mean monthly sales volume in a downtown location. In summary, the mall location seems to give a higher mean monthly sales volume than either the street or downtown location.

BI

Part 5: Predicting a future sales volume Suppose that Electronics World wishes to predict the sales volume in a future month for an individual store that has 200,000 households in its area and is located in a shopping mall. The point prediction of this sales volume is (since $D_M = 1$

FIGURE 14.16   **Geometrical Interpretation of the Sales Volume Model**
$$y = \beta_0 + \beta_1 x + \beta_2 D_M + \beta_3 x D_M + \varepsilon$$

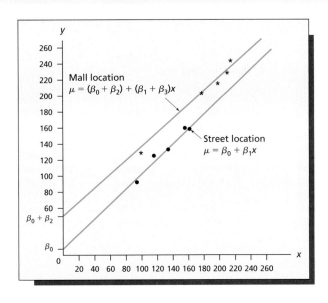

and $D_D = 0$ when a store is in a shopping mall)

$$\hat{y} = b_0 + b_1(200) + b_2(1) + b_3(0)$$
$$= 14.978 + .8686(200) + 28.374(1)$$
$$= 217.07$$

This point prediction is given at the bottom of the MINITAB output in Figure 14.15(a). The corresponding 95 percent prediction interval, which is [201.69, 232.45], says we are 95 percent confident that the sales volume in a future sales period for an individual mall store that has 200,000 households in its area will be between \$201,690 and \$232,450.

Part 6: Interaction models   Consider the Electronics World data for street and mall locations given in Table 14.8 (page 595) and the model

$$y = \beta_0 + \beta_1 x + \beta_2 D_M + \beta_3 x D_M + \varepsilon$$

This model uses the *cross-product,* or *interaction, term* $x D_M$ and implies that

1   For a street location, mean sales volume equals (since $D_M = 0$)

$$\beta_0 + \beta_1 x + \beta_2(0) + \beta_3 x(0) = \beta_0 + \beta_1 x$$

2   For a mall location, mean sales volume equals (since $D_M = 1$)

$$\beta_0 + \beta_1 x + \beta_2(1) + \beta_3 x(1) = (\beta_0 + \beta_2) + (\beta_1 + \beta_3)x$$

As illustrated in Figure 14.16, if we use this model, then the straight lines relating mean sales volume to x for street and mall locations have *different y-intercepts* and *different slopes*. Therefore, we say that this model assumes *interaction* between x and store location. Such a model is appropriate if the relationship between mean sales volume and x depends on (that is, is different for) the street and mall store locations. In general, **interaction** exists between two independent variables if the relationship between (for example, the slope of the line relating) the mean value of the dependent variable and one of the independent variables depends upon the value (or level) of the other independent variable. Figure 14.17 gives the MegaStat output of a regression analysis of the sales volume data using the interaction model. Here D_M and $x D_M$ are labeled as DM and XDM, respectively, on the output. The MegaStat output tells us that the p-value related to the significance of $x D_M$ is .5886. This large p-value tells us that the interaction term is not significant. It follows that the no-interaction model on page 595 seems best.

FIGURE 14.17   **MegaStat Output Using the Interaction Model**
$$y = \beta_0 + \beta_1 x + \beta_2 D_M + \beta_3 x D_M + \varepsilon$$

Regression Analysis

R^2	0.984		
Adjusted R^2	0.975	n	10
R	0.992	k	3
Std. Error	7.709	Dep. Var.	**Sales**

ANOVA table

Source	SS	df	MS	F	p-value
Regression	21,431.1861	3	7,143.7287	120.20	9.53E-06
Residual	356.5933	6	59.4322		
Total	21,787.7795	9			

Regression output

					confidence interval	
variables	coefficients	std. error	t (df = 6)	p-value	95% lower	95% upper
Intercept	7.9004	19.3142	0.409	.6967	-39.3598	55.1607
X	0.9207	0.1399	6.579	.0006	0.5783	1.2631
DM	42.7297	24.3812	1.753	.1302	-16.9290	102.3885
XDM	-0.0917	0.1606	-0.571	.5886	-0.4846	0.3012

Next, consider the Electronics World data for street, mall, and downtown locations given in Table 14.9 (page 597). In modeling these data, if we believe that interaction exists between the number of households in a store's area and store location, we might consider using the model

$$y = \beta_0 + \beta_1 x + \beta_2 D_M + \beta_3 D_D + \beta_4 x D_M + \beta_5 x D_D + \varepsilon$$

Similar to Figure 14.16, this model implies that the straight lines relating mean sales volume to x for the street, mall, and downtown locations have *different y-intercepts* and *different slopes*. If we perform a regression analysis of the sales volume data using this interaction model, we find that the p-values related to the significance of $x D_M$ and $x D_D$ are large $-.5334$ and $.8132$, respectively. Since these interaction terms are not significant, it seems best to employ the no-interaction model on page 596.

In general, if we wish to model the effect of a qualitative independent variable having a levels, we use $a - 1$ dummy variables. The parameter multiplied by a particular dummy variable expresses the effect of the level represented by that dummy variable with respect to the effect of the level that is not represented by a dummy variable. For example, if we wish to compare the effects on sales, y, of four different types of advertising campaigns—television (T), radio (R), magazine (M), and mailed coupons (C)—we might employ the model

$$y = \beta_0 + \beta_1 D_T + \beta_2 D_R + \beta_3 D_M + \varepsilon$$

Since this model does not use a dummy variable to represent the mailed coupon advertising campaign, the parameter β_1 is the difference between mean sales when a television advertising campaign is used and mean sales when a mailed coupon advertising campaign is used. The interpretations of β_2 and β_3 follow similarly. As another example, if we wish to employ a confidence interval and a hypothesis test to compare the mall and downtown locations in the Electronics World example, we can use the model

$$y = \beta_0 + \beta_1 x + \beta_2 D_S + \beta_3 D_M + \varepsilon$$

Here the dummy variable D_M is as previously defined, and

$$D_S = \begin{cases} 1 & \text{if a store is in a street location} \\ 0 & \text{otherwise} \end{cases}$$

Since this model does not use a dummy variable to represent the downtown location, the parameter β_2 expresses the effect on mean sales of a street location compared to a downtown location, and the parameter β_3 expresses the effect on mean sales of a mall location compared to a downtown location.

The Excel output of the least squares point estimates of the parameters of this model is as follows:

	Coefficients	Standard Error	t Stat	P-value	Lower 95%	Upper 95%
Intercept	21.8415	8.5585	2.5520	0.0269	3.0044	40.6785
Households (x)	0.8686	0.0405	21.4520	2.52E-10	0.7795	0.9577
DummyStreet	-6.8638	4.7705	-1.4388	0.1780	-17.3635	3.6360
DummyMall	21.5100	4.0651	5.2914	0.0003	12.5628	30.4572

Since the least squares point estimate of β_3 is $b_3 = 21.51$, we estimate that for any given number of households in a store's area, the mean monthly sales volume in a mall location is \$21,510 higher than the mean monthly sales volume in a downtown location. The Excel output tells us that a 95 percent confidence interval for β_3 is [12.5628, 30.4572]. Therefore, we are 95 percent confident that for any given number of households in a store's area, the mean monthly sales volume in a mall location is between \$12,562.80 and \$30,457.20 greater than the mean monthly sales volume in a downtown location. The Excel output also shows that the t statistic and p-value for testing $H_0: \beta_3 = 0$ versus $H_a: \beta_3 \neq 0$ in this model are, respectively, 5.2914 and .0003. Therefore, we have very strong evidence that there is a difference between the mean monthly sales volumes in mall and downtown locations.

In some situations dummy variables represent the effects of unusual events or occurrences that may have an important impact on the dependent variable. For instance, suppose we wish to build a regression model relating quarterly sales of automobiles (y) to automobile prices (x_1), fuel prices (x_2), and personal income (x_3). If an autoworkers' strike occurred in a particular quarter that had a major impact on automobile sales, then we might define a dummy variable D_S to be equal to 1 if an autoworkers' strike occurs and to be equal to 0 otherwise. The least squares point estimate of the regression parameter multiplied by D_S would estimate the effect of the strike on mean auto sales. Finally, dummy variables can be used to model the impact of regularly occurring *seasonal* influences on time series data—for example, the impact of the hot summer months on soft drink sales (see Exercises 14.41 and 14.42 in the Supplementary Exercises at the end of this chapter).

Exercises for Section 14.7

CONCEPTS

14.22   What is a qualitative independent variable?

14.23   How do we use dummy variables to model the effects of a qualitative independent variable?

14.24   What does the parameter multiplied by a dummy variable express?

METHODS AND APPLICATIONS

14.25   Neter, Kutner, Nachtsheim, and Wasserman (1996) relate the speed, y, with which a particular insurance innovation is adopted to the size of the insurance firm, x, and the type of firm. The dependent variable y is measured by the number of months elapsed between the time the first firm adopted the innovation and the time the firm being considered adopted the innovation. The size of the firm, x, is measured by the total assets of the firm, and the type of firm—a qualitative independent variable—is either a mutual company or a stock company. The data in Table 14.10 are observed.   ● InsInnov

    a   Discuss why the data plot in the page margin indicates that the model

$$y = \beta_0 + \beta_1 x + \beta_2 D_S + \varepsilon$$

might appropriately describe the observed data. Here D_S equals 1 if the firm is a stock company and 0 if the firm is a mutual company.

    b   The model of part *a* implies that the mean adoption time of an insurance innovation by mutual companies having an asset size x equals

$$\beta_0 + \beta_1 x + \beta_2(0) = \beta_0 + \beta_1 x$$

and that the mean adoption time by stock companies having an asset size x equals

$$\beta_0 + \beta_1 x + \beta_2(1) = \beta_0 + \beta_1 x + \beta_2$$

connect™

Plot of the Insurance Innovation Data

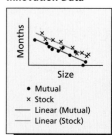

Size

● Mutual
× Stock
—— Linear (Mutual)
—— Linear (Stock)

TABLE 14.10   The Insurance Innovation Data   ● InsInnov

Firm	Number of Months Elapsed, y	Size of Firm (Millions of Dollars), x	Type of Firm	Firm	Number of Months Elapsed, y	Size of Firm (Millions of Dollars), x	Type of Firm
1	17	151	Mutual	11	28	164	Stock
2	26	92	Mutual	12	15	272	Stock
3	21	175	Mutual	13	11	295	Stock
4	30	31	Mutual	14	38	68	Stock
5	22	104	Mutual	15	31	85	Stock
6	0	277	Mutual	16	21	224	Stock
7	12	210	Mutual	17	20	166	Stock
8	19	120	Mutual	18	13	305	Stock
9	4	290	Mutual	19	30	124	Stock
10	16	238	Mutual	20	14	246	Stock

FIGURE 14.18   Excel Output of a Regression Analysis of the Insurance Innovation Data Using the Model $y = \beta_0 + \beta_1 x + \beta_2 D_S + \varepsilon$

Regression Statistics

Multiple R	0.9461
R Square	0.8951
Adjusted R Square	0.8827
Standard Error	3.2211
Observations	20

ANOVA	df	SS	MS	F	Significance F
Regression	2	1,504.4133	752.2067	72.4971	4.77E-09
Residual	17	176.3867	10.3757		
Total	19	1,680.8			

	Coefficients	Standard Error	t Stat	P-value	Lower 95%	Upper 95%
Intercept	33.8741	1.8139	18.6751	9.15E-13	30.0472	37.7010
Size of Firm (x)	-0.1017	0.0089	-11.4430	2.07E-09	-0.1205	-0.0830
DummyStock	8.0555	1.4591	5.5208	3.74E-05	4.9770	11.1339

The difference between these two means equals the model parameter β_2. In your own words, interpret the practical meaning of β_2.

c Figure 14.18 presents the Excel output of a regression analysis of the insurance innovation data using the model of part a. Using the output, test H_0: $\beta_2 = 0$ versus H_a: $\beta_2 \neq 0$ by setting $\alpha = .05$ and .01. Interpret the practical meaning of the result of this test. Also, use the computer output to find, report, and interpret a 95 percent confidence interval for β_2.

d If we add the interaction term xD_S to the model of part a, we find that the p-value related to this term is .9821. What does this imply?

14.26   THE FLORIDA POOL HOME CASE   ● PoolHome

Table 3.12 (page 161) gives the selling price (Price, expressed in thousands of dollars), the square footage (SqrFt), the number of bathrooms (Bathrms), and the niceness rating (Niceness, expressed as an integer from 1 to 7) of 80 homes randomly selected from all homes sold in a Florida city during the last six months. (The random selections were made from homes having between 2,000 and 3,500 square feet.) Table 3.12 also gives values of the dummy variable Pool?, which equals 1 if a home has a pool and 0 otherwise. Figure 14.19 presents the MegaStat output of a regression analysis of these data using the model

$$\text{Price} = \beta_0 + \beta_1 \cdot \text{SqrFt} + \beta_2 \cdot \text{Bathrms} + \beta_3 \cdot \text{Niceness} + \beta_4 \cdot \text{Pool?} + \varepsilon$$

a Noting that β_4 is the effect on mean sales price of a home having a pool, find (on the output) a point estimate of this effect. If the average current purchase price of the pools in the sample is $32,500, find a point estimate of the percentage of a pool's cost that a customer buying a pool can expect to recoup when selling his (or her) home.

FIGURE 14.19   MegaStat Output of a Regression Analysis of the Florida Pool Home Data Using the Model Price = $\beta_0 + \beta_1 \cdot$ SqrFt + $\beta_2 \cdot$ Bathrms + $\beta_3 \cdot$ Niceness + $\beta_4 \cdot$ Pool? + ε

Regression Analysis

R^2	0.874		
Adjusted R^2	0.868	n	80
R	0.935	k	4
Std. Error	13.532	Dep. Var.	**Price**

ANOVA table

Source	SS	df	MS	F	p-value
Regression	95,665.2412	4	23,916.3103	130.61	5.41E-33
Residual	13,733.7327	75	183.1164		
Total	109,398.9739	79			

Regression output

variables	coefficients	std. error	t (df=75)	p-value	confidence interval 95% lower	95% upper
Intercept	24.9760	16.6267	1.502	.1373	-8.1460	58.0980
SqrFt	0.0526	0.0066	7.982	1.29E-11	0.0395	0.0658
Bathrms	10.0430	3.7287	2.693	.0087	2.6151	17.4710
Niceness	10.0420	0.7915	12.687	2.38E-20	8.4653	11.6188
Pool?	25.8623	3.5747	7.235	3.36E-10	18.7411	32.9835

b   If we add various combinations of the interaction terms SqrFt · Pool?, Bathrooms · Pool?, and Niceness · Pool? to the above model, we find that the *p*-values related to these terms are greater than .05. What does this imply?

14.27 THE SHELF DISPLAY CASE   ◉ BakeSale

The Tastee Bakery Company supplies a bakery product to many supermarkets in a metropolitan area. The company wishes to study the effect of the height of the shelf display employed by the supermarkets on monthly sales, *y* (measured in cases of 10 units each), for this product. Shelf display height has three levels—bottom (*B*), middle (*M*), and top (*T*). For each shelf display height, six supermarkets of equal sales potential will be randomly selected, and each supermarket will display the product using its assigned shelf height for a month. At the end of the month, sales of the bakery product at the 18 participating stores will be recorded. When the experiment is carried out, the data in Table 14.11 are obtained. Here we assume that the set of sales amounts for each display height is a sample that has been randomly selected from the population of all sales amounts that could be obtained (at supermarkets of the given sales potential) when using that display height. To compare the population mean sales amounts μ_B, μ_M, and μ_T that would be obtained by using the bottom, middle, and top display heights, we use the following dummy variable regression model:

$$y = \beta_B + \beta_M D_M + \beta_T D_T + \varepsilon$$

Here D_M equals 1 if a middle display height is used and 0 otherwise; D_T equals 1 if a top display height is used and 0 otherwise. Figure 14.20 presents the MINITAB output of a regression analysis of the bakery sales study data using this model.[1]

a   By using the definitions of the dummy variables, show that

$$\mu_B = \beta_B \qquad \mu_M = \beta_B + \beta_M \qquad \mu_T = \beta_B + \beta_T$$

b   Use the overall *F* statistic to test $H_0: \beta_M = \beta_T = 0$, or, equivalently, $H_0: \mu_B = \mu_M = \mu_T$. Interpret the practical meaning of the result of this test.

c   Show that your results in part *a*, imply that

$$\mu_M - \mu_B = \beta_M \qquad \mu_T - \mu_B = \beta_T \qquad \mu_M - \mu_T = \beta_M - \beta_T$$

TABLE 14.11
Bakery Sales Study Data (Sales in Cases)
◉ BakeSale

Shelf Display Height		
Bottom (*B*)	Middle (*M*)	Top (*T*)
58.2	73.0	52.4
53.7	78.1	49.7
55.8	75.4	50.9
55.7	76.2	54.0
52.5	78.4	52.1
58.9	82.1	49.9

---

[1]In general, the regression approach of this exercise produces the same comparisons of several population means that are produced by **one-way analysis of variance** (see Section 11.2).

FIGURE 14.20   MINITAB Output of a Dummy Variable Regression Analysis of
                the Bakery Sales Data in Table 14.11

```
The regression equation is
Bakery Sales = 55.8 + 21.4 DMiddle - 4.30 DTop

Predictor    Coef    SE Coef      T       P
Constant    55.800     1.013    55.07   0.000
DMiddle     21.400     1.433    14.93   0.000
DTop        -4.300     1.433    -3.00   0.009

S = 2.48193    R-Sq = 96.1%    R-Sq(adj) = 95.6%

Analysis of Variance
Source           DF      SS      MS       F       P
Regression        2   2273.9  1136.9   184.57   0.000
Residual Error   15     92.4     6.2
Total            17   2366.3

Values of Predictors for New Obs      Predicted Values for New Observations
New Obs   DMiddle   DTop           New Obs    Fit   SE Fit     95% CI            95% PI
      1         1      0                 1   77.200   1.013  (75.040, 79.360)  (71.486, 82.914)
```

TABLE 14.12

**Advertising
Campaigns Used
by Enterprise
Industries**

🌢 Fresh3

Sales Period	Advertising Campaign
1	B
2	B
3	B
4	A
5	C
6	A
7	C
8	C
9	B
10	C
11	A
12	C
13	C
14	A
15	B
16	B
17	B
18	A
19	B
20	B
21	C
22	A
23	A
24	A
25	A
26	B
27	C
28	B
29	C
30	C

Then use the least squares point estimates of the model parameters to find a point estimate of each of the three differences in means. Also, find a 95 percent confidence interval for and test the significance of each of the first two differences in means. Interpret your results.

d   Find a point estimate of mean sales when using a middle display height, a 95 percent confidence interval for mean sales when using a middle display height, and a 95 percent prediction interval for sales at an individual supermarket that employs a middle display height (see the bottom of the MINITAB output in Figure 14.20).

e   Consider the following alternative model

$$y = \beta_T + \beta_B D_B + \beta_M D_M + \varepsilon$$

Here D_B equals 1 if a bottom display height is used and 0 otherwise. The MINITAB output of the least squares point estimates of the parameters of this model is as follows:

```
Predictor    Coef      SE Coef       T         P
Constant    51.500      1.013      50.83     0.000
DBottom      4.300      1.433       3.00     0.009
DMiddle     25.700      1.433      17.94     0.000
```

Since β_M expresses the effect of the middle display height with respect to the effect of the top display height, β_M equals $\mu_M - \mu_T$. Use the MINITAB output to calculate a 95 percent confidence interval for and test the significance of $\mu_M - \mu_T$. Interpret your results.

14.28   THE FRESH DETERGENT CASE 🌢 Fresh3

Recall from Exercise 14.4 that Enterprise Industries has observed the historical data in Table 14.5 (page 579) concerning y (demand for Fresh liquid laundry detergent), x_1 (the price of Fresh), x_2 (the average industry price of competitors' similar detergents), and x_3 (Enterprise Industries' advertising expenditure for Fresh). To ultimately increase the demand for Fresh, Enterprise Industries' marketing department is comparing the effectiveness of three different advertising campaigns. These campaigns are denoted as campaigns A, B, and C. Campaign A consists entirely of television commercials, campaign B consists of a balanced mixture of television and radio commercials, and campaign C consists of a balanced mixture of television, radio, newspaper, and magazine ads. To conduct the study, Enterprise Industries has randomly selected one advertising campaign to be used in each of the 30 sales periods in Table 14.5. Although logic would indicate that each of campaigns A, B, and C should be used in 10 of the 30 sales periods, Enterprise Industries has made previous commitments to the advertising media involved in the study. As a result, campaigns A, B, and C were randomly assigned to, respectively, 9, 11, and 10 sales periods. Furthermore, advertising was done in only the first three weeks of each sales period, so that the carryover effect of the campaign used in a sales period to the next sales period would be minimized. Table 14.12 lists the campaigns used in the sales periods.

To compare the effectiveness of advertising campaigns A, B, and C, we define two dummy variables. Specifically, we define the dummy variable D_B to equal 1 if campaign B is used in a

FIGURE 14.21　MegaStat Output of a Dummy Variable Regression Model Analysis of the Fresh Demand Data

Regression Analysis

	R^2 0.960			
	Adjusted R^2 0.951		n 30	
	R 0.980		k 5	
	Std. Error 0.150		Dep. Var. **Demand**	

ANOVA table

Source	SS	df	MS	F	p-value
Regression	12.9166	5	2.5833	114.39	6.24E-16
Residual	0.5420	24	0.0226		
Total	13.4586	29			

Regression output

variables	coefficients	std. error	t (df = 24)	p-value	confidence interval 95% lower	95% upper
Intercept	8.7154	1.5849	5.499	1.18E-05	5.4443	11.9866
X1	−2.7680	0.4144	−6.679	6.58E-07	−3.6234	−1.9127
X2	1.6667	0.1913	8.711	6.77E-09	1.2718	2.0616
X3	0.4927	0.0806	6.110	2.60E-06	0.3263	0.6592
DB	0.2695	0.0695	3.880	.0007	0.1262	0.4128
DC	0.4396	0.0703	6.250	1.85E-06	0.2944	0.5847

Predicted values for: Demand

Predicted	95% Confidence Interval lower	upper	95% Prediction Interval lower	upper	Leverage
8.61621	8.51380	8.71862	8.28958	8.94285	0.109

sales period and 0 otherwise. Furthermore, we define the dummy variable D_C to equal 1 if campaign C is used in a sales period and 0 otherwise. Figure 14.21 presents the MegaStat output of a regression analysis of the Fresh demand data by using the model

$$y = \beta_0 + \beta_1 x_1 + \beta_2 x_2 + \beta_3 x_3 + \beta_4 D_B + \beta_5 D_C + \varepsilon$$

a　In this model the parameter β_4 represents the effect on mean demand of advertising campaign B compared to advertising campaign A, and the parameter β_5 represents the effect on mean demand of advertising campaign C compared to advertising campaign A. Use the regression output to find and report a point estimate of each of the above effects and to test the significance of each of the above effects. Also, find and report a 95 percent confidence interval for each of the above effects. Interpret your results.

b　The prediction results at the bottom of the MegaStat output correspond to a future period when the price of Fresh will be $x_1 = 3.70$, the competitor's average price of similar detergents will be $x_2 = 3.90$, the advertising expenditure for Fresh will be $x_3 = 6.50$, and advertising campaign C will be used. Show how $\hat{y} = 8.61621$ is calculated. Then find, report, and interpret a 95 percent confidence interval for mean demand and a 95 percent prediction interval for an individual demand when $x_1 = 3.70$, $x_2 = 3.90$, $x_3 = 6.50$, and campaign C is used.

c　Consider the alternative model

$$y = \beta_0 + \beta_1 x_1 + \beta_2 x_2 + \beta_3 x_3 + \beta_4 D_A + \beta_5 D_C + \varepsilon$$

Here D_A equals 1 if advertising campaign A is used and equals 0 otherwise. Describe the effect represented by the regression parameter β_5.

d　The MegaStat output of the least squares point estimates of the parameters of the model of part c is as follows.

Regression output

variables	coefficients	std. error	t (df = 23)	p-value	confidence interval 95% lower	95% upper
Intercept	8.9849	1.5971	5.626	8.61E-06	5.6888	12.2811
X1	−2.7680	0.4144	−6.679	6.58E-07	−3.6234	−1.9127
X2	1.6667	0.1913	8.711	6.77E-09	1.2718	2.0616
X3	0.4927	0.0806	6.110	2.60E-06	0.3263	0.6592
DA	−0.2695	0.0695	−3.880	.0007	−0.4128	−0.1262
DC	0.1701	0.0669	2.543	.0179	0.0320	0.3081

FIGURE 14.22   **MegaStat Output of a Regression Analysis of the Fresh Demand Data Using the Model**
$$y = \beta_0 + \beta_1x_1 + \beta_2x_2 + \beta_3x_3 + \beta_4D_B + \beta_5D_C + \beta_6x_3D_B + \beta_7x_3D_C + \varepsilon$$

R^2 0.960
Adjusted R^2 0.948
R 0.980
Std. Error 0.156

Regression output variables	coefficients	std. error	t (df = 22)	p-value	confidence interval 95% lower	95% upper
Intercept	8.7619	1.7071	5.133	3.82E-05	5.2216	12.3021
X1	−2.7895	0.4339	−6.428	1.81E-06	−3.6894	−1.8895
X2	1.6365	0.2062	7.938	6.72E-08	1.2089	2.0641
X3	0.5160	0.1288	4.007	.0006	0.2489	0.7831
DB	0.2539	0.8722	0.291	.7737	−1.5550	2.0628
DC	0.8435	0.9739	0.866	.3958	−1.1762	2.8631
X3DB	0.0030	0.1334	0.023	.9822	−0.2736	0.2797
X3DC	−0.0629	0.1502	−0.419	.6794	−0.3744	0.2486

Predicted values for: Demand

Predicted	95% Confidence Interval lower	upper	95% Prediction Interval lower	upper	Leverage
8.61178	8.50372	8.71984	8.27089	8.95266	0.112

Use the MegaStat output to test the significance of the effect represented by β_5 and find a 95 percent confidence interval for β_5. Interpret your results.

14.29   THE FRESH DETERGENT CASE   ● Fresh3

Figure 14.22 presents the MegaStat output of a regression analysis of the Fresh demand data using the model

$$y = \beta_0 + \beta_1x_1 + \beta_2x_2 + \beta_3x_3 + \beta_4D_B + \beta_5D_C + \beta_6x_3D_B + \beta_7x_3D_C + \varepsilon$$

where the dummy variables D_B and D_C are defined as in Exercise 14.28.
a   This model assumes that there is interaction between advertising expenditure x_3 and type of advertising campaign. What do the p-values related to the significance of the cross-product terms x_3D_B and x_3D_C say about the need for these interaction terms and about whether there is interaction between x_3 and type of advertising campaign?
b   The prediction results at the bottom of Figure 14.22 are for a future sales period in which $x_1 = 3.70$, $x_2 = 3.90$, $x_3 = 6.50$, and advertising campaign C will be used. Use the output to find and report a point prediction of and a 95 percent prediction interval for Fresh demand in such a sales period. Is the 95 percent prediction interval given by this model shorter or longer than the 95 percent prediction interval given by the model that utilizes D_B and D_C in Exercise 14.28? What are the implications of this comparison?

14.8 Model Building and the Effects of Multicollinearity ● ● ●

● SalePerf

CHAPTER 17

Multicollinearity   Recall the sales territory performance data in Table 14.3 (page 575). These data consist of values of the dependent variable y (SALES) and of the independent variables x_1 (TIME), x_2 (MKTPOTEN), x_3 (ADVER), x_4 (MKTSHARE), and x_5 (CHANGE). The complete sales territory performance data analyzed by Cravens, Woodruff, and Stomper (1972) consist of the data presented in Table 14.3 and data concerning three additional independent variables. These three additional variables are defined as follows:

x_6 = number of accounts handled by the representative (we will sometimes denote this variable as ACCTS)

FIGURE 14.23　MINITAB Output of a Correlation Matrix for the Sales Territory Performance Data

	Sales	Time	MktPoten	Adver	MktShare	Change	Accts	WkLoad
Time	0.623							
	0.001							
MktPoten	0.598	0.454						
	0.002	0.023						
Adver	0.596	0.249	0.174		Cell Contents: Pearson correlation			
	0.002	0.230	0.405		P-Value			
MktShare	0.484	0.106	-0.211	0.264				
	0.014	0.613	0.312	0.201				
Change	0.489	0.251	0.268	0.377	0.085			
	0.013	0.225	0.195	0.064	0.685			
Accts	0.754	0.758	0.479	0.200	0.403	0.327		
	0.000	0.000	0.016	0.338	0.046	0.110		
WkLoad	-0.117	-0.179	-0.259	-0.272	0.349	-0.288	-0.199	
	0.577	0.391	0.212	0.188	0.087	0.163	0.341	
Rating	0.402	0.101	0.359	0.411	-0.024	0.549	0.229	-0.277
	0.046	0.631	0.078	0.041	0.911	0.004	0.272	0.180

x_7 = average workload per account, measured by using a weighting based on the sizes of the orders by the accounts and other workload-related criteria (we will sometimes denote this variable as WKLOAD)

x_8 = an aggregate rating on eight dimensions of the representative's performance, made by a sales manager and expressed on a 1–7 scale (we will sometimes denote this variable as RATING)

Table 14.13 gives the observed values of x_6, x_7, and x_8, and Figure 14.23 presents the MINITAB output of a **correlation matrix** for the sales territory performance data. Examining the first column of this matrix, we see that the simple correlation coefficient between SALES and WKLOAD is $-.117$ and that the p-value for testing the significance of the relationship between SALES and WKLOAD is .577. This indicates that there is little or no relationship between SALES and WKLOAD. However, the simple correlation coefficients between SALES and the other seven independent variables range from .402 to .754, with associated p-values ranging from .046 to .000. This indicates the existence of potentially useful relationships between SALES and these seven independent variables.

While simple correlation coefficients (and scatter plots) give us a preliminary understanding of the data, they cannot be relied upon alone to tell us which independent variables are significantly related to the dependent variable. One reason for this is a condition called *multicollinearity*. **Multicollinearity** is said to exist among the independent variables in a regression situation if these independent variables are related to or dependent upon each other. One way to investigate multicollinearity is to examine the correlation matrix. To understand this, note that all of the simple correlation coefficients not located in the first column of this matrix measure the **simple correlations between the independent variables.** For example, the simple correlation coefficient between ACCTS and TIME is .758, which says that the ACCTS values increase as the TIME values increase. Such a relationship makes sense because it is logical that the longer a sales representative has been with the company, the more accounts he or she handles. Statisticians often regard multicollinearity in a data set to be severe if at least one simple correlation coefficient between the independent variables is at least .9. Since the largest such simple correlation coefficient in Figure 14.23 is .758, this is not true for the sales territory performance data.

The most important problem caused by multicollinearity is that, even when multicollinearity is not severe, it can hinder our ability to use the t statistics and related p-values to assess the importance of the independent variables. Recall that we can reject H_0: $\beta_j = 0$ in favor of H_a: $\beta_j \neq 0$ at level of significance α if and only if the absolute value of the corresponding t statistic is greater than $t_{\alpha/2}$ based on $n - (k + 1)$ degrees of freedom, or, equivalently, if and only if the related p-value is less than α. Thus the larger (in absolute value) the t statistic is and the smaller the p-value is, the stronger is the evidence that we should reject H_0: $\beta_j = 0$ and the stronger is the evidence that the independent variable x_j is significant. When multicollinearity exists, the sizes of the t

TABLE 14.13
Values of ACCTS, WKLOAD, and RATING
SalePerf2

Accounts, x_6	Work-load, x_7	Rating, x_8
74.86	15.05	4.9
107.32	19.97	5.1
96.75	17.34	2.9
195.12	13.40	3.4
180.44	17.64	4.6
104.88	16.22	4.5
256.10	18.80	4.6
126.83	19.86	2.3
203.25	17.42	4.9
119.51	21.41	2.8
116.26	16.32	3.1
142.28	14.51	4.2
89.43	19.35	4.3
84.55	20.02	4.2
119.51	15.26	5.5
80.49	15.87	3.6
136.58	7.81	3.4
78.86	16.00	4.2
136.58	17.44	3.6
138.21	17.98	3.1
75.61	20.99	1.6
102.44	21.66	3.4
76.42	21.46	2.7
136.58	24.78	2.8
88.62	24.96	3.9

FIGURE 14.24   MegaStat Output of the *t* Statistics and *p*-Values for the Sales Territory Performance
Model $y = \beta_0 + \beta_1 x_1 + \beta_2 x_2 + \beta_3 x_3 + \beta_4 x_4 + \beta_5 x_5 + \beta_6 x_6 + \beta_7 x_7 + \beta_8 x_8 + \varepsilon$

Regression output variables	coefficients	std. error	t (df = 16)	p-value	confidence interval 95% lower	95% upper
Intercept	−1,507.8137	778.6349	−1.936	.0707	−3,158.4457	142.8182
Time	2.0096	1.9307	1.041	.3134	−2.0832	6.1024
MktPoten	0.0372	0.0082	4.536	.0003	0.0198	0.0546
Adver	0.1510	0.0471	3.205	.0055	0.0511	0.2509
MktShare	199.0235	67.0279	2.969	.0090	56.9307	341.1164
Change	290.8551	186.7820	1.557	.1390	−105.1049	686.8152
Accts	5.5510	4.7755	1.162	.2621	−4.5728	15.6747
WkLoad	19.7939	33.6767	0.588	.5649	−51.5975	91.1853
Rating	8.1893	128.5056	0.064	.9500	−264.2304	280.6090

statistic and of the related *p*-value **measure the additional importance of the independent variable x_j over the combined importance of the other independent variables in the regression model.** Since two or more correlated independent variables contribute redundant information, multicollinearity often causes the *t* statistics obtained by relating a dependent variable to a set of correlated independent variables to be smaller (in absolute value) than the *t* statistics that would be obtained if separate regression analyses were run, where each separate regression analysis relates the dependent variable to a smaller set (for example, only one) of the correlated independent variables. Thus multicollinearity can cause some of the correlated independent variables to appear less important—in terms of having small absolute *t* statistics and large *p*-values—than they really are.

● SalePerf   For example, Figure 14.24 tells us that when we perform a regression analysis of the sales territory performance data using a model that relates *y* to all eight independent variables, the *p*-values related to TIME, MKTPOTEN, ADVER, MKTSHARE, CHANGE, ACCTS, WKLOAD, and RATING are, respectively, .3134, .0003, .0055, .0090, .1390, .2621, .5649, and .9500. By contrast, recall from Figure 14.5 (page 576) that when we perform a regression analysis of the sales territory performance data using a model that relates *y* to the first five independent variables, the *p*-values related to TIME, MKTPOTEN, ADVER, MKTSHARE, and CHANGE are, respectively, .0065, .0001, .0025, .0001, and .0530. Note that TIME (*p*-value = .0065) seems **highly significant** and CHANGE (*p*-value = .0530) seems **somewhat significant** in the five independent variable model. However, when we consider the model that uses all eight independent variables, TIME (*p*-value = .3134) seems **insignificant** and CHANGE (*p*-value = .1390) seems **somewhat insignificant.** The reason that TIME and CHANGE seem more significant in the five independent variable model is that, since this model uses fewer variables, TIME and CHANGE contribute less overlapping information and thus have additional importance in this model.

Comparing regression models on the basis of R^2, *s*, adjusted R^2, prediction interval length, and the *C* statistic   We have seen that when multicollinearity exists in a model, the *p*-value associated with an independent variable in the model measures the additional importance of the variable over the combined importance of the other variables in the model. Therefore, it can be difficult to use the *p*-values to determine which variables to retain in and which variables to remove from a model. The implication of this is that we need to evaluate more than the **additional importance** of each independent variable in a regression model. We also need to evaluate how well the independent variables **work together** to accurately describe, predict, and control the dependent variable. One way to do this is to determine if the **overall** model gives a high R^2 and $\overline{R}^2$, a small *s*, and short prediction intervals.

It can be proved that **adding any independent variable to a regression model, even an unimportant independent variable, will decrease the unexplained variation and will increase the explained variation.** Therefore, since the total variation $\Sigma(y_i - \overline{y})^2$ depends only on the observed *y* values and thus remains unchanged when we add an independent variable to a regression model, it follows that **adding any independent variable to a regression model will increase R^2 = (Explained variation)/(Total variation).** This implies that R^2 cannot tell us (by decreasing) that adding an independent variable is undesirable. That is, although we wish to obtain a model with a large R^2, there are better criteria than R^2 that can be used to **compare** regression models.

One better criterion is the standard error

$$s = \sqrt{\frac{SSE}{n - (k + 1)}}$$

When we add an independent variable to a regression model, the number of model parameters $(k + 1)$ increases by one, and thus the number of degrees of freedom $n - (k + 1)$ decreases by one. If the decrease in $n - (k + 1)$, which is used in the denominator to calculate s, is proportionally more than the decrease in SSE (the unexplained variation) that is caused by adding the independent variable to the model, then s will increase. **If s increases, this tells us that we should not add the independent variable to the model.** To see one reason why, consider the formula for the prediction interval for y

$$[\hat{y} \pm t_{\alpha/2}s\sqrt{1 + \text{Distance value}}]$$

Since **adding an independent variable** to a model decreases the number of degrees of freedom, adding the variable will increase the $t_{\alpha/2}$ point used to calculate the prediction interval. To understand this, look at any column of the t table in Table A.4 (pages 642–643) and scan from the bottom of the column to the top—you can see that the t points increase as the degrees of freedom decrease. It can also be shown that adding any independent variable to a regression model will not decrease (and usually increases) the distance value. Therefore, since adding an independent variable increases $t_{\alpha/2}$ and does not decrease the distance value, **if s increases, the length of the prediction interval for y will increase.** This means the model will predict less accurately and thus we should not add the independent variable.

On the other hand, if adding an independent variable to a regression model **decreases s,** the length of a prediction interval for y will decrease if and only if the decrease in s is enough to offset the increase in $t_{\alpha/2}$ and the (possible) increase in the distance value. Therefore, **an independent variable should not be included in a final regression model unless it reduces s enough to reduce the length of the desired prediction interval for y.** However, we must balance the length of the prediction interval, or in general, the "goodness" of any criterion, against the difficulty and expense of using the model. For instance, predicting y requires knowing the corresponding values of the independent variables. So we must decide whether including an independent variable reduces s and prediction interval lengths enough to offset the potential errors caused by possible inaccurate determination of values of the independent variables, or the possible expense of determining these values. If adding an independent variable provides prediction intervals that are only slightly shorter while making the model more difficult and/or more expensive to use, we might decide that including the variable is not desirable.

Since a key factor is the length of the prediction intervals provided by the model, one might wonder why we do not simply make direct comparisons of prediction interval lengths (without looking at s). It is useful to compare interval lengths, but these lengths depend on the distance value, which depends on how far the values of the independent variables we wish to predict for are from the center of the experimental region. We often wish to compute prediction intervals for several different combinations of values of the independent variables (and thus for several different values of the distance value). Thus we would compute prediction intervals having slightly different lengths. However, the standard error s is a constant factor with respect to the length of prediction intervals (as long as we are considering the same regression model). Thus it is common practice to compare regression models on the basis of s (and s^2). Finally, note that it can be shown that the standard error s decreases if and only if $\overline{R}^2$ (adjusted R^2) increases. It follows that, if we are comparing regression models, the model that gives the smallest s gives the largest $\overline{R}^2$.

EXAMPLE 14.10 **The Sales Territory Performance Case**   💧 SalePerf   **C**

Figure 14.25 gives MINITAB and MegaStat output resulting from calculating R^2, $\overline{R}^2$, and s for some of the best regression models in the sales territory performance situation (the values of C_p on the output will be explained after we complete this example). The MINITAB output gives the

FIGURE 14.25 MINITAB and MegaStat Output of Some of the Best Sales Territory Performance Regression Models

(a) The MINITAB output of the two best models of each size

Vars	R-Sq	R-Sq(adj)	Mallows C-p	S	Time	MktPoten	Adver	MktShare	Change	Accts	WkLoad	Rating
1	56.8	55.0	67.6	881.09						X		
1	38.8	36.1	104.6	1049.3	X							
2	77.5	75.5	27.2	650.39			X			X		
2	74.6	72.3	33.1	691.10		X		X				
3	84.9	82.7	14.0	545.51		X	X	X				
3	82.8	80.3	18.4	582.64		X	X			X		
4	90.0	88.1	5.4	453.84		X	X	X		X		
4	89.6	87.5	6.4	463.95	X	X	X	X				
5	91.5	89.3	4.4	430.23	X	X	X	X	X			
5	91.2	88.9	5.0	436.75		X	X	X	X			
6	92.0	89.4	5.4	428.00	X	X	X	X	X			
6	91.6	88.9	6.1	438.20		X	X	X	X	X		
7	92.2	89.0	7.0	435.67	X	X	X	X	X	X		
7	92.0	88.8	7.3	440.30	X	X	X	X	X	X		X
8	92.2	88.3	9.0	449.03	X	X	X	X	X	X	X	X

(b) The MegaStat output of the best single model of each size

Nvar	Time	MktPoten	Adver	MktShare	Change	Accts	WkLoad	Rating	s	Adj R²	R²	Cp	p-value
1						.0000			881.093	.550	.568	67.558	1.35E-05
2			.0002			.0000			650.392	.755	.775	27.156	7.45E-08
3		.0000	.0011	.0000					545.515	.827	.849	13.995	8.43E-09
4		.0001	.0001	.0011		.0043			453.836	.881	.900	5.431	9.56E-10
5	.0065	.0000	.0025	.0000	.0530				430.232	.893	.915	4.443	1.59E-09
6	.1983	.0001	.0018	.0004	.0927	.2881			428.004	.894	.920	5.354	6.14E-09
7	.2868	.0002	.0027	.0066	.0897	.2339	.5501		435.674	.890	.922	7.004	3.21E-08
8	.3134	.0003	.0055	.0090	.1390	.2621	.5649	.9500	449.026	.883	.922	9.000	1.82E-07

(c) The MegaStat output of the best eight models

Nvar	Time	MktPoten	Adver	MktShare	Change	Accts	WkLoad	Rating	s	Adj R²	R²	Cp	p-value
6	.1983	.0001	.0018	.0004	.0927	.2881			428.004	.894	.920	5.354	6.14E-09
5	.0065	.0000	.0025	.0000	.0530				430.232	.893	.915	4.443	1.59E-09
7	.2868	.0002	.0027	.0066	.0897	.2339	.5501		435.674	.890	.922	7.004	3.21E-08
5		.0001	.0006	.0006	.1236	.0089			436.746	.889	.912	4.975	2.10E-09
6		.0002	.0006	.0098	.1035	.0070	.3621		438.197	.889	.916	6.142	9.31E-09
7	.2204	.0002	.0040	.0006	.1449	.3194		.9258	440.297	.888	.920	7.345	3.82E-08
6	.0081	.0000	.0054	.0000	.1143			.7692	440.936	.887	.915	6.357	1.04E-08
6	.0083	.0000	.0044	.0000	.0629		.9474		441.966	.887	.915	6.438	1.08E-08

two best models of each size in terms of s and $\overline{R}^2$—the two best one-variable models, the two best two-variable models, the two best three-variable models, and so on. The first MegaStat output gives the best single model of each size, and the second MegaStat output gives the eight best models of any size, in terms of s and $\overline{R}^2$. The MegaStat output also gives the p-values for the variables in each model. Examining the output, we see that the three models having the smallest values of s and largest values of $\overline{R}^2$ are

1   The six-variable model that contains

TIME, MKTPOTEN, ADVER, MKTSHARE, CHANGE, ACCTS

and has $s = 428.004$ and $\overline{R}^2 = 89.4$; we refer to this model as Model 1.

2   The five-variable model that contains

TIME, MKTPOTEN, ADVER, MKTSHARE, CHANGE

and has $s = 430.232$ and $\overline{R}^2 = 89.3$; we refer to this model as Model 2.

3   The seven-variable model that contains

TIME, MKTPOTEN, ADVER, MKTSHARE, CHANGE, ACCTS, WKLOAD

and has $s = 435.674$ and $\overline{R}^2 = 89.0$; we refer to this model as Model 3.

To see that s can increase when we add an independent variable to a regression model, note that s increases from 428.004 to 435.674 when we add WKLOAD to Model 1 to form Model 3. In this case, although it can be verified that adding WKLOAD decreases the unexplained variation from 3,297,279.3342 to 3,226,756.2751, this decrease has not been enough to offset the change in the denominator of

$$s^2 = \frac{SSE}{n - (k + 1)}$$

which decreases from $25 - 7 = 18$ to $25 - 8 = 17$. To see that prediction interval lengths might increase even though s decreases, consider adding ACCTS to Model 2 to form Model 1. This decreases s from 430.232 to 428.004. However, consider a questionable sales representative for whom TIME $= 85.42$, MKTPOTEN $= 35,182.73$, ADVER $= 7,281.65$, MKTSHARE $= 9.64$, CHANGE $= .28$, and ACCTS $= 120.61$. The 95 percent prediction interval given by Model 2 for sales corresponding to this combination of values of the independent variables is [3,233.59, 5,129.89] and has length $5,129.89 - 3,233.59 = 1,896.3$. The 95 percent prediction interval given by Model 1 for such sales is [3,193.86, 5,093.14] and has length $5,093.14 - 3,193.86 = 1,899.28$. In other words, the slight decrease in s accomplished by adding ACCTS to Model 2 to form Model 1 is not enough to offset the increases in $t_{\alpha/2}$ and the distance value (which can be shown to increase from .109 to .115), and thus the length of the prediction interval given by Model 1 increases. In addition, the extra independent variable ACCTS in Model 1 has a p-value of .2881. Therefore, we conclude that Model 2 is better than Model 1 and is, in fact, the "best" sales territory performance model (using only linear terms).

Another quantity that can be used for comparing regression models is called the **C statistic** (also often called the **C_p statistic**). To show how to calculate the C statistic, suppose that we wish to choose an appropriate set of independent variables from p potential independent variables. We first calculate the mean square error, which we denote as s_p^2, for the model using all p potential independent variables. Then, if SSE denotes the unexplained variation for another particular model that has k independent variables, it follows that the C statistic for this model is

$$C = \frac{SSE}{s_p^2} - [n - 2(k + 1)]$$

For example, consider the sales territory performance case. It can be verified that the mean square error for the model using all $p = 8$ independent variables is 201,621.21 and that the SSE for the model using the first $k = 5$ independent variables (Model 2 in the previous example) is 3,516,812.7933. It follows that the C statistic for this latter model is

    ● SalePerf

$$C = \frac{3,516,812.7933}{201,621.21} - [25 - 2(5 + 1)] = 4.4$$

Since the C statistic for a given model is a function of the model's SSE, and since we want SSE to be small, **we want C to be small.** Although adding an unimportant independent variable to a regression model will decrease SSE, adding such a variable can increase C. This can happen when the decrease in SSE caused by the addition of the extra independent variable is not enough to offset the decrease in $n - 2(k + 1)$ caused by the addition of the extra independent variable (which increases k by 1). It should be noted that although adding an unimportant independent variable to a regression model can increase both s^2 and C, there is no exact relationship between s^2 and C.

While we want C to be small, it can be shown from the theory behind the C statistic that **we also wish to find a model for which the C statistic roughly equals $k + 1$,** the number of parameters in the model. **If a model has a C statistic substantially greater than $k + 1$, it can be shown that this model has substantial *bias* and is undesirable.** Thus, although we want to find a model for which C is as small as possible, if C for such a model is substantially greater than $k + 1$, we may prefer to choose a different model for which C is slightly larger and more nearly equal to the number of parameters in that (different) model. **If a particular model has a small value of C and C for this model is less than $k + 1$, then the model should be considered desirable.** Finally, it should be noted that for the model that includes all p potential independent variables (and thus utilizes $p + 1$ parameters), it can be shown that $C = p + 1$.

● SalePerf

If we examine Figure 14.25, we see that Model 2 of the previous example has the smallest C statistic. The C statistic for this model equals 4.4. Since $C = 4.4$ is less than $k + 1 = 6$, the model is not biased. Therefore, this model should be considered best with respect to the C statistic.

Exercises for Section 14.8

CONCEPTS

connect™

14.30 What is multicollinearity? What problems can be caused by multicollinearity?

14.31 Discuss how we compare regression models.

METHODS AND APPLICATIONS

Load	Pop
15.57	18.0
44.02	9.5
20.42	12.8
18.74	36.7
49.20	35.7
44.92	24.0
55.48	43.3
59.28	46.7
94.39	78.7
128.02	180.5
96.00	60.9
131.42	103.7
127.21	126.8
409.20	169.4
463.70	331.4
510.22	371.6

14.32 THE HOSPITAL LABOR NEEDS CASE ● HospLab2

Recall that Table 14.6 (page 580) presents data concerning the need for labor in 16 U.S. Navy hospitals. This table gives values of the dependent variable Hours (monthly labor hours) and of the independent variables Xray (monthly X-ray exposures), BedDays (monthly occupied bed days—a hospital has one occupied bed day if one bed is occupied for an entire day), and Length (average length of patients' stay, in days). The data in Table 14.6 are part of a larger data set analyzed by the navy. The complete data set consists of two additional independent variables—Load (average daily patient load) and Pop (eligible population in the area, in thousands)—values of which are given on the page margin. Figures 14.26 and 14.27 give MINITAB and MegaStat output of multicollinearity analysis and model building for the complete hospital labor needs data set.

a Find the three largest simple correlation coefficients between the independent variables in Figure 14.26(a).

b Based on your answer to part *a*, which independent variables are most strongly involved in multicollinearity?

c Do any least squares point estimates in Figure 14.26(b) have a sign (positive or negative) that is different from what we would intuitively expect—another indication of multicollinearity?

F I G U R E   14.26   MINITAB and MegaStat Output of Multicollinearity Analysis for the Hospital Labor Needs Data

(a) The MegaStat output of a correlation matrix

	Load	Xray	BedDays	Pop	Length	Hours
Load	1.0000					
Xray	.9051	1.0000				
BedDays	.9999	.9048	1.0000			
Pop	.9353	.9124	.9328	1.0000		
Length	.6610	.4243	.6609	.4515	1.0000	
Hours	.9886	.9425	.9889	.9465	.5603	1.0000

16 sample size

±.497 critical value .05 (two-tail)
±.623 critical value .01 (two-tail)

(b) The MINITAB output of a regression analysis relating hours to all five potential independent variables

Predictor	Coef	SE Coef	T	P
Constant	2270.4	670.8	3.38	0.007
LOAD	-9.30	60.81	-0.15	0.882
XRAY	0.04112	0.01368	3.01	0.013
BEDDAYS	1.413	1.925	0.73	0.480
POP	-3.223	4.474	-0.72	0.488
LENGTH	-467.9	131.6	-3.55	0.005

FIGURE 14.27   MegaStat Output of Model Building for the Hospital Labor Needs Data

(a) The MegaStat output of the best single model of each size

Nvar	Load	Xray	BedDays	Pop	Length	s	Adj R²	R²	Cp	p-value
1			.0000			856.707	.976	.978	52.313	5.51E-13
2			.0000		.0001	489.126	.992	.993	9.467	7.41E-15
3		.0120	.0000		.0012	387.160	.995	.996	3.258	9.92E-15
4		.0091	.0000	.2690	.0013	381.555	.995	.997	4.023	1.86E-13
5	.8815	.0132	.4799	.4878	.0052	399.712	.995	.997	6.000	5.65E-12

(b) The MegaStat output of the best five models

Nvar	Load	Xray	BedDays	Pop	Length	s	Adj R²	R²	Cp	p-value
4		.0091	.0000	.2690	.0013	381.555	.995	.997	4.023	1.86E-13
3		.0120	.0000		.0012	387.160	.995	.996	3.258	9.92E-15
4	.3981	.0121	.1381		.0018	390.876	.995	.996	4.519	2.43E-13
4	.0000	.0097		.1398	.0011	391.236	.995	.996	4.538	2.45E-13
5	.8815	.0132	.4799	.4878	.0052	399.712	.995	.997	6.000	5.65E-12

d   The *p*-value associated with *F*(model) for the model in Figure 14.26(b) is less than .0001. In general, if the *p*-value associated with *F*(model) is much smaller than any of the *p*-values associated with the independent variables, this is another indication of multicollinearity. Is this true in this situation?

e   Figures 14.27(a) and (b) indicate that the two best hospital labor needs models are the model using Xray, BedDays, Pop, and Length, which we will call Model 1, and the model using Xray, BedDays, and Length, which we will call Model 2. Which model gives the smallest value of *s* and the largest value of $\bar{R}^2$? Which model gives the smallest value of *C*? Consider a questionable hospital for which Xray = 56,194, BedDays = 14,077.88, Pop = 329.7, and Length = 6.89. The 95 percent prediction intervals given by Models 1 and 2 for labor hours corresponding to this combination of values of the independent variables are, respectively, [14,888.43, 16,861.30] and [14,906.24, 16,886.26]. Which model gives the shortest prediction interval? Which model has all of the *p*-values for its independent variables less than .05? Overall, which model seems best?

TABLE 14.14   Prescription Sales Data   ● PreSales

Pharmacy	Sales, y	Floor Space, x_1	Prescription Percentage, x_2	Parking, x_3	Income, x_4	Shopping Center, x_5
1	22	4,900	9	40	18	1
2	19	5,800	10	50	20	1
3	24	5,000	11	55	17	1
4	28	4,400	12	30	19	0
5	18	3,850	13	42	10	0
6	21	5,300	15	20	22	1
7	29	4,100	20	25	8	0
8	15	4,700	22	60	15	1
9	12	5,600	24	45	16	1
10	14	4,900	27	82	14	1
11	18	3,700	28	56	12	0
12	19	3,800	31	38	8	0
13	15	2,400	36	35	6	0
14	22	1,800	37	28	4	0
15	13	3,100	40	43	6	0
16	16	2,300	41	20	5	0
17	8	4,400	42	46	7	1
18	6	3,300	42	15	4	0
19	7	2,900	45	30	9	1
20	17	2,400	46	16	3	0

F I G U R E   **14.28**   **The MegaStat Output of the Single Best Model of Each Size for the Prescription Sales Data**

Nvar	FloorSpace	Presc.Pct	Parking	Income	ShopCntr?	s	Adj R^2	R^2	Cp	p-value
1		.0014				4.835	.408	.439	10.171	.0014
2	.0035	.0000				3.842	.626	.666	1.606	.0001
3	.1523	.0002			.2716	3.809	.633	.691	2.436	.0002
4	.1997	.0003	.5371		.3424	3.883	.618	.699	4.062	.0008
5	.2095	.0087	.5819	.8066	.3564	4.010	.593	.700	6.000	.0025

14.33   Market Planning, Inc., a marketing research firm, has obtained the prescription sales data in Table 14.14 for $n = 20$ independent pharmacies.[2] In this table y is the average weekly prescription sales over the past year (in units of \$1,000), x_1 is the floor space (in square feet), x_2 is the percentage of floor space allocated to the prescription department, x_3 is the number of parking spaces available to the store, x_4 is the weekly per capita income for the surrounding community (in units of \$100), and x_5 is a **dummy variable** that equals 1 if the pharmacy is located in a shopping center and 0 otherwise. Use the MegaStat output in Figure 14.28 to discuss why the model using FloorSpace and Pres.Pct might be the best model describing prescription sales. The least squares point estimates of the parameters of this model can be calculated to be $b_0 = 48.2909$, $b_1 = -.003842$, and $b_2 = -.5819$. Discuss what b_1 and b_2 say about obtaining high prescription sales.   ● PreSales

CHAPTER 17

14.9 Residual Analysis in Multiple Regression ● ● ●

In Section 13.8 we showed how to use residual analysis to check the regression assumptions for a simple linear regression model. In multiple regression we proceed similarly. Specifically, for a multiple regression model we plot the residuals given by the model against (1) values of each independent variable, (2) values of the predicted value of the dependent variable, and (3) the time order in which the data have been observed (if the regression data are time series data). A fanning-out pattern on a residual plot indicates an increasing error variance; a funneling-in pattern indicates a decreasing error variance. Both violate the constant variance assumption. A curved pattern on a residual plot indicates that the functional form of the regression model is incorrect. If the regression data are time series data, a cyclical pattern on the residual plot versus time suggests positive autocorrelation, while an alternating pattern suggests negative autocorrelation. Both violate the independence assumption. On the other hand, if all residual plots have (at least approximately) a horizontal band appearance, then it is reasonable to believe that the constant variance, correct functional form, and independence assumptions approximately hold. To check the normality assumption, we can construct a histogram, stem-and-leaf display, and normal plot of the residuals. The histogram and stem-and-leaf display should look bell-shaped and symmetric about 0; the normal plot should have a straight-line appearance.

● SalePerf   To illustrate these ideas, consider the sales territory performance data in Table 14.3 (page 575). Figure 14.5 (page 576) gives the MegaStat output of a regression analysis of these data using the model

$$y = \beta_0 + \beta_1 x_1 + \beta_2 x_2 + \beta_3 x_3 + \beta_4 x_4 + \beta_5 x_5 + \varepsilon$$

The least squares point estimates on the output give the prediction equation

$$\hat{y} = -1{,}113.7879 + 3.6121 x_1 + .0421 x_2 + .1289 x_3 + 256.9555 x_4 + 324.5334 x_5$$

Using this prediction equation, we can calculate the predicted sales values and residuals given on the MegaStat output of Figure 14.29. For example, observation 10 on this output corresponds to a sales representative for whom $x_1 = 105.69$, $x_2 = 42{,}053.24$, $x_3 = 5{,}673.11$, $x_4 = 8.85$, and $x_5 = .31$. If we insert these values into the prediction equation, we obtain a predicted sales value of $\hat{y}_{10} = 4{,}143.597$. Since the actual sales for the sales representative are $y_{10} = 4{,}876.370$, the residual e_{10} equals the difference between $y_{10} = 4{,}876.370$ and $\hat{y}_{10} = 4{,}143.597$, which is 732.773. The

[2]This problem is taken from an example in L. Ott, *An Introduction to Statistical Methods and Data Analysis*, 2nd ed. (Boston: PWS-KENT Publishing Company, 1987). Used with permission.

FIGURE 14.29   **MegaStat Output of the Sales Territory Performance Model Residuals**

Observation	Sales	Predicted	Residual
1	3,669.880	3,504.990	164.890
2	3,473.950	3,901.180	−427.230
3	2,295.100	2,774.866	−479.766
4	4,675.560	4,911.872	−236.312
5	6,125.960	5,415.196	710.764
6	2,134.940	2,026.090	108.850
7	5,031.660	5,126.127	−94.467
8	3,367.450	3,106.925	260.525
9	6,519.450	6,055.297	464.153
10	4,876.370	4,143.597	732.773
11	2,468.270	2,503.165	−34.895
12	2,533.100	1,827.065	706.245
13	2,408.110	2,478.083	−69.973
14	2,337.380	2,351.344	−13.964
15	4,586.950	4,797.688	−210.738
16	2,729.240	2,904.099	−174.859
17	3,289.400	3,362.660	−73.260
18	2,800.780	2,907.376	−106.596
19	3,264.200	3,625.026	−360.826
20	3,453.620	4,056.443	−602.823
21	1,741.450	1,409.835	331.615
22	2,035.750	2,494.101	−458.351
23	1,578.000	1,617.561	−39.561
24	4,167.440	4,574.903	−407.463
25	2,799.970	2,488.700	311.270

FIGURE 14.30   **MegaStat Residual Plots for the Sales Territory Performance Model**

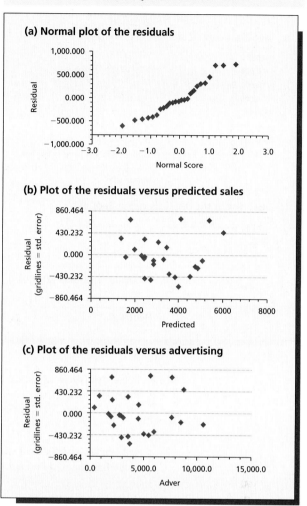

(a) Normal plot of the residuals

(b) Plot of the residuals versus predicted sales

(c) Plot of the residuals versus advertising

normal plot of the residuals in Figure 14.30(a) has a straight-line appearance. The plot of the residuals versus predicted sales in Figure 14.30(b) has a horizontal band appearance, as do the plots of the residuals versus the independent variables [the plot versus x_3, advertising, is shown in Figure 14.30(c)]. We conclude that the regression assumptions approximately hold for the sales territory performance model (note that since the data are cross-sectional, a residual plot versus time is not appropriate).

Exercises for Section 14.9

CONCEPTS

14.34 Discuss how we use residual plots to check the regression assumptions for a multiple regression model.

14.35 Discuss how we check the normality assumption for a multiple regression model.

METHODS AND APPLICATIONS

14.36 **THE HOSPITAL LABOR NEEDS CASE**   ● HospLab

Consider the hospital labor needs data in Table 14.6 (page 580). Figure 14.31 gives residual plots that are obtained when we perform a regression analysis of these data by using the model

$$y = \beta_0 + \beta_1 x_1 + \beta_2 x_2 + \beta_3 x_3 + \varepsilon$$

   a   Interpret the normal plot of the residuals.
   b   Interpret the residual plots versus predicted labor hours, BedDays (x_2), and Length (x_3).

connect

FIGURE 14.31   **MegaStat and Excel Residual Analysis for the Hospital Labor Needs Model**
$$y = \beta_0 + \beta_1 x_1 + \beta_2 x_2 + \beta_3 x_3 + \varepsilon$$

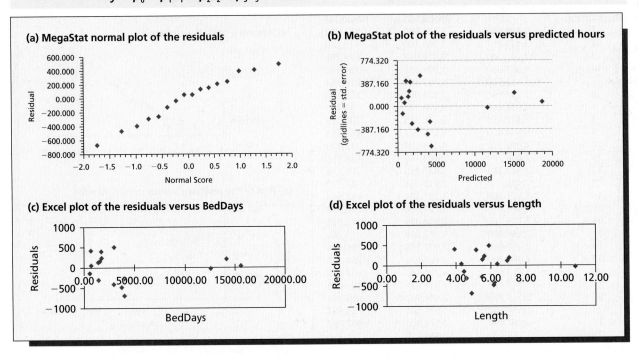

14.37   Recall that Figure 13.28(a) (page 547) gives $n = 16$ weekly values of Pages' Bookstore sales (y), Pages' advertising expenditure (x_1), and a competitor's advertising expenditure (x_2). Use MINITAB, Excel, or MegaStat to fit the model

$$y = \beta_0 + \beta_1 x_1 + \beta_2 x_2 + \varepsilon$$

and plot the model's residuals versus time. Does the residual plot indicate that using x_2 in the model has removed the autocorrelation that is apparent in Figure 13.28(b)?

Chapter Summary

This chapter has discussed **multiple regression analysis.** We began by considering the **multiple regression model** and the assumptions behind this model. We next discussed the **least squares point estimates** of the model parameters and some ways to judge **overall model utility**—the **standard error,** the **multiple coefficient of determination,** the **adjusted multiple coefficient of determination,** and the **overall F test.** Then we considered testing the significance of a single independent variable in a multiple regression model, calculating a **confidence interval** for the mean value of the dependent variable, and calculating a **prediction interval** for an individual value of the dependent variable. We

continued this chapter by discussing the use of **dummy variables** to model **qualitative** independent variables. We then considered **multicollinearity,** which can adversely affect the ability of the t statistics and associated p-values to assess the importance of the independent variables in a regression model. For this reason, we need to determine if the overall model gives a **high R^2,** a **small s,** a **high adjusted R^2,** short prediction intervals, and a **small C.** We discussed how to compare regression models on the basis of these criteria. We concluded this chapter by showing how to use **residual analysis** to check the regression assumptions for multiple regression models.

Glossary of Terms

dummy variable: A variable that takes on the values 0 or 1 and is used to describe the effects of the different levels of a qualitative independent variable in a regression model. (page 595)

interaction: The situation in which the relationship between the mean value of the dependent variable and an independent variable is dependent on the value of another independent variable. (page 599)

multicollinearity: The situation in which the independent variables used in a regression analysis are related to each other. (page 607)

multiple regression model: An equation that describes the relationship between a dependent variable and more than one independent variable. (page 574)

Important Formulas and Tests

The multiple regression model: page 574

The least squares point estimates: page 574

Point estimate of a mean value of y: page 574

Point prediction of an individual value of y: page 574

Mean square error: page 582

Standard error: page 582

Total variation: page 583

Explained variation: page 583

Unexplained variation: page 583

Multiple coefficient of determination: page 583

Multiple correlation coefficient: page 583

Adjusted multiple coefficient of determination: page 584

An F test for the multiple regression model: page 585

Standard error of the estimate b_j: page 588

Testing the significance of an independent variable: page 588

Confidence interval for β_j: page 590

Distance value (in multiple regression): page 593

Confidence interval for a mean value of y: page 593

Prediction interval for an individual value of y: page 593

C statistic: page 611

Supplementary Exercises

14.38 In a September 1982 article in *Business Economics*, C. I. Allmon related y = Crest toothpaste sales in a given year (in thousands of dollars) to x_1 = Crest advertising budget in the year (in thousands of dollars), x_2 = ratio of Crest's advertising budget to Colgate's advertising budget in the year, and x_3 = U.S. personal disposable income in the year (in billions of dollars). The data analyzed are given in Table 14.15. When we perform a regression analysis of these data using the model

$$y = \beta_0 + \beta_1 x_1 + \beta_2 x_2 + \beta_3 x_3 + \varepsilon$$

we find that the least squares point estimates of the model parameters and their associated p-values (given in parentheses) are $b_0 = 30{,}626(.156)$, $b_1 = 3.893(.094)$, $b_2 = -29{,}607(.245)$, and $b_3 = 86.52(<.001)$. Suppose it was estimated at the end of 1979 that in 1980 the advertising budget for Crest would be 28,000; the ratio of Crest's advertising budget to Colgate's advertising budget would be 1.56; and the U.S. personal disposable income would be 1,821.7. Using the model, a point prediction of and a 95 percent prediction interval for Crest sales in 1980 are 251,059 and [221,988, 280,130]. Show how the point prediction has been calculated. ● Crest

14.39 The trend in home building in recent years has been to emphasize open spaces and great rooms, rather than smaller living rooms and family rooms. A builder of speculative homes in the college community of Oxford, Ohio, had been building such homes, but his homes had been taking many months to sell and selling for substantially less than the asking price. In order to determine what types of homes would attract residents of the community, the builder contacted a statistician at a local college. The statistician went to a local real estate agency and obtained the data in Table 14.16. This table presents the sales price y, square footage x_1, number of rooms x_2, number of bedrooms x_3, and age x_4 for each of 63 single-family residences recently sold in the community. When we perform a regression analysis of these data using the model

$$y = \beta_0 + \beta_1 x_1 + \beta_2 x_2 + \beta_3 x_3 + \beta_4 x_4 + \varepsilon$$

we find that the least squares point estimates of the model parameters and their associated p-values (given in parentheses) are $b_0 = 10.3676(.3710)$, $b_1 = .0500(<.001)$, $b_2 = 6.3218(.0152)$, $b_3 = -11.1032(.0635)$, and $b_4 = -.4319(.0002)$. Discuss why the estimates $b_2 = 6.3218$ and $b_3 = -11.1032$ suggest that it might be more profitable when building a house of a specified square footage (1) to include both a (smaller) living room and family room rather than a (larger) great room and (2) to not increase the number of bedrooms (at the cost of another type of room) that would normally be included in a house of the specified square footage. ● OxHome

Note: Based on the statistical results, the builder realized that there are many families with children in a college town and that the parents in such families would rather have one living area for the children (the family room) and a separate living area for themselves (the living room). The builder started modifying his open-space homes accordingly and greatly increased his profits.

14.40 In the article "The Effect of Promotion Timing on Major League Baseball Attendance" (*Sport Marketing Quarterly*, December 1999), T. C. Boyd and T. C. Krehbiel use data from six major league baseball teams having outdoor stadiums to study the effect of promotion timing on major league baseball attendance. One of their regression models describes game attendance in 1996 as follows (p-values less than .10 are shown in parentheses under the appropriate

TABLE 14.15   Crest Toothpaste Sales Data ● Crest

Year	Crest Sales, y	Crest Budget, x_1	Ratio, x_2	U.S. Personal Disposable Income, x_3
1967	105,000	16,300	1.25	547.9
1968	105,000	15,800	1.34	593.4
1969	121,600	16,000	1.22	638.9
1970	113,750	14,200	1.00	695.3
1971	113,750	15,000	1.15	751.8
1972	128,925	14,000	1.13	810.3
1973	142,500	15,400	1.05	914.5
1974	126,000	18,250	1.27	998.3
1975	162,000	17,300	1.07	1,096.1
1976	191,625	23,000	1.17	1,194.4
1977	189,000	19,300	1.07	1,311.5
1978	210,000	23,056	1.54	1,462.9
1979	224,250	26,000	1.59	1,641.7

Source: C. I. Allmon, "Advertising and Sales Relationships for Toothpaste: Another Look," *Business Economics* (September 1982), pp. 17, 58. Reprinted by permission. Copyright © 1982 National Association for Business Economics.

TABLE 14.16   Measurements Taken on 63 Single-Family Residences ● OxHome

Residence	Sales Price, y (× \$1,000)	Square Feet, x_1	Rooms, x_2	Bedrooms, x_3	Age, x_4	Residence	Sales Price, y (× \$1,000)	Square Feet, x_1	Rooms, x_2	Bedrooms, x_3	Age, x_4
1	53.5	1,008	5	2	35	33	63.0	1,053	5	2	24
2	49.0	1,290	6	3	36	34	60.0	1,728	6	3	26
3	50.5	860	8	2	36	35	34.0	416	3	1	42
4	49.9	912	5	3	41	36	52.0	1,040	5	2	9
5	52.0	1,204	6	3	40	37	75.0	1,496	6	3	30
6	55.0	1,204	5	3	10	38	93.0	1,936	8	4	39
7	80.5	1,764	8	4	64	39	60.0	1,904	7	4	32
8	86.0	1,600	7	3	19	40	73.0	1,080	5	2	24
9	69.0	1,255	5	3	16	41	71.0	1,768	8	4	74
10	149.0	3,600	10	5	17	42	83.0	1,503	6	3	14
11	46.0	864	5	3	37	43	90.0	1,736	7	3	16
12	38.0	720	4	2	41	44	83.0	1,695	6	3	12
13	49.5	1,008	6	3	35	45	115.0	2,186	8	4	12
14	105.0	1,950	8	3	52	46	50.0	888	5	2	34
15	152.5	2,086	7	3	12	47	55.2	1,120	6	3	29
16	85.0	2,011	9	4	76	48	61.0	1,400	5	3	33
17	60.0	1,465	6	3	102	49	147.0	2,165	7	3	2
18	58.5	1,232	5	2	69	50	210.0	2,353	8	4	15
19	101.0	1,736	7	3	67	51	60.0	1,536	6	3	36
20	79.4	1,296	6	3	11	52	100.0	1,972	8	3	37
21	125.0	1,996	7	3	9	53	44.5	1,120	5	3	27
22	87.9	1,874	5	2	14	54	55.0	1,664	7	3	79
23	80.0	1,580	5	3	11	55	53.4	925	5	3	20
24	94.0	1,920	5	3	14	56	65.0	1,288	5	3	2
25	74.0	1,430	9	3	16	57	73.0	1,400	5	3	2
26	69.0	1,486	6	3	27	58	40.0	1,376	6	3	103
27	63.0	1,008	5	2	35	59	141.0	2,038	12	4	62
28	67.5	1,282	5	3	20	60	68.0	1,572	6	3	29
29	35.0	1,134	5	2	74	61	139.0	1,545	6	3	9
30	142.5	2,400	9	4	15	62	140.0	1,993	6	3	4
31	92.2	1,701	5	3	15	63	55.0	1,130	5	2	21
32	56.0	1,020	6	3	16						

Source: RE/MAX Alpha Real Estate, Oxford, Ohio.

TABLE 14.17   Estimated Attendance Increases Due to Promotions under Different Conditions

Day	Weekday		Weekend	
	Nonrival	**Rival**	**Nonrival**	**Rival**
Day	Promotion + (Promo*DayGame)	Promotion + (Promo*DayGame) + (Promo*Rival)	Promotion + (Promo*DayGame) + (Promo*Weekend)	Promotion + (Promo*DayGame) + (Promo*Weekend) + (Promo*Rival)
	9,804	10,500	5,114	5,810
Night	Promotion	Promotion + (Promo*Rival)	Promotion + (Promo*Weekend)	Promotion + (Promo*Weekend) + (Promo*Rival)
	4,745	5,441	55	751

independent variables):

$$\text{Attendance} = 2{,}521 + 106.5\ Temperature + 12.33\ Winning\ \% + .2248\ OpWin\ \%$$

$$(<.001) \qquad\qquad (<.001) \qquad\qquad (<.001)$$

$$-\ 424.2\ DayGame + 4{,}845\ Weekend + 1{,}192\ Rival + 4{,}745\ Promotion$$

$$(<.001) \qquad\qquad (<.10) \qquad\qquad (<.001)$$

$$+\ 5{,}059\ Promo*DayGame - 4{,}690\ Promo*Weekend + 696.5\ Promo*Rival$$

$$(<.001) \qquad\qquad (<.001)$$

In this model, *Temperature* is the high temperature recorded in the city on game day; *Winning %* is the home team's winning percentage at the start of the game; *OpWin %* is a dummy variable that equals 1 if the opponent's winning percentage was .500 or higher and 0 otherwise; *DayGame* is a dummy variable that equals 1 if the game was a day game and 0 otherwise; *Weekend* is a dummy variable that equals 1 if the game was on a Friday, Saturday, or Sunday and 0 otherwise; *Rival* is a dummy variable that equals 1 if the opponent was a rival and 0 otherwise; *Promotion* is a dummy variable that equals 1 if the home team ran a promotion during the game and 0 otherwise. Using the model, which is based on 475 games and has an R^2 of .6221, Boyd and Krehbiel obtain Table 14.17, which gives estimated attendance increases due to promotions under different conditions. Use the model to verify the estimated increases (that is, show how these estimates have been calculated). Then discuss why Boyd and Krehbiel conclude that "promotions run during day games and on weekdays are likely to result in greater attendance increases."

14.41 TREND AND SEASONAL PATTERNS: PART 1

Time series data sometimes exhibit **trend** and/or **seasonal patterns. Trend** refers to the upward or downward movement that characterizes a time series over time. Thus trend reflects the long-run growth or decline in the time series. Trend movements can represent a variety of factors. For example, long-run movements in the sales of a particular industry might be determined by changes in consumer tastes, increases in total population, and increases in per capita income. **Seasonal variations** are periodic patterns in a time series that complete themselves within a calendar year or less and then are repeated on a regular basis. Often seasonal variations occur yearly. For example, soft drink sales and hotel room occupancies are annually higher in the summer months, while department store sales are annually higher during the winter holiday season. Seasonal variations can also last less than one year. For example, daily restaurant patronage might exhibit within-week seasonal variation, with daily patronage higher on Fridays and Saturdays.

As an example, Table 14.18 presents quarterly sales of the TRK-50 mountain bike for the previous four years at a bicycle shop in Switzerland. The MINITAB plot in Figure 14.32 shows that the bike sales exhibit a linear trend and a strong seasonal pattern, with bike sales being higher in the spring and summer quarters than in the winter and fall quarters. If we let y_t denote the number of TRK-50 mountain bikes sold in time period t at the Swiss bike shop, then a regression model describing y_t is

$$y_t = \beta_0 + \beta_1 t + \beta_{Q2}Q_2 + \beta_{Q3}Q_3 + \beta_{Q4}Q_4 + \varepsilon_t$$

Here the expression $(\beta_0 + \beta_1 t)$ models the linear trend evident in Figure 14.32. Q_2, Q_3, and Q_4 are dummy variables defined for quarters 2, 3, and 4. Specifically, Q_2 equals 1 if quarterly bike sales were observed in quarter 2 (spring) and 0 otherwise; Q_3 equals 1 if quarterly bike sales were observed in quarter 3 (summer) and 0 otherwise; Q_4 equals 1 if quarterly bike sales were observed in quarter 4 (fall) and 0 otherwise. Note that we have not defined a dummy variable for quarter 1

TABLE 14.18	Quarterly Sales of the TRK-50 Mountain Bike ● BikeSales		
Year	Quarter	t	Sales, y_t
1	1 (Winter)	1	10
	2 (Spring)	2	31
	3 (Summer)	3	43
	4 (Fall)	4	16
2	1	5	11
	2	6	33
	3	7	45
	4	8	17
3	1	9	13
	2	10	34
	3	11	48
	4	12	19
4	1	13	15
	2	14	37
	3	15	51
	4	16	21

FIGURE 14.32   MINITAB Plot of TRK-50 Bike Sales

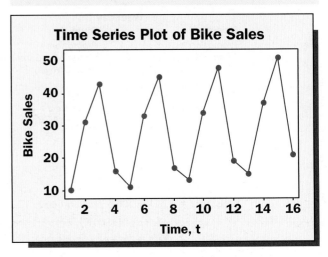

FIGURE 14.33   MINITAB Output of an Analysis of the Quarterly Bike Sales by Using Dummy Variable Regression

```
The regression equation is
BikeSales = 8.75 + 0.500 Time + 21.0 Q2 + 33.5 Q3 + 4.50 Q4


Predictor      Coef   SE Coef       T      P
Constant     8.7500    0.4281   20.44  0.000
Time         0.50000  0.03769   13.27  0.000
Q2          21.0000    0.4782   43.91  0.000
Q3          33.5000    0.4827   69.41  0.000
Q4           4.5000    0.4900    9.18  0.000


S = 0.674200   R-Sq = 99.8%   R-Sq(adj) = 99.8%


Values of Predictors for New Obs    Predicted Values for New Observations
New Obs   Time    Q2    Q3    Q4    New Obs    Fit   SE Fit      95% CI              95% PI
      1   17.0     0     0     0          1  17.250   0.506  (16.137, 18.363)   (15.395, 19.105)
      2   18.0     1     0     0          2  38.750   0.506  (37.637, 39.863)   (36.895, 40.605)
      3   19.0     0     1     0          3  51.750   0.506  (50.637, 52.863)   (49.895, 53.605)
      4   20.0     0     0     1          4  23.250   0.506  (22.137, 24.363)   (21.395, 25.105)
```

(winter). It follows that the regression parameters β_{Q2}, β_{Q3}, and β_{Q4} compare quarters 2, 3, and 4 with quarter 1. Intuitively, for example, β_{Q4} is the difference, excluding trend, between the level of the time series (y_t) in quarter 4 (fall) and the level of the time series in quarter 1 (winter). A positive β_{Q4} would imply that, excluding trend, bike sales in the fall can be expected to be higher than bike sales in the winter. A negative β_{Q4} would imply that, excluding trend, bike sales in the fall can be expected to be lower than bike sales in the winter.

Figure 14.33 gives the MINITAB output of a regression analysis of the quarterly bike sales by using the dummy variable model. The MINITAB output tells us that the linear trend and the seasonal dummy variables are significant (every t statistic has a related p-value less than .01). Also, notice that the least squares point estimates of β_{Q2}, β_{Q3}, and β_{Q4} are, respectively, $b_{Q2} = 21$, $b_{Q3} = 33.5$, and $b_{Q4} = 4.5$. It follows that, excluding trend, expected bike sales in quarter 2 (spring), quarter 3 (summer), and quarter 4 (fall) are estimated to be, respectively, 21, 33.5, and 4.5 bikes greater than expected bike sales in quarter 1 (winter). Furthermore, using all of the least squares point estimates in Figure 14.33, we can compute point forecasts of bike sales in quarters 1 through 3 of next year (periods 17 through 19) as follows:

$$\hat{y}_{17} = b_0 + b_1(17) + b_{Q2}(0) + b_{Q3}(0) + b_{Q4}(0) = 8.75 + .5(17) = 17.250$$

$$\hat{y}_{18} = b_0 + b_1(18) + b_{Q2}(1) + b_{Q3}(0) + b_{Q4}(0) = 8.75 + .5(18) + 21 = 38.750$$

$$\hat{y}_{19} = b_0 + b_1(19) + b_{Q2}(0) + b_{Q3}(1) + b_{Q4}(0) = 8.75 + .5(19) + 33.5 = 51.750$$

These point forecasts are given at the bottom of the MINITAB output, as is the point forecast of bike sales in quarter 4 of next year. Identify the quarter 4 bikes sales point forecast, and show how it has been calculated.

Note: The MINITAB output also gives 95 percent prediction intervals for y_{17}, y_{18}, y_{19}, and y_{20}. The upper limits of these prediction intervals suggest that the bicycle shop can be reasonably sure that it will meet demand for the TRK-50 mountain bike if the numbers of bikes it stocks in quarters 1 through 4 are, respectively, 19, 41, 54, and 25 bikes.

14.42 TREND AND SEASONAL PATTERNS: PART 2

Table 14.19 gives the monthly international passenger totals over the last 11 years for an airline company. A plot of these passenger totals reveals an upward trend with increasing variation, and the natural logarithmic transformation is found to best equalize the variation (see Figure 14.34(a) and (b)). Figure 14.34(c) gives the MINITAB output of a regression analysis of the monthly international passenger totals by using the model

$$\ln y_t = \beta_0 + \beta_1 t + \beta_{M1}M_1 + \beta_{M2}M_2 + \cdots + \beta_{M11}M_{11} + \varepsilon_t$$

Here $M_1, M_2, \ldots, M_{11}$ are appropriately defined dummy variables for January (month 1) through November (month 11). Let y_{133} denote the international passenger totals in month 133 (January of next year). The MINITAB output tells us that a point forecast of and a 95 percent prediction interval for $\ln y_{133}$ are, respectively, 6.08610 and [5.96593, 6.20627]. Using the least squares point estimates on the MINITAB output, show how the point forecast has been calculated. Then, by calculating $e^{6.08610}$ and $[e^{5.96593}, e^{6.20627}]$, find a point forecast of and a 95 percent prediction interval for y_{133}. AirPass

TABLE 14.19   Monthly International Passenger Totals (Thousands of Passengers)   AirPass

Year	Jan.	Feb.	Mar.	Apr.	May	June	July	Aug.	Sept.	Oct.	Nov.	Dec.
1	112	118	132	129	121	135	148	148	136	119	104	118
2	115	126	141	135	125	149	170	170	158	133	114	140
3	145	150	178	163	172	178	199	199	184	162	146	166
4	171	180	193	181	183	218	230	242	209	191	172	194
5	196	196	236	235	229	243	264	272	237	211	180	201
6	204	188	235	227	234	264	302	293	259	229	203	229
7	242	233	267	269	270	315	364	347	312	274	237	278
8	284	277	317	313	318	374	413	405	355	306	271	306
9	315	301	356	348	355	422	465	467	404	347	305	336
10	340	318	362	348	363	435	491	505	404	359	310	337
11	360	342	406	396	420	472	548	559	463	407	362	405

Source: *FAA Statistical Handbook of Civil Aviation* (several annual issues). These data were originally presented by Box and Jenkins (1976).

FIGURE 14.34   Analysis of the Monthly International Passenger Totals

(a) Plot of the passenger totals

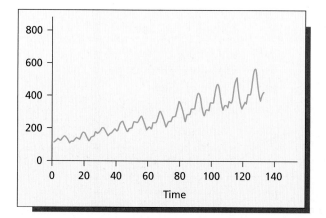

(b) Plot of the natural logarithms of the passenger totals

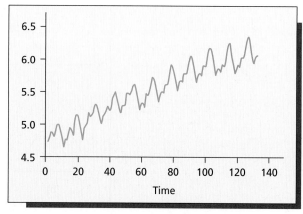

FIGURE 14.34(c)   **MINITAB Output of a Regression Analysis of the Monthly International Passenger Totals Using the Dummy Variable Model**

Predictor	Coef	SE Coef	T	P		Predicted Values for New Observations			
Constant	4.69618	0.01973	238.02	0.000	Time	Fit	SE Fit	95% PI	
Time	0.0103075	0.0001316	78.30	0.000	133	6.08610	0.01973	(5.96593,	6.20627)
Jan	0.01903	0.02451	0.78	0.439	134	6.07888	0.01973	(5.95871,	6.19905)
Feb	0.00150	0.02451	0.06	0.951	135	6.22564	0.01973	(6.10547,	6.34581)
March	0.13795	0.02450	5.63	0.000	136	6.19383	0.01973	(6.07366,	6.31400)
April	0.09583	0.02449	3.91	0.000	137	6.20008	0.01973	(6.07991,	6.32025)
May	0.09178	0.02449	3.75	0.000	138	6.33292	0.01973	(6.21276,	6.45309)
June	0.21432	0.02448	8.75	0.000	139	6.44360	0.01973	(6.32343,	6.56377)
July	0.31469	0.02448	12.85	0.000	140	6.44682	0.01973	(6.32665,	6.56699)
Aug	0.30759	0.02448	12.57	0.000	141	6.31605	0.01973	(6.19588,	6.43622)
Sept	0.16652	0.02448	6.80	0.000	142	6.18515	0.01973	(6.06498,	6.30531)
Oct	0.02531	0.02447	1.03	0.303	143	6.05455	0.01973	(5.93438,	6.17472)
Nov	-0.11559	0.02447	-4.72	0.000	144	6.18045	0.01973	(6.06028,	6.30062)

S = 0.0573917   R-Sq = 98.3%   R-Sq(adj) = 98.1%   Durbin-Watson statistic = 0.420944

14.43   THE QUADRATIC REGRESSION MODEL

The quadratic regression model relating y to x is written as

$$y = \beta_0 + \beta_1 x + \beta_2 x^2 + \varepsilon$$

where β_0, β_1, and β_2 are regression parameters relating the mean value of y to x and ε is an error term that describes the effects on y of all factors other than x and x^2. The quadratic equation $\beta_0 + \beta_1 x + \beta_2 x^2$ that relates $\mu_{y|x}$ to x is the equation of a **parabola.** Two parabolas are shown in Figure 14.35(a) and (b) and help to explain the meanings of the parameters β_0, β_1, and β_2. Here β_0 is the **y-intercept** of the parabola (the value of $\mu_{y|x}$ when $x = 0$). Furthermore, β_1 is the **shift parameter** of the parabola: the value of β_1 shifts the parabola to the left or right. Specifically, increasing the value of β_1 shifts the parabola to the left. Lastly, β_2 is the **rate of curvature** of the parabola. If β_2 is greater than 0, the parabola opens upward [see Figure 14.35(a)]. If β_2 is less than 0, the parabola opens downward [see Figure 14.35(b)]. If a scatter plot of y versus x shows points scattered around a parabola, or a part of a parabola [some typical parts are shown in Figure 14.35(c), (d), (e), and (f)], then the quadratic regression model might appropriately relate y to x.

Suppose an oil company wishes to improve the gasoline mileage obtained by cars that use its premium unleaded gasoline. Company chemists suggest that an additive, ST-3000, be blended with the gasoline. In order to study the effects of this additive, mileage tests are carried out in a laboratory using test equipment that simulates driving under prescribed conditions. The amount of additive ST-3000 blended with the gasoline is varied, and the gasoline mileage for each test run is recorded. Table 14.20 gives the results of the test runs. Here the dependent variable y is

FIGURE 14.35   **The Mean Value of the Dependent Variable Changing in a Quadratic Fashion as x Increases** $(\mu_y = \beta_0 + \beta_1 x + \beta_2 x^2)$

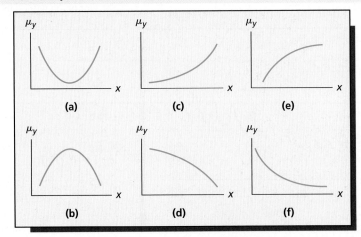

TABLE 14.20	The Gasoline Mileage Study Data GasAdd

Number of Units, x, of Additive ST-3000	Gasoline Mileage y (Miles per Gallon)
0	25.8
0	26.1
0	25.4
1	29.6
1	29.2
1	29.8
2	32.0
2	31.4
2	31.7
3	31.7
3	31.5
3	31.2
4	29.4
4	29.0
4	29.5

FIGURE 14.36 Scatter Plot of Gasoline Mileage (y) versus Number of Units (x) of Additive ST-3000

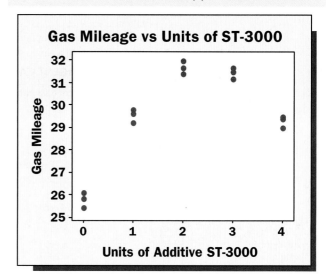

FIGURE 14.37 MINITAB Output of a Regression Analysis of the Gasoline Mileage Data Using the Quadratic Model

```
The regression equation is
Mileage = 25.7 + 4.98 Units - 1.02 UnitsSq

Predictor      Coef    SE Coef      T       P
Constant    25.7152     0.1554  165.43   0.000
Units         4.9762     0.1841   27.02   0.000
UnitsSq      -1.01905   0.04414  -23.09   0.000

S = 0.286079    R-Sq = 98.6%    R-Sq(adj) = 98.3%

Analysis of Variance
Source           DF      SS      MS       F       P
Regression        2  67.915  33.958  414.92   0.000
Residual Error   12   0.982   0.082
Total            14  68.897

Values of Predictors for New Obs    Predicted Values for New Observations
New Obs   Unit    UnitsSq          New Obs     Fit   SE Fit       95% CI             95% PI
      1   2.44    5.9536                 1  31.7901   0.1111  (31.5481, 32.0322)  (31.1215, 32.4588)
```

gasoline mileage (in miles per gallon) and the independent variable x is the amount of additive ST-3000 used (measured as the number of units of additive added to each gallon of gasoline). One of the study's goals is to determine the number of units of additive that should be blended with the gasoline to maximize gasoline mileage. The company would also like to predict the maximum mileage that can be achieved using additive ST-3000.

Figure 14.36 gives a scatter plot of y versus x. Since the scatter plot has the appearance of a quadratic curve (that is, part of a parabola), it seems reasonable to relate y to x by using the quadratic model

$$y = \beta_0 + \beta_1 x + \beta_2 x^2 + \varepsilon$$

Figure 14.37 gives the MINITAB output of a regression analysis of the data using this quadratic model. Here the squared term x^2 is denoted as UNITSSQ on the output.

a Find the least squares point estimates b_0, b_1, and b_2 of the model parameters β_0, β_1, and β_2. Use these estimates to write the least squares prediction equation.

b Find the p-values related to x and x^2 on the computer output. What do these p-values say about the significance of x and x^2? Based on these results, is there a quadratic relationship between y and x?

c Using calculus (taking the derivative of the prediction equation with respect to x, setting it equal to zero, and solving for x), it can be shown that $x = 2.44$ maximizes predicted mileage.

Verify that using this amount of additive ST-3000 will result in a predicted gas mileage equal to 31.7901 mpg as indicated at the bottom of the MINITAB output.

d On the computer output find and interpret a 95 percent interval for the mean mileage obtained by using a large number of gallons of gasoline containing 2.44 units of additive ST-3000 per gallon.

e On the computer output find and interpret a 95 percent interval for the mileage that would be obtained by using a single gallon of gasoline containing 2.44 units of additive ST-3000.

14.44   THE FRESH DETERGENT CASE   ● Fresh2

Consider the historical data concerning demand for Fresh detergent in Table 14.5 (page 579). Also, consider the model

$$y = \beta_0 + \beta_1 x_4 + \beta_2 x_3 + \beta_3 x_3^2 + \beta_4 x_4 x_3 + \varepsilon$$

Here, y is demand for Fresh; x_4 is the price difference; and x_3 is Enterprise Industries' advertising expenditure for Fresh. If we use this model to perform a regression analysis of the data in Table 14.5, we obtain the following partial Excel and MegaStat outputs:

	Coefficients	Standard Error	t Stat	P-value	Regression Statistics	
Intercept	29.1133	7.4832	3.8905	0.0007	Multiple R	0.9596
PriceDif (x4)	11.1342	4.4459	2.5044	0.0192	R Square	0.9209
AdvExp (x3)	-7.6080	2.4691	-3.0813	0.0050	Adjusted R Square	0.9083
x3sq	0.6712	0.2027	3.3115	0.0028	Standard Error	0.2063
x4x3	-1.4777	0.6672	-2.2149	0.0361	Observations	30

Predicted values for: Y

	95% Confidence Interval		95% Prediction Interval		
Predicted	lower	upper	lower	upper	Leverage
8.32725	8.21121	8.44329	7.88673	8.76777	0.075

a Do the quadratic term x_3^2 and the interaction term $x_4 x_3$ seem important in the model? Justify your answer.

b The predicted demand $\hat{y} = 8.32725$ on the output is for a future sales period when the price difference will be $.20 ($x_4 = .20$) and the advertising expenditure will be $650,000 ($x_3 = 6.50$). Show how this predicted demand has been calculated.

14.45   Internet Exercise   ● AlbHome

How do home prices vary with square footage, age, and a variety of other factors? The Data and Story Library (DASL) contains data, including the sale price, for a random sample of 117 homes sold in Albuquerque, New Mexico. Go to the DASL website (http://lib.stat.cmu.edu/DASL/) and retrieve the home price data set (http://lib.stat.cmu.edu/DASL/Datafiles/homedat.html). There are a number of ways to capture the home price data from the DASL site. One simple way is to select just the rows containing the data values (and not the labels), copy, paste directly into an Excel or MINITAB worksheet, add your own variable labels, and save the resulting worksheet. It is possible to copy the variable labels from DASL as well, but the differences in alignment and the intervening blank line add to the difficulty (data sets: AlbHome.xlsx, AlbHome.MTW).

a Construct plots of PRICE versus SQFT and PRICE versus AGE. Describe the nature and apparent strength of the relationships between PRICE and the variables SQFT and AGE. Construct box plots of PRICE versus each of the qualitative/dummy variables NE (northeast location), CUST (custom built), and COR (corner location). What do the box plots suggest about the effect of these features on home prices?

b Using MINITAB, Excel, MegaStat, or other available statistical software, develop a multiple regression model of the dependent variable PRICE versus independent variables SQFT, AGE, NE, CUST, and COR. Identify and interpret the key summary measures $-R^2$, the standard error, and the F statistic from the ANOVA table. Identify and interpret the p-values for the estimated regression coefficients. Which of the independent variables appear to be most important for predicting Albuquerque home prices? Compute and interpret a point prediction and a 95 percent prediction interval for a five-year-old, 2,500 square foot, custom-built home located in the northeast sector of the city (not on a corner lot). Prepare a brief summary of your observations.

c Using MINITAB, Excel, MegaStat, or other available statistical software, develop a multiple regression model of the dependent variable PRICE versus independent variables SQFT, NE, and SQFT*NE (an interaction variable formed as the product of SQFT and NE). Identify and interpret the estimated regression coefficients to describe how the relationship between PRICE and SQFT varies by location (NE sector or not). You may find it helpful to construct a scatter plot of PRICE versus SQFT using two different plot symbols depending on whether the home is in the northeast sector.

Appendix 14.1 ■ Multiple Regression Analysis Using MINITAB

The instruction blocks in this section each begin by describing the entry of data into the MINITAB Data window. Alternatively, the data may be loaded directly from the data disk included with the text. The appropriate data file name is given at the top of each instruction block. Please refer to Appendix 1.1 for further information about entering data, saving data, and printing results when using MINITAB.

Multiple regression in Figure 14.4(a) on page 572 (data file: FuelCon2.MTW):

- In the Data window, enter the fuel consumption data from Table 14.1 (page 569)—the average hourly temperatures in column C1 with variable name Temp, the chill indexes in column C2 with variable name Chill, and the weekly fuel consumptions in column C3 with variable name FuelCons.

- Select **Stat : Regression : Regression**

- In the Regression dialog box, select FuelCons into the Response window.

- Select Temp and Chill into the Predictors window.

To compute a **prediction** for fuel consumption when the temperature is 40° F and the chill index is 10:

- In the Regression dialog box, click on the Options... button.

- In the "Regression—Options" dialog box, enter 40 and 10 into the "Prediction intervals for new observations" window. (The number and order of values in this window must match the Predictors list in the Regression dialog box.)

- Click OK in the Regression—Options dialog box.

To obtain **residual plots:**

- Click on the Graphs... button and check the desired plots (see Appendix 13.1).

- Click OK in the Regression—Graphs dialog box.

To see the regression results in the Session window and the high-resolution graphs:

- Click OK in the Regression dialog box.

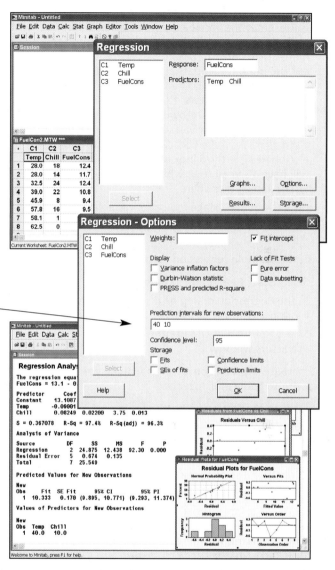

Multiple regression with indicator (dummy) variables in Figure 14.15(a) on page 598 (data file: Electronics2.MTW):

- In the Data window, enter the sales volume data from Table 14.9 on page 597 with sales volume in column C1, location in column C2, and number of households in column C3 with variable names Sales, Location, and Households.

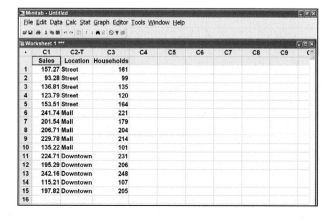

To **create indicator/dummy variable predictors:**

- Select **Calc : Make Indicator Variables**

- In the "Make Indicator Variables" dialog box, enter Location into the "Indicator variables for" window.

- The "Store indicator variables in columns" window lists the distinct values of Location in alphabetical order. Corresponding to each distinct value, enter the variable name to be used for that value's indicator variable—here we have used the names DDowntown, DMall, and DStreet (or you can use default names that are supplied by MINITAB if you wish). The first indicator variable (DDowntown) will have 1's in all rows where the Location equals Downtown and 0's elsewhere. The second indicator variable (DMall) will have 1's in all rows where Location equals Mall and 0's elsewhere. The third indicator variable (DStreet) will have 1's in all rows where Location equals Street and 0's elsewhere.

- Click OK in the "Make Indicator Variables" dialog box to create the indicator variables in the Data window.

To **fit the multiple regression** model:

- Select **Stat : Regression : Regression**

- In the Regression dialog box, select Sales into the Response window.

- Select Households DMall DDowntown into the Predictors window.

To compute a **prediction** of sales volume for 200,000 households and a mall location:

- Click on the Options… button.

- In the "Regression—Options" dialog box, type 200 1 0 in the "Prediction intervals for new observations" window.

- Click OK in the "Regression—Options" dialog box.

- Click OK in the Regression dialog box.

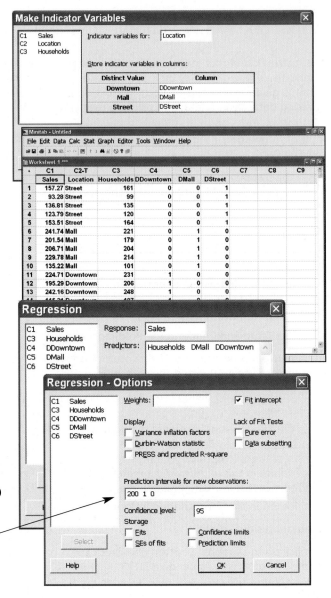

Correlation matrix in Figure 14.23 on page 607 (data file: SalePerf2.MTW):

- In the Data window, enter the sales territory performance data from Tables 14.3 (page 575) and 14.13 (page 607) into columns C1–C9 with variable names Sales, Time, MktPoten, Adver, MktShare, Change, Accts, WkLoad, and Rating.

- Select **Stat : Basic Statistics : Correlation**

- In the Correlation dialog box, enter all variable names into the Variables window.

- If *p*-values are desired, make sure that the "Display *p*-values" checkbox is checked.

- Click OK in the Correlation dialog box.

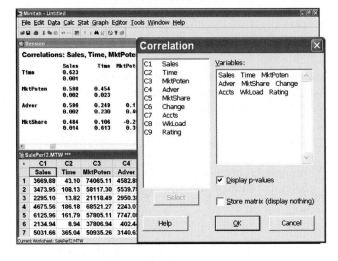

Best subsets regression in Figure 14.25(a) on page 610 (data file: SalePerf2.MTW):

- In the Data window, enter the sales territory performance data from Tables 14.3 (page 575) and 14.13 (page 607) into columns C1–C9 with variable names Sales, Time, MktPoten, Adver, MktShare, Change, Accts, WkLoad, and Rating.

- Select **Stat : Regression : Best Subsets**

- In the Best Subsets Regression dialog box, enter Sales into the Response window.

- Enter the remaining variable names into the "Free predictors" window.

- Click on the Options… button.

- In the "Best Subsets Regression—Options" dialog box, enter 2 in the "Models of each size to print" window.

- Click OK in the "Best Subsets Regression—Options" dialog box.

- Click OK in the Best Subsets Regression dialog box.

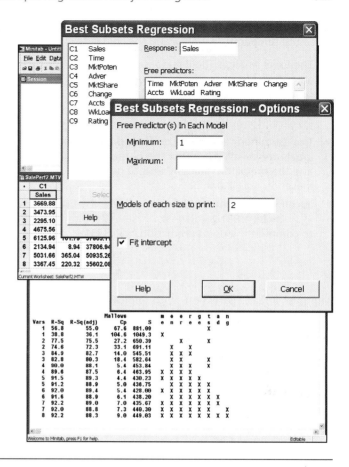

Appendix 14.2 ■ Multiple Regression Analysis Using Excel

The instruction blocks in this section each begin by describing the entry of data into an Excel spreadsheet. Alternatively, the data may be loaded directly from the data disk included with the text. The appropriate data file name is given at the top of each instruction block. Please refer to Appendix 1.2 for further information about entering data, saving data, and printing results when using Excel.

Multiple regression in Figure 14.4(b) on page 572 (data file: FuelCon2.xlsx):

- Enter the fuel consumption data from Table 14.1 (page 569)—temperatures (with label Temp) in column A, chill indexes (with label Chill) in column B, and fuel consumptions (with label FuelCons) in column C.

- Select **Data : Data Analysis : Regression** and click OK in the Data Analysis dialog box.

- In the Regression dialog box:
  Enter C1.C9 into the "Input Y Range" window.
  Enter A1.B9 into the "Input X Range" window.

- Place a checkmark in the Labels checkbox.

- Be sure that the "Constant is Zero" checkbox is NOT checked.

- Select the "New Worksheet Ply" output option.

- Click OK in the Regression dialog box to obtain the regression output in a new worksheet.

Note: The independent variables must be in adjacent columns because the "Input X Range" must span the range of the values for all of the independent variables.

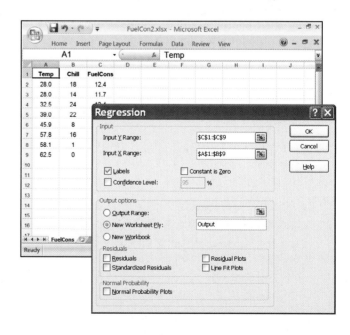

To compute a point prediction for fuel consumption when the temperature is 40° F and the chill index is 10:

- The Excel Analysis ToolPak does not provide an option for computing point or interval predictions. A point prediction can be computed from the regression results using Excel cell formulas as follows.

- The estimated regression coefficients and their labels are in cells A8.B10 of the output worksheet and the predictor values 40 and 10 have been placed in cells I2 and I3.

- In cell I4, enter the Excel formula
  = B8 + B9*I2 + B10*I3
  to compute the point prediction (=10.3331).

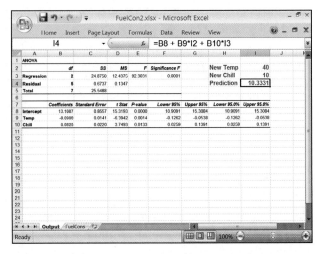

Multiple linear regression with indicator (dummy) variables in Figure 14.15(b) on page 598 (data file: Electronics2.xlsx):

- Enter the sales volume data from Table 14.9 (page 597)—sales volumes (with label Sales) in column A, store locations (with label Location) in column B, and number of households (with label Households) in column C. (The order of the columns is chosen to arrange for an adjacent block of predictor variables.)

- Enter the labels DM and DD in cells D1 and E1.

- Following the definitions of the dummy variables DM and DD in Example 14.9 (pages 597 and 598), enter the appropriate values of 0 and 1 for these two variables into columns D and E.

- Select **Data : Data Analysis : Regression** and click OK in the Data Analysis dialog box.

- In the Regression dialog box:
  Enter A1.A16 into the "Input Y Range" window.
  Enter C1.E16 into the "Input X Range" window.

- Place a checkmark in the Labels checkbox.

- Select the "New Worksheet Ply" output option.

- Click OK in the Regression dialog box to obtain the regression results in a new worksheet.

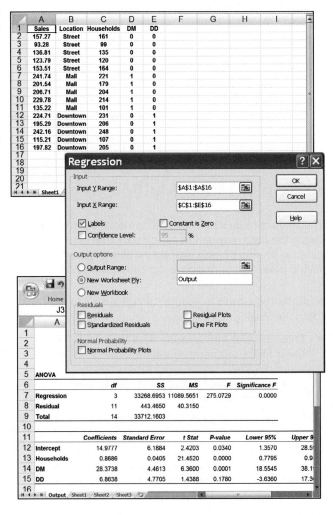

Appendix 14.3 ■ Multiple Regression Analysis Using MegaStat

The instructions in this section begin by describing the entry of data into an Excel worksheet. Alternatively, the data may be loaded directly from the data disk included with the text. The appropriate data file name is given at the top of each instruction block. Please refer to Appendix 1.2 for further information about entering data, saving data, and printing results in Excel. Please refer to Appendix 1.3 for more information about using MegaStat.

Multiple regression similar to Figure 14.4 on page 572 (data file: FuelCon2.xlsx):

- Enter the fuel consumption data in Table 14.1 (page 569) as shown—temperatures (with label Temp) in column A, chill indexes (with label Chill) in column B, and fuel consumptions (with label FuelCons) in column C. Note that Temp and Chill are contiguous columns (that is, they are next to each other). This is not necessary, but it makes selection of the independent variables (as described below) easiest.

- Select **Add-Ins : MegaStat : Correlation/ Regression : Regression Analysis**

- In the Regression Analysis dialog box, click in the Independent variables window and use the AutoExpand feature to enter the range A1.B9. Note that if the independent variables are not next to each other; hold the CTRL key down while making selections and then AutoExpand.

- Click in the Dependent variable window and enter the range C1.C9.

- Check the appropriate Options and Residuals checkboxes as follows:

  1 Check "Test Intercept" to include a y-intercept and to test its significance.

  2 Check "Output Residuals" to obtain a list of the model residuals.

  3 Check "Plot Residuals by Observation," and "Plot Residuals by Predicted Y and X" to obtain residual plots versus time, versus the predicted values of y, and versus the values of each independent variable (see Section 14.9).

  4 Check "Normal Probability Plot of Residuals" to obtain a normal plot (see Section 14.9).

To obtain a **point prediction** of y when the temperature equals 40 and the chill index equals 10 (as well as a confidence interval and prediction interval):

- Click on the drop-down menu above the predictor values window and select "Type in predictor values."

- Type 40 and 10 (separated by at least one blank space) into the predictor values window.

- Select a desired level of confidence (here 95%) from the Confidence Level drop-down menu or type in a value.

- Click OK in the Regression Analysis dialog box.

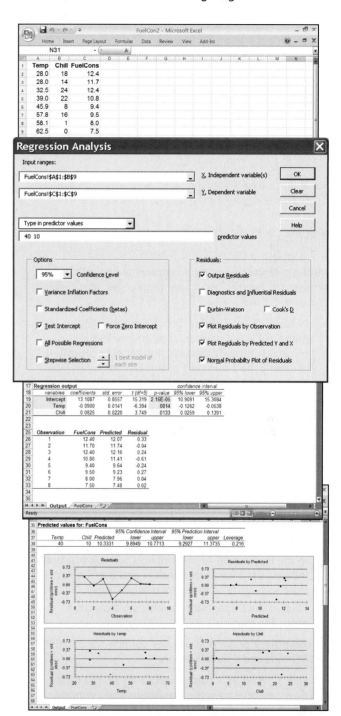

Predictions can also be obtained by placing the values of the predictor variables into spreadsheet cells. For example, suppose that we wish to compute predictions of y for each of the following three temperature–chill index combinations: 50 and 15; 55 and 20; 30 and 12. To do this:

- Enter the values for which predictions are desired in spreadsheet cells as illustrated in the screenshot—here temperatures are entered in column F and chill indexes are entered in column G. However, the values could be entered in any adjacent columns.

- In the drop-down menu above the predictor values window, select "Predictor values from spreadsheet cells."

- Select the range of cells containing the predictor values (here F1.G3) into the predictor values window.

- Select a desired level of confidence from the Confidence Level drop-down menu or type in a value.

- Click OK in the Regression Analysis dialog box.

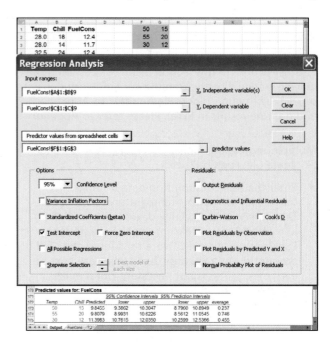

Multiple regression with indicator (dummy) variables similar to Figure 14.15 on page 598 (data file: Electronics2.xlsx):

- Enter the sales volume data from Table 14.9 (page 597)—sales volumes (with label Sales) in column A, store locations (with label Location) in column B, and numbers of households (with label Households) in column C. Again note that the order of the variables is chosen to allow for an adjacent block of predictor variables.

- Enter the labels DM and DD into cells D1 and E1.

- Following the definitions of the dummy variables DM and DD in Example 14.9 (pages 597 and 598), enter the appropriate values of 0 and 1 for these two variables into columns D and E as shown in the screen.

- Select **Add-Ins : MegaStat : Correlation/ Regression : Regression Analysis**

- In the Regression Analysis dialog box, click in the Independent variables window and use the Auto-Expand feature to enter the range C1.E16.

- Click in the Dependent variable window and enter the range A1.A16.

To compute a prediction of sales volume for 200,000 households and a mall location:

- Select "Type in predictor values" from the drop-down menu above the predictor values window.

- Type 200 1 0 into the predictor values window.

- Select or type a desired level of confidence (here 95%) in the Confidence Level box.

- Click the Options and Residuals checkboxes as shown (or as desired).

- Click OK in the Regression Analysis dialog box.

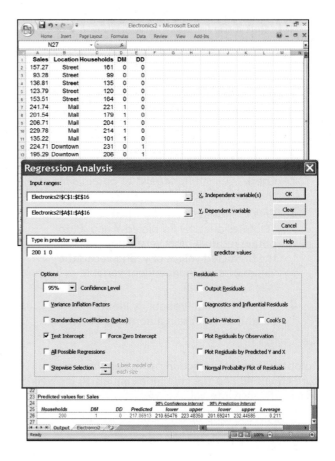

Stepwise selection in Figure 14.25(b) on page 610 and **all possible regressions** in Figure 14.25(c) on page 610 (data file: SalePerf2.xlsx):

- Enter the sales performance data in Tables 14.3 (page 575) and 14.13 (page 607) into columns A through I with labels as shown in the screen.

- Select **Add-Ins : MegaStat : Correlation/ Regression : Regression Analysis**

- In the Regression Analysis dialog box, click in the Independent variables window and use the AutoExpand feature to enter the range B1.I26.

- Click in the Dependent variable window and use the AutoExpand feature to enter the range A1.A26.

- Check the "Stepwise Selection" checkbox.

- Click OK in the Regression Analysis dialog box.

Stepwise selection will give the best model of each size (1, 2, 3, and more independent variables). The default gives one model of each size. For more models, use the arrow buttons to request the desired number of models of each size.

- Check the "All Possible Regressions" checkbox to obtain the results for all possible regressions. This option will handle up to 12 independent variables.

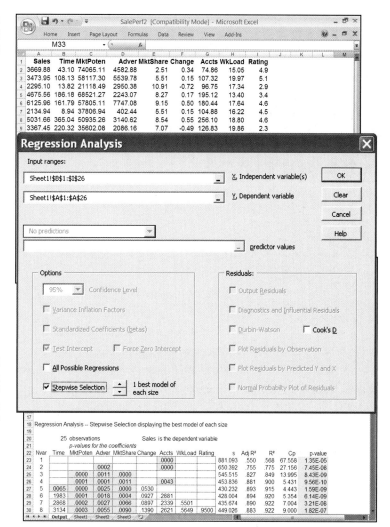

Appendix **A**

Statistical Tables

Table A.1   A Binomial Probability Table

Table A.2   A Poisson Probability Table

Table A.3   Cumulative Areas under the Standard Normal Curve

Table A.4   A t Table: Values of t_α

Table A.5   An F Table: Values of $F_{.10}$

Table A.6   An F Table: Values of $F_{.05}$

Table A.7   An F Table: Values of $F_{.025}$

Table A.8   An F Table: Values of $F_{.01}$

Table A.9   Percentage Points of the Studentized Range

Table A.10 A Chi-Square Table: Values of χ^2_α

Table A.11 A Table of Areas under the Standard Normal Curve

TABLE A.1   **A Binomial Probability Table:**
Binomial Probabilities (*n* between 2 and 6)

n = 2   *p*

x↓	.05	.10	.15	.20	.25	.30	.35	.40	.45	.50	
0	.9025	.8100	.7225	.6400	.5625	.4900	.4225	.3600	.3025	.2500	2
1	.0950	.1800	.2550	.3200	.3750	.4200	.4550	.4800	.4950	.5000	1
2	.0025	.0100	.0225	.0400	.0625	.0900	.1225	.1600	.2025	.2500	0
	.95	.90	.85	.80	.75	.70	.65	.60	.55	.50	*x*↑

n = 3   *p*

x↓	.05	.10	.15	.20	.25	.30	.35	.40	.45	.50	
0	.8574	.7290	.6141	.5120	.4219	.3430	.2746	.2160	.1664	.1250	3
1	.1354	.2430	.3251	.3840	.4219	.4410	.4436	.4320	.4084	.3750	2
2	.0071	.0270	.0574	.0960	.1406	.1890	.2389	.2880	.3341	.3750	1
3	.0001	.0010	.0034	.0080	.0156	.0270	.0429	.0640	.0911	.1250	0
	.95	.90	.85	.80	.75	.70	.65	.60	.55	.50	*x*↑

n = 4   *p*

x↓	.05	.10	.15	.20	.25	.30	.35	.40	.45	.50	
0	.8145	.6561	.5220	.4096	.3164	.2401	.1785	.1296	.0915	.0625	4
1	.1715	.2916	.3685	.4096	.4219	.4116	.3845	.3456	.2995	.2500	3
2	.0135	.0486	.0975	.1536	.2109	.2646	.3105	.3456	.3675	.3750	2
3	.0005	.0036	.0115	.0256	.0469	.0756	.1115	.1536	.2005	.2500	1
4	.0000	.0001	.0005	.0016	.0039	.0081	.0150	.0256	.0410	.0625	0
	.95	.90	.85	.80	.75	.70	.65	.60	.55	.50	*x*↑

n = 5   *p*

x↓	.05	.10	.15	.20	.25	.30	.35	.40	.45	.50	
0	.7738	.5905	.4437	.3277	.2373	.1681	.1160	.0778	.0503	.0313	5
1	.2036	.3281	.3915	.4096	.3955	.3602	.3124	.2592	.2059	.1563	4
2	.0214	.0729	.1382	.2048	.2637	.3087	.3364	.3456	.3369	.3125	3
3	.0011	.0081	.0244	.0512	.0879	.1323	.1811	.2304	.2757	.3125	2
4	.0000	.0005	.0022	.0064	.0146	.0284	.0488	.0768	.1128	.1563	1
5	.0000	.0000	.0001	.0003	.0010	.0024	.0053	.0102	.0185	.0313	0
	.95	.90	.85	.80	.75	.70	.65	.60	.55	.50	*x*↑

n = 6   *p*

x↓	.05	.10	.15	.20	.25	.30	.35	.40	.45	.50	
0	.7351	.5314	.3771	.2621	.1780	.1176	.0754	.0467	.0277	.0156	6
1	.2321	.3543	.3993	.3932	.3560	.3025	.2437	.1866	.1359	.0938	5
2	.0305	.0984	.1762	.2458	.2966	.3241	.3280	.3110	.2780	.2344	4
3	.0021	.0146	.0415	.0819	.1318	.1852	.2355	.2765	.3032	.3125	3
4	.0001	.0012	.0055	.0154	.0330	.0595	.0951	.1382	.1861	.2344	2
5	.0000	.0001	.0004	.0015	.0044	.0102	.0205	.0369	.0609	.0938	1
6	.0000	.0000	.0000	.0001	.0002	.0007	.0018	.0041	.0083	.0156	0
	.95	.90	.85	.80	.75	.70	.65	.60	.55	.50	*x*↑

(table continued)

TABLE A.1   *(continued)*
Binomial Probabilities (*n* between 7 and 10)

n = 7   p

x↓	.05	.10	.15	.20	.25	.30	.35	.40	.45	.50	
0	.6983	.4783	.3206	.2097	.1335	.0824	.0490	.0280	.0152	.0078	7
1	.2573	.3720	.3960	.3670	.3115	.2471	.1848	.1306	.0872	.0547	6
2	.0406	.1240	.2097	.2753	.3115	.3177	.2985	.2613	.2140	.1641	5
3	.0036	.0230	.0617	.1147	.1730	.2269	.2679	.2903	.2918	.2734	4
4	.0002	.0026	.0109	.0287	.0577	.0972	.1442	.1935	.2388	.2734	3
5	.0000	.0002	.0012	.0043	.0115	.0250	.0466	.0774	.1172	.1641	2
6	.0000	.0000	.0001	.0004	.0013	.0036	.0084	.0172	.0320	.0547	1
7	.0000	.0000	.0000	.0000	.0001	.0002	.0006	.0016	.0037	.0078	0
	.95	.90	.85	.80	.75	.70	.65	.60	.55	.50	x↑

n = 8   p

x↓	.05	.10	.15	.20	.25	.30	.35	.40	.45	.50	
0	.6634	.4305	.2725	.1678	.1001	.0576	.0319	.0168	.0084	.0039	8
1	.2793	.3826	.3847	.3355	.2670	.1977	.1373	.0896	.0548	.0313	7
2	.0515	.1488	.2376	.2936	.3115	.2965	.2587	.2090	.1569	.1094	6
3	.0054	.0331	.0839	.1468	.2076	.2541	.2786	.2787	.2568	.2188	5
4	.0004	.0046	.0185	.0459	.0865	.1361	.1875	.2322	.2627	.2734	4
5	.0000	.0004	.0026	.0092	.0231	.0467	.0808	.1239	.1719	.2188	3
6	.0000	.0000	.0002	.0011	.0038	.0100	.0217	.0413	.0703	.1094	2
7	.0000	.0000	.0000	.0001	.0004	.0012	.0033	.0079	.0164	.0313	1
8	.0000	.0000	.0000	.0000	.0000	.0001	.0002	.0007	.0017	.0039	0
	.95	.90	.85	.80	.75	.70	.65	.60	.55	.50	x↑

n = 9   p

x↓	.05	.10	.15	.20	.25	.30	.35	.40	.45	.50	
0	.6302	.3874	.2316	.1342	.0751	.0404	.0207	.0101	.0046	.0020	9
1	.2985	.3874	.3679	.3020	.2253	.1556	.1004	.0605	.0339	.0176	8
2	.0629	.1722	.2597	.3020	.3003	.2668	.2162	.1612	.1110	.0703	7
3	.0077	.0446	.1069	.1762	.2336	.2668	.2716	.2508	.2119	.1641	6
4	.0006	.0074	.0283	.0661	.1168	.1715	.2194	.2508	.2600	.2461	5
5	.0000	.0008	.0050	.0165	.0389	.0735	.1181	.1672	.2128	.2461	4
6	.0000	.0001	.0006	.0028	.0087	.0210	.0424	.0743	.1160	.1641	3
7	.0000	.0000	.0000	.0003	.0012	.0039	.0098	.0212	.0407	.0703	2
8	.0000	.0000	.0000	.0000	.0001	.0004	.0013	.0035	.0083	.0176	1
9	.0000	.0000	.0000	.0000	.0000	.0000	.0001	.0003	.0008	.0020	0
	.95	.90	.85	.80	.75	.70	.65	.60	.55	.50	x↑

n = 10   p

x↓	.05	.10	.15	.20	.25	.30	.35	.40	.45	.50	
0	.5987	.3487	.1969	.1074	.0563	.0282	.0135	.0060	.0025	.0010	10
1	.3151	.3874	.3474	.2684	.1877	.1211	.0725	.0403	.0207	.0098	9
2	.0746	.1937	.2759	.3020	.2816	.2335	.1757	.1209	.0763	.0439	8
3	.0105	.0574	.1298	.2013	.2503	.2668	.2522	.2150	.1665	.1172	7
4	.0010	.0112	.0401	.0881	.1460	.2001	.2377	.2508	.2384	.2051	6
5	.0001	.0015	.0085	.0264	.0584	.1029	.1536	.2007	.2340	.2461	5
6	.0000	.0001	.0012	.0055	.0162	.0368	.0689	.1115	.1596	.2051	4
7	.0000	.0000	.0001	.0008	.0031	.0090	.0212	.0425	.0746	.1172	3
8	.0000	.0000	.0000	.0001	.0004	.0014	.0043	.0106	.0229	.0439	2
9	.0000	.0000	.0000	.0000	.0000	.0001	.0005	.0016	.0042	.0098	1
10	.0000	.0000	.0000	.0000	.0000	.0000	.0000	.0001	.0003	.0010	0
	.95	.90	.85	.80	.75	.70	.65	.60	.55	.50	x↑

TABLE A.1 *(continued)*
Binomial Probabilities (*n* equal to 12, 14, and 15)

n = 12   p

x↓	.05	.10	.15	.20	.25	.30	.35	.40	.45	.50	
0	.5404	.2824	.1422	.0687	.0317	.0138	.0057	.0022	.0008	.0002	12
1	.3413	.3766	.3012	.2062	.1267	.0712	.0368	.0174	.0075	.0029	11
2	.0988	.2301	.2924	.2835	.2323	.1678	.1088	.0639	.0339	.0161	10
3	.0173	.0852	.1720	.2362	.2581	.2397	.1954	.1419	.0923	.0537	9
4	.0021	.0213	.0683	.1329	.1936	.2311	.2367	.2128	.1700	.1208	8
5	.0002	.0038	.0193	.0532	.1032	.1585	.2039	.2270	.2225	.1934	7
6	.0000	.0005	.0040	.0155	.0401	.0792	.1281	.1766	.2124	.2256	6
7	.0000	.0000	.0006	.0033	.0115	.0291	.0591	.1009	.1489	.1934	5
8	.0000	.0000	.0001	.0005	.0024	.0078	.0199	.0420	.0762	.1208	4
9	.0000	.0000	.0000	.0001	.0004	.0015	.0048	.0125	.0277	.0537	3
10	.0000	.0000	.0000	.0000	.0000	.0002	.0008	.0025	.0068	.0161	2
11	.0000	.0000	.0000	.0000	.0000	.0000	.0001	.0003	.0010	.0029	1
12	.0000	.0000	.0000	.0000	.0000	.0000	.0000	.0000	.0001	.0002	0
	.95	.90	.85	.80	.75	.70	.65	.60	.55	.50	x↑

n = 14   p

x↓	.05	.10	.15	.20	.25	.30	.35	.40	.45	.50	
0	.4877	.2288	.1028	.0440	.0178	.0068	.0024	.0008	.0002	.0001	14
1	.3593	.3559	.2539	.1539	.0832	.0407	.0181	.0073	.0027	.0009	13
2	.1229	.2570	.2912	.2501	.1802	.1134	.0634	.0317	.0141	.0056	12
3	.0259	.1142	.2056	.2501	.2402	.1943	.1366	.0845	.0462	.0222	11
4	.0037	.0349	.0998	.1720	.2202	.2290	.2022	.1549	.1040	.0611	10
5	.0004	.0078	.0352	.0860	.1468	.1963	.2178	.2066	.1701	.1222	9
6	.0000	.0013	.0093	.0322	.0734	.1262	.1759	.2066	.2088	.1833	8
7	.0000	.0002	.0019	.0092	.0280	.0618	.1082	.1574	.1952	.2095	7
8	.0000	.0000	.0003	.0020	.0082	.0232	.0510	.0918	.1398	.1833	6
9	.0000	.0000	.0000	.0003	.0018	.0066	.0183	.0408	.0762	.1222	5
10	.0000	.0000	.0000	.0000	.0003	.0014	.0049	.0136	.0312	.0611	4
11	.0000	.0000	.0000	.0000	.0000	.0002	.0010	.0033	.0093	.0222	3
12	.0000	.0000	.0000	.0000	.0000	.0000	.0001	.0005	.0019	.0056	2
13	.0000	.0000	.0000	.0000	.0000	.0000	.0000	.0001	.0002	.0009	1
14	.0000	.0000	.0000	.0000	.0000	.0000	.0000	.0000	.0000	.0001	0
	.95	.90	.85	.80	.75	.70	.65	.60	.55	.50	x↑

n = 15   p

x↓	.05	.10	.15	.20	.25	.30	.35	.40	.45	.50	
0	.4633	.2059	.0874	.0352	.0134	.0047	.0016	.0005	.0001	.0000	15
1	.3658	.3432	.2312	.1319	.0668	.0305	.0126	.0047	.0016	.0005	14
2	.1348	.2669	.2856	.2309	.1559	.0916	.0476	.0219	.0090	.0032	13
3	.0307	.1285	.2184	.2501	.2252	.1700	.1110	.0634	.0318	.0139	12
4	.0049	.0428	.1156	.1876	.2252	.2186	.1792	.1268	.0780	.0417	11
5	.0006	.0105	.0449	.1032	.1651	.2061	.2123	.1859	.1404	.0916	10
6	.0000	.0019	.0132	.0430	.0917	.1472	.1906	.2066	.1914	.1527	9
7	.0000	.0003	.0030	.0138	.0393	.0811	.1319	.1771	.2013	.1964	8
8	.0000	.0000	.0005	.0035	.0131	.0348	.0710	.1181	.1647	.1964	7
9	.0000	.0000	.0001	.0007	.0034	.0116	.0298	.0612	.1048	.1527	6
10	.0000	.0000	.0000	.0001	.0007	.0030	.0096	.0245	.0515	.0916	5
11	.0000	.0000	.0000	.0000	.0001	.0006	.0024	.0074	.0191	.0417	4
12	.0000	.0000	.0000	.0000	.0000	.0001	.0004	.0016	.0052	.0139	3
13	.0000	.0000	.0000	.0000	.0000	.0000	.0001	.0003	.0010	.0032	2
14	.0000	.0000	.0000	.0000	.0000	.0000	.0000	.0000	.0001	.0005	1
15	.0000	.0000	.0000	.0000	.0000	.0000	.0000	.0000	.0000	.0000	0
	.95	.90	.85	.80	.75	.70	.65	.60	.55	.50	x↑

(table continued)

TABLE A.1　**(continued)**
Binomial Probabilities (*n* equal to 16 and 18)

n = 16　　　　　　　　　　　　　　　　　**p**

x↓	.05	.10	.15	.20	.25	.30	.35	.40	.45	.50	
0	.4401	.1853	.0743	.0281	.0100	.0033	.0010	.0003	.0001	.0000	16
1	.3706	.3294	.2097	.1126	.0535	.0228	.0087	.0030	.0009	.0002	15
2	.1463	.2745	.2775	.2111	.1336	.0732	.0353	.0150	.0056	.0018	14
3	.0359	.1423	.2285	.2463	.2079	.1465	.0888	.0468	.0215	.0085	13
4	.0061	.0514	.1311	.2001	.2252	.2040	.1553	.1014	.0572	.0278	12
5	.0008	.0137	.0555	.1201	.1802	.2099	.2008	.1623	.1123	.0667	11
6	.0001	.0028	.0180	.0550	.1101	.1649	.1982	.1983	.1684	.1222	10
7	.0000	.0004	.0045	.0197	.0524	.1010	.1524	.1889	.1969	.1746	9
8	.0000	.0001	.0009	.0055	.0197	.0487	.0923	.1417	.1812	.1964	8
9	.0000	.0000	.0001	.0012	.0058	.0185	.0442	.0840	.1318	.1746	7
10	.0000	.0000	.0000	.0002	.0014	.0056	.0167	.0392	.0755	.1222	6
11	.0000	.0000	.0000	.0000	.0002	.0013	.0049	.0142	.0337	.0667	5
12	.0000	.0000	.0000	.0000	.0000	.0002	.0011	.0040	.0115	.0278	4
13	.0000	.0000	.0000	.0000	.0000	.0000	.0002	.0008	.0029	.0085	3
14	.0000	.0000	.0000	.0000	.0000	.0000	.0000	.0001	.0005	.0018	2
15	.0000	.0000	.0000	.0000	.0000	.0000	.0000	.0000	.0001	.0002	1
	.95	.90	.85	.80	.75	.70	.65	.60	.55	.50	x↑

n = 18　　　　　　　　　　　　　　　　　**p**

x↓	.05	.10	.15	.20	.25	.30	.35	.40	.45	.50	
0	.3972	.1501	.0536	.0180	.0056	.0016	.0004	.0001	.0000	.0000	18
1	.3763	.3002	.1704	.0811	.0338	.0126	.0042	.0012	.0003	.0001	17
2	.1683	.2835	.2556	.1723	.0958	.0458	.0190	.0069	.0022	.0006	16
3	.0473	.1680	.2406	.2297	.1704	.1046	.0547	.0246	.0095	.0031	15
4	.0093	.0700	.1592	.2153	.2130	.1681	.1104	.0614	.0291	.0117	14
5	.0014	.0218	.0787	.1507	.1988	.2017	.1664	.1146	.0666	.0327	13
6	.0002	.0052	.0301	.0816	.1436	.1873	.1941	.1655	.1181	.0708	12
7	.0000	.0010	.0091	.0350	.0820	.1376	.1792	.1892	.1657	.1214	11
8	.0000	.0002	.0022	.0120	.0376	.0811	.1327	.1734	.1864	.1669	10
9	.0000	.0000	.0004	.0033	.0139	.0386	.0794	.1284	.1694	.1855	9
10	.0000	.0000	.0001	.0008	.0042	.0149	.0385	.0771	.1248	.1669	8
11	.0000	.0000	.0000	.0001	.0010	.0046	.0151	.0374	.0742	.1214	7
12	.0000	.0000	.0000	.0000	.0002	.0012	.0047	.0145	.0354	.0708	6
13	.0000	.0000	.0000	.0000	.0000	.0002	.0012	.0045	.0134	.0327	5
14	.0000	.0000	.0000	.0000	.0000	.0000	.0002	.0011	.0039	.0117	4
15	.0000	.0000	.0000	.0000	.0000	.0000	.0000	.0002	.0009	.0031	3
16	.0000	.0000	.0000	.0000	.0000	.0000	.0000	.0000	.0001	.0006	2
17	.0000	.0000	.0000	.0000	.0000	.0000	.0000	.0000	.0000	.0001	1
	.95	.90	.85	.80	.75	.70	.65	.60	.55	.50	x↑

TABLE A.1 *(concluded)*
Binomial Probabilities (*n* equal to 20)

n = 20   **p**

x↓	.05	.10	.15	.20	.25	.30	.35	.40	.45	.50	
0	.3585	.1216	.0388	.0115	.0032	.0008	.0002	.0000	.0000	.0000	20
1	.3774	.2702	.1368	.0576	.0211	.0068	.0020	.0005	.0001	.0000	19
2	.1887	.2852	.2293	.1369	.0669	.0278	.0100	.0031	.0008	.0002	18
3	.0596	.1901	.2428	.2054	.1339	.0716	.0323	.0123	.0040	.0011	17
4	.0133	.0898	.1821	.2182	.1897	.1304	.0738	.0350	.0139	.0046	16
5	.0022	.0319	.1028	.1746	.2023	.1789	.1272	.0746	.0365	.0148	15
6	.0003	.0089	.0454	.1091	.1686	.1916	.1712	.1244	.0746	.0370	14
7	.0000	.0020	.0160	.0545	.1124	.1643	.1844	.1659	.1221	.0739	13
8	.0000	.0004	.0046	.0222	.0609	.1144	.1614	.1797	.1623	.1201	12
9	.0000	.0001	.0011	.0074	.0271	.0654	.1158	.1597	.1771	.1602	11
10	.0000	.0000	.0002	.0020	.0099	.0308	.0686	.1171	.1593	.1762	10
11	.0000	.0000	.0000	.0005	.0030	.0120	.0336	.0710	.1185	.1602	9
12	.0000	.0000	.0000	.0001	.0008	.0039	.0136	.0355	.0727	.1201	8
13	.0000	.0000	.0000	.0000	.0002	.0010	.0045	.0146	.0366	.0739	7
14	.0000	.0000	.0000	.0000	.0000	.0002	.0012	.0049	.0150	.0370	6
15	.0000	.0000	.0000	.0000	.0000	.0000	.0003	.0013	.0049	.0148	5
16	.0000	.0000	.0000	.0000	.0000	.0000	.0000	.0003	.0013	.0046	4
17	.0000	.0000	.0000	.0000	.0000	.0000	.0000	.0000	.0002	.0011	3
18	.0000	.0000	.0000	.0000	.0000	.0000	.0000	.0000	.0000	.0002	2
	.95	.90	.85	.80	.75	.70	.65	.60	.55	.50	x↑

Source: Computed by D. K. Hildebrand. Found in D. K. Hildebrand and L. Ott, *Statistical Thinking for Managers,* 3rd ed. (Boston, MA: PWS-KENT Publishing Company, 1991).

TABLE A.2   A Poisson Probability Table
Poisson Probabilities (μ between .1 and 2.0)

μ

x	.1	.2	.3	.4	.5	.6	.7	.8	.9	1.0
0	.9048	.8187	.7408	.6703	.6065	.5488	.4966	.4493	.4066	.3679
1	.0905	.1637	.2222	.2681	.3033	.3293	.3476	.3595	.3659	.3679
2	.0045	.0164	.0333	.0536	.0758	.0988	.1217	.1438	.1647	.1839
3	.0002	.0011	.0033	.0072	.0126	.0198	.0284	.0383	.0494	.0613
4	.0000	.0001	.0003	.0007	.0016	.0030	.0050	.0077	.0111	.0153
5	.0000	.0000	.0000	.0001	.0002	.0004	.0007	.0012	.0020	.0031
6	.0000	.0000	.0000	.0000	.0000	.0000	.0001	.0002	.0003	.0005

μ

x	1.1	1.2	1.3	1.4	1.5	1.6	1.7	1.8	1.9	2.0
0	.3329	.3012	.2725	.2466	.2231	.2019	.1827	.1653	.1496	.1353
1	.3662	.3614	.3543	.3452	.3347	.3230	.3106	.2975	.2842	.2707
2	.2014	.2169	.2303	.2417	.2510	.2584	.2640	.2678	.2700	.2707
3	.0738	.0867	.0998	.1128	.1255	.1378	.1496	.1607	.1710	.1804
4	.0203	.0260	.0324	.0395	.0471	.0551	.0636	.0723	.0812	.0902
5	.0045	.0062	.0084	.0111	.0141	.0176	.0216	.0260	.0309	.0361
6	.0008	.0012	.0018	.0026	.0035	.0047	.0061	.0078	.0098	.0120
7	.0001	.0002	.0003	.0005	.0008	.0011	.0015	.0020	.0027	.0034
8	.0000	.0000	.0001	.0001	.0001	.0002	.0003	.0005	.0006	.0009

(table continued)

TABLE A.2   *(continued)*
Poisson Probabilities (μ between 2.1 and 5.0)

μ

x	2.1	2.2	2.3	2.4	2.5	2.6	2.7	2.8	2.9	3.0
0	.1225	.1108	.1003	.0907	.0821	.0743	.0672	.0608	.0550	.0498
1	.2572	.2438	.2306	.2177	.2052	.1931	.1815	.1703	.1596	.1494
2	.2700	.2681	.2652	.2613	.2565	.2510	.2450	.2384	.2314	.2240
3	.1890	.1966	.2033	.2090	.2138	.2176	.2205	.2225	.2237	.2240
4	.0992	.1082	.1169	.1254	.1336	.1414	.1488	.1557	.1622	.1680
5	.0417	.0476	.0538	.0602	.0668	.0735	.0804	.0872	.0940	.1008
6	.0146	.0174	.0206	.0241	.0278	.0319	.0362	.0407	.0455	.0504
7	.0044	.0055	.0068	.0083	.0099	.0118	.0139	.0163	.0188	.0216
8	.0011	.0015	.0019	.0025	.0031	.0038	.0047	.0057	.0068	.0081
9	.0003	.0004	.0005	.0007	.0009	.0011	.0014	.0018	.0022	.0027
10	.0001	.0001	.0001	.0002	.0002	.0003	.0004	.0005	.0006	.0008
11	.0000	.0000	.0000	.0000	.0000	.0001	.0001	.0001	.0002	.0002

μ

x	3.1	3.2	3.3	3.4	3.5	3.6	3.7	3.8	3.9	4.0
0	.0450	.0408	.0369	.0334	.0302	.0273	.0247	.0224	.0202	.0183
1	.1397	.1304	.1217	.1135	.1057	.0984	.0915	.0850	.0789	.0733
2	.2165	.2087	.2008	.1929	.1850	.1771	.1692	.1615	.1539	.1465
3	.2237	.2226	.2209	.2186	.2158	.2125	.2087	.2046	.2001	.1954
4	.1733	.1781	.1823	.1858	.1888	.1912	.1931	.1944	.1951	.1954
5	.1075	.1140	.1203	.1264	.1322	.1377	.1429	.1477	.1522	.1563
6	.0555	.0608	.0662	.0716	.0771	.0826	.0881	.0936	.0989	.1042
7	.0246	.0278	.0312	.0348	.0385	.0425	.0466	.0508	.0551	.0595
8	.0095	.0111	.0129	.0148	.0169	.0191	.0215	.0241	.0269	.0298
9	.0033	.0040	.0047	.0056	.0066	.0076	.0089	.0102	.0116	.0132
10	.0010	.0013	.0016	.0019	.0023	.0028	.0033	.0039	.0045	.0053
11	.0003	.0004	.0005	.0006	.0007	.0009	.0011	.0013	.0016	.0019
12	.0001	.0001	.0001	.0002	.0002	.0003	.0003	.0004	.0005	.0006
13	.0000	.0000	.0000	.0000	.0001	.0001	.0001	.0001	.0002	.0002

μ

x	4.1	4.2	4.3	4.4	4.5	4.6	4.7	4.8	4.9	5.0
0	.0166	.0150	.0136	.0123	.0111	.0101	.0091	.0082	.0074	.0067
1	.0679	.0630	.0583	.0540	.0500	.0462	.0427	.0395	.0365	.0337
2	.1393	.1323	.1254	.1188	.1125	.1063	.1005	.0948	.0894	.0842
3	.1904	.1852	.1798	.1743	.1687	.1631	.1574	.1517	.1460	.1404
4	.1951	.1944	.1933	.1917	.1898	.1875	.1849	.1820	.1789	.1755
5	.1600	.1633	.1662	.1687	.1708	.1725	.1738	.1747	.1753	.1755
6	.1093	.1143	.1191	.1237	.1281	.1323	.1362	.1398	.1432	.1462
7	.0640	.0686	.0732	.0778	.0824	.0869	.0914	.0959	.1002	.1044
8	.0328	.0360	.0393	.0428	.0463	.0500	.0537	.0575	.0614	.0653
9	.0150	.0168	.0188	.0209	.0232	.0255	.0281	.0307	.0334	.0363
10	.0061	.0071	.0081	.0092	.0104	.0118	.0132	.0147	.0164	.0181
11	.0023	.0027	.0032	.0037	.0043	.0049	.0056	.0064	.0073	.0082
12	.0008	.0009	.0011	.0013	.0016	.0019	.0022	.0026	.0030	.0034
13	.0002	.0003	.0004	.0005	.0006	.0007	.0008	.0009	.0011	.0013
14	.0001	.0001	.0001	.0001	.0002	.0002	.0003	.0003	.0004	.0005
15	.0000	.0000	.0000	.0000	.0001	.0001	.0001	.0001	.0001	.0002

TABLE A.2   *(concluded)*
Poisson Probabilities (μ between 5.5 and 20.0)

x	5.5	6.0	6.5	7.0	7.5	8.0	8.5	9.0	9.5	10.0
0	.0041	.0025	.0015	.0009	.0006	.0003	.0002	.0001	.0001	.0000
1	.0225	.0149	.0098	.0064	.0041	.0027	.0017	.0011	.0007	.0005
2	.0618	.0446	.0318	.0223	.0156	.0107	.0074	.0050	.0034	.0023
3	.1133	.0892	.0688	.0521	.0389	.0286	.0208	.0150	.0107	.0076
4	.1558	.1339	.1118	.0912	.0729	.0573	.0443	.0337	.0254	.0189
5	.1714	.1606	.1454	.1277	.1094	.0916	.0752	.0607	.0483	.0378
6	.1571	.1606	.1575	.1490	.1367	.1221	.1066	.0911	.0764	.0631
7	.1234	.1377	.1462	.1490	.1465	.1396	.1294	.1171	.1037	.0901
8	.0849	.1033	.1188	.1304	.1373	.1396	.1375	.1318	.1232	.1126
9	.0519	.0688	.0858	.1014	.1144	.1241	.1299	.1318	.1300	.1251
10	.0285	.0413	.0558	.0710	.0858	.0993	.1104	.1186	.1235	.1251
11	.0143	.0225	.0330	.0452	.0585	.0722	.0853	.0970	.1067	.1137
12	.0065	.0113	.0179	.0263	.0366	.0481	.0604	.0728	.0844	.0948
13	.0028	.0052	.0089	.0142	.0211	.0296	.0395	.0504	.0617	.0729
14	.0011	.0022	.0041	.0071	.0113	.0169	.0240	.0324	.0419	.0521
15	.0004	.0009	.0018	.0033	.0057	.0090	.0136	.0194	.0265	.0347
16	.0001	.0003	.0007	.0014	.0026	.0045	.0072	.0109	.0157	.0217
17	.0000	.0001	.0003	.0006	.0012	.0021	.0036	.0058	.0088	.0128
18	.0000	.0000	.0001	.0002	.0005	.0009	.0017	.0029	.0046	.0071
19	.0000	.0000	.0000	.0001	.0002	.0004	.0008	.0014	.0023	.0037
20	.0000	.0000	.0000	.0000	.0001	.0002	.0003	.0006	.0011	.0019
21	.0000	.0000	.0000	.0000	.0000	.0001	.0001	.0003	.0005	.0009
22	.0000	.0000	.0000	.0000	.0000	.0000	.0001	.0001	.0002	.0004
23	.0000	.0000	.0000	.0000	.0000	.0000	.0000	.0000	.0001	.0002

μ

x	11.0	12.0	13.0	14.0	15.0	16.0	17.0	18.0	19.0	20.0
0	.0000	.0000	.0000	.0000	.0000	.0000	.0000	.0000	.0000	.0000
1	.0002	.0001	.0000	.0000	.0000	.0000	.0000	.0000	.0000	.0000
2	.0010	.0004	.0002	.0001	.0000	.0000	.0000	.0000	.0000	.0000
3	.0037	.0018	.0008	.0004	.0002	.0001	.0000	.0000	.0000	.0000
4	.0102	.0053	.0027	.0013	.0006	.0003	.0001	.0001	.0000	.0000
5	.0224	.0127	.0070	.0037	.0019	.0010	.0005	.0002	.0001	.0001
6	.0411	.0255	.0152	.0087	.0048	.0026	.0014	.0007	.0004	.0002
7	.0646	.0437	.0281	.0174	.0104	.0060	.0034	.0019	.0010	.0005
8	.0888	.0655	.0457	.0304	.0194	.0120	.0072	.0042	.0024	.0013
9	.1085	.0874	.0661	.0473	.0324	.0213	.0135	.0083	.0050	.0029
10	.1194	.1048	.0859	.0663	.0486	.0341	.0230	.0150	.0095	.0058
11	.1194	.1144	.1015	.0844	.0663	.0496	.0355	.0245	.0164	.0106
12	.1094	.1144	.1099	.0984	.0829	.0661	.0504	.0368	.0259	.0176
13	.0926	.1056	.1099	.1060	.0956	.0814	.0658	.0509	.0378	.0271
14	.0728	.0905	.1021	.1060	.1024	.0930	.0800	.0655	.0514	.0387
15	.0534	.0724	.0885	.0989	.1024	.0992	.0906	.0786	.0650	.0516
16	.0367	.0543	.0719	.0866	.0960	.0992	.0963	.0884	.0772	.0646
17	.0237	.0383	.0550	.0713	.0847	.0934	.0963	.0936	.0863	.0760
18	.0145	.0255	.0397	.0554	.0706	.0830	.0909	.0936	.0911	.0844
19	.0084	.0161	.0272	.0409	.0557	.0699	.0814	.0887	.0911	.0888
20	.0046	.0097	.0177	.0286	.0418	.0559	.0692	.0798	.0866	.0888
21	.0024	.0055	.0109	.0191	.0299	.0426	.0560	.0684	.0783	.0846
22	.0012	.0030	.0065	.0121	.0204	.0310	.0433	.0560	.0676	.0769
23	.0006	.0016	.0037	.0074	.0133	.0216	.0320	.0438	.0559	.0669
24	.0003	.0008	.0020	.0043	.0083	.0144	.0226	.0328	.0442	.0557
25	.0001	.0004	.0010	.0024	.0050	.0092	.0154	.0237	.0336	.0446
26	.0000	.0002	.0005	.0013	.0029	.0057	.0101	.0164	.0246	.0343
27	.0000	.0001	.0002	.0007	.0016	.0034	.0063	.0109	.0173	.0254
28	.0000	.0000	.0001	.0003	.0009	.0019	.0038	.0070	.0117	.0181
29	.0000	.0000	.0001	.0002	.0004	.0011	.0023	.0044	.0077	.0125
30	.0000	.0000	.0000	.0001	.0002	.0006	.0013	.0026	.0049	.0083
31	.0000	.0000	.0000	.0000	.0001	.0003	.0007	.0015	.0030	.0054
32	.0000	.0000	.0000	.0000	.0001	.0001	.0004	.0009	.0018	.0034
33	.0000	.0000	.0000	.0000	.0000	.0001	.0002	.0005	.0010	.0020

Source: Computed by D. K. Hildebrand. Found in D. K. Hildebrand and L. Ott, *Statistical Thinking for Managers,* 3rd ed. (Boston, MA: PWS-KENT Publishing Company, 1991).

TABLE A.3   Cumulative Areas under the Standard Normal Curve

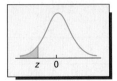

z	0.00	0.01	0.02	0.03	0.04	0.05	0.06	0.07	0.08	0.09
−3.9	0.00005	0.00005	0.00004	0.00004	0.00004	0.00004	0.00004	0.00004	0.00003	0.00003
−3.8	0.00007	0.00007	0.00007	0.00006	0.00006	0.00006	0.00006	0.00005	0.00005	0.00005
−3.7	0.00011	0.00010	0.00010	0.00010	0.00009	0.00009	0.00008	0.00008	0.00008	0.00008
−3.6	0.00016	0.00015	0.00015	0.00014	0.00014	0.00013	0.00013	0.00012	0.00012	0.00011
−3.5	0.00023	0.00022	0.00022	0.00021	0.00020	0.00019	0.00019	0.00018	0.00017	0.00017
−3.4	0.00034	0.00032	0.00031	0.00030	0.00029	0.00028	0.00027	0.00026	0.00025	0.00024
−3.3	0.00048	0.00047	0.00045	0.00043	0.00042	0.00040	0.00039	0.00038	0.00036	0.00035
−3.2	0.00069	0.00066	0.00064	0.00062	0.00060	0.00058	0.00056	0.00054	0.00052	0.00050
−3.1	0.00097	0.00094	0.00090	0.00087	0.00084	0.00082	0.00079	0.00076	0.00074	0.00071
−3.0	0.00135	0.00131	0.00126	0.00122	0.00118	0.00114	0.00111	0.00107	0.00103	0.00100
−2.9	0.0019	0.0018	0.0018	0.0017	0.0016	0.0016	0.0015	0.0015	0.0014	0.0014
−2.8	0.0026	0.0025	0.0024	0.0023	0.0023	0.0022	0.0021	0.0021	0.0020	0.0019
−2.7	0.0035	0.0034	0.0033	0.0032	0.0031	0.0030	0.0029	0.0028	0.0027	0.0026
−2.6	0.0047	0.0045	0.0044	0.0043	0.0041	0.0040	0.0039	0.0038	0.0037	0.0036
−2.5	0.0062	0.0060	0.0059	0.0057	0.0055	0.0054	0.0052	0.0051	0.0049	0.0048
−2.4	0.0082	0.0080	0.0078	0.0075	0.0073	0.0071	0.0069	0.0068	0.0066	0.0064
−2.3	0.0107	0.0104	0.0102	0.0099	0.0096	0.0094	0.0091	0.0089	0.0087	0.0084
−2.2	0.0139	0.0136	0.0132	0.0129	0.0125	0.0122	0.0119	0.0116	0.0113	0.0110
−2.1	0.0179	0.0174	0.0170	0.0166	0.0162	0.0158	0.0154	0.0150	0.0146	0.0143
−2.0	0.0228	0.0222	0.0217	0.0212	0.0207	0.0202	0.0197	0.0192	0.0188	0.0183
−1.9	0.0287	0.0281	0.0274	0.0268	0.0262	0.0256	0.0250	0.0244	0.0239	0.0233
−1.8	0.0359	0.0351	0.0344	0.0336	0.0329	0.0322	0.0314	0.0307	0.0301	0.0294
−1.7	0.0446	0.0436	0.0427	0.0418	0.0409	0.0401	0.0392	0.0384	0.0375	0.0367
−1.6	0.0548	0.0537	0.0526	0.0516	0.0505	0.0495	0.0485	0.0475	0.0465	0.0455
−1.5	0.0668	0.0655	0.0643	0.0630	0.0618	0.0606	0.0594	0.0582	0.0571	0.0559
−1.4	0.0808	0.0793	0.0778	0.0764	0.0749	0.0735	0.0721	0.0708	0.0694	0.0681
−1.3	0.0968	0.0951	0.0934	0.0918	0.0901	0.0885	0.0869	0.0853	0.0838	0.0823
−1.2	0.1151	0.1131	0.1112	0.1093	0.1075	0.1056	0.1038	0.1020	0.1003	0.0985
−1.1	0.1357	0.1335	0.1314	0.1292	0.1271	0.1251	0.1230	0.1210	0.1190	0.1170
−1.0	0.1587	0.1562	0.1539	0.1515	0.1492	0.1469	0.1446	0.1423	0.1401	0.1379
−0.9	0.1841	0.1814	0.1788	0.1762	0.1736	0.1711	0.1685	0.1660	0.1635	0.1611
−0.8	0.2119	0.2090	0.2061	0.2033	0.2005	0.1977	0.1949	0.1922	0.1894	0.1867
−0.7	0.2420	0.2389	0.2358	0.2327	0.2296	0.2266	0.2236	0.2206	0.2177	0.2148
−0.6	0.2743	0.2709	0.2676	0.2643	0.2611	0.2578	0.2546	0.2514	0.2482	0.2451
−0.5	0.3085	0.3050	0.3015	0.2981	0.2946	0.2912	0.2877	0.2843	0.2810	0.2776
−0.4	0.3446	0.3409	0.3372	0.3336	0.3300	0.3264	0.3228	0.3192	0.3156	0.3121
−0.3	0.3821	0.3783	0.3745	0.3707	0.3669	0.3632	0.3594	0.3557	0.3520	0.3483
−0.2	0.4207	0.4168	0.4129	0.4090	0.4052	0.4013	0.3974	0.3936	0.3897	0.3859
−0.1	0.4602	0.4562	0.4522	0.4483	0.4443	0.4404	0.4364	0.4325	0.4286	0.4247
−0.0	0.5000	0.4960	0.4920	0.4880	0.4840	0.4801	0.4761	0.4721	0.4681	0.4641

TABLE A.3 Cumulative Areas under the Standard Normal Curve (*concluded*)

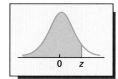

z	0.00	0.01	0.02	0.03	0.04	0.05	0.06	0.07	0.08	0.09
0.0	0.5000	0.5040	0.5080	0.5120	0.5160	0.5199	0.5239	0.5279	0.5319	0.5359
0.1	0.5398	0.5438	0.5478	0.5517	0.5557	0.5596	0.5636	0.5675	0.5714	0.5753
0.2	0.5793	0.5832	0.5871	0.5910	0.5948	0.5987	0.6026	0.6064	0.6103	0.6141
0.3	0.6179	0.6217	0.6255	0.6293	0.6331	0.6368	0.6406	0.6443	0.6480	0.6517
0.4	0.6554	0.6591	0.6628	0.6664	0.6700	0.6736	0.6772	0.6808	0.6844	0.6879
0.5	0.6915	0.6950	0.6985	0.7019	0.7054	0.7088	0.7123	0.7157	0.7190	0.7224
0.6	0.7257	0.7291	0.7324	0.7357	0.7389	0.7422	0.7454	0.7486	0.7518	0.7549
0.7	0.7580	0.7611	0.7642	0.7673	0.7704	0.7734	0.7764	0.7794	0.7823	0.7852
0.8	0.7881	0.7910	0.7939	0.7967	0.7995	0.8023	0.8051	0.8078	0.8106	0.8133
0.9	0.8159	0.8186	0.8212	0.8238	0.8264	0.8289	0.8315	0.8340	0.8365	0.8389
1.0	0.8413	0.8438	0.8461	0.8485	0.8508	0.8531	0.8554	0.8577	0.8599	0.8621
1.1	0.8643	0.8665	0.8686	0.8708	0.8729	0.8749	0.8770	0.8790	0.8810	0.8830
1.2	0.8849	0.8869	0.8888	0.8907	0.8925	0.8944	0.8962	0.8980	0.8997	0.9015
1.3	0.9032	0.9049	0.9066	0.9082	0.9099	0.9115	0.9131	0.9147	0.9162	0.9177
1.4	0.9192	0.9207	0.9222	0.9236	0.9251	0.9265	0.9279	0.9292	0.9306	0.9319
1.5	0.9332	0.9345	0.9357	0.9370	0.9382	0.9394	0.9406	0.9418	0.9429	0.9441
1.6	0.9452	0.9463	0.9474	0.9484	0.9495	0.9505	0.9515	0.9525	0.9535	0.9545
1.7	0.9554	0.9564	0.9573	0.9582	0.9591	0.9599	0.9608	0.9616	0.9625	0.9633
1.8	0.9641	0.9649	0.9656	0.9664	0.9671	0.9678	0.9686	0.9693	0.9699	0.9706
1.9	0.9713	0.9719	0.9726	0.9732	0.9738	0.9744	0.9750	0.9756	0.9761	0.9767
2.0	0.9772	0.9778	0.9783	0.9788	0.9793	0.9798	0.9803	0.9808	0.9812	0.9817
2.1	0.9821	0.9826	0.9830	0.9834	0.9838	0.9842	0.9846	0.9850	0.9854	0.9857
2.2	0.9861	0.9864	0.9868	0.9871	0.9875	0.9878	0.9881	0.9884	0.9887	0.9890
2.3	0.9893	0.9896	0.9898	0.9901	0.9904	0.9906	0.9909	0.9911	0.9913	0.9916
2.4	0.9918	0.9920	0.9922	0.9925	0.9927	0.9929	0.9931	0.9932	0.9934	0.9936
2.5	0.9938	0.9940	0.9941	0.9943	0.9945	0.9946	0.9948	0.9949	0.9951	0.9952
2.6	0.9953	0.9955	0.9956	0.9957	0.9959	0.9960	0.9961	0.9962	0.9963	0.9964
2.7	0.9965	0.9966	0.9967	0.9968	0.9969	0.9970	0.9971	0.9972	0.9973	0.9974
2.8	0.9974	0.9975	0.9976	0.9977	0.9977	0.9978	0.9979	0.9979	0.9980	0.9981
2.9	0.9981	0.9982	0.9982	0.9983	0.9984	0.9984	0.9985	0.9985	0.9986	0.9986
3.0	0.99865	0.99869	0.99874	0.99878	0.99882	0.99886	0.99889	0.99893	0.99897	0.99900
3.1	0.99903	0.99906	0.99910	0.99913	0.99916	0.99918	0.99921	0.99924	0.99926	0.99929
3.2	0.99931	0.99934	0.99936	0.99938	0.99940	0.99942	0.99944	0.99946	0.99948	0.99950
3.3	0.99952	0.99953	0.99955	0.99957	0.99958	0.99960	0.99961	0.99962	0.99964	0.99965
3.4	0.99966	0.99968	0.99969	0.99970	0.99971	0.99972	0.99973	0.99974	0.99975	0.99976
3.5	0.99977	0.99978	0.99978	0.99979	0.99980	0.99981	0.99981	0.99982	0.99983	0.99983
3.6	0.99984	0.99985	0.99985	0.99986	0.99986	0.99987	0.99987	0.99988	0.99988	0.99989
3.7	0.99989	0.99990	0.99990	0.99990	0.99991	0.99991	0.99992	0.99992	0.99992	0.99992
3.8	0.99993	0.99993	0.99993	0.99994	0.99994	0.99994	0.99994	0.99995	0.99995	0.99995
3.9	0.99995	0.99995	0.99996	0.99996	0.99996	0.99996	0.99996	0.99996	0.99997	0.99997

TABLE A.4   A *t* Table: Values of t_α for *df* = 1 through 48

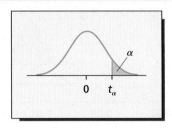

df	$t_{.100}$	$t_{.05}$	$t_{.025}$	$t_{.01}$	$t_{.005}$	$t_{.001}$	$t_{.0005}$
1	3.078	6.314	12.706	31.821	63.657	318.309	636.619
2	1.886	2.920	4.303	6.965	9.925	22.327	31.599
3	1.638	2.353	3.182	4.541	5.841	10.215	12.924
4	1.533	2.132	2.776	3.747	4.604	7.173	8.610
5	1.476	2.015	2.571	3.365	4.032	5.893	6.869
6	1.440	1.943	2.447	3.143	3.707	5.208	5.959
7	1.415	1.895	2.365	2.998	3.499	4.785	5.408
8	1.397	1.860	2.306	2.896	3.355	4.501	5.041
9	1.383	1.833	2.262	2.821	3.250	4.297	4.781
10	1.372	1.812	2.228	2.764	3.169	4.144	4.587
11	1.363	1.796	2.201	2.718	3.106	4.025	4.437
12	1.356	1.782	2.179	2.681	3.055	3.930	4.318
13	1.350	1.771	2.160	2.650	3.012	3.852	4.221
14	1.345	1.761	2.145	2.624	2.977	3.787	4.140
15	1.341	1.753	2.131	2.602	2.947	3.733	4.073
16	1.337	1.746	2.120	2.583	2.921	3.686	4.015
17	1.333	1.740	2.110	2.567	2.898	3.646	3.965
18	1.330	1.734	2.101	2.552	2.878	3.610	3.922
19	1.328	1.729	2.093	2.539	2.861	3.579	3.883
20	1.325	1.725	2.086	2.528	2.845	3.552	3.850
21	1.323	1.721	2.080	2.518	2.831	3.527	3.819
22	1.321	1.717	2.074	2.508	2.819	3.505	3.792
23	1.319	1.714	2.069	2.500	2.807	3.485	3.768
24	1.318	1.711	2.064	2.492	2.797	3.467	3.745
25	1.316	1.708	2.060	2.485	2.787	3.450	3.725
26	1.315	1.706	2.056	2.479	2.779	3.435	3.707
27	1.314	1.703	2.052	2.473	2.771	3.421	3.690
28	1.313	1.701	2.048	2.467	2.763	3.408	3.674
29	1.311	1.699	2.045	2.462	2.756	3.396	3.659
30	1.310	1.697	2.042	2.457	2.750	3.385	3.646
31	1.309	1.696	2.040	2.453	2.744	3.375	3.633
32	1.309	1.694	2.037	2.449	2.738	3.365	3.622
33	1.308	1.692	2.035	2.445	2.733	3.356	3.611
34	1.307	1.691	2.032	2.441	2.728	3.348	3.601
35	1.306	1.690	2.030	2.438	2.724	3.340	3.591
36	1.306	1.688	2.028	2.434	2.719	3.333	3.582
37	1.305	1.687	2.026	2.431	2.715	3.326	3.574
38	1.304	1.686	2.024	2.429	2.712	3.319	3.566
39	1.304	1.685	2.023	2.426	2.708	3.313	3.558
40	1.303	1.684	2.021	2.423	2.704	3.307	3.551
41	1.303	1.683	2.020	2.421	2.701	3.301	3.544
42	1.302	1.682	2.018	2.418	2.698	3.296	3.538
43	1.302	1.681	2.017	2.416	2.695	3.291	3.532
44	1.301	1.680	2.015	2.414	2.692	3.286	3.526
45	1.301	1.679	2.014	2.412	2.690	3.281	3.520
46	1.300	1.679	2.013	2.410	2.687	3.277	3.515
47	1.300	1.678	2.012	2.408	2.685	3.273	3.510
48	1.299	1.677	2.011	2.407	2.682	3.269	3.505

TABLE A.4   *(concluded)*
A *t* Table: Values of t_α for *df* = 49 through 100, 120, and ∞

df	$t_{.100}$	$t_{.05}$	$t_{.025}$	$t_{.01}$	$t_{.005}$	$t_{.001}$	$t_{.0005}$
49	1.299	1.677	2.010	2.405	2.680	3.265	3.500
50	1.299	1.676	2.009	2.403	2.678	3.261	3.496
51	1.298	1.675	2.008	2.402	2.676	3.258	3.492
52	1.298	1.675	2.007	2.400	2.674	3.255	3.488
53	1.298	1.674	2.006	2.399	2.672	3.251	3.484
54	1.297	1.674	2.005	2.397	2.670	3.248	3.480
55	1.297	1.673	2.004	2.396	2.668	3.245	3.476
56	1.297	1.673	2.003	2.395	2.667	3.242	3.473
57	1.297	1.672	2.002	2.394	2.665	3.239	3.470
58	1.296	1.672	2.002	2.392	2.663	3.237	3.466
59	1.296	1.671	2.001	2.391	2.662	3.234	3.463
60	1.296	1.671	2.000	2.390	2.660	3.232	3.460
61	1.296	1.670	2.000	2.389	2.659	3.229	3.457
62	1.295	1.670	1.999	2.388	2.657	3.227	3.454
63	1.295	1.669	1.998	2.387	2.656	3.225	3.452
64	1.295	1.669	1.998	2.386	2.655	3.223	3.449
65	1.295	1.669	1.997	2.385	2.654	3.220	3.447
66	1.295	1.668	1.997	2.384	2.652	3.218	3.444
67	1.294	1.668	1.996	2.383	2.651	3.216	3.442
68	1.294	1.668	1.995	2.382	2.650	3.214	3.439
69	1.294	1.667	1.995	2.382	2.649	3.213	3.437
70	1.294	1.667	1.994	2.381	2.648	3.211	3.435
71	1.294	1.667	1.994	2.380	2.647	3.209	3.433
72	1.293	1.666	1.993	2.379	2.646	3.207	3.431
73	1.293	1.666	1.993	2.379	2.645	3.206	3.429
74	1.293	1.666	1.993	2.378	2.644	3.204	3.427
75	1.293	1.665	1.992	2.377	2.643	3.202	3.425
76	1.293	1.665	1.992	2.376	2.642	3.201	3.423
77	1.293	1.665	1.991	2.376	2.641	3.199	3.421
78	1.292	1.665	1.991	2.375	2.640	3.198	3.420
79	1.292	1.664	1.990	2.374	2.640	3.197	3.418
80	1.292	1.664	1.990	2.374	2.639	3.195	3.416
81	1.292	1.664	1.990	2.373	2.638	3.194	3.415
82	1.292	1.664	1.989	2.373	2.637	3.193	3.413
83	1.292	1.663	1.989	2.372	2.636	3.191	3.412
84	1.292	1.663	1.989	2.372	2.636	3.190	3.410
85	1.292	1.663	1.988	2.371	2.635	3.189	3.409
86	1.291	1.663	1.988	2.370	2.634	3.188	3.407
87	1.291	1.663	1.988	2.370	2.634	3.187	3.406
88	1.291	1.662	1.987	2.369	2.633	3.185	3.405
89	1.291	1.662	1.987	2.369	2.632	3.184	3.403
90	1.291	1.662	1.987	2.368	2.632	3.183	3.402
91	1.291	1.662	1.986	2.368	2.631	3.182	3.401
92	1.291	1.662	1.986	2.368	2.630	3.181	3.399
93	1.291	1.661	1.986	2.367	2.630	3.180	3.398
94	1.291	1.661	1.986	2.367	2.629	3.179	3.397
95	1.291	1.661	1.985	2.366	2.629	3.178	3.396
96	1.290	1.661	1.985	2.366	2.628	3.177	3.395
97	1.290	1.661	1.985	2.365	2.627	3.176	3.394
98	1.290	1.661	1.984	2.365	2.627	3.175	3.393
99	1.290	1.660	1.984	2.365	2.626	3.175	3.392
100	1.290	1.660	1.984	2.364	2.626	3.174	3.390
120	1.289	1.658	1.980	2.358	2.617	3.160	3.373
∞	1.282	1.645	1.960	2.326	2.576	3.090	3.291

Source: Provided by J. B. Orris using Excel.

T A B L E   A . 5   **An *F* Table: Values of *F*.10**

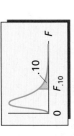

Numerator Degrees of Freedom (df_1)

df_2 \ df_1	1	2	3	4	5	6	7	8	9	10	12	15	20	24	30	40	60	120	∞
1	39.86	49.50	53.59	55.83	57.24	58.20	58.91	59.44	59.86	60.19	60.71	61.22	61.74	62.00	62.26	62.53	62.79	63.06	63.33
2	8.53	9.00	9.16	9.24	9.29	9.33	9.35	9.37	9.38	9.39	9.41	9.42	9.44	9.45	9.46	9.47	9.47	9.48	9.49
3	5.54	5.46	5.39	5.34	5.31	5.28	5.27	5.25	5.24	5.23	5.22	5.20	5.18	5.18	5.17	5.16	5.15	5.14	5.13
4	4.54	4.32	4.19	4.11	4.05	4.01	3.98	3.95	3.94	3.92	3.90	3.87	3.84	3.83	3.82	3.80	3.79	3.78	3.76
5	4.06	3.78	3.62	3.52	3.45	3.40	3.37	3.34	3.32	3.30	3.27	3.24	3.21	3.19	3.17	3.16	3.14	3.12	3.10
6	3.78	3.46	3.29	3.18	3.11	3.05	3.01	2.98	2.96	2.94	2.90	2.87	2.84	2.82	2.80	2.78	2.76	2.74	2.72
7	3.59	3.26	3.07	2.96	2.88	2.83	2.78	2.75	2.72	2.70	2.67	2.63	2.59	2.58	2.56	2.54	2.51	2.49	2.47
8	3.46	3.11	2.92	2.81	2.73	2.67	2.62	2.59	2.56	2.54	2.50	2.46	2.42	2.40	2.38	2.36	2.34	2.32	2.29
9	3.36	3.01	2.81	2.69	2.61	2.55	2.51	2.47	2.44	2.42	2.38	2.34	2.30	2.28	2.25	2.23	2.21	2.18	2.16
10	3.29	2.92	2.73	2.61	2.52	2.46	2.41	2.38	2.35	2.32	2.28	2.24	2.20	2.18	2.16	2.13	2.11	2.08	2.06
11	3.23	2.86	2.66	2.54	2.45	2.39	2.34	2.30	2.27	2.25	2.21	2.17	2.12	2.10	2.08	2.05	2.03	2.00	1.97
12	3.18	2.81	2.61	2.48	2.39	2.33	2.28	2.24	2.21	2.19	2.15	2.10	2.06	2.04	2.01	1.99	1.96	1.93	1.90
13	3.14	2.76	2.56	2.43	2.35	2.28	2.23	2.20	2.16	2.14	2.10	2.05	2.01	1.98	1.96	1.93	1.90	1.88	1.85
14	3.10	2.73	2.52	2.39	2.31	2.24	2.19	2.15	2.12	2.10	2.05	2.01	1.96	1.94	1.91	1.89	1.86	1.83	1.80
15	3.07	2.70	2.49	2.36	2.27	2.21	2.16	2.12	2.09	2.06	2.02	1.97	1.92	1.90	1.87	1.85	1.82	1.79	1.76
16	3.05	2.67	2.46	2.33	2.24	2.18	2.13	2.09	2.06	2.03	1.99	1.94	1.89	1.87	1.84	1.81	1.78	1.75	1.72
17	3.03	2.64	2.44	2.31	2.22	2.15	2.10	2.06	2.03	2.00	1.96	1.91	1.86	1.84	1.81	1.78	1.75	1.72	1.69
18	3.01	2.62	2.42	2.29	2.20	2.13	2.08	2.04	2.00	1.98	1.93	1.89	1.84	1.81	1.78	1.75	1.72	1.69	1.66
19	2.99	2.61	2.40	2.27	2.18	2.11	2.06	2.02	1.98	1.96	1.91	1.86	1.81	1.79	1.76	1.73	1.70	1.67	1.63
20	2.97	2.59	2.38	2.25	2.16	2.09	2.04	2.00	1.96	1.94	1.89	1.84	1.79	1.77	1.74	1.71	1.68	1.64	1.61
21	2.96	2.57	2.36	2.23	2.14	2.08	2.02	1.98	1.95	1.92	1.87	1.83	1.78	1.75	1.72	1.69	1.66	1.62	1.59
22	2.95	2.56	2.35	2.22	2.13	2.06	2.01	1.97	1.93	1.90	1.86	1.81	1.76	1.73	1.70	1.67	1.64	1.60	1.57
23	2.94	2.55	2.34	2.21	2.11	2.05	1.99	1.95	1.92	1.89	1.84	1.80	1.74	1.72	1.69	1.66	1.62	1.59	1.55
24	2.93	2.54	2.33	2.19	2.10	2.04	1.98	1.94	1.91	1.88	1.83	1.78	1.73	1.70	1.67	1.64	1.61	1.57	1.53
25	2.92	2.53	2.32	2.18	2.09	2.02	1.97	1.93	1.89	1.87	1.82	1.77	1.72	1.69	1.66	1.63	1.59	1.56	1.52
26	2.91	2.52	2.31	2.17	2.08	2.01	1.96	1.92	1.88	1.86	1.81	1.76	1.71	1.68	1.65	1.61	1.58	1.54	1.50
27	2.90	2.51	2.30	2.17	2.07	2.00	1.95	1.91	1.87	1.85	1.80	1.75	1.70	1.67	1.64	1.60	1.57	1.53	1.49
28	2.89	2.50	2.29	2.16	2.06	2.00	1.94	1.90	1.87	1.84	1.79	1.74	1.69	1.66	1.63	1.59	1.56	1.52	1.48
29	2.89	2.50	2.28	2.15	2.06	1.99	1.93	1.89	1.86	1.83	1.78	1.73	1.68	1.65	1.62	1.58	1.55	1.51	1.47
30	2.88	2.49	2.28	2.14	2.05	1.98	1.93	1.88	1.85	1.82	1.77	1.72	1.67	1.64	1.61	1.57	1.54	1.50	1.46
40	2.84	2.44	2.23	2.09	2.00	1.93	1.87	1.83	1.79	1.76	1.71	1.66	1.61	1.57	1.54	1.51	1.47	1.42	1.38
60	2.79	2.39	2.18	2.04	1.95	1.87	1.82	1.77	1.74	1.71	1.66	1.60	1.54	1.51	1.48	1.44	1.40	1.35	1.29
120	2.75	2.35	2.13	1.99	1.90	1.82	1.77	1.72	1.68	1.65	1.60	1.55	1.48	1.45	1.41	1.37	1.32	1.26	1.19
∞	2.71	2.30	2.08	1.94	1.85	1.77	1.72	1.67	1.63	1.60	1.55	1.49	1.42	1.38	1.34	1.30	1.24	1.17	1.00

Denominator Degrees of Freedom (df_2)

Source: M. Merrington and C. M. Thompson, "Tables of Percentage Points of the Inverted Beta (*F*)-Distribution," *Biometrika* 33 (1943), pp. 73–88. Reproduced by permission of the Biometrika Trustees.

TABLE A.6   An F Table: Values of $F_{.05}$

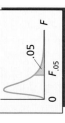

Numerator Degrees of Freedom (df_1)

df_2 \ df_1	1	2	3	4	5	6	7	8	9	10	12	15	20	24	30	40	60	120	∞
1	161.4	199.5	215.7	224.6	230.2	234.0	236.8	238.9	240.5	241.9	243.9	245.9	248.0	249.1	250.1	251.1	252.2	253.3	254.3
2	18.51	19.00	19.16	19.25	19.30	19.33	19.35	19.37	19.38	19.40	19.41	19.43	19.45	19.45	19.46	19.47	19.48	19.49	19.50
3	10.13	9.55	9.28	9.12	9.01	8.94	8.89	8.85	8.81	8.79	8.74	8.70	8.66	8.64	8.62	8.59	8.57	8.55	8.53
4	7.71	6.94	6.59	6.39	6.26	6.16	6.09	6.04	6.00	5.96	5.91	5.86	5.80	5.77	5.75	5.72	5.69	5.66	5.63
5	6.61	5.79	5.41	5.19	5.05	4.95	4.88	4.82	4.77	4.74	4.68	4.62	4.56	4.53	4.50	4.46	4.43	4.40	4.36
6	5.99	5.14	4.76	4.53	4.39	4.28	4.21	4.15	4.10	4.06	4.00	3.94	3.87	3.84	3.81	3.77	3.74	3.70	3.67
7	5.59	4.74	4.35	4.12	3.97	3.87	3.79	3.73	3.68	3.64	3.57	3.51	3.44	3.41	3.38	3.34	3.30	3.27	3.23
8	5.32	4.46	4.07	3.84	3.69	3.58	3.50	3.44	3.39	3.35	3.28	3.22	3.15	3.12	3.08	3.04	3.01	2.97	2.93
9	5.12	4.26	3.86	3.63	3.48	3.37	3.29	3.23	3.18	3.14	3.07	3.01	2.94	2.90	2.86	2.83	2.79	2.75	2.71
10	4.96	4.10	3.71	3.48	3.33	3.22	3.14	3.07	3.02	2.98	2.91	2.85	2.77	2.74	2.70	2.66	2.62	2.58	2.54
11	4.84	3.98	3.59	3.36	3.20	3.09	3.01	2.95	2.90	2.85	2.79	2.72	2.65	2.61	2.57	2.53	2.49	2.45	2.40
12	4.75	3.89	3.49	3.26	3.11	3.00	2.91	2.85	2.80	2.75	2.69	2.62	2.54	2.51	2.47	2.43	2.38	2.34	2.30
13	4.67	3.81	3.41	3.18	3.03	2.92	2.83	2.77	2.71	2.67	2.60	2.53	2.46	2.42	2.38	2.34	2.30	2.25	2.21
14	4.60	3.74	3.34	3.11	2.96	2.85	2.76	2.70	2.65	2.60	2.53	2.46	2.39	2.35	2.31	2.27	2.22	2.18	2.13
15	4.54	3.68	3.29	3.06	2.90	2.79	2.71	2.64	2.59	2.54	2.48	2.40	2.33	2.29	2.25	2.20	2.16	2.11	2.07
16	4.49	3.63	3.24	3.01	2.85	2.74	2.66	2.59	2.54	2.49	2.42	2.35	2.28	2.24	2.19	2.15	2.11	2.06	2.01
17	4.45	3.59	3.20	2.96	2.81	2.70	2.61	2.55	2.49	2.45	2.38	2.31	2.23	2.19	2.15	2.10	2.06	2.01	1.96
18	4.41	3.55	3.16	2.93	2.77	2.66	2.58	2.51	2.46	2.41	2.34	2.27	2.19	2.15	2.11	2.06	2.02	1.97	1.92
19	4.38	3.52	3.13	2.90	2.74	2.63	2.54	2.48	2.42	2.38	2.31	2.23	2.16	2.11	2.07	2.03	1.98	1.93	1.88
20	4.35	3.49	3.10	2.87	2.71	2.60	2.51	2.45	2.39	2.35	2.28	2.20	2.12	2.08	2.04	1.99	1.95	1.90	1.84
21	4.32	3.47	3.07	2.84	2.68	2.57	2.49	2.42	2.37	2.32	2.25	2.18	2.10	2.05	2.01	1.96	1.92	1.87	1.81
22	4.30	3.44	3.05	2.82	2.66	2.55	2.46	2.40	2.34	2.30	2.23	2.15	2.07	2.03	1.98	1.94	1.89	1.84	1.78
23	4.28	3.42	3.03	2.80	2.64	2.53	2.44	2.37	2.32	2.27	2.20	2.13	2.05	2.01	1.96	1.91	1.86	1.81	1.76
24	4.26	3.40	3.01	2.78	2.62	2.51	2.42	2.36	2.30	2.25	2.18	2.11	2.03	1.98	1.94	1.89	1.84	1.79	1.73
25	4.24	3.39	2.99	2.76	2.60	2.49	2.40	2.34	2.28	2.24	2.16	2.09	2.01	1.96	1.92	1.87	1.82	1.77	1.71
26	4.23	3.37	2.98	2.74	2.59	2.47	2.39	2.32	2.27	2.22	2.15	2.07	1.99	1.95	1.90	1.85	1.80	1.75	1.69
27	4.21	3.35	2.96	2.73	2.57	2.46	2.37	2.31	2.25	2.20	2.13	2.06	1.97	1.93	1.88	1.84	1.79	1.73	1.67
28	4.20	3.34	2.95	2.71	2.56	2.45	2.36	2.29	2.24	2.19	2.12	2.04	1.96	1.91	1.87	1.82	1.77	1.71	1.65
29	4.18	3.33	2.93	2.70	2.55	2.43	2.35	2.28	2.22	2.18	2.10	2.03	1.94	1.90	1.85	1.81	1.75	1.70	1.64
30	4.17	3.32	2.92	2.69	2.53	2.42	2.33	2.27	2.21	2.16	2.09	2.01	1.93	1.89	1.84	1.79	1.74	1.68	1.62
40	4.08	3.23	2.84	2.61	2.45	2.34	2.25	2.18	2.12	2.08	2.00	1.92	1.84	1.79	1.74	1.69	1.64	1.58	1.51
60	4.00	3.15	2.76	2.53	2.37	2.25	2.17	2.10	2.04	1.99	1.92	1.84	1.75	1.70	1.65	1.59	1.53	1.47	1.39
120	3.92	3.07	2.68	2.45	2.29	2.17	2.09	2.02	1.96	1.91	1.83	1.75	1.66	1.61	1.55	1.50	1.43	1.35	1.25
∞	3.84	3.00	2.60	2.37	2.21	2.10	2.01	1.94	1.88	1.83	1.75	1.67	1.57	1.52	1.46	1.39	1.32	1.22	1.00

Denominator Degrees of Freedom (df_2)

Source: M. Merrington and C. M. Thompson, "Tables of Percentage Points of the Inverted Beta (F)-Distribution," Biometrika 33 (1943). pp. 73–88. Reproduced by permission of the Biometrika Trustees.

TABLE A.7   An *F* Table: Values of $F_{.025}$

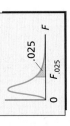

df_2 \ df_1	1	2	3	4	5	6	7	8	9	10	12	15	20	24	30	40	60	120	∞
1	647.8	799.5	864.2	899.6	921.8	937.1	948.2	956.7	963.3	968.6	976.7	984.9	993.1	997.2	1,001	1,006	1,010	1,014	1,018
2	38.51	39.00	39.17	39.25	39.30	39.33	39.36	39.37	39.39	39.40	39.41	39.43	39.45	39.46	39.46	39.47	39.48	39.49	39.50
3	17.44	16.04	15.44	15.10	14.88	14.73	14.62	14.54	14.47	14.42	14.34	14.25	14.17	14.12	14.08	14.04	13.99	13.95	13.90
4	12.22	10.65	9.98	9.60	9.36	9.20	9.07	8.98	8.90	8.84	8.75	8.66	8.56	8.51	8.46	8.41	8.36	8.31	8.26
5	10.01	8.43	7.76	7.39	7.15	6.98	6.85	6.76	6.68	6.62	6.52	6.43	6.33	6.28	6.23	6.18	6.12	6.07	6.02
6	8.81	7.26	6.60	6.23	5.99	5.82	5.70	5.60	5.52	5.46	5.37	5.27	5.17	5.12	5.07	5.01	4.96	4.90	4.85
7	8.07	6.54	5.89	5.52	5.29	5.12	4.99	4.90	4.82	4.76	4.67	4.57	4.47	4.42	4.36	4.31	4.25	4.20	4.14
8	7.57	6.06	5.42	5.05	4.82	4.65	4.53	4.43	4.36	4.30	4.20	4.10	4.00	3.95	3.89	3.84	3.78	3.73	3.67
9	7.21	5.71	5.08	4.72	4.48	4.32	4.20	4.10	4.03	3.96	3.87	3.77	3.67	3.61	3.56	3.51	3.45	3.39	3.33
10	6.94	5.46	4.83	4.47	4.24	4.07	3.95	3.85	3.78	3.72	3.62	3.52	3.42	3.37	3.31	3.26	3.20	3.14	3.08
11	6.72	5.26	4.63	4.28	4.04	3.88	3.76	3.66	3.59	3.53	3.43	3.33	3.23	3.17	3.12	3.06	3.00	2.94	2.88
12	6.55	5.10	4.47	4.12	3.89	3.73	3.61	3.51	3.44	3.37	3.28	3.18	3.07	3.02	2.96	2.91	2.85	2.79	2.72
13	6.41	4.97	4.35	4.00	3.77	3.60	3.48	3.39	3.31	3.25	3.15	3.05	2.95	2.89	2.84	2.78	2.72	2.66	2.60
14	6.30	4.86	4.24	3.89	3.66	3.50	3.38	3.29	3.21	3.15	3.05	2.95	2.84	2.79	2.73	2.67	2.61	2.55	2.49
15	6.20	4.77	4.15	3.80	3.58	3.41	3.29	3.20	3.12	3.06	2.96	2.86	2.76	2.70	2.64	2.59	2.52	2.46	2.40
16	6.12	4.69	4.08	3.73	3.50	3.34	3.22	3.12	3.05	2.99	2.89	2.79	2.68	2.63	2.57	2.51	2.45	2.38	2.32
17	6.04	4.62	4.01	3.66	3.44	3.28	3.16	3.06	2.98	2.92	2.82	2.72	2.62	2.56	2.50	2.44	2.38	2.32	2.25
18	5.98	4.56	3.95	3.61	3.38	3.22	3.10	3.01	2.93	2.87	2.77	2.67	2.56	2.50	2.44	2.38	2.32	2.26	2.19
19	5.92	4.51	3.90	3.56	3.33	3.17	3.05	2.96	2.88	2.82	2.72	2.62	2.51	2.45	2.39	2.33	2.27	2.20	2.13
20	5.87	4.46	3.86	3.51	3.29	3.13	3.01	2.91	2.84	2.77	2.68	2.57	2.46	2.41	2.35	2.29	2.22	2.16	2.09
21	5.83	4.42	3.82	3.48	3.25	3.09	2.97	2.87	2.80	2.73	2.64	2.53	2.42	2.37	2.31	2.25	2.18	2.11	2.04
22	5.79	4.38	3.78	3.44	3.22	3.05	2.93	2.84	2.76	2.70	2.60	2.50	2.39	2.33	2.27	2.21	2.14	2.08	2.00
23	5.75	4.35	3.75	3.41	3.18	3.02	2.90	2.81	2.73	2.67	2.57	2.47	2.36	2.30	2.24	2.18	2.11	2.04	1.97
24	5.72	4.32	3.72	3.38	3.15	2.99	2.87	2.78	2.70	2.64	2.54	2.44	2.33	2.27	2.21	2.15	2.08	2.01	1.94
25	5.69	4.29	3.69	3.35	3.13	2.97	2.85	2.75	2.68	2.61	2.51	2.41	2.30	2.24	2.18	2.12	2.05	1.98	1.91
26	5.66	4.27	3.67	3.33	3.10	2.94	2.82	2.73	2.65	2.59	2.49	2.39	2.28	2.22	2.16	2.09	2.03	1.95	1.88
27	5.63	4.24	3.65	3.31	3.08	2.92	2.80	2.71	2.63	2.57	2.47	2.36	2.25	2.19	2.13	2.07	2.00	1.93	1.85
28	5.61	4.22	3.63	3.29	3.06	2.90	2.78	2.69	2.61	2.55	2.45	2.34	2.23	2.17	2.11	2.05	1.98	1.91	1.83
29	5.59	4.20	3.61	3.27	3.04	2.88	2.76	2.67	2.59	2.53	2.43	2.32	2.21	2.15	2.09	2.03	1.96	1.89	1.81
30	5.57	4.18	3.59	3.25	3.03	2.87	2.75	2.65	2.57	2.51	2.41	2.31	2.20	2.14	2.07	2.01	1.94	1.87	1.79
40	5.42	4.05	3.46	3.13	2.90	2.74	2.62	2.53	2.45	2.39	2.29	2.18	2.07	2.01	1.94	1.88	1.80	1.72	1.64
60	5.29	3.93	3.34	3.01	2.79	2.63	2.51	2.41	2.33	2.27	2.17	2.06	1.94	1.88	1.82	1.74	1.67	1.58	1.48
120	5.15	3.80	3.23	2.89	2.67	2.52	2.39	2.30	2.22	2.16	2.05	1.94	1.82	1.76	1.69	1.61	1.53	1.43	1.31
∞	5.02	3.69	3.12	2.79	2.57	2.41	2.29	2.19	2.11	2.05	1.94	1.83	1.71	1.64	1.57	1.48	1.39	1.27	1.00

Numerator Degrees of Freedom (df_1)

Denominator Degrees of Freedom (df_2)

Source: M. Merrington and C. M. Thompson, "Tables of Percentage Points of the Inverted Beta (*F*)-Distribution," *Biometrika* 33 (1943), pp. 73–88. Reproduced by permission of the Biometrika Trustees.

TABLE A.8　An *F* Table: Values of $F_{.01}$

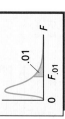

Numerator Degrees of Freedom (df_1)

df_2	1	2	3	4	5	6	7	8	9	10	12	15	20	24	30	40	60	120	∞
1	4,052	4,999.5	5,403	5,625	5,764	5,859	5,928	5,982	6,022	6,056	6,106	6,157	6,209	6,235	6,261	6,287	6,313	6,339	6,366
2	98.50	99.00	99.17	99.25	99.30	99.33	99.36	99.37	99.39	99.40	99.42	99.43	99.45	99.46	99.47	99.47	99.48	99.49	99.50
3	34.12	30.82	29.46	28.71	28.24	27.91	27.67	27.49	27.35	27.23	27.05	26.87	26.69	26.60	26.50	26.41	26.32	26.22	26.13
4	21.20	18.00	16.69	15.98	15.52	15.21	14.98	14.80	14.66	14.55	14.37	14.20	14.02	13.93	13.84	13.75	13.65	13.56	13.46
5	16.26	13.27	12.06	11.39	10.97	10.67	10.46	10.29	10.16	10.05	9.89	9.72	9.55	9.47	9.38	9.29	9.20	9.11	9.02
6	13.75	10.92	9.78	9.15	8.75	8.47	8.26	8.10	7.98	7.87	7.72	7.56	7.40	7.31	7.23	7.14	7.06	6.97	6.88
7	12.25	9.55	8.45	7.85	7.46	7.19	6.99	6.84	6.72	6.62	6.47	6.31	6.16	6.07	5.99	5.91	5.82	5.74	5.65
8	11.26	8.65	7.59	7.01	6.63	6.37	6.18	6.03	5.91	5.81	5.67	5.52	5.36	5.28	5.20	5.12	5.03	4.95	4.86
9	10.56	8.02	6.99	6.42	6.06	5.80	5.61	5.47	5.35	5.26	5.11	4.96	4.81	4.73	4.65	4.57	4.48	4.40	4.31
10	10.04	7.56	6.55	5.99	5.64	5.39	5.20	5.06	4.94	4.85	4.71	4.56	4.41	4.33	4.25	4.17	4.08	4.00	3.91
11	9.65	7.21	6.22	5.67	5.32	5.07	4.89	4.74	4.63	4.54	4.40	4.25	4.10	4.02	3.94	3.86	3.78	3.69	3.60
12	9.33	6.93	5.95	5.41	5.06	4.82	4.64	4.50	4.39	4.30	4.16	4.01	3.86	3.78	3.70	3.62	3.54	3.45	3.36
13	9.07	6.70	5.74	5.21	4.86	4.62	4.44	4.30	4.19	4.10	3.96	3.82	3.66	3.59	3.51	3.43	3.34	3.25	3.17
14	8.86	6.51	5.56	5.04	4.69	4.46	4.28	4.14	4.03	3.94	3.80	3.66	3.51	3.43	3.35	3.27	3.18	3.09	3.00
15	8.68	6.36	5.42	4.89	4.56	4.32	4.14	4.00	3.89	3.80	3.67	3.52	3.37	3.29	3.21	3.13	3.05	2.96	2.87
16	8.53	6.23	5.29	4.77	4.44	4.20	4.03	3.89	3.78	3.69	3.55	3.41	3.26	3.18	3.10	3.02	2.93	2.84	2.75
17	8.40	6.11	5.18	4.67	4.34	4.10	3.93	3.79	3.68	3.59	3.46	3.31	3.16	3.08	3.00	2.92	2.83	2.75	2.65
18	8.29	6.01	5.09	4.58	4.25	4.01	3.84	3.71	3.60	3.51	3.37	3.23	3.08	3.00	2.92	2.84	2.75	2.66	2.57
19	8.18	5.93	5.01	4.50	4.17	3.94	3.77	3.63	3.52	3.43	3.30	3.15	3.00	2.92	2.84	2.76	2.67	2.58	2.49
20	8.10	5.85	4.94	4.43	4.10	3.87	3.70	3.56	3.46	3.37	3.23	3.09	2.94	2.86	2.78	2.69	2.61	2.52	2.42
21	8.02	5.78	4.87	4.37	4.04	3.81	3.64	3.51	3.40	3.31	3.17	3.03	2.88	2.80	2.72	2.64	2.55	2.46	2.36
22	7.95	5.72	4.82	4.31	3.99	3.76	3.59	3.45	3.35	3.26	3.12	2.98	2.83	2.75	2.67	2.58	2.50	2.40	2.31
23	7.88	5.66	4.76	4.26	3.94	3.71	3.54	3.41	3.30	3.21	3.07	2.93	2.78	2.70	2.62	2.54	2.45	2.35	2.26
24	7.82	5.61	4.72	4.22	3.90	3.67	3.50	3.36	3.26	3.17	3.03	2.89	2.74	2.66	2.58	2.49	2.40	2.31	2.21
25	7.77	5.57	4.68	4.18	3.85	3.63	3.46	3.32	3.22	3.13	2.99	2.85	2.70	2.62	2.54	2.45	2.36	2.27	2.17
26	7.72	5.53	4.64	4.14	3.82	3.59	3.42	3.29	3.18	3.09	2.96	2.81	2.66	2.58	2.50	2.42	2.33	2.23	2.13
27	7.68	5.49	4.60	4.11	3.78	3.56	3.39	3.26	3.15	3.06	2.93	2.78	2.63	2.55	2.47	2.38	2.29	2.20	2.10
28	7.64	5.45	4.57	4.07	3.75	3.53	3.36	3.23	3.12	3.03	2.90	2.75	2.60	2.52	2.44	2.35	2.26	2.17	2.06
29	7.60	5.42	4.54	4.04	3.73	3.50	3.33	3.20	3.09	3.00	2.87	2.73	2.57	2.49	2.41	2.33	2.23	2.14	2.03
30	7.56	5.39	4.51	4.02	3.70	3.47	3.30	3.17	3.07	2.98	2.84	2.70	2.55	2.47	2.39	2.30	2.21	2.11	2.01
40	7.31	5.18	4.31	3.83	3.51	3.29	3.12	2.99	2.89	2.80	2.66	2.52	2.37	2.29	2.20	2.11	2.02	1.92	1.80
60	7.08	4.98	4.13	3.65	3.34	3.12	2.95	2.82	2.72	2.63	2.50	2.35	2.20	2.12	2.03	1.94	1.84	1.73	1.60
120	6.85	4.79	3.95	3.48	3.17	2.96	2.79	2.66	2.56	2.47	2.34	2.19	2.03	1.95	1.86	1.76	1.66	1.53	1.38
∞	6.63	4.61	3.78	3.32	3.02	2.80	2.64	2.51	2.41	2.32	2.18	2.04	1.88	1.79	1.70	1.59	1.47	1.32	1.00

Denominator Degrees of Freedom (df_2)

Source: M. Merrington and C. M. Thompson, "Tables of Percentage Points of the Inverted Beta (*F*)-Distribution," *Biometrika* 33 (1943), pp. 73–88. Reproduced by permission of the Biometrika Trustees.

TABLE A.9 Percentage Points of the Studentized Range
(Note: r is the "first value" and v is the "second value" referred to in Chapter 11.)

Entry is $q_{.10}$

v	r 2	3	4	5	6	7	8	9	10	11	12	13	14	15	16	17	18	19	20
1	8.93	13.4	16.4	18.5	20.2	21.5	22.6	23.6	24.5	25.2	25.9	26.5	27.1	27.6	28.1	28.5	29.0	29.3	29.7
2	4.13	5.73	6.77	7.54	8.14	8.63	9.05	9.41	9.72	10.0	10.3	10.5	10.7	10.9	11.1	11.2	11.4	11.5	11.7
3	3.33	4.47	5.20	5.74	6.16	6.51	6.81	7.06	7.29	7.49	7.67	7.83	7.98	8.12	8.25	8.37	8.48	8.58	8.68
4	3.01	3.98	4.59	5.03	5.39	5.68	5.93	6.14	6.33	6.49	6.65	6.78	6.91	7.02	7.13	7.23	7.33	7.41	7.50
5	2.85	3.72	4.26	4.66	4.98	5.24	5.46	5.65	5.82	5.97	6.10	6.22	6.34	6.44	6.54	6.63	6.71	6.79	6.86
6	2.75	3.56	4.07	4.44	4.73	4.97	5.17	5.34	5.50	5.64	5.76	5.87	5.98	6.07	6.16	6.25	6.32	6.40	6.47
7	2.68	3.45	3.93	4.28	4.55	4.78	4.97	5.14	5.28	5.41	5.53	5.64	5.74	5.83	5.91	5.99	6.06	6.13	6.19
8	2.63	3.37	3.83	4.17	4.43	4.65	4.83	4.99	5.13	5.25	5.36	5.46	5.56	5.64	5.72	5.80	5.87	5.93	6.00
9	2.59	3.32	3.76	4.08	4.34	4.54	4.72	4.87	4.99	5.13	5.23	5.33	5.42	5.51	5.58	5.66	5.72	5.79	5.85
10	2.56	3.27	3.70	4.02	4.26	4.47	4.64	4.78	4.91	5.03	5.13	5.23	5.32	5.40	5.47	5.54	5.61	5.67	5.73
11	2.54	3.23	3.66	3.96	4.20	4.40	4.57	4.71	4.84	4.95	5.05	5.15	5.23	5.31	5.38	5.45	5.51	5.57	5.63
12	2.52	3.20	3.62	3.92	4.16	4.35	4.51	4.65	4.78	4.89	4.99	5.08	5.16	5.24	5.31	5.37	5.44	5.49	5.55
13	2.50	3.18	3.59	3.88	4.12	4.30	4.46	4.60	4.72	4.83	4.93	5.02	5.10	5.18	5.25	5.31	5.37	5.43	5.48
14	2.49	3.16	3.56	3.85	4.08	4.27	4.42	4.56	4.68	4.79	4.88	4.97	5.05	5.12	5.19	5.26	5.32	5.37	5.43
15	2.48	3.14	3.54	3.83	4.05	4.23	4.39	4.52	4.64	4.75	4.84	4.93	5.01	5.08	5.15	5.21	5.27	5.32	5.38
16	2.47	3.12	3.52	3.80	4.03	4.21	4.36	4.49	4.61	4.71	4.81	4.89	4.97	5.04	5.11	5.17	5.23	5.28	5.33
17	2.46	3.11	3.50	3.78	4.00	4.18	4.33	4.46	4.58	4.68	4.77	4.86	4.93	5.01	5.07	5.13	5.19	5.24	5.30
18	2.45	3.10	3.49	3.77	3.98	4.16	4.31	4.44	4.55	4.65	4.75	4.83	4.90	4.98	5.04	5.10	5.16	5.21	5.26
19	2.45	3.09	3.47	3.75	3.97	4.14	4.29	4.42	4.53	4.63	4.72	4.80	4.88	4.95	5.01	5.07	5.13	5.18	5.23
20	2.44	3.08	3.46	3.74	3.95	4.12	4.27	4.40	4.51	4.61	4.70	4.78	4.85	4.92	4.99	5.05	5.10	5.16	5.20
24	2.42	3.05	3.42	3.69	3.90	4.07	4.21	4.34	4.44	4.54	4.63	4.71	4.78	4.85	4.91	4.97	5.02	5.07	5.12
30	2.40	3.02	3.39	3.65	3.85	4.02	4.16	4.28	4.38	4.47	4.56	4.64	4.71	4.77	4.83	4.89	4.94	4.99	5.03
40	2.38	2.99	3.35	3.60	3.80	3.96	4.10	4.21	4.32	4.41	4.49	4.56	4.63	4.69	4.75	4.81	4.86	4.90	4.95
60	2.36	2.96	3.31	3.56	3.75	3.91	4.04	4.16	4.25	4.34	4.42	4.49	4.56	4.62	4.67	4.73	4.78	4.82	4.86
120	2.34	2.93	3.28	3.52	3.71	3.86	3.99	4.10	4.19	4.28	4.35	4.42	4.48	4.54	4.60	4.65	4.69	4.74	4.78
∞	2.33	2.90	3.24	3.48	3.66	3.81	3.93	4.04	4.13	4.21	4.28	4.35	4.41	4.47	4.52	4.57	4.61	4.65	4.69

T A B L E A . 9 (continued)

Entry is $q_{.05}$

v	2	3	4	5	6	7	8	9	10	11	12	13	14	15	16	17	18	19	20
													r							
1	18.0	27.0	32.8	37.1	40.4	43.1	45.4	47.4	49.1	50.6	52.0	53.2	54.3	55.4	56.3	57.2	58.0	58.8	59.6
2	6.08	8.33	9.80	10.9	11.7	12.4	13.0	13.5	14.0	14.4	14.7	15.1	15.4	15.7	15.9	16.1	16.4	16.6	16.8
3	4.50	5.91	6.82	7.50	8.04	8.48	8.85	9.18	9.46	9.72	9.95	10.2	10.3	10.5	10.7	10.8	11.0	11.1	11.2
4	3.93	5.04	5.76	6.29	6.71	7.05	7.35	7.60	7.83	8.03	8.21	8.37	8.52	8.66	8.79	8.91	9.03	9.13	9.23
5	3.64	4.60	5.22	5.67	6.03	6.33	6.58	6.80	6.99	7.17	7.32	7.47	7.60	7.72	7.83	7.93	8.03	8.12	8.21
6	3.46	4.34	4.90	5.30	5.63	5.90	6.12	6.32	6.49	6.65	6.79	6.92	7.03	7.14	7.24	7.34	7.43	7.51	7.59
7	3.34	4.16	4.68	5.06	5.36	5.61	5.82	6.00	6.16	6.30	6.43	6.55	6.66	6.76	6.85	6.94	7.02	7.10	7.17
8	3.26	4.04	4.53	4.89	5.17	5.40	5.60	5.77	5.92	6.05	6.18	6.29	6.39	6.48	6.57	6.65	6.73	6.80	6.87
9	3.20	3.95	4.41	4.76	5.02	5.24	5.43	5.59	5.74	5.87	5.98	6.09	6.19	6.28	6.36	6.44	6.51	6.58	6.64
10	3.15	3.88	4.33	4.65	4.91	5.12	5.30	5.46	5.60	5.72	5.83	5.93	6.03	6.11	6.19	6.27	6.34	6.40	6.47
11	3.11	3.82	4.26	4.57	4.82	5.03	5.20	5.35	5.49	5.61	5.71	5.81	5.90	5.98	6.06	6.13	6.20	6.27	6.33
12	3.08	3.77	4.20	4.51	4.75	4.95	5.12	5.27	5.39	5.51	5.61	5.71	5.80	5.88	5.95	6.02	6.09	6.15	6.21
13	3.06	3.73	4.15	4.45	4.69	4.88	5.05	5.19	5.32	5.43	5.53	5.63	5.71	5.79	5.86	5.93	5.99	6.05	6.11
14	3.03	3.70	4.11	4.41	4.64	4.83	4.99	5.13	5.25	5.36	5.46	5.55	5.64	5.71	5.79	5.85	5.91	5.97	6.03
15	3.01	3.67	4.08	4.37	4.59	4.78	4.94	5.08	5.20	5.31	5.40	5.49	5.57	5.65	5.72	5.78	5.85	5.90	5.96
16	3.00	3.65	4.05	4.33	4.56	4.74	4.90	5.03	5.15	5.26	5.35	5.44	5.52	5.59	5.66	5.73	5.79	5.84	5.90
17	2.98	3.63	4.02	4.30	4.52	4.70	4.86	4.99	5.11	5.21	5.31	5.39	5.47	5.54	5.61	5.67	5.73	5.79	5.84
18	2.97	3.61	4.00	4.28	4.49	4.67	4.82	4.96	5.07	5.17	5.27	5.35	5.43	5.50	5.57	5.63	5.69	5.74	5.79
19	2.96	3.59	3.98	4.25	4.47	4.65	4.79	4.92	5.04	5.14	5.23	5.31	5.39	5.46	5.53	5.59	5.65	5.70	5.75
20	2.95	3.58	3.96	4.23	4.45	4.62	4.77	4.90	5.01	5.11	5.20	5.28	5.36	5.43	5.49	5.55	5.61	5.66	5.71
24	2.92	3.53	3.90	4.17	4.37	4.54	4.68	4.81	4.92	5.01	5.10	5.18	5.25	5.32	5.38	5.44	5.49	5.55	5.59
30	2.89	3.49	3.85	4.10	4.30	4.46	4.60	4.72	4.82	4.92	5.00	5.08	5.15	5.21	5.27	5.33	5.38	5.43	5.47
40	2.86	3.44	3.79	4.04	4.23	4.39	4.52	4.63	4.73	4.82	4.90	4.98	5.04	5.11	5.16	5.22	5.27	5.31	5.36
60	2.83	3.40	3.74	3.98	4.16	4.31	4.44	4.55	4.65	4.73	4.81	4.88	4.94	5.00	5.06	5.11	5.15	5.20	5.24
120	2.80	3.36	3.68	3.92	4.10	4.24	4.36	4.47	4.56	4.64	4.71	4.78	4.84	4.90	4.95	5.00	5.04	5.09	5.13
∞	2.77	3.31	3.63	3.86	4.03	4.17	4.29	4.39	4.47	4.55	4.62	4.68	4.74	4.80	4.85	4.89	4.93	4.97	5.01

(table continued)

TABLE A.9　*(concluded)*

Entry is $q_{.01}$

v	2	3	4	5	6	7	8	9	10	11	12	13	14	15	16	17	18	19	20
1	90.0	135	164	186	202	216	227	237	246	253	260	266	272	277	282	286	290	294	298
2	14.0	19.0	22.3	24.7	26.6	28.2	29.5	30.7	31.7	32.6	33.4	34.1	34.8	35.4	36.0	36.5	37.0	37.5	37.9
3	8.26	10.6	12.2	13.3	14.2	15.0	15.6	16.2	16.7	17.1	17.5	17.9	18.2	18.5	18.8	19.1	19.3	19.5	19.8
4	6.51	8.12	9.17	9.96	10.6	11.1	11.5	11.9	12.3	12.6	12.8	13.1	13.3	13.5	13.7	13.9	14.1	14.2	14.4
5	5.70	6.97	7.80	8.42	8.91	9.32	9.67	9.97	10.2	10.5	10.7	10.9	11.1	11.2	11.4	11.6	11.7	11.8	11.9
6	5.24	6.33	7.03	7.56	7.97	8.32	8.61	8.87	9.10	9.30	9.49	9.65	9.81	9.95	10.1	10.2	10.3	10.4	10.5
7	4.95	5.92	6.54	7.01	7.37	7.68	7.94	8.17	8.37	8.55	8.71	8.86	9.00	9.12	9.24	9.35	9.46	9.55	9.65
8	4.74	5.63	6.20	6.63	6.96	7.24	7.47	7.68	7.87	8.03	8.18	8.31	8.44	8.55	8.66	8.76	8.85	8.94	9.03
9	4.60	5.43	5.96	6.35	6.66	6.91	7.13	7.32	7.49	7.65	7.78	7.91	8.03	8.13	8.23	8.32	8.41	8.49	8.57
10	4.48	5.27	5.77	6.14	6.43	6.67	6.87	7.05	7.21	7.36	7.48	7.60	7.71	7.81	7.91	7.99	8.07	8.15	8.22
11	4.39	5.14	5.62	5.97	6.25	6.48	6.67	6.84	6.99	7.13	7.25	7.36	7.46	7.56	7.65	7.73	7.81	7.88	7.95
12	4.32	5.04	5.50	5.84	6.10	6.32	6.51	6.67	6.81	6.94	7.06	7.17	7.26	7.36	7.44	7.52	7.59	7.66	7.73
13	4.26	4.96	5.40	5.73	5.98	6.19	6.37	6.53	6.67	6.79	6.90	7.01	7.10	7.19	7.27	7.34	7.42	7.48	7.55
14	4.21	4.89	5.32	5.63	5.88	6.08	6.26	6.41	6.54	6.66	6.77	6.87	6.96	7.05	7.12	7.20	7.27	7.33	7.39
15	4.17	4.83	5.25	5.56	5.80	5.99	6.16	6.31	6.44	6.55	6.66	6.76	6.84	6.93	7.00	7.07	7.14	7.20	7.26
16	4.13	4.78	5.19	5.49	5.72	5.92	6.08	6.22	6.35	6.46	6.56	6.66	6.74	6.82	6.90	6.97	7.03	7.09	7.15
17	4.10	4.74	5.14	5.43	5.66	5.85	6.01	6.15	6.27	6.38	6.48	6.57	6.66	6.73	6.80	6.87	6.94	7.00	7.05
18	4.07	4.70	5.09	5.38	5.60	5.79	5.94	6.08	6.20	6.31	6.41	6.50	6.58	6.65	6.72	6.79	6.85	6.91	6.96
19	4.05	4.67	5.05	5.33	5.55	5.73	5.89	6.02	6.14	6.25	6.34	6.43	6.51	6.58	6.65	6.72	6.78	6.84	6.89
20	4.02	4.64	5.02	5.29	5.51	5.69	5.84	5.97	6.09	6.19	6.29	6.37	6.45	6.52	6.59	6.65	6.71	6.76	6.82
24	3.96	4.54	4.91	5.17	5.37	5.54	5.69	5.81	5.92	6.02	6.11	6.19	6.26	6.33	6.39	6.45	6.51	6.56	6.61
30	3.89	4.45	4.80	5.05	5.24	5.40	5.54	5.65	5.76	5.85	5.93	6.01	6.08	6.14	6.20	6.26	6.31	6.36	6.41
40	3.82	4.37	4.70	4.93	5.11	5.27	5.39	5.50	5.60	5.69	5.77	5.84	5.90	5.96	6.02	6.07	6.12	6.17	6.21
60	3.76	4.28	4.60	4.82	4.99	5.13	5.25	5.36	5.45	5.53	5.60	5.67	5.73	5.79	5.84	5.89	5.93	5.98	6.02
120	3.70	4.20	4.50	4.71	4.87	5.01	5.12	5.21	5.30	5.38	5.44	5.51	5.56	5.61	5.66	5.71	5.75	5.79	5.83
∞	3.64	4.12	4.40	4.60	4.76	4.88	4.99	5.08	5.16	5.23	5.29	5.35	5.40	5.45	5.49	5.54	5.57	5.61	5.65

r

Source: *The Analysis of Variance*, pp. 414–16, by Henry Scheffe, ©1959 by John Wiley & Sons, Inc. Reprinted by permission of John Wiley & Sons, Inc.

TABLE A.10   A Chi-Square Table: Values of χ^2_α

df	$\chi^2_{.995}$	$\chi^2_{.99}$	$\chi^2_{.975}$	$\chi^2_{.95}$	$\chi^2_{.90}$	$\chi^2_{.10}$	$\chi^2_{.05}$	$\chi^2_{.025}$	$\chi^2_{.01}$	$\chi^2_{.005}$
1	.0000393	.0001571	.0009821	.0039321	.0157908	2.70554	3.84146	5.02389	6.63490	7.87944
2	.0100251	.0201007	.0506356	.102587	.210720	4.60517	5.99147	7.37776	9.21034	10.5966
3	.0717212	.114832	.215795	.341846	.584375	6.25139	7.81473	9.34840	11.3449	12.8381
4	.206990	.297110	.484419	.710721	.063623	7.77944	9.48773	11.1433	13.2767	14.8602
5	.411740	.554300	.831211	1.145476	1.61031	9.23635	11.0705	12.8325	15.0863	16.7496
6	.675727	.872085	1.237347	1.63539	2.20413	10.6446	12.5916	14.4494	16.8119	18.5476
7	.989265	1.239043	1.68987	2.16735	2.83311	12.0170	14.0671	16.0128	18.4753	20.2777
8	1.344419	1.646482	2.17973	2.73264	3.48954	13.3616	15.5073	17.5346	20.0902	21.9550
9	1.734926	2.087912	2.70039	3.32511	4.16816	14.6837	16.9190	19.0228	21.6660	23.5893
10	2.15585	2.55821	3.24697	3.94030	4.86518	15.9871	18.3070	20.4831	23.2093	25.1882
11	2.60321	3.05347	3.81575	4.57481	5.57779	17.2750	19.6751	21.9200	24.7250	26.7569
12	3.07382	3.57056	4.40379	5.22603	6.30380	18.5494	21.0261	23.3367	26.2170	28.2995
13	3.56503	4.10691	5.00874	5.89186	7.04150	19.8119	22.3621	24.7356	27.6883	29.8194
14	4.07468	4.66043	5.62872	6.57063	7.78953	21.0642	23.6848	26.1190	29.1413	31.3193
15	4.60094	5.22935	6.26214	7.26094	8.54675	22.3072	24.9958	27.4884	30.5779	32.8013
16	5.14224	5.81221	6.90766	7.96164	9.31223	23.5418	26.2962	28.8454	31.9999	34.2672
17	5.69724	6.40776	7.56418	8.67176	10.0852	24.7690	27.5871	30.1910	33.4087	35.7185
18	6.26481	7.01491	8.23075	9.39046	10.8649	25.9894	28.8693	31.5264	34.8053	37.1564
19	6.84398	7.63273	8.90655	10.1170	11.6509	27.2036	30.1435	32.8523	36.1908	38.5822
20	7.43386	8.26040	9.59083	10.8508	12.4426	28.4120	31.4104	34.1696	37.5662	39.9968
21	8.03366	8.89720	10.28293	11.5913	13.2396	29.6151	32.6705	35.4789	38.9321	41.4010
22	8.64272	9.54249	10.9823	12.3380	14.0415	30.8133	33.9244	36.7807	40.2894	42.7956
23	9.26042	10.19567	11.6885	13.0905	14.8479	32.0069	35.1725	38.0757	41.6384	44.1813
24	9.88623	10.8564	12.4011	13.8484	15.6587	33.1963	36.4151	39.3641	42.9798	45.5585
25	10.5197	11.5240	13.1197	14.6114	16.4734	34.3816	37.6525	40.6465	44.3141	46.9278
26	11.1603	12.1981	13.8439	15.3791	17.2919	35.5631	38.8852	41.9232	45.6417	48.2899
27	11.8076	12.8786	14.5733	16.1513	18.1138	36.7412	40.1133	43.1944	46.9630	49.6449
28	12.4613	13.5648	15.3079	16.9279	18.9392	37.9159	41.3372	44.4607	48.2782	50.9933
29	13.1211	14.2565	16.0471	17.7083	19.7677	39.0875	42.5569	45.7222	49.5879	52.3356
30	13.7867	14.9535	16.7908	18.4926	20.5992	40.2560	43.7729	46.9792	50.8922	53.6720
40	20.7065	22.1643	24.4331	26.5093	29.0505	51.8050	55.7585	59.3417	63.6907	66.7659
50	27.9907	29.7067	32.3574	34.7642	37.6886	63.1671	67.5048	71.4202	76.1539	79.4900
60	35.5346	37.4848	40.4817	43.1879	46.4589	74.3970	79.0819	83.2976	88.3794	91.9517
70	43.2752	45.4418	48.7576	51.7393	55.3290	85.5271	90.5312	95.0231	100.425	104.215
80	51.1720	53.5400	57.1532	60.3915	64.2778	96.5782	101.879	106.629	112.329	116.321
90	59.1963	61.7541	65.6466	69.1260	73.2912	107.565	113.145	118.136	124.116	128.299
100	67.3276	70.0648	74.2219	77.9295	82.3581	118.498	124.342	129.561	135.807	140.169

TABLE A.11   A Table of Areas under the Standard Normal Curve

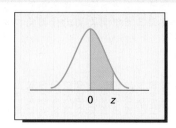

z	.00	.01	.02	.03	.04	.05	.06	.07	.08	.09
0.0	.0000	.0040	.0080	.0120	.0160	.0199	.0239	.0279	.0319	.0359
0.1	.0398	.0438	.0478	.0517	.0557	.0596	.0636	.0675	.0714	.0753
0.2	.0793	.0832	.0871	.0910	.0948	.0987	.1026	.1064	.1103	.1141
0.3	.1179	.1217	.1255	.1293	.1331	.1368	.1406	.1443	.1480	.1517
0.4	.1554	.1591	.1628	.1664	.1700	.1736	.1772	.1808	.1844	.1879
0.5	.1915	.1950	.1985	.2019	.2054	.2088	.2123	.2157	.2190	.2224
0.6	.2257	.2291	.2324	.2357	.2389	.2422	.2454	.2486	.2517	.2549
0.7	.2580	.2611	.2642	.2673	.2704	.2734	.2764	.2794	.2823	.2852
0.8	.2881	.2910	.2939	.2967	.2995	.3023	.3051	.3078	.3106	.3133
0.9	.3159	.3186	.3212	.3238	.3264	.3289	.3315	.3340	.3365	.3389
1.0	.3413	.3438	.3461	.3485	.3508	.3531	.3554	.3577	.3599	.3621
1.1	.3643	.3665	.3686	.3708	.3729	.3749	.3770	.3790	.3810	.3830
1.2	.3849	.3869	.3888	.3907	.3925	.3944	.3962	.3980	.3997	.4015
1.3	.4032	.4049	.4066	.4082	.4099	.4115	.4131	.4147	.4162	.4177
1.4	.4192	.4207	.4222	.4236	.4251	.4265	.4279	.4292	.4306	.4319
1.5	.4332	.4345	.4357	.4370	.4382	.4394	.4406	.4418	.4429	.4441
1.6	.4452	.4463	.4474	.4484	.4495	.4505	.4515	.4525	.4535	.4545
1.7	.4554	.4564	.4573	.4582	.4591	.4599	.4608	.4616	.4625	.4633
1.8	.4641	.4649	.4656	.4664	.4671	.4678	.4686	.4693	.4699	.4706
1.9	.4713	.4719	.4726	.4732	.4738	.4744	.4750	.4756	.4761	.4767
2.0	.4772	.4778	.4783	.4788	.4793	.4798	.4803	.4808	.4812	.4817
2.1	.4821	.4826	.4830	.4834	.4838	.4842	.4846	.4850	.4854	.4857
2.2	.4861	.4864	.4868	.4871	.4875	.4878	.4881	.4884	.4887	.4890
2.3	.4893	.4896	.4898	.4901	.4904	.4906	.4909	.4911	.4913	.4916
2.4	.4918	.4920	.4922	.4925	.4927	.4929	.4931	.4932	.4934	.4936
2.5	.4938	.4940	.4941	.4943	.4945	.4946	.4948	.4949	.4951	.4952
2.6	.4953	.4955	.4956	.4957	.4959	.4960	.4961	.4962	.4963	.4964
2.7	.4965	.4966	.4967	.4968	.4969	.4970	.4971	.4972	.4973	.4974
2.8	.4974	.4975	.4976	.4977	.4977	.4978	.4979	.4979	.4980	.4981
2.9	.4981	.4982	.4982	.4983	.4984	.4984	.4985	.4985	.4986	.4986
3.0	.4987	.4987	.4987	.4988	.4988	.4989	.4989	.4989	.4990	.4990

Source: A. Hald, *Statistical Tables and Formulas* (New York: Wiley, 1952), abridged from Table 1. Reproduced by permission of the publisher.

Appendix B: Counting Rules

Consider the situation in Example 4.3 (page 174) in which a student takes a pop quiz that consists of three true–false questions. If we consider our experiment to be answering the three questions, each question can be answered correctly or incorrectly. We will let C denote answering a question correctly and I denote answering a question incorrectly. Figure B.1 depicts a tree diagram of the sample space outcomes for the experiment. The diagram portrays the experiment as a three-step process—answering the first question (correctly or incorrectly—that is, C or I), answering the second question (correctly or incorrectly—that is, C or I), and answering the third question (correctly or incorrectly—that is, C or I). The tree diagram has eight different branches, and the eight distinct sample space outcomes are listed at the ends of the branches.

In general, a rule that is helpful in determining the number of experimental outcomes in a multiple-step experiment is as follows:

A Counting Rule for Multiple-Step Experiments

If an experiment can be described as a sequence of k steps in which there are n_1 possible outcomes on the first step, n_2 possible outcomes on the second step, and so on, then the total number of experimental outcomes is given by $(n_1)(n_2) \cdots (n_k)$.

For example, the pop quiz example consists of three steps in which there are $n_1 = 2$ possible outcomes on the first step, $n_2 = 2$ possible outcomes on the second step, and $n_3 = 2$ possible outcomes on the third step. Therefore, the total number of experimental outcomes is $(n_1)(n_2)(n_3) = (2)(2)(2) = 8$, as is shown in Figure B.1. Now suppose the student takes a pop quiz consisting of five true–false questions. Then, there are $(n_1)(n_2)(n_3)(n_4)(n_5) = (2)(2)(2)(2)(2) = 32$ experimental outcomes. If the student is totally unprepared for the quiz and has to blindly guess the answer

FIGURE B.1   A Tree Diagram of Answering Three True–False Questions

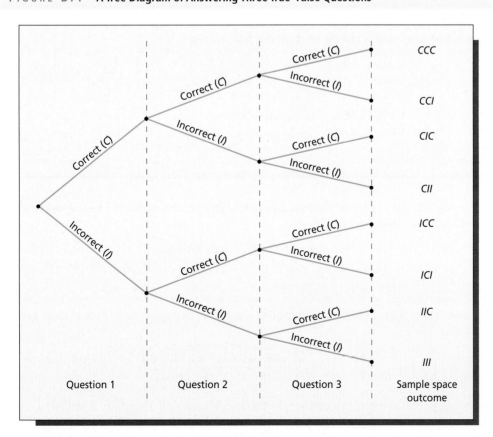

to each question, the 32 experimental outcomes might be considered to be equally likely. There-fore, since only one of these outcomes corresponds to all five questions being answered correctly, the probability that the student will answer all five questions correctly is 1/32.

As another example, suppose a bank has three branches; each branch has two departments, and each department has four employees. One employee is to be randomly selected to go to a convention. Since there are $(n_1)(n_2)(n_3) = (3)(2)(4) = 24$ employees, the probability that a particular one will be randomly selected is 1/24.

Next, consider the population of the percentage returns for last year of six high-risk stocks. This population consists of the percentage returns $-36, -15, 3, 15, 33$, and 54 (which we have arranged in increasing order). Now consider randomly selecting without replacement a sample of $n = 3$ stock returns from the population of six stock returns. Below we list the 20 distinct samples of $n = 3$ returns that can be obtained:

Sample	n = 3 Returns in Sample	Sample	n = 3 Returns in Sample
1	−36, −15, 3	11	−15, 3, 15
2	−36, −15, 15	12	−15, 3, 33
3	−36, −15, 33	13	−15, 3, 54
4	−36, −15, 54	14	−15, 15, 33
5	−36, 3, 15	15	−15, 15, 54
6	−36, 3, 33	16	−15, 33, 54
7	−36, 3, 54	17	3, 15, 33
8	−36, 15, 33	18	3, 15, 54
9	−36, 15, 54	19	3, 33, 54
10	−36, 33, 54	20	15, 33, 54

Since each sample is specified only with respect to what returns are contained in the sample, and therefore not with respect to the different orders in which the returns can be randomly selected, each sample is called a **combination of $n = 3$ stock returns selected from $N = 6$ stock returns.** In general, the following result can be proven:

A Counting Rule for Combinations

The number of combinations of n items that can be selected from N items is

$$\binom{N}{n} = \frac{N!}{n!(N-n)!}$$

where

$$N! = N(N-1)(N-2)\cdots 1$$
$$n! = n(n-1)(n-2)\cdots 1$$

Note: 0! is defined to be 1.

For example, the number of combinations of $n = 3$ stock returns that can be selected from the six previously discussed stock returns is

$$\binom{6}{3} = \frac{6!}{3!(6-3)!} = \frac{6!}{3!\,3!} = \frac{6\cdot 5\cdot 4\,(3\cdot 2\cdot 1)}{(3\cdot 2\cdot 1)\,(3\cdot 2\cdot 1)} = 20$$

The 20 combinations are listed above. As another example, the Ohio lottery system uses the random selection of 6 numbers from a group of 47 numbers to determine each week's lottery winner. There are

$$\binom{47}{6} = \frac{47!}{6!\,(47-6)!} = \frac{47\cdot 46\cdot 45\cdot 44\cdot 43\cdot 42\,(41!)}{6\cdot 5\cdot 4\cdot 3\cdot 2\cdot 1\,(41!)} = 10{,}737{,}573$$

combinations of 6 numbers that can be selected from 47 numbers. Therefore, if you buy a lottery ticket and pick six numbers, the probability that this ticket will win the lottery is 1/10,737,573.

Exercises for Appendix B

B.1   A credit union has two branches; each branch has two departments, and each department has four employees. How many total people does the credit union employ? If you work for the credit union, and one employee is randomly selected to go to a convention, what is the probability that you will be chosen?

B.2   How many combinations of two high-risk stocks could you randomly select from eight high-risk stocks? If you did this, what is the probability that you would obtain the two highest-returning stocks?

Appendix C: The Hypergeometric Distribution

Suppose a population consists of N items (for example, stocks); r of these items are "successes" (for example, stocks with positive returns for a year), and $(N - r)$ of these items are "failures" (for example, stocks with zero or negative returns for the year). If we randomly select n of the N items without replacement, it can be shown that the probability that x of the n randomly selected items will be successes is given by the **hypergeometric distribution**

$$p(x) = \frac{\binom{r}{x}\binom{N - r}{n - x}}{\binom{N}{n}}$$

For example, recall from Appendix B that $N = 6$ high-risk stocks gave the following returns last year: $-36, -15, 3, 15, 33,$ and 54. Note that $r = 4$ of these returns are positive, and $N - r = 2$ of these returns are negative. Suppose you randomly selected $n = 3$ of the six stocks to invest in at the beginning of last year, and let x denote the number of the three stocks that gave positive returns. It follows that the probability that x is at least 2 (that is, the probability that x is either 2 or 3) is

$$p(2) + p(3) = \frac{\binom{4}{2}\binom{2}{1}}{\binom{6}{3}} + \frac{\binom{4}{3}\binom{2}{0}}{\binom{6}{3}} = \frac{\left(\frac{4!}{2!\,2!}\right)\left(\frac{2!}{1!\,1!}\right)}{\frac{6!}{3!\,3!}} + \frac{\left(\frac{4!}{3!\,1!}\right)\left(\frac{2!}{0!\,2!}\right)}{\frac{6!}{3!\,3!}}$$

$$= \frac{(6)(2)}{20} + \frac{(4)(1)}{20} = .8$$

Note that, on the first random selection from the population of N items, the probability of a success is r/N. Since we are making selections **without replacement,** the probability of a success changes as we continue to make selections. However, if the population size N is "much larger" than the sample size n (say, at least 20 times as large), then making the selections will not substantially change the probability of a success. In this case, we can assume that the probability of a success stays essentially constant from selection to selection, and the different selections are essentially independent of each other. Therefore, we can approximate the hypergeometric distribution by the easier-to-compute binomial distribution:

$$p(x) = \frac{n!}{x!\,(n - x)!}\,p^x(1 - p)^{n - x} = \frac{n!}{x!\,(n - x)!}\left(\frac{r}{N}\right)^x\left(1 - \frac{r}{N}\right)^{n - x}$$

The reader will use this approximation in Exercise C.2.

Exercises for Appendix C

C.1   Suppose that you purchase (randomly select) 3 TV sets from a production run of 10 TV sets. Of the 10 TV sets, 9 are destined to last at least five years without needing a single repair. What is the probability that all three of your TV sets will last at least five years without needing a single repair?

C.2   Suppose that you own an electronics store and purchase (randomly select) 15 TV sets from a production run of 500 TV sets. Of the 500 TV sets, 450 are destined to last at least five years without needing a single repair. Set up an expression using the hypergeometric distribution for the probability that at least 14 of your 15 TV sets will last at least five years without needing a single repair. Then, using the binomial tables, approximate this probability by using the binomial distribution. What justifies the approximation? Hint: $p = r/N = 450/500 = .9$.

Answers to Most Odd-Numbered Exercises

Chapter 1

1.3 a. Quantitative
b. Quantitative
c. Qualitative
d. Quantitative
e. Qualitative

1.7 Coca-Cola; Coca-Cola Enterprises; Reynolds American; Pepsi Bottling Group, Sara Lee

1.9 a. 33276 58586
03427 09998
08178 14346
51259 24200
60268 07351
b. Between 36 and 48
$46/65 = .708$

1.11 a. People who oppose TV sex and violence
b. Doubtful
c. Highly doubtful

1.13 a. Yes. The plot suggests the breaking strengths exhibit a relatively constant amount of variation around a constant level.
b. Between 46.8 and 54.0

1.17 Ordinal; nominative; ordinal; nominative; ordinal; nominative

1.31 Cable rates are increasing in an approximately linear fashion.

Chapter 2

2.5 a. 144
b. 36

2.7 a.

Pizza Chain	Frequency	Relative Frequency
Domino's	5	.20
Godfather's	3	.12
Little Caesar's	2	.08
Papa John's	9	.36
Pizza Hut	6	.24
	25	1.00

2.21 a. Between 42 and 62.
b. Slightly skewed with a tail to the left.

2.23 a. Between 48 and 54.
b. Symmetrical

2.29 Although most growth rates are $\leqslant 61\%$, 7 of the companies have growth rates of 70% or higher.

2.37 The distribution has a tail to the right.

2.39 That was a highly unusual year for Maris.

2.41 b. Slightly skewed with tail to left.
c. No. 19 of 65 customers (29.2%) had scores below 42.

2.45 a. 17
b. 14
c. Those who prefer Rola seem to have purchased it while those who prefer Koka have not tended to purchase Rola.

2.47 a. 22
b. 4
c. Those who prefer Rola appear to consume more Cola.

2.49 b. 1st row: 79.7%, 20.3%, 100%
2nd row: 65.8%, 34.2%, 100%
c. 1st column: 50.2%, 49.8%, 100%
2nd column: 33.0%, 67.0%, 100%
d. Viewers concerned with violence are more likely to say quality has declined.

2.51 The more generous a person is, the less likely they are to leave without tipping.

2.57 There is a positive linear relationship between home size and price.

2.59 To respond to competition from satellite TV. As satellite rates increased, cable rates could increase and still remain competitive.

2.61 Consumers tend to give better taste ratings to the restaurants they prefer.

2.65 a. No.
b. Yes, strong trend.
c. The line graph is better because it makes the growth apparent, but it exaggerates the trend.
d. No.

2.67 The most frequent manufacturing quality rating is average (20 out of 37). Only Lexus received best rating.

2.69 All three regions have about 20% of their automobiles receiving ratings of better or higher. About average is the most frequent rating for all three regions. The US has the lowest percentage in the worst category.

2.71 See answer to 2.69.

2.73 Although the Pacific Rim and European regions have higher percentages of cars receiving better or best design ratings, they also have higher percentages of cars receiving the worst ratings. US cars consistently receive average ratings.

2.75 a. $k = 6$.
d. Skewed with a tail to the left.

2.77 26%. Probably.

2.79 The distribution is skewed with a tail to the right.

2.81 The distribution is skewed with a tail to the right.

2.83 The distribution has a tail to the right with one outlying value.

2.85 a. Heights: 12, 4.8, 3.8, 4.4, .84

2.87 The vertical scale has been broken, exaggerating the Chevy advantage.

Chapter 3

3.3 a. 9.6, 10, 10
b. 103.33, 100, 90

3.5 a. Yes, $\bar{x} = 42.954 > 42$
b. $\bar{x} <$ median $= 43$. There is a slight skewness to the left.

3.7 a. Yes, $\bar{x} = 50.575 > 50$.
b. median $= 50.650$. They are close because the distribution is nearly symmetric.

3.9 Slight skewness to left; US is lowest.

3.11 Skewed to right; US is highest.

3.13 Skewed to right. US is above mean and median.

3.15 a. Skewed right.
b. About 33%; about 50%.

3.19 range $= 10$; $\sigma^2 = 11.6$; $\sigma = 3.4059$

3.21 a. Revenue: 20.2; 44.6641; 6.6831
Profit: 29,079; 54693193.81; 7395.48

b. z-scores: −.176; 2.886; −1.046; −.161; −.590; −.166; −.140; −.214; −.187; −.207

3.23 a. The rule is appropriate.
b. [48.9312, 52.2188]; [47.2875, 53.8626]; [45.6436, 55.5064]
c. Yes
d. 67.5%, 95%, 100% Yes

3.25 a. Somewhat reasonable
b. [40.3076, 45.5924]; [37.6652, 48.2348]; [35.0228, 50.8772]
c. Yes
d. 63%, 98.46%, 100%; Yes

3.27 a. [−72.99, 94.85], [−5.72, 31.72], [−47.87, 116.77]
c. 383.9, 72, 119.4
RS Internet Age is most risky; Franklin Income A is least risky

3.31 a. 192   c. 141   e. 132
b. 152   d. 171   f. 30

3.33 30 year rates higher; variability similar; Average of differences is .444

3.35 a. All categories
b. Most: strategic quality planning; quality and operational results. Least: Info. and analysis; human

3.39 a. Strong positive linear association between x and y.
b. ŷ = 134.4751

3.43 a. Weighted mean = 13.56%
b. Unweighted mean = 10.72%

3.45 a. 4.6 lb.
b. 3.8289

3.47 a. 51.5; 81.61; 9.0338

3.51 .4142

3.53 a. 0.39436
b. $2139

3.57 a. about 70%
b. about 410 UKL

3.59 a. 151.24%
b. Pools might be installed in homes that are larger and nicer than ordinary.

Chapter 4

4.3 b1. AA
b2. AA, BB, CC
b3. AB, AC, BA, BC, CA, CB
b4. AA, AB, AC, BA, CA
b5. AA, AB, BA, BB
c. 1/9, 1/3, 2/3, 5/9, 4/9

4.5 b1. PPPN, PPNP, PNPP, NPPP
b2. Outcomes with ≤2 P's (11)
b3. Outcomes with ≥1 P (15)
b4. PPPP, NNNN
c. 1/4, 11/16, 15/16, 1/8

4.7 .15

4.11 a1. .25
a2. .40
a3. .10
c1. .55
c2. .45
c3. .45

4.13 a. 5/8
b. 21/40
c. 19/40
d. 3/8
e. 31/40

4.15 a. .205
b. .698
c. .606
d. .303

4.19 a. .6
b. .4
c. Dependent

4.21 .55

4.23 .1692

4.25 .31

4.27 b. .40
c. Yes, $P(FRAUD|FIRE) = P(FRAUD)$

4.29 a. .874
b. .996
c. .004

4.31 a. .10
b. .059, .068, .049, .037
c. .0256
d. .0151, .0174, .0125, .0095
e. .0801

4.33 a. .0295
b. .9705
c. Probably not

4.37 0.098, 0.610, 0.292

4.39 a. 0.089
b. No

4.41 0.247, 0.616, 0.137

4.45 0.36, 0.09, 0.42

4.47 0.5455

4.49 0.902867

4.51 0.943647

4.53 0.721

4.55 0.362

4.57 0.502

4.59 Slight dependence

4.61 a. 0.317
b. Yes

4.63 0, 0.0635, 0.4118, 0.1176, 0.4118

4.65 0.2967, 0.3077, 0.0879, 0.1099

4.67 a. 0.1327, 0.1089. America West has a smaller percent of flights delayed.
b. Alaska: 0.1109, 0.0515, 0.0862, 0.1686, 0.1421
Am. W: 0.1443, 0.0790, 0.1451, 0.2873, 0.2328
Alaska has a smaller percentage of flights delayed at each airport.

Chapter 5

5.3 a. Discrete
b. Discrete
c. Continuous
d. Discrete
e. Discrete
f. Continuous
g. Continuous

5.5 $p(x) \geq 0$, each x
$$\sum_{all\ x} p(x) = 1$$

5.9 a. .8, .4
b. 1.15, .90967
c. 1.6, 2.1071

5.11 a. .667, .444, .667, [−.667, 2.001], [−1.334, 2.668]
b. 1.5, .75, .866, [−.232, 3.232], [−1.098, 4.098]
c. 2, 1, 1, [0, 4], [−1, 5]

5.13 b. $500

5.15 a.

x	p(x)
$400	.995
−$49,600	.005

b. $150
c. $1,250

5.17 −$4.20

5.19 a. p(x) = .1099, .0879, .3077, .2967, .1978
b. 3.38

5.23 a. $p(x) = \dfrac{5!}{x!\,(5-x)!}(.3)^x(.7)^{5-x}$
$x = 0, 1, 2, 3, 4, 5$
c. .1323
d. .9692
e. .8369
f. .0308
g. .1631
h. $\mu_x = 1.5$, $\sigma_x^2 = 1.05$, $\sigma_x = 1.024695$
i. [−.54939, 3.54939], .9692

5.25 a. $p(x) = \dfrac{15!}{x!\,(15-x)!}(.9)^x(.1)^{15-x}$
b1. .4509
b2. .9873
b3. .5491
b4. .1837
b5. .0022
c. No, $P(x \leq 9)$ is very small

5.27 a1. .0625
a2. .3125
b1. .4119
b2. .2517
b3. .0059
c. No, $P(x < 5)$ is very small

5.29 a. .9996, .0004
b. .4845, .5155
c. p = 1/35
d. .000040019

5.33 a. $\mu_x = 2$, $\sigma_x^2 = 2$, $\sigma_x = 1.414$
b. [−.828, 4.828], .9473
[−2.242, 6.242], .9955

5.35 a. .7851
b. .2149
c. .1912
d. .0088

5.37 a. Approximately zero
b. Rate of comas unusually high.

5.39 a.

x	p(x)
0	4/9
1	4/9
2	1/9

b. p(x) = .16, .48, .36
c. p(x) = .12, .56, .32

5.41 a. 2/3, 2/3
b. 1.2, .693
c. 1.2, .632
d. b and c
e. b

5.43 a. $12,000
b. At least $6,000

5.45 a. Binomial
n = 8, p = .8
b. .0104
c. No, probability is very small

5.47 a. .0498
b. .9962
c. .0038
d. .9574
e. .1157

5.49 .9995
5.51 .3232
Not much evidence against it
5.53 .0293
Claim probably not true

Chapter 6
6.7 $h = 1/125$
6.9 a. 3, 3, 1.73205
b. [1.268, 4.732], .57733
6.11 a. $f(x) = 1/20$ for $120 \leq x \leq 140$
c. .5
d. .25
6.13 $c = 1/6$
6.15 a. 4.5
b. 1.0, .57733
6.23 a. -1, one σ below μ
b. -3, three σ below μ
c. 0, equals μ
d. 2, two σ above μ
e. 4, four σ above μ
6.25 a. 2.33   d. -2.33
b. 1.645   e. -1.645
c. 2.05   f. -1.28
6.27 a. 696   f. 335.5
b. 664.5   g. 696
c. 304   h. 700
d. 283   i. 300
e. 717
6.29 a1. .9830
a2. .0033
a3. .0456
b. 947
6.31 a. .0013
b. Claim probably not true
6.33 .0424
6.35 a. 10%, 90%, -13.968
b. -1.402, 26.202
6.37 a. $[\mu \pm 2.33\sigma]$
b. [46.745, 54.405]
6.39 a. A: .3085
B: .4013
B is investigated more often
b. A: .8413
B: .6915
A is investigated more often
c. B
d. Investigate if cost variance
exceeds \$5,000
.5987
6.41 $\mu = 700, \sigma = 100$
6.43 Both np and $n(1-p) \geq 5$
6.45 a. $np = 80$ and
$n(1-p) = 120$
both ≥ 5
b1. .0558
b2. .9875
b3. .0125
b4. .0025
b5. .0015
6.47 a1. $np = 200$ and
$n(1-p) = 800$
both ≥ 5
a2. 200, 12.6491
a3. Less than .001
b. No
6.49 a. Less than .001
b. No
6.55 a. $3e^{-3x}$ for $x \geq 0$
c. .9502
d. .4226
e. .0025

f. 1/3, 1/9, 1/3
g. .9502
6.57 a. $(2/3)e^{-(2/3)x}$ for $x \geq 0$
c1. .8647
c2. .2498
c3. .0695
c4. .2835
6.59 a1. .1353
a2. .2325
a3. .2212
b. Probably not, probability is .2212
6.61 That the data come from a normal
population.
6.65 .0062
6.67 a. .8944
b. 73
6.69 a. .8944
b. .7967
c. .6911
6.71 298
6.73 .9306
6.77 2/3
6.79 a. .0062
b. .6915
c. 3.3275%
6.81 .7745

Chapter 7
7.7 a. 10, .16, .4
b. 500, .0025, .05
c. 3, .0025, .05
d. 100, .000625, .025
7.9 a. Normally distributed
No, sample size is large (≥ 30)
b. $\mu_{\bar{x}} = 20, \sigma_{\bar{x}} = .5$
c. .0228
d. .1093
7.11 a. Normal distribution because $n \geq 30$
b. 6, .247
c. .0143
d. 1.43%, conclude $\mu < 6$
7.13 a. .2206
b. .0027
c. Yes
7.19 a. .5, .001, .0316
b. .1, .0009, .03
c. .8, .0004, .02
d. .98, .0000196, .004427
7.21 a. Approximately normal
b. .9, .03
c. .0228, .8664, .6915
7.23 a. .0823
b. Perhaps, evidence not very strong
7.25 a1. .7372
a2. .9756
7.27 a. Less than .001
b. Yes
7.29 a. .3085
b. .0013
c. More difficult for average.
Yes.
7.31 a. .0014
b. Yes
7.33 a. .9544
b. .0062
7.35 a. Less than .00003
b. Yes, conclude that $p < .5$
7.37 a. [49.151, 52.049]
b. [50.088, 51.112]
c. $n = 40$
7.39 a. Less than .00003
b. Yes

7.41 a. Less than .00003
b. Yes

Chapter 8
8.3 a. Longer
b. Shorter
c. Shorter
d. Longer
8.5 a. [49.608, 50.392]
b. [49.485, 50.515]
c. [49.566, 50.434]
d. [49.744, 50.256]
e. [49.4, 50.6]
8.7 a. [4.976, 5.944], [4.824, 6.096]
b. Yes, 95% interval is below 6
c. No, 99% interval extends above 6
8.9 a. [3.653, 7.707]
b. 3.653
8.11 a. [76.132, 89.068]
b. [85.748, 100.252]
c. Mean audit delay for public
owner-controlled companies
appears to be shorter
8.15 1.363, 2.201, 4.025
1.440, 2.447, 5.208
8.17 a. [3.442, 8.558]
b. Can be 95% confident, cannot be
99% confident
8.19 a. [6.832, 7.968]
b. Yes, 95% interval is below 8.
8.21 a. [786.609, 835.391]
b. Yes, 95% interval is above 750
8.23 [4.969, 5.951]; Yes
8.29 a. $n = 262$
b. $n = 452$
8.31 a. $n = 47$
b. $n = 328$
8.33 $n = 54$
8.35 a. $p = .5$
b. $p = .3$
c. $p = .8$
8.37 Part a. [.304, .496],
[.286, .514],
[.274, .526]
Part b. [.066, .134],
[.060, .140],
[.055, .145]
Part c. [.841, .959],
[.830, .970],
[.823, .977]
Part d. [.464, .736],
[.439, .761],
[.422, .778]
8.39 a. [.473, .610]
b. No, the interval extends below .5.
8.41 a. [.3804, .4596], no
b. [.5701, .6299], yes
c. 95% margin of error is .03
8.43 a. [.611, .729]
b. Yes, interval above .6
8.45 [.264, .344]
Yes, 95% interval exceeds .20.
8.47 a. $\hat{p} = .02$, [.0077, .0323]
b. $\hat{p} = .054$, [.034, .074]
c. Yes
8.49 Using $p = .73754$ and $z_{.005} = 2.576$,
$n = 1429.13$ (or $n = 1430$)
8.55 68.26%: [2.985, 7.935]
95.44%: [.510, 10.410]
99.73%: [0, 12.885]
95% CI: [4.969, 5.951]

8.57 a. [63.590, 72.490]
b. [52.287, 61.193]
c. Yes. The entire CI for the financial companies is below the CI for the industrial companies.

8.59 a. [.572, .648] Yes
b. $.04 \approx 1.96 \sqrt{\dfrac{.61(.39)}{622}}$

8.61 a. [56.47, 59.13]
b. 144

8.63 a. [25.1562, 27.2838]
b. Yes, not much more than 25

8.65 fa: [7.685%, 7.975%]; differs from 8.31%
dlcs: [9.108%, 17.732%]; does not differ from 11.71%
dms: [9.788%, 20.272%]; does not differ from 13.64%
dscs: [16.327%, 28.693%]; differs from 14.93%

8.67 [.61025, .66975]

8.69 a. [.796, .856]
b. Yes, interval is above .75

Chapter 9

9.1 H_0 status quo
H_a hoped for or suspected condition exists

9.5 Type I

9.7 The probability of Type II error becomes too large

9.9 a. H_0: $\mu \geq 6$ versus H_a: $\mu < 6$
b. Type I: decide $\mu < 6$ when $\mu \geq 6$
Type II: decide $\mu \geq 6$ when $\mu < 6$

9.11 a. H_0: $\mu = 16$ versus H_a: $\mu \neq 16$
b. Type I: readjust filler when not necessary
Type II: do not readjust when needed

9.13 The company should use $\alpha = .05$ so that β, the probability of failing to shut down when necessary, is not too high.

9.17 1.28; reject H_0

9.19 2.33; reject H_0

9.21 p-value $= .0062$; reject H_0 at all α's except .001

9.23 $z = -2$

9.25 -1.645; reject H_0

9.27 -3.09; do not reject H_0

9.29 Strong

9.31 ± 1.645; reject H_0

9.33 ± 2.575; reject H_0.

9.35 p-value $= .0026$; reject H_0 at all α's except .001.

9.37 a. H_0: $\mu \leq 42$ versus H_a: $\mu > 42$
b. $z = 2.91$; rejection points are 1.28, 1.645, 2.33, and 3.09. Reject H_0 at all α's except .001.
c. p-value $= .0018$. Reject H_0 at all α's except .001.
d. Very strong

9.39 H_0: $\mu \geq 90$ versus H_a: $\mu < 90$;
p-value $= .1492$; little evidence

9.41 $z = 1.31 <$ rejection point;
p-value $= .0951 > \alpha = .05$.
Do not shut down.

9.43 a. H_0: $\mu = 3$ versus H_a: $\mu \neq 3$
b. $z = 2.37 > 1.96$;
p-value $= .0178 < .05$.
The team should be assigned.

9.45 [16.017, 16.083]; reject H_0 because 16 is not in the interval

9.47 [56.49, 59.11]. While there is evidence $\mu < 60$, it may not be enough lower to be of practical importance.

9.51 $t = 2.33$; reject H_0 at .10 and .05 but not at .01 or .001.

9.53 H_0: $\mu \geq 8$ versus H_a: $\mu < 8$;
$t = -2.26 < -1.761$. Reject H_0 and decide the mean alert time with the new panel is less than 8 seconds.

9.55 a. H_0: $\mu \leq 3.5$ versus H_a: $\mu > 3.5$
b. $t = 3.62$; reject H_0 at $\alpha = .10$, .05, and .01 but not .001. There is very strong evidence.
d. Since the p-value is very low, we can be very confident $\mu > 3.5$.

9.57 b. Since $|t|$ exceeds 2.131, 2.776, and 4.604, reject H_0 at $\alpha = .10$, .05, .01. Cannot reject H_0 at $\alpha = .001$.

9.59 a. Reject H_0 at $\alpha = .10$, .05, .01
b. There is extremely strong evidence.

9.61 $t = 2.90 > 1.669$. Reject H_0. Since p-value $= .0025$, we have very strong evidence.

9.67 Yes for a, c, d, e, g, h; no for b, f.

9.69 a. $z = -2.18$; do not reject H_0
b. p-value $= .0292$
c. Reject H_0 at $\alpha = .10$ and .05; do not reject H_0 at .01 or .001

9.71 a. H_0: $p \leq .5$ versus H_a: $p > .5$
b. $z = 1.19$. Do not reject H_0 at any α. There is little evidence.

9.73 a. H_0: $p \leq .18$ versus H_a: $p > .18$
b. $z = 1.84$; p-value $= .0329$. Reject H_0 at $\alpha = .10$ and .05; do not reject H_0 at $\alpha = .01$, .001. There is strong evidence.
c. Possibly.

9.75 a. H_0: $p \geq .95$ versus H_a: $p < .95$
b. $z = -14.68$. Reject H_0 at every value of α. There is extremely strong evidence.
c. Yes. $\hat{p} = .79$ is well below .95.

9.81 a. $\beta = .0084, .4168, .4168, .0084$
b. No. $\beta = .4168$ is large. We must increase the sample size n.
c. The power increases as μ moves away from 3.

9.83 $n = 275$

9.87 [.000085, .000271]

9.89 [.000074, .000340]

9.91 a. H_0: $p \geq .05$ versus H_a: $p < .05$
b. $z = -2.43$. Reject H_0 at $\alpha = .10$, .05, .01 but not at .001. There is very strong evidence.
c. p-value $= .0075$. Reject H_0 at $\alpha = .10$, .05, .01 but not at .001.
d. Yes. A 2.12% reduction in improper checks translates into cost savings of $424,000.

9.93 a. H_0 would be rejected at $\alpha = .10$, .05, .01, but not at .001.
b. Very strong evidence.

9.95 a. H_0: $\mu \leq 1200$ versus H_a: $\mu > 1200$
b. $t = 2.20$. Reject H_0 at $\alpha = .10$, .05 but not at .01 or .001.
c. $t = 3.72$. Reject H_0 at every α. The sample of 100.
d. Each sample suggests an extra 41.2 hours of performance, which might translate into several months more useage (since remotes are not used constantly).

9.97 a. [.0157, .0419]
b. [22.641, 24.685]
c. [1203.14, 1279.26]

9.99 b. fa: $t = -6.66$; reject H_0
dlcs: $t = .80$; do not reject H_0
dmcs: $t = .53$; do not reject H_0
dscs: $t = 2.46$; reject H_0

9.101 Some evidence since H_0 can be rejected at $\alpha = .10$.

9.103 a. $t = 4.92$. Reject H_0 at each α. There is extremely strong evidence.
b. Probably. Over the long run, an increase of .44% in mutual fund fees can impact an investor's account balance.

Chapter 10

10.1 a. less   d. greater
b. equal   e. greater
c. less   f. not equal

10.5 a. [4.02, 5.98] Yes.
b. $z = 10$. Reject H_0 and decide $\mu_1 > \mu_2$.
c. p-value $= .0228$. Reject H_0 at $\alpha = .10$, .05, but not .01 or .001.

10.7 a. $[-20.12, -.68]$. Yes, by between .68 and 20.12 days.
c. $z = -2.10$. Decide $\mu_1 < \mu_2$.
d. p-value $= .0179$. Reject H_0 at $\alpha = .10$, .05 but not .01 or .001; strong evidence

10.9 a. $[-.05, .31]$
b. No
c. H_0: $\mu_1 - \mu_2 \leq 0$ versus H_a: $\mu_1 - \mu_2 > 0$
d. $z = 1.41$. Do not reject H_0; there is insufficient evidence to claim association.

10.11 a. H_0: $\mu_1 - \mu_2 = 0$ versus H_a: $\mu_1 - \mu_2 \neq 0$
b. $z = 5.06$. Reject H_0 and decide the means differ.
c. p-value $< .00003$. Reject H_0 at each level of α; extremely strong evidence.
d. [.44, 1.36]

10.17 $t = 3.39$; reject H_0 at $\alpha = .10$, .05, .01 but not .001; very strong evidence.

10.19 Assuming unequal variances in all three problems: for 10.16 the interval is [23.503, 36.497] and we can be 95% confident. For 10.17, $t = 3.39$ with 11 $d.f.$; reject H_0 at $\alpha = .10$, .05, .01 but not .001; very strong. For 10.18, $t = 3.39$ with 11 $d.f.$; reject H_0 at $\alpha = .10$, .05, .01 but not .001; very strong

10.21 a. H_0: $\mu_1 - \mu_2 \leq 0$ versus H_a: $\mu_1 - \mu_2 > 0$
b. $t = 1.97$; reject H_0 at .10 and .05 but not .01 or .001; strong evidence.
c. $[-12.01, 412.01]$. A's mean could be anywhere from $12.01 lower to $412.01 higher than B's.

10.23 a. H_0: $\mu_1 - \mu_2 = 0$ versus H_a: $\mu_1 - \mu_2 \neq 0$
b. Reject H_0 at $\alpha = .10$, .05 but not .01 or .001; strong evidence
c. [$1.10, $100.90]

10.29 a. [100.141, 106.859]; yes. [98.723, 108.277]; no
b. $t = 2.32$; reject H_0 at $\alpha = .05$ but not .01; strong
c. $t = -4.31$; reject H_0 at $\alpha = .05$, .01; extremely strong.

10.31 a. $H_0: \mu_d = 0$ versus $H_a: \mu_d \neq 0$
b. $t = 9.22$; reject H_0 at each level of α; extremely strong.
c. p-value = .000; reject H_0 at each α; extremely strong.
d. [.1678, .2796]; 30 year loan rates are between .1678% and .2796% higher

10.33 a. $t = 6.18$; decide there is a difference.
b. A 95% confidence interval is [2.01, 4.49], so we can estimate the minimum to be 2.01 and the maximum to be 4.49.

10.35 a. $H_0: \mu_d = 0$ versus $H_a: \mu_d \neq 0$
b. $t = 3.89$; reject H_0 at all α except .001; yes
c. p-value = .006; reject H_0 at all α except .001; very strong evidence

10.39 $z = -10.14$; reject H_0 at each value of α; extremely strong evidence

10.41 a. $H_0: p_1 - p_2 = 0$ versus $H_a: p_1 - p_2 \neq 0$
b. $z = 3.63$; reject H_0 at each value of α
c. $H_0: p_1 - p_2 \leq .05$ versus $H_a: p_1 - p_2 > .05$
$z = 1.99$ and p-value = .0233; strong evidence
d. [.0509, .1711]; yes

10.43 p-value = .004; very strong evidence [−.057, −.011]; −.057

10.45 a. $z = 3.72$; reject $H_0: p_1 - p_2 = 0$ at $\alpha = .001$; [.201, .079]; largest: .091; smallest: .029
b. $z = -4.435$; reject $H_0: p_1 - p_2 = 0$ at $\alpha = .001$; [−.201, −.079]; largest: .079; smallest: .201

10.49 a. 2.96
b. 4.68
c. 3.16
d. 8.81

10.51 a. $F = 3.24$; do not reject
b. $F = 3.24$; do not reject

10.53 a. $F = 2.06$; do not reject H_0
b. p-value = .5052; do not reject H_0
c. Yes
d. $F = 2.06$

10.55 a. $H_0: \mu_T - \mu_B = 0$ versus $H_a: \mu_T - \mu_B \neq 0$
$t = 1.54$; cannot reject H_0 at any values of α; little or no evidence
b. [−.09, .73]

10.57 a. $H_0: \mu_d = 0$ versus $H_a: \mu_d > 0$
b. $t = 10.00$; reject H_0 at all levels of α
c. p-value = .000; reject H_0 at all levels of α; extremely strong evidence

10.59 a. $t = 8.251$; reject $H_0: \mu_O - \mu_{JVC} = 0$ at $\alpha = .001$
b. [$32.69, $55.31]; probably
c. $t = 2.627$; reject $H_0: \mu_O - \mu_{JVC} \leq 30$ at $\alpha = .05$

Chapter 11 (Answers to an Even-Numbered Exercise also given)

11.1 Factor = independent variables in a designed experiment
treatments = values of a factor (or combination of factors)
experimental units = entities to which treatments are assigned
response variable = the dependent variable (or variable of interest)

11.3 Response: time to stabilize emergency condition
Factor: display panel
Treatments: panels A, B, C
Experimental units: air traffic controllers

11.5 Constant variance, normality, independence

11.7 To determine which treatment means differ and to estimate how large the differences are.

11.9 a. $F = 184.57$, p-value = .000; reject H_0 and decide shelf height affects sales.
b. Point estimate of $\mu_M - \mu_B$ is 21.4; [17.681, 25.119]. $\mu_T - \mu_B$: −4.3; [−8.019, −.581]. $\mu_T - \mu_M$: −25.7; [−29.419, −21.981].
c. $\mu_M - \mu_B$: [18.35, 24.45]
d. μ_B: [53.65, 57.96]
μ_M: [75.04, 79.36]
μ_T: [49.34, 53.66]

11.11 a. $F = 43.36$, p-value = .000; reject H_0; designs affect sales
b. B − A: [11.56, 20.84]
C − A: [3.56, 12.84]
C − B: [−12.64, −3.36]
c. B − A: [12.41, 19.99]
C − A: [4.41, 11.99]
C − B: [−11.79, −4.21]
d. μ_A: [13.92, 19.28]
μ_B: [30.12, 35.48]
μ_C: [22.12, 27.48]

11.12 $F = 16.42$; p-value < .001; reject H_0; brands differ

11.13 Divot − Alpha: [38.41, 127.59]
Divot − Century: [50.21, 139.39]
Divot − Best: [−14.39, 74.79]
Century − Alpha: [−56.39, 32.79]
Century − Best: [−109.19, −20.01]
Best − Alpha: [8.21, 97.39]
Best and Divot appear to be most durable
Divot: [313.26, 359.94]
Best: [283.06, 329.74]
Alpha: [230.26, 276.94]
Century: [218.46, 265.14]

11.15 When differences between experimental units may be concealing any true differences between the treatments.

11.17 a. $F = 36.23$; p-value = .000; reject H_0; sales methods differ
b. $F = 12.87$; p-value = .007; reject H_0; salesman effects differ
c. Method 1 − Method 2: [−2.30, 2.96]
Method 1 − Method 3: [2.37, 7.63]
Method 1 − Method 4: [3.70, 8.96]
Method 2 − Method 3: [2.04, 7.30]
Method 2 − Method 4: [3.37, 8.63]
Method 3 − Method 4: [−1.30, 3.96]
Methods 1 and 2

11.19 a. $F = 441.75$ and p-value =.000; reject H_0; keyboard brand effects differ.

b. $F = 107.69$ and p-value =.000; reject H_0; specialist effects differ.
c. A − B: [8.55, 11.45]
A − C: [12.05, 14.95]
B − C: [2.05, 4.95]
Keyboard A

11.21 a. $F = 5.78$ and p-value =.0115; reject H_0; soft drink brands affect sales.
b. Coke Classic − New Coke: [7.99, 68.01]
Coke Classic − Pepsi: [−.71, 59.31]
New Coke − Pepsi: [−38.71, 21.31]
c. Yes, mean sales of Coke Classic were significantly higher than those for New Coke.

11.23 a. $F = 4.67$; reject
b. Group 1 − Group 2: [−5.45, −0.55]
Group 1 − Control: [−3.35, 1.55]
Group 2 − Control: [0.55, 5.45]
Group 2 is the largest.

11.25 Computer model effects differ (p-value = 0.0002) and compiler effects differ (p-value = 0.0001).
3h − 1h: [−3.47, −2.67]
2h − 1h: [−2.27, −1.47]
3h − 2h: [−1.60, −0.80]
1435 − 1235: [0.47, 1.27]
1335 − 1235: [2.00, 2.80]
1435 − 1335: [−1.93, −1.13]

Chapter 12

12.7 a. Each $E_i \geq 5$
b. $\chi^2 = 300.605$; reject H_0

12.9 a. $\chi^2 = 137.14$; reject H_0
b. Differences between brand preferences

12.11 a1. $(-\infty, 10.185)$
a2. $(10.185, 14.147)$
a3. $(14.147, 18.108)$
a4. $(18.108, 22.069)$
a5. $(22.069, 26.030)$
a6. $(26.030, \infty)$
b. 1.5, 9, 22, 22, 9, 1.5
c. Can use χ^2 test
e. 1, 9, 30, 15, 8, 2
$\chi^2 = 5.581$
f. Fail to reject; normal

12.13 Fail to reject H_0; normal

12.17 a. | | 40%
 | | 60%
b. 20% | 80%
16% | 24%
40% | 60%
80% | 30%
4% | 56%
6.67% | 93.33%
20% | 70%
c. $\chi^2 = 16.667$; reject H_0
d. Yes

12.19 a. | | 24.24%
 | | 22.73%
 | | 53.03%
51.515% | 48.485%
b. For Heavy/Yes cell: cell: 18.18%; row: 75%; column: 35.29%
c. $\chi^2 = 6.86$; fail to reject H_0
d. Possibly; can reject H_0 at $\alpha = .05$

12.21 a. $\chi^2 = 16.384$; reject H_0
b. $[-.216, -.072]$
12.23 $\chi^2 = 65.91$; reject H_0:
$[.270, .376]$
12.25 b. $\chi^2 = 20.941$; reject H_0
c. Dependent
12.27 $\chi^2 = 71.48$; reject H_0

Chapter 13

13.1 When the plot suggests a linear relationship between x and y.
13.3 In each case, we use $\hat{y} = b_0 + b_1 x$.
13.5 a. $b_0 = 14.82$; $b_1 = 5.707$
b_0 is the estimated mean salary of graduates having GPA = 0 (ridiculous).
b_1 is the estimated change in mean salary corresponding to a 1 point increase in GPA.
b. 33.368 or \$33,368.
13.7 a. $b_0 = 7.814$; $b_1 = 2.665$
b_0 is the estimated mean demand when x, the price difference, is 0. Yes.
b_1 is the estimated change in mean demand when x increases by 1 unit.
b. 8.0805 or 808,050 bottles.
13.9 b. b_0 is the estimated mean price of home of 0 square feet (nonsense).
b_1 is the estimated change in mean price when x increases 1 unit (100 sq ft).
c. $\hat{y} = 48.02 + 5.700x$
d. 162.02 or \$162,020
13.11 σ^2; σ
13.13 21.3002; 4.6152
13.15 74.6762; 8.6415
13.17 27.8530; 5.2776
13.21 a. $b_0 = 11.4641$; $b_1 = 24.6022$
b. $SSE = 191.7017$;
$s^2 = 21.3002$; $s = 4.615$
c. $s_{b_1} = .8045$; $t = 30.580$
d. $t > 2.262$; reject H_0: $\beta_1 = 0$; strong evidence that regression relationship is significant.
e. $t > 3.250$; reject H_0: $\beta_1 = 0$; very strong evidence that regression relationship is significant.
f. p-value = .000; reject H_0: $\beta_1 = 0$ at all values of α. Extremely strong evidence regression relationship is significant.
g. [22.782, 26.422]
h. [21.987, 27.217]
i. $s_{b_0} = 3.4390$; $t = 3.334$
j. p-value = .0087; reject H_0: $\beta_0 = 0$ at all values of α except .001. Very strong evidence that the intercept is significant.
k. $SS_{xx} = 32.909$, $s_{b_0} = 3.439$, $s_{b_1} = .8045$
13.23 a. $b_0 = 18.4875$; $b_1 = 10.1463$
b. $SSE = 746.7624$; $s^2 = 74.6762$; $s = 8.6415$
c. $s_{b_1} = .0866$; $t = 117.1344$
d. Reject H_0: $\beta_1 = 0$ with $\alpha = .05$. Regression relationship is significant (strong evidence).

e. Reject H_0: $\beta_1 = 0$ with $\alpha = .01$. Regression relationship is significant (very strong evidence).
f. p-value = .000; reject H_0: $\beta_1 = 0$ at all values of α. Regression relationship is significant (extremely strong evidence).
g. [9.9533, 10.3393]
h. [9.872, 10.421]
i. $s_{b_0} = 4.6766$; $t = 3.9532$
j. p-value = .0027; reject H_0: $\beta_0 = 0$ at all values of α except $\alpha = .001$. Intercept is significant (very strong evidence).
13.25 [3.091, 5.770]
13.27 A confidence interval estimates a mean value of y; a prediction interval predicts an individual value of y.
13.29 a. 33.362; [32.813, 33.911]
b. 33.362; [31.878, 34.846]
c. .1583
13.31 a. 8.0806; [7.9479, 8.2133]
b. 8.0806; [7.4187, 8.7425]
c. .041902
d. [7.9016, 8.2596]; [7.1878, 8.9734]
e. (i) 8.4804; [8.3604, 8.6004]
(ii) 8.4804; [7.8209, 9.1398]
(iii) .034267
(iv) [8.3185, 8.6423]; [7.5909, 9.3699]
13.33 a. 162.03; [154.04, 170.02]
b. 162.03; [136.34, 187.72]
c. The second.
13.37 19918.8428;
$r^2 = .990$, $r = .995$
13.39 1,024,592.904;
$r^2 = .999$, $r = .9995$
13.41 Exp. Var. = 5.1817
UnExp. Var. = 0.1343
Total Var. = 5.3160; $r^2 = .975$
13.45 Reject H_0: $\rho = 0$ at all four values of α
13.47 t-test for significance of β_1
13.49 a. $F = 935.149$
b. Reject H_0 with $\alpha = .05$; significant
c. Reject H_0 with $\alpha = .01$; significant
d. p-value less than .001; reject H_0 at all values of α; significant
13.51 a. $F = 13,720.4877$
b. Reject H_0 with $\alpha = .05$; significant
c. Reject H_0 with $\alpha = .01$; significant
d. p-value = .000; reject H_0 at all values of α; significant
13.53 a. $F = 154.2792$
b. Reject H_0 with $\alpha = .05$; significant
c. Reject H_0 with $\alpha = .01$; significant
d. p-value = .0002; reject H_0 at all values of α; significant
13.57 Approximate horizontal band appearance. No violations indicated.
13.59 No violations indicated.
13.61 Cyclical plot
13.63 a. yes, plot appears linear
b. $b_0 = 306.619$; $b_1 = -27.714$
c. $\hat{y} = 306.619 - 27.714x$
d. p-value = .000; significant
e. for \$2.10: 248.420; [244.511, 252.327]
for \$2.75: 230.405; [226.697, 234.112]
for \$3.10: 220.705; [216.415, 224.994]

13.65 a. We cannot
b. Possibly not; don't take up smoking
13.67 a. 10.0045; [8.494, 11.514]
b. 10.0045; [−.310, 20.318]
13.69 Aggressive: [.00750, .02510]
Estimate of β_1 increases with return time.
Defensive: [−.00661, −.00263]
Estimate decreases with return time.
Neutral: [.00509, .01236] Estimate increases with return time.

Chapter 14

14.3 a. $b_1 = 5.6128$; $b_2 = 3.8344$
b. 172.278 or \$172,278
14.5 a. $b_1 = .0386$; $b_2 = 1.0394$; $b_3 = -413.7578$
b. $\hat{y} = 15,896.25$
c. It is 1311.06 hours higher.
14.9 1. SSE = 73.6; $s^2 = 10.5$; $s = 3.24164$
2. SSTO = 7447.5; SSE = 73.6; SSR = 7374.0
3. $R^2 = 99.0\%$; $\bar{R}^2 = 98.7\%$
4. $F(\text{model}) = 350.87$
5. $350.87 > F_{.05} = 4.74$. Decide at least one of β_1, β_2 is not 0.
6. $350.87 > F_{.01} = 9.55$
7. $p = .000$. The model is significant at each level of α.
14.11 1. SSE = 1,798,712.2; $s^2 = 149,892.7$; $s = 387.1598$
2. SSTO = 464,126,601.6; SSE = 1,798,712.2; SSR = 462,327,889.4
3. $R^2 = 99.61\%$; $\bar{R}^2 = 99.52\%$
4. $F(\text{model}) = 1028.1309$
5. $1028.1309 > F_{.05} = 3.49$. Decide at least one of β_1, β_2, β_3 is not 0.
6. $1028.1309 > F_{.01} = 5.95$
7. $p = .000$. The model is significant at each level of α.
14.15 1. $b_0 = 7.5891$,
$s_{b_0} = 2.4450$, $t = 3.104$;
$b_1 = -2.3577$,
$s_{b_1} = .6379$, $t = -3.696$;
$b_2 = 1.6122$,
$s_{b_2} = .2954$, $t = 5.459$;
$b_3 = .5012$,
$s_{b_3} = .1259$, $t = 3.981$;
2. β_0: $t = 3.104 > t_{.025} = 2.056$; reject H_0: $\beta_0 = 0$ with $\alpha = .05$;
β_1: $|t| = 3.696 > 2.056$; reject H_0: $\beta_1 = 0$ with $\alpha = .05$;
β_2: $t = 5.459 > 2.056$; reject H_0: $\beta_2 = 0$ with $\alpha = .05$;
β_3: $t = 3.981 > 2.056$; reject H_0: $\beta_3 = 0$ with $\alpha = .05$;
β_0, x_1, x_2, x_3 all significant with $\alpha = .05$
3. In each case, $|t| > t_{.005} = 2.779$; reject appropriate H_0 with $\alpha = .01$; β_0, x_1, x_2, x_3 all significant with $\alpha = .01$
4. For H_0: $\beta_0 = 0$, p-value = .0046 < $\alpha = .01$; reject H_0 at each α except $\alpha = .001$;
For H_0: $\beta_1 = 0$, p-value = .0010 < $\alpha = .01$; reject H_0 at each α except $\alpha = .001$;

For H_0: $\beta_2 = 0$,
  p-value $< .0001 < \alpha = .001$;
  reject H_0 at each value of α;
  For H_0: $\beta_3 = 0$, p-value $=$
  $.0005 < \alpha = .001$; reject H_0
  at each value of α;
  β_0 and x_1 significant at $\alpha = .01$;
  x_2 and x_3 significant at $\alpha = .001$;
5. 95% intervals: $[b_j \pm 2.056\, s_{b_j}]$;
  β_0: [2.5622, 12.6160];
  β_1: $[-3.669, -1.046]$;
  β_2: [1.0049, 2.2195];
  β_3: [.2423, .7601];
6. 99% intervals: $[b_j \pm 2.779\, s_{b_j}]$;
  For example,
  β_1: $[-4.1304, -0.5850]$

14.19 a. 172.28; [168.56, 175.99]
  b. 172.28; [163.76, 180.80]
  c. [166.79, 177.77]; [159.68, 184.88]

14.21 [14,906.24; 16,886.26] Unusually high

14.25 a. Parallel linear plots with different intercepts.

b. $\beta_2 =$ mean difference between adoption times of stock and mutual companies of the same size.
  c. $|t_2| = 5.5208$; p-value $< .001$. Reject H_0 at both α values. Significant difference between company types. [4.9770, 11.1339]
  d. Slopes equal; no interaction.

14.27 b. $F = 184.57$; p-value $< .001$; reject H_0. Display heights affect sales.
  c. 21.4; [18.35, 24.45]; $|t_M| = 14.93$. Reject H_0: $\beta_M = 0$. Middle and bottom heights yield different mean sales.
  -4.3; $[-7.35, -1.25]$; $|t_T| = 3.00$. Reject H_0: $\beta_T = 0$. Top and bottom heights yield different mean sales. Estimate of $\beta_M - \beta_T$ is 25.7.
  d. 77.2; [75.04, 79.36]; [71.486, 82.914]
  e. [22.65, 28.75]; $|t| = 17.94$, p-value $< .001$. Reject H_0: $\beta_M = 0$. Middle and top heights yield different mean sales.

14.29 a. No interaction between expenditure and campaign type.
  b. 8.61178; [8.27089, 8.95266]; slightly longer.

14.33 s is close to its minimum; $\bar{R}^2$ is near its maximum; C_p is small.

14.37 Yes, adding x_2 has reduced the pattern in the plot of the residuals against time.

14.39 The significant positive coefficient on x_2 implies more rooms are desirable while the negative coefficient on bedrooms indicates that more bedrooms are not.

14.41 $\hat{y} = 8.75 + .5(20) + 4.5 = 23.25$

14.43 a. $\hat{y} = 25.7152 + 4.9762x - 1.01905x^2$
  b. x: $p = 0$; x^2: $p = 0$. Both x and x^2 are highly significant. Yes.
  c. $\hat{y} = 25.7152 + 4.9762(2.44) - 1.01905(2.44)^2 = 31.7901$
  d. (31.5481, 32.0322)
  e. (31.1215, 32.4588)

References

Abraham, B., and J. Ledolter. *Statistical Methods for Forecasting*. New York, NY: John Wiley & Sons, 1983.

Akaah, Ishmael P., and Edward A. Riordan. "Judgments of Marketing Professionals about Ethical Issues in Marketing Research: A Replication and Extension." *Journal of Marketing Research*, February 1989, pp. 112–20.

Ashton, Robert H., John J. Willingham, and Robert K. Elliott. "An Empirical Analysis of Audit Delay." *Journal of Accounting Research* 25, no. 2 (Autumn 1987), pp. 275–92.

Axcel, Amir. *Complete Business Statistics*. 3rd ed. Burr Ridge, IL: Irwin/McGraw-Hill, 1996.

Bayus, Barry L. "The Consumer and Durable Replacement Buyer." *Journal of Marketing* 55 (January 1991), pp. 42–51.

Beattie, Vivien, and Michael John Jones. "The Use and Abuse of Graphs in Annual Reports: Theoretical Framework and Empirical Study." *Accounting and Business Research* 22, no. 88 (Autumn 1992), pp. 291–303.

Blauw, Jan Nico, and Willem E. During. "Total Quality Control in Dutch Industry." *Quality Progress* (February 1990), pp. 50–51.

Blodgett, Jeffrey G., Donald H. Granbois, and Rockney G. Walters. "The Effects of Perceived Justice on Complainants' Negative Word-of-Mouth Behavior and Repatronage Intentions." *Journal of Retailing* 69, no. 4 (Winter 1993), pp. 399–428.

Bowerman, Bruce L., and Richard T. O'Connell. *Forecasting and Time Series: An Applied Approach*. 3rd ed. Belmont, CA: Duxbury Press, 1993.

Bowerman, Bruce L., and Richard T. O'Connell. *Linear Statistical Models: An Applied Approach*. 2nd ed. Boston, MA: PWS-KENT Publishing Company, 1990, pp. 457, 460–64, 729–974.

Bowerman, Bruce L., Richard T. O'Connell, and Emily S. Murphree, *Business Statistics in Practice*. 5th ed. Burr Ridge, IL: McGraw-Hill, Irwin, 2009.

Box, G. E. P., and G. M. Jenkins. *Time Series Analysis: Forecasting and Control*. 2nd ed. San Francisco, CA: Holden-Day, 1976.

Boyd, Thomas C., and Timothy C. Krehbiel. "The Effect of Promotion Timing on Major League Baseball Attendance." *Sport Marketing Quarterly* 8, no. 4 (1999), pp. 23–34.

Brown, R. G. *Smoothing, Forecasting and Prediction of Discrete Time Series*. Englewood Cliffs, NJ: Prentice Hall, 1962.

Carey, John, Robert Neff, and Lois Therrien. "The Prize and the Passion." *Business Week* (Special 1991 bonus issue: The Quality Imperative), January 15, 1991, pp. 58–59.

Carslaw, Charles A. P. N., and Steven E. Kaplan. "An Examination of Audit Delay: Further Evidence from New Zealand." *Accounting and Business Research* 22, no. 85 (1991), pp. 21–32.

Cateora, Philip R. *International Marketing*. 9th ed. Homewood, IL: Irwin/McGraw-Hill, 1993, p. 262.

Clemen, Robert T. *Making Hard Decisions: An Introduction to Decision Analysis*. 2nd ed. Belmont, CA: Duxbury Press, 1996, p. 443.

Conlon, Edward J., and Thomas H. Stone. "Absence Schema and Managerial Judgment." *Journal of Management* 18, no. 3 (1992), pp. 435–54.

Cooper, Donald R., and C. William Emory. *Business Research Methods*. 5th ed. Homewood, IL: Richard D. Irwin, 1995, pp. 434–38, 450–51, 458–68.

Cuprisin, Tim. "Inside TV & Radio." *The Milwaukee Journal Sentinel*, April 26, 1995.

Dawson, Scott. "Consumer Responses to Electronic Article Surveillance Alarms." *Journal of Retailing* 69, no. 3 (Fall 1993), pp. 353–62.

Deming, W. Edwards. *Out of the Crisis.* Cambridge, MA: Massachusetts Institute of Technology Center for Advanced Engineering Study, 1986, pp. 18–96, 312–14.

Dielman, Terry. *Applied Regression Analysis for Business and Economics.* Belmont, CA: Duxbury Press, 1996.

Dillon, William R., Thomas J. Madden, and Neil H. Firtle. *Essentials of Marketing Research.* Homewood, IL: Richard D. Irwin Inc., 1993, pp. 382–84, 416–17, 419–20, 432–33, 445, 462–64, 524–27.

Dondero, Cort. "SPC Hits the Road." *Quality Progress,* January 1991, pp. 43–44.

Draper, N., and H. Smith. *Applied Regression Analysis.* 2nd ed. New York, NY: John Wiley & Sons, 1981.

Farnum, Nicholas R. *Modern Statistical Quality Control and Improvement.* Belmont, CA: Duxbury Press, 1994, p. 55.

Fitzgerald, Neil. "Relations Overcast by Cloudy Conditions." *CA Magazine,* April 1993, pp. 28–35.

Garvin, David A. *Managing Quality.* New York, NY: Free Press/ Macmillan, 1988.

Gibbons, J. D. *Nonparametric Statistical Inference.* 2nd ed. New York, NY: McGraw-Hill, 1985.

Gitlow, Howard, Shelly Gitlow, Alan Oppenheim, and Rosa Oppenheim. *Tools and Methods for the Improvement of Quality.* Homewood, IL: Richard D. Irwin, 1989, pp. 14–25, 533–53.

Guthrie, James P., Curtis M. Grimm, and Ken G. Smith. "Environmental Change and Management Staffing: A Reply." *Journal of Management* 19, no. 4 (1993), pp. 889–96.

Kuhn, Susan E. "A Closer Look at Mutual Funds: Which Ones Really Deliver?" *Fortune,* October 7, 1991, pp. 29–30.

Kumar, V., Roger A. Kerin, and Arun Pereira. "An Empirical Assessment of Merger and Acquisition Activity in Retailing." *Journal of Retailing* 67, no. 3 (Fall 1991), pp. 321–38.

Magee, Robert P. *Advanced Managerial Accounting.* New York, NY: Harper & Row, 1986, p. 223.

Mahmood, Mo Adam, and Gary J. Mann. "Measuring the Organizational Impact of Information Technology Investment: An Exploratory Study." *Journal of Management Information Systems* 10, no. 1 (Summer 1993), pp. 97–122.

Martocchio, Joseph J. "The Financial Cost of Absence Decisions." *Journal of Management* 18, no. 1 (1992), pp. 133–52.

Mendenhall, W., and J. Reinmuth. *Statistics for Management Economics.* 4th ed. Boston, MA: PWS-KENT Publishing Company, 1982.

The Miami University Report. Miami University, Oxford, OH, vol. 8, no. 26, 1989.

Moore, David S. *The Basic Practice of Statistics.* 2nd ed. New York: W. H. Freeman and Company, 2000.

Moore, David S., and George P. McCabe. *Introduction to the Practice of Statistics.* 2nd ed. New York: W. H. Freeman, 1993.

Morris, Michael H., Ramon A. Avila, and Jeffrey Allen. "Individualism and the Modern Corporation: Implications for Innovation and Entrepreneurship." *Journal of Management* 19, no. 3 (1993), pp. 595–612.

Neter, J., M. Kutner, C. Nachtsheim, and W. Wasserman. *Applied Linear Statistical Models.* 4th ed. Homewood, IL: Irwin/ McGraw-Hill, 1996.

Neter, J., W. Wasserman, and M. H. Kutner. *Applied Linear Statistical Models.* 2nd ed. Homewood, IL: Richard D. Irwin, 1985.

Nunnally, Bennie H., Jr., and D. Anthony Plath. *Cases in Finance.* Burr Ridge, IL: Richard D. Irwin, 1995, pp. 12–1–12–7.

Olmsted, Dan, and Gigi Anders. "Turned Off." *USA Weekend,* June 2–4, 1995.

Ott, Lyman. *An Introduction to Statistical Methods and Data Analysis.* 2nd ed. Boston, MA: PWS-Kent, 1987.

Schaeffer, R. L., William Mendenhall, and Lyman Ott. *Elementary Survey Sampling.* 3rd ed. Boston, MA: Duxbury Press, 1986.

Scherkenbach, William. *The Deming Route to Quality and Productivity: Road Maps and Roadblocks.* Washington, D.C.: Ceepress Books, 1986.

Seigel, James C. "Managing with Statistical Models." SAE Technical Paper 820520. Warrendale, PA: Society for Automotive Engineers, Inc., 1982.

Sichelman, Lew. "Random Checks Find Loan Application Fibs." *The Journal-News* (Hamilton, Ohio), Sept. 26, 1992 (originally published in *The Washington Post*).

Siegel, Andrew F. *Practical Business Statistics.* 2nd ed. Homewood, IL: Richard D. Irwin, 1990, p. 588.

Silk, Alvin J., and Ernst R. Berndt. "Scale and Scope Effects on Advertising Agency Costs." *Marketing Science* 12, no. 1 (Winter 1993), pp. 53–72.

Stevenson, William J. *Production/Operations Management.* 6th ed. Homewood, IL: Irwin/McGraw-Hill, 1999, p. 228.

Thomas, Anisya S., and Kannan Ramaswamy. "Environmental Change and Management Staffing: A Comment." *Journal of Management* 19, no. 4 (1993), pp. 877–87.

Von Neumann, J., and O. Morgenstern. *Theory of Games and Economic Behavior.* 2nd ed. Princeton, NJ: Princeton University Press, 1947.

Walton, Mary. *The Deming Management Method.* New York, NY: Dodd, Mead & Company, 1986.

Weinberger, Marc G., and Harlan E. Spotts. "Humor in U.S. versus U.K. TV Commercials: A Comparison." *Journal of Advertising* 18, no. 2 (1989), pp. 39–44.

Wright, Thomas A., and Douglas G. Bonett. "Role of Employee Coping and Performance in Voluntary Employee Withdrawal: A Research Refinement and Elaboration." *Journal of Management* 19, no. 1 (1993) pp. 147–61.

Photo Credits

Chapter 1
Page 2: © Photographer's Choice/RF/Getty Images.
Page 5: © Stephen Simpson/Getty Images.
Page 7: © Bonnie Kamin/PhotoEdit.
Page 15: © Dave Robertson/Masterfile.
Page 21: © Brand X Pictures/PunchStock/DAL.
Page 22: © Michael N. Paras/age fotostock.

Chapter 2
Page 48: © SuperStock/age fotostock.
Page 49: © Stan Honda/AFP/Getty Images.
Page 70: © Gary Conner/PhotoEdit.
Page 75: © Digital Vision/Getty Images/DAL.
Page 84: © Comstock/Jupiterimages/DAL.

Chapter 3
Page 114: © Comstock/PunchStock/DAL.
Page 116: © Stockbyte-Platinum/Getty Images/RF.
Page 130: © Andy Ridder/VISUM/The Image Works.

Chapter 4
Page 170: © Spencer Grant/PhotoEdit.
Page 178: © The McGraw-Hill Companies, Inc./John Flournoy, photographer/DAL.
Page 189: © Royalty-Free/Corbis.

Chapter 5
Page 206: AP Photo/Marcio Jose Sanchez.
Page 213: © Don Smetzer/Getty Images.
Page 220: © Claro Cortes IV/Reuters/Corbis.
Page 231: © Jeff Hunter/Getty Images.

Chapter 6
Page 242: © Chris P. Batson/Alamy/RF.
Page 258: AP Photo/Rick Bowmer.

Chapter 7
Page 284: © Pictor International/Jupiterimages/RF.
Page 294: © Royalty-Free/Corbis.

Chapter 8
Page 308: © Purestock/SuperStock/RF.
Page 315: © Jeff Greenberg/The Image Works.
Page 330: © Brian Pieters/Masterfile.

Chapter 9
Page 346: © Tony Freeman/PhotoEdit.
Page 348: © Yellow Dog Productions/Getty Images.
Page 349: © Steve Cole/Getty Images.
Page 357: © NBC Inc. Used with permission.

Chapter 10
Page 394: © Comstock Images/Getty Images.
Page 395: © Digital Vision/Getty Images/DAL.
Page 409: © Spencer Grant/PhotoEdit.

Chapter 11
Page 440: © C. Borland/Photolink/Getty Images/DAL.

Chapter 12
Page 470: © Business Wire/Getty Images.

Chapter 13
Page 498: © Fisher/Thatcher/Getty Images.
Page 500: Reprinted courtesy of Columbia Gas System.
Page 504: © Royalty-Free/Corbis/DAL.

Chapter 14
Page 568: © Royalty-Free/Corbis/DAL.
Page 575: © Ryan McVay/Getty Images/DAL.
Page 597: © Ryan McVay/Getty Images/DAL.

Chapter 15
Page 632: © Adam Crowley/Photodisc/Getty Images/DAL.

Index

Page numbers followed by n refer to notes.

A

Accenture, 56
Addition rule, 183, 184, 185
Adjusted multiple coefficient of
 determination, 584
Akaah, Ishmael P., 330
Alam, Pervaiz, 488, 489
Allen, Jeffrey, 316
Allmon, C. I., 617, 618
Alson, Jeff, 10n
Alternative (research) hypothesis, 347–349;
 see also Hypothesis testing
 definition, 385
 greater than, 353–356
 less than, 358–359
 not equal to, 359–361
 one-sided, 349, 353–363
 two-sided, 349, 379–381
Analysis of covariance, 453
Analysis of variance (ANOVA), 441
 one-way, 444–453
 randomized block design, 455–460
Analysis of variance table, 449, 457–458
Anders, Gigi, 14
Andrews, R. L., 577
ANOVA; *see* Analysis of variance
Ashton, Robert H., 339
Autocorrelation
 negative, 546
 positive, 545–546
Avila, Ramon A., 316

B

Back-to-back stem-and-leaf displays, 72–73
Bar charts, 50–51, 87; *see also* Pareto charts
Barlev, Benzion, 558, 559
Barnett, A., 209
Bayes' theorem, 198–200, 202
Bayesian statistics, 200, 202
Bayus, Barry L., 317, 365, 400
Beattie, Vivien, 340
Bell-shaped curve, 128; *see also* Normal curve
Berndt, Ernst R., 316
Between-treatment variability, 446–447
Binomial distribution, 219–228, 235
 mean, variance, and standard deviation,
 227–228
 normal approximation of, 266–269
Binomial experiments, 221, 235
Binomial formula, 221–222
Binomial random variables, 221, 235
Binomial tables, 224–225, 235, 633–637
Bissell, H. H., 556
Bivariate normal probability distribution, 536
Blauw, Jan Nico, 323
Block, Stanley B., 91, 217, 218
Blodgett, Jeffrey G., 341

Bloomberg, 21
Bonett, Douglas G., 399
Boundaries, class, 57
Bowerman, Bruce L., 19, 200, 323, 369, 406,
 413, 453, 536
Box-and-whiskers displays (box plots),
 138–141, 156
Boyd, Thomas C., 617
Branch, Shelly, 335n

C

C statistic, 611–612
Carslaw, Charles A. P. N., 317, 399
Categorical (qualitative) variables, 3, 17, 26
Categories, 471
Cateora, Philip R., 422, 423
CBS, 357
Cell frequencies, 480, 481
Cell percentages, 480–481
Cells, 471
Censuses, 4, 26
Central Limit Theorem, 288, 292–293, 302
Central tendency, 115–122
 definition, 115, 156
 mean, 115–117, 119–122
 median, 117–118, 119–122
 mode, 118, 119–122
Chambers, S., 560
Charts; *see* Graphs
Chebyshev's Theorem, 131–132, 156
Chi-square distribution, 382–383, 385
Chi-square goodness of fit tests, 471
 for multinomial probabilities, 471–474
 for normality, 475–477
Chi-square point, 382
Chi-square statistic, 472
Chi-square table, 382–383, 651
Chi-square test for independence, 471,
 480–485, 488
Class boundaries, 57
Class lengths, 56–57, 59, 60
Class midpoints, 59, 87
Cleary, Barbara A., 55
Cluster sampling, 19, 26
Coates, R., 28
Coefficient of variation, 133, 156
Colavito, Rocky, 28
Column percentages, 77, 480
Comparisonwise error rate, 450
Complement, of event, 180, 202
Completely randomized experimental design,
 441–442, 453
Conditional probability, 187–188
 definition, 202
 real-world example, 192–195
Confidence coefficient, 311–312, 338
Confidence intervals, 309
 compared to tolerance intervals, 336–337

definition, 338
 formula justification, 314–315
 general formula, 311–313
 multiple regression model, 590, 591–594
 one-sided, 361–362
 for population mean, known standard
 deviation, 309–315
 for population mean, unknown standard
 deviation, 317–323
 for population proportion, 329–333
 randomized block design, 459
 sample sizes, 325–328
 simple linear regression, 520, 525–527
 simultaneous, 450–451
 testing hypotheses with, 361–362
 two-sided, 361–362
Confidence level, 310, 312, 338
Constant variance assumption
 multiple linear regression, 581
 residual analysis, 542, 545
 simple linear regression model, 514
Contingency tables, 182, 471, 480–483, 488
Continuity correction, 267, 268
Continuous probability distribution,
 247–248, 276
Continuous random variables, 207–208, 235
Control group, 455
Cooper, Donald R., 142, 370, 407, 486, 489
Corbette, M. F., 301n
Correlation
 auto-, 545–546
 causation and, 535
 negative, 147, 534
 positive, 147, 534
Correlation coefficient
 definition, 156
 multiple, 583
 population, 147, 536
 sample, 146–147
 simple, 533–535
Correlation matrix, 607
Counting rules, 178–179, 653–654
Covariance
 analysis of, 453
 definition, 145, 156
 population, 147
 sample, 145–146
Covariates, 453
Cravens, David W., 575
Critical value rule, 353–355, 357, 361, 366
Critical values, 354, 385
Cross-sectional data, 504, 555
Crosstabulation tables, 75–78, 87
Cumulative frequency distributions, 63–64, 87
Cumulative normal table, 250–255, 276
Cumulative percent frequencies, 64
Cumulative percent frequency distribution, 87
Cumulative percentage point, 53
Cumulative relative frequencies, 64

Cumulative relative frequency distribution, 87
Cuprisin, Tim, 27

D

D'Ambrosio, P., 560
Data; *see also* Observations; Variables
    definition, 3, 26
    sources, 20–21
Decision theory, 200, 202; *see also*
    Bayes' theorem
Degrees of freedom (*df*), 318, 338, 382–383
Deloitte & Touche Consulting, 56
Denman, D. W., 90
Dependent events, 190, 202
Dependent variables; *see also* Regression
    analysis; Response variables
    definition, 555
    predicted values, 506
    in simple linear regression, 499
    transformation, 548–551
Descriptive statistics, 4, 26, 49; *see also*
    Central tendency; Variance
    grouped data, 151–152
    variation measures, 125–133
Designed experiments, 441; *see also*
    Experiments
df; *see* Degrees of freedom
Dichotomous questions, 22
Dillon, William R., 7n, 83, 186, 187, 303, 330,
    375, 400, 415, 421, 432, 487
Discrete random variables, 207
    definition, 235
    mean (expected value), 211–214
    probability distributions, 208–216
    standard deviation, 214–216
    variance, 214–215
Distance values, 525–526, 555, 593
Distributions; *see* Frequency distributions
Dot plots, 68–69, 87
Dow Jones & Company, 21
Dummy variables, 594–601, 616
Dun & Bradstreet, 21
During, Willem E., 323

E

Educational Testing Service, 21
Elber, Lynn, 196, 300
Elliott, Robert K., 339
Emenyonu, Emmanuel N., 486
Emory, C. William, 142, 370, 407, 486, 489
Empirical Rule
    areas under normal curve and, 249, 255
    definition, 157
    for normally distributed population, 128
    skewness and, 130–131
Environmental Protection Agency (EPA), 9,
    10, 130
Equality, 349
Ernst & Young Consulting, 56
Error mean square (MSE), 448
Error sum of squares (SSE), 447, 457
Error term, 502, 503, 555
Errors
    of non-observation, 23–24, 26
    of observation, 23–25, 26
    sampling, 23–24
    in surveys, 23–25
Estimated regression line, 505
Events, 174–175
    complement, 180

definition, 174, 202
    dependent, 190
    independent, 190–192
    intersection of, 183
    mutually exclusive, 183–185
    probability, 175–178
    union of, 183
Excel applications
    analysis of variance, 449, 467–468
    bar charts, 50–51, 103
    binomial probabilities, 239
    chi-square tests, 493–494
    confidence intervals, 322, 344
    crosstabulation tables, 108–109
    experimental design, 467–468
    frequency histograms, 61, 104–107
    frequency polygons, 107
    getting started, 36–41
    hypothesis testing, 391
    least squares line, 165
    least squares point estimates, 572
    multiple linear regression, 627–628
    normal distribution, 281–282
    numerical descriptive statistics, 164–166
    ogives, 108
    Pareto charts, 52–53
    pie charts, 51, 52, 104
    Poisson probabilities, 240
    runs plot, 39–40
    sample correlation coefficient, 167
    sample covariance, 166
    scatter plots, 109
    simple linear regression analysis, 519,
        564–565
    tabular and graphical methods, 102–109
    two-sample hypothesis testing, 437–438
Expected value of random variable,
    211–214, 235
Experimental outcomes, 171–172, 653–654
Experimental region, 508–509, 510, 555
Experimental studies, 21, 26
Experimental units, 441
Experiments
    basic design concepts, 441–443
    binomial, 221
    definition, 171, 202
    independent samples, 399, 442
    paired differences, 409–413
    randomized, 441–442, 453
    randomized block design, 455–460
    sample spaces, 173
Experimentwise error rate, 450
Explained variation, 532, 555, 608
Exponential distribution, 270–271,
    276–277
Extreme outliers, 139, 157

F

F distribution, 424–425, 430
F point, 424–425
F table, 424–425, 644–647
F test, 429
    differences between treatment means, 448
    overall, 585–586
    simple linear regression model, 537–539
Factors, 441
Farnum, Nicholas R., 158, 233
Federal Trade Commission (FTC), 376–379
Ferguson, J. T., 577
Finite populations, 9, 26
First quartile, 137, 157

Firtle, Neil H., 7n, 83, 186, 187, 303, 330, 375,
    400, 415, 421, 432, 487
Fitzgerald, Neil, 335
Five-number summary, 137–138
Ford, John K., 287
Frames, 5, 7, 26
Freeman, L., 28
Frequencies; *see also* Relative frequencies
    cumulative, 63–64
    definition, 49
    finding, 58
Frequency bar charts, 51
Frequency distributions, 49–50, 58
    constructing, 59
    cumulative, 63–64
    definition, 87
    mound-shaped, 61, 130–131
    shapes, 61–62, 119
    skewness, 61–62, 119–120, 130–131
Frequency histograms; *see* Histograms
Frequency polygons, 62–63, 87
Frommer, F. J., 230n

G

Gallup, George, 9
Gaudard, M., 28
General multiplication rule, 189
Geometric mean, 154–155, 157
Giges, Nancy, 279
Goodness of fit tests
    for multinomial probabilities, 471–474, 488
    for normality, 475–477, 488
Graduate Management Admission Council, 21
Granbois, Donald H., 341
Graphs
    bar charts, 50–51
    box-and-whiskers displays, 138–141
    dot plots, 68–69
    frequency polygons, 62–63
    histograms, 56–61
    misleading, 84–85
    normal probability plots, 273–276
    ogives, 64
    Pareto charts, 51–53
    pie charts, 51, 52
    residual plots, 541–542
    scatter plots, 81–82, 499
    stem-and-leaf displays, 70–73, 544, 545
Gray, Sidney J., 486
Greater than alternative hypothesis, 349,
    353–356, 385
Grouped data, 151–152, 157
Gunn, E. P., 301n
Gupta, S., 478

H

Hald, A., 652
Hartley, H. O., 319
Heller, Jeffrey, 143, 144
Hildebrand, D. K., 637, 639
Hirt, Geoffrey A., 91, 217, 218
Histograms, 56
    constructing, 56–61
    definition, 87
    percent frequency, 59
    relative frequency, 59
Homogeneity, test for, 474, 488
Horizontal bar charts, 51
Howard, Theresa, 7n
Hypergeometric distribution, 228, 655

Hypothesis testing, 347
    about population mean, 353–363
    about population proportion, 371–374
    alternative hypothesis, 347–349
    confidence intervals, 361–362
    critical value rule, 353–355, 357, 361
    legal system and, 350
    null hypothesis, 347–349, 362–363
    one-sided alternative hypothesis, 349,
        353–363
    p-values, 355–356, 357, 361
    steps, 357
    t tests, 366–369
    two-sided alternative hypothesis, 379–381
    Type I and Type II errors, 350–351, 353,
        376–381
    weight of evidence, 362–363
    z tests, 353–363, 371–374

I

Independence assumption
    chi-square test, 471, 480–485
    multiple linear regression, 581
    residual analysis, 545–547
    simple linear regression model, 514
Independent events, 190–192, 202
Independent samples, 395–398
    comparing population proportions, 417–420
    comparing population variances, 423–429
Independent samples experiment,
    399, 430, 442
Independent variables; see also Regression
    analysis
    adding to models, 608–609
    definition, 26, 555
    in experimental studies, 21
    interaction, 599
    multicollinearity, 606–608
    significance, 587–590
    in simple linear regression, 499
Indicator variables; see Dummy variables
Infinite populations, 9, 26
Information Resources, Inc., 21
Inner fences, 138, 157
Interaction, 599, 616
Interquartile range (IQR), 138, 157
Intersection, of events, 183
Interval variables, 17, 26
Intervals of values, 247
IQR; see Interquartile range

J

Jones, Michael John, 340

K

Kaplan, Steven E., 317, 399
Kerrich, John, 172n
Kerwin, Roger A., 387, 431
Krehbiel, Timothy C., 617
Krohn, Gregory, 416
Kruskal-Wallis H test, 453
Kuehn, Harvey, 28
Kumar, V., 387, 431
Kutner, M., 601

L

Landon, Alf, 8–9
Least squares line, 147–148, 157, 506

Least squares plane, 573
Least squares point estimates
    definition, 555
    means, 573–574
    multiple regression model, 571–573
    simple linear regression model, 505–510
Least squares prediction equation,
    507–508, 573
Leaves, 70–71
Left-hand tail area, 253, 261–262
Less than alternative hypothesis, 349,
    358–359, 385
Level of significance, 353
Levy, Haim, 558, 559, 561
Liebeck, Stella, 15
Line charts; see Runs plots
Line of means, 501–502
Linear regression models; see Multiple
    regression model; Simple linear
    regression model
Linear relationships, 81, 144–145
Literary Digest poll (1936), 8–9, 24
Logarithmic transformation, 548
Long-run relative frequencies, 172

M

Ma, Lan, 21
Madden, Thomas J., 7n, 83, 186, 187, 303,
    330, 375, 400, 415, 421, 432, 487
Magee, Robert P., 265
Mahmood, Mo Adam, 341
Mail surveys, 23
Makridakis, S., 553
Mann, Gary J., 341
Mann-Whitney test; see Wilcoxon rank
    sum test
Margin of error, 312, 332–333, 338
Martocchio, Joseph J., 297
Mason, J. M., 556
Matrix algebra, 572
Mazis, M. B., 90
McCabe, George P., 474, 484
McGee, V. E., 553
Mean; see also Population mean
    binomial random variable, 227–228
    compared to median and mode, 119–122
    discrete random variable, 211–214
    geometric, 154–155
    least squares point estimates, 573–574
    normal distribution, 248
    Poisson random variable, 233
    sample, 116, 151
    weighted, 150–151
Mean level, 501–502, 570
Mean square error, 515–516, 582
Mean squares, 446, 448
Measure of variation, 125, 157
Measurement, 3, 17, 26
Median, 117–118,
    119–122, 157
MegaStat applications
    analysis of variance, 468–469
    bar charts, 110
    binomial probabilities, 245
    box-and-whiskers display, 139–141, 168
    chi-square tests, 495–497
    confidence intervals, 322, 345
    contingency tables, 480–481
    crosstabulation tables, 112–113
    dot plots, 112
    experimental design, 468–469

frequency histograms, 60–61
frequency polygons, 111
getting started, 41–46
histograms, 110–111
hypergeometric probabilities, 245
hypothesis testing, 367–368, 373–374,
    392–393
least squares line, 169
multiple linear regression, 629–631
multiple regression analysis, 576–577
normal distribution, 282–283
numerical descriptive statistics, 168–169
ogives, 111
Poisson probabilities, 245
runs plot, 44–45
sample correlation coefficient, 169
scatter plots, 113
simple linear regression analysis, 547,
    566–567
stem-and-leaf display, 71–72, 112
tabular and graphical methods, 110–113
two-sample hypothesis testing, 438–439
unequal variances procedure, 405–406
Meier, Heidi Hylton, 488, 489
Mendenhall, William, 19
Merrington, M., 425, 644–647
Mild outliers, 139, 157
Minimum-variance unbiased point estimate,
    295, 302
MINITAB applications
    analysis of variance, 449, 466–467
    bar charts, 51, 94–95
    binomial probabilities, 222–224, 238
    box-and-whiskers display, 139, 163
    chi-square tests, 490–492
    confidence intervals, 322, 342–343
    contingency tables, 480–481
    crosstabulation tables, 100
    dot plots, 99
    experimental design, 466–467
    frequency histograms, 60, 97–98
    frequency polygons, 98
    getting started, 29–35
    hypothesis testing, 367–368, 389–390
    least squares line, 163
    least squares point estimates, 572
    multiple linear regression, 625–627
    normal distribution, 279–280
    normal plot, 544
    numerical descriptive statistics, 162–164
    ogives, 99
    pie charts, 96
    Poisson distribution, 231–232, 238
    randomized block ANOVA, 458
    runs plot, 31–32
    sample correlation coefficient, 164
    sample covariance, 164
    sampling distribution of sample mean, 293
    sampling distributions, 307
    scatter plots, 101
    simple linear regression analysis, 519,
        563–564
    stem-and-leaf display, 71–72, 100
    tabular and graphical methods, 94–101
    two-sample hypothesis testing, 434–436
Mode, 118, 119–122, 157
Model building
    adding independent variables, 608–609
    comparing models, 608–612
    multicollinearity, 606–608
Moore, David S., 474, 484
Morris, Michael H., 316

Mound-shaped distributions, 61, 130–131, 157
MSE; *see* Error mean square
MST; *see* Treatment mean square
Multicollinearity, 606–608, 616
Multinomial experiments, 471–472, 488
Multiple-choice questions, 22
Multiple coefficient of determination, 583–584
Multiple correlation coefficient, 583
Multiple regression model, 548, 569–577, 616
    assumptions, 581–582
    confidence intervals, 590, 591–594
    dummy variables, 594–601
    least squares point estimates, 571–573
    mean square error, 582
    multicollinearity, 606–608
    multiple coefficient of determination, 583–584
    multiple correlation coefficient, 583
    overall F test, 585–586
    point estimation, 573–574
    point prediction, 574
    prediction intervals, 591–594
    regression parameters, 570–571, 574
    residual analysis, 614–615
    significance of independent variable, 587–590
    standard error, 582
Multiplication rule
    general, 189
    for independent events, 191
Multistage cluster sampling, 19
Murphree, Emily S., 19, 323, 369, 406, 413, 453, 536
Mutually exclusive events, 183–185, 202
Myers, Dale H., 143, 144

N

Nachtsheim, C., 601
NBC, 357
Negative autocorrelation, 546, 555
Negative correlation, 147
Neter, J., 601
Nominative variables, 17, 26
Nonparametric methods, 322–323, 369
    Kruskal-Wallis H test, 453
    Spearman's rank correlation coefficient, 536
    Wilcoxon rank sum test, 406
    Wilcoxon signed ranks test, 413
Nonresponse, 24, 26
Normal curve, 128
    areas under, 249–255
    cumulative areas under, 250–255
    definition, 157
    left-hand tail area, 253, 261–262
    points on horizontal axis, 259–260, 261
    properties, 248
    right-hand tail area, 252, 253–254, 259–261
Normal distribution, 128
    approximation of binomial distribution, 266–269
    bivariate, 536
    goodness of fit test, 475–477
Normal probability distribution, 248, 257, 277
Normal probability plot, 273, 544
    constructing, 273–274, 276
    definition, 277, 555
    interpreting, 274–276
Normal table, 249, 652
    cumulative, 250–255, 640–641
Normality assumption
    chi-square goodness of fit test, 475–477
    multiple linear regression, 581

residual analysis, 544
    simple linear regression model, 514
Not equal to alternative hypothesis, 349, 359–361, 385
Null hypothesis, 347–349, 362–363, 385; *see also* Hypothesis testing
Nunnally, Bennie H., Jr., 336, 421

O

Observational studies, 21–22, 26
Observations, 4, 171, 441
O'Connell, Richard T., 19, 200, 323, 369, 406, 413, 453, 536
O'Connor, Catherine, 416
Ogives, 64, 87
Olmsted, Dan, 14
One-sample hypothesis testing; *see* Hypothesis testing
One-sided alternative hypothesis, 349, 353–363, 385
One-sided confidence intervals, 361–362
One-way ANOVA, 444–453
    assumptions, 445
    between-treatment variability, 446–447
    estimation, 451
    pairwise comparisons, 450–452
    testing for significant differences between treatment means, 445–448
    within-treatment variability, 446, 447
Open-ended questions, 22
Ordinal variables, 17, 26
Orris, J. B., 41, 643
Ott, L., 19, 613, 614n, 637, 639
Outer fences, 138, 157
Outliers
    definition, 87, 139
    detecting, 69, 73, 139
    mild and extreme, 139
Overall F test, 585–586
Ozanne, M. R., 301n

P

Paired differences experiment, 409–413, 430
Pairwise comparisons, 450–452
Parameters, binomial distribution, 227–228
Pareto, Vilfredo, 52
Pareto charts, 51–53, 87
Pareto principle, 52
Pearson, E. S., 319
Pearson, Michael A., 488, 489
Percent bar charts, 51
Percent frequencies, 50
    cumulative, 64
Percent frequency distributions, 50, 87
Percent frequency histograms, 59
Percentage points, 332–333
Percentiles, 136, 157; *see also* Quartiles
Pereira, Arun, 387, 431
Perry, E. S., 90
Phone surveys, 22–23
Pie charts, 51, 52, 87
Pilkington, G. B., II, 556
Plane of means, 570, 573
Plath, D. Anthony, 336, 421
Point estimates, 115, 574; *see also* Least squares point estimates
    definition, 157
    minimum-variance unbiased, 295
    randomized block design, 459
    unbiased, 289, 295–296

Point prediction, 574
Poisson distribution, 230–233, 235
Poisson probability table, 637–639
Poisson random variable, 230, 233, 235
Polls; *see* Surveys
Pooled estimates, 401
Population correlation
    coefficient, 147, 536
Population covariance, 147
Population mean, 115, 116–117
    comparing using independent samples, variances known, 395–398
    comparing using independent samples, variances unknown, 401–406
    confidence intervals, known standard deviation, 309–315
    confidence intervals, unknown standard deviation, 317–323
    definition, 157
    grouped data, 152
    paired differences experiment, 409–413
    t tests, 366–369
    z tests, 353–363
Population parameter, 115, 157
Population proportion
    comparing using large, independent samples, 417–420
    confidence intervals, 329–333
    z tests, 371–374
Population standard deviation, 125–126, 157
Population variance, 125–126
    comparing with independent samples, 423–429
    definition, 157
    grouped data, 152
    statistical inference, 383–384
Populations, 3–4, 26
    comparing, 395
    finite, 9
    infinite, 9
Positive autocorrelation, 545–546, 555
Positive correlation, 147
Posterior probability, 198, 202
Power, of statistical test, 379, 385
Prediction intervals, 525–528, 591–594
Preliminary samples, 326–327
Prior probability, 198, 202
Probability, 171–173
    classical, 172
    conditional, 187–188, 192–195
    of event, 175–178, 202
    subjective, 172–173
Probability curves, 247
Probability density function, 247
Probability distributions; *see also* Binomial distribution; Normal distribution
    continuous, 247–248
    of discrete random variable, 208–216, 235
    uniform, 245–247
Probability rules, 180
    addition rule, 183, 184, 185
    multiplication rule, 189, 191
    rule of complements, 180
Processes, 9, 26
    sampling, 9–11
    statistical control, 10–11
Proportion; *see* Population proportion; Sample proportion
pth percentile, 136
p-value (probability value)
    compared to critical value method, 357
    definition, 385

greater than alternative hypothesis testing, 355–356
less than alternative hypothesis testing, 358–359
not equal to alternative hypothesis testing, 360–361
t tests, 366
testing null hypothesis, 362–363

Q

Qualitative data, graphical summaries; *see* Bar charts; Pie charts
Qualitative variables, 3, 26
  dummy variables, 594–601
  measurement scales, 17
Quality, Pareto principle, 52
Quantitative data, graphical summaries; *see* Frequency distributions; Histograms
Quantitative variables, 3, 17, 26
Quartic root transformation, 548
Quartiles, 137–138
Queueing theory, 271, 277
Queues, 271

R

Random number table, 4, 5–6, 26
Random samples
  completely randomized experimental design, 441–442, 453
  definition, 4, 26
  frames, 5
  importance, 8–9
  sampling with replacement, 4–5
  sampling without replacement, 5
  stratified, 18–19
Random variables; *see also* Discrete random variables
  binomial, 221
  continuous, 207–208
  definition, 207, 235
Randomized block design, 455–460
  confidence intervals, 459
  point estimates, 459
Ranges, 125
  definition, 157
  interquartile, 138
Ranking, 17
Rare event approach, 225
Ratio variables, 17, 26
Recording errors, 25
Regression analysis, 499; *see also* Multiple regression model; Simple linear regression model
  analysis of covariance, 453
  comparing models, 608–612
Regression assumptions, 514–515
Regression model, 501
Regression parameters, 503, 570–571, 574
Regression residuals, 540; *see also* Residuals
Rejection point; *see* Critical value rule
Relative frequencies
  cumulative, 64
  definition, 50, 58
  long-run, 172
Relative frequency distributions, 50, 87
Relative frequency histograms, 59
Replication, 441
Research hypothesis; *see* Alternative (research) hypothesis

Residual analysis
  assumption of correct functional form, 544, 545
  constant variance assumption, 542, 545
  independence assumption, 545–547
  multiple regression model, 614–615
  normality assumption, 544
  simple linear regression model, 540–547
  transformation of dependent variable, 548–551
Residual plots, 541–542, 555
Residuals, 506, 540, 555, 571
Response bias, 25, 26
Response rates, 23, 26
Response variables, 21, 26, 441
Right-hand tail area, 252, 253–254, 259–261
Ringold, D. J., 90
Riordan, Edward A., 330
Roosevelt, Franklin D., 8–9
Row percentages, 77, 480
Rule of complements, 180
Runs plots, 11, 26, 82

S

Sample block means, 456
Sample correlation coefficient, 146–147
Sample covariance, 145–146
Sample frames, 5, 7, 23, 26
Sample mean, 116, 151, 157; *see also* Sampling distribution of sample mean
Sample proportion, sampling distribution of, 298–299
Sample sizes, 116
  for confidence interval for population proportion, 331–333
  definition, 157
  determination, 22, 325–328
  sampling distribution and, 292–293
  Type I and Type II error probabilities, 380
Sample space outcomes, 173–174, 178–179, 202
Sample spaces, 173, 202
Sample standard deviation, 126–127, 157
Sample statistic
  definition, 115–116, 157
  sampling distribution of, 295
Sample treatment means, 456
Sample variance, 126–127, 151–152, 157
Samples; *see also* Random samples
  cluster, 19
  definition, 4, 26
  independent, 442
  preliminary, 326–327
  systematic, 7–8, 19–20
  voluntary response, 9, 24
Sampling
  with replacement, 4–5, 26
  without replacement, 5, 26
  for surveys, 18–20
  undercoverage, 24
Sampling distribution comparing population means, 396, 430
Sampling distribution comparing population proportions, 417–420, 430
Sampling distribution comparing population variances, 424, 430
Sampling distribution of sample mean, 285–292, 302
  Central Limit Theorem, 288, 292–293
  unbiasedness and minimum-variance estimates, 295–296

Sampling distribution of sample proportion, 298–299, 302
Sampling distribution of sample statistic, 295, 302
Sampling error, 23–24, 26
Scatter plots, 81–82, 87–88, 499, 541–542
Schaeffer, R. L., 19
Scheffe, Henry, 650
Second quartile, 137
Selection bias, 24, 26
Sichelman, Lew, 334
Silk, Alvin J., 316
Sills, Jonathan, 124
Simonoff, Jeffrey S., 21
Simple coefficient of determination, 530–533, 555
Simple correlation coefficient, 533–535, 555
Simple linear regression model, 499–505
  assumptions, 514–515
  confidence intervals, 520, 525–527
  definition, 555
  distance values, 525–526
  F test, 537–539
  least squares point estimates, 505–510
  mean square error, 515–516
  point estimation, 510
  point prediction, 510
  prediction intervals, 525–528
  residual analysis, 540–547
  significance of slope, 517–519
  significance of y-intercept, 520–521
  simple coefficient of determination, 530–533
  simple correlation coefficient, 533–535
  standard error, 515–516
Simpson, O. J., 200
Simultaneous confidence intervals, 450–451
Skewed to left, 61–62, 88, 120
Skewed to right, 61–62, 88, 119
Skewness, Empirical Rule and, 130–131
Slope, 147
Slope, of simple linear regression model, 501–502, 503
  confidence interval, 520
  definition, 555
  least squares point estimates, 506
  significance, 517–519
Spearman's rank correlation coefficient, 536
Spotts, Harlan E., 335, 421
Square root transformation, 548
SSE; *see* Error sum of squares
SST; *see* Treatment sum of squares
SSTO; *see* Total sum of squares
Stamper, Joseph C., 575
Standard deviation
  binomial random variable, 227–228
  normal distribution, 248
  Poisson random variable, 233
  population, 125–126
  of random variable, 214–216, 235
  sample, 126–127
Standard error, 515–516, 525, 582, 593
Standard error of the estimate, 322, 339, 517, 588
Standard normal curve, areas under, 259–261, 640–641, 652
Standard normal distribution, 250, 277
Standardized normal quantile value, 273–274
Standardized value; *see* z-scores
States of nature, 199
Statistical control, 10–11, 26

Statistical inference
    definition, 4, 26
    generalizing, 171
    for population variance, 383–384
    rare event approach, 225
Statistical process control (SPC), 11, 26
Statistical significance, 354, 385
Statistics, 3
Stem-and-leaf displays, 70–71, 88
    back-to-back, 72–73
    constructing, 71–72
    of residuals, 544, 545
    symmetrical, 71
Stems, 70
Stevens, Doug L., 5n
Straight-line relationships; *see* Linear
        relationships
Strata, 18, 26
Stratified random samples, 18–19, 26–27
Studentized range, percentage points of,
        648–650
Subjective probability, 172–173, 202
Sum of squared residuals (errors), 506,
        554, 571
Sums of squares, 446
Surveys
    definition, 27
    errors, 23–25
    Literary Digest poll (1936), 8–9, 24
    mail, 23
    margins of error, 332–333
    nonresponse, 24
    phone, 22–23
    pilot, 22
    questions, 22
    response rates, 23
    sample sizes, 22
    sampling designs, 18–20
Symmetrical distributions, 61, 88, 119, 120
Systematic samples, 7–8, 19–20, 27

T

t distribution, 317–318, 339, 366
t points, 318–320, 339
t table, 318–320, 339,
        642–643
t tests, 366–369
Target population, 23, 27
Test statistic, 349
    definition, 385
    unequal variance, 405–406
    z tests, 353–354

Third quartile, 137, 157
Thompson, C. M., 425, 644–647, 651
Time series data, 504
    autocorrelation, 545–546
    definition, 555
Time series plots, 11; *see also* Runs plots
Tolerance intervals, 129–130, 262
    compared to confidence intervals, 336–337
    definition, 157
Total sum of squares (SSTO), 447, 457
Total variation, 532, 555, 608
Transformation of dependent variable, 548–551
Travel Industry of America, 21
Treatment mean square (MST), 448
Treatment means, 444
    sample, 456
Treatment sum of squares (SST), 446–447, 457
Treatments, 441, 444
Tukey formula, 450–451
Two-sided alternative hypothesis, 349,
        379–381, 386
Two-sided confidence intervals, 361–362
Two-way cross-classification tables; *see*
        Contingency tables
Type I errors, 350–351, 353, 386
Type II errors, 350–351, 376–381, 386

U

Unbiased point estimate, 289, 295–296, 302
Undercoverage, 24, 27
Unequal variance test statistic, 405–406
Unexplained variation, 532, 555, 608
Unger, L., 7n
Uniform distribution, 245–247, 277
Union, of events, 183
U.S. Department of Energy, 9
U.S. Bureau of the Census, 20

V

Values of variables, 3
Variables, 3, 27; *see also* Dependent variables;
        Discrete random variables; Independent
        variables; Qualitative variables
    quantitative, 3, 17, 26
    random, 207, 221, 235
Variables, relationships between
    crosstabulation tables, 75–78
    linear, 81, 144–145
    scatter plots, 81–82
Variance; *see also* Analysis of variance
        (ANOVA); Population variance

binomial random variable, 227–228
    minimum-variance unbiased point
        estimate, 295
    normal distribution, 248
    Poisson random variable, 233
    of random variable, 214–215, 235
    sample, 126–127, 151–152
Variation
    coefficient of, 133
    explained, 532, 555, 608
    measures of, 125–133
    total, 532, 555, 608
    unexplained, 532, 555, 608
Venn diagrams, 180
Vertical bar charts, 51
Voluntary response samples, 9
Voluntary response surveys, 24, 27

W

Wainer, Howard, 86
Walters, Rockney G., 341
Wasserman, W., 601
Weight of evidence, 362–363
Weighted mean, 150–151, 157
Weinberger, Marc G., 335, 421
Wheelwright, S. C., 553
Whiskers, 138–139
Wilcoxon rank sum test, 406
Wilcoxon signed ranks test, 413
Willingham, John J., 339
Within-treatment variability, 446, 447
Woodruff, Robert B., 575
Woods, D. L., 556
Wright, Thomas A., 399

Y

y-intercept, 147
y-intercept, of simple linear regression model,
        501–502, 503
    definition, 555
    least squares point estimates, 506
    significance, 520–521

Z

z_α point, 259–260, 277
$-z_\alpha$ point, 261, 277
z tests, 353–363
    about population proportion, 371–374
z values, 250, 263, 277; *see also* Normal table
z-scores, 132, 157

Case Index

A

AccuRatings Case, 171, 177–178, 179, 185, 187, 192–195, 197, 212–213, 219
Advertising Media Case, 395, 417, 418, 420
Air Traffic Control Case, 324, 328, 369

B

Bank Customer Waiting Time Case, 14, 16, 66, 122–123, 134, 297, 316, 325, 338, 352, 364, 371, 397, 398, 479

C

Car Mileage Case, 3, 9–10, 70–72, 116–117, 127, 129–130, 207–208, 243, 255–258, 285, 290–292, 309–310, 313–314, 327–328, 337, 475–476
Catalyst Comparison Case, 395, 401–402, 403–404, 426–427, 428–429
Cell Phone Case, 3, 5–6, 121–122
Cheese Spread Case, 243, 268–269, 285, 299, 309, 329–330, 347, 371, 372
Cigarette Advertisement Case, 90, 341, 387
Client Satisfaction Case, 49, 480–483, 484–485
Coffee Temperature Case, 15, 243, 258–259
Commercial Response Case, 441, 443, 455

D

Defective Cardboard Box Case, 441, 456, 460
Direct Labor Cost Case, 513, 517, 523, 530, 535, 540
Disk Brake Case, 340, 365

E

Electronic Article Surveillance Case, 347, 373

F

Fast-Food Restaurant Rating Case, 83, 524, 535, 540
Florida Pool Home Case, 160–161, 602–603

Fresh Detergent Case, 507, 512–513, 516, 523, 529–530, 535, 540, 552, 577–579, 591, 594, 604–606, 624
Fuel Consumption Case, 82, 148–149, 499–502, 507–510, 516, 518–519, 520, 526–527, 533, 534, 536, 538, 551–552, 569–574, 585–586, 589, 590, 591–592

G

Gasoline Mileage Case, 441, 442, 444, 448–450, 451–452

H

Hospital Labor Needs Case, 507, 580–581, 591, 594, 612–613, 615–616
Household Income Case, 119

I

Insurance Information Institute Case, 120
International Business Travel Expense Case, 160, 305, 341
Investment Case, 158–159, 278, 341, 388
Investor Satisfaction Case, 75–78

M

Marketing Ethics Case, 309, 330–331, 334, 374–375
Marketing Research Case, 3, 7–8, 65, 120, 309, 322
Microwave Oven Preference Case, 472–473

O

Oil Drilling Case, 199–200

P

Payment Time Case, 49, 56–59, 120–121, 127–128, 285, 294–295, 309, 310, 347, 348

Q

QHIC Case, 499, 504, 510, 520, 528, 533, 541–542, 548–551

R

Real Estate Sales Price Case, 82, 507, 513–514, 517, 523, 530, 535, 540, 577, 591, 594
Repair Cost Comparison Case, 395, 409–410, 411, 412–413
Risk Analysis Case: Game Shows and Stock Returns, 285–288

S

Sales Territory Performance Case, 569, 574–577, 589–590, 592, 609–611
Service Time Case, 149, 511, 516, 522, 529, 535, 536, 539, 552–553
Shelf Display Case, 443, 453, 603–604, D-1–D-2, D-8
Starting Salary Case, 511, 516, 522, 529, 535, 536, 539

T

Trash Bag Case, 16, 67, 74, 123, 134, 265, 304, 315–316, 324, 338, 347, 348

U

United Kingdom Insurance Case, 160, 306, 342, 388

V

Valentine's Day Chocolate Case, 347, 348–349, 379–380
VALIC Case, 141
Video Game Satisfaction Rating Case, 13–14, 66, 75, 122, 134–135, 297, 316, 325, 338, 352, 363–364, 371, 489

MegaStat® – Statistical Software for Excel

MegaStat is a full featured statistical add-in that is included on the CD-ROM with
Bowerman/O'Connell/Orris/Murphree, *Essentials of Business Statistics, Third Edition.*

MegaStat is always available from Excel's main menu.
Selecting a menu item pops up an easy to use dialog box. Regression analysis is shown below.

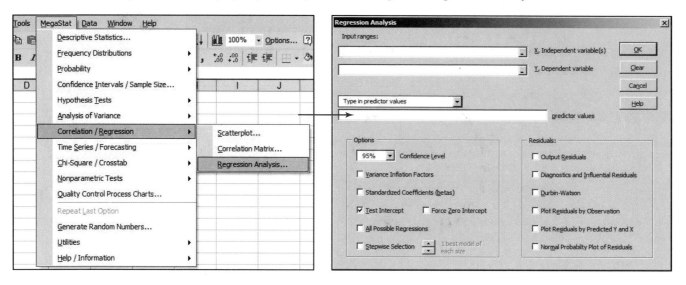

MegaStat includes the following features:

- Creates output sheets with carefully formatted output.
- AutoExpand feature allows quick data selection.
- Automatic detection of data labels.
- Completely separate from Excel's Data Analysis Tools. (The Data Analysis add-in does not have to be installed.)
- MegaStat corrects several computational problems with Excel and Data Analysis Tools.
- Computations involving factorials can handle factorials in excess of 1,000,000!
- The Stepwise Selection procedure provides a powerful new alternative to traditional stepwise regression.

MegaStat Contents:

Descriptive Statistics – standard output plus box plot, runs plot, stem & leaf, empirical rule, normal plot, normal curve, goodness of fit, etc.

Frequency Distributions – qualitative and quantitative (auto selection of interval width)

Probability – counting rules, discrete distributions (binomial, hypergeometric, Poisson), continuous distributions (normal, t, chi-square, and F)

Confidence Intervals & Sample Size – Intervals for means & proportions. Sample size determination for confidence intervals and hypothesis testing.

Hypothesis Tests – one and two group tests and confidence intervals for mean and proportion; tests for variances

ANOVA – One Factor, Randomized Blocks, Two-Factor (Includes graphical display and Tukey post-hoc analysis)

Regression – Scatterplot, Correlation Matrix, and Regression. Options for prediction intervals, VIFs and residual diagnostics. All Possible Regressions and Stepwise Selection. Non-contiguous independent variables can be selected without rearranging data.

Time Series / Forecasting – Curve Fit, Deseasonalization, Moving Average, and Exponential Smoothing

Chi-Square – Contingency Table, Crosstabulation, Goodness of Fit Test

Nonparametric Tests – includes nine of the most commonly used procedures

Quality Control Process Charts – charts for variables, proportion defective, and number of defects

Generate Random Numbers – fixed values or live functions for Uniform, Normal or Exponential distributions

MegaStat is a registered trademark of J. B. Orris, Butler University